DISCARD

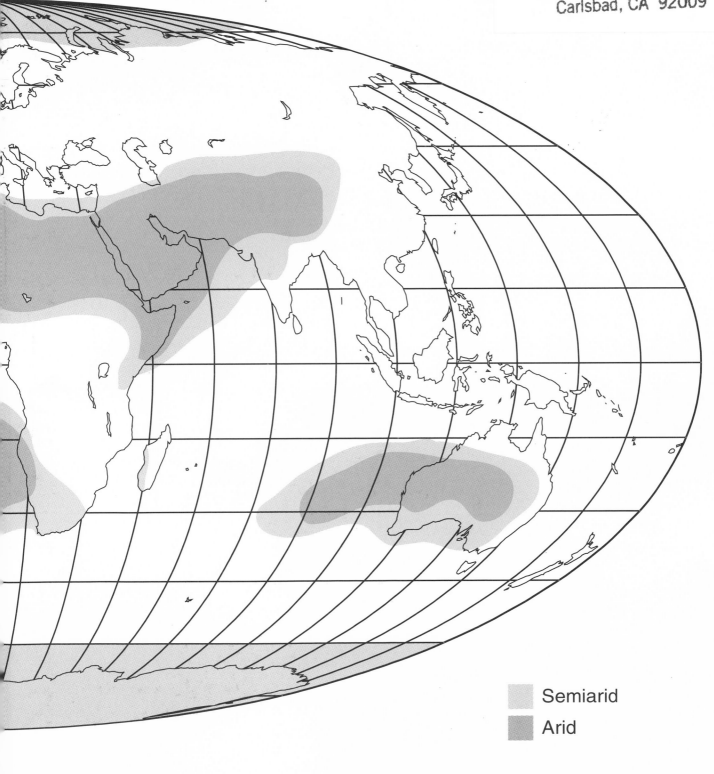

Semiarid

Arid

ENCYCLOPEDIA OF DESERTS

ENCYCLOPEDIA OF DESERTS

Edited by Michael A. Mares

University of Oklahoma Press : Norman

Published in collaboration with the Oklahoma Museum of Natural History, University of Oklahoma

Library of Congress Cataloging-in-Publication Data
Encyclopedia of deserts / edited by Michael A. Mares.
   P. cm.
  "Published in collaboration with the Oklahoma Museum of Natural History, University of Oklahoma."
  Includes bibliographical references and index.
  ISBN 0–8061–3146–2 (cloth : alk. paper)
  1. Deserts—Encyclopedias. 2. Arid regions—Encyclopedias.
I. Mares, Michael A. II. Oklahoma Museum of Natural History (Norman, Okla.)
GB611.E65 1999
910'.02154'03—dc21   98–4437
                             CIP

On the endpapers: The arid and semiarid world, both land and sea.
All base maps from MapArt.
All maps designed by Patrick Fisher
Text design by Laurie J. Vitt. Formatted with Adobe FrameMaker 5.5® in New Caledonia font.

The paper in this book meets the guidelines for permanence and durability of the Committee on Production Guidelines for Book Longevity of the Council on Library Resources, Inc. ∞

There is a silence where hath been no sound . . .
In the cold grave . . .
Or in wide desert where no life is found.
Thomas Hood

Geographers . . . crowd into the edges of their maps parts of the world which they do not know about, adding notes in the margins . . . that beyond this lies nothing but sandy deserts full of wild beasts.
Plutarch

Full many a flower is born to blush unseen,
And waste its sweetness on the desert air.
Thomas Gray

Far in the desert we have been
Where Nature, still to poets kind,
Admits no vegetable green
To soften the determined mind.
Roy Campbell

Robert Ryan: *God Almighty! I've known heat before, but this is . . . I hate the desert! It's got no . . . pity . . .*
Lee Marvin: *Yea, it takes gettin' used to it.*
Robert Ryan: *Broiling by day. Freezing at night. Alkali dust choking every hole in your body. How in the name of God does anybody live long enough to get used to it?*
Lee Marvin: *Men tempered like steel. Tough breed. Men who learn how to endure.*
The Professionals

What man calls civilization always results in deserts.
Donald Marquis

The desert shall rejoice, and blossom as the rose.
Song of Solomon

DUST DEVIL

Whirling animator of stillness,
Disrupting the desert serenity,
Cholla wave with arms akimbo,
And pebbles quicken to mobility.

Transient dervish of aridity,
Evanescent path mapped in shadows,
Your nimble dance on ballerina feet
Granting voice to mute saguaros.

Ephemeral spirit of the sere!
Exultant plants gesticulate,
Then cacti meditate anew,
And desert silence fills your wake.

Michael A. Mares

CONTENTS

PREFACE

Deserts are special places. They occur on all continents, in the open sea, at the poles, and along the equator. They may be cold or hot. They occur below sea level, on the highest mountains, along coasts, and in the middle of continents. Deserts grade imperceptibly into semideserts and together form the extensive drylands of the world.

People have long inhabited the arid lands of the world, first as small tribes skilled at living in the harsh environment and more recently as city dwellers who must go to heroic lengths to obtain water to sustain modern civilization. We affect the desert, and it affects us. Deserts are an integral part of the story of humanity and thus are the object of fascination for many of us. Until now there has been no single source that addresses all the complex factors that constitute desert ecosystems.

I invited researchers from throughout the world to produce a volume that would give a broad overview of major aspects of the deserts and semideserts of the world. We attempted to provide, in a single reference, a clear and concise presentation of a wide range of topics: the causes of arid lands, the types of arid lands that exist, their unique flora and fauna, native peoples, history, geology, geography, and climate. Our goal has been to produce a book that would be a single source of easily understood information on the arid lands of the world. It is written at a level that a high school student or college freshman can appreciate, although it will also be of use to the specialist, as it ranges widely across disciplines. One need not be a specialist, however, to use or understand the book. All that is required is an interest in some aspect of deserts.

This volume has a geographic bias. Much of what we know about deserts and semideserts, especially their ecology, comes from work that has been conducted in North America. Thus the arid lands of North America are covered in greater depth than those of other regions of the world. However, no desert or semidesert area has been intentionally ignored. A particular region that is not given individual attention is covered in discussions of entire countries or continents.

There is a second bias: vertebrates are given more attention than invertebrates. Perhaps this is because I am a vertebrate biologist, or because humans and their domestic animals are vertebrates.

Certainly it has nothing to do with the species diversity or abundance of invertebrates, for they are far more diverse and numerous than vertebrates. Attempting to deal on an individual basis with the vast numbers of invertebrates that inhabit deserts would have been an awesome undertaking, and I am sure that the hats of all vertebrate biologists are tipped in salute to desert researchers who work with this important and remarkably speciose group of organisms. Ditto for botanists, who may find more species existing in a single quadrat than there are mammals over the entire desert.

These caveats notwithstanding, no group of plants or animals has been intentionally ignored, and entries are provided for all major taxonomic groups (e.g., arthropods, insects, plants) which discuss aspects of their diversity and adaptation to aridity. Some groups (e.g., annual plants, ants, bees, beetles, butterflies, cacti) have individual entries. I hope this is a good middle ground for such a vast undertaking. I would have welcomed an encyclopedia of Old World or New World deserts, or of desert organisms in general. Alas, none is available. So this book serves as a beginning, perhaps to stimulate other authors to come together and develop those volumes that will continue to provide additional information on the remarkable diversity of the arid lands of the world.

I thank all of the contributors who labored to produce accounts that are interesting, complete, and accessible. Several anonymous reviewers lent considerable expertise to improving the manuscript. Pat Smith and Brigid Brink assisted with typing and formatting several accounts. Patrick Fisher produced the maps. Kris Grau assisted with editorial matters. Dr. Laurie J. Vitt was of inestimable help in providing photographs, authoring many accounts, and producing the camera-ready copy for the press. Finally, I thank Dr. Janet K. Braun, not only a major contributor to the volume, but also the person who, using her significant organizational skills and unbounded optimism, kept the project on track.

Like the noble century plant that inhabits the deserts of the southwestern United States, this book appeared to be quiescent for a long period before flowering and fruiting. I hope that you will find the fruit enjoyable.

HOW TO USE THIS BOOK

In this book deserts and semideserts are viewed as part of a continuum of aridity, with deserts being drier than semideserts. The term "desert" will thus generally refer to both arid and semiarid lands, although specific semidesert areas will be discussed in individual accounts or in overviews of the drylands of a country or region. Thus, for example, in the account on DESERTS, both arid and semiarid areas are discussed. There are good reasons for doing this. First, deserts and semideserts often grade imperceptibly one to the other. Second, while deserts may have plants and animals that are endemic (i.e., occur only in that particular desert), more commonly deserts share the majority of their flora and fauna with surrounding semiarid areas. While the use of "desert" to refer to arid and semiarid areas will be maintained throughout the *Encyclopedia*, in accounts of specific desert and semidesert areas the degree of aridity will be discussed, as will similarities and differences among the arid and semiarid areas of the world. From the perspective of people in the desert, whether an area is semiarid or arid is often a semantic, more than a practical, distinction. Even a semiarid area can be extremely challenging to humans, for we are not adapted to life in the desert—or even the semidesert.

The *Encyclopedia of Deserts* is arranged alphabetically, with 665 major topics. I examined a large number of major works on deserts that included biological, historical, climatological, geological, anthropological, ecological, and other disciplinary information and drew on my experience in working in many of the world's deserts over more than three decades to select those topics for inclusion in the *Encyclopedia* that are most important to understanding the broad sweep of the deserts of the world. Rather than have short contributions of a sentence or two on thousands of topics, I decided to request inclusive essays that would cover many topics at once. Thus, for example, rather than divide the subject of plant adaptations to deserts into 50 or more discrete topics, an overarching essay, PLANT ADAPTATIONS, is included.

At the conclusion of each entry, topics of related interest are cross-referenced. For example, the second entry in the *Encyclopedia* is AARDWOLF, a hyena that has specialized for a diet of termites.

The aardwolf is an unusual member of a family of rather large carnivorous mammals that has evolved to become a termite eater in the drylands of Africa. At the end of the account are several cross-references: AARDVARK; ARMADILLO; CARNIVORES; ECHIDNA; HYENA; MAMMALS; PANGOLIN. The aardvark, some armadillos, the echidna, and the pangolin are ant or termite specialists that live in various deserts and semideserts around the world and share some characteristics with the aardwolf (they are ecological equivalents in some sense; that is, they share a part of their ecological niche with one another). By looking up HYENA, the reader will learn about other hyenas in deserts as well as about hyenas in general. Moreover, the distinctive habits of the aardwolf will become apparent in comparing it to other species that are its close relatives. The entry CARNIVORES will provide an overview of the order to which the aardwolf belongs, an assemblage of diverse, usually meat-eating mammals, but with notable exceptions (such as the aardwolf). Since the aardwolf is a mammal, turning to MAMMALS will provide a wealth of information on the class Mammalia, a group of major importance in deserts, especially considering that humans are also mammals.

Of course, each of the cross-referenced entries has cross-references to additional entries. So the reader will be led on a desert expedition by looking up a single word and following the cross-referenced items through the *Encyclopedia*. This format not only provides an abundance of information on any single topic but also illustrates the complexity and interrelatedness of the organisms and the nonbiological factors that constitute the world's desert and semidesert ecosystems (ECOSYSTEM).

A second example might prove useful. We know from watching westerns, if nothing else, that deserts have cacti. Do all deserts have cacti? For that matter, why are so many westerns set in deserts? First, the reader can look up CACTI. Here is a large amount of information on the diversity and distribution of the members of this family of succulent plants. Moreover, one of these, the saguaro, is especially common in the Sonoran Desert. A perusal of the entries SAGUARO and SONORAN DESERT will provide a wealth of information on both this unusual species of cactus and the type of desert in which it occurs. By following the cross-references at the end of the accounts, the reader will be led to MONTE DESERT, SUCCULENTS, and CONVERGENT EVOLUTION. These accounts will provide information about a southern desert in Argentina that looks much like the Sonoran Desert of North America, so much so that a western supposedly set in the Sonoran Desert was filmed there. The reader also will learn of succulent plants that have developed in deserts of Africa which look and function much like cacti, although they are not closely related, and why plants have frequently developed the succulent life form to inhabit arid areas (PLANT ADAPTATIONS). Finally, by examining the account MOVIES IN DESERTS, one will learn why deserts have been so important not only to our beloved and uniquely American western film genre but also to many other types of films that have been set in deserts throughout the world.

Each account has a Further Reading section in which literature is listed which serves as a source of detailed information on that subject. Where possible, literature that is broadly oriented and readily accessible is cited so that the reader may be led gently into greater depth on the topic. In some cases, of course, specialized literature has been cited because it provides the only available detailed information. Because deserts occur throughout the world, the literature that is cited may be based on research that was published in other countries. Most of the literature cited in this volume can be obtained in a good city library, and certainly in most college or university libraries. The suggested readings are rich sources of general and specialized information and allow readers to pursue their interest on any topic to any depth desired.

AN INTRODUCTION TO DESERTS provides basic information on deserts that orients the reader to the formation of deserts and semideserts, their distribution, and their importance. The section deals with everything from geography to geology and from biology to climate. It provides a basic understanding of why arid and semiarid areas develop, where they occur, and what they are like. Finally, the comprehensive INDEX at the end of the volume contains key phrases, words, scientific names, and subject areas that were dealt with in the *Encyclopedia*. The index is a gift: it is a compass to lead you into the desert.

SUBJECT LIST BY TOPIC

GEOGRAPHIC AREAS AND DESERT REGIONS

NEW WORLD

ANTARCTIC DESERT. *See* AN INTRODUCTION TO DESERTS

ANZA-BORREGO DESERT

ARCTIC DESERT. *See* AN INTRODUCTION TO DESERTS; ASIA, DESERTS OF

ARGENTINA, DESERTS OF. *See* SOUTH AMERICA, DESERTS OF

ARIZONA DESERT

ATACAMA DESERT

BAJA CALIFORNIA, DESERTS OF

BOLIVIA, DESERTS OF. *See* SOUTH AMERICA, DESERTS OF

BORREGO DESERT. *See* ANZA-BORREGO DESERT

BRAZIL SEMIDESERT. *See* CAATINGA

CAATINGA

CALIFORNIA DESERT

CHACO

CHIHUAHUAN DESERT

CHILE, DESERTS OF

COLORADO DESERT

DEATH VALLEY

DEEP CANYON DESERT

GREAT AMERICAN DESERT

GREAT BASIN DESERT

GUAJIRA

MEXICO, DESERTS OF

MOHAVE DESERT. *See* MOJAVE DESERT

MOJAVE DESERT

MONTANA DESERT

MONTE DESERT

NEVADA DESERT

NEW MEXICO DESERT

OREGON DESERT

PAINTED DESERT

PAMPAS

PATAGONIA

PERU, DESERTS OF

PUNA

SECHURA DESERT

SONORAN DESERT

SOUTH AMERICA, DESERTS OF

TEXAS DESERT

TULAROSA BASIN. *See* NEW MEXICO DESERT

UNITED STATES, DESERTS OF

UTAH DESERT

WASHINGTON DESERT

YUMA DESERT

OLD WORLD

AFGHANISTAN, DESERTS OF

AFRICA, DESERTS OF

ALA-SHAN-GOBI DESERT. *See* ASIA, DESERTS OF

ARABIAN DESERT. *See* SAUDI ARABIA, DESERTS OF

ARABIAN GULF, DESERTS OF

ARCTIC DESERT. *See* AN INTRODUCTION TO DESERTS; ASIA, DESERTS OF

ASIA, DESERTS OF

AUSTRALIA, DESERTS OF

ETHIOPIA, DESERTS OF. *See* AFRICA, DESERTS OF

GOBI DESERT. *See* ASIA, DESERTS OF

GREAT KAVIR. *See* IRAN, DESERTS OF

GREAT SANDY DESERT. *See* AUSTRALIA, DESERTS OF

GREAT VICTORIA DESERT. *See* AUSTRALIA, DESERTS OF

INDIA, DESERTS OF. *See* INDO-PAKISTAN DESERTS

INDO-PAKISTAN DESERTS

IRAN, DESERTS OF

MOUNTAINS, RIVERS, PLAINS, AND PLACES

LIFE FORMS IN DESERTS

BEHAVIOR, ECOLOGY, EVOLUTION

BACTERIA

PLANTS

GENERAL

DECOMPOSITION

DESERT BLOOM

DESERT GRASSLAND

EPHEMERAL PLANTS. *See* ANNUAL
  PLANTS

EPIPHYTES

FOREST

FUNGI. *See* PLANTS

GERMINATION

GOURDS

GRASSES

GRASSLAND

GROWING SEASON

HALOPHYTES

HERBS

MALLEE

PERENNIAL PLANTS

PLANT ADAPTATIONS

PLANT COVER

PLANT GEOGRAPHY

PLANTS

PRAIRIE

PRIMARY PRODUCTIVITY

PSAMMOPHYTES

PSAMMOPHYTIC SCRUB

RIPARIAN COMMUNITIES

SAVANNA

SHRUBS

STEPPE

SUCCESSION

SUCCULENTS

THORN FOREST. *See* CHACO

XENOPHYTES

XEROPHYLLOUS FOREST

XEROPHYTES

DESERT TAXA

ACACIA

AGAVE

ALGAE. *See* PLANTS

ALGARROBO. *See* MESQUITE

ARROWWEED

ARTEMISIA

BACTERIA

BEARGRASS

BOOJUM

BRITTLEBUSH

BROMELIADS

CACTACEAE. *See* CACTI

CACTI

CACTUS, COLUMNAR

CARDÓN

CATCLAW

CHAPARRAL

CHENOPODS. *See*
  CHENOPODIACEAE

CHENOPODIACEAE

CHOLLA

COTTONWOOD

CREOSOTE BUSH

CRYPTOGAMS

DESERT BROOM

DEVIL'S CLAW

EUPHORBIACEAE

FUNGI. *See* PLANTS

GOURDS

GRASSES

GREASEWOOD

GUAYULE

GUM ARABIC TREE. *See* LEGUMES

IRONWOOD

JOJOBA

JOSHUA TREE

LEGUMES

LICHENS

LOCOWEED

MESQUITE

MISTLETOE

MOSSES

OCOTILLO

ORGAN PIPE CACTUS

PALMS
PALOVERDE
POPPY
PRICKLY PEAR
PROSOPIS. *See* MESQUITE
RESURRECTION PLANT
SAGEBRUSH
SAGUARO
SALTBUSH
SALT CEDAR
TAMARISK. *See* SALT CEDAR
TUMBLEWEED
WELWITSCHIA
YUCCA

MORPHOLOGY, PHYSIOLOGY

ADVENTITIOUS ROOTS. *See* PLANT ROOTS, ADVENTITIOUS
BULBS
C$_3$ PLANTS
C$_4$ PLANTS
CAM PLANTS
FLOWERS
FRUITS
GERMINATION
LEAVES
METABOLIC WATER
MICROPHYLLY. *See* LEAVES
NITROGEN-FIXING PLANTS
PATHOGENS
PHOTOSYNTHESIS
PHREATOPHYTES
PHYSIOLOGY
PLANT ADAPTATIONS
PLANT DISPERSAL BY WIND. ANEMO-CHORY
PLANT ROOTS, ADVENTITIOUS
PLANTS
POLLINATION
PSAMMOPHYTES
ROOTS

SALT BALANCE
SEED DISPERSAL BY ANIMALS. ZOO-CHORY
SEEDS
STOMA
THORN
TRANSPIRATION
XENOPHYTES
XEROPHYTES

ANIMALS

GENERAL

ACTIVITY CYCLES, ANIMALS
ANIMAL ADAPTATIONS
BREEDING SEASON
BURROWING ANIMALS
CARRION EATERS
CARRYING CAPACITY
COLORATION
CONVERGENT EVOLUTION
COUNTERSHADING
CRESPUSCULAR
CRYPSIS
CYCLES. *See* ACTIVITY CYCLES, ANI-MALS
DIET
DORMANCY
ENDEMISM
FOSSORIAL ANIMALS. *See* BURROW-ING ANIMALS
GRANIVORY
HERBIVORY
HOWLING
LOCOMOTION
METAMORPHOSIS
NESTS, BIRD
NOCTURNAL
OMNIVORY
PARALLEL EVOLUTION
PIGMENT
REPRODUCTION

BUZZARD
CARACARA
CARRION EATERS
CONDOR
CROW
DOVE. *See* PIGEON
EMU
FINCH
FLAMINGO
FLICKER
GILA WOODPECKER
GRAY GULL
GUINEA FOWL
HAWK. *See* RAPTORS
HERON
HORNBILL
HUMMINGBIRD
IBIS
LARK
MALLEEFOWL
MOCKINGBIRD
MOUSEBIRD
NIGHTJAR
ORIOLES
OSTRICH
OVENBIRD
OWL
PARROT
PENGUIN
PIGEON
QUAIL
RAPTORS
RAVEN. *See* CROW
RHEA
ROADRUNNER
SANDGROUSE
SHRIKE
SPARROWS
STORK
SWIFT

TAPACULO
TINAMOU
VULTURE
WAXBILL
WEAVER
WOODPECKERS
WREN

MAMMALS

AARDVARK
AARDWOLF
ADDAX
AFRICAN LION
ANTELOPE
ARGALI
ARMADILLO
ASS
ATLAS BROWN CATTLE
AWASSI SHEEP
BABOON
BADGER
BARBARY DEER
BARBARY LION
BARBARY SHEEP
BAT
BIGHORN SHEEP
BLACKBUCK
BOBCAT
BURRO. *See* ASS
CAMEL
CAMELS, SOUTH AMERICAN
CARACAL
CARNIVORES
CARRION EATERS
CATS
CATTLE. *See* DOMESTIC ANIMALS
CAVY
CHEETAH
COATI
COYOTE
CYNOMYS. *See* PRAIRIE DOG

DASSIE RAT
DEER
DIK-DIK
DINGO
DOG, WILD
DOMESTIC ANIMALS
DONKEY. *See* ASS; DOMESTIC
    ANIMALS
ECHIDNA
ELAND
ELEPHANT
FENNEC
FERRET
FOX
GAZELLE
GEMSBOK
GENET
GERBIL
GERENUK
GIRAFFE
GOAT
GOPHER
GRASSHOPPER MOUSE
GROUND SQUIRREL
GUANACO. *See* CAMELS, SOUTH
    AMERICAN
GUNDI
HAMSTER
HARE
HARTEBEEST
HEDGEHOG
HETEROMYIDS
HUEMUL
HYENA
HYRAX
IBEX
JACKAL
JACKRABBIT
JAGUAR
JERBOA
KANGAROO

KANGAROO MOUSE
KANGAROO RAT
KLIPSPRINGER
KUDU
LION
LYNX. *See* BOBCAT; CARACAL
MAMMALS
MARA
MARSUPIALS
MEERKAT
MICE. *See* RODENTS
MOLE, GOLDEN
MOLE RAT
MONGOOSE
MONKEYS IN DESERTS
MOUFLON SHEEP
NYALA
ORYX
PACKRAT. *See* WOODRAT
PANGOLIN
PATAGONIAN "HARE". *See* MARA
PECCARY
PIKA
POCKET MOUSE
PORCUPINE
PRAIRIE DOG
PRONGHORN
PSAMMOMYS. *See* SAND RAT
PUMA
QUOKKA
RABBIT
RHINOCEROS
RINGTAIL
RODENTS
SAND RAT
SEA LION
SEAL
SERVAL
SHEEP
SHREW

NATIVE PEOPLES

CLIMATE

AN INTRODUCTION TO DESERTS

The men who first walked on the moon in 1969 returned with a famous picture that showed earthrise over the moon. We saw a gloriously blue planet dusted with white clouds and suspended in a lifeless black void. This photograph provided humanity with a new appreciation for the rarity of life and its incongruous persistence on this lonely planet fixed in the vastness of the solar system. It is instructive to view the earth from a distance to appreciate its rich diversity of life. If an alien scientist were to take a random sample of the earth's biota at only a single point on its surface, that point would very likely be an ocean, for oceans cover 71 percent of the earth and are thus its most extensive habitat. The earth's oceans are rich, both in diversity of species and in abundance of individual species, but the varied life forms of the sea that might be recorded by the alien biologist would provide only an incomplete view of life on our planet, for the sea poses stringent requirements for existence. The marine environment is full of challenges for organisms that live there, challenges that involve, among other things, water availability, salt balance, light, and temperature. Nevertheless, the alien's sample would show a wide range of organisms, from tiny algae to giant mammals.

What if our alien scientist took a second sample of the earth's species from a terrestrial habitat? That sample likely would be taken from a desert or semidesert area, for after oceans, these are one of the most common habitats on earth, encompassing more than 35 percent of the world's land area, or 61 million square kilometers. From this additional sample, the alien scientist would learn that life on land is certainly quite different from life in the sea, but the desert samples would also show a great diversity of species and a wide range of organisms, from tiny algae to giant mammals. Moreover, among the major challenges facing desert organisms are also water, salt balance, light, and temperature.

Thus a desert, which might be considered the antithesis of the sea, actually poses similar challenges to the evolution of life. Like the sea, deserts are not well studied. Like the sea, they are rich in species. Like the sea, they are unforgiving to

humans: without water, people stranded at sea or in the desert will die of thirst.

Humans and deserts have been inextricably linked across the ages, and it is important that we understand these marvelous areas, for they are a major component of our world. Deserts have been important throughout human history. The cradle of civilization is located in a dryland situated near the confluence of two great rivers. Indeed, agriculture was developed to deal with the sporadic rainfall and general aridity of the southern portion of the Tigris-Euphrates Valley (TIGRIS-EUPHRATES), and agriculture was what led to the development of modern civilization. Moreover, our very system of written laws dates back to Hammurabi, king of Babylonia from 1792 to 1750 B.C., whose first laws were written to deal with the use of water for agricultural purposes. Thus modern systems of codified laws were developed to permit people to live in an arid area and use its water to grow their crops. Humanity entered the nuclear age in the deserts of New Mexico (WHITE SANDS NATIONAL MONUMENT), and the Great Basin Desert of Nevada (GREAT BASIN DESERT) was selected for obliteration in the nuclear testing program that followed.

Deserts have been the scene for the development of great religions (RELIGION IN DESERTS) and theaters for great wars. They have inspired poets and artists, writers and scientists, philosophers and generals. Indeed, much of human history has taken place in deserts. Deserts make a major contribution to the remarkable nature of our planet and provide a home for innumerable species that are unknown outside the boundaries of arid lands. Far from being wastelands, deserts are habitats that are filled with unique forms of life. Ironically, the world's drylands are today considered threatened and fragile ecosystems—threatened by the very species, *Homo sapiens*, whose oldest civilizations were first formed there (CONSERVATION IN DESERTS).

Most of the world's deserts and semideserts form along both sides of the 30° latitudinal band in the Northern and Southern hemispheres. This occurs because as the warm tropical latitudes are heated, their moist air rises and cools and its moisture condenses, resulting in enormous quantities of rain falling in the tropics. As the cool air loses its moisture, it travels toward the poles at high altitudes. For a number of complex meteorological reasons, the cool, dry air descends at about 30° north and south latitudes. As it descends, it becomes hotter and its relative humidity drops (DESERTS). The great deserts of northern Africa, Australia, southern Africa, and the semiarid and arid areas of temperate North and South America are the result of these high pressure zones of descending warm air (*Subtropical Deserts*).

Deserts form for other reasons as well, including aridity that is due to cool offshore ocean currents (*Cool Coastal Deserts*). In western coastal regions in the Southern Hemisphere, where cold ocean currents abut a warm landmass, little moisture is transferred from the cold waters of the ocean to the air reaching the land. In these regions, the descending air mass, which is already dry, becomes even drier, resulting in some of the most arid deserts in the world. This is the case with the Sechura/Atacama desert system in Chile (CHILE, DESERTS OF) and Peru (PERU, DESERTS OF) and the Namib Desert in southwestern Africa (NAMIBIA, DESERTS OF). In the Northern Hemisphere, this same factor accounts for a part of the desert system of Baja California (BAJA CALIFORNIA, DESERTS OF).

In some places, deserts may form because they are located at the center of vast continents (*Continental Deserts*). As moist air travels from the sea over land, it begins to lose its moisture as rain. If the continent is sufficiently large, most of the water is lost before the winds reach the central parts of the continent. The arid deserts of central Asia are in part the result of their continental isolation, as are portions of the Australian Desert.

Rain Shadow Deserts may also form where barriers to wind and rain occur (DESERTS, RAIN SHADOW). For example, if a mountain range causes the prevailing winds to rise to higher altitudes—thus cooling the air and condensing the moisture in the form of rain—the air becomes quite dry as it travels over the mountain range and descends on the other side to lower elevations, warming as elevation decreases. Deserts form in zones where the moisture in the winds is removed by such significant geological barriers. Various deserts in North and South America and India, for example, are the result of being in the rain shadow of significant mountain chains.

We do not deal with the frigid deserts extensively in this volume, but it is important to note that at the polar regions the air is exceedingly cold and dry, resulting in *Polar Deserts* (in the Northern Hemisphere, the *Arctic Desert*; in the Southern Hemisphere, the *Antarctic Desert*). Because of the cold air, rain does not fall in these areas. Although snow and ice may fall, technically these areas are, in fact, frigid, arid deserts.

The drylands of the world exist along a continuum of environmental factors, including especially precipitation, although temperature, evaporation, and pattern of rainfall play important roles in characterizing the aridity of an area as well. A general rule has been that deserts receive irregular precipitation of less than 250 millimeters annually while experiencing high evaporation, and this value still serves as a loose definition of a desert. Various authors have distinguished between *hyperarid areas* (which some call true deserts), that is, zones receiving less than 25 millimeters of precipitation annually and having no rainy season, and *semiarid areas*, that is, zones receiving less than 600 millimeters of precipitation annually. The latter definition includes not only the most arid deserts within the broad category of drylands but also areas that experience long droughts and that may support grasses or shrubs. Included within hyperarid areas are parts of the Sahara of Africa, the Mojave of North America, the Namib of southern Africa, and the Atacama of Chile. Other zones falling within the more inclusive definition of a desert (e.g., the 250-millimeter precipitation zone) are the Great Basin, Chihuahuan, and Sonoran deserts of North America, much of the Australian Desert, the deserts of Argentina, portions of northern and southern Africa, and large parts of the Asian deserts. Semiarid areas, which pose challenges to existence similar to those of desert areas, include the scrublands and drier grasslands of the world. When the first European explorers crossed the Great Plains of North America, they referred to it as the Great American Desert, and a trek through the semiarid portions of New Mexico by the Spaniards was called the Dead Man's Journey (JORNADA DEL MUERTO).

Some of the oldest habitats on earth are deserts (the Namib Desert is a good example), and some of the oldest-known living organisms are species inhabiting deserts. An example is an ancient creosote bush that grows in the Mojave Desert and may be more than 11,000 years old—a single living organism that was more than 6,000 years old when the Great Pyramid of Cheops was constructed in the Sahara Desert.

Deserts and semideserts may support vast fields of dunes, extensive gallery forests, sparse scrublands, and salt lakes. One popular view of a desert is that of a wasteland containing mainly snakes and scorpions and a few sparse plants, but the world's deserts are rich in both animals and plants. The diverse flora of the desert includes highly unusual plants, such as the giant saguaro cactus of North America (SAGUARO), which can weigh up to 20 tons and live for 200 years, or the bizarre ground-hugging *Welwitschia* of Africa's Namib Desert, which has been called the weirdest plant on earth and which may live for more than 2,000 years (WELWITSCHIA). Depending on which desert one visits, a traveler may encounter armadillos or aardvarks, camels or cacti, elephants or emus, kangaroo rats or kangaroos, polar bears or penguins, rhinoceroses or rheas, vicuñas or velvet mites. The desert air may be filled with the soft cooing of mourning doves, the screeching of parrots, or the low thumping sounds of the burrowing tucu-tuco rodents of South America. Bighorn sheep, flamingos, camel spiders, aardwolves, and gemsbok all grace the desert landscape, as do fish, amphibians, and even shrimp that appear suddenly and miraculously after summer thundershowers, filling short-lived pools with teeming life in the midst of years of apparently lifeless aridity.

In this volume the reader will encounter many unusual and memorable phenomena, among them the world's fastest mammal (CHEETAH) and fastest rodent (MARA) and an Australian frog that remains buried under the arid desert soil in a state of torpor for up to five years during extended droughts and then suddenly appears on the surface in large numbers after an exceedingly rare rainfall (DORMANCY). There is a gull (GRAY GULL) that forages at sea but nests in the Atacama Desert of interior Chile, following a habit that was initiated by its ancestors long ago when Pleistocene lakes filled the area that is today among the most arid and barren habitats on the planet. In the deserts of North America, small rodents abound which are, in effect, climatologists and paleobotanists; they gather leaves, seeds, and sticks and cement these together in piles called MIDDENS, which provide an irreplaceable record of plant distribution and climatic change over thousands of years. In the Patagonian Desert of Argentina, penguins nest in burrows alongside desert rodents and guanacos (South American camels)(CAMELS, SOUTH AMERICAN; PENGUIN). The Devils Hole pupfish of the Mojave Desert (FISHES) has a geographic distribution of only 20 square meters, the smallest range of any species of vertebrate in the world. In this volume are reports of sand dunes more than 1,000 meters high (ASIA, DESERTS OF) and gypsum dunes as blindingly white as snow (WHITE SANDS NATIONAL MONUMENT). The people of the desert have included Jesus Christ and Muhammad (RELIGION IN DESERTS) and regionally important historical figures such as COCHISE and GERONIMO. The desert has always challenged organisms, whether as the Dead Man's Journey of the Spaniards in New Mexico or the *trekbookken* of millions of SPRINGBOK across southern Africa. In their adaptation to the challenges of aridity, desert organisms have evolved into some of most extraordinary plants and animals in the world, making deserts magically rich places filled with remarkable, but largely hidden, life.

Today deserts throughout the world are under a variety of threats from human activities. If the nomadic Bedouins of North Africa traveled across the desert leaving nothing but their ephemeral tracks, the armies of the allies and Iraq that fought the Gulf War left marks on the desert that will be visible for centuries. Vast agricultural projects use water from distant sources to make the desert bloom with extensive monocultures of plants destined for the dinner table, but the use of pesticides and of irrigation water that deposits salts on the desert soil drive native species from the farmlands and into ever-decreasing geographic ranges. Enormous cities that survive on irreplaceable fossil water continue to expand and destroy increasing amounts of desert habitats, leading to the disappearance of many desert species from a region. To survive in the desert heat, these cities eventually require water from other areas, and heroic plans have been implemented to aid their continued growth and insatiable need for water. Water conservation is seldom attempted. In Argentina, goats are grazed freely in the most arid habitats, reducing native species of plants and animals and leading to increased erosion and other habitat damage. In the deserts of the Middle East and North America, off-road vehicles destroy pristine sand dunes that support life forms that cannot live elsewhere, trampling plants that have survived since before Columbus landed in the New World. Despite the threat to deserts and their plants and animals on all continents, few countries have set aside sufficient land in reserves to protect the biota of these unique areas. Deserts have been ignored, their needs subordinated to the needs of habitats that appear more picturesque, richer in species, greener, wetter, and more popular in the public mind. But deserts are a part of our own history as a species, and if we lose these wondrous habitats, we will lose a part of our own history, a part of ourselves.

By visiting deserts and understanding them, we are privileged to witness life in all its variety and all its tenacity. Deserts, for all their climatological rigors, give us hope for renewed life—hope that life will find a way, regardless of the challenges it may face. Perhaps some of the world's great religions began in deserts because deserts, more than any other habitat, show us that life can overcome all obstacles to persist. Life in deserts can instruct us all in surmounting barriers, adapting to challenges, and waxing rich in isolation. Deserts are thus places of hope and wonder, places where we can appreciate nature and cultivate our humanity.—Michael A. Mares

See also **ANIMAL ADAPTATIONS; DESERTS; PLANT ADAPTATIONS**

Further Reading

Adolph, E. F. 1969. *Physiology of Man in the Desert*. New York: Hafner.

Alcock, J. 1985. *Sonoran Desert Spring*. Chicago: University of Chicago Press.

Allan, T., and A. Warren, eds. 1993. *Deserts: The Encroaching Wilderness*. New York: Oxford University Press.

Amiran, D. H. K., and A. W. Wilson, eds. 1973. *Coastal Deserts: Their Natural and Human Environments*. Tucson: University of Arizona Press.

Arritt, S. 1993. *The Living Earth Book of Deserts*. New York: Reader's Digest Assoc.

Axelrod, D. I. 1950. Evolution of desert vegetation in western North America. *Contributions to Paleontology, Carnegie Institution of Washington Publication* 590:215-306.

———. 1958. Evolution of the Madro-Tertiary Geoflora. *Botanical Review* 24(7):433-509.

Barbour, M. G., and W. D. Billings. 1988. *North American Terrestrial Vegetation*. Cambridge: Cambridge University Press.

Barker, W. R., and P. J. M. Greenslade. 1982. *Evolution of the Flora and Fauna of Arid Australia*. Adelaide: Peacock.

Bender, G. L., ed. 1982. *Reference Handbook on the Deserts of North America*. Westport, Conn.: Greenwood Press.

Blume, H.-P., and S. M. Berkowicz. 1995. *Arid Ecosystems*. Cremlingen-Destedt, Germany: Catena.

Brown, G. W., Jr., ed. 1968. *Desert Biology: Special Topics on the Physical and Biological Aspects of Arid Regions*. Vol. 1. New York: Academic Press.

———. 1974. *Desert Biology: Special Topics on the Physical and Biological Aspects of Arid Regions*. Vol. 2. New York: Academic Press.

Camacho, J. H. 1995. *Desiertos: Zonas áridas y semiáridas de Colombia*. Cali: Banco de Occidente Credencial.

Cloudsley-Thompson, J. L. 1996. *Biotic Interactions in Arid Lands*. New York: Springer.

Cloudsley-Thompson, J. L., and M. J. Chadwick. 1964. *Life in Deserts*. London: Foulis.

Cooke, R., A. Warren, and A. Goudie. 1993. *Desert Geomorphology*. London: University College London Press. Pp. 168-186.

Crawford, C. S. 1981. *Biology of Desert Invertebrates*. New York: Springer.

Evenari, M., I. Noy-Meir, and D. W. Goodall, eds. 1985. *Ecosystems of the World, Hot Deserts and Arid Shrublands*. Vol. 12 (2 pts.). New York: Elsevier.

Evenari, M., L. Shanan, and T. Naphtali. 1971. *The Negev*. Cambridge, Mass.: Harvard University Press.

Ferrari, M. 1996. *Deserts*. New York: Smithmark.

Flegg, J. 1993. *Deserts: A Miracle of Life*. New York: Facts on File; Blandford Press.

Glantz, M. H. 1977. *Desertification: Environmental Degradation in and Around Arid Lands*. Boulder, Colo.: Westview Press.

Goodall, D. W., and R. A. Perry, eds. 1979. *Arid-Land Ecosystems: Structure, Functioning and Management*. New York: Cambridge University Press.

Goodin, J. R., and D. K. Northington, eds. 1985. *Plant Resources of Arid and Semiarid Lands: A Global Perspective*. New York: Academic Press.

Gosh, P. K., and I. Prakash. 1988. *Ecophysiology of Desert Vertebrates*. Jodhpur: Scientific Publishers.

Hastings, J. R., and R. M. Turner. 1965. *The Changing Mile*. Tucson: University of Arizona Press.

Heathcote, R. L. 1983. *The Arid Lands: Their Use and Abuse*. New York: Longman.

Hills, E. S., ed. 1966. *Arid Lands: A Geographical Appraisal*. London: Methuen.

Ingram, D. L., and L. E. Mount. 1975. *Man and Animals in Hot Environments*. New York: Springer.

Jaeger, E. C. 1957. *The North American Deserts*. Stanford: Stanford University Press.

———. 1961. *Desert Wildlife*. Stanford: Stanford University Press.

Kerslake, D. 1972. *The Stress of Hot Environments*. London: Cambridge University Press.

Lane, B. C. 1998. *The Solace of Fierce Landscapes: Exploring Desert and Mountain Spirituality*. Oxford: Oxford University Press.

Leopold, A. S. 1962. *Life Nature Library. The Desert*. New York: Time Inc.

Louw, G. N., and M. K. Seely. 1982. *Ecology of Desert Organisms*. London: Longman.

Lovegrove, B. 1993. *The Living Deserts of Southern Africa*. Vlaeberg: Fernwood.

Mabbutt, J. A. 1977. *Desert Landforms*. Cambridge, Mass.: MIT Press.

Mabry, T. J., J. H. Hunziker, and D. R. DiFeo, Jr., eds. 1977. *Creosote Bush: Biology and Chemistry of Larrea in New World Deserts*. Stroudsburg, Pa.: Dowden, Hutchinson, and Ross.

McClaran, M. P., and T. R. Van Devender. 1995. *The Desert Grassland*. Tucson: University of Arizona Press.

McGinnies, W. G., B. J. Goldman, and P. Paylore, eds. 1968. *Deserts of the World: An Appraisal of Research into Their Physical and Biological Environments*. Tucson: University of Arizona Press.

MacMahon, J. A. 1985. *Deserts*. New York: Knopf.

McNamee, G. 1996. *A Desert Bestiary: Folklore, Literature, and Ecological Thought from the World's Dry Places*. Boulder, Colo.: Johnson Books.

McNeely, J. A. and V. M. Neronov, eds. 1991. *Mammals in the Palaeoarctic Desert: Status and Trends in the Sahara-Gobian Region*. Moscow: UNESCO Man and Biosphere Programme (MAB).

Millington, A. C., and K. Pye, eds. 1994. *Environmental Change in Drylands: Biogeographical and Geomorphological Perspectives*. New York: Wiley.

Nabhan, G. P. 1985. *Gathering the Desert*. Tucson: University of Arizona Press.

Noy-Meir, I. 1973. Desert ecosystems: Environment and producers. *Annual Review of Ecology and Systematics* 4:25-51.

———. 1974. Desert ecosystems: Higher trophic levels. *Annual Review of Ecology and Systematics* 5:195-214.

Owens, M., and D. Owens. 1984. *Cry of the Kalahari*. Glasgow: HarperCollins.

Petrov, M. P. 1976. *Deserts of the World*. New York: Wiley.

Polis, G. A., ed. 1991. *The Ecology of Desert Communities*. Tucson: University of Arizona Press.

Pond, A. W. 1962. *The Desert World*. New York: Nelson.

Prakash, I., and P. K. Ghosh, eds. 1975. *Rodents in Desert Environments*. Monographiae Biologicae. The Hague: Junk.

Pye, K., and H. Tsoar. 1990. *Aeolian Sand and Sand Dunes*. London: Unwin Hyman.

Quezel, P. 1965. *La vegetation du Sahara, du Tchad a la Mauritanie*. Stuttgart: Gustav Fischer.

Reisner, M. 1986. *Cadillac Desert: The American West and Its Disappearing Water*. New York: Viking Penguin.

Schmidt-Nielsen, K. 1964. *Desert Animals: Physiological Problems of Heat and Water*. New York: Oxford University Press.

Sears, E. 1935. *Deserts on the March*. Norman: University of Oklahoma Press.

Seely, M. 1992. *The Namib*. Windhoek, Namibia: Meinert.

Shephard, M. 1995. *The Great Victoria Desert*. Chatswood, NSW, Australia: Reed Books.

Shreve, F., and I. L. Wiggins. 1964. *Vegetation and Flora of the Sonoran Desert*. Vols. 1 and 2. Stanford: Stanford University Press.

Simpson, B. B., ed. 1977. *Mesquite: Its Biology in Two Desert Ecosystems*. Stroudsburg, Pa.: Dowden, Hutchinson, and Ross.

Takhtajan, A. 1986. *Floristic Regions of the World*. Berkeley: University of California Press.

Thomas, D. S. G. 1989. *Arid Zone Geomorphology*. London: Belhaven Press.

Thomas, D. S. G., and P. A. Shaw. 1991. *The Kalahari Environment*. New York: Cambridge University Press.

Trimble, S. 1995. *The Sagebrush Ocean: Natural History of the Great Basin*. Reno: University of Nevada Press.

United Nations Environment Programme. 1992. *World Atlas of Desertification*. London: Edward Arnold.

Walter, H. 1983. *Vegetation of the Earth*. New York: Springer.

Webb, R. H., and H. G. Wilshire, eds. 1983. *Environmental Effects of Off-Road Vehicles: Impacts and Management in Arid Regions*. New York: Springer.

Weissleder, W., ed. 1978. *The Nomadic Alternative: Modes and Models of Interaction in the African-Asian Deserts and Steppes*. Chicago: Aldine.

West, N. E., ed. 1983. *Ecosystems of the World: Temperate Deserts and Semi-deserts*. Vol. 5. New York: Elsevier.

Wickens, G. E., J. R. Goodin, and D. V. Field, eds. 1985. *Plants for Arid Lands*. London: Unwin Hyman.

Zohary, M. 1973. *Geobotanical Foundations of the Middle East*. Vols. 2 and 3. Amsterdam: Gustav Fischer.

CONTRIBUTORS

Dr. Rafiq Ahmad
Biosaline Research Programme
Department of Botany
University of Karachi
Karachi 75270, Pakistan
e-mail: biosal@biruni.erum.com

Ms. Juana Susana Barroso
Documentation and Information Service
Centro de Economía, Legislación y Administración
Instituto Nacional del Agua y del Ambiente
  (CELAA-INA)
Belgrano 210 (Oeste)
5500 Mendoza, Argentina
email: celaa@piemza.edu.ar

Dr. Janet K. Braun
Oklahoma Museum of Natural History
University of Oklahoma
Norman, OK 73019
e-mail: jkbraun@ou.edu

Lic. Antonia Paniza Cabrera
Instituto de Desarrollo Regional (Universidad de
  Granada)
Dr. Lopez Argueta s/n
18071 Granada, Spain
e-mail: fcorodri@goliat.ugr.es

Dr. Janalee P. Caldwell
Oklahoma Museum of Natural History and Depart-
  ment of Zoology
University of Oklahoma
Norman, OK 73019
e-mail: caldwell@ou.edu

Ing. Roberto Juan Candia
Instituto Argentino de las Zonas Áridas (IADIZA)
Parque General San Martín
5500 Mendoza, Argentina

Dr. Rob Channell
Department of Zoology
University of Oklahoma
Norman, OK 73019
e-mail: rchannell@ou.edu

Ms. Amanda Renner Charles
Department of Biological Sciences
Fort Hays State University
Hays, KS 67601-4099

Dr. Nicholas J. Czaplewski
Oklahoma Museum of Natural History
University of Oklahoma
Norman, OK 73019
e-mail: nczaplewski@ou.edu

Dr. Harold E. Dregne
Horn Professor Emeritus
International Center for Arid and Semiarid Land
  Studies
P.O. Box 41036
Texas Tech University
Lubbock, TX 79409-1036
e-mail: a1hed@ttacs.ttu.edu

Dr. John F. Eisenberg
Ordway Chair of Ecosystem Conservation
Florida Museum of Natural History
University of Florida
Gainesville, FL 32611-7800
e-mail: jfe@flmnh.ufl.edu

Dr. Kristina A. Ernest
Department of Biological Science
Central Washington University
Ellensburg, WA 98926-7537
e-mail: ernestk@cwu.edu

Dr. James R. Estes
Department of Botany and Microbiology
University of Oklahoma
Norman, OK 73019
Current address
Nebraska State Museum
Lincoln, NE 68588-0338
e-mail: jestes@unl.edu

Lic. Jorge M. Gonnet
Biodiversity Research Group
Instituto Argentino de las Zonas Áridas (IADIZA)
Parque General San Martín
5500 Mendoza, Argentina
e-mail: ctcricyt@criba.edu.ar

Dr. E. Annette Halpern
Biology Department
California State University
Bakersfield, CA 93311-1099
e-mail: ahalpern@csubak.edu

Dr. Ahmad K. Hegazy
Department of Botany
Faculty of Science
Cairo University
Giza, Egypt
e-mail: ahkhegazy@frcu.eun.eg

Dr. David S. Hinds
Biology Department
California State University
Bakersfield, CA 93311-1099
e-mail: dhinds@csubak.edu

Dr. Bruce W. Hoagland
Oklahoma Biological Survey and Department of
    Geography
University of Oklahoma
Norman, OK 73019
e-mail: bhoagland@ou.edu

Dr. Gary K. Hulett
Department of Biological Sciences
Fort Hays State University
Hays, KS 67601-4099
e-mail: bigh@fhsuvm.fhsu.edu

Dr. Thomas E. Lacher, Jr.
Caesar Kleberg Chair in Wildlife Biology
Department of Wildlife and Fisheries Sciences
Texas A&M University
College Station, TX 77843-2258
e-mail: tlacher@tamu.edu

Dr. A. Dennis Lemly
USDA, Forest Service
Southern Forest Experiment Station
Virginia Tech University
Blacksburg, VA 24061-0321

Dr. Stephen C. Lougheed
Director, International Summer School on Biodi-
    versity and Systematics
Department of Biology
Queen's University
Kingston, Ontario
Canada K7L 3N6
e-mail: lougheed@biology.queensu.ca

Dr. Barry G. Lovegrove
Department of Zoology
University of Natal
Pietermaritzburg, South Africa
e-mail: lovegrove@zoology.unp.ac.za

Dr. Richard E. MacMillen
705 Foss Road
Talent, OR 97540
e-mail: bidmac@jeffnet.org

Dr. E. A. (Tony) Mares
English Department
University of New Mexico
Albuquerque, NM 87131-2006
e-mail: tmares@unm.edu

Dr. Michael A. Mares
Oklahoma Museum of Natural History and Depart-
    ment of Zoology
University of Oklahoma
Norman, OK 73019
e-mail: mamares@ou.edu

Dr. Edie Marsh-Matthews
Oklahoma Museum of Natural History and Depart-
    ment of Zoology
University of Oklahoma
Norman, OK 73019
e-mail: emarsh@ou.edu

Dr. Federico Norte
Jefe de Unidad de Meteorología
Centro Regional de Investigaciones Científicas y
    Técnicas (CRICYT)
Parque General San Martín
5500 Mendoza, Argentina
e-mail: norte@cpsarg.com

Dr. Orlando Ocampo
Department of Foreign Language and Literature
Reilly Hall 208
Le Moyne College
Syracuse, NY 13214-1399
e-mail: ocampo@maple.lemoyne.edu

Dr. Ricardo A. Ojeda
Biodiversity Research Group
Instituto Argentino de las Zonas Áridas (IADIZA)
Parque General San Martín
5500 Mendoza, Argentina
e-mail: ctcricyt@criba.edu.ar

Dr. Richard A. Pailes
Department of Anthropology
University of Oklahoma
Norman, OK 73019
e-mail: rapailes@ou.edu

Ing. Virgilio G. Roig
Instituto Argentino de las Zonas Áridas (IADIZA)
Parque General San Martín
5500 Mendoza, Argentina
e-mail: vroig.planet.losandes.com.ar

Dr. Duane A. Schlitter
Executive Director, Museum Park
P.O. Box 28088
Sunnyside, Pretoria 0132, South Africa
e-mail: schlitda.nchm.co.za

Dr. Ernest M. Steinauer
Department of Botany and Microbiology
University of Oklahoma
Norman, OK 73019
Current address
153 Hummock Pond Road
Nantucket, MA 02554

Dr. Vatche P. Tchakerian
Department of Geography
Texas A&M University
College Station, TX 77843-3147
e-mail: vpt7728@venus.tamu.edu

Dr. Gordon E. Uno
Department of Botany and Microbiology
University of Oklahoma
Norman, OK 73019
e-mail: unobotany@ou.edu

Dr. Dan R. Upchurch
USDA-ARS Cropping Systems Research Laboratory
Route 3, Box 215
Lubbock, TX 79401
e-mail: dupchurch@mail.csrl.ars.usda.gov

Ing. Alberto I. J. Vich
Ecological Watershed Management Unit
Instituto Argentino de Nivología, Glaciología y Ciencias Ambientales (IANIGLA-CONICET)
Bajada del Cerro s/n, Parque General San Martín
5500 Mendoza, Argentina
e-mail: aijvich@cricyt.edu.ar

Dr. Laurie J. Vitt
Oklahoma Museum of Natural History and Department of Zoology
University of Oklahoma
Norman, OK 73019
e-mail: vitt@ou.edu

Dr. Linda L. Wallace
Department of Botany
University of Oklahoma
Norman, OK 73019
e-mail: lwallace@ou.edu

Dr. Ted M. Zobeck
USDA-ARS Cropping Systems Research Laboratory
Route 3, Box 215
Lubbock, TX 79401
e-mail: tzobeck@mail.csrl.ars.usda.gov

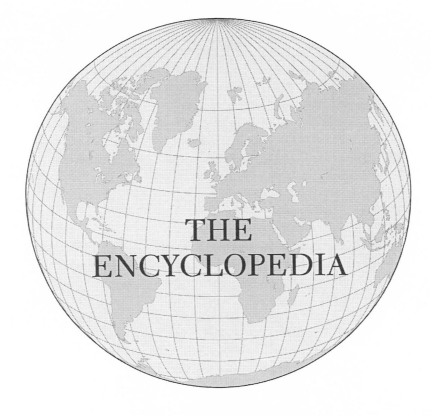

THE
ENCYCLOPEDIA

AARDVARK

One of the most unusual mammals (*Orycteropus afer*), loosely resembling a long-eared, long-snouted pig. The aardvark, also called antbear, is the only member of the family Orycteropodidae (order Tubulidentata). It has a long skull with small teeth that serve no apparent function. Aardvarks are distributed widely in Africa south of the Sahara (except in tropical western Africa and the Ethiopian horn). They occur in association with termite mounds in many habitats but are particularly common in open woodlands, savannas, scrub habitats and disturbed areas. The animals may stand 65 centimeters high at the shoulder and weigh up to 65 kilograms. "Aardvark" means "earth pig" in Afrikaans.

Aardvarks are solitary and nocturnal. They live in burrows that can be long and complex and frequently contain a large chamber. They emerge from their burrows late in the evening to forage almost exclusively on termites and ants, although several researchers have reported that they also consume small quantities of fruits and succulents. Indeed, there is a wild cucumber (*Cucumis humifructus*; known as the aardvark pumpkin) that grows 30 centimeters below the ground which is consumed by aardvarks for its moisture, highest in the maturing fruits during the driest part of the year. The aardvark is the only animal that can disseminate the seeds of this cucumber through its feces; thus the two species appear to be mutualists (i.e., they benefit one another through their association). Food is apparently found by smell. The termite mounds, when located, are excavated rapidly using the forefeet and claws. Aardvarks capture their prey by extending their very long tongue, which is covered by a slimy saliva, into the termite mounds. The tongue is retracted into the mouth with the ants or termites stuck to it. The major predators of aardvarks are large African cats, hyenas, hunting dogs, and humans.—Thomas E. Lacher, Jr.

See also **AFRICA, DESERTS OF; ANTS; BURROWING ANIMALS; MAMMALS; TERMITES**

Further Reading

Dorst, J., and P. Dandelot. 1980. A Field Guide to the Larger Mammals of Africa. London: Collins.

Nowak, R. M. 1991. Walker's Mammals of the World. 5th ed. Baltimore: Johns Hopkins University Press.

Shoshani, J., C. A. Goldman, and J. G. M. Thewissen. 1988. Orycteropus afer. Mammalian Species 300:1–8.

Skinner, J. D., and R. H. N. Smithers. 1990. The Mammals of the Southern African Subregion. Pretoria: University of Pretoria.

AARDWOLF

Insect-eating hyena (*Proteles cristatus*; mammalian family Hyaenidae, order Carnivora). This unusual hyena is found in Africa in two separate populations. The northern population extends in a band along the African coast from extreme southeastern Egypt to Central Tanzania; the southern population is distributed from southern Angola and southern Zambia to the Cape of Good Hope. Aardwolves are an indicator species of the Somalia-Kalahari semidesert, the two sections of which were joined during drier periods but are now separated by mesic (moist) forests in Zambia. Aardwolves prefer open sandy plains and savannas with a mean annual rainfall of 100–800 millimeters; they do not occur in forests or true deserts.

Aardwolves have a shoulder height of 450–500 millimeters and weigh 9–14 kilograms. The forelimbs have five digits and are longer than the hind limbs, which have four digits; the limbs are slender. The general coloration of the aardwolf is yellowish gray with black stripes. The legs have black bands above the knee and are completely black below the knee. A well-developed mane extends from behind the head to the black tip of the tail. The claws are blunt and do not retract. Both sexes have well-developed anal scent glands that are used for marking territories. The skull and jaw are not as robust as those of other species of hyenas, and, in contrast to all other hyenas, the teeth are reduced, small, and widely separated. The carnassials (the shearing molariform teeth that are present in many meat eaters, such as dogs) are not well developed, but the canines are large and sharp.

The diet of this nocturnal species consists of termites, primarily the nasute harvester termite, *Trinervitermes*, and the aardwolf may consume up to 300,000 termites in a single night. Hearing and smell may be used to locate foraging parties of termites. The southern African aardwolf may switch to the larger diurnal (active during the day) harvester termite, *Hodotermes*, in winter when it is too cold for *Trinervitermes* to be active. The broad spatulate tongue and production of large amounts of saliva help in obtaining large numbers of termites. Aardwolves are not carnivores in the sense that they are meat eaters, although they often use carrion as a source of insects.

Aardwolves do not generally dig their own dens. They may modify and use abandoned burrows of the springhare and, less commonly, those of the aardvark and African porcupine. They are generally water independent; most of the water they need is obtained from their termite diet. Pairs and family groups have been observed, but the aardwolf is generally solitary. The hairs of the mane are erected during interactions with other aardwolves or predators to give the appearance of larger size. One to five young are born after a gestation period of 90–110 days. Aardwolves are threatened by hunting and habitat destruction, and they may be rare in parts of the species' range.—Janet K. Braun

See also **AARDVARK; AFRICA, DESERTS OF; ARMADILLO; CARNIVORES; ECHIDNA; HYENA; MAMMALS; PANGOLIN; TERMITES**

Further Reading

Estes, R. D. 1991. *The Behavior Guide to African Mammals*. Berkeley: University of California Press.

Grzimek's Encyclopedia of Mammals. Vol. 3. 1990. New York: McGraw-Hill.

Kingdon, J. 1984. *East African Mammals: An Atlas of Evolution in Africa (Carnivores)*. Vol. 2A. Chicago: University of Chicago Press.

Koehler, C. E., and P. R. K. Richardson. 1990. Proteles cristatus. *Mammalian Species* 363:1–6.

Macdonald, D., ed. 1984. *The Encyclopedia of Mammals*. New York: Facts on File.

Nowak, R. M. 1991. *Walker's Mammals of the World*. 5th ed. Baltimore: Johns Hopkins University Press.

Skinner, J. D., and R. H. N. Smithers. 1990. *The Mammals of the Southern African Subregion*. Pretoria: University of Pretoria.

ABORIGINES. *See* DESERT PEOPLES

ACACIA

Large genus (about 17,000 species) of woody plants in the legume family (Fabaceae or Leguminosae) commonly found in deserts and warm desert grasslands throughout the world. Acacias are the flat-topped trees that characterize African savannas and semideserts. Acacia trees also compose a large part of the desert scrub community of the American Southwest, which consists of open stands of low-branching trees and shrubs, interspersed with short-lived herbaceous plants, and bare ground. Like other members of the family, acacias have compound, deciduous leaves and pods (legumes) as fruits. Whitethorn, or mescat acacia (*Acacia constricta*), is a locally abundant shrub along washes, slopes, and mesas from 700 to 1,500 meters in the Chihuahuan Desert. Deep rooted, growing up to three meters tall, and armed with paired white spines over three centimeters long, this species has small, fragrant, golden yellow flowers, with many stamens clustered into conspicuous balls extending from the stem on long stalks. Unlike many other legumes, whitethorn has little forage value and has become a weedy pest that encroaches on grasslands. In addition to its spines, whitethorn also produces poisonous hydrocyanic acid under certain conditions.

Other common acacias in North American deserts are the viscid acacia (*Acacia neovernicosa*) and the catclaw acacia (*Acacia greggii*), which has numerous short curved thorns like a cat's claws. Catclaw acacia flowers are small and yellowish and grow in cylindrical spikes. The seeds of the catclaw acacia were eaten by Native American tribes of Arizona and Mexico after first being ground into a meal and then converted into mush or cakes.

In the lowlands of southern Texas and adjacent Mexico acacia shrubs and mesquite trees have modified and, in many places, replaced the grasslands dominated by grama grass (*Bouteloua trifida*) and other grasses. This area receives from 40 to 75 centimeters of precipitation each year and has been commonly called the Texas semidesert. The introduction of cattle on the grasslands of this area has promoted the invasion of woody plants and *Opuntia* cacti. Cattle eat pods of legumes but do not digest the beans inside, which are then spread into the areas where the grass is overgrazed. A similar situation of overgrazing has allowed mesquite and acacia to replace grassland in southern Arizona. The spread of catclaw acacia has also been aided by its ability to resprout after fire in the desert grasslands.

Species of *Acacia* are of some economic importance. Australian species provide wattle bark, which is used in tanning. Several species are the source of useful timbers, and two species, *Acacia stenocarpa* and *Acacia senegal*, produce gum arabic that contributes to the production of many household products.—Gordon E. Uno

See also **ARIZONA DESERT; CACTI; CALIFORNIA DESERT; CATCLAW; COLORADO DESERT; LEGUMES; MESQUITE; MONTE DESERT; PAMPAS; PHREATOPHYTES; PLANT ADAPTATIONS; PLANTS; SHRUBS; SONORAN DESERT; XEROPHYLLOUS FOREST**

Further Reading

Bailey, L. H. 1935. *The Standard Cyclopedia of Horticulture*. New York: Macmillan.

Barbour, M. G., and W. D. Billings. 1988. *North American Terrestrial Vegetation*. New York: Cambridge University Press.

Brown, D. E., ed. 1994. *Biotic Communities: Southwestern United States and Northwestern Mexico*. Salt Lake City: University of Utah Press.

Heywood, V. H., ed. 1993. *Flowering Plants of the World*. Updated edition. New York: Oxford University Press.

McClaran, M. P., and T. R. Van Devender, eds. 1995. *The Desert Grassland*. Tucson: University of Arizona Press.

ACTIVITY CYCLES, ANIMALS

Divisions of the day or year wherein animals carry out behavioral activities such as sleeping, feeding, and mating. Animals have daily as well as seasonal activity cycles. In addition, most are either diurnal (active during the day), crepuscular (active at dawn or dusk), or nocturnal (active at night); relatively few species are active for more than one of these major periods. Activity cycles differ greatly among different organisms and depend on such factors as whether the climate is severe enough to warrant hibernation or estivation(dormancy during the summer), whether an organism is endothermic (warm blooded) or ectothermic (cold blooded), and the activity cycles of their predators and prey. Birds and mammals, which are endotherms, are active most of the year, except in cold northern deserts, where some mammals may hibernate and some birds may migrate to escape cold temperatures. Other mammals and birds are behaviorally adapted to withstand cold temperatures. In hot deserts diurnal species may be less active during the hottest part of the day, perhaps having a bimodal period of activity in the early morning and late afternoon (crepuscular). The desert iguana, *Dipsosaurus dorsalis*, lives in the harsh desert of the southwestern United States and has a preferred body temperature ranging from 38°C to 43°C. In summer extreme daytime temperatures permit this lizard to be active only for short periods early in the morning and late in the evening; however, the more favorable springtime conditions allow it to be active almost all day; thus activity cycles may change throughout the year, particularly in temperate deserts. Cactus wrens, common birds in deserts of the American Southwest, remain active during hot summer days but confine their daytime foraging to the shade of bushes and small trees. The length of time a cactus wren is active on a given day is dependent on light intensity, not on temperature.

For amphibians, activity cycles are highly dependent on rainfall. Many desert amphibians remain inactive throughout much of the year, coming to the surface only when seasonal rainfall begins. Amphibians are typically nocturnal, carrying out their breeding and feeding throughout the night. Desert amphibians often breed explosively during the first few days of rain after a prolonged drought; however, they may remain active for a month or two after breeding to feed and replenish nutrient reserves for the upcoming periods of estivation.

Desert insects also have activity periods. Some species of termites, for example, reduce aboveground activity considerably during hot summer periods and are not active at all above ground in the winter, when colder temperatures prevail. Thus most foraging above ground occurs in late summer and fall in conjunction with seasonal rain and cooler temperatures. Experiments with termites have revealed that soil moisture is the most important factor in regulating aboveground activity. Activity of desert ants generally increases after rainfall. Moreover, when temperatures drop, nocturnal ants become diurnal.—Janalee P. Caldwell

See also **ACTIVITY CYCLES, PLANTS (PHENOLOGY); AMPHIBIANS; ANIMAL ADAPTATIONS; BIRDS; CREPUSCULAR; ECTOTHERMY; ESTIVATION; HIBERNA-**

TION; INSECTS; LIZARDS; MAMMALS; NOCTURNAL; SNAKES

Further Reading

Anderson, A. H., and A. Anderson. 1973. *The Cactus Wren*. Tucson: University of Arizona Press.

Brown, G. W., Jr., ed. 1968. *Desert Biology: Special Topics on the Physical and Biological Aspects of Arid Regions*. Vol. 1. New York: Academic Press.

Cloudsley-Thompson, J. L. 1996. *Biotic Interactions in Arid Lands*. Berlin: Springer.

Schmidt-Nielsen, K. 1964. *Desert Animals: Physiological Problems of Heat and Water*. New York: Oxford University Press.

Vitt, L. J. 1991. Desert reptile communities. *In* G. Polis, ed., *The Ecology of Desert Communities*, 247–277. Tucson: University of Arizona Press.

Wiens, J. 1991. The ecology of desert birds. *In* G. Polis, ed., *The Ecology of Desert Communities*, 278–310. Tucson: University of Arizona Press.

ACTIVITY CYCLES, PLANTS (PHENOLOGY)

Divisions of time (daily, seasonal, yearly) during which biological activities of plants are carried out. The study of periodicity in plant activity is termed phenology. Various aspects of the biology of plants occur in diurnal (daily) or annual (yearly) cycles. Many desert species bloom in the late winter; others flower in spring or fall. Although the summer is often hot and dry, a few species, such as those in the genera *Wislizenia* and *Oxystylis* of the caper family, bloom even during that season. Furthermore, most individual plants within a species come into flower over a relatively short time span. This mass flowering increases the opportunity for cross-pollination. Seasonal flowering is typically controlled by temperature, moisture, or day length. Temperature and moisture may exert their control by determining when growth is initiated, although they may also provide false seasonal cues, such as a warm spell in late winter or aseasonal summer rains. Day length, in contrast, is very regular, with the shortest day of the year (in the Northern Hemisphere) always falling on or about December 21, and the longest on June 21. Therefore, changing day length can be used as a signal of seasonally associated phenomena to initiate a number of growth responses, including seed germination, bud break, sugar transport, leaf fall, and onset of flowering.

The effect of day length is complex and remains the subject of much research; however, the broad outlines are reasonably well understood. It is known that plants have pigments in their leaves called phytochromes that exist in two forms, each of which absorbs light at different wavelengths. One form (*Pr*) absorbs red light, and the other (*Pfr*) absorbs far red wavelengths. These two pigment forms are reversible, and each is converted to the other when it absorbs light. In the dark the far red form also slowly reverts to the red form. Plants use the phytochrome system to mark day length, and they may use this system to trigger responses that are seasonally dependent.

With respect to flowering, the periodicity of plants may be categorized as short-day, long-day, or day-neutral. The last group does not use the phytochrome system to regulate time of flowering. Short-day plants flower when darkness exceeds a critical length. Short-day plants, such as chrysanthemums, flower in the fall, when the day length is decreasing. Long-day plants, such as many lilies, flower in the spring, when the day length is increasing. Long-day plants flower when the dark period is shorter than a critical length. The conversion of *Pfr* to *Pr* in the dark is used by plants as a clock to measure the length of the dark period. Low temperature (vernalization) is also used by some plants to prevent premature flowering or bud bursting. Thus a sufficient period of cold temperature is required before processes such as growth and flowering can be initiated.

In addition to seasonal changes, some plants also change on a daily schedule. The showy white flowers of *Cnidoscolus*, an armed herb of dry, sandy habitats, first open at dusk; they are highly fragrant and produce a very sweet nectar. Other desert plants, including evening primrose, have similar patterns of flowering. Flowers of other species (e.g., dayflowers, *Commelina*) open in the early morning and close before evening. This diurnal behavior is helpful in coordinating the cycles of flowers with those of specific pollinators. For instance, *Cnidoscolus* and evening primrose are pollinated by night-flying hawkmoths that seek flowers by odor and need large amounts of sugar water to maintain their ability to fly at night. Dayflowers are visited primarily by day-flying bees and flies. Daily cycles have been studied in less detail than seasonal ones, but often they appear to be triggered by specific levels of light intensity. For some flowers, however, pollination initiates changes in color, shape, odor, and nectar production.—James R. Estes

See also **ACTIVITY CYCLES, ANIMALS; ANNUAL PLANTS; BEES; BULBS; DESERT BLOOM; FLOWERS; GERMINATION; GROWING SEASON; INSECTS; PLANT ADAPTATIONS; PLANTS; SEEDS**

Further Reading

Cloudsley-Thompson, J. L. 1996. *Biotic Interactions in Arid Lands*. Berlin: Springer.

Goodin, J. R., and D. K. Northington, eds. 1985. *Plant Resources of Arid and Semiarid Lands: A Global Perspective*. New York: Academic Press.

Hills, E. S., ed. 1966. *Arid Lands: A Geographical Appraisal*. London: Methuen.

Leopold, A. S. 1962. *Life Nature Library: The Desert*. New York: Time Inc.

Orians, G. H., and O. T. Solbrig, eds. 1977. *Convergent Evolution in Warm Deserts*. Stroudsburg, Pa.: Dowden, Hutchinson, and Ross.

ADAPTATIONS, ANIMALS. See ANIMAL ADAPTATIONS

ADAPTATIONS, PLANTS. See PLANT ADAPTATIONS

ADAPTIVE STRATEGIES, ANIMALS. See ANIMAL ADAPTATIONS

ADAPTIVE STRATEGIES, PLANTS. See PLANT ADAPTATIONS

ADDAX

Species of hoofed mammal (*Addax nasomaculatus*) in the family Bovidae of the order Artiodactyla. The Bovidae is a large taxon that includes antelopes, goats, sheep, and cattle. Addax are restricted to desert and semidesert areas of the western Sahara; and once ranged from Mauritania to Egypt and perhaps as far east as the Arabian Peninsula. Addax now are classified by the International Union for the Conservation of Nature (IUCN) as one of the world's most endangered mammals . The only known remaining wild population occurs in northeastern Niger and numbers fewer than 200 individuals. There are approximately 400 individuals in captivity.

Addax are extremely well adapted to desert life. They are able to exist without drinking free water and obtain all their water from the plants they consume. At one time they were common across the Sahara in herds of 20 to 200 animals. They do not establish territories; rather, they are nomadic and migrate over great distances in search of food. Males and females are similar, and both sexes have long, spiraling horns that can reach a length of 90 centimeters. Their color changes with the seasons; in winter they are grayish brown, but they turn almost white in the summer. Wild populations give birth in late winter, and the offspring mature in two to three years. They have lived as long as 19 years in captivity.

The current status of the addax in their native habitat is extremely precarious. They are heavily persecuted by hunters and have been severely affected by recent droughts. It is not known whether they will be able to survive in the wild.—Thomas E. Lacher, Jr.

See also **ANTELOPE; MAMMALS; SAHARA DESERT; UNGULATES**

Further Reading

Dorst, J., and P. Dandelot. 1980. *A Field Guide to the Larger Mammals of Africa*. London: Collins.

Estes, R. D. 1991. *The Behavior Guide to African Mammals*. Berkeley: University of California Press.

Grzimek's Encyclopedia of Mammals. Vol. 5. 1990. New York: McGraw-Hill.

Haltenorth, T., and H. Diller. 1980. *A Field Guide to the Mammals of Africa, Including Madagascar*. London: Collins.

Nowak, R. M. 1991. *Walker's Mammals of the World*. 5th ed. Baltimore: Johns Hopkins University Press.

ADDER

Common name for venomous snakes (order Squamata) of the Old World that are in the genera *Acanthophis*, *Bitis*, *Vipera*, and *Causus*. These genera are in two very different families: *Acanthophis* is in the family Elapidae and occurs in Australia; the others are in the family Viperidae and occur in Africa, Europe, and Asia. None of the New World viperids (e.g., rattlesnakes) are called adders. Elapids are highly venomous snakes with fixed front fangs (e.g., coral snakes and cobras); viperids are also highly venomous snakes but with movable front fangs.

Although most species of adder do not occur in deserts, a few are confined to desert habitats and share sets of adaptations with other desert snakes. For example, the dwarf sand adder (*Bitis peringueyi*) lives in areas of fine, windblown sand in the Namib Desert of Namibia and Angola in southwestern Africa. With the exception of lacking the "horns" above the eyes, it is very similar ecologically and behaviorally to the horned vipers (*Cerastes*) of North African deserts and to the sidewinder (*Crotalus cerastes*) of the southwestern deserts of North America. These small-bodied snakes use sidewinding locomotion to move across the sand and can disappear into the sand within a few seconds. Other desert species include the horned adder, *Bitis caudalis,* which occurs in southern Africa from Angola to Zimbabwe and Namaqualand, and the hornsman adder, *Bitis cornuta,* which occurs in desert areas of the Cape Province. These latter two species are morphologically and ecologically similar to the desert species described above, and both have enlarged scales over the eyes forming "horns."—Laurie J. Vitt

See also **ANIMAL ADAPTATIONS; COBRA; CORAL SNAKE; DEFENSIVE ADAPTATIONS, ANIMALS; POISONOUS ANIMALS; RATTLESNAKE; SIDEWINDER; SNAKES; VENOM**

Further Reading

Broadley, D. G. 1983. *Fitzsimons' Snakes of Southern Africa.* Johannesburg: Delta Books.

Shine, R. 1991. *Australian Snakes: A Natural History.* Sydney: Reed.

ADIABATIC PROCESSES

Atmospheric energy conversions that take place without a transfer of heat occurring within a system (such as an air parcel and its surroundings); that is, neither heat gain nor heat loss occurs. The most common adiabatic atmospheric phenomena are those that involve a change in air temperature due to a change in the pressure of the air. If the pressure of an air mass decreases (such as by moving up a mountain), the air will expand. If no heat is taken from the surrounding air to accomplish this, the energy required to do the work is taken from the heat energy of the rising air mass itself, resulting in a decrease in the temperature of the air mass (i.e., rising air becomes cooler). If a rising air parcel of unsaturated (dry) air expands and cools adiabatically, the cooling rate of the air is called the dry adiabatic lapse rate and amounts to 10°C for every 1,000 meters of increase in elevation. In a rising parcel of air, the point at which the relative humidity approaches 100 percent and condensation takes place results in the ascending air no longer cooling at the dry adiabatic rate (since heat was obtained

from the condensation of water). Thus, when moist, air cools more slowly at the moist adiabatic lapse rate of about 6°C per 1,000-meter increase in elevation. In a similar manner, as less dense air descends to lower elevations its pressure increases and the air becomes warmer and drier through adiabatic processes.

An example of how air movement over a mountain can have profound effects on vegetation will illustrate the importance of these processes. As fairly dry air approaches a mountain, it is deflected upward. It expands and cools as it rises, eventually reaching a point at which the water in the air condenses, forming clouds, fog, or rain. Increased precipitation and cooler temperatures at the higher elevations lead to increased vegetation on the mountain on the windward side. As the air travels over the mountain, it descends on the leeward side, becoming drier and warmer at lower elevations. In these areas the exceedingly dry, hot air can lead to the formation of rain shadow deserts. Similarly, air descending around 30° north and south latitudes that is heated adiabatically is one of the major reasons that deserts form in these regions.—Federico Norte

See also **AN INTRODUCTION TO DESERTS; BAROMETRIC PRESSURE (ATMOSPHERIC PRESSURE); CLIMATE; CLOUDS; CONVECTIVE STORM; DESERTS; DESERTS, MONTANE; DESERTS, RAIN SHADOW; FOG DESERT; HEAT; LOW PRESSURE**

Further Reading

Day, J. A., and V. J. Schaefer. 1991. *Clouds and Weather.* Boston: Houghton Mifflin.

Gates, D. M. 1972. *Man and His Environment: Climate.* New York: Harper and Row.

Oliver, J. E., and R. W. Fairbridge, eds. 1987. *The Encyclopedia of Climatology.* New York: Chapman and Hall.

Schaefer, V. J., and J. A. Day. 1981. *A Field Guide to the Atmosphere.* Boston: Houghton Mifflin.

Schneider, S. H., ed. 1996. *Encyclopedia of Climate and Weather.* 2 vols. New York: Oxford University Press.

ADOBE

A common clay containing quartz and many other minerals, which, when water is added to it, becomes soft and malleable. The adobe clay is then mixed with straw or horse hair and shaped into an adobe brick (commonly called an "adobe"). When the brick dries, it is very hard and suitable for con-

Relatively modern adobe building in the Monte Desert of northwestern Argentina, with pre-Andean mountains in the background. (Photo: M. A. Mares)

struction, particularly in dry climates, where it is not subjected to rapid erosion by rain.

Adobe is found in abundance in arid and semiarid parts of Africa, the Middle East, and the American Southwest, where it is frequently used in construction. When the Spaniards first explored what was later to become the American Southwest in 1540, they encountered agrarian Indians living in villages constructed of adobe. The Spaniards were well acquainted with adobe from their North African experience. Seeing the well-ordered villages, usually located near the Rio Grande and its tributaries, they used the Spanish word *pueblos* to refer to them. The name stuck. The pueblos of the Southwest, in addition to their ethnic, cultural, political, and social significance, are also fine examples of large structures built of adobe.

There are many advantages to adobe construction in an appropriate climate. The clay acts as a natural insulator, so that an adobe house remains cool in summer and warm in winter with minimal heating. Despite the existence of many other modern building materials, adobe continues to be very popular in the American Southwest and elsewhere.—E. A. Mares

See also **DESERT PEOPLES; HOPI; JORNADA DEL MUERTO; NAVAJO (DINE'É); RIO GRANDE**

Further Reading

McHenry, P. G. 1985. *Adobe: Build It Yourself*. Tucson: University of Arizona Press.

———. 1989. *Adobe and Rammed Earth Buildings*. Tucson: University of Arizona Press.

Rudofsky, B. 1969. *Architecture Without Architects*. New York: Doubleday.

ADVENTITIOUS ROOTS. *See* PLANT ROOTS, ADVENTITIOUS

AEOLIAN DEPOSITS. *See* WIND EROSION

AEOLIAN EROSION. *See* WIND TRANSPORT

AESTIVATION. *See* ESTIVATION

AFGHANISTAN, DESERTS OF

Country situated on the eastern side of the Irano-Afghan Plateau, a southward extension of the Central Asian mountain ranges, and bordered by Tajikistan, Uzbekistan, Turkmenistan, Iran, and Pakistan. It occupies an area of 650,000 square kilometers at an average elevation of 600–3,000 meters. The climate is a typical semiarid steppe (grassy) that is extremely cold in winter and hot in summer. Winter is strongly influenced by northerly and northwesterly winds coming from the Arctic and Atlantic oceans which bring snowfall and severe cold weather to the highlands and rain to lower elevations. Winter temperatures drop to -15°C; summer temperatures of 35°C have been recorded in the drought-ridden southwestern plateau. Annual precipitation increases from west to east. An average of about 400 millimeters per year has been recorded in mountainous areas, whereas in the arid region of Farah, annual rainfall is only 75 millimeters. Sandy deserts are situated in southern Afghanistan. Brief descriptions of some of the major desert areas follow.

The *Sistan Depression* (sometimes called the Sistan Desert) is located in southwestern Afghanistan in the region where the Helmand and Farah rivers enter Hamu-i-Salbari Lake. The water in the area of the delta evaporates, leaving behind salts. The Sistan Depression occupies an area of about 2,500 square kilometers at an altitude of 300–350 meters. The northern portion of the delta is converted into a large marsh during periods of flooding, whereas the southern delta is less swampy. Winter temperatures often fall below zero, and the summer

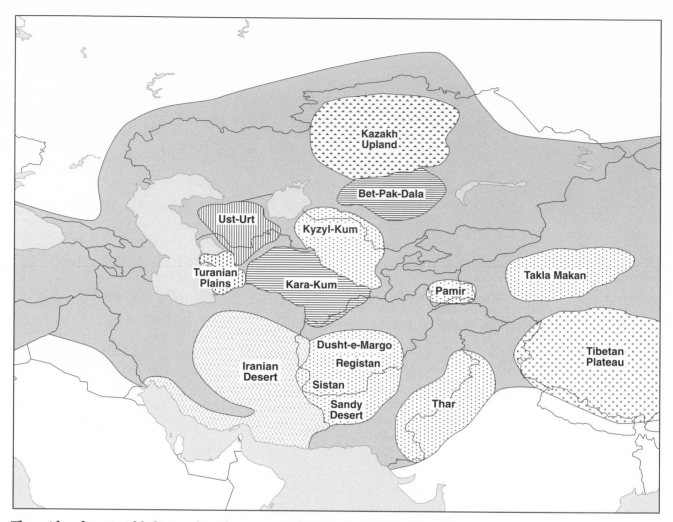

The arid and semiarid habitats of southwestern and central Asia, including major deserts. Shading indicates desert and semidesert limits. The dark shading covers a region that includes both arid and semiarid habitats.

is hot and dry. Much of the area near Helmand in the Norun region is covered by moving sand. Herbaceous shrubs (e.g., *Lagonychium farcatum*, *Lasiagrostis megastachya*, and *Schanginia baccata*), are found growing in this area, along with *Heliotropium lasiocarpum*. Many species of *Tamarix* grow in areas supporting saline swamps.

Registan, a sandy desert, is situated on the eastern side of the Halmand River below Kandhar at an elevation of 500–1,500 meters. It extends over an area of 40,000 square kilometers between mountain ranges and continues southward to Chagai in the region of Kalat in Pakistan. It is a hot, hyperarid region consisting mainly of sand dunes, with loose sand blowing south in response to the northerly winds. Riverbeds in the area are buried under accumulations of shifting sand. Summer mean monthly temperatures are around 32°C.

The *Dusht-e-Margo* (= Dasht-i-Margo) is another clayey-gravelly desert situated between the Khash Bud and Helmand rivers at elevations from 450 to 1,000 meters. There are many dry sandy river basins in the region, and takyrs and solonchaks (enclosed depressions in which salts accumulate) in the southwestern part of this desert. Vegetation is mostly halophytes.—Rafiq Ahmad

See also **ASIA, DESERTS OF; DESERTIFICATION; HALOPHYTES; INDUS RIVER; IRRIGATION DRAINAGE; PLAYA; SALT; STONE PAVEMENT**

Further Reading

Chouhan, T. S., ed. 1993. *Natural and Human Resources of Rajasthan*. Jodhpur: Scientific Publishers.

Hills, E. S., ed. 1966. *Arid Lands: A Geographical Appraisal*. London: Methuen.

McGinnies, W. G., B. J. Goldman, and P. Paylore, eds. 1968. *Deserts of the World: An Appraisal of Research into Their Physical and Biological Environments.* Tucson: University of Arizona Press.

Nir, D. 1974. *The Semi-arid World: Man on the Fringe of the Desert.* London: Longman.

Petrov, M. P. 1976. *Deserts of the World.* New York: Wiley.

Walter, H. 1983. *Vegetation of the Earth.* Berlin: Springer.

West, N. E., ed. 1983. *Ecosystems of the World: Temperate Deserts and Semi-deserts.* Vol. 5. New York: Elsevier.

AFRICA, DESERTS OF

Second-largest continent after Asia, lying to the south of Europe (from which it is separated by the Mediterranean Sea) and to the southwest of Asia (from which it is separated by the Red Sea) and bounded by the Indian Ocean on the east and the Atlantic Ocean on the west. The African continent approaches a land connection with another continent only in the northwest, where it is separated from Asia by the Suez Canal, the Gulf of Suez, and the Red Sea. The great continent of Africa, with more than 30.3 million square kilometers of territory, is built on ancient granites (3.2 billion years old) and other rocks and extends across more than 70° of latitude (37° north to almost 37° south latitude) and longitude (18° west to about 51° east longitude), crossing the equator and including vast deserts and semideserts within its boundaries. In the north the continent mainly includes the enormous Sahara Desert, the world's largest desert (approximately 7.4 million square kilometers), which is continuous with the desert of the Arabian Peninsula and southern Asia. The Sahara, which has vast sand seas as well as immense areas that are essentially devoid of vegetation, also contains significant mountain chains: the Atlas Mountains in the northwest, the Ahaggar Mountains in the west central region, and the Tibesti Mountains in the east central region. In Sudan and Ethiopia, at its eastern extreme, the Sahara is called the Nubian Desert. The only major river that traverses the Sahara is the Nile, the longest river in the world (6,650 kilometers).

North of the Sahara, along the Mediterranean coast, are various semiarid scrublands. The Sahel, an extensive semidesert scrub, is situated south of the Sahara and extends across the breadth of the continent in a narrow band. South of the Sahel is another, wider band of vegetation that crosses the continent from west to east and includes steppe vegetation, and south of this band is an even wider belt of grassland vegetation. Various types of rain forest vegetation are found within the tropics on both sides of the equator. South of the tropical rain forest, grassland and semiarid scrubland again appear, grading to the Kalahari and Namib deserts and the complex vegetation types (including the fynbos) that characterize the southern tip of Africa.

The band of aridity in northern Africa that includes the Sahara developed because of the zone of descending dry air that occurs around 30° north and 30° south latitude. The desert habitats of southern Africa also developed along the 30° south latitudinal band. In addition, the Namib Desert has resulted in part from its position along a western coastline with cold offshore water and dry air over the land, making this a cool, coastal desert, subject to fogs and extremely arid.

Africa supports an extremely complex and rich flora and fauna, including large numbers of endemic (found nowhere else) families, genera, and species. This is suggestive of both ancient age over which speciation could have occurred and the effects of isolation, as the continent was effectively an island for at least two extended periods (from about 90 million to 30 million years ago and again from about 23 million to 17 million years ago). Human populations on the continent have been large and growing for thousands of years. Their numbers and the widespread use of domestic livestock have had a profound effect on the flora and fauna of the continent, so that few unmodified habitats remain.

Africa is the only place on earth where a hint of the ancient megafauna still survives to any significant degree, and those species most characteristic of the continent (e.g., elephants, rhinoceroses, zebras, giraffes, antelopes) reflect the rich Pleistocene fauna of North and South America and Eurasia before massive extinctions occurred.

Most of the African continent is desert, semidesert, or grassland, and the unique adaptations of the plants and animals of the continent reflect this long association with aridity.—Michael A. Mares

See also **AN INTRODUCTION TO DESERTS; ARABIAN GULF, DESERTS OF; DESERTS; FYNBOS; ISRAEL, DESERTS OF; JORDAN, DESERTS OF; KALAHARI**

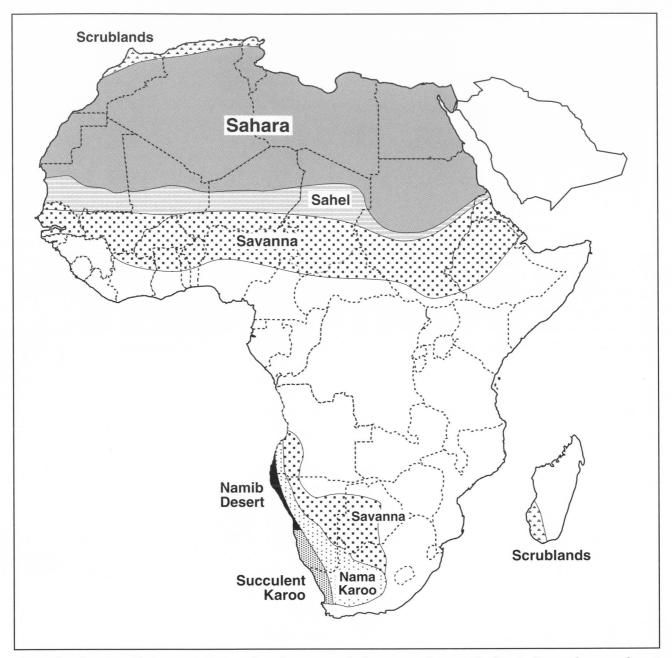

The arid and semiarid habitats of Africa and Madagascar, including major deserts. Shading indicates desert and semi-desert limits.

DESERT; KAROO; LEBANON, DESERTS OF; LIBYA, DESERTS OF; MIDDLE EAST, DESERTS OF; NAMIBIA, DESERTS OF; SAHARA DESERT; SAUDI ARABIA, DESERTS OF; SOUTH AFRICA, DESERTS OF

Further Reading

Cloudsley-Thompson, J. L., ed. 1984. *Key Environments: Sahara Desert.* New York: Pergamon Press, in collaboration with the International Union for the Conservation of Nature and Natural Resources.

Cowling, R. M., D. M. Richardson, and S. M. Pierce. 1997. *Vegetation of Southern Africa.* Oxford: Cambridge University Press.

Grenot, C. J. 1974. Physical and vegetational aspects of the Sahara Desert. *In* G. W. Brown Jr., ed., *Desert Biology: Special Topics on the Physical and Biological Aspects of Arid Regions,* 2:103–164. New York: Academic Press.

Haltenorth, T., and H. Diller. 1980. *A Field Guide to the Mammals of Africa, Including Madagascar.* London: Collins.

Kingdon, J. 1989. *Island Africa*. Princeton: Princeton University Press.

Lovegrove, B. 1993. *The Living Deserts of Southern Africa*. Vlaeberg: Fernwood.

McGinnies, W. G., B. J. Goldman, and P. Paylore, eds. 1968. *Deserts of the World: An Appraisal of Research into Their Physical and Biological Environments*. Tucson: University of Arizona Press.

Nir, D. 1974. *The Semi-arid World: Man on the Fringe of the Desert*. London: Longman.

Swearingen, W. D., and A. Bencherifa. 1996. *The North African Environment at Risk*. Boulder, Colo.: Westview Press.

Walter, H. 1983. *Vegetation of the Earth*. Berlin: Springer.

AFRICAN LION

Largest cat species (*Panthera leo*) of the family Felidae (mammalian order Carnivora) found in Africa. The current distribution of the African lion is between approximately 20° north latitude and 23° south latitude, extending to about 27° south latitude in Natal and in northern Namibia. In all cases the lion is restricted to open forests and savannas, including dry savanna and semidesert. Lions can occur at high elevations up to 4,500 meters in East Africa. Male and female lions are easily distinguished. Males are larger (up to 250 kilograms) and have a large mane covering the head and neck. Females lack the mane and are much smaller, reaching only 180 kilograms.

Lions are the largest predators in Africa. They have a complex social system of groups, or prides, consisting of one or more adult males, several females, and large numbers of subadults and juveniles. The breeding system is polygamous, with one male mating with the various females in the pride. The adult females do much of the hunting. The dominant male arrives at the end of the hunt and often will chase other lions away while it feeds. Lions prey on a variety of animals but prefer larger prey, especially antelopes, giraffes, zebras, and buffalo. They hunt primarily at night but may be active during the day. Lions are almost without enemies; the only animals that will occasionally attack an adult lion are packs of African wild dogs and hyenas. Outside of protected areas the African lion is declining rapidly in numbers as natural habitat gives way to the expansion of agriculture.—Thomas E. Lacher, Jr.

See also **CARNIVORES; CATS; NAMIBIA, DESERTS OF**

Further Reading

Dorst, J., and P. Dandelot. 1980. *A Field Guide to the Larger Mammals of Africa*. London: Collins.

Estes, R. D. 1991. *The Behavior Guide to African Mammals*. Berkeley: University of California Press.

Haltenorth, T., and H. Diller. 1980. *A Field Guide to the Mammals of Africa, Including Madagascar*. London: Collins.

Nowak, R. M. 1991. *Walker's Mammals of the World*. 5th ed. Baltimore: Johns Hopkins University Press.

Schaller, G. B. 1972. *The Serengeti Lion: A Study of Predator-Prey Relations*. Chicago: University of Chicago Press.

Skinner, J. D., and R. H. N. Smithers. 1990. *The Mammals of the Southern African Subregion*. Pretoria: University of Pretoria.

AGAVE

Common and scientific name of one of the most economically important plant genera in the family Agavaceae. About 300 species of agaves exist worldwide in arid climates, and several live in the deserts of the southwestern United States and northern Mexico. Agaves are succulents, storing water in large, stiff, fleshy, and sharp-pointed leaves that grow from a basal rosette. Larger agaves are commonly called century plants because of the extended length of time (10–15 years) that individuals remain in a vegetative state before producing a tall flowering stalk (up to eight meters) with many flowers. On flowering and producing seeds, the plant dies. If the young flowering stalk of *Agave americana* is removed, a sweet sap may be collected and fermented to produce pulque, an alcoholic beverage that can be drunk immediately or distilled to produce mescal. Mexican Indians also used the sticky fluid from the agave leaves as a healing salve. Smaller *Agave* species are commonly called lechuguillas, because of their resemblance to a head of lettuce (*lechuga* is the Spanish word for lettuce). These agaves produce shorter flowering stalks than the century plants and are species indicative of the Chihuahuan Desert.

A number of agaves produce strong, durable fibers used for a variety of purposes, including cordage, fishnets, and floor matting. The two most important species in fiber production are *Agave sisalana*, which produces true sisal, and *Agave fourcroydes*, which produces henequen, another fiber that is often called sisal. These fibers are classified as "hard" because their cells are impregnated with

Century plant, *Agave*, near Colima, Mexico. (Photo: M. A. Mares)

lignin (an important celluloselike substance found in wood). Leaves are cut from mature plants and crushed between large rollers, or soaked in water and pounded. The soft mush of the leaves is scraped away to reveal long fibers (up to one meter in length), which are then washed, dried, and made into cords, twine, or rope. Most ropes used in sailing today are synthetic; however, sisal fibers are sometimes still used even though they are not as strong as synthetic fibers. Sisal cordage is hard wearing, has low stretch characteristics, and is resistant to heat and sunlight. Commercial production of these hard agave fibers centers in Central America and eastern Africa. Agave plants may produce up to 300 leaves during their lifetime. Lechuguilla also produces a less important fiber, istle or Tampico fiber. These fibers are coarse and stiff and often are used to make scrubbing brushes as well as rough cordage.—Gordon E. Uno

See also **CHIHUAHUAN DESERT; PLANT ADAPTATIONS; PLANTS; SUCCULENTS; TEXAS DESERT**

Further Reading

Lewington, A. 1990. *Plants for People*. New York: Oxford University Press.
Schery, R. W. 1972. *Plants for Man*. Englewood Cliffs, N.J.: Prentice-Hall.

AGRICULTURALISTS. *See* DESERT PEOPLES

AGRICULTURE IN DESERTS

Agricultural activities, including the production of grain, fruit, and other crops, demand significant amounts of water. Thus aridity and agriculture would appear to be incompatible; however, desert habitats, under the proper circumstances, can be quite productive, leading to significant commercial production of various food and other products. Indeed, the oldest agriculture known has occurred in deserts, and desert agricultural activities today range from subsistence farming to massive agribusiness.

Arid and semiarid habitats account for 30 percent of the world's land area, and more than 850 million people inhabit such regions, fully 20 percent of the world population. In all such areas evapotranspiration exceeds rainfall, meaning that more water is lost to the atmosphere than is gained from rain. Geoclimatic factors have led to the formation of arid and semiarid zones in five major regions: *North Africa—Eurasia*, including the great deserts of the Sahara, the arid steppes of the former Soviet Union, China, and Mongolia, and the deserts of eastern Africa, the Arabian and Persian gulfs, and the Indo-Pakistan region; *South America*, including an arid and semiarid zone extending along the western portions of the continent, mainly to the west of the great Andean mountain chain, and the arid and semiarid portions of Argentina (Monte Desert, Chaco, Patagonia) and Chile; *Southern Africa*, with its broad zone of aridity consisting mainly of the Namib Desert, the Kalahari, and the Karoo; *North America*, including the desert Southwest of the United States, northern Mexico, and the Baja California peninsula; and *Australia*, especially the central and western parts of this largely desert continent.

Although deserts and semideserts are primarily zones with little water, there are several sources of water that can be used in each area for agricultural purposes. For example, in mountainous regions runoff water from orographic (mountain) rains can be captured through dams and stored for later use. The water is moved from the dam to the crops through irrigation ditches, canals, or underground pipes. This mechanism of water capture and later distribution is known as water spreading or spate irrigation, and has been used for more than 4,000 years, beginning in the Middle East (e.g., the Negev Desert of Israel and adjacent countries). Similar practices have been in place in the arid southwestern United States (e.g., New Mexico, where the Hopi termed this type of irrigation agriculture *akchin*) for more than 1,000 years. In Argentina, when the Spanish invaders arrived in the arid region of Mendoza (today a rich agricultural area and the country's major wine-producing region), they discovered an irrigation system designed by the Incas that was based on capturing and distributing rainwater to crops such as squash, corn, and potatoes. A disadvantage of this type of water management is that water is primarily available for a short period following rains, rather than over a longer period, and is often unpredictable; however, depending on the extent of the system of canals and holding tanks, even very small amounts of rain can be taken directly to individual plants, thus permitting agriculture to be sustained in areas of great aridity. In the Negev Desert of Israel, for example, fruit trees are cultivated using a water capture and conservation system that transfers small amounts of runoff to crops.

A second source of water in deserts is also associated with mountainous regions that receive snow and involves the capture of water resulting from snowmelt. This type of water leads to the formation of rivers that may extend into the periphery of arid lowlands or even into the arid region proper. Such rivers, such as the Rio Grande or Colorado River of the desert Southwest, can provide year-round access to water for agricultural purposes, and, using series of irrigation canals, the water can be transported well away from the river to outlying agricultural areas. Depending on the amount of water that flows through the river, enormous agricultural activity may be possible using the largely predictable water from snowmelt.

A third source of water in dry regions is subterranean water, wherein underground water that is either fossil in nature (i.e., deposited thousands of years ago and not replenished through rain or other mechanisms) or at varying depths and replenished over time depending on rainfall and other factors can be brought to the surface and used for crops. Underground water is a major source of both drinking water and agricultural water in many parts of the world, including the desert Southwest. In some cases fossil aquifers are being depleted, which has led to various water projects to import water into arid regions from regions having greater water availability.

A fourth source of water in arid regions, but one that is not widely used in agriculture because of its high monetary cost, is desalinized seawater. While costly, several countries in the Middle East and elsewhere convert salt water to fresh water, but primarily to produce drinking water.

Some examples of agricultural activities carried out in various desert regions will illustrate the variety, extent, and importance of agriculture in the dry zones of the world, the arid climate notwithstanding, as well as the mechanisms used to collect and store water for agricultural uses. *Africa.* The African continent contains 15 million square kilometers of arid habitats, constituting 37 percent of the world total (by comparison, South America contains 3 million square kilometers, or 6 percent of the world total). African deserts are among the most extensive and most arid on earth. Away from permanent rivers, agricultural practices in African deserts involve underground dams to capture subsurface water that flows below surface channels such as dry riverbeds. Small surface dams are also used to store surface runoff and then channel this to crops. In mountainous areas, such as parts of Zimbabwe, runoff water is captured on steep slopes and stored in tanks of up to 100-cubic-meter storage capacity. *Australia.* In Australian semiarid areas that receive up to 300 millimeters of annual rainfall, enough runoff water can be obtained from a surface area of 2,400 square meters to meet the water needs of up to 6 people, 10 horses, 2 cows, and 150 sheep for a year. To capture and hold this amount, plastic sheeting is used, or the ground surface is lined with impermeable clay, to keep water from seeping into the ground, and covered holding tanks for water storage are required. Nevertheless, this illustrates how efficient capture and storage of water in a semiarid area can yield significant water to meet many needs. In Western Australia subsurface waters down to a depth of about 30 meters are often saline (high in dissolved salts), and these salts must be removed or reduced if agriculture is to be effective. Among other techniques, trees such as *Prosopis* (mesquite) and salt-concentrating plants such as members of the sagebrush genus *Atriplex* are used to remove salts from the groundwater.

In well-managed desert areas where mountains are present to provide runoff from rain or snowmelt, the careful harvesting and storing of water, with later precise distribution of it to crops, has resulted in the development of extremely productive and economically important agricultural lands. Thus, for example, the vineyards in the Mendoza region of Argentina, as well as the fruits and other crops grown there, are possible only because of the careful monitoring and use of water, a use that occurs under tight government control. Similarly, the productive farmlands of large portions of California and Arizona that would normally be arid or semiarid are made possible by the rationed use of water from the Colorado River, from underground aquifers, or from distant lakes and rivers. The result has been one of the most economically important agricultural regions in the United States. Where water is more scarce, agricultural uses of desert land may be marginal at best, often only supporting subsistence agriculture, with productivity being limited to that required by small numbers of people and their domestic animals. Because of the high rates of evaporation of surface water, desert areas are particularly prone to the deposition of dissolved salts on or near the soil surface. This process, termed leaching, results over time in subsurface salts being brought to the surface, thereby making the upper soil layers too salty to support agricultural crops.

Desert agriculture has always been challenging, whether because water scarcity and unpredictability make farming difficult or because intense evaporation and sunlight lead to soil degradation from salt deposition. Nevertheless, given the wise use of water and modern, ecologically sensitive agricultural practices, desert lands can be very productive and economically important.—Roberto Juan Candia

See also **AFRICA, DESERTS OF; ARTESIAN BASIN; AUSTRALIA, DESERTS OF; COLORADO RIVER; DAM; DESERT PEOPLES; GROUNDWATER; HYDROLOGY; IRRIGATION DRAINAGE; ISRAEL, DESERTS OF; NILE RIVER; RIO GRANDE; RIVERS; RUNOFF; SAHARA DESERT; SALINIZATION; SALINITY; SALT; SALT PAN; SOUTH AFRICA, DESERTS OF; WATER OF RETENTION**

Further Reading

Clemings, R. 1996. *Mirage: The False Promise of Desert Agriculture*. San Francisco: Sierra Club Books.

Goodin, J. R., and D. K. Northington, eds. 1985. *Plant Resources of Arid and Semiarid Lands: A Global Perspective*. Orlando, Fla.: Academic Press.

Hills, E. S., ed. 1966. *Arid Lands: A Geographical Appraisal*. London: Methuen.

Hinman, C. W., and J. W. Hinman. 1992. *The Plight and Promise of Arid Land Agriculture*. New York: Columbia University Press.

Mortimore, M. 1998. *Roots in the African Dust: Sustaining the Sub-Saharan Drylands*. New York: Cambridge University Press.

National Academy of Science. 1974. *More Water for Arid Lands: Promising Technologies and Research Opportunities*. Washington, D.C.: National Academy Press.

Nir, D. 1974. *The Semi-arid World: Man on the Fringe of the Desert*. London: Longman.

Wickens, G. E., J. R. Goodin, and D. V. Field, eds. 1985. *Plants for Arid Lands*. London: Unwin Hyman.

ALA-SHAN-GOBI DESERT. *See* ASIA, DESERTS OF

ALGAE. *See* PLANTS

ALGARROBO. *See* MESQUITE

ALLUVIAL FAN

Landform created as streams leave confined channels at the outlet of a mountain front and deposit their alluvial materials (materials deposited through the erosional action of water) in a fan-shaped pattern. Best developed in arid and semiarid regions, alluvial fans have a conical surface originating at the apex—the point where the stream emerges from the mountain catchment—and radiating outward away from the apex toward the toe (base). Deposition of alluvial materials takes place as a result of the sudden decrease in stream velocity as the stream leaves its confined channel. Alluvial fans are classified as wet or dry. Wet fans are formed by perennial flows; dry fans are formed by ephemeral

Massive alluvial fan descending from arid pre-Andean mountain chains in the Monte Desert of northwestern Argentina. (Photo: M. A. Mares)

flows. Almost all alluvial fans found in deserts are of the dry type. Alluvial fan slopes range from five to ten degrees at the apex to less than two degrees at the toe. Variations in fan area and slope are the result of lithologic (rock substrate) differences within the drainage basin. Coarser debris, typically derived from metamorphic rocks (rocks produced under great heat and pressure), produce fans with steeper gradients, whereas materials eroded from sedimentary rocks (rocks formed under seas from sediments) form fans with gentler slopes. Particle size generally decreases with increasing distance from the fan apex. In addition to stream flow, mudflows, debris flows, and sheet floods also transport and deposit materials on alluvial fans.

The occurrence of alluvial fans is determined by several factors. A lack of vegetation results in stream channels that move over time. The movement of the channels allows for diversion of sediment deposition to different areas, thus facilitating fan growth. A long period between flooding events, as is common in desert environments, allows weathered debris to accumulate in the mountains, ready for transport once the flooding occurs. Climate change or changes in discharge can lead to the entrenchment of fans, the abandonment of previous channels, and the formation of desert pavement (a surface feature of concentrated stones, ranging in size from boulders to finest gravel and overlying a layer of sand, silt, or clay). Pebbles and cobbles on abandoned alluvial fan surfaces often develop

extensive coatings of rock varnish (a thin coating of manganese and iron oxides and hydroxides, minerals, and other elements). All these conditions are especially prominent in the Basin and Range Province of the southwestern United States, where spectacular fans can be found in such areas as Death Valley National Monument in eastern California.

As alluvial fans grow laterally, they eventually merge to form bajadas. These landforms no longer possess the typical cone shape of an alluvial fan but resemble a nondescript depositional slope, often referred to as an alluvial apron.—Vatche P. Tchakerian

See also **COLLUVIAL DEPOSITS (COLLUVIUM); DESERT SLOPES; ROCK VARNISH; STONE PAVEMENT**

Further Reading

Blair, T. C., and J. G. McPherson. 1994. Alluvial fan processes and forms. *In* A. D. Abrahams and A. J. Parsons, eds., *Geomorphology of Desert Environments*, 354–402. London: Chapman and Hall.

Cooke, R., A. Warren, and A. Goudie. 1993. *Desert Geomorphology*. London: University College Press.

Rundel, P. W., and A. C. Gibson. 1996. *Ecological Communities and Processes in a Mojave Desert Ecosystem: Rock Valley, Nevada*. Cambridge: Cambridge University Press.

ALLUVIAL SOILS

Poorly developed soils derived from recent erosion caused by runoff of water and flooding of waterways. In general, the upper part of the soil profile is well aerated during the dry season, and organic matter is mineralized rapidly. Pronounced variation in the depth of the water table leads to the maintenance of high levels of dissolved oxygen in the water, thus avoiding phenomena related to the chemical reduction of compounds. Regardless of the characteristics shared by alluvial soils, they may be quite different in their state of development and in chemical composition. In 1953 these soils were grouped into three major categories: (1) AC alluvial soils, low in calcium and cations and poorly developed and acidic; (2) calciform AC alluvial soils, rich in carbonates and humus-containing calcium, lumpy in texture, and generally dry due to the deep water table in alluvial areas; and (3) A(B)(C) alluvial soils, better developed than the other two types, with greater alteration of minerals (the presence of iron oxides make this layer dark colored).—Alberto I. J. Vich and Juana Susana Barroso

See also **ALLUVIAL FAN; COLLUVIAL DEPOSITS (COLLUVIUM); GROUNDWATER; MINERALS; SOILS, DESERT**

Further Reading

Bates, R. L., ed. 1987. *Glossary of Geology*. 3d ed. Alexandria, Va.: American Geological Institute.

Cooke, R., A. Warren, and A. Goudie. 1993. *Desert Geomorphology*. London: University College London Press.

Fuller, W. H. 1974. Desert soils. *In* G. W. Brown Jr., ed., *Desert Biology: Special Topics on the Physical and Biological Aspects of Arid Regions*, 2:31–101. New York: Academic Press.

Suh-Shiaw, Lo. 1992. *Glossary of Hydrology*. Taipei: Sheng Te.

Walter, H. and E. Stadelmann. 1974. A new approach to the water relations of desert plants. *In* G. W. Brown Jr., ed., *Desert Biology: Special Topics on the Physical and Biological Aspects of Arid Regions*, 2:213–310. New York: Academic Press.

ALTIPLANO

Elevated plateau (generally 3,600–4,600 meters) between the western Andes (Cordillera Occidental) and the main Andean ranges (Cordillera Real) that extends along their length, encompassing an area of about 100,000 square kilometers. The altiplano is mostly situated within Bolivia, but it extends northward as far as Peru and southward into Chile and Argentina. It is formed in a great depression between the massive mountain chains that has been filled through erosional processes that have been occurring since the Miocene, about 20 million years ago. The altiplano is rather uniform in aspect, but its uniformity is broken occasionally by isolated mountain ranges and closed drainage systems. The altiplano is essentially a closed drainage system with many interconnected alpine lakes, such as the massive Lake Titicaca that empties into the Poopó River via the Desaguadero River. In the southern portions of the altiplano low rainfall leads to the formation of salt lakes and saline flats, such as the Coipasa or Uyuni in southwestern Bolivia.

The climate is cold and dry; most of the region is a true desert. Rainfall may be as little as 50 millimeters per year or as much as 600 millimeters per year. There is a single rainy season occurring in the summer (October–March). There are tremendous fluc-

Pampa de las Avestruzes (Plain of the Rheas), a high arid plain (4,000 meters elevation) in the Andes of Mendoza Province, Argentina. (Photo: M. A. Mares)

tuations in daily temperature, with frequent freezes, even in summer, occurring at night.

The dominant vegetation is shrub steppe comprising vegetation mats that are 30–150 centimeters high, with bare ground between them. During the rainy season many annual plants appear, as do perennial plants that grow from underground storage organs. Even during the rainy season, however, ground cover is never complete. In some moist areas there are many grasses, and in some locations, especially ravines and rocky hillsides from 3,800 to 4,000 meters elevation, there are open forests of queñoa (*Polylepis tomentella*, family Rosaceae). In northern and eastern portions of the altiplano, where annual precipitation is greater than 400 millimeters, there are tola steppes (*Parastrephia lepidophyla*, family Asteraceae). South and west of this community are zones whose plants include various composites, such as species in the genera *Baccharis* and *Fabiana*, and shrubs such as *Adesmia*. The altiplano also has a number of endemic plants, including members of the families Asteraceae, Verbenaceae, and Cactaceae. Endemic species are found in the genera *Parastrephia* (Asteraceae), *Lampaya* (Verbenaceae), *Oreocereus* (Cactaceae), and *Lophopappus* (Poaceae).

The altiplano supports a number of endemic anamil species. Camels (mammalian family Camelidae, order Artiodactyla), such as the vicuña, are the most notable because of their historical economic importance. Today the vicuña is a highly visible endangered species. The guanaco, another camelid, although occurring in low-elevation desert scrublands outside of the altiplano, is most abundant in the high plain of the Andes. The taruca (or huemul) deer, *Hippocamelus antisensis* (family Cervidae, order Artiodactyla), is another large-bodied altiplano mammal that is threatened with extinction. Other mammals characteristic of this high plain are the endemic wild cat, *Oreailurus jacobita*, and such wide-ranging species as the puma (*Puma concolor*) and the fox (*Pseudalopex culpaeus*). There are also many small mammals that characterize the altiplano, including species, and even genera, that are endemic to the zone. Among the common taxa are such rodent genera as *Andinomys*, *Akodon*, *Phyllotis*, *Galenomys* (endemic), *Neotomys* (endemic), *Calomys*, *Galea*, *Microcavia*, *Ctenomys*, *Abrocoma* (endemic), *Punomys* (endemic), and *Lagidium* (endemic). A few vespertilionid bats (i.e., members of the family Vespertilionidae) in the genera *Myotis*, *Eptesicus*, and *Histiotus* also occur in the altiplano.

The altiplano has a wealth of birds, including tinamous (*Nothoprocta*, *Tinamotis*), seedsnipes (*Attagis*), doves (*Metriopelia*), owls (*Speotytus*), hummingbirds (*Oreotrochilus*, *Patagona*), woodpeckers (*Colaptes*), ducks (*Lophonetta*), coots (*Fulica*), plovers (*Charadrius*), gulls (*Larus*), vultures (*Coragyps*, *Cathartes*), falcons (*Milvago*), and eagles (*Polyborus*, *Geranoaetus*).

Amphibians are also common in wet areas, especially frogs (*Hyla*) and toads (*Telmatobius* and *Bufo*). Unusual for deserts, several fish are also present, including *Orestia*, (family Cyprinodontidae), *Pygidium* (family Trichomycteridae), *Ancistrus* (family Loricariidae), and *Astroblepus* (family Astroblepidae).

The invertebrates of the altiplano have not been well studied, but the area has many taxa representing many orders and families.

The altiplano was home to the great Inca civilization that began in the 14th century and waned after the Spanish conquest. The Incan Empire extended from northern Peru to southern Argentina throughout the high Andean habitats, as well as in the lowland deserts of the Pacific Coast. Lands were taken through conquest by the Incan army as well as through negotiated alliances. The Incas were primarily people of the desert who worshiped the sun and believed that their rulers were descendants of the Sun God (several attempts to conquer tropical forest lands were unsuccessful). Internal strife led to a weakening of the empire in the 1530s just as the Spanish conquistador Francisco Pizarro arrived in Peru in 1532 with perhaps 150 soldiers. The arrival of the Spanish marked the end of the Incan Empire, one of the greatest desert civilizations that ever existed. The Incas had a society in which politics and economic activity were tightly intertwined and in which various societal functions (e.g., military activities, bureaucratic administration, road building, architectural activity, agriculture through irrigation) were highly organized. Today many descendants of the Incas still inhabit the altiplano of Central and southern South America.—Virgilio G. Roig

See also **ANDEAN GRASSLANDS; ANDES; AMPHIBIANS; ANIMAL ADAPTATIONS; CAMELS, SOUTH AMERICAN; DESERT GRASSLAND; DESERTS, MONTANE; GRASSLAND; HERBIVORY; MAMMALS; PAMPAS; PLANT ADAPTATIONS; PRAIRIE; PUMA; PUNA; REPTILES; SOUTH AMERICA, DESERTS OF**

Further Reading

Allan, T., and A. Warren, eds. 1993. *Deserts: The Encroaching Wilderness*. New York: Oxford University Press.

Cabrera, A. L. 1957. La vegetación de la puna, Argentina. *Revista de Investigaciones Agrícolas*. Buenos Aires.

Cabrera, A. L., and A. Willink. 1973. Biogeografía de América Latina. Organization of American States, Monograph No. 13. Washington, D.C.

Fjeldså, J., and N. Krabbe. 1990. *Birds of the High Andes*. Svendborg, Denmark: Apollo.

Mares, M. A., J. Morello, and G. Goldstein. 1985. The Monte Desert and other subtropical semi-arid biomes of Argentina, with comments on their relation to North American arid areas. *In* M. Evenari, I. Noy-Meir, and D. W. Goodall, eds., *Ecosystems of the World: Hot Deserts and Arid Shrublands*, 12B:203–237. Amsterdam: Elsevier.

Morello, J. 1984. *Pérfil ecológico de Sudamérica*. Barcelona: Ediciones Cultura Hispánica, Instituto de Cooperación Iberoamericana.

Ojeda, R. A., and M. A. Mares. 1989. A biogeographic analysis of the mammals of Salta Province, Argentina: Patterns of species assemblage in the Neotropics. *Special Publications, The Museum, Texas Tech University* 27:1–66.

AMPHIBIANS

Vertebrate animals (members of the class Amphibia) that first evolved in the Devonian Period, more than 400 million years ago. Amphibians lack external scales and have glandular skin, gills present during larval development or as adults, and eggs encased in jelly membranes. There are three lineages of amphibians living today, the caecilians (Gymnophiona), the salamanders (Urodela), and the frogs and toads (Salientia). Many more species of amphibians are extinct (being known only from fossils) than are extant (living). Systematists currently recognize 6 extant families of caecilians, 10 families of salamanders, and 25 families of frogs and toads.

Amphibians possess many unique characteristics that distinguish them from other vertebrates. In terms of skeletal features, the skull articulates with the vertebral column by a specialized vertebra called the atlas, and the ribs are bicapitate (two pronged); ribs are lacking in most frogs. Many amphibians have a two-phase life history, an aquatic larval stage and a terrestrial adult stage; some species may be entirely terrestrial or entirely aquatic. Respiration usually is supplemented by means of the skin, which is porous and freely permits the exchange of oxygen and carbon dioxide. Gills are used in aquatic larvae and adults, and terrestrial species have lungs (except in plethodontid salamanders). The exchange of gases across the skin is so efficient that some groups (e.g., plethodontid salamanders) have secondarily lost lungs.

Two types of glands (mucous and granular) are present in the skin of all amphibians. Mucous glands continuously secrete mucopolysaccharides (complex hydrocarbon molecules) that function to keep the skin moist, thereby facilitating cutaneous respiration (respiration through the skin). Granular glands are also called poison glands. The toxicity of the secretions of the granular glands ranges from slightly irritating to highly toxic or lethal and serves as a defense mechanism. In certain amphibians these glands coalesce, forming macroglands. For example, in toads the parotoid glands (large glands located on the sides of the head) are conglomerations of granular glands that secrete a milky, toxic substance when the animal is disturbed.

Salamanders and most frogs and toads have external fertilization, wherein eggs and sperm are shed from the body and unite externally, although a few species have internal fertilization. Reproduction must occur in water, or at least in a moist environment, to prevent desiccation of the eggs and sperm. Amphibians have anamniotic eggs; that is,

the eggs do not have shells as they do in reptiles and birds. Instead the ova (eggs) are enclosed by several membranes and are subject to rapid desiccation if not in water or in a moist habitat. The membranes are very thin at the time that eggs are deposited in water, but they absorb water and quickly form a tough protective coat around the ovum.

Frogs and toads are unique among amphibians in that the young, called tadpoles, are very different from adults in morphology and physiology. Tadpoles typically have a round, globular body, with a long, tapering tail. After a period of time that ranges from one to two weeks to several years, depending on the species, the larval forms undergo metamorphosis and change into adult frogs. Many radical changes, initiated by the hormone thyroxin, occur during this period. The most obvious is loss of the tail, which is gradually absorbed, and growth of the limbs. The hind limbs begin to develop early in the tadpole stage but are held flat against the body and are not used until they are quite large. The front limbs develop at the same rate but are hidden beneath the operculum, a thin layer of skin that covers the gills. At metamorphosis, as the tail is absorbed, the hind limbs enlarge and the forelimbs break through the operculum.

The tadpoles of most species of frogs are herbivorous (plant eating) or detritivorous (foraging on detritus), and the digestive system consists of a long, coiled intestine. At transformation the digestive system undergoes a radical modification, and the long, coiled intestine becomes greatly shortened and divided into a distinct esophagus, stomach, small intestine, and large intestine. The internal gills of the tadpole are lost, and the lungs become fully functional. In many species the lungs begin to develop and become partially functional long before metamorphosis. Tadpoles of these species are frequently seen rising to the surface of the water to gulp air. Many other physiological changes occur at metamorphosis.

Relatively few amphibians occur in deserts because of the extreme dependence of these animals on water; however, some of the species that are present in arid areas have unique adaptations for desert life, notably the spadefoot toads (family Pelobatidae, genera *Scaphiopus* and *Spea*) of the deserts of the southwestern United States. Spadefoot toads have many adaptations for dealing with arid conditions. Individuals emerge from underground retreats and breed in one or two nights after heavy rains. The eggs hatch in less than two days, and the tadpole stage is extremely short, lasting only 12–16 days. The desert ponds in which tadpoles develop may last only a short time, and many dry before the tadpoles can complete metamorphosis. In addition, large numbers of tadpoles are present at one time, and resources for tadpole growth and development can become depleted quickly. These ponds also can have populations of fairy shrimp, a small invertebrate adapted for desert life and having a very short life cycle. In any given pond some tadpoles become carnivorous in response to the density of fairy shrimp. These carnivores are morphologically distinct from their omnivorous counterparts. Their beaks become enlarged and heavily serrated, and they develop powerful jaw muscles. The shrimp provide a high-quality, but short-lasting, food supply that allows the carnivorous tadpoles to develop faster than their omnivorous counterparts.

Adult amphibians have novel mechanisms for controlling rates of evaporative water loss. Some species form cocoons that completely encase the body and reduce the amount of water loss. Cocoons first were recognized and described in several species of Australian frogs. The cocoon is formed from many layers of the stratum corneum (the epidermal layer of the skin). Instead of the old skin sloughing off, it remains attached, forming an envelope, but with tiny openings at the nostrils to facilitate breathing. In *Pternohyla fodiens,* a species of tree frog that occurs from the southwestern United States to Michoacan, Mexico, a cocoon can consist of as many as 43 layers of the stratum corneum. In addition, experiments with other species of frogs that form cocoons revealed that water loss was reduced by 20–50 percent because of the presence of the cocoon. Currently, 12 species in six families of frogs are known to form cocoons.

One group of Australian frogs in the genus *Cyclorana* is known as "water-holding" frogs. Representatives of this genus are found throughout most of continental Australia. Most species are burrowers and are only seen above ground after heavy rains. *Cyclorana platycephala* is the best known. As the soil begins to dry individuals of this species burrow deep underground and form cocoons around their bodies. The bladder remains filled, providing the animal with a source of water. Several years may

elapse between rains, and the frogs do not emerge or feed during this time.

Some species of tree frogs in the genus *Phyllomedusa* withstand arid conditions by producing secretions that provide a protective layer over their bodies. These frogs are found in arid areas in Bolivia, Argentina, Paraguay, and southern Brazil. All frogs have mucous and granular glands in their skin, but these frogs are unique in having lipid glands. As a frog begins to dry out, the glands secrete lipids (fat-based molecules), and the frog methodically spreads these secretions over its body with its hands and feet. After it has covered its body it assumes a folded posture and can remain on a perch in a tree for the duration of the day without desiccating. Experiments have shown that water loss in these species of *Phyllomedusa* is reduced by 5–10 percent over that of other frogs in the same genus that lack the lipid glands and lipid-spreading behavior.

Amphibians that live in deserts estivate (become dormant) underground during extremely dry conditions, emerging only to breed and feed when seasonal rains occur. Some species estivate for more than one year, and they must be able to withstand this period without desiccating. In addition to the formation of cocoons, species accumulate high concentrations of urea in body fluids. This accumulation changes the osmolarity (concentration) of the body fluids and reduces water loss. Many species of aquatic amphibians can store urea, but desert amphibians are capable of storing much greater amounts compared to aquatic amphibians. Spadefoot toads store large amounts of urea in their body fluids. Tiger salamanders (*Ambystoma tigrinum*), which also occur in deserts in the southwestern United States, spend considerable time underground during dry periods and store urea at the same rate as spadefoot toads.

Studies on *Phyllomedusa sauvagei*, a tree frog in the family Hylidae that inhabits deserts in Central Argentina, and *Chiromantis xerampelina*, a rhacophorid tree frog (a member of the family Rhacophoridae) that occurs in the Namib Desert in Africa, have shown that these two species excrete the majority of their nitrogen as uric acid. Although in different families, these two species are ecological equivalents (i.e., fill similar niches), living in dry, arboreal habitats. Their evaporative water losses are very low, equal to those of desert reptiles. Uric acid precipitates when water is reabsorbed and therefore requires little water for excretion. Until the 1970s it was thought that amphibians were incapable of producing uric acid as a nitrogenous waste product, but these frogs are indeed uricotelic, eliminating nitrogenous waste as uric acid, like birds or reptiles do.

African reed frogs in the genus *Hyperolius*, when deprived of water, store excess nitrogen in their iridophores, a pigment found in their skin. Iridophores contain large amounts of guanine, which is a nitrogen-containing purine (crystalline molecules formed from atoms of carbon, hydrogen, and nitrogen). During dry periods these frogs deposit enough iridophores in their skin to eliminate about 35 percent of the excess nitrogen from their body fluids.—Janalee P. Caldwell

See also **ANIMAL ADAPTATIONS; BREEDING SEASON; DEHYDRATION; DESICCATION-RESISTANT SPECIES; DORMANCY; ECTOTHERMY; ESTIVATION; EXCRETORY SYSTEM; FOAM NEST; FROGS; HIBERNATION; LIFE HISTORY STRATEGY (ITEROPARITY); MELANIN; REPRODUCTION; SPADEFOOT TOAD; TADPOLES; TOADS; WATER BALANCE; WATER STRESS**

Further Reading

Blaylock, L. A., R. Ruibal, and K. Platt-Aloia. 1976. Skin structure and wiping behavior of phyllomedusine frogs. *Copeia* 1976:283–295.

Duellman, W. E., and L. Trueb. 1986. *Biology of Amphibians*. New York: McGraw-Hill.

Ford, L. S., and D. C. Cannatella. 1993. The major clades of frogs. *Herpetological Monographs* 7:94–117.

Frost, D. R., ed. 1985. *Amphibian Species of the World: A Taxonomic and Geographical Reference*. Lawrence, Kan.: Allen Press and Association of Systematics Collections.

Pfennig, D. 1990. The adaptive significance of an environmentally cued developmental switch in an anuran tadpole. *Oecologia* 85:101–107.

Trueb, L., and R. Cloutier. 1991. A phylogenetic investigation of the inter- and intrarelationships of the Lissamphibian (Amphibia: Temnospondyli). *In* H.-P. Schultze and L. Trueb, eds., *Origins of the Higher Groups of Tetrapods: Controversy and Consensus*, 223–313. Ithaca: Cornell University Press.

Warburg, M. R. 1997. *Ecophysiology of Amphibians Inhabiting Xeric Environments*. New York: Springer.

Woodward, B. D. 1982. Tadpole competition in a desert anuran community. *Oecologia* 54:96–100.

———. 1987. Clutch parameters and pond use in some Chihuahuan Desert anurans. *Southwestern Naturalist* 32:13–19.

Guanacos (***Lama guanicoe***), South American camels, grazing on bunchgrass in the high Andean grasslands (above 3,500 meters elevation) of Mendoza Province, Argentina, along the Chilean border. (Photo: M. A. Mares)

ANDEAN GRASSLANDS (ANDEAN STEPPES)

Grasslands occurring at various elevations throughout the length of the Andes Mountains of South America as a consequence of local and regional climatic and edaphic (soil) conditions. In the Colombian Andes montane grasslands are found as high as 4,300 meters, where they include species such as the grasses *Festuca sublimis*, *Calamagrostis lingulata*, and *Agrostis nigritella* and several species of *Poa*; dicotyledonous plants (flowering plants having two seed leaves) such as *Loricata colombiana*; and herbs such as *Senecio repens*, *Hypochoeris sessiflora*, and *Cerastium caespitosum*. Other grasses that characterize the Andean steppes in other areas are *Aciachme pulvinata*, *Deyeuxia cephalanta*, *Stipa ichu*, and *Poa gymnantha*.

Farther south, in the Andes of Mendoza and San Juan provinces, Argentina, the steppe vegetation is composed of species of grass in the genus *Stipa*, as well as species of *Adesmia* (family Leguminosae), *Ephedra* (family Ephedraceae), *Nassauvia* (family Asteraceae), and *Senecio* (family Asteraceae).

Common mammals in the montane steppe grassland habitats are rodents (*Akodon*, *Eligmodontia*, *Phyllotis*, *Andinomys*, *Ctenomys*), camelids (*Lama* and *Vicugna*), and carnivores (*Pseudalopex* and *Puma*). Birds are boreal (occurring in far northern latitudes around the world) or Patagonian.

The high elevation grasslands and shrublands of the Andes of Central and southern South America were the home of the Incas, a civilization that existed from the 14th century until 1532, when it was conquered by the Spanish.—Virgilio G. Roig

See also **ALTIPLANO; AMPHIBIANS; ANDES; ANIMAL ADAPTATIONS; CAMELS, SOUTH AMERICAN; DESERT GRASSLAND; DESERTS, MONTANE; GRASSLAND; HERBIVORY; MAMMALS; PAMPAS; PLANT ADAPTATIONS; PRAIRIE; PUMA; PUNA; REPTILES; RODENTS; SOUTH AMERICA, DESERTS OF**

Further Reading

Allan, T., and A. Warren, eds. 1993. *Deserts: The Encroaching Wilderness*. New York: Oxford University Press.

Cabrera, A. L. 1957. La vegetación de la puna, Argentina. *Revista de Investigaciones Agrícolas*, Buenos Aires.

Cabrera, A. L., and A. Willink. 1973. *Biogeografía de América Latina*. Organization of American States, Monograph No. 13. Washington, D.C.

Fjeldså, J., and N. Krabbe. 1990. *Birds of the High Andes*. Svendborg, Denmark: Apollo.

Mares, M. A., J. Morello, and G. Goldstein. 1985. The Monte Desert and other subtropical semi-arid biomes of Argentina, with comments on their relation to North American arid areas. *In* M. Evenari, I. Noy-Meir, and D. W. Goodall, eds., *Ecosystems of the World: Hot Deserts and Arid Shrublands*, 12B:203–237. Amsterdam: Elsevier.

Morello. J. 1984. *Pérfil ecológico de Sudamérica*. Barcelona: Ediciones Cultura Hispánica, Instituto de Cooperación Iberoamericana.

Ojeda, R. A., and M. A. Mares. 1989. A biogeographic analysis of the mammals of Salta Province, Argentina: Patterns of species assemblage in the Neotropics. *Special Publications, The Museum, Texas Tech University* 27:1–66.

ANDES

South American mountain range extending generally along the west coast of the continent for more than 8,000 kilometers in length and up to 800 kilometers in width from northernmost South America (Venezuela) to Tierra del Fuego (Argentina, Chile). The component materials of the Andes derive from a Mesozoic geosyncline (large depression in the earth), with the basal materials being Paleozoic in origin, although these alpine mountains, with their simple erosional features, are relatively quite young, having arisen primarily during the late Miocene and Pliocene, about 20 million years ago.

Aerial view of the arid Andes Mountains along the central Chile-Argentine border, with peaks reaching over 6,700 meters. (Photo: M. A. Mares)

Because these mountains are continuous for such a great latitudinal extent, from well north to far south of the equator, no specific Andean climate can be defined. Arid and semiarid climates appear in western portions of the Central Andes, and great desert areas are associated with the mountains south of this area. In the lowlands along the eastern face of the Andes are the extremely arid coastal deserts of Peru (Sechura Desert) and Chile (Atacama Desert).

At the highest elevations in the Central Andes mountains the desertic puna vegetation extends southward through much of Peru, Bolivia, Chile, and Argentina, to as far as 40° south latitude. Because of its high elevational limits (above 3,400 meters), the arid portion of the high Andes is a cold desert, with snow in the winter months. The vegetation is of low aspect and is sparse, with arid-adapted grasses (e.g., *Poa, Stipa, Festuca*) and dicotyledonous cushion plants (e.g., *Azorella, Adesmia*). A wide diversity of plant communities occurs along the Andean ranges and includes numerous endemic genera and species of plants. In some mesic (wet) areas, *Oxycloe* (family Juncaginaceae) and members of the families Ciperaceae, Poaceae, and Dicotyledonae form unusual wetlands within this arid montane region.

It is difficult to define any faunistic regions within the Andean habitats, but all Andean habitats are rather poor in numbers of species of mammals, reptiles, and amphibians (although they are rich in birds and invertebrates).

The high elevation grasslands and shrublands of the Andes of Central and southern South America were home to the great Inca civilization. Their descendants still inhabit the area today.—Virgilio G. Roig

See also **ALTIPLANO; AMPHIBIANS; ANDEAN GRASS-LANDS; ANIMAL ADAPTATIONS; CAMELS, SOUTH AMERICAN; CHILE, DESERTS OF; DESERT GRASS-LAND; DESERTS, MONTANE; DOMESTIC ANIMALS; GRASSLAND; HERBIVORY; MAMMALS; PAMPAS; PLANT ADAPTATIONS; PUMA; PUNA; REPTILES; RODENTS; SECHURA DESERT; SOUTH AMERICA, DESERTS OF**

Further Reading

Allan, T., and A. Warren, eds. 1993. *Deserts: The Encroaching Wilderness*. New York: Oxford University Press.

Cabrera, A. L. 1957. La vegetación de la puna, Argentina. *Revista de Investigaciones Agrícolas*, Buenos Aires.

Cabrera, A. L., and A. Willink. 1973. *Biogeografía de América Latina*. Organization of American States, Monograph No. 13. Washington, D.C.

Fjeldså, J., and N. Krabbe. 1990. *Birds of the High Andes*. Svendborg, Denmark: Apollo.

Mares, M. A., J. Morello, and G. Goldstein. 1985. The Monte Desert and other subtropical semi-arid biomes of Argentina, with comments on their relation to North American arid areas. *In* M. Evenari, I. Noy-Meir, and D. W. Goodall, eds., *Ecosystems of the World: Hot Deserts and Arid Shrublands*, 12B:203–237. Amsterdam: Elsevier.

Morello, J. 1984. *Perfil ecológico de Sudamérica*. Barcelona: Ediciones Cultura Hispánica, Instituto de Cooperación Iberoamericana.

Ojeda, R. A., and M. A. Mares. 1989. A biogeographic analysis of the mammals of Salta Province, Argentina: Patterns of species assemblage in the Neotropics. *Special Publications, The Museum, Texas Tech University* 27:1–66.

ANIMAL ADAPTATIONS

Genetically controlled (and sometimes learned) characteristics that enhance the chances of animals contributing their genes to the next generation. Animals have many adaptations for living in the extreme environmental conditions often found in deserts. Adaptations may include morphological, behavioral, and physiological features. Organisms are composed of conglomerations of adaptations, but many special ones have evolved for being able to persist in deserts.

Among the physical factors with which animals have to contend in deserts are extreme temperatures, both hot and cold, and lack of standing water throughout most of the year, except for a short time after a seasonal rainfall. Reflections of solar radiation on uneven surfaces on the desert floor create local areas of extreme heat. In some northern deserts cold temperatures throughout part of the year require animals to go into prolonged periods of hibernation.

Behaviorally, many desert organisms will avoid extreme temperatures by escaping to less harsh parts of the environment. They may retreat to burrows beneath the ground, to crevices in rocks or plants, or to the shade beneath desert shrubs. Depending on the activity cycles of the organisms, they may retreat either during the hottest part of the day or during all the daylight hours. Among birds, the North American rock wren uses crevices in rocks and the elf owl uses cavities in trees or saguaro cacti to avoid extreme temperatures. Small mammals living in deserts are typically nocturnal and avoid hot daytime temperatures altogether. Many amphibians, including *Breviceps* and *Pyxicephalus* from African deserts and *Scaphiopus* and *Spea* from North American deserts, have well-developed tubercles on their hind feet with which they dig their own burrows. Desert lizards frequently use burrows of other animals, although a few species dig their own burrows. Skinks, species of the lizard genus *Angolosaurus*, are adept at simply burying themselves in the sand; they use swimming motions to accomplish this and can disappear from sight in less than a second.

Kangaroo rats in the genus *Dipodomys* exemplify some of the extreme adaptations of mammals for living in deserts. Approximately 10 species of kangaroo rats live in arid grasslands or deserts of the western United States and northwestern Mexico. These animals get their common name from their mode of travel; they hop quickly from spot to spot, often holding their front feet up like tiny kangaroos. When frightened by a rattlesnake or another potential predator, these 10-centimeter-long rats may cover 1.5–2.5 meters in a single jump. Like real kangaroos, they also have a long tail, which stores fat to help them get through long periods of hibernation in the northern part of their range and helps them to keep their balance as they leap about.

Water is scarce or nonexistent at certain times of the year in deserts, but this is not a problem for kangaroo rats because they never drink water. Yet, like other mammals, they must keep their internal fluids in balance so that their cells do not desiccate. They are nocturnal and forage at night for seeds, their primary food. Seeds are rich in carbohydrates and, as these are broken down and digested, they provide ATP (adenosine triphosphate, chemical energy needed at the cellular level for activity) as well as metabolic water. For comparison, humans get approximately 12 percent of their daily water needs from metabolic water, whereas kangaroo rats satisfy 90 percent of their water needs from this source.

During the warmer months of the year, kangaroo rats spend the daylight hours in deep burrows in the sand, a microhabitat that is much cooler than the desert surface. Kangaroo rats lack sweat glands, which in other mammals normally play a role in cooling the body when temperatures are high. A kangaroo rat could lose a large part of its body weight from water loss if it were exposed to the desert sun, so the behavioral adaptation of spending daylight hours in a cool burrow avoids this danger. In addition, this retreat provides another mechanism for conserving water. As the animal breathes in cool air in its burrow, water vapor condenses on the epithelial (outer) layer of its nasal passages. Here some of the precious water is resorbed into the body instead of being lost into the air. Dry seeds stored in the burrow will also absorb moisture from the air in the humid burrow and return it to the kangaroo rat when the seeds are eaten. Kangaroo rats also have special adaptations in their kidneys that greatly concentrate the urine and prevent excess water from being lost by that route. This is accomplished by having extremely long loops of Henle, tubules in the kidneys that facilitate reabsorption of water. The volume of urine is greatly reduced by this mechanism. For comparison, the urine of kangaroo rats is three to five times more concentrated than that of humans.

Birds are another group of animals that are conspicuous inhabitants of desert environments. Most are active in the early part of the day and avoid the extreme daytime temperatures by moving into the shade and becoming relatively inactive; however, birds have many physiological adaptations for enduring heat. They are endotherms (warm

blooded) and maintain a relatively high body temperature, usually about 40°C, so they do not begin to be overheated until the ambient temperature reaches this point. Some birds can lose heat by erecting the feathers on their bodies, thereby increasing the thickness of the insulation on their bodies. Evaporative cooling (a cooling method somewhat wasteful of water) may occur through the skin, by panting, or by gular flapping, a behavior in which birds rapidly move the skin of the throat and cause air to cool the damp surfaces of the mouth and throat.

Birds, like other animals, must also deal with the scarcity of water in the desert. Unlike the kangaroo rats described above, birds tend not to be physiologically adapted to use metabolic water to meet their needs. One way in which they decrease their usage of water is by excreting uric acid, rather than urea, as a waste product. It has been calculated that by doing this birds lose only one-tenth as much water as mammals during excretion. Birds, however, are dependent on freestanding water and can often be seen in large numbers at the few places in deserts where water is found.

Lizards are some of the most abundant and conspicuous vertebrates in deserts, and many are diurnal (active during the day). The abdominal cavity of nearly all desert lizards has a black peritoneal lining, whereas nocturnal or fossorial (burrowing) lizards lack this black lining. The black lining is apparently an adaptation to prevent damage to the internal organs, including the testes and ovaries, from the high incidence of short-wave ultraviolet radiation in deserts. Experiments using a range of wavelengths showed that skin, muscles, and the black peritoneum, in that order, are effective in reducing the amount of ultraviolet light that penetrates to the body cavity. This adaptation may be coevolved with the tendency for the skin of some lizards to blanch or lighten as a mechanism for radiating heat on very hot, sunny days. More ultraviolet light would penetrate the skin of light-colored animals, and the protection of the internal organs by the black peritoneum would be especially effective during that time.

Many desert lizards have toe fringes that allow them to maneuver more efficiently on sand. Morphologically, toe fringes are formed from the lateral projection of elongated scales on the sides of the toes. The fringes appear to have significance in aiding the lizard to escape prey.

Snakes are another abundant group of vertebrates in deserts. Snakes, because of their lack of limbs, have specialized types of locomotion, one of which, called sidewinding, is an adaptation to moving on a sandy substrate. In sidewinding, the neck is placed on the ground and bent laterally. The rest of the body is moved parallel to the head but is placed on the ground anterior to the point at which the neck touches the ground. As the rear of the body is moved forward, the neck is moved laterally and forward. Thus the body moves sideways, seemingly by loops being raised and lifted laterally. The mode of locomotion is very rapid and may aid in helping the snake to escape predators as well as in reducing the time spent with the body pressed on a hot substrate.

In many ways amphibians seem less likely to inhabit deserts than other groups of vertebrates because of their porous skin and their dependence on water for reproduction. Although relatively few species of amphibians live in deserts, those that do have some remarkable adaptations for survival in an inhospitable environment. Several of these involve the skin. One of the most unusual adaptations is the ability of many species of amphibians to form cocoons. Because amphibians are dependent on water, they generally spend most of the year in burrows below ground. Individuals of some species that have been excavated during estivation (dormancy during summer) were found to be enclosed in a parchmentlike wrapping. On microscopic examination this covering was found to consist of multiple layers of stratum corneum, the outer dead layer of skin that would normally be shed; however, instead of shedding the skin, the layers remain intact and completely enclose the frog. In *Pterno-hyla fodiens*, a fossorial hylid frog (family Hylidae) occurring in the desert of the southwestern United States, it was found that the cocoon of one individual frog consisted of 43 layers of shed skin. Numerous studies have shown that the function of the cocoon is to reduce evaporative water loss. Water loss is reduced incrementally as the number of layers of shed skin accumulate.

The skin of many amphibians contains numerous chromatophores (pigment-containing granules) that interact in various ways to produce brilliant color; however, one type of chromatophore, the iri-dophore, also plays a role in osmoregulation (water balance) in an arid-adapted African frog in the genus *Hyperolius*. The iridophores are part of the dermal chromatophore unit, a particular arrangement of chromatophores in the skin. The iridophores are white or silvery and give certain frogs a metallic or bright color. Guanine is the primary pigment in iridophores, forming 80–90 percent of the composition. These frogs excrete nitrogen as urea, rather than uric acid, a process that requires relatively more water. When water is not available the iridophores take up and store enough of the excess nitrogen, about 35 percent of the total, to serve an osmoregulatory function.

Still another adaptation of the skin to prevent water loss is the ability to produce a waterproof layer in some species of New World tree frogs in the genus *Phyllomedusa*. The skin of these frogs contains a special type of gland that produces a lipid (fatty) secretion that has a waxy character. When they begin to desiccate these frogs undergo a stereotypic behavior in which they contort their bodies and pass their limbs over their back, the primary location of the lipid glands, where they pick up the lipid secretions and wipe them over the entire skin. This produces a waxy covering that prevents evaporative water loss.

The larvae of two amphibians that live in the southwestern deserts of the United States have an unusual morphological adaptation for existence in ephemeral ponds. Some individuals within the cohort in the pond may develop into cannibalistic or carnivorous morphs. In tiger salamanders, *Ambystoma tigrinum*, the cannibalistic morphs differ from the normal morphs in having disproportionately large heads with wide mouths and elongate vomerine teeth (teeth that grow from the vomer bone of the mouth). These features facilitate the capture and ingestion of smaller siblings, although these salamanders feed on other prey as well as conspecifics (members of their own species). Ingestion of other salamanders facilitates rapid growth in tiger salamander cannibals and may provide higher-quality nutrients and thus faster development in these and remaining noncannibalistic individuals.

Carnivorous morphs also develop in four species of spadefoot toads, *Spea*. In these species the carnivorous morphs develop greatly enlarged jaw muscles and a large, serrated beak (part of the mouth of the tadpole). Morph determination in at least one species, *Spea multiplicatus*, appears to be environmentally induced not by the presence of conspecifics but by the ingestion of live fairy shrimp, a small invertebrate that can become very abundant in temporary desert ponds.

Invertebrate animals, particularly predaceous arthropods, are among the most successful animals adapted to desert conditions. Desert scorpions are capable of tolerating higher temperatures than any other arthropod, their rate of water loss is lower than other arthropods, and their metabolic rates are among the lowest of any in the animal kingdom. Both scorpions and spiders are capable of going for long periods (up to one year) without feeding.—Janalee P. Caldwell

See also **AMPHIBIANS; ARTHROPODS; BIPEDALITY; BIRDS; BURROWING ANIMALS; CAMEL; CAMEL'S HUMP; CONVERGENT EVOLUTION; COUNTERCURRENT HEAT EXCHANGE; DESICCATION-RESISTANT SPECIES; DEHYDRATION; ECTOTHERMY; ENDOTHERMY; ESTIVATION; EXCRETORY SYSTEM; HEAT BALANCE; HEAT EXCHANGE; HIBERNATION; INSECTS; KIDNEY FUNCTION, DESERT RODENTS; LIZARDS; MAMMALS; METABOLIC WATER; RENAL PAPILLA; RESPIRATORY WATER LOSS; SALT BALANCE; SHIVERING; SNAKES; SPIDERS; SURVIVAL IN DESERTS; SWEAT GLANDS; THERMOREGULATION; TORPOR; TYMPANIC BULLAE; WATER BALANCE; WATER STRESS**

Further Reading

Bradshaw, S. D. 1997. *Homeostasis in Desert Reptiles.* New York: Springer.

Brown, G. W., Jr., ed. 1968. *Desert Biology: Special Topics on the Physical and Biological Aspects of Arid Regions.* Vol. 1. New York: Academic Press.

Carothers, J. H. 1986. An experimental confirmation of morphological adaptation: Toe fringes in the sand-dwelling lizard *Uma scoparia. Evolution* 40:871–874.

Costa, G. 1995. *Behavioural Adaptations of Desert Animals.* New York: Springer.

Crump, M. L. 1992. Cannibalism in amphibians. *In* M. A. Elgar and B. J. Crespi, eds., *Cannibalism: Ecology and Evolution among Diverse Taxa*, 256–276. Oxford: Oxford University Press.

Degan, A. A. 1997. *Ecophysiology of Small Desert Mammals.* New York: Springer.

Heatwole, H. 1996. *Energetics of Desert Invertebrates.* New York: Springer.

Luke, C. 1986. Convergent evolution of lizard toe fringes. *Biological Journal of the Linnean Society* 27:1–16.

Polis, G. A., and T. Yamashita. 1991. The ecology and importance of predaceous arthropods in desert communities. *In* G. Polis, ed., *The Ecology of Desert Communities*, 383–437. Tucson: University of Arizona Press.

Wiens, J. 1991. The ecology of desert birds. *In* G. Polis, ed., *The Ecology of Desert Communities*, 278–310. Tucson: University of Arizona Press.

ANIMAL HUSBANDRY. *See* DOMESTIC ANIMALS

ANNUAL PLANTS

Life history strategy type among flowering plants wherein a plant (also known as a therophyte) completes its life cycle in one year, during which time it germinates, grows, matures, flowers, produces seeds, and dies. Some annual plants evade the hot, dry desert summers by laying dormant below the soil surface as seeds until adequate precipitation falls. Other annual plants will grow and flower immediately following summer rains, as in the Sonoran Desert of North America. Annual plants that lie quiescent as seeds and germinate when rain falls are termed aridopassive pluviotherophytes. Winter annuals will germinate following late winter and early spring precipitation. They are long-lived but experience high mortality after germination. They grow both under desert shrubs and in the areas between shrubs. Summer annuals, in contrast, are short-lived and grow mostly in the spaces between desert shrubs. Following germination desert annuals grow rapidly and quickly flower and set seed. In wet years the desert is carpeted by the growth of annuals. But in dry years desert annuals may be absent. The number of annual species in deserts exceeds the more conspicuous perennials, in some cases by a ratio of up to 10:1. The actual productivity of biomass by annual plants can exceed that of perennials in wet years. For example, 20–30 species of annuals account for 80 percent of the seeds produced in the desert and 90 percent of the total seed biomass. Annuals that grow under shrubs are the most abundant group of annuals in years with little rainfall. Annual plants can be quite diverse. For example, in the Kara-Kum Desert of Asia there are 143 species of annauls, 98 of which bloom in spring.

The seeds of annual plants provide an important food source to desert animals, particularly rodents, ants, and some species of birds. Because these animals feed primarily on seeds, they are referred to as granivores. The plant seed is an energy storage unit, full of complex compounds intended to help the plant embryo germinate and grow. There is a close link between granivore population size and the amount of annual plant seeds available. Granivore populations will decline in years when there are few seeds. At the regional level granivore abundance and diversity has been shown to decrease in desert regions where precipitation is sufficient to turn desert vegetation into perennial grassland.—Bruce W. Hoagland

See also **ANIMAL ADAPTATIONS; BIPEDALITY; DESERT BLOOM; DESERT GRASSLAND; FLOWERS; GRANIVORY; GRASSES; GRASSLAND; HERBIVORY; KANGAROO RAT; PLANT ADAPTATIONS; PLANTS; RODENTS; SEEDS**

Further Reading

Archibold, O. W. 1995. *Ecology of World Vegetation.* New York: Chapman and Hall.

Brown, J. H., O. J. Reichman, and D. W. Davidson. 1979. Granivory in desert ecosystems. *Annual Review of Ecology and Systematics* 10:201–227.

MacMahon, J. A. 1988. Warm deserts. *In* M. G. Barbour and W. D. Billings, eds., *North American Terrestrial Vegetation*, 231–264. Cambridge: Cambridge University Press.

Samson, D. A., T. E. Philippi, and D. W. Davidson. 1992. Granivory and competition as a determinant of annual plant diversity in the Chihuahuan desert. *Oikos* 65:61–80.

ANTARCTIC DESERT. *See* AN INTRODUCTION TO DESERTS

ANTELOPE

Common name referring to a large group of 90–100 species of herbivorous hoofed animals belonging to the family Bovidae (mammalian order Artiodactyla). (The North American pronghorn, often called an antelope, is not a member of the bovid family but is in its own family, Antilocapridae.) All bovids share certain characteristics: horns that have bony cores covered with a keratinized sheath (keratin is the substance that forms such structures as hair, teeth, and nails), cloven hooves, a stomach with three or four chambers, and the behavior of chewing their cud. Other animals in this family are bison, cattle, sheep, and goats.

Bovids are naturally distributed almost worldwide; they are absent only from South America and Australia, although domesticated species are found everywhere. They are most common and most diverse in the subtropical and tropical regions of Africa and Asia. Two-thirds of all bovid species (including most of the bovids loosely classified as antelopes) occur in Africa, with another 18 percent occurring in India. In Africa antelopes are found in a wide variety of habitats, including tropical rain forest, wet and dry savannas, deserts, mountains, and swamps, but they attain their greatest diversity and abundance in savannas.

For many people, antelopes are the symbol of the East African savannas. These savannas have a variety of types of antelopes, such as the eland, kob, duiker, wildebeest, gazelle, impala, sable, oryx, hartebeest, and dik-dik.

Several species are particularly well adapted to semiarid and desert conditions. The northern horn of Africa is inhabited by addax and scimitar-horned oryx, both of which are true desert-adapted species capable of surviving for long periods with little water. Both species are now extremely rare. Damas, dorcas, and Loder's gazelles can also be found in North African deserts. The deserts of southern and southwestern Africa support a diverse antelope fauna, including the klipspringer, gerenuk, beisa oryx, gemsbok, springbok, and common duiker. The gerenuk is completely independent of free water.—Thomas E. Lacher, Jr.

See also **ADDAX; AFRICA, DESERTS OF; ASIA, DESERTS OF; BLACKBUCK; DIK-DIK; ELAND; GAZELLE; GEMSBOCK; HARTEBEEST; IBEX; KLIPSPRINGER; KUDU; MAMMALS; NYALA; ORYX; PRONGHORN; SOUTH AFRICA, DESERTS OF; SPRINGBOK; UNGULATES; WATER HOLE; WILDLIFE**

Further Reading

Dorst, J., and P. Dandelot. 1980. *A Field Guide to the Larger Mammals of Africa.* London: Collins.

Estes, R. D. 1991. *The Behavior Guide to African Mammals.* Berkeley: University of California Press.

Nowak, R. M. 1991. *Walker's Mammals of the World.* 5th ed. Baltimore: Johns Hopkins University Press.

Spinage, C. A. 1986. *The Natural History of Antelopes.* New York: Facts on File.

ANTICYCLONE

Area of high pressure in which the wind blows in a clockwise direction in the Northern Hemisphere and counterclockwise in the Southern Hemisphere. This direction is the opposite of that which usually characterizes cyclonic circulation. Because anticyclonic circulation and relative atmospheric pressure usually are correlated, the terms "anticyclone" and "high" generally are used interchangeably. Clouds usually do not form within highs, and skies are clear. Highs are common in desert regions, where high insolation (sunshine) occurs during the day and pronounced radiative heat loss occurs at night. Thus in many deserts the days are hot and the nights are cool, or even cold. Large desert animals, such as the camel, may use the clear desert nights to unload through radiation the heat that was gained and stored during the day.—Federico Norte

See also **ADIABATIC PROCESSES; BAROMETRIC PRESSURE; CAMEL; CLIMATE; CLOUDS; CONVECTIVE STORM; CYCLONE; HEAT BALANCE; INSOLATION; LOW PRESSURE; THERMOREGULATION**

Further Reading

Day, J. A., and V. J. Schaefer. 1991. *Clouds and Weather.* Boston: Houghton Mifflin.

Oliver, J. E., and R. W. Fairbridge, eds. 1987. *The Encyclopedia of Climatology.* New York: Chapman and Hall.

Schaefer, V. J., and J. A. Day. 1981. *A Field Guide to the Atmosphere.* Boston: Houghton Mifflin.

Schneider, S. H., ed. 1996. *Encyclopedia of Climate and Weather.* 2 vols. New York: Oxford University Press.

ANTLIONS

Larvae of insects in the family Myrmeleontidae (insect order Neuroptera), which also contains lacewings, snakeflies, owlflies, dobsonflies, fishflies, and alderflies. The name derives from the habits of antlions, which attack ants and other small insects either on the surface of the ground or within pits that the antlions construct.

There are three subfamilies of antlions, the Acanthoclisinae, the Dendroleontinae, and the Myrmeleontinae. All are tanklike in morphology and possess a pair of long, sharp, pincerlike, sickle-shaped mandibles. Larvae in the first two subfamilies typically lie in wait for small insect prey on the surface of the ground or just under the surface. Many larvae of the Myrmeleontinae live in funnel-like pits that they dig in sand by moving in concentric circles. The pits appear nearly perfectly symmetrical, with smooth sides. The antlion positions itself at the apex of the pit, hidden in the sand. When a small insect, such as an ant, falls into the pit and tries to escape by climbing the walls, the antlion uses flicks of its head to throw sand at its victim,

which ultimately falls to the bottom of the pit, is grabbed by the large pincers of the antlion, and is dragged under the sand. The antlion then feeds on body fluids of the prey. Antlion larvae in all three subfamilies leave apparently aimless trails in the sand, which gave antlions the common name doodlebugs.

Antlions are common primarily in North American, African, and Australian deserts, with the Myrmeleontidae being most conspicuous due to their funnellike traps. They are most often found in soft sand just under the overhang of cliffs or under the edge of tree or shrub canopies. As adults antlions have four membranous wings that are held tentlike over the body when at rest. Although they superficially resemble damselflies, they can be distinguished easily on the basis of how the wings are held while at rest, their flight behavior, and their antennae. Adult antlions generally fly slowly and flutter while in flight, whereas damselflies fly rapidly and are capable of astonishing maneuvers. In addition, adult antlions typically have clubbed antennae about as long as the head, whereas damselflies have very short antennae without clubs.—Laurie J. Vitt

See also **ANIMAL ADAPTATIONS; ANTS; ARTHROPODS; INSECTS; PREDATION**

Further Reading

Borror, D. J., C. A. Triplehorn, and N. F. Johnson. 1992. *An Introduction to the Study of Insects.* New York: Harcourt Brace.

Crawford, C. S. 1981. *Biology of Desert Invertebrates.* New York: Springer.

ANTS

Insects in the family Formicidae of the order Hymenoptera, which also contains bees, wasps, and many other common species. Ants usually can be distinguished from other hymenopterans by the structure of their antennae, which have a very long first segment and then are bent to about a 90° angle.

Ants are social insects that usually live in groups and have a caste system in which different individuals perform different functions within the nest. The caste system of ants (and other hymenopterans) is different from that of termites in that different castes have different chromosome numbers. Queens are the females that produce eggs, and they are diploid (having two sets of chromosomes).

Males fertilize eggs of the females and are haploid (having one set of chromosomes). Workers are diploid sterile females that do the work for the colony. Soldiers are a large-bodied worker caste usually with relatively enlarged heads and mandibles. In some species there are other castes that are intermediate between those mentioned, and these are diploid as well.

Ants differ considerably in colony size, diets, where and how they nest, how they forage, and even in their annual cycles of activity and reproduction. Some colonies exceed a million individuals; others contain very few. Many ants live in elaborate burrow systems in the ground with chambers used for a variety of functions. Some live in tree cavities, some live in leaf litter, and others live in nearly every imaginable microhabitat. Still others are nomadic at least part of the time. Ants eat almost any edible material. Many are predaceous. Others feed on nectar, seeds, carrion, vegetative parts of plants, fruits, and nuts. Some species forage individually; others form immense blankets of advancing animals that take almost everything they encounter. Some enter nests of other ants and, in addition to food, often capture other ants, which they then use as "slaves."

Ants communicate by a variety of means, but chemical communication appears to be most important. Airborne chemicals (pheromones) are used to identify food, elicit grooming behavior, mark trails, and even signal danger. Chemical signals produced by a disturbed individual can induce attack by many more individuals, for example, the swarming of fire ants when just a few individuals have been disturbed. Many of the chemicals produced by ants, especially those in the subfamily Myrmicinae, are noxious or toxic and used to discourage predators. Some of the vertebrates that eat ants (e.g., horned lizards and poison dart frogs) appear to co-opt the chemicals produced by ants and use them in their own defense.

Ants are among the most common insects in deserts. Moreover, ants can be found in nearly every desert microhabitat. Within deserts there is a relationship between mean annual rainfall (which is an indicator of primary production, or the amount of energy stored in plant tissues produced by plants) and the number of ant species. Typically, desert areas with approximately 20 millimeters of rainfall per year have 6 to 8 species of ants, whereas desert areas receiving more than 90 millimeters of annual rainfall may have more than 20 ant species. Like many other arthropods inhabiting desert regions, desert ants are not morphologically much different from ants in other environments. They have been successful in deserts because their activity has been adjusted to avoid extremes of temperature and drought. Some species do, however, have adaptations that function specifically in the context of desert environments. For example, some desert ants have fringes of hairs on the head, called psammophores, that are used to move fine-grained sand.

The feeding ecology of desert ants differs considerably among species. Some feed primarily on seeds that are collected, returned to the nest, and eaten during periods when seeds cannot be harvested. Others are predaceous, feeding on arthropods and other desert invertebrates. Still other species harvest plant parts, which are then taken to the nest and used as substrates on which to grow fungi, which are eaten by the ants. Finally, some desert species harvest nectar collected from aphids and other homopterans, return to the nest, and transfer the nectar to individual ants that function as miniature storage tanks. These "repletes" hang from the ceiling of cavities within the nest, essentially storing energy to be used by nest members when other resources are in short supply.

Desert ants are also important as seed dispersers. For example, ants are responsible for dispersing seeds of more than 1,000 plant species in South Africa. Ants collect nearly 20 percent of all seeds produced by plants in parts of the Australian deserts and up to 10 percent of the seeds produced in the Chihuahuan Desert. Construction and maintenance of ant colonies can affect the composition of the soil because deeper soils are brought to the surface. In addition, in instances in which ants clear areas immediately associated with the nest, ants can directly modify plant species composition. The tunnels that ants make may be important in the filtration of water through the soil. Finally, ant density and its influence on seed harvest may directly affect populations of seed-eating birds and rodents through competition.

One species of ant, *Camponotus detritus*, is restricted to sand dunes in the Namib Desert, one of the most extreme deserts on earth. It feeds on detritus but also receives a major portion of its nutritional requirements from scale insects (Homoptera) that live on perennial plants.

There are a few other insects and some spiders that resemble ants. In some instances winged forms of ants resemble wasps; the best example is the wasp family Mutilidae, in which wingless females (velvet ants) look like hairy ants.—Laurie J. Vitt

See also **ANIMAL ADAPTATIONS; ANTLIONS; ARTHROPODS; BEES; HYMENOPTERA; INSECTS; POISONOUS ANIMALS; TERMITES; VELVET ANTS; VENOM; WASPS**

Further Reading

Borror, D. J., C. A. Triplehorn, and N. F. Johnson. 1992. *An Introduction to the Study of Insects*. New York: Harcourt Brace.

Buckley, R. C., ed. 1982. *Ant-Plant Interactions in Australia*. The Hague: W. Junk.

Huxley, C. R., and D. F. Cutler. 1991. *Ant-Plant Interactions*. New York: Oxford University Press.

MacKay, W. P. 1991. The role of ants and termites in desert ecosystems. *In* G. A. Polis, ed., *The Ecology of Desert Communities*, 111–150. Tucson: University of Arizona Press.

Milne, L., and M. Milne. 1980. *The Audubon Society Field Guide to North American Insects and Spiders*. New York: Knopf.

Seeley, M. K. 1991. Sand dune communities. *In* G. A. Polis, ed., *The Ecology of Desert Communities*, 348–382. Tucson: University of Arizona Press.

Wheeler, G. C., and J. Wheeler. 1973. *Ants of Deep Canyon*. Riverside, Calif.: Philip L. Boyd Deep Canyon Desert Research Center, University of California.

Wilson, E. O. 1971. *The Insect Societies*. Cambridge, Mass.: Harvard University Press.

ANZA-BORREGO DESERT

Beautiful and diverse desert region west of the Colorado River in extreme southern California; a subdivision of the more extensive Colorado Desert. This desert is named after the famous Spanish explorer Juan Bautista de Anza, who traversed and explored the area in 1775 while traveling northward to establish San Francisco.

Anza-Borrego, which is west of the productive Imperial Valley and bordered on the west by the Laguna Mountains and on the north and east by the Santa Rosa Mountains, is a diverse mosaic of arid plains and hills, badlands, and native palm oases. Most of the region is dominated by the ubiquitous creosote bush (*Larrea tridentata*) and associated species such as ocotillo (*Fouquieria splendens*) and burro bush (*Franseria dumosa*), as well as the only

natural occurrence in California of the small-leafed elephant plant, or torote (*Bursera microphylla*).

The Anza-Borrego Desert State Park was designated California's first desert state park in 1933 and encompasses more than 600,000 acres. An area of privately owned land occurs in the central portion of the park. This desert is famed for the colorful annual blooms that occur during years of heavy rain. The most recent and spectacular bloom was associated with the El Niño event of late 1997 and early 1998, when the park received much larger than normal amounts of rainfall and the annual plants produced a remarkable ground cover of colorful annuals.—Gary K. Hulett and Amanda Renner Charles

See also **AN INTRODUCTION TO DESERTS; ANNUAL PLANTS; CALIFORNIA DESERT; CHENOPODIACEAE; COLORADO DESERT; CREOSOTE BUSH; DESERT BLOOM; DESERTS; DESERTS, HOT; DESERTS, TEMPERATE; PLANT ADAPTATIONS; PLANTS; OCOTILLO; SEMIARID ZONES; UNITED STATES, DESERTS OF**

Further Reading

Barbour, M. G., and J. Major, eds. 1977. *Terrestrial Vegetation of California*. New York: Wiley.

Brown, D. E., ed. 1994. *Biotic Communities: Southwestern United States and Northwestern Mexico*. Salt Lake City: University of Utah Press.

Lindsay, L. 1998. *The Anza-Borrego Desert Region: A Guide to the State Park and Adjacent Areas of the Western Colorado Desert*. Berkeley, Calif.: Wilderness Press.

Parish, S. B. 1930. Vegetation of the Mohave and Colorado deserts of southern California. *Ecology* 3:481–499.

Shreve, F. 1925. Ecological aspects of the deserts of California. *Ecology* 6:93–103.

Vogl, R. J., and L. T. McHargue. 1966. Vegetation of California Fan Palm oases on the San Andreas Fault. *Ecology* 47:532–540.

Wauer, R. H. 1964. Ecological distribution of the birds of the Panamint Mountains, California. *Condor* 66:287–301.

Weir, K. 1998. *Southern California Handbook: Including Greater Los Angeles, Disneyland, San Diego, Death Valley and other Desert Parks*. Emeryville, Calif.: Moon Publications.

APACHE

North American Indian people primarily inhabiting the desert Southwest and adjacent Mexico and related to the Navajo, with both groups being members of the Athapascan linguistic family. After entering North America across the Bering Land Bridge later than most other Indian groups, the Apaches eventually migrated southward (perhaps as late as A.D. 1,500) to the arid and semiarid parts of North America, where they developed many adaptations to life in a hot, dry region. The term "Apache" is from the Zuñi word meaning enemy. The Apaches called themselves *Dini*, *Indé*, or *Tindé*, terms meaning "the people." The Apaches were divisible into six main groups (Kiowa Apache, Lipan, Jicarilla, Mescalero, Chiricahua, and Western Apache) that had regional affinities, although many different smaller bands existed within the broader groups. As a people, the Apache ranged from the plains of Oklahoma, Texas, eastern Colorado, and eastern New Mexico (the Kiowa Apache) to eastern Arizona (the Western Apache). Between these two extremes, various groups inhabited the mountains and deserts of New Mexico, Colorado, and Arizona and the desert states of Chihuahua and Sonora, Mexico.

Apache social organization was centered on the extended family, often with an older woman, such as a mother-in-law, assuming an important role in the functioning of the group. Although some Apaches did limited farming (40 percent of the diet of the Western Apache was composed of vegetables and fruits, and they raised such crops as corn, beans, and squash), most Apaches were hunters, and meat (antelope, deer, rabbits, hares, and rodents) was a regular part of their diet. The hunting groups supplemented their diet with wild fruits and vegetables (e.g., piñon nuts, mesquite beans, potatoes, cactus fruits).

The Apaches were a fierce, warrior people, and although they did not number more than 5,000 and did not function as a unified nation, they were difficult to subdue by the Spaniards, then the Mexicans, and finally the troops of the U.S. Army. Apaches engaged in a great deal of raiding to obtain horses, food, and other booty and escape without detection. Apaches also engaged in warfare, in which warriors avenging the deaths of Apaches who had been killed would attack an enemy without mercy. The history of the Apaches is one filled with atrocities on all sides. The Apaches produced many great warriors in the 19th century, including Cochise, Mangas Coloradas, and Geronimo. The bellicose activities between the Apaches and immigrants to the Southwest extended in one form or another

over several centuries. The Apaches were not defeated and did not cede their desert territory over this extended period. Their small war parties with their intimate knowledge of the terrain and their significant military acumen challenged thousands of organized troops of the U.S. Army for many decades before the final surrender of their aging chief, Geronimo, in 1868. This ended the Apache wars. Today most Apaches live on reservations in New Mexico and Arizona.—Michael A. Mares

See also **COCHISE; DESERT PEOPLES; GERONIMO; HOHOKAM; HOPI; JORNADA DEL MUERTO; LLANO ESTACADO; NAVAJO; RIO GRANDE**

Further Reading

Ball, E. 1988. *Indeh: An Apache Odyssey*. Norman: University of Oklahoma Press.

Debo, A. 1976. *Geronimo: The Man, His Time, His Place*. Norman: University of Oklahoma Press.

Geronimo, with S. M. Barrett. 1989. *Geronimo's Story of His Life*. Williamstown, Mass.: Cornerhouse Publishers.

Melody, M. E. 1989. *The Apache*. New York: Chelsea House.

Opler, M. 1971. *Apachean Culture History and Ethnology*. Tucson: University of Arizona Press.

Roberts, D. 1993. *Once They Moved Like the Wind*. New York: Simon and Schuster.

Schwarz, M. 1992. *Cochise: Apache Chief*. New York: Chelsea House.

Smith, P. C. 1996. Geronimo. *In* P. C. Smith and P. G. Allen, eds., *As Long As The River Flows*, 34–71. New York: Scholastic Books.

Sweeney, E. R. 1991. *Cochise Chiricahua Apache Chief*. Norman: University of Oklahoma Press.

Worcester, D. E. 1979. *The Apaches: Eagles of the Southwest*. Norman: University of Oklahoma Press.

AQUATIC HABITATS

Surface waters sufficiently large and permanent to support populations of organisms. In deserts aquatic habitats may be lotic (flowing) systems that range in size from large rivers (such as the Nile) to small, intermittent streams or lentic (standing) systems such as lakes, spring pools, and marshes.

Large rivers that flow through deserts originate at higher elevations where rainfall and snowmelt control the volume and rate of flow. In desert areas flow rates are affected by the rate of evaporation as well. Annual variation in water flow may result in the development of isolated pools that persist only where evaporation is reduced, such as in deep, shaded canyons. Smaller tributary streams in deserts are typically intermittent. In spring-fed tributaries surface flow may cease when high air temperatures increase the rate of evaporation, but subsurface flow through porous substrates may sustain standing water in isolated pools downstream in areas where nonporous substrates force water to the surface. Very small, runoff streams, or arroyos, may be dry most of the time, with water only accumulating during and immediately after flash floods. Because of the variable and unpredictable flow regimes in lotic habitats, temperature, salinity, and total dissolved solids also vary dramatically.

Lentic habitats differ considerably in size and characteristics. There are very few large, natural lakes in deserts, but those that do exist, such as Pyramid Lake in Nevada, are remnants of much larger, ancient lakes that developed in times of wetter climate (Plio-Pleistocene, approximately 1.6 million years before the present). Many smaller, shallower desert lakes also represent remnants of now-extinct playa lakes that deposited extensive salt flats on the desert floor as they evaporated, possibly as recently as 10,000 years ago. The persistence of present-day desert lakes depends on accumulation of water from runoff and seepage in endorheic basins (closed basins with no outflow). Like desert rivers and streams, desert lakes are subject to large-scale fluctuations in water level, temperature, and chemistry.

In deserts springs are the only aquatic habitats that exhibit nearly constant conditions of discharge, temperature, and chemistry. Those conditions, however, often represent extremes, and spring environments may harbor only a few, highly tolerant species. Thermal springs emit water that passes through volcanic or other geothermal zones and may have water that outflows at temperatures in excess of 46°C. Desert springs also frequently emit mineralized waters containing extremely high concentrations of bicarbonates, and mineralized spring pools are often lined with travertine deposits (layered calcium carbonate deposits).

Marshes (*cienegas* in Spanish) are shallow, marginal waters that may be associated with both lentic and lotic systems. They are often filled with emergent vegetation and exhibit wide fluctuations in depth, temperature, and water chemistry, and in many ways resemble coastal lagoons. Conditions may be so extreme that at times marshes are uninhabitable.—Edie Marsh-Matthews

See also **ARROYO; ARTESIAN BASIN; BOLSÓN; FISHES; FLOOD; FLOODPLAIN; HYDROLOGICAL CYCLE; HYDROLOGY; NILE RIVER; PLAYA; PLEISTOCENE; PLIOCENE; RIPARIAN COMMUNITIES; RIO GRANDE; RIVERS; RUNOFF; SALT PAN; WATER; WATER HOLE; WELL**

Further Reading

Alcock, J. 1985. *Sonoran Desert Spring*. Chicago: University of Chicago Press.

Brown, D. E., ed. 1994. *Biotic Communities: Southwestern United States and Northwestern Mexico*. Salt Lake City: University of Utah Press.

Cole, G. A. 1981. Habitats of North American desert fishes. *In* R. J. Naiman and D. L. Soltz, eds., *Fishes in North American Deserts*, 477–492. New York: Wiley.

Deacon, J. E., and W. L. Minckley. 1974. Desert fishes. *In* G. W. Brown, Jr., ed., *Desert Biology: Special Topics on the Physical and Biological Aspects of Arid Regions*, 2:385–488. New York: Academic Press.

AQUIFER. *See* ARTESIAN BASIN

ARABIAN DESERT. *See* SAUDI ARABIA, DESERTS OF

ARABIAN GULF, DESERTS OF

Westward extension of the Arabian Sea (also called the Persian Gulf) that is bounded by Iraq, Kuwait, Saudi Arabia, Bahrain, Qatar, the United Arab Emirates, and Oman on the west; and Iran on the east. (See map of Arabian Gulf area, p. 361.)

Vegetation in the Arabian Gulf is typical of arid deserts. The southeastern lower desert of Iraq is situated at the head of the Gulf and constitutes part of the flat floodplain of the Tigris and Euphrates rivers. The climate in the southeastern part of Iraq is influenced by the Gulf, with low annual rainfall ranging from 75 to 150 millimeters. The natural desert landscape in Iraq supports plant communities of *Acacia gerrardii, Ziziphus nummularia, Rhanterium epapposum, Cymbopogon parkeri*, and *Haloxylon salicornicum*. Salt-affected lands are characterized by *Suaeda vermiculata, Binertia cycloptera, Limonium spicatum, Halocnemum strobilaceum*, and *Aeluropus littoralis*.

The state of Kuwait, with a land area of about 17,820 square kilometers, is located in the northwestern Gulf between 28°30′–30°05′ north latitude and 46°33′–48°30′ east longitude. Summers are hot and dry, and winters are mild to cold. Mean annual rainfall is about 115 millimeters; mean monthly minimum temperature of the coldest month (January) is 7.7°C, and mean monthly maximum temperature of the hottest month (July) is 44.7°C. Dust and sandstorms, locally known as toaz, are common, particularly in summer. The general topography is flat or gently undulating.

Kuwait's desert vegetation consists of steppe (treeless plain) or scrub, with only slight differences in the sparse plant coverage between sites. The major plant communities are dominated by *Haloxylon salicornicum*, *Rhanterium epapposum*, *Cyperus conglomeratus*, *Stipagrostis plumosa*, *Zygophyllum coccineum*, and *Panicum turgidum*. Coastal salt marshes and salt-affected lands are dominated by *Salicornia europaea*, *Juncus rigidus*, *Halocnemum strobilaceum*, *Seidlitztia rosmarinus*, *Nitraria retusa*, *Tamarix passerinoides*, *Aeluropus littoralis*, and *Cressa cretica*.

Bahrain consists of an archipelago of 33 islands (26° north latitude and 50°28′–50°38′ east longitude) on the western side of the Arabian Gulf, with a total area of about 620 square kilometers; the main island constitutes about 85 percent of the total area. The climate is characterized by hot summers and mild winters; mean annual temperature is 27°C, with a mean daily minimum of 14°C in January and a maximum of 38.5°C in August. The average annual rainfall is less than 80 millimeters.

The main island of Bahrain is divisible into five physiographic zones having different floristic compositions. Starting from the island's coast toward its center, these zones are (1) coastal salt-affected lowlands, dominated by *Zygophyllum quatarense*, *Halopeplis perfoliata*, *Halocnemum strobilaceum*, and *Schanginia aegyptiaca*; (2) backslopes, with soils varying from loose to gravelly sand and with vegetation including *Anabasis setifera*, various *Cyperus*, *Sporobolus arabicus*, *Suaeda vermiculata*, and *Helianthemum kahiricum*; (3) the escarpment zone, an essentially barren zone heavily disturbed as a result of the presence of gypsum quarries; (4) the interior basin, which is characterized by relatively rich vegetation dominated by *Zygophyllum quatarense*, *Heliotropium bacciferum*, and *Helianthemum kahiricum*; and (5) the central plateau, with rocky and gravelly soils supporting sparse vegetation of *Ochradenus baccatus*, *Lycium shawii*, *Erodium bryoniifolium*, and *Glossonema edule*.

The peninsula of Qatar, with an area of about 11,600 square kilometers, projects into the Gulf from the Arabian shore and lies between 50°45′–51°40′ east longitude and 24°40′–26°10′ north latitude. It has a slightly undulating topography with scattered large depressions (locally known as rhodat). Mean annual rainfall is about 80 millimeters; mean annual temperature is 26.5°C, with the mean daily minimum being 12.7°C in January and the mean daily maximum being 41.2°C in August.

Qatar's landscapes are varied and depend on the general topography and substrate. Rocky or gravel habitats (hamada desert) are barren and sometimes support very sparse shrubby vegetation of *Zygophyllum quatarense*, *Acacia tortilis*, and *Lycium shawii*. Large depressions, ranging from a few hundred meters to more than two kilometers in diameter and which collect fine soils and runoff water, may support forest growth of shrubs and trees over three meters in height. Common species in these areas are *Ziziphus nummularia*, *Lycium shawii*, and *Acacia tortilis*. Shallow depressions support plant growth of *Francoeuria crispa* and *Cymbopogon parkeri*. The sandy plains are characterized by *Panicum turgidum*, *Haloxylon salicornicum*, *Stipagrostis plumosa*, and *Zygophyllum quatarense*. Fields of mobile sand dunes are concentrated primarily in southeastern Qatar. The dunes are barren, with vegetation developed only on dune bases and on interdune connections. Common sand dune species are *Cyperus conglomeratus*, *Seidlitzia rosmarinus*, *Zygophyllum quatarense*, and *Haloxylon salicornicum*. Coastal and inland salt marshes (sabkhas) support plant communities dominated by *Halopeplis perfoliata*, *Halocnemum strobiolaceum*, *Arthrocnemum glaucum*, *Limonium axillare*, *Sporobolus arabicus*, *Aeluropus lagopoides*, and *Zygophyllum quatarense*. Wadi and runnel (gullies) habitat types occur mainly in southwestern Qatar; their vegetation includes *Acacia* species, *Lycium shawii*, *Pennisetum divisum*, *Chrysopogon aucheri*, and *Glossonema edule*.

Mangroves and their characteristic coastal vegetation occupy only small areas of the Arabian Gulf coast. Their location between the terrestrial and marine ecosystems renders these habitat types an important ecological transition zone in such an extremely arid environment. *Avicennia marina* is the only natural mangrove species in the Gulf region.

Humans have occupied the Gulf region for millennia. By the 10th century A.D. the Arabs of the Gulf had established a trade network to China and eastern Asia. Cargos of textiles and spices were accompanied by the exchange of new ideas, science, and religion. Nomadic pastoralism had been the traditional land use practice before the discovery of oil in the 1930s, but oil is largely responsible for the immense economic wealth and strategic importance associated with much of the Arabian Gulf today. Rapid socioeconomic changes have increased the pressure on almost every part of the terrestrial and marine ecosystems of the Gulf region, and are likely to have far-reaching environmental effects beyond the Middle East.

Environmental impacts associated with oil exploration, production, transportation, and processing (refining) in the Gulf region come from both onshore and offshore fields. Onshore exploration and production of oil affects the biotic (living) and abiotic (nonliving) components of desert ecosystems due to the mechanical and other procedures used and to accidents such as fires, explosions, and oil spills. In the production of oil, large amounts of brine (salt water) are associated with oil in an emulsion form and the brine is separated by chemical agents or electrostatic operations. The disposal of the separated brine is normally carried out by injection into the earth or disposal in nearby marine waters. This procedure has serious negative effects on the desert ecosystem.

Onshore oil transportation by pipelines may also result in accidental oil spills, and the pipelines disturb wildlife and affect land use. Potential hazards may come also from transportation and liquefaction of natural gas due to the discharge of heat into the atmosphere and the occasional emission or flaring of excess components. If the liquefied natural gas is spilled, it boils rapidly and affects the atmosphere.

The impacts of oil processing come from airborne and liquid effluent emissions, accidental spills from stored crude oil or refined products, and the potential nuisance of the odor around the refinery. Refineries require large amounts of water in various process operations; the wastewaters thus produced are loaded with pollutants. A 300,000–barrel-per-day refinery requires 520 hectares of land for direct use and an additional 520 hectares as an exclusion area. The combination of pollutant emissions, wastewaters, and the large land area occupied by the refinery conflicts with traditional land use and disturbs wildlife, particularly in small countries such as Kuwait, Bahrain, and Qatar.

Coastal reclamation represents one of the major impacts on deserts of the Arabian Gulf, particularly in small countries. Extensive infilling of coastal marshes has been undertaken to increase the land available for residential developments, ports, bridges, causeways, roads, and other purposes. Dredging in the Gulf provides much of the infill material needed for coastal expansion. These activities have serious detrimental effects on the natural habitats. In recent decades dredging of shallow coastal waters has occurred over more than 20 square kilometers in Bahrain, about 50 square kilometers in Saudi Arabia, and about 50 square kilometers in Qatar.

Because of the great wealth and the lack of environmental awareness in the societies located along the Gulf, almost every adult male owns an off-road vehicle. The widespread use of these vehicles has increased soil erosion and destroyed large areas of the natural landscape, along with associated vegetation and wildlife. Every piece of land in Qatar, Bahrain, and Kuwait seems to be affected by off-road vehicle driving; and vehicles used in the 1991 Gulf War created serious impacts in Kuwait as well as in Iraq and Saudi Arabia.

Groundwater resources in the Arabian Gulf region are overexploited due to expansion of urbanization and agricultural activities. The lowering of the groundwater table has resulted in increased saltwater penetration of the freshwater aquifer and a consequent increase of water salinity. Because of improper agricultural practices in the arid desert environment, the rate of deterioration of arable land has increased, and many farms have been abandoned because of the increased soil and water salinity and lack of water.—Ahmad K. Hegazy

See also **ACACIA; AFRICA, DESERTS OF; CHENOPODIACEAE; ISRAEL, DESERTS OF; JEDDAH; JORDAN, DESERTS OF; LEBANON, DESERTS OF; LIBYA, DESERTS OF; MIDDLE EAST, DESERTS OF; OFF-ROAD VEHICLES; PALESTINE, DESERTS OF; POLLUTION; SAHARA DESERT; SAUDI ARABIA, DESERTS OF; SYRIA, DESERTS OF; UNITED ARAB EMIRATES, DESERTS OF; YEMEN, DESERTS OF**

Further Reading

Guest, E., and A. Al-Rawi. 1966. *Flora of Iraq.* Vol. 1. Baghdad: Ministry of Agriculture.

Halwagy, R., A. F. Moustafa, and S. M. Kamel. 1982. On the ecology of the desert vegetation in Kuwait. *Journal of Arid Environments* 5:95–107.

Hegazy, A. K. 1995. Phytomonitoring and management of tar piles on the Qatari coastal marshes, Arabian Gulf. *Environmental Pollution* 90:187–190.

International Union for the Conservation of Nature. 1982. *Management Requirements for Natural Habitats and Biological Resources on the Arabian Gulf Coast of Saudi Arabia.* IUCN/University of York Report to Meteorology and Environmental Protection Administration.

McNeely, J. A., and V. M. Neronov, eds. 1991. *Mammals in the Palaeoarctic Desert: Status and Trends in the Sahara-Gobian Region.* Moscow: UNESCO Man and Biosphere Programme (MAB).

Nir, D. 1974. *The Semi-arid World: Man on the Fringe of the Desert.* London: Longman.

Obeid, M. 1975. *Qatar: Study of the Natural Vegetation.* Rome: Food and Agriculture Organization.

United Nations Environment Programme. 1981. *The Environmental Impacts of Production and Use of Energy.* Dublin: Tycooly Press.

Virgo, K. J. 1980. *An Introduction to the Vegetation of Bahrain.* Manama, Bahrain: Natural History Society.

ARABS. *See* DESERT PEOPLES

ARACHNIDS

Diverse group of invertebrate animals in the phylum Arthropoda (arthropods) having six pairs of appendages. The first pair is modified into chelicerate mouthparts, the second pair is modified in a number of ways and called pedipalps, and the next four typically (but not always) serve as walking legs. There are eleven orders (called subclasses by some authorities) of arachnids, and almost all have representatives in deserts. Spiders are the most diverse and abundant arachnids in deserts. In some deserts scorpions are also abundant, but they are less diverse than spiders.

The order Scorpiones contains the scorpions, arachnids easily recognized by the combination of a large pair of pedipalps modified into pincerlike structures used to capture and hold prey, a flattened body (mesosoma) composed of seven segments, and an elongate five-segmented taillike structure (metasoma) with a sharp, recurved stinger on the end.

The order Palpigradi contains the micro whipscorpions, which are tiny arachnids with an elongate segmented taillike structure and pedipalps modified similar to walking legs.

The order Uropygi contains the whipscorpions, which are much larger in size than micro whipscorpions, have pedipalps that are greatly enlarged, powerful, and used to subdue prey, and have a long and very thin taillike structure (the last segment is whiplike) that is waved in defense while acetic acid is squirted from glands located at the base of the tail. The first pair of walking legs is modified into a set of antennalike structures. Because of the vinegary smell of their defensive chemicals, species occurring in the United States are referred to as vinegaroons. These nocturnal species are common in the Chihuahuan Desert.

The order Schizomida, also known as short-tailed whipscorpions, are similar in form to whipscorpions but are smaller and more slender. The last appendage of the tail is not long and whiplike. A species found in deserts of southern California typically is found under rocks or in litter.

The order Amblypygi consists of the tailless whipscorpions, which are flat, spiderlike arachnids easily recognized by the structure of their pedipalps and first pair of walking legs. The pedipalps are large structures covered with sharp spines and are used to capture and impale prey. The first pair of walking legs is extremely long, flexible, and carried over the body continually moving; they are apparently used like antennae.

The order Araneae consists of the spiders, a very large group of arachnids. The body is composed of two major parts: the cephalothorax and the abdomen. Spiders have four pairs of walking legs.

The order Ricinulei is a very small group of tropical arthropods.

The order Opiliones consists of the harvestmen, also known as daddy longlegs in the United States. The body is oval, and in many species the four pairs of legs are inordinately long (hence daddy longlegs). The pedipalps are very small. In deserts they are nocturnal and found under surface objects or in crevices by day.

The order Acari consists of the mites and ticks.

The order Pseudoscorpiones consists of the pseudoscorpions, small scorpionlike arachnids lacking the elongate tail and stinger. These tiny arachnids occur under the bark of desert trees and are carried on the bodies of other insects, particularly large beetles.

The order Solifugae comprises the sun spiders or whipscorpions. They are fast-moving, usually nocturnal arachnids with the first pair of walking legs modified into sensory structures that are carried above the front part of the body. They are very common in deserts.—Laurie J. Vitt

See also **ARTHROPODS; BLACK WIDOW SPIDER; DEFENSIVE ADAPTATIONS, ANIMALS; POISONOUS ANIMALS; RED VELVET MITE; SCORPIONS; SPIDERS; SUN SPIDER; TARANTULA; TICKS; VENOM**

Further Reading

Borror, D. J., C. A. Triplehorn, and N. F. Johnson. 1992. *An Introduction to the Study of Insects.* New York: Harcourt Brace.

Polis, G. A., and T. Yamashita. 1991. The ecology and importance of predaceous arthropods in desert communities. *In* G. Polis, ed., *The Ecology of Desert Communities,* 383–437. Tucson: University of Arizona Press.

Smith, R. L. 1982. *Venomous Animals of Arizona.* Tucson: Cooperative Extension Service, University of Arizona.

ARCTIC DESERT. *See* AN INTRODUCTION TO DESERTS; ASIA, DESERTS OF

ARENOSOL. *See* SOILS, DESERT, ARENOSOL

ARGALI

Large, wild sheep (*Ovis ammon,* mammalian order Artiodactyla, family Bovidae) native to mountainous or arid regions of Central and southern Asia, including Siberia, Kazakhstan, Kirgizia, Tadzhikistan, Afghanistan, Pakistan, China, India, Nepal, and Mongolia. Argalis (also known as Marco Polo sheep) are the world's largest sheep. Although typically light brown, individuals vary in color from pale brown to dark gray. Argalis have striking markings: a white neck ruff, white patch on the rear, and white socks from the knees to the hooves. Rams have large curled horns that may approach two meters in length over the greater curvature. Although argalis prefer to eat grasses and herbs having a high moisture content, they often resort to eating dry or woody plant material to survive in deserts. These animals are most common, particularly in the desert portions of the range, in and around steep outcroppings of rock, because of the increased concentration of plants, greater view, and

protective cover afforded by rocky areas. Males and females live in separate herds and only congregate during the breeding season (October–December). Unlike other species of sheep, argali rams establish harems and defend them from other males. One or two lambs are born after a gestation of 22 weeks. Lambs are weaned at four months of age. Young ewes reach sexual maturity at 18 months; young rams reach sexual maturity at 30 months. In Pakistan these sheep occur at elevations of from 4,500 to 6,100 meters in sparsely vegetated mountains. Their numbers have declined in some areas due to hunting, although they are protected in several countries (e.g., the former Soviet Union and Afghanistan).—Rob Channell

See also **ASIA, DESERTS OF; BARBARY SHEEP; GOAT; MAMMALS; MOUFLON SHEEP; SHEEP; UNGULATES**

Further Reading

Clark, J. L. 1964. *The Great Arc of the Wild Sheep.* Norman: University of Oklahoma Press.

Demidov, E. P. 1966. *After Wild Sheep in the Altai and Mongolia.* New York: Ambercrombie and Fitch.

Roberts, T. J. 1977. *The Mammals of Pakistan.* London: Ernest Benn.

Schaller, G. B., and G. Binyuan. 1994. Comparative ecology of ungulates in the Aru Basin of Northwest Tibet. *Research and Exploration* 10:266–293.

ARGENTINA, DESERTS OF. *See* SOUTH AMERICA, DESERTS OF

ARIDITY

Term that refers to factors associated with dryness, such as drought and low relative humidity. In deserts aridity generally is caused by low annual precipitation, high evaporation, and low vegetative cover. Because of aridity, agriculture in deserts is difficult at best, usually accomplished with irrigation or through the use of underground water. Aridity can be quantified through various indices, such as $I = P/T \times 10$, where I = the Index of Aridity, T = the average annual temperature in degrees Centigrade, and P = average annual precipitation in millimeters. Despite many such indices, however, there is little agreement as to the complex array of factors that lead to aridity in a desert, or how arid areas can best be compared using such indices. In addition, other factors, such as soil type, time of year in which precipitation falls, drainage, and grazing, can influence the degree of aridity of an area.—Virgilio G. Roig

See also **AN INTRODUCTION TO DESERTS; ARIDITY INDEX; CLIMATE; CLIMATE CLASSIFICATION; DESERTS; DROUGHT; HEAT; HOLDRIDGE LIFE ZONES; INSOLATION; MOISTURE INDEX; PRECIPITATION**

Further Reading

Oliver, J. E., and R. W. Fairbridge, eds. 1987. *The Encyclopedia of Climatology*. New York: Chapman and Hall.

ARIDITY INDEX

Relative quantitative index of aridity based on the percentage of water deficiency and water need during a particular season and at any particular point that is calculated as ARIDITY INDEX = 100 $\times$ d/n, where d = water deficiency and represents the sum of the absolute values of the monthly differences between rainfall and potential evapotranspiration, when rainfall is less than potential evapotranspiration, and n = the water needed at a particular site, which is calculated as the sum of the monthly values of potential evapotranspiration for months having a water deficiency.

The converse of the aridity index is the humidity index, which is also a percentage relationship to express excess water at a site. It is calculated as HUMIDITY INDEX = 100 $\times$ s/m, where s = excess water, representing the sum of the monthly differences between rainfall and potential evapotranspiration for those months when precipitation exceeds evapotranspiration, and m = the water needed at a site, which is calculated as the sum of the monthly values for evapotranspiration during those months when there is excess rainfall. Both indices are calculated independently. The higher their value, the drier (for the aridity index) or wetter (for the humidity index) a particular site is determined to be.

In 1948 the above indices were combined into a single index by Thornthwaite, who called it the MOISTURE INDEX. This index is a measure of precipitation effectiveness for plant growth and takes into account both the excess and the deficiency of water at a particular site. The moisture index is calculated as follows: MOISTURE INDEX = HUMIDITY INDEX − 0.60 $\times$ ARIDITY INDEX. Based on the moisture index (*MI*), Thornthwaite developed his system of climatic classification, with the different vegetational climatic types resulting as follows: *MI* > 100 = perhumid; 20 < *MI* < 100 = humid; 0 < *MI* < 20 = subhumid; −40 < *MI* < 0 = semiarid; and *MI* < −40 = arid.—Alberto I. J. Vich and Juana Susana Barroso

See also **AN INTRODUCTION TO DESERTS; ARIDITY; CLIMATE; CLIMATE CLASSIFICATION; DESERTS; DROUGHT; HEAT; HOLDRIDGE LIFE ZONES; INSOLATION; MOISTURE INDEX; PRECIPITATION**

Further Reading

Oliver, J. E., and R. W. Fairbridge, eds. 1987. *The Encyclopedia of Climatology*. New York: Chapman and Hall.

Suh-Shiaw, Lo. 1992. *Glossary of Hydrology*. Taipei: Sheng Te.

Schneider, S. H., ed. 1996. *Encyclopedia of Climate and Weather*. 2 vols. New York: Oxford University Press.

Thornthwaite, C. D., and J. R. Mather. 1967. *Instrucciones y tablas para el cómputo de la evapotranspiración potencial y el balance hídrico*. Buenos Aires: INTA-Instituto de Suelos y Agrotécnica, Publication No. 46.

ARIDOSOL. *See* SOILS, DESERT, ARIDOSOL

ARID ZONES DEFINED. *See* AN INTRODUCTION TO DESERTS; DESERTS

ARIZONA DESERT

Northeasternmost portion of the Sonoran Desert lying within the United States. This desert is the home of the saguaro cactus and is usually referred to as the Arizona Upland Desert. It is considered the most picturesque portion of the Sonoran Desert.

The Arizona Desert occurs on sloping plains that are highly dissected and broken. Much of the area is traversed by shallow arroyos that carry water only after torrential desert thunderstorms. There are two rainy seasons in this desert, one in the summer and one in the winter. The Arizona Desert receives the most precipitation of any of the hot deserts in North America.

The vegetation of the Arizona Desert has a definite shrubland appearance and is dominated by leguminous trees and perennial succulents. The state tree of Arizona, paloverde (*Cercidium*), is a conspicuous member of the diverse flora of this desert, and its yellow blooms brighten the landscape. Other common trees are ironwood (*Olneya tesota*), mesquite (*Prosopis*), and catclaw acacia (*Acacia greggii*). These important nitrogen-fixing plants contribute their nutrient-rich leaves and pods to the desert floor, where they decay and thus enrich the desert soils. The most extensive portion of this desert is dominated by the little-leaf, or foothill, paloverde (*Cercidium microphyllum*) and the columnar cactus (*Carnegiea gigantea*).

In much of the Arizona Desert, particularly on well-drained bajadas, many other species of cacti are extremely common. In fact, cacti are so characteristic of this desert that the famous desert ecologist Forrest Shreve referred to it as a crassicaulescent, or stem-succulent, desert. Some of the more recognizable species of cacti are teddy bear cholla (*Opuntia bigelovii*), chain-fruited cholla (*Opuntia fulgida*), buckhorn cholla (*Opuntia acanthocarpa*), pencil cholla (*Opuntia arbuscula*), organ pipe cactus (*Stenocereus thurberi*), and senita (*Lophocereus schottii*) and fish-hook barrel cactus (*Ferocactus wislizenii*).

The most remarkable and most photographed of all the cacti is the giant saguaro (sometimes spelled sahuaro), which often reaches a height of 15 meters. It is a classic example of the adaptation of a plant to arid desert environments. The huge fluted stem of the saguaro contains sufficient water reserves to enable it to survive harsh dry periods that may last for many months.

Grasses also form an important part of the Arizona Desert. Common genera are *Bouteloua*, *Hilaria*, and *Sporobolus*. Many of the grass species are of great forage value and provide grazing for domestic livestock as well as wild animals.

Numerous animals are characteristic of the Arizona Desert: white-throated woodrat (*Neotoma albigula*), desert cottontail (*Sylvilagus audubonii*), Gila woodpecker (*Melanerpes uropygialis*), cactus wren (*Heleodytes brunneicapillus couesi*), and Gambel's quail (*Lophortyx gambelii*). In addition, there are a variety of snakes, lizards, and invertebrates.

Some of the more accessible and especially beautiful scenic areas of the Arizona Desert are the Saguaro National Monument near Tucson, Arizona, and the Organ Pipe Cactus National Monument near Ajo, Arizona. Also, west of Tucson in the Tucson Mountains is the Arizona-Sonora Desert Museum, which houses a spectacular array of Sono-

ran Desert flora and fauna.—Gary K. Hulett and Amanda Renner Charles

See also **AN INTRODUCTION TO DESERTS; BIRDS; CACTI; CHOLLA; CALIFORNIA DESERT; CHIHUAHUAN DESERT; CLIMATE; DESERTS; DESERTS, HOT; DESERTS, TEMPERATE; LIZARDS; MAMMALS; MESQUITE; ORGAN PIPE CACTUS; ORGAN PIPE CACTUS NATIONAL MONUMENT; PALOVERDE; PLANT GEOGRAPHY; REPTILES; SAGUARO; SEMI-ARID ZONES; SNAKES; SONORAN DESERT**

Further Reading

Brown, D. E. 1978. The vegetation and occurrence of chaparral and woodland flora on isolated mountains within the Sonoran and Mojave deserts in Arizona. *Journal of the Arizona-Nevada Academy of Science* 13:7–12.

Brown, D. E., ed. 1994. *Biotic Communities: Southwestern United States and Northwestern Mexico.* Salt Lake City: University of Utah Press.

Lowe, C. H., and D. E. Brown. 1973. *The Natural Vegetation of Arizona.* State of Arizona, Arizona Resources Information System. ARIS Cooperative Publication 2. Phoenix.

Niering, W. A. R., H. Whittaker, and C. H. Lowe. 1963. The saguaro: A population in relation to environment. *Science* 142:15–23.

Steenbergh, W. F., and P. L. Warren. 1977. *Preliminary Ecological Investigations of Natural Community Status at Organ Pipe Cactus National Monument.* USDI Cooperative National Park Resources Studies Unit, University of Arizona Technical Report 3.

Turner, R. M. 1974. Quantitative and historical evidence of vegetation changes along the Upper Gila River, Arizona. U.S. Geological Survey Professional Paper 655-H.

Whittaker, R. H., and W. A. Niering. 1965. Vegetation of the Santa Catalina Mountains, Arizona. *Ecology* 46:429–452.

ARKOSIC SAND. *See* SOILS, DESERT, ARKOSIC SAND

ARMADILLO

Unusual mammal whose body is covered with armor; member of the mammalian order Xenarthra, family Dasypodidae. There are 20 living species in 8 genera; all 20 are restricted to the Americas, and only 2 are found outside of South America. The range of *Cabassous centralis* extends northward from Colombia into Mexico. The nine-banded armadillo (*Dasypus novemcinctus*) has the most extensive distribution in the family, ranging from northern Argentina to the southern United States;

the species continues to expand its distribution and now occurs as far north as Central Oklahoma and South Carolina.

Armadillos are primarily species of tropical and subtropical regions. Several species occur in rain forest habitats; however, most armadillos, including the giant armadillo (*Priodontes maximus*), inhabit savannas, arid scrublands, and deserts. Two genera are particularly adapted to arid regions. The genus *Chaetophractus*, hairy armadillos, contains three species that are found in the high altitude puna desert, the semiarid Chaco thorn scrub, the Monte Desert, and the Pampas (or grasslands) habitats found from Bolivia through Paraguay and Chile to Argentina. The genus *Chlamyphorus*, fairy armadillos, contains two species that are restricted to the arid Chaco and Monte Desert regions of Bolivia, Paraguay, and Argentina. The southern three-banded armadillo (*Tolypeutes matacus*) also is primarily an arid habitat specialist whose range overlaps species in the previous two genera. Its sister species, *Tolypeutes tricinctus*, was once thought to be extinct but has been rediscovered in the semiarid Caatinga of northeastern Brazil;, a habitat similar to the Chaco but thousands of kilometers distant.

All armadillos have similar morphology. The back is covered by an armor of bony plates. The plates on the shoulders and rump are rigid, but there are a varying number of flexible bands between plates. The tail, head, and limbs also have some armor. The claws, especially on the forelimbs, are well developed for digging. The teeth are peg-like and usually number 14–18 (the giant armadillo has 80–100, the most of any mammal), and the tongue is long and protrusible. The range in size in this family is impressive: head-body length ranges from 125 to 1,000 millimeters, and weight ranges from 80 grams to 60 kilograms. Armadillos use their armor for protection, usually by drawing the legs in under the body and pulling the head in against the shoulder armor. The three-banded armadillos (*Tolypeutes*) are able to roll their body into an armored ball.

All species are primarily nocturnal. They feed mostly on insects and invertebrates but also select small vertebrates, fungi, vegetable material, and carrion. They search for food by sense of smell. Armadillos are solitary except during the mating season. Species in the genus *Dasypus* give birth to four young (with the exception of *Dasypus hybridus*, which has from 8 to 12 young); other genera have litters of one or two, but in many cases there is no information on reproduction in the wild. Many species of armadillos are considered delicacies and are hunted heavily. Of the 20 species, only 2 are endangered: the giant armadillo and the Brazilian three-banded armadillo. Habitat destruction has created concern for the status of the fairy armadillos.—Thomas E. Lacher, Jr.

See also **AARDVARK; ANTS; CAATINGA; CHACO; MAMMALS; MONTE DESERT; PANGOLIN; PAMPAS; SAVANNA; SOUTH AMERICA, DESERTS OF; TERMITES; TYMPANIC BULLAE**

Further Reading

Macdonald, D., ed. 1984. *The Encyclopedia of Mammals*. New York: Facts on File.

Montgomery, G. G., ed. 1985. *The Evolution and Ecology of Armadillos, Sloths, and Vermilinguas*. Washington, D.C.: Smithsonian Institution Press.

Nowak, R. M. 1991. *Walker's Mammals of the World*. 5th ed. Baltimore: Johns Hopkins University Press.

ARROWWEED

Shrublike perennial plant (*Pluchea servicea*) of the sunflower family (Asteraceae) commonly found in southwestern U.S. deserts. Arrowweed grows to three meters tall, often forming dense thickets along streambeds and in moist, saline soils. A common constituent of Sonoran Desert riparian vegetation, arrowweed frequently grows between willows and mesquites along river channels. The leaves of arrowweed emit an agreeable fragrance until the plants dry, at which time their odor becomes rank and unpleasant.

Arrowweed is browsed by deer and sometimes by livestock. Native Americans used its straight stems to make arrow shafts, thereby contributing to its common name. The straight stems of arrowweed also made the plant useful as a construction material in walls and roofs of mud huts. Native Americans used stems to make storage bins, animal cages, and baskets. Pima Indians brewed a tea from the leaves of the stem tips.—Gordon E. Uno

See also **CHIHUAHUAN DESERT; MESQUITE; O'ODHAM; PLANT ADAPTATIONS; PLANTS; RIPARIAN COMMUNITIES; SONORAN DESERT**

Further Reading

Dodge, N. N. 1961. *Flowers of the Southwest Deserts*. Globe, Ariz.: Southwestern Monuments Association.

ARROYO

Ephemeral or intermittent stream channel found in semiarid and arid regions. The term was first used in the southwestern United States and is of Spanish origin. It is typically associated with dry stream channels in New Mexico, Arizona, southern California, and West Texas and throughout the drier parts of Latin America. Some arroyos are also found in badlands, such as in Badlands National Monument, South Dakota. The arroyo begins as a narrow, steep-sided, flat-bottomed channel in alluvium (material deposited by flowing water), gradually getting wider and shallower downstream, and terminates when it intersects the main channel bed and bank. The terminal end of the arroyo is characterized by a spread of alluvial deposits often covered by vegetation. Headward arroyo extension results from upstream erosion because of piping (pipes are subsurface channels found in steep slopes on gullies and arroyos into which surface waters and sediments enter and reemerge elsewhere in the hillslope system; they can serve as subsurface conduits for waters and sediments), sapping (a groundwater seepage or spring-controlled erosional process responsible for the development of amphitheater-shaped dry valleys and canyons; the process takes place at the junction between different rock strata and is especially pronounced between impermeable rocks, such as shale, overlain by more permeable strata, such as sandstone), or surface erosion.

Entrenching (cutting down vertically, such as a stream cutting through its own floodplain sediments) occurs in unconsolidated alluvium commonly found in floodplains and is attributed to the erosional forces of surface runoff. Arroyo formation as a consequence of climatic change results primarily from an increase in the frequency of high-magnitude summer rainstorms and a decrease in the low-intensity rains, the latter responsible for plant growth. These intense rainfalls produce erosional forces that overcome the weakened vegetation. Anthropogenic (human-related) activities that contribute to arroyo formation include ranching, burning, clearing, and poor agricultural practices. Overgrazing by livestock during the late 19th century is believed to have been responsible for the initiation of many arroyos in New Mexico and Arizona.

Arroyos are also prominent in semiarid areas of southern Africa, India, the Iberian Peninsula, Australia, and South America. Regional synonyms for arroyo are donga (Southeast Africa), gully, wadi or oued (North Africa and the Middle East), and wash.—Vatche P. Tchakerian

See also **ALLUVIAL FAN; COLLUVIAL DEPOSITS (COLLUVIUM); FLOOD; FLOODPLAIN; HYDROLOGICAL CYCLE; HYDROLOGY; IRRIGATION DRAINAGE; RIPARIAN COMMUNITIES; RIVERS; RUNOFF**

Further Reading

Campbell, I. A. 1989. Badlands and badland gullies. In D. S. G. Thomas, ed., Arid Zone Geomorphology, 159–183. London: Belhaven.

Cooke, R., A. Warren, and A. Goudie. 1993. Desert Geomorphology. London: University College London Press.

ARTEMISIA

Abundant shrub commonly called sagebrush (several species are included under the common name) belonging to the large family Asteraceae (sunflowers), with the most important species in North America being big sagebrush (Artemisia tridentata). These aromatic herbs and shrubs are grown for their foliage and potential medicinal content. Wormwood, a common European garden herb in this relatively large genus, is the source of absinthe. Artemisia is found mostly in the Northern Hemisphere, including across much of western North America. It is also both abundant and diverse in Old World deserts; for example, there are more than 100 species of Artemisia in the deserts of Middle Asia alone. Wild Artemisia afra at one time supplied commercial quantities of essential oils in deserts of South Africa. These woody shrubs grow to one meter in height and perhaps are the most characteristic and widespread dominant plant in the intermountain deserts and desert grasslands of the Great Basin between the Rocky Mountains and the Sierra Nevada. In some areas sagebrush commonly makes up more than 70 percent of the vegetation cover and more than 90 percent of the plant biomass.

In general sagebrush density increases, but the size of the plants decreases on more xeric sites. Sagebrush also increases with overgrazing and lowered fire frequency. Sagebrush has the ability to photosynthesize almost year-round because it produces two sets of leaves. One set is large and ephemeral, developing in the spring and remaining on the plant until the summer drought arrives. The plant also produces smaller, persistent leaves that last through the winter. The leaves and the dominance of sagebrush in the Great Basin produce the characteristic grayish-green color of the entire plant community. The leaves possess low palatability because of a bitter, pungent taste; however, the shrub is a somewhat valuable forage plant for livestock during the winter and when alternative foliage is unavailable.—Gordon E. Uno

See also **GREAT BASIN DESERT; CHENOPODIACEAE; MONTANA DESERT; MONTE DESERT; NEVADA DESERT; OREGON DESERT; PAMPAS; PERENNIAL PLANTS; PLANT ADAPTATIONS; PLANT GEOGRAPHY; PLANTS; SAGEBRUSH; SEMIDESERT; UNITED STATES, DESERTS OF; UTAH DESERT**

Further Reading

Bailey, L. H. 1935. *The Standard Cyclopedia of Horticulture*. New York: Macmillan.

Brown, D. E., ed. 1994. *Biotic Communities: Southwestern United States and Northwestern Mexico*. Salt Lake City: University of Utah Press.

Heywood, V. H., ed. 1993. *Flowering Plants of the World*. Updated ed. New York: Oxford University Press.

USDA Forest Service. 1988. *Range Plant Handbook*. New York: Dover.

ARTESIAN BASIN

Depositional basin or syncline (a U-shaped downfold in sedimentary strata) within which is located an aquifer or series of aquifers. Aquifers are divided into three zones: the recharge area, the discharge area, and the transitional area.

The area of highest elevation at which the aquifer is exposed at the surface is known as the recharge area. Here water penetrates the exposed aquifer and replenishes the groundwater. Both precipitation and surface runoff contribute to the recharge of the aquifer. The recharge area is often fed by the local drainage patterns or outflows of neighboring aquifers.

In the discharge area the aquifer is exposed to the surface at an elevation below that of the recharge area. The discharge site can be either natural or artificial. The natural discharge sites can be distinguished as either open or hidden. Artesian, or free-flowing, springs are examples of open natural sites. Hidden natural sites include those located in river channels or on the seafloor. In some basins hidden discharge may occur as flow from one aquifer to another. Artificial discharge sites are favorable locations for wells intended for human use.

The portion of the aquifer between the recharge and discharge areas is known as the transitional area. The difference in elevations between the recharge and discharge areas (termed the piezometric surface) establishes the isopotential level, or artesian water level. Water in a well drilled in this area will reach the height of the isopotential level at that site.

Artesian basins occur in all parts of the world, including arid lands such as around Roswell, New Mexico, in the southwestern United States. An extensive artesian basin is located in Central Australia. Here Jurassic sandstones underlie 1.3 million square kilometers of land, with a recharge area in the Eastern Highlands of the continent. Other prominent artesian basins occur in North Africa (Sudan, Egypt, Libya) and the Arabian Peninsula.—Vatche P. Tchakerian

See also **AQUATIC HABITATS; GROUNDWATER; IRRIGATION DRAINAGE; RUNOFF; WATER**

Further Reading

Dunne, T., and L. B. Leopold. 1978. *Water in Environmental Planning*. New York: Freeman. Pp. 192–235.

ARTESIAN WATER. See ARTESIAN BASIN

ARTESIAN WELL. See ARTESIAN BASIN

ARTHROPODS

Living and extinct invertebrates having an articulated chitinous exoskeleton (external skeleton) covering the entire body, metamerism (the body is divided into a linear series of segments), and a pair of appendages associated with each metamere (segment). The word "arthropod" derives from the phylum Arthropoda, a taxonomic grouping that contains all of the arthropods. "Arthro" refers to jointed, and "poda" ("foot" in Greek) refers to appendage. The phylum Arthropoda contains two currently living evolutionary groups, the Chelicerata (spiders, mites, ticks, scorpions, sun spiders) and the Mandibulata (crustaceans, millipedes, centipedes, and insects). Some authors divide the arthropods into three groups, the Chelicerata, the Crustacea (crustaceans), and the Tracheata (millipedes, centipedes, and insects).

The chitinous exoskeleton separates the arthropods from other segmented invertebrates. Most arthropods can be easily recognized as such because they have jointed appendages. Anterior body segments are fused into a head region (cephalon), which contains compound eyes and several pairs of modified appendages (antennae, antennules, maxillae, and mandibles). Included in the arthropods are millipedes, centipedes, scorpions, spiders, mites, ticks, insects, crabs, shrimp, lobsters, barnacles, and many other groups. Arthropods are among the most evolutionarily diverse living organisms, with about 100,000 species of noninsect arthropods described and more than a million species of insects named.

Their economic importance is immeasurable. They maintain biological diversity on a global scale, as they form the basis of food chains for large numbers of invertebrates and vertebrates; many are harvested in large quantities and eaten by humans; some are agricultural pests ;contributing substantially to the cost of food production; some have been used to control agricultural pests; and some are vectors of the most important diseases affecting humans. Perhaps more than 95 percent of the species of organisms in the world are arthropods.

A remarkably diverse group, the arthropods have adapted to nearly every imaginable habitat and microhabitat. Many crustaceans live in oceans, while most insects, spiders, scorpions, centipedes, and millipedes live in terrestrial environments. A large number of insect and mite species are aquatic (fresh water) throughout their lives, whereas many insects have aquatic larvae and terrestrial or aerial adults. Ticks, many mites, and some insects are parasitic on other animals, although many mites are free living. Many arthropods have high reproductive rates due to a combination of early sexual maturity and production of large numbers of eggs or offspring. Consequently, populations of arthropods can grow extremely rapidly given the proper conditions. Familiar examples are the rapid growth of cockroach populations in human habitations, fruit flies in rotting fruit, and spiders in hard-to-clean areas of buildings. Rapid growth of populations of arthropods that transmit human disease can have grim results, for example, fleas and bubonic plague.

Appendages of arthropods have undergone striking adaptations. In addition to being involved in flight, some appendages, such as the legs of swimming insects, have evolved into oars, facilitating locomotion in water. Still others have been modified into defensive structures, such as the biting jaws of centipedes, spiders, and many insects. In many marine arthropods, such as barnacles, appendages have become modified for oxygen uptake, becoming functional gills.

Among the most spectacular evolutionary advances found in arthropods is the ability to fly, which apparently has evolved only once in the history of the group—in the large class Insecta. The evolution of flight undoubtedly led to a rapid diversification of insects and assisted them in locating new microhabitats, food, and mates while offering a means of escaping predation. Flight in insects influenced diversification in many other groups of organisms as well. For example, flying insects are the primary pollinators of most plants; many of the plants with which we are familiar today simply would never have evolved in the absence of flying insects. Many of the orb-weaving spiders have nests especially designed to capture flying insects, and consequently insects may have played an important role in the diversification of spiders as well.

The eyes of arthropods vary from simple light detectors to complex compound structures capable of forming images and detecting even the slightest motion. Spiders have many eyes (usually four pairs) that reflect blue or green when viewed at night with artificial light.

Because the body of arthropods is covered by a series of platelike structures comprising the chitinous exoskeleton, growth is possible only by shedding (molting) the rigid exoskeleton and replacing it with a larger exoskeleton. Molting is a complex physiological process involving hormonal mediation such that (1) a new exoskeleton is developed underneath the original exoskeleton, but the new exoskeleton is not hardened, (2) the old exoskeleton splits open such that the arthropod can climb out of it, and (3) the new, larger exoskeleton then hardens. Adding to this complexity is the fact that many arthropods undergo dramatic metamorphosis as they grow, such that great morphological changes occur coincident with molting. Examples are the spectacular changes that occur when a caterpillar transforms into a chrysalis and later emerges from the chrysalis as a moth or butterfly.

Arthropod defense mechanisms are extremely diverse, ranging from production of injected toxins, sprayed chemicals, urticating (irritating) hairs, and a hard cuticle to group behavior and swarming in response to potential intruders.

The evolutionary history of arthropods is complex. Terrestrial arthropods date back to at least the Paleozoic, and preceded the evolution of vascular plants. Arthropods are extremely important in all ecosystems. As prey, many form the basis of complex food webs involving other arthropods, amphibians, reptiles, mammals, and birds. Predaceous arthropods are often the prey of other predaceous arthropods, or of vertebrate species. Many arthropods (primarily insects) are the carriers of pollen from male to female reproductive organs of plants and consequently assume critical importance for maintenance of plant diversity. In some instances only one (or a few) species of insects is responsible for pollination of a particular plant species.

Life cycles and reproductive behavior of arthropods vary from simple to extremely complex. In those with simple life cycles, juveniles hatch from eggs or are born with a morphology nearly identical to that of adults. For example, in scorpions, all of which are viviparous (live bearing), the newly born scorpions are identical to adults but smaller. Extended parental care occurs in scorpions, and the juveniles are carried on the back of the female. Throughout their lives they increase in size as a result of feeding and a series of moltings. The feeding behavior of juveniles is identical to that of adults; they simply feed on much smaller prey.

At the other extreme are certain insects that undergo drastic metamorphoses during their life cycles. Butterflies, for example, hatch from eggs as tiny larvae called caterpillars. The caterpillars feed on green vegetation, increasing in size as they grow and molt. After a set number of moltings the caterpillars either construct a cocoon or simply remain in a protected microhabitat and undergo a molting that transforms them from a mobile, feeding caterpillar to a stationary, nonfeeding chrysalis. During the chrysalis stage the insect slowly transforms from a juvenile into an adult. In the final molt the chrysalis exoskeleton is broken open and the adult emerges. At emergence the wings of the adult are not inflated and the entire body is soft. The adult usually hangs on to the exoskeleton of the chrysalis, or the cocoon, and inflates its wings as its new adult exoskeleton hardens. The adult then flies off in search of a mate to continue the cycle. Most butterflies feed as adults, taking nectar from plants rather than feeding on the green leaves that they ate as caterpillars.

Arthropods are by far the most diverse group of animals in deserts of the world. They live in nearly every imaginable desert microhabitat, from the tips of branches in trees to deep caverns in the burrows of vertebrates. Some are even ectoparasites of vertebrates (fleas, ticks, mites). Those most frequently observed in deserts are scorpions, centipedes, millipedes (especially following rains), spiders, and myriad insects. Many desert arthropods have evolved behavior, morphology, and/or physiology to deal with thermal extremes and extreme water shortages. Desert arthropods are the primary food of most desert lizards and amphibians, many birds, and some mammals. Even some of the fishes that live in desert aquatic systems feed on arthropods.—Laurie J. Vitt

See also **ANTLIONS**; **ANTS**; **ARACHNIDS**; **BAGWORMS**; **BLACK WIDOW SPIDER**; **BEES**; **BEETLES**; **BUGS**; **BUTTERFLIES**; **CATERPILLARS**; **CENTIPEDE, GIANT**; **EARWIGS**; **FLIES**; **GRASSHOPPERS**; **HYMENOPTERA**; **INSECTS**; **MILLIPEDES**; **MOLT**; **MOTHS**; **POISONOUS ANIMALS**; **SCORPIONS**; **SPIDERS**; **SUN SPIDER**; **TARANTULA**; **TENEBRIONIDAE**; **TERMITES**; **TICKS**; **VELVET ANT**; **VENOM**

Further Reading

Barnes, R. D. 1980. *Invertebrate Zoology.* 4th ed. Philadelphia: W. D. Saunders.

Cloudsley-Thompson, J. L. 1991. *Ecophysiology of Desert Arthropods and Reptiles.* New York: Springer.

Crawford, C. S. 1981. *Biology of Desert Invertebrates.* New York: Springer.

Edney, E. B. 1974. Desert arthropods. *In* G. W. Brown, Jr., ed., *Desert Biology: Special Topics on the Physical and Biological Aspects of Arid Regions,* 2:312–384. New York: Academic Press.

Eisenbeis, G., and W. Wichard. 1985. *Atlas on the Biology of Soil Arthropods.* New York: Springer.

Heatwole, H. 1996. *Energetics of Desert Invertebrates.* New York: Springer.

Milne, L., and M. Milne. 1980. *The Audubon Society Field Guide to North American Insects and Spiders.* New York: Knopf.

Nielsen, C. 1995. *Animal Evolution: Interrelationships of the Living Phyla.* New York: Oxford University Press.

Savory, T. 1977. *Arachnida.* New York: Academic Press.

Seeley, M. K. 1991. Sand dune communities. *In* G. A. Polis, ed., *The Ecology of Desert Communities,* 348–382. Tucson: University of Arizona Press.

Shear, W. A. 1991. The early development of terrestrial ecosystems. *Nature* 351:283–289.

Somme, L. 1995. *Invertebrates in Hot and Cold Arid Environments*. New York: Springer.

ASIA, DESERTS OF

Major portion of the Asian continent that encompasses an area of 16.5 million square kilometers occupied by deserts of varying levels of aridity, with 6 percent being extremely arid (hyperarid), 48 percent arid, and 46 percent semiarid. In addition, about 3 million square kilometers of the Arctic Tundra of North Siberia are completely devoid of forests and are known as the polar desert, or Arctic Desert. A series of more or less arid regions stretch with few breaks from the west coast of North Africa to northeastern Mongolia. The Saharan, Arabian, and Persian deserts form a broad belt of warm tropical and subtropical drylands that extends as far as the Thar Desert in the Indo-Pakistan subcontinent. The present classification of deserts in Middle Asiatic and Central Asiatic regions varies depending on the expert consulted. The deserts of eastern China, although situated in the eastern part of the continent, are included by many among Central Asiatic deserts. Hence it appears more logical to classify them according to longitude: Midwestern, Central, and Mideastern. Although even under this scenario the boundaries of some deserts extend beyond regional longitudinal limits, their major distribution still falls within the ranges specified. Hence the following classification has been adopted here to describe the geographic location and to discuss the deserts.

I. Deserts of Siberia (polar deserts)
   A. Ice cap
   B. Tundra
   C. Taiga (or boreal forest)
II. Midwestern deserts (50°–75° east longitude)
   A. Southern Irano-Turanian physiographic unit: Ust-Urt Plateau and Turanian Lowland. Kazyl-Kum and Kara-Kum deserts of Uzbekistan and Turkmenistan.
   B. Northern Kazakhistan physiographic unit: Bet-Pak-Dala Plateau and Kazakh Uplands
   C. Pamir Plateau
III. Central deserts (75°–95° east longitude)
   A. Tibetan Plateau
   B. Takla Makan Desert
   C. Tsaidam Desert
IV. Mideastern deserts (95°–120° east longitude)
   A. Ala-Shan Desert
   B. Gobi Desert
   C. Ordos Plateau

On the basis of lithoedaphic (rock substrate and soil) characters, Asian deserts can be differentiated into (i) alluvial plains on desert sand sierozems (soils having a brownish-gray surface horizon and a light-colored subsurface horizon overlaying a carbonaceous hardpan layer); (ii) sandy-pebble deserts on gypsiferous (gypsum soils—calcium sulfate), gray-brown soil of Tertiary and Cretaceous plateaus; (iii) gypsiferous gravel deserts on gray-brown soil of Tertiary plateaus and piedmont plains; (iv) loamy desert on weakly carbonated soil; (v) clay-loess and pans on piedmont plains and ancient deltas; (vi) solonchaks (= playas, or salt flats forming in enclosed basins) and coastal salt pans.

The basin and range topography (= shield and platform topography) is present in relatively tectonically stabilized regions and is visible over much of the Saudi Arabian Peninsula and parts of the Central and Mideastern Asian deserts. Basin and range topography is dominated by alternating mountain ranges and associated basins and is most common in areas that have experienced tectonic activity (e.g., Iran, Afghanistan, Indo-Pakistan, and part of Central and Mideastern Asia). It is characterized by steep-sided valleys leading to exposed piedmont plains filled with sandy/sandy-pebbly proluvial deposits (complex sediments that form at the base of slopes).

Such level plains in basins are commonly known as playas and occur in drainage basins that are formed by blocking the flow of water through faulting (displacement of geological strata due to tectonic activities), folding (undulation of the land surface, curving, bending as a result of displacement or compression), or subsidence (mass downward settling of a surface). Sandy-pebbly deserts of Central and Mideastern Asian regions are found in Ordos, Alashan, western Tsaidam, Mongolian Gobi, Dzungaria, and the Tarim depressions. They are mostly Cretaceous plateaus on piedmont plains and depressions where surface deposits are gravel and pebble.

Deserts on piedmont plains in the Midwestern Asian region have sandy or sandy-pebbly proluvial deposits found along the foothills of Kopet Dagh, the Zaunguzskre Neogene Plateau, and the Kyzyl-Kum. Deserts of the Kara-Kum Lowland, Sary-Ishik-Otran, Muyunkum, and Aral Kara-Kum in the Midwestern Asian region, the Thar in Indo-Pakistan, and the Nafunds and Rub' Al-Khāli in the Arabian Peninsula are composed of sand masses on ancient alluvial plains. The Rub' Al-Khāli (empty quarter) of Saudi Arabia is an example of an area where drainage is blocked by aeolian (windblown) deposits on sandstone strata.

The solonchak deserts (enclosed depressions in which salts accumulate), namely, the Tsaidam depressions, the Lop Nor, and Gashun Nur lacustrine (pertaining to lake sediments) basins, the Tarim and Mongolian Gobi lowlands, and the Alashan are situated in Central and Mideastern Asia, whereas Sarykamysh, Balkhash, Zai-san, Dengizkul, and other lacustrine depressions are found in Midwestern Asia. Patches of the coastal lowlands along the Caspian Sea, Persian Gulf, and Oman coast are also solonchaks.

Deserts of Siberia (Polar Deserts)

This region encompasses about 6.5 million square kilometers of frozen desert (polar desert), marshy plains, desolate plateaus, and vast forests occupying about half of the former Soviet Union. The extensive polar ice sheet in the Northern Hemisphere is a frozen biological desert that supports virtually no life. An area of about 3 million square kilometers in northern Siberia called taundra (= tundra) is completely devoid of forest. The sub-Arctic includes vast areas of forested country called taiga (a Russian term used for dwarf open coniferous forests; the equivalent term in the New World is boreal forest). The southern limit of the Arctic is differentiated by the timberline. Categories of climates that prevail in Siberia are as follows:

1) Ice cap (polar climate): Temperature remains below zero all year, and the permafrost (permanently frozen ground) extends far into the ground.

2) Tundra (Arctic climate): Mean temperature during most of the year is below 10°C and remains below zero at least for one month. The growing season in the southern tundra commences in June and lasts only until September.

3) Taiga (sub-Arctic climate): Mean temperature is above 10°C for not more than four months and is below zero for one or more months.

Most of the polar desert receives less than 100–250 millimeters of precipitation per year, including both rain and snow. Additional water is unable to percolate below the ground due to the permafrost, hence swamps form over extensive areas. The northern tundra outside the limits of the ice cap supports some lichens and cushion-type vegetation. The central tundra is rich in herbaceous plants. Dwarf shrubs start to appear in the southern tundra. Open areas in the forest-tundra zone are generally occupied by shrub tundra with dwarf birch and dwarf willows. Spruce forests constitute most of the vegetation of Siberia. Deciduous forests (oak) and steppe-meadows along with grass and sagebrush steppe appear farther south. One or more timberline species replace others across Siberia.

The reindeer (*Rangifer tarandus*) of Eurasia is equivalent to the caribou of North America. In autumn they gather in large herds and destroy lichens and dwarf shrubs. Lemmings (a rodent of northern regions) remain active beneath the hard covering of snow and colonize under well-drained southern slopes, destroying about 90–94 percent of the vegetation in the area. Burrowing ground squirrels, arctic fox, polar bears, Siberian tigers, geese, swans, ducks, and whales are some members of the Siberian fauna; these animals inhabit one of the coldest deserts on earth.

Deserts of Midwestern Asia

The western border of the Midwest Asian deserts begins at the Caspian Sea and extends through Turkmenistan and Uzbekistan to the eastern borders of Tajekistan and Kirgistan. Kazakhistan extends from the upper part of the Caspian Sea to the western border of China. In the south these deserts are bordered by the mountains of Iran (Elburz and Kopet Bagh ranges) and Afghanistan (Pamir and Hindu Kush ranges); in the north they merge through the Kazakh hills and the intermittent clayey-loamy-gravelly plains of the Russian steppes. Topography over this huge area is varied. The northern Kazakhistan and southern Irano-Turanian regions appear to be two different physiographic units. (See map of southwestern and central Asia deserts, p. 10.)

The northern portion along the eastern side of the Caspian Sea is occupied by the Ust-Urt gravelly gypsiferous desert; farther south there are two vast sandy deserts, the Kyzyl-Kum and the Kara-Kum in

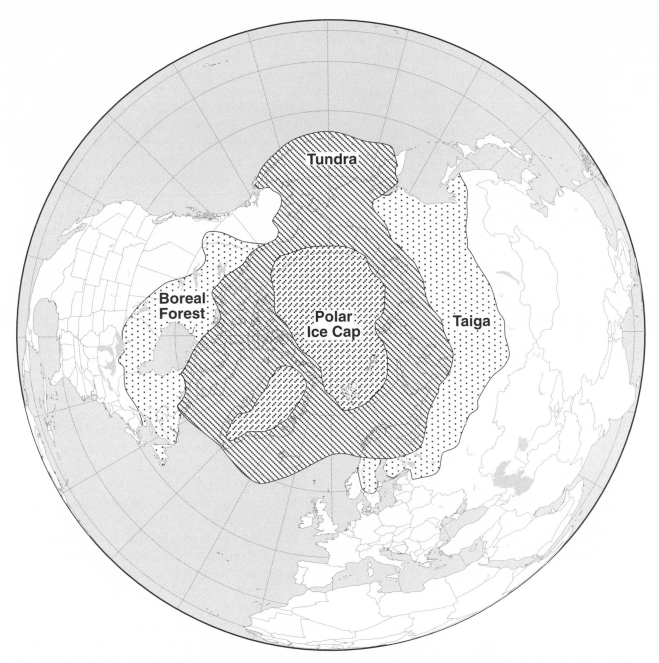

The semiarid habitats of the northern polar region, including the taiga and the boreal forest. Shading indicates desert and semidesert limits.

Uzbekistan and Turkmenistan, respectively. The stony desert of Bet-Pak-Dala is located on the eastern end of Kazakhistan by the side of Balkhash Lake. The mountainous districts of Dzungarian Ala-Tan, Tien Shan, and Pamir-Alai are situated at their eastern and southeastern boundaries.

Several solonchaks are found along the coast of the Caspian Sea and in lake basins. Prolonged irrigation practices coupled with inadequate leaching in the sandy plains have resulted in excessive salt accumulation in the irrigated lands of Turkmenistan.

There are two large rivers in the area, the Amu-Darya (Darya is Persian for "river") and the Syr Darya. The former arises from the eastern mountains (Pamir and Hindu Kush ranges) and flows northwest along the border of Turkmenistan and Uzbekistan before reentering Uzbekistan and flowing into the Aral Sea. The Syr Darya arises from the Alai Range in Kirgistan and flows northwest through Kazakhistan and into the northeastern corner of the Aral Sea. Two small rivers, the Ili and Kara-Tal, arise from the Tian Shan range and empty into the eastern side of Balkhash Lake.

The groundwater is of good quality under the piedmont, though it may be somewhat saline under the alluvial plains. A Mediterranean type of climate prevails in these regions, with summers generally hot and dry and winters cold; however, the winter in the northern portions of this desert can become very cold (mean monthly temperature about -14°C) due to the influx of Arctic winds. The drop in winter temperatures in the southern areas is not as great as that in the northern areas (mean monthly temperature about 4.8°C). Summer temperatures in both physiographic units range from 25°C to 32°C. Rainfall depends on the Mediterranean cyclones. Annual precipitation ranges from 100 to 150 millimeters in desert areas. Higher amounts of annual precipitation have been observed near mountain ranges along the Iranian border (240 millimeters). Brief descriptions of the main deserts of this region follow.

Irano-Turanian Region (Ust-Urt Plateau, Turanian Plain, Kyzyl-Kum Desert, and Kara-Kum Desert)

The main part of the Ust-Urt Plateau is situated between the eastern upper half of the Caspian Sea and the western part of the Aral Sea. It is a gravelly gypsiferous desert composed of almost horizontal Tertiary strata of limestone, marl, clay, sandstone, and crystalline gypsum. Some scattered solonchaks are also present. Sloping piedmonts merge in the south through the Kara-Kal Pak Lowlands, with the Turanian Plain spreading from the eastern side of the lower half of the Caspian Sea to the southern and southeastern side of the Aral Sea. The hillocks in the Turanian Lowlands are covered with clayey and stony material. The vast sandy desert called the Kyzyl-Kum (meaning "Red Sand") is situated east of the Turanian Plain in the northern part of Uzbekistan and has an area of 19 million hectares composed of Neogene sandstone, clay, and conglomerates alternating with sand-filled lowland hillocks and saline depressions. The second largest desert, the Kara-Kum (meaning "Black Sand"), encompasses 35 million hectares beginning at the southern Turanian Plain and extending eastward to the Amu River, covering more than half of Turkmenistan. It bears underground strata of a thick homogeneous sand intercalated (one or more layers occur between other layers) with clays. It is composed of sand dunes and alluvial plains interspersed with sandstone, marls, limestone, and conglomerate, along with clayey material. Between the sand dunes are scattered takyrs (lowlands having thick [8–19 meters] layers of heavy clay and loam, often with a desiccated polygonal cracked surface) and lakes of a solonchak nature. Fertile irrigated land of the ancient alluvial basin has been converted into barren wasteland due to overirrigation with brackish water, which resulted in salt accumulating in the soil. Solonchak depressions are common along the Caspian coast.

Northern Kazakhistan (Kazakh Upland and Bet-Pak-Dala Plateau)

Bet-Pak-Dala is a large plateau of stony desert situated to the west of Balkhash Lake. It gradually merges in the north with the Kazakh Upland. Barren rocky hills of Quaternary to Precambrian age occur across the elevated plains, as well as riverbeds and small lakes in the northern Kazakhistan Desert. The region is situated in the arid and semiarid cold winter climatic zone. The northern portions of this large semidesert area merge with the southern parts of the Siberian steppe.

Vegetation is sparse in the Midwestern Asian deserts, and only a few shrubs and grasses are found scattered in the area. Among ephemeral herbaceous plants are *Poa bulbosa*, *Carex hostii*, and *Ferula foetida* in the lowlands. Among xerophytic flora found on the slopes and foothills are *Calligonum*, *Artemisia arenaria*, *Alhagi camelorum*, *Salsola siebri*, *Haloxylon persicum*, *Aristida karelini*, *Carex physodes*, and *Agropyron sibiricum*.

Pamir Plateau

The Pamir Plateau, known as the roof of the world is situated between 72°–75° east longitude and 3°–39° north latitude in the high mountains in Tajekistan. It is an interwoven cluster of high mountains radiating to form the Hindu Kush toward the southwest, Karakoram toward the southeast, Kunlun Shan eastward, and Tien Shan northeastward. The Trans-Alai ranges (highest point is Lenin Peak, elevation 7,134 meters) and Mount Communism (elevation 7,495 meters) situated at the northern limits of the plateau are associated with many glaciers descending from the permanent snow line at 4,600 meters. The Wakhan River valley extends along the southern border of Afghanistan through the Hindu Kush range.

The Pamir experiences an extremely cold climate for most of the year. Average winter temperature remains below zero (-17°C), and temperatures frequently drop to -46°C. July is the warmest month; the average monthly temperature reaches 14°C and may go as high as 21°C. Annual precipitation is about 25–75 millimeters in the east and 230 millimeters in the west. The climate of the valley in summer is suitable for growing barley, vegetables, and fruits. Dwarf shrubs 10–15 centimeters high (*Eurasia creations*, *Artemisia skorniakovii*, *Tanacetum pamiricum*) grow scattered on the slopes of the foothills, and there are alpine meadows along streams.

Deserts of Central and Mideastern Asia

Since the deserts of the Central and Mideastern regions of Asia differ from the other deserts of Asia in climate, topography, structure, elevation, and origin, and since they constitute one huge continuous geomorphic mass stretching from Central to eastern Asia, they are considered together as a unit. They extend over 1.1 million square kilometers from 75° to 120° east longitude and from 35° to 50° north latitude, mainly in China and Mongolia. The rocky and pebbly deserts are called "gobi," and the sandy deserts are called "shamo." These deserts are spread over (i) the Tarim Basin, including the Takla Makan; (ii) the Dzungarian Basin; (iii) the Xinjiang-Gansu; (iv) the Tsaidam Basin; and (v) the Ala-Shan Basin. Semidesert regions are found in Ningxia and central Mongolia, whereas steppe vegetation characterizes eastern Mongolia and the eastern slopes of the Hinggan Mountains.

The deserts of China appear to have been formed during the late Cretaceous and early Tertiary when the Tibetan Plateau was uplifted during the great Himalayan orogeny (mountain building). The landmass is differentiated into recent inland alluvial basins (Takla Makan, Dzungarian, Tarim, and Tsaidam basins) and a high Cretaceous sedimentary plateau (elevations ranging from 500 to 1,500 meters). The Turfan and Hami depressions are below sea level. The region lacks almost any external drainage. The area remains extremely dry, with average annual precipitation less than 100 millimeters. Winter temperatures can reach as low as -6°C to -9°C, and average summer temperature may range from 24°C to 26°C.

Tibetan Plateau

Tibet is a plateau of rugged mountains spread over an area of about 1,221,000 square kilometers, between 80°–95° east longitude and 28°–36° north latitude in Central Asia at an elevation of 4,000–6,000 meters. It is surrounded by high mountain ranges and crossed by almost parallel mountain chains that separate the northern and central regions of high altitude from the southeastern portion, which is an area of narrow, deep valleys. In the north it is bordered by the Kunlun Shan Mountains, with elevations from 5,500 to 6,100 meters, and in the south by the high Himalayan crest, which reaches 6,600 meters. The Karakoram and Ladakh ranges demarcate its western and southwestern borders. A series of extremely rugged ranges extend north to south, separating its eastern border with China. The area can be divided into four major physiographic regions.

The Tibetan Plateau, called Chang Tang (Northern Plains), extends for 1,300 kilometers from west to east at an elevation of 4,600 meters. It is an arid, barren wasteland lacking vegetation. Flat depressions along the foothills of the northern mountains are filled with stony, pebbly material over the rugged piedmont. The area lacks any true river systems and is characterized by the presence of many saline lakes. Since the water-laden monsoons are intercepted by the southern Himalayan ranges, the Tibetan Plateau receives only 250–400 of millimeters annual precipitation. Daily temperatures in winter range from -10°C to 7°C, and in summer from 10°C to 24°C. Grasses appear in summer and are used by grazing animals.

The second physiographic unit is that of northwestern Tibet adjoining Kashmir. The headwaters of the Indus (known as Sengge Zanglro), the Sutlej (called Langqen Kanbab), and the Brahmaputra (called Tsangpo) originate from Lake Manasarowar situated at the highest reaches of the Trans-Himalayan Mountains (elevation 6,714 meters).

The third major physiographic region is that of the deep valley situated between the Himalayan and Trans-Himalayan ranges. The Brahamputra River flows in the valley in an easterly direction across southern Tibet before entering India.

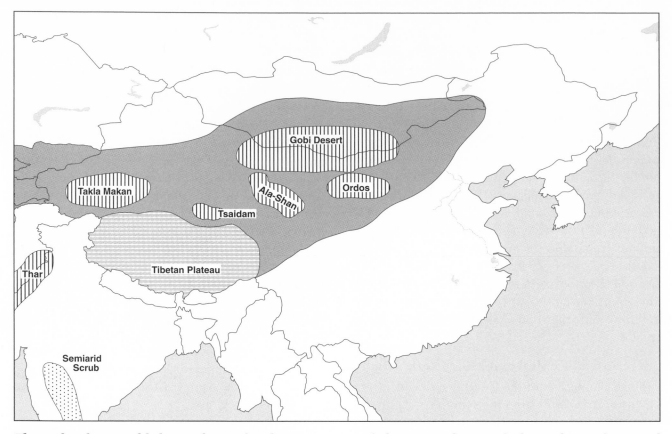

The arid and semiarid habitats of central and eastern Asia, including major deserts. Shading indicates desert and semidesert limits. The dark shading covers a region that includes both arid and semiarid habitats.

The fourth physiographic region is situated on the eastern side of Tibet on the Sichuan border of China. It has parallel valleys with a north-south orientation which contain the headwaters of the great South Asian rivers (the Salween, Mekong, and Yangtze). The climate is comparatively less extreme in the south and southeastern valleys than on the plateau, and mean monthly temperatures range from 3°C to 10°C during winter months and 18°C–24°C during summer months. Cultivation of rice, tea, apples, and bananas occurs on a limited scale. Climatic severity is reduced due to the warm and humid summer monsoon. Lhasa (elevation 3,600 meters), the capital of Tibet, is located in this region. Some root crops, vegetables, and barley are grown during the short summer in the basins of nearby seasonal streams. Yaks, sheep, goats, horses, mules, and ponies are raised in the region.

The Takla Makan Desert

This is the largest sandy desert of Central Asia and is in the Tarim Depression, where it is bordered by high mountains. The ancient lakes in the Tarim Depression and in other inland basins dried out gradually during the late Cretaceous and early Tertiary periods, and the sands of the Takla Makan engulfed the area. In the west it is surrounded by the Pamir Mountains, and in the east it gradually enters into the Lop Nor Lake Basin. The northern boundary is formed by the Tien Shan mountains, the southern boundary by the Kunlun Mountains. Between the Kunlun and Pamir mountains (in the southwest) there is a sloping strip of alluvial pebble-gravel sediment. The lacustrine alluvial deposits (deposited in association with a lake) extend north to the Tarim River valley. As the high Tibetan Plateau does not permit moisture from the Indian Ocean to reach this area, the climate remains extremely dry.

All the rivers arising from the Kunlun Mountains flow northward. Less conspicuous rivers disappear in the valleys filled with aeolian sand, whereas comparatively larger rivers (Khotan and Charchan) maintain their course through the desert up to the Tarim Depression. The sand mass in the north touches the border of the Tarim River valley, which gradually slopes eastward to the Lop Nor Lake Basin. The area of Takla Makan sand is about 271,000 square kilometers; its elevation to the west and south is 1,200–1,500 meters, and to the east and north the elevation is 800–1,000 meters. The length of sand mass from east to west is about 1,000 kilometers, and its maximum width in the center from north to south is about 420 kilometers.

A Quaternary alluvium several hundred meters thick is hidden under up to 300 meters of wind-blown sand. Sand dunes on the eastern side are mostly crescent shaped, and on the western side they are transverse and longitudinal. The dunes in general are 250–500 meters wide and 30–150 meters high, though some pyramidal-shaped barchan sand dunes 200–300 meters high are also present. Eroded ancient river channels half-filled with sand appear between sand dunes, partly exposing the gravel structure. Soils vary from medium texture in alluvial fans to fine texture near river-beds. Coarse-textured gravelly sand with surface stones (gobi) is found along the foothills of mountain slopes. Some farming is practiced along river-banks at the foothills in medium-textured soils, which vary from almost nonsaline to slightly saline in nature.

Problems with salinity have arisen due to soluble salts being carried by stream water flowing through salt-loaded rocks and depositing them in low-lying areas of the desert. Hence the underground water has been rendered saline both on the periphery and in central portions of the sandy desert. The degree of salinity in groundwater may vary from low to high.

The water table may be only 6–10 meters deep in the desert, whereas in piedmont districts it can reach a depth of 100–150 meters. One may find thickets of herbaceous vegetation with trees (i.e., Toghrak poplar) along riparian valleys and moist depressions. The groundwater emerges at the surface in a few places to form either good-quality or saline lakes. The vegetation in these lakes varies from hydrophytes (i.e., *Phragmites* and *Lasiagrostis*) to halophytes (i.e., *Tamarix* and *Nitraria*). Plants such as *Nitraria*, *Reaumuria*, *Calligonum* and *Poteninia* (fruticulose; i.e., low, flat, and with many fruits and semishrubby) are found on sandy-pebbly substrates. Low mountains and hills bear dry steppe (grassland) vegetation (e.g., *Stipa*,

Aneurolepidium, *Agropyrum*, and *Astragalus*). Large stabilized dunes support some herbaceous vegetation and some trees. Halophytic vegetation (*Salsola*, *Suaeda*, *Haloxylon*) is abundant at saline depressions.

Tsaidam Desert

This is an elevated basin at an altitude of 2,600–3,000 meters surrounded by high mountains. In the north it is bordered by the Altyn Tag (elevation 5,400 meters) and Nan Shan (elevation greater than 5,000 meters) ranges and in the south by the Kun-lun ranges (elevation greater than 6,000 meters). The average monthly temperature in winter months varies between -9°C and 13°C and in summer months between 17°C and 18°C at different points in the Tsaidam Basin. Annual precipitation is extremely low, ranging from 13 to 34 millimeters. The lowland flat plain is filled with clayey, pebbly, and sandy strata. In the central part of the basin there was a large Pleistocene lake (Dewsan Nur) that today is loaded with crusted solonchaks devoid of any kind of vegetation. *Artemisia* bushes grow on the sandy soils of the foothills and slopes.

Ala-Shan Desert

This desert is situated in a depression toward the west of Ordos adjoining the great bend of the Hwang-Ho River. The Bei-Shan Desert joins its western boundary, which is connected with the Tarim Basin through the Lop Nor depression in the west. The Ala-Shan Plateau has a complex heterogeneous geomorphology. In the north there are isolated low tectonic ranges; in the center there are aggradational (built up through deposition), chalky, sandy-pebbly plains giving the characteristic gobi structure. Most of the southern portion is occupied by eroded dry riverbeds filled with aeolian sand. The southern region is composed of three main sand masses in addition to many smaller dunes, which, due to lack of stabilization, are moved by the wind. Rainfall varies from 49 millimeters in the east to 68 millimeters in the west. The average monthly winter temperature varies from -6°C to -10°C; average monthly summer temperatures vary from 22°C to 24.5°C. Groundwater is present in dune regions. This desert is characterized by the presence of many freshwater or saline lakes that support shrubby swamp-meadow vegetation on their peripheries. Mesophytic shrubs such as *Lonicera*, *Rosa*, *Rhamnus*, and *Potentilla* appear at elevations from 1,900 to 2,500 meters, and grassy steppes supporting *Picea, Pinus,* and *Juniperus* are found from 2,500 to 3,000 meters.

Gobi Desert

The term "gobi" in the Mongolian and Manchu languages is defined as vast, flat areas of Mongolian Plateau where the ground is covered with coarse substances and the human population is scarce. The deserts of Central Asia include mountains that gently merge with stony slopes and gravelly sandy plains producing the flat, pebbly-rocky plains known as gobi deserts. They occur over Outer Mongolia and the mainland of China, including Gashun. The Dzungarian and Trans-Altai regions of the Gobi Desert occupy a strip of dissected rugged plains (elevation 900–1,200 meters) 1,750 kilometers long and 600 kilometers wide which is predominantly Tertiary-Cretaceous in origin. The dry riverbeds often terminate in closed saline dry or waterlogged depressions. Brown-colored sand is found mainly in the Mongolian Gobi, although small masses of moving sand dunes also occur in the Chinese portion of the desert. The average monthly winter temperature in the Mongolian Gobi may reach -18°C, and the average monthly summer temperature is 23°C; about 100 millimeters of rainfall each year.

Many of the rocky and gravelly deserts of Asia carry the common name "gobi." They may differ somewhat in elevation, width of their sloping piedmont plains, number of dry riverbeds, degree of topographic relief, and amount of annual precipitation, but overall they all bear the gobi characteristic of being flat, pebbly-rocky plains. Gashun Gobi, for example, is situated in Siankiang Ulgar of the Chinese People's Republic between the eastern spurs of the Tien Shan Mountains in the north and the Beishan Mountains in the south. The Trans-Altai Gobi occurs between the eastern spurs of the Mongolian and Gobi Altai in the northeast and the Beishan Mountains in the south. The eastern Gobi (in fact, the main Gobi Desert) occupies the area between the eastern spurs of the Gobi Altai, the volcanic region of Darigange, and the highlands of Jeho and Yin Shan. The Dzungarian Gobi is located between the eastern spurs of the Mongolian Altai and the easternmost portion of the Tien Shan Mountains.

Vegetation in gobi deserts depends on texture of sandy-pebbly plains (which is responsible for the retention of moisture), basic material piedmont (gypsiferous, carbonaceous, or solonchak type), ambient temperatures, and amount of precipitation; however, fruticulose vegetation (e.g., *Reaumuria soongorica, Poteninia mongolica, Calligonum mongolicum*) occurs on sandy-pebbly plains and *Stipa, Aneurole pidium, Artemisia, Agropyron,* and *Astragalus* grow on lower slopes in mountainous regions. As in other deserts, halophytic (salt-loving) vegetation (e.g., *Salsola drbusenla, Nitraria sibirica, Haloxylon ammonendran*) is found in saline depressions.

Ordos Desert

This desert is situated in the bend of the Hwang-Ho River and occurs on a plateau of soft sandstone and on a base of slightly eroded plains and lakes. The surface is covered with a layer of alluvium that is comparatively thinner on the plateau and thicker in the depressions. Series of sand dunes (up to 1,000 meters high) alternate with sand-filled flat plains. Some sand dunes have been fixed by the natural vegetation; in other regions the dunes are in continuous movement from the wind. The depressions often contain saline lakes bearing halophytic vegetation along their edges. A steppe region of the loessial plain (a deposit of porous, calcareous material) is situated at the upper Hwang-Ho and is under cultivation. Xeromorphic hard leaf grass (*Stipa tenacisia*) grows in abundance. *Artemisia ordosica* and *Pycnostelma* cover about 30–40 percent of the sandy plains.—Rafiq Ahmad

See also **AFGHANISTAN, DESERTS OF; AN INTRODUCTION TO DESERTS; DESERTIFICATION; DESERT PEOPLES; GAZELLE; GRASSLAND; HAMSTER; HIMALAYA MOUNTAINS; INDO-PAKISTAN DESERTS; INDUS RIVER; IRAN, DESERTS OF; IRRIGATION DRAINAGE; JERBOA; PAMPAS; PLAYA; PSAMMOPHYTES; PSAMMOPHYTIC SCRUB; RODENTS; SABKHA; SALT; SALT PAN; SAVANNA; STEPPE; STONE PAVEMENT; UNGULATES**

Further Reading

Blackmore, C. 1995. *The Worst Desert on Earth: Crossing the Taklamakan.* London: John Murray.

Chouhan, T. S., ed. 1993. *Natural and Human Resources of Rajasthan.* Jodhpur: Scientific Publishers.

Man, J. 1997. *Gobi: Tracking the Desert.* London: Weidenfeld and Nicholson.

McGinnies, W. G., B. J. Goldman, and P. Paylore, eds. 1968. *Deserts of the World: An Appraisal of Research into Their Physical and Biological Environments*. Tucson: University of Arizona Press.

McNeely, J. A., and V. M. Neronov, eds. 1991. *Mammals in the Palaeoarctic Desert: Status and Trends in the Sahara-Gobian Region*. Moscow: UNESCO Man and Biosphere Programme (MAB).

Petrov, M. P. 1976. *Deserts of the World*. New York: Wiley.

Walter, H. 1983. *Vegetation of the Earth*. New York: Springer.

West, N. E., ed. 1983. *Ecosystems of the World: Temperate Deserts and Semi-deserts*. Vol. 5. New York: Elsevier.

Wielgolaski, F. E., ed. 1997. *Polar and Alpine Tundra*. New York: Elsevier.

Young, S. B. 1989. *To the Arctic*. New York: Wiley.

Zohary, M. 1963. *On the Geobotanical Structure of Iran*. Research Council of Israel. Vol. 11D. Supplement, sec. D, Botany. Jerusalem: Weizman Science Press.

ASPHALT. *See* STONE PAVEMENT

ASS

Native ungulate of the horse family (mammalian order Perissodactyla, family Equidae) of the deserts and semiarid regions of Africa and Eurasia. The ass resembles a small horse but with much longer, rounded ears and relatively shorter legs. The long ears facilitate the radiation of excess heat to the environment, acting as cooling structures that help maintain body temperature in hot regions. Asses demonstrate an impressive ability to find food in arid habitats. They feed on grasses, leaves, and bark. They are able to tolerate dehydration (loss of body water) of up to one-third of body weight. A dehydrated ass can drink a quarter of its body weight in water in a few minutes. This ability to withstand dehydration rivals that of the camel, but asses are unable to tolerate the extreme fluctuations in body temperature that a camel can endure. The relatively thin coat of hair of the ass provides little in the way of protecting insulation against extreme desert temperatures. Wild asses tend to avoid the heat of the day by spending time in the shade and limiting feeding and drinking periods to the evening and dawn.

Wild asses typically live in herds of 10–12 individuals. During the breeding season herds consist of a single stallion, several mares, and a few young; however, during autumn and winter many herds may band into larger groups of 100–300 animals. Stallions are territorial during the breeding season.

Mating takes place in spring. Single foals are born after a gestation of one year. Weaning takes place after six to eight months, and it takes the young ass two years to reach sexual maturity.

The donkey, also referred to as jackass or burro, was domesticated from the North African wild ass (*Equus asinus*), possibly with some genetic contributions from the Asiatic wild ass (*Equus hemionus*) in the Middle East. (There is no difference between a donkey and a burro. In common usage "burro" refers to a Mexican- or Spanish-bred ass, or an ass of small size.) There are many regional breeds of domesticated ass, but all seem to derive from the same original stock, with possible later contributions to the bloodline from captured wild asses. The hardy nature of the donkey makes it an important beast of burden around the world but particularly in the desert, where its ability to withstand desiccation and high temperatures make it an ideal pack animal.

African and Asiatic wild asses were once widely distributed, but now only a few populations of each species remain, and the sizes of the populations are declining. The major threats to wild asses come from humans. The wild ass is hunted for meat and hides, and the introduction of domesticated asses into regions containing the remaining populations of wild asses threatens their genetic distinctiveness through interbreeding.

Feral descendants of domesticated asses threaten the natural habitats of many arid regions. In the southwestern United States asses and horses have been implicated in the decline of bighorn sheep through the habitat degradation they caused. Despite the threat to native wildlife, people have been critical of management techniques to control ass populations. To manage feral populations, the U.S. government has established a program to allow private citizens to adopt horses and asses.—Rob Channell

See also **AFRICA, DESERTS OF; ASIA, DESERTS OF; CAMEL; DOMESTIC ANIMALS; MAMMALS; PINNAE; UNGULATES; ZEBRA**

Further Reading

Brookshier, F. 1974. *The Burro*. Norman: University of Oklahoma Press.

Dent, A. 1972. *Donkey: The Story of the Ass from East to West*. London: Harrap.

Estes, R. D. 1991. *The Behavior Guide to African Mammals*. Berkeley: University of California Press.

ASWAN. *See* MIDDLE EAST, DESERTS OF

ATACAMA DESERT

Narrow strip of desert extending for nearly 1,000 kilometers along the western coast of South America from the northern border of Chile to Copiapó (27° south latitude), reaching a maximum width of 180 kilometers. In vast areas of this desert rainfall has never been recorded. Consequently an extremely arid, desolate, and barren landscape predominates. Despite the aridity there are plants in the desert, such as cacti (*Eulychnia*) and perennials (e.g., *Nolana*) and mesquite (*Prosopis*) in basins where some water catchment occurs, but in general the area is almost devoid of life. Even bacteria are scarce, and in many portions of the most arid parts of the desert insects and fungi are absent. In general, there is no rainfall from sea level to about 3,000 meters elevation on the high Andean slopes, where a belt of tufted grass and "tola" shrubs (*Lepidophyllum quadrangulare* and *Baccharis tola*) offer some fuel and forage to local populations and their livestock.

From Copiapó northward to Arica there is a succession of dry basins, alluvial fans, and extensive salt beds interrupted by only three tropical oases (Arica, Calama, and Atacama). These appear in the form of green strips along the courses of the only rivers in the region with sufficient volume to reach the Pacific Ocean. In the area south of Copiapó, which stretches for about 650 kilometers as far south as Illapel (31.5° south latitude), some rain may fall occasionally. (See map of South American deserts, p. 533.)

The interior of the Atacama Desert is practically devoid of vegetation; only some brushlike forms of plants occur along the coastal plateaus, dependent for survival on the moisture of persistent fog banks. In places away from the area of fog formation the desert is almost lifeless. Even decomposition does not occur; dead vegetation may be thousands of years old, and human burials also persist as mummified remains for millennia (more than 9,000 years). Among the few animals are several birds, a small mouse (*Phyllotis darwini*), and a fox (*Pseudalopex griseus*).

A few port towns exist in this desert. Iquique, Caldera, and Antofagasta are located on precarious sea-eroded terraces at the base of coastal cliffs. These towns are the outlet for the numerous mining centers in the interior tectonic basins. The wealth of the region lies in its mineral resources (copper, sodium chloride, sodium nitrate, iodine salts), not in its sparse biotic resources.—Virgilio G. Roig

See also **ANDES; AN INTRODUCTION TO DESERTS; CHILE, DESERTS OF; DESERTS; PERU, DESERTS OF; SECHURA DESERT; SOUTH AMERICA, DESERTS OF**

Further Reading

Allan, T., and A. Warren, eds. 1993. *Deserts: The Encroaching Wilderness*. New York: Oxford University Press.

Amiran, D. H. K., and A. W. Wilson, eds. 1973. *Coastal Deserts: Their Natural and Human Environments*. Tucson: University of Arizona Press.

Cabrera, A. L., and A. Willink. 1973. Biogeografía de América Latina. Organization of American States, Monograph No. 13. Washington, D.C.

Rauh, W. 1985. The Peruvian-Chilean deserts. *In* M. Evenari, I. Noy-Meir, and D. W. Goodall, eds., *Ecosystems of the World: Hot Deserts and Arid Shrublands*, 12B:239–267. Amsterdam: Elsevier.

ATLAS BROWN CATTLE

Dominant and traditional form of livestock (domestic cattle, *Bos taurus*) raised north and west of the Atlas Mountains. Cows do not exceed 340 kilograms, and bulls rarely exceed 400 kilograms. Bulls and cows both have short horns that may curve upward or downward. The breed was derived from the short-horned, humpless cattle of the pharaohs of ancient Egypt and was transported from the Nile Valley by successive migrations of people. Atlas brown cattle are extremely hardy and capable of surviving in harsh conditions and with poor fodder. Many other breeds of cattle have been introduced into the arid areas of North Africa, but Atlas brown cattle maintain dominance because of their natural resistance to many of the diseases that occur in the region. These cattle are not good milk producers but do produce fair meat under very poor conditions.—Rob Channell

See also **AFRICA, DESERTS OF; DOMESTIC ANIMALS; MAMMALS; UNGULATES; ZEBU CATTLE**

Further Reading

Rouse, J. E. 1970. *World Cattle*. Vol. 2. Norman: University of Oklahoma Press.

ATMOSPHERIC CIRCULATION. *See*
AN INTRODUCTION TO DESERTS

AUSTRALIA, DESERTS OF

Continent (world's smallest) lying between 10°–40° south latitude and 120°–155° east longitude and bounded by the Indian Ocean on the west and south and the Pacific Ocean on the east. New Guinea and Tasmania are very close to Australia and repeatedly came into contact with the mainland with each major lowering of sea level; these three landmasses, therefore, act as a single biogeographic unit. The mainland of Australia is approximately 7,270,000 square kilometers; New Guinea, 652,600 square kilometers; and Tasmania, 67,328 square kilometers. Mainland Australia extends from the tropical York Peninsula in the north, southward to the temperate state of Victoria. The eastern portion of Australia is forested, ranging from tropical to temperate in climate. The northern rim of Australia is characterized by seasonal rainfall, with varying degrees of forest cover. The southwestern portion of the continent is also seasonally mesic (wet) and supports a shrublike vegetation interspersed with trees. The central portion of the continent is extremely dry. Indeed, Australia is the driest of the world's continents.

Australia was not always as dry as it is today. When it was joined with Antarctica and South America, 135 million years ago, the climate of Australia was rather moist. But with the breakup of Gondwanaland (the southern supercontinent), commencing in the late Mesozoic (85 million years ago), Australia began to drift toward the northwest. A combination of the gradual formation of the ice cap in Antarctica and the development of ocean currents that could circulate polar waters began a change of the overall climate of the earth. Indeed, the final separation of Antarctica from South America led to the development of new ocean currents and contributed to the change in the earth's climate, with a pronounced cooling in the high latitudes of the Northern and Southern hemispheres. This global transition began at the close of the Oligocene, 24 million years ago. Australia continued to drift northward, and the major portion of the continent was exposed to a failure of the rain-laden westerly winds. The moist winds of the westerlies being denied, aridity increased; thus the drying out of the

Desert scrub vegetation on a red sandhill near Sandringham Station, southwestern Queensland. (Photo: R. E. MacMillen)

continent with subsequent changes in the proportion of its vegetative cover commenced in the Miocene, 24 million years ago, and has continued to the present.

When viewing the mainland of Australia, one can appreciate that the center of the continent is extremely dry, surrounded by an intermediate zone that is semiarid and, finally, a peripheral zone that is in part transitional to those areas occurring along the rim of the continent that support forests. In the central portion of the continent rainfall averages less than 150 millimeters per year, and the mean annual evaporation may exceed 3,000 millimeters per year.

Proceeding in the opposite direction, from the periphery to the center from the east coast of Australia, one passes from a forested zone dominated by *Eucalyptus* over the Great Dividing Range of mountains to an intermediate savanna zone dominated by *Acacia* and then into an area referred to as the Mallee. This is an area of widely spaced shrubs, interspersed with some trees and grasses and experiencing pronounced seasonal rainfall. Toward the center one encounters the Mulga vegetational formation, which is a mixture of shrubs and saltbush. Together both of these may be considered shrublands, although the Mulga formation is more steppelike (treeless, often grassy, plain). The driest portion is irregularly distributed in the center of the continent and may, under favorable conditions, sup-

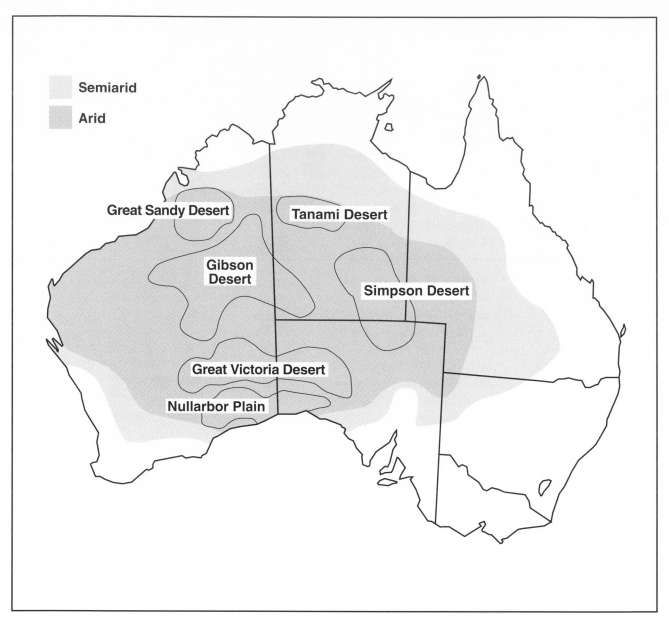

Map of major Australian deserts, including both arid and semiarid habitats. Shading indicates desert and semidesert limits.

port grass cover, but much of it is bare rock and sand dunes.

True deserts with minimum vegetative cover are the Simpson Desert north of Lake Eyre in Central Australia; the Great Sandy Desert located in far northwestern Australia; the Gibson Desert located south of the Great Sandy Desert in west central Australia; the Tanami Desert located due east of the Great Sandy Desert; and the Great Victoria Desert located south of the Gibson Desert in southwest central Australia (in southeastern West Australia, southwestern Northern Territory, and western South Australia). The Simpson Desert is separated from the more western deserts by a mosaic of *Acacia* woodlands and shrub steppes. Immediately south of the Great Victoria Desert along the south central rim of the continent of Australia is the Nullarbor Plain, a desert occurring on a limestone substrate.

The soil substrate of the arid portions of Australia varies from a pebble surface to red soils and, finally, to windblown sand. It shows variations in soil formation almost identical to those experienced in the great deserts of central Asia and the southwestern United States, with the exception that there are no large mountain ranges in the center of Australia. Most of the former mountains have been eroded, and in fact Australia demonstrates the least effect of recent orogeny (mountain building) of any of the major continents. In certain low-lying areas of central Australia there may be small saline lakes or lake basins. Some of these basins, such as Lake Eyre, may, on a cycle of 20 years or so, fill with rainwater and form temporary breeding sites for numerous water birds. Without doubt, during the glaciation episodes of the Pleistocene (1 million–10,000 years ago), mesic and dry phases alternated in the areas of the Mallee and Mulga shrublands. But the central portion of the continent had clearly experienced extreme aridity for a considerable period.—John F. Eisenberg

See also **ACACIA; AN INTRODUCTION TO DESERTS; CLIMATE; CONVERGENT EVOLUTION; ECHIDNA; KANGAROO; MALLEE; MARSUPIALS; PLATE TECTONICS; QUOKKA; RODENTS**

Further Reading

Archer, M., and G. Clayton, eds. 1984. *Vertebrate Zoogeography and Evolution in Australia*. Carlisle, W. Australia: Hesperian.

Beard, J. S. 1990. *Plant Life of Western Australia*. Kenthurst, NSW, Australia: Kangaroo Press.

Cogger, H. G., and E. E. Cameron, eds., 1984. *Arid Australia*. Sydney: Australian Museum.

Pyne, S. J. 1991. *Burning Bush: A Fire History of Australia*. Sydney: Allen and Unwin.

Shephard, M. 1995. *The Great Victoria Desert*. Chatswood, NSW, Australia: Reed Books.

United Nations Environment Programme. 1992. *World Atlas of Desertification*. London: Edward Arnold.

AWASSI SHEEP

Popular, hardy, fat-tailed breed of sheep raised throughout the Near East, where it thrives on the sparse desert scrub. In warm deserts retaining body heat generally is not a problem, but ridding the body of excess heat is difficult. The most common way in which animals dissipate excess heat is to increase the surface area from which the heat can be radiated. The insulating properties of fat inhibit the radiation of excess heat, but the variable environment of the desert requires storage of large reserves of energy when plant material is available for use when the area is drier and less productive. By concentrating fat deposits in the tail (5–10 kilograms of fat may be stored in the tail alone), awassi sheep can use more of their body to radiate excess heat and still have the energy they require during periods when food is scarce. Awassi sheep must drink water daily but are able to travel long distances from water to graze. They have been common in the Near East since at least 800 B.C.—Rob Channell

See also **BARBARY SHEEP; DESERT PEOPLES; DOMESTIC ANIMALS; HEAT BALANCE; HEAT EXCHANGE; MAMMALS; MIDDLE EAST, DESERTS OF; MOUFLON SHEEP; SHEEP; THERMOREGULATION; UNGULATES**

Further Reading

Epstein, H. 1985. *The Awassi Sheep with Special Reference to the Improved Dairy Type*. Rome: Food and Agriculture Organization.

BABBLER

Small to medium-sized, thrushlike Old World songbird (order Passeriformes, family Timaliidae). The evolutionary affinities and taxonomic rank of this group are somewhat controversial. Between 252 and 279 species in approximately 50 genera are recognized. Babblers reach maximum species diversity in tropical Asia, with a few taxa occurring in Africa and northern Eurasia and one species occurring in North America. Most taxa inhabit a range of deciduous woodlands (forests where leaves are shed each year due to seasonal or climatic changes) and evergreen woodlands, often humid, although some (e.g., the Arabian babbler, *Turdoides squamiceps*, of the Arabian and Sinai peninsulas) occur in arid scrub and wadis (dry stream washes). In Africa the timaliids are represented by the chatterers (genus *Turdoides*), species inhabiting drier scrub and savanna (grasslands, often with sparse trees) environments.

Babblers have relatively stocky bodies. Total lengths range from 10 to 35 centimeters. The legs and toes are typically quite robust, and the legs are somewhat elongated in less arboreal species. The wings are short and rounded, and flight is generally weak. Most species are not migratory. Plumage is highly variable across species, although many are colored cryptically (i.e., to provide concealment). Sexes are usually similar. The majority of babblers are insectivorous (insect eaters) and frugivorous (fruit eaters), although some also consume small vertebrates and seeds. Some babblers store large seeds.

Many babblers are highly sociable, holding group territories and nesting communally, with helpers (usually related juveniles) giving aid to adult breeding pairs. Nests are either domes or open cups constructed of various types of plant material, located in trees, or bushes, or on the ground. Clutch size ranges from two to six. Incubation lasts approximately 15 days. Incubation duties and care of chicks are generally shared by both sexes.—Stephen C. Lougheed

See also **AFRICA, DESERTS OF; ASIA, DESERTS OF; BIRDS; ISRAEL, DESERTS OF; JORDAN, DESERTS OF; LEBANON, DESERTS OF; LIBYA, DESERTS OF; MIDDLE EAST, DESERTS OF; PALESTINE, DESERTS OF; SAHARA DESERT; SAUDI ARABIA, DESERTS OF; SYRIA, DESERTS OF; UNITED ARAB EMIRATES, DESERTS OF; YEMEN, DESERTS OF**

Further Reading

Cramp, S., and C. M. Perrins, eds. 1993. *Handbook of the Birds of Europe the Middle East and North Africa. The Birds of the Western Palearctic.* Vol. 7. Oxford: Oxford University Press.

Delacour, J. 1946. Les timaliinés. *Oiseau* 16:14–31.

Zahavi, A. 1990. Arabian babblers: The quest for social status in a cooperative breeder. *In* P. B. Stacey and W. D. Koenig, eds., *Cooperative Breeding in Birds*, 105–130. Cambridge: Cambridge University Press.

BABOON

Primates (mammalian order Primates, family Cercopithecidae) adapted to foraging on the ground and consisting of the genera *Papio* and *Theropithecus*; the latter also referred to as the gelada baboon. Baboons have relatively short tails, and the muzzle is elongated, giving them a doglike face. The gelada is somewhat exceptional in having a shorter, rounded muzzle. There is a great disparity in the size of adults when sexes are compared: males are generally three times the weight of females. These animals typically live in troops, and savanna-dwelling forms have a social structure characterized by several adult males accompanying groups of females and their offspring of various ages. The hamadryas baboon and the gelada baboon have a social structure based on a single male and several females; however, these patriarchal units are often accompanied by subgroups of adult males.

Baboons are typically omnivorous (animal and plant eaters) and in open country make use of roots and tubers as well as the seeds of graminaceous (grass) plants. They also consume fruits, arthropods, and small vertebrates. The tendency to form troops, especially those with several adult males, permits an active defense against ground predators. The large males, often weighing more than 25 kilograms and acting as a group, can displace a terrestrial predator such as a hyena or leopard.

Nevertheless, all baboons seek out trees or rocky hillsides as sleeping places. Usually the home range (area where an animal normally carries out its daily activities) of a baboon includes a feeding and foraging area and a permanent water source as well as appropriate sleeping areas.

A female baboon produces one young after a seven-month gestation period. The young is dependent on the mother, who transports it for the first six months of its life. Baboons mature rapidly, and the female may bear a young every two years. Sexual maturity of males occurs at approximately seven years of age, and females mature at four to five years of age.

Baboons are found throughout Africa south of the Sahara. Some show adaptations to savannas, and some baboon species, such as the hamadryas, occupy extremely arid areas, generally in the vicinity of some permanent water source. Indeed, hamadryas baboons also occur in Yemen in the southwestern portion of peninsular Arabia, a very dry region.—John F. Eisenberg

See also **AFRICA, DESERTS OF; MAMMALS; MONKEYS IN DESERTS; SOUTH AFRICA, DESERTS OF**

Further Reading

Estes, R. D. 1991. *The Behavior Guide to African Mammals*. Berkeley: University of California Press.

Nowak, R. M. 1991. *Walker's Mammals of the World*. 5th ed. Baltimore: Johns Hopkins University Press.

Richard, A. 1985. *Primates in Nature*. New York: Freeman.

BACTERIA

Ubiquitous microorganisms that are prokaryotic (lack a nucleus and reproduce through cell splitting) and heterotrophic (obtain nutrients from organic material outside the cell). Desert soils, by definition, receive less than 250 millimeters of precipitation per year. In addition, many deserts also experience extreme daily temperature fluctuations. Thus any microorganisms living in arid desert soils must be able to tolerate long periods of desiccation and extremely high temperatures. Many bacteria possess adaptations that allow them to survive in a dormant condition during periods unfavorable to growth. These bacteria actively grow only during the brief time when conditions are favorable, such as after a rainstorm. Such desert-dwelling species have the ability to switch their metabolic activities on and off in response to changes in the environ-

ment. Desert-dwelling bacteria and fungi also form spores that allow them to exist for many years between periods of growth. After a rain these spores may germinate and the organisms actively grow and reproduce before the soil dries again.

Desert crusts are mats of cyanobacterial cells covering undisturbed parts of the deserts of the southwestern United States and other deserts as well. These mats are important in stabilizing desert sand and in paving the way for other successional species such as lichens and mosses but are, however, extremely fragile and easily destroyed by grazing and trampling. The mats are formed as cyanobacterial cells secrete a slimy, mucopolysaccharide sheath in which they live and grow. In dry weather this sheath becomes brittle, protecting the cyanobacteria and stabilizing the sand. In wet weather the microorganisms grow and secrete new sheath material.—Gordon E. Uno

See also **DECOMPOSITION; NITROGEN-FIXING PLANTS; PATHOGENS; PHOTOSYNTHESIS; PLANT COVER; PLANTS; ROCK VARNISH**

Further Reading

Atlas, R. M., and R. Bartha. 1993. *Microbial Ecology*. Redwood City, Calif.: Benjamin/Cummings.

BADGER

Carnivorous mammal (*Taxidea taxus*) closely related to weasels (order Carnivora, family Mustelidae, subfamily Taxidiinae) and occurring in grasslands, shrublands, and deserts of North America and Mexico from central Canada to central Mexico. The badger is characterized by a stocky, strong body (exceeding 11 kilograms for large males), a wedge-shaped skull, long claws on the forefeet, shovellike claws on the hind feet, short ears, powerful jaws, and teeth adapted for crushing. The body gives the appearance of being dorsoventrally flattened (i.e., the body is depressed), and the animals, with their short legs, are wider than they are tall. The American badger (*Taxidea taxus*) is brownish gray (but may vary from yellowish to silvery), with a distinctive white stripe running from its nose to its forehead and, occasionally, down its back. Males are up to 25 percent larger than females.

Badgers are ferocious and fearless as they forage through the deserts and grasslands for prey that are hidden in underground burrows. They also possess an extraordinary sense of smell, but sources disagree on their visual acuity (it is assumed that because of their small eyes they do not see well). The badger lives a seminomadic life. They are excellent diggers, constructing and abandoning numerous burrow systems as they search for food. Indeed, badgers are one of the major diggers in the prairies and scrub deserts of North America, digging up gophers, squirrels, and other small mammals and building elaborate dens in which the young are born. They have a nictitating membrane that can cover the eye and protect it when they are digging.

The diet of the American badger consists primarily of rodents (at least 29 species of rodent prey have been recorded), rabbits and jackrabbits, and even coyotes and skunks. In addition, badgers also eat carrion, insects, birds, reptiles, and whatever other food they encounter in their opportunistic foraging bouts. American badgers are solitary, coming together to breed only in summer or autumn. Badgers have been observed cooperating with a coyote to hunt prey. This unusual cross-specific hunting behavior has not been explored in any detail. Birth takes place in March or April. Litters consist of two or three cubs. The majority of females breed as yearlings, but males do not breed until their second year. In the wild the life span of the American badger may exceed 14 years.—Rob Channell

See also **BURROWING ANIMALS; CARNIVORES; GRASSLAND; PRAIRIE; PRAIRIE DOG; PREDATION**

Further Reading

Lindzey, F. G. 1982. Badger. *In* J. A. Chapman and G. A. Feldhamer, eds., *Wild Mammals of North America: Biology, Management, and Economics*, 653–663. Baltimore: Johns Hopkins University Press.

Long, C. A. 1973. Taxidea taxus. *Mammalian Species* 26:1–4.

Long, C. A., and C. A. Killingley. 1983. *The Badgers of the World*. Springfield, Ill.: Thomas.

Macdonald, D., ed. 1984. *The Encyclopedia of Mammals*. New York: Facts on File.

Neal, E. 1986. *The Natural History of Badgers*. New York: Facts on File.

BADLANDS

Intricately dissected landscapes located in areas with limited precipitation and long dry periods and formed on soft, highly erodible (subject to erosion), impervious, and poorly consolidated materials, such as shales, volcanic ash, and lacustrine sediments

Badlands area in the high Monte Desert (above 2,500 meters elevation) near Cafayate, Salta Province, northwestern Argentina. (Photo: M. A. Mares)

(sediments deposited in a lake). Badlands lack vegetative cover and tend to have steep smooth slopes and dense and intricate drainage networks. Early settlers of the western United States applied the term to widely scattered barren regions that proved difficult to cross and that were agriculturally unproductive.

Although badlands are common in arid and semiarid environments, they also are found in wetter environments, such as the humid tropics, owing to the fact that their formation is primarily controlled by the nature of the substrate (lithology). These distinct landforms can also form as a result of anthropogenic (human-related) activities, including poor agricultural practices, strip mining, or waste and soil heap deposition, which tends to accelerate erosion.

Both surface and subsurface erosion contribute to the formation of badlands. The unvegetated and unconsolidated surface materials are highly susceptible to rainsplash and slopewash processes, which leads to accelerated erosion. The shrink-swell nature of many clays, especially montmorillonite and bentonite (clays susceptible to both swelling and shrinking as a result of alternating wetting and drying during the year), contributes to desiccation cracking, which subsequently leads to subsurface processes, such as cracks and micropipes (small subsurface channels for water and sediments found on steep slopes). In badlands accelerated erosion from intense runoff, characteristic of desert thunderstorms, may result in drainage pattern densities from 25 to 350 kilometers in length per square kilometer, a density 10–20 times greater than those found in more humid areas. The rapid erosion prevents formation of soils suitable for vegetative growth, thus exacerbating the susceptibility to erosion. In some areas continuous uplift keeps badland topography from being completely destroyed by rapid erosion. Erosion in badlands is transport limited, meaning the rate of erosion is dependent on the frequency and magnitude of fluvial (water-related) events of sufficient energy to move the abundant preweathered sediment.

In North America excellent examples of badlands are found in Dinosaur Provincial Park, Alberta, Canada; Badlands National Monument, South Dakota; the Cretaceous Mancos Shale in Arizona and Utah; and Anza-Borrego Desert State Park in southern California. Badlands occur in many deserts around the world, including those of Asia and South America.—Vatche P. Tchakerian

See also **ANZA-BORREGO DESERT; ARROYO; EROSION; IRRIGATION DRAINAGE; SOILS, DESERT; WEATHERING, DESERT**

Further Reading

Campbell, I. A. 1989. Badlands and badland gullies. *In* D. S. G. Thomas, ed., *Arid Zone Geomorphology*, 159–183. London: Belhaven.

Howard, A. D. 1994. Badlands. *In* A. D. Abrahams and A. J. Parsons, eds., *Geomorphology of Desert Environments*, 213–242. London: Chapman and Hall.

BAGWORMS

Larvae or pupae of insects (moths) in the family Psychidae, order Lepidoptera. Larvae construct bags of silk combined with twigs or pieces of leaves, climb into the bags, and move around feeding and growing while remaining in the bags. Eventually they seal the bags, which remain hanging from twigs in trees. They transform into pupae that remain in the bags until they transform into adults. Females metamorphose into wormlike adults that are wingless and legless and remain in the bag. Males transform into moths with wings and legs. Males seek out females, mate with them, and leave. The female then deposits eggs in the bag, and the eggs spend the winter protected there. In spring the eggs hatch and the larvae leave the bag and construct their own bags.

Bagworms are not the same as tent caterpillars, which are in a different family of moths (Lasiocampidae) and form large tentlike nets in trees which contain from tens to hundreds of individuals.—Laurie J. Vitt

See also **ARTHROPODS; CATERPILLARS; HERBIVORY; INSECTS; LIFE HISTORY STRATEGY (ITEROPARITY); MOTHS**

Further Reading

Borror, D. J., C. A. Triplehorn, and N. F. Johnson. 1992. *An Introduction to the Study of Insects*. New York: Harcourt Brace.

Borror, D. J., and R. E. White. 1970. *A Field Guide to the Insects*. Boston: Houghton Mifflin.

Davis, D. R. (1964) Bagworm moths of the western hemisphere. *U.S. National Museum Bulletin* 244:1–233.

BAJA CALIFORNIA, DESERTS OF

Southern extension of the Sonoran Desert from the southwestern United States into the Baja California peninsula in northwestern Mexico. Although Baja California exhibits many features of the Sonoran Desert, there also are many unique ecological characteristics that result from its highly variable geography and from its isolation on a peninsula. (See map of the deserts of the United States and Mexico, p. 356.)

The physiography of Baja California is formed by the Peninsular Range Province that extends from the Sierra Nevada of California to the tip of Baja California. The elevations are highest at the northern end of Baja, with peaks over 3,000 meters in the San Pedro Martir Mountains. Elevations then decrease progressing southward toward the lower end of Baja, where they rise again at the Sierra de la Giganta and Sierra de la Laguna ranges.

Climatic conditions in Baja California are varied but generally arid. Summer temperatures are very hot and precipitation is scanty and episodic, although there are distinctive influences from monsoonal moisture patterns in the autumn and winter. Because of the narrowness of the Baja peninsula, Pacific Ocean and Sea of Cortez water currents and temperatures influence the climatic and weather conditions along the eastern and western coasts, and it is a cool, coastal desert.

Many of the faunal and floral elements occurring in Baja California result from migrations that were driven south into refugia (areas where isolated populations of organisms persist) during Pleistocene glacial periods. It is likely that some of these moved back north during subsequent hot, dry interglacial periods, suggesting that the complex vegetational patterns of the deserts of Baja California are the result of a dynamic interaction between the biota, physiography, and both recent and geological climatic conditions.

Two of the most famous Sonoran Desert biologists, Forrest Shreve and Ira L. Wiggins, described in great detail the vegetational subdivisions of the Baja California portion of the Sonoran Desert: the Lower Colorado Valley Desert, the Central Gulf Coast Desert, the Vizcaino Desert, and the Magdalena Desert. Subsequent ecological research has modified this classification somewhat, but the classic communities of Shreve and Wiggins remain the basis for understanding the deserts of Baja California.

The Lower Colorado Valley Desert, which is an extension of what is called the Colorado Desert in the United States, extends into Baja California as far south as Bahía de los Angeles on the Gulf side of the peninsula. This desert, which is also known as the microphyllous desert because of the dominance of small-leafed shrubs, is dominated by creosote bush (*Larrea tridentata*) and burro bush (*Franseria dumosa*) and is ecologically similar to the Colorado Desert of southern California. It is relatively simple in composition, particularly on the gravelly and sandy plains that comprise much of this area; however, the upper portions of the numerous bajadas, volcanic fields (malpais), and low hills support a richer diversity of plants, including mesquite (*Prosopis juliflora* var. *Torreyana*), paloverde (*Cercidium floridum, Cercidium microphyllum*) and ironwood (*Olneya tesota*). There are also many ephemeral species that flourish after winter rains, creating desert blooms of great floral beauty.

The Central Gulf Coast Desert is found in two areas on either side of the Sea of Cortez (Gulf of California). In Baja California this extremely dry desert extends from Isla Angel de la Guarda, in a narrow strip along the east coast, to the tip of Baja at San José del Cabo. Rainfall in this region is scant because of the effects of the peninsular rain shadow. Temperatures are very high in summer except along the coast where some moderating effects of the Gulf waters are apparent.

The Gulf Coast Desert is also known as the Sarcocaulescent Desert because of the prevalence of stem-succulent trees that have exaggerated fleshy trunks. Common plants are the elephant tree or torchwood (*Bursera microphylla, Bursera hindsiana*), ashy jatropha (*Jatropha cinerea*), ironwood (*Olneya tesota*), paloverde (*Cercidium floridum*), ocotillo (*Fouquieria splendens*), mesquite (*Prosopis juliflora* var. *Torreyana*), and an assortment of shrubs. The succulent cardón (*Pachycereus pringlei*) also is found here. In general the vegetation of this desert is heterogeneous and spaced widely over the rocky landscape. The mammals, birds, and reptiles of the Central Gulf Coast Desert are similar to those in most of the Sonoran Desert.

A third distinctive arid region in Baja California is the Vizcaino Desert, which is named after Sebastian Vizcaino, an early Spanish explorer. The Vizcaino Desert is located on the coastal plain on the Pacific side of Baja California and consists of nearly level plains, low hills, sandy plains, low mountain ridges, and a variety of volcanic features. Most of the terrain is less than 500 meters above sea level. This region is cooler than other parts of the Sonoran Desert because of the moderating effect of the Pacific Ocean. Shreve and Wiggins referred to this desert as sarcophyllous (fleshy-leafed) desert, but a variety of low microphyllous (small-leafed) shrubs, leaf succulents, and stem succulents are also common in the area. Important plant genera include *Agave, Yucca,* and *Dudleya* as well as the boojum (*Fouquieria columnaris*), torote blanco (*Pachycormus discolor*), and *Ambrosia (= Franseria) dumosa.* The giant succulent cardón (*Pachycereus pringlei*) is the dominant cactus of this desert, much like the saguaro (*Carnegiea gigantea*) that is so conspicuous in the Arizona Upland Desert of the more northern part of the Sonoran Desert.

The Magdalena Desert occupies the southern third of Baja California on the western side of the peninsula from San Ignacio to Todos Santos. Most of this area is found in the Llano de la Magdalena, a low-lying plain in the southwestern part of Baja California. This region consists of broad and sandy valleys and plains, granitic hills, and occasional volcanic features. There are also numerous large and small playas dotting the region.

The vegetation of the Magdalena Desert is less striking than that of the Vizcaino Desert to the north because of the absence of *Idria* and *Pachycormus*, as well as the infrequency of *Pachycereus*, *Yucca*, and *Agave*. The vegetation is dominated by microphyllous shrubs and trees and has a definite desert scrub appearance. The mammals, birds, and reptiles of the Vizcaino/Magdalena region include many genera common to deserts of the southwestern United States. Foxes, coyotes, jackrabbits, woodrats, quail, skunks, horned lizards, snakes, and numerous rodents are found in the area.—Gary K. Hulett and Amanda Renner Charles

See also **AGAVE; ALLUVIAL FAN; AN INTRODUCTION TO DESERTS; BIRDS; CACTI; CACTUS, COLUMNAR; CALIFORNIA DESERT; COLORADO DESERT; CREOSOTE BUSH; DESERTS; DESERTS, HOT; DESERTS, TEMPERATE; IRONWOOD; LIZARDS; MAMMALS; MEXICO, DESERTS OF; PALOVERDE; PLANT GEOGRAPHY; REPTILES; SEMIARID ZONES; SNAKES; SONORAN DESERT; UNITED STATES, DESERTS OF; YUCCA; YUMA DESERT**

Further Reading

Anonymous. 1976. *Baja California*. Los Angeles: Automobile Club of Southern California.

Barco, M. 1980. *The Natural History of Baja California*. Los Angeles: Dawson's Book Shop.

Krutch, J. W. 1970. *The Forgotten Peninsula: A Naturalist in Baja California*. New York: William Morrow.

MacMahon, J. A. 1985. *Deserts*. New York: Knopf.

Wiggins, I. L. 1980. *Flora of Baja California*. Stanford: Stanford University Press.

BAJADA. *See* ALLUVIAL FAN

BARBARY DEER

Small subspecies of the red deer (*Cervus elaphus*) in the mammalian order Artiodactyla, family Cervidae (called elk in North America), that is confined to forests on the border of Algeria and Tunisia. Small size and simple antler structure characterize this subspecies. The antlers are thin with short tines (prongs). The poor quality of available forage in this arid region may have evolutionarily selected for the small size of the Barbary sheep. The small population size, limited distribution, large-scale habitat loss, and continued poaching make the Barbary deer; vulnerable to extinction. A population of Barbary deer has been introduced into the southwestern United States in Texas on a game farm.—Rob Channell

See also **AFRICA, DESERTS OF; DEER; MAMMALS; UNGULATES**

Further Reading

Kowalski, K. 1991. *Mammals of Algeria*. Krakow: Polish Academy.

BARBARY LION

Extinct subspecies of lion (*Panthera leo leo*), also known as the Atlas or Berber lion (mammalian order Carnivora, family Felidae). Barbary lions once occurred across Africa north of the Sahara from Egypt to Morocco, where they inhabited semiarid regions and open forests. They are commonly featured in the art of pharaonic tombs and temples. They were reported from Algeria and Tunisia in the 1880s and from Morocco in 1920. The last reported Tunisian lion was shot in 1891. The Barbary lion is the subspecies from which the species was originally described.

Little reliable information is available on the Barbary lion. It is believed that they were quite common at one time, especially during the Roman era, as these were the lions used in the gladiator matches pitting man against animal during which thousands of animals from throughout the Roman Empire were slaughtered. The Roman trade in wild animals is believed to be responsible for the decline in many species of wild animals in North Africa.—Thomas E. Lacher, Jr.

See also **AFRICA, DESERTS OF; AFRICAN LION; CARNIVORES; CATS; CONSERVATION IN DESERTS; MAMMALS; PREDATION; WILDLIFE**

Further Reading

Grzimek's Encyclopedia of Mammals. Vol. 3. 1990. New York: McGraw-Hill.

Haltenorth, T., and H. Diller. 1980. *A Field Guide to the Mammals of Africa, Including Madagascar*. London: Collins.

Nowak, R. M. 1991. *Walker's Mammals of the World*. 5th ed. Baltimore: Johns Hopkins University Press.

BARBARY PARTRIDGE

Stocky, medium-sized game bird (*Alectoris barbara*) native to extreme northern Africa (order Galliformes, family Phasianidae). These partridges range throughout arid and semiarid scrub and woodlands, from sea level to more than 3,000 meters above sea level. Plumage of the head and throat, as in other *Alectoris* species, is strongly patterned. Flanks are vertically barred and underparts plain. Body length is usually 32–34 centimeters, and wingspan ranges from 46 to 49 centimeters. Males are, on average, slightly larger than females. Although capable of flying, Barbary partridges do so reluctantly; they prefer to run to escape danger. Their diet includes seeds, fruit, leaves, and insects (e.g., ants). Barbary partridges apparently derive all water requirements from food items as they do not appear to require freestanding water. *Alectoris barbara* is primarily sedentary, although populations in higher elevations may descend to lower elevations during periods of inclement weather. Hunting pressure and habitat loss have caused local population declines, but the species remains common in remoter areas.

Barbary partridges are probably monogamous. Eggs are laid in shallow nest-scrapes usually located under a bush. Clutch size averages 11 eggs but may range from 6 to 20. The incubation period is likely similar to congeners—20–25 days. Incubation duties are probably performed by the female. The young are precocial, leaving the nest as soon as their down feathers are dry.—Stephen C. Lougheed

See also **AFRICA, DESERTS OF; ANIMAL ADAPTATIONS; ANTS; BIRDS; WATER BALANCE**

Further Reading

Cramp, S., and K. E. L. Simmons, eds. 1980. *Handbook of the Birds of Europe the Middle East and North Africa. The Birds of the Western Palearctic*. Vol. 2. Oxford: Oxford University Press.

Urban, E. K., C. H. Fry, and S. Keith, eds. 1986. *The Birds of Africa*. Vol. 2. New York: Academic Press.

Valverde, J. A. 1957. *Aves del Sahara español*. Madrid: Consejo Superior de Investigaciones Científicas.

BARBARY SHEEP

Species of goatlike sheep; (mammalian order Artiodactyla, family Bovidae) living in rocky desert areas of northern Africa;. Barbary sheep (*Ammotragus lervia*) resemble a goat more than a sheep in many ways, but biochemical analysis indicates that they are more closely related to sheep. Impressive horns, triangular in cross-section, are possessed by both males (85 centimeters long) and females (40 centimeters long). Females (30–60 kilograms) are approximately half the size of males (100–145 kilograms). Barbary sheep have bodies that are stocky with a short tail. Their hair is short and ranges from tan to brown-red in color. Especially long hair forms a ruff on the underside of the neck and pantaloons on the front legs.

The underside of the Barbary sheep is naked, allowing increased efficiency in radiating excess body heat to the ambient environment. The sheep avoid the high temperatures of their desert habitat by spending a great deal of time in the shade and feeding on desert shrubs or mountain herbs primarily during the evening and, occasionally, nighttime hours. Barbary sheep live in small troops. Mating occurs from September to November, and a single lamb is born after a gestation period of five months. Barbary sheep are estimated to live 10 years in the wild. Being hunted for meat, hair, and horns has eliminated this species from all but the most inaccessible parts of its range; the species is classified as vulnerable to extinction.—Rob Channell

See also **AFRICA, DESERTS OF; ANIMAL ADAPTATIONS; BODY TEMPERATURE; GOAT; HEAT BALANCE; HEAT STRESS; HYPERTHERMIA; MAMMALS; PHYSIOLOGY; SHEEP; THERMOREGULATION; WATER BALANCE**

Further Reading

Clark, J. L. 1964. *The Great Arc of the Wild Sheep*. Norman: University of Oklahoma Press.

BARCHAN (BARKHAN) DUNE. *See* DUNES

BAROMETRIC PRESSURE(ATMOSPHERIC PRESSURE)

Pressure exerted by the atmosphere as a consequence of the force of gravity acting on a column of air lying above any particular point over the earth's surface. Like any gas, the pressure exerted by the atmosphere can be described in terms of the movement of gas molecules. Barometric pressure is usually measured using a barometer. The most common unit of measurement is the Pascal (Pa), which is the force exerted by one Newton on an area of one meter square. Until very recently millibars were used to measure barometric pressure, where one millibar was equal to 1,000 dynes per square centimeter (one dyne is the force that will accelerate a one-gram mass by one centimeter per second per second). Meteorologists also use millimeters (or inches) of mercury as units of barometric pressure. These refer to the height of a column of mercury that counterbalances the pressure from a column of air that displaces the mercury to the height indicated. To avoid misunderstandings in usage of terms, a standard atmosphere is defined in terms equivalent to common systems of measurement. For example, one atmosphere is equal to 1,013.3 hecto-pascals (hPa, where 1 hPa = 100 Pa) is equal to 1,013.3 millibars is equal to 760.3 millimeters of mercury is equal to 29.43 inches of mercury.—Federico Norte

See also **CLIMATE; CONVECTIVE STORM; ISOHYET; LOW PRESSURE; PREVAILING WESTERLIES; WIND**

Further Reading

Day, J. A., and V. J. Schaefer. 1991. *Clouds and Weather.* Boston: Houghton Mifflin.

Oliver, J. E., and R. W. Fairbridge, eds. 1987. *The Encyclopedia of Climatology.* New York: Chapman and Hall.

Schaefer, V. J., and J. A. Day. 1981. *A Field Guide to the Atmosphere.* Boston: Houghton Mifflin.

Schneider, S. H., ed. 1996. *Encyclopedia of Climate and Weather.* 2 vols. New York: Oxford University Press.

BASIN AND RANGE TOPOGRAPHY. *See* ASIA, DESERTS OF; GREAT BASIN DESERT

BAT

Mammal (order Chiroptera) characterized by the possession of forelimbs that are modified into wings, and which are capable of sustained flapping flight. Bats reach their highest diversity and abundance in tropical regions, especially in moist habitats. Relatively few kinds of bats are specially adapted to inhabit deserts. Most of the approximately 925 living species are nocturnal (active at night) insect eaters, although many species have adapted to feeding on other kinds of foods, including fruit, nectar, pollen, leaves, the blood of birds or mammals, and the flesh of small vertebrates (fish, frogs, lizards, birds, and mammals). Some nectar- and pollen-feeding bats of the family Phyllostomidae (e.g., *Leptonycteris, Choeronycteris, Platalina*) are major pollinators of certain cacti and other desert plants in North and South America. Most desert bats catch insects in midair during flight using echolocation (high-pitched, usually ultrasonic cries that are reflected by the prey back to the bat, thus indicating the location of the prey as well as its identity and its movements). A few kinds of bats that inhabit deserts in different parts of the world are adept at passively detecting flightless, ground-dwelling arthropods, such as scorpions, order Solifugae, crickets, ground beetles, and grasshoppers, seizing them on the ground. These bats include, in the family Vespertilionidae, *Otonycteris hemprichi* in southwestern Asia and northern Africa, *Nyctophilus* species in Australia, and *Antrozous pallidus* in North America; in the family Nycteridae, African *Nycteris thebaica* feed in this manner.

Most bats require a drink of water every day they are active. Thus many bats, including some species that are not highly adapted to arid environments, are able to live at least in the margins of deserts if drinking water is available within flying distance of their daytime roost. Normally the water must be calm (oases, ephemeral pools along arroyos or wadis) and sufficiently unobstructed to permit the bats to drink from it by flying over it slowly and dropping their lower jaw to scoop up a mouthful of water. Insectivorous bats that regularly inhabit the driest deserts have kidneys that are specialized to help them conserve water by producing highly concentrated urine. These include members of the families Rhinopomatidae (mouse-tailed bats, genus *Rhinopoma*, of northern Africa and southwestern Asia), Molossidae (free-tailed bats, such as *Sauromys petrophilus* in the Namib Desert and *Tadarida brasiliensis* in southwestern North America and central and southern South America), and several members of the Vespertilionidae (evening bats, such as *Eptesicus zuluensis* in the Namib Desert, *Antrozous pallidus, Euderma maculatum*, and the tiny [4-gram] *Pipistrellus hesperus* and *Myotis californicus* in southwestern North America). These species drink water when they can find it, but some of them are able to go for long periods without drinking.

Desert-dwelling bats avoid the worst of the heat and aridity by roosting during the day mostly in caves or rock crevices, but a few kinds roost in the dead leaves of palms or in cavities made by woodpeckers in columnar cacti, such as saguaro (*Carnegiea gigantea*) and cardón (genus *Pachycereus*). Some species of tomb bats (family Emballonuridae, genus *Taphozous*) are most unusual in that they roost in tombs in the desert, such as the Great Pyramids near Giza in the Egyptian desert. Like other desert mammals, certain bats (e.g., tomb bats [family Emballonuridae], mouse-tailed bats [family Rhinopomatidae]) put on body fat that helps them to survive the seasonal periods of greatest environmental stress. At these seasons they can lessen or avoid the energetic expenditures for flying, foraging, and coping with heat stress or cold by becoming dormant. They may also avoid starvation by surviving on the stored fat. Some species that inhabit desert areas with cold winters (e.g., *Pipistrellus hesperus*) may periodically go into torpor—but may also be incapable of prolonged hibernation and therefore must remain active during the winter. In southwestern North America several species of Vespertilionidae and one of Molossidae were found to be flying in near-freezing and subfreezing air temperatures when few insects were available to eat. California leaf-nosed bats (*Macrotus californicus*, family Phyllostomidae) inhabit the low-elevation Sonoran and Mojave deserts of North America. They, too, are incapable of hibernating, or even of using torpor, and are intolerant of cold temperatures, dying if their body temperature falls below 26°C for too long. This species is able to survive in winter by using geothermally heated roost sites (caves or mines) that have very stable, warm (about 29°C) year-round temperatures.

In South America the Atacama Desert of the Peruvian-Chilean coast has been hyperarid since at least the middle Miocene epoch (for about 15 million years) and arid or semiarid since the early Miocene; several genera and species of bats have become adapted to the arid Atacama and are endemic there. These are *Platalina genovensium*, *Lonchophylla hesperia*, and *Artibeus fraterculus* (family Phyllostomidae), *Amorphochilus schnablii* (smoky bats, family Furipteridae), *Myotis atacamensis* (family Vespertilionidae), *Mormopterus kalinowskii* (family Molossidae), and *Tomopeas ravus*; the latter is the sole member of a subfamily (Tomopeatinae) of the family Molossidae. The high degree of endemism among Atacama Desert bats probably reflects their early arrival in the region, their long-term isolation west of the uplifting Andes Mountains, and their association with and adaptation to the desert environment. The basic natural history of most of these species, as with many of the world's desert bats, is very poorly known.—Nicholas J. Czaplewski

See also **ANIMAL ADAPTATIONS; AN INTRODUCTION TO DESERTS; ATACAMA DESERT; CACTI; CACTUS, COLUMNAR; CARDÓN; CHILE, DESERTS OF; INSECTS; MAMMALS; MOTHS; PERU, DESERTS OF; POLLINATION; THERMOREGULATION; TORPOR; WATER BALANCE**

Further Reading

Alpers, C. N., and G. H. Brimhall. 1988. Middle Miocene climatic change in the Atacama Desert, northern Chile: Evidence from supergene mineralization at La Escondida. *Geological Society of America Bulletin* 100:1640–1656.

Arlettaz, R., G. Dändliker, E. Kasybekov, J.-M. Pillet, S. Rybin, and J. Zima. 1995. Feeding habits of the long-eared desert bat, *Otonycteris hemprichi* (Chiroptera: Vespertilionidae). *Journal of Mammalogy* 76:873–876.

Bell, G. P. 1982. Behavioral and ecological aspects of gleaning by a desert insectivorous bat, *Antrozous pallidus* (Chiroptera: Vespertilionidae). *Behavioral Ecology and Sociobiology* 10:217–223.

Bell, G. P., G. A. Bartholomew, and K. E. Nagy. 1986. The roles of energetics, water economy, foraging behavior, and geothermal refugia in the distribution of the bat, *Macrotus californicus*. *Journal of Comparative Physiology B* 156:441–450.

Findley, J. S. 1993. *Bats: A Community Perspective*. Cambridge: Cambridge University Press.

Geluso, K. N. 1978. Urine-concentrating ability and renal structure of insectivorous bats. *Journal of Mammalogy* 59:312–323.

Nowak, R. M. 1991. *Walker's Mammals of the World*. 5th ed. Baltimore: Johns Hopkins University Press.

O'Shea, T. J., and T. A. Vaughan. 1977. Nocturnal and seasonal activities of the pallid bat, *Antrozous pallidus*. *Journal of Mammalogy* 58:269–284.

Ruffner, G. A., R. M. Poché, M. Meierkord, and J. A. Neal. 1979. Winter bat activity over a desert wash in southeastern Utah. *Southwestern Naturalist* 24:447–453.

Sudman, P. D., L. J. Barkley, and M. S. Hafner. 1994. Familial affinity of *Tomopeas ravus* (Chiroptera) based on protein electrophoresis and cytochrome *b* sequence data. *Journal of Mammalogy* 75:365–377.

BEARGRASS

Perennial grasslike plant in the lily family (Liliaceae) characterized by a reduced shoot and numerous linear, nonsucculent leaves. These plants are not true grasses; they resemble yuccas, but the leaves are more like those of a grass. Beargrass may refer more generally to the genus *Nolina* or, more specifically, to *Nolina microcarpa* (as used here). The stem lies entirely below ground, with a rosette of leaves at the ground surface. Leaves are six to nine millimeters wide and approximately a meter long. Bisexual or unisexual flowers are borne in a panicle (open, branching flower) at the end of a stalk one to two meters high. Sepals and petals are white or greenish and about two millimeters long.

Beargrass (*Nolina*) prairie south of Silver City, in southwestern New Mexico. (Photo: M. A. Mares)

The fruit is a three-lobed capsule about five millimeters long, with one seed per lobe.

Beargrass grows on mountainsides and mesa tops and along washes and canyons in well-drained soils. It can be found in the Mojave, Sonoran, and Chihuahuan deserts, desert grassland, and oak woodlands of the southwestern United States and northwestern Mexico from 900 to 2,000 meters elevation.

The leaves and flower stalks are browsed by cattle during dry periods. Fibers from the leaves are woven into baskets and mats by Native Americans. Both *Nolina microcarpa* and *N. texana* may be called sacahuista in Mexico.—Kristina A. Ernest

See also **CHIHUAHUAN DESERT; DESERT GRASSLAND; MOJAVE DESERT; PLANT ADAPTATIONS; SONORAN DESERT; YUCCA**

Further Reading

Benson, L., and R. A. Darrow. 1981. *Trees and Shrubs of the Southwestern Deserts*. Tucson: University of Arizona Press.

BEDOUINS. *See* DESERT PEOPLES

BEES

Common name for a variety of insect families (containing more than 20,000 species) in the order Hymenoptera, superfamily Apoidea. Typically when one thinks of bees, honeybees and bumblebees come to mind. The vision is one of a squat-bodied flying insect that stings and lives in large social colonies that should not be disturbed. True bees are in the superfamily Apoidea. Most are associated with flowers, where they feed on nectar and collect pollen that is used to provision their nests. The larvae of most bees feed on the pollen that is brought back to the nest. A side benefit of the former activity is that the bees transport pollen from flower to flower, resulting in pollination and consequent seed production.

Most bees are actually solitary. Each female constructs a nest, deposits an egg in each cell, provisions the cell with pollen, closes the cell, and constructs additional cells with no further feeding of larvae. The eusocial bees not only construct the nest, lay eggs, and provision the cells but also provide pollen or honey to the developing larvae. Honey is formed by concentrating the collected nectar through evaporation.

Some of the more obvious bees in deserts are honeybees and bumblebees (family Apidae), leaf-cutting bees (family Megachilidae), and halictid bees (family Halictidae). The halictid bees can be recognized because of their brilliant metallic blue or green coloration. In most eusocial bees workers have ovipositors modified for injecting painful toxins. Typically stinging is used to defend the nest, but restraining or harassing individual bees outside of a nest can result in attack and stinging.—Laurie J. Vitt

See also **ARTHROPODS; DEFENSIVE ADAPTATIONS, ANIMALS; FLOWERS; HYMENOPTERA; INSECTS; POISONOUS ANIMALS; POLLINATION; VELVET ANTS; VENOM; WASPS**

Further Reading

Borror, D. J., C. A. Triplehorn, and N. F. Johnson. 1992. *An Introduction to the Study of Insects*. New York: Harcourt Brace.

Borror, D. J., and R. E. White. 1970. *A Field Guide to the Insects*. Boston: Houghton Mifflin.

von Frisch, K. 1967. *The Dance Language and Orientation of Bees*. Cambridge, Mass.: Belknap Press.

Wilson, E. O. 1971. *The Insect Societies*. Cambridge, Mass.: Harvard University Press.

BEETLES

Insects in the immense order Coleoptera, which contains more than 250,000 species and is characterized by forewings that are thickened and cover the rear wings and abdomen (secondarily reduced in some) and meet at the midline of the dorsal surface of the abdomen. Beetles are among the most diverse insect groups taxonomically and ecologically, and they occur in nearly all environments inhabited by insects. All beetles have a life history characterized by egg laying, hatching into one of several larval types depending on species, a series of instars (developmental stages) during the larval period, followed by complete metamorphosis ultimately resulting in an adult stage drastically different from the larva.

Although the mouthparts of beetles in general are considered chewing mouthparts, they are modified to varying degrees among the many families. In some the mandibles are effective in breaking seeds; in others they are used for cutting leaves. In a few beetle families the mandibles are elongate, sharpened, and used for subduing other arthropods. Many beetles produce sounds in a variety of contexts. Some sounds are produced for defense, some are used to attract mates, and some are used during courtship. Because of the great taxonomic and morphological diversity of beetles, a variety of characteristics are used in identification, including the structure of the antennae, legs, elytra, mouthparts, and reproductive parts. Although most beetles have the elytra covering the entire abdomen, some, such as the rove beetles (family Staphylinidae), have very short elytra, so that the abdomen is exposed.

Some of the more common beetles observed in deserts are the darkling beetles (family Tenebrionidae), tiger beetles (family Cicindelidae), blister beetles (family Meloidae), and ground beetles (family Carabidae). Darkling beetles (especially those in the genus *Eleodes*) are active on the surface at night and early in the day; when disturbed they raise the abdomen off the ground and expel noxious chemicals (quinones) for defense. The predaceous tiger beetles are often brilliantly colored and run rapidly across the ground, flying short distances when approached too close. Desert blister beetles often march about on the desert floor in the morning and late afternoon and are particularly conspicuous. The ground beetles are primarily nocturnal in deserts and search the desert floor for arthropod prey at night, retreating under surface objects or into crevices during the day. Careful searching of stems and leaves of desert plants reveals an abundance of snout beetles (family Curculionidae), and searching through decaying cacti produces a variety of life history stages of hister beetles (family Histeridae) and others. The larvae of hister beetles feed on the larvae of other insects

(including many species of flies) that feed on the decaying plant material. Desert trees often contain the wood-eating larvae of click beetles (family Elateridae), metallic wood-boring beetles (family Buprestidae), and long-horned beetles (family Cerambycidae). Dung beetles (family Scarabaeidae) can often be found in deserts rolling balls of animal feces across the ground early in the morning or late in the afternoon. The carcasses of dead animals attract numerous beetles as well, including carrion beetles (family Silphidae) and rove beetles (family Staphylinidae).—Laurie J. Vitt

See also **ANIMAL ADAPTATIONS; ARTHROPODS; DEFENSIVE ADAPTATIONS, ANIMALS; INSECTS**

Further Reading

Borror, D. J., C. A. Triplehorn, and N. F. Johnson. 1992. *An Introduction to the Study of Insects*. New York: Harcourt Brace.

Borror, D. J., and R. E. White. 1970. *A Field Guide to the Insects*. Boston: Houghton Mifflin.

BENGUELA CURRENT

Cold ocean current of relatively low salinity that moves north from the South Atlantic along the west coast of Africa. The current intensifies the aridity of the Namib Desert by providing less water from evaporation (thus decreasing the water vapor available for precipitation) than would occur if the ocean water off the coast were warm. The Benguela Current also cools the air above it, causing morning fogs along the coast and relatively cool air temperatures in one of the world's most arid regions. The movement of water from the deep Atlantic Ocean to the continental shelf of Africa causes an upwelling of nutrient-rich water that is ideal for the development of plankton. The plankton-rich waters of the Benguela Current are thus an excellent fishing area, supporting a fishing industry based along a desert coastline.—Rob Channell

See also **HUMBOLDT CURRENT; NAMIBIA, DESERTS OF; OCEAN CURRENTS; SOUTH AFRICA, DESERTS OF; WELWITSCHIA**

Further Reading

Neumann, G. 1968. *Ocean Currents*. Amsterdam: Elsevier.

BIG BEND NATIONAL PARK

U.S. national park established in 1944 in the northern section of the Chihuahuan Desert called the Trans-Pecos. The park is located in the southern

Trans-Pecos region of southwestern Texas. The southern border of the park is the Rio Grande, which separates the United States and Mexico. Big Bend National Park is the seventh largest national park in the United States, encompassing 287,000 hectares.

The characteristic high elevations of the Chihuahuan Desert are in evidence in the park and appear as rugged mountains rising out of the surrounding desert. Emory Peak, in the Chisos Mountains, is the highest point at 2,388 meters. Douglas fir, ponderosa pine, and Arizona cypress are found at the higher elevations, whereas pinyon pine, juniper, and oaks occur on slopes. At lower elevations, characteristic Chihuahuan Desert plants such as creosote bush, ocotillo, yucca, and many species of cactus can be seen. Along the Rio Grande are some of the lowest elevations of the Chihuahuan Desert. These low areas are dominated by riverine communities of mesquite, cane, willow, and cottonwood. Some areas of the park are desert grassland.

A diverse fauna inhabits the park: 10 species of amphibians (frogs and toads); 55 species of reptiles (30 species of snakes, 21 of lizards, and 4 of turtles); 398 species of birds; 74 species of mammals (28 rodents, 19 bats, 17 carnivores, 5 ungulates, 3 rabbits, 1 opossum, and 1 shrew); and a wide variety of invertebrates.—Janet K. Braun

See also **AN INTRODUCTION TO DESERTS; CHIHUAHUAN DESERT; CONSERVATION IN DESERTS; DESERTS; DESERTS, HOT; TEXAS DESERT; UNITED STATES, DESERTS OF**

Further Reading

MacMahon, J. A. 1985. *Deserts*. New York: Knopf.

Medellín-Leal, F. 1982. The Chihuahuan Desert. *In* G. L. Bender, ed., *Reference Handbook on the Deserts of North America*, 321–382. Westport, Conn.: Greenwood.

Steele, D. G. 1998. *Land of the Desert Sun: Texas' Big Bend Country*. College Station: Texas A&M University Press.

Wauer, R. H., and D. H. Riskind, eds. 1977. *Transactions of the Symposium on the Biological Resources of the Chihuahuan Desert Region, United States and Mexico*. U.S. Dept. of Interior, National Park Service, Transactions and Proceedings No. 3.

Wright, B. 1998. *Portraits from the Desert: Bill Wright's Big Bend*. Austin: University of Texas Press.

Desert bighorn rams (*Ovis canadensis*) near Red Rock, New Mexico. (Photo: K. A. Ernest)

BIGHORN SHEEP

Wild mountain sheep (mammalian order Artiodactyla, family Bovidae); of western North America, named for the massive, curled horns of the rams. Bighorn sheep (*Ovis canadensis*) are relatively large-bodied, social animals. During much of the year rams remain in bachelor herds, while ewes often occur in groups with juveniles. During the rut (breeding season) rams join the ewe-juvenile groups. Larger rams, particularly those with larger horns, are dominant over younger, smaller rams. Occasionally two rams vie for dominance in spectacular fights in which the rams charge at each other on their hind legs and clash horns, producing a reverberating boom.

"Desert bighorn" usually refers to the four (of seven) subspecies that live in desert regions—common names are Nelson, Mexican, Peninsular, and Weems bighorn—but this distinction is ecological rather than taxonomic. Desert bighorn historically occurred in the southernmost part of the Great Basin Desert and through most of the Mojave, Sonoran, and Chihuahuan deserts. These desert mammals usually inhabit very rugged terrain with canyons, rocky cliffs, or low desert mountains. Habitats suitable for desert bighorn include piñon-juniper woodland, sagebrush desert, and desert scrub. Bighorn eat a wide variety of grasses, forbs, shrubs, and cacti.

Desert bighorn breed during the summer or fall. Most mature ewes (older than 21 months) breed every year and give birth to a single lamb after a gestation period of six months. Lambs are precocial, covered with hair at birth and able to follow their mothers in a day or two. During the day ewes may leave their older lambs in nursery groups, guarded by other ewes, while they forage. Lambs are weaned by the age of six months; females remain in the family unit with their mothers. Males remain with the family group for one to three years, then join bachelor groups.

The horn is a permanent sheath of keratin covering a bony core (keratin is the substance that forms such structures as hair and nails). The horn grows more or less continuously, but a lapse during the rut leaves annual rings, by which a sheep's age can be determined. Bighorn can live 15–16 years in the wild. The main causes of death are predation (by mountain lions, bobcats, coyotes), disease, accidents, and ingestion of poisonous plants.

Bighorn once were common over much of the western mountain and desert areas from southern Canada to northern Mexico. Hunting, competition with domestic livestock, and disease transmitted from livestock have severely reduced their populations in some areas, though recent efforts to increase herds and transplant bighorn sheep back into their traditional range have improved their conservation status.—Kristina A. Ernest

See also **ANIMAL ADAPTATIONS; CHIHUAHUAN DESERT; CONSERVATION IN DESERTS; GREAT BASIN DESERT; MAMMALS; MEXICO, DESERTS OF; MOJAVE DESERT; SHEEP; SONORAN DESERT; THERMOREGULATION; UNGULATES; UNITED STATES, DESERTS OF; WATER BALANCE; WILDLIFE**

Further Reading

Krausman, P. R., J. R. Morgart, and M. E. Chilelli. 1984. *Annotated Bibliography of Desert Bighorn Sheep Literature, 1897–1983*. Phoenix: Southwest Natural History Association.

Monson, G., and L. Sumner, eds. 1980. *The Desert Bighorn: Its Life History, Ecology and Management*. Tucson: University of Arizona Press.

Shackleton, D. M. 1985. Ovis canadensis. *Mammalian Species* 230:1–9.

BILHARZIA

Parasitic disease caused by trematode flukes (genus *Schistosoma*). The complex life cycle of the parasite begins when the egg, deposited into water, releases an early ciliated larval stage, a miracidium. The miracidium then finds and burrows into a snail (genus *Limnea*). The parasite multiplies during several intermediate larval stages (sporocysts) in the snail host and then escapes into the water as a late larval stage with a forked tail, the cercaria. People who are bathing, washing, or drinking attract the cercaria that then burrow into the skin of the new host. The parasite matures in the circulatory system of the infected individual. After mating the female parasite ejects fertilized eggs into the body of the host, and these are later released into the environment in the host's urine or feces. Eggs deposited in water containing appropriate snail hosts repeat the life cycle.

The most common symptoms of bilharzia are fever, extreme fatigue, distended abdomen from enlargement of the spleen or liver, and discharge of blood in urine or feces. Impactment of eggs in organs causes a fibrous thickening of tissues and impairs organ function. Attempted controls on bilharzia include limiting snail populations and improved sanitation. Infections of bilharzia may be treated with appropriate drugs. While schistosomes are not limited to deserts, the incidence of infection is particularly high in arid areas because of limited sources of water and the often unsanitary conditions prevailing in underdeveloped arid areas. Increased use of irrigation has increased the size of regions infected with bilharzia.—Rob Channell

See also **AFRICA, DESERTS OF; CONTAMINATION; IRRIGATION DRAINAGE; POLLUTION**

Further Reading

Basch, P. F. 1991. *Schistosomes: Development, Reproduction, and Host Relations*. New York: Oxford University Press.

BIODIVERSITY. See DIVERSITY

BIOME

Biotic community with homogeneous life forms and characteristic plant and animal species. The term is used to denote large natural units of terrestrial landscape. Biomes usually are not based on species composition but rather on the dominant life form of the vegetation, which gives the landscape a special appearance and homogeneity (e.g., grassland, forest, desert, woodland). The term was introduced in 1939 by the American ecologists Frederic E. Clements and Victor E. Shelford.

Ecologists have tried many approaches to classifying and describing the terrestrial landscape of the earth. Most have focused on vegetation as the major criterion for classification. The term "biome" was an early attempt to integrate the principal vegetation types with the distinctive and interacting animal life, climatic regimes, and soils over relatively large geographic areas. Although plants give a biome most of its distinguishing character, animals have morphological, physiological, and behavioral traits that are adaptive to the dominant vegetation, climate, and physiography of the biome. Because the life form of the vegetation reflects the major features of climate and soils and provides habitat for animals, a classification system based primarily on vegetation provides a sound basis for an ecological classification. Similar terms are plant formation, biotic region, life zone, major life zone, biotic province.

A biome is the largest terrestrial community-scale unit used by ecologists, and there are many subdivisions within each biome. The use of the term is less common today than earlier in the century, having been replaced by the more integrative term "ecosystem." Major biomes are tundra, coniferous forest, temperate deciduous forest, temperate grassland, woodland, tropical savanna, desert, and tropical rain forest. All biomes together constitute the biosphere (the zones of the earth that support life), the largest ecological unit.—Gary K. Hulett and Amanda Renner Charles

See also ECOLOGY; ECOSYSTEM; ECOTYPE; HOLDRIDGE LIFE ZONES; PLANT GEOGRAPHY; PRIMARY PRODUCTIVITY

Further Reading

Clements, F. E., and V. E. Shelford. 1939. *Bioecology.* New York: Wiley.

Golley, F. B. 1993. *A History of the Ecosystem Concept in Ecology.* New Haven: Yale University Press.

Shelford, V. E. 1963. *The Ecology of North America.* Urbana: University of Illinois Press.

BIOSPHERE RESERVE

Biological reserve developed by the Man and the Biosphere (MAB) Program created by the General Conference of the United Nations Educational, Scientific, and Cultural Organization (UNESCO). The concept first was proposed at the sixteenth session of the UNESCO General Conference in 1970. The goal of MAB is to develop, using scientific principles, a strategy for the rational use and conservation of biospheric resources and to improve the ways in

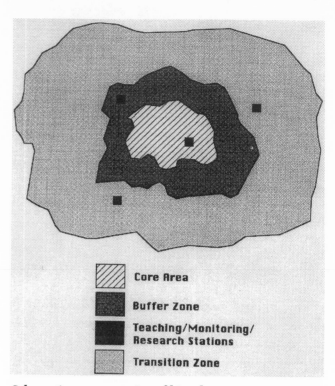

Core Area

Buffer Zone

Teaching/Monitoring/Research Stations

Transition Zone

Schematic representation of biosphere reserve concept: Transition Zone (light shading); Buffer Zone (dark shading); Core Area (crosshatched); Teaching/Monitoring/Research Stations (black squares).

which people deal with the environment. A second goal is to be able to predict how today's actions on the natural world will affect the future of that world, thus providing the ability to manage more effectively the natural resources of the biosphere. The program differs from those dedicated to basic ecological research in that it seeks to examine both the impact of humans on the environment and the impact of the environment on humans. National Committees of the MAB Program are established in nearly 100 countries.

The MAB mandate to generate scientific knowledge on the conservation of natural areas and biodiversity required a framework that allows for research on the interaction between humans and the environment. In 1974 a special task force of the MAB Program developed a set of criteria and objectives for the creation of a number of protected sites where such long-term research could be conducted. These reserves, termed biosphere reserves, serve several functions. They conserve for present and future use the diversity and integrity of biotic communities within natural and seminatural ecosystems. This would protect the genetic diversity of constituent populations in perpetuity. Reserves also provide sites for basic and applied ecological research, both within and outside protected area boundaries. Educational and training activities also are supported at MAB sites.

The biosphere reserve concept required a special design consisting of a system of zones of activity. The central *core area* is generally a national park or wilderness area, theoretically subject to strict protection. This area should ideally be large enough to support a full complement of the biodiversity typical of the ecosystem under protection. The next layer, the *buffer zone,* serves to protect the core area from destructive human activity. Activities prescribed for buffer zones include research and monitoring, recreational activities such as ecotourism, traditional land use by rural populations, and environmental education. The outer layer of the biosphere reserve is an undemarcated transitional area that should contain human activities that are more intensive than those occurring in the buffer zone but still not excessively destructive to the natural environment. Activities such as agriculture and forestry conducted by low-density human settlements would be acceptable.

The first biosphere reserves were designated in 1976; by 1987, 266 reserves existed in 70 countries. More reserves and countries continue to be added to the list. An attempt has been made to place biosphere reserves in all of the world's major ecosystems on all continents. Many biosphere reserves have been established in semiarid and arid lands in North and South America, Africa, Asia, and Australia. A scientific advisory panel establishes research priorities in biosphere reserves to guarantee that MAB objectives are met. Biosphere reserves continue to receive strong global support; the practical approach of integrating conservation with human activities is in large part responsible for the success of the program.—Thomas E. Lacher, Jr.

See also **BIOME; CONSERVATION IN DESERTS; DIVERSITY; ECOSYSTEM**

Further Reading

CNPPA. 1979. *The Biosphere Reserve and its Relationship to other Protected Areas.* Commission Report. Morges: International Union for Conservation of Nature and Natural Resources.

Gregg, W. P., Jr., S. L. Krugman, and J. D. Wood, Jr., eds. 1989. *Proceedings of the Symposium on Biosphere Reserves, Fourth World Wilderness Congress, September 14–17, 1987, YMCA at the Rockies, Estes Park, Colorado, USA.* Atlanta: U.S. Department of Interior, National Park Service.

Robertson Vernhes, J. (1986) Biosphere reserves: The beginnings, the present, and the future challenges. *In* W. P. Gregg, Jr., S. L. Krugman, and J. D. Wood, Jr., eds., *Proceedings of the Symposium on Biosphere Reserves, Fourth World Wilderness Congress, September 14–17, 1987, YMCA at the Rockies, Estes Park, Colorado, USA,* 7–20. Atlanta: U.S. Department of Interior, National Park Service.

Unrau, H. D. 1997. *A History of the Lands Added to Death Valley Monument by the California Desert Protection Act of 1994: A Special History Study.* Denver: Denver Service Center.

BIPEDALITY

Condition referable to either posture or locomotion, wherein a four-footed animal stands on its two hind feet (posture) or moves (locomotion) either by hopping on the two hind feet or alternately striding from one hind foot to the other. Short strides may be referred to as a shuffle, and there are many variations. Bipedal hopping is often referred to as bipedal ricochetal locomotion.

Animals that are specialized for bipedal locomotion generally exhibit an elongation of segments of the hind limb, whereas the forelimbs may be modified for grasping and are often reduced in length. Herein bipedal ricochetal locomotion is considered to be a special case of locomotor adaptation in small desert mammals. Reptiles, birds, and amphibians also exhibit modifications of the hind legs for leaping or bipedal progression, but these are not necessarily tied to semiarid or desert habitats (although some lizards in arid areas will use bipedal locomotion to escape predators, e.g., the zebra-tailed lizard, *Callisaurus draconoides,* of the American Southwest or the fringed lizard, *Chlamydosaurus kingii,* of dry woodlands of northern Australia); however, most bipedal mammals exhibit this locomotor syndrome in savanna (grassy plain, often with scattered trees) or desert conditions. Kangaroos of the mammalian marsupial family Macropodidae are exceptional in that bipedal locomotion in this group is not confined solely to xeric (arid) habitats but is found in species inhabiting all types of areas, including secondarily arboreal (tree-dwelling) species in the absence of competing arboreal animals (New Guinea).

Bipedal ricochetal locomotion has evolved convergently (similar traits have developed in distantly related lineages) within the order Rodentia, especially in those families that show adaptations to xeric habitats. The bipedal locomotor adaptation in rodents is accompanied by modifications in the skeleton, including lengthening of the hind feet, shortening of the forelimbs, and elongation of the tail; the latter serves as a counterbalance when the animal is hopping at high speed. The neck is often shortened, and in some cases the cervical vertebrae are fused or partially fused. The vertebral column is somewhat shortened and strengthened to withstand the stresses that normally accompany a hopping gait. Extreme adaptations among rodents for bipedal locomotion are exhibited by the kangaroo rats of the family Heteromyidae and the jerboas of the family Dipodidae.

Bipedal ricochetal locomotion permits an animal to travel at great speed, and the long tail provides a way for the animal to turn sharply, even in midair. It has been suggested that this type of locomotion evolved in part under natural selection to avoid predators. When rodents exceeding 30 grams in weight forage in rather open habitats, such as those that characterize most deserts, they may be conspicuous, thus increasing their vulnerability to attack by owls, snakes, and other predators. Bipedality may thus have evolved to permit rapid and erratic movement in sparsely vegetated open habitats.—John F. Eisenberg

See also **ANIMAL ADAPTATIONS; CONVERGENT EVOLUTION; HETEROMYIDS; JERBOA; KANGAROO; KANGAROO MOUSE; KANGAROO RAT; LOCOMOTION; MAMMALS; PREDATION; RODENTS; SPRINGHARE; TYMPANIC BULLAE**

Further Reading

Genoways, H., and J. H. Brown, eds. 1993. *Biology of the Heteromyidae*. Special Publication No. 10. American Society of Mammalogists. Lawrence, Kan.: Allen Press.

Mares, M. A. 1993. Desert rodents, seed consumption, and convergence: The evolutionary shuffling of adaptations. *BioScience* 43:372–379.

Prakash, I., and P. K. Ghosh, eds. 1975. *Rodents in Desert Environments*. Monographiae Biologicae. The Hague: W. Junk.

Schmidt-Nielsen, K. 1964. *Desert Animals: Physiological Problems of Heat and Water*. New York: Oxford University Press.

BIRDS

All species (more than 9,000 living species are recognized) in the vertebrate class Aves, one of the most speciose classes of terrestrial vertebrates. Phylogenetic (evolutionary) relationships still are not delineated clearly, and this uncertainty is reflected in current, sometimes rancorous, taxonomic debate. Traditional classifications group birds into approximately 27 orders and 173 families. The order Passeriformes (so-called perching birds) contains more than 60 percent of all bird species, classified into 74 families and about 1,160 genera. The remaining 26 orders, which contain approximately 4,000 species in about 900 genera, are collectively referred to as nonpasserines. Charles Sibley and his co-workers, based on data derived from DNA-DNA hybridization experiments, have recently challenged much of the avian taxonomic orthodoxy. Although some of Sibley and colleagues' recommendations await corroboration from analyses using independent genetic data sets (many have already been confirmed), their results underscore the necessity of not assuming that current systematics (the scientific association of taxa based on shared relationships) is necessarily representative of actual phylogeny (shared evolutionary relationships).

The earliest acknowledged avian fossil is that of *Archaeopteryx lithographica*, dated to the late Jurassic, approximately 150 million years before present. *Archaeopteryx* possessed a mosaic of avian and reptilian features and thus constituted a remarkable form, intermediate between two living vertebrate classes (Aves and Reptilia). Two theories predominate as to the ancestry of birds. One suggests that the avian lineage originated directly from the pseudosuchian thecodonts, the ancestors of all reptiles, approximately 230 million years ago. Advocates of the alternate theory propose that the avian lineage arose somewhat later from a saurischian (reptile-hipped) dinosaur ancestor.

Although birds inhabit, and are adapted to, a diverse array of habitats, all taxa are quite similar in body plan. All extant (living) birds are warm blooded (endothermic) and maintain a core body temperature within a narrow range (homeothermic). Like mammals, birds have a four-chambered heart, but this feature has probably evolved independently in each group. The highly efficient respiratory system comprises paired, small, highly vascularized lungs and a series of interconnected air sacs. Both the appendicular skeleton (containing the appendages) and axial skeleton (located along the long axis and including the skull and spine) of birds have become exceptionally modified to meet the competing demands of flying and walking. Many birds have bones that are highly "pneumatized" (containing air-filled spaces). Reduction of weight, while maintaining the rigidity and strength required for flying, is also achieved through fusion or elimination of bones. The furcula (= wishbone), for example, is the result of the fusion of the clavicles; it prevents lateral compression of the pectoral (shoulder) girdle when flight muscles are contracted. Avian forelimbs have also become highly modified to form wings; all currently flightless avian species are undoubtedly descended from flying progenitors (ancestors). A body covering of feathers is one of the diagnostic characteristics of birds. All living birds have bills that lack teeth. Bill morphology is particularly variable across bird species, reflecting a diversity of food types and corresponding foraging methods.

Reproduction in birds is oviparous (egg laying), embryos developing outside of the mother within calcareous-shelled eggs. Fertilization is internal. The majority of bird species were once considered to be truly monogamous, but it has become increasingly clear, based on evidence from DNA fingerprinting, that this is not the case and that, while many species may be socially monogamous, individuals often engage in extrapair copulations.

Numerous bird species inhabit arid and semiarid environments; however, a relatively low proportion of these taxa may be considered to be truly desert adapted. A significant percentage of the avifauna that occurs in true deserts also ranges over a wide variety of other habitats (e.g., crows, flickers, owls), occupies ecological islands, such as oases (e.g., bulbuls), or ranges throughout deserts only when conditions are favorable (e.g., parrots, emus). Organisms that inhabit deserts must endure extreme temperatures and scarcity of water; accordingly we may divide a discussion of avian adaptations to desert conditions into sections dealing with each of these major factors.

When ambient temperatures exceed that of a homeotherm's body, excess heat must be dissipated to prevent a marked, critical, and potentially fatal increase of core temperature. Birds, in this sense, may be considered to be "preadapted" to conditions of extreme heat. Birds have, on average, a higher core body temperature (by 2°–4°C) than do mammals. Thus during periods of extreme heat birds will experience fewer daily hours when the ambient temperature exceeds body temperature than will a mammal of comparable size. Moreover, birds generally seem capable of tolerating elevations of core body temperatures for short periods (facultative hyperthermia). Birds do, however, possess a variety of mechanisms for dissipating heat.

Evaporative cooling methods result in heat loss from moist body surfaces. Birds do not have sweat glands so must use other mechanisms to rid themselves of excess heat. Many birds pant, which involves rapid inhalation and exhalation of air and a concomitant heat loss from the lining of the trachea (windpipe), lungs, and air sacs. Gular fluttering, used by a small percentage of bird groups (e.g., herons, nightjars, owls, pigeons, roadrunners), involves rapid vibration of the upper air passages only; heat is lost from the surfaces of the buccal (mouth) cavity and esophagus. Some avian taxa, notably the storks and New World vultures, excrete dilute urine onto their legs, presumably to facilitate heat loss through evaporation. Finally, bathing during periods of extreme heat may be considered a behavioral adaptation that may lead to evaporative cooling from the moist integument (skin).

One of the primary functions of feathers is to provide a protective, insulating layer; in desert birds feathers must function both as a thermal shield against insolation and as insulation preventing heat loss during sometimes cold nights. Feathers must also permit heat loss when core temperature becomes elevated. The ostrich (*Struthio camelus*) provides an instructive example as to how these competing demands may be met. Dorsal feathers are long but sparsely distributed. When ambient temperatures are high these feathers are elevated, increasing the thickness of the barrier against solar radiation but allowing for lateral movement of air at the skin's surface. If nights are cold, interlocking feathers are depressed against the body, trapping an insulating layer of air. During periods of heat stress some bird species (e.g., the black vulture, *Coragyps atratus*) may increase the surface area of exposed skin by raising their wings to expose the more sparsely feathered underwing and flank. Probably the most obvious adaptation to extreme heat is simply avoidance; many species of birds confine their foraging activities to short periods at dawn and dusk (termed crespuscular activity) or are nocturnal (active at night) and seek shelter during the hottest parts of the day.

Populations of birds in desert regions tend to be less heavily pigmented than their counterparts in more humid habitats (termed Gloger's ecogeographic rule). Two hypotheses, not necessarily mutually exclusive, have been advanced as explanations for this trend. The first proposes that light coloration serves a thermoregulatory function in desert birds; thus pale plumage may acquire a lower radiative heat load than darker plumage. The second hypothesis suggests that this pattern is a result of selection for cryptic coloration in environments where the background is generally quite pale (i.e., to reduce the probability of detection by predators or prey).

There are notable exceptions to Gloger's ecogeographic rule that caution against gross generalizations regarding the adaptive significance of plumage coloration. Some species, for example, the common raven (*Corvus corax*) and the black vulturevulture, black;, have completely black plumage. Birds with darker plumages may actually acquire significantly less radiative heat load when wind speeds exceed three meters per second and when feathers are erected. Moreover, some birds appear to use dark plumage to enhance absorption of radiant solar energy. For example, the greater roadrunner (*Geococcyx californianus*) exposes black dorsal plumage and skin to solar radiation during sunning behavior. Finally, black coloration may serve a social function in some bird species inhabiting open habitats in enhancing conspicuousness over large distances.

Although the popular conception of deserts is one of areas with extreme high daily temperatures, inhabitants of such environments may also face quite frigid nightly temperatures. Several groups of birds (e.g., roadrunner, swift, hummingbird), some of which are found in deserts, have independently evolved the ability to enter torpor, which allows core body temperature, heart rate, oxygen uptake, and respiratory frequency to decrease when food is at a premium, or during periods of cold. This mechanism presumably minimizes the energy expenditure necessary to maintain an elevated body temperature.

Obviously one of the defining characteristics of deserts is scarcity of freestanding water and low annual precipitation. One of the major challenges for an inhabitant of an arid zone is procurement of adequate amounts of water and water conservation. Birds, like other desert organisms, obtain water from three sources. First, many desert birds derive a substantial portion of their water needs from their food (e.g., insects, invertebrates, or foliage of succulent plants). A second source of water is that obtained from metabolic processes, so-called metabolic water. Although a number of birds derive some of their requirements via these mechanisms, none approach the efficiency of some rodent species (e.g., kangaroo rats, *Dipodomys*), which are essentially independent of permanent sources of drinking water. The most obvious supply of water for desert birds is that of freestanding fresh water, either ephemeral or permanent. Many desert water sources are saline to varying degrees; however, most terrestrial birds (unlike marine species) lack nasal glands adapted for removal of salt and generally have only low to moderate tolerances for salt intake. There are a few notable exceptions, however. For example, chicks of the ground-nesting Rueppell's bustard (*Eupodotis vigorsii rueppellii*) of southern Africa minimize water loss through the use of efficient salt glands. Some species (e.g., the greater roadrunner) secrete salt actively from their salt glands during incubation, presumably enhancing water conservation. The zebra finch (*Poephila guttata*) of Australia, although lacking a salt gland, is able to drink water with sodium chloride concentrations exceeding that of seawater because of increased renal efficiency.

Spatial and temporal distribution of water supplies are important correlates of the occurrence, breeding schedules, and migration of many desert bird species. Patterns of precipitation in arid regions may be roughly classified as either irregular and unpredictable or predictable and seasonal. In arid zones where precipitation is sporadic many of the bird species are nomadic, moving into these areas only when ephemeral water sources are present after rains. Unpredictable rainfall also has implications for timing of breeding. For example, many birds of western and central Australia have quite flexible breeding schedules that are tied to the erratic occurrence of precipitation. In desert zones with predictable, often bimodal, precipitation patterns birds may exhibit breeding periodicity closely related to the rainy seasons.

One of the most remarkable adaptations to limited water supply can be found in the sandgrouse (family Pteroclididae) of arid regions of Africa and Asia. Males of these species have belly feathers that are structurally modified for transporting water, often from distant sources, to their offspring. Calculations suggest that males of some species may be capable of delivering up to 18 grams of water per trip to their chicks.

Reduction of water requirements reduces the frequency with which desert organisms must seek a water source. Thus mechanisms that aid in conservation of water must be considered to be important factors in ensuring survival. Many birds of desert areas seem quite tolerant of dehydration. A number of studies have shown that individuals of some species may survive for a number of weeks at elevated temperatures with no water and incur little weight loss. Probably the ultimate mechanism in water conservation is that of excretion of concentrated wastes with low water content. As was the case in the consideration of tolerance to extreme heat, birds would appear to be, in a sense, preadapted to survival in water-stressed environments. Avian "urine" contains a preponderance of insoluble uric acid, rather than water-soluble urea. Uric acid allows for the elimination of about twice as much nitrogen (a major product of metabolic processes) per molecule of water as urea. Water also is conserved in desert birds through increased kidney efficiency via reduced glomerular filtration rates.

Nest structure and placement are often critical for maintaining a constant and optimal microclimate for incubation of eggs. Nests may be placed beneath shrubs, on rock ledges, or in burrows, oriented so as to protect the eggs from the impact of wind and direct solar radiation. The nest structure itself may serve the same function, the material used in construction acting as insulation. The porous, calcareous-shelled eggs provide protection for the developing embryo, the number of pores in the eggshell being a compromise between the relative rates of oxygen intake and water loss. Although incubation itself often is perceived as a mechanism for heating eggs when temperatures are subnormal, it is also a method for removing excess heat from developing embryos via the parents' bloodstream when temperatures are excessive. A number of arid-nesting birds (e.g., some shorebirds, sandgrouse, and storks) frequently moisten their eggs, either by applying water directly or by using wet vegetation; this presumably both cools the eggs and prevents desiccation. If there are periods of direct sun during the incubation period, parents may also stand over the nest to provide shade. Chicks, once hatched, often use the shade of the parent as protection against direct sun.—Stephen C. Lougheed

See also **BULBULS; CROW; DOVE; EMU; FEATHERS; FINCH; FLAMINGO; FLICKER; GRAY GULL; HAWK; HEAT BALANCE; HEAT EXCHANGE; HERON; HORNBILL; HUMMINGBIRD; MELANIN; NIGHTJAR; OSTRICH; OWL; PARROT; PIGEON; PIGMENT; RAPTORS; RHEA; ROADRUNNER; SANDGROUSE; STORK; SWIFT; WATER BALANCE; WAXBILL**

Further Reading

Cook, W. E. 1997. *Avian Desert Predators.* New York: Springer.

Feduccia, A. 1980. *The Age of Birds.* Cambridge, Mass.: Harvard University Press.

Hadley, N. F. 1979. Thermal and water relations of desert animals. *In* D. W. Goodall and R. A. Perry, eds., *Arid-land Ecosystems: Structure, Functioning and Management,* 1:743–768. Cambridge: Cambridge University Press.

Howard. R., and A. Moore. 1991. *A Complete Checklist of the Birds of the World.* 2nd ed. New York: Academic Press.

Low, W. A. 1979. Spatial and temporal distribution and behaviour. *In* D. W. Goodall and R. A. Perry, eds., *Arid-land Ecosystems: Structure, Functioning and Management,* 1:769–822. Cambridge: Cambridge University Press.

Maclean, G. L. 1996. *Avian Adaptations to Deserts of the Northern and Southern Hemispheres: A Comparison.* Perth, Western Australia: Curtin University of Technology.

Miller, A. H. 1963. Desert adaptations in birds. *In Proceedings of the XIII International Ornithological Congress 1962,* 666–674.

Schmidt-Nielsen, K. 1964. *Desert Animals: Physiological Problems of Heat and Water.* New York: Oxford University Press.

Schodde, R. 1982. Origin, adaptation and evolution of birds in arid Australia. *In* W. R. Barker and P. J. M. Greenslade, eds., *Evolution of the Flora and Fauna of Arid Australia,* 191–224. Frewville, South Australia: Peacock.

Serventy, D. L. 1971. Biology of desert birds. *In* D. S. Farner, and J. R. King, eds., *Avian Biology,* 1:287–339. New York: Academic Press.

Sibley, C. G., and J. E. Ahlquist. 1990. *Phylogeny and Classification of Birds. A Study in Molecular Evolu-*

tion. New Haven: Yale University Press.

Walsberg, G. E., G. S. Campbell, and J. R. King. 1978. Animal coat color and radiative heat gain: A re-evaluation. *Journal of Comparative Physiology* 126B:211–222.

BIRDS OF PREY. *See* RAPTORS

BLACKBUCK

Species of gazelle (mammalian order Artiodactyla, family Bovidae) indigenous to the open, flat lands of India, Pakistan, and Bangladesh. The blackbuck (*Antilope cervicapra*) is so named because the color of males of the species fluctuates between brown and pitch black and is contrasted with the white of the chin, around the eye, and on the underparts. Females and juveniles are light tan. Although the females are hornless, horns that are impressively long (35–75 centimeters), deeply grooved, and twisted adorn the males. Blackbucks feed on grass and leaves and can survive a relatively long period without drinking free water. Males and females form small social groups. Mating is not seasonal but takes place year-round. After a gestation of five to six months, one kid is born. It takes the kid two years to reach sexual maturity. Life spans in the wild are estimated to be 10–12 years. Natural predators of the blackbuck include wolves, cheetahs, and pariah dogs. In the past century populations of blackbuck have seen precipitous declines. They were reintroduced into Pakistan following their extirpation there. Populations have also been introduced into Argentina, Nepal, and Texas.—Rob Channell

See also **ANIMAL ADAPTATIONS; ANTELOPE; GAZELLE; HERBIBORY; INDO-PAKISTAN DESERTS; UNGULATES**

Further Reading

Schaller, G. B. 1967. *The Deer and the Tiger: A Study of Wildlife in India.* Chicago: University of Chicago Press.

Sinha, N. K. 1986. Study on Blackbuck, *Antilope cervicapra* (Linnaeus) around Jodhpur (Rajasthan). *In* T. C. Majupuria, ed., *Wildlife Wealth of India: Resources and Management,* 467–477. Bangkok: Tecpress Service.

BLACK WIDOW SPIDER

Any of the spiders in the genus *Latrodectus* (family Theridiidae) in which the female has a bulbous, glossy black body characterized by a red hourglass marking on the ventral surface. Black widows vary in size from about 1 to 1.5 centimeters, with leg spans approaching four centimeters. Legs are long and thin. Males are small and spindly, with long legs and a mottled (red, brown, and cream) abdomen.

Black widow webs can be found naturally at interfaces between rocks and ground, logs and ground, and in numerous kinds of crevices. Webs are often common in similar structural microhabitats around buildings. Webs are irregular in shape. There are at least five species distributed throughout much of the world, with the best-known species being *Latrodectus mactans*, of the United States.

About 150 eggs are deposited by females in small cuplike structures constructed of webbing. The cup is covered with silk following egg deposition and remains in the spider web for about 30 days before hatching. Tiny juvenile spiders often disperse by producing a long strand of webbing from an elevated perch such that wind carries the spider to a new location, a process called ballooning. Food consists of arthropods and, rarely, small vertebrates. Prey are detected as they enter the web by vibrations of the strands. The spider approaches the prey backward, spraying silk to entangle it, after which the helpless prey is bitten and killed. Body fluids then are sucked up by the black widow.

Black widows are best known because they produce a highly toxic venom. Although black widows seldom bite and certainly do not seek out people, their bites have been known to cause death in humans. The neurotoxic venom; they produce can cause extreme pain, respiratory distress, anxiety, shock, and numerous other symptoms. Acute effects of the bite may last two to three days or even longer.—Laurie J. Vitt

See also **ARACHNIDS; ARTHROPODS; DEFENSIVE ADAPTATIONS, ANIMALS; DESERTS; POISONOUS ANIMALS; SPIDERS; RED VELVET MITE; VENOM**

Further Reading

Hermes, W. B., and M. T. James. 1964. *Medical Entomology.* New York: Macmillan.

Kaston, B. J. 1970. Comparative biology of American black widow spiders. *Transactions San Diego Natural History* 16:33–82.

Kaston, B. J. 1978. *How to Know the Spiders.* Dubuque: W. C. Brown.

Levi, H. W., and H. S. Levi. 1968. *A Guide to Spiders.* New York: Golden Press.

Milne, L., and M. Milne. 1980. *The Audubon Society*

Field Guide to North American Insects and Spiders. New York: Knopf.

Smith, R. L. 1982. *Venomous Animals of Arizona.* Tucson: Cooperative Extension Service, University of Arizona.

BOBCAT

Species of cat (*Lynx rufus*) in the subfamily Felinae (mammalian order Carnivora, family Felidae) that is closely related to the lynx. Bobcats are found over an extensive geographic area from southern Canada, throughout most of the continental United States, and south to Oaxaca, Mexico. Given such a broad distribution, bobcats can occur in many different habitats, including coniferous and deciduous forests, grasslands, and deserts. They are also found in areas of mixed agriculture and forest and are occasionally observed near human dwellings and in small towns and the suburbs of large cities. This species has adapted the best to disturbance of any of the North American cats.

Bobcats range in size from 750 to 1,000 centimeters and weigh approximately 6–11 kilograms. They have a very short tail of only 125–155 millimeters. Bobcats have a characteristic external appearance: a short body with stout legs, small black tufts on the tip of the ears, and a short tail with black bars on the tip. They have thick fur that is yellowish to reddish brown and is darker on the back. The face and back have black streaking that becomes distinct black spots on the belly.

They are active day and night and are among the most diurnal of the cats. Bobcats are not desert specialists and occur in a diverse array of habitats. Where they occur in the western deserts of North America, they are especially common in canyons, rocky woodlands, and forest patches, although they are also seen in open desert scrub. The bobcat present in the southwestern deserts of the United States is somewhat smaller than other subspecies. Rocky areas in caves and crevices are preferred for dens and rest sites, but desert bobcats will range widely to hunt. They feed on a variety of small mammals, birds, and lizards and, occasionally, young deer. They reproduce in late winter, and the young are born in the spring. There are from one to four young that are born with their eyes closed; they take about two months to be weaned. Bobcats live up to 20 years.—Thomas E. Lacher, Jr.

See also **CARNIVORES; CATS; MAMMALS; PREDATION**

Further Reading

Gittleman, J. L., ed. 1989. *Carnivore Behavior, Ecology, and Evolution.* Ithaca: Cornell University Press.

Hoffmeister, D. F. 1971. *Mammals of the Grand Canyon.* Urbana: University of Illinois Press.

National Wildlife Federation. 1979. *Bobcat Research Conference Proceedings; Current Research on Biology and Management of* Lynx rufus. Washington, D.C.: National Wildlife Federation, Scientific and Technical Series 6.

Nowak, R. M. 1991. *Walker's Mammals of the World.* 5th ed. Baltimore: Johns Hopkins University Press.

BODY TEMPERATURE

Term typically applied to a representative temperature of an animal, usually its deep rectal or cloacal temperature in vertebrates. Because animals are often in circumstances in which the body temperature differs from the immediate external environment, resulting in heat exchange with that environment, the peripheral portions of the body maintain a less constant temperature than do the inner, core portions. Therefore, the core temperature is the most representative temperature of the animal, and the terms "body temperature" and "core temperature" are synonymous.

Animals, including desert forms, may be categorized according to body temperature characteristics. Ectotherms are animals that lack surface insulation, and whose body temperatures result from exogenous thermal sources; their body temperatures may therefore be labile (variable). Such species include most arthropods, fish, amphibians, and reptiles. Endotherms are animals that possess good surface insulation (feathers or fur) and rely on endogenous heat production to maintain fairly high, constant body temperatures; these include birds and mammals. Some birds and mammals maintain high, constant body temperatures during periods of activity but lapse into ectothermy while inactive, as do certain insects; these animals are aptly referred to as heterotherms or facultative heterotherms. The process of controlling body temperature, whether in an endotherm, ectotherm, or heterotherm, is called thermoregulation.—Richard E. MacMillen

See also **CLOTHING; DEHYDRATION; ECTOTHERMY; ENDOTHERMY; ESTIVATION; EXCRETORY SYSTEM; EXPLOSIVE HEAT DEATH; HEAT BALANCE; HEAT EXCHANGE; HEAT STRESS; HEATSTROKE; HIBER-**

NATION; HUMAN PHYSIOLOGY IN DESERTS; HYPERTHERMIA; HYPOTHERMIA; KIDNEYS; PERSPIRATION; PHYSIOLOGY; SALT BALANCE; SHIVERING; SUNSTROKE; SURVIVAL IN DESERTS; SWEAT GLANDS; THERMOREGULATION; TORPOR; TRANSPIRATION; VAN'T HOFF EFFECT; WATER BALANCE

Further Reading

Gordon, M. S., G. A. Bartholomew, A. D. Grinnell, C. B. Jorgensen, and F. N. White. 1982. *Animal Physiology: Principles and Adaptations.* New York: Macmillan.

Schmidt-Nielsen, K. 1990. *Animal Physiology: Adaptation and Environment.* 4th ed. New York: Cambridge University Press.

BOLIVIA, DESERTS OF. *See* SOUTH AMERICA, DESERTS OF

BOLSÓN

Enclosed drainage basin found at both high and low elevations and surrounded by mountains. In desert areas bolsones (a word of Spanish origin) frequently lead to the formation of salt lakes or saline flats, areas with high evaporation and siltation that may be seasonally flooded or may have generally shallow water throughout the year. Bolsones are common in most desert areas where mountain ranges are extensive and interlocking ranges form the requisite closed drainage system. In Argentina, for example, such enclosed basins are found throughout the high altiplano, as well as in the low-elevation Monte Desert. Bolsones are also common in the deserts of the southwestern United States and other regions having complicated series of desertic mountain ranges (e.g., a number of Old World deserts). Extensive research has been carried out on bolsones in Mexico as well.

Bolsones often support plants and animals that are specialized for life in saline areas, including various halophytic (salt-loving) plants and animals that may be capable of processing high salt loads. In some cases the very isolation of these valleys may lead to speciation of both plants and animals. In Argentina, for example, bolsones have likely led to the isolation and development of mammalian genera (e.g., the phyllotine rodent genus *Andalgalomys*) as well as taxa that are able to consume quantities of salt water that exceed levels of salinity found in the ocean (e.g., rodents of the South American phyllotine genera *Eligmodontia* and *Sali-*

nomys, the octodontid rodent *Tympanoctomys*). These patterns of speciation and adaptation also characterize other bolsón situations.—Virgilio G. Roig

See also ALLUVIAL FAN; ALTIPLANO; ANDES; ANIMAL ADAPTATIONS; CAMELS, SOUTH AMERICAN; DESERT SLOPES; HALOPHYTES; LANDSCAPE; MAMMALS; PLANT ADAPTATIONS; PLAYA; RODENTS; SALINITY; SALT BALANCE; SALT CRUST; SALT DESERT; SALT PAN; WEATHERING, DESERT; WIND EROSION

Further Reading

Braun, J. K., and M. A. Mares. 1995. A new genus and species of phyllotine rodent (Rodentia: Muridae: Sigmodontinae) from South America. *Journal of Mammalogy* 76:504–521.

Cooke, R., A. Warren, and A. Goudie. 1993. *Desert Geomorphology.* London: University College London Press.

Grenot, C. J. 1983. *Desierto Chihuahuense: Fauna del Bolsón de Mapimí.* Chapingo, Mexico: Universidad Autónoma, Departamento de Zonas Áridas.

Mares, M. A., J. Morello, and G. Goldstein. 1985. The Monte Desert and other subtropical semi-arid biomes of Argentina, with comments on their relation to North American arid areas. *In* M. Evenari, I. Noy-Meir, and D. W. Goodall, eds., *Ecosystems of the World: Hot Deserts and Arid Shrublands*, 12B:203–237. Amsterdam: Elsevier.

Morello. J. (1984) *Perfil ecológico de Sudamérica.* Barcelona: Ediciones Cultura Hispánica, Instituto de Cooperación Iberoamericana.

Ojeda, R. A., and M. A. Mares. 1989. A biogeographic analysis of the mammals of Salta Province, Argentina: Patterns of species assemblage in the Neotropics. *Special Publications, The Museum, Texas Tech University* 27:1–66.

BONNEVILLE

Region, encompassing parts of Utah, Nevada, and Idaho, that was prehistorically covered by Lake Bonneville, which formed approximately 17,000 years ago from the water of retreating glaciers. The size of the lake would increase with the decline of the glaciers and decrease with the advance of the glaciers. At its maximum the lake covered approximately 19,000 square miles. With the last retreat of the glaciers 9,000 years ago, the lake dried up, remaining only as an extensive basin, Bonneville Salt Flats, and relatively small lakes (Utah Lake, Great Salt Lake;, Sevier Dry Lake, and Little Salt Lake).

Of the expansive region once covered by Lake Bonneville, one of the best-known areas is the Bonneville Salt Flats, which refers to an area of 100 square miles in northwestern Utah. The potential annual evaporation exceeds the annual precipitation through most of the former area of Lake Bonneville. This imbalance of evaporation and precipitation causes salts dissolved in water to accumulate in the low-lying areas of the former lake. At the Bonneville Salt Flats this salt causes the ground to become as hard as concrete during the dry season. It is this level, hard surface that attracts racing enthusiasts, many of whom have taken advantage of the natural pavement to set new world speed records.

The Bonneville region was named after Benjamin E. Bonneville. Beginning in 1831, while on leave from the army, Bonneville explored the Great Basin and parts of California. Bonneville's journals of his explorations were later used by Washington Irving; as the basis of the book *The Adventures of Captain Bonneville.*—Rob Channell

See also **BOLSÓN; DESERT SLOPES; LAKES, PLUVIAL; PLAYA; RUNOFF; SALINITY; SALT CRUST; SALT DESERT; SALT PAN; UNITED STATES, DESERTS OF; UTAH DESERT; WEATHERING, DESERT**

Further Reading

Irving, W. 1852. *The Adventures of Captain Bonneville, U.S.A., in the Rocky Mountains and the Far West.* New York: Putnam.

Pack, F. J. 1939. *Lake Bonneville, a Popular Treatise Dealing with the History and Physical Aspects of Lake Bonneville.* Salt Lake City: University of Utah Press.

BOOJUM

Tall tree of the Sonoran Desert (*Fouquieria columnaris*) in the candlewood family (Fouquieriaceae) which resembles an upside-down carrot with wavy arms and is related to ocotillo, another common Sonoran Desert plant. The boojum, or "cirio" as it is known in Spanish, can reach a height of up to 20 meters, but in exposed locations mature trees may be a mere 50 centimeters tall. The columnar trunk tapers gradually; it may bear small lateral branches or be unbranched. Near the Pacific Coast of Baja California some trees are covered with lichens. The oldest common name, milapá, was used by the Cochimí Indians. Godfrey Sykes of the Desert Botanical Laboratory in Tucson, who had read

Boojum tree (*Fouquieria columnaris*) in the desert of Baja California, Mexico. (Photo: D. Beck)

Lewis Carroll's *The Hunting of the Snark*, took the name from Carroll's "boojum," a mythical thing from a desolate region.

Boojums grow in the central part of Baja California and coastal Sonora, Mexico. In Baja they occur as dominant plants in the Vizcaino subdivision of the Sonoran Desert in communities with agaves, yuccas, and the columnar cardón cactus. Their range is more restricted in coastal Sonora, where they grow on bajadas within the Central Gulf Coast subdivision. They can be found on granitic (granite-based), basaltic (fine-grained, crystalline, igneous rock), and volcanic soils having a high clay content.

Boojums are xerophytes, well adapted to arid regions. Although the Vizcaino subdivision has low precipitation, moisture is available in the form of fog, especially during winter. Boojums are drought deciduous and bear leaves primarily during the winter.

Boojums begin reproducing when they are about two meters tall. Mature trees produce fruits nearly every year during the summer rainy season. The yellow flowers are clustered in panicles (open, branching flowers) at the top of the trunk. Floral visitors include moths, butterflies, bees, true bugs, flies and other insects, and hummingbirds. The seeds mature by fall and are wind dispersed for short distances from the parent plant. Germination can occur rapidly in rocky crevices or beneath shrubs.—Kristina A. Ernest

See also **BAJA CALIFORNIA, DESERTS OF; MEXICO, DESERTS OF; OCOTILLO; PLANT ADAPTATIONS; PLANT DISPERSAL BY WIND (ANEMOCHORY); PLANTS; SONORAN DESERT**

Further Reading

Humphrey, R. R. 1974. *The Boojum and Its Home.* Tucson: University of Arizona Press.

Shreve, F., and I. L. Wiggins. 1964. *Vegetation and Flora of the Sonoran Desert.* Vols. 1 and 2. Stanford: Stanford University Press.

BORREGO DESERT. *See* ANZA-BORREGO DESERT

BRACKISH WATER. *See* IRRIGATION DRAINAGE

BRAZIL, SEMIDESERT. *See* CAATINGA

BREEDING SEASON

Period during which organisms reproduce. In temperate regions the breeding season of many animals is frequently associated with seasonal changes in the weather. Many animals reproduce during spring, when temperatures begin to moderate and when food becomes more readily available for the young, perhaps because of plant growth or increased insect activity. Amphibians may breed during the spring because of the combination of moderating temperatures and rainfall, which are necessary for reproduction in these animals. Deserts may have broadly predictable times of the year when rainfall occurs, and many organisms reproduce during these periods. The breeding season in some animals is extended because of the complex behavior associated with reproduction. For example, birds frequently must establish territories, form mating pairs, construct nests, lay eggs, and care for their young for a long period. Cactus wren males in the southwestern United States defend territories as early as January, and the first eggs are laid in March. While the first clutch is being cared for, a male cactus wren may construct a secondary nest nearby in which the female will deposit a second clutch of eggs after the first brood is fledged. In mild areas of the southwestern deserts the breeding season of some mammals may extend throughout the year. Kangaroo rats, for example, may have three litters of young during the year, although the frequency of breeding is reduced in the winter. In one well-studied species, *Dipodomys ordii*, breeding may be correlated with the availability of food (seeds, fruits, leaves, insects), declining during periods of drought and increasing during wet periods. In the deserts of the southwestern United States summer rains bring out many species of frogs and toads that form explosive breeding aggregations, taking advantage of the small vernal pools that are present for only a brief time. In contrast to birds and mammals, breeding seasons may be very abbreviated in some desert amphibians because of the scarcity of rainfall and other resources. For example, spadefoot toads (genera *Scaphiopus* and *Spea*) remain buried underground for most of the year, but heavy rains stimulate individuals to come above ground. Males congregate in large numbers at newly formed pools and call to attract females to the site. Intense competition occurs among males for access to the females as they arrive at the ponds. The eggs are deposited within a day or two; thus the breeding season in these species may last only a few days each year.—Janalee P. Caldwell

See also **AMPHIBIANS; ANIMAL ADAPTATIONS; ARTHROPODS; BIRDS; FROGS; INSECTS; MAMMALS; REPTILES; REPRODUCTION; SPADEFOOT TOAD; TOADS**

Further Reading

Duellman, W. E., and L. Trueb. 1986. *Biology of Amphibians.* New York: McGraw-Hill.

Wells, K. D. 1977. The courtship of frogs. *In* D. H. Taylor and S. I. Guttman, eds., *The Reproductive Biology of Amphibians,* 233–262. New York: Plenum.

BRITTLEBUSH

Short, rounded shrub (*Encelia farinosa*) in the daisy family (Asteraceae) with soft, but brittle, woody branches and bright yellow flowers. It also grows along washes and on plains and mesas in the Mojave and Sonoran deserts and extends into the thorn forest of western Mexico. Brittlebush is usually 40–60 centimeters high but can reach 1 meter (and, occasionally, 1.5 meters) in height. The whitish, hairy stems and branches exude a brownish resin. The leaves are whitish or light greenish gray, growing mainly near the ends of branches. Leaves are produced twice yearly, with distinct morphological differences between the summer and winter crops. The compound flowers, also produced twice yearly, occur in heads clustered on stalks. Flowers of the disc (flower head) are usually yellow but sometimes purple. Brittlebush is common on volcanic soils and rocky slopes, where its bright flowers are strikingly beautiful in the spring.

Brittlebush, a very hardy desert plant, is dehydration tolerant as well as drought tolerant. It is an example of a desert semishrub and can be distinguished from true shrubs by its soft wood, plentiful branches, and ability to respond to extremes in moisture conditions. One such response is dropping leaves during periods of drought. Another adaptation for xeric conditions is leaf pubescence, which increases the amount of light that is reflected (rather than absorbed) from the leaf surface, thus lowering leaf temperature and reducing evaporative water loss. Leaves may vary in size, pubescence, and absorptance depending on moisture conditions.

The resin of the brittlebush is burned as an incense (thus the common Spanish name, *incenso*), chewed as a gum, and used as glue and varnish. The branches, resin, and leaves are used medicinally to relieve aches and pains (especially arthritis), as well as for colds.—Kristina A. Ernest

See also **DESERTS; MOJAVE DESERT; PLANT ADAPTATIONS; PLANTS; SHRUBS; SONORAN DESERT; UNITED STATES, DESERTS OF**

Further Reading

Sandquist, D. R., and J. R. Ehleringer. 1998. Intraspecific variation of drought adapatation in brittlebush: leaf pubescence and timing of leaf loss vary with rainfall. *Oecologia* 113:162–169.

Shreve, F., and I. L. Wiggins. 1964. *Vegetation and Flora of the Sonoran Desert.* Vols. 1 and 2. Stanford: Stanford University Press.

BROMELIADS

Herbaceous plants in the family Bromeliaceae having thick, daggerlike leaves. This is a large family, occurring in the warmer parts of North and South America (only one species occurs in the Old World,

Ground bromeliads (*Tillandsia*) in the lowland desert of Peru. (Photo: V. G. Roig)

in Africa). Bromeliads are found in lush, moist areas but are important desert inhabitants, particularly in South American and South African deserts. Representative genera are *Puya, Abromeitiella, Aechmea, Dyckia, Ochagavia,* and *Navia.* Desert bromeliads, such as *Hechtia,* occur in the Chihuahuan Desert of southern Texas. Bromeliads can live either rooted in the soil or as epiphytes, plants that grow on the branches of other plants without parasitizing them. Most of their water is stored in small cups formed by the basal portions of their stiff leaves, which makes them adept at trapping moisture from fog, the prevalent form of precipitation in some of their native habitats. In North America members of the lily family (e.g., yuccas) have an appearance similar to the bromeliads of South America, an example of convergent evolution.—Linda L. Wallace

See also **CHIHUAHUAN DESERT; CONVERGENT EVOLUTION; MONTE DESERT; PLANT ADAPTATIONS; PLANTS; SOUTH AFRICA, DESERTS OF; SOUTH AMERICA, DESERTS OF; SUCCULENTS; YUCCA**

Further Reading

Benzing, D. H. 1980. *The Biology of the Bromeliads.* Eureka, Calif.: Mad River Press.

Martin, C. E. 1994. Physiological ecology of the Bromeliaceae. *The Botanical Review* 60:1–82.

Puente, Maria-Ester. 1994. The desert epiphyte, *Tillandsia recurvata,* harbours the nitrogon-fixing bacterium, *Pseudomonas stutzeri. Canadian Journal of Botany* 72:406–408.

BUGS

Common name for insects in the order Hemiptera. True bugs are distinguished from other insects by the structure of their front wings. The base of the front wings is typically thickened and leathery in texture and membranous at the apex. The hind wings, usually covered by the front wings when the insect is not flying, are membranous. Wings are held flat against the upper surface of the abdomen when not being used in flight. Mouth parts of hemipterans are of the piercing-sucking type. Compound eyes are well developed, and, at least in most terrestrial species, the antennae are long.

Most true bugs found in deserts occur on vegetation. Many of these feed on plant juices by piercing the surface of plants and sucking out the juices. Some of the more common herbivorous families of bugs on desert plants are the Miridae (plant or leaf bugs), the Aradidae (flat bugs), the Coreidae (leaf-footed bugs), the Pentatomidae (stinkbugs), and the Lygaeidae (seed bugs). Plant bugs differ considerably in morphology, depending on species. Some are long and spindly, and others are rather short and robust. These bugs typically are found on leaves or stems of plants, and some are extremely cryptic in morphology and coloration. The flat bugs are extremely flattened dorsoventrally and most often are encountered under the bark of trees, such as mesquite (*Prosopis*). Leaf-footed bugs can often be found in large numbers on flowers of various species of *Yucca*. Stinkbugs are usually encountered on leafy vegetation, but some species are found on stems of desert perennials. Although stinkbugs produce aromatic chemicals (which, interestingly, smell sweet to some people and sour to others) when disturbed, many other hemipterans also produce similar-smelling compounds. Seed bugs are typically associated with seeds of desert plants.

Not all true bugs are herbivores. For example, desert species in the family Reduviidae (assassin bugs) are predaceous on other insects and spiders. This family is particularly interesting because of the incredible morphological diversity among species. Some species are elongate with front legs that aid in capturing insects. Others are short and robust and extremely cryptic in morphology. Still others cover their bodies with dust particles in the nymph stage so that they look like moving dust balls. Several species (e.g., *Triatoma*) suck blood of mammals, including humans. They are recognized as "kissing bugs" or "assassin" bugs because they often bite humans while they are asleep and may carry and transmit trypanosomes that cause Chagas disease. Assassin bugs often live in mammal nests in deserts, particularly the nests of woodrats (*Neotoma*).

In addition to the many terrestrial and arboreal bugs in deserts, many species are associated with water, both permanent and temporary. Because most bugs can fly, temporary ponds that fill during the rainy season in deserts become infested with bugs, many of which are predaceous and take advantage of the high abundance of other invertebrates, and even vertebrates, in the high-nutrient temporary ponds. The most common families observed in aquatic situations in deserts are the Belostomatidae (giant water bugs), Corixidae (water boatmen), Gelastocoridae (toad bugs), Naucoridae (creeping water bugs), Notonectidae (backswimmers), and Gerridae (water striders). Giant water bugs are well known by humans because of their very painful bites, large size, predaceous habits, and interesting life history. They not only feed on invertebrates but also commonly capture and eat small fish, tadpoles, and frogs. In some species the female deposits eggs on the back of the male who then carries the eggs around during development. Water boatmen swim around in the water column preying on smaller insects. Toad bugs live on the damp banks of streams and pools hopping about like miniature toads. Creeping water bugs literally "creep" through aquatic vegetation searching for prey and, if handled, inflict extremely painful bites. They reach their highest levels of local species diversity in streams in the semiarid Southwest. Backswimmers swim about in the water column and on the surface upside down using their long hind legs like giant oars. Water striders skip across the surface of the water using the surface tension as their substrate. Tiny hairs on the tarsi of their legs allow them to remain on the surface without getting wet. They are extremely rapid and often move in groups across the surface.

True bugs are important components of desert ecosystems as herbivores, predators, and prey for many other species of invertebrates and vertebrates.—Laurie J. Vitt

See also **ANIMAL ADAPTATIONS; ARTHROPODS; DEFENSIVE ADAPTATIONS, ANIMALS; INSECTS; MESQUITE; PREDATION; SPIDERS; WOODRAT; YUCCA**

Further Reading

Borror, D. J., C. A. Triplehorn, and N. F. Johnson. 1992. *An Introduction to the Study of Insects*. New York: Harcourt Brace.

Borror, D. J., and R. E. White. 1970. *A Field Guide to the Insects*. Boston: Houghton Mifflin.

Henry, T. J., and R. C. Froeschner, eds. 1988. *Catalogue of the Heteroptera, or True Bugs, of Canada and the Continental United States*. Leiden: E. J. Brill.

Wisdom, C. S. 1991. Patterns of heterogeneity in desert herbivorous insect communities. *In* G. A. Polis, ed., *The Ecology of Desert Communities*, 151–179. Tucson: University of Arizona Press.

BULBS

Underground, perenniating organs (perennial organs) with short disklike stems that are enclosed by highly modified, usually fleshy, storage leaves. Bulbs usually have dry, scaly outer protective leaves. They form the overwintering organ for most perennial species in the lily family (Liliaceae), and they occur in a variety of other monocot (flowering plants having only one seed leaf) groups as well. Bulbs occur only rarely among dicots (flowering plants having two seed leaves). Bulbs may be mistaken for corms, tubers, or fleshy rhizomes (underground stems), which are also belowground perenniating organs; however, in corms, tubers, and rhizomes the stem is fleshy and enclosing leaves are dry, scalelike, or vestigial. These organs are solid in cross-section, whereas bulbs are layered.

Plants with bulbs and bulblike structures are abundant members of most deserts, such as the African, Iranian-Turanian, Jordanian, Arabian, and South American deserts. With their large stores of food and water, they are able to respond quickly to environmental cues and grow rapidly, a distinct advantage in areas, such as deserts, with extreme climatic conditions and long periods of heat and drought when conditions are not conducive to plant growth. For instance, rain lilies (*Cooperia*) produce a belowground stem somewhat intermediate between bulbs and corms, and they flower approximately five to seven days after a heavy rain. This adaptation permits them to withstand long periods of drought, and then to respond and reproduce quickly when adequate rain falls. The bulb of *Allium rothii*, a member of the onion genus, is also effective at gathering and storing water.

Cultivated plants that exhibit true buds include lily, tulip, wake robin, and onion. A corm-bearing plant is the crocus. Many irises have fleshy rhizomes. White (or Irish) potatoes are tubers.—James R. Estes

See also **HERBS; IRAN, DESERTS OF; PERENNIAL PLANTS; PHOTOSYNTHESIS; PLANT ADAPTATIONS; PLANTS; SAUDI ARABIA, DESERTS OF; SOUTH AMERICA, DESERTS OF**

Further Reading

Heywood, V. H., ed. 1993. *Flowering Plants of the World*. Updated ed. New York: Oxford University Press.

Kamenetsky, R. 1994. Life cycle, flower initiation, and propagation of the desert geophyte *Allium rothii*. *International Journal of Plant Science* 155:596–606.

Rees, A. R. 1972. *The Growth of Bulbs*. New York: Academic Press.

BULBULS

Group of small to medium-sized, primarily arboreal Old World songbirds (order Passeriformes, family Pycnonotidae). Approximately 120 species in 14 genera are recognized, depending on the author cited. Pycnonotids range throughout Africa and southern Asia and for the most part are nonmigratory. The majority of species are associated with forest and parkland habitats in tropical regions. A few species, notably some members of the genus *Pycnonotus*, inhabit semiarid habitats. For example, the white-cheeked bulbul, *Pycnonotus leucogenys*, occurs in dry tracts of thorn scrub in southern Asia (Pakistan and India). Some arid-land bulbul taxa, notably the common bulbul (*Pycnonotus barbatus*) of Africa, are quick to exploit new water sources associated with human settlement. Bulbuls have moderately slender bodies, short rounded wings, longish tails, short necks, and narrow bills. Plumage coloration is generally quite dull. Some species possess an erectile crest. Sexes are generally similar, although males may be slightly larger. Length varies from 15 to 28 centimeters. Bulbuls are primarily frugivorous (fruit eaters) and insectivorous (insect eaters); some species supplement their diet with pollen and nectar.

Most bulbul species defend territories, either as a solitary pair or in small groups. Breeding systems are variable and include monogamy, polygyny, and cooperative breeding (i.e., a number of nonparental birds aid in the care of the chicks). Nests are constructed of twigs and leaves, usually between one and nine meters above the ground in trees or bushes. Clutch size ranges from two to five eggs. Both sexes share in incubation duties, this period lasting 11–14 days. Chicks are fed by both parents. Many species produce more than one brood per year.—Stephen C. Lougheed

See also **AFRICA, DESERTS OF; ANIMAL ADAPTATIONS; ASIA, DESERTS OF; BIRDS**

Further Reading

Cramp, S., ed. 1988. *Handbook of the Birds of Europe the Middle East and North Africa. The Birds of the Western Palearctic*. Vol. 5. Oxford: Oxford University Press.

Keith, S., E. K. Urban, and C. H. Fry, eds. 1992. *The Birds of Africa*. Vol. 4. New York: Academic Press.

Roberts, T. J. 1992. *The Birds of Pakistan*. Vol. 2. Karachi: Oxford University Press.

BURRO. *See* ASS

BURROWING ANIMALS

Animals specialized for underground existence in burrows (fossorial species, such as gophers) or that use burrows extensively for shelter or foraging (e.g., kangaroo rats). Many terrestrial vertebrates and invertebrates are adapted for constructing burrows; insects, spiders, amphibians, reptiles, and mammals immediately come to mind. Mammals illustrate the concept of a burrow existence. Many species are adapted for constructing burrows as refuges or sites for rearing their young. Insectivores (members of the mammalian order Insectivora, including shrews and moles), carnivores, and rodents show many adaptations for constructing burrows. A burrow in the soil provides a refuge from rainfall and intense sunlight. Indeed, a deep burrow may maintain a stable internal temperature well below that of the soil surface temperature, while keeping relative humidity high, thus reducing water loss due to respiration. Burrows, when plugged by the occupant, are an effective refuge against certain types of predators. Mammals with burrowing adaptations usually have rather long stout claws and, in the case of rodents, may also have heavy incisors adapted for biting into the soil, thus loosening it and making it easier for the forepaws to move soil about. The degree of specialization for excavating burrows will, of course, vary with the soil type in which the species normally occurs. Digging in sandy soil presents different problems from constructing burrows in hard compacted soils, for example.

A special case of burrowing ability involves mammals that use tunnels and their chambers not only as nest sites and refuges but also for the collection of food. A mole, for example, spends most of its life underground. Its foraging tunnels are near the surface, where it preys on various soil invertebrates associated with the root systems of the plants. North American pocket gophers, although they are herbivores (plant eaters), as opposed to the insectivorous moles, use their tunnels to obtain underground (and aboveground) plant parts.

In desert habitats burrowing animals can forage while remaining well protected from the extremes of temperature. Species that feed on invertebrates that forage underground in desert habitats include such specialists as the Namib Desert golden mole, *Eremitalpa*, and the marsupial mole of central Australia, *Notoryctes*. Rodents that forage underground in desert habitats include the African blind mole rat, *Heterocephalus*; rodents of the genera *Geomys* and *Thomomys* in semiarid habitats of North America; and the tucu-tuco (*Ctenomys*) in South America. Extreme specialization for foraging and living underground (e.g., fossorial species) entails the following morphological characteristics: shortening of the neck; reduction in the size of the external ear; reduction in the size of the eyes; shortening of the tail; and elongation of the claws of the forepaws. The fur tends to be short, since the necessity for thermoregulation is reduced, and in the case of *Heterocephalus*, the hair is essentially lost except for a few vibrissae (whiskers). Highly fossorial species, such as moles, gophers, and mole rats, share these and many other traits that have evolved in response to an underground existence.—John F. Eisenberg

See also **ANIMAL ADAPTATIONS; CHIHUAHUAN DESERT; CONVERGENT EVOLUTION; DESERTS; DESSICATION-RESISTANT SPECIES; GOPHER; MAMMALS; MOLE, GOLDEN; MOLE RAT; MONTE DESERT; NAMIBIA, DESERTS OF; RODENTS; SHREW; SONORAN DESERT; SOUTH AFRICA, DESERTS OF; SOUTH AMERICA, DESERTS OF; TUCU-TUCO**

Further Reading

Sherman, P. W., J. U. M. Jarvis, and R. D. Alexander, eds. 1991. *Biology of the Naked Mole Rat*. Princeton: Princeton University Press.

BUSHMEN. *See* DESERT PEOPLES

BUSTARD

Medium to large-sized terrestrial bird of open arid and semiarid habitats of the Old World (order Gruiformes, family Otididae). Evolutionary relationships of this ancient family are unclear, although DNA-DNA hybridization experiments (experiments that test the genetic similarity of organisms) suggest that it is closely allied to the cranes and limpkins. Twenty-one to 24 species in 4–11 genera are recognized, depending on the author cited. The majority of species occur in Africa, with the remainder found in parts of Eurasia and Australia. Bustards occupy a wide range of dry habitats, including desert, open grassland and scrub, savanna, and dense brush. Bustards have robust bodies, relatively long legs, broad rounded wings, long necks, and flattened heads with short bills. Length varies from 40 to 120 centimeters. Smaller bustard species show little sexual dimorphism (differences between the sexes) in size, whereas in larger species the female is markedly smaller than the male. Plumage coloration varies substantially across species. Bustards lack the gland that in other avian species provides oil for preening; therefore, they clean their plumage by dust bathing. The diet consists of insects, plant matter, and small vertebrates.

In many desert bustard species the timing of breeding coincides with the occurrence of rains, although some species are able to nest and successfully raise young in extreme conditions (e.g., genus *Chlamydotis*). The breeding system for most species is poorly studied, but bustards may generally be quite promiscuous. Male courtship behavior often involves intricate aerial or ground displays. Bustards nest on the ground in sparsely lined scrapes (depressions in the ground) excavated by the female. Clutches usually consist of one or two eggs but in some smaller species may contain up to six eggs. Incubation is undertaken solely by the female and lasts from 20 to 28 days. The chicks are precocial (well developed and able to move about) and, once hatched, are primarily cared for and fed by the female; males may contribute to these activities in some species.—Stephen C. Lougheed

See also **AFRICA, DESERTS OF; ANIMAL ADAPTATIONS; ASIA, DESERTS OF; AUSTRALIA, DESERTS OF; BIRDS; BREEDING SEASON**

Further Reading

Cramp, S., and K. E. L. Simmons, eds. 1980. *Handbook of the Birds of Europe the Middle East and North Africa. The Birds of the Western Palearctic*, Vol. 2. Oxford: Oxford University Press.

Johnsgard, P. A. 1991. *Bustards, Hemipodes and Sandgrouse: Birds of Dry Places.* Oxford: Oxford University Press.

Urban, E. K., C. H. Fry, and S. Keith, eds. 1986. *The Birds of Africa*. Vol. 2. New York: Academic Press.

BUTTERFLIES

All insects in the order Lepidoptera (which includes both butterflies and moths) having slender antennae that are knobbed at the tip. The remainder of lepidopterans (moths) have filiform (hairlike or threadlike), setaceous (bristlelike), or plumose (featherlike) antennae. As in moths, the wings are usually opaque and covered with fine scales. Most butterflies are diurnal, the adults feed on nectar (if they feed), and the larvae, which are typically called caterpillars, feed on leaves and stems of plants. Most of a butterfly's life is spent in the egg, larval, or pupal stage. The greatest diversity of butterflies occurs in tropical and subtropical habitats of the world, but many species are found in deserts as well. Adult butterflies are most conspicuous in deserts when annual plants are flowering or when perennial plants are producing flowers.

Common families in deserts are the Lycaenidae (coopers, hairstreaks, metalmarks, blues, etc.) and the Nymphalidae (mourning cloaks, angelwings, etc.), but others can be found in deserts as well. The lycaenids are often brightly colored as adults and usually have a circle of white around the antennae. These are often fast-flying butterflies, and some can hover. The larvae are short, robust, and often flattened. Honeydew produced by some of the larvae is harvested by ants, and there are even some lycaenid larvae that live in ant colonies. When wings of the nymphalids are folded up over the body, they may appear to mimic dead leaves, and most species have a light-colored spot on the underside of the hind wing that resembles a "C." Monarch butterflies (*Danaus plexippus*, family Danaidae) are often seen in North American deserts as they migrate between Canada and Mexico.—Laurie J. Vitt

See also **ANNUAL PLANTS; ARTHROPODS; INSECTS; FLOWERS; MOTHS; PERENNIAL PLANTS; POLLINATION**

Further Reading

Borror, D. J., C. A. Triplehorn, and N. F. Johnson. 1992. *An Introduction to the Study of Insects*. New York: Harcourt Brace.

Smart, P. 1989. *The Illustrated Encyclopedia of the Butterfly World*. New York: Crescent Books.

Vane-Wright, R. I., and P. R. Ackery. 1984. *The Biology of Butterflies*. New York: Academic Press.

Wisdom, C. S. 1991. Patterns of heterogeneity in desert herbivorous insect communities. *In* G. A. Polis, ed., *The Ecology of Desert Communities*, 151–179. Tucson: University of Arizona Press.

BUZZARD

Large diurnal bird of prey (order Falconiformes, family Accipitridae) with a cosmopolitan (worldwide) distribution, except for Antarctica, Australia, and the Malay Peninsula. The buzzards (referred to as "hawks" in the New World) are confined to the genus *Buteo* (25 species) and a few related genera (e.g., *Parabuteo* and *Buteogallus*). In combination, the term "buzzard" encompasses some other birds of prey (e.g., the buzzard eagles, genus *Butastur*). It is also often used colloquially in North America to refer to vultures (family Cathartidae), or sometimes the crested caracara (*Polyborus plancus*). Buzzards range over a wide variety of habitats, including deserts. Some species exhibit broad habitat preferences. For example, the red-tailed hawk (*Buteo jamaicensis*) shows probably the broadest ecological tolerance of any buzzard, ranging throughout North and Central America, from prairies and alpine meadows through woodlands to deserts. Other species are more specific in their habitat preferences. The long-legged buzzard (*Buteo rufinus*), for example, occupies drier habitats in mountains, steppes (treeless, generally grassy, plains), and plains of southeastern Europe, North Africa, and Asia Minor.

Length varies from approximately 40 to 100 centimeters. Females generally exceed males in size by a slight margin. Buzzards have broad wings and tails that are well adapted for soaring. Species of high latitudes are usually migratory to some degree, whereas most tropical and subtropical species are year-round residents. Plumage pattern is typically quite distinctive, consisting of brown, white, and rusty brown, or black and white, often with barring. Plumage is not sexually dimorphic (different between sexes). The bill, as in other raptors, is sharply decurved and powerful. Legs generally are not feathered, although there are exceptions (e.g., the rough-legged buzzard, *Buteo lagopus*), and the feet are equipped with strong talons for the capture of prey. The diet consists largely of mammals and reptiles but may also include birds and insects. Some species also feed on carrion (e.g., the jackal buzzard, *Buteo rufofuscus*, of southern and eastern Africa).

The majority of buzzards are described as socially monogamous. Some species are known to breed cooperatively with multiple adult groups (e.g., the Galapagos hawk, *Buteo galapagoensis*, and the Harris' hawk, *Parabuteo unicinctus*). Buzzards are usually highly territorial. Nests are constructed of sticks and located in trees. Clutch size varies from one to five eggs. Females perform the majority of incubation duties, although in some species the male also incubates. During incubation the female may be fed by the male. Females brood and feed the newly hatched chicks while males do most of the hunting. As the young develop, females progressively increase the time spent hunting away from the nestlings.—Stephen C. Lougheed

See also **BIRDS; CARRION EATERS; RAPTORS**

Further Reading

Brown, L., and D. Amadon. 1968. *Eagles, Hawks and Falcons of the World*. Vol. 2. London: Country Life.

Brown, L. H., E. K. Urban, and K. Newman. 1982. *The Birds of Africa*. Vol. 1. New York: Academic Press.

Faaborg, J., and J. C. Bednarz. 1990. Galápagos and Harris' hawks: Divergent causes of sociality in two raptors. *In* P. B. Stacey and W. D. Koenig (eds.): *Cooperative Breeding in Birds*, 357–383. Cambridge: Cambridge University Press.

Mader, W. J. 1975. Biology of the Harris' hawk in southern Arizona. *Living Bird* 14:59–85.

C₃ PLANTS

Plants that use the C_3 photosynthetic pathway, the most common photosynthetic pathway that occurs in plants of all habitats. The relative abundance of C_3 plants is greatest in cool, shady habitats such as forest understories and least in hot, sunny habitats such as deserts and temperate and tropical grasslands and savannas. In general the relative abundance of C_3 plants increases from the equator to the poles. Many C_3 plants in deserts are annuals or deciduous shrubs that avoid, rather than tolerate, drought.

In C_3 plants CO_2 is combined with a five-carbon sugar, ribulose-1,5-bisphosphate (RuBP), during the Calvin cycle to form a six-carbon compound that breaks into two three-carbon molecules, 3-phosphoglyceric acid (3-PGA). This reaction is catalyzed by the enzyme ribulose bisphosphate carboxylase (rubisco). The principle limitation to C_3 photosynthesis is photorespiration in which rubisco catalyzes the oxidation of RuBP to CO_2 and 3-PGA at an energy cost. Photorespiration rates are greatest at high O_2 and low CO_2 concentrations in the leaf mesophyll, for example, at high light and temperature levels. Therefore, CO_2 fixation rates for C_3 plants peak at light intensities considerably below full sunlight; however, C_3 plants are more energy efficient in low light than either C_4 or CAM plants. C_3 plants are generally not as drought tolerant as C_4 or CAM plants because their stomata close when soil moisture is low, but even partial stomatal closure increases mesophyll O_2 concentrations, thus increasing photorespiration.—Ernest M. Steinauer

See also **ANNUAL PLANTS; C₄ PLANTS; CAM PLANTS; DESERT GRASSLAND; DESERTS; PAMPAS; PHOTOSYNTHESIS; PLANT ADAPTATIONS; PLANTS; STOMA**

Further Reading

Calvin, M. 1989. Forty years of photosynthesis and related research. *Photosynthesis Research* 21:3–16.

Larcher, W. 1995. *Physiological Plant Ecology.* Berlin: Springer.

Salisbury, F. B., and C. W. Ross. 1992. *Plant Physiology.* Belmont, Calif.: Wadsworth.

C₄ PLANTS

Plants with thick-walled bundle sheath cells (Krantz leaf anatomy) which, during photosynthesis, spatially separate CO_2 fixation from sugar production in the Calvin cycle. C_4 species occur in many plant families, especially among monocots (flowering plants having only one seed leaf), but account for only about 0.4 percent of plant species. Abundance of C_4 plants increases in warm, sunny, dry habitats and from the poles to the tropics. C_4 plants are important members of desert communities and are dominants in tropical and temperate grasslands and savannas. Many crops are C_4 plants (e.g., maize).

Carbon fixation in C_4 plants occurs only in mesophyll cells where CO_2 is combined with three-carbon phosphoenolpyruvate (PEP) to form four-carbon oxaloacetic acid (OAA) using the enzyme PEP carboxylase. OAA is then converted to malic or aspartic acid and transferred to the bundle sheath cells where CO_2 is released into the Calvin cycle. PEP carboxylase has a high affinity for CO_2. This maintains high CO_2 concentrations in bundle sheath cells, even under conditions favoring rapid photosynthesis (high light and temperature levels), which deplete CO_2 in C_3 plants. In addition, C_4 plants tend to be drought tolerant as they can partially close stomata but still retain high CO_2 concentrations in bundle sheath cells, even though mesophyll CO_2 concentrations are reduced. This gives C_4 plants a competitive advantage over C_3 plants in high light, high temperature, or dry habitats; however, energy costs associated with acid production and transfer place C_4 plants at a disadvantage compared to C_3 plants in low light environments.—Ernest M. Steinauer

See also **ANNUAL PLANTS; C₃ PLANTS; CAM PLANTS; DESERT GRASSLAND; DESERTS; PAMPAS; PHOTOSYNTHESIS; PLANT ADAPTATIONS; PLANTS; STOMA**

Further Reading

Hatch, M. D., and N. K. Boardman, eds. 1987. *Photosynthesis: The Biochemistry of Plants.* Vol. 10. New York: Academic Press.

Cactus-scrub habitat with granite outcrops in the semiarid Caatinga of northeastern Brazil, near Exu, Pernambuco. (Photo: T. E. Lacher, Jr.)

Hatch, M. D., and C. R. Slack. 1967. Further studies on a new pathway of photosynthetic carbon dioxide fixation in sugar-cane and its occurrence in other plant species. *Biochemical Journal* 102:417–422.

Larcher, W. 1995. *Physiological Plant Ecology.* Berlin: Springer.

Salisbury, F. B., and C. W. Ross. 1992. *Plant Physiology.* Belmont, Calif.: Wadsworth.

CAATINGA

Large (650,000-square-kilometer) semiarid biome that dominates the easternmost horn of Brazil, between 3°–16° south latitude and 35°–45° west longitude. Generally, tropical habitats dominate the landscape in the equatorial regions between 20° north and south latitude. Rain forests dominate the areas between 10° north and south of the equator, and savannas or tropical grasslands can be found in the band of latitudes from 10° to 20° degrees north and south of the equator. The Caatinga is a puzzling exception to this general rule in northeastern Bra-zil. This irregularly shaped region is surrounded on all sides by tropical ecosystems: the palm savannas of the Amazon Basin on the west, the mesic grass-lands of the Cerrado savannas on the southwest and south, and the tropical Atlantic Rain Forest in the east. The Caatinga is unique in South America in its ecology, its history, and its people. (See map of South American deserts, p. 533.)

Much of the Caatinga was once a prehistoric ocean bottom. The landscape is dominated by Cre-taceous sandstone deposits that rest on a basement of Precambrian crystalline rock. The landscape is old and weathered, and in many areas the sand-stone has eroded, exposing the basement either as an expansive exposed rock shelf (*lajeiro* in Portu-guese, or as a series of boulder piles and small rocky hills (*serras* or *serrotes*). This results in considerable topographic relief throughout much of the Caat-inga. There are several areas where the sandstone deposits remain in large contiguous plateaus (*cha-*

padas in Portuguese) that can be several hundred miles long. The plateaus have a much different soil than the surrounding plains. The plateaus and the serras are also important sites of orographic precipitation (related to significant differences in elevation, such as a mountain range) and are wetter than the surrounding lowlands.

The limits of the Caatinga closely follow the 800-millimeter (approximately 31.5 inches) isohyet (a graphical representation delineating a geographic area that receives the same amount of precipitation, in this case, 800 millimeters) of precipitation. Within this larger boundary, precipitation varies from more than 1,600 millimeters on some of the high plateaus to less than 300 millimeters in the most arid regions. Rainfall is highly seasonal and occurs between May and November. The annual variation in amount and timing of rainfall is very high, and the dry season may extend for as long as 10 months during exceptionally dry years. Precipitation can range from extremely heavy rainfall (e.g., exceeding 600 millimeters in a single month) to no rain during very dry years. The occurrence of such severe dry conditions in this irregularly shaped region has earned the Caatinga the names "the Polygon of Drought" and "the Zone of Calamities."

The harsh climate of the Caatinga places a strain on the organisms that occur there. The plants, in particular, must be able to survive both annual and long-term droughts and show numerous morphological and physiological adaptations to arid conditions. The Caatinga flora contains many species of cacti with large spines, thorny shrubs and trees, terrestrial waxy-leafed bromeliads, and barrel-trunked trees. These represent adaptations to water conservation and protection against herbivores. Desert-adapted trees frequently have hard, waxy leaves (sclerophyllous leaves) as an adaptation to predictable drought. Most Caatinga trees have thin, soft leaves that are easily shed. Botanists feel that this is an adaptation to the high unpredictability in precipitation that characterizes the area. The overall level of specialization of the Caatinga plants to drought suggests a long history of evolution under unpredictably arid conditions.

In contrast, the vertebrate animals of the Caatinga do not possess many specialized adaptations to either aridity or an unpredictable climate. Although there are many species of plants that are endemic to (limited to) the Caatinga, there is a very low level of endemism in the vertebrate fauna: only one species of lizard, ten or fewer species of birds, and two species of mammals can be considered to be Caatinga endemics.

The Caatinga has not received sufficient attention by conservationists in Brazil. There are several small national parks that protect Caatinga habitat, but the region is underrepresented in the conservation network in Brazil. The most significant protected area in the Caatinga is the Raso da Catarina Biological Reserve in the state of Bahía. This large reserve (200,000 hectares) protects a part of some of the most arid habitat in the Caatinga. It also is the last stronghold for two highly endangered species: Lear's macaw (*Anodorhynchus leari*) and the three-banded armadillo (*Tolypeutes tricinctus*).

The unique climate of the Caatinga has also had effects on the human population of the region. Northeastern Brazil remains the poorest region in the country, economically speaking, in part because of the highly unpredictable climate. The periodic droughts have brought great hardship and poverty to the area, resulting in a depressed standard of living, in great contrast to the wealthy states of the south. The major urban centers of northeastern Brazil—Forteleza, Recife, and Salvador—are on the coast and have been placed under tremendous stress by the periodic immigration of poor rural families fleeing drought. The Caatinga has been a source of social unrest several times during the history of Brazil. The isolation of the Caatinga has also resulted in the development of a distinct cultural region. The inhabitants of the Caatinga, called *nordestinos*, have a distinctive accent easily distinguishable from other Brazilians. The region also has a rich folklore, with characteristic music, dances, art, and handicrafts. Many of Brazil's greatest composers are nordestinos, and the award-winning author Jorge Amado writes almost exclusively on northeastern themes.—Thomas E. Lacher, Jr.

See also **BAT; BIRDS; CAVY; CHACO; CLIMATE; CRETACEOUS; DESERT SLOPES; EL NIÑO; MAMMALS; PARROT; PLANT ADAPTATIONS; PLATE TECTONICS; PRECAMBRIAN; REPTILES; SOUTH AMERICA, DESERTS OF**

Further Reading

Bucher, E. H. 1982. Chaco and Caatinga: South American arid savannas, woodlands and thickets. *In* B. J. Huntley and B. H. Walker, eds., *Ecology of Tropical Savannas* 48–79. New York: Springer.

Mares, M. A., M. R. Willig, and T. E. Lacher, Jr. 1985. The Brazilian Caatinga in South American zoogeography: Tropical mammals in a dry region. *Journal of Biogeography* 12:57–69.

Nir, D. 1974. *The Semi-arid World: Man on the Fringe of the Desert.* London: Longman.

Paiva, M. P., and E. Campos. 1995. *Fauna do Nordeste do Brasil: Conhecimento científico e popular.* Fortaleza: Banco de Nordeste do Brasil, S.A.

Solbrig, O. T., E. Medina, and J. F. Silva, eds. 1996. *Biodiversity and Savanna Ecosystem Processes.* Berlin: Springer.

Vasconselos Sobrinho, J. 1971. *As regiões naturais do nordeste, o meio e a civilização.* Recife: Conselho do Desenvolvimento de Pernambuco.

Webb, K. 1974. *The Changing Face of Northeast Brazil.* New York: Columbia University Press.

CACTACEAE. *See* CACTI

CACTI

Large (87 genera, 2,000 species) plant family (Cactaceae) made up mostly of succulent, spiny perennial plants of arid regions and distributed mainly in warm, arid, and semiarid regions from southern Canada to the tip of South America, from sea level to about 4,000 meters elevation. Members of the family have been introduced into Australia and other parts of the world (one genus occurring in Africa and Sri Lanka may be introduced). Although cacti are characteristic plants of warm deserts in the New World, they also occur in semiarid regions, grasslands, dry forests, and even in the canopies of tropical forests. They are susceptible to damage from freezing, which limits their distribution (and size) in more northerly or southerly localities. Cacti commonly grow on rocky slopes or well-drained soils. Cacti can be recognized by their large fleshy stems, which are usually leafless, and by the presence of spines (at least in young plants). Spines are modified leaves that are hardened and dry and do not function in photosynthesis (chemical process that combines carbon dioxide and water, in the presence of light energy, to form carbohydrates and oxygen). They are clustered within spirally arranged, specialized areas called areoles, as are the branches and flowers. Photosynthesis in cacti occurs in the large, green, succulent stems, where the plant stores water during the long periods of desert drought.

Most members of this family are xerophytes (plants that are adapted to dry or drought condi-

Pincushion cactus (*Mammilaria*) in flower in Arizona. (Photo: K. A. Ernest)

tions). Cacti tolerate drought because of their succulent, or water-storing, tissues. A waxy cuticle covering the thick epidermis (outermost cell layer of tissue) of the stems helps to reduce evaporative water loss. The cuticle is thickest on the side of the cactus most exposed to sunlight. To perform photosynthesis, plants must open stomatal pores to let in carbon dioxide from the air. While most plants absorb carbon dioxide during the day, cacti (and some other succulents) reduce water loss by opening these pores at night. The stem contains many water storage cells, a trait that allows these plants to live in areas with low and unpredictable rainfall. In some ribbed cacti (e.g., the saguaro cactus of the Sonoran Desert) the stem can expand and contract considerably as moisture availability changes. Most cacti have fleshy roots that are shallow but spread widely from the plant base. This form of root system allows cacti to absorb water from rain showers quickly and over a large area. A few cacti have tuberlike roots.

The cactus spines, which are modified leaves, come in a variety of forms: simple and straight, bristlelike, short and conical, bent like fishhooks, curved and hornlike, and sometimes hairy or feathery. Although not involved in photosynthesis, the spines protect the succulent tissues of the cactus from potential herbivores and help prevent the cactus from overheating by reducing incident solar radiation and providing a boundary layer around the plant that reduces convective heat transfer (transfer of heat from the heated environment to the plant).

Cactus flowers, which are usually solitary, sessile, and bisexual, with an inferior ovary, blossom in rose, crimson, purple, yellow, or orange. Some of the largest flowers of this family bloom at night, such as those of the saguaro, *Carnegiea*. These white, fragrant flowers are pollinated by bats seeking nectar and pollen from the numerous stamens. The long (30 centimeters) flower of *Hylocereus*, an epiphytic shrub (a shrub that lives on another plant without parasitizing it) in Costa Rica, is one of the largest flowers in the world. Pollinators of cactus flowers include moths, bees, and other insects; hummingbirds and other birds; and bats. The cactus fruit is a berry that is frequently juicy and eaten by humans, including those of the prickly pear, or tuna, cactus (*Opuntia*). Certain *Echinocereus* species are known as strawberry cacti because of the flavor of their fruit's juicy pulp. Other cactus fruits of economic importance are those of the giant *Cereus*, the *Carnegiea gigantea*, known locally as *pitahayas de sahuara* and the organ pipe cactus (*Myrtillocactus geometrizans*), which are sold in markets as the garambulla. Cactus fruits are readily eaten and dispersed by desert tortoises, birds, rodents, coyotes, peccaries, and other mammals. Although spines also may provide some protection from browsing mammals, many types of animals feed on cacti. Insects, rabbits, hares, rodents, peccaries (*Tayassu tajacu*), deer, and bighorn sheep feed on the green portions of the plants. Some cacti are susceptible to soft rots, caused by yeast and bacteria. These rots attract cactophilic (cactus-loving) fruit flies.

The growth form of cacti is variable but generally consists of an enlarged stem. This may be swollen and unbranched, as in the barrel cactus, or branched, as in the saguaro. The stems of some cacti are jointed, such as the prickly pear with its flattened joints (pads) and the cholla with its cylindrical joints. The surface of the stem (ignoring the spines) may be smooth (e.g., prickly pear) or have bumpy tubercles (e.g., cholla) or vertical ribs (e.g., saguaro, barrel cactus). Cacti range in height from a few centimeters tall to more than 20 meters.

Some species of cacti develop hard, woody stems as the plant becomes older, while a few, such as *Rhipsalis*, are epiphytes with many jointed and spineless stems. The Cactaceae has no close relatives. Many unrelated xerophytes, however, such as members of the family Euphorbiaceae, evolved adaptations similar to those of cacti, including succulence and spines, and also occupy arid habitats. Spiny or fleshy plants in the Euphorbiaceae and other families have been commonly misnamed "cacti." The counterparts of cacti in other deserts present an interesting case of convergent evolution, in which unrelated organisms have similar appearances. Plants in Africa and Asia that have an appearance and ecology similar to that of cacti are actually members of the spurge and milkweed families.

Cacti have a few economic uses. Besides being eaten raw, some fleshy fruits of cacti may be made into jams or syrups. Prickly pear cacti (*Opuntia*) are grown commercially for their fruits in Mexico and California. Cacti may be eaten by domestic livestock during periods of drought. Species of all genera are cultivated by collectors and gardeners. The narcotic peyote, or mescal button, is the stem of the *Lophophora williamsii* cactus. Used as an intoxicant and febrifuge by certain Native Americans, this plant plays a major role in the religious rituals of the Native American Church. The frequent uprooting of cacti for transplantation as ornamentals in some parts of the United States has led to serious reductions in the population sizes of cacti, and state and federal governments have enacted laws to protect cacti in the field.—Kristina A. Ernest and Gordon E. Uno

See also **ARIZONA DESERT; BAJA CALIFORNIA, DESERTS OF; BAT; C₃ PLANTS; C₄ PLANTS; CAATINGA; CACTUS, COLUMNAR; CAM PLANTS; CARDÓN; CHACO; CHIHUAHUAN DESERT; DESERT GRASSLAND; DESERTS, HOT; FLOWERS; MEXICO, DESERTS OF; MONTE DESERT; NEVADA DESERT; ORGAN PIPE CACTUS; PECCARY; PERENNIAL PLANTS; PHOTOSYNTHESIS; PLANT ADAPTATIONS; PLANT GEOGRAPHY; PLANT ROOTS, ADVENTITIOUS; PLANTS; POLLINATION; SAGUARO; SOUTH AMERICA, DESERTS OF; THORNS; UNITED STATES, DESERTS OF; XENOPHYTES; WOODRAT**

Further Reading

Britton, N. L., and J. N. Rose. 1963. *The Cactaceae. Descriptions and Illustrations of Plants of the Cactus Family.* 4 vols. New York: Dover.

Gibson, A. C., and P. S. Nobel. 1986. *The Cactus Primer.* Cambridge, Mass.: Harvard University Press.

Heywood, V. H., ed. 1993. *Flowering Plants of the World.* Updated ed. New York: Oxford University Press.

Hoffman J., A. E. 1989 *Cactáceas en la flora silvestre de Chile.* Santiago: Fundación Claudio Gay.

Lamb, B. M. 1991. *A Guide to Cacti of the World.* New York: Angus and Robertson (HarperCollins).

Marshall, W. T. 1941. *Cactaceae*. Pasadena: Abbey Garden Press.

Slaba, R. 1992. *The Illustrated Guide to Cacti*. New York: Sterling.

Weniger, D. (n.d) *Cacti of the Southwest*. Austin: University of Texas Press.

CACTUS, COLUMNAR

Group of large, arborescent (treelike) cacti with succulent, massive, columnlike stems, including forms with unbranched stems or plants with arms branching either from the base or from higher up a central trunk. Several genera of cacti contain columnar species, including *Carnegiea* (saguaro), *Cereus* (queen of the night), *Lophocereus* (e.g., senita), *Lemaireocereus* (e.g., organ pipe cactus), *Trichocereus, Echinopsis, Escontria, Mitrocereus, Neobuxbaumia, Cephalocereus, Stetsonia,* and *Pachycereus*. Some authors consider barrel cacti (*Ferocactus*) to be columnar, but these are generally considered a separate form (barrel type) of stem succulent. Because the columnar species occur in several unrelated genera, the columnar growth form is the result of convergent evolution.

The Mexican genus *Pachycereus* contains about 20 species, all of which are treelike and tall. The hecho, *Pachycereus pecten-aboriginum*, and cardón, *Pachycereus pringlei*, are common columnar cacti of the Sonoran Desert and thorn forest that often reach heights of 10–12 meters. Cardón, occasionally reaching 20 meters in height, may be the largest cactus in the world.

The root systems of columnar cacti are generally relatively shallow but extend laterally for distances of 20 meters or more. Vertical woody "ribs" help support the mass of the cactus. The irregular stem surface, in accordionlike vertical folds, helps to scatter solar radiation. These massive plants have extremely large thermal inertias, heating up relatively slowly but reaching temperatures 10°–15°C above air temperatures if exposed to high temperatures for long periods. The columnar cacti tend to be less tolerant of cold temperatures than are the smaller cacti, and many columnar species are frost sensitive. The flowers are often large, showy, white, and nocturnal and are pollinated by insects, birds, and bats. A diversity of alkaloids (organic compounds, frequently with alkaline properties, that

Large, columnar, cardón cactus (*Pachycereus*) in the desert of Sonora, Mexico. (Photo: D. Beck)

form salts; they are often toxic) are produced by columnar cacti.

Columnar cacti occur from the southwestern United States southward into Mexico, Central America, and South America. Although typically desert species (giving the characteristic appearance to the Sonoran Desert, for example), they also are found in thorn forest, dry tropical deciduous (experiencing leaf loss during parts of the year) forest, tropical semideciduous forest, and other tropical habitats. They grow on deep granitic soils, sandy soils, finer-grained silty soils, volcanic malpais (rough lava), and shallow calcareous soils of desert valleys, plains, bajadas (lower slopes built from water erosion), and mesas (tablelands).

One of the well-developed vegetational associations with columnar cacti in the Sonoran Desert lies in the Central Gulf Coast Subdivision on the coastal plain. Here five columnar cacti grow in the cactus-mesquite-saltbush series: saguaro (*Carnegiea gigantea*), senita (*Lophocereus schottii*), hecho (*Pachycereus pecten-aboriginum*), organ pipe cactus (*Stenocereus thurberi*), and the related *Stenoc-*

ereus alamosensis. Other shrubs and small trees co-occurring with the columnar cacti include elephant tree (*Bursera*), limber bush, mesquite, and paloverde.

Ribs of the columnar cacti are used in fences and furniture. The fruits are usually edible and are harvested by Native Americans for use in preserves and wine.—Kristina A. Ernest

See also **ANZA-BORREGO DESERT; ARIZONA DESERT; BAJA CALIFORNIA, DESERTS OF; BAT; C₃ PLANTS; C₄ PLANTS; CAM PLANTS; CAATINGA; CACTI; CARDÓN; CHACO; CHIHUAHUAN DESERT; COLORADO DESERT; CONVERGENT EVOLUTION; DESERT GRASSLAND; DESERTS, HOT; FLOWERS; GILA WOODPECKER; MEXICO, DESERTS OF; MONTE DESERT; NEVADA DESERT; ORGAN PIPE CACTUS; PERENNIAL PLANTS; PHOTOSYNTHESIS; PLANT ADAPTATIONS; PLANT GEOGRAPHY; PLANT ROOTS, ADVENTITIOUS; PLANTS; POLLINATION; PRICKLY PEAR; SAGUARO; SOUTH AMERICA, DESERTS OF; THORN; UNITED STATES, DESERTS OF; WOODPECKERS; XENOPHYTES**

Further Reading

Bravo-Hollis, H. 1978. *Las Cactáceas de México.* 2d ed. Vol. 1. Mexico City: Universidad Nacional Autónoma de México.

Lamb, B. M. 1991. *A Guide to Cacti of the World.* New York: Angus and Robertson (HarperCollins).

Nobel, P. S. 1980. Morphology, surface temperatures, and northern limits of columnar cacti in the Sonoran Desert. *Ecology* 61:1–7.

Shreve, F., and I. L. Wiggins. 1964. *Vegetation and Flora of the Sonoran Desert.* Vols. 1 and 2. Stanford: Stanford University Press.

Weniger, D. (n.d.) *Cacti of the Southwest.* Austin: University of Texas Press.

CALCAREOUS SOILS. *See* SOILS, DESERT, CALCAREOUS

CALCIFEROUS HARDPAN. *See* DURICRUSTS

CALCRETE. *See* SOILS, DESERT, CALCRETE

CALICHE. *See* SOILS, DESERT, CALICHE

CALIFORNIA DESERT

Southeastern part of California characterized by Sonoran Desert vegetation. Although this region is sometimes referred to as the California Desert, it is usually divided into the Colorado Desert and the Mojave Desert. It is perhaps best represented by the desert found in the Anza-Borrego region.—Gary K. Hulett and Amanda Renner Charles

See also **ANZA-BORREGO DESERT; COLORADO DESERT; SONORAN DESERT; UNITED STATES, DESERTS OF**

Further Reading

Latting, J., and P. G. Rowlands, eds. 1995. *The California Desert: An Introduction to Natural Resources and Man's Impact.* Riverside, Calif.: June Latting Books.

Munz, P. A. 1962. *California Desert Wildflowers.* Berkeley: University of California Press.

Weir, K. 1998. *Southern California Handbook: Including Greater Los Angeles, Disneyland, San Diego, Death Valley and other Desert Parks.* Emeryville, Calif.: Moon Publications.

CAMEL

Large mammal in the order Artiodactyla, family Camelidae, that is popularly associated with deserts. The one-hump camel (*Camelus dromedarius*) is an animal universally associated with successful desert existence and remarkable endurance. The domesticated dromedary camel, also called the Arabian or Indian camel, is found in almost all the desert areas of the world, including parts of India, Australia, and Asia, although it is found primarily in the Sahara of North Africa. The Bactrian, or two-hump, camel lives in the colder mountains of Afghanistan, northern China, and the former southern Soviet Union. Dromedary camels were domesticated about 4,000 years ago, probably in Arabia, and their wild one-hump ancestor is extinct. Today camels play a key role in the desert economy and social relations of the peoples of northern Africa.

The camel is well adapted to its harsh environment. It is able to withstand the heat, sparse vegetation, and limited water of the desert. The camel's ability to travel for days without water or food is legendary. Camels have large padded feet that are well suited to travel over soft desert sand, translucent eyelids that allow them to see relatively well with their eyes shut, and nostrils that close to keep out sand; however, unlike smaller inhabitants of deserts, the camel (adults weigh 250–680 kilograms) cannot escape the sun and heat by burrowing underground or even by seeking shade, since little shade is available over vast areas. Indeed, its large size can be viewed as an important advantage

Camel (*Camelus dromedarius*) grazing in the scrublands of the Rajasthan Desert of northwestern India near Jodhpur. (Photo: M. A. Mares)

for desert living since it retards heat gain. The camel's noteworthy success results principally from its ability to tolerate elevated body temperatures, to minimize several avenues for water loss, and to reduce heat gain from the environment.

Camels have a remarkable tolerance for increased body temperature. A dehydrated camel can withstand body temperature fluctuations of up to 8°C (from a normal of 34°C to a maximum of about 42°C). Such fluctuation would be lethal to most mammals, which have preferred resting body temperatures of 36°–38°C. This tolerance spares the camel from having to use unacceptable amounts of water for keeping cool. If a 500-kilogram camel were instead to resist body temperature change by employing evaporative cooling, rather than tolerating heat gain, it would require more than five liters of water to dissipate the heat.

By allowing body temperature to increase, a camel is therefore able to save water, as well as energy, which would otherwise be lost by evaporative cooling. In addition, an elevated body temperature decreases the temperature gradient between the camel and its surroundings, further reducing environmental heat gain. The camel takes advantage of the relative coolness of the evening, when temperature gradients are favorable, to transfer body heat back to the environment by radiation, conduction (transfer of heat energy from particle to particle), and convection (transfer of heat energy through the movements of many particles at once, as in the flow of a liquid). The camel's long legs are

an asset in this heat transfer. Their considerable blood flow aids in heat dissipation.

Unlike many mammals, such as dogs, camels do not rely on respiratory evaporative cooling to reduce body temperature. Their rate of respiration increases minimally in response to higher temperatures. As a result less body water is lost to evaporation, and they do not generate the additional body heat that would normally accompany increased respiration. In hot weather camels rely on sweating to remove body heat and keep body temperature within an acceptable range; however, they do not sweat continuously, an obvious advantage for water conservation, and they do not wet the fur at the outer surface. Therefore, evaporation takes place directly at the skin surface, which means that the heat of vaporization (heat energy required to vaporize water) is provided by body heat, not by the environment. Avoiding wet fur is also advantageous because it prevents the loss of the fur's insulative properties.

In addition to maintaining dry fur, the coat thickness varies with the season. In summer a light-colored fur both protects from sunburn and is highly reflective, scattering incoming solar radiation. The fur's characteristics, coupled with sweating at the skin surface, result in the skin on the camel's back being 30°C cooler than the surface of the fur just above it, which is exposed to the desert sun.

During the cooler months in the Sahara camels often do not need to drink water at all, receiving adequate water solely from their diet. Camels eat a varied diet of plant foods, dry grass, and even thorn bushes with a high salt content. Unlike other animals, the camel's appetite does not seem to be affected by dehydration, which assures a supply of energy, even when water availability is minimal. When temperatures are 30°–35°C, camels are able to go 10–15 days without water, but during the hottest weeks of summer water is required more frequently.

Camels are able to tolerate significant dehydration. Furthermore, their ability to conserve water improves with increasing dehydration. This is accomplished mainly by decreasing water loss due to sweating. While many mammals cannot survive water loss beyond 12–14 percent of body weight (10 percent loss is debilitating for humans, for example), camels can tolerate double that amount of water loss—to more than 25 percent of body weight—without ill effects. This tolerance is no doubt possible because camels reduce water loss from the blood volume at the expense of water loss from the alimentary tract (digestive tract) and the intracellular spaces. A dehydrated human loses significant water from the plasma, which imposes severe circulatory strain on the heart due to the thickened blood. This can be fatal.

Camels can rehydrate rapidly when given the opportunity. Interestingly, though, they drink only enough to restore the original water loss. Their rehydration ability is notable, both for its speed and because the water is transferred quickly to the circulation without damaging the osmotic balance of the animal. For example, a 600-kilogram camel can consume 200 kilograms of water in only three minutes. This intake represents more than 30 percent of its original body weight. Most mammals would suffer lethal hemolysis (destruction of red corpuscles) with this rate of intake. The camel avoids osmotic damage by possessing unique red blood cells that are particularly resistant to volume changes in concentrated or dilute plasma.

The kidney of the camel is also designed for water conservation. When dehydrated, the camel can reduce its already minimal urinary flow by up to 76 percent, and the kidneys can further concentrate the salts in the urine to twice the level of seawater. Finally, a camel can conserve water by excreting very dry feces. A dehydrated camel can cut fecal water loss in half, saving 13 percent of its total water use.—E. Annette Halpern

See also **ANIMAL ADAPTATIONS; BODY TEMPERATURE; CAMEL'S HUMP; CAMELS, SOUTH AMERICAN; ENDOTHERMY; HEAT BALANCE; HEAT EXCHANGE; HEAT STRESS; HYPERTHERMIA; MAMMALS; METABOLISM; PERSPIRATION; PHYSIOLOGY; SALT BALANCE; SWEAT GLANDS; THERMOREGULATION; UNGULATES; WATER BALANCE**

Further Reading

Gauthier-Pilters, H., and A. I. Dagg. 1981. *The Camel: Its Evolution, Ecology, Behavior and Relationship to Man.* Chicago: University of Chicago Press.

Gordon, M. S., G. A. Bartholomew, A. D. Grinell, C. B. Jorgensen, and F. N. White. 1982. *Animal Physiology: Principles and Adaptations.* New York: Macmillan.

Gosh, P. K., and I. Prakash. 1988. *Ecophysiology of Desert Vertebrates.* Jodhpur: Scientific Publishers.

Schmidt-Nielsen, K. 1964. *Desert Animals: Physiological Problems of Heat and Water.* New York: Oxford University Press.

Wilson, R. T. 1989. *Ecophysiology of the Camelidae and Desert Ruminants.* New York: Springer.

CAMEL'S HUMP

Large store of adipose (fat) tissue (10–15 kilograms) located in the middorsal (back) region of the desert-dwelling dromedary camel (*Camelus dromedarius*). By contrast, the cold-region Bactrian camel (*Camelus bactrianus*) has two humps.

Fat is the preferred form for energy storage in animals because of its high caloric (energy) content per gram. A fat-filled hump enables a camel to venture far from food sources for lengthy periods. When food is in short supply, fat is metabolized and the hump almost disappears.

According to legend, the camel's hump and stomach are filled with water, but this is not the case. Some have conjectured that the oxidation of fat found in the hump supplies the camel with extra water, as fat metabolism yields metabolic water (water resulting from the breakdown of fat molecules); however, the "burning" of fat requires extra oxygen, which in turn means more ventilation and water loss by evaporation from the lungs. This respiratory water loss exceeds any water that is produced from the metabolism of fat. Therefore, fat in a camel's hump yields no net gain in water when it is metabolized.

Though the camel's hump can store considerable fat for future energy needs, fat is not stored elsewhere on the camel's body. Subcutaneous fat would act as insulation and would, therefore, retard heat loss from the body. This would clearly be a disadvantage for a desert animal with the need to dissipate considerable body heat. Therefore, it is important that energy reserves be stored as fat somewhere on the body that would not interfere with heat loss. The camel accomplishes this is by restricting fat storage to the hump.—E. Annette Halpern

See also **ANIMAL ADAPTATIONS; BODY TEMPERATURE; CAMEL; CAMELS, SOUTH AMERICAN; ENDOTHERMY; HEAT BALANCE; HEAT EXCHANGE; HEAT STRESS; HYPERTHERMIA; MAMMALS; METABOLISM; PERSPIRATION; PHYSIOLOGY; SALT BALANCE; SWEAT GLANDS; THERMOREGULATION; UNGULATES; WATER BALANCE**

Further Reading

Gauthier-Pilters, H., and A. I. Dagg. 1981. *The Camel, Its Evolution, Ecology, Behavior and Relationship to Man.* Chicago: University of Chicago Press.

Gosh, P. K., and I. Prakash. 1988. *Ecophysiology of Desert Vertebrates.* Jodhpur: Scientific Publishers.

Schmidt-Nielsen, K. 1964. *Desert Animals: Physiological Problems of Heat and Water.* New York: Oxford University Press.

Wilson, R. T. 1989. *Ecophysiology of the Camelidae and Desert Ruminants.* New York: Springer.

CAMEL SPIDER. *See* SUN SPIDER

CAMELS, SOUTH AMERICAN

Two genera and four species of the mammalian order Artiodactyla, family Camelidae (which also includes the dromedary and Bactrian camels of the Old World). The New World camels are distributed in western South America from Peru to Argentina. There are two wild species, vicuña and guanaco, and two domesticated species, llama and alpaca. The llama, alpaca, and vicuña are found at relatively high elevations (2,000–5,000 meters) from central Peru to central Argentina. The guanaco is more widely distributed in desert grasslands and shrublands (0–4,500 meters) from central Peru to southernmost Chile and Argentina. Both wild species are considered threatened or endangered, and extensive conservation efforts are under way by the Peruvian, Chilean, and Argentine governments, as well as by many private organizations.

Although the South American camels are the largest mammalian herbivores in the arid habitats of the continent, they are smaller and more delicate than the Old World camels. The hump, characteristic of Old World camels, is absent. The vicuña is slender and very delicate (the smallest camelid), whereas guanacos are heavier and more robust. Both wild species are brownish above and whitish below. Llamas and alpacas (the domestic species) are multicolored or solid in color, and they have long, fine fur. As with all camels, each foot has two toes (the third and fourth digit), the body rests not on hooves but on thick cutaneous (skin) pads, and only the front ends of the hooves, which are small and flattened like nails, touch the ground. A split upper lip, long, curved neck, and lack of connective tissue between the thigh and the body are characteristics of all camels. Camels are unique among mammals in having elliptical red blood cells. In the

Guanaco (*Lama guanicoe*) in the Patagonian Desert of easternmost Chubut Province, Argentina. (Photo: M. A. Mares)

upper jaw the incisors are absent, except the third, which is placed posteriorly and is hooked and sharp edged. The canines are tusklike. The teeth are ever-growing with open roots. Vicuñas and guanacos have relatively large hearts. In the vicuñas of the high mountains the heart is 50 percent larger than in other mammals of the same size (an adaptation for living at high elevations). In guanacos, which occur from sea level to mountaintops, the heart is only 15 percent larger than in mammals of similar body size.

Camels are noted for two unusual behaviors. They mate while lying down, and they "spit." When excited, camels will raise their head, flatten their ears against their head, and expel air, which sometimes includes moisture or food.

Vicuña are grazers of the puna grasslands and need to drink water daily. They are sedentary, non-migratory, and defend separate feeding and sleeping territories. The corridors between the two territories are not defended. Territories are marked by urine and feces placed in dung piles that are used by both sexes and all age groups.

Guanacos are browsers and grazers of the grasses and shrubs of grasslands, savannas, deserts, and the puna. Populations can be sedentary or migratory, and they are flexible in their habitat needs. Unlike the vicuña, they are water independent. Their social system is similar to that of the vicuña.

Llamas and alpacas were probably domesticated from the guanaco more than 4,000 years ago. These animals, raised for wool, transportation, meat, and fuel, were, and continue to be, an important part of the lives of the people of the high Andes. Today the llama is used primarily for transportation and wool, whereas the alpaca is raised primarily for its wool, which is much finer than that of the llama.—Janet K. Braun

See also **ALTIPLANO; ANDEAN GRASSLANDS; ANDES; ANIMAL ADAPTATIONS; BODY TEMPERATURE; CAMEL; CAMEL'S HUMP; ENDOTHERMY; HEAT BALANCE; HEAT EXCHANGE; HEAT STRESS; HYPERTHERMIA; MAMMALS; METABOLISM; PATAGONIA; PERSPIRATION; PHYSIOLOGY; PUNA; SALT BALANCE; SOUTH AMERICA, DESERTS OF; SWEAT GLANDS; THERMOREGULATION; UNGULATES; WATER BALANCE**

Further Reading

Grzimek's Encyclopedia of Mammals. Vol. 5. 1990. New York: McGraw-Hill.

Macdonald, D., ed. 1984. *The Encyclopedia of Mammals.* New York: Facts on File.

Nowak, R. M. 1991. *Walker's Mammals of the World.* 5th ed. Baltimore: Johns Hopkins University Press.

Redford, K. H., and J. F. Eisenberg. 1992. *Mammals of the Neotropics: The Southern Cone, Chile, Argentina, Uruguay, Paraguay.* Vol. 2. Chicago: University of Chicago Press.

Torres, H., ed. 1992. *South American Camelids: An Action Plan for Their Conservation.* Gland, Switzerland: International Union for the Conservation of Nature (IUCN).

CAM PLANTS

Plants that temporally separate CO_2 fixation from the Calvin cycle (the biochemical pathway by which glucose is regenerated in plant cells), typically found in water-limited environments including deserts, salt marshes, and tropical forest canopies. Crassulacean acid metabolism (CAM) is found in at least 26 angiosperm families, including the Agavaceae, Bromeliaceae, Cactaceae, Crassulaceae, Euphorbeaceae, and Orchidaceae, in a gymnosperm, *Welwitschia*, and in *Isoetes*, an aquatic relative of club mosses. Most CAM plants are succulents with thickened leaves or stems and cells with large vacuoles for water storage. Water use efficiency is high in CAM plants, but photosynthetic efficiency is low because of the costs associated with acid storage (see below). Therefore, CAM plants are generally not competitive with either C_3 or C_4 plants except in severely water-limited environments.

CAM plants reduce transpiration by opening stomates only at night. CO_2 is then combined with phosphoenolpyruvate (PEP) to form oxaloacetic acid (OAA) using the enzyme PEP carboxylase. OAA is converted to malic acid and stored in vacuoles. This is evidenced by lowered cell sap pH. Malic acid is decarboxylated during the day to PEP and CO_2 for use in the Calvin cycle. In contrast to C_4 plants, the entire photosynthetic process occurs within individual cells. Many CAM plants are facultative, switching from C_3 photosynthesis (stomates, or pores, open in the day) when water is plentiful to CAM when water becomes scarce. Some CAM plants close stomates permanently during droughts but combine respiratory CO_2 with PEP and store it in vacuoles for later use in photosynthesis. They can thus capture some solar energy while conserving water.—Ernest M. Steinauer

See also **ANNUAL PLANTS; BAJA CALIFORNIA, DESERTS OF; BROMELIADS; C_3 PLANTS; C_4 PLANTS; CACTI; CACTUS, COLUMNAR; CARDÓN; CHIHUAHUAN DESERT; DESERT GRASSLAND; DESERTS; EUPHORBIACEAE; MEXICO, DESERTS OF; PHOTOSYNTHESIS; PLANT ADAPTATIONS; PLANTS; SONORAN DESERT; STOMA; SOUTH AMERICA, DESERTS OF; SUCCULENTS; UNITED STATES, DESERTS OF; WELWITSCHIA**

Further Reading

Hatch, M. D., and N. K. Boardman, eds. 1987. *Photosynthesis: The Biochemistry of Plants.* Vol. 10. New York: Academic Press.

Larcher, W. 1995. *Physiological Plant Ecology.* Berlin: Springer.

Salisbury, F. B., and C. W. Ross. 1992. *Plant Physiology.* Belmont, Calif.: Wadsworth.

Winter, K., and J. A. C. Smith, eds. 1996. *Crassulacean Acid Metabolism: Biochemistry, Ecophysiology, and Evolution.* Berlin: Springer.

CARACAL

Medium-sized, wide-ranging cat (*Caracal caracal*; mammalian order Carnivora, family Felidae) that occurs from southern Africa to India. The caracal is absent from rain forests of western Africa and from the central Sahara Desert. Caracals are distinctive, with sleek, muscular bodies and long, pointed ears that are black on the outside with a thin, black tuft on the tip. The rest of the body is reddish brown on the back and white on the throat and underbelly. Caracals inhabit a variety of habitats from deserts to savannas and can be found in both lowlands and mountains.

Caracals prey on a wide range of mammals, birds, and reptiles, including poisonous snakes. They occasionally take domestic animals, such as goats and poultry, and are considered to be pests in parts of their range. They are fast runners over short distances and usually attack prey with a quick dash after stalking or waiting in hiding. They hunt primarily at night. They appear to be largely solitary and only form pairs to mate. The female gives birth to one to six young. In captivity caracals have lived as long as 17 years.

People have long recognized caracals for their hunting prowess, and they have been raised in captivity in Iran and India for hunting. They were revered in ancient Egypt and were featured in Egyptian art. Bronzed sculptures of caracals were placed as guardians of Egyptian tombs. They are currently declining in abundance in North Africa, South Africa, and parts of Asia.—Thomas E. Lacher, Jr.

See also **AFRICA, DESERTS OF; ASIA, DESERTS OF; CARNIVORES; CATS; KALAHARI DESERT; KAROO; MAMMALS; NAMIBIA, DESERTS OF; PREDATION; SAHARA DESERT; SOUTH AFRICA, DESERTS OF**

Further Reading

Dorst, J., and P. Dandelot. 1980. *A Field Guide to the Larger Mammals of Africa*. London: Collins.

Haltenorth, T., and H. Diller. 1980. *A Field Guide to the Mammals of Africa, Including Madagascar*. London: Collins.

Kingdon, J. 1989. *East African Mammals: An Atlas of Evolution in Africa*. Vol. 3A. Chicago: University of Chicago Press.

Skinner, J. D., and R. H. N. Smithers. 1990. *The Mammals of the Southern African Subregion*. Pretoria: University of Pretoria.

CARACARA

Medium-sized group of scavenging birds ranging from southern North America through Central and South America (order Falconiformes, family Falconidae). Nine species in two to four genera are recognized. Habitat preferences are variable. Species of the genus *Daptrius* prefer tropical forest zones, whereas the remaining taxa of caracaras are associated with more open country. Some species, notably the crested caracara (*Polyborus plancus*), are associated with arid and semiarid habitats. One species, the Guadalupe caracara (*Polyborus luto-*

sus), which formerly occupied desert habitat on Guadalupe Island off the west coast of Mexico, is now extinct.

Caracaras are long-legged raptors, with rather long wings and tails. Total length ranges from 35 to 65 centimeters. They spend much time perched or walking rather than flying and soar very little. The head is partially bare, especially at the base of the strongly hooked bill. Plumage is generally dark, often with fine barring or pale coloration on the face, chest, and belly. Sexes are similar in external appearance. Caracaras are predominantly carnivorous (e.g., feeding on small vertebrates, insects, and carrion), but one species, the red-throated caracara (*Daptrius americanus*), specializes on wasp larvae, fruits, and seeds. Generally, caracaras are important scavengers and often are found feeding with New World vultures on carcasses. Some species, especially the crested caracara, engage in piratical attacks on other birds, including conspecifics (members of their own species), to rob them of their prey.

Caracaras construct untidy nests of sticks in trees, on cliff ledges, or, rarely, on the ground. Clutch size usually consists of two or three eggs. The incubation period lasts approximately 30 days. Both parents probably contribute to incubation and perform parental duties.—Stephen C. Lougheed

See also **BIRDS; CAATINGA; CARRION EATERS; CHACO; MEXICO, DESERTS OF; MONTE DESERT; RAPTORS; SOUTH AMERICA, DESERTS OF; UNITED STATES, DESERTS OF; VULTURE**

Further Reading

Bent, A. C. 1938. Life histories of North American birds of prey. *U.S. National Museum Bulletin* No. 170.

Blake, E. R. 1977. *Manual of Neotropical Birds*. Vol. 1. Chicago: University of Chicago Press.

Brown, L., and D. Amadon. 1968. *Eagles, Hawks and Falcons of the World*. Vol. 2. London: Country Life.

Fjeldså, J., and N. Krabbe. 1990. *Birds of the High Andes*. Svendborg, Denmark: Apollo.

Johnson, A. W. 1965. *The Birds of Chile and Adjacent Regions of Argentina, Bolivia and Peru*. Vol. 1. Buenos Aires: Platt.

CARBONATES

Group of minerals having the negatively charged carbonate anion $(CO_3)^{2-}$ as the fundamental component. The most common carbonates can be classified into three broad groups based on the combinations of the negatively charged carbonate compound (anion) with positively charged compounds (cations) and/or the mineral crystal form. The Calcite Group has the carbonate anion combined with a single small cation and has a hexagonal structure. Calcite ($CaCO_3$) is the most common member of this group. The Dolomite Group has the carbonate anion combined with two small cations alternating in position in the crystal structure as found in dolomite ($CaMg[CO_3]$). The third group, the Aragonite Group, has the carbonate anion combined with a single cation in an orthorhombic (three unequal axes at right angles) structure as found in aragonite ($CaCO_3$). Calcium carbonate ($CaCO_3$) is by far the most common carbonate found in desert environments and the dominant compound in limestone. The general reaction for calcium carbonate formation is $Ca^{2+} + 2HCO_3$ $<=> CaCO_3 + H_2O + CO_2$. In soils carbonates are inherited from the parent geologic material, or have formed from secondary accumulations. Calcification is the accumulation of carbonates in soils due to soil formation processes. In arid regions, where water is scarce and temperature relatively high, leaching of carbonate is much reduced and the precipitation of carbonate is favored. Soils rich in carbonate often have limited water-holding capacity and develop surface crusts that impede water movement and plant emergence. Carbonates in soils also restrict plant nutrient and micronutrient uptake and may form dense impervious layers in the soil.—Ted M. Zobeck and Dan R. Upchurch

See also **ALLUVIAL SOILS; DESERT SLOPES; DURICRUSTS; LIMESTONE; SOILS, DESERT; SOILS, DESERT, CALCAREOUS; SOILS, DESERT, CALICHE; SOILS, DESERT, PEDOCAL; SOIL TAXONOMY; WEATHERING, DESERT**

Further Reading

Birkeland, P. W. 1974. *Pedology, Weathering, and Geomorphological Research.* New York: Oxford University Press.

Dixon, J. B., and S. B. Weed, eds. 1977. *Minerals in Soil Environments.* Madison: Soil Science Society of America.

Tennison, A. C. 1974. *Nature of Earth Materials.* Englewood Cliffs, N.J.: Prentice-Hall.

Wilding, L. P., N. E. Smeck, and G. F. Hall. 1983. *Pedogenesis and Soil Taxonomy II: The Soil Orders.* Vol 11B: *Developments in Soil Science.* New York: Elsevier.

Cardón cactus (*Trichocereus*) in the Monte Desert, Catamarca Province, Argentina. (Photo: M. A. Mares)

CARDÓN

Common name given to several genera and species of arborescent cacti that occur throughout many of the arid and semiarid parts of North and South America. These are large cacti that are found from the semiarid habitats of northernmost South America through portions of the high Andean puna and into the great thorn forest (Chaco) of Paraguay, Bolivia, and Argentina and the extensive Monte Desert of Argentina. Other species occur in semiarid areas of northern and eastern South America (e.g., Caatinga) and northward through Mexico. Common genera of cardones include *Trichocereus, Cereus, Neoraimondia, Lemaireocereus, Cephalocereus, Stetsonia,* and *Pachycereus.*

These cacti may occur in vast groupings, as in the branched cactus forests of the Monte Desert, which look very much like the saguaro cactus forests (or organ pipe cactus community) of the Sonoran Desert of North America. They may also occur solitarily. Cardones may reach five meters or more in height, may have as few as one or two branches, or may be plants with a complex many-branched aspect.

Cardones are a major botanical component of South American drylands and are an important contributor to the ecology of these areas. Their spiny branches provide protected places for the nests of many species of birds, such as dendrocolaptids (wood creepers), and some birds (e.g., the white-fronted woodpecker, *Melanerpes cactorum*) actually hollow out nests within the structure of the thick cactus trunk itself. In their basic ecology cardones are quite similar (and related to) the saguaro (*Carnegiea gigantea*) of the North American Sonoran Desert.—Virgilio G. Roig

See also **ALTIPLANO; BAJA CALIFORNIA, DESERTS OF; BIRDS; C$_3$ PLANTS; C$_4$ PLANTS; CAATINGA; CACTI; CACTUS, COLUMNAR; CAM PLANTS; CHACO; MONTE DESERT; ORGAN PIPE CACTUS; SAGUARO; SONORAN DESERT; SOUTH AMERICA, DESERTS OF; WOODPECKERS**

Further Reading

Britton, N. L., and J. N. Rose. 1963. *The Cactaceae. Descriptions and Illustrations of Plants of the Cactus Family.* 4 vols. New York: Dover.

Cabrera, A. L. 1976. *Regiones fitogeográficas Argentinas: Enciclopedia Argentina de agricultura y jardinería.* Buenos Aires: ACME.

Gibson, A. C., and P. S. Nobel. 1986. *The Cactus Primer.* Cambridge, Mass.: Harvard University Press.

Lamb, B. M. 1991. *A Guide to Cacti of the World.* New York: Angus and Robertson (HarperCollins).

Morello, J. 1958. La provincia fitogeográfica del Monte. *Opera Lilloana* 2:1–155.

CARNIVORES

Term applied to organisms which has both a functional (dietary) and an evolutionary (taxonomic) definition. The functional definition of a carnivore is any animal (or in some rare cases, any plant) that consumes the tissues of another animal for sustenance. The animals consumed are vertebrates, in the strictest definition of carnivore. The broadest definition of carnivore includes animals that consume invertebrates, the body fluids of live organisms, and the tissues of dead organisms (carrion). The terms "carnivore" and "predator" are used as synonyms by some authors, but predation usually has a much broader definition. The functional definition of carnivore encompasses mammals, birds, fish, other vertebrates, many invertebrates, and

Large spotted genet (*Genetta tigrina*, family Viverridae) in northern Kwazulu-Natal Province, South Africa, at the Itala Game Reserve. (Photo: M. A. Mares)

even some plants like the Venus's-flytrap and the pitcher plants.

The term "carnivore" can also refer specifically to the animals classified by taxonomists (scientists who name organisms and determine their evolutionary relationships) as members of the mammalian order Carnivora. The taxonomic definition is restricted to the 271 species of the 11 families currently in the order (families include those of the dogs, cats, mongooses, hyenas, weasels, walruses, fur seals, true seals, raccoons, bears, and civets). The taxonomic definition covers only mammals, and many of these do not eat other animals for sustenance. For example, the giant panda (*Ailuropoda melanoleuca*; family Ursidae) feeds almost exclusively on bamboo, and the kinkajou (*Potus flavus*; family Procyonidae) eats only fruit, nectar, and honey.

The characteristics that link the species classified in the order Carnivora are morphological and historical, not functional or behavioral. The most primitive carnivores, the creodonts, were first observed in the early Paleocene, making this order of mammals one of the oldest known. All carnivores share certain morphological traits. Several small bones in the wrists of carnivores (the scaphoid, the lunar, and the centrale) are fused into the scapholunar bone. The collarbone is also greatly reduced and suspended on ligaments lodged within the shoulder muscles. The most important feature is the possession of modified teeth, the carnassials, for shearing and cutting through flesh. The last upper premolars on each side are modified to shear past the lower first molars, like the blades of scissors. This trait was present in the ancestors of all modern Carnivora; however, in many of the contemporary species, such as pandas, the carnassials have reverted to grinding structures for chewing plant material.

Many of the species in the order Carnivora are among the world's most endangered mammals. Large predators, such as the cats, have been heavily persecuted for their skins. Cats, foxes, wolves, and bears are also killed as pests by farmers and ranchers in many parts of the world. Finally, because large carnivores require extensive areas of undisturbed habitat, many species have been severely affected by habitat destruction. The survival of the largest carnivores will only be guaranteed through the protection of sufficient undisturbed habitat.—Thomas E. Lacher, Jr.

See also **BADGER; BARBARY LION; CARACAL; CATS; CHEETAH; COATI; COYOTE; DINGO; DOG, WILD; FENNEC; FERRET; FOX; GENET; GRASSHOPPER MOUSE; HOWLING; HYENA; JACKAL; JAGUAR; LION; MAMMALS; MONGOOSE; PALEOCENE; PREDATION; PUMA; RINGTAIL; SEA LION; WEASEL; WILDLIFE**

Further Reading

Bothma, J. du P. 1998. *Carnivore Ecology in Arid Lands.* New York: Springer.

Estes, R. D. 1991. *The Behavior Guide to African Mammals.* Berkeley: University of California Press.

Ewer, R. F. 1973. *The Carnivores.* London: Weidenfeld and Nicolson.

Gittleman, J. L., ed. 1989. *Carnivore Behavior, Ecology, and Evolution.* Ithaca: Cornell University Press.

Macdonald, D., ed. 1984. *The Encyclopedia of Mammals.* New York: Facts on File.

CARRION EATERS

Organisms that derive all or part of their food from animal carcasses. Carrion is a common food source for a variety of arid-land organisms, including many mammals, birds, insects, and microorganisms. Decomposition is generally slower in xeric (dry) than in humid environments. Carrion eaters, therefore, perform an important ecological role in accelerating the breakdown of animal matter. Relatively few species feed only on carrion. This trend is probably based on two factors influencing carrion availability. First, in some areas the occurrence of animal carcasses is unpredictable. Second, in others

regular migration of herds of some herbivorous mammals (e.g., the wildebeest of Africa, *Connochaetes*) generate an adequate local carrion supply only seasonally. Thus carrion, at least among vertebrates, is a reliable food source only for organisms that are extremely mobile (e.g., vultures). Numerous organisms scavenge on animal carcasses opportunistically, the carrion forming only a portion of their diet. For example, the bat-eared fox (*Otocyon megalotis*) of arid zones of eastern and southern Africa primarily eats termites but may include other insects, fruit, and carrion in its diet. Even some species of hyenas are primarily hunters and consume carrion only occasionally. The diet of some invertebrate species consists of carrion only during one stage of their life cycle. For example, the larvae of some species of skin beetles (Dermestidae) consume carrion whereas the adults feed on flowers.

The dominant scavengers of carcasses vary with the size of the corpse. Most large carcasses (e.g., large ungulates) are consumed primarily by vertebrates, whereas smaller carcasses (e.g., rodents and birds) often provide food for necrophagous fly larvae (larvae that develop on carcasses) and beetles. Large carcasses usually permit the possibility of the development of more diverse scavenging communities than do the bodies of small animals.—Stephen C. Lougheed

See also **ARMADILLO; BEETLES; BIRDS; BUZZARD; CARACARA; CONDOR; CROW; HYENA; MAMMALS; RAPTORS; VULTURE**

Further Reading

Cloudsley-Thompson, J. L., and M. J. Chadwick. 1964. *Life in Deserts.* London: Foulis.

Doube, B. M. 1987. Spatial and temporal organization in communities associated with dung pads and carcasses. *In* J. H. R. Gee and P. S. Giller, eds., *Organization of Communities Past and Present,* 255–280. Oxford: Blackwell.

Houston, D. C. 1980. The adaptations of scavengers. *In* A. R. E. Sinclair and M. Norton-Griffiths, eds., *Serengeti: Dynamics of an Ecosystem,* 263–286. Chicago: University of Chicago Press.

Wallace, M. P., and S. A. Temple. 1987. Competitive interactions within and between species in a guild of avian scavengers. *Auk* 104:290–295.

Zimmerman, D. R. 1975. Vulture restaurant. *Natural History* 84:26–31.

CARRYING CAPACITY

Maximum number of individuals of a particular species that can be supported by the resource base of the environment. Carrying capacity may be influenced by both biotic factors (resulting from the effects of organisms) and abiotic factors (resulting from the nonliving component of the environment). A common biotic factor that controls population size is the relative number of predator and prey species. For instance, if there is a sharp increase in the numbers of jackrabbits in a southwestern desert grassland, the numbers of coyotes would most likely also increase in response to the increased food supply. The increase in numbers of predators would then lead to a decrease in the numbers of jackrabbits the following year. Some species might impinge on overall community structure through their control over several species. Species that influence the numbers of many species are referred to as keystone species. Population size may also be influenced by physical or nonbiological factors. As an example, a sustained increase in precipitation in the Chihuahuan Desert could result in a surge of herbaceous perennials. If the weather change proved to be long term (i.e., if the climate changes), it could be disastrous for some species and a boon to others.

Carrying capacity may be influenced by parameters of population density. Population density of plants may be controlled through factors that are density dependent (the number of individuals in one generation affects the carrying capacity of the next generation) or density independent (where population sizes of generations are independent of one another). If a rapidly expanding population were to exceed the carrying capacity of an area, it would most likely result in a precipitous drop in the population size the next generation. Similarly, in a population that is density independent the limits on density are set by factors other than the population's density. For example, the number of sand dunes most certainly influences the number of sand-dwelling kangaroo rats, and the number of saguaro cacti with holes in them sets limits on the numbers of saguaro owls that can nest there.

The parched conditions of deserts might seem to favor abiotic or density-independent controls on population size, because it seems intuitive that the numbers of individuals of desert species will be lower than corresponding numbers in rain forest species; however, some species, such as ground-dwelling bees, are highly adapted to the dry climates of deserts, and they prosper there, as do many other kinds of organisms. Carrying capacity is thus a complex result of interacting factors that serve to limit the size of populations in a given area.—James R. Estes

See also **ARTHROPODS; CACTUS, COLUMNAR; DECOMPOSITION; ECOLOGY; ENERGY FLOW; PHOTOSYNTHESIS; PRIMARY PRODUCTIVITY; PRODUCTIVITY, AQUATIC ECOSYSTEMS**

Further Reading

Odum, E. P. 1983. *Basic Ecology.* Philadelphia: Saunders.

Whittaker, R. H. 1975. *Communities and Ecosystems.* New York: Macmillan.

CATCLAW

Desert shrub or tree of the pea family (Leguminosae) with prickles along the branches resembling the claws of a cat. The common name catclaw usually refers to *Acacia greggii*, which is also called wait-a-minute, although it may also refer to *Mimosa biuncifera*. *Acacia greggii* is a shrub or tree commonly only one to two meters tall but occasionally reaching eight meters. It is considered a winter-deciduous plant (loses its leaves during the winter), but the compound leaves, with three to five pairs of leaflets, remain on the plant except during severe cold. The pale yellow flowers are arranged in cylindrical spikes four to five centimeters long. The pods are long and thin (6–13 centimeters x 1 centimeter), usually constricted between the seeds, and curved.

Catclaw occurs in thickets along washes, streams, and canyon bottoms and, individually, on mesas (tablelands) and hillsides in the Mojave, Sonoran, and Chihuahuan deserts and in desert grassland from sea level to 1,500 meters. Because of the stout, curved prickles on these plants, thickets are difficult and painful to traverse on foot.

New leaves are browsed by cattle in the spring, and mature leaves are browsed when little other forage is available. Nectar from the flowers is an important source of honey. The hard wood of catclaw is used for firewood. Pods are crushed into a meal used in cooking by Native Americans. Catclaw is used medicinally for conjunctivitis, diarrhea, bleeding, diaper rash, sore throat, and coughing, and as a sedative. In Mexico this plant is called *uña de gato*, a literal translation of cat's claw.—Kristina A. Ernest

See also **ACACIA; ARIZONA DESERT; CHIHUAHUAN DESERT; DESERTS; LEGUMES; MEXICO, DESERTS**

OF; MOJAVE DESERT; PLANT ADAPTATIONS; PLANT GEOGRAPHY; PLANTS; SONORAN DESERT; THORN; UNITED STATES, DESERTS OF

Further Reading

Benson, L., and R. A. Darrow. 1981. *Trees and Shrubs of the Southwestern Deserts*. Tucson: University of Arizona Press.

MacMahon, J. A. 1985. *Deserts*. New York: Knopf.

CATERPILLARS

Larvae of insects in the order Lepidoptera (moths and butterflies). Caterpillars are elongate larvae with six pairs of walking legs (thoracic legs), additional abdominal prolegs, a well-developed head, and very short antennae. They are herbivorous (plant eaters) and in large numbers are capable of causing considerable damage to crops and natural vegetation.

Caterpillars vary considerably in overall appearance depending on species. Many are smooth, with no apparent external features except various color patterns. Others are covered by hairs of varying lengths and sizes, which, when brushed against or inhaled by potential predators, cause considerable irritation. These urticating (irritating) hairs function like tiny spears that penetrate the skin. Yet other caterpillars have large knobs or spines that may also contain urticating hairs.

Caterpillars eat continually, undergo a series of molts during which they increase in size, and ultimately transform into a chrysalis stage, which later transforms into an adult. Because of their abundance and the ease with which they can be captured, caterpillars are important prey for many species of wasps and numerous vertebrates, including birds and lizards.—Laurie J. Vitt

See also ANIMAL ADAPTATIONS; ARTHROPODS; BAGWORMS; BUTTERFLIES; DEFENSIVE ADAPTATIONS, ANIMALS; HAWKMOTH; INSECTS; LIFE HISTORY STRATEGY (ITEROPARITY); METAMORPHOSIS; MOTHS; WASPS

Further Reading

Borror, D. J., C. A. Triplehorn, and N. F. Johnson. 1992. *An Introduction to the Study of Insects*. New York: Harcourt Brace.

Borror, D. J., and R. E. White. 1970. *A Field Guide to the Insects*. Boston: Houghton Mifflin.

CATS

Refers to all species in the mammalian order Carnivora, family Felidae. There are 36 species in 18 genera. Cats have a near-cosmopolitan (worldwide) distribution and are absent only from Greenland and some northern Canadian islands, northern Siberia, Madagascar, Australia, New Zealand, and other Pacific islands.

All species within the family are fairly uniform in external morphology and anatomy. Cats are the most carnivorous of the Carnivora and are highly specialized to pursue, capture, and kill vertebrate prey. The skull of cats is rounded with a very short rostrum. This allows for a powerful bite. The orbits are enlarged to hold the large eyes, an adaptation for animals that hunt by sight. They have binocular color vision, and their visual acuity at night is six times that of humans. The senses of hearing and smell are also well developed. All felids have the specialized carnassial shearing teeth typical of the order Carnivora. The last upper premolars on each side are modified to shear past the lower first molars, like the blades of scissors. They also have short, strongly built forelimbs, and the paws have recurved, completely retractile claws (only partially retractile in the cheetah).

Felids are sometimes split into two groups by natural historians: the big and small cats. The big cats (subfamilies Acinonychinae and Pantherinae) are those species that can roar but not purr, and the small cats can purr continuously but not roar. The ability to roar is conferred by the replacement of a bone in the throat (the hyoid) with cartilage, which allows greater freedom of movement.

More than 75 percent of all cat species are forest dwellers and very good climbers. There are several species that are adapted to arid and semiarid zones. Of the larger cats, cheetahs, jaguars, lions, leopards, and tigers can all occur in savannas, semideserts, and dry forests. Some even occur in deserts at their margins. A number of species of small cats are arid-land specialists. These include the sand cat (*Felis margarita*), the caracal (*Caracal caracal*), and the serval (*Leptailurus serval*). The puma or mountain lion (*Puma concolor*) has one of the broadest distributions of all vertebrates, occurring from Alaska to Tierra del Fuego. It occurs in virtually all habitats in the Western Hemisphere, including wet tropical forest and deserts.

Cats are among the most threatened of the large vertebrates. Twenty-two of the 36 species are endangered in at least part of their range.—Thomas E. Lacher, Jr.

See also **BARBARY LION; CARACAL; CARNIVORES; CHEETAH; FENNEC; JAGUAR; LION; MAMMALS; PREDATION; PUMA; WILDLIFE**

Further Reading

Estes, R. D. 1991. *The Behavior Guide to African Mammals*. Berkeley: University of California Press.

Ewer, R. F. 1973. *The Carnivores*. London: Weidenfeld and Nicolson.

Gittleman, J. L., ed. 1989. *Carnivore Behavior, Ecology, and Evolution*. Ithaca: Cornell University Press.

Macdonald, D., ed. 1984. *The Encyclopedia of Mammals*. New York: Facts on File.

Nowak, R. M. 1991. *Walker's Mammals of the World*. 5th ed. Baltimore: Johns Hopkins University Press.

CATTLE. *See* DOMESTIC ANIMALS

CAVY

Group of related species of rodents (mammalian order Rodentia, family Caviidae) that contains two subfamilies: the Caviinae, or the cavies, and the Dolichotinae, or the maras. Currently, 12 species of cavies in four genera are recognized. The five species in the genus *Cavia* are the guinea pigs, including the domestic guinea pig, *Cavia porcellus*. Guinea pigs occur in a range of savanna and scrub habitats from sea level to montane grasslands. The genus *Microcavia* contains the three species of desert cavies, all of which are found in arid regions of Argentina and Bolivia. The genus *Galea* (three species) is the most generalized of the cavies and occurs in all of the above habitats as well as in forest edges. The rock cavy, or mocó, *Kerodon rupestris*, is the most specialized of the cavies. It is restricted to rocky outcrops and boulder piles in the arid Caatinga region of northeastern Brazil.

All cavies are herbivorous (plant eaters). *Galea* and *Cavia* consume grasses and most other types of plant material. *Microcavia* and *Kerodon* are somewhat more specialized and forage on leaves in shrubs and trees (i.e., they are browsers). *Kerodon* is an especially agile climber and will go high into trees on the slenderest of limbs in search of tender leaves. The sight of a nearly two-pound "guinea pig" creeping along a pencil-thin branch is surprising.

The red-rumped rock cavy (*Kerodon rupestris*) of the semiarid, tropical Caatinga scrubland of northeastern Brazil. (Photo: M. A. Mares)

All species of cavies give birth to small litters of very precocial (well-developed) young. *Galea* and *Microcavia* average about three young per litter, whereas *Kerodon* rarely has more than one offspring. The young are mobile and can consume solid food within a few days of birth.

Cavies are hunted throughout their range. Indeed, the domestic guinea pig continues to be raised in captivity for food. These animals are generally common where they occur. An exception is *Kerodon*, which, because of its highly specialized habitat requirements, is becoming increasingly rare in northeastern Brazil.—Thomas E. Lacher, Jr.

See also **ALTIPLANO; ANDEAN GRASSLANDS; ANDES; CAATINGA; CHACO; CONVERGENT EVOLUTION; HERBIVORY; MARA; MAMMALS; MONTE DESERT; PAMPAS; PUNA; RODENTS**

Further Reading

Lacher, T. E., Jr. 1981. The comparative social behavior of *Kerodon rupestris* and *Galea spixii* and the evolution of behavior in the Caviidae. *Bulletin of the Carnegie Museum* 17:1–71.

Macdonald, D., ed. 1984. *The Encyclopedia of Mammals*. New York: Facts on File.

Rood, J. P. 1970. Ecology and social behavior of the desert cavy (*Microcavia australis*). *American Midland Naturalist* 83:415–453.

———. 1972. Ecological and behavioural comparisons of three genera of Argentine Cavies. *Animal Behavior Monographs* 5:1–83.

CENOZOIC

Era of geologic time extending from the end of the Mesozoic era (65 million years ago) to the present.

This era is often called the Age of Mammals (or sometimes the Age of Birds) because of the dominance of this group in the continental fossil record and its evolutionary diversification during this era. The term "Cenozoic" means "recent life" or "recent animals" (relative to the Paleozoic's "ancient life" and Mesozoic's "middle life"). Fossils in Cenozoic rocks include many types closely related to modern forms, increasingly so as modern times are approached. This era is subdivided in one of two different ways: into two periods or suberas, Tertiary and Quaternary, or into two nonequivalent periods, Paleogene and Neogene. By the first method the Tertiary spans a period from about 65 million years ago to 1.8 million years ago, and the Quaternary spans 1.8 million years ago to the present. By the second method the Paleogene extends from 65 million years ago to 23 million years ago, and the Neogene extends from 23 million years ago to the present (or sometimes only to the beginning of the Pleistocene).

Tectonic activity that was occurring in the Mesozoic continued uninterrupted into the Cenozoic. During this era the continents moved into their present positions and acquired their present forms. Following a period in the Late Cretaceous when sea levels were exceedingly high, global sea levels generally regressed (became lowered) throughout the Cenozoic to very low levels in the Pleistocene. Perhaps most notable among the tectonic events of this era are the northward movements of the Indian subcontinent and of Africa, resulting in the closure of the former Tethys Sea and the uplift of the Alps and the Himalayas. General widening of the Atlantic Ocean by seafloor spreading and westward tectonic movements (movement of the earth's geologic plates) of the Americas uplifted the American cordilleras (mountain ranges). These various tectonic and orogenic (mountain-building) developments affected oceanic and atmospheric circulation, contributing in turn to the development of modern arid regions on the lee sides of the resulting mountain ranges, thus resulting in the formation of deserts and semideserts as well as grasslands.—Nicholas J. Czaplewski

See also **AN INTRODUCTION TO DESERTS; DESERTS; EOCENE; GLACIAL PERIODS; INTERGLACIALS; MIDDEN; MIOCENE; NEOGENE; OLIGOCENE; PALEOCENE; PALEOCLIMATE; PLATE TECTON-**

Giant centipede (*Scolopendra heros*). (Photo: L. J. Vitt)

ICS; PLEISTOCENE; PLIOCENE; QUATERNARY; RECENT (HOLOCENE); TERTIARY

Further Reading

Cocks, L. R. M. 1981. *The Evolving Earth*. London: British Museum (Natural History).

Levin, H. L. 1988. *The Earth Through Time*. 3d ed. Philadelphia: Saunders.

Rogers, J. J. W. 1993. *A History of the Earth*. Cambridge: Cambridge University Press.

Smith, A. G., and J. C. Briden. 1977. *Mesozoic and Cenozoic Paleocontinental Maps*. Cambridge: Cambridge University Press.

CENTIPEDE, GIANT

Large (10–15 centimeters), flat, elongate, segmented, terrestrial arthropod with a single pair of legs on each body segment. Giant centipedes have a large pair of fangs (called gnathopods) on the undersurface of the head and long antennae on the dorsal surface of the head. The posterior end of the body contains a pair of long appendages (cerci) that resemble the antennae. These impressive arthropods are in the genus *Scolopendra*. The most impressive species in North American deserts is *Scolopendra heros*, which, in the Sonoran Desert, typically is yellow with bluish black on both ends of the body. Other species of desert centipedes are orange with black cross-bands.

When disturbed these centipedes often raise the tail off the ground to mimic the head. Predators may thus attack the wrong end, providing the centipede an opportunity to attack a would-be predator with the toxic fangs. Movement is rapid and snakelike. Centipedes are voracious predators, feeding on invertebrates and small vertebrates, which they kill with their venom and masticate with their jaws. They are generally nocturnal (active at night) but may be active on the surface on cloudy days following rain. During the day they remain hidden under surface objects and in burrows of other animals. The venom of desert centipedes varies in toxicity depending on the species, but most are not considered threatening to humans. Bites produce symptoms similar to those of wasp stings.—Laurie J. Vitt

See also **ARTHROPODS; DEFENSIVE ADAPTATIONS, ANIMALS; MILLIPEDES; POISONOUS ANIMALS; SCORPIONS; VENOM**

Further Reading

Lewis, J. G. E. 1981. *The Biology of Centipedes*. Cambridge: Cambridge University Press.

CERASTES

Genus name for the "horned" vipers occurring in sandy areas of North Africa (from western Morocco and Arabia eastward to western Iran). Horned vipers are in the snake family Viperidae and consequently possess movable front fangs that are capable of injecting large doses of venom produced in venom glands located at the rear of the head. There are currently three recognized species, *Cerastes cerastes*, occurring from Morocco eastward to the Negev of Israel; *Cerastes gasperettii*, occurring throughout most of the Arabian Peninsula into western Iran; and *Cerastes vipera*, occurring in the Sahara Desert from Morocco to the Negev Desert of Israel.

The horned vipers are restricted to areas of fine, windblown sand. Their morphology, behavior, and ecology is convergent with the sidewinder rattlesnake of the southwestern United States (i.e., they have evolved to look and function alike, although they are not closely related). Most have a hornlike scale above each eye, and all use a form of locomotion called sidewinding. Individuals bury themselves in sand by undulating the body such that the posterior end disappears into the sand first and is followed by the remainder of the body. Frequently, all that remains visible at the surface is the pair of

The Old World sidewinder (*Cerastes*) in Wadi Natroun, Egypt. (Photo: M. A. Mares)

eyes with the protruding horns. Prey are bitten, envenomed, and swallowed whole.—Laurie J. Vitt

See also **ANIMAL ADAPTATIONS; CONVERGENT EVOLUTION; DEFENSIVE ADAPTATIONS, ANIMALS; DUNES; IRAN, DESERTS OF; ISRAEL, DESERTS OF; JORDAN, DESERTS OF; MIDDLE EAST, DESERTS OF; PIT VIPER; POISONOUS ANIMALS; PREDATION; REPTILES; SAHARA DESERT; SIDEWINDER; SNAKES; VENOM**

Further Reading

Mehrtens, J. M. 1987. *Living Snakes of the World in Color*. New York: Sterling.

Werner, Y. H., A. Le Verdier, D. Rosenman, and N. Sivan. 1991. Systematics and zoogeography of *Cerastes* (Ophidia: Viperidae) in the Levant: 1. Distinguishing Arabian from African "*Cerastes cerastes*." *Snake* 23:90–100.

Werner, Y. H., and N. Sivan. 1992. Systematics and zoogeography of *Cerastes* (Ophidia: Viperidae) in the Levant: 2. Taxonomy, Ecology, and Zoogeography. *Snake* 24:34–39.

CHACO

Vast thorn scrub (the Chaco Domain) extending across parts of southern Bolivia, western Paraguay, and much of northern Argentina, from the Andean piedmont to the banks of the Paraná River. It comprises vast plains and occasional low mountains, or sierras. The climate is continental, with precipitation coming mainly as summer rains. Annual rain-

Complex, dense, Chacoan thorn scrub vegetation consisting of tall shrubs, trees, and columnar cacti in northern Catamarca Province, Argentina. (Photo: M. A. Mares)

fall ranges from as little as 500 millimeters in the west to 1,200 millimeters in the east. Mean annual temperature is 20°–23°C. In the western Chaco rainfall occurs mostly in summer (November to March), whereas in the east extreme rains occur throughout much of the year. Over most of this area a deciduous xerophytic forest prevails (trees with a mass shedding of leaves in response to climate or time of the year). There is an herbaceous layer of grasses and a number of Cactaceae and terrestrial Bromeliaceae, although palm groves, savannas, and halophytic shrub steppes also are found in the Chaco. The most typical trees are quebracho colorado (*Schinopsis*), which is usually associated with *Aspidosperma quebrachoblanco* (quebracho blanco), *Caesalpinia paraguayensis* (guayacón tropical), *Patagonula americana* (guayaibu), and *Tabebuia avellanedae* (lapacho). In some areas there are palo santo groves of *Bulnesia sarmientoi*, or palm groves of *Copernicia australis*, as well as colonies of the palm *Trithrinax campestris*. Grasses of the genera *Setaria*, *Digitaria*, and *Pennisetum* and thorny bromeliads, such as *Bromelia serra*, *Bromelia hieronymi*, *Dyckia ferox* (commonly known as chaguares), as well as a number of cacti of the genera *Cleistocactus*, *Eriocereus*, and *Opuntia* are dominant in the lower layer. On the banks of rivers and marshes *Salix humboldtiana* is dominant, associated with a tree composite, *Tesaria integrifolia*.

Argentine authors usually distinguish four districts in the Chaco: a more humid eastern district with *Schinopsis balansae* dominant; a drier eastern district with *Schinopsis lorentzii* dominant; a mountain, or serrano, district on the western edge of the province, with predominance of *Schinopsis haenkeana*; and a southern, or savanna, district, which is bare of trees but has many grasses, including *Elionurus muticus* and *Leptochloa chloridiformis*.

The mammal fauna of the Chaco is diverse and includes several marsupials, such as the widespread *comadreja overa* opossum (*Didelphis azarae*), the *comadreja colorada*, or red opossum (*Lutreolina crassicaudata*), and several mouse opossums (genus *Thylamys*). There are many species of bats and foxes (*Cerdocyon*, *Pseudalopex*). The *aguará-guazú*, or maned wolf (*Chrysocyon brachyurus*), also occurs in the Chaco and is one of its most characteristic animals. Several carnivores and monkeys also occur in this region. Among the many rodents of the Chaco are the nutria (*Myocastor coypu*) and the marsh rat (*Holochilus brasiliensis*). Among the Cervidae, or deer, are the largest South American deer, the *ciervo de los pantanos*, or marsh deer (*Blastocerus dichotomus*), and the *venado de las pampas*, or pampas deer (*Ozotoceros bezoarticus*). Many mammals of the order Xenarthra also are found in the region, such as the *pichiciego chaqueño*, or fairy armadillo (*Chlamyphorus retusus*); the *peludo grande*, or six-lined armadillo (*Euphractus sexcinctus*); the *oso hormiguero*, or giant anteater (*Myrmecophaga*); the *oso melero*, or tamandua (*Tamandua*); and the *perezozo*, or sloth (*Bradypus*).

More than 200 species of birds have been reported from the Chaco, the most characteristic being the two species of *chuñas*, or seriemas (*Chunga burmeisteri* and *Cariama cristata*), tinamous of the genera *Nothura* and *Eudromia*, the *charata* (*Ortalis*), and a number of species of parrots. Similarly, the reptile fauna is rich in turtles, *yacarés* (caimans), snakes (boas and anacondas), and two species of iguanas (*Tupinambis*). The amphibian fauna is rich and exceeds 30 species. There are also about 30 species of fish known from the Chaco. Chaco invertebrates are also diverse, with one of the most evident being the large termites (*Cornitermes*), which build termitaria, or *tacuríes*, up to 1.5 meters in height.—Virgilio G. Roig

See also **AMPHIBIANS; ARMADILLO; BIRDS; CACTI; CARDÓN; CLIMATE; MAMMALS; MESQUITE;**

MONTE DESERT; PAMPAS; PLANT ADAPTATIONS; REPTILES; SOUTH AMERICA, DESERTS OF; THORN; XEROPHYLLOUS FOREST; XEROPHYTES

Further Reading

Allan, T., and A. Warren, eds. 1993. *Deserts: The Encroaching Wilderness*. New York: Oxford University Press.

Cabrera, A. L. 1976. *Regiones fitogeográficas Argentinas. Enciclopedia Argentina de agricultura y jardinería*. Buenos Aires: ACME.

Cabrera, A. L., and A. Willink. 1973. Biogeografía de América Latina. Organization of American States, Monograph No. 13. Washington, D.C.

Mares, M. A. 1993. Heteromyids and their ecological counterparts: a pandesertic view of rodent ecology. *In* H. H. Genoways and J. H. Brown, eds., *The Biology of the Family Heteromyidae*, 652–713. Special Publication No. 10, American Society of Mammalogists.

Mares, M. A., J. Morello, and G. Goldstein. 1985. The Monte Desert and other subtropical semi-arid biomes of Argentina, with comments on their relation to North American arid areas. *In* M. Evenari, I. Noy-Meir, and D. W. Goodall, eds., *Ecosystems of the World: Hot Deserts and Arid Shrublands*, 12B:203–237. Amsterdam: Elsevier.

Morello, J. 1984. *Pérfil ecológico de Sudamérica*. Barcelona: Ediciones Cultura Hispánica, Instituto de Cooperación Iberoamericana.

Ojeda, R. A., and M. A. Mares. 1989. A biogeographic analysis of the mammals of Salta Province, Argentina: Patterns of species assemblage in the Neotropics. *Special Publications, The Museum, Texas Tech University* 27:1–66.

CHAPARRAL

Biome of Mediterranean climates dominated by chaparral shrubs that possess evergreen sclerophyllous, or hard, leaves that help prevent wilting during periods of extreme drought. Chaparral is a shrubland community found in regions around the world typically characterized by cool, wet winters and hot, dry summers. Chaparral exists in countries that border the Mediterranean Sea, central Chile, South Africa, southwestern and southern Australia, and the southwestern part of the United States and adjacent parts of Mexico. The Coastal Chaparral community dominates southern California and Baja California mountain slopes and foothills. The Interior Chaparral covers similar areas in Arizona and parts of northern Mexico. In both chaparral communities drought occurs every year. In the Coastal Chaparral seasonal high temperatures coincide with the six-month dry period. These dry conditions combine with the Santa Ana winds to produce dangerous fire situations each year. Plant species inhabiting this community are well adapted to the frequent fires, possessing such characteristics as stump-sprouting, which allows shrubs whose aboveground parts have been burned to the ground to quickly resprout from the living stump that remains safe from the fire just below the ground's surface. Typical species of the Coastal Chaparral of California are manzanita (*Arctostaphylos*), buckthorn (*Rhamnus*), scrub oak (*Quercus dumosa*), chamise (*Adenostoma fasciculatum*), and *Ceanothus* species, and of the Interior Chaparral, shrub live oak (*Quercus turbinella*).

One of the most detailed studies of comparative ecology and evolution between chaparral biome sites was conducted in Chile and California in the 1970s. Investigators found that the vegetation of these two widely separated plant communities had converged in both form and function, even though the species composition of the two areas was different, given their different histories. Indeed, none of the dominant plant genera were shared. Dominant Chilean chaparral plants included *Lithraea caustica*, *Trevoa trinervis*, *Kageneckia oblonga*, *Colliguaya odorifera*, *Satureja gilliesii*, *Cryptocarya alba*, and *Quillaja saponaria*. The animals occurring between the two sites were quite different in their overall ecology and species diversity when the entire chaparral biome was considered, although the diversity of species of similar taxonomic groups of animals in habitat patches was similar between the two study areas.—Gordon E. Uno

See also **BAJA CALIFORNIA, DESERTS OF; CLIMATE; DESERTS; PLANT ADAPTATIONS; PLANT GEOGRAPHY; PLANTS; PRECIPITATION; SANTA ANA WINDS; SEMIARID ZONES; SHRUBS**

Further Reading

Barbour, M. G., and W. D. Billings. 1988. *North American Terrestrial Vegetation*. New York: Cambridge University Press.

Brown, D. E., ed. 1994. *Biotic Communities: Southwestern United States and Northwestern Mexico*. Salt Lake City: University of Utah Press.

di Castri, F., and H. Mooney, eds. 1973. *Mediterranean-type Ecosystems: Origin and Structure*. New York: Springer.

Mooney, H. A., ed. 1977. *Convergent Evolution in Chile and California: Mediterranean Climate Ecosystems*. Stroudsburg, Pa.: Dowden, Hutchinson, and Ross.

CHEETAH

Large species of cat, *Acinonyx jubatus* (mammalian order Carnivora, family Felidae), that originally ranged from Tajikistan and India westward throughout most of Africa is absent only from the tropical forest zones of West Africa and the central Sahara. Cheetahs are now extinct in India, and have declined in numbers across much of Africa. Cheetahs inhabit open savannas and savanna woodlands but can be found in semiarid habitats and along the fringes of desert areas. They maintain home ranges whose size varies inversely with prey density.

Cheetahs are skillful predators that hunt by slowly stalking their prey and then charging when they get within several hundred meters. Over short distances cheetahs are the fastest of all terrestrial mammals. They can achieve speeds of 80–112 kilometers per hour. Most chases rarely exceed 100 meters, however, and cheetahs can maintain such high velocities for a maximum of only about 500 meters. Cheetahs do not dissipate the heat generated in their muscles during a pursuit, so their body temperature would exceed lethal limits after 500 meters. Cheetahs prey primarily on small and medium-bodied antelopes. Humans have long recognized the hunting skill of the cheetah and first domesticated them more than 4,000 years ago.

Cheetahs occur alone or in small groups of either a mother and offspring or several related males. Females give birth to three to five young. Cheetahs are considered to be especially susceptible to extinction because of the extremely low levels of genetic variability that have been detected in wild populations. They also have a very poor record of breeding in captivity, although several zoos have recently had success in captive breeding.—Thomas E. Lacher, Jr.

See also **BARBARY LION; CARACAL; CARNIVORES; CATS; FENNEC; JAGUAR; LION; MAMMALS; PREDATION; PUMA; WILDLIFE**

Further Reading

Dorst, J., and P. Dandelot. 1980. *A Field Guide to the Larger Mammals of Africa*. London: Collins.

Estes, R. D. 1991. *The Behavior Guide to African Mammals*. Berkeley: University of California Press.

Haltenorth, T., and H. Diller. 1980. *A Field Guide to the Mammals of Africa, Including Madagascar*. London: Collins.

Kitchener, A. 1991. *The Natural History of the Wild Cats*. Ithaca: Comstock.

Nowak, R. M. 1991. *Walker's Mammals of the World*. 5th ed. Baltimore: Johns Hopkins University Press.

CHENOPODES. *See* CHENOPODIACEAE

CHENOPODIACEAE

Family of annual or perennial herbs, shrubs, or (rarely) small trees, commonly known as the Goosefoot family, consisting of about 100 genera and 1,400 species worldwide which is particularly abundant in xerophytic (dry) and halophytic (saline) areas. Leaves are mostly alternate or sometimes opposite, sometimes scalelike, often succulent, simple, and without stipules, and the blades are entire, toothed, or lobed. Flowers are apetalous, small, inconspicuous, and often greenish. The family is distinguished by the scurfy (i.e., having small scale or branchlike particles on the leaf epidermis) character of the leaves and branches.

Members of the family are predominately herbaceous, but in deserts there are a significant number of important shrubs. Important desert genera include *Atriplex* (saltbush), *Chenopodium* (goosefoot), *Cycloloma* (winged pigweed), *Kochia* (summer cypress), *Salsola* (Russian thistle), *Sarcobatus* (greasewood), *Grayia* (hopsage), *Corispermum* (bugseed), *Salicornia* (grasswort), *Suaeda* (sea blight), and *Ceratoides* (eurotia, winterfat) as well as *Halogeton, Monolepis, Bassia, Roubieva*, and *Axyris*.

Cultivated members of the family include the garden beet (*Beta vulgaris*) and spinach (*Spinacea oleracea*). Members of the family also occur as weeds in cultivated soil or in waste places near towns. The Russian thistle (*Salsola*) is a common tumbleweed in semiarid regions.—Gary K. Hulett and Amanda Renner Charles

See also **DESERTS; DESERTS, HOT; DESERTS, TEMPERATE; GREAT BASIN DESERT; PERENNIAL PLANTS; PHREATOPHYTES; PLANT ADAPTATIONS; PLAYA; SAGEBRUSH; SALINITY; SALT CRUST; SALT DESERT; SALT PAN; SEMIARID ZONES; SHRUBS; TUMBLEWEED; WEATHERING, DESERT**

Further Reading

Clemants, S. E. 1992. *Chenopodiaceae and Amaranthaceae of New York State*. Albany: New York State Education Department.

West, N. E., ed. 1983. *Ecosystems of the World: Temperate Deserts and Semi-deserts*. Vol. 5. New York: Elsevier.

CHIHUAHUAN DESERT

Inland warm desert centered in north central Mexico between the Sierra Madre Occidental (to the west), which casts a rain shadow over the region, and the Sierra Madre Oriental (to the east). The Chihuahuan Desert is the southeasternmost of the deserts of North America and covers approximately 500,000 square kilometers between 21°–34° north latitude and 100°-109° west longitude, extending from the southern parts of Texas, New Mexico, and Arizona through parts of the Mexican states of Chihuahua, Coahuila, San Luis Potosí, Nuevo León, Zacatecas, Durango, and Sonora. This is a high-elevation desert, ranging from about 600 meters to more than 2,000 meters. (See map of deserts of the United States and Mexico, p. 356.)

Chihuahuan Desert habitat with yuccas near Dragoon, Arizona. (Photo: D. Beck)

The Chihuahuan Desert is typical basin and range landscape, with mountain ranges, bajadas (lower slopes formed by erosion due to the action of water), plains, and basins. One of the unique features of this desert is that much of the land lacks external drainage. Water in about a dozen internal drainages flows into closed basins (basins that have no outlet) called bolsones. One of the largest is the Bolsón de Mapimí in Mexico. Shallow saline lakes (playas) in the centers of larger bolsones become seasonally flooded. These are the remnants of Pleistocene or Holocene pluvial lakes.

The geology of the region is dominated by the volcanic Sierra Madre Occidental and the limestone of the Sierra Madre Oriental. In between, much of the Chihuahuan Desert (more than 80 percent) lies on limestone, which was formed under the sea millions of years ago by marine organisms that secreted calcium carbonate. This limestone gives rise to calcareous soils, which commonly contain caliche, a hardened layer of calcium carbonate. The soils of the foothills are gravelly, while finer-grained soils are found on the mesas (tablelands) and in basins. Sand dunes (médanos) are especially common on the leeward edge of playas. The enormous Samalayuca Dunes of northern Chihuahua are a splendid example. Saline soils develop in playas, on buried salt deposits, and near hot springs.

Gypsum (calcium sulfate) deposits are abundant in the Chihuahuan Desert. In its pure form this rock is known as selenite, but most deposits of gypsum contain impurities such as oxides and carbonates. Gypsum soils are usually white or gray. An unusual feature is that pounding on these soils produces a hollow sound. This may be caused by the abundant water channels that penetrate the soils. Gypsum deposits are responsible for one of the most spectacular dune areas of the Chihuahuan Desert, the White Sands of southern New Mexico. Several species of animals have light-colored races that reside on these immaculate white dunes, including earless lizards, grasshopper mice, spotted ground squirrels, and Ord's kangaroo rats. White dunes also occur in Cuatro Ciénegas, Coahuila.

On the edge of the desert are several lava fields, or malpais. These occur in the Tularosa Basin of New Mexico and the Guadiana of Durango, Mexico. The Guadiana lava flow occurred less than 10,000 years ago, but some volcanic rocks in the region derived from volcanic events 13–58 million years ago.

Precipitation in the Chihuahuan Desert falls predominantly during the summer as thunderstorms (sometimes fierce) from the Gulf of Mexico, but low-intensity rains or snow from Pacific storms contribute some moisture during the winter. The mean annual precipitation is 20–30 centimeters (extreme sites may receive fewer than 10 centimeters or more than 35 centimeters in a year), but, total precipitation notwithstanding, rainfall varies tremendously from year to year. Summers are hot (> 40°C) and, surprisingly, winters can be quite cold (-30°C) with many days below freezing.

The major drainage out of the Chihuahuan Desert is the Rio Grande (or Rio Bravo, as it is known in Mexico), which empties into the Gulf of

Mexico, thus mixing its waters with the Atlantic Ocean. This is unique among North American deserts: all others lie west of the continental divide and drain into the Pacific Ocean. The main tributaries of the Rio Grande are the Pecos River and the Rio Conchos. Two main river systems with no exterior drainage are the Rio Nazas and Rio Aguanaval near the west central edge of the desert. Most rivers experience substantial seasonal variation in water flow, with flooding following the summer rainstorms and reduced or even interrupted flow during dry periods. As with rivers of most North American deserts, those of the Chihuahuan Desert are commonly bordered by riparian forests of cottonwood, willow, and sycamore.

The vegetation of the Chihuahuan Desert is dominated by shrubs, particularly creosote bush (*Larrea tridentata*) and tarbush (*Flourensia cernua*). Grasses and succulents are also important elements. Small cacti (e.g., chollas and prickly pears of the genus *Opuntia*) are common. The northern portion of the Chihuahuan Desert lacks the spectacular columnar cacti typical of the Sonoran Desert, but some species of columnar cacti are abundant in its southern portions. This is a floristically varied and rich desert, with more than 1,000 endemic (occurring only there) plant species.

There are three main vegetation types: desert scrub, saxicolous scrub, and desert grassland. Desert scrub is the predominant vegetation type. Creosote bush is the dominant shrub, especially in lower plains. In this desert creosote bush is diploid (it is polyploid in the Sonoran and Mojave Deserts) and has straighter stems with less dense foliage. (Diploid refers to having two sets of chromosomes, polyploid is having more than two sets of chromosomes.) Tarbush and mariola (*Parthenium incanum*) are the other dominant shrubs. Tarbush is a good indicator species of Chihuahuan Desert because its distribution follows closely the borders of the desert. Other common shrubs are saltbush (*Atriplex*), whitethorn acacia (*Acacia constricta*), allthorn (*Koeberlinia spinosa*), and mesquite (*Prosopis juliflora*).

Saxicolous (rock-associated) scrub vegetation commonly grows along hillsides. Main components are the leaf and stem succulents, particularly agaves (*Agave*), yuccas (*Yucca*), sotol (*Dasylirion*), beargrass (*Nolina*), and ocotillo (*Fouquieria splendens*). Lechuguilla (*Agave lechuguilla*) is a typical Chihua-huan Desert succulent. Other succulents include barrel cacti (*Ferocactus*, *Echinocactus*) and peyote (*Lophophora williamsii*). Dried peyote buttons are hallucinogenic, and have been so heavily harvested in the U.S. portions of their range that they are nearly exterminated. Peyote is used in religious ceremonies of the Native American Church.

Desert grassland is dominated by grama grasses (*Bouteloua*), tobosa (*Hilaria mutica*), and fluff grass (*Erioneuron*). Other frequently encountered grasses are burro grass, ear and bush muhly, and Bigelow desert grass. The predominance of grasses in the Chihuahuan Desert gives it a much different character and appearance than the Sonoran Desert, where grasses are a much less conspicuous component.

One distinctive type of vegetation in the southern portion of the Chihuahuan Desert is the nopalera. In these areas prickly pear cacti (*Opuntia* spp.) grow in very dense clusters. Scattered yucca, acacia, mesquite, creosote bush, and other smaller plants occur among the prickly pears. One theory to account for the nopaleras suggests that these areas were heavily browsed by large mammals, such as camels, ground sloths, and glyptodonts, that are now extinct. The desert scrub was thus converted to a cactus desert.

Several types of specialized plants occur in the Chihuahuan Desert, exhibiting adaptations to extreme soil or rock conditions. The saline soils are sparsely vegetated, mainly colonized by halophytic (salt-tolerant) grasses, saltbush relatives, and members of the caper family. The Chihuahuan Desert supports 40 halophytic species, more than half of which are endemic. Several hundred species of gypsophilic (gypsum-loving) plants are known to inhabit gypsum soils. Some of these are quite bizarre and may have very localized distributions. Another interesting plant is the resurrection plant (*Selaginella*), which quickly sports new growth after rains, rendering whole hillsides green.

The Chihuahuan Desert contains a splendid diversity of animals. A frequently seen invertebrate is the desert millipede. This detritivore feeds on soil surface organic matter. A wide variety of invertebrate predators, including centipedes and spiders, occur in this desert (and others). Many herbivorous insects are common residents. Grasshoppers are locally abundant and include the larger horse lubber (Mexican general) and a variety of slant-faced grasshoppers that feed mainly on grasses. Ants make up another group of conspicuous insects. Harvester ants (*Pheidole, Pogonomyrmex*) are abundant consumers of seeds. Termites are important decomposers in the Chihuahuan Desert. These subterranean insects are responsible for the decomposition of a variety of dead plant parts and animal fecal material (especially cattle dung) and are important in the cycling of nutrients such as nitrogen, phosphorus, and sulfur.

More than 100 native species of fishes live in streams of the Chihuahuan Desert. Pupfish live in saline streams, in springs, and in the Pecos River. The damming of streams to create water storage reservoirs, diversion of water for municipal uses and agriculture, pollution of waterways, and introduction of exotic species have had disastrous effects on the indigenous fishes, eliminating a majority of these species. A number of exotic species of fish have been introduced, including minnows, suckers, catfishes, mosquitofish, sunfishes, and cichlids.

Among amphibians, tiger salamanders and spadefoot toads are the most likely to be seen in the Chihuahuan Desert. A high diversity of lizards are supported, including the Texas banded gecko, horned lizards, crevice spiny lizards, and whiptails. The New Mexico whiptail and Chihuahuan spotted whiptail are parthenogenetic species, species whose populations are composed solely of females that can reproduce without mating. Most of the snakes of this desert also inhabit other deserts, but one endemic species is the Trans-Pecos rat snake. Other resident snakes include the rock rattlesnake, Mexican kingsnake, Texas blind snake, and Big Bend patchnose snake. An unusual reptile is a species of box turtle (*Terrapene*) that is an aquatic resident of spring-fed bolsón lakes. All other members of this genus are terrestrial.

The bird fauna of the Chihuahuan Desert is not particularly diverse. Local areas typically contain 10–20 breeding species. Apparently there are no endemic species. Among the most typical are the scaled quail and Chihuahuan raven. Other common species are poorwills, Lucifer hummingbirds, woodpeckers and flickers, kingbirds and flycatchers, cactus wrens, thrashers, gnatcatchers, shrikes, orioles, pyrrhuloxias, house finches, towhees, and black-throated sparrows.

Approximately 120 species of mammals reside in this desert. Among the most conspicuous are the black-tailed jackrabbits, a variety of ground squirrels, mice, and woodrats; mule deer; peccaries; coyotes; kit and gray foxes; and skunks. Before the arrival of Europeans, bison, pronghorn, and bighorn sheep were abundant. Chihuahuan Desert endemics include the desert pocket gopher (*Geomys arenarius*), Nelson's kangaroo rat (*Dipodomys nelsoni*), Mexican ground squirrel (*Spermophilus mexicanus*), and Texas antelope squirrel (*Ammospermophilus interpres*).

The Chihuahuan Desert is a relatively young desert geologically. During the Pleistocene much of what is now covered by creosote bush was a mixture of pinyon pine, oak, and juniper. Desert conditions probably developed only 11,000–12,000 years ago. The boundaries of the Chihuahuan Desert are not static. The current desert scrub is bounded on the east by interior chaparral and on the west by short grama (*Bouteloua*) grassland. Desert grades into grassland in transitional zones near the borders. In fact, the desert scrub has been extending into grassland areas. Controversy exists surrounding the causes of this expansion, but overgrazing and fire suppression probably played a role. The main plants that have expanded their ranges are creosote bush, mesquite, ocotillo, and prickly pear.

One of the major prehistoric cultural traditions in southwestern North America, the Mogollon, began about A.D. 200 and extended through much of the Chihuahuan Desert. This country was home to a number of Indian tribes, most of which were hunter-gatherers. Many were nomadic or seminomadic, living in small family groups. A few tribes living along river valleys established pueblos and were more agrarian. Tribes of the region include the Chiso, Apache (Chiricahua and Mimbreño bands), Jumano (Shuman), Manso, Concho, Toboso, Salinero-Cabeza, and Coahuileo. From the early 1700s to the mid-1800s the Comanches from the southwestern plains of the United States made trips into the Chihuahuan Desert along the Comanche Trail to take livestock and foods.

Economic resources of the Chihuahuan Desert include livestock grazing and mining (lead, zinc, silver, gold, copper, iron). Several desert plants have economic importance. Wax extracted from candelilla produces shoe polish, floor wax, and chewing gum. Rubber from the guayule shrub was harvested for use during World War II when other sources became scarce, and attempts are still being made to extract commercial rubber from this plant. Major human effects, besides water diversion, grazing, and mining, include fire suppression (which influences the vegetation) and overhunting of big game (e.g., mule deer, desert bighorn, black bear).—Kristina A. Ernest

See also **AGAVE; AMPHIBIANS; ANTS; ARROWWEED; ARTEMISIA; ARTHROPODS; BAJADA; BEARGRASS; BIRDS; BLACK WIDOW SPIDER; BOLSÓN; BROMELIADS; BULBS; CACTI; CENOZOIC; CENTIPEDE, GIANT; COCHISE; CREOSOTE BUSH; DESERT GRASSLAND; DUNES; GERONIMO; GRASSES; GREASEWOOD; GROWING SEASON; GUAYULE; HALOPHYTES; HORNED LIZARD; INSECTS; JORNADA DEL MUERTO; LEGUMES; LIMESTONE; MAMMALS; MESQUITE; MEXICO, DESERTS OF; MILLIPEDES; NEW MEXICO DESERT; OCOTILLO; OVERGRAZING; PLAYA; PLANT ADAPTATIONS; PLANT GEOGRAPHY; PLEISTOCENE; REPTILES; RESURRECTION PLANT; RIO GRANDE; RIPARIAN COMMUNITIES; SEMIARID ZONES; SOILS, DESERT, CALICHE; SONORAN DESERT; SPIDERS; SUCCULENTS; TEXAS DESERT; TUMBLEWEED; UNITED STATES, DESERTS OF; YUCCA; WILDLIFE; WOODRAT**

Further Reading

Barbault, R., and G. Halffter. 1981. *Ecology of the Chihuahuan Desert*. Mexico, D.F.: Instituto de Ecología.

Bender, G. L., ed. 1982. *Reference Handbook on the Deserts of North America*. Westport, Conn.: Greenwood Press.

Brown, D. E., ed. 1994. *Biotic Communities: Southwestern United States and Northwestern Mexico*. Salt Lake City: University of Utah Press.

Grenot, C. J. 1983. *Desierto Chihuahuense: Fauna del Bolsón de Mapimí*. Chapingo, Mexico: Universidad Autónoma, Departamento de Zonas Áridas.

Griffen, W. B. 1969. *Culture Change and Shifting Populations in Central Northern Mexico*. Anthropological Papers of the University of Arizona, No. 13. Tucson: University of Arizona Press.

MacMahon, J. A. 1985. *Deserts*. New York: Knopf.

———. 1988. Warm deserts. *In* M. G. Barbour and W. D. Billings, eds., *North American Terrestrial Vegetation*, 231–264. Cambridge: Cambridge University Press.

MacMahon, J. A., and F. H. Wagner. 1985. The Mojave, Sonoran and Chihuahuan deserts of North America. *In* M. Evenari, I. Noy-Meir, and D. W. Goodall (eds.), *Ecosystems of the World, Hot Deserts and Arid Shrublands*, 12A:105–202. Amsterdam: Elsevier.

Native Plant Society of Texas. 1996. *The Chihuahuan Desert and Its Many Ecosystems: 1996 Symposium Proceedings, October 17–20, 1995, El Paso, Texas*.

Waco: Native Plant Society of Texas.

Wauer, R. H., and D. H. Riskind. 1977. *Transactions of the Symposium on the Biological Resources of the Chihuahuan Desert Region, United States and Mexico*. U.S. Dept. of Interior, National Park Service, Transactions and Proceedings No. 3.

CHILE, DESERTS OF

Narrow deserts that extend in the lowlands along the Pacific Coast of Chile from the border with Peru to as far south as 30° south latitude. These deserts are extremely arid (e.g., rainfall has never been recorded in Arica or Iquique, and only 6 millimeters fall each year in Antofagasta) and hot in the northern regions and somewhat wetter (e.g., 20 millimeters annual precipitation in Caldera and 110 millimeters per year in Coquimbo) and less extreme in temperatures at the southern limits.

As in other cold coastal deserts (e.g., Baja California, Namib), fog is an important factor in parts of the Chilean deserts. The fog is associated with the cold Humboldt Current that sweeps cold water northward from the southern polar regions along the west coast of South America. Warm winds blowing out to sea from the land blow over the cold ocean water and are cooled. This leads to the formation of fog, as the moisture in the air condenses with atmospheric cooling. This fog moves inland for several kilometers without producing rain. Rain does not fall until the moisture-laden air meets the Andes and rises, thus further cooling the air and leading to orographic precipitation (precipitation that is related to the uplifting of air masses caused by the presence of mountains). (See map of South American deserts, p. 533.)

The Chilean desert system is an extension of the Peruvian Sechura Desert to the north. In northern Chile this desert is called the Atacama Desert and is characterized by an absolute lack of vegetation from the base of the Andes to the ocean. In parts of the northern desert relatively mesic (wet) valleys dissect the arid desert. These valleys support plant communities that are composed of the trees *Prosopis chilensis*, *Prosopis tamarugo*, *Salix humboldtiana*, *Schinus areira*, *Acacia macrantha*, and *Caesalpinia tinctoria* and other shrubby and herbaceous plants.

South of Antofagasta, where rain begins to fall, masses of ephemeral plants (e.g., *Calandrinia* [family Portulacaceae], *Tretagonia* [family Chenopodi-

Hyperarid Atacama Desert habitat near Antofagasta, Chile. (Photo: P. Meserve)

aceae], and *Tarasa* [family Malvaceae]) may appear, grow, flower, and fruit over a period of only a few days, leaving seeds to await the next rain, which may not occur for many years. From just south of Antofagasta, through the region of Atacama, and to about the city of Ovalle, plant communities appear with many trees, among them *Balbisia peduncularis*, *Heliotropium stenophyllum*, and *Oxalys gigantea*. In rocky areas in this region ground bromeliads (*Puya*) are common.

The mammal fauna of the lowland deserts of Chile is adapted to live in extremely arid habitats, and only a relatively few species are able to inhabit this region. The fauna includes members of the marsupial genus *Thylamys*, foxes (*Pseudalopex*), skunks (*Conepatus*), weasels (*Galictis*), bats (*Myotis, Histiotus, Amorphochilus, Tadarida*), rodents (*Eligmodontia, Phyllotis, Akodon, Octodon, Ctenomys*), and several other species.

Birds are not abundant in this extreme desert, but there are an array of species, including doves (*Zenaida, Columbina*), parrots (*Aratinga, Forpus*), woodpeckers (*Chrysoptilus, Picumnus*), hummingbirds (*Rhodopis, Myrtis, Thaumastura, Leucippus, Hylocharis*), the black vulture (*Coragyps*), the burrowing owl (*Speotytus cunicularia*), and a number of passeriforms (the huet huet, *Pteroptochus*; mockingbirds, *Mimus*; thrushes, *Turdus*; ovenbirds, *Furnarius*; rhinocryptids, *Melanopareia*; and spinetails, *Synallaxis*).

There are also several reptiles and amphibians that occur in this desert region, including the lizards *Liolaemus, Gonatodes, Callopistes*, and *Tropidurus* and the toads *Telmatobius* and *Bufo*.

Chile's deserts also include a rich array of invertebrates, such as spiders and beetles.—Virgilio G. Roig

See also **ALTIPLANO; ANDEAN GRASSLANDS; ANDES; AMPHIBIANS; AN INTRODUCTION TO DESERTS; ARIDITY; ATACAMA DESERT; BAT; BIRDS; CACTI; CARDÓN; HUMBOLDT CURRENT; INSECTS; MAMMALS; MESQUITE; PUNA; REPTILES; RODENTS; SECHURA DESERT**

Further Reading

Cabrera, A. L., and A. Willink. 1973. Biogeografía de América Latina. Organization of American States, Monograph No. 13. Washington, D.C.

Mares, M. A. 1993. Heteromyids and their ecological counterparts: a pandesertic view of rodent ecology. *In* H. H. Genoways and J. H. Brown, eds., *The Biology of the Family Heteromyidae*, 652–713. Special Publication No. 10, American Society of Mammalogists.

Nir, D. 1974. *The Semi-arid World: Man on the Fringe of the Desert*. London: Longman.

Osgood, W. H. 1943. The Mammals of Chile. *Zoological Series, Field Museum of Natural History*. Vol. 30.

Rauh, W. 1985. The Peruvian-Chilean deserts. *In* M. Evenari, I. Noy-Meir, and D. W. Goodall, eds., *Ecosystems of the World: Hot Deserts and Arid Shrublands*, 12B:239–267. Amsterdam: Elsevier.

Redford, K. H., and J. F. Eisenberg. 1992. *Mammals of the Neotropics: The Southern Cone, Chile, Argentina, Uruguay, Paraguay*. Vol. 2. Chicago: University of Chicago Press.

CHINOOK. *See* SANTA ANA WINDS

CHOLLA

Plants in the genus *Opuntia* (subgenus *Cylindropuntia*), family Cactaceae, having cylindrical stem segments. These cacti are generally erect, many-branched, shrubby or arborescent (treelike) forms (up to five meters tall) with stems segmented into short joints of circular cross-section. Each joint results from growth during a single season. Both glochids (small bristles with barbs) and finely barbed spines are present on stems or fruits. The flowers are diurnal (open during the day) and showy, often pink or purple. The fruit may be fleshy or dry, often with spines or glochids, but the seeds are often absent or sterile. Plants reproduce vegetatively when joints become detached or chains of sterile fruits drop a section to the ground. These can then form roots and produce new plants. These

Teddy bear cholla cactus (*Opuntia bigelovii*) in the Saguaro National Monument, Tucson, Arizona (Sonoran Desert). Visible at left is ocotillo (*Fouquieria splendens*). (Photo: M. A. Mares)

spine-covered cactus joints bounce when they hit the ground, giving the cactus a reputation for "jumping." Indeed, one species, *Opuntia fulgida*, is known as jumping cholla.

Chollas are characteristic plants of the North American deserts. They are abundant and speciose and occur in the Mojave, Sonoran, Chihuahuan, Great Basin, and Altar deserts. They are typical cacti of the desert of Sonora, Mexico, where they co-occur with paloverde, brittlebush, ocotillo, bur sage, creosote bush, ironwood, mesquite, yucca, barrel cactus, and columnar cacti. Chollas also extend into Central America, the West Indies, and South America, and may occur in habitats outside of deserts, including desert grassland, thorn scrub, thorn forest, chaparral, and tropical dry deciduous forest. Chollas grow on sandy or alluvial soils (deposited after erosion by water), in arroyos (gullies), and on bajadas (lower slopes resulting from deposition of materials due to erosion by water).

Chollas are very drought resistant, more so than their congeners (related species in the same genus), the prickly pears. The spines may play a role in decreasing radiation to the plant, thus reducing its surface temperature, especially in particularly spiny species such as the teddy bear cholla (*Opuntia bigelovii*). Chollas contribute to the stability and fertility of the soil; however, they may be considered a pest on rangelands, where they proliferate in response to overgrazing by cattle. The fruits serve as forage for cattle during drought. The fruits and stems are eaten by a variety of wild animals, including peccaries and desert tortoises. Chollas play an important role in vegetative communities by protecting other cacti and nonsucculent plants from solar radiation and herbivory by small mammals. Packrats sequester cholla joints for protection of their nests and pathways. Cactus wrens, mourning doves, and roadrunners frequently build nests in cholla.

The stems are used for fuel and furniture. The roots, juice, and fruits are used medicinally by the Seris (and probably other Native Americans) for dropsy, gallstones, kidney stones, kidney pain, fever, diarrhea, and toothache.—Kristina A. Ernest

See also C$_3$ PLANTS; C$_4$ PLANTS; CACTI; CAM PLANTS; CHIHUAHUAN DESERT; COLORADO DESERT; DESERT GRASSLAND; GRASSLAND; NEW MEXICO DESERT; OVERGRAZING; PECCARY; PLANT ADAPTATIONS; PRICKLY PEAR; REPTILES; SONORAN DESERT; SUCCULENTS; TORTOISE; UNITED STATES, DESERTS OF; WOODRAT

Further Reading

Benson, L. 1981. *The Cacti of Arizona*. 3d ed. Tucson: University of Arizona Press.

Bravo-Hollis, H. 1978. *Las Cactáceas de México*. 2d ed. Vol. 1. México, D. F.: Universidad Nacional Autónoma de México.

CHUCKWALLA

Large, flattened, rough-skinned lizard (*Sauromalus obesus*; family Iguanidae) generally associated with rocky areas in deserts of the southwestern United States (southern Nevada and Utah, southeastern California, and western Arizona) and northwestern Mexico. Chuckwallas can be distinguished easily from other desert lizards of North America by a combination of their size of up to 20 centimeters snout-vent length (body length measured from the tip of the snout to the cloacal "vent"), color (generally brown, black, or tan), granular scales, stout body, and heavy, blunt tail. Males are black on the head, neck, throat, chest, and legs, with red, orange, or yellow, often in flecks, on the back. The tail of adult males is yellow or tan. Adult females are drab brown. Juveniles vary in color but usually have a black-and-yellow banded tail.

Chuckwallas are usually associated with rocky areas, often where there are large boulders. They feed on vegetation and, occasionally, insects at the edge of rocky areas. When disturbed or retreating

Chuckwalla (*Sauromalus obesus*) near Burro Creek in the Sonoran Desert of Arizona. (Photo: L. J. Vitt)

for the night, they enter narrow crevices in rocks. For defense they inflate their lungs and wedge themselves in narrow crevices from which they are nearly impossible to remove. Mating occurs in spring, and eggs are deposited from June through August. Hatchlings first appear in late August, and sexual maturity is reached in their second summer.—Laurie J. Vitt

See also **CALIFORNIA DESERT; COLORADO DESERT; CREOSOTE BUSH; HERBIVORY; LIZARDS; MEXICO, DESERTS OF; NEVADA DESERT; PHYSIOLOGY; REPTILES; THERMOREGULATION; UNITED STATES, DESERTS OF; UTAH DESERT; WATER BALANCE**

Further Reading

Abst, M. L. 1987. Environment and variation in life history traits of the chuckwalla, *Sauromalus obesus*. *Ecological Monographs* 57:215–232.

Stebbins, R. C. 1985. *A Field Guide to Western Reptiles and Amphibians*. Boston: Houghton Mifflin.

CICADA

Plant-eating (herbivorous) insect in the family Cicadidae in the insect order Homoptera. Cicadas are large insects (up to 50 millimeters) that are flylike in overall appearance. They are best known by their long larval periods (e.g., the 17-year cicada) and the loud sounds that are produced by the males. The sound varies among species, but for the most part it can be described as a shrill and nearly deafening buzz. Often cicada calls are heard late in the day during summer months. In parts of the southern United States cicadas are called July flies because they become most abundant during July.

Male calls are produced to lure females for mating. Following mating, females deposit eggs into twigs on live trees, often causing the twig to die. Some eggs remain as eggs over the winter, but others hatch during the same season, depending on species and locality. Nymphs drop off the twigs, enter the ground, and begin feeding on the roots of perennial plants. The nymph period varies among species but is generally quite long. Some of the species are periodical, with synchronized emergences occurring at 13- to 17-year intervals. When a synchronized emergence occurs there can be literally millions of cicadas in an area. The nymphs crawl up on tree trunks or the sides of buildings and metamorphose into adults. The adult stage only lives about a month. In deserts many of the cicada species are quite small, but they can be easily found by tracking down the characteristic loud buzzing sound made by the males.—Laurie J. Vitt

See also **ARTHROPODS; BREEDING SEASON; HERBIVORY; INSECTS; METAMORPHOSIS**

Further Reading

Borror, D. J., C. A. Triplehorn, and N. F. Johnson. 1992. *An Introduction to the Study of Insects*. New York: Harcourt Brace.

Borror, D. J., and R. E. White. 1970. *A Field Guide to the Insects*. Boston: Houghton Mifflin.

Dybas, H. S., and M. Lloyd. 1974. The habits of 17-year periodical cicadas (Homoptera, *Auchenorrhyncha*), 1956–1980. *Ecological Monographs* 44:279–324.

CITIES IN DESERTS

Major centers of population that have developed in the deserts of the world. Some date to biblical times, others are recent developments of modern societies. Some have millions of inhabitants, others are smaller cities of a few hundred thousand people. Some desert cities were holy cities in the remote past, others were way stations for travelers and could hardly be considered cities at all. Some desert cities (e.g., Mecca, Jerusalem) are still considered holy places, even with the encroachment of the modern, more secular, world. Today both Mecca and Jerusalem support a population of 500,000. As the world's population continues to expand and as rural populations decline, an ever-higher percentage of people are living in cities.

Some of these cities place heavy burdens on land and water resources.

Most of the large desert cities are located along major rivers in the Old World, particularly in the Middle Eastern region. Cairo, Egypt, situated on the banks of the Nile, has a population of 10.1 million people, and Alexandria, Egypt, at the mouth of the Nile, has 2.9 million inhabitants. Both cities are ancient and owe their existence to the water carried by the Nile. Similarly, Baghdad, Iraq, a city of 3.4 million people, is situated on the banks of the Tigris River. In the New World, the El Paso, Texas-Juarez, Mexico, complex, with a population of more than 2 million, has developed along the Rio Grande, as has Albuquerque, New Mexico.

Other large desert or semidesert cities have developed along coastlines where the moderating effects of the ocean minimize climatic extremes. Several large cities fall into this category, including Karachi, Pakistan (5.9 million inhabitants); Casablanca, Morocco (2.6 million); Beirut, Lebanon (1.1 million); and Lima, Peru (5.8 million). Lima obtains much of its water from runoff from the snow-covered Andes Mountains to the east, a similar strategy used by Mendoza, Argentina, a desert city of 500,000 people that obtains water year-round from runoff from the Andes Mountains immediately to the west. Jeddah, Saudi Arabia, a city of 1.2 million people situated on the coast of the Red Sea, uses reservoirs that retain rainwater as well as large-scale desalinization of seawater to provide water to its people and industry.

Phoenix and Tucson, Arizona, southwestern desert cities of 1.2 million and 0.8 million people, respectively, well illustrate the problems faced by large population centers that develop in arid regions. Both cities have grown rapidly in recent decades, and although they originally obtained their water from runoff and aquifers, the water needs of their expanding populations have proven too great to be met by these traditional sources. Thus Arizona instituted a plan (the central Arizona Project) to bring water across the desert in large canals from the distant Colorado River, a waterway that already fills tremendous demands from several states and two nations. The water has been brought to Phoenix and Tucson at great cost, both to the environment and in terms of actual costs needed to collect, transport, and distribute the water. Moreover, the quality of the water has caused problems as well, so

much so that the City of Tucson restricted the use of the water for domestic consumption and continued to rely on the use of groundwater, a rapidly diminishing resource. The aridity and heat of the desert pose challenges to population centers that develop in desert regions. There are no easy answers to meet the water needs of cities in deserts.

Some desert communities today have entertainment as their primary economic base (e.g., Las Vegas, Nevada). Although entertainment is necessary and even desirable, it is legitimately questionable whether extensive resorts should be built in desert environments, where water needs remain a severe challenge and where great environmental damage can be done to fossil water resources, or to the few waterways that exist in arid areas. For ancient peoples, deserts were areas for reflection and contemplation. Major religions were founded in deserts. In the modern world deserts, if treated with respect, could continue to be special spaces for people who wish to develop their contemplative natures there. It is a peculiarly modern dilemma that desert cities exist simultaneously at the two extremes of meeting expectations for worldly pleasure and for spiritual growth.—Michael A. Mares and E. A. Mares

See also **AN INTRODUCTION TO DESERTS; AQUATIC HABITATS; COLORADO RIVER; CONSERVATION IN DESERTS; DAMS; DESERTIFICATION; ECOLOGY; FLOOD; ISRAEL, DESERTS OF; JEDDAH; MIDDLE EAST, DESERTS OF; NILE RIVER; PRODUCTIVITY, AQUATIC ECOSYSTEMS; RELIGION IN DESERT; RIO GRANDE; RIVERS; RUNOFF; SAUDI ARABIA, DESERTS OF; WATER**

Further Reading

Allan, T., and A. Warren, eds. 1993. *Deserts: The Encroaching Wilderness*. New York: Oxford University Press.

Glantz, M. H. 1977. *Desertification: Environmental Degradation in and Around Arid Lands*. Boulder, Colo.: Westview Press.

Heathcote, R. L. 1983. *The Arid Lands: Their Use and Abuse*. New York: Longman.

Lane, B. C. 1998. *The Solace of Fierce Landscapes: Exploring Desert and Mountain Spirituality*. Oxford: Oxford University Press.

Millington, A. C., and K. Pye, eds. 1994. *Environmental Change in Drylands: Biogeographical and Geomorphological Perspectives*. New York: Wiley.

Reisner, M. 1986. *Cadillac Desert: The American West and Its Disappearing Water*. New York: Viking Penguin.

Sears, E. 1935. *Deserts on the March*. Norman: University of Oklahoma Press.

United Nations Environment Programme. 1992. *World Atlas of Desertification*. London: Edward Arnold.

CLAY. *See* SOILS, DESERT, CLAY

CLIMATE

Defined simply as the weather over long spans of time (e.g., decades) for any particular region for which statistics on various climatic factors (e.g., wind, temperature, insolation, cloud cover, humidity) are available. The word *climate* derives from the Greek *klima*, which means "inclination" and refers to the angle of the sun over the horizon. This angle varies throughout the year and is thus an important factor in climate. Climate is correlated with the collective influence of the sun, ocean temperatures, ocean currents, and the topography of the earth. These fundamental controls on climate have led to a climatic classification that uses terms such as "Arctic climate," "maritime climate," and "montane (mountainous) climate," each reflecting the major factors influencing climate.

Distinctions are also made between the general climate of a region, which is termed the macroclimate, and the local climate at a much smaller scale, which is termed the microclimate. The need to describe climate in a detailed manner for geographic, agricultural, and biological purposes has led to the development of various classifications of climate. To understand climate better, it is necessary to define several terms.

Climatic controls are factors that always affect climate. These include solar radiation, as well as its variation with latitude, the distribution of land and water on the earth, topographic relief at large scales (e.g., the presence of mountain ranges), and ocean currents. Although atmospheric circulation can be considered a basic factor in controlling climate, the movement of the atmosphere is itself controlled by these four factors. Thus wind circulation is a secondary control on climate rather than a primary one.

Climatic cycles (*climatic oscillations*) refer to long-term periods over which climate varies with some regularity, although not with strict periodicity. The term "cycle" is used somewhat loosely in climatology, and refers to the fact that a climatic event is more likely to occur at the peak of an oscillation than during the low point of an oscillation (e.g., if there is a general trend to mean annual temperatures in an area being higher than the long-term average, then it is more likely that the subsequent year will also be warmer than average). Various cycles having an influence on climate are recognized, such as cycles in sunspot activity (which vary from 7 to 17 years) and the Brücken cycle, which is a 35-year cycle between periods of cold, moist weather and periods of warm, dry weather. Curiously, cycles varying from 33 to 37 years have been described for various meteorological phenomena, including rainfall (which is reflected in tree ring formation), but the variation in the cycles is great, ranging from 15 to 50 years. Consequently such cycles are of little use in predicting weather during any particular year.

Climatic diagram refers to a graphic representation of climate, usually based on the variation in two major parameters of climate (e.g., temperature and rainfall) over a one-year period. Such diagrams are used to compare climates for overall similarities.

Climatic factors are similar to climatic controls but also include local factors that influence climate, such as pollution or smoke from a city or the extent of a surface that supports buildings rather than vegetation.

Climatic forecasts are predictions of climate for a region over the course of a year or for any portion of the year (e.g., summer) and are statistically based. Since so many factors affect the climate in any area (e.g., temperature, precipitation, wind, humidity, evaporation, sunshine), and since these interact in complex ways, it is difficult to predict the climate with any degree of certainty. Generally, climatic forecasts are made by examining long-term data on climate (e.g., two decades or more) and examining the mean data on each parameter for a particular season (e.g., average summer rainfall or average winter temperature).

Because *solar radiation* is the primary control on climate (the sun provides 99.97 percent of the energy that is involved in the earth-atmosphere system), variations in solar energy are of primary importance in determining climate. How much solar radiation is absorbed by a system is affected by the surface on which the sunlight falls. Thus if there is snow cover in an area, for example, little energy is absorbed, whereas water and highways absorb great amounts of solar energy. Absorption of solar radiation will lead to differential heating of the substrate, a factor that will affect air movements and atmospheric pressure as the air above the surface is heated or cooled. For a given area darker substrates absorb more solar energy than do lighter-colored substrates. In deserts, where soils are often light colored, there is a great deal of solar radiation reflected back to the atmosphere. This reflectivity, or albedo, may reduce cloud formation and the amount of rain that falls in an area.

Climatic controls help to generate differences in air pressure when they interact with other factors that lead to differential heating of the atmosphere. If a surface is heated to a high temperature, the air above it will also be heated and become less dense (since air expands as it is warmed) and its pressure will drop. If a nearby region has higher atmospheric pressures, there will be a pressure gradient that develops, and wind movements will occur from the area of high pressure to the area of low pressure. Information on climatic controls and associated climatic factors is used in developing climatic maps based on mean atmospheric pressures over the surface of the earth. Analyses of climatic models indicate that low pressure forms over the land in summer and high pressure forms over the oceans. In winter the significant cooling of the earth at high latitudes in the Northern Hemisphere generates areas of extreme high pressure. There are also centers of relatively constant high pressure over the oceans in the subtropical latitudes of both hemispheres, as well as a band of permanent low pressure along a line near the equator that is associated with the region of maximum solar radiation (the Intertropical Convergence Zone, or ITCZ). The great pressure differences over these large areas of the earth's surface are responsible for the movements of large air masses around the world, and this helps to determine the climate for any region.

Air masses are generally classified by their temperature and humidity, which are measured in their region of origin. For example, T = tropical (warm), P = polar (cold), A = Arctic or Antarctic (cold to very cold), M = mountainous (humid), and C = continental (dry). An example of a very special air mass that is of great importance to desert formation is the T_s air mass (T_s stands for tropical descending air). This is a mass of warm, dry air that tends to be located in the subtropical zones along western continental coasts (Baja California, Chile, Namibia) and is partially responsible for the formation of some of the world's most arid deserts.

Front is used to describe the limits between different air masses (e.g., cold front, warm front). For the great Intertropical Convergence Zone, however, which is the area near the equator where the northern and southern trade winds collide, the term "front" is not used, as in reality the zone is a phenomenon that includes a mix of clouds and storms that develop over a region where great masses of air from the Northern and Southern hemispheres converge.

Temperature is an important component of climate which has a fundamental impact on living organisms. It influences many human activities, for example, and is reflected in the types of clothing worn by people in a particular region, the energy requirements to heat or cool their dwellings, the efficiency and cost of agricultural activities, and many other factors. The interaction of temperature and moisture influences which organisms can survive in a desert, as well as the types of adaptations they must develop if they are to inhabit successfully the arid zones of the world. The variation of temperature in space and time in a region is a major determinant of the weather for that area.

Humidity in meteorological terms refers to the amount of water vapor in the atmosphere or the total quantity of water in the atmosphere in any form (gaseous, liquid, solid). The presence or absence of humidity in a particular area is a determinant of the weather in that area, as well as a determinant of the climate over time. Two aspects of the hydrologic cycle are related to humidity, evaporation and precipitation. Precipitation may be caused by many factors, but it basically requires that a volume of air be cooled until it falls below the dew point to the point of saturation, such that clouds form and precipitation develops.—Federico Norte

See also **AN INTRODUCTION TO DESERTS; ADIABATIC PROCESSES; ANTICYCLONE; ARIDITY; BAROMETRIC PRESSURE (ATMOSPHERIC PRESSURE); CLIMATE CLASSIFICATION; CLOUDS; CLOTHING; CONVECTIVE STORM; DESERTS; DESERTS, MONTANE; DESERTS, RAIN SHADOW; DROUGHT; DUST DEVIL; EL NIÑO; FOG DESERT; HAIL; HEAT; ISOHYET; LOW PRESSURE; MOISTURE INDEX; MONSOON; PRECIPITATION; PREVAILING WESTERLIES; RELATIVE HUMIDITY; ROARING**

FORTIES; SANTA ANA WINDS; TRADE WINDS; WIND

Further Reading

Day, J. A., and V. J. Schaefer. 1991. *Clouds and Weather.* Boston: Houghton Mifflin.

Gates, D. M. 1972. *Man and His Environment: Climate.* New York: Harper and Row.

Guerzoni, S., and R. Chester. 1996. *The Impact of Desert Dust across the Mediterranean.* Boston: Kluwer Academic Publisher.

Oliver, J. E., and R. W. Fairbridge, eds. 1987. *The Encyclopedia of Climatology.* New York: Chapman and Hall.

Schaefer, V. J., and J. A. Day. 1981. *A Field Guide to the Atmosphere.* Boston: Houghton Mifflin.

Schneider, S. H., ed. 1996. *Encyclopedia of Climate and Weather.* 2 vols. New York: Oxford University Press.

CLIMATE CLASSIFICATION

Process of grouping climates so as to reflect similarities in various parameters, such as total rainfall and temperature. No two places on earth have exactly the same climate, but it is possible to identify regions that are similar to a greater or lesser degree. The complexity of identifying similar climatic regions can be appreciated when one considers the great number of variables that affect the climate of an area. When so many variables are taken together, it becomes very difficult to agree on a definition of what constitutes "similar" climates. Consequently systems of climatic classification have been developed which attempt to define regions wherein there is some homogeneity of climatic elements.

The oldest climatic classification is that of the Greeks, who simply divided each hemisphere into three major zones that were defined by variations in day length. They described climates as being summerlike, intermediate, and winterlike based on the latitudinal position of the sun. Two centuries later, in the 4th century B.C., Aristotle modified the earlier description, defined the tropics of Cancer and Capricorn (23.5° north and south latitude, respectively) and the Arctic and Antarctic circles (66.5° north and south latitude, respectively) as limiting latitudes for the climatic zones (frigid, temperate, and torrid), with only the temperate zone being fit for human existence.

The next major advance in climatic classification was introduced in the 19th century (1879) by Alexander Supan, who developed a map based on mean annual temperatures and the mean temperature during the warmest month. He designated thermal zones (hot, temperate, and cold) on the surface of the earth. Supan also divided the world into 34 climatic zones that could relate climates in different parts of the globe to one another. Later, climatic variation came to include more factors than merely the position of the sun. The climatic classifications that resulted were termed polar, temperate, tropical, continental, maritime, and mountainous, as well as some others. With some variations these climatic classifications are still used today.

The climatic classifications most commonly used at present, however, were developed by Wladimir Köppen in 1918 and Charles Thornthwaite in 1931. Köppen's is the system that is most used by meteorologists because it is based on climatic data that are easily measured (i.e., temperature and precipitation). To identify climates, it uses capital and lowercase letters that refer to the climatic classifications (in German, which was Köppen's native language).

In essence Köppen divided climates into five major groups: A, for tropical rainy climates; B, for dry climates; C, for warm temperate rainy climates; D, for cold snow forest climates; and E, for polar climates. In addition, he devised subdivisions of climate that were based on precipitation and were related to vegetation. These included A_f for tropical rain forest; A_w for tropical savanna; and A_m for tropical monsoon. The C and D climates also use a third letter to refine the delineation of climate and indicate temperature variation (a = hot summers, with mean T of the warmest month > 22°C; b = warm summers, with mean T of the warmest month < 22°C, but with at least four months with mean T > 10°C; and c = cool summers, with fewer than four months with T > 10°C). The D climate also uses the third letter "d" (d = short summers and cold winters, the coldest monthly T < -38°C). Köppen's climatic classification thus transcended a simple climatic division to include the influence of climate on vegetation as well. He used various levels of temperature and precipitation variables to define a wide range of climatic (and botanic) types.

Use of Köppen's classification resulted in the ability to describe and map both world climate and world vegetation. Thus climates that were A_f described rain forests, those that were A_w described savannas, and those that were B_w described deserts. Moreover, it was possible to show this relationship based simply on two parameters (rainfall and temperature) and their variation throughout the year and in different seasons.

Nevertheless, for all of their utility, Köppen's climatic regions did not always reflect the dominant vegetation types of an area when his formulas were applied. Thus Thornthwaite (in 1931, modified in 1948) added the additional parameter of evaporation to the formulas, with an index of evaporation known as the precipitation-effectiveness index (or P-E index) that eventually was calculated using data on mean monthly temperature and mean monthly precipitation. Thornthwaite then used these indices to describe the limits of the major vegetation zones: A' = tropical; B' = temperate; C' = cold; D' = taiga (or boreal forest); E' = tundra; and F' = frost. He also developed the T-E index (based on a formulation that used mean monthly temperature values), which described the growth-limiting effects of low temperatures on plants and the growth-enhancing effects of high temperatures on plants (without reaching the very high temperatures that inhibit plant growth). Using a combination of data on precipitation and temperature, and their variation, as well as the two indices, Thornthwaite was able to develop a system of climate classification that strongly reflected the dominant vegetation in each region of the earth. The Thornthwaite system is widely used today by biologists, as it describes global vegetation patterns using only climatic data.—Federico Norte

See also **AN INTRODUCTION TO DESERTS; ADIABATIC PROCESSES; ANTICYCLONE; ARIDITY; BAROMETRIC PRESSURE (ATMOSPHERIC PRESSURE); CLOUDS; CONVECTIVE STORM; DESERTS; DROUGHT; EL NIÑO; HEAT; HOLDRIDGE LIFE ZONES; ISOHYET; LOW PRESSURE; MOISTURE INDEX; MONSOON; PRECIPITATION; PREVAILING WESTERLIES; RELATIVE HUMIDITY; ROARING FORTIES; SANTA ANA WINDS; TRADE WINDS; WIND**

Further Reading

Day, J. A., and V. J. Schaefer. 1991. *Clouds and Weather*. Boston: Houghton Mifflin.

Gates, D. M. 1972. *Man and His Environment: Climate*. New York: Harper and Row.

Oliver, J. E., and R. W. Fairbridge, eds. 1987. *The Encyclopedia of Climatology*. New York: Chapman and Hall.

Schaefer, V. J., and J. A. Day. 1981. *A Field Guide to the Atmosphere*. Boston: Houghton Mifflin.

Schneider, S. H., ed. 1996. *Encyclopedia of Climate and Weather*. 2 vols. New York: Oxford University Press.

CLOTHING

Material worn as a covering by people in the desert which can have a direct effect on thermoregulation (maintenance of body temperature). The desert can be harsh, not only because of its high temperatures, but also because of large diurnal (daily) temperature fluctuations. Proper clothing is essential for protection against hypothermia and hyperthermia. Hypothermia is a reduction in body temperature; hyperthermia is an increase in body temperature. Either condition could be fatal. A cloth covering reduces heat gained from solar radiation, reflected environmental radiation, and convection (transfer of heat energy through the movements of many particles at once, as in the flow of a liquid, i.e., heat transfer) from the surroundings. With reduced heat gain from the environment, there is also reduced evaporative water loss, which is otherwise needed to dissipate the heat that has been gained. Loose-fitting clothing is advantageous because it allows evaporation at the surface of the skin, not the cloth. A clothed person in the desert can reduce heat gained from the environment by 55 percent and reduce water loss by evaporation to about two-thirds of that which would be lost without clothing.

Loose-fitting, long-sleeved shirts and long pants in light colors (preferably white) will protect skin from sunburn and reflect solar radiation in the visible range; however, white clothing is not effective in the infrared range, which accounts for about one-half the energy of solar radiation. All colors of cloth absorb virtually all of the infrared radiation that falls on them. Therefore, white clothing will not protect the person from heat radiated from the ground. Bedouins are known to wear black robes, and it has been shown that heat gained by the Bedouins wearing either black or white robes is the same, as long as air can pass through the robe readily.

Wool is the best fabric choice in the desert environment. Nomadic Bedouins in the Middle East wear loose wool garments year-round. Wool has dead air spaces between fibers that maintain their insulating value even when wet. Furthermore, wool contains lanolin, which sheds water. Cotton, in contrast, does not shed water, and wet cotton gives 90 percent less protection from hypothermia than dry cotton. Therefore, for hiking in the desert a loosely knit wool sweater is a better clothing choice than a cotton sweatshirt.—E. Annette Halpern

See also **DESERT PEOPLES; EXPLOSIVE HEAT DEATH; HEAT BALANCE; HEAT EXCHANGE; HEAT STRESS; HUMAN PHYSIOLOGY IN DESERTS; HYPERTHERMIA; HYPOTHERMIA; PERSPIRATION; SALT BALANCE; SHIVERING; SUNBURN; SUNSTROKE; SURVIVAL IN DESERTS; THERMOREGULATION; URINE; WATER BALANCE; WATER STRESS**

Further Reading

Kerslake, D. 1972. *The Stress of Hot Environments.* London: Cambridge University Press.

Lehman, C. A. 1988. *Desert Survival Handbook.* Phoenix: Primer.

Schmidt-Nielsen, K. 1964. *Desert Animals: Physiological Problems of Heat and Water.* New York: Oxford University Press.

Shkolnik, A., C. R. Taylor, V. Finch, and A. Borut. 1980. Why do Bedoins wear black robes in hot deserts? *Nature* 283:373–375.

CLOUDS

Meteorological phenomenon wherein visible drops of water and/or particles of ice in the atmosphere form and coalesce above a particular point on the earth. The particles of a cloud are usually extremely small and cannot be discerned individually by the human eye. Therefore, clouds appear to be solid masses when in fact they are composed of enormous numbers of small particles. Clouds are distinguished from fog only in that fog is in close contact with the surface of the land or water, whereas clouds are higher in the atmosphere. Clouds may be thick or thin, high or low, and there are many different varieties of clouds. They are an important component of the weather and the climate in any particular region. And, especially important in deserts, where water is the main limiting factor to productivity, they produce rain. Although not all clouds produce rain, all clouds affect the energy balance of the atmosphere and influence wind, large-scale climate, and local weather. The condensation of water in clouds or the formation of ice crystals affects the temperature in regions surrounding the clouds, and this can have effects on the habitats below. The energy in clouds can lead to monsoonal rains in desert areas when it is dissipated as torrential rains. The opaque nature of clouds can also affect the absorption and reflection of the sun's rays, thus modifying the insolation of desert habitats.—Federico Norte

See also **ADIABATIC PROCESSES; ANTICYCLONE; BAROMETRIC PRESSURE (ATMOSPHERIC PRESSURE); CLIMATE; CLIMATE CLASSIFICATION; CONVECTIVE STORM; CYCLONE; DEW; DROUGHT; ECOLOGY; EL NIÑO; FOG DESERT; HAIL; HEAT; HYDROLOGICAL CYCLE; HYDROLOGY; INSOLATION; LOW PRESSURE; MOISTURE INDEX; MONSOON; PRECIPITATION; RELATIVE HUMIDITY; SNOW**

Further Readings

Day, J. A., and V. J. Schaefer. 1991. *Clouds and Weather.* Boston: Houghton Mifflin.

Oliver, J. E., and R. W. Fairbridge, eds. 1987. *The Encyclopedia of Climatology.* New York: Chapman and Hall.

Schaefer, V. J., and J. A. Day. 1981. *A Field Guide to the Atmosphere.* Boston: Houghton Mifflin.

Schneider, S. H., ed. 1996. *Encyclopedia of Climate and Weather.* 2 vols. New York: Oxford University Press.

COASTAL DESERTS. *See* AN INTRODUCTION TO DESERTS

COATI

Two species of mammals in the genus *Nasua*, order Carnivora, family Procyonidae (the raccoon family). *Nasua narica* occurs from the southwestern United States through Mexico and Central America to northern Colombia. *Nasua nasua* is found throughout South America east of the Andes, south to northern Argentina. Coatis are about one meter in length, approximately half being the length of the body and the other half being the tail. They can weigh up to seven kilograms. They are generally a dark rusty brown color above and buffy below. There are several small white spots above, below, and behind the eyes. The tail is dark brown with pale or buffy rings. Coatis have a long, thin face with an upturned snout.

Coatis are among the most gregarious and noisy animals of the Americas. They are active during the day and can be seen alone or in groups of up to 40. They climb well and frequently forage high in trees. They occur in a wide range of different habitats, from deserts to tropical rain forest. In deserts they tend to be found in forested ravines or scrubby areas.

Coatis feed on virtually everything that they encounter, from fruits and other plant material to invertebrates and small vertebrates. They use their long snouts to seek out food in cracks and under rocks. When disturbed they give a loud warning whoop. They are extremely amusing to watch and are tolerant of observers. Females give birth to two to six young, which they often raise in a tree. The behavior and biology of the two species differs little.—Thomas E. Lacher, Jr.

See also **CARNIVORES; CHACO; MAMMALS; MEXICO, DESERTS OF; MONTE DESERT; OMNIVORY; SONORAN DESERT; SOUTH AMERICA, DESERTS OF**

Further Reading

Emmons, L. H. 1990. *Neotropical Rainforest Mammals: A Field Guide.* Chicago: University of Chicago Press.

Gittleman, J. L., ed. 1989. *Carnivore Behavior, Ecology, and Evolution.* Ithaca: Cornell University Press.

Kaufmann, J. H. 1962. Ecology and social behavior of the coati, *Nasua narica,* on Barro Colorado Island, Panama. *University of California Publications in Zoology* 60:95–222.

Nowak, R. M. 1991. *Walker's Mammals of the World.* 5th ed. Baltimore: Johns Hopkins University Press.

COBRA

Old World snake in the family Elapidae that typically raises the anterior portion of the body off the ground and expands the neck laterally, forming a hood that is two to three times the width of the neck. Cobras are highly venomous, having nonmovable front fangs through which they inject venom. The venom, which is primarily neurotoxic (i.e., affects nerve function), is transported to the hollow fangs from the venom glands in the back of the head via ducts. There are three commonly recognized genera of cobras: *Naja,* including most typical cobras; *Ophiophagus,* the king cobra; and *Hemachatus,* the ringhals, or spitting, cobra. The latter is common in riverine habitats and rocky areas in the Namib Desert. Most cobras are moderate in size (1–1.5 meters), but the king cobra can reach 6 meters in length. Cobras feed primarily on cold-blooded prey, such as other species of snakes, but also may eat mammals and birds.

Cobras occur across a diversity of habitats, ranging from the tropical forests of Southeast Asia to the savannas (grasslands) of East Africa. None are true desert snakes, but a few occur within the boundaries of deserts, such as the arid and semiarid areas of Asiatic (e.g., portions of the former Soviet Union) as well as North African deserts. The best-known desert cobra is the Egyptian cobra, *Naja haje.* This species has been particularly important in

ancient religious history, particularly in Egypt. Snakes resembling cobras were even engraved in some Egyptian monuments. The "asp" of Cleopatra fame is believed to have been an Egyptian cobra. Another species, the yellow, or Cape, cobra (*Naja nivea*), enters the Kalahari Desert and parts of Namibia. One of the most fearsome cobras, the black mamba (*Dendroaspis polylepis*), a snake reaching almost 4 meters in length and with extremely toxic venom, is found in semiarid and arid parts of eastern and southern Africa, from Kenya to Namibia.—Laurie J. Vitt

See also **AFRICA, DESERTS OF; DEFENSIVE ADAPTATIONS, ANIMALS; INDO-PAKISTAN DESERTS; IRAN, DESERTS OF; KALAHARI DESERT; KAROO; MIDDLE EAST, DESERTS OF; NAMIBIA, DESERTS OF; PIT VIPER; POISONOUS ANIMALS; PREDATION; REPTILES; RODENTS; SAHARA DESERT; SNAKES; SOUTH AFRICA, DESERTS OF; VENOM**

Further Reading

Broadley, D. G. 1983. *Fitzsimons' Snakes of Southern Africa.* Johannesburg: Delta Books.

Mehrtens, J. M. 1987. *Living Snakes of the World in Color.* New York: Sterling.

Minton, S. A., and M. R. Minton. 1969. *Venomous Reptiles.* New York: Scribner's.

COCHISE

One of the greatest of the 19th-century Apache chiefs. Cochise's fame was second only to that of Geronimo, although historians such as Edwin R. Sweeney, the biographer of Cochise, consider Cochise (ca. 1810–1874) to be a more significant figure in Apache history.

To understand Cochise, one must understand the Apache tribe. The term "Apache" was applied to this tribe by their enemies, probably deriving from a Zuñi word, *apachu,* meaning "enemy." The Apaches used several terms to refer to themselves, including Dine'é, which translates loosely as "the people."

The Apache, like their cousins, the Navajo, are members of the southern geographic division of the Athapascan linguistic family of western Canada. They may have migrated into the American Southwest by 1400. The Southern Athapascans, in turn, are divided into seven major groupings, one of which is the western division made up of the Navajo, Mescalero, Western Apache, and Chiricahua tribes. These tribes were made up of several bands subdivided into "local groups." The bands had family, social, and cultural ties, and their relations were for the most part peaceful.

There were four bands of Chiricahua: the eastern Chiricahua (Chihenne, or Red Paint People to the Apaches), the Southern Chiricahua (Nednhi, or Enemy People to the Apaches), the Central Chiricahua (known as the Chokonen, as well as the Chiricahua, by the Apache) and the Bedonkohe (smallest of the bands). Cochise was a member of and rose to prominence in the Central Chiricahua band. Geronimo was a member of the Bedonkohes, but as this was such a small band it was assimilated into other bands in the early 1860s, the majority going to the Chiricahuas led by Cochise.

Tensions between a nomadic, Stone Age culture, such as that of the Apache, and a European culture, such as that of the Spanish and the partially Hispanicized Mexicans, were bound to be high. After Mexico gained its independence from Spain in 1821, the Mexican government, facing severe internal problems, found it difficult to continue the policies of pacification of the Apaches, which involved the regular supplying of food and other goods to the Indians. The Apaches, moreover, had become historically accustomed to ranging freely over a vast arid area that included territories located today in the northern Mexican border states of Chihuahua and Sonora and the southern portions of two U.S. border states, New Mexico and Arizona.

The United States, in a war against Mexico (1846–1848), followed by the Gadsden Purchase in 1854, incorporated the northern range of the Apaches into its own territory. After 1854 there was a repetitive pattern to Apache history. The Apaches would raid on both sides of the new border between the United States and Mexico, live in brief periods of peace negotiated either by the Mexican or American authorities, and then, after a betrayal of some sort or another, usually by Mexican or American authorities but not always so, there would be a renewal of fighting. In a larger sense the older pattern of raiding northern Mexican communities and then retreating into the relative security of the mountains of Arizona and New Mexico continued after 1854. The difference was that the Apaches faced a much larger and better armed foe in the Americans.

It was in this tumultuous border ambience of the 1850s that Cochise rose to power. He was athletic of build and highly intelligent, and his years of

fighting primarily against Mexicans in the 1830s and 1840s alongside such noted Apache warriors as Pisago Cabezón (possibly Cochise's father), Miguel Narbona, and Mangas Coloradas had honed his leadership and military skills.

Initial contacts between Cochise and the Americans were friendly. Nevertheless, the American government, prompted in part by Mexican complaints, but also by its own internal security needs, wanted to prevent further Apache raiding into Mexico. The Americans combined both diplomacy and military action to achieve their ends with the Apaches. Dr. Michael Steck was appointed by the U.S. Bureau of Indian Affairs to be the Indian agent for all the southwestern tribes. Steck pursued a policy of peaceful coexistence, but at the same time Colonel R. C. Bonneville launched a campaign in 1857 against the White Mountain Apache (Chihenne). Cochise, nevertheless, kept a relatively stable peace with the Butterfield Overland Mail Company whose major route ran through the heart of Apache country. Moreover, in the 1850s it was in the Apaches' best interests to remain at peace with the United States, since otherwise the Indians would have to wage war simultaneously against Mexican and American forces. In December 1858 Cochise met with Steck and indicated a desire to live in harmony with the Americans.

Despite occasional flare-ups along the border with both Mexicans and Americans, a fragile peace was maintained until February 1861. At this point an event occurred which was to forever alter relations between the Apaches and the Americans.

On 4 February 1861 Cochise arrived at a prearranged meeting with 2d Lt. George N. Bascom of the U.S. Seventh Infantry at Apache Pass. Bascom had been detailed to try to obtain the release of a young boy who had been kidnapped from a ranch by Apaches. Neither Cochise nor the Chiricahuas had been involved in the kidnapping, but Bascom suspected Cochise of involvement. Cochise knew nothing of Bascom's suspicions. Cochise arrived at the meeting with his brother, Coyuntura, his wife, Dos-teh-seh, two of his children, and two or three warriors, possibly nephews. Cochise's lack of suspicion was obvious from this entourage. Bascom proceeded to discuss the kidnapping. Cochise indicated that although he did not have power over the band suspected of taking the boy, he would try to obtain his release. Bascom accused Cochise of lying and informed him that he and his party would be held prisoner until the boy and some missing cattle were returned. Cochise then managed to escape by slashing his way out of the tent where the meeting was held and dodging a hail of bullets as he ran up a nearby hill. In the days that followed Bascom said that Cochise's relatives would only be released when the boy was returned. Soon the relatives of Cochise were executed by Bascom. Dosteh-seh and Cochise's young son Naiche were spared.

Bascom, by actions that can only be charitably described as ignorant and inept, had unwittingly ignited the Cochise Wars that were to last for ten years. From 1861 until 1871 Cochise and other Apache warriors attacked American troops and settlers at every opportunity. Operating out of his home base in the mountain ranges of southern Arizona, Cochise and his followers were far too knowledgeable and skillful to be trapped by the U.S. Cavalry. This was also the period of the American Civil War (1861–1865), and so American troops were not as readily available for the Indian wars as they had been earlier. The Apaches, in fact, thought that the retreating American troops in 1861 meant that their attempts to drive out the Americans had been successful. Subsequent military actions in the region by both Confederate and Union troops showed the Apaches how false their hopes had been.

Two figures emerge from this period on the American side who understood the tragic plight of the Apaches and the mistaken and inhumane practices of their fellow countrymen. They were Thomas Jeffords, a former Butterfield Company employee, and Gen. Oliver Otis Howard, an American Civil War veteran and a newly appointed peace commissioner in 1872.

Tom Jeffords, through courageous efforts and honesty, was able to establish a deep friendship with Cochise. At times, when Jeffords acted as an Indian agent, he was able to relieve some of the Apache distress on various reservations.

General Howard, who had lost his right arm in the Civil War and was a deeply religious man, had a genuine desire to negotiate a fair peace with Cochise. He met with Cochise and by early October 1872 the two parties had arrived at a peace settlement. The Chiricahuas were given a reservation on their own homeland and Jeffords was appointed agent to the Chiricahuas. Cochise promised, in return, not to raid within the United States, to stay on the reservation, and to allow travelers to move safely through Apache country.

Apache raiding across the border into Mexico continued to be a problem, however, and this raised the threat that Gen. George Crook, a fierce Indian fighter who wanted a military solution, not a peaceful settlement with the Apaches, would prevail with the War Department. Under pressure from General Crook, Cochise agreed in November 1873 to order a halt to all Apache raiding into Mexico. By now Cochise was a dying chief. He had suffered from a stomach ailment for years. Breaking with tradition because of the crisis with the U.S. government, Cochise named his son Taza as his successor and admonished him and the Apaches in general to live at peace with the Americans. Cochise died on the morning of 8 June 1874.

Within two years the United States broke its promises once again, and the Chiricahuas were uprooted and transported to the San Carlos Reservation in central Arizona. Those few Apaches who refused to follow Taza opted instead to continue fighting under Geronimo. The new round of warfare would continue until 1886. After Geronimo surrendered in that year, a majority of the surviving Chiricahuas were imprisoned in Florida and later at Fort Sill, Oklahoma. Most of them never saw their homeland in Arizona again.—E. A. Mares

See also **CHIHUAHUAN DESERT; DESERT PEOPLES; GERONIMO; HOPI; JORNADA DEL MUERTO; NAVAJO (DINE'É); NEW MEXICO DESERT; SONORAN DESERT**

Further Reading

Roberts, D. 1993. *Once They Moved Like the Wind.* New York: Simon and Schuster.

Schwarz, M. 1992. *Cochise: Apache Chief.* New York: Chelsea House.

Sweeney, E. R. 1991. *Cochise: Chiricahua Apache Chief.* Norman: University of Oklahoma Press.

COLLUVIAL DEPOSITS (COLLUVIUM)

General term referring to weathered earthen materials moved by gravity, mass movement of soil, and local wash and accumulated at the base of slopes. The materials are generally poorly sorted, consisting of a variety of grain sizes. The definition of "colluvium" may vary in different disciplines.

Geologists describe the movement of colluvial material as predominantly due to gravitational forces, but it can be accelerated by the presence of water and ice. In this context colluvial deposits may occur in deserts as steep sloping accumulations of angular fragments (talus or scree) that have formed by accumulation of weathered materials from adjacent steep, bedrock slopes. The accumulations are primarily the result of gravitational forces acting on weathered material. Soil scientists also recognize gravity as the primary agent of movement of the weathered material but also include materials moved by water not associated with defined stream channels over short distances. In this context colluvial deposits also include fine-grained material usually found at the base of hills.—Ted M. Zobeck and Dan R. Upchurch

See also **ALLUVIAL FAN; ALLUVIAL SOILS; DESERT SLOPES; DURICRUSTS; FLOOD; RIVERS; RUNOFF; SOILS, DESERT; SOILS, DESERT, LITHOSOL; SOIL TAXONOMY; WEATHERING, DESERT; WIND EROSION; WIND TRANSPORT**

Further Reading

Chorley, R. J., S. A. Schumm, and D. E. Sugden. 1985. *Geomorphology.* New York: Methuen.

Goudie, A. S. 1981. *Geomorphological Techniques.* London: George Allen and Unwin.

Soil Survey Division Staff. 1993. *Soil Survey Manual.* USDA Agricultural Handbook No. 18. Washington, D.C.: U.S. Government Printing Office.

COLORADO DESERT

Northernmost part of the Sonoran Desert, bounded on the west by the Peninsular Ranges and on the east by the California-Arizona state line, which is the Colorado River and is generally considered transitional to the larger Mojave Desert to the north. This region of southeastern California is often referred to as the California Desert and is sometimes divided into the Mojave Desert and the Colorado Desert. Although the latter is not located in the state of Colorado, it bears its name because of its proximity to the Colorado River.

The Colorado Desert occurs at low elevations along the Colorado and Gila rivers and around the Salton Sea, extending into Baja California as far south as Bahía de Los Angeles and low-lying Sonora, south to the Rio Magdalena on the east side of the Gulf of California.

Although the precipitation is similar to the Mojave Desert, the temperatures are higher in the Colorado Desert, particularly in the winter. The southern part of the Colorado Desert is moderated by the Gulf of California and rarely experiences freezing temperatures.

The physiography of this region is varied, although most of the region consists of bajadas and nearly level plains. Important geologic features include the Algodones Sand Dunes east of the Salton Basin between Yuma, Arizona, and El Centro, California, and dunes near the head of the Gulf of California. In addition, there are numerous malpais (lava flows) and volcanic hills, which create additional topographic and vegetational diversity in the region.

The Colorado Desert has less biotic diversity overall than the Mojave Desert, but there is a much greater arborescent (treelike) component in the former. The vegetation is relatively homogeneous and simple in composition over much of the region, although the upper portions of the bajadas, the low hills, and the small mountains are more diverse.

The vegetation of the Colorado Desert is dominated by creosote bush (*Larrea tridentata*), burro bush (*Franseria dumosa*), brittlebush (*Encelia farinosa*), teddy bear cholla (*Opuntia bigelovii*), and catclaw (*Acacia greggii*), with *Larrea* and *Franseria* composing 90–100 percent of the vegetational composition. Vegetation on the Algodones Dunes (*algodones* is Spanish for "cotton") includes Indian rice grass (*Oryzopsis hymenoides*) and wild buckwheat (*Eriogonum deserticola*).

The numerous arroyos and waterways in the Colorado Desert support trees that are more typical of upland bajadas in the Sonoran Desert of Arizona. These include *Prosopis juliflora, Cercidium floridum, Cercidium microphyllum, Olneya tesota, Dalea spinosa, Prosopis glandulosa,* and *Chilopsis linearis.* Saline areas often support a saltbush scrub community dominated by *Atriplex polycarpa.*

Although the Colorado River is an artificial eastern boundary of the Colorado Desert, it does mark the approximate distributional limit of the saguaro, *Carnegiea gigantea,* and *Cercidium microphyllum,* which is probably related to precipitation. Many Colorado Desert plants also occur in the Mojave and the Arizona portion of the Sonoran Desert; however, some species such as California fan palm (*Washingtonia filifera*) and *Beleperone californica* are limited to protected and isolated habitats in the Colorado Desert, where the microclimate is favorable.

Although a sizable segment of the Colorado Desert is presently protected by the Anza-Borrego Desert State Park, much of the region of the Coachella and Imperial valleys of the Colorado Desert has been transformed by extensive agricultural production of vegetables and fruits from irrigated lands.—Gary K. Hulett and Amanda Renner Charles

See also **ALLUVIAL FAN; AMPHIBIANS; ANTS; ANZA-BORREGO DESERT; ARTEMISIA; ARTHROPODS; BIRDS; BLACK WIDOW SPIDER; BOLSÓN; CACTI; CACTUS, COLUMNAR; CALIFORNIA DESERT; CREOSOTE BUSH; DESERTS; DESERTS, HOT; DESERTS, TEMPERATE; DUNES; GREASEWOOD; GROWING SEASON; GUAYULE; HALOPHYTES; HORNED LIZARD; INSECTS; LEGUMES; LIZARDS; MAMMALS; MEXICO, DESERTS OF; MILLIPEDES; OCOTILLO; PALOVERDE; PLANT ADAPTATIONS; PLANT GEOGRAPHY; REPTILES; SEMIARID ZONES; SNAKES; SONORAN DESERT; SPIDERS; SUCCULENTS; UNITED STATES, DESERTS OF; WILDLIFE; WOODRAT; YUCCA; YUMA DESERT**

Further Reading

Jaeger, E. C. 1938. *The California Deserts: A Visitor's Handbook*. Stanford: Stanford University Press.

———. 1957. *The North American Deserts*. Stanford: Stanford University Press.

MacMahon, J. A. 1985. *Deserts*. New York: Knopf.

Marks, J. B. 1950. Vegetation and soil relations in the lower Colorado Desert. *Ecology* 31:176–193.

COLORADO RIVER

System of rivers that drains approximately 637,000 square kilometers of the central and southwestern United States and northwestern Mexico and includes the Colorado River itself and its major tributaries—the Bill Williams, Gila, Green, Little Colorado, San Juan, and Virgin rivers. The Colorado River begins at 4,300 meters in central Colorado and traverses portions of Wyoming, Colorado, Utah, New Mexico, Nevada, Arizona, California, and Mexico on its 2,330-kilometer trip to the Gulf of California.

The most impressive feature of the Colorado River is the Grand Canyon in northwestern Arizona (which lies in the Great Basin Desert-Colorado Plateau Semidesert). The Colorado River carved the Grand Canyon out of desert when the area was uplifted, thereby increasing the velocity of the river and its load of gravel and rock. This increased water speed and gravel load allowed the Colorado River to create the Grand Canyon through increased erosion. The aridity of the region kept erosion and precipitation from softening the canyon walls and destroying this natural wonder.

Because the Colorado River flows through an arid region, it is a valuable resource for water. It was among the first river systems to be developed for multiple uses. More than 20 major dams have been constructed on it and its tributaries. Hoover Dam, impounding Lake Mead, was completed for the purpose of supplying electricity to southern California. The Imperial Dam was constructed to provide water for the Imperial Valley of California via the All American Canal. The purpose of Parker Dam, impounding Lake Havasu, was to provide water for Los Angeles and San Diego. The alleviation of electricity shortages in Arizona required the construction of Davis Dam. Glen Canyon Dam, impounding Lake Powell, was completed with the intent of slowing siltation downstream in Lake Mead. Two other dams, Bridge Canyon and Marble Gorge, were halted when it became known that their completion would flood portions of Grand Canyon National Park. On the Mexican portion of the Colorado River is the Morelos Diversion Dam, which provides water to the Mexicali Valley for irrigation and to the Mexican border cities of Mexicali and Tijuana. Major dams on the tributaries of the Colorado include Flaming Gorge Dam on the Green River and the Navajo Dam on the San Juan River. As a consequence of all this development, the Colorado River no longer flows into the Gulf of California. The dams have changed the ecosystem of the river, and everything from the water temperature and flooding regime to the vegetation on the riverbanks has been altered. It is not surprising, considering the large-scale development of the river, that many species of animals and plants endemic (limited) to the Colorado River system and its valleys are now threatened with extinction.—Rob Channell

See also **ARIZONA DESERT; COLORADO DESERT; CONSERVATION IN DESERTS; CONTAMINATION; DAM; GRAND CANYON; GREAT BASIN DESERT; HABITAT DEGRADATION; HYDROLOGICAL CYCLE; HYDROLOGY; INSECTICIDES; IRRIGATION DRAINAGE; PESTICIDES; RIO GRANDE; RIPARIAN COMMUNITIES; RIVERS; RUNOFF; SONORAN DESERT; WATER; YUMA DESERT**

Further Reading
Fradkin, P. L. 1968. *A River No More.* New York: Knopf.

COLORATION

Color or pattern of a particular organism's skin, pelage (fur), or plumage (feathers). Although many desert organisms display light colors, there are many others that are all black, or have parts or their plumage or pelage black. The reasons for this are complex, and more than one factor is frequently involved. In some, crypsis (blending with the environment to avoid detection) may be involved: a light animal against a light background may be more difficult for predators to see. Body temperature must be closely regulated in desert environments, and coloration is intimately related to thermoregulation (temperature balance). It is well known that black objects absorb heat, whereas light objects radiate heat. Desert environments are not continuously hot, as one is sometimes led to believe by the popular literature. In fact, night and early mornings can be quite cold, especially in deserts located in temperate zones.

Many tenebrionid beetles in the Namib Desert are black, and much study of the behavior of the beetles and of environmental temperatures was required to understand this coloration. Experiments revealed that optimal body temperature for these beetles was 36°–40°C. The beetles cannot be active during midday because surface temperatures may exceed 60°C. Early morning temperatures may be as low as 20°C, which is not warm enough for the beetles to be active; however, because they are black and therefore can readily absorb heat, they can position themselves in sunlight in the mornings and quickly attain a body temperature of 36°C. They are able to be active while it is relatively cool, and at midday they retreat to cooler areas beneath the sand. In late afternoon they again emerge, and, although the temperature is cooling, their black coloration enables them to take advantage of the last remaining sunlight to maintain their body temperature. Many lizards and other kinds of organisms interact with the desert environment in a similar way.

Among birds and mammals, the conflict between light coloration for crypsis and heat reflectance and dark or black coloration has been solved in a number of clever ways. Roadrunners, for example, have black feathers underlying outer light, cryptically colored feathers. They have the ability to deflect the outer feathers, exposing the black underfeathers. This behavior is commonly observed during cool mornings, suggesting that they are using the black coloration to increase their body heat. At other times the light outer coloration allows a degree of background matching and provides protection from predators. Some ground squirrels have a similar adaptation. Their skin is black beneath a light-colored pelage, and they use this feature behaviorally to thermoregulate by exposing their bellies to the sun.

Skin color in amphibians is mediated through hormonal changes on the dermal chromatophore unit, an arrangement of three distinct types of chromatophores (pigment granules) in the dermal layer of the skin. The melanophores are the most basal of the three types and are responsible for darkening and lightening the skin. The iridophores and xanthophores lie above the melanophores. Xanthophores are most superficial, and these contain pteridines (color-reflecting chemicals), which impart red, orange, or yellow coloration. The iridophores cause bright coloration. They are white or silvery and can reflect light of certain wavelengths. Iridophores are stacked in layers in the African frogs of the genera *Chiromantis* and *Hyperolius* and may play a role in slowing the loss of water across the skin in these frogs.—Janalee P. Caldwell

See also **AMPHIBIANS; ANIMAL ADAPTATIONS; ARTHROPODS; BEETLES; BIRDS; CROW; CRYPSIS; ECOLOGY; FROGS; MAMMALS; NAMIBIA, DESERTS OF; PIGMENT; REPTILES; ROADRUNNER; SOUTH AFRICA, DESERTS OF; WARNING COLORATION**

Further Reading

Endler, J. A. 1989. On the measurement and classification of colour in studies of animal colour pattern. *Biological Journal of the Linnean Society* 41:315–352.

Fox, D. L. 1979. *Biochromy: Natural Coloration of Living Things.* Berkeley: University of California Press.

Hamilton, W. J., III. 1973. *Life's Color Code.* New York: McGraw-Hill.

Shoemaker, V. H., S. S. Hillman, S. D. Hillyard, D. C. Jackson, L. L. McClanahan, P. C. Withers, and M. L. Wygoda. 1992. Exchange of water, ions, and respiratory gases in terrestrial amphibians. *In* M. E. Feder and W. W. Burggren, eds., *Environmental Physiology of the Amphibians*, 125-150. Chicago: University of Chicago Press.

Andean condor (*Vultur gryphus*). (Photo: M. A. Mares)

CONDOR

Two species of immense New World vultures (order Ciconiiformes, family Cathartidae). The endangered California condor (*Gymnogyps californianus*) formerly ranged throughout rocky and brushy mountainous terrain and savannas (grasslands), from southern Washington State south to northern Baja California on the west coast of North America. All remaining wild individuals were taken into captivity by 1987 to initiate a captive breeding program. The Andean condor (*Vultur gryphus*) is distributed throughout a variety of typically desolate montane habitats, including deserts, in the Andes Mountains and may range down to sea level at southern latitudes. It has become locally extinct in some areas. Condors have broad, long wings (spans may exceed three meters), and weight can reach 12 kilograms. The Andean condor is generally slightly larger than its North American counterpart. Because of their great size, condors are dependent on suitable rising air thermals to permit soaring flight.

The head and upper neck are mostly bare. Bare skin is colored orange in *G. californianus* and blackish red in *V. gryphus*. Adult plumage is primarily black. Both species have a ruff of feathers at the base of the neck. In Andean condors the ruff is prominent and white. Male Andean condors are also distinguished by a prominent comb on the top of the head. Condor diets consist almost entirely of carrion, primarily of larger mammals. Condors, like other carrion eaters, perform the important function of scavenging carcasses before putrescence.

Condors have a low reproductive rate, with a usual clutch size of one, and often breed only in alternate years. The pair bond is probably of long duration. Although both species tend to breed on inaccessible cliffs, California condors prefer protected ledges, caves, or cavities in giant sequoias, whereas Andean condors use open ledges. Incubation and parental duties are shared.—Stephen C. Lougheed

See also **ANZA-BORREGO DESERT; BAJA CALIFORNIA, DESERTS OF; BIRDS; CARRION EATERS; RAPTORS; VULTURE**

Further Reading

Brown, L., and D. Amadon. 1968. *Eagles, Hawks and Falcons of the World*. Vol. 2. London: Country Life.

Fjeldså, J., and N. Krabbe. 1990. *Birds of the High Andes*. Svendborg, Denmark: Apollo.

Gailey, J., and N. Bolwig. 1973. Observations on the behavior of the Andean condor (*Vultur gryphus*). *Condor* 75:60–68.

Snyder, N. F. R., R. B. Ramey, and F. C. Sibley. 1986. Nest-site biology of the California condor. *Condor* 88:228–241.

Snyder, N. F. R., and H. A. Snyder. 1989. Biology and conservation of the California condor. *Current Ornithology* 6:175–267.

CONSERVATION IN DESERTS

Process of retarding environmental degradation in desert regions using a variety of strategies, such as designating ecological reserves, conducting research to reduce species loss or to recover populations of declining species, and minimizing adverse human impacts on organisms and their habitats. Interest in conserving the natural environment has gained strength over the last several decades as people have become concerned about the state of the world's ecosytems. Still, deserts are often viewed as wastelands—areas to be "recovered" or "improved." Conservation efforts in many developing countries emphasize tropical and subtropical wet habitats. As a consequence, semiarid and arid habitats are given little attention as areas requiring extensive conservation efforts.

Deserts worldwide are subject to various threats. Perhaps the greatest threat is to semiarid grasslands and shrublands through overgrazing and improper agricultural practices. Irrigation of arid lands can result in salinization of the soils. Both grazing and agricultural activities have increased in recent years as the number of people living in arid and semiarid areas worldwide has increased; approximately 14 percent of the world's population—840 million people—now occupies these habitats. This has not only increased the extent and intensity of agricultural activities, it also has resulted in changes in the lifestyles of the people. Traditional activities that were often more sustainable are being abandoned for imported technologies often not suited for arid environments.

As population densities increase in arid and semiarid areas, deforestation for firewood has increased, an especially serious problem in semiarid woodlands. Deserts also contain important deposits of many valuable minerals (such as uranium, iron ore, phosphates, and copper) as well as petroleum. Although areas of exploitation of these resources are often localized, there can be total devastation of the area near the mine, and mine tailings are not always properly disposed of. Petroleum spills can contaminate large areas of desert, as occurred in Kuwait after the Gulf War or is occurring in Azerbaijan.

The earliest conservation literature in the United States focused on temperate forests (Thoreau) or the mountain west (John Muir), but the works of authors such as the late Edward Abbey (*Desert Solitaire: A Season in the Wilderness*, 1968, and *Cactus Country*, 1973) raised the consciousness of North Americans about desert conservation. The United States now has an extensive network of national parks, wildlife sanctuaries, and national preserves in arid habitats, including the recently created (1994) 607,000-hectare Mojave National Preserve.

Protected areas already exist in desert habitats in several other countries, including Argentina, Australia, Iran, Mexico, Namibia, South Africa, Tunisia, Turkmenistan, and Uzbekistan. There is at least some level of protection in most of the major deserts, but many parks are not patrolled, and protection of wildlife can be lax. The amount of land set aside is also not sufficient to guarantee the long-term viability of many species of larger, desert-adapted mammals. At the 1992 United Nations Conference on Environment and Development in Rio de Janeiro participants argued for a "Convention on Desertification" that would address issues on arid lands in much the same manner that Rio 1992 brought tropical forest issues to the fore; however, a coordinated, multinational plan to deal with

conservation in the deserts of the world is yet to be developed.—Thomas E. Lacher, Jr.

See also **BIOSPHERE RESERVE; CONTAMINATION; DESERTIFICATION; DESERT PEOPLES; DIRT BIKES; INSECTICIDES; IRRIGATION DRAINAGE; MIDDLE EAST, DESERTS OF; OFF-ROAD VEHICLES; PESTICIDES; POLLUTION; SALINIZATION; WILDLIFE**

Further Reading

Allan, T., and A. Warren, eds. 1993. *Deserts: The Encroaching Wilderness*. New York: Oxford University Press.

Arritt, S. 1993. *The Living Earth Book of Deserts*. New York: Reader's Digest Assoc.

Fisher, R. 1984. *Our Threatened Inheritance: Natural Treasures of the United States*. Washington, D.C.: National Geographic Society.

Flegg, J. 1993. *Deserts: A Miracle of Life*. New York: Facts on File; Blandford Press.

Kuletz, V. 1998. *Tainted Desert: Environmental Ruin in the American West*. New York: Routledge.

Swearingen, W. D., and A. Bencherifa. 1996. *The North African Environment at Risk*. Boulder, Colo.: Westview Press.

Williams, M., ed. 1993. *Planet Management*. New York: Oxford University Press.

CONTAMINATION

Term referring to the presence of products in the natural environment that are generated by human activities. These products can be synthetic chemicals from chemical plants and agricultural fields or natural organic material from human waste or fertilizer. The terms "contamination" and "pollution" are often used as synonyms, but there are some subtle differences between them. "Pollution" refers primarily to solid wastes, but contamination does not. "Contamination" is used to describe natural processes, such as the contamination of water by soil mineral residues or the contamination of soil with high levels of (naturally-occurring) aluminum. It is used in the context of diseases and epidemiology as well.

A primary concern in arid lands is the contamination of water supplies. When water is drawn from rivers in arid regions for irrigation or drinking water, the rate of flow in rivers declines and the rate of evaporation increases. The salinity of the water can far exceed limits for human consumption set by the World Health Organization. So much water is drawn from the Colorado River in the western

United States, for example, that the rate of flow at the mouth is essentially zero. The contamination of the water supply with excess salts can be exacerbated when combined with the runoff of agricultural pesticides and fertilizers from irrigated agricultural lands.

Many arid regions are rich in mineral resources, and mining activities result in the contamination of soils with toxic mine tailings. Air pollution can also be a problem as far as 20 kilometers downwind from copper and lead smelters. Deposition of these airborne contaminants can kill vegetation and totally alter the ecosystem.—Thomas E. Lacher, Jr.

See also **BIOSPHERE RESERVE; COLORADO RIVER; CONSERVATION IN DESERTS; DESERTIFICATION; DIRT BIKES; INSECTICIDES; IRRIGATION DRAINAGE; MIDDLE EAST, DESERTS OF; OFF-ROAD VEHICLES; PESTICIDES; POLLUTION; SALINIZATION; WILDLIFE**

Further Reading

Moriarity, F. 1988. *Ecotoxicology: The Study of Pollutants in Ecosystems.* 2d. ed. London: Academic Press.

Southwick, C. H. 1976. *Ecology and the Quality of our Environment.* New York: Van Nostrand.

Williams, M., ed. 1993. *Planet Management.* New York: Oxford University Press.

Zakrzewski, S. F. 1991. *Principles of Environmental Toxicology.* Washington, D.C.: American Chemical Society.

CONTINENTAL DRIFT. See PLATE TECTONICS

CONVECTIVE STORM

Perturbed state of the atmosphere that is associated with a parcel of air moving upward, usually due to surface heating, and the subsequent cooling of these parcels, which, if they contain appreciable amounts of moisture, will have that moisture condense and fall to the earth as rain, hail, or even snow. Convective storms may be quite short-lived over any particular point and may unleash significant amounts of precipitation over very short periods. Such storms are usually characterized by lightning and thunder. In many of the deserts of the world, much of the rainfall that is received is from convective storms that can be quite violent and that can release great amounts of water over a relatively small area. This is one reason that deserts are characterized by high rates of erosion, sudden flash floods, and large amounts of surface runoff that is rapidly removed from the system or transferred to lower elevations. Because of the great movements of air masses into and out of a convective storm, and because of the great energy flux that is associated with the storm (particularly cooling of the air as precipitation increases), such a storm can also have significant effects on the thermal profile of desert habitats. Convective storms can also bring strong gusty winds to the desert, and this also influences erosion, vegetation, heat transfer, and evaporation.

Frequently in deserts relatively isolated clouds undergo rapid vertical development with subsequent thunder and lightning and rainfall, and these are known as cumulonimbus clouds. Such clouds can form as long lines of isolated storms extending for more than 100 kilometers. These storms are born and develop as humid air is heated and begins to rise, becoming unstable as it does so. Factors of topography and differential heating can affect this rising column of air. Usually many factors interact to form a convective storm. In some areas, particularly on the grasslands of the United States, convective storms may become extremely violent and produce tornadoes, some of the most destructive storms in nature. Tornadoes are not common in desert areas, however.—Federico Norte

See also **ADIABATIC PROCESSES; AN INTRODUCTION TO DESERTS; ANTICYCLONE; ARIDITY; BAROMETRIC PRESSURE (ATMOSPHERIC PRESSURE); CLIMATE; CLIMATE CLASSIFICATION; CLOUDS; DESERTS; DESERTS, MONTANE; DESERTS, RAIN SHADOW; DROUGHT; DUST DEVIL; EL NIÑO; FLOOD; HABOOB; HAIL; HEAT; ISOHYET; LOW PRESSURE; MOISTURE INDEX; MONSOON; PRECIPITATION; PREVAILING WESTERLIES; RELATIVE HUMIDITY; ROARING FORTIES; RUNOFF; SANTA ANA WINDS; TRADE WINDS; WEATHERING, DESERT; WIND**

Further Reading

Day, J. A., and V. J. Schaefer. 1991. *Clouds and Weather.* Boston: Houghton Mifflin.

Oliver, J. E., and R. W. Fairbridge, eds. 1987. *The Encyclopedia of Climatology.* New York: Chapman and Hall.

Schaefer, V. J., and J. A. Day. 1981. *A Field Guide to the Atmosphere.* Boston: Houghton Mifflin.

Schneider, S. H., ed. 1996. *Encyclopedia of Climate and Weather.* 2 vols. New York: Oxford University Press.

CONVERGENT EVOLUTION

Similarity in form that does not necessarily derive from a common ancestral genetic heritage but occurs because of similar pressures of natural selection acting on organisms over time (such similar species would be considered ecological equivalents). Thus, for example, the animals that develop in two desert areas on different continents having plants with similar life forms and ecology face similar evolutionary challenges. These similar selective pressures are derived not only from the similar climates and landforms but from the similar life forms of the plants as well. In such a situation the pressures of natural selection are likely to be similar at several different scales, leading to the development of similar ecological, morphological, physiological, and other traits in the faunas that develop in each desert. When two animal or plant lineages have been reproductively isolated for a considerable period (millions of years) and yet resemble one another in form and/or function, we speak of the processes that have produced similar forms as resulting from convergent evolution.

To use an example within desert rodents, the similarity in form and function of the bipedal (animals that move primarily by using the hind feet), ricochetal (hopping) locomotion of jerboas compared to similar locomotor modes in kangaroo rats is considered to be the result of convergent evolution. Jerboas belong to the family Dipodidae, and kangaroo rats are members of the family Heteromyidae. The families are not closely related, and the morphologically more conservative members of each family are adapted to mesic (wet) habitats and are not bipedal; however, in the evolutionary history of both lineages there has been a tendency to exploit a diverse array of arid habitats. Thus similar selective pressures in Old World deserts and in New World deserts have shaped the form of the desert-dwelling lineages—in this case, jerboas and kangaroo rats. They resemble one another in body proportions and locomotor type, even though they differ in diet and other traits.

This argument can be extended to include the evolution of bipedal locomotion exhibited by even more distantly related mammals living in xeric (dry) landscapes, including the southern African springhare (*Pedetes*) and the desert-inhabiting kangaroos (Macropodidae). There may be convergences in morphology, physiology, and behavior. Plant, animals, and other organisms can all develop a host of similar characteristics that develop over time due to the force of convergent evolution.—John F. Eisenberg

See also **ANIMAL ADAPTATIONS; BIPEDALITY; BURROWING ANIMALS; DEFENSIVE ADAPTATIONS, ANIMALS; ECOLOGY; GOPHER; KANGAROO; KANGAROO RAT; KANGAROO MOUSE; MAMMALS; PARALLEL EVOLUTION; PHYSIOLOGY; RODENTS; SPRINGHARE; TUCU-TUCO; TYMPANIC BULLAE; WATER BALANCE**

Further Reading

Degan, A. A. 1997. *Ecophysiology of Small Desert Mammals*. New York: Springer.

Maclean, G. L. 1996. *Avian Adaptations to Deserts of the Northern and Southern Hemispheres: A Comparison*. Perth, Western Australia: Curtin University of Technology.

Mares, M. A. 1993. Desert rodents, seed consumption, and convergence: The evolutionary shuffling of adaptations. *BioScience* 43:372–379.

Mares, M. A. 1993. Heteromyids and their ecological counterparts: a pandesertic view of rodent ecology. *In* H. H. Genoways and J. H. Brown, eds., *The Biology of the Family Heteromyidae*, 652–713. Special Publication No. 10, American Society of Mammalogists.

Schluter, D., and R. E. Ricklefs. 1993. Convergence and the regional component of species diversity. *In* R. E. Ricklefs and D. Schluter, eds., *Species Diversity in Ecological Communities*, 230–240. Chicago: University of Chicago Press.

Simpson, G. G. 1949. *The Meaning of Evolution*. New Haven: Yale University Press.

CORAL SNAKE

New World venomous snakes in the genera *Micrurus* and *Micruroides* (family Elapidae), usually with highly contrasting rings of various combinations of red, black, and yellow. Fifty-three species are recognized in the genus *Micrurus*, and one species is recognized in the genus *Micruroides*. Coral snakes are distributed across a variety of habitats, from the southeastern United States to Argentina. The greatest number of species is found in the tropical forests of Central and South America. Coral snakes can be active at any time of day or night. In deserts they are usually nocturnal (active at night), whereas in tropical forests they may be either diurnal (active during the day) or nocturnal.

The biology of coral snakes is as varied as the habitats in which they live. Most feed on elongate vertebrates, including other reptiles, amphibians, and fishes. Coral snakes are believed to be the model in a fascinating mimicry complex in which

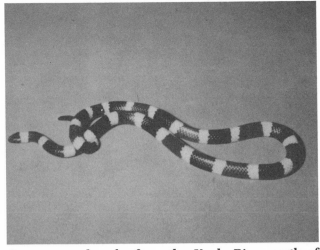

Sonoran coral snake from the Verde River north of Mesa, Arizona (*Micrurus euryxanthus*). (Photo: L. J. Vitt)

many nonvenomous snakes are thought to gain an evolutionary advantage in terms of predation by having color patterns similar to the highly venomous coral snakes. Thus predators are fooled into perceiving the nonvenomous snake as the dangerous coral snake, thus allowing the nonpoisonous snake to escape predation.

Coral snakes, like other snakes in the family Elapidae, possess fixed, nonmovable fangs located at the front of the upper jaw. The hollow fangs deliver neurotoxic venom (venom that affects nerve function) through ducts from venom glands located on either side of the head. The venom is used for subduing prey and in defense. Envenomation (injecting venom) of humans by coral snakes causes progressive muscle paralysis, and the symptoms can take considerable time to develop. In severe cases death can occur from respiratory arrest.—Laurie J. Vitt

See also **ARIZONA DESERT; COLORADO DESERT; DEFENSIVE ADAPTATIONS, ANIMALS; MEXICO, DESERTS OF; MONTE DESERT; POISONOUS ANIMALS; REPTILES; SNAKES; SONORAN DESERT; SOUTH AMERICA, DESERTS OF; VENOM**

Further Reading

Campbell, J. A., and W. W. Lamar. 1989. *The Venomous Reptiles of Latin America*. Ithaca: Cornell University Press.

Greene, H. W., and R. W. McDiarmid. 1981. Coral snake mimicry: Does it occur? *Science* 213:1207–1212.

Minton, S. A., and M. R. Minton. 1969. *Venomous Reptiles*. New York: Scribner's.

Roze, J. A. 1996. *Coral Snakes of the Americas: Biology, Identification, and Venoms*. Malabar, Fla.: Krieger.

Isolated leafy cottonwood (*Populus*) along the Gila River in New Mexico. (Photo: D. Beck)

COTTONWOOD

Tree of the willow family (Salicaceae) with a broad crown and drooping branches, including several species in the genus *Populus*. Cottonwoods commonly grow along streams and rivers, thus surviving in the deserts of North America by evading drought rather than by possessing xeric (arid) adaptations. The large, spade-shaped or linear leaves are winter deciduous (the leaves are lost in winter). The flowers, clustered in separate female and male catkins (inflorescence of unisexual flowers), appear prior to, or concurrent with, leaf development and are wind pollinated. The fruit is a simple, dry capsule, with tufted, silky seeds. The ease with which cottonwoods can be propagated from branch cuttings has resulted in their introduction to areas outside their native range.

Fremont cottonwood, *Populus fremontii*, is abundant around springs, along canyons on desert slopes, and in bottomlands. This species has a broad distribution across the deserts of the western United States and northern Mexico at elevations up to 2,000 meters. Fremont cottonwood also occurs in chaparral, pinyon-juniper woodland, and grass-lands but requires water close to its root zone.

Narrowleaf cottonwood, *Populus angustifolia*, is smaller than Fremont cottonwood and occurs at higher elevations. It grows along streams in the Sonoran, Chihuahuan, and Great Basin deserts but also extends into nondesert areas in the northern United States and Canada. Narrowleaf cottonwoods are one of the preferred foods of beavers. Other species of cottonwood (*alamo* in Spanish) are *Populus acuminata* (lanceleaf cottonwood), *Populus trichocarpa* (black cottonwood), *Populus dimorpha*, and *Populus monticola*.

The wood of cottonwoods is soft and subject to breaking during windstorms but can be used for fencing. Native Americans use the leaves, cortex, sprouts, and roots for chest ailments, stomach cramps, inflammation, dysentery, kidney pain, burns, scurvy, and ulcers. Pima Indians used the branches for baskets and ate the catkins. Cotton-woods provide browse for cattle. The carpenter bee (*Xylocarpa californica*) tunnels through the wood of cottonwoods and other trees.—Kristina A. Ernest

See also **DESERT SLOPES; DESSICATION-RESISTANT SPECIES; ECONOMIC VALUE OF DESERT PRODUCTS; FOREST; LEAVES; PERENNIAL PLANTS; PHREATOPHYTES; PLANT ADAPTATIONS; PLANTS; RIO GRANDE; RIPARIAN COMMUNITIES**

Further Reading

Benson, L., and R. A. Darrow. 1981. *Trees and Shrubs of the Southwestern Deserts*. Tucson: University of Arizona Press.

Kearney, T. H., and R. H. Peebles. 1960. *Arizona Flora*. Berkeley: University of California Press.

Lanner, R. M. 1984. *Trees of the Great Basin: A Natural History*. Reno: University of Nevada Press.

COUNTERCURRENT HEAT EXCHANGE

Heat transfer between arterial and venous blood when the vessels lie in close proximity to one another and the blood flow in each vessel is in opposite directions (countercurrent). Heat moves by conduction (transfer of heat energy from particle to particle) from the regions of high temperature, typically the artery, to the regions of low temperature, typically the vein. Thus cool venous blood returning from peripheral structures (e.g., limbs in a cool environment) may be rewarmed to a higher temperature by heat coming from warmer arterial

blood on its way to the periphery. This conserves the amount of metabolic heat that otherwise would be expended to reheat the cool venous blood. Countercurrent heat transfer can also occur in hot climates, with the heat exchange occurring between venous blood warmed to high temperatures and arterial blood cooled by central evaporative cooling (i.e., panting). In either case there is a decrease in the effect of the environmental temperature on the animal.

The amount of heat transfer is dependent on the rate of blood flow and the degree of contact between arteries and veins, which is enhanced in some animals by an extensive network of fine vessels called a rete mirabile (literally, wonderful net). In many animals the countercurrent system can be bypassed if it is advantageous for the animal to exchange heat with its environment rather than retain it in the body. The bypass is made possible by the existence of two sets of veins, one deep and part of the countercurrent exchange system, the other superficial and not in close proximity to the major arteries. Appropriate vasomotor adjustments (muscular adjustments to vessel thickness) control the volume of blood returned through the alternate return vessels, thereby precisely regulating heat transfer with the environment. For example, an animal exposed to a cold night in the desert would primarily return venous blood from appendages through the deep countercurrent veins. In the warm portion of the day the superficial veins would be used to dissipate heat from the hotter body core to the cooler environment. In the hottest portion of the day, when the animal is forced to use evaporative cooling, the countercurrent veins would again be used.

Some animals in hot environments make use of countercurrent heat transfer to keep specific structures cool. For example, the 100-kilogram oryx is extremely tolerant of hot, dry conditions, primarily because it can withstand body temperatures of 46°C (115°F). It does this by keeping the brain temperature 3°C cooler using a countercurrent heat transfer between warm arterial and cool venous blood. The external carotid artery supplying the brain loses heat as it passes through a complex network, the carotid rete, filled with venous blood cooled because of evaporation from the mucous membranes in the nasal passages. The carotid rete plays a role in reducing brain temperatures of many mammals.

In the North American kangaroo rat, a small desert rodent, water is conserved as a result of a countercurrent heat transfer in the nasal passage. During inhalation the walls of the nasal passageway are cooled by evaporation from the nasal surfaces. During exhalation, as warm moist air from the lungs passes over these cool surfaces, the air is cooled. Consequently water in the exhaled air condenses as it cools and remains in the body. Thus the evaporative water loss is remarkably low. Countercurrent heat transfer occurs here because of temporal separation, as opposed to spatial separation, of arterial and venous blood flow.—David S. Hinds

See also **ANIMAL ADAPTATIONS; CAMEL; ELEPHANT; GEMSBOK; HEAT BALANCE; HEAT EXCHANGE; HEAT STRESS; JACKRABBIT; KIDNEYS; RENAL PAPILLA; THERMOREGULATION; WATER BALANCE**

Further Reading

Hill, R. W., and G. A. Wyse. 1989. *Animal Physiology.* New York: Harper and Row.

Folk, G. E., Jr. 1974. *Introduction to Environmental Physiology.* 2d ed. Philadelphia: Lea and Febiger.

Schmidt-Nielsen, K. 1964. *Desert Animals: Physiological Problems of Heat and Water.* New York: Oxford University Press.

———. 1972. *How Animals Work.* London: Cambridge University Press.

COUNTERSHADING

Process of optical flattening that confers camouflage to animals. When sunlight illuminates an object from above, the object will be brightest on top (dorsum) and will gradually shade to a darker color toward the bottom (ventrum). This shading gives the object depth and allows the viewer to distinguish its shape. Thus even if an animal is exactly, but uniformly, the same color as the substrate, it will be easily visible when illuminated.

Most animals are darker above than they are below. When they are illuminated from above, the darker back is lightened and the lighter belly is shaded. The animal thus appears to be of a single color (appears monochromatic) and easily blends in with the substrate. This pattern of coloration, or countershading, destroys the impression of shape in the organism and allows the animal to blend in with its background.

Countershading is most common in organisms that are active during the day and are subject to bright sunlight. The most dramatic countershading occurs in marine and freshwater fishes. An interesting case is the Nile catfish (*Synodontis batensoda*), which swims upside down. The belly is colored dark, and the back is light; perfect countershading in reverse.

Countershading is observed in arid-land animals that inhabit regions with low vegetation. Many species common to arid grasslands have countershading (e.g., lions, cheetahs, antelopes, and some small mammals). Animals that occur on bright sandy substrates (and are active during the day) often have less pronounced countershading because the sand reflects light onto the belly during daylight.—Thomas E. Lacher, Jr.

See also **ANIMAL ADAPTATIONS; BIPEDALITY; CHEETAH; COLORATION; CRYPSIS; JERBOA; KANGAROO RAT; OWL; PIGMENT; PREDATION; RODENTS**

Further Reading

Fogden, M., and P. Fogden. 1974. *Animals and Their Colors.* New York: Crown.

Herán, I. 1976. *Animal Coloration: The Nature and Purpose of Colours in Vertebrates.* London: Hamlyn.

COYOTE

Medium-sized mammalian carnivore of the dog family, Canidae, with rather long, gray hair tinged with reddish or black. Adults weigh 8–20 kilograms. Females are slightly smaller than males, and desert coyotes are generally smaller than are individuals from other regions. The scientific name, *Canis latrans*, means "barking dog." The common name derives from the Aztec *coyotyl*.

Coyotes are generalist feeders whose diet includes rodents, rabbits, deer, and other vertebrates; insects and other invertebrates; carrion; fruits; and grasses and other vegetation. Lagomorphs (rabbits, hares) account for a large proportion of the diet in some regions. Coyotes are less specialized in diet and other features than are other members of the genus *Canis*. They can be active during the day or at night. They often dig holes to use as dens but may also occupy burrows dug by other mammals, or situate their dens in brush piles, logs, shrubs, or abandoned buildings. The breeding season varies geographically but generally occurs during winter months. Females undergo estrus (period of reproductive activity) only once each year,

Coyote (*Canis latrans*) in a cactus scrubland near Red Rock, New Mexico. (Photo: D. Beck)

between January and March. After a gestation period of 60–63 days, females give birth to a litter of four to six pups, on average (a litter of up to 17 pups has been reported). The altricial (helpless) pups are fed by both male and female. Young are weaned when four to seven weeks old, and most disperse from the territory of their parents during the first fall. Males and females can reproduce in their first winter. Wild coyotes generally live 6 to 8 years, but they have been known to live up to 14 years. Coyotes can hybridize with dogs and wolves.

This canid may travel widely and have a fairly large home range (area in which the animal carries out its normal activities): approximately 20–68 square kilometers for males and 8–16 square kilometers for females. Although they often travel alone or in pairs, coyotes can be very social. They sometimes live in temporary or permanent groups of three to seven individuals. Packs may defend territories of five to seven square kilometers. One advantage of group living is the enhanced ability to take larger prey. The communication system of coyotes is one of the most complex known for mammals. Especially well developed are their visual and vocal communication. The morning and evening yips and howls of coyotes are a familiar sound of the deserts of the American Southwest.

Coyotes live in a variety of habitats, including woodlands, forest, grasslands, and cultivated areas. They are among the most abundant and conspicuous carnivores of the North American deserts. Historically coyotes primarily inhabited the western grasslands, but they now range from Alaska across most of Canada and the continental United States to Mexico and Central America. Range expansion was promoted by the reduction in wolf populations and by forest clearing, especially in the late 1800s to early 1900s but continuing today.

Because they prey on livestock, coyotes have long been persecuted by humans. Common control methods are trapping, shooting, and poisoning; however, most control efforts have not been successful. Coyotes are trapped for their fur, despite its relatively low economic value.—Kristina A. Ernest

See also **CARNIVORES; CHIHUAHUAN DESERT; DESERT GRASSLAND; FOX; GREAT BASIN DESERT; HOWLING; MAMMALS; MOJAVE DESERT; OMNIVORY; PRAIRIE; PRAIRIE DOG; PREDATION; ROADRUNNER; SONORAN DESERT**

Further Reading

Bekoff, M. 1978. *Coyotes: Biology, Behavior, and Management.* New York: Academic Press.

Bekoff, M., ed. 1977. Canis latrans. *Mammalian Species* 79:1–9.

Dolnick, E. H., R. L. Medford, and R. J. Schied. 1976. *Bibliography on the Control and Management of the Coyote and Related Canids with Selected References on Animal Physiology, Behavior, Control Methods, and Reproduction.* Beltsville, Md.: Agricultural Research Service.

CREOSOTE BUSH

Dominant shrub (family Zygophyllaceae, genus *Larrea*) of the North and South American warm deserts, characterized by resinous, olive green leaves that remain on the plant even after turning yellow or brown during periods of drought. In North American deserts *Larrea tridentata* is generally 0.5 to 2 meters tall. The numerous ascending or upright stems grow from the root crown at the soil surface, commonly forming an inverted cone shape. The five-petaled yellow flowers are abundant on these shrubs after warm rains.

Technically creosote bush (its common name) occurs only in the United States and Mexico (where it is called *gobernadora* or *hediondilla*), but it is closely related to similar shrubs in the Monte Desert of Argentina and arid and semiarid regions of Chile, Peru, and Bolivia. (Some authors also refer to other members of the genus *Larrea* as "creosote bush," whether or not it grows in North America.) *Larrea* provides an excellent example of a transtropical disjunct distribution, divided by a

Creosote bush (*Larrea cuneifolia*) flat in the Monte Desert of northwestern Argentina. (Photo: M. A. Mares)

large gap across Central America and northern South America. *Larrea* probably evolved in South America, where there are four species. The distribution of *Larrea tridentata* coincides closely with the distribution of the warm deserts of North America and covers an elevational range from -73 to 2,625 meters. The three chromosomal races—diploid (or normal number of chromosomes, which are in two sets) in the Chihuahuan Desert, tetraploid (doubled complement, or four sets of chromosomes) in the Sonoran Desert, and hexaploid (tripled complement, or six sets of chromosomes) in the Mojave Desert—are associated with distinct morphological and physiological traits. Creosote bush, like several other desert shrubs, has been expanding its range into desert grassland areas during the past century. Potential factors in this distributional change are warming and drying climate, livestock grazing, and fire suppression.

Creosote bush is perhaps the most drought-tolerant plant of North America's deserts, remaining productive even during hot, dry periods. Features contributing to this drought tolerance include the presence of both a tap (deep) and lateral roots, small resin-coated leaves, desiccation-tolerant cells, and the ability to withstand very low internal water content. This hardy shrub grows in diverse soil types, from rocky volcanic slopes and soils with a hardened caliche layer to sand dunes and wash channels. Typical habitats include sloped bajadas (alluvial fans) and well-drained sandy flats. Creosote bush often occurs on alkaline limestone-

derived soils but is susceptible to phosphorus toxicity in acidic soils.

Creosote bush occurs in various plant communities, as the dominant woody perennial in desert grasslands and creosote "flats," as a codominant with other perennials such as bur sage, or in mixed communities with paloverde, mesquite, acacia, saguaro, barrel cactus, cholla, prickly pear, rabbit brush, bur sage, brittlebush, or ocotillo. Creosote bush acts as a nurse plant, providing protection for germinating cacti and annual plants that grow in its shade. Where creosote bush grows as essentially a monoculture (plant community where mainly a single plant is present), shrubs appear to be equally spaced. Explanations for this pattern of distribution between plants have been controversial. Is this spacing caused by competition for water, by toxic chemicals secreted by the roots, or by faulty perceptions of clumps of shrubs as individual plants? Such questions have not yet been answered satisfactorily.

This species may reproduce either asexually, via clones formed by underground root extensions, or sexually, via seeds. Clones in the Mojave Desert form "fairy rings," starting from a central plant that dies back as younger, genetically identical clones grow progressively farther out from the center. One large clone in the Mojave Desert, estimated to be almost 11,000 years old, may be the world's oldest living organism.

Flowering is opportunistic: a shrub may bloom several times a year if rain is adequate. Flowers are pollinated by a variety of bees, wasps, flies, and beetles, and perhaps also by birds. The numerous small, white, hairy fruits may remain on the plant until the following year, but many are consumed by insects, pocket mice, kangaroo rats, and ground squirrels.

The leaves and stems are eaten by a variety of insects, many of which feed exclusively on creosote bush. One such insect, the lac scale, produces a lacquerlike substance used by Native Americans for sealing and patching pottery and baskets. The desert iguana and chuckwalla are exceptional among reptiles in their consumption of the flowers and fruits of creosote bush. The generalist desert packrat (*Neotoma lepida*) and black-tailed jackrabbit (*Lepus californicus*) eat the stems and leaves during dry periods. In arid areas of Argentina creosote bush leaves and stems are eaten by burrowing rodents (tucu-tuco) of the genus *Ctenomys*, South American equivalents of North American pocket gophers, and the unusual chinchilla rat of the South American Andes, *Abrocoma* (family Abrocomidae), has been shown to be a creosote bush specialist.

After rain in creosote bush flats, a distinctive aroma fills the air. Volatile oils on the leaves and stems of creosote bush are responsible. Several hundred chemical compounds are produced by this plant, functioning as antioxidants, protectors from radiation, antidesiccants, and herbivore deterrents. Perhaps because of this great chemical diversity, creosote bush has been used for a wide variety of medicinal purposes by Native Americans. *Larrea* is used as an emetic, antiseptic, expectorant, and pain reliever and in the treatment of venereal disease, tuberculosis, sores and wounds, and cancer. Extracts are currently being investigated for potential uses against AIDS. Creosote bush is known in some regions as greasewood, a name usually referring to plants in the genus *Sarcobatus*.—Kristina A. Ernest

See also **ALLUVIAL FAN; BAJA CALIFORNIA, DESERTS OF; CALIFORNIA DESERT; CHACO; CHIHUAHUAN DESERT; CHUCKWALLA; DEATH VALLEY; DESERT GRASSLAND; ECONOMIC VALUE OF DESERT PRODUCTS; GREASEWOOD; HERBIVORY; IGUANA, DESERT; JACKRABBIT; MOJAVE DESERT; MONTE DESERT; NEW MEXICO DESERT; PLANT ADAPTATIONS; SONORAN DESERT; TEXAS DESERT; TUCU-TUCO**

Further Reading

Campos López, E., T. J. Mabry, and S. Fernández Tavizon, eds. 1981. *Larrea*. Mexico City: Consejo Nacional de Ciencia y Tecnología. (In English)

Dalton, P. D. 1961. Ecology of the creosotebush *Larrea tridentata* (DC.) Cov. Ph.D. dissertation, University of Arizona.

Mabry, T. J., J. H. Hunziker, and D. R. DiFeo Jr., eds. 1977. *Creosote Bush: Biology and Chemistry of Larrea in New World Deserts*. Stroudsburg, Pa.: Dowden, Hutchinson, and Ross.

McCraw, D. J. 1985 A phytogeographic history of *Larrea* in southwestern New Mexico illustrating the historical expansion of the Chihuahuan Desert. M. A. thesis, University of New Mexico.

Nabhan, G. P. 1985. *Gathering the Desert*. Tucson: University of Arizona Press.

CREPUSCULAR

Type of rhythmic or cyclic activity pattern wherein animals are active during the twilight hours (dusk and dawn). This activity cycle, because it is based on a 24-hour clock, also is termed a circadian rhythm. In deserts animals that confine their activity to dawn and/or dusk avoid the stresses associated with high temperatures. Cycles of activity may show a seasonal shift or be correlated with metabolic rate. Activity cycles differ greatly between species. The temporal spacing of activity may allow the coexistence of more species by reducing the competition for resources between animals that are similar ecologically if the resources differ at different times. Carnivores or predators may adjust their circadian cycle to that of their prey. For example, coyotes (*Canis latrans*) are crepuscular because their primary prey, rabbits and rodents, are active mainly at dusk and dawn.—Janet K. Braun

See also **ACTIVITY CYCLES, ANIMALS; ANIMAL ADAPTATIONS; NOCTURNAL**

CRETACEOUS

Geologic period at the end of the Mesozoic era spanning the time from 146 million years ago until 65 million years ago. The term also refers to the system of rocks that correspond with this time period. The Cretaceous is perhaps best known as the end of the Age of Reptiles, terminating with the extinction of many groups of organisms, including the dinosaurs. It is also important as the time during which angiosperms (flowering plants) underwent their greatest evolutionary radiation. At the same time there was a great diversification of many major groups of insects.

The Cretaceous was a time when climatic conditions were warm and stable around the world. Latitudinal temperature gradients were low, and the earth was probably ice-free or nearly so, with sea levels possibly higher than at any other time during the last 600 million years. Flora and fauna were remarkably similar over much of the earth, with subtropical plants and animals existing at latitudes 70° from the equator.—Nicholas J. Czaplewski

See also **AN INTRODUCTION TO DESERTS; DESERTS; EOCENE; FOSSILS; MIOCENE; NEOGENE; OLIGOCENE; PALEOCENE; PALEOCLIMATE; PLATE TECTONICS; PLEISTOCENE; PLIOCENE; QUATERNARY; RECENT (HOLOCENE); TERTIARY**

Further Reading

Levin, H. L. 1988. *The Earth Through Time*. 3d ed. Philadelphia: Saunders.

Rogers, J. J. W. 1993. *A History of the Earth*. Cambridge: Cambridge University Press.

CROTALUS

Generic name for most species of rattlesnakes (reptile family Viperidae, subfamily Crotalinae). There are two genera of rattlesnakes, *Crotalus* and *Sistrurus*. *Sistrurus* contains the pigmy rattlesnakes and the massasauga. All other rattlesnakes are in the genus *Crotalus*. With the exception of the desert massasauga (*Sistrurus catenatus edwardsii*), all rattlesnakes found in deserts are in the genus *Crotalus*. Rattlesnakes can easily be distinguished from all other snakes by the presence of a cornified (hardened) structure on the tail made of overlapping scales that makes a characteristic buzzing sound, or rattle. The genus *Crotalus* can be readily distinguished from the genus *Sistrurus* by the structure of head scales. Rattlesnakes in the genus *Crotalus* have numerous small, irregular scales on the dorsal surface of the head, whereas rattlesnakes in the genus *Sistrurus* have nine large scales on the dorsal surface of the head.

There are 26 species in the genus *Crotalus*, many of which occur in deserts of the southwestern United States and northern Mexico (although rattlesnakes of this genus extend as far south as the deserts and drylands of central Argentina). The best-known species in North American deserts are the prairie rattlesnake (*Crotalus viridis viridis*), the western diamondback (*Crotalus atrox*), the sidewinder (*Crotalus cerastes*), the Mojave rattlesnake (*Crotalus scutulatus*), and the black-tailed rattlesnake (*Crotalus molossus*).—Laurie J. Vitt

See also **BADGER; BIPEDALITY; CHIHUAHUAN DESERT; DEFENSIVE ADAPTATIONS, ANIMALS; DESERT GRASSLAND; KANGAROO RAT; MOJAVE DESERT; PIT VIPER; POISONOUS ANIMALS; PRAIRIE; PRAIRIE DOG; PREDATION; RATTLESNAKE; SIDEWINDER; SNAKES; SONORAN DESERT; VENOM**

Further Reading

Campbell, J. A., and W. W. Lamar. 1989. *The Venomous Reptiles of Latin America*. Ithaca: Cornell University Press.

Klauber, L. M. 1972. *Rattlesnakes: Their Habits, Life Histories and Influence on Mankind*. 2d ed. 2 vols. Berkeley: University of California Press.

Mehrtens, J. M. 1987. *Living Snakes of the World in Color*. New York: Sterling.

CROW

General name for all members of the avian family Corvidae (order Passeriformes). Corvidae consists of jays, nutcrackers, magpies, choughs, and "typical crows." Corvids have a cosmopolitan (worldwide) distribution and are only absent from the high Arctic, Antarctica, southern South America, and most oceanic islands. Approximately 116 species from 23 genera are recognized. The "typical crows" of the genus *Corvus* number approximately 40 and contain the largest passerine species in the world, the ravens. Corvids have strong legs and feet, relatively long, robust bills, often with terminal hooks, and tails of moderate length. Total length ranges from 20 to 65 centimeters and weight ranges from 80 to 1,500 grams. Corvids are generally strong fliers. Plumage is frequently all or mostly black, although many jays are brightly marked with blues, greens, and shades of brown or chestnut. Most species are quite gregarious, will commonly roost communally, and may be seen mobbing predators. Diet is usually varied and includes fruit, seeds, small invertebrates and vertebrates, bird eggs, and carrion. Typically larger food items are held in a foot, or under both feet, so that they may be torn apart using the bill. Hiding of surplus food is also a characteristic behavior displayed by many corvids.

The most geographically widespread genus within the Corvidae is *Corvus*, members of which are absent only from South America. These "typical crows" inhabit a wide array of habitats ranging from forest through tundra to true deserts. Many *Corvus* species, like the raven, *Corvus corax*, are highly visible members of the desert fauna with diets consisting largely of carrion. Numerous taxa of this genus have quite successfully adapted to the presence of human habitation and actively scavenge from human refuse.

In some corvid species pairs defend breeding territories. Others nest colonially. Cooperative breeding, with helpers giving aid to adult breeding pairs, is present in some species. Generally both sexes are involved in nest construction. Nests are typically rather untidy cups made of twigs and branches. Clutch sizes range from two to eight eggs. The female usually performs all incubation duties and is fed by her mate during this period. Both sexes are involved in feeding the chicks.—Stephen C. Lougheed

See also **ANIMAL ADAPTATIONS; BIRDS; CARRION EATERS; CHIHUAHUAN DESERT; COLORATION; PIGMENT; SONORAN DESERT**

Further Reading

Bent, A. C. 1946. Life histories of North American jays, crows and titmice. *U.S. National Museum Bulletin* No. 191.

Coombs, F. 1978. *The Crows: A Study of the Corvids of Europe*. London: Batsford.

Cramp, S., and C. M. Perrins, eds. 1994. *Handbook of the Birds of Europe the Middle East and North Africa*. Vol. 8. *The Birds of the Western Palearctic*. Oxford: Oxford University Press.

Goodwin, D. 1976. *Crows of the World*. Ithaca: Cornell University Press.

Heinrich, B. 1989. The raven's feast. *Natural History* 2:44–51.

CRYPSIS

Ability of an organism to blend with its background so as to be invisible to predators. Visual crypsis is the most prevalent type and is frequently studied by biologists, who are themselves members of a visual species, but crypsis can pertain to other sensory modalities (i.e., senses other than vision can be involved in masking the presence of an animal). For example, an organism may emit an odor that masks the site of its nest, resulting in olfactory crypsis. Two types of visual crypsis have been noted: (1) blending with the environment, as in nearly white lizards or rodents living on a light sandy soil in a desert, and (2) masquerading as a certain object not subject to predation, as in certain katydids that resemble dead leaves. Cryptic animals may also adopt behaviors that enhance their crypticity. In order for crypsis to work, an animal must remain motionless much of the time. Thus sit-and-wait desert lizards (predators that remain motionless, waiting for their prey to appear) are often pale in coloration to match their background. Locomotion in these lizards typically consists of quick bursts of speed, then a sudden stop, after which they vanish from a predator's sight by blending with their background. Horned lizards, genus *Phrynosoma*, are slow-moving, pancake-shaped desert lizards that are difficult to detect because of a multicolored brown, dark brown, and black-spotted dorsum and a disruptive body outline caused by rows of fringe scales along its sides. If disturbed, these lizards run a short distance, then stop and flatten themselves against the substrate and virtually disappear. They frequently bury themselves deeper in the sand by scooping sand with their bodies as they tilt from side to side, leaving only their eyes and nostrils exposed.—Janalee P. Caldwell

See also **ANIMAL ADAPTATIONS; ARTHROPODS; COLORATION; DEFENSIVE ADAPTATIONS, ANIMALS; HORNED LIZARD; INSECTS; LIZARDS; PIGMENT; PREDATION; RODENTS; WARNING COLORATION**

Further Reading

Duellman, W. E., and L. Trueb. 1986. *Biology of Amphibians*. New York: McGraw-Hill.

Edmunds, E. 1974. *Defense in Animals*. New York: Longman.

Fox, D. L. 1979. *Biochromy: Natural Coloration of Living Things*. Berkeley: University of California Press.

Hamilton, W. J., III. 1973. *Life's Color Code*. New York: McGraw-Hill.

CRYPTOGAMS

Primitive plants that do not produce true flowers or seeds include cyanobacteria, algae, fungi, mosses and liverworts, and fern allies and ferns. Two groups of cryptogams, the cyanobacteria and algae, are important in the formation and maintenance of cryptogamic soil crusts. Cryptogamic soil crusts form a hardened layer at the soil surface inhabited and generated by cyanobacteria and algae. These crusts occur most often on clay or silty soils, where they stabilize soil surfaces, provide low quantities of nitrogen, and help retain moisture. The nitrogen is provided by members of the cyanobacteria that are capable of fixing nitrogen and making it available to other plants. Desert ecosystems are low in nitrogen, and although the amount of nitrogen fixed by cyanobacteria is low, it is a significant source for some deserts. Desert soils are low in nitrogen, and most of what is present is in nonusable forms. Typically nitrogen is most available during wet periods, when microbial activity is highest.—Bruce W. Hoagland

See also **BACTERIA; NITROGEN-FIXING PLANTS; PLANT ADAPTATIONS; PLANTS**

Further Reading

Archibold, O. W. 1995. *Ecology of World Vegetation*. New York: Chapman and Hall.

Skujins, J. 1984. Microbial ecology of desert soils. *Advances in Microbial Ecology* 7:49–91.

CYCLES. *See* ACTIVITY CYCLES, ANIMALS

CYCLONE

Area of low atmospheric pressure with counterclockwise rotation of air masses in the Northern Hemisphere and clockwise rotation of air masses in the Southern Hemisphere. Modern meteorology restricts the use of the term "cyclone" to air masses having a cyclonic circulation, although the true cyclone is generally of enormous proportions. Tornadoes, waterspouts, and dust devils are developed by similar processes, although these are not called cyclones. Cyclones, developing around significant lows, are usually associated with torrential rains and are often characteristic of the tropical zones. Large cyclones occurring within the tropics are usually called hurricanes or typhoons when they are intense, and they have a classic, well-defined cyclonic structure. When storms of similar structure occur in the higher latitudes they are called extratropical cyclones or extratropical storms. Cyclones and hurricanes do not generally extend into desert areas, although as these storms break up over land and become more diffuse, the convective storms associated with the cyclones and the broad masses of moist air that are a part of the leading edge of the storms may have pronounced effects in coastal, or even inland, deserts.—Federico Norte

See also **ANTICYCLONE; BAROMETRIC PRESSURE (ATMOSPHERIC PRESSURE); CLIMATE; CLIMATE CLASSIFICATION; CLOUDS; CONVECTIVE STORM; DESERTS; EL NIÑO; ISOHYET; LOW PRESSURE; MOISTURE INDEX; MONSOON; PRECIPITATION**

Further Reading

Day, J. A., and V. J. Schaefer. 1991. *Clouds and Weather.* Boston: Houghton Mifflin.

Oliver, J. E., and R. W. Fairbridge, eds. 1987. *The Encyclopedia of Climatology.* New York: Chapman and Hall.

Schaefer, V. J., and J. A. Day. 1981. *A Field Guide to the Atmosphere.* Boston: Houghton Mifflin.

Schneider, S. H., ed. 1996. *Encyclopedia of Climate and Weather.* 2 vols. New York: Oxford University Press.

CYNOMYS. *See* PRAIRIE DOG

DAM

Barrier to water flow constructed transversely across a watercourse or valley for one or more purposes, including flood control, recreation, irrigation, and hydroelectric power, and employing various materials in its construction (e.g., concrete, earth, rocks). Dams can be classified according to their function, their hydraulic characteristics, and the construction materials used. Based on function, dams can be classified as impounding dams, diversion dams, or detention dams.

In general dams are built to permit the storage of water during periods of water abundance for use during periods of water scarcity. On a global scale about 5 percent of surface water is regulated by dams and their reservoirs; in North America 8 percent of all surface water is regulated by dams.

Diversion dams are designed to elevate the water level and permit the water to be diverted through canals or pipes to other areas where it is used; these are also termed overflow dams. Such dams are typically used where water is needed for agricultural or industrial purposes. Other dams are built to diminish the effects of flooding (detention dams; also termed flood dams or check dams, depending on size, construction, and exact function) by causing water that would normally flood an area after a rainfall to be detained temporarily and released gradually through an undersluice (floodgate) to minimize the deleterious effects of floodwaters. Dams may also be built to retain sediments (check dams), to decrease the effects of torrents that transport large amounts of sediments downstream. Depending on its hydraulic characteristics, a dam may allow water to flow over its crest or release water through other means, such as sluiceways. As their name implies, overflow dams are composed of materials that are not easily eroded by water flowing over their crest, and they usually contain outlet works (e.g., weir, sluiceway, spillway). Such dams are frequently constructed of concrete, masonry, steel, or wood.

The most common classification system used for dams is based on the materials that are used in their construction. Such dams are described as earthen dams, rock-fill dams, or concrete dams. The most common dams are made of rock, gravel, or similar materials. Earthen dams are quite common in arid and semiarid areas, and were used by early civilizations. For example, an earthen dam constructed in Ceylon in 504 B.C. was 17.7 kilometers long and 21.3 meters high. Some earthen dams are quite high, such as the one at Oroville, California, which is 236 meters. Although such dams may be enormous, they are also secure. This is not the case with smaller earthen dams, which frequently give way to the force of the water because of inadequate maintenance and poor construction. Rock-filled dams are constructed of all sizes of rocks, which assures their stability, as well as an impervious membrane, generally of concrete, asphalt, or some other material that stops the movement of water through the permeable rock fill.

The gravity dam is a structure whose massive weight is capable of resisting the great forces acting on it. Such dams may be straight or curved depending on their width and height. When built on a strong foundation, this type of dam is especially long lived and requires little maintenance. The oldest gravity dam known was built of masonry without mortar in Egypt in 4,000 B.C. and apparently functioned effectively for 4,500 years. The arch dam is also constructed of concrete. In this type of dam the water load is transmitted by arch action alone to the abutments that are built into solid rock.—Alberto I. J. Vich and Juana Susana Barroso

See also **COLLUVIAL DEPOSITS (COLLUVIUM); COLORADO RIVER; FLOOD; HYDROLOGICAL CYCLE; HYDROLOGY; IRRIGATION DRAINAGE; RIVERS; RUNOFF; WATER**

Further Reading

Linsley, R. K., and J. B. Franzini. 1972. *Water-resources Engineering*. New York: McGraw-Hill.

Moore, G. W. 1978. *Dictionary of Geography: Definitions and Explanation of Terms used in Physical Geography*. New York: Harper and Row.

Parker, A. D. 1971. *Planning and Estimating Dam Construction*. New York: McGraw-Hill.

Suh-Shiaw, Lo. 1992. *Glossary of Hydrology*. Taipei: Sheng Te.

U.S. Department of Interior, Bureau of Reclamation. 1977. *Design of Small Dams*. 2d ed. Washington, D.C.: U.S. Government Printing Office.

DARCY'S LAW

One of the laws of groundwater or subsurface water motion. Groundwater or subsurface water can be induced to move by several factors acting alone or in combination: differences in heat, surface tension, electrical potentials, pressure, gravity, and water chemistry. These forces attain importance based on whether they are acting above the water table (surface tension and gravity) or below the water table (pressure and gravity). Of all the forces listed above, only electrical potentials may be of limited effect in deserts.

In deserts movement of soil moisture due to a temperature gradient is a common occurrence. The accumulation of moisture on the underside of flat rocks, dark pavement, or other objects found on the surface results from their rapid, radiant cooling after their exposure to several warm days.

The Darcy's law mathematical equation calculates the quantity of water flowing in the subsurface. Although Darcy's law is usually applied to situations of saturated water flow, it can be used in calculations of moisture flow in deserts, which are generally areas of unsaturated moisture flow. The equation is as follows:

$$Q = -KA \cdot \frac{\partial h}{\partial s}$$

where Q is the volume of water flowing per unit time; K is hydraulic conductivity, a constant; A is the area of the cross-section normal to the flow direction; and $\partial h/\partial s$ is the hydraulic gradient.—Janet K. Braun

See also **GROUNDWATER; HYDROLOGICAL CYCLE; HYDROLOGY; IRRIGATION DRAINAGE; RUNOFF; WATER; WATER POTENTIAL**

Further Reading

Davis, S. N. 1974. Hydrogeology of arid regions. *In* G. W. Brown, Jr., ed., *Desert Biology: Special Topics on the Physical and Biological Aspects of Arid Regions*, 2:1–30. New York: Academic Press.

Dregne, H. E. 1968. Appraisal of research on surface materials of desert environments. *In* W. G. McGinnies, B. J. Goldman, and P. Paylore, eds., *Deserts of the World*, 287–377. Tucson: University of Arizona Press.

DASSIE RAT

Species of rodent (*Petromus typicus*) that is the sole member of the mammalian family Petromuridae (order Rodentia). Dassie rats are found only in the Namib Desert region of western Angola, Namibia, and South Africa. They are extremely specialized animals and occur only in areas of rocky outcrops and rocky hills where they live in crevices or under piles of boulders. Dassie rats are squirrellike in their body shape, but their tail is long and thin rather than bushy. They have numerous morphological adaptations to their rocky habitat. The soles of their feet are covered with leathery pads to facilitate movement on the rocky surface. The skull is flat, and the ribs are so flexible that dassie rats can squeeze their bodies into extremely tight crevices. They move with agility, often bounding from rock to rock.

Dassie rats are herbivores (plant eaters) and consume grasses, leaves, and fruits. They also climb trees to reach leaves, which they pluck from the branches and carry to the rocks. They are active during the day and spend hours sunning themselves on the rocks. When alarmed they dart for cover and then often give a high-pitched whistling call that appears to function as a warning. Little is known of their social system, but they exhibit many traits typical of other rock-dwelling mammals that have harem-based polygynous mating systems; (i.e., mating systems in which a male mates with several females). Females give birth to one or two well-developed young.—Thomas E. Lacher, Jr.

See also **CONVERGENT EVOLUTION; MAMMALS; NAMIBIA, DESERTS OF; RODENTS; SOUTH AFRICA, DESERTS OF**

Further Reading

Mares, M. A., and T. E. Lacher, Jr. 1987. Ecological, morphological, and behavioral convergence in rock-dwelling mammals. *Current Mammalogy* 1:307–348.

Nowak, R. M. 1991. *Walker's Mammals of the World*. 5th ed. Baltimore: Johns Hopkins University Press.

Skinner, J. D., and R. H. N. Smithers. 1990. *The Mammals of the Southern African Subregion*. Pretoria: University of Pretoria.

DEAD SEA

Large salt lake situated at the northern end of the Great Rift Valley of Africa (an area termed the Arava Rift) on the Israeli-Jordanian border and including the lowest point on earth (394 meters

The Dead Sea in Israel, with salt deposits visible along the shore and in the water. (Photo: M. A. Mares)

Eroded landscape in Death Valley National Park. (Photo: M. A. Mares)

below sea level) in its shoreline. The Dead Sea is 1,049 square kilometers in area—46 kilometers long by 16 kilometers wide—with water depth varying from 3 to 400 meters (it is deeper at the northern end). The Dead Sea, a remnant of Pleistocene Lake Lisan, has an extremely high concentration of salts (approximately seven times that of seawater) that accumulate through erosion of the surrounding arid hillsides, influent flow through salt beds, evaporation from Lake Tiberias (Sea of Galilee) located 112 kilometers to the north, and evaporation in the Dead Sea itself. Few organisms can survive in its salty water. Although the freshwater Jordan River flows from the Sea of Galilee into the Dead Sea, the Dead Sea is landlocked and subject to extremely high evaporation rates (1.4 meters/year); thus salt concentrations increase over time. Without a regular infusion of water, the sea would eventually evaporate.—Michael A. Mares

See also **HEAT; HYDROLOGICAL CYCLE; HYDROLOGY; ISRAEL, DESERTS OF; JORDAN, DESERTS OF; MIDDLE EAST, DESERTS OF; SALINITY; SALT; SALT CRUST; SALT PAN; WEATHERING, DESERT**

Further Reading

Brown, G. W., Jr., ed. 1968. *Desert Biology: Special Topics on the Physical and Biological Aspects of Arid Regions.* Vol. 1. New York: Academic Press.

Evenari, M., I. Noy-Meir, and D. W. Goodall, eds. 1985. *Ecosystems of the World, Hot Deserts and Arid Shrublands.* Vol. 12 (2 pts.). New York: Elsevier.

Evenari, M., L. Shanan, and T. Naphtali. 1971. *The Negev.* Cambridge, Mass.: Harvard University Press.

DEATH VALLEY

Relatively young desert basin located in southern California between the Panamint Mountains on the west and the Black Mountains on the east. Death Valley is perhaps the most famous desert basin in the basin and range physiographic region of western North America.

Great alluvial fans, which are immense fan-shaped deposits of waterborne debris at canyon mouths, slope from the adjacent high mountains to the Death Valley floor, a broad, flat, salt-crusted dry bed (playa) of an ancient Pleistocene lake. These alluvial fans are mainly on the west side of the valley and can be six miles long and 450 meters higher than the playa. The lowest spot in the Western Hemisphere is in Death Valley, where the elevation ranges from 85 meters below sea level to more than 3,000 meters above sea level in surrounding mountains. The floor of Death Valley is about 518 square kilometers in area, with a salt crust that is up to a meter thick and underlain by deep deposits of silt and clay. A part of the larger Mojave Desert of California and southeastern Nevada, Death Valley has many other outstanding geologic features: active sand dunes, canyons, mountains, volcanic pits, and salt.

Death Valley National Monument, which was created by presidential proclamation in February 1933, is now Death Valley National Park as a result of the California Desert Protection Act of 1994. It encompasses approximately 7.4 million acres.

The first non-Native American to see Death Valley was probably John C. Frémont, noted frontier explorer, who was guided by Kit Carson. A detailed and graphic account of the journey of a party of immigrants who became lost in Death Valley was written by William Lewis Manly in his journal *Death Valley in '49.*

Death Valley is the site of an ancient lake named after the explorer William Lewis Manly. Lake Manly was 182 meters deep and more than 160 kilometers long and existed during the Pleistocene epoch more than 10,000 years ago. As the climate became more arid, this ancient lake, along with many others in western North America, diminished and left behind alkali-crusted playas or flat clay beds on the valley floors. Old shorelines of the ancient lakes can still be seen high on the adjacent mountains.

The hydrologic basin draining into Death Valley is about 23,300 square kilometers. The salty Amargosa River (*amargosa* is Spanish for "bitter"), which formerly joined with the Mojave River, occasionally drains into Death Valley when intense storms produce flash floods. The most recent Death Valley lake resulted from snowmelt and heavy rains in surrounding mountains in 1969; approximately 207 square kilometers of the playa were flooded to a depth of a meter by this runoff.

Death Valley is famous as the home of the 20-mule teams that were used to haul borax (sodium borate) from borax mines. Borax was discovered there in 1881.

Death Valley is notorious for its extremely hot and dry climate. The highest temperature ever recorded in Death Valley was 56.7°C (134°F) on 10 July 1913 at Greenland Ranch. This is the highest temperature ever recorded for North America and is only 2 degrees cooler than the world record of 136°F recorded in Libya. Precipitation is less than 50 millimeters per year and occurs mainly in the winter. Evaporation rates are high, about 3.7 meters per year.

The basin is home to approximately 600 plant species, including many endemics (species found nowhere else), such as Death Valley sage (*Salvia funerea*), which occurs on limestone in canyons flanking Death Valley. These plants are extremely well adapted to the high temperatures and arid conditions. Some, such as honeysweet (*Tidestromia oblongifolia*), are able to photosynthesize at tem-

peratures of over 50°C. Though infrequent, rainstorms often induce rapid and massive germination of perennials and annuals, creating a desert bloom. The vegetation at higher elevations in the surrounding mountains includes bristlecone pine (*Pinus aristata*), limber pine (*Pinus flexilis*), and piñon pine (*Pinus monophylla*). The gravel alluvial fans extending from the mountains support xerophytic (dry) vegetation, including nearly pure stands of desert holly (*Atriplex hymenelytra*), along with honeysweet (*Tidestromia oblongifolia*), cattle spinach (*Atriplex polycarpa*), burroweed (*Franseria dumosa*), brittlebush (*Encelia farinosa*), and creosote bush (*Larrea tridentata*). The ubiquitous creosote bush, with its dark green, resinous leaves and yellow flowers, often contrasts with the surrounding stark and gray desert landscape.

Closer to the valley floor the vegetation consists of a variety of phreatophytes (plants whose roots reach into the capillary fringe of the water table). Typical genera are *Baccharis*, *Salix*, *Prosopis*, *Phragmites*, *Pluchea*, *Atriplex*, *Tamarisk*, and *Suaeda*. Some plants, such as *Allenrolfea*, *Juncus*, *Distichlis*, *Suaeda*, *Tamarix*, *Sporobolus*, *Atriplex*, and *Pluchea*, are noted for their tolerance to salty conditions. The playa of Death Valley is an extremely hostile environment and is usually devoid of any vegetation.

Death Valley has populations of feral burros, bighorn sheep, deer, coyote, puma, bobcat, kit fox, and a surprising variety of small mammals, reptiles, birds, and fishes. The Devils Hole pupfish (*Cyprinodon diabolis*) exists only in Death Valley.—Gary K. Hulett and Amanda Renner Charles

See also **AN INTRODUCTION TO DESERTS; ANNUAL PLANTS; ARIDITY; ASS; BIGHORN SHEEP; BIRDS; CACTI; CACTUS, COLUMNAR; CALIFORNIA DESERT; CHUCKWALLA; COLORADO DESERT; CREOSOTE BUSH; DESERTS; DESERTS, HOT; DESERTS, TEMPERATE; DROUGHT; FISHES; HEAT; JOSHUA TREE; LIZARDS; MEXICO, DESERTS OF; PALOVERDE; PHREATOPHYTES; PLANT GEOGRAPHY; PLEISTOCENE; PRECIPITATION; REPTILES; SALTBUSH; SALT CEDAR; SALT PAN; SEMIARID ZONES; SNAKES; SONORAN DESERT; WEATHERING, DESERT; YUCCA; YUMA DESERT**

Further Reading

Brown, D. E., ed. 1994. *Biotic Communities: Southwestern United States and Northwestern Mexico.* Salt Lake City: University of Utah Press.

Caruthers, W. 1951. *Loafing along Death Valley Trails: A*

Personal Narrative of People and Places. Palm Desert, Calif.: Desert Magazine Press.

Ferris, R. S. 1974. *Death Valley Wildflowers.* Bishop, Calif.: Chalfant Press.

Hunt, C. B. 1975. *Death Valley: Geology, Ecology, Archaeology.* Berkeley: University of California Press.

Kirk, R. 1956. *Exploring Death Valley: A Guide for Tourists.* Stanford: Stanford University Press.

Leadabrand, R. 1966. *A Guidebook to the Mojave Desert of California, including Death Valley, Joshua Tree National Monument, and the Antelope Valley.* Los Angeles: Ritchie Press.

Manly, W. L. 1966. *Death Valley in '49.* Ann Arbor: March of America Facsimile Series, No. 90.

Sharp, R. P. 1976. *Field Guide to Southern California.* Dubuque: Kendall/Hunt Publishing Co.

Unrau, H. D. 1997. *A History of the Lands Added to Death Valley Monument by the California Desert Protection Act of 1994: A Special History Study.* Denver: Denver Service Center.

Weir, K. 1998. *Southern California Handbook: Including Greater Los Angeles, Disneyland, San Diego, Death Valley and other Desert Parks.* Emeryville, Calif.: Moon Publications.

DECOMPOSITION

Biological breakdown of organic molecules into simple molecules through the action of enzymes (organic substances that are produced by organisms and cause changes in other substances) secreted into the external environment by some fungi and bacteria. This process returns basic materials to the soil, water, and air and contributes to natural recycling of minerals and essential compounds.

Autotrophic organisms are organisms that produce their own foods (e.g., green plants, photosynthetic bacteria, blue-green bacteria). All other organisms are heterotrophic; that is, they obtain their energy-rich molecules from other organisms. Among the heterotrophs some groups—carnivores (meat eaters) and herbivores (plant eaters)—ingest their food, but others (decomposers) break down organic molecules by secreting digestive compounds into their environment. These decomposers are heterotrophic bacteria and fungi (saprophytes), which decay the long-chain organic molecules of plants, herbivores, and carnivores when they die. In fact, some bacteria and fungi (parasites) are capable of attacking plants and animals while they are still living.

When they render organic materials into carbon dioxide (CO_2), water (H_2O), and other simple molecules, saprophytes extract energy in the form of molecules of adenosine triphosphate (ATP) for their own biological processes. Decomposition is also vital for all ecosystems, and the entire biosphere, because decomposers return inorganic molecules to the soil, water, and atmosphere. This recycling is necessary for the circulation of carbon, oxygen, nitrogen, phosphorus, and other essential elements. When these essential elements are returned to the environment, they can be absorbed by plants and once again reassembled into the molecules of life. Both bacteria and fungi decompose lipids, proteins, and carbohydrates. However, only fungi and a limited array of bacteria are able to break down lignin, the primary component of vascular plants and one of the most abundant organic molecules on earth (lignin is the compound that provides the strength in wood).

Desert soils are moisture deficient, and with the extreme temperatures that occur in deserts, decomposition is often relatively slow. For example, the Atacama-Sechura Desert of coastal Chile and Peru is so hot and dry that fallen leaves often do not decompose. Rather they are finally pulverized by the action of the wind. Similarly, in the Namib Desert of southern Africa, standing dead trees may remain undecomposed for centuries. However, with lower levels of productivity, the rapid turnover of essential elements is probably not as crucial in deserts as it is in forests and grasslands.—James R. Estes

See also **BACTERIA; ECOLOGY; ECOSYSTEM; ENERGY FLOW; HUMUS; PHOTOSYNTHESIS; PLANTS**

Further Reading

Crawford, C. S. 1991. The community ecology of macroarthropod detritivores. *In* G. A. Polis, ed., *The Ecology of Desert Communities*, 89–112. Tucson: University of Arizona Press.

Ehleringer, J. R., et al. 1992. Lack of nitrogen cycling in the Atacama Desert. *Nature* 359:316–319.

Odum, E. P. 1983. *Basic Ecology.* Philadelphia: Saunders.

Zak, J. C., and W. W. Freckman. 1991. Soil communities in deserts: microarthropods and nematodes. *In* G. A. Polis, ed., *The Ecology of Desert Communities*, 55–88. Tucson: University of Arizona Press.

DEEP CANYON DESERT

Canyon in southern California on western edge of Colorado Desert and center of the 5,666-hectare P.

L. Boyd Deep Canyon Desert Research Center. Deep Canyon links the Santa Rosa Mountains of southern California to the Colorado Desert, draining the eastern slopes of the Santa Rosa Mountains into the Salton Trough, the low point of the Colorado Desert. Intermittently flowing Deep Creek cuts through this spectacular canyon that consists of metamorphic, igneous, and sedimentary rocks. Recorded history for the area is limited; however, the oral history of the Cahuilla, the descendants of the first known people to inhabit the area, suggests that Deep Canyon was used simply as a seasonal route between the desert and the mountains. The lowest part of the canyon is characterized by creosote bush (*Larrea tridentata*), mesquite (*Prosopis juliflora*), teddy bear cholla (*Opuntia bigelovii*) and various cacti. Forty-five percent of the Deep Canyon desert flora is made up of annual plants whose appearance and relative abundance fluctuate greatly from year to year and locality to locality. Piñon pines (*Pinus monophylla*), junipers (*Juniperus californica*), and yuccas yield to coniferous forest that includes Jeffrey pine (*Pinus jeffreyi*) and white fir (*Abies concolor*) at higher elevations. Mature fan palms (*Washingtonia filifera*) occur in the steep side canyons of Deep Canyon where water has been trapped just below the surface of the ground. Characteristic animals are the desert bighorn, coyote, pocket mouse, and jackrabbit.— Gordon E. Uno

See also **BIGHORN SHEEP; CALIFORNIA DESERT; CACTI; COLORADO DESERT; COYOTE; CREOSOTE BUSH; JACKRABBIT; MESQUITE; PALMS; POCKET MOUSE; SALINITY; SALT PAN**

Further Reading

Ryan, R. M. 1968. *Mammals of Deep Canyon. Colorado Desert, California.* Palm Springs, Calif.: Desert Museum.

Ting, I. P., and B. Jennings, eds. 1976. *Deep Canyon: A Desert Wilderness for Science.* Berkeley: University of California Press.

DEER

Large herbivorous (plant-eating) mammals in the family Cervidae (order Artiodactyla). Typical habitat for many deer species is forest, woodland, or savanna (grasslands). Two species of deer, both in the genus *Odocoileus*, can be found in the deserts of North America. The mule deer (*Odocoileus hemionus*) is named for its large ears, a distinctive

Young mule deer (*Odocoileus hemionus*) in desert scrubland near Red Rock, New Mexico. (Photo: D. Beck)

feature by which these animals can be identified. Mule deer occur over much of western North America, inhabiting all biomes of this region (except tundra), including all four major deserts and adjacent semiarid habitats. The smaller white-tailed deer (*Odocoileus virginianus*) occurs over most of North America, except parts of the southwestern United States, and extends southward into northern South America. This species is less common in desert regions, but its range overlaps that of the mule deer in parts of the Great Basin, Sonoran, and Chihuahuan deserts. In historic zones of overlap white-tailed deer generally occupied higher elevations or moister sites, but human alteration of habitats has increased contact between these two species.

Although deer can be large (adult males, 70–150 kilograms), they are more slender than many of the bulkier artiodactyls (such as bison). Their long legs are well suited to running, and some deer can bound on all four legs at once, a movement called stotting. One conspicuous physical trait of deer is the presence of antlers on males. Permanent, bony pegs arising from the skull provide a supporting base for the antlers, which are grown and shed every year. While the antlers are growing, skin supplied with blood vessels and covered with dense, fine hairs surrounds their bony core. Once the antlers have stopped growing, the deer rubs its antlers against shrubs and trees to shed this velvet. Fully developed, naked antlers are present during rut (the mating season) and are shed in winter following the rut season.

Most deer are social to some degree. The breeding system is polygynous, with dominant males (stags or bucks) mating with several females (does). Bucks display or fight for dominance within the group; the most dominant bucks (usually the largest ones, with the largest antlers) gain access to does. Adult males and females generally remain in separate groups except during the breeding season (late fall-winter) and temporary winter feeding aggregations. Does give birth to one or two (occasionally three or four) fawns in the late spring or summer. Gestation averages just under seven months (200–208 days). The precocial (helpless) fawns are well camouflaged with a spotted pelage until they are three or four months old.

Deer are often considered browsers (animals that forage on leaves) but are more accurately described as mixed feeders, including both herbaceous and woody vegetation in their diets. Grasses and forbs can be important dietary components during the summer. When these plants become less available during the winter or dry season, deer rely more on browse from shrubs and trees and may migrate to a different area. In the desert seasonal changes in precipitation may also initiate mule deer migration. Succulents (including cacti) may compose up to 70 percent of the dry season diet.

The main predators of deer in desert regions are coyotes, bobcats, mountain lions, eagles, and domestic dogs. Deer are hunted as a game animal in many regions. Deer tend to be most active during the morning and evening (crepuscular) but may be active during winter afternoons or at night during the heat of the summer. They have keen senses of vision and smell. The large ears of mule deer give them especially acute hearing. Individuals communicate by visual displays, pheromones (chemicals used to communicate information to other animals; in deer the pheromones are spread by rubbing scent glands located on the forehead, feet, legs, and near the eyes and by urination), and vocalizations. A variety of vocal and other sounds (e.g., foot stomping) facilitate communication among white-tailed deer.—Kristina A. Ernest

See also **CHIHUAHUAN DESERT; HERBIVORY; MAMMALS; PINNAE; PREDATION; PUMA; SONORAN DESERT; UNGULATES**

Further Reading

Anderson, A. E., and O. C. Wallmo. 1984. Odocoileus hemionus. *Mammalian Species* 219:1–9.

Putman, R. 1988. *The Natural History of Deer*. Ithaca: Cornell University Press.

Smith, W. P. 1991. Odocoileus virginianus. *Mammalian Species* 388:1–13.

Wemmer, C. M., ed. 1982. *Biology and Management of the Cervidae*. Washington, D.C.: Smithsonian Institution Press.

DEFENSIVE ADAPTATIONS, ANIMALS

Behavioral, morphological, and physiological characteristics designed to decrease the probability that a predator will be successful. There are nearly as many defensive adaptations as there are species of animals, but most fall within several general categories.

Crypsis, or background matching, is when an animal takes on the color or pattern of its background. It is an effective defensive adaptation used by many species. Often some of the most intricate and striking color patterns render animals nearly invisible in their natural habitats. Crypsis can include color matching, disruptive coloration, and immobility. Color matching can make an animal seem "invisible," whereas disruptive coloration makes it difficult to detect the outline of an organism against structurally complex microhabitats. Lack of movement alone can render animals difficult to detect, especially in complex environments. The function of these adaptations in defense is to reduce detectability of the prey by the predators.

Flight, or the act of fleeing, is used by most animals, either when a predator is first detected or after other mechanisms, such as crypsis, have failed. Depending on the species in question, animals may run, crawl, hop, or fly. Often flash displays are associated with the initiation of flight. Such displays involve the rapid display of bright colors or eye spots that momentarily distract the attention of a predator, thus affording the prey the opportunity to escape.

Structural morphological weaponry is common in animals and serves to interfere with the predation process while having the potential for actually harming the predator. Among the best-known examples is the use of quills by porcupines and urticating hairs by spiders and caterpillars. Animals that attack porcupines can be stuck with a large number of quills that penetrate the skin and are held in by numerous tiny barbs that cause extreme pain and possibly death. Urticating hairs are similar to quills but much smaller. Tarantulas, for example, when disturbed by predators, use their hind legs to rub hair from the dorsal surface of the abdomen. The hairs land on the skin or eyes of predators, causing severe itching, or may actually be inhaled into the respiratory tract, causing sneezing and coughing. The effects of urticating hairs can last from hours to days, but the immediate effect provides the prey the opportunity to escape. Other morphological characteristics designed for other uses, such as teeth and claws, may also be used for defense. Most vertebrates, for example, bite, kick, and scratch as last-ditch responses to predation attempts.

Chemical weaponry includes the production of noxious and bad-tasting substances from the skin, ejection of chemicals into the air—usually directed at the face of a predator—and the injection of venoms. Most of these cause immediate responses by the predator and offer the prey the opportunity to escape. Some prey may maim or kill the predator through chemicals. Examples of chemicals released on external surfaces are parotoid gland products of toads and cyanotoxins of millipedes. Many animals simply defecate or urinate on a predator when grabbed, and noxious smelling or bad-tasting secretions from cloacal glands may often be mixed with the exudate (material that is excreted), making them even more offensive. Certain species of horned lizards (*Phrynosoma*) squirt blood from the eye sinuses when grasped by canids (coyotes or foxes), causing the predator to release them. Vinegaroons, or whipscorpions (class Uropygida), spray acetic acid into the eyes of predators, and spitting cobras eject venom directly at the eyes of predators. Ants, wasps, bees, velvet ants, and venomous snakes inject complex chemicals into predators, causing immediate extreme pain and, in some instances, death.—Laurie J. Vitt

See also **ADDER; ANIMAL ADAPTATIONS; ANTS; BURROWING ANIMALS; COBRA; COLORATION; CORAL SNAKE; COUNTERSHADING; CRYPSIS; GILA MONSTER; MILLIPEDES; PIGMENT; PIT VIPER; RATTLESNAKE; SCORPIONS; TAIL LOSS; VELVET ANT; VENOM; WOODRAT**

Further Reading

Cloudsley-Thompson, J. L. 1996. *Biotic Interactions in Arid Lands*. Berlin: Springer.

Endler, J. A. 1986. Defense against predators. *In* M. E. Feder and G. V. Lauder, eds., *Predator-Prey Relationships: Perspectives and Approaches from the Study of Lower Vertebrates*, 109–134. Chicago: University of Chicago Press.

Greene, H. W. 1988. Antipredator mechanisms in reptiles. *In* C. Gans and R. B. Huey, eds., *Biology of the Reptilia, Ecology B, Defense and Life History*, 16:1–152. New York: Liss.

DEHYDRATION

Process of losing water. Deserts are regions where the potential for water loss is great because the potential for evaporation generally exceeds actual precipitation, yielding a net drying effect. These conditions result in relatively low amounts of water vapor in the atmosphere, promoting maximal solar surface heating by day and maximal surface cooling by night. Since dehydration is typically greater under warmer daytime conditions than cooler nighttime conditions during the same 24-hour period, many desert animals restrict their surface activity to these cooler periods, thereby reducing exposure to dehydration. In addition to behavioral avoidance, dehydration in desert animals is further reduced by combinations of structural and functional mechanisms. Humans, in contrast, must rely almost exclusively on behavioral adjustments; they are very vulnerable to excessive dehydration.

Desert plants, which in their vegetative phases are immobile on the surface, must resort to other means to avoid excessive dehydration. Desert annual plants spend most of their lives as dehydration-resistant seeds, with germination and vegetative growth restricted to periods immediately following precipitation, when water lost by evaporation is readily replaced by uptake of soil moisture. Perennial desert plants avoid excessive dehydration by one or more of the following adaptations: having deep tap roots that penetrate to the underground water table; being drought deciduous (losing their leaves during droughts) and substantially reducing their leafy surface areas of water loss; having resinous outer-leaf coatings that retard water loss; restricting gas exchange to the evening hours. Thus many, if not most, desert organisms avoid, rather than tolerate, dehydration.—Richard E. MacMillen

See also **ANIMAL ADAPTATIONS; DESICCATION; DESICCATION-RESISTANT SPECIES; PERSPIRATION; PHYSIOLOGY; PLANT ADAPTATIONS; RESPIRATORY WATER LOSS; SALT BALANCE; STOMA;**

Carpet of wildflowers (mostly *Heliotropium* of the family Boraginaceae) in a *Bulnesia* woodland in the Monte Desert near Andalgalá, Catamarca Province, Argentina. (Photo: M. A. Mares)

SURVIVAL IN DESERTS; TRANSPIRATION; WATER BALANCE

Further Reading

Hadley, N. F., ed. 1975. *Environmental Physiology of Desert Organisms*. Stroudsburg, Pa.: Dowden, Hutchinson and Ross.

MacMahon, J. A. 1985. *Deserts*. New York: Knopf.

Polis, G. A., ed. 1991. *The Ecology of Desert Communities*. Tucson: University of Arizona Press.

DESERT BLOOM

Sudden appearance of large numbers of flowers in arid desert habitats following rains, mainly due to the germination, growth, and flowering of desert annual plants (ephemerals; also called therophytes) in response to heavy, seasonal precipitation. Desert plants consist of both perennials and annuals. The former are mainly shrubs, trees, cacti, and the like, whereas the latter are generally herbaceous plants that survive as green plants for a relatively short period, sometimes only weeks or months, and spend most of their lives as seeds that are produced during their brief growing season. These seeds, which are an important food resource for such species as rodents, birds, and ants, may remain viable for years, or even decades, awaiting the next major rainfall event. Sporadic rains of lesser intensity may lead to the seed bank in the soil building up as the seeds produced by annual plants from various years combine to increase their number. Eventually unusually heavy and widespread rainfall will occur in the desert, and the resultant sudden initiation of seed germination with subsequent growth of desert annual plants will cover the desert with small green plants. These plants generally grow and flower over a period of only a few weeks, so soon after heavy rain the desert will become covered with a carpet of multicolored flowers. Such spectacular blooms occur only sporadically over extensive areas. One of the most impressive blooms of desert annual plants was associated with the El Niño climatic event of 1998, when carpets of desert annuals covered the arid habitats of the southwestern deserts of the United States. Such blooms are particularly pronounced in the Anza-Borrego Desert of southern California.—Michael A. Mares

See also **ACTIVITY CYCLES, PLANTS (PHENOLOGY); ANNUAL PLANTS; ANTS; ANZA-BORREGO DESERT; BULBS; CACTI; CONVECTIVE STORM; EL NIÑO; FLOWERS; GERMINATION; GRANIVORY; GROWING SEASON; HETEROMYIDS; KANGAROO RAT; MONSOON; PERENNIAL PLANTS; PLANT ADAPTATIONS; POCKET MOUSE; PRIMARY PRODUCTIVITY; SEED DISPERSAL BY ANIMALS (ZOOCHORY)**

Further Reading

Brown, J. H., O. J. Reichman, and D. W. Davidson. 1979. Granivory in desert ecosystems. *Annual Review of Ecology and Systematics* 10:201–227.

Cloudsley-Thompson, J. L. 1996. *Biotic Interactions in Arid Lands*. Berlin: Springer.

Goodin, J. R., and D. K. Northington, eds. 1985. *Plant Resources of Arid and Semiarid Lands: A Global Perspective*. New York: Academic Press.

MacMahon, J. A. 1988. Warm deserts. *In* M. G. Barbour and W. D. Billings, eds., *North American Terrestrial Vegetation*, 231–264. Cambridge: Cambridge University Press.

Samson, D. A., T. E. Philippi, and D. W. Davidson. 1992. Granivory and competition as a determinant of annual plant diversity in the Chihuahuan Desert. *Oikos* 65:61–80.

DESERT BROOM

Evergreen shrub in the daisy family (Asteraceae), 1–3 meters tall, named for its broomlike branches. The dark, angled branches of *Baccharis sarothroides* have five to seven ridges. The small, linear leaves remain on the plant year-round but are more abundant during the summer rainy season. The white or cream-colored flowers are clustered in heads. Desert broom is dioecious (having separate male and female plants).

Desert broom (*romerillo* in Mexico) grows in the Mojave, Sonoran, and Chihuahuan deserts and the desert grassland, from about 300 to 1,500 meters. It is commonly found in sandy or gravelly washes but also on hillsides and bottomlands. It can tolerate saline soils.

Both leaves and stems are resinous and therefore not generally browsed by livestock (they are potentially toxic). The branches are used by Seri and Mayan Indians for colds and muscular aches and chewed for toothache. Desert broom is used as an ornamental plant.—Kristina A. Ernest

See also **CHIHUAHUAN DESERT; DESERT GRASSLAND; HALOPHYTES; MOJAVE DESERT; PLANTS; SONORAN DESERT**

Further Reading

Benson, L., and R. A. Darrow. 1981. *Trees and Shrubs of the Southwestern Deserts*. Tucson: University of Arizona Press.

DESERT DISTRIBUTION. *See* AN INTRODUCTION TO DESERTS

DESERT FORMATION. *See* AN INTRODUCTION TO DESERTS

DESERT GRASSLAND

Area found in semiarid regions that supports various species of grasses (family Poaceae) as the major plant cover. In North America desert grasslands are scattered across the southwestern United States and northern Mexico. They are part of a complex mosaic of warm desert habitats that include the Sonoran and Chihuahuan deserts. However, they are considered by most authors to be separate from either the hot or cold deserts. In fact, some authors call them semideserts, rather than true deserts, because the average annual precipitation exceeds that of other warm desert communities. (Many authors also refer to most of the deserts of the United States and Mexico as semideserts, distinguishing them from the extremely arid deserts of Asia, Africa, parts of South America, and very limited areas in North America.)

Occurring in a physiographic province called the Mexican Highlands, the average elevation of the desert grasslands in North America is above 1,000 meters. Prior to the introduction of cattle, these sites were dominated by short bunchgrasses of the genera *Bouteloua*, *Hilaria*, *Muhlenbergia*, and

Desert grassland near Albuquerque, New Mexico. (Photo: M. A. Mares)

Oryzopsis. Since grazing and fire suppression have been practiced for a long period, grasses are being replaced by shrubs such as *Larrea*, *Flourensia*, and *Prosopis*. This latter genus, also known as mesquite, is particularly invasive following cattle grazing as cattle can act as seed vectors. Cattle eat the large beanlike pods but are unable to digest the seeds themselves. The mesquite seeds, which require passage through a mammalian intestine to germinate, then pass through their digestive tracts and are deposited some distance from the parent plant.

Like most desert species the original grass flora of desert grasslands was incapable of tolerating excessive herbivory (consumption by plant eaters). Repeated grazing by cattle caused the demise of the desert grasslands. Although not as well documented as in North America, similar events are thought to have occurred in the sub-Saharan grasslands of the Sahel region of Africa. These were once grasslands that attracted nomadic peoples with large numbers of livestock. Although human and livestock populations increased, thus increasing the pressure on the grasslands, some observers feel that this was insufficient to cause the decline in these grasslands until it was coupled with a general climatic shift in the region. Regardless of the proximal cause, the result has been a shift from desert grassland to a more arid desert shrubland.

In South America desert grasslands are rare but consist of adventitious (with roots sprouting from stems) annual grass species. These regions receive most of their precipitation in the winter and could support sclerophyllous (leathery-leafed) shrubs. However, annual grasses dominate. These species grow only during the moist period of the year and survive drought as seeds.

Grassland areas can also be found in small sites scattered within other desert vegetation types. Frequently these are found in riparian areas (next to streams or river courses) or other locations where water may accumulate. These small grasslands are also sought out by grazing animals and may be subjected to degradation through grazing.—Linda L. Wallace

See also **AFRICA, DESERTS OF; ANDEAN GRASS-LANDS; CHIHUAHUAN DESERT; CREOSOTE BUSH; GRASSLAND; GREAT BASIN DESERT; MESQUITE; OVERGRAZING; PAMPAS; PLANT GEOGRAPHY; PRAIRIE; RIPARIAN COMMUNITIES; SAHARA DESERT; SAVANNA; STEPPE**

Further Reading

Brown, D. E., ed. 1994. *Biotic Communities: Southwestern United States and Northwestern Mexico*. Salt Lake City: University of Utah Press.

Humphrey, R. H. 1958. *The Desert Grassland*. Tucson: University of Arizona Press.

———. 1970. *Arizona Range Grasses*. Tucson: University of Arizona Press.

Joern, A., and K. H. Keeler, eds. 1995. *The Changing Prairie*. New York: Oxford University Press.

Lowe, C. H., ed. 1964. *The Vertebrates of Arizona*. Tucson: University of Arizona Press.

McClaran, M. P., and T. R. Van Devender. 1995. *The Desert Grassland*. Tucson: University of Arizona Press.

Samson, F. B., and F. L. Knopf, eds. 1996. *Prairie Conservation*. Washington, D.C.: Island Press.

Sims, P. L. 1988. Grasslands. *In* M. G. Barbour and W. D. Billings, eds., *North American Terrestrial Vegetation*, 266–286. Cambridge: Cambridge University Press.

Vankat, J. L. 1979. *The Natural Vegetation of North America*. New York: John Wiley.

Walter, H. 1983. *Vegetation of the Earth*. Berlin: Springer.

DESERTIFICATION

Phenomenon in which there is a relative increase in aridity or in factors associated with aridity in a particular region, which thus becomes increasingly arid, or desertic—a form of ecosystem deterioration. It may involve changes in climate, soils, flora, fauna, or drainage patterns and may be caused by activities associated with humans. The significance of the process of desertification derives from its magnitude in the amount of land and the numbers of people that are affected, the rate at which it occurs, and its implications for the future well-being of people as well as ecosystem integrity.

A precise definition of desertification is difficult because of differences in opinion regarding the impact of desertification on habitats or regions. Desertification arises from the fragility of dryland ecosystems, which, under excessive pressure of human usage, changes in land use, or climatic change, decline in productivity and in their ability to recover from perturbations. Stability and resilience are major factors in the viability of all systems, whether social, cultural, physical, or biological. Although desertification can develop solely from natural causes (non-human induced) and can occur in any climatic zone (not only arid habitats are affected), present international efforts are concerned mainly with desertification that derives from the interaction of human activities in natural ecosystems in arid, semiarid, and subhumid lands.

Where the integrity (the ability of the system to sustain itself in a particular ecological state) of these systems breaks down due to the effects of desertification, it is difficult to restore their primary productivity. As a result, while the productivity of natural resources is partially lost through desertification, this productivity may in fact enter a spiral of decreasing productivity that will result in the system's productivity becoming unavailable to humans.

In recent years detailed definitions of desertification have been provided. The first comes from the United Nations Plan of Action to Combat Desertification, wherein desertification is defined as the degradation or destruction of the biological potential of the land leading to desertlike conditions; this is particularly important when increased productivity is required to support increasing human populations. The effects of habitat deterioration are especially pronounced in the fragile ecosystems found at the desert's margins. Desertification is a self-accelerating process, and the costs of rehabilitating desert lands increase exponentially as desertification progresses.

A second definition was provided by Harold Dregne in 1976. He described desertification as the impoverishment of arid, semiarid, and some subhumid ecosystems by the combined impacts of human activities and drought. Habitat degradation manifests itself through reduced productivity of desirable plants, decreases in biomass and the diversity of the flora and fauna, and accelerated deterioration of the soil.

In the 1982 UN report on desertification, the ultimate irreversibility of the process of desertification was noted. Thus if steps are not taken early on to reduce the deleterious effects of desertification, it may not be possible to recover the productive semiarid habitats at a later date.—Virgilio G. Roig

See also **ARIDITY INDEX; CLIMATE; COLORADO RIVER; DESERT GRASSLAND; DESERTS; DROUGHT; EL NIÑO; HABITAT DEGRADATION; HEAT; MIDDLE EAST, DESERTS OF; OFF-ROAD VEHICLES; PLANT GEOGRAPHY; POLLUTION; PRIMARY PRODUCTIVITY; SAUDI ARABIA, DESERTS OF; SEMIDESERTS**

Further Reading

Allan, T., and A. Warren, eds. 1993. *Deserts: The Encroaching Wilderness*. New York: Oxford University Press.

Cloudsley-Thompson, J. L. 1977. Animal life and desertification. *Environmental Conservation* 4:199–204.

Evers, Y. D. 1996. *The Social Dimensions of Desertification: Annotated Bibliography and Literature Review*. Nairobi: United Nations Environment Programme.

Glantz, M. H. 1977. *Desertification: Environmental Degradation in and Around Arid Lands*. Boulder, Colo.: Westview Press.

Mortimore, M. 1998. *Roots in the African Dust: Sustaining the Sub-Saharan Drylands*. New York: Cambridge University Press.

Nir, D. 1974. *The Semi-arid World: Man on the Fringe of the Desert*. London: Longman.

Swearingen, W. D., and A. Bencherifa. 1996. *The North African Environment at Risk*. Boulder, Colo.: Westview Press.

United Nations Environment Programme. 1992. *World Atlas of Desertification*. London: Edward Arnold.

Williams, M., ed. 1993. *Planet Management*. New York: Oxford University Press.

DESERT PATINA. *See* ROCK VARNISH

DESERT PAVEMENT. *See* DURICRUSTS

DESERT PEOPLES

Humans (*Homo sapiens*; mammalian order Primates, family Hominidae) who inhabit or have inhabited desert regions throughout the world and use or have used similar or different strategies to survive in arid and semiarid environments. Anthropologists often classify peoples according to their mode of production, that is, how they get their food, resulting in three basic categories: foragers, agriculturalists, and pastoralists. This classification is appropriate when dealing with desert peoples, because life in the desert is basically an ecological problem (obtaining food, water, and shelter in an arid environment having low productivity), and all three categories are represented.

Foragers

In the past all peoples were hunter-gatherers who foraged for whatever necessities nature could provide. The production of food by domestication of plants and animals is a relatively recent phenomenon that occurred independently in both the Old and New worlds. Although agriculture was developed about 10,000 years ago, many hunter-gatherer groups were still living during the age of discovery, when Europeans were exploring and describing the New World. In recent times hunter-gatherers were found only in areas that were marginal or useless for either agriculture or pastoralism. The !Kung San (the *!* stands for a clicklike sound that does not appear in English), also known as the Bushmen, were still following their traditional way of life in the Kalahari Desert of southern Africa as recently as the mid-twentieth century, as were the Australian Aborigines.

Western North America supported many hunter-gatherers, such as the Western Shoshoni, Northern Paiute, and Ute throughout the Great Basin; the Shoshonean-speaking Serrano, Cahuila, Luiseño, and related tribes in central and southern California; Hokan-speaking tribes such as the Mojave, Diegueño, and Indians of Lower California; and the Karankawa, Coahuiltec, and other tribes in southern Texas and northern Mexico. These areas are all arid and lacked agriculture before modern irrigation technology.

What makes deserts especially important in the history of human development is the fact that the earliest appearance of the domestication of plants and animals in both the Old and New worlds consistently occurred in arid lands. The end of the Pleistocene, and gradual disappearance of continental glaciers, was a major worldwide environmental transition that took place over a period of time roughly dated between 15,000 and 8,000 years ago.

Habitat changes across vast regions were pronounced. In areas that eventually became the arid zones of today, cultural adaptation necessarily took a different course. Initially the Mesolithic in these zones was not unlike that of northern latitudes. But as aridity intensified and desert areas expanded, hunter-gatherer adaptations had to change too, taking on patterns that were still evident as recently as the eighteenth century in marginal arid zones.

Two factors important in understanding hunter-gatherer adaptations and the eventual development of agriculture involved the unique biotic characteristics of arid-adapted plants and animals and the patterns of rainfall in arid zones. The specific pattern of rainfall varies from one desert to another, but all are characterized by seasonality, scarcity, and unreliability. In most deserts the rains come in well-defined wet seasons alternating with fairly predictable dry periods.

North American Desert People

In western North America there are two rainy seasons, summer and winter, alternating with spring and fall dry seasons. The winter precipitation is associated with the movement of large air masses covering whole regions, and may last for several days at a time. In upper elevations it comes in the form of snow, which melts into runoff in the spring, causing flooding downstream. In contrast, summer rains are in the form of localized thunderstorms that deliver large amounts of water in a restricted area in a brief period. It is not unusual for a single thunderstorm to deliver locally more than half the annual precipitation in one afternoon. Summer storms run off rapidly, causing flash floods and erosion, and contribute little to the ground water table. From the perspective of hunter-gatherer adaptations, the most significant factor is not the scarcity of rains but rather the unreliability of rainfall. In a summer storm one valley can experience drought while an adjacent valley is flooded. It is this unpredictability that conditions hunter-gatherer adaptations.

Plant productivity is lower in deserts, and this is related to the sparse rainfall and the high evaporation. Consequently there is less biomass in a desert than in an area of comparable size that is more mesic (wet). This lowered productivity results in a lower carrying capacity of the environment for humans and other organisms. Further, large animals tend to be few in number, and the most abundant animals are small and nocturnal. As a result desert-dwelling hunter-gatherers depend primarily on plant resources for their subsistence needs, with meat being an occasional supplement rather than a staple.

In the arid zones of western North America, a significant factor in hunter-gatherer adaptations is the presence of at least one tree-borne fruit that can be used as a food source and that is capable of prolonged storage. In California this is the acorn; in the Great Basin and adjacent plateau country it is the pinyon pine nut; and in the lowland deserts of Baja California and the Sonoran Desert it is the mesquite bean.

Shoshoni, Paiute, and Ute

For hunter-gatherers with a simple food procurement technology, the environment cannot support dense populations. While hunter-gatherer bands vary in size according to specific local conditions, they seldom exceed 19 people per square kilometer. In the Great Basin and adjacent plateaus the Shoshoni, Paiute, and Ute were characterized by a family-level organization. The typical functioning social unit consisted of a man and woman, their children, and perhaps one or two single relatives who otherwise would be unattached, moving seasonally to harvest a variety of desert plant resources as these became available. No single locality could provide sufficient resources year-round to support a resident population, so mobility was the norm. Movements coincided with seasonal availability of resources. The Shoshoni knew and used close to 100 species of plants, but different species were found in dispersed locales. The small group would have to make decisions on where to go next, based on their knowledge of plant life, and when and where particular resources would be ready to harvest. A wrong decision could be disastrous. The unreliability of localized rainfall could result in a group traveling many kilometers to gather food from a stand of some particular species of edible seeds only to find that the supply was limited due to a lack of rain in that locale.

Information, therefore, had great importance. In addition, pronounced territoriality would be disadvantageous. To claim a certain territory for exclusive use would result in limiting the group's range of movement in response to patchy rainfall and resource availability. Instead of claiming territory, the premium was on marriage exogamy, creating a network of kinship over a broad area. In effect, everyone was related to everyone else in some way, facilitating movement from one locale to another according to need and also facilitating the exchange of information on the potential availability of resources.

Most of the food resources in arid lands were small, xerophytic hard-shelled seeds, which were gathered in baskets, roasted, and ground into a flour. The Great Basin of Nevada and Utah is characterized by a basin and range topography, and isolated piñon groves are found on the flanks of the ranges at about 2,800–3,800 meters elevation. A given stand of piñon comes into harvest only once every several years. Consequently it was important to know which groves were ready to produce seeds in any given year.

After moving around from one resource area to another gathering edible seeds and roots through the spring and summer, the family groups would come together into larger aggregates in October or November to harvest the pine nuts. Since the piñon nuts were relatively abundant and could be stored, the encampment would remain through most of the winter, breaking up again in the spring to repeat the mobile pattern until the following fall. Pronghorn and jackrabbit were the main sources of animal protein, although small mammals, locusts, fly larvae, and lizards were also eaten. When it was known that the jackrabbit population was high in a given locality, several families would congregate there for a cooperative hunt, provided at least one family had in its possession a rabbit net. The latter was a simple device a meter or less in height and about a hundred meters in length, with a 7- to 10-centimeter mesh. The net would be stretched across a small valley floor, supported by brush. Everyone would form a line across the valley and walk toward the net, driving rabbits ahead of them into the net where they could be clubbed easily.

!Kung Bushmen

In the past anthropologists tended to describe hunter-gatherer organization as patrilocal bands, membership of which was organized around a group of related males, their spouses and sons, together with their son's spouses and children as well as unmarried daughters. Most hunter-gatherer bands are composite, in which members of different kin groups, either patrilineal (tracing descent through the male line) or matrilineal (tracing descent through the female line), but more likely bilateral (tracing descent through both the male and female lines), are likely to be present. The Hadza of East Africa, the Bushmen of southern Africa, the Australian Aborigines, and the various Native American hunter-gatherer bands of California and Baja all exhibit similar characteristics.

Band composition is fluid, with individuals or groups of individuals able to disperse, or bud off to join other bands pretty much at will. Indeed, some anthropologists are hesitant to use the term "bands," preferring instead to describe hunter-gatherer organization as an unstructured aggregate of individuals and families, reflecting the fluidity of membership.

The organization of the !Kung Bushmen of the Dobi area in the northwest region of the Kalahari in Botswana consists of a number of camps associated with permanent water holes, each camp having from 20 to 40 people. The actual composition and size of the camps changes literally from day to day as individuals or families come and go, joining relatives in one camp, visiting friends in another.

!Kung subsistence patterns are similar to those described for the Shoshoni, reflecting the common problems of adapting to arid conditions. However, the Kalahari is characterized by a single dry season, from May to October. Residents in a given camp harvest resources within a day's walk, which is about a 10-kilometer radius around the camp. In general the women gather vegetable resources, and the men hunt medium and large game. Food is plentiful, such that they are able to pick and choose from some 85 edible species, many of which are collected only during times of relative scarcity. The principle vegetable resource is the mongongo nut, which is both abundant and nutritious and makes up as much as 50 percent of the diet. Distances greater than 10 kilometers from camp are traveled only near the end of the dry season, when resources are relatively scarce.

Although the men do some gathering of vegetable resources, they devote most of their efforts to hunting. However, in this they are less successful than the women in their gathering activity, and meat makes up only about 20 percent of the diet. Sharing of meat is a regular occurrence, which offsets the fact that on any given day most of the men will have been unsuccessful.

The Hadza of Tanzania

In contrast to the !Kung, the Hadza do not seem to share food or to cooperate in either gathering or hunting. The Hadza are hunter-gatherers in the Rift Valley of Tanzania, east and west of Lake Eyasi. Their environment is mostly savanna, with thorn scrub and acacia being the dominant vegetation, but with an abundance of wildlife. The area is also infested with the tsetse fly, which explains why the East African cattle complex has not penetrated the area. The vegetable resources consist of a variety of edible roots, berries, and the fruit of the baobab tree, which are abundant even during periods of drought. Like the !Kung, the bulk of their diet is vegetable. The women forage daily, gathering berries in the dry season and edible roots in the wet season, most of which are prepared and eaten as they are gathered. Meanwhile the men gather vegetable resources and hunt, each man going out on his own rather than cooperatively. They use strong bows and arrows tipped with poison and are successful more frequently than are the !Kung hunters. When a man kills game he cooks and eats it on the spot if it is small, bringing some meat back to camp only if it is a large animal. A possible explanation for the difference in behavior between the !Kung and the Hadza may be the sheer abundance of game in the Hadza homeland, as contrasted with the scarcity of game in the harsh desert of the !Kung.

Hunter-Gatherers of the Desert

At one time it was thought that hunter-gatherers lived a harsh and difficult life, always on the verge of starvation. Recent research has shown that quite the opposite is the case, however. The !Kung Bushmen, for example, are found to have a relatively easy life. !Kung women need to forage for vegetable resources only about 3 or 4 days a week, and (normally) at no time do they suffer from a scarcity of food. All hunter-gatherers in arid lands are characterized by a stable albeit low-density population, with about 20–50 persons per aggregate, except for special occasions. Studies have shown that their health is no worse than that of the people of most industrialized nations. Indeed, one anthropologist described them as the original affluent society, if one defines affluence as leisure time.

Agriculturalists

The earliest appearance of agriculture occurred in arid or semiarid lands in southwestern Asia in the Old World and in the central Mexican highlands in the New World. In the Near East during the latter half of the last glaciation, and in the millennia following (20,000–12,000 B.C.), the climate was colder and drier than it is today. Initially much of the area was deforested due to the cold, limiting resources and the size of the human population that could be supported. For the first several millennia after 12,000 B.C., summers actually became longer, hotter, and drier than they are today. With the onset of the warming trend, nut-bearing groves of trees and associated cereal grasses spread widely, and with them the cereal grains/tree-borne nut subsistence pattern.

Barley, the most widespread of the cereal grasses, does not tolerate cold but does tolerate heat and aridity and thus was found in lower elevations, along stream courses, and as a component of the oak woodland zone. In addition, it spreads readily in disturbed soils, and thus was easily spread by human activity. Wild einkorn wheat tolerates cold and is found in dense stands in the upland plateaus of Turkey and the Zagros Mountains of Iran and Iraq. Wild emmer wheat tolerates neither cold nor heat, and was the most localized, being found mainly in the Levant (the eastern Mediterranean, including Greece, Lebanon, Israel, the Jordan Valley, Turkey, Syria, and Egypt). All varieties of cereal grasses could be found in dense stands, an important trait if human populations are to be supported by these plants.

Cereal grasses, such as wheat, have a rachis, a part of the stalk that holds the seeds, which becomes brittle when the seeds are ripened and shatters in the breeze, dispersing the seeds. This occurs during a brief period in the spring, lasting only about three weeks immediately before the beginning of the long, hot, dry season. However, if the dry season comes early, this period of ripening could be as brief as a few days. Thus for prehistoric peoples hoping to harvest wild grains, timing was of the utmost importance. Attempting to harvest the grain too early would result in unripe grains, but waiting too long would result in the seeds having already been dispersed and becoming impossible to collect.

The rewards for successful harvesting were great. Estimates based on harvesting rates using a hand sickle of the sort found as archaeological artifacts suggest that, under ideal conditions, a family of four could harvest as much as a metric ton of grain during a three-week period—a year's supply of food. Since the xerophytic seed grains are naturally storable, they provide a reliable food supply throughout the year if adequate storage facilities are developed.

The various cereal grains that were used by agriculturists have distinctive characteristics that presented problems that had to be solved before a total reliance on them as a staple food supply could be achieved. In addition to the problem of timing the harvest, the prehistoric grain collectors had to develop tools for harvesting (sickles), adequate facilities for dry storage of the harvested grains, and tools for processing the grains. Processing equipment consisted of milling stones by which the grains were abraded to separate them from the glumes, or husks, and reduce them to a flour. The glumes of wild cereals adhere firmly to the seed and are difficult to separate; the seeds either had to be roasted or soaked to loosen the glumes prior to milling. In general seed grains were not initially the food resource of choice among hunter-gatherers but rather served as resources to fall back on during periods of scarcity, when preferred resources were unavailable. The latter included the various tree-borne nuts (pistachios, almonds, walnuts, and acorns) and legumes. However, the cereals had certain favorable characteristics that promoted their increased use: they could be harvested in abundance and would survive prolonged storage; they thrived on disturbed soils, such as would be present on and around temporary camps and permanent settlements; and they were susceptible to genetic modification that increased their productivity.

The investment in nonmovable facilities, such as heavy grain-processing equipment and storage structures, promoted the repeated use of favorably located sites on a permanent basis. Sometime during this period the earliest permanent or semipermanent settlements developed, where the inhabitants were harvesting a variety of wild cereal grains, principally wheat, barley, and ryegrass, and locally abundant tree-borne fruits. Nuts were harvested in the autumn, cereals in late spring. Meat protein was obtained by hunting herding ungulates,

such as sheep, goats, and deer, supplemented by smaller animals, such as tortoises, land snails, and freshwater marine animals, including fish and shellfish.

By 10,000 B.C. the pattern of permanent and semipermanent settlement and processing of cereal grains was well established and the formerly stable population began to expand rapidly. The population increase appears to have been a direct consequence of permanent settlement in the optimal habitat, the cereal grain/oak-pistachio uplands. Beginning with a population of about 100,000 people in 8000 B.C., it is estimated that the human population reached 3.2 million by 4000 B.C.

However, this exploitation of cereal grains, coupled with permanent habitation, does not alone explain the domestication of the cereal grasses, as people could have continued to harvest wild grasses. There is evidence that after 10,000 B.C. obsidian-bladed sickles were used for harvesting the wild wheat. As noted, as the seeds ripen, the rachis becomes brittle, allowing the seeds to break off the stalk and disperse. However, some of the seeds have a relatively tough rachis, a trait that would have been maladaptive for the plant as those seeds could not be dispersed.

Harvesting the wild cereal grasses with a sickle causes many of the seeds to break off the stalks in the process. The effect was that the seeds actually gathered by the prehistoric harvesters, those seeds remaining on the stalk after being cut with the sickle, disproportionately tended to include grains with a tough rachis. Thus the early Neolithic harvesters were unknowingly selecting for cereals with a tough rachis. It has been postulated that as populations expanded and eventually exceeded the carrying capacity for the optimal habitat, the overflow population was forced to occupy otherwise marginal areas, or habitats at lower elevations outside the cereal grain/oak-pistachio zone. The cereal grains they would have carried with them would include a high proportion of those having a tough rachis, which, when dropped either deliberately or accidentally in the disturbed soils around their habitations, produced stands of cereal grasses in which the tough rachis was predominant. Another important change was a selection for seeds with husks that did not adhere firmly, thereby facilitating the processing of the grain.

A risk in relying on wild cereal grains would have been the pronounced variation in rainfall from one year to the next in arid and semiarid areas. One way of reducing the risk was to manipulate the natural water supply by constructing simple rock alignments across hill slopes or small rock check dams across dry streambeds to direct occasional rain runoff to harvestable plants. Another strategy was the dispersal of seeds in areas that were likely to receive runoff naturally, such as areas subject to periodic flooding and the humid soils of lower valleys.

The Natufians

The expansion of human populations outside the optimal habitat for wild cereal grasses, together with the manipulation of plants, water, and soil, resulted in increasing crop yields in zones less susceptible to rainfall variation and favored the continued selection of the most productive varieties of grains. This process ultimately led to full-time reliance on cultivation and permanent settlements in lower valleys and tributaries of larger main streams, such as the Tigris and Euphrates in Mesopotamia and the Nile in Egypt. The Natufians are the first society known to rely primarily on the cultivation of wild cereals. They were a Neolithic society found in the Levant from 10,000 to 7,000 B.C. at sites such as Ain Mallaha in the Jordan Valley, where excavations have revealed circular stone house foundations and plaster-lined pits dating to 10,000 B.C. Typical Natufian sites have bell-shaped pits lined with lime plaster to provide waterproofing, the presence of cereal grains, and numerous stone sickle blades.

Animal Domestication

Evidence indicates that the domestication of animals, particularly sheep and goats and, later, cattle, came about concurrently with the domestication of cereals and as part of the same process. The wild stands of cereal grasses were prime pasture for wild sheep and goats. As Neolithic peoples settled into permanent villages in and around the stands of cereal grasses, they came into continuous close association with the animals, and a new relationship between the two developed. Previously sheep and goats had been hunted. Now their proximity would have made hunting easier, but coupled with the increasing human population and the spread of incipient agriculture that reduced the food supply of wild grains available to the animals, it would also cause a decline in the sheep and goat populations.

The response was to pen and herd the animals, allowing them to feed on the stupple after the grains had been harvested, leading eventually to domestication. Thus plant and animal domestication proceeded as complementary adjustments to the increasing aridity of the Near East beginning some 12,000 years ago, in a great arc from the Egyptian Nile, northward through the eastern Mediterranean lands of Palestine and Jordan, to the Anatolian Peninsula, and southeastward through Iraq and Iran.

Notable archaeological sites from this period are Zawi Chemi Shanidar in Iraq, dating from 9,000 B.C., which had domesticated sheep; and Ali Kosh in southwestern Iran, dating from 7,500 B.C., Jericho in Jordan, dating from 7,000 B.C., and Jarmo in Iraq, dating from 6,800 B.C., all with domesticated wheat, barley, and goats. Çatal Hüyük, a true town in present-day Turkey, dates from 6,000 B.C. and covers some 13 hectares; it had a population of about 6,000, with numerous art objects and murals and evidence of domesticated wheat, barley, sheep, cattle, and goats.

By 3,500 B.C. or earlier, cattle were being used to draw the plow, which made it possible to cultivate the broad valley floors, such as the Tigris and Euphrates in Mesopotamia, a necessary development to keep pace with the burgeoning human population. But cultivating the major valleys required irrigation, which in turn led to ever-increasing social differentiation. An important characteristic of arid lands is that even with modern irrigation the land that can be cultivated is a relatively small proportion of the total land in a region. Most of the land is either infertile or at too high an elevation to bring in irrigation water and receives insufficient rainfall for agriculture. Hence populations tend to be distributed unevenly, with relatively narrow zones of dense populations, such as along the Nile or in the Tigris and Euphrates valleys, separated by large tracts with thinly dispersed populations of pastoral nomads. By 3,800 B.C. at Uruk (located in Iraq between the lower Tigris and Euphrates rivers), the first recognizable city appeared and civilization flowered.

Unfortunately civilizations in arid lands, dependent on intensive agriculture and large-scale irrigation, contain the seeds of their own downfall. Agriculture in arid lands leads to erosion and soil depletion, and irrigation brings in salts and alkalis that are left behind as the water evaporates, until eventually the soils are too saline to support plant life. Major cities once close to the Persian Gulf are now buried under silt many kilometers inland, left behind by the expanding river delta whose growth was fed by the upstream erosion, and large areas of once-fertile valleys are now useless due to their salt content.

New World Agriculture

In the New World agriculture developed independently of the Old World in the semiarid uplands of what is now modern Mexico. Although once again the beginnings of cultivation appear to be responses to the problem of surviving in an increasingly arid environment, the conditions were not quite the same. There were two important differences that made New World agriculture different from that of the Old World: (1) the lack of extensive stands of wild cereal grains comparable to those of the Near East and (2) the absence of animals susceptible to domestication that could serve as draft animals. The llama was used as a pack animal in the South American Andes, but it could not carry heavy loads and was too small to pull a plow. Consequently agriculture in the New World developed in a somewhat different way. The sequence of cultural development representing the transition from hunting-gathering to incipient cultivation to full-scale agriculture was first worked out for the Tehuacan Valley in the state of Puebla, Mexico, and subsequent research in neighboring states indicates that it is representative of what was happening concurrently throughout the highlands of Mexico.

Beginning sometime before 7,200 B.C. the inhabitants of Tehuacan Valley were essentially similar to the description given above for the Great Basin Shoshoni. Organization consisted of seminomadic families, or microbands, that moved seasonally in response to the availability of plant food resources, with meat, which was obtained through hunting, being a secondary food source. A wide variety of plants were used, including agaves, chilis, avocados, piñon nuts, mesquite beans, acorns, various squashes, and several grasses gathered for their seeds. The latter included teosinte, a subtropical arid-lands grass that has been identified as the wild progenitor of corn, or *Zea mays*.

In its natural habitat teosinte is found from Chihuahua south through Mexico and Guatemala, and throughout this region it still grows wild around cultivated fields and readily back-crosses with corn, resulting in a hardier hybrid. Similar to Old World grains, teosinte has a brittle rachis that easily shatters when its 9–10 seeds are ripe, and the seeds are encased in a tough glume. Because of the difficulties of harvesting and processing, it was not favored as a staple but was relied on as a "famine" food, to supplement other, easier to use grains during dry years.

Teosinte is a weedy plant that thrives on disturbed soil. Hence when a mobile hunter-gatherer band, as part of its seasonal round, returned to a previous campsite a year later, they probably would find it covered with a stand of harvestable teosinte. One of the attributes of domestication is an increase in yield, and experiments have shown that the yields of other grasses being used by the prehistoric peoples of highland Mexico several thousand years ago do not increase with cultivation. Teosinte has a tendency to mutate, and a series of genetic changes leading toward *Zea mays* made it increasingly more productive. In addition wild runner beans (*Paseolus* sp.) and wild squash (*Cucurbita* sp.) occur naturally with teosinte, and were among the early domesticates in the Tehuacan Valley. Squashes were originally used for their seeds; their flesh became edible only later as a result of domestication. Archaeological evidence for their use goes back as far as 8,000–7,000 B.C., but domesticated varieties are difficult to recognize from archaeologically preserved fragments and are not identified with any certainty until well after 3,000 B.C. The association of these plants is important for the diet of the prehistoric peoples of Mexico, and the corn-beans-squash complex later spread throughout the New World where native agriculture was practiced. Corn is deficient in lysine, an essential amino acid, whereas beans are rich in lysine; taken together they make for better nutrition than would be the case if either food were eaten alone.

After 7,200 B.C. there is evidence of incipient cultivation, including various strategies that were used to manipulate the natural water supply, such as the crude construction of rock alignments across hillsides to direct natural runoff water to desirable plants and the construction of simple rock dams across arroyo beds to obstruct the flow of water and cause it to spread out across the cultivated plot. Among the seeds and other plant parts recovered from archaeological sites of this period are squash, chilis, and avocados, and among the artifacts are a variety of ground stone milling utensils and mortars for processing hard-shelled seeds.

By 5,000 B.C. fragmentary plant remains show signs of domestication, and by 3400 B.C. small pit-house settlements, each with five to ten houses, are located along the river terraces. Still the population continued to rely on wild plants and animals for 70 percent of their subsistence. It is not until after 1500 B.C. that we find evidence of substantial communities relying on agriculture, and thereafter cultural developments appear in rapid succession, paralleling the development of civilization in the Old World arid zones but with the absence of pastoralism due to the lack of suitable livestock.

By A.D. 300 the great city of Teotihuacan dominated the Valley of Mexico, and agriculture spread northward into the arid zones of what is now northern Mexico and the southwestern United States, eastward into southeastern North America, and southward through Middle America and into South America. When Europeans reached the New World agriculture was found throughout eastern, central, and southwestern portions of North America and south into most of South America, with the corn-beans-squash complex in much of that area. Thus agriculture and the organized communities that were associated with it began in the semiarid uplands of Mesoamerica, now called Mexico, as a means of reducing the risks imposed by an arid environment where rainfall was extremely variable and unpredictable.

In both the Old and New worlds the rise of the state followed similar paths due to similar causes, and, just as with agriculture, it occurred first in arid zones. Once agriculture became a reliable mode of subsistence, a number of new factors entered: (1) people settled in permanent locations, as arable land now became a valuable asset; (2) populations began to increase rapidly, necessitating an intensification of agricultural production; (3) geography became important, as not all land was equally arable and resources were not concentrated, some resources or land being more valuable or strategic than others; and (4) the loss of mobility meant the loss of direct access to some resources and led to the development of complex exchange networks and economic specialization. In addition certain food crops, cereals in the Old World, corn and beans in the New World, were readily storable. Hence surpluses could be accumulated and used in exchange (barter), resulting in differential access to wealth and power, all of which led to the development of a political-military-religious hierarchy, the initial ingredients for the formation of the state.

Pastoralists

There is disagreement as to which came first in domestication, animals or food crops. However, it is likely that they developed together as a single process. In the Middle East the dense stands of wild cereal grasses not only attracted human foragers but were also prime pasture for wild sheep and goats, the same animals the foragers hunted for meat. As the early Neolithic hunter-gathers became increasingly dependent on the cereals for subsistence and began establishing permanent communities in the cereal grains/oak-pistachio uplands, goats, sheep, and humans came into increasingly closer and continuous contact. Thus it was only a matter of time before the animals would be penned, manipulated, and controlled. The early Neolithic sites with sheep and goat remains in association with early cultivation support this.

In arid and semiarid areas a relatively small percentage of the land is arable, consisting of land that is either naturally watered by rainfall and runoff or near enough to a water source and low enough to be amenable to irrigation. The intervening areas, taking up the largest share of the landmass, consist of vast tracts of grasslands, wastelands of sand and rock, mountains, and low-lying saline playas. The southern portion of the Arabian Peninsula is a dry, barren wasteland known as the Empty Quarter, where few have reason to venture. The bulk of the population is concentrated in the river valleys and oases, green ribbons and isolated dots of fertile soil and vegetation in an otherwise inhospitable landscape. Those seemingly unusable lands are not empty (or lacking a human presence), however, but are thinly populated by pastoralists.

Pastoralism is defined as a pattern of economic-subsistence activity specializing in the care and utilization of herds of large animals and the concomitant cultural adaptations associated with such activity. The animals that figure in pastoralism are principally sheep, horses, cattle, and camels. Typically pastoralists specialize in the herding of only one species, with the exception of the horse. Hence

Bedouins are commonly camel herders but also keep horses for riding; in East Africa pastoralists keep cattle; and in central Asia Mongol pastoralists specialize in horses. Because of the lack of appropriate animals, pastoralism did not develop independently in the New World. In the Old World arid-lands pastoralism as a way of life is found across North Africa, sub-Saharan East Africa, the Middle East, and central Asia. Pastoralism can be found in those areas having sufficient vegetation, principally grasses, to support livestock but with insufficient water to support agriculture. Two patterns of pastoralism are recognized: transhumance, which is by far the more common, and nomadism.

Transhumance

Peoples practicing transhumance have permanent villages and practice horticulture along with pastoralism. Typically women, adolescents, and old people are responsible for cultivation, while the men travel with the animal herds. The animals are moved seasonally in response to the localized availability of water and grass. They are taken to upland pastures in the summer and then gradually moved to lower pastures near the village for winter pasture.

The Jie of Uganda are a typical example of transhumance. They live in villages in the western part of their territory, where water is available throughout the year, and the women practice hoe horticulture. During the rainy season the men take the herds of cattle eastward to take advantage of the seasonally available grass there. Near the end of the dry season they begin shifting the herds westward, where there is water and grass, and finally as the pasture is used up they move to the vicinity of their village where grass and water continue to be available for the rest of the year. The essential characteristic of transhumance is that only a part of the group is mobile, adjusting its movements according to the needs of the animals, while the remainder stay at a home base, where they cultivate food crops. By moving their herds away from the home base, they avoid overgrazing that part of the range.

Nomads

Nomads do not have a home base, and when they move their herds the entire community moves. Not surprisingly, the material possessions of nomadic pastoralists are meager, light, and highly transportable. They live in tents furnished with blankets, carpets, tapestries, and cushions, use basketry more than pottery, and avoid the accumulation of heavy, nonportable goods.

Contrary to popular belief, nomads do not roam aimlessly but follow well-established routes through known country. As with transhumance, their movements are in response to the needs of their animals, and territorial claims focus on pasture and water sources at specific times of the year. Hence it is quite possible for two or more groups to claim the same territory, but at different times. An example are the Basseri and Qashqa'i in Iran. The Basseri are pastoral nomads, the Qashqa'i practice transhumance. They move their horse herds from near sea level by the Persian Gulf some 300 miles northward to summer pastures ranging from 1,900 to 3,300 meters elevation. The move requires coordination, planning, and tight scheduling. Each group has a leader, called khan. The Basseri are a relatively small group, and their khan holds his authority only by virtue of his leadership ability and the loyalty of fellow tribesmen. He decides when segments of his tribe will move and where they will pasture. The Qashqa'i are a much larger group, numbering some 400,000, with many subtribes. The Qashqa'i khan has considerable authority and leads a hierarchy of minor khans, and together they coordinate the scheduling of the Qashqa'i. The movement of both tribes must be carefully coordinated so that they do not come into conflict over pasture. If a tribe or subtribe arrives late at their assigned pasturage, they lose their right to pasture their herds, as their lateness will result in a conflict with the scheduling of other tribes.

Bedouins

The Bedouin tribes of the Arabian Peninsula herded camels and horses. The horses were kept for prestige and for raiding and defense. The camels were kept for their milk, hides, occasionally for their meat, and as assets to be sold in the village markets. When on the move camels were also used for transport, both as riding and pack animals. They were bred with specific purposes in mind, and blood lines were carefully controlled, with some bred as fast riding animals, some for carrying women, and others as pack animals, for carrying supplies or water.

For most of the year the Bedouin remained in the interior of Arabia, their movements a response to the needs of their camel herds. Different areas would have pasturage at different seasons on a fairly regular basis but with year-to-year variation. Bedouin would spend the late, hot summer at oases villages, where they could obtain supplies and water and perhaps pasture their animals on the stubble of agricultural fields after the harvest. In September they would move out toward the winter pasture, their camels loaded with a year's supply of grains, dates, and other agricultural products, and they continued such movements in a roughly circular route until they returned to the villages again the following August.

The main food and often the only food for months, particularly among poorer Bedouins, was camel milk. Since neither cheese nor butter could be made from it, camel milk could be consumed only in liquid form. When in the larger villages, or when visited by itinerant traders, some camels would be sold to purchase food stores of wheat, barley, dried dates, and coffee or purchase needed manufactured goods.

Warfare and raiding were a constant occurrence in the life of the Bedouin. Horses, although impractical in the deserts and steppes of Arabia, were nevertheless prized possessions. Every Bedouin man of any stature owned a horse, a wealthy sheikh owned several, and even a poor Bedouin would arrange to own a share of a horse. They demanded constant care, with much of the grain purchased in town being intended for the horses. Water had to be transported to the camp as it was dangerous to take the horses to water for fear of theft. Horses were used for raiding and defense. Although ultimately all Bedouin were related, the more distant the relationship, the more likely that hostilities were the norm, particularly during drought years. The men rode fast camels on a raid and led their horses beside them, because horses were ineffective over any distance in the desert and too valuable to use merely for travel. When nearing the enemy camp they would switch to their horses for the attack. Warfare between tribes and subtribes were based on old hostilities and feuds but ultimately were the results of competition for scarce resources, particularly water and pasturage.

Social Organization

Social organization among pastoralists is kinship based, with a strong male bias in the form of patrilineal segmentary lineages. As lineages grow in membership they tend to divide, forming new lineages that maintain the original relationship. Hence one can think of the lineages as segments in a dendritic (family tree) system of kin relations, or as a hierarchy of lineage relationships. One's loyalty is first to one's own lineage, second to a group of related lineages, third to a larger grouping of related lineages, and so on. Often, as with the nomadic Bedouin, marriage preferences are endogamous; that is, a young man marries the daughter of his father's brother or the daughter of some other male member of the lineage structure. What are often referred to in the literature on pastoralists as tribes are really groups of related lineages forming subgroupings of larger ethnic groups. The male bias is reflected in the position of women and the association of males with the animal herds. A Bedouin's wealth is measured in his camels and horses, an East African Masai's in his cattle. Among nomadic pastoralists usually only men own the animals, and women have low status. Polygyny is not uncommon, although most men cannot afford many wives.

Pastoralist Economies

Pastoralists' subsistence is based on their animals, and typically the animals are not raised for their meat. Rather animal by-products are used for everything from food to tent covers. Camels, horses, and cattle are milked, and milk by-products such as cheese, butter, and yogurt make up the main part of the diet. In East Africa, where transhumance is practiced, cattle are bled through an artery in the neck and the blood is either cooked or mixed with milk. Although meat is eaten, often on special occasions, it seldom makes up a major portion of the diet. In addition pastoralists require agricultural products and manufactured items. Those who practice transhumance cultivate garden crops. Pastoral nomads typically maintain a symbiotic relationship with village-dwelling agriculturalists, with whom they trade animal products, such as milk products and hides, in exchange for agricultural produce and manufactured items.

Historically, in addition to trading with agricultural communities, pastoral nomads have taken advantage of their greater mobility, which often gave them military superiority, to raid the sedentary village and town dwellers. In some cases such raiding ultimately led to the conquest of agriculturally based civilizations by nomads. The Mongol hordes, the Huns, and the Arabs are well-known examples. Usually such nomadic conquerors ended up being absorbed by the conquered as they themselves became sedentary in the process of administering the complex civilizations they had taken over.

The Modern Age

The societies and social groupings described above are changing rapidly. Modern technology and the globalization of Euro-American culture has affected even the remotest corners of the earth. A !Kung San is more likely to slake his thirst with a Coca-Cola than with water stored in an ostrich shell. The Saudi has given up his camels in favor of a Mercedes and rides his horse only to play polo. The Kuwaiti receives a free university education in a nation artificially created by British imperialism to guarantee a supply of oil for Great Britain.

Still the desert is a fragile and demanding environment, and much of modern human adaptation has yet to be tested over long spans of time. The rapid growth of the human population is having its impact in many ways. Modern American culture includes a great deal of leisure activity, which is a significant factor in the American economy. Visitors and residents alike in the desert Southwest enjoy the outdoors. Indeed outdoor living is one of the area's main attractions. But the excessive use of the natural environment can cause serious damage. Off-road vehicles have started erosion cycles that the perpetrators never see. Construction of new homes and businesses take up an ever-increasing share of the desert environment, disrupting natural watercourses, erasing natural vegetation, and re-forming the landscape. Euro-Americans migrating from the East have attempted to re-create eastern environments in the desert, planting bermuda grass lawns that require constant watering and introducing foreign vegetation. The tamarisk, or salt cedar tree, was introduced from the Near East, ostensibly to control erosion along the Gila River in Arizona. It has taken over the riverine environment and spread downstream to the Colorado River and upstream on the Colorado even as far as the Grand Canyon, crowding out native species of plants on which the native wildlife depend. The introduction of this one tree alone has massively altered the riverine environment of the Colorado.

Massive irrigation projects have turned former desert lands into lush fields of agricultural production, but this has not been accomplished without a price being paid. Desert soils lack a developed humus layer and require artificial fertilizers, much of which eventually reaches the water supply. Irrigation water carries salts and alkalis that remain on the land as the water evaporates. If allowed to accumulate, the land eventually becomes useless, but if flushed out, which requires additional large amounts of water, the salts are concentrated downstream, rendering the downstream water unusable. For many years the water of the Colorado River flowing across the border into Mexico was too saline for Mexican farmers to use, and the problem was resolved only after an international treaty was negotiated which guaranteed Mexico its share of clean water.

Too often our modern technological marvels produce unanticipated results, creating problems as bad as or worse than those they were intended to solve. The high Aswan Dam in Egypt, which created the huge Lake Nasser on the Nile, has provided control of the annual Nile floods and increased the area of Nile Valley land that can be irrigated. For millennia before the construction of the dam the Nile flooded on an annual basis, watering the land and also depositing a heavy load of silt that was rich in nutrients that replenished the soil. In addition the silt load of the Nile continued to expand the river delta, which provided the richest and most productive zone of agricultural land in that arid region. But now the Nile dumps its load of silt behind the Aswan Dam, in Lake Nasser, and clear water flows below the dam. Without the heavy load of silt, the water flows rapidly, causing downcutting of the riverbed, which in turn lowers the water table in the valley. Meanwhile, because the river no longer deposits its silt on the land, artificial fertilizers are needed to enrich the soil, which most Egyptian farmers cannot afford. Downstream the delta is now being eroded away by the fast-flowing river and the sea, resulting in the loss of some of the richest agricultural lands. Finally, the great Nile River once carried nutrients into the eastern Mediterranean, which nurtured one of the world's richest fisheries. But since the construction of the Aswan Dam, the clear water of the Nile no longer empties nutrients into the sea, and throughout the eastern Mediterranean the fishing industry has suffered significant losses.

It remains to be seen how modern populations can adapt to desert conditions and whether or not modern societies can be as successful at inhabiting the desert over the long term as the many societies that came before.—Richard A. Pailes

See also **AN INTRODUCTION TO DESERTS; ASIA, DESERTS OF; CLIMATE; CLIMATE CLASSIFICATION; COCHISE; COLORADO RIVER; CONSERVATION IN DESERTS; CONVECTIVE STORM; DAM; DESERTS; DIRT BIKES; DOMESTIC ANIMALS; DROUGHT; DUNE BUGGIES; FLOOD; GERONIMO; HEAT; IRAN, DESERTS OF; IRRIGATION DRAINAGE; JACKRABBIT; JORDAN, DESERTS OF; MIDDLE EAST, DESERTS OF; NAMIBIA, DESERTS OF; NILE RIVER; PRONGHORN; OFF-ROAD VEHICLES; OVERGRAZING; PLEISTOCENE; PRECIPITATION; RIO GRANDE; SAHARA DESERT; SALT CEDAR; SALT DESERT; SAUDI ARABIA, DESERTS OF; SOUTH AFRICA, DESERTS OF; TIGRIS-EUPHRATES; WATER HOLE**

Further Reading

Adams, R. M. 1966. *The Evolution of Urban Society: Early Mesopotamia and Mexico*. Chicago: Aldine.

Cordell, L. 1998. *Prehistory of the Southwest*. 2d ed. New York: Academic Press.

Dregne, H. E., ed. 1970. *Arid Lands In Transition*. Washington, D.C.: American Association for the Advancement of Science Publication No. 90.

Dunbier, R. 1968. *The Sonoran Desert*. Tucson, Arizona: University of Arizona Press.

Fontana, B. L. 1974. Man in arid lands: The Piman Indians of the Sonoran Desert. *In* G. W. Brown, ed., *Desert Biology: Special Topics on the Physical and Biological Aspects of Arid Regions*, 2:489–528. New York: Academic Press.

Hills, E. S., ed. 1966. *Arid Lands: A Geographical Appraisal*. London: Methuen.

Konczacki, Z. A. 1978. *The Economics of Pastoralism: A Case Study of Sub-Saharan Africa*. London: F. Cass.

Lee, R. B., and I. DeVore, eds. 1968. *Man The Hunter*. Chicago: Aldine Press.

MacNeish, R. S., ed. 1967–1972. *The Prehistory of the Tehuacan Valley*. 5 vols. Austin: University of Texas Press.

Martin, P. S., and F. Plog. 1973. *The Archaeology of Arizona: A Study of the Southwest Region*. Garden City, N.Y.: Doubleday/Natural History Press.

Mellart, J. 1975. *The Earliest Civilizations in the Near East*. London: Thames and Hudson.

Nir, D. 1974. *The Semi-arid World: Man on the Fringe of the Desert*. London: Longman.

Price, D. T., and A. B. Gebauer, eds. 1995. *Last Hunters, First Farmers*. Santa Fe, New Mex.: School of American Research.

Smith, A. B. 1992. *Pastoralism in Africa: Origins and Development Ecology*. Athens: Ohio University Press.

Spencer, B., and F. J. Gillen. [1899] 1968. *The Native Tribes of Central Australia*. New York: Dover.

Steward, J. H. 1938. Basin-Plateau sociopolitical groups. *Bureau of American Ethnology Bulletin* 120.

Struever, S., ed. 1971. *Prehistoric Agriculture*. Garden City, N.Y.: Natural History Press.

Warren, S. S. 1997. *Desert Dwellers: Native People of the American Southwest*. San Francisco: Chronicle Books.

Weissleder, W., ed. 1978. *The Nomadic Alternative: Modes and Models of Interaction in the African-Asian Deserts and Steppes*. Chicago: Aldine.

DESERT SLOPES

Inclined faces of hills in deserts that can be classified as either rock slopes or debris-mantled slopes. The development of slopes on steep, bare rock faces is primarily controlled or limited by how much materials can be detached from the slope, hence they are weathering limited. Gravity is the main driving force, and most mass movement takes place as rockfalls or rock slides. Rocks falling down the cliff face accumulate below and form a talus or scree slope at or near the angle of repose (generally about 45°). The talus slope can get progressively longer as long as material is removed at a slower rate than the rate of accumulation. On less steep slopes debris produced by weathering is generally finer (smaller in size) than that on steeper slopes and often covers the slopes with a thin veneer of soil or regolith (weathered soil/rock). These slopes are considered to be transport limited, the mobility of the materials is contingent on slopewash, rainsplash, and other localized mass movement processes. Some debris-covered slopes have a unique triangular facet shape and are armored by surface boulders and cemented with extensive rock varnish coatings. These talus flatirons are considered relict features from a more humid climate, as the talus protects the underlying debris. The debris is from a more humid episode, when slopewash processes were more active, whereas the talus that covers it is from an arid period when rockfalls were the only significant slope process.

In areas with alternating layers of permeable (such as sandstone) and impermeable (such as

Slick rock formation in Arches National Park, Utah. (Photo: M. A. Mares)

shale) sedimentary rocks (formed through the deposition of sediment), differential weathering and erosion, combined with scarp retreat and basal sapping processes, produce compound or complex slopes. Basal sapping is a groundwater, seepage, and/or spring-controlled erosional process responsible for the development of amphitheater-shaped dry valleys and canyons. The process takes place at the junction between different rock strata. It is especially pronounced between impermeable rocks, such as shale, overlain by more permeable strata, such as sandstone. The more resistant sandstone rock face is undermined and collapses in the form of rockfalls, as moisture accumulates at the sandstone/shale boundary. Repeated cycles of wetting and drying, combined with frost and salt weathering, are thought to be the primary weathering processes responsible for the weakening in the contact area. Basal sapping is widespread among the sedimentary rocks (such as the Navajo Sandstone) of the Colorado Plateau in the southwestern United States (basal sapping is also invoked to explain some of the dry canyons on Mars).

Deserts have a higher proportion of bare rock hillslopes than other environments, owing primarily to the fact that the rate of removal of weathered debris is greater than the rate of debris production. Lithology and the bedding characteristics of the rocks determine the shape of the slope. Resistant rocks tend to exhibit rectilinear (sharp-angled) faces, while less-resistant rocks tend to have more rounded upper slopes, the result of rock or soil

creep, rainsplash erosion, and slopewash. Even massive sandstone cliffs show different slope configurations because of discontinuities and lithological variations (partings) within the sandstone layers. Rounded and smoothed sandstone cliffs, such as those in Arches National Park in Utah (which lies in the Great Basin Desert-Colorado Plateau Semidesert), are also referred to as slick rock. The term "segmented cliff" is also sometimes used to denote the different slope forms ranging from straight-faced cliffs to the more rounded slick rocks.

The combination of fluvial (water) erosion, parallel cliff or scarp retreat, and mass movement processes is thought to be responsible for the formation of the characteristic mesa and butte topography of much of the Colorado Plateau, as seen around Monument Valley in northeastern Arizona (which lies in the Great Basin Desert-Colorado Plateau Semidesert). The mesas are steep-sided, nearly horizontal, plateaus of rock, made up mostly of alternating layers of sedimentary rocks, capped by a resistant layer or unit (caprock). Buttes are small, isolated, flat-topped hills, mostly the result of scarp retreat and erosion of the surrounding mesas. Ultimately an isolated pinnacle or a pedestal rock is all that remains, such as Balanced Rock in Arches National Park, where the great American naturalist-novelist Edward Abbey worked as a park ranger and wrote his now-classic *Desert Solitaire*. In addition, cliffs or scarps developed on alternating layers of resistant and less-resistant sedimentary rocks exhibit unequal stairway-type slopes, called compound slopes, as seen from the south rim of Grand Canyon National Park in Arizona.

One of the most unique desert slopes is the pediment. This is a gently sloping (usually less than 10°) bedrock surface, separated from the mountain by an abrupt change in slope, called the piedmont angle. Pediments are best developed on coarse intrusive igneous (formed through volcanic action) rocks, especially granite. They are considered an erosional feature (as opposed to such depositional features as alluvial fans) and lack significant surficial deposits. There are two major types: rock pediments (mostly granites), whereby the erosional surface is of the same composition as the mountain behind it, and glacis pediments (coined by the French), where the pediment cuts across a mesa-type, caprock escarpment (mostly sedimentary rocks) truncating the less-resistant strata overlain by the resistant caprock formation. Pediments are believed to be the result of a number of geomorphic processes, including parallel retreat of the mountain front and with it the extension of the pediment and fluvial activity, whereby streams as they leave the confines of their mountain channels begin to spread laterally and form the pediment surface. Another hypothesis favored by some researchers is the notion that pediments are initiated underground by deep chemical weathering processes as moisture preferentially infiltrates at the sharp piedmont angle. Subsequently the overlying materials are stripped away (change in climate or base level) and the pediment exposed. No single explanation accounts for the formation of pediments. Excellent examples of rock and glacis pediments are found in the Mojave and Sonoran deserts of North America and the Sahara Desert of North Africa, respectively.—Vatche P. Tchakerian

See also **ALLUVIAL FAN; BADLANDS; CARBONATES; DURICRUSTS; GRAND CANYON; INSELBERG; MOJAVE DESERT; MONUMENT VALLEY; ROCK VARNISH; SAHARA DESERT; SOILS, DESERT, CALCRETE; SONORAN DESERT; WEATHERING, DESERT**

Further Reading

Cooke, R., A. Warren, and A. Goudie. 1993. *Desert Geomorphology.* London: University College London Press. Pp. 168–186.

Howard, A. D., and M. J. Selby. 1994. Rock slopes. *In* A. D. Abrahams and A. J. Parsons, eds., *Geomorphology of Desert Environments,* 123–172. London: Chapman and Hall.

Jenney, J. P., and C. Stone. 1980. *Studies in Western Arizona.* Tucson: Arizona Geological Society.

Oberlander, T. M. 1989. Slope and pediment systems. *In* D. S. G. Thomas, ed., *Arid Zone Geomorphology,* 56–84. London: Belhaven.

DESERTS

Areas of sparse rainfall (generally less than 250 millimeters per year) that support a vegetation type that has widely scattered plants dominated by xerophytic (drought-adapted) shrubs and succulents, with bare substrate predominating in the landscape. Deserts may also be defined on the basis of the relative levels of precipitation and evapotranspiration. Evapotranspiration is the total water vapor lost from the soil surface (evaporation) and plant surfaces (transpiration). Of evaporation and transpiration, the latter is the most profuse. That is why farmers in dry climates attempt to keep fallow fields weed-free. True deserts occur in arid (annual precipitation less than 200 millimeters per year) or hyperarid (annual precipitation less than 25 millimeters per year) climates. In such areas moisture usually falls as rain. These conditions are common in the Northern and Southern hemispheres between 20° and 30° latitude.

The most common factor in determining climate is the intense equatorial solar radiation, which heats the air and generates high levels of humidity. Warm tropical air rises; as it does it cools, and the atmospheric moisture condenses. That results in high rainfall patterns in the equatorial region. The rotating earth causes these air masses to move away from the equator toward both poles, and the air begins to descend on either side of the Tropic of Capricorn and the Tropic of Cancer around the 30° latitudinal band. As the air descends it warms and relative humidity declines, resulting in a warm, dry belt of aridity around the globe. Summer high temperatures in these areas are usually above 30°C and may reach 50°C. That results in high levels of evapotranspiration and massive water deficits. The sparse vegetation, low moisture levels, and cloudless skies, however, result in extensive heat radiation during the night, so evening temperatures are often cool.

Arid climates and/or desert vegetation result from four additional causes: (1) rain shadows that result from high mountains that intercept the prevailing winds and moisture; (2) great distance from bodies of water that generate moist atmospheric conditions; (3) proximity to cold ocean currents; and (4) soil conditions that reduce the availability of moisture that is present. The first three produce a climatic zone that is often identical to that found in true deserts, and not surprisingly, the vegetation is similar. Depending on the mitigating lithic (substrate) and atmospheric circumstances, the vegetation may differ in the fourth case. Hyperarid (i.e., extremely arid) conditions prevail when two or more of the causes of deserts coincide. In these circumstances, the biota is extremely sparse. (See map on end papers.)

Rain Shadows. For most regions of the globe, weather fronts move from west to east, resulting in prevailing westerly winds. As these fronts move onshore from seas or lakes, they often carry moist air. Mountains at right angles to the flow of air intercept the fronts, and the air is forced up and over the mountain range. The air cools when it rises, and it holds less moisture. Therefore, precipitation falls on the windward side of the mountains. Descending air is warmer and holds more moisture, and much of the moisture was already removed on the western slopes. The consequence for the lee side of the mountains is a dry climate, and the higher the mountain chain, the drier the downwind slope will be.

Continental Climates. In general oceanic air is most moist when it first moves onto land. This often creates dense vegetation on continental margins. As the air mass pushes inland, an increasing amount of the moisture is released as precipitation and the air becomes successively drier. Therefore, the interiors of large continents are often dry simply because they are so far from the moisture-spawning oceans. This phenomenon most often produces semiarid grasslands but can result in desert conditions. The best examples of such continental deserts are in central Asia, but those deserts also are affected by mountain ranges. Most deserts located near the centers of large continents owe at least a portion of their aridity to their distance from an oceanic water source.

Cold Ocean Currents. Water currents moving from polar regions toward the equator carry cold water. These colder seas do not provide as much moisture to the atmosphere as warm currents do because surface evaporation is less over cold water. If the cold current is close to shore, the oceanic fronts that move inland bear relatively little moisture. Thus the adjacent coastal areas are drier than typical coastlines. This set of circumstances can result in a Mediterranean climate, with warm dry summers and mild rainy winters if there is a moist season, or can lead to the development of a hyperarid coastal desert. Examples of a Mediterranean climate are southern California, Western Australia, the Cape region of South Africa, and the Chilean coast. Because so little moisture comes ashore, the prevailing weather fronts are drier and the moisture is bled from them at shorter distances inland. Examples of coastal deserts are the Chilean-Peruvian Atacama-Sechura Desert of South America and the Namib Desert of Namibia and South Africa.

Soil Type. Physical restriction of water availability may produce conditions that mimic true deserts.

The most common of these is the presence of high levels of salt in the water or soil. If salt levels are sufficiently high, water can actually migrate from root hairs into the soil, unless the plants have energy-driven mechanisms for pumping water against this diffusion gradient. Clay soils also hold moisture tenaciously and reduce water potentials, but most clay soils occur under grassland vegetation and do not appear in deserts. Water may also be tied up in ice. For instance, Antarctica is a desert-like region (polar desert) with very little liquid water available, even if vascular plants did occur there. It is, in essence, the Antarctic Desert. Tundra and alpine regions are not usually considered deserts, although the North Polar region, termed the Arctic Desert, is also a polar desert.

The most extreme deserts—hyperarid regions—occur when two or more of those factors coincide. In such areas there is almost no vegetation, and sand, gravel, and rock predominate. Sand dunes often develop because of the lack of vegetative cover and high winds. In such a climate vegetation is possible only where moisture is available. Subsurface water might, however, be available in aquifers or below dry watercourses. Therefore, some plants with deep taproots are able to exist. Water tables may reach the surface and create oases, which often have a lush and diverse flora. This pattern is common in the African and Middle Eastern deserts. In areas such as the Wadi Araba in the Jordanian desert, high rainfall in the mountains forms streams that flow to the desert. A rich tropical or semitropical vegetation persists along these watercourses.

Primary productivity in deserts is low relative to the other major vegetation types (grasslands and forests). This results because the vegetation is sparse and much of the desert floor is exposed rather than covered by plants. Not surprisingly, vegetation cover is governed largely by water availability, with the hot, dry deserts having little vegetation—for instance the Sahara and Middle Eastern deserts—and the cooler, wetter deserts, such as the Great Basin Desert, being relatively productive.

The number of plants per hectare (abundance) and total biomass produced per hectare (net productivity) are both low in desert biomes. However, number of species per unit area (diversity) may be quite high. As an example, the Wadi Araba of Israel and Jordan is exceptionally dry, but it has a high level of endemic plant species (species that occur nowhere else). The Sonoran Desert of the southwestern United States and northwestern Mexico has a high level of plant diversity, in part because of the number of habitats that are available.

A number of strategies are employed by plants to survive in desert climates, but most plants survive by avoiding the dry conditions (annual plants, phreatophytes). Only xerophytes (arid-adapted species) and succulents are true desert plants. They are regularly exposed to the nearly perpetual drought of many deserts. Both types of plants conserve water by reducing the numbers of stomata (leaf pores), controlling their opening and closing, producing waxy epidermal layers, and reducing or even eliminating leaves for part of the year, or even permanently, as with cacti and many euphorbias.—James R. Estes

See also **AN INTRODUCTION TO DESERTS; ARIDITY; CHIHUAHUAN DESERT; CLIMATE; CLIMATE CLASSIFICATION; DESERT GRASSLAND; DESERTS, HOT; DESERTS, MONTANE; DESERTS, RAIN SHADOW; DESERTS, SUBTROPICAL; DESERTS, TEMPERATE; FOREST; GRASSLAND; HALOPHYTES; HEAT; HOLDRIDGE LIFE ZONES; HIMALAYA MOUNTAINS; PLANT ADAPTATIONS; SALT DESERT; SEMIDESERT; UNITED STATES, DESERTS OF**

Further Reading

Allen, T., and A. Warner, eds. 1993. *Deserts: The Encroaching Wilderness. A World Conservation Atlas.* New York: Oxford University Press.

Bender, G. L., ed. 1982. *Reference Handbook on the Deserts of North America.* Westport, Conn.: Greenwood Press.

Brown, D. E., ed. 1994. *Biotic Communities: Southwestern United States and Northwestern Mexico.* Salt Lake City: University of Utah Press.

Evenari, M., I. Noy-Meir, and D. W. Goodall, eds. 1985. *Ecosystems of the World, Hot Deserts and Arid Shrublands.* Vol. 12 (2 pts.). New York: Elsevier.

MacMahon, J. A. 1988. Warm deserts. *In* M. G. Barbour and W. D. Billings, eds., *North American Terrestrial Vegetation,* 231–264. Cambridge: Cambridge University Press.

Priscu, J. C., ed. 1998. *Ecosystem Dynamics in a Polar Desert: The McMurdo Dry Valleys, Antarctica.* Washington, D.C.: American Geophysical Union.

Sears, E. 1935. *Deserts on the March.* Norman: University of Oklahoma Press.

West, N. E. 1988. Intermountain deserts, shrub steppes, and woodlands. *In* M. G. Barbour and W. D. Billings, eds., *North American Terrestrial Vegetation,* 209–230. New York: Oxford University Press.

DESERTS, COASTAL. *See* AN INTRODUCTION TO DESERTS

DESERTS, COLD. *See* AN INTRODUCTION TO DESERTS

DESERTS, HOT

Deserts with high diurnal summer and winter temperatures. Hot deserts occur in the desert belt between 20° and 30° latitude on either side of the equator. These deserts result from the heating of air at the equator. The heated air is less dense; therefore, it rises, cools, and moves north and south from the equator. The cool air descends and heats as it becomes more dense with decreasing altitude. This warm, dry air settles between 20° and 30° north and south latitudes. These regions are hot because of their proximity to the equator and because of the influx of warm air. Many of the great deserts of the world occur in this region of the globe (Saharan, Arabian, Iranian, Australian, Kalahari, Atacama, Sonoran, and Chihuahuan deserts).

In true hot deserts daytime temperatures in summer can reach 50°C. Because of the dry air, sparse vegetation, and clear skies, even hot deserts cool rapidly at night. The exposed soils and generally strong winds result in extensive and high dune fields that continually shift. Evaporation rates exceed precipitation so that many hot deserts also have high concentrations of salts ($NaCl$, $CaSO_4$) in the soil, further exacerbating the dry conditions.

Shrubs and succulents form the dominant vegetation of hot deserts. The succulents store water and conduct CAM-photosynthesis (CAM = crassulacean acid metabolism). Shrubs are either evergreen or drop their leaves during hot, dry periods (or during winter). Often the leaves of the shrubs are hard and dry, or waxy. Both shrubs and succulents may be protected against herbivory by thorns, spines, or prickles, and many of the shrubs have bitter chemicals, including salt, in the tissues. Some of the woody shrubs also produce chemical compounds that inhibit the growth of potential competitors (allelopathy). Allelopathy results in widespread vegetation with little ground cover between the shrubs. These chemicals may also cement the soil particles to produce what is called desert pavement, further restricting germination of competing seeds.—James R. Estes

See also **AN INTRODUCTION TO DESERTS; ARIDITY; AUSTRALIA, DESERTS OF; BAJA CALIFORNIA, DESERTS OF; CACTI; CAM PLANTS; CHIHUAHUAN DESERT; CLIMATE; CLIMATE CLASSIFICATION; DESERTS, MONTANE; DESERTS, RAIN SHADOW; DESERTS, SUBTROPICAL; DESERTS, TEMPERATE; GERMINATION; HALOPHYTES; HEAT; HOLDRIDGE LIFE ZONES; IRAN, DESERTS OF; MOJAVE DESERT; PHOTOSYNTHESIS; PLANT ADAPTATIONS; SAHARA DESERT; SALT DESERT; SEMIDESERT; SHRUBS; SOILS, DESERT, CALCAREOUS; SONORAN DESERT; SUCCULENTS; STONE PAVEMENT; THORN; UNITED STATES, DESERTS OF; XEROPHYTES**

Further Reading

Allen, T., and A. Warner, eds. 1993. *Deserts: The Encroaching Wilderness. A World Conservation Atlas.* New York: Oxford University Press.

Bender, G. L., ed. 1982. *Reference Handbook on the Deserts of North America.* Westport, Conn.: Greenwood Press.

Evenari, M., I. Noy-Meir, and D. W. Goodall, eds. 1985. *Ecosystems of the World, Hot Deserts and Arid Shrublands.* Vol. 12 (2 pts.). New York: Elsevier.

DESERTS, MONTANE

Arid zones in mountainous areas that support desert vegetation. Because air cools as it rises, mountains are cooler than the surrounding lowlands. Cooling air results in condensation and precipitation. Accordingly it is unexpected to find deserts on mountains. However, mountain ranges that occur in the rain shadow of other mountains may have more moisture than the surrounding plain but still have too little moisture to support grasslands or forests. Furthermore, the dry side of very high mountains may be quite dry, as air flowing over the mountain drops its moisture on the windward side and becomes drier on the leeward side. Therefore, it is not uncommon to have montane deserts, and a number of them exist downwind from the world's major mountain ranges in North America, South America, Asia, Africa, and Australia. The dry sides of massive mountains on the equator, such as Mount Kilimanjaro in Africa, exhibit very harsh climatic conditions in which every day is hot summer and every night is cold winter. The vegetation adapted to such areas often has highly unusual growth forms. There are great montane deserts, termed orobiomes in Asia, including the Himalayan Mountain chain, and an extensive montane desert extending for more than 8,000 kilometers in west-

ern South America along the Andes Mountains.—James R. Estes

See also **ANDES; AN INTRODUCTION TO DESERTS; ARIDITY; ASIA, DESERTS OF; BAJA CALIFORNIA, DESERTS OF; CLIMATE; CLIMATE CLASSIFICATION; DESERTS, RAIN SHADOW; HIMALAYA MOUNTAINS; HOLDRIDGE LIFE ZONES; PHOTOSYNTHESIS; PLANT ADAPTATIONS; UNITED STATES, DESERTS OF**

Further Reading

Evenari, M., I. Noy-Meir, and D. W. Goodall, eds. 1985. *Ecosystems of the World, Hot Deserts and Arid Shrublands.* Vol. 12 (2 pts.). New York: Elsevier.

Trimble, S. 1995. *The Sagebrush Ocean: Natural History of the Great Basin.* Reno: University of Nevada Press.

DESERTS, POLAR. *See* AN INTRODUCTION TO DESERTS

DESERTS, RAIN SHADOW

Deserts that occur on the leeward (downwind) side of a mountain range. Vegetation differs dramatically between the sides of mountain ranges that interrupt the prevailing winds and moisture. This occurs because the air is cooled as the wind flows over the mountains, resulting in increased precipitation, either rain or snow, on the windward side. However, as the air warms on the backside, its ability to hold moisture increases and the region immediately below the mountains receive little precipitation. The Cascade Mountains in Washington, Oregon, and northern California intercept extremely moist air in the winter months. The result is heavy snow on the western flank of these mountains. The eastern slope is much drier and the vegetation more sparse. A large, high basin desert, the Great Basin occurs east of the foot of the Cascades. Other north-south mountains occur in the Great Basin and create even drier and more desolate deserts, such as the Alvord Desert in the shadow of the Steens Mountains of south central Oregon. The Steens Mountains themselves receive only about 250 millimeters of precipitation annually at the summit. Plants are extremely sparse in the Alvord Desert, which is in the shadow of 2,700-meter peaks and receives less than 50 millimeters of annual precipitation.

The Gobi and Mongolian deserts of Asia are isolated from the moisture of the Asian subcontinent by the Himalayas, and in South America the Andes are a formidable barrier to moisture, creating desert conditions well beyond the desert latitudes. Remarkably the lee sides of the Hawaiian Islands are desertlike and support a vegetation of xerophytes and succulents, even though the windward side may record 5,000–15,000 millimeters of rain each year.—James R. Estes

See also **ANDES; AN INTRODUCTION TO DESERTS; ARIDITY; ASIA, DESERTS OF; DESERTS; CACTI; CLIMATE; DESERTS, MONTANE; DESERTS, SUBTROPICAL; DESERTS, TEMPERATE; GERMINATION; HALOPHYTES; HOLDRIDGE LIFE ZONES; MOJAVE DESERT; MONTE DESERT; OREGON DESERT; PHOTOSYNTHESIS; PLANT ADAPTATIONS; SALT DESERT; SHRUBS; SUCCULENTS; THORN; UTAH DESERT; WASHINGTON DESERT; UNITED STATES, DESERTS OF; XEROPHYTES**

Further Reading

Bender, G. L., ed. 1982. *Reference Handbook on the Deserts of North America*. Westport, Conn.: Greenwood Press.

Brown, J. H., and A. C. Gibson. 1983. *Biogeography*. St. Louis: Mosby.

Cronquist, A., A. H. Holmgren, N. H. Holmgren, and J. L. Reveal. 1972. *Intermountain Flora: Vascular Plants of the Intermountain West, U.S.A.* New York: Hafner.

Osmond, C. B., L. F. Pitelka, and G. M. Hidy, eds. 1990. *Plant Biology of the Basin and Range*. New York: Springer.

Takhtajan, A. 1986. *Floristic Regions of the World*. Berkeley: University of California Press.

DESERTS, SUBTROPICAL

Deserts that occur at the higher latitudes of the tropical zones. True deserts are common in a band around 30° north and south latitudes; however, some desertlike, semiarid areas occur deeper into the tropics in what normally would be forested zones. Rainfall in these areas is interrupted by north-south oriented mountain ranges that intercept the prevailing winds and moisture. Fronts moving onto land from the oceans usually are moisture laden. As the air passes over the mountains, it cools, causing the moisture to condense and fall as rain or snow (even in the tropics). As the air flows down the opposite slope, it is compressed and warmed. Warm air is capable of holding more moisture than cooling air. This deprives the downwind area of rainfall and snowfall, and the climate is much drier in that zone. Although these regions in the rain shadow are at latitudes and altitudes that would typically support tropical rain forest, most

are grasslands or thorn-shrublands. Thus the rain shadow does not typically result in the formation of true deserts. Examples of such areas are the Chaco thorn scrub of northern South America, which is an extensive grassland and thorn scrub region, and the xeroscapes (extremely arid areas) on the southwestern sides of the Hawaiian Islands and some islands of the Indonesian Archipelago.—James R. Estes

See also **AN INTRODUCTION TO DESERTS; ARIDITY; AUSTRALIA, DESERTS OF; BAJA CALIFORNIA, DESERTS OF; CACTI; CHACO; CHIHUAHUAN DESERT; CLIMATE; CLIMATE CLASSIFICATION; DESERTS; HOT; DESERTS, TEMPERATE; DESERTS, MONTANE; DESERTS, RAIN SHADOW; GERMINATION; HALOPHYTES; HOLDRIDGE LIFE ZONES; IRAN, DESERTS OF; MIDDLE EAST, DESERTS OF; MOJAVE DESERT; PHOTOSYNTHESIS; PLANT ADAPTATIONS; SAHARA DESERT; SALT DESERT; SEMIDESERT; SHRUBS; SONORAN DESERT; SUCCULENTS; UNITED STATES, DESERTS OF**

Further Reading

Evenari, M., I. Noy-Meir, and D. W. Goodall, eds. 1985. *Ecosystems of the World, Hot Deserts and Arid Shrublands*. Vol. 12 (2 pts.). New York: Elsevier.

DESERTS, TEMPERATE

Deserts that occur north or south of the tropical zone and north or south of the subtropical deserts. Most true deserts occur at the southern boundary of the temperate zones of the world (straddling 30° north and south latitude). However, the Great Basin Desert, the Gobi Desert, the Mongolian Desert, Patagonia, and the deserts of southern Australia occur at higher latitudes. These tend to be cold deserts, with some precipitation falling as snow. In each of these instances the desert region occurs in the rain shadow of mountains that intercept the prevailing winds and moisture. As the air passes over the mountains it expands and cools, causing it to release the moisture at higher elevations. The air flowing down the reverse side becomes drier and warmer. Therefore, precipitation is less than expected for the latitude. The climate is also drier in the center of a continent, and the Gobi and Mongolian deserts are in the center of a massive continental landmass, as well as on the lee side of the highest mountain range in the world.—James R. Estes

See also **AN INTRODUCTION TO DESERTS; ARIDITY; ASIA, DESERTS OF; CACTI; CLIMATE; CLIMATE CLASSIFICATION; DESERTS; DESERTS, MONTANE; DESERTS, RAIN SHADOW; DESERTS, SUBTROPI-**

CAL; HALOPHYTES; HOLDRIDGE LIFE ZONES; PHOTOSYNTHESIS; PLANT ADAPTATIONS; SALT DESERT; SEMIDESERT; SHRUBS; SUCCULENTS; UNITED STATES, DESERTS OF

Further Reading

Evenari, M., I. Noy-Meir, and D. W. Goodall, eds. 1985. *Ecosystems of the World, Hot Deserts and Arid Shrublands.* Vol. 12 (2 pts.). New York: Elsevier.

DESERT WEATHERING. *See* WEATHERING, DESERT

DESICCATION

Process of losing water completely; complete dehydration. Deserts are desiccating environments, yet most desert organisms avoid the potential stresses by combinations of behavioral, morphological, and physiological adaptations; they become desiccated only by continued exposure to surface conditions, after dying from other causes. A very few desert dwellers, however, can withstand nearly complete desiccation, including lichens among the plants and the egg stages of certain aquatic crustaceans among animals. In both respiration and metabolism are greatly reduced while desiccated but are resumed again with rehydration when moisture becomes available.—Richard E. MacMillen

See also ANIMAL ADAPTATIONS; DEHYDRATION; DESICCATION-RESISTANT SPECIES; PERSPIRATION; PHYSIOLOGY; PLANT ADAPTATIONS; RESPIRATORY WATER LOSS; SALT BALANCE; STOMA; SURVIVAL IN DESERTS; TRANSPIRATION; WATER BALANCE

Further Reading

Belk, D., and G. A. Cole. 1975. Adaptational biology of desert temporary-pond inhabitants. *In* N. F. Hadley, ed., *Environmental Physiology of Desert Organisms,* 207–226. Stroudsburg, Pa.: Dowden, Hutchinson and Ross.

Lange, O. L., E. D. Schulze, L. Kappen, U. Buschbom, and M. Evenari. 1975. Adaptations of desert lichens to drought and extreme temperatures. *In* N. F. Hadley, ed., *Environmental Physiology of Desert Organisms,* 20–37. Stroudsburg, Pa.: Dowden, Hutchinson, and Ross.

DESICCATION-RESISTANT SPECIES

Species existing in drought-prone areas that resist temporal (occasional) conditions of extreme dryness through behavioral, physiological, morphological, or even life history adaptations that offset the challenges of becoming desiccated. The problem that organisms in deserts must solve is how to keep from losing body water to the environment at a faster rate than they can regain it. In the absence of water for drinking, most water that desert animals ingest is contained in their food. Conditions of drought in most deserts are associated with high temperatures; as a result adaptations for resistance to drought often serve to offset effects of temperature as well.

Behavior

Among animals the most common behavioral response to desiccating conditions, whether magnified by low humidity or high temperature, is to select microhabitats (small patches of habitat) that offer relatively higher humidity and lower temperatures. Among desert arthropods the most conspicuous mechanism to offset water loss is the timing of activity to periods of relatively low temperatures and high humidity. Many scorpions, spiders, sun spiders, millipedes, centipedes, and insects, for example, are nocturnal and avoid extremely desiccating conditions. Many desert insects reduce water loss by limiting respiration to very short periods and keeping the openings to the respiratory tract (spiracles) closed most of the time, effectively sealing off the wet surfaces of the tracheal system. Predaceous arthropods gain water from the invertebrates they eat, whereas many homopterans and hemipterans acquire water by piercing plants with their proboscis and sucking juices. A South African desert beetle, *Lepidochora discoidalis,* constructs tiny trenches in sand on dunes facing the ocean. Water settles in the trenches and is ingested by the beetles. Some arthropods avoid dry seasons by producing life history stages, such as eggs, that essentially remain undeveloped during the dry season and hatch when conditions become more favorable.

Most desert snakes and mammals are nocturnal (active at night), thus avoiding desiccating conditions associated with exposure to the sun and high daytime temperatures. Some lizards, including most desert geckos and the Gila monster, are generally nocturnal. Even desert lizards and snakes that are typically diurnal (active during the day) limit much of their activity to morning and late afternoon to avoid the hottest and driest part of the day. Moreover, desert lizards and snakes spend large portions of time in the shade to regulate their body temperatures and reduce water loss. Desert amphibians are not only nocturnal, they remain almost totally inactive except during rainy periods, thus avoiding both daytime and seasonal conditions that contribute to desiccation. In addition, because desert amphibians rely on water for reproduction, all behavior related to reproduction is cued to rainy periods. During prolonged droughts the problems of water retention are magnified because food may become scarce as a direct result of drought. Consequently the primary water source for many animals (preformed water in food) becomes extremely limited. Many desert species cease activity during extended droughts, thus reducing metabolic rates so that large amounts of water are unnecessary.

Physiology

A number of physiological mechanisms aid desert plants in retaining water. For example, waxy substances may be produced to cover leaf surfaces, thus reducing evaporative water loss. Some plants are tolerant of extremely high salt concentrations in tissues, making them capable of withstanding high desiccation levels. The problem most desert animals face is eliminating nitrogenous wastes produced by metabolism from the body without using large amounts of water to do so. Nitrogenous waste products are toxic in high concentrations, and, under normal circumstances, when water loss is not a problem, these wastes are carried from the body in dilute urine. Among the most obvious physiological adaptations to desiccating conditions in animals is water retention in the kidneys while at the same time releasing salts so that osmotic balance can be maintained within the organism. This can be accomplished in several ways. One is to simply retain water through resorption (reabsorbing it, usually in the kidneys) and produce highly concentrated urine. In desert birds the production of uric acid, rather than urine, as a urinary waste product reduces metabolic water loss. Some desert rodents, for example, produce urine so concentrated that crystals are formed as rapidly as urine is produced. In many turtles, lizards, snakes, crocodilians, and birds, extrarenal (literally, outside the kidney) salt glands release highly concentrated salts using almost no water. The actual location of salt glands varies among vertebrate groups. In desert lizards lateral nasal glands secrete salt into the nasal cavities; salts are then extruded by sneezing or head shaking. Some desert frogs, such as the spadefoot (Scaphiopus), take advantage of their permeable skin to absorb water during the rainy season and produce dilute urine to release nitrogenous wastes. As conditions begin to dry, the frogs enter burrows, where the soil moisture potential is high enough that they can continue to absorb water. As the soil moisture potential decreases to the point that the frog can no longer absorb water, the frog retains urea (a nitrogenous waste product), causing high osmotic concentrations in the body fluids. The high osmotic concentration of body fluids offsets external desiccating conditions (effectively reduces the gradient between the frog and its environment), such that water is not lost to the external environment. Indeed, the osmotic concentration of body fluids may be high enough that the frogs actually continue to absorb water from relatively dry soil. Physiological adjustments in some arthropods allow them to withstand extremes of desert conditions. In the Sudan desert the scorpion Leiurus quinquestriatus can withstand temperatures of 48°C with a relative humidity of 10 percent for as much as 24 hours.

Morphology

Water can be lost directly to the environment by evaporation from external body surfaces. Plants have evolved a diversity of morphological adaptations to offset potential effects of desiccation. The most obvious adaptations are structural; many desert plants (e.g., the family Cactaceae) have a morphology that drastically reduces the surface to volume ratio, thereby reducing water loss through transpiration. Many of these plants are succulent; they contain a cell type (palisade parenchyma) that aids in water retention. Many other desert plants reduce surface to volume ratios simply by reducing leaf size. Some plants shed leaves during the driest seasons, such as the ocotillo (Fouquieria splendens) and the creosote bush (Larrea tridentata). The cuticle of many desert arthropods (including scorpions) is highly waterproof, aiding water conservation. Some desert amphibians have developed morphological adaptations that greatly reduce such water loss, particularly when coupled with the animals' behavior. For example, wax frogs (Phyllomedusa) living in South American deserts have specialized glands in the skin that secrete a waxy substance that they spread over the entire body surface, much like a sunbather spreads suntan oil. The waxy material (a lipid, or fatty substance) reduces water loss in much the same way that waxing of apples in grocery stores does. In addition, the frogs assume a compact posture on the underside of leaves, effectively reducing the surface area that is exposed to the desiccating air. Other desert frogs, such as the burrowing tree frog (*Pternohyla fodiens*) of the Sonoran Desert, molt several times when they cease activity following the rainy season and position themselves on walls of mammal burrows with the legs tucked under the body. In addition to reducing exposed surface area, they reduce evaporative water loss from the skin by retaining the keratanized (hardened) layers of molted skin.

Life histories

The timing of fruit production or seed production in desert plants can significantly offset potential losses due to desiccation. In addition, many plant species produce seeds that remain undeveloped until moisture conditions are optimal. This effect is most obvious when desert wildflowers bloom following unpredictable winter rainfall, often after years of little or no rain. Reproducing in desert environments presents special challenges for species of animals having eggs that are not resistant to desiccation (i.e., permeable eggs), or species having aquatic larvae (amphibians). Reptile eggs, like those of the desert iguana (*Dipsosaurus dorsalis*), for example, will only develop within a specific range of soil moisture potentials and temperatures. Most lizards and snakes with permeable eggs simply place their eggs in soil with high enough water potentials to facilitate development. The actual timing of reproductive events is undoubtedly critical to ensure that physical conditions necessary for development exist.

Desert amphibians time their breeding to seasonal availability of water, and the exact breeding season depends on the type of water supply required. Some species breed early in the year when temporary but predictable seasonal streams are full of water. Their larval development is short enough that tadpoles usually metamorphose before the streams dry up. Among the most spectacular examples of life history adaptations to deserts are the amphibian species that breed in unpredictable temporary ponds that form during summer rainstorms. Typically these amphibian species migrate to ponds in great numbers and breed in a single night (or at least over a period of not more than several nights). This is called explosive breeding. Eggs are deposited in the water and hatch within a day or so, and larval development is extremely rapid. Larval development can be viewed as a race to metamorphose before the pond dries. In some spadefoot toads, certain tadpoles develop carnivorous mouthparts and begin devouring other tadpoles, as well as invertebrates, in the rapidly drying ponds. These carnivorous tadpoles. carnivorous; have an added advantage in that growth rates are increased and time to metamorphosis reduced.—Laurie J. Vitt

See also **AMPHIBIANS; ANIMAL ADAPTATIONS; BIRDS; BREEDING SEASON; BURROWING ANIMALS; DEHYDRATION; DESICCATION; ESTIVATION; FOAM NEST; FROGS; IGUANA, DESERT; INSECTS; MAMMALS; PERSPIRATION; PHYSIOLOGY; PLANT ADAPTATIONS; RESPIRATORY WATER LOSS; SALT BALANCE; SNAKES; SPADEFOOT TOAD; STOMA; SURVIVAL IN DESERTS; TRANSPIRATION; WATER BALANCE; WATER STRESS**

Further Reading

Brown, G. W., Jr., ed. 1968. *Desert Biology: Special Topics on the Physical and Biological Aspects of Arid Regions.* Vol. 1. New York: Academic Press.

———. 1974. *Desert Biology: Special Topics on the Physical and Biological Aspects of Arid Regions.* Vol. 2. New York: Academic Press.

Gordon, M. S., G. A. Bartholomew, A. D. Grinnell, C. B. Jorgensen, and F. N. White. 1982. *Animal Physiology: Principles and Adaptations.* New York: Macmillan.

Gosh, P. K., and I. Prakash. 1988. *Ecophysiology of Desert Vertebrates.* Jodhpur: Scientific Publishers.

Lovegrove, B. 1993. *The Living Deserts of Southern Africa.* Vlaeberg: Fernwood.

Muth, A. 1980. Physiological ecology of the desert iguana (*Dipsosaurus dorsalis*) eggs: Temperature and water relations. *Ecology* 61:1335–1343.

Petrov, M. P. 1976. *Deserts of the World.* New York: Wiley.

Schmidt-Nielsen, K. 1964. *Desert Animals: Physiological Problems of Heat and Water.* New York: Oxford University Press.

DEVIL'S CLAW

Low, spreading annual or perennial herb of the genus *Proboscidea* (family Martyniaceae), whose fleshy fruits dry as a woody pod split into two long, curved horns (hence the common name Devil's horn). Also called unicorn plants, these glandular or viscid-pubescent herbs have large leaves. The large, showy, bell- or funnel-shaped flowers appear in terminal racemes (individual flowers are borne on the stem and form an infloresence). The flowers are pollinated by solitary bees (*Perdita*), which use them as a mating site. The long claws of the mature pod easily catch on animal fur, thereby aiding in dispersal.

Five species are present in the Sonoran and Chihuahuan deserts, four of which are annuals. *Proboscidea parviflora* has a whitish to reddish purple flower, commonly with dark spots. It grows on sandy or gravelly plains and mesas and along roads from 300 to 1,500 meters elevation. The flowers of *Proboscidea arenaria* are copper colored or yellow with purple or brownish spots. This species grows on sandy plains and mesas and gravelly slopes from 900 to 1,200 meters. The only perennial devil's claw, *Proboscidea altheaefolia*, has a yellow or copper-colored flower with red or brown spots. It grows 30–50 centimeters tall on sandy soils below 800 meters. The flowers of *Proboscidea louisianica* vary from whitish to yellowish to reddish purple. This annual species of disturbed sites occurs only rarely in the Sonoran Desert; it is more common in the southeastern United States. *Proboscidea sinaloensis* is an annual with a purplish flower. It grows along arroyos and valley floors in northwestern Mexico.

The Papago Indians and other southwestern tribes cultivate *Proboscidea parviflora* and use fibers from the dried pods to weave designs into baskets. The large, tuberous roots of devil's claw were eaten by Seri Indians, and the seeds were eaten by various Indian groups. Cattle graze on the green plants.—Kristina A. Ernest

See also **BEES; CHIHUAHUAN DESERT; ECONOMIC VALUE OF DESERT PRODUCTS; HERBS; INSECTS; MEXICO, DESERTS OF; O'ODHAM; PLANT ADAPTATIONS; SONORAN DESERT**

Further Reading

Kearney, T. H., and R. H. Peebles. 1960. *Arizona Flora*. Berkeley: University of California Press.

Nabhan, G. P., A. Whiting, H. Dobyns, R. Hevly, and R. Euler. 1978. Devil's claw domestication: Evidence from southwestern Indian fields. *Journal of Ethnobiology* 1(1):135–164.

Shreve, F., and I. L. Wiggins. 1964. *Vegetation and Flora of the Sonoran Desert*. Vols. 1 and 2. Stanford: Stanford University Press.

DEW

Deposition of droplets of water that are formed through condensation of water vapor in the atmosphere when the cooled air comes in contact with surfaces that also have been cooled through radiation cooling, that is, when heat is transferred from a warmer surface to the cooler atmosphere, during clear nights. Such surfaces include leaves of plants and the soil. If the surface temperature is below freezing, water vapor forms a thin layer of ice that is called hoarfrost. Dew also may freeze as the temperature descends below 0°C, and in this case, it is called white dew.

It is not exactly known how much dew forms on plants in desert areas, although it can range from 10 millimeters in cold climates to as much as 75 millimeters per year in subhumid warm areas. In some desert areas, especially semiarid and Mediterranean habitats, dew may contribute a significant percentage of the total precipitation that is available in the area during the year for plants and animals. In certain conditions dew formation may play an important role as a factor influencing the weathering of rocks. In fog deserts, such as those in Namibia and in Chile (Atacama Desert), dew is among the primary sources of water for animals and plants. Various organisms have special adaptations to capture dew and use it to supply their water needs.—Alberto I. J. Vich and Juana Susana Barroso

See also **AN INTRODUCTION TO DESERTS; ATACAMA DESERT; BAJA CALIFORNIA, DESERTS OF; CHILE, DESERTS OF; CLIMATE; CLOUDS; FOG DESERT; MOISTURE INDEX; NAMIBIA, DESERTS OF; PERU, DESERTS OF; RELATIVE HUMIDITY; WATER BALANCE**

Further Reading

Hofmann, G. 1955. Die Thermodynamik der Taubildung. Cited in Dew. *The New Encyclopaedia Britannica*. 1974. 15th ed. Chicago: University of Chicago Press. Pp. 679–680.

Huschke, R., ed. 1980. *Glossary of Meteorology*. Boston: American Meteorological Society.

Moore, G. W. 1978. *Dictionary of Geography: Definitions and Explanation of Terms used in Physical Geography*. New York: Harper and Row.

Moran, J. M., and M. D. Morgan. 1991. *Meteorology. The Atmosphere and the Science of Weather*. New York: MacMillan.

Oliver, J. E., and R. W. Fairbridge, eds. 1987. *The Encyclopedia of Climatology*. New York: Chapman and Hall.

Schneider, S. H., ed. 1996. *Encyclopedia of Climate and Weather*. 2 vols. New York: Oxford University Press.

Walter, H., and E. Stadelmann. 1974. A new approach to the water relations of desert plants. *In* G. W. Brown

Jr., ed., *Desert Biology: Special Topics on the Physical and Biological Aspects of Arid Regions*, 2:213–310. New York: Academic Press.

DIET

Combination of food items that individuals or species consume to acquire nutrients. All energy to fuel the activities of living organisms comes ultimately from the sun. Autotrophs (self-feeders), typically plants, convert water and carbon dioxide in the atmosphere to carbohydrates in the presence of sunlight in a process called photosynthesis. These carbohydrates form the basis for all food molecules used by plants and animals. Animals, called heterotrophs, cannot synthesize their own food and must eat plants or other heterotrophs that eat autotrophs (i.e., herbivores) to acquire their nutrients. Examination of the diets of all organisms in an ecosystem (all interacting plants and animals in a given geographic region) reveals that intricate food webs are formed, as most organisms feed on more than one kind of food item. These organisms are called generalists, whereas the smaller number of species that feed only on one or a few types of food items are called specialists.

Diets of individuals may change seasonally as different resources (food items) become available or disappear. For example, some desert lizards are herbivores when rainfall is high enough to cause plants to grow, flower, and set fruit, but these same lizards become insectivorous when dry conditions cause plants to become dormant at the same time that insects are abundant. Individuals of some species show ontogenetic changes in their diets; that is, they may feed on one type of food during one stage of their lives and feed on entirely different types of food during other life stages. Tadpoles, for example, are largely herbivorous, but adult frogs are insectivorous.

As in other ecosystems, food webs in deserts are very complex. Desert rodents feed on seeds, grasses, spiders, and insects, and in turn are fed on by snakes, owls and other birds, badgers, and foxes. Snakes eat various vertebrates and invertebrates, including rodents, lizards, birds and bird eggs, other snakes, ants, termites, and other small invertebrates. Snakes in turn are part of the diet for certain birds, other snakes, and some mammals. Desert frogs feed on insects of various kinds, and their tadpoles feed on algae and detritus.

Although it is rare in most ecosystems for simple food chains to occur (i.e., where each type of organism feeds on only one other food type), the paucity of resources in certain very arid deserts has resulted in this situation. For example, harsh conditions in certain areas in the Namib Desert in southwestern Africa permit no vegetation to grow. However, vegetation blows in from other regions, and soil samples may have as much as 36 percent organic matter from this source. Insects, particularly beetles, feed on this organic matter and are in turn consumed by lizards, which in turn are consumed by snakes.

Desert communities typically have a high diversity of predaceous arthropods, including spiders, scorpions, insects, and parasitoids. In fact, the biomass of desert arthropods exceeds that of desert vertebrates. Arthropods, even though many are generalists, may regulate the abundance of their prey populations. More data are available for spiders and scorpions than for other arthropod groups. Removal experiments revealed that decreasing the population size of one species of scorpion allowed their spider prey populations to more than double.—Janalee P. Caldwell

See also **ANIMAL ADAPTATIONS; ARTHROPODS; CARNIVORES; ECOLOGY; ECOSYSTEM; ENERGY FLOW; GRANIVORY; HERBIVORY; INSECTS; KANGAROO RAT; NAMIBIA, DESERTS OF; OMNIVORY; PREDATION; PRIMARY PRODUCTIVITY; RODENTS; SCORPIONS; SEED DISPERSAL BY ANIMALS (ZOOCHORY); SEEDS; SNAKES; SPIDERS**

Further Reading

Brown, G. W., Jr., ed. 1968. *Desert Biology: Special Topics on the Physical and Biological Aspects of Arid Regions.* Vol. 1. New York: Academic Press.

Polis, G. A. 1991. Food webs in desert communities. *In* G. Polis, ed., *The Ecology of Desert Communities*, 383–437. Tuscon, Arizona: University of Arizona Press.

Polis, G. A., and T. Yamashita. 1991. The ecology and importance of predaceous arthropods in desert communities. *In* G. Polis, ed., *The Ecology of Desert Communities*, 383–437. Tucson: University of Arizona Press.

DIK-DIK

Common name applied to a number of closely related, small African antelopes in the genus *Madoqua* (mammalian order Artiodactyla, family Bovidae). There are currently four recognized species distributed in East Africa from the Sudan and Somalia south to Tanzania. One species, Kirk's dik-

Damara (Kirk's) dik-dik (*Madoqua kirkii*) browsing in the semiarid shrub habitat of Etosha National Park, northern Namibia. (Photo: M. A. Mares)

dik, has a disjunct distribution, occurring in East Africa as well as in Angola and Namibia. Dik-diks are very petite antelopes; the females are slightly larger than the males and average only slightly more than 60 centimeters in length and weigh less than six kilograms. All dik-diks are similar in morphology and habits. Only the males have horns, which are small and often concealed by a tuft of hair on the head. All species possess a highly specialized nose that is modified into a mechanism for cooling arterial blood via evaporation. Dik-diks are specialized for arid climates and are found primarily in dry steppe and semidesert. They appear able to go without free water for long periods.

The name dik-dik comes from the call of these small antelopes, described as a "zick-zick." They are active in the early morning and late afternoon, and occasionally at night. They forage on leaves, fruit, and buds of shrubs and small trees and are very dependent on salt. They are heavily preyed on by a variety of carnivores, including eagles and large lizards, and are hunted by humans for meat and leather, which is used to make gloves. Dik-diks mate for life, and the male defends their small territory. Dik-diks live for up to 10 years in captivity but survive for less than half this time in the wild.—Thomas E. Lacher, Jr.

See also **ADDAX; AFRICA, DESERTS OF; BLACKBUCK; COUNTERCURRENT HEAT EXCHANGE; ELAND; GAZELLE; GEMSBOCK; HARTEBEEST; IBEX; KLIPSPRINGER; KUDU; MAMMALS; NAMIBIA, DESERTS OF; NYALA; ORYX; SOUTH AFRICA,** DESERTS OF; SPRINGBOK; UNGULATES; WATER HOLE; WILDLIFE

Further Reading

Dorst, J., and P. Dandelot. 1980. *A Field Guide to the Larger Mammals of Africa.* London: Collins.

Estes, R. D. 1991. *The Behavior Guide to African Mammals.* Berkeley: University of California Press.

Haltenorth, T., and H. Diller. 1980. *A Field Guide to the Mammals of Africa, Including Madagascar.* London: Collins.

Kingdon, J. 1989. *East African Mammals: An Atlas of Evolution in Africa.* Vol. 3C. Chicago: University of Chicago Press.

Nowak, R. M. 1991. *Walker's Mammals of the World.* 5th ed. Baltimore: Johns Hopkins University Press.

DINGO

Subspecies of the domestic dog found in Australia (*Canis familiaris dingo*; mammalian order Carnivora, family Canidae). Dingoes probably descended from feral dogs of the Aborigines. White patches cover their predominantly yellow to brown bodies. Breeding takes place in April or May. Four to five pups are born after a gestation of two months. The life span of dingoes in the wild is estimated to be 15 years. Dingoes feed on small mammals, lizards, and carrion. They are solitary by nature, but occasionally form small hunting packs. They do not bark but can growl, howl, and whimper.

A loose association with Aborigines has been maintained throughout the dingo's history. Dingoes were undoubtedly introduced into Australia by Aborigines, who used the dogs for warmth, security, and possibly food. Today Aborigines will capture young pups and tame them for pets. While dingos do pose a threat to sheep, this threat is outweighed by the dingo's contribution in limiting introduced European rabbit populations. Extensive dingo control programs of bounties, poisoning, and fencing exist throughout Australia. While not internationally recognized as endangered, dingoes are threatened by feral dogs that, through interbreeding, dilute the genetic distinctiveness of the dingo subspecies.—Rob Channell

See also **AUSTRALIA; CARNIVORES; DESERT PEOPLES; MAMMALS; MARSUPIALS; PREDATION; QUOKKA**

Further Reading

Bueler, L. E. 1973. *Wild Dogs of the World.* New York: Stein and Day.

Sheldon, J. W. 1992. *Wild Dogs: The Natural History of the Nondomestic Canidae.* San Diego: Academic Press.

DIRT BIKES

Motorcycles (also referred to as trail bikes) that are modified for off-road use. They are stripped of all nonessential parts to make them lighter. The engine is mounted higher above the ground than in traditional motorcycles, and the gear box is modified to have a wider range of speeds. The suspension is heavier, the handlebars are wider, and the steering is quicker and more sensitive. The sale of all motorcycles increased dramatically in the 1970s and 1980s, and several million are sold each year. Approximately 40 percent of all motorcycles sold are used for off-road activities.

Trail bikes are heavily used in the California Desert. Organized races are held on Bureau of Land Management lands, and numerous conflicts have developed between motorcycle clubs and other interest groups. Environmental groups are concerned about the damage the bikes cause to desert vegetation and wildlife, as well as the noise and air pollution that result from heavy use. Archaeologists have been fighting to protect important archaeological sites. Indigenous groups want to keep tribal lands off-limits to off-road vehicle use. Hikers and nature groups object to the noise, erosion, and occasional vandalism. As is the case with all off-road vehicles, new management plans attempt to accommodate all users of public lands, but balancing such conflicting uses as motorcycle racing and backpacking is challenging. There is more concern about motorcycle use in arid lands because the process of restoration of desert soils is so complex and difficult. Deserts are especially fragile ecosystems and show scars of habitat destruction for very long periods. Thus should errors be made in how desert lands are used, the consequences could be long-term damage to these habitats. More research is needed to measure the impact of all off-road vehicles on drylands, especially in developed countries, such as the United States, where economic levels permit widespread recreational use of desert habitats.—Thomas E. Lacher, Jr.

See also **ARABIAN GULF, DESERTS OF; COLLUVIAL DEPOSITS (COLLUVIUM); CONSERVATION IN DESERTS; CONTAMINATION; DUNE BUGGIES; DUNES; HABITAT DEGRADATION; OFF-ROAD VEHICLES; POLLUTION; WILDLIFE**

Further Reading

Andrews, R. N. L., and P. F. Nowak, eds. 1980. *Off-Road Vehicle Use: A Management Challenge.* Washington, D.C.: Office of Environmental Quality, U.S. Department of Agriculture.

Heath, R. 1974. *The Environmental Consequences of the Off-Road Vehicle: With Profiles of the Industry and the Enthusiast.* Washington, D.C.: Defenders of Wildlife.

Webb, R. H., and H. G. Wilshire, eds. 1983. *Environmental Effects of Off-Road Vehicles: Impacts and Management in Arid Regions.* New York: Springer.

DISTRIBUTION OF DESERTS. *See* AN INTRODUCTION TO DESERTS

DIVERSITY

Term used to denote the variety and richness of living organisms. Diversity may refer to the number of species in a defined area (forest, mountain range, political unit, etc.), in which case it is known as species richness. Species diversity is often represented by a mathematical formulation (i.e., an index) that includes not only the number of species but also the relative abundances of individuals in each species. Thus if there are 10 species in an area and 91 individuals pertain to one species while each of the other species is represented by only a single individual, the area would have a lower species diversity index than an area that also supported 10 species but that had each species represented by 10 individuals. The number of species (species richness) in the two areas would be the same (10), but the evenness with which the species are represented is an important component of true species diversity, thus the species diversity would be higher in the area in which species were equally abundant.

Other terms have also come to be used in studies of diversity. Because it is so difficult to determine the abundance of each species in a geographic area, the term "species diversity" is commonly used to refer to the number of species in an area (or species richness), which is also termed alpha (α) diversity (within-habitat diversity). At a larger scale, gamma (γ) diversity is used to describe the number of species in a region, thus differing from alpha diversity only in the scale that is considered. As species diversity differs from point to point, with different species reaching their limits and other species replacing them, the rate at which species accumulate along a line extending away from the point at which alpha diversity is measured is called beta (β) diversity (or species diversity between habitats).

In recent years the term "biodiversity" has come to be synonymous with diversity. The prefix *bio-* is superfluous, because species diversity has always considered the diversity of life forms of all types. However, whereas species diversity could refer to the diversity of only a single taxon, such as the species of mammals in an area, or the species of rodents in an area, or even all life forms in an area, the "biodiversity" is an inclusive term that is not limited to single taxa. Thus one does not speak of the biodiversity of birds or the biodiversity of insects. Rather one refers to an area as having a high biodiversity, meaning a richness of plant, animal, and other life forms considered together, without distinguishing finer taxonomic divisions.

Deserts have been shown to be exceptionally rich in terms of species and, especially, in terms of higher taxa. Deserts are also homes to endemic (occurring nowhere else) taxa. Thus desert areas often contain species, genera, or even families of organisms that do not occur in other habitats. Such specialized organisms have evolved over great spans of time to exist in the harsh desert environment. Unlike tropical forest organisms, for example, which can inhabit an array of non-rain forest habitats, desert organisms often are limited to deserts. The diversity of life in deserts has been unappreciated, especially with the recent emphasis on the richness of life in the tropical rain forests. When higher-order diversity is considered, such as that of genera or families of organisms, and when genetic uniqueness is considered, deserts have been shown to be among the richest and most diverse habitats on earth.—Michael A. Mares

See also **BIOME; CONSERVATION IN DESERTS; ECOLOGY; ECOSYSTEM; LANDSCAPE; SPECIATION; WILDLIFE**

Further Reading

Brown, J. H., and A. C. Gibson. 1983. *Biogeography*. St. Louis: Mosby.

Cody, M. L., and J. M. Diamond, eds. 1974. *Ecology and Evolution of Communities*. Cambridge, Mass.: Belknap Press.

MacArthur, R. H. 1972. *Geographical Ecology*. New York: Harper and Row.

Ricklefs, R. E., and D. Schluter, eds. 1993. *Species Diversity in Ecological Communities*. Chicago: University of Chicago Press.

Rosenzweig, M. L. 1995. *Species Diversity in Space and Time*. Cambridge: Cambridge University Press.

DOG, WILD

Doglike predator (*Lycaon pictus*; mammalian order Carnivora, family Canidae) of sub-Saharan Africa, also known as the African hunting dog or Cape dog. Wild dogs have short hair and show a wide variation in color but are usually covered with irregularly shaped blotches of yellow and white. The tail is covered in longer hair and tipped in white. Long legs are an adaptation for speed in this predator, and its large round ears help it radiate excess body heat. Ideally a savanna species, wild dogs can be found in a variety of habitats, from the arid Sahara into mountainous areas.

Wild dogs are cooperative predators specializing in hunting small gazelles and antelopes, but they are capable of killing larger prey, such as zebras. On average a hunting pack consists of 10 individuals. Packs hunt over a large home range (1,500 square kilometers), only establishing a base when pups are present. Hunting is concentrated in the morning and evening hours, thus avoiding the hot afternoons. Social hierarchies exist in both males and females.

Once a year the dominant male mates with the dominant female. Two to 14 pups are born after a gestation period of two to two and a half months. The entire pack provides care for the pups. Care of pups establishes or reinforces female social dominance and can escalate to fighting among the females in a pack. Males provide a large amount of care to the pups. Ten to 12 weeks after birth, pups are weaned and begin to roam with the hunting pack. Pups reach sexual maturity at 18 months. Females leave their birth pack, join another pack having unrelated males, and try to establish their dominance in the new pack. Wild dogs are thought to live for 10 years.

The wild dog is considered an endangered species and is threatened by habitat loss, persecution by humans, and introduced diseases, such as canine distemper.—Rob Channell

See also **AFRICA, DESERTS OF; CARNIVORES; MAMMALS; PINNAE; PREDATION; SOUTH AFRICA, DESERTS OF**

Further Reading

Bueler, L. E. 1973. *Wild Dogs of the World*. New York: Stein and Day.

Sheldon, J. W. 1992. *Wild Dogs: The Natural History of the Nondomestic Canidae*. San Diego: Academic Press.

DOMESTIC ANIMALS

Animals that are selectively bred in captivity and genetically modified in some way from their wild ancestors for use by people. Breeding individuals are selected on the basis of docility, color, horn size, and meat or milk production. Most domestic animals are dependent on man for protection and food throughout their lives. Domestic animals should be distinguished from tame animals. Tame animals are animals that are caught in the wild and learn from experience that people can provide food and shelter; such animals have lost their fear of people. Tame animals are not usually bred in captivity for specific traits. The distinction between taming and domestication was probably lost on primitive people, and domestication probably occurred initially by taming, with later unintentional domestication by breeding of favored animals having specific qualities. The earliest domestications probably resulted from animals that were caught and tamed for their hides and meat. The additional benefits of domestication, milk, wool, transportation, and fertilizer, were welcome but unplanned.

Not all animals are amenable to domestication. Certain qualities make some animals more likely to be domesticated than others. Among large mammals two important qualities are living in herds and not being territorial. An early breeder would try to maximize the number of animals that could be tended in a given amount of time or with a given amount of effort. This is easily accomplished if all the animals can be maintained together and the shepherd does not have to separate animals to discourage territorial fighting.

Many of these species also follow, in the wild, a dominant individual or pair of individuals. These individuals determine when and how the group will move and who will mate and may help to determine the status of the other individuals in their group. The person caring for the animals takes the place of the dominant member of the group. In this way people are able to exploit the social structure of the animals to provide a better living situation for them.

It seems to be important that the animals have an even temperament. Animals prone to viciousness would endanger their caretakers and would not be likely candidates for domestication. Also, animals that are particularly prone to panic may endanger themselves and their owners in attempting to escape some perceived threat. This selection of docile, but not panic-prone, animals has resulted in the perception that many species of domesticated animals are not as intelligent or lively as their wild ancestors or other closely related species.

Interestingly, the major domestications occurred between 8000 B.C. and 2500 B.C. and no additional domestications of significant species has occurred since that time, despite continued efforts at additional domestication. Equally impressive is the fact that most domestications of large mammals occurred in the Middle East, a particularly arid region. It was in this same region, at about the same time, that the first civilizations arose. Some scholars have argued that the rise of these civilizations and the development of domesticated plants and animals were not a coincidence but that such domestications helped to provide the foundations of these early civilizations.

Except for the domestication of the dog;, the first domestication of other animals was likely conducted by sedentary farmers trying to supplement their diet of grains with meat. Unlike hunters, the other group often associated with the domestication of animals, farmers possessed a number of advantages. First, nomadic hunters would have had to deal with moving large wild animals, at least early in the domestication process. This would not be a problem for sedentary farmers, who could construct a pen for the animals and leave them there indefinitely. Second, farmers, unlike hunters, could supplement the diet of the animals with surplus grain. Third, domestication is a lengthy process, requiring the selection of animals and their traits by selective breeding over many generations. The hunters, typically with no idea of where or when their next meal would be obtained, could not have invested the time required for domestication. Only the predictable sedentary lifestyle of the farmer could have provided the commitment of time and resources that domestication requires.

Farmers are then thought to have come to rely increasingly on their animals as the climate of much of the world became drier. These drier conditions made grain crops unreliable and unprofitable, so that the farmers came to rely almost completely on their domestic animals. Further deteriorating conditions would cause the farmers to adopt a nomadic or pastoral lifestyle to maintain their herds. Such nomadic herding occurs in arid and semiarid areas to this day.

Domesticated animals can provide a livelihood for people living in regions without adequate water to sustain crop-based agriculture. The unpredictable rains of the deserts make vegetation quality vary from area to area; the people who tend animals in the desert often are nomadic to provide their animals with the forage and water that they require. Over the centuries that nomadic shepherds have used the various deserts of the world to raise their animals, they have learned to guide their migrations to regions that provide the best forage at each season.

Among all the domesticated animals, probably none invokes the image of the desert more than the camel. There are actually two types of camels: the Bactrian, or two-humped, camel (*Camelus bactrianus*) and the dromedary, or one-humped, camel (*Camelus dromedarius*). The wild distribution of the Bactrian camel includes much of central Asia extending from the Mediterranean to near the Pacific Ocean. The wild distribution of the dromedary included northern Africa and a part of the Middle East. The distribution of the wild forms of camels meets in the northern part of the Middle East, and it was here approximately 7,500–5,000 years ago that domestication took place. Of the two species the dromedary is better adapted for dry conditions with high temperatures. The camel is the major beast of burden in the deserts of the Old World. Many scholars credit the stamina of the camel with the development and maintenance of many of the transdesert trade routes that were so important throughout the history of civilization;. The camel is also valued for the coarse yet strong wool it provides.

The llama and alpaca, close relatives of the Old World camels, served the same uses in the arid highlands of the South American Andes;. The llama was domesticated from the wild llama (*Lama glama*) 6,000–4,000 years ago in what is now Peru. The alpaca (*Lama paca*) is thought to be the result of a hybridization between domesticated llamas and their close relative, the vicuña (*Vicugna vicugna*).

Both are hardy animals capable of living in the harsh, cold, arid regions of the high Andes. Their split upper lip allows them to graze on the short grasses that characterize the region. Llamas and their relatives have been used by indigenous peoples and later settlers as a beast of burden and a source of wool.

The ass is also a particularly important transport animal in many arid regions of the world. Asses, also referred to as burros, jackasses, or donkeys, were domesticated from the North African wild ass; (*Equus asinus*) in the Middle East or northern Africa about 6,000 years ago. It is likely that some forms of ass have been bred with Asian wild asses (*Equus hemionus*) to form local variants. The ass's ability to withstand dehydration and survive on meager forage makes it an excellent source of transportation in arid regions. The ass is particularly favored among the nomadic shepherds in desert regions of the Old World for carrying equipment and people.

Cattle are not particularly well suited to desert conditions. They are, however, a common feature of the river valleys that traverse deserts. It was in this type of valley in the Near East that scientists believe that cattle were first domesticated from a now-extinct wild form (*Bos primigenius*) more than 8,000 years ago. Several breeds of cattle are able to survive in warm, arid regions. Such breeds are epitomized by the Zebu cattle with their characteristic hump of fat over their shoulders. In addition to being important sources of milk (and butter and cheese), cattle have also been used for transportation, labor, and leather.

Swine are poorly adapted for desert climates but can be found near rivers and water holes throughout the deserts of Asia and northern Africa. Pigs were probably domesticated multiple times throughout much of Asia and Europe. Several of these domestications probably have contributed to today's domesticated pig. The earliest-known domestication of swine was 9,000 years ago in the Middle East. Hide and meat are major products obtained from swine.

Despite the variety of animals found in the desert regions of the world, goats and sheep are the major economic livestock of most arid regions. Their hardiness and ability to survive on almost any vegetation make them particularly valued by desert shepherds. Sheep and goats provide an ample source of meat and dairy products as well as produce wool that can be used directly or sold to generate cash.

The domesticated goat was derived from the wild goat (*Capra hircus*) more than 9,000 years ago in the Middle East. The long period over which the goat has been domesticated has resulted in the development of more than 200 breeds that differ in size, hair length and texture, horn shape, ability to produce milk, and hardiness.

Sheep were domesticated from the mouflon (*Ovis aries*), a wild type of sheep, in western Asia or the Middle East more than 10,000 years ago. There have undoubtedly been contributions from other species of wild sheep, but most of the genetic makeup of domesticated sheep originates from the mouflon. Many of the 800 breeds of domesticated sheep are adapted to the local environments or to fulfill the needs of the local people. Sheep breeds differ in their sizes, presence and size of horns, ear size and shape, and color and texture of wool. Of all the domesticated animals, the sheep is probably the one most dependent on man for its survival.

The cumulative effect of centuries of grazing by nomadic herds around the Mediterranean, in the Near East, and in Africa has decreased plant growth to such a degree that the plants' roots can no longer stabilize the soil. This soil then becomes susceptible to erosion from the infrequent but often intense desert rain showers or the dry winds. This decrease in the amount of soil further decreases the ability of the desert to support plants, and the number of plants declines further, with the cycle feeding on itself. The net effect of this decline in quality and amount of soil and in plant cover is expansion of desert regions and intensification of the desert within arid regions. This process is known as desertification.

Domesticated animals can be detrimental to native species of animals found in deserts. In addition to altering the environment by increased desertification, domesticated animals compete with native species for the limited forage available in the desert. The stocking of large numbers of domesticated animals in a region can rapidly deplete forage to such a level that the native species starve to death.—Rob Channell

See also **ALTIPLANO; ANDES; ASS; ATLAS BROWN CATTLE; AWASSI SHEEP; CAMEL; DESERT GRASSLAND; DESERTIFICATION; DESERT PEOPLES;** **DINGO; GOAT; ISRAEL, DESERTS OF; JORDAN, DESERTS OF; LEBANON, DESERTS OF; LIBYA, DESERTS OF; MIDDLE EAST, DESERTS OF; MOUFLON SHEEP; PUNA; SAHARA DESERT; SAUDI ARABIA, DESERTS OF; SOILS, DESERT; SOUTH AFRICA, DESERTS OF; SYRIA, DESERTS OF; UNITED ARAB EMIRATES, DESERTS OF; YEMEN, DESERTS OF; ZEBU CATTLE**

Further Reading

Cole, H. H., and M. Ronning. 1974. *Animal Agriculture: The Biology of Domestic Animals and Their Use by Man.* San Francisco: Freeman.

Diamond, J. 1994. Zebras and the Anna Karenina principle. *Natural History*, Sept.:4–10.

Hills, E. S., ed. 1966. *Arid Lands: A Geographical Appraisal.* London: Methuen.

Isaac, E. 1970. *Geography of Domestication.* Englewood Cliffs: Prentice-Hall.

DONKEY. *See* ASS; DOMESTIC ANIMALS

DORMANCY

State of inactivity or torpidity in which an organism avoids inhospitable environmental conditions. A number of different terms have been proposed for this condition, and not all researchers agree on which terms are most appropriate. Some of the proposed terms are hibernation, estivation, brumation, cold torpor, and overwintering. The state of being dormant, or in "suspended animation," has apparently evolved independently in many unrelated groups of organisms, and many subtle and not so subtle differences have been discovered in how this condition comes about and how it is maintained. These differences therefore make it difficult to discretely categorize the physiological state of dormancy among different animals. Some animals enter a period of deep dormancy, which is called hibernation if it occurs in winter and estivation if it occurs in summer. Other animals may enter shorter periods of dormancy lasting only a few hours a day or slightly longer. The physiological aspects of dormancy involve slowing down many body functions, including endocrine activity, circulation, and respiration. The number of red blood cells increases, enabling the blood to carry more oxygen per volume. Body temperature drops to ambient temperatures in some organisms such as amphibians and reptiles but is usually regulated to some degree in birds and mammals.

Long periods of estivation are characteristic of most amphibians that live in desert environments. Typically periods of rain are necessary to stimulate emergence and breeding in these animals. However, if rains do not materialize, emergence and breeding may be bypassed, possibly with a reduced survivorship as time goes on. Eric Van Beurden found that the water-holding Australian frog, *Cyclorana platycephala*, could estivate for up to five years in sequence when summer rains failed to arrive, yet populations of these frogs continue to exist in the Simpson, Gibson, and Great Sandy deserts of central and western Australia. An energetics model predicted that 10 percent of these frogs would survive after five years of estivation. The meteorological data from this region indicate that populations of this frog would not be able to exist here were it not for the long-term survivors. Van Beurden found that these frogs survive because the fat bodies that store lipid reserves (fats that are present in the body cavity of all amphibians) can be up to 24 percent of the total body weight. This is much different from the North American desert frog, *Scaphiopus*, in which slightly more than 2 percent of the body weight is stored in the fat bodies prior to estivation. Estivating *Scaphiopus*, which live in a desert with more frequent rains, do not survive for more than two years.—Janalee P. Caldwell

See also **ACTIVITY CYCLES, ANIMALS; AMPHIBIANS; ANIMAL ADAPTATIONS; BAT; BREEDING SEASON; DEHYDRATION; DESICCATION; ESTIVATION; FROGS; HEAT; HIBERNATION; HUMMINGBIRD; INSECTS; MAMMALS; MARSUPIALS; METABOLISM; TOADS; TORPOR; WATER BALANCE**

Further Reading

Pinder, A. W., K. B. Storey, and G. R. Ultsch. 1992. Estivation and hibernation. *In* M. E. Feder and W. W. Burggren, eds., *Environmental Physiology of the Amphibians*, 250–274. Chicago: University of Chicago Press.

Seymour, R. S. 1973. Energy metabolism of dormant spadefoot toads (*Scaphiopus*). *Copeia* 1973:435–445.

Van Beurden, E. K. 1980. Energy metabolism of dormant Australian water-holding frogs (*Cyclorana platycephalus*). *Copeia* 1980:787–799.

DOVE. *See* PIGEON

DRAINAGE. *See* IRRIGATION DRAINAGE

DRINKING WATER

Water used for human consumption and domestic use, including personal hygiene. Generally this definition would cover only water that does not injure or otherwise negatively affect human beings and would thus have the proper physical, chemical, biological, and radioactive characteristics so that it would not cause illness. Additional factors that are also taken into account in describing water quality are taste, smell, color, and turbidity. Definitions of water quality around the world may vary, but certain basic parameters related to human health must be met for water to be considered adequate drinking water. Generally the most important factors relating to water quality and potability are its chemical and bacteriological makeup. In desert and semidesert areas drinking water is often in short supply or of marginal utility (e.g., in many deserts drinking water can be quite salty).—Alberto I. J. Vich and Juana Susana Barroso

See also **COLORADO RIVER; DAM; EXPLOSIVE HEAT DEATH; HEAT STRESS; HUMAN PHYSIOLOGY IN DESERTS; IRRIGATION DRAINAGE; SUNSTROKE; SURVIVAL IN DESERTS; WATER**

Further Reading

Custodio, E. 1976. *Hidrología subterránea*. Barcelona: Omega.

Davis, S. N. 1974. Hydrogeology of arid regions. *In* G. W. Brown, Jr., ed., *Desert Biology: Special Topics on the Physical and Biological Aspects of Arid Regions*, 2:1–30. New York: Academic Press.

Suh-Shiaw, Lo. 1992. *Glossary of Hydrology*. Taipei: Sheng Te.

World Health Organization. 1993. *Guidelines for Drinking-Water Quality*. 2d ed. Geneva: World Health Organization.

DROUGHT

Abnormally dry and sufficiently long period without rain that there are deleterious effects on the hydrologic balance of an area (e.g., agricultural damage, water scarcity, electrical scarcity due to lack of water in hydroelectric plants, damage to vegetation or animals). The severity of a drought depends on lack of rain, low humidity, the duration of the drought, and the size of the area affected. In general the term "drought" should be used to describe periods of water deficit that are relatively extensive compared with what might be considered the normal period of aridity in a region. Thus "drought" is a relative term.

Drought and aridity should not be confused. Although arid areas may be subject to droughts, they have aridity as a long-term characteristic. Droughts are temporary and may appear in any part of the world, including regions that are not generally subjected to aridity. Droughts are generally divided into two categories, one with a basis in meteorology and another with a basis in agriculture. Droughts are considered meteorological phenomena when they are defined and compared with a limit of rainfall that is a percentage of the long-term mean rain received in any particular area. In agricultural terms, a drought is a condition in which the moisture in the soil of a region is not available to plant roots and the plants are unable to grow. A meteorological drought may not have significant negative effects on the vegetation of an area if it occurs before plant growth, whereas a period of aridity that does not qualify as a meteorological drought may, for all practical purposes, be a drought as far as plant growth is concerned.

Droughts are predominantly associated with anticyclones that persist for extended periods. However, aridity and drought are phenomena that are complex and involve not only meteorological factors but hydrological, environmental, social, and other factors as well. For any particular point on the earth, rainfall totals vary, as does the pattern of rainfall. To understand the causes of drought, one must examine atmospheric pressure, movement of air masses, temperature, and other climatological parameters. Many things can lead to the initiation or intensification of a drought, including the albedo (the reflectivity of the soil), vegetative cover, the presence of human dwellings, the existence of a dense layer of dust in the atmosphere (such as might be related to windstorms or volcanic activity), changes in the temperature of the superficial waters of the oceans, such as the El Niño phenomenon, and increases in the concentration of carbon dioxide in the atmosphere.

An example of how substrate and human activities can affect a drought can be shown by vegetative cover and desert soils. If there are light-colored soils in a desert (as there frequently are) and if the area is covered with vegetation, any removal of vegetation over large areas will increase the albedo of the area (because of the light-colored soils) and lead to lower atmospheric humidity and reduced formation of clouds. Thus an area that is already arid could be changed to one of hyperaridity due to a change in the surface albedo related to the removal of vegetation.—Federico Norte

See also **ADIABATIC PROCESSES; AN INTRODUCTION TO DESERTS; BAROMETRIC PRESSURE (ATMOSPHERIC PRESSURE); CLIMATE; CLIMATE CLASSIFICATION; DAM; DESERTS; DESERTS, MONTANE; DESERTS, RAIN SHADOW; FLOOD; GROUNDWATER; HEAT; HYDROLOGICAL CYCLE; HYDROLOGY; INSOLATION; MONSOON; PRECIPITATION; RIVERS; RUNOFF; WELL**

Further Reading

Day, J. A., and V. J. Schaefer. 1991. *Clouds and Weather.* Boston: Houghton Mifflin.

Nir, D. 1974. *The Semi-arid World: Man on the Fringe of the Desert.* London: Longman.

Oliver, J. E., and R. W. Fairbridge, eds. 1987. *The Encyclopedia of Climatology.* New York: Chapman and Hall.

Schaefer, V. J., and J. A. Day. 1981. *A Field Guide to the Atmosphere.* Boston: Houghton Mifflin.

Schneider, S. H., ed. 1996. *Encyclopedia of Climate and Weather.* 2 vols. New York: Oxford University Press.

DUNE BUGGIES

Motor vehicles equipped with large balloon tires that allow the vehicle to "float" on loose sand. They generally have an open cockpit with a roll bar. They can be purchased already manufactured, but more often small cars, especially old Volkswagen Beetles, are converted to dune buggies in auto body shops. The number of users of dune buggies has increased dramatically in recent years, but it is difficult to obtain accurate figures on the number in use. Use is particularly heavy in the California Desert, where thousands will be in use on public and private lands on any given weekend. Much of the use occurs on Bureau of Land Management (BLM) lands. There are 17,000 square miles of BLM land in the California Desert alone.

Dune buggies are used primarily on sand dunes. This can be especially destructive in coastal areas, where dune buggies destroy sensitive dune vegetation and crush the nests and eggs of dune-nesting birds. Little is known about the ecology of desert dunes; but there are many species of invertebrates and vertebrates that are known to use sand dune habitats. The ecological impact of dune buggies in these habitats is not well understood. There is a clear physical impact, however. Dune buggies, like most off-road vehicles, have come under increasing regulation in recent years.—Thomas E. Lacher, Jr.

See also **ARABIAN GULF, DESERTS OF; CALIFORNIA DESERT; COLLUVIAL DEPOSITS; CONSERVATION IN DESERTS; CONTAMINATION; DIRT BIKES; DUNES; ECOLOGY; HABITAT DEGRADATION; OFF-ROAD VEHICLES; POLLUTION; WILDLIFE**

Further Reading

Andrews, R. N. L., and P. F. Nowak, eds. 1980. *Off-Road Vehicle Use: A Management Challenge.* Washington, D.C.: Office of Environmental Quality, U.S. Department of Agriculture.

Heath, R. 1974. *The Environmental Consequences of the Off-Road Vehicle: With Profiles of the Industry and the Enthusiast.* Washington, D.C.: Defenders of Wildlife.

Webb, R. H., and H. G. Wilshire, eds. 1983. *Environmental Effects of Off-Road Vehicles: Impacts and Management in Arid Regions.* New York: Springer.

DUNES

The most common type of aeolian (windblown) depositional landforms in desert areas (other types include sand ripples and large-scale dunes, called megadunes or draas). Dunes are formed because sand moving near the ground surface encounters an obstacle (rock, vegetation), which increases surface roughness. The wind velocity drops below the minimum speed necessary to transport sand and the sand loses momentum and is deposited, forming a sand patch (atmospheric instabilities can also cause sand deposition). As this process continues the sand patch traps incoming saltating grains and prevents their further movement downwind. Ultimately the wind aerodynamically shapes the sand patch into a sand dune.

A dune formed by winds from a single direction will have a gently sloping windward side (10°–12°), a crest (highest elevation on the dune), and a steeply sloping slipface at the angle of repose for dry sand (30°–32°). The junction of the slipface with the main dune body is the brink. Most sand dunes are made up of fine-sorted (uniform size), quartz sand, although some dunes can have gypsum or clay. Once established dunes migrate in the direction of the most effective sand-transporting winds. Typical dune heights range from 3 to 100

Sand dune "sea" at the Namib Desert Research Station, Gobabeb, Namibia; the riparian woodlands of the Kuiseb River are visible at the base of the dunes. (Photo: M. A. Mares)

meters, although dunes of greater height are known.

As the wind transports sand from the windward slope (the erosional side) to the crest, sand is piled up and a threshold condition is reached, whereby further accumulation sends the sand avalanching down the slipface (the depositional side) as the angle of repose for dry sand is exceeded. This pattern is repeated and causes the dune to migrate downwind, maintaining its aerodynamic shape. As the dune grows in height, it begins to influence the airflow over it. Thus a dune is in a constant dynamic equilibrium as wind regime, sand supply, and dune form are always changing, their interactions representing the extent of dune erosion and deposition and hence net downwind movement. Dunes occur in a variety of forms, and numerous names have been proposed. Three primary classes can be distinguished: crescentic, linear, and star dunes.

Crescentic dunes form in areas characterized by consistently dominant and fairly unidirectional wind regimes, the latter fluctuating 15°–20° or less around a mean compass value or direction. Three major types can be recognized: barchan, transverse, and parabolic. *Barchans* are crescentic dunes with elongated horns pointing downwind and are considered the classic desert dune type. The crescent shape of the dune is largely the result of sands moving faster at the edges (thus forming the horns of the dune) than they do along the main body of the barchan. They tend to form best in areas having a sparse supply of sand, limited vegetation cover, a surface of bedrock or desert pavement, and strong unidirectional winds. They exhibit some of the highest downwind migration rates of any dunes. As sand supply increases and/or the directional wind regime changes or fluctuates significantly, barchans may coalesce to form complex barchanoid ridges and transverse dunes. *Transverse dunes* are asymmetric in shape and form at right angles (normal or transverse) to the strong unidirectional wind regime in areas with abundant sand supply, both in desert and coastal environments. *Parabolic* (or U-shaped) dunes are crescentic in plan with the arms (horns) pointing upwind or into the direction of the prevailing winds (opposite form of barchans). Vegetation or moisture anchors the trailing arms of the dune while the central section is selectively deflated and eroded, thus enabling the dune to be elongated. Parabolic dunes with parallel arms one to two kilometers long are found near Pismo Beach in central California as well as in the Thar Desert of India and Pakistan. They are common in coastal environments, along with blowouts (erosional hollows or depressions carved by wind in vegetated coastal dunes), where vegetation, high water tables, and strong unidirectional winds contribute to their formation and preservation.

Linear dunes (or *longitudinal dunes*) are characterized by straight to sinuous sand ridges oriented parallel to the prevailing or dominant wind directions and are the most common desert dune type. These parallel sand ridges are separated from one another by sand-free interdune surfaces. Linear dunes are usually about 15–20 meters high and up to a kilometer apart. In cross-section they have a triangular profile, with a sharp crest and one or two slipfaces on either side, depending on the seasonality of the winds. Two major types are recognized: vegetated linear dunes and seifs. *Vegetated linear dunes*, which consist of long, straight, and rather narrow sand ridges, with clumps of vegetation on the sides and even occasionally on the crest, are especially prominent in the Simpson Desert of Australia and the Kalahari Desert of southern Africa. Some exhibit branching patterns resulting in mergers at Y junctions. Vegetation is an integral part of this dune type. *Seifs* (from the Arabic word for sword) are more massive, sharp-crested, and sinuous, without significant vegetation and generally higher and wider than vegetated linear dunes. The

origin of linear dunes and their dynamics have been the focus of considerable debate. Earlier views held that they formed as a result of parallel roll-vortex flow patterns in the interdune flats. Recent field data indicate that linear dunes most likely form in areas characterized by wide bimodal wind regimes and extend parallel to the direction of the dominant sand transporting winds. According to another field-tested model, airflow that strikes the linear dune crest obliquely gets separated and blows parallel to the dune axis on the lee side. Not all vegetated linear dunes are fossil or relict, even though vegetation is a major component of certain linear dunes, as sand can be (and is) transported on the crest and flanks.

Star dunes are pyramid-shaped sand ridges with three or more arms radiating outward from a central peak, with multiple slipfaces. They tend to form in the interior of many sand seas (ergs) or other large depositional basins. They are the largest of the many dune types, with some attaining heights greater than 300 meters. They are best formed in areas that exhibit a complex or a multidirectional wind regime. In addition, topography and/or the converging sand transport paths seem to play a role in their formation, as most star dunes seem to grow vertically once established. Excellent examples are found in the Gran Desierto del Altar in the Sonoran Desert of Mexico and in the Namib Desert in Namibia.—Vatche P. Tchakerian

See also **ARABIAN GULF, DESERTS OF; ASIA, DESERTS OF; AUSTRALIA, DESERTS OF; CALIFORNIA DESERT; DIRT BIKES; DUNE BUGGIES; DUNES, LUNETTE; DUNES, NABKHA; JORDAN, DESERTS OF; MIDDLE EAST, DESERTS OF; MOJAVE DESERT; NAMIBIA, DESERTS OF; OFFROAD VEHICLES; PALESTINE, DESERTS OF; PSAMMOPHYTES; PSAMMOPHYTIC SCRUB; SAHARA DESERT; SAND RAMP; SAUDI ARABIA, DESERTS OF; SOILS, DESERT; SOILS, DESERT, ARKOSIC SAND; WHITE SANDS NATIONAL MONUMENT; WIND TRANSPORT; WIND**

Further Reading

Cooke, R., A. Warren, and A. Goudie. 1993. *Desert Geomorphology.* London: University College London Press.

Lancaster, N. 1994. Dune morphology and dynamics. *In* A. D. Abrahams and A. J. Parsons, eds., *Geomorphology of Desert Environments*, 474–505. London: Chapman and Hall.

Pye, K., and H. Tsoar. 1990. *Aeolian Sand and Sand Dunes.* London: Unwin Hyman.

Thomas, D. S. G. 1989. Aeolian sand deposits. *In* D. S. G. Thomas, ed., *Arid Zone Geomorphology*, 284–307. London: Belhaven.

DUNES, LUNETTE

Crescentic-shaped, vegetated, lakeshore dunes found on the lee (downwind) side of playas and pans. Their composition ranges from mostly fine sand to mostly clays and/or clay pellets (clay dunes). Pelletization is the result of the aggregation of fine silts and clays into sand-size particles by salts and carbonates. Clay content ranges from 10 to 75 percent. They form best in areas characterized by strong seasonality of precipitation. During the dry season aeolian activity entrains the lake sediments and the clay pellets, and during the wet season when the pan or playa is full, cementing agents are able to bind the pellets and anchor the dune. The crescentic shape of the lunette is also influenced by wave processes on the downwind end of the lake. They also tend to be found in association with other geomorphic features, such as lakeshore beach ridges and vegetated dunes. Typical lunette heights range from 5 to 50 meters.

In Australia, the Kalahari Desert, and Tunisia, significant concentrations of lunettes are found downwind of playas and pans that often have water after the rainy season. In some pans both clay-rich and sand-rich lunettes are found superimposed or fringed together, indicating changes in source regions or climate. Most lunettes exhibit paleosols and other postdepositional aggregates, indicating both seasonal and long term environmental changes. Both their internal structures and their deposits are useful for deciphering paleoclimatic information.—Vatche P. Tchakerian

See also **ARABIAN GULF, DESERTS OF; ASIA, DESERTS OF; AUSTRALIA, DESERTS OF; DIRT BIKES; DUNE BUGGIES; DUNES; DUNES, NABKHA; JORDAN, DESERTS OF; MIDDLE EAST, DESERTS OF; MOJAVE DESERT; NAMIBIA, DESERTS OF; OFF-ROAD VEHICLES; PALESTINE, DESERTS OF; PLAYA; PSAMMOPHYTES; PSAMMOPHYTIC SCRUB; SAHARA DESERT; SALT PAN; SAND RAMP; SAUDI ARABIA, DESERTS OF; SOILS, DESERT; SOILS, DESERT, ARKOSIC SAND; WHITE SANDS NATIONAL MONUMENT; WIND; WIND TRANSPORT**

Further Reading

Cooke, R., A. Warren, and A. Goudie. 1993. *Desert Geomorphology*. London: University College London Press.

Goudie, A., and G. L. Wells. 1995. The nature, distribution and formation of pans in arid zones. *Earth Science Reviews* 38:1–69.

Pye, K., and H. Tsoar. 1990. *Aeolian Sand and Sand Dunes*. London: Unwin Hyman.

DUNES, NABKHA

Type of dune anchored by vegetation and composed of sands, silts, and clays. They are elliptical in plan, and the vegetation serves as loci for the trapping and deposition of windblown materials within the plant foliage by reducing the wind velocities near the ground. Springs or near-surface groundwater provides the necessary moisture for the vegetation. To trap the windblown materials effectively, plants must be at least 10–15 centimeters in height. The anchoring vegetation stabilizes the dune, rendering it immobile yet allowing for downwind growth. The size of the nabkha depends on the size and density of the anchoring vegetation. Nabkhas up to three meters high may form downwind of low shrubs, while meganabkhas up to 10 meters high and one kilometer long may form around clumps of trees. Wind velocities between neighboring nabkhas increase because of concentrated wind flow, often resulting in greater erosion in interdune areas. Occasionally nabkhas kill the vegetation by covering it or raising its roots above the groundwater. Once the vegetation has been destroyed, the nabkha is vulnerable to deflation (gradual disappearance by wind).

Nabkha initiation and development is strongly linked to land degradation (and desertification) in drylands as a result of both natural stresses, such as climate change and drought, and anthropogenic stresses on the ecosystem. Such human-induced activities as grazing, cultivation, and burning can lead to the development of nabkhas, as the remaining clumps of vegetation trap the windblown materials. These dunes are also referred to as coppice or shrub-coppice dunes.—Vatche P. Tchakerian

See also **ARABIAN GULF, DESERTS OF; ASIA, DESERTS OF; AUSTRALIA, DESERTS OF; DESERTIFICATION; DIRT BIKES; DUNE BUGGIES; DUNES; GROUNDWATER; JORDAN, DESERTS OF; MIDDLE EAST, DESERTS OF; MOJAVE DESERT; NAMIBIA, DESERTS OF; OFF-ROAD VEHICLES; OVERGRAZING; PALESTINE, DESERTS OF; PLAYA; PSAMMOPHYTES; PSAMMOPHYTIC SCRUB; SAHARA DESERT; SALT PAN; SAND RAMP; SAUDI ARABIA, DESERTS OF; SHRUBS; SOILS, DESERT; SOILS, DESERT, ARKOSIC SAND; WIND; WIND TRANSPORT**

Further Reading

Cooke, R., A. Warren, and A. Goudie. 1993. *Desert Geomorphology.* London: University College London Press.

Nickling, W. G., and S. A. Wolfe. 1994. The morphology and origin of nabkhas, region of Mopti, Mali, West Africa. *Journal of Arid Environments* 28:13–30.

DURICRUSTS

Hardened surface (and near-surface) of chemically precipitated crusts or horizons typically composed of high concentrations of minerals, such as iron, aluminum, silica, calcium carbonate, or gypsum. Duricrusts are named after the primary mineral forming it. The most common types are calcrete (calcium), silcrete (silica), ferricrete (iron), and gypcrete (gypsum). Other types are alcrete (aluminum), salcrete (sodium chloride), halcrete (halite), and dolocrete (magnesium carbonate). Average thickness ranges from 1 to 10 meters. Their presence in arid and semiarid environments generally indicates formation during more humid conditions and thus are considered relict landforms. Duricrusts are often found as caprocks and/or overlying mesa- and butte-type topography in desert environments.

Concentration levels necessary for the formation of duricrusts result from either sedimentation or pedogenic (soil-forming) processes. Aeolian (windblown), alluvial (deposited by water), or colluvial (material transported and deposited by mass movement processes, such as by dry slides) processes can be responsible for the surface accumulation of the particular mineral involved, usually in the lowest topographic areas. Likewise, pedogenic processes, including illuviation (subsurface weathering and leaching), create the enriched horizon necessary for duricrust formation.

Duricrusts composed of pure calcium carbonate are known as calcretes. These formations often form prominent scarps or caprocks. Most calcretes are formed by pedogenic processes, as percolating rainwater infiltrates the soil and mobilizes carbonate from upper horizons (with high carbon dioxide content) and deposits it in lower horizons (with low carbon dioxide content). The carbonate is deposited as coatings on pebbles. The coatings grow and eventually fill the interparticle voids. Some calcretes were formed in areas where the parent material did not have sufficient calcium content. In these

Duricrust caprock formations along the Arizona-Utah border. (Photo: M. A. Mares)

instances the influx of calcium-rich aeolian dust seems to be the major factor for the formation of the calcrete. Absolute dating methods determined that many calcretes are ancient. Ages range from 30,000 to 15,000 years before the present in Namibia and Spain. Some duricrusts in the southwestern United States started to form during the late Miocene. Since many calcic (containing calcium) horizons in the southwestern United States are too deep to be attributed to current precipitation, well-developed calcretes most likely formed during wetter than present climates.

Silcrete duricrusts are very hard and brittle. Silica content is commonly as high as 90 percent. Like other duricrusts, silcretes often form caprocks in arid environments. Weathering of the silcrete mesas produces the very distinct gibber stony plains of the Australian arid zone. Silcrete duricrusts are often ancient in age and most likely formed during wetter environments, owing to the fact that high amounts of water (and high temperatures) is required to mobilize silica. A warm, humid climate would be required to produce weathering that could release the necessary silica from silicate minerals. Extensive silcretes occur in Australia, South Africa, and the Sahara. Some Australian silcretes are late Jurassic in age. Silcretes in the Sahara date from the Oligocene, a period characterized by high amounts of moisture in that region. Southern Africa silcretes may be Cretaceous in age.

Ferricretes are relict features that originated in humid tropical environments with iron concentrations of up to 80 percent. They can be from 1 to 10 meters thick and formed because of the intense leaching of iron-bearing compounds from the soil and weathered rock (regolith). Ferricrete is formed as iron is oxidized and immobilized after it is released by deep weathering and percolates toward the surface. Ferricretes and silcretes are often found together in some regions owing to the fact that they were most likely derived from the same weathering profiles, but with different chemistries and modes of formation. Good examples of ferricretes are found along the edges of the Australian deserts and in the southern Sahel in Africa.

Gypcrete is an indurated (hard) crust with the mineral gypsum constituting from 50 to 90 percent of the total deposit. Because gypsum is highly soluble and less widespread than silica or calcium carbonate, it has a limited geographic distribution. It is typically found in the more hyperarid regions of drylands, such as in parts of Algeria and Tunisia in the Sahara Desert, where average precipitation values are less than 100 millimeters. Massive gypcretes are also found in the central Namib Desert, in parts of southern and western Australia, and in central Asia. Gypcrete in the southwestern United States is limited to a few large hydrologic basins where gypsum accumulates as a result of the deflation (lowering of a surface by wind) of sand, dust, and other minerals from dry lake surfaces. Because gypsum is highly susceptible to dissolution by water, gypcrete rarely creates the mesa and butte or caprock cuesta landscapes typical with other duricrusts. As a result most gypcretes are Pliocene or younger in age.—Vatche P. Tchakerian

See also **COLLUVIAL DEPOSITS (COLLUVIUM); DESERT SLOPES; MIOCENE; PLIOCENE; ROCK VARNISH; SALT; SALT CRUST; SALT PAN; SOILS, DESERT; SOILS, DESERT, CALCAREOUS; SOILS, DESERT, CALCRETE; SOILS, DESERT, CALICHE; STONE PAVEMENT; WHITE SANDS NATIONAL MONUMENT**

Further Reading

Cooke, R., A. Warren, and A. Goudie. 1993. *Desert Geomorphology.* London: University College London Press.

Dixon, J. C. 1994. Duricrusts. *In* A. D. Abrahams and A. J. Parsons, eds., *Geomorphology of Desert Environments,* 82–105. London: Chapman and Hall.

Watson, A. 1989. Desert crusts and rock varnish. *In* D. S. G. Thomas, ed., *Arid Zone Geomorphology,* 25–41. London: Belhaven.

DUST DEVIL

Phenomenon in which a small but vigorous whirlwind (rapidly spinning column of air), usually of very short duration, lifts soil and other matter into the air. Dust devils are often visible for long distances across the desert. The diameter of whirlwinds ranges from 3 to 33 meters, and their mean height is approximately 200 meters. Nevertheless, in some cases dust devils have reached altitudes of several hundred meters. The direction of rotation of dust devils may be anticyclonic or cyclonic (counterclockwise or clockwise). They develop primarily on hot days with clear skies in arid zones, where the very hot soil causes an unstable temperature gradient that is particularly pronounced in the first 200 meters of the atmosphere. Whirlwinds may affect the electrical charge in the atmosphere. In such cases they may develop into electrified tubes in which the electrical charge of the atmosphere has been separated due to the effects of the friction of the whirling column of air within the dust devil. In many desert areas dust devils are particularly common in spring and summer. More powerful dust devils, often approaching the scale of small tornadoes, can develop in association with strong convective storms in desert areas.—Federico Norte

See also **ANTICYCLONE; BAROMETRIC PRESSURE (ATMOSPHERIC PRESSURE); CLIMATE; CLIMATE CLASSIFICATION; CONVECTIVE STORM; CYCLONE; DESERTS; HEAT; LOW PRESSURE; WIND**

Further Reading

Day, J. A., and V. J. Schaefer. 1991. *Clouds and Weather.* Boston: Houghton Mifflin.

Oliver, J. E., and R. W. Fairbridge, eds. 1987. *The Encyclopedia of Climatology.* New York: Chapman and Hall.

Schaefer, V. J., and J. A. Day. 1981. *A Field Guide to the Atmosphere.* Boston: Houghton Mifflin.

Schneider, S. H., ed. 1996. *Encyclopedia of Climate and Weather.* 2 vols. New York: Oxford University Press.

DUST STORM. *See* HABOOB; SAHARA DESERT; SANTA ANA WINDS

E

EARS. *See* PINNAE

EARWIGS

Insects in the order Dermaptera characterized by the possession of forcepslike pincers located at the posterior end of the abdomen. When they have wings, they are small and covered, at least partially, by short wing covers (elytra). The most common earwigs are terrestrial and vary in size from about 5 to 30 millimeters. Some, however, are very small and are parasitic on bats or rodents. Terrestrial earwigs are not easily observed in deserts because they spend much of their time under rocks and other surface debris. They may become terrestrially active at night. Earwigs feed primarily on decaying vegetation but occasionally feed on plants or other insects. They are of considerable biological interest because they have extended parental care, an unusual attribute in a small invertebrate. Females construct nests in which they deposit eggs. They attend the eggs until they hatch, and, in some species, the female remains with the young earwigs for an extended period. In addition to using the pincers for defense, some species produce noxious chemicals that may be sprayed from glands on the dorsal side of the third and fourth abdominal segments.—Laurie J. Vitt

See also **ARTHROPODS; DEFENSIVE ADAPTATIONS, ANIMALS; INSECTS; VENOM**

Further Reading

Borror, D. J., C. A. Triplehorn, and N. F. Johnson. 1992. *An Introduction to the Study of Insects*. New York: Harcourt Brace.

Borror, D. J., and R. E. White. 1970. *A Field Guide to the Insects*. Boston: Houghton Mifflin.

Eisner, T. 1960. Defense mechanisms of arthropods. 2. The chemical and mechanical weapons of an earwig. *Psyche* 67:62–70.

ECHIDNA

Spiny anteater belonging to one of two families of egg-laying mammals, the Tachyglossidae (subclass Prototheria, order Monotremata). The short-beaked echidna, genus *Tachyglossus*, occurs in Australia, including the Australian desert, Tasmania, and New Guinea. The long-beaked echidna, genus *Zaglossus*, is found in the mountains of New Guinea. Length of the head and body ranges from 30 to 45 centimeters, and weight ranges from two to seven kilograms. Echidnas have a long, naked, tubular snout with a small mouth at the tip and a long (up to 18 centimeters), sticky tongue. *Zaglossus* feeds on termites and ants, whereas *Tachyglossus* prefers earthworms and solitary insects. Although echidnas lack teeth, pads of horny spines on the back of the tongue and on the palate help to crush food. Spines, which cover all but the belly and the limbs, are a protective device. The second toe of the hind foot is enlarged and used for grooming. Males have a large horny spur on the ankle of the hind limb, but a functional venom gland is absent.

A single soft-shelled egg is laid in a pouch formed from the enlarged folds of skin and muscle on each side of the abdomen. The egg hatches after 10 days, and the young echidna remains in the pouch until spines develop at about six months. Echidnas nurse for one year from hairy patches known as milk areolae—although echidnas lack true teats or nipples, these patches develop into a nipplelike structure.

Echidnas are solitary and take refuge in shallow burrows, hollow logs, or underbrush. When threatened they roll into a ball or dig quickly into soft dirt, so that only the spiny back is visible. Superficially echidnas resemble the hedgehogs (family Erinaceidae) of the Old World deserts. Short-beaked echidnas have few sweat glands and generally avoid high temperatures by seeking refuge during the day and being active at dusk and dawn. Echidnas do not hibernate, but some may enter torpor. Echidnas are long-lived and may live in the wild for up to 20 years.—Janet K. Braun

See also **ANTS; AUSTRALIA; BURROWING ANIMALS; CONVERGENT EVOLUTION; HEDGEHOG; MAMMALS; MARSUPIALS; PERSPIRATION; SWEAT GLANDS; TERMITES; THERMOREGULATION; TORPOR; WATER BALANCE**

Further Reading

Augee, M. L. 1983. Short-beaked echidna. *In* R. Strahan, ed., *The Complete Book of Australian Mammals*, 8–9. London: Angus and Robertson.

Griffiths, M. 1989. Tachyglossidae. *In* D. W. Walton and B. J. Richardson, eds., *Fauna of Australia, Mammalia*, 1B:407–435. Canberra: Australian Government Publishing Service.

Grzimek's Encyclopedia of Mammals. Vol. 1. 1990. New York: McGraw-Hill.

Macdonald, D., ed. 1984. *The Encyclopedia of Mammals*. New York: Facts on File.

Ride, W. D. L. 1980. *A Guide to the Native Mammals of Australia*. Oxford: Oxford University Press.

ECOLOGY

Study of the interactions between organisms and their environment for the purpose of understanding patterns of distribution, abundance, and associations of organisms. Ecology as a discipline in science is relatively new, with its modern approach dating from the 1930s. Ecology has its roots in natural history observations of organisms, a methodology that dates from the time of Aristotle (384–322 B.C.), but the modern discipline goes beyond observation in an attempt to document, quantify, or experimentally test patterns of interest in terms of cause and effect.

Ecology is studied at many different levels. Autecology is the study of single–species' patterns of habitat and food use, reproduction, migration, and physiological adaptations to the abiotic (nonliving) environment. The specific study of physiological adaptations is often called physiological ecology and usually focuses on ranges of tolerance of organisms to specific environmental conditions such as temperature, water availability, salinity, photoperiod, light conditions, or soil type. Population ecology is the study of interactions among organisms of the same species which influence the number and distribution of individuals of that species. Population ecology is an example of a subdiscipline of ecology that examines biotic (living) interactions. Community ecology studies the biotic interactions among different species that occur in the same place. Community-level interactions include food web dynamics, predation, competition among similar species for resources in limited supply, parasitism, cooperation, and other higher-order interactions that influence the types and number of species that can live in the same area. Ecosystem ecology examines interactions of biotic and abiotic factors that together influence flow of energy and cycling of materials in specific regions. Studies in ecosystem ecology focus on one particular type of habitat, such as ocean, coral reef, temperate forest, or desert, that is easily distinguishable from surrounding habitat types.—Edie Marsh-Matthews

See also **BIOME; BIOSPHERE RESERVE; CARRYING CAPACITY; DIVERSITY; ECOSYSTEM; ECOTYPE; ENERGY FLOW; INTERNATIONAL BIOLOGICAL PROGRAM; LANDSCAPE; PRODUCTIVITY, AQUATIC ECOSYSTEMS; SUCCESSION**

Further Reading

Cloudsley-Thompson, J. L. 1996. *Biotic Interactions in Arid Lands*. Berlin: Springer.

Krebs, C. J. 1995. *Ecology: The Experimental Analysis of Distribution and Abundance*. 4th ed. New York: Harper and Row.

Odum, E. P. 1983. *Basic Ecology*. Philadelphia: Saunders.

ECONOMIC VALUE OF DESERT PRODUCTS

Plants and plant products having commercial value that are produced commercially or grow naturally in arid climates. Although temperate and tropical regions provide most of the world's economically important products, the unique but depauperate flora of deserts includes a few plant species that are of economic value. Members of several families are of considerable importance: in the Agavaceae, *Agave* for fiber and food and *Yucca* for fiber and steroids; in the Cactaceae, *Opuntia* for food, sugars, and alkaloids; in the Euphorbiaceae, *Euphorbia* for wax and natural rubber; in the Fabaceae, *Acacia* for tannins and *Prosopis* for proteins; in the Poaceae, various species for cattle fodder; and in the Solanaceae, *Solanum* for food, medicines, and alkaloids.

The growing human population requires the search for additional sources of food. One way to produce enough food in the future is to convert arid and semiarid rangelands into farmlands. People of semiarid regions of the world rely heavily on a relatively small number of food crops, most of which are also grown in temperate climates. Agriculture in arid and semiarid regions often requires extensive irrigation, placing high demands on already-strained aquifers and other sources of water. An alternative to developing irrigation-based farmland is to cultivate plants already adapted to xeric conditions. Species that tolerate low soil moisture conditions are being investigated as potential widespread crops.

Two potential candidates for future cultivation in arid regions are the tepary bean (*Phaseolus acutifolius*) and amaranth (*Amaranthus*), which have been used for years by native peoples in the southwestern United States and Mexico. The tepary bean, whose range includes much of Arizona, New Mexico, and northwestern Mexico, is one of the most drought- and heat-adapted food crops known. The beans (seeds) of the tepary contain more protein than most current commercial beans, and the seeds are produced in good quantity, especially after a rainfall. Amaranth, whose native range includes Arizona and much of western and southern Mexico, is an ancient crop that was revered by the Aztecs. Amaranth plants grow to one meter in height, while requiring little care, and produce large seed heads that can weigh 2.7–3.6 kilograms and contain half a million seeds. The seeds burst open at high cooking temperatures like popcorn and can also be milled into a flour that is rich in certain essential amino acids. The leaves of the amaranth are edible and rich in vitamins and minerals and have the flavor of spinach.

Another problem in the agriculture system in semiarid regions is the buildup of salt in the soil due to irrigation practices. As irrigation waters are brought to the field, they pick up dissolved natural salts from the soils in which they flow. In warm and hot climates water that does not percolate into the ground evaporates into the air, but the salt that is dissolved in the water remains at or near the surface of the soil. Most crops cannot tolerate the salt and die; however, there are a few salt-resistant plants that may become more valuable as crops in the future. One such plant is the Chilean tamarugo tree, which can survive in exceptionally salty conditions. The pods and leaves of the tamarugo have been used as fodder for sheep. In China, where salinization of irrigated farmland has also increased, species of salt-tolerant *Artemisia* have been employed to stabilize nearby dunes and to act as windscreens.

Millet is the common name for many small-seeded cereal and forage grasses used for food, feed, or forage. Millets tolerate a wide range of environmental conditions including semiarid climates and will grow where more desirable grains, such as corn, wheat, and rice, will not. Although they have a relatively high nutritional value compared to noncereal sources of starch, millet grain yields are often low due to the marginal conditions in which they are grown. Millets, however, are often a staple of the poorest people of the poorest countries in the world. In some semiarid parts of northern Africa, native farmers clear the scrub from the acacia-grassland savanna and plant crops such as millet, sorghum, and sesame. After a few years the nutrient-poor soil no longer supports the production of these crops, and the farmers allow the fields to lay fallow. Native plants then return to the area, among them the acacia tree (*Acacia senegal*), a legume that helps to restore fertility to the soil. Farmers then plant their grass crops in the soil for a few years until the nutrients again diminish to the point where productivity drops off.

Plants are not only economically important for the food and fodder that they provide for humans and their livestock; they are also the source of many extracts and natural products of commercial value. Gum arabic is a widely used exudate gum from the *Acacia senegal* tree of northeastern Africa. Most of the world's supply is still collected from wild trees that have been cut or punctured to cause a wound reaction in the trees. The gum arabic that exudes from the wound dries and is then collected and sent to processing plants around the world. Gum arabic finds its way into a wide variety of products, including candy, in which it prevents crystallization of the sugar, and hand lotions and liquid soaps, where it acts as a fat emulsifier.

Several species of *Agave* provide strong, durable fibers that are woven into ropes, cords, mats, and fishing nets. *Agave sisalana*, *Agave fourcroydes* (sisal hemp), and *Agave heteracantha* (istle fiber) are three of the most important fiber plants in this genus. In Mexico a sweet sap is collected from the stems of several different species of *Agave* which, when fermented, becomes a mild alcoholic wine called pulque. Tequila and mescal are both alcoholic beverages distilled from pulque, depending on the *Agave* used. *Agave tequilana* is the source for tequila, but several species may be used for the production of mescal.

The jojoba shrub, *Simmondsia chinensis*, grows in the Great Basin and Sonoran deserts of North America and produces an economically important oil. Jojoba oil is actually a liquid wax, with a chemical structure similar to that of sperm whale oil, which had been used extensively as a lubricant for fine machinery. Because of the depletion of sperm whales, jojoba oil was once seen as a potential replacement lubricant and savior for the whale; however, oil yields have been low and the economic value of jojoba has not yet met its initial potential.

During World War II the supply of natural rubber to the United States was cut off because of the occupation of many Asian rubber plantations by the Japanese. This caused an intensified search for alternative sources of rubber as well as intensified experimentation in the process for producing synthetic rubber. Although the use of synthetic rubber has greatly increased since its development during World War II, the demand for natural rubber from plants remains high because its properties remain superior to those of synthetic rubber. For instance, natural rubber is still desired in the manufacture of tires. Although most natural rubber is still obtained from tropical trees of the genus *Hevea*, one potential source of natural rubber from semiarid regions is guayule, *Parthenium argentatum*, a member of the sunflower family.

Guayule is a native shrub of the Chihuahuan Desert of southwestern Texas and northwestern Mexico. The rubber made from guayule is very similar to that from the *Hevea* rubber plant, and almost 20 percent of the dry weight of the guayule is rubber. Although a guayule processing plant has been built in Mexico, the development of guayule as an important crop has been hampered by the fact that the rubber cannot be harvested from the plants until they are about seven years old. The shrubs are cut down or uprooted, dipped in hot water to aid the processing, and then ground up in water. The rubber is skimmed from the liquid, purified, and then sent to manufacturing plants. Another plant species that is capable of producing natural rubber in commercial quantities is the Mexican slipper spurge (*Pedilanthus macrocarpus*), a member of the Euphorbiaceae. Investigations into the cultivation of the plant and the utility of its rubber are being conducted.

Kenaf (*Hibiscus cannabinus*) is an annual species of the mallow family (Malvaceae). Kenaf is quick growing, tolerates saline and dry soils, and has the potential to reduce the reliance on trees as a source of pulp for making paper. The paper made from kenaf is strong, does not yellow quickly, and holds ink well, and the plants can be cultivated in many southern states without irrigation. Kenaf newsprint is now available at half the cost of wood pulp.

Around the world increasing population pressure has forced countries to explore the use of arid and semiarid habitats and the plant resources therein to supply the ever-increasing food, fuel, and shelter needs of people. People have altered the landscape dramatically in some places, promoting the spread of plants unfavorable to livestock. As people remove woody species for fuelwood, they denude the land and reduce the water-holding capability of the soil in which the plants once grew. This greatly accelerates the desertification process, turning once-productive soils into desert wastelands. The introduction of multipurpose plants into these fragile habitats is being attempted to slow or reverse the desertification process. These are species that grow quickly, that produce both fodder for domesticated animals and fuelwood for people, and that can be harvested at a sustainable level without damaging the soil or habitat. Several species of *Casuarina* trees have been introduced into parts of Africa for fuelwood. In South America species of *Prosopis* and *Acacia* have the greatest potential for fuelwood species, and *Chenopodium quinua* and *Amaranthus caudatus* are potential food crops. In other countries such as Australia, investigations continue into the increased use of dry areas with the intensified domestication of such forage plants as *Acacia* and *Casuarina*. The search for xerophytic (drought-loving) forage plants is under way all over the world, and in the Middle East species including *Atriplex* and *Opuntia* could provide, with minimal irrigation, the necessary protein and carbohydrate resources for domesticated animals. In North America the increased use of arid and semiarid regions due to population pressure is greatest in Mexico; however, in the United States huge metropolitan areas continue to grow in the desert Southwest, placing great demands on water supplies, the environment, and plant resources of the region. Potential industrial plant sources in the United States include guayule and jojoba, and a possible food plant is *Cucurbita foetidissima*, the buffalo gourd. Other candidates for economically important plants are *Aloe vera* and *Asclepias* species for their medicinal value; *Atriplex* and bitterbrush (*Purshia tridentata*) as potential forage plants; and saltbush (*Atriplex canescens*), rabbit brush (*Chrysothamnus nauseosus*), black greasewood (*Sarcobatus vermiculatus*), and big sagebrush (*Artemisia tridentata*) as possible fuel plants. Extensive studies have been conducted on desert plants from the southwestern United States and northwestern Mexico to determine their possible economic potential as producers of biocrude, the hydrocarbon and hydrocarbonlike chemical fraction of plants that may be used to make liquid fuels and a variety of chemical products. In addition to guayule, potential hydrocarbon crops from the semiarid parts of the world include various species of the genus *Euphorbia*.

A growing economic use of desert plants has developed in the horticulture and landscape businesses for people who live in arid or semiarid climates and wish to incorporate drought-tolerant plant species into the landscape plan around their homes or workplaces. These xeric-adapted (arid-adapted) plants bring a pleasant aesthetic quality associated with a southwestern lifestyle while requiring little supplemental irrigation. The demand for these xeric landscapes has placed pressure on suppliers of the larger, slow-growing species of plants, such as the giant saguaro cactus. These plants now must be protected from plant poachers, who have removed large individuals, each worth thousands of dollars, from restricted areas in the wild. Other important xeric landscape species and ornamentals are various species of yucca, cacti, and agave, ocotillo (*Fouquieria splendens*), and sotol (*Dasylirion leiophyllum*).—Gordon E. Uno

See also **ACACIA; ADOBE; AGAVE; AGRICULTURE IN DESERTS; BEES; BIOME; BIOSPHERE RESERVE; BROMELIADS; CACTI; CACTUS, COLUMNAR; COTTONWOOD; CREOSOTE BUSH; DESERT BROOM; DESERTIFICATION; DIRT BIKES; DOMESTIC ANIMALS; DUNE BUGGIES; FELDSPAR; FRUITS; GOURDS; GREASEWOOD; GREAT BASIN DESERT; GUAYULE; GYPSUM; HABITAT DEGRADATION; HERBS; INSECTS; IRONWOOD; IRRIGATION DRAINAGE; JOJOBA; LEGUMES; MESQUITE; MIDDLE EAST, DESERTS OF; MINERALS; MOVIES IN DESERTS; OFF-ROAD VEHICLES; OVERGRAZING; PALMS; PARROT; PLANTS; POTASH; PRIMARY PRODUCTIVITY; RIO GRANDE; RIPARIAN COMMUNITIES; SAGEBRUSH; SALT; SEEDS; SONORAN DESERT; SUNBURN; VENOM; WILDLIFE; YUCCA**

Further Reading

Goodin, J. R., and D. K. Northington, eds. 1985. *Plant Resources of Arid and Semiarid Lands: A Global Per-* *spective*. New York: Academic Press.

Hills, E. S., ed. 1966. *Arid Lands: A Geographical Appraisal*. London: Methuen.

Hinman, C. W., and J. W. Hinman. 1992. *The Plight and Promise of Arid Land Agriculture*. New York: Columbia University Press.

Nir, D. 1974. *The Semi-arid World: Man on the Fringe of the Desert*. London: Longman.

Scherer, C. A. K. 1997. *The Alchemy of the Desert: A Comprehensive Guide to Desert Flower Essences for Professional & Self-Help Use*. Tucson: Desert Alchemy Editions.

Wickens, G. E., J. R. Goodin, and D. V. Field, eds. 1985. *Plants for Arid Lands*. London: Unwin Hyman.

ECOSYSTEM

Term generally used to describe the functional system of the biotic (living) and abiotic (nonliving) components of some defined area. An ecosystem includes not only all of the animal, plant, fungi, and bacterial species but also the climate and its interactions with the organisms and the nonliving system, the soils and sediments, and even the nutrients that cycle through the biotic and abiotic environment. Conceptually an ecosystem has parameters that are not characteristic of individual organisms, or even populations, but rather includes the processes having to do with the transfer of energy (and matter) between producers (green plants) and consumers (herbivores, parasites, decomposers, and predators) and the nonbiotic portions of the system. Nutrient cycles, such as the nitrogen and carbon cycles, are properties of ecosystems. Individual organisms or populations do not have nitrogen or carbon cycles, but they are important components of those cycles in ecosystems.

Ecosystems can be small or large. For example, a temporary pond in the Sonoran Desert is an ecosystem that may contain tadpoles of various frog species, fairy shrimp, algal blooms, detritus, processes such as competition and predation, and cycling of nutrients like nitrogen. The water that the organisms live in is part of the temporary pond ecosystem, as are the soils underlying the pond, the soil runoff from erosion, and the atmosphere and climate that affect the pond. On a larger scale the Sonoran Desert itself could be considered an ecosystem, consisting of all living species (e.g., amphibians, reptiles, birds, mammals, invertebrates, plants, and bacteria) combined with geomorphologic factors (e.g., rocky hillsides, sandy flats, alluvial outwash plains, desert washes, and temporary streams), and biological processes (e.g., species interactions), weather patterns, predictability of climatological events, and even urbanization. In fact, the entire planet can be considered to be a single ecosystem, which is termed the biosphere. An ecosystem is thus a conceptual framework that describes an interactive system within which information at a variety of levels is integrated.—Laurie J. Vitt

See also **BIOME; BIOSPHERE RESERVE; CARRYING CAPACITY; DIVERSITY; ECOLOGY; ECOTYPE; ENERGY FLOW; INTERNATIONAL BIOLOGICAL PROGRAM; LANDSCAPE; PRODUCTIVITY, AQUATIC ECOSYSTEMS; SUCCESSION**

Further Reading

Blume, H.-P., and S. M. Berkowicz. 1995. *Arid Ecosystems*. Cremlingen-Destedt, Germany: Catena.

Golley, F. B. 1993. *A History of the Ecosystem Concept in Ecology*. New Haven: Yale University Press.

Odum, E. P. 1968. Energy flow in ecosystems: A historical review. *American Zoologist* 8:11–18.

———. 1969. The strategy of ecosystem development. *Science* 164:262–270.

Pianka, E. R. 1988. *Evolutionary Ecology*. 4th ed. San Francisco: Harper and Row.

Whittaker, R. H. 1975. *Communities and Ecosystems*. New York: Macmillan.

ECOTYPE

Populations within a species that are adapted to local environmental conditions. Environmental conditions often differ greatly across the distribution of a widely ranging species. For instance, Douglas fir (*Pseudostuga menziesii*), a major timber tree of western North America, extends from Alaska to northern Mexico and from the coast range of northern Washington State, an area with more than 2,000 millimeters of rain per year, to areas with only about 380 millimeters per year. Some populations of Douglas fir grow near sea level in the Willamette Valley of Oregon, whereas other populations grow high on nearby Mount Hood. Even on a single mountain the climate varies greatly depending on the elevation, angle of the slope, and facing (orientation) of the slope. Plants are largely immobile, and they must adapt to local conditions. As a consequence local populations of species carry morphological and physiological features that permit them to survive those conditions. Therefore, Douglas fir has a wide array of types, each locally adapted. These local adaptations are a result of natural selection. Plants on a south-facing slope, for example, will be more drought resistant than those from an adjacent, but cooler and wetter, north-facing slope.

Perhaps the most thoroughly studied ecotypes are within the genus *Achillea* (family Asteraceae or Asteraceae). *Achillea lanulosa* occurs throughout California, from the Great Basin Desert on the eastern side of the Sierra Nevada, through the mountains, across the dry Central Valley to the Coast Range, and finally to the beaches of the Pacific Ocean. At least 11 ecotypes have been identified on an east-west transect across the state. Some ecotypes are frost resistant, others are frost intolerant; some flourish in the winter, others in the summer, and others do well year-round.

Rather than have a monotonous landscape, deserts are heterogeneous with numerous habitats that support different moisture and temperature regimes. Therefore, deserts are equally likely to have ecotypes form within species. When environmental conditions change dramatically across short distances, distinct ecotypes are favored. However, when conditions change gradually over a span greater than the potential for gene flow, the ecotypic variation is clinal (gradually changing over space). Under these conditions discrete ecotypes may not originate, even though the local populations are adapting to local surroundings.—James R. Estes

See also **BIOME; BIOSPHERE RESERVE; CARRYING CAPACITY; DESERTS; DIVERSITY; ECOLOGY; ECOSYSTEM; ENERGY FLOW; INTERNATIONAL BIOLOGICAL PROGRAM; LANDSCAPE; PLANT ADAPTATIONS; PLANT GEOGRAPHY; PRODUCTIVITY, AQUATIC ECOSYSTEMS; SUCCESSION**

Further Reading

Clausen, J., D. D. Keck, and W. M. Hiesey. 1958. *Experimental Studies on the Nature of Species. 3. Environmental Responses of Climatic Races of Achillea*. Washington, D.C.: Carnegie Institution of Washington, Publication No. 581.

Jordan, N. 1992. Path analysis of local adaptation in two ecotypes of the annual plant *Diodia teres* Walt (Rubiaceae). *American Naturalist* 140:149–166.

ECTOTHERMY

Condition in organisms wherein the body temperature approximates very closely the surrounding temperature. Although the term is applied largely to vertebrate animals other than birds and mammals, it may be applied just as aptly to almost all plants and all animals except for birds and mammals. Ectothermic organisms lack an exterior insulative coat, such that the heat produced internally by oxidative metabolism is lost to a cooler external medium (air or water) nearly as fast as it is produced. Correspondingly, if these organisms enter a warmer environment, they gain heat very rapidly, lacking a heat-retardant coat, until the body temperature equilibrates with ambient conditions. Ectothermy simply means that the body temperature of an ectothermic organism is determined by external thermal influences. Essentially comparable (but less accurate) terms are cold-bloodedness and poikilothermy; the former means that an organism is cool or cold to the human touch, whereas the latter means that an organism's body temperature is variable.

In ectothermic animals at rest, the rate of metabolism is positively related to body temperature and therefore is dictated by external thermal conditions. While active, ectotherms have elevated metabolic rates that reflect the level of activity, but the heat that is produced by this activity rarely is sufficient to offset the high rate of heat exchange with the environment; consequently this heat of activity seldom yields a body temperature that differs from ambient conditions. This is especially true of smaller ectothermic animals, whose large surface areas (where heat is exchanged) relative to volumes (where heat is produced) yield maximal rates of heat exchange with the environment. Larger ectotherms have reduced surface areas relative to their volumes and possess the potential of slight, momentary elevations of body temperatures above ambient levels during bursts of activity, but these are inconsequential without additional thermoregulatory refinement.

Certain larger lizards, snakes, and fish possess unusual circulatory refinements that prolong retention of blood, heated by activity metabolism, within internal core areas, resulting at least temporarily in elevated body temperatures. Furthermore certain flying insects, even though small, have elevated body temperatures during flight, generated from heat produced by highly active flight muscles; but as soon as these insects come to rest, their high rates of heat exchange result in body temperatures that reflect external conditions.

The most remarkable ectotherms are many day-active (diurnal) lizards that engage in behavioral thermoregulation, resulting in precise control over body temperatures as long as they have access to solar radiation. These "heliotherms" shuttle in and out of the sun, shade, and different portions of the thermal environment during the day, typically maintaining body temperatures that approach those of birds and mammals, around 35°–42°C. Each species has its own "preferred body temperature" that it regulates very precisely during the day, even though encumbered with ectothermic limitations. The champion of these is the North American desert iguana (*Dipsosaurus dorsalis*), which regulates body temperature during its midmorning period of activity in spring and summer right at 42°C, nearly comparable both in precision and in magnitude to an endothermic bird.—Richard E. MacMillen

See also **AMPHIBIANS; ARTHROPODS; BODY TEMPERATURE; ENDOTHERMY; ESTIVATION; HEAT BALANCE; HEAT EXCHANGE; HIBERNATION; IGUANA, DESERT; INSECTS; MARSUPIALS; METABOLISM; PHYSIOLOGY; REPTILES; THERMOREGULATION; TORPOR; VAN'T HOFF EFFECT**

Further Reading

Gordon, M. S., G. A. Bartholomew, A. D. Grinnell, C. B. Jorgensen, and F. N. White. 1982. *Animal Physiology: Principles and Adaptations*. New York: Macmillan.

Schmidt-Nielsen, K. 1990. *Animal Physiology: Adaptation and Environment*. 4th ed. New York: Cambridge University Press.

ELAND

Large, spiral-horned antelope in the mammalian family Bovidae (order Artiodactyla), including the common eland (*Tragelaphus oryx*) and the giant eland, or Derby's eland (*Tragelaphus derbianus*). Common elands prefer forests, brush, semideserts, savannas (grasslands), and woodlands from Ethiopia and southern Zaire to South Africa. Derby's eland, closely associated with woodlands, is distributed from Senegal to southern Sudan. Elands have disappeared from much of their historical range due to hunting, habitat destruction, and domestic animal diseases, especially rinderpest. They are the most frequently represented animal depicted in the primitive rock art of southern Africa. *Eland* is a Dutch word meaning "moose."

Males and females differ in size and appearance. Males may weigh twice as much as females (1,000 kilograms) and have a large dewlap (flap of skin hanging from the throat) and longer (60–123 centimeters), thicker, and more tightly screwed horns. Besides being smaller, females are more slender, with longer, thinner horns, and a small, tufted dewlap.

Unlike cattle elands have a small mouth and pointed muzzle. Elands are foliage gleaners: they eat grasses and herbs as well as leaves of trees and bushes, which they select from poor-quality vegetation. Derby's eland is a browser, eating shoots and leaves from its woodland habitat. The renowned wanderers of the arid regions of Africa, they travel great distances seeking fresh vegetation produced by the unpredictable and localized rainfall. During the rainy season large groups of up to several hundred individuals may form.

Elands will drink water if it is available, but they generally are water independent. To conserve water they eat plants with a high water content, excrete dry feces and concentrated urine, and confine their activity to the coolest parts of the day (morning and evening). During the hottest part of the day, elands lay down in a sheltered environment. When water-stressed, a blood-flow "radiator," or carotid rete system, allows the body temperature to increase but keeps the brain temperature cooler.—Janet K. Braun

See also **AFRICA, DESERTS OF; ANIMAL ADAPTATIONS; ANTELOPE; BODY TEMPERATURE; COUNTERCURRENT HEAT EXCHANGE; ENDOTHERMY; HEAT BALANCE; HEAT EXCHANGE; HEAT STRESS; HERBIVORY; HYPERTHERMIA; MAMMALS; NAMIBIA, DESERTS OF; PINNAE; SOUTH AFRICA, DESERTS OF; UNGULATES; WATER BALANCE; WATER STRESS; XEROPHYLLOUS FOREST**

Further Reading

Estes, R. D. 1991. *The Behavior Guide to African Mammals*. Berkeley: University of California Press.

Grzimek's Encyclopedia of Mammals. Vol. 1. 1990. New York: McGraw-Hill.

Kingdon, J. 1989. *East African Mammals: An Atlas of Evolution in Africa*. Vol. 3C. Chicago: University of Chicago Press.

Macdonald, D., ed. 1984. *The Encyclopedia of Mammals*. New York: Facts on File.

ELEPHANT

Largest living land mammal, belonging to the family Elephantidae in the order Proboscidea. There are two living species, each in a separate genus (*Elephas maximus*, the Asian elephant, and *Loxodonta africana*, the African elephant). The human demand for ivory, desertification, and human pressures on the land have severely fragmented the once-extensive ranges of both the Asian and the African elephant. Many populations are now restricted to protected areas.

The Asian elephant (*Elephas*) was found from the Tigris-Euphrates River system throughout the Indian subcontinent, Indochina, Malaysia, Indonesia, and southern China. It prefers dry thorn scrub and evergreen forest habitats. The African elephant (*Loxodonta*) inhabited all of sub-Saharan Africa and occurred in North Africa before becoming extinct during the Middle Ages. Although the African elephant is found in many types of habitat from sea level to 4,500 meters, including the great sand dune areas of the Namib Desert of coastal southern Africa, desert and desert steppes are not preferred.

African elephants are the larger of the two species. The length of the head and body ranges from five to six meters and the length of the tail ranges from one to two meters. They stand 2–4 meters at the shoulder and weigh 2,000–6,000 kilograms. The skull is enlarged, but many sinuses help to make it lighter; the neck is short. In African elephants the trunk, which is used in communication, feeding, drinking, digging, and as a "hand," has two finger-like projections at the tip. The limbs are elongate; the joints have limited flexibility, resulting in slow and deliberate movements. The soles of the feet are flattened. Female elephants have two teats located between the forelegs; in males a scrotum is lacking and the testes remain in the body cavity.

Elephants have distinctive teeth. Two incisors and 12 molars are present in the upper jaw, and 12 molars are present in the lower jaw. The molars have transverse ridges for grinding coarse vegetation. Unlike most mammals, the molars form at the back of the jaw and move forward as the others are worn down; only one molar at a time is functional. Tusks are elongated incisors and are found in both sexes of African elephants. They are used in fighting, digging, eating, and marking. Tushes (deciduous premaxillary incisors 5–12 centimeters long) are present at birth and are replaced by the continually growing tusks after one year. Record tusk length is 3.45 meters. The ivory or dentine is found beneath a layer of enamel.

The thick (3–4 centimeters), sparsely haired skin lacks sweat glands. Elephants can survive temperatures from 49°C to -29°C but may suffer serious effects from sunstroke and dehydration. To dissipate heat from the body, the large ears of the African elephant have a fanlike arrangement of subcutaneous blood vessels on the medial side and are fanned to increase heat loss.

Elephants continue to grow throughout their life span of 55–60 years, a life span approximating that of humans. The largest individuals are generally the oldest. A single calf, born 22 months after conception, nurses for an average of two to three years. Puberty is reached between 8 and 13 years of age.

Elephants are social animals. The basic family unit consists of a female and her offspring, usually three to five members. Clans, numbering from 6 to 70 individuals, are composed of families of sisters and daughters and are led by the dominant sister. Males from 12 to 15 years of age are forced from families and join loose associations of males. Seasonal migrations of African elephant herds formerly occurred between areas. Distribution fragmentation and restriction to protected areas has limited this behavior and the associated dietary habits, resulting in reduced viability.

The African elephant diet consists of bark, fruit, grass, herbs, tree foliage, and up to 225 liters of water per day. Salt licks are also used. In desert areas elephants seek green vegetation and water near rivers and pools.

Elephants were first domesticated by Ptolemy II near the Red Sea. Unlike the Asian elephant, there is no indigenous tradition of African elephant domestication. Hannibal used African elephants from the Atlas Mountains against the Romans before his defeat in 202 B.C.—Janet K. Braun

See also **AFRICA, DESERTS OF; ANIMAL ADAPTATIONS; ANTELOPE; BODY TEMPERATURE; COUNTERCURRENT HEAT EXCHANGE; ENDOTHERMY; HEAT BALANCE; HEAT EXCHANGE; HEAT STRESS; HEATSTROKE; HERBIVORY; HYPERTHERMIA; MAMMALS; METABOLISM; NAMIBIA, DESERTS OF; PINNAE; SOUTH AFRICA, DESERTS OF; THERMOREGULATION; UNGULATES; WATER BALANCE; WATER STRESS; XEROPHYLLOUS FOREST**

Further Reading

Estes, R. D. 1991. *The Behavior Guide to African Mammals*. Berkeley: University of California Press.

Grzimek's Encyclopedia of Mammals. Vol. 4. 1990. New York: McGraw-Hill.

Laursen, L., and M. Bekoff. 1978. Loxodonta africana. *Mammalian Species* 92:1–8.

Macdonald, D., ed. 1984. *The Encyclopedia of Mammals*. New York: Facts on File.

Shoshani, J., and J. F. Eisenberg. 1982. Elephas maximus. *Mammalian Species* 182:1–8.

EL NIÑO

Oceanic/meteorological phenomenon in which a warm equatorial ocean countercurrent flows toward the coast of Peru, covering the cold waters of the Humboldt Current that normally lie offshore and having pronounced effects on atmospheric circulation and rainfall patterns. This shift in the ocean current generally occurs around Christmas, which in Hispanic America is known as the festival of the Christ Child, or El Niño. The El Niño phenomenon occurs approximately every four years, but it may occur after only two years or may be delayed for up to seven years. It is associated with the Intertropical Convergence Zone (ITCZ), which El Niño causes to shift southward. As a result intense rainfall occurs in southern regions that are normally arid and semiarid. When warm ocean waters expand eastward during an El Niño event, equatorial wind currents flow eastward (an equatorial jet), carrying moisture far inland over parts of South America. El Niño also has significant effects in the Northern Hemisphere.

Although El Niño is an oceanic phenomenon of local and regional occurrence, it also is related to global atmospheric circulation through the southern oscillation. The southern oscillation is a phenomenon wherein when atmospheric pressure is high in the central Pacific Ocean, it tends to be low between the Indian Ocean and Australia. These lows are associated with rainfall whose intensity is related inversely to atmospheric pressure. The differences in pressure between Tahiti, French Polynesia, and the Port of Darwin in northern Australia are usually used as the index of the intensity of the southern oscillation. Positive values mean that there will be an intensification of convective rainstorms throughout Australia, Indonesia, the Philippines, and Southeast Asia, whereas a negative index corresponds to a decrease in rain for that region and an increase in rain over the Central Pacific. The relationship between the El Niño ocean current and the southern oscillation is so strong that it has been considered a single phenomenon called the El Niño/southern oscillation, or ENSO.

El Niño also can have profound influences throughout much of the world. For example, the 1982–1983 El Niño event was exceptionally strong and led to very high precipitation in regions as diverse as California, Texas, Louisiana, Oklahoma, Europe, Peru, Ecuador, Chile, and central and eastern Argentina. At the same time there were zones of intense drought in northeastern Brazil, the high Andes of Bolivia, Madagascar, South Africa, Manchuria, northern China, Australia, and New Zealand.

The opposite phenomenon of El Niño has come to be known as La Niña. When the warm water of the tropical oceans moves westward, there is greater rainfall in the eastern Pacific and much less rainfall in eastern regions, such as South America.—Federico Norte

See also **ANNUAL PLANTS; ANTICYCLONE; BAROMETRIC PRESSURE (ATMOSPHERIC PRESSURE); BENGUELA CURRENT; CLIMATE; CLIMATE CLASSIFICATION; CLOUDS; CONVECTIVE STORM; CYCLONE; DESERT BLOOM; DESERTS; DROUGHT; FLOOD; HEAT; HUMBOLDT CURRENT; HYDROLOGICAL CYCLE; HYDROLOGY; LOW PRESSURE; MONSOON; OCEAN CURRENTS; PRECIPITATION; WATER**

Further Reading

Day, J. A., and V. J. Schaefer. 1991. *Clouds and Weather.* Boston: Houghton Mifflin.

Oliver, J. E., and R. W. Fairbridge, eds. 1987. *The Encyclopedia of Climatology.* New York: Chapman and Hall.

Schaefer, V. J., and J. A. Day. 1981. *A Field Guide to the Atmosphere.* Boston: Houghton Mifflin.

Schneider, S. H., ed. 1996. *Encyclopedia of Climate and Weather.* 2 vols. New York: Oxford University Press.

EMU

Large flightless bird (*Dromaius novaehollandiae*; family Dromaiidae, order Casuariiformes) occurring throughout the open eucalyptus forests, woodlands, and desert shrublands of Australia. *Dromaius novaehollandiae* is the sole surviving member of the family. The smaller, island species, the King Island emu (*Dromaius ater*) and the Kangaroo Island emu (*Dromaius baudinianus*), were extirpated (eliminated) by humans in the late 18th century. Among living birds the emu is second only to the ostrich in stature (1.5–1.85 meters) and weight (up to 50 kilograms). Like the ostrich emus are ratites lacking a sternal keel on which flight muscles attach in flying birds. The long powerful legs and feet with three toes are well adapted for traveling over great distances. Plumage is loose and coarse, consisting of long feathers lacking barbs. Although tied to permanent sources of fresh water, emus inhabit arid and semiarid habitats. The varied diet consists of fruits, seeds, flowers, plant shoots, insects, and small vertebrates. Emus are both social and nomadic in the nonbreeding season, and will range over hundreds of kilometers each year.

Emus appear to be monogamous in the wild. They nest on the ground in shallow, poorly lined scrapes. Clutch sizes range from 5 to 11. Emus exhibit exclusive male incubation and parental care. The average incubation period is 56 days, during which time males generally forgo eating and drinking. The young are precocial, leaving the nest soon after hatching. Females may remain with a single male or may abandon the family during incubation. In captivity females have been observed to seek additional mates and produce additional clutches of eggs, although the extent of such sequential polyandry in nature is undetermined. Males remain with chicks for up to seven months until the onset of the subsequent breeding season.—Stephen C. Lougheed

See also **AUSTRALIA, DESERTS OF; BIRDS; OMNIVORY; OSTRICH; RHEA; WATER BALANCE**

Further Reading

Davies, S. J. J. F. 1978. The food of emus. *Australian Journal of Ecology* 3:411–422.

Dawson, T. J., D. Read, E. M. Russell, and R. M. Herd. 1984. Seasonal variation in daily activity patterns, water relations and diet of emus. *Emu* 84:93–102.

Handford, P., and M. A. Mares. 1985. The mating systems of ratites and tinamous: An evolutionary perspective. *Biological Journal of the Linnean Society* 25:77–104.

Marchant, S., and P. J. Higgins, eds. 1990. *Handbook of Australian, New Zealand and Antarctic Birds.* Vol. 1 (pt. A). Melbourne: Oxford University Press.

Pizzey, G. 1988. *A Field Guide to the Birds of Australia.* Sydney: Collins.

ENDEMISM

Absolute limitation of the occurrence of a species, or some other taxonomic category (e.g., family), to a particular geographic region. During the course of geologic time, new species are continually arising. When a new species arises, whether by the gradual accumulation of genetic changes typical of animals or by the more abrupt ploidy (increasing the number of chromosomes) common in plants, that species must compete and interact with its environment and with other species already in existence. Some species have characteristics that allow successful competition with other species, and their ranges will expand. Other species may continue to be locally successful and to persist but remain confined to a relatively restricted geographic location, thus becoming endemics to that region. Endemism is a relative term and is used from the perspective of the geographic region or habitat type in question. Thus it is common to speak of species that are endemic to islands or grasslands or other specific regions. Species that range over large areas are not usually referred to as endemic, although species may be viewed as being endemic to a country or a continent. Deserts typically have many endemic species, in part because they tend to have environmental conditions that differ abruptly from surrounding habitats, making it more difficult for an animal or plant that is adapted for surviving in a desert to adapt also to the surrounding habitats.

In recent years, as rigorous cladistic methods (system of determining the relatedness of organisms by examining characteristics that are shared or unique) have been developed to determine phylogenetic (evolutionary) relationships among organisms, attempts have been made to define endemism in a more rigorous way. Using cladistic methods the origin of species distributions and the relationships among species in a given area should be considered in defining areas of endemism.—Janalee P. Caldwell

See also **BIOSPHERE RESERVE; CONSERVATION IN DESERTS; ECOLOGY; ECOSYSTEM; ECOTYPE; DESERTS; DIVERSITY; FISHES; SPECIATION**

Further Reading

Axelius, B. 1991. Areas of distribution and areas of endemism. *Cladistics* 7:197–199.

Harold, A. S., and R. D. Mooi. 1994. Areas of endemism: definition and recognition criteria. *Systematic Biology* 43:261–266.

Thirgood, S. J., and M. F. Heath. 1994. Global patterns of endemism and the conservation of biodiversity. *In* P. L Forey, C. J. Humphries, and R. I. Vane-Wright, eds., *Systematics and Conservation Evaluation*, 207–227. Oxford: Clarendon Press.

Wiley, E. O. 1988. Vicariance biogeography. *Annual Review of Ecology and Systematics* 19:513–542.

ENDOTHERMY

Condition, typically in birds and mammals, in which a high and rather constant body temperature is maintained regardless of external thermal conditions. In birds this body temperature is usually around 40°–42°C and in mammals around 36°–38°C, with the lower temperatures more typical of the usual periods of inactivity (at night in most birds; during the day in many mammals) and the higher temperatures occurring during the usual periods of activity (birds by day; mammals at night).

The source of heat that results in these high body temperatures is predominantly internal and is derived as a product of energy metabolism. To retain this heat within the body (and to retard heat loss to the external environment) birds and mammals have very effective insulative coats in the form of feathers or fur, respectively. In addition, these endotherms have very efficient circulatory systems that tend to shunt the blood away from the body surfaces during cold weather, thereby retarding heat loss further. Depending on the external temperature, metabolic rate will vary such that the ensuing heat production will offset heat lost to the environment, resulting in a relatively constant body temperature.

During hot conditions the only physiological means of preventing excessive heat gain, either from internal or external sources, is to dissipate this heat by evaporative cooling, which, in desert endotherms, involves mobilizing precious body water to externally exposed surfaces to promote evaporation. In mammals evaporative cooling is usually achieved by panting or by spreading saliva over the forelimbs. In some birds evaporative cooling is achieved by a process called gular flutter, in which air is drawn rapidly over the mouth and throat surfaces, independent of the respiratory process.

Typically desert endotherms avoid the need to employ evaporative cooling for thermoregulation by behavioral means, escaping to more moderate thermal climates where precious body fluids will be conserved. Day-active birds seek shady shelters during periods of high external temperatures, relying on their inherently high body temperatures, inactivity, and mild hyperthermia to preclude the need of evaporative cooling; if these water-conserving mechanisms fail under excessively high environmental temperatures, birds have the option of merely flying to more moderate thermal environments. The less mobile desert mammals are usually active at night, spending the hotter daytime hours in cooler underground burrows or other shelters, thereby almost completely escaping the stresses of the hot desert days.

Certain very large desert mammals, such as camels, burros, and some African gazelles, cannot readily escape to cooler shelters during the day because of their size and the paucity of cool microclimates. Instead they have to face the hot days directly, relying on combinations of a small surface area to volume ratio to minimize heat gain as well as effective heat-retardant insulation, a tolerance of mild hyperthermia that allows for heat storage by day and passive dissipation at night, and relative inactivity during the hottest periods of the day. In addition, some African gazelles have specialized circulatory adaptations that maintain cooler brain temperatures during periods of excessive hyperthermia, thereby ensuring that the brain temperature is maintained within tolerable limits while the temperature of the less sensitive body rises to higher levels.

Under conditions of excessive cold, both birds and mammals typically employ behavioral avoidance by retreating to more moderate shelters or by migrating to more thermally moderate climates. Many small mammals combine the use of underground thermal shelters with temporary abandonment of endothermy by undergoing hibernation; thus these endotherms have the capability of temporarily approaching an ectothermic state. Other terms that are frequently, but less aptly, applied to the endothermic state are warm-blooded and homeothermic (or homoiothermic).—Richard E. MacMillen

See also **ANIMAL ADAPTATIONS; BIRDS; BODY TEMPERATURE; CAMEL; CAMEL'S HUMP; COUNTERCURRENT HEAT EXCHANGE; ECTOTHERMY; ELEPHANT; EXPLOSIVE HEAT DEATH; HEAT BALANCE; HEAT EXCHANGE; HEAT STRESS; HEAT-** **STROKE; HIBERNATION; HYPERTHERMIA; MAMMALS; METABOLISM; SHIVERING; THERMOREGULATION; TORPOR; WATER BALANCE**

Further Reading

Gordon, M. S., G. A. Bartholomew, A. D. Grinnell, C. B. Jorgensen, and F. N. White. 1982. *Animal Physiology: Principles and Adaptations*. New York: Macmillan.

Schmidt-Nielsen, K. 1990. *Animal Physiology: Adaptation and Environment*. 4th ed. New York: Cambridge University Press.

ENERGY FLOW

Transfer of energy among trophic (feeding) levels in an ecosystem, and between the nonliving and the living parts of the environment. In most ecosystems solar energy is the ultimate source for all energy available to support metabolism (life processes). Solar energy is transformed and fixed into complex carbon molecules during photosynthesis by plants. The energy fixed in the chemical bonds of the plant tissues is the only energy available to all heterotrophic organisms (organisms that consume other organisms to gain energy) in the ecosystem. Plants are therefore called primary producers, and all other organisms are called consumers.

The classical view of energy flow in ecosystems has been that of a pyramid, with energy at each trophic level only a fraction of that at the level below. In the pyramid primary producers are at the base, primary consumers (herbivores) at the next level, secondary consumers (predators) at the next level, and so on. The reduction in available energy from base to apex is due to the loss of energy at each step of transfer up the pyramid. Energy is lost at each level due to basal metabolic costs of the organisms at that level, including costs of growth, foraging, reproduction, and defense. The energy is lost as heat and cannot be recovered and made available to higher trophic levels. The only energy available to higher trophic levels, therefore, is that stored in chemical bonds of the tissues of organisms.

The actual efficiency of transfer of energy between trophic levels has proved to be difficult to measure but in most cases is estimated to be less than 10 percent. This low efficiency limits the numbers of trophic levels in most ecosystems to two or three above the level of primary producers.—Edie Marsh-Matthews

See also **ECOLOGY; ECOSYSTEM; PRIMARY PRODUCTIVITY; PRODUCTIVITY, AQUATIC ECOSYSTEMS**

Further Reading

Krebs, C. J. 1995. *Ecology: The Experimental Analysis of Distribution and Abundance.* 4th ed. New York: Harper and Row.

Phillipson, J. 1966. *Ecological Energetics.* London: Edward Arnold.

EOCENE

Second epoch of the Tertiary period representing geologic time between 58 million and about 34 million years ago. A globally uniform, warm humid climate that had prevailed since the late Cretaceous period continued into the early part of the Eocene, when it reached its zenith. However, by the middle Eocene (about 40 million–37 million years ago) a major marine transgression (rise in sea level), major changes in ocean circulation due in part to the breakup of the supercontinent Gondwana, and significant climatic deterioration occurred. Year-round ice might have been present in Antarctica by this time. The northern continents also underwent a marked cooling and drying after the middle Eocene, resulting in changes in vegetation from warm subtropical forests to dry woodland by the latest Eocene. A number of diverse groups of warmth-adapted organisms, both marine and terrestrial, underwent concomitant extinction in the middle and late Eocene.

Based on a wide diversity of sources of evidence not evenly available from all continents (geological, sedimentological, paleontological, paleobotanical, marine and terrestrial isotopic), the Oligocene brought about increased seasonality and an overall cooling and drying in the global paleoclimate. In most cases it is not yet possible to identify Eocene "deserts" in the modern sense of the word. However, evidence of semiarid to arid landscapes, sometimes including abundant aeolian (windblown) deposits occurred during this 10-million-year interval which indicates the presence of at least incipient drylands.

In parts of North America fossil root traces and soil profiles indicate that the humid forests of the Cretaceous and Paleocene gave way to dry woodlands or wooded "savannas" or scrublands. Loss of the forest canopy of wind-pollinated conifers was followed by paleofloras dominated by wind-pollinated angiosperms. Grass pollen and grass fossils are absent from the Eocene record during the early development of savannas, suggesting that Eocene–Oligocene drylands were dominated by low-growing woody scrub vegetation lacking grasses ("rangelands"), rather similar to modern, seasonally dry *Ephedra*-saltbush communities of the Great Basin or bluebush-saltbush communities of central Australia. Terrestrial paleofaunas of snails, amphibians, and reptiles preserved in western and central North America also reflect increased aridification.

On other continents the geological record is less well studied. In Europe data from paleobotany and fossil vertebrates show no obvious drying trend, but such a trend is present by the Oligocene. A drying trend is recorded in the middle Eocene fossil pollen record in Asia, where the Gobi Desert and parts of China were arid or subarid. No detailed record of Eocene paleoclimate has yet been developed in Africa, South America, or Antarctica, but Oligocene data indicate that the drying trend had occurred by then (e.g., in South America the beginning of the Andean uplift changed vegetation from subtropical woodlands to scrubby arid savanna woodlands; in Australia microphyllous and sclerophyllous plants greatly increased in importance).

The early Eocene high-latitude forests and warm climates allowed forest-dwelling vertebrates to expand their distributional ranges into Arctic zones. For example, a fossil vertebrate fauna from Ellesmere and Axel Heiberg islands (northernmost part of North America; paleolatitude about 75°N) included catfish, bowfin, several kinds of turtles, crocodilians, and several kinds of mammals, including primates; living relatives of all these groups inhabit primarily tropical and warm temperate regions today.

During at least the late Eocene a land connection or near-connection existed between South America and Antarctica, as evidenced by the occurrence of certain kinds of fossil mammals on Seymour Island, Antarctic Peninsula, that have evolutionary affinities with South American mammals. At this time cool, temperate rain forests occupied the Antarctic Peninsula.—Nicholas J. Czaplewski

See also **CENOZOIC; CRETACEOUS; FOSSILS; MADRO-TERTIARY GEOFLORA; MIOCENE; NEOGENE; OLIGOCENE; PALEOCENE; PALEOCLIMATE; PERMIAN; PLATE TECTONICS; PLIOCENE;**

PRECAMBRIAN; QUATERNARY; RECENT (HOLO-CENE); TERTIARY

Further Reading

Case, J. A. 1988. Paleogene floras from Seymour Island, Antarctic Peninsula. *Geological Society of America Memoir* 169:523–530.

Cocks, L. R. M. 1981. *The Evolving Earth*. London: British Museum (Natural History).

Dawson, M. R., M. C. McKenna, K. C. Beard, and J. H. Hutchison. 1993. An early Eocene plagiomenid mammal from Ellesmere and Axel Heiberg Islands, Arctic Canada. *Kaupia, Darmstädter Beiträge zur Naturgeschichte* 3:179–192.

Goin, F. J., and A. A. Carlini. 1995. An early Tertiary microbiotheriid marsupial from Antarctica. *Journal of Vertebrate Paleontolology* 15:205–207.

McKenna, M. C. 1980. Eocene paleolatitude, climate, and mammals of Ellesmere Island. *Palaeogeography, Palaeoclimatology, Palaeoecology* 30:349–362.

Pascual, R., and E. Ortiz Jaureguizar. 1990. Evolving climates and mammal faunas in Cenozoic South America. *In* J. G. Fleagle and A. L. Rosenberger, eds., *The Platyrrhine Fossil Record*, 23–60. London: Academic Press.

Pomerol, C., and I. Premoli-Silva, eds. 1986. *Terminal Eocene Events*. Amsterdam: Elsevier.

Prothero, D. R. 1994. *The Eocene–Oligocene Transition: Paradise Lost*. New York: Columbia University Press.

———. 1994. The late Eocene–Oligocene extinctions. *Annual Reviews of Earth and Planetary Sciences* 22:145–165.

Prothero, D. R., and W. A. Berggren, eds. 1992. *Eocene–Oligocene Climatic and Biotic Evolution*. Princeton: Princeton University Press.

Wolfe, J. A. 1978. A paleobotanical interpretation of Tertiary climates in the Northern Hemisphere. *American Scientist* 66:694–703.

———. 1994. Tertiary climatic changes at middle latitudes of western North America. *Palaeogeography, Palaeoclimatology, Palaeoecology* 108:195–205.

Woodburne, M. O., and W. J. Zinsmeister. 1982. Fossil land mammal from Antarctica. *Science* 218:284–286.

Zachos, J. C, J. R. Breza, and S. W. Wise. 1992. Early Oligocene ice-sheet expansion on Antarctica. *Geology* 20:569–573.

EPHEMERAL PLANTS. *See* ANNUAL PLANTS

EPIPHYTES

Plants that use other plants for physical support. Epiphytes grow on other plants so that they are raised above the ground; however, they do not receive any water, minerals, or photosynthate (sug-ars) from their supporting plants and so are different from parasitic plants. Epiphytes and the plants on which they grow have a commensalistic relationship, one in which the epiphyte benefits from the interaction, but the supporting plant is unaffected. Without a connection to the ground, epiphytes must obtain their water and nutrients from the air and rainwater. Thus many epiphytes flourish in communities with a high annual precipitation, such as the tropical rain forest. They may still be found in regions with less precipitation where the above-ground habitat is arid. In such areas many epiphytes will possess adaptations characteristic of xero-phytes, plants that grow in arid conditions. Desert environments lack precipitation and humidity to support numerous epiphytes, but cyanobacteria, algae, mosses, and lichens occur on the cooler, moister side of many trees and shrubs in these xeric communities. Lichens are unique organisms made up of a species of fungus and a species of either alga or cyanobacteria living together in a mutualistic relationship in which both organisms benefit from their interaction. The fungus protects the photosynthetic algal or cyanobacterial species, which provides food for both. Lichens colonize and grow on extremely dry surfaces, including rock faces and the bark of trees and shrubs.—Gordon E. Uno

See also **BACTERIA; DIVERSITY; LICHENS; MOSSES; PLANT ADAPTATIONS; PLANTS**

Further Reading

Barbour, M. G., and W. D. Billings. 1988. *North American Terrestrial Vegetation*. Cambridge: Cambridge University Press.

Barbour, M. G., J. H. Burk, and W. D. Pitts. 1980. *Terrestrial Plant Ecology*. Menlo Park, Calif.: Benjamin/ Cummings.

Friedmann, E. I., and M. Galun. 1974. Desert algae, lichens, and fungi. *In* G. W. Brown, ed., *Desert Biology: Special Topics on the Physical and Biological Aspects of Arid Regions*, 2:166–212. New York: Academic Press.

ERG (SAND SEA). *See* DUNES

ESTIVATION

Seasonal torpor employed by mammals and birds during the summer. This phenomenon occurs while environmental temperatures are moderate, with reductions of body temperature and energy metabolism being much less pronounced than in hibernators. As summer is a period when food is relatively abundant, it is difficult to view estivation largely as an energy-conserving mechanism. The resource in shortest supply in summer in various deserts is water, both because of low rainfall and because of higher rates of water loss while animals are active. Estivation in desert animals, therefore, may be viewed primarily as a water-conserving mechanism that enables escape in shelters from potentially dehydrating surface conditions; secondarily, energy savings likely prolongs escape by extending the fasting period. The documentation of estivation in desert mammals and birds has been infrequent, with no thoroughly documented instance in birds and only a single one in mammals. The best-documented endothermic estivator is the North American cactus mouse (*Peromyscus eremicus*), an inhabitant of the southwestern deserts. Field studies show that individuals do not engage in surface activity during the summer periods of highest temperature and least water availability, retreating instead to underground burrows. Laboratory studies show individuals readily enter torpor during the summer, reducing body temperatures, metabolic rates, and water expenditures. In addition, torpid cactus mice can only tolerate moderate lowerings of their body temperatures; when their temperatures get too low, such as under colder winter conditions, death ensues. In this instance estivation serves as an important survival mechanism, facilitating avoidance of otherwise life-threatening summer conditions. Further research will likely reveal additional desert estivators.—Richard E. MacMillen

See also **ANIMAL ADAPTATIONS; BIRDS; DESSICATION-RESISTANT SPECIES; HEAT BALANCE; HEAT STRESS; HIBERNATION; HYPOTHERMIA; MAMMALS; MARSUPIALS; METABOLISM; PHYSIOLOGY; POCKET MOUSE; RODENTS; THERMOREGULATION; TORPOR; WATER BALANCE; WATER STRESS**

Further Reading

Gordon, M. S., G. A. Bartholomew, A. D. Grinnell, C. B. Jorgensen, and F. N. White. 1982. *Animal Physiology: Principles and Adaptations*. New York: Macmillan.

MacMillen, R. E. 1965. Aestivation in the Cactus Mouse, *Peromyscus eremicus*. *Comparative Biochemistry and Physiology* 16:227–247.

Schmidt-Nielsen, K. 1990. *Animal Physiology: Adaptation and Environment*. 4th ed. New York: Cambridge University Press.

Large, cactuslike, columnar euphorb in the Itala Game Reserve, northern Kwazulu-Natal Province, South Africa. (Photo: M. A. Mares)

ETHIOPIA, DESERTS OF. *See* AFRICA, DESERTS OF

EUPHORBIACEAE

Large worldwide plant family of about 300 genera and 8,000 species often referred to as spurges or milkweeds. Euphorbs are common in the tropics but also extend into temperate regions north and south of the equator. Fifteen genera have more than 100 species each, and the largest genus, *Euphorbia*, has more than 1,600 species. The Euphorbiaceae exhibit a diversity of growth forms, including rain forest trees, shrubs, perennial and annual herbs, and succulents. Many members of the family are known to be poisonous and often contain a bitter, pungent, milky white sap. The use of many euphorbs for medicinal purposes by humans is well documented. Chemicals found in some species are severe skin irritants or even carcinogenic, but other substances found in some genera (e.g., *Jatropha*) may be inhibitory for human carcinoma cells.

This family has significant economic importance because it includes the rubber tree (*Hevea* spp.), castor bean (*Ricinus communis*), and poinsettia (*Euphorbia pulcherrima*). Several species of *Manihot*, the genus of cassava, manioc, and tapioca, are important sources of food in the tropics, despite their toxic chemical constituents. In recent years various species of *Euphorbia* have been studied as possible energy sources to replace diminishing petroleum supplies.

In the presence of similar environments, widely divergent taxonomic groups can come to resemble each other in one or more morphological traits, an evolutionary process called convergent evolution. One such example of convergent evolution involves the Euphorbiaceae and the cactus family (Cactaceae). Many succulent species of Euphorbiaceae are extremely difficult to distinguish from cacti because certain members of these two important plant families have evolved the same type of spines and similar succulent growth forms in response to the hot, dry climates of the Eastern and Western hemispheres, particularly in the deserts of southern Africa (Euphorbiaceae) and southwestern North America (Cactaceae). In the succulent Karoo of South Africa, euphorbs are dominants and account for most of the biomass.—Gary K. Hulett and Amanda Renner Charles

See also **AFRICA, DESERTS OF; CACTI; CACTUS, COLUMNAR; CONVERGENT EVOLUTION; KALAHARI DESERT; KAROO; NAMIBIA, DESERTS OF; PLANTS; SONORAN DESERT; SOUTH AFRICA, DESERTS OF**

Further Reading

Calvin, M. 1977. Hydrocarbons via photosynthesis. *Energy Research* 1:299–327.

———. 1985. Fuel oils from higher plants. *Annual Proceedings of the Phytochemical Society of Europe* 26:147–160.

Jury, S. L., T. Reynolds, D. F. Cutler, and F. J. Evans, eds. 1987. *The Euphorbiales: Chemistry, Taxonomy and Economic Botany.* New York: Academic Press.

EUPHRATES. *See* TIGRIS-EUPHRATES

EVAPORATION. *See* IRRIGATION DRAINAGE

EVOLUTION, CONVERGENT. *See* CONVERGENT EVOLUTION

EVOLUTION, PARALLEL. *See* PARALLEL EVOLUTION

EXCRETORY SYSTEM

Organs involved with regulating the composition and concentration of internal body fluids. The substances regulated by the excretory system are quite diverse, as are the organs of excretion themselves. Excretory structures invariably require that some water be lost as regulation is accomplished. Animals that have successfully colonized deserts usually have excretory adaptations that minimize water loss as they remove waste products. For example, the camel is noteworthy for its ability to reduce excretory water loss by concentrating salts in the urine and by reducing urinary flow by as much as 76 percent when dehydrated. The water that is retained contributes significantly to the camel's success when environmental water is scarce.

All animals must get rid of nitrogen-containing wastes from the normal turnover of protein within the body. A breakdown product is ammonia (NH_3), which is toxic even in low concentrations. In terrestrial animals ammonia is rapidly converted by one of the excretory organs (the liver) into less toxic compounds: uric acid in birds, reptiles, and insects, for example, and urea in mammals. The kidneys then remove and excrete the waste products of uric acid and/or urea.

Uric acid is a relatively insoluble substance and is expelled as a white paste called guano with very little water loss to the animal. Therefore, birds, reptiles, and insects may be considered to be pre-adapted for desert life because of their ability to excrete uric acid. The excretion of urea in urine, however, requires at least some water for its disposal.

The kidney of vertebrates is well known for its production of urine. However, only birds and mammals have kidneys that can produce urine more concentrated than (hyperosmotic to) blood, which can be an important water-conserving mechanism. In birds the concentrating ability, expressed as the urine/plasma concentration ratio, is limited to about two. In mammals the ratio may be considerably greater (e.g., 4 in humans, 10 in cats, and 14 in the desert kangaroo rat). The highest ratios are found in mammals from desert habitats. The kangaroo rat is exceptional, but it is outperformed by the sand rat (*Psammomys*) of the North African desert with a ratio of 17 and the Australian hopping mouse (*Notomys*) with urine 25 times more concentrated than plasma.

The ability of mammals to produce a concentrated urine is associated with the anatomy of the functional unit of the kidney, the nephron. In particular, concentrating ability correlates with the length of the nephron structure called the loop of Henle. Long loops are found in animals that produce the most highly concentrated urine, for example, desert rodents, camels, and desert antelopes. Short loops are found in nephrons of animals that require abundant water, for example, beavers, muskrats, and pigs.

Though efficient excretory systems are clearly of benefit to many desert animals, this avenue of water conservation is not necessarily a prerequisite for desert life. If water savings are sufficient from other mechanisms (e.g., by reductions in cutaneous water loss, or water lost through the skin), animals with less efficient kidneys may still successfully make a home in the desert.—E. Annette Halpern

See also **ANIMAL ADAPTATIONS; BIRDS; CAMEL; CAMEL'S HUMP; COUNTERCURRENT HEAT EXCHANGE; DEHYDRATION; DESICCATION; DESICCATION-RESISTANT SPECIES; ENDOTHERMY; HEAT BALANCE; HEAT EXCHANGE; HEAT STRESS; HUMAN PHYSIOLOGY IN DESERTS; KANGAROO RAT; KIDNEY FUNCTION, DESERT RODENTS; KIDNEYS; METABOLIC WATER; METABOLISM; PERSPIRATION; PHYSIOLOGY; RENAL PAPILLA; RESPIRATORY WATER LOSS; SAND RAT; SWEAT GLANDS; THERMOREGULATION; TRANSPIRATION; URIC ACID; URINE; WATER BALANCE; WATER STRESS**

Further Reading

Hickman, C. P., Jr., and L. S. Roberts. 1994. *Biology of Animals.* Dubuque, Iowa: Brown.

MacMillen, R. E., and A. K. Lee. 1967. Australian desert mice: independence of exogenous water. *Science* 158:383–385.

Schmidt-Nielsen, K. 1990. *Animal Physiology: Adaptation and Environment.* 4th ed. New York: Cambridge University Press.

Wilson, R. T. 1989. *Ecophysiology of the Camelidae and Desert Ruminants.* New York: Springer.

EXPLOSIVE HEAT DEATH

Death resulting from an extremely rapid rise in body temperature to a level incompatible with life. Explosive heat rise and the resulting death occur very quickly, in contrast with death from dehydration, which is characterized by a general, steady decrease in bodily functions.

The rapid rise in an organism's temperature is thought to occur because the blood no longer carries sufficient amounts of heat away from the internal core to the cooling surfaces. The failure of circulation to move the heat is due to a decrease in blood water volume, which in turn follows extreme vasodilation and dehydration. The ability of the blood to transfer heat lies in the high specific heat of the water in the blood. Obviously when the water content of blood is reduced, so is its capacity to transfer heat. Also when water is lost from the blood, resistance to flow (viscosity) increases. This puts a strain on the heart, which in turn further reduces blood flow. The reduced blood volume, increased viscosity, and strain on the heart puts an animal into circulatory shock, a generalized inadequacy of blood flow throughout the body to the extent that cells are damaged. In explosive heat rise a positive feedback cycle results, whereby the shock itself causes additional shock. The condition becomes a vicious cycle, and the circulatory system deteriorates so that cardiac output becomes greatly decreased. Death ensues because the cells, particularly neural tissues, simply cannot obtain enough oxygen to derive the energy necessary to sustain life.

It is presumed that explosive heat death occurs in animals that depend on circulation to move heat from deep core regions to cooling surfaces. A further consideration is the source of water lost in evaporative cooling. In humans, for example, dehydration in a hot environment reduces the plasma volume out of proportion to the total water loss. In fact, the reduction in circulating plasma volume can be 2.5 times greater than expected based on whole-body losses. This obviously increases the circulatory strain to a greater extent than if the water had been lost from elsewhere. In some animals (e.g., camels and donkeys) water loss comes primarily from water outside the circulatory system, and the plasma loses much less than its proportional share of the total water lost. The maintenance of high plasma volume facilitates circulation and allows these animals to tolerate a water loss of up to 27 percent of body weight. This loss is twice the dehydration that would bring other mammals into lethal explosive heat rise.—David S. Hinds

See also **ANIMAL ADAPTATIONS; BIRDS; CAMEL; CAMEL'S HUMP; COUNTERCURRENT HEAT EXCHANGE; DEHYDRATION; DESICCATION; DESICCATION-RESISTANT SPECIES; ENDOTHERMY; HEAT BALANCE; HEAT EXCHANGE; HEAT STRESS; HEATSTROKE; HUMAN PHYSIOLOGY IN DESERTS; KANGAROO RAT; KIDNEY FUNCTION, DESERT RODENTS; KIDNEYS; METABOLIC WATER; METABOLISM; PERSPIRATION; PHYSIOLOGY; RENAL**

PAPILLA; RESPIRATORY WATER LOSS; SAND RAT; SURVIVAL IN DESERTS; SWEAT GLANDS; THERMOREGULATION; TRANSPIRATION; URIC ACID; URINE; WATER BALANCE; WATER STRESS

Further Reading

Daniels, F., Jr. 1974. Solar radiation. *In* N. B. Slonim, ed., *Environmental Physiology*, 276–286. Saint Louis: Mosby.

Folk, G. E., Jr. 1974. *Introduction to Environmental Physiology*. 2d ed. Philadelphia: Lea and Febiger.

Lee, D. H. K. 1968. Human adaptations to arid environments. *In* G. W. Brown Jr., ed., *Desert Biology: Special Topics on the Physical and Biological Aspects of Arid Regions*, 1:517–556. New York: Academic Press.

Schmidt-Nielsen, K. 1964. *Desert Animals: Physiological Problems of Heat and Water*. New York: Oxford University Press.

Schmidt-Nielsen, K. 1990. *Animal Physiology: Adaptation and Environment*. 4th ed. New York: Cambridge University Press.

EXTREME DESERTS. *See* DESERTS

FEATHERS

Characteristic covering structures of all living birds. Fossils of *Archaeopteryx* (the first "avian" fossil), dated at approximately 150 million years before the present, indicate an organism that was a mosaic of dinosaurian and avian characteristics and show clear impressions of well-developed feathers. Feathers are of epidermal origin and, like reptilian scales or human fingernails, are constructed primarily of keratin. Feathers play a major role in the adaptation of birds to the wide range of environments in which they exist. They can be classified into six types based on their morphology, location on the body, and function. Flight and contour feathers (so-called typical feathers) consist of a central shaft (the rachis), lateral branches called barbs, and interlocking barbules that extend from the barbs. Flight feathers of the wing and tail are large, strong, and shaped so as to provide efficient flying or swimming surfaces. Contour feathers constitute the major covering of the body; they provide protection for the skin and contribute to streamlining. Down and semiplume feathers lack the interlocking barbules and provide insulation. Bristle feathers consist of a single rachis and are found around the eyes and mouth; these act as guard structures and, in some species (e.g., the insectivorous nightjars), are involved in capture of prey. Finally, filoplumes, always associated with contour feathers, function as sensory organs. Pigmentation of feathers also serves a number of functions ranging from camouflage (e.g., the cryptically colored tinamous and nightjars) to mate attraction and territorial defense (e.g., many species of hummingbirds).

Feathers can perform key functions in the adaptation of birds to xeric (dry), hot environments. In desert birds the body covering of feathers functions both as a thermal barrier against insolation (heat from the sun) and as an insulating layer during the often cold desert nights. Pale plumage coloration of desert birds, as well as being important in crypsis (camouflage), may reduce heat load. This latter proposed function may be somewhat simplistic, as birds with darker plumages may actually acquire

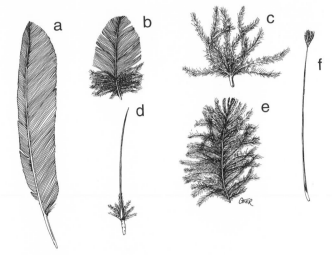

Types of feathers: a, flight; b, body contour; c, down; d, semiplume; e, bristle; f, filoplume. (Artist: Ken Otter)

significantly less radiative heat load when wind speeds exceed three meters per second and when feathers are erected.

Arid environments present some novel challenges with respect to feather care. For example, a number of desert taxa (e.g., larks, sandgrouse, bustards) engage in dust bathing, wherein dry particles of earth and sand are rubbed into the plumage. This behavior has been reported as a mechanism for dislodging external parasites and also possibly for cleaning the plumage when water is scarce. Some arid-land species have been shown to molt more frequently than related taxa living in environments where feather wear is less of a problem. For example, some African lark species (family Alaudidae) undergo two complete molts annually, whereas their European counterparts molt only once a year.

Finally, in some desert birds feather structure has evolved to perform key specialized roles that enhance survival in these extreme environments. One of the most spectacular examples of this may be found in the sandgrouse (family Pteroclididae) of arid regions of Africa and Asia. Males of these species have belly feathers that have been structurally modified for transport of water, from sometimes distant sources, to their offspring.—Stephen C. Lougheed

See also **ANIMAL ADAPTATIONS; BIRDS; CROW; ENDOTHERMY; FLICKER; GILA WOODPECKER; GUINEA FOWL; HEAT BALANCE; HEAT STRESS; MALLEEFOWL; MOLT; PHYSIOLOGY; OSTRICH; OWL; ROADRUNNER; SANDGROUSE; TINAMOU; THERMOREGULATION; WATER BALANCE; WOODPECKERS**

Further Reading

Maclean, G. L. 1983. Water transport by sandgrouse. *BioScience* 33:365–369.

Spearman, R. I. C., and J. A. Hardy. 1985. Integument. *In* A. S. King and J. McLelland, eds., *Form and Function in Birds*, 3:1–56. New York: Academic Press.

Stettenheim, P. 1972. The integument of birds. *In* D. S. Farner and J. R. King, eds., *Avian Biology*, 2:1–63. New York: Academic Press.

Walsberg, G. E., G. S. Campbell, and J. R. King. 1978. Animal coat color and radiative heat gain: A re-evaluation. *Journal of Comparative Physiology* 126:211–222.

FELDSPAR

Family of aluminosilicate minerals with a repeating pattern of linked SiO_4 and AlO_4 tetrahedra forming a crystalline structure. Varying amounts of Na, K, and Ca (sodium, potassium, and calcium, respectively) may be included in the structure, balancing the electrostatic charge. Occasionally other cations may be included. Feldspars are present in most soils and the parent material from which they form. The type of feldspar present in a soil is a function of the parent material and the degree of weathering (age) of the soil. In general the amount of feldspar decreases with increasing weathering of the soil.

The family of feldspars may be represented by the end points of a continuum of the inclusion of Na, K, and Ca into the structure. Potassium-feldspar is the end point with inclusions of K, exclusively. Albite and anorthite are the end points with pure Na and Ca, respectively. Potassium-feldspar is highly resistant to weathering, whereas anorthite is relatively easily weathered during soil formation. In soils the feldspars exist primarily in the sand and silt-sized fractions. However, the clay fraction of less weathered soils may contain alkali feldspars (those in the group between K-feldspar and albite). Most soils in arid regions contain alkali feldspars.

Other than from the addition of fertilizer, feldspars are second to micas as a natural source of potassium for plant growth. Weathering also releases Ca and Na to the soil solution, representing the natural source of these nutrients.—Dan R. Upchurch and Ted M. Zobeck

See also **MINERALS; NUTRIENTS; SOILS, DESERT; SOILS, DESERT, CALCAREOUS; SOILS, DESERT, CALICHE; SOILS, DESERT, CLAY; SOIL TAXONOMY; WEATHERING, DESERT**

Further Reading

Bohn, H. L., B. L. McNeal, and G. A. O'Connor. 1985. *Soil Chemistry.* 2d ed. New York: Wiley.

Buol, S. W., F. D. Hole, and R. J. McCracken. 1980. *Soil Genesis and Classification.* 2d ed. Ames: Iowa State University Press.

Fuller, W. H. 1975. *Soils of the Desert Southwest.* Tucson: University of Arizona Press.

Huang, P. M. 1977. Feldspars, olivines, pyroxenes, and amphiboles. *In* J. B. Dixon, S. B. Weed, J. A. Kitterick, M. H. Milford, and J. L. White, eds., *Minerals in Soil Environments*, 553–602. Madison, Wis.: Soil Science Society of America.

Tisdale, S. L., and W. L. Nelson. 1975. *Soil Fertility and Fertilizers.* 3d ed. New York: Macmillan.

FENNEC

Distinctive small fox (*Vulpes zerda*) of northern Africa; that is placed by some taxonomists in a separate genus (*Fennecus*) in the mammalian order Carnivora, family Canidae. The fennec is the smallest of all foxes, at 40 centimeters in length with an additional 30 centimeters of tail. An adult weighs a mere 1–1.5 kilograms. Fennec foxes are strict desert inhabitants, occurring in the arid lands of North Africa, the Sinai, and the Arabian Peninsula. Fennecs are very efficient diggers and construct burrows in the sand. They are particularly common in dune habitats.

Fennecs have several adaptations to life in sandy deserts. They have densely furred soles to protect the feet from hot desert sands and pale, thick fur to keep them warm during cold desert nights. They also have exceptionally large ears that serve to radiate body heat. They are able to survive indefinitely without free water. They have weakly developed dentition and feed heavily on insects. They also consume small vertebrates, eggs, roots, and fruits.

Fennecs are nocturnal (active at night) and live in social groups of mated pairs and their offspring. They purr like cats, like the very similar North American species, the kit fox. They squeak when near other familiar fennecs or human keepers, and they also bark like small domestic dogs. Females give birth to litters varying from one to six offspring. Birth occurs in the spring in the wild.

The fennec fox is heavily hunted in the Sahara; they are also captured live and marketed as food. As a consequence they are declining in abundance in many parts of their range.—Thomas E. Lacher, Jr.
See also **ANIMAL ADAPTATIONS; CARNIVORES; FOX; MAMMALS; PINNAE; SAHARA DESERT**

Further Reading

Gittleman, J. L., ed. 1989. *Carnivore Behavior, Ecology, and Evolution*. Ithaca: Cornell University Press.

Macdonald, D., ed. 1984. *The Encyclopedia of Mammals*. New York: Facts on File.

Nowak, R. M. 1991. *Walker's Mammals of the World*. 5th ed. Baltimore: Johns Hopkins University Press.

Sheldon, J. W. 1992. *Wild Dogs: The Natural History of the Nondomestic Canidae*. San Diego: Academic Press.

FERRET

Term used to refer to the domesticated form of the European polecat (*Mustela putorius*) and to a single wild species, the black-footed ferret (*Mustela nigripes*) in the mammalian order Carnivora, family Mustelidae. The black-footed ferret was once a common species throughout the semiarid, short-grass prairies of the western United States. It is a highly specialized mammal, feeding exclusively on prairie dogs. Its numbers declined dramatically in this century as prairie dogs were eliminated by ranchers and farmers. It was officially listed as an endangered species in 1967 and was included under the U.S. Endangered Species Act in 1973.

Black-footed ferrets were actually considered extinct for many years until a small population was discovered in 1981 near Meeteetse, Wyoming. The population reached a maximum of 129 in 1984. In 1985 the U.S. Fish and Wildlife Service decided to remove a number of adult ferrets from the wild population to begin a captive breeding colony. All these captive individuals ultimately died from canine distemper that was contracted in the wild. The wild population also began to decline from the effects of canine distemper;, and by 1987 all 18 remaining wild ferrets had been captured and placed in a captive breeding colony.

The captive population bred successfully, and in 1991 a program of reintroduction of ferrets to the wild began. Even though there was a high level of initial mortality in the reintroduced population, several litters subsequently were produced in the wild. The reintroduction program is continuing, and wildlife officials are optimistic that wild populations of black-footed ferrets will eventually be reestablished.—Thomas E. Lacher, Jr.
See also **BADGER; CARNIVORES; CONSERVATION IN DESERTS; COYOTE; FOX; GRASSLAND; MAMMALS; PRAIRIE; PRAIRIE DOG; WEASEL**

Further Reading

Gittleman, J. L., ed. 1989. *Carnivore Behavior, Ecology, and Evolution*. Ithaca: Cornell University Press.

Macdonald, D., ed. 1984. *The Encyclopedia of Mammals*. New York: Facts on File.

Nowak, R. M. 1991. *Walker's Mammals of the World*. 5th ed. Baltimore: Johns Hopkins University Press.

Seal, U. S., E. T. Thorne, M. A. Bogan, and S. H. Anderson, eds. 1989. *Conservation Biology and the Black-footed Ferret*. New Haven: Yale University Press.

FIELD CAPACITY OF SOILS

Amount of water maintained in the soil after any excess water has been drained away through the action of gravity and the remaining water has been redistributed in the soil profile, which generally occurs two to three days after a saturating rain. The concept of field capacity was developed after observing how water moves through different types of soils—more rapidly through some soils than through others and generally more rapidly immediately after rain than after time has passed. The field capacity thus defines the ability of the soil to retain water after its initial input and outflow from a particular patch of soil. Field capacity is an important concept, because it describes the water that is available for use by plants. Field capacity is thus a physical property of the soil itself and is a constant. It is technically defined as the amount of water that is maintained in the soil at 0.1–0.3 atmospheres of pressure (measured under laboratory conditions).

Although water movement through the soil diminishes progressively over time, it does not stop. In soils with coarse texture the difference between rapid and slow movement is very pronounced. In medium to fine soils water movement may persist at similar rates for long periods. In most cases, however, water will move rapidly through the soil and be used by plants during this period.—Alberto I. J. Vich and Juana Susana Barroso
See also **GROUNDWATER; HYDROLOGICAL CYCLE; HYDROLOGY; IRRIGATION DRAINAGE; PLANT**

ADAPTATIONS; PLANT ROOTS, ADVENTITIOUS; PLANTS; ROOTS; RUNOFF; SOILS, DESERT; WATER BALANCE; WATER OF RETENTION; WATER POTENTIAL

Further Reading

Dochaufour, P. 1978. *Manual de edafología*. Barcelona: Toray-Masson.

Fuller, W. H. 1974. Desert soils. *In* G. W. Brown Jr., ed., *Desert Biology: Special Topics on the Physical and Biological Aspects of Arid Regions*, 2:31–101. New York: Academic Press.

Peters, D. B. 1965. Water availability. *In* C. C. Black et al., eds., *Methods of Soil Analysis. Pt. 1: Physical and Mineralogical Properties, Including Statistics of Measurement and Sampling*, 279–285. Madison, Wis.: ASAE (Agronomy Monograph 9).

Suh-Shiaw, Lo. 1992. *Glossary of Hydrology*. Taipei: Sheng Te.

Walter, H. and E. Stadelmann. 1974. A new approach to the water relations of desert plants. *In* G. W. Brown Jr., ed., *Desert Biology: Special Topics on the Physical and Biological Aspects of Arid Regions*, 2:213–310. New York: Academic Press.

FINCH

Small, seed-eating songbird (order Passeriformes, family Fringillidae) with an almost cosmopolitan distribution, absent only from Australia and Antarctica. The term "finch" is often used to refer to some member species of the Emberizidae (subfamily Emberizinae, the New World sparrows), the Estrildidae (waxbills), and the Ploceidae (weavers). This discussion will be restricted to only the fringillid finches. Fringillidae, with approximately 150 species in 33 genera, is divided into three subfamilies: Fringillinae (three species in the genus *Fringilla*; e.g., the common chaffinch, *Fringilla coelebs*, of western Europe and northwestern Africa), Carduelinae (e.g., the house finch, *Carpodacus mexicanus*, of western North America), and the Drepanidinae (the Hawaiian finches; e.g., the apapane, *Himatione sanguinea*). The Fringillidae reach maximum species diversity in Eurasia.

The habitats of fringillids range from humid forests to deserts. The species that inhabit arid and semiarid environments are numerous. The house finch, for example, breeds in arid scrub, oak-juniper, pine-oak, chaparral, open woodland, and savanna habitats from British Columbia, Canada, to Baja California, Mexico. The white-throated canary (*Serinus albogularis*) breeds in arid scrub environments of southwestern Africa. Generally fringillids require permanent sources of water, even in xeric environments. However, some fringillids possess various behavioral and physiological adaptations for desert existence. For example, *Carpodacus mexicanus*, a year-round resident of deserts, can tolerate high temperatures by employing respiratory cooling mechanisms, whereas its congener, the Cassin's finch (*Carpodacus cassinii*), cannot.

Fringillids generally have robust bills, and correspondingly strong skulls and associated musculature, for cracking the coats of seeds, which constitute a significant proportion of their diet; however, bill morphology differs among species (especially within the Drepanidinae), reflecting specializations on different food types. Finches also have muscular gizzards to assist in digesting seeds. Fringillids are typically fairly small, ranging from 10 to 30 centimeters in length, but often are quite robust. Among species, plumage is highly variable, from drab to brightly colored. In addition to seeds, the diet may include fruit, buds, insects, and, in some specialized Hawaiian finches, nectar.

Timing of breeding is closely tied to food supplies. The dates of onset and duration of the breeding season in cardueline finches are quite variable. Fringillids may nest solitarily or in colonies. Nests are cup-shaped and constructed of grasses, twigs, and other vegetation, usually placed in a tree or bush. Clutch size ranges from two to five. Females typically perform incubation duties but are often fed by the male. Generally both parents participate in feeding of the young.—Stephen C. Lougheed

See also **AFRICA, DESERTS OF; ASIA, DESERTS OF; BAJA CALIFORNIA, DESERTS OF; BIRDS; CHIHUAHUAN DESERT; DESERT GRASSLAND; DESERTS; GRANIVORY; MOJAVE DESERT; PHYSIOLOGY; SAHARA DESERT; SEED DISPERSAL BY ANIMALS (ZOOCHORY); SONORAN DESERT; SOUTH AFRICA, DESERTS OF; UNITED STATES, DESERTS OF; WAXBILL; WEAVER**

Further Reading

Bent, A. C. 1968. Life histories of North American cardinals, grosbeaks, buntings, towhees, finches, sparrows, and allies. *U.S. National Museum Bulletin* No. 237.

Cramp, S., and C. M. Perrins, eds. 1994. *Handbook of the Birds of Europe the Middle East and North Africa.* Vol. 8. *The Birds of the Western Palearctic.* Oxford: Oxford University Press.

Hill, G. E. 1993. House finch (*Carpodacus mexicanus*). *In* A. Poole and F. Gill, eds., *The Birds of North America*, No. 46. Philadelphia: Academy of Natural

Sciences; Washington, D.C.: American Ornithologists' Union.

Ridgely, R. S., and G. Tudor. 1989. *The Birds of South America.* Vol. 1. Austin: University of Texas Press.

Salt, G. W. 1952. The relation of metabolism to climate and distribution in three finches of the genus *Carpodacus. Ecological Monographs* 22:121–152.

FIRE

Physicochemical process producing heat and light by combustion of pyrogean material (fuel); in terrestrial ecosystems plants are the main fuel. There are various consequences of fire on abiotic and biotic components of ecosystems. In most shrublands fire plays a significant role in the maintenance of community structure and function, and has been an important selective force in the evolution of plant form and life history. Variations in intensity and extent of fires are determined by abiotic factors, such as weather and topography, as well as by characteristics of the fuel (shrubs, grasses, forests). Frequency of fire, seasonality in rain, and general climatic conditions are other factors that play an important role in fires.

The aboveground portions of most shrubs are killed during fires, although only 60–80 percent of aboveground biomass may be consumed. Heat transfer down through the soil profile is quickly attenuated, so that temperatures rarely rise above 100°C at soil depths greater than three centimeters. In moister temperate shrublands increased light following fire may greatly influence seedling success. The postfire shrublands may be considerably more heterogeneous with respect to resources due to changes in nutrient availability, for example. Surface soil moisture availability may increase above prefire conditions once sufficient leaf area is available to provide shade. Thus, in some shrublands, conditions for seedling establishment may be most favorable in the second or third year following burning. Fire is thought to cause the downward migration of hydrophobic chemicals, thus increasing surface soil wettability and the potential for surface erosion, which plays an important role in postfire vegetation patterns.

Shrubland species show a wide range of adaptations to fire, such as lignotubers (woody tubers from which plants can regrow), fire-stimulated germination and flowering, and greater investment in seed production. Herbaceous species are the primary contributors to shrubland production in the years immediately following a fire, although this varies among shrublands. In general species richness and equitability (the evenness with which species are represented in an area) tend to be highest immediately following a fire and decline rather quickly thereafter. Fires affect shrubland herbivore populations and grazing patterns. Increased insect abundance and diversity after chaparral fires have been attributed to increased floristic diversity. However, populations of phytophagous (leaf-eating) insects and small mammals were reduced immediately after chaparral fires, although small mammals increased to a peak five years after burning. The decreased levels of herbivory (leaf eating) seen after a fire may have been a significant selective force in the evolution of mechanisms that concentrate reproductive effort among shrubland plants in the immediate postfire years.—Jorge M. Gonnet

See also **ECOLOGY; ECOSYSTEM; GRASSLAND; LANDSCAPE; PRIMARY PRODUCTIVITY; SUCCESSION**

Further Reading

Christensen, N. L. 1985. Shrubland fire regimes and their evolutionary consequences. *In* S. T. A. Pickett and P. S. White, eds., *The Ecology of Natural Disturbances and Patch Dynamics*, 86–100. New York: Academic Press.

Collins, S. L., and L. L. Wallace, eds. 1990. *Fire in North American Tallgrass Prairies.* Norman: University of Oklahoma Press.

de Van Booysen, P., and N. M. Tainton, eds. 1984. *Ecological Effects of Fire in South African Ecosystems.* New York: Springer.

Mooney, H. A., et al. 1981. *Fire Regimes and Ecosystem Properties.* U.S. Forest Service General Technical Report WO 26.

FISHES

Aquatic vertebrates that breathe by means of gills and use fins for locomotion. Animals called fishes constitute a diverse group of organisms that are more similar in overall ecology than in evolutionary relatedness. Within the subphylum Vertebrata of the phylum Chordata, there are two superclasses that include fishes: Agnatha (jawless vertebrates) and Gnathostomata (jawed vertebrates). Gnathostome groups with living representatives are the cartilaginous fishes, such as sharks, skates, and rays (class Chondrichthyes), and the bony fishes, such as minnows, basses, herrings, and tunas (class Osteichthyes).

Diversity of extant fishes is estimated to be 25,000 species. By far the greatest diversity is within the bony fishes, and in particular within the teleosts (a subgroup of bony fishes). Approximately 60 percent of described fish species are marine (occurring only in salt or brackish water environments), and approximately 40 percent are found only in freshwater; a small percentage of species use both habitats at different times in the life cycle (these species are said to be diadromous).

Diversity of species is also reflected in diversity of morphology (form), physiology (internal function), life history, and ecology. Size of adult fishes spans more than four orders of magnitude, from the Indian goby that matures at 10 millimeters to the whale shark that reaches 12 meters. Fishes vary in form from the torpedo-shaped, fast-swimming tuna to laterally compressed types such as angelfishes to the dorsoventrally compressed skates and rays. There are typically two sets of paired fins (pectoral and pelvic) and several unpaired, median fins that include one or more dorsal (back) fins, one anal fin, and the caudal (tail) fin. Fin size and placement, and even the presence of certain fins, vary dramatically among fishes.

Physiological adaptations of fishes reflect the range of aquatic habitats in which they are found. There are general adaptations to life in water, such as use of the gills to extract oxygen from the medium. Gills develop as outpouchings of the alimentary canal (gut) in the posterior region of the head. Water passes over the gills in only one direction in most fishes. The flow of blood within the gills is opposite in direction to that of water flow over the gills, and this arrangement allows maximum extraction of oxygen from the medium with minimal energy. Efficiency of oxygen extraction is extremely important because, even at maximum saturation, oxygen concentration in water is approximately 1/30 of that in air and water density is 800 times that of air, making movement of water over the gills energetically expensive. Fish species that live in oxygen-poor environments often have accessory breathing organs that allow them to use atmospheric oxygen. Such organs include lungs (as in the lungfishes), swimbladders (as in gars and catfishes that gulp air at the surface), and modifications of the internal lining of the buccal (mouth) cavity (such as those found in the labyrinth fishes and electric eels).

Regardless of whether a fish lives in salt water or freshwater, body fluid concentration in most fishes differs from that of the surrounding medium. Fishes that live in marine environments typically have ion concentrations lower than that of seawater (the exception is hagfishes, which have ion concentration equal to that of seawater), and fishes in freshwater have body fluid concentrations higher than that of freshwater. Because of these concentration differences, fishes in salt water tend to lose water and gain salts across all permeable surfaces, and those in freshwater tend to gain water and lose salts. Maintenance of internal fluid concentration is achieved in several ways. Many fishes exhibit adaptations (such as scales and a coat of mucus covering external body surfaces) that reduce the surface area permeable to water and salts. Other species reduce the concentration difference between internal and external fluids by sequestering urea in body fluids (as do sharks). Despite such adaptations, however, flux of water and ions still occurs, and maintenance of internal fluid concentrations within the tolerance levels of the species requires mechanisms to restore body fluid concentration. Fishes that lose water to the medium drink water and do not urinate; those that gain water from the medium do not drink and produce large volumes of dilute urine. Despite direction of ion flux between fish and medium, ion concentrations are regulated by specialized cells in the gills that actively pump ions into or out of the body. Kidneys may also assist in maintaining ion concentrations.

Most fishes are poikilothermic ectotherms; that is, body temperature is variable (*poikilo-*) and tracks the temperature of the external (*ecto-*) environment. Ranges of thermal tolerance vary dramatically among fishes, with some species restricted to narrow temperature ranges (stenothermal environments) and others able to tolerate a wide range of thermal fluctuation (eurythermal environments). Tolerance of particular thermal regimes by fishes often has an underlying biochemical basis such as the presence of "antifreeze" molecules in Antarctic fishes and of heat-tolerant enzymes in fishes found in hot-spring environments. Body temperature regulation is primarily behavioral, with fishes moving between available thermal environments.

Reproduction in fishes varies from oviparity (egg laying) to viviparity (giving live birth to offspring that have developed with ongoing energy contribution from the mother). In addition, many species exhibit ovoviviparity, in which live offspring develop within the mother's body but entirely from energy stored in eggs. Fish species in ephemeral environments, such as tropical marsh pools, may reproduce within weeks of hatching and then die, while other long-lived species may not reproduce until they are several years old and then breed every year for decades.

Fishes occupy almost every available aquatic habitat on earth, from polar seas to desert hot springs. Distributions of particular species may be worldwide, as is that of some herrings, tunas, and other oceanic forms, but more typically species are restricted in distribution to single continents and often single drainages, lakes, or springs.

Fishes of several different families occur in desert environments, but the most common families represented are Cyprinodontidae (killifishes and pupfishes), Cyprinidae (minnows), and Cichlidae (cichlids). Desert fish communities are typically depauperate (having few species) compared to fish communities of adjacent mesic (wet) regions. Desert rivers may support communities of long-lived, large-bodied species, such as the squawfish and humpbacked chub of the Colorado River in the American West. Fishes in desert spring habitats, in contrast, are typically small species with life spans of no more than a year (e.g., pupfishes).

Fishes that occupy desert aquatic habitats are often exposed to extreme environmental conditions. These species exhibit physiological adaptations such as the ability to withstand extreme temperatures (greater than 43°C in some desert springs of the American West), high salinities (up to four times the concentration of seawater), and severe oxygen deficits. Aquatic desert environments are also highly variable, and many desert fishes tolerate rapid changes in conditions. One of the most unusual desert fish is an endemic clariid catfish (*Clarias cavernicola*) of the Kalahari Desert, which lives in a dark sinkhole and survives by feeding on fecal matter and other materials deposited by baboons inhabiting a cave above it.

Another important and well-studied group of desert fishes are the desert pupfishes, and an extensive discussion of their biology is merited. This unusual group of fishes are in the genus *Cyprinodon* and are found in aquatic habitats (primarily springs, sinkholes, and marshes) in deserts of the American West and northern Mexico. Of the 36 described species in the genus, approximately 20 are found only in desert environments.

Desert pupfishes are small (6–8 centimeters in length as adults) and deep bodied and exhibit sexual dimorphism in size, with males typically being longer and more deep bodied than females. There may also be sexual dimorphism in coloration, with females having a mottled or barred pattern and mature males having a plainer body coloration, except during the breeding season when males develop dark bars on the edges of fins (primarily the caudal fin) and iridescent body hues.

Pupfishes have small, upturned mouths with tricuspid (three-cusped) teeth in the jaw. They are generalized feeders; they eat aquatic insect larvae if these are available but consume mostly algae, vascular plants, and bottom debris rich in organic matter.

Pupfishes have a prolonged spawning period and in some desert springs may spawn year-round. At spawning females lay eggs in the substrate, which then may be guarded by a territorial male (depending on population size and substrate availability). Eggs hatch in a few days, and the young grow quickly. If water temperatures are warm and food is abundant, some species may reach sexual maturity in six weeks. Pupfishes live about a year under natural conditions.

Pupfishes are among the most tolerant of extreme environments of all fishes. There are pupfish species that inhabit waters with temperatures as high as 45°C and salinities four times that of seawater. Pupfishes may also occur in habitats nearly devoid of oxygen. Species that live in such anoxic conditions have enlarged gills and frequently gulp air at the surface of the water. Because of their tolerance of extreme conditions, pupfishes are often the only vertebrate inhabitants of desert aquatic ecosystems.

Desert pupfishes may have distributions limited to individual springs, sinkholes, or marshes. The Devils Hole pupfish, for example, has a known distribution on only one ledge with a total area of 20 square meters in Devils Hole, Nevada—the smallest known range of any vertebrate species. Despite the limited distribution, population densities in these small habitats may be as high as 150 fish per square meter.

Because of their limited distribution, desert pupfishes are among the most endangered of all North American fishes. Desert habitats that support pupfish populations are vulnerable to human alteration by groundwater pumping and surface irrigation, and several major springs that once harbored pupfishes have gone dry in this century because of such activities.

Conservation of desert fishes is of major concern. Aquatic desert habitats are highly vulnerable to human impacts such as dewatering for irrigation and urbanization, and such activities in the American West have caused partial or complete extinction of many desert fishes. The introduction of nonnative fishes has also resulted in the loss of pure stocks of several desert species and the entire elimination of others through the effects of competition, predation, and hybridization.—Edie Marsh-Matthews

See also **AQUATIC HABITATS; BODY TEMPERATURE; BUGS; CALIFORNIA DESERT; COLORADO RIVER; CONSERVATION IN DESERTS; DAM; ECTOTHERMY; ENDEMISM; HEAT BALANCE; INSECTICIDES; IRRIGATION DRAINAGE; METABOLISM; MOJAVE DESERT; POLLUTION; PRIMARY PRODUCTIVITY; SALT BALANCE; SALT PAN; WATER; WATER BALANCE**

Further Reading

Cole, G. A. 1968. Desert limnology. *In* G. W. Brown, Jr., ed., *Desert Biology: Special Topics on the Physical and Biological Aspects of Arid Regions*, 2:423–486. New York: Academic Press.

Deacon, J. E., and W. L. Minckley. 1974. Desert fishes. *In* G. W. Brown, Jr., ed., *Desert Biology: Special Topics on the Physical and Biological Aspects of Arid Regions*, 2:385–488. New York: Academic Press.

Kodric-Brown, A. 1981. Variable breeding systems in pupfishes (Genus *Cyprinodon*): Adaptations to changing environments. *In* R. J. Naiman and D. L. Soltz, eds., *Fishes in North American Deserts*, 205–235. New York: Wiley.

Miller, R. R. 1981. Coevolution of deserts and pupfishes (Genus *Cyprinodon*) in the American southwest. *In* R. J. Naiman and D. L. Soltz, eds., *Fishes in North American Deserts*, 39–94. New York: Wiley.

Moyle, P. B., and J. J. Cech, Jr. 1995. *Fishes: An Introduction to Ichthyology*, 3d ed. Englewood Cliffs, N.J.: Prentice-Hall.

Nelson, J. S. 1994. *Fishes of the World*. 3d ed. New York: Wiley.

Page, L. M., and B. M. Burr. 1991. *A Field Guide to Freshwater Fishes of North America North of Mexico*. Boston: Houghton Mifflin.

Weedman, D. A. 1997. *Status of the Gila Topminnow and Desert Pupfish in Arizona*. Phoenix: Arizona Game and Fish Department.

Flamingo (*Pheonicopterus*). (Photo: M. A. Mares)

FLAMINGO

Large, conspicuous wading bird with unique feeding adaptations (order Ciconiiformes, family Phoenicopteridae). Four to six species in one to three genera are recognized. Flamingos range discontinuously throughout tropical and subtropical zones in Europe, Asia, Africa, and the Americas. In some cases populations of phoenicopterids are found in arid high-altitude regions. For example, both the Andean flamingo and James' flamingo (*Phoenicopterus andinus* and *Phoenicopterus jamesi*, respectively) inhabit shallow saline lakes of the high-altitude (4,000 meters above sea level) dry altiplano of the South American Andes. Other species are associated with bodies of water at lower-altitude dry regions. For example, the Chilean flamingo (*Phoenicopterus chilensis*) is commonly found in salt flats of the lowland deserts of Argentina. All species are invariably associated with brackish, saline, or alkaline bodies of water.

Flamingos have ovate bodies, short tails, and exceptionally long necks and legs. The wings are long and broad. Flamingos are strong fliers, and some populations undertake substantial migrations. Most species are probably nomadic, engaging in local movements in search of limited resources. The plumage is primarily pink and red, with black flight feathers. The red colors of flamingo plumage are derived from carotenoid pigments found in some food items. Captive-reared flamingos not fed a carotenoid-rich diet often appear quite pale. The bill is strongly decurved, with a small upper mandible and a large, troughlike lower mandible, both edged with lamellae (thin plates). To feed, flamingos immerse their bills upside down in water. The fleshy tongue acts as a piston, bringing water in and expelling it across the lamellae. This action allows for the retention of food particles within the bill. Algae and diatoms are important food items for all species, but the diet of larger species includes many small invertebrates.

Flamingos are typically monogamous and have pair-bonds that are of long duration. Nesting is colonial, with breeding colonies of up to 900,000 pairs having been recorded in the Rift Valley of East Africa. Initiation of egg laying is highly synchronized within a colony. Nesting may not occur in some years. Nests consist of mounds of mud with a shallow depression at their apex. Clutch size is usually one. Incubation periods range from 27 to 31 days, and duties are shared by both parents. Young are initially cared for by both parents and are fed a regurgitated secretion from the crop. At between 7 and 12 days the chicks form large groups (creches) that remain together until after fledging.—Stephen C. Lougheed

See also **ALTIPLANO; ANDEAN GRASSLANDS; ANDES; ARTHROPODS; BIRDS; CHILE, DESERTS OF; DIET; KAVIR; PLANTS; PLAYA; PUNA; SABKHA; SALINITY; SALT PAN; SHRIMP, DESERT; WATER BALANCE**

Further Reading

Brown, L. H., E. K. Urban, and K. Newman. 1982. *The Birds of Africa*. Vol. 1. New York: Academic Press.

Cramp, S., and K. E. L. Simmons, eds. 1977. *Handbook of the Birds of Europe, the Middle East and North Africa. The Birds of the Western Palearctic*. Vol. 1. Oxford: Oxford University Press.

Fjeldså, J., and N. Krabbe. 1990. *Birds of the High Andes*. Svendborg, Denmark: Apollo.

Johnson, A. W. 1965. *The Birds of Chile and Adjacent Regions of Argentina, Bolivia and Peru*. Vol. 1. Buenos Aires: Platt.

Kear, J., and N. Duplaix-Hall, eds. 1975. *Flamingos*. Berkhamstead, England: Poyser.

Ogilvie, M., and C. Ogilvie. 1989. *Flamingos*. Wolfeboro, N.H.: Sutton.

FLICKER

Genus (*Colaptes*) of medium-sized, largely terrestrial woodpeckers (bird order Piciformes, family Picidae) distributed throughout the Americas. Eight or nine species of *Colaptes* are recognized, ranging in length from 20 centimeters (the spot-breasted flicker, *Colaptes punctigula*) to 30 centimeters (e.g., the Andean flicker, *Colaptes rupicola*). Flickers are believed to be descended from arboreal ancestors; thus their terrestrial habits are the result of secondary adaptation. Flickers are characterized by the presence of yellow or orange feather shafts, comparatively large feet, a narrow bill, and a skull that is less robust than in other woodpeckers. Vocal displays are loud and conspicuous.

Flickers generally avoid environments that are densely treed as they forage extensively on the ground. Some, however, range throughout a wide variety of open habitats. For example, western populations of the black-necked flicker (*Colaptes atricollis*) inhabit scrub woodland and forests of the western slopes of the Peruvian Andes up to an elevation of 2,800 meters. Eastern populations of this same species are associated with deserts and scrub vegetation between altitudes of 1,700 and 3,400 meters above sea level. Although primarily insectivorous (insect eating), some *Colaptes* species (e.g., the northern flicker, *Colaptes auratus*) may supplement their diet with plant matter.

Most flickers appear to be monogamous and territorial. Nest cavities are generally excavated in trees, columnar cacti, telephone poles, or fence posts. The Andean flicker, in contrast, nests in burrows excavated in cliff faces, rocky ledges, or banks along watercourses or roadbeds and may be found in colonies of up to 12 pairs. Clutch sizes generally range from four to six eggs. In northern flickers, however, clutch size, positively correlated with latitude, varies from 3 to 12 eggs. Incubation duties and care of young are shared by both sexes.—Stephen C. Lougheed

See also **ANDES; ARGENTINA, DESERTS OF; BIRDS; CACTUS, COLUMNAR; CARDÓN; FOREST; MONTE DESERT; RIPARIAN COMMUNITIES; SAGUARO; SONORAN DESERT; WOODPECKERS**

Further Reading

Bent, A. C. 1939. Life histories of North American

woodpeckers. *U.S. National Museum Bulletin* No. 174.

Short, L. L. 1972. The systematics and behavior of South American flickers (Aves: *Colaptes*). *Bulletin of the American Museum of Natural History* No. 149.

———. 1982. *Woodpeckers of the World*. Greenville: Delaware Museum of Natural History.

FLIES

Insects (order Diptera) characterized by one pair of front wings, with rear wings reduced to knoblike structures called the halteres. Flies rank as one of the largest insect groups in terms of the number of species. In this group are gnats, mosquitoes, houseflies, flesh flies, sand flies, blowflies, and many more. Several groups are particularly common in deserts.

Flies in the family Asilidae are called robber flies because of their unusual feeding habits. Common in deserts, these flies are predaceous on other insects, including bees and wasps, and usually capture prey while it is flying. They can often be observed perched on surface objects or branches of vegetation holding the insect that they captured. The larvae are predaceous as well, feeding on insects living in decaying plant material. Robber flies can inflict painful bites if handled.

Flies in the family Syrphidae, often known as flower flies, are extremely common in deserts and easily recognized by their flight patterns. Adult flower flies hover in midair like tiny helicopters, remaining motionless except for rapid wing movements, often within inches of an observer's face, frequently darting to a new midair position. They often are banded yellow and black, resembling small wasps. The larvae differ in feeding behaviors. Some live in decaying plant material, including cacti, others live in nests of social insects, and yet others are predaceous.

Flies in the family Calliphoridae, commonly known as blowflies, are metallic colored (blue or green) and usually associated with dead animals or animal feces. Adults lay eggs on the decaying material, and the larvae feed on carrion. Although most desert species are beneficial in that they help remove rotting dead animals from the environment, one species, the screwworm fly (*Cochliomyia hominivorax*), lays eggs in open wounds on animals, and the larvae literally eat the victim alive. Infection by screwworm larvae produces a characteristic smell that attracts more flies to the wound.

Flies in the family Culcidae, the mosquitoes, are common near ephemeral bodies of water in deserts. Their larvae are aquatic and can appear in very small containers of water. Consequently, in addition to being common near natural water sources, they are often found near human habitations. For example, mosquitoes often breed in the pools of water that form inside abandoned tires following rain. Because females feed on blood and many species transmit a variety of diseases, mosquitoes are considered pest insects at a variety of levels.

Flies in the family Psychodidae, the moth flies and sand flies, vary considerably in ecology. Moth flies are typically harmless to humans and are often seen in showers because larvae may develop in drains. These are the small flies that rest on walls with their wings horizontal to the surface on which they sit and in which the wings appear fuzzy. One group of psychodids, the phlebotomine sand flies, feed on blood and in many regions have a major impact on man. These flies are vectors for leishmaniasis, a disease caused by the microorganism *Leishmania*.

Flies in the family Mydaidae, the mydas flies, are particularly common in South African and Australian deserts.—Laurie J. Vitt

See also **ARTHROPODS; BIRDS; CARRION EATERS; DECOMPOSTION; DIVERSITY; ECOLOGY; ECOSYSTEM; INSECTS; RIVERS; RUNOFF; WATER; WATER HOLE**

Further Reading

Borror, D. J., C. A. Triplehorn, and N. F. Johnson. 1992. *An Introduction to the Study of Insects*. New York: Harcourt Brace.

Borror, D. J., and R. E. White. 1970. *A Field Guide to the Insects*. Boston: Houghton Mifflin.

Wilson, E. O. 1971. *The Insect Societies*. Cambridge, Mass.: Harvard University Press.

FLOOD

Rapid elevation of the level of water in a watercourse to a maximum level for either shorter or longer periods, with a later reduction to a lower velocity. The term "flood" also refers to any rise in water that causes a watercourse to flow out of its normal bed. This results when the capacity of the watercourse to convey water is exceeded and surrounding areas are flooded. Some hydrologists con-

Flash flood in an arroyo in the Monte Desert of northwestern Argentina following sudden thunderstorms. (Photo: M. A. Mares)

sider a flood to be defined by comparison with regular water flow (e.g., a flood may be said to occur when the flow is 3–5 times greater than the average). Floods are frequently associated with human catastrophes, as damage is caused to human constructions, although in many cases floods may be a very positive force of nature that enriches soils in desert areas. For example, the regular flooding of the Nile River valley led to the deposition of nutrient-rich soils along the Nile and permitted this arid area to support significant agricultural-based civilizations.

Floods are generally characterized by the maximum amount of water that flows past a particular point at any instant, the length of time during which a waterway is in flood stage, the total volume of water that has been transported by the waterway, and the distribution of the floods throughout the year (termed the hydrograph), as well as by the total area that is flooded. By describing each of these characteristics, a greater understanding of the flood and its effects is possible. For example, by studying how high the water rises in any particular waterway over time, it is possible to develop structures such as dams that can mitigate the effects of floods or use floodwaters in a positive manner. Programs of water conservation and canal management may also be developed to mitigate flood damage. Strategies for eliminating flood damage might include deviating floodwaters to areas that are more distant and where water is needed yet unavailable.

Many of the calculations that describe a flood are based on determining the probable maximum flood. This value corresponds to the greatest flood that can be expected to occur with some degree of certainity over a long period (e.g., the 50-year flood, or the 100-year flood). This is not to say that it is the largest flood that might ever be or has ever been experienced by an area.

Floods in deserts can be spectacular because of the intensity, duration, and extent of rains. In mountainous regions where there is snow cover, a sudden increase in temperature may lead to a rapid rise in runoff due to snowpack melting, which causes sudden floods in drylands located far from the mountains. In fact, floods may occur in arid regions even if they have not received rain if there have been heavy rains far from the arid habitat in question (tens of kilometers). Such floods will often arrive in a spectacularly sudden fashion (flash floods), giving no warning of their arrival as gullies and dry riverbeds become rushing torrents of silt-filled water and uprooted vegetation. Even boulders may be transported from the highlands into lower areas if the force of the water is sufficient. In heavily populated areas such as the southwestern United States, it is not uncommon for people in desert cities such as Tucson or Phoenix, Arizona, to be drowned when crossing a wash as a sudden flash flood arrives.

In mountainous areas large blocks of ice may suddenly break loose and block downward-rushing waters, thus building up large masses of water behind the blockage until the dam is broken suddenly by the force of the water, leading to a flash flood in the arid lands below, even when no rain has fallen either in the mountains or in the lowlands.

In general, sudden rainfall in desert areas leads to short-lived floods of high intensity, as dry streams become swollen with runoff from the rain. These flash floods generally occur in small- to medium-sized streams, gullies, and rivers whose physical characteristics, particularly degree of steepness of channels, as well as biological characteristics (type and density of the surrounding vegetation), play a great role in the intensity and duration of the flood. Such floods are difficult to predict.—Alberto I. J. Vich and Juana Susana Barroso

See also **CLIMATE; CLOUDS; CONVECTIVE STORM; CYCLONE; DROUGHT; EL NIÑO; FLOODPLAIN; GROUNDWATER; IRRIGATION DRAINAGE; MOIS-**

TURE INDEX; PRECIPITATION; RIVERS; RUNOFF; WATER

Further Reading

Anonymous. 1974. *Symposium on Flash Floods.* Proceedings. Paris, International Association of Hydrological Science (IAHS), Publication No. 112.

Dalrymple, T. 1982. Hydrology of flow control. Pt. 1: Flood characteristics and flow determination. *In* T. C. Ven, ed., *Handbook of Applied Hydrology: A Compendium of Water-resources Technology.* New York: McGraw-Hill.

Davis, S. N. 1974. Hydrogeology of arid regions. *In* G. W. Brown, Jr., ed., *Desert Biology: Special Topics on the Physical and Biological Aspects of Arid Regions*, 2:1–30. New York: Academic Press.

Walter, H. and E. Stadelmann. 1974. A new approach to the water relations of desert plants. *In* G. W. Brown Jr., ed., *Desert Biology: Special Topics on the Physical and Biological Aspects of Arid Regions*, 2:213–310. New York: Academic Press.

FLOODPLAIN

Low-lying, generally flat plain bordering a waterway that is formed by deposition of sediments carried by the stream or river and inundated during periods when the river floods. Each time the river overflows its banks, a new layer of sediments leads to a gradual increase of the initial topographic level of the floodplain. The closer the floodplain to the river, the greater the amount of sediments deposited there, giving rise to a levee or bank along the river's edges. Floodplains are characterized by having one principal channel that is usually quite long and meanders; stream flow varies periodically over the floodplain and may move from one part of the channel to another depending on the volume of water that is moving through the channel. In some cases small lakes, called oxbow lakes, may form as meandering channels are cut off from the main waterflow. Floodplains may be extremely fertile areas for agricultural crops. Certainly the floodplain of the Nile is a classic example of the types of remarkably rich floodplains that can develop after periodic floods.—Alberto I. J. Vich and Juana Susana Barroso

See also **ALLUVIAL SOILS; FLOOD; GROUNDWATER; HYDROLOGICAL CYCLE; HYDROLOGY; RIPARIAN COMMUNITIES; RIVERS; RUNOFF; WATER**

Further Reading

Cooke, R., A. Warren, and A. Goudie. 1993. *Desert Geomorphology.* London: University College London Press.

Davis, S. N. 1974. Hydrogeology of arid regions. *In* G. W. Brown, Jr., ed., *Desert Biology: Special Topics on the Physical and Biological Aspects of Arid Regions*, 2:1–30. New York: Academic Press.

Gregory, K. J., and D. E. Walling. 1973. *Drainage Basin: Form and Process: A Geomorphological Approach.* Kent: Arnold.

FLOWERS

Sexual reproductive structures of flowering plants, or angiosperms. Flowers often attract animal pollinators that aid in the transfer of pollen from one flower to another. The attractive appendages of flowers are usually the brightly colored petals, with the shape, size, and odor of each flower being important factors in drawing particular animal species to them. Animal visitors receive a variety of rewards, including sweet nectar, protein-rich pollen, and fleshy flower parts that may be eaten. Not all angiosperms, however, possess flowers with showy petals, or any nectar or odor; these flowers may be pollinated by the wind. All flower visitors are not actually pollinators, because the body of the animal may be too small, or its body shaped inappropriately, to receive or transfer pollen to the stigma (part of the female's reproductive organs) of another flower. Nevertheless, flowers are a rich source of food for many animals, including humans.

In the desert the problem of sexual reproduction is great for all plants but especially for annuals—plants whose entire life span is less than one year. Once the seed of an annual plant germinates, it has only one opportunity to reproduce before it dies, unlike a perennial, which may flower and reproduce each year from maturity until death. It is critical that annuals not grow, or flower, in times of extreme environmental stress. A group of desert plants, called ephemeral annuals, escape drought conditions by completing their life cycle within a period of two months or less, flowering in the spring while there is still moisture left in the soil after winter rains, or in the summer after summer rains. These ephemeral annuals have water-soluble germination inhibitors in their seeds that prevent the young embryo from developing. After a light rain only part of the inhibitor is removed from the seed, and thus the seed does not germinate. This prevents the annual from starting its life when there is insufficient water to support it throughout its life. After heavy winter rains, however, the inhibitor is washed

Large cactus flower in the Sonoran Desert of Arizona. (Photo: M. A. Mares)

out completely, and the seed germinates. With a heavy rain the groundwater is ample, and the ephemeral annual is able to reproduce before soil moisture diminishes. Because each plant produces hundreds of seeds, in some years thousands of ephemeral annual plants grow and reproduce at the same time, carpeting the desert floor with spectacular floral shows of red, yellow, orange, and white blossoms—a phenomenon termed desert bloom. Some of the more conspicuous annuals are the desert dandelion (*Rafinesquia neomexicana*), tackstem (*Calycoseris wrightii, Calycoseris parryi*), Arizona poppy (*Kallstroemia grandiflora*), goldfields (*Baeria chrysostoma*), and owlclover (*Orthocarpus purpurascens*). Among perennials, some of the most familiar desert flowering plants are the giant saguaro (*Carnegiea gigantea*), an indicator species of the Sonoran Desert with waxy white flowers and also the state flower of Arizona; the Joshua tree (*Yucca brevifolia*), an indicator of the Mojave Desert with green-white flowers; and the lechuguilla (*Agave*), an indicator of the Chihuahuan Desert with lavender-brown flowers. The larger rel-

atives of lechuguilla are sometimes referred to as century plants because of the years (10–15) required to store sufficient plant food before they develop a huge flowering stalk up to eight meters tall, producing seed and then dying.—Gordon E. Uno

See also **AGAVE; ANNUAL PLANTS; BAT; BEES; BUTTERFLIES; CACTi; CHIHUAHUAN DESERT; DESERT BLOOM; FLIES; FRUITS; INSECTS; JOSHUA TREE; MOJAVE DESERT; MOTHS; PLANT ADAPTATIONS; PLANTS; POLLINATION; SAGUARO; SEEDS; SONORAN DESERT; YUCCA**

Further Reading

Dodge, N. N. 1961. *Flowers of the Southwest Deserts*. Globe, Ariz.: Southwestern Monuments Association.

Munz, P. A. 1962. *California Desert Wildflowers*. Berkeley: University of California Press.

Taylor, R. J. 1998. *Desert Wildflowers of North America*. Missoula, Mont.: Mountain Press.

FLUVISOL. *See* SOILS, DESERT, FLUVISOL

FOAM NEST

Frothy substance in which eggs are deposited; a behavior characterizing certain species of frogs in the families Leptodactylidae, Rhacophoridae, and Myobatrachidae. Foam nests are constructed on land in depressions or burrows, in trees, or on the surface of the water in temporary ponds. The foam comprises polysaccharides (carbohydrate molecules made up of at least three monosaccharides) present in the seminal fluid of the male and the jelly and eggs of the female. Actual construction of a foam nest differs among species, but in leptodactylids males typically move their hind legs rapidly as eggs and seminal fluid are secreted during amplexus, the mating position in frogs wherein the male grips the female around the waist or behind the arms. In myobatrachids females construct the nest by rapidly moving their arms and rapidly beating secretions and eggs emitted from the juxtaposed cloacae. The foam is generated in the same way as meringue: rapid beating causes the polysaccharides to become thick and frothy.

Foam nests have two primary functions: (1) providing protection of the vulnerable eggs from predators that have a difficult time moving through the foam and (2) protecting eggs from drying in arid conditions. When environmental conditions are dry,

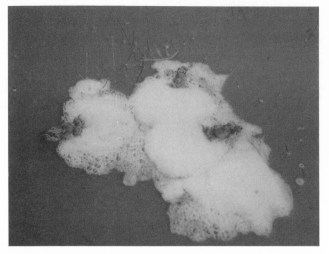

Three pair of leptodactylid frogs, *Physalaemus*, in the high semiarid grasslands of northwestern Argentina (Tucuman Province) kicking their hind legs to whip up a foam nest, which will enclose their eggs and protect them from desiccation until hatching. (Photo: M. A. Mares)

the outer portion of the foam nest may become dry and crusty, whereas the interior portion and the eggs remain moist. After hatching larvae may continue to remain in the moist foam until rains wash them into pools, where they complete their development in water. Several species of leptodactylid frogs in the genera *Leptodactylus*, *Physalaemus*, and *Pleurodema* inhabit arid areas in Argentina and construct foam nests in which the eggs and larvae are protected until the seasonal rains begin. Several studies have demonstrated that certain ephydrid flies occasionally enter the foam and prey on eggs of some species of leptodactylid frogs.—Janalee P. Caldwell

See also **AMPHIBIANS; ANIMAL ADAPTATIONS; BREEDING SEASON; DESICCATION; DESICCATION-RESISTANT SPECIES; DORMANCY; DROUGHT; FROGS; METAMORPHOSIS; PHYSIOLOGY; SOUTH AMERICA, DESERTS OF; TOADS; WATER; WATER HOLE**

Further Reading

Cei, J. M. 1980. Amphibians of Argentina. *Monitore Zoologico Italiano Monografiche* 2:1–609.

Duellman, W. E., and L. Trueb. 1986. *Biology of Amphibians*. New York: McGraw-Hill.

Hödl, W. 1990. An analysis of foam nest construction in the Neotropical frog *Physalaemus ephippifer* (Leptodactylidae). *Copeia* 1990:547–554.

Villa, J. 1980. "Frogflies" from Central and South America with notes on other organisms of the amphibian egg microhabitat. *Brenesia* 17:49–68.

FOEHN. *See* SANTA ANA WINDS

FOG DESERT

Type of desert in which fog, which forms due to factors related to the geographic position of the desert as well as to offshore ocean currents, is the major source of moisture for plants and animals. Fog is essentially a stratus cloud that forms close to the surface of the land or water. Horizontal visibility in fog is reduced to no more than one kilometer and may be much less than that, only a few meters. A fog is formed by small droplets of water whose size varies from 10 to 50 microns with a concentration of drops in the size category of 10–100 microdrops per cubic centimeter. Air in fog has a high relative humidity, generally above 95 percent. When the fog consists of ice crystals, it is called ice fog. Radiation fogs are produced as air cools during the night, and advection fogs develop when warm, humid air is displaced by a barrier such as a mountain and rises, thus causing it to cool and form fog. This type of fog is common in desert areas. Sea fog forms when warm, moist air moves above cold water. Such fog forms along the coast of the Pacific Ocean in the Atacama Desert of coastal Chile and Peru as the prevailing winds carry moist air from the interior Pacific over the waters of the cold Humboldt Current. For similar reasons, these types of fog also form along the coasts of Baja California and Namibia. These fogs are the major water source for organisms in these deserts, which are some of the most arid on earth.—Federico Norte

See also **AN INTRODUCTION TO DESERTS; ATACAMA DESERT; BAJA CALIFORNIA, DESERTS OF; CHILE, DESERTS OF; CLIMATE; CLIMATE CLASSIFICATION; CLOUDS; DESERTS; HUMBOLDT CURRENT; NAMIBIA, DESERTS OF; OCEAN CURRENTS; PERU, DESERTS OF; SECHURA DESERT; SOUTH AFRICA, DESERTS OF**

Further Reading

Day, J. A., and V. J. Schaefer. 1991. *Clouds and Weather*. Boston: Houghton Mifflin.

Oliver, J. E., and R. W. Fairbridge, eds. 1987. *The Encyclopedia of Climatology*. New York: Chapman and Hall.

Schaefer, V. J., and J. A. Day. 1981. *A Field Guide to the Atmosphere*. Boston: Houghton Mifflin.

Schneider, S. H., ed. 1996. *Encyclopedia of Climate and Weather*. 2 vols. New York: Oxford University Press.

FOREST

Type of vegetation dominated by trees (vascular plants that have one primary stem and exceed three meters in height). Trees need more water than shrubs or grasses; therefore, forests occur in climates that have equitable levels of rainfall in all seasons or that have extensive rainfall in the winter months. The woody plants that occur in deserts are generally shrubs, and most woody vegetation types under desert conditions are shrublands rather than forests. True forests occur in deserts only under circumstances when transpiration rates are much reduced, that is, in cold climates. For instance, the Steens Mountains in Oregon harbor a montane desert dominated by sagebrush, but a fir forest occurs in protected areas. Taiga (or boreal) forests of northern Canada also have low levels of precipitation, but in general the taiga and fir forests are not deserts. These vegetation types do not have a predominance of bare substrate, and precipitation equals or exceeds evapotranspiration. In Australia the *Eucalyptus* forests and *Acacia* woodlands are more forestlike than shrublike, as are the pistachio forests of central Asian deserts.

Genera of trees that occur in shrublands at the margins of deserts in the United States include junipers (*Juniperus*), piñon pine (*Pinus edulis*), and oaks (*Quercus*), especially shinnery oaks. These genera include numerous members that occur in semiarid habitats, and they are often abundant in adjoining woodlands, especially in the Great Basin.—James R. Estes

See also **BIOME; CHACO; COTTONWOOD; DESERTS; DESERTS, MONTANE; ECOLOGY; ECOSYSTEM; GRASSLAND; HOLDRIDGE LIFE ZONES; LEGUMES; LICHENS; PHREATOPHYTES; PLANT GEOGRAPHY; SAGEBRUSH; SHRUBS; RIO GRANDE; RIPARIAN COMMUNITIES; XEROPHYLLOUS FOREST; XEROPHYTES; WOODPECKERS**

Further Reading

Barbour, M. G., and W. D. Billings. 1988. *North American Terrestrial Vegetation*. Cambridge: Cambridge University Press.

Rost, T. L., M. G. Barbour, R. M. Thornton, T. E. Weier, and C. R. Stocking. 1984. *Botany*. 2d ed. New York: John Wiley.

FOSSILS

Evidence of past life—whether plant, animal, fungal, or bacterial—naturally preserved in the earth's crust since some past geologic time. The evidence may consist of remains of the organism or derivative parts (e.g., pollen or spores), of impressions of the organism (natural molds or casts), or of tracks or traces left by animals. Fossils occur in abundance mainly in sedimentary rocks (rocks that were originally deposited as sediments) but are found rarely in igneous (formed through volcanic action) and metamorphic rocks (rocks that have changed form due to such factors as heat, pressure, and water) as well. They are most common in rocks deposited during the last 600 million years. Among the oldest fossils on earth are bacteria and blue-green "algae" (cyanobacteria), about 3.2 billion years old, and stromatolites (algal or bacterial mats), about 3.4 billion years old, both in southern Africa. Cyanobacteriumlike prokaryotes (primitive organisms lacking a nucleus and reproducing via a simple splitting of the cell) also are known from about 3.5 billion years ago in what is now Western Australia.

The fossil record of ancient life on earth is incomplete; only the hard parts of organisms that had hard parts when alive are preserved readily. Preservation of soft-bodied organisms or soft parts of organisms is extremely rare. Also, only a small fraction of all the organisms that ever lived on earth have been detected as fossils. Nevertheless, fossils have contributed tremendously to the understanding of the evolution of life on earth.

The earth's geologic time scale was developed by using the record of sedimentary rocks and fossils they contained. These records can be correlated between and among continents by identifying synchronous events in earth history and can be developed into a relative chronological sequence. This relative sequence can then be correlated and refined further using other independent sources of geochronological information, especially by radiometric dating (the absolute dating of rocks using radioisotopes of certain elements). The radioactive elements in various minerals and rocks allow us to determine with great accuracy the number of years that have passed since the minerals in the rocks crystallized.

Fossils help to reconstruct paleoclimatic information for various parts of the earth over long periods of geologic time. They indicate radical changes in paleoclimate in some areas and relative stability in others. Fossils also are used to help interpret the existence and timing of connections between landmasses during earth history. Fossils aid in the reconstruction of ancient floras and faunas and of phylogenetic relationships, or evolutionary histories, for living and extinct organisms. They do so primarily by helping to determine primitive characteristics and evolutionary trends and patterns. Scientists examine major groups of fossils and trends in their occurrence through geologic time to address questions about evolutionary radiations and extinctions; they attempt to determine whether major extinctions and diversifications are related and what their causes might be.

The scarcity of vegetation in deserts and in semiarid areas sometimes affords opportunities to find fossils of terrestrial organisms, as in recent spectacular discoveries of vertebrate fossils of Cretaceous age in Mongolia (in part of what is now the Gobi Desert). There the exceptional preservation and completeness of skeletons of various dinosaurs (including eggs and juveniles), birds, reptiles, and mammals was due in many cases to quick burial by aeolian (wind-formed) dune sands. In some instances small herds or groups of dinosaurs likely were killed and buried by ancient sandstorms.—Nicholas J. Czaplewski

See also **AMPHIBIANS; AN INTRODUCTION TO DESERTS; ARTHROPODS; ASIA, DESERTS OF; BIRDS; CENOZOIC; CRETACEOUS; DESERTS; DUNES; EOCENE; LITHOSPHERE; MADRO-TERTIARY GEOFLORA; INSECTS; MAMMALS; MIDDEN; MIOCENE; NEOGENE; OLIGOCENE; PALEOCENE; PALEOCLIMATE; PLANTS; PLATE TECTONICS; PLEISTOCENE; PLIOCENE; PRECAMBRIAN; QUATERNARY; RECENT (HOLOCENE); REPTILES; TERTIARY**

Further Reading

Behrensmeyer, A. K., J. D. Damuth, W. A. DiMichele, R. Potts, H.-D. Sues, and S. L. Wing. 1992. *Terrestrial Ecosystems Through Time*. Chicago: University of Chicago Press.

Eldredge, N. 1987. *Life Pulse: Episodes from the Story of the Fossil Record*. New York: Facts of File.

Grzimek's Encyclopedia of Evolution. 1976. New York: Van Nostrand Reinhold.

Lipps, J. H. 1993. *Fossil Prokaryotes and Protists*. Cambridge, Mass.: Blackwell.

Novacek, M. J. 1997. *Dinosaurs of the Flaming Cliffs*. New York: Anchor Books.

Rudwick, M. J. S. 1985. *The Meaning of Fossils: Episodes in the History of Palaeontology*. 2d ed. Chicago: University of Chicago Press.

Schopf, J. W. 1993. Microfossils of the early Archean Apex Chert: New evidence of the antiquity of life. *Science* 260:640–646.

FOSSORIAL ANIMALS. *See* BURROWING ANIMALS

FOX

Member of the dog family, Canidae, of the mammalian order Carnivora. According to recent taxonomy, eight genera containing 22 species are recognized: *Alopex* (1 species), *Atelocynus* (1 species), *Cerdocyon* (1 species), *Dusicyon* (1 species, extinct), *Otocyon* (1 species), *Pseudalopex* (5 species), *Urocyon* (2 species), and *Vulpes* (10 species). Foxes are found worldwide, except Australia (where the red fox has been introduced), New Zealand, and Antarctica. They inhabit almost all habitat types, including deserts. As with many carnivores, foxes are threatened throughout much of the world by indiscriminate hunting and habitat disruption.

Size varies from a length of head and body of 24 centimeters, length of tail of 18 centimeters, and weight of 1.5 kilograms (in the smallest canid, the fennec fox, *Vulpes zerda*) to a length of head and body of 100 centimeters, length of tail of 35 centimeters, and weight of 9 kilograms (in the small-eared dog, *Atelocynus microtis*). In general foxes are small and have pointed muzzles, flattened slender skulls, large ears, and long bushy tails.

As opportunistic feeders, foxes will consume almost all available food resources, including fruits and leaves, carrion, birds, invertebrates, rodents, and fish. Only the bat-eared fox (*Otocyon*) of Africa has a specialized diet; more than 80 percent of its diet consists of insects (harvester termites, *Hodotermes*) and dung beetles (family Scarabidae). As with so many termite-eating mammals, the teeth of the bat-eared fox are reduced in size.

Foxes are generally nocturnal (active at night), except during the breeding season. They may be monogamous or solitary or form groups of one male and several vixens (female foxes). Breeding occurs once a year. Litter size ranges from one to six; gestation is 50–63 days. The young are born in dens or rock crevices. Ranges and territories are scent marked (foxes have a strong peculiar odor, which makes it difficult to keep them as house pets). Foxes will communicate by yapping and howling.

A number of foxes have adapted to life in arid or semiarid environments. Among these are the "sand foxes," *Vulpes chama, Vulpes pallida, Vulpes rueppelli*, and *Vulpes zerda*. The Cape fox (*Vulpes chama*) is found in Africa south of the equator. It inhabits savannas and semiarid regions, including the Namib Desert of southwestern Africa. The pale fox (*Vulpes pallida*) prefers nonrocky habitats in the semiarid areas of the steppes and savannas of the Sahel south of the Sahara from Senegal to Somalia. Rueppel's fox (*Vulpes rueppelli*) inhabits sand dunes and rocky desert regions in Africa north of the Sahara, as well as Arabia, Iran, Afghanistan, and Pakistan. The fennec fox (*Vulpes zerda*), the smallest-known canid, inhabits the deserts in North Africa, the Sinai, and Arabia. It is well adapted to living in arid environments. Its large ears (the longest in relation to its body size) and pointed nose help to radiate heat. The pale fur also aids in temperature regulation; the fur is dense, which is important for withstanding the cold nighttime temperatures. The soles of the feet are hairy, an important asset in traveling over loose sand. Like other foxes and carnivores, the fennec lacks sweat glands. It confines its activities to the night and uses a den during the day. Fennecs will drink water, but they can survive long periods on water obtained from their food.

The bat-eared fox, *Otocyon megalotis*, although not a desert specialist, occurs in grasslands, savannas, and forest edges from South Africa northward to Botswana, Angola, Rhodesia, and Somalia; a second population is found in Ethiopia, Sudan, and Tanzania. The large ears that characterize this species are used for locating insects and dissipating heat. This fox is usually found near herds of zebras, wildebeest, and buffalo, which assist it in locating a ready source of food, such as dung beetles.

Other fox species inhabit the arid and semiarid region of the Middle East and Asia. The hairy-pawed Tibetan sand fox (*Vulpes ferrilata*) occurs in alpine desert habitats above 3,000 meters on the high plateaus of Nepal and Tibet. Blanford's fox (*Vulpes cana*) prefers the steep cliffs and rocky terrain of the mountain-steppe habitat of Afghanistan, Iran, Pakistan, and Turkmenistan. The steppes and subdeserts of China, Mongolia, Manchuria, Iran, and Afghanistan are the home of the Corsac fox (*Vulpes corsac*).

In North America the kit fox (*Vulpes macrotis*) inhabits arid and semiarid regions of the Southwest. In South America at least three species are known to occur in arid environments. The culpeo, *Pseudalopex culpaeus*, is distributed from southern Ecuador southward along the Andes to Tierra del Fuego. It is found in open dry habitats at elevations ranging from sea level to the high Andes. There is considerable variation in size. In colder areas *P. culpaeus* is large with dense fur; individuals occurring at high altitudes have enlarged hearts. The Sechura fox, *Pseudalopex sechurae*, occurs in one of the driest regions on earth, the arid coastal desert of southwestern Ecuador and northwestern Peru. The pampas fox, *Pseudalopex gymnocercus*, is found in open plains, pampas, and semiarid regions from Peru southward along the Andes to Chile, in all but southernmost Argentina, Uruguay, Paraguay, and southern Brazil.—Janet K. Braun

See also **ACTIVITY CYCLES, ANIMALS; AFRICA, DESERTS OF; ATACAMA DESERT; BURROWING ANIMALS; CARNIVORES; CARRION EATERS; CHACO; CHIHUAHUAN DESERT; CHILE, DESERTS OF; HEAT BALANCE; HOWLING; KALAHARI DESERT; KAROO; MAMMALS; MOJAVE DESERT; MONTE DESERT; NAMIBIA, DESERTS OF; PINNAE; SONORAN DESERT; SOUTH AFRICA, DESERTS OF; SOUTH AMERICA, DESERTS OF; UNITED STATES, DESERTS OF; WATER BALANCE**

Further Reading

Estes, R. D. 1991. *The Behavior Guide to African Mammals*. Berkeley: University of California Press.

Grzimek's Encyclopedia of Mammals. Vol. 4. 1990. New York: McGraw-Hill.

Macdonald, D., ed. 1984. *The Encyclopedia of Mammals*. New York: Facts on File.

Nowak, R. M. 1991. *Walker's Mammals of the World*. 5th ed. Baltimore: Johns Hopkins University Press.

Sheldon, J. W. 1992. *Wild Dogs: The Natural History of the Nondomestic Canidae*. San Diego: Academic Press.

FROGS

Vertebrate animals characterized by many morphological distinctions, including a shortened vertebral column (spine), a urostyle formed from fused tail vertebrae, and long hind limbs. The latter contribute to their great jumping ability, a trait used by many frogs to escape from predators. The general term "frogs" is applicable to many anuran families, whereas toads are members of the family Bufonidae. Male frogs (and toads) do not have a copulatory organ, and reproduction in most species consists of simultaneously releasing eggs and sperm that unite outside the body, a process called external fertilization. Frogs have a complex life history in which the eggs develop into tadpoles, soft-bodied organisms usually with a round body and long tapering tail. Tadpoles spend from one week to several years in water (depending on species) before metamorphosing into froglets, small replicates of the adult form. Many tropical species of frogs have life history adaptations that omit the tadpole stage, ostensibly to reduce dependence on a life history stage that is quite vulnerable to predators. Most frogs have permeable skin and are dependent on moist environmental conditions to prevent water loss and, ultimately, death from desiccation; thus desert frogs in particular must have adaptations that allow them to survive arid conditions. Some arid-adapted species accomplish this by burrowing underground and forming a "cocoon," accumulations of layers of shed skin that prevent water from being readily lost through the skin. Other species have lipid glands in the skin and secrete waxes that they wipe over their bodies, effectively waterproofing themselves. As of 1992 authorities recognized 3,967 species of frogs and toads classified in 25 families.—Janalee P. Caldwell

See also **ACTIVITY CYCLES, ANIMALS; AMPHIBIANS; ANIMAL ADAPTATIONS; BREEDING SEASON; BURROWING ANIMALS; COLORATION; DESICCATION; DESICCATION-RESISTANT SPECIES; DORMANCY; FOAM NEST; LIFE HISTORY STRATEGY (ITEROPARITY); MELANIN; METAMORPHOSIS; PHYSIOLOGY; PIGMENT; REPRODUCTION; SPADEFOOT TOAD; TADPOLES; TOADS; WARNING COLORATION; WATER BALANCE; WATER HOLE**

Further Reading

Duellman, W. E. 1993. *Amphibian Species of the World: Additions and Corrections.* Special Publication No. 21, Museum of Natural History, University of Kansas, Lawrence.

Duellman, W. E., and L. Trueb. 1986. *Biology of Amphibians.* New York: McGraw-Hill.

Frost, D. R., ed. 1985. *Amphibian Species of the World: A Taxonomic and Geographical Reference.* Lawrence, Kan.: Allen Press and Association of Systematics Collections.

Shoemaker, V. H., S. S. Hillman, S. D. Hillyard, D. C. Jackson, L. L. McClanahan, P. C. Withers, and M. L. Wygoda. 1992. Exchange of water, ions, and respiratory gases in terrestrial amphibians. *In* M. E. Feder and W. W. Burggren, eds., *Environmental Physiology of the Amphibians*, 125–150. Chicago: University of Chicago Press.

FRUITS

Seed-containing, ripened ovaries of flowers. A wide variety of fruit types exist, mostly reflecting the type of dispersal agent involved in distributing the seeds from the plant on which they were produced. Fruits may be one- to many-seeded and fleshy or dry at maturity. Fleshy fruits are often dispersed by animals that eat the fruit and seeds, digesting the flesh of the fruit and passing the tough seeds unharmed through the digestive tract, or eating the fruit and dropping the seeds in the process. Wind is also a major disperser of seeds and fruits for such plants as milkweeds, dandelions, and tumbleweeds. The weak stem of the tumbleweed breaks off during a windstorm, and the plant drops seeds as it bounces along the ground. Animals of all kinds, including humans, eat fruits for their nutrients and carbohydrates and for the seeds inside, which are high in carbohydrates, protein, and oil. In the desert fruits commonly eaten by Native Americans were the legume pods of the honey and screwbean mesquites (*Prosopis*), the prickly pear cactus (*Opuntia*), the jojoba (*Simmondsia chinensis*), and occasionally the large egg-shaped fruits of the buffalo gourd and its relatives (*Cucurbita*).—Gordon E. Uno

See also **ANNUAL PLANTS; CACTI; CACTUS, COLUMNAR; DESERT PEOPLES; DIET; ECONOMIC VALUE OF DESERT PRODUCTS; FLOWERS; GOURD; HOHOKAM; HOPI; JOSHUA TREE; LEGUMES; NAVAJO (DINE'É); O'ODHAM; PLANT ADAPTATIONS; PLANT DISPERSAL BY WIND (ANEMOCHORY); PLANTS; SAGUARO; SEEDS; SONORAN DESERT; TUMBLEWEED; YUCCA**

Further Reading

Balls, E. K. 1970. *Early Uses of California Plants.* Berkeley: University of California Press.

Dodge, N. N. 1961. *Flowers of the Southwest Deserts.* Globe, Ariz.: Southwestern Monuments Association.

FUNGI. *See* PLANTS

FYNBOS

Vegetation type restricted to extreme southern Africa; in the Cape Floristic Region. The origin of the term is the Dutch word *fijnbosch*, which refers to the small, fine leaves that are typical of the plants that are dominant in this biome. The Cape Floristic Region occupies an area of approximately 90,000 square kilometers in South Africa; about 85 percent of this region is fynbos vegetation. The Cape Floristic Region is primarily a coastal and near-coastal association of vegetation communities that extends north from the Cape (34° south latitude) to 32° south latitude in the west and from the Atlantic Coast (18° east longitude) to about 26° east longitude on the southern edge of the continent. The city of Cape Town, South Africa, is located within the fynbos vegetation.

The Cape region is dominated by steep coastal mountains that capture rains on the west-facing slopes during the Southern Hemisphere winter. Summers are warm and dry. The climate is also characterized by transient weather systems and substantial day-to-day variability in temperature and precipitation. The presence of the warm Agulhas Current in the southeast generates a misty rain that is carried up into the tabletop highlands.

The vegetation of southern Africa is among the richest in the world. There are 18,550 species in a 2.6-million-square-kilometer area; approximately 14,800, or 80 percent, of these are endemic (occurring nowhere else) species. In the Cape Floristic Region (90,000 square kilometers), 68 percent of the 8,578 species are endemic. This exceeds the rate of endemism on many islands. More than 2,000 species have been documented in a 2,000-hectare area of the Jonkershoek Nature Reserve. The vegetation is dominated by several extremely speciose (containing many species) genera: 600 species of the genus *Erica*, 108 species of *Cliffortia*, 115 species of *Muraltia*, 117 species of *Restio*, and 100 species of *Protea*. The latter genus and other species of the family Proteaceae are especially common in the sclerophyllous (hard-leafed) vegetation of the fynbos. There are few important tree species. The silver tree (*Leucadendron argenteum*) is restricted to the more humid slopes and wet ravines of Table Mountain. Several exotic species, especially *Pinus radiata* and *Acacia cyclops*, have successfully invaded mountain fynbos and watercourses, respectively.

The leaves of fynbos plants are covered with a hard cuticle (sclerophyllum) to conserve water during the dry summer. The plants are deep rooted and are able to draw moisture from the water table. The soils are generally low in nutrients and acidic, which in part explains the dominance of the families Proteaceae and Ericaceae. Fire remains an important ecological factor, and the disturbance caused by fire is partly responsible for maintaining the high species richness in the fynbos. Burned-over areas are invaded by colonizing species such as *Gladiolus* and *Watsonia*. They are replaced by herbaceous species, which are succeeded by a dwarf shrub community. After about seven years the typical sclerophyllous vegetation of the fynbos begins to return. Unfortunately, fire also facilitates the colonization of the fynbos by exotic species. Although several extensive areas of fynbos remain in southern Africa, urbanization and agricultural expansion are taking their toll on this unique and extremely diverse biome.—Thomas E. Lacher, Jr.

See also **AFRICA, DESERTS OF; BIOSPHERE RESERVE; CONSERVATION IN DESERTS; DIVERSITY; ECOLOGY; ENDEMISM; PLANT ADAPTATIONS; PLANTS; SOUTH AFRICA, DESERTS OF; SPECIATION**

Further Reading

Cowling, R., ed. 1992. *The Ecology of Fynbos*. Cape Town: Oxford University Press.

Cowling, R. M., D. M. Richardson, and S. M. Pierce. 1997. *Vegetation of Southern Africa*. Oxford: Cambridge University Press.

Van Wilgen, B. W., D. M. Richardson, F. J. Kruger, and H. J. van Hensbergen, eds. 1992. *Fire in South African Mountain Fynbos: Ecosystem, Community and Species Response at Swartboskloof*. Berlin: Springer.

Walter, H. 1983. *Vegetation of the Earth*. Berlin: Springer.

GAZELLE

Ungulate (23 species in 6 genera) in the mammalian subfamily Antilopinae (family Bovidae) that occurs in semideserts, deserts, savannas, steppes, and rocky outcrops, primarily in Africa but also in the Middle East, India, and China. In Africa most gazelles live on the edge of the Sahara Desert, although some may be found in the desert proper. East Africa is the center of species diversity for the group. Only three species, the gerenuk (*Litocranius walleri*), Thompson's gazelle (*Gazella thomsonii*), and Grant's gazelle (*Gazella granti*), are found south of the equator, and only one species, the springbok (*Antidorcas marsupialis*), occurs in southern Africa.

Outside of Africa gazelles occur in Mongolia and China (Tibetan gazelle, Mongolian gazelle, and Przewalski's gazelle; genus *Procapra*), the Indian subcontinent (blackbuck, *Antilope cervicapra*), the Arabian Peninsula and the Middle East (mountain gazelle *Gazella gazella*), and from the Middle East and Saudi Arabia east to Iran and Turkestan into eastern China (goitered gazelle, *Gazella subgutturosa*). Others species found outside of Africa are *Gazella arabica* (Saudi Arabia), *Gazella bennettii* (Iran to northwest India), *Gazella bilkis* (Yemen), and the extinct *Gazella saudiya* (Saudia Arabia, Kuwait, and Iraq). A number of species and subspecies are considered extinct, endangered, or threatened due to hunting and habitat deterioration.

Gazelles are generally similar in shape; they have long legs, long necks, and slender bodies, and most have annulated (ringed) horns. Males are larger than females and typically have S-shaped (lyre-shaped) horns; females have thinner, more weakly ringed horns that are more variable in shape. All species are generally brownish above and whitish below; the blackbuck of India is an exception, as males turn black above when about three years old. Some species have blackish or brownish bands along the side of the body; most species have white buttocks, and some are black on the tip of the tail. The blaze is dark, with a white band on either side; a dark band extends from the eyes to the muzzle; and a white eye ring is present.

Gazelles have well-developed sight and hearing and are highly adapted for life in an arid environment. To conserve body water, they exhibit nasal panting, concentrate urine, produce dry feces, and have reflective pelage. They browse on green vegetation at night or in early morning when plants have a higher water content and when temperatures are lower. They are inactive during the warmest parts of the day. They have long limbs for efficient long-distance travel; many species are nomadic or have seasonal migrations, which allow for the seasonal exploitation of resources.

Gazelles, when playing or alarmed, may exhibit a stotting or pronking gait. This stiff-legged bouncing that occurs with all four legs at once is most pronounced in the springbok. Gazelles typically form small herds, although large aggregations of gazelles and other species form during some parts of the year. Males and females typically are segregated when resident in an area but integrate during migrations. Males establish territories during the breeding season by marking boundaries with urine and dung piles and, in some species, with secretions from the preorbital glands (scent glands located anterior to the eye) which they daub onto twigs or grass stems.—Janet K. Braun

See also **AFRICA, DESERTS OF; ANTELOPE; ASIA, DESERTS OF; BLACKBUCK; HEAT BALANCE; HEAT EXCHANGE; HERBIVORY; IRAN, DESERTS OF; MAMMALS; MIDDLE EAST, DESERTS OF; NAMIBIA, DESERTS OF; PHYSIOLOGY; SAHARA DESERT; SOUTH AFRICA, DESERTS OF; SPRINGBOK; THERMOREGULATION; UNGULATES; WATER BALANCE**

Further Reading

Alden, P. C., R. D. Estes, D. Schlitter, and B. McBride. 1995. *National Audubon Society Field Guide to African Wildlife*. New York: Knopf.

Dorst, J., and P. Dandelot. 1980. *A Field Guide to the Larger Mammals of Africa*. London: Collins.

Estes, R. D. 1991. *The Behavior Guide to African Mammals*. Berkeley: University of California Press.

Grzimek's Encyclopedia of Mammals. Vol. 5. 1990. New York: McGraw-Hill.

Haltenorth, T., and H. Diller. 1980. *A Field Guide to the Mammals of Africa, Including Madagascar.* London: Collins.

Macdonald, D., ed. 1984. *The Encyclopedia of Mammals.* New York: Facts on File.

Nowak, R. M. 1991. *Walker's Mammals of the World.* 5th ed. Baltimore: Johns Hopkins University Press.

Skinner, J. D., and R. H. N. Smithers. 1990. *The Mammals of the Southern African Subregion.* Pretoria: University of Pretoria.

GECKO

Lizard in the reptilian families Gekkonidae and Eublepharidae. About 850 species are currently recognized. No single set of obvious external characteristics distinguishes geckos from all other lizards; as a group (the Gekkota) they share highly modified internal ear structures that separate them from other lizard assemblages. The popular image of a gecko is that of a flattened lizard with a spectacle (transparent scale) over the eye, large adhesive toe pads on the feet, and skin having a rubbery texture. This image corresponds to most members of the gecko subfamily Gekkoninae (family Gekkonidae). Another group is snakelike in morphology, lacks front limbs, and has flaplike appendages for hind limbs. These are the flapfoots of Australia, in the subfamily Pygopodinae (family Gekkonidae). Other geckos have eyelids, lack toe pads, and have granular skin (family Eublepharidae), or lack eyelids and toe pads (family Gekkonidae, subfamily Sphaerpdactylinae).

Geckos are well-known inhabitants of the deserts of the world, often forming a major component of the lizard fauna. A majority of desert geckos are nocturnal (active at night). The best-known North American geckos are the banded geckos, members of the genus *Coleonyx*. They have been used as a model system in studies dealing with the evolution and ecology of tail autotomy (tail loss). The only other gecko in North American deserts is in the genus *Phyllodactylus*, the leaf-toed gecko, which is restricted to deserts of extreme southern California and Baja California, Mexico. The greatest diversity of desert geckos occurs in arid Australia, where they form a major part of the lizard fauna. Many of the Australian desert geckos are highly specialized. For example, *Diplodactylus elderi* appears to be restricted to tussocks of the spinifex grasses, and the flapfoot, *Delma fraseri*, is commonly associated with *Triodia* grass clumps.

Banded gecko (*Coleonyx variegatus*) of the deserts of the southwestern United States. (Photo: L. J. Vitt)

The Australian geckos are among the best-studied species ecologically, primarily as the result of the extensive research conducted by Eric R. Pianka of the University of Texas.—Laurie J. Vitt

See also **ARIZONA DESERT; AUSTRALIA, DESERTS OF; BAJA CALIFORNIA, DESERTS OF; CALIFORNIA DESERT; DEFENSIVE ADAPTATIONS, ANIMALS; LIZARDS; MOJAVE DESERT; PREDATION; REPTILES; SONORAN DESERT; TAIL LOSS**

Further Reading

Cogger, H. G. 1992. *Reptiles and Amphibians of Australia.* Ithaca: Cornell University Press.

Loveridge, A. 1972. Revision of the African lizards of the Family Gekkonidae. *Bulletin of the Museum of Comparative Zoology* 98:1–469.

Pianka, E. R. 1986. *Ecology and Natural History of Desert Lizards: Analyses of the Ecological Niche and Community Structure.* Princeton: Princeton University Press.

GEMSBOK

Ungulate of the species *Oryx gazella* (mammalian order Artiodactyla, family Bovidae) that inhabits the arid plains and deserts from Ethiopia and Somalia to Namibia and eastern South Africa. They are large (length of body 180–235 centimeters), have a long tufted tail (length of 80–90 centimeters), stand 115–140 centimeters at the shoulder, and weigh 180–225 kilograms. The ears are short and broad, with rounded tips. A mane extends from the head to the shoulders. The coloration is grayish or brownish, with a black-and-white face mask, a black stripe on the back and flanks, and black marks on

Gemsbok (*Oryx gazella*) in the Etosha Pan, Etosha National Park, northern Namibia. (Photo: M. A. Mares)

the legs. Males have a tuft of hair on the throat. Both sexes have long (90–127 centimeters), straight, backward-directed horns.

Gemsbok are well adapted to living in arid environments. They prefer a diet of perennial grasses, but when vegetation deteriorates they switch to selectively browsing on shrubs and trees. Their ability to be selective is enhanced by a narrow mouth—the narrowest of all large African ungulates. Gemsbok do not seek shade during the hottest parts of the day. They sweat to maintain constant temperature and restrict their activities to mornings and evenings, when air temperatures are coolest. If they become water stressed and cannot spare water for evaporative cooling by sweating from the skin, the body temperature is allowed to increase (up to 43°C), but the brain temperature remains cool (they accomplish this through the carotid rete system, what is essentially a "radiator" that cools the blood flowing to the brain). Because of their large body size, the body heats up slowly and reaches the maximum body temperature toward the end of the day, as desert temperatures begin to decrease. Gemsbok are often seen standing on the tops of dunes or hills at the end of a hot day. At such times they are catching the cool evening breezes and "off-loading" the heat stored in the body during the day. The thin fur and poor insulation allow rapid cooling. In the Namib Desert gemsbok feed at night to take advantage of the increased moisture content of the plants due to fog-induced changes in the relative humidity. Gemsbok drink at streams and water

holes, but during droughts additional moisture is obtained from melons or juicy bulbs. Despite the bitter taste, they will consume the geophyte gemsbok cucumber (containing 70 percent water and weighing 670 grams [= 0.5 liter] of water). Cucumbers are dug up, the water extracted, and the fibers spit out.

This ungulate is gregarious and is often seen in groups of 2–20, although herds of 100–200 have been observed. A single young is born after a gestation period of 8.5–10 months; weaning occurs at 3.5 months. Sexual maturity is reached at 1.5–2 years of age. Gemsbok may exhibit aggressive behavior, especially during encounters at water holes when resources are limited. Although still common, some populations have been extirpated by hunting.—Janet K. Braun

See also **AFRICA, DESERTS OF; ANIMAL ADAPTATIONS; ANTELOPE; COUNTERCURRENT HEAT EXCHANGE; HEAT BALANCE; HEAT EXCHANGE; HEAT STRESS; HERBIVORY; MAMMALS; NAMIBIA, DESERTS OF; ORYX; PHYSIOLOGY; SOUTH AFRICA, DESERTS OF; THERMOREGULATION; UNGULATES; WATER BALANCE**

Further Reading

Estes, R. D. 1991. *The Behavior Guide to African Mammals.* Berkeley: University of California Press.

Grzimek's Encyclopedia of Mammals. Vol. 5. 1990. New York: McGraw-Hill.

Kingdon, J. 1989. *East African Mammals: An Atlas of Evolution in Africa (Bovids).* Vol. 3D. Chicago: University of Chicago Press.

Lovegrove, B. 1993. *The Living Deserts of Southern Africa.* Vlaeberg: Fernwood.

Macdonald, D., ed. 1984. *The Encyclopedia of Mammals.* New York: Facts on File.

Nowak, R. M. 1991. *Walker's Mammals of the World.* 5th ed. Baltimore: Johns Hopkins University Press.

Skinner, J. D., and R. H. N. Smithers. 1990. *The Mammals of the Southern African Subregion.* Pretoria: University of Pretoria.

GENET

Members of the family Viverridae, a taxon of mammalian carnivores that also includes the mongoose and the meerkat. There are nine species of genets, all in the genus *Genetta*, but only one species, the common genet (*Genetta genetta*), regularly occurs in arid habitats. The common genet is found from southern Africa north through the East African savannas to the edge of the Sahara. It also occurs in

North Africa along the Mediterranean and in western Europe.

The common genet looks much like a cross between a ferret and a spotted cat. It has a slender body approximately one meter long, half of the length being the tail. Genets weigh approximately two kilograms. The body is yellowish brown with rows of black spots, and the tail is banded with a black tip. Their claws are retractile, like those of a cat.

All genets are adapted to an arboreal lifestyle, but the common genet spends a great deal of time on the ground where it occurs in arid regions. In the dry woodlands south of the Sahara they are most common in rocky areas. They coexist with another species in these regions, the blotched genet (*Genetta tigrina*); however, the blotched genet tends to occur in the moister valleys. Genets prey on a wide variety of small vertebrates and invertebrates and consume fruit as well. They are nocturnal (active at night) and use scent marking as an important means of communication. Females give birth to a litter of two to four young that take up to six months to wean. They can reproduce year-round, but in drier areas reproduction is more seasonal. Genets are still fairly common and are often domesticated as pets.—Thomas E. Lacher, Jr.

See also **AFRICA, DESERTS OF; CARNIVORES; MAMMALS; MEERKAT; MIDDLE EAST, DESERTS OF; PREDATION; SAHARA DESERT; SOUTH AFRICA, DESERTS OF; SPAIN, DESERTS OF**

Further Reading

Estes, R. D. 1991. *The Behavior Guide to African Mammals*. Berkeley: University of California Press.

Gittleman, J. L., ed. 1989. *Carnivore Behavior, Ecology, and Evolution*. Ithaca: Cornell University Press.

Kingdon, J. 1989. *East African Mammals: An Atlas of Evolution in Africa*. Vol. 3A. Chicago: University of Chicago Press.

Macdonald, D., ed. 1984. *The Encyclopedia of Mammals*. New York: Facts on File.

Nowak, R. M. 1991. *Walker's Mammals of the World*. 5th ed. Baltimore: Johns Hopkins University Press.

GERBIL

Mouse to rat-sized rodent (order Rodentia) in the mammalian family Muridae, subfamily Gerbillinae, a group that also includes jirds and sand rats. The 15 or so genera and more than 80 described species occur throughout Africa and are distributed eastward to Turkey, the southwestern Russian republics, and northern China. Although this is the largest group of rodents in Africa and Asia that is adapted to desert habitats, these species also inhabit savannas (grasslands with scattered trees), steppes (grasslands), rocks, and farmlands.

There is considerable variation in size, body shape, and coloration. Length of head and body ranges from 6 to 20 centimeters, length of tail from 7 to 22 centimeters, and weight from 8 to 190 grams. A number of species have grooved incisors, the purpose of which is unknown. As an adaptation against predation, gerbil coloration generally matches the color of the surrounding habitat; populations found on light-colored sands are blond, those on dark sands are dark, and those on red sands are reddish. Many species have a contrastingly colored tail tuft that may act as a predator decoy. The eyes are positioned so as to give a wide field of view. The middle ear is large, enhancing the hearing of low-frequency sounds such as owl wing beats.

Some species have elongate hind limbs and are saltatorial (having a leaping locomotion), whereas others do not and are quadrupedal. The soles of the hind feet of many of the sand-dwelling species are well haired. These hairs provide traction in the sand and may also provide insulation from hot surfaces, even though most species are nocturnal (active at night).

Nearly all species live in areas where high daytime temperatures can cause severe stress. Because of their size, gerbils have a large surface to volume ratio and must therefore find and efficiently use water resources and minimize water loss. Gerbils are unable to withstand high temperatures even for several hours. During the hottest parts of the day they remain in their burrows, which may be up to 50 centimeters below the surface and where the temperature is a constant 20°–25°C. They usually block the entrance with dirt in order to deter predators, maintain burrow humidity, and keep out hot, dry air. Daytime activity is restricted to species that have more northern distributions where temperatures are milder, or to the winter months. Water is conserved by its efficient extraction from food, water loss in the feces is minimized, and the kidneys are so efficient that wastes are reduced to only a few drops of highly concentrated urine. Seed-eating gerbils (i.e., granivores) gather seeds at night when they are covered with dew; their water content is further increased by transporting the seeds back to the high humidity of the burrow.

Gerbils are generally vegetarians, consuming various plant parts, including seeds, fruits, leaves, stems, roots, and bulbs. Some are omnivorous or insectivorous. Many have specialized diets. *Gerbillus* is a seed specialist. Great gerbils and antelope rats are herbivores. Fat sand rats (*Psammomys*) only eat the salty succulent plants of the family Chenopodiaceae. These plants contain 80–90 percent water but are extremely salty (concentrations well above that of seawater), and many also contain high concentrations of oxalic acid. Fat sand rats are able to consume these plants, produce a highly concentrated urine, and process the oxalic acid, which may cause serious poisoning and is sometimes lethal to species that lack the specialized ability to use this compound. Wagner's gerbils also eat snails; snail shells can be seen piled up outside their burrows.

Gerbils living in areas with cold winters hoard food. A Mongolian gerbil was found with 20 kilograms of seeds in its burrow. The great gerbil hoards and also constructs large (one meter high, three meters long) stacks of desert plants outside its burrow (up to 60 kilograms of plant matter). One species, the fat-tailed gerbil (*Pachyuromys duprasi*), stores fat in its tail.

Gerbils have numerous types of social systems. Species inhabiting deserts tend to be solitary, although their burrows may be in close proximity and colonies may exist. Savanna species are more social—pair-bonds are formed, and there are family structures. Species living in cold deserts, such as members of the *Meriones* group, have complex social systems. Large groups gather in single burrows, perhaps to keep warm or to protect food stores. The social group of the Mongolian gerbil consists of one to three adult males, two to seven adult females, and a number of subadults and juveniles. To deter inbreeding, females in heat leave the group, travel to another group to breed, and return to give birth (after a gestation of 21–28 days) and raise the young protected by uncles and the mother.

Desert gerbils reproduce after the rainy season; in other habitats gerbils may produce litters all year. Litter size ranges from 1 to 12; the life span is 1–2 years.

The common pet store gerbil is the Mongolian gerbil. In some areas gerbils are considered pests because they damage crops. The fleas from gerbils have also been known to transmit diseases such as plague and leishmaniasis.—Janet K. Braun

See also **AFRICA, DESERTS OF; ANIMAL ADAPTATIONS; BURROWING ANIMALS; CONVERGENT EVOLUTION; EXCRETORY SYSTEM; GRANIVORY; JERBOA; KIDNEY FUNCTION, DESERT RODENTS; KIDNEYS; MAMMALS; METABOLIC WATER; MIDDLE EAST, DESERTS OF; NAMIBIA, DESERTS OF; RENAL PAPILLA; RODENTS; SAHARA DESERT; SEED DISPERSAL BY ANIMALS (ZOOCHORY); SEEDS; SOUTH AFRICA, DESERTS OF; SWEAT GLANDS; THERMOREGULATION; TYMPANIC BULLAE; WATER BALANCE**

Further Reading

Grzimek's Encyclopedia of Mammals. Vol. 3. 1990. New York: McGraw-Hill.

Harrison, D. L., and P. J. J. Bates. 1991. *The Mammals of Arabia*. Kent, England: Sevenoaks/Harrison Zoological Museum.

Macdonald, D., ed. 1984. *The Encyclopedia of Mammals*. New York: Facts on File.

Nowak, R. M. 1991. *Walker's Mammals of the World*. 5th ed. Baltimore: Johns Hopkins University Press.

Osborn, D. J., and I. Helmy. 1980. The contemporary land mammals of Egypt (including Sinai). *Fieldiana: Zoology* 5:1–579.

GERENUK

Species of antelope, *Litocranius walleri*, in the mammalian order Artiodactyla, family Bovidae, also known as the giraffe gazelle; or Waller's gazelle. Two or three subspecies are recognized. Gerenuks are found from East Africa southward to Tanzania, and were known historically in Egypt and Sudan. The common name giraffe gazelle derives from the long limbs and neck. The S- or lyre-shaped horns of the males are 25–44 millimeters long and curve sharply forward at the tips; horns are absent in females.

Gerenuks inhabit desert to dry bush savanna. Adaptations of the skeleton and musculature enable them to browse on tall bushes by standing on their hind legs, and the long neck allows access to food that is inaccessible to other gazelles. Mobile lips and a narrow, pointed muzzle facilitate feeding on plant parts, particularly those with high water content, including tender leaves, young shoots, flowers, and fruits. Gerenuks are independent of free water and obtain all of their water from their food.

Animals such as gerenuks that feed on widely spaced food items must spend considerable time and energy in acquiring food. High-energy activities, such as fighting, migration, and energy loss due to bad weather, are minimized. Gerenuks lie down in strong wind, thus reducing the body's surface area that is exposed to water loss or heat gain. Population densities are low. Gerenuks do not form migratory aggregations, but they do form small groups of one to five individuals, generally with one highly territorial dominant male. Secretions from scent glands in front of the eyes are used in marking territories. When alarmed gerenuks will stand motionless with their necks erect. When frightened they will leave the area in a crouched trot, with the neck and tail carried horizontally. Their predators include cheetahs, leopards, lions, Cape hunting dogs, and hyenas. Young are prey for servals, caracals, ratels, and eagles.—Janet K. Braun

See also **AFRICA, DESERTS OF; ANTELOPE; HEAT BALANCE; HEAT EXCHANGE; HERBIVORY; MAMMALS; SOUTH AFRICA, DESERTS OF; THERMOREGULATION; UNGULATES; WATER BALANCE; XEROPHYLLOUS FOREST**

Further Reading

Estes, R. D. 1991. *The Behavior Guide to African Mammals.* Berkeley: University of California Press.

Grzimek's Encyclopedia of Mammals. Vol. 5. 1990. New York: McGraw-Hill.

Kingdon, J. 1989. *East African Mammals: An Atlas of Evolution in Africa.* Vol. 3D. *Bovids.* Chicago: University of Chicago Press.

Macdonald, D., ed. 1984. *The Encyclopedia of Mammals.* New York: Facts on File.

GERMINATION

Initiation of growth or bursting of pollen, seed, spores (tiny reproductive bodies), or zygotes (fertilized eggs). Pollen is a male gametophyte (a plant that reproduces through the production of male and/or female sex cells, or gametes, and union, or fertilization, of the two types of gametes). At maturity a pollen grain has three cells, two of which are sperm. In the flowering plants (the most common group of plants in deserts) pollen is produced in the anthers (upper part of the stamen) of flowers, and germination of pollen takes place on receptive stigmas (pollen-receptive surface of the pistil, the central flower organ enclosing the ovules, which develop into seeds), usually but not always of the same species.

Because plants are immobile, it is necessary for pollen to be distributed by wind, water, or animals from one flower to another. In desert plants insects and birds—not the wind as might be expected—are the most common pollinators. Solitary bees are excellent pollinators in deserts. They are abundant, and they dwell in burrows they dig in the soil. Female bees usually restrict their flower visits to members of a single species, or genus, of plants when they collect pollen. Therefore, there is relatively little pollen wasted by the bee.

Recognition proteins in the stigma and pollen wall are necessary for the pollen grain to burst and for the pollen tube to initiate growth down the style to the ovule. The sperm cells migrate down the pollen tube, and one enters the embryo sac, which is a 4- to 16-celled female gametophyte within an ovule. Two of the cells within the female gametophyte are the egg and the fusion nucleus. One sperm fertilizes the egg, and the other fertilizes the fusion nucleus (a process known as double fertilization, which occurs only in the flowering plants).

The zygote divides and grows to become the embryo within the seed (mature ovule). The fertilized fusion cell becomes the endosperm, a nutritive tissue that is consumed by the embryo as it grows. During this phase the ovule matures and becomes a seed borne within the maturing ovary of the pistil. The mature ovary is a fruit. (If a plant structure produces seeds within it, it is a fruit, although some commercial fruits are bred to be seedless. Therefore, many common vegetables [e.g., tomatoes, squash, cucumbers, green beans, and eggplants] are, in fact, fruits.) The fruit is blown by the wind, floated by water, propelled, or carried by an animal to a new location. Wind and water are two common means of transporting fruits and seeds in desert floras. Animals may carry fruits on their fur or feathers, cache them as potential food, or even eat the fruit and carry the seed within their digestive tracts.

Regardless of the mechanism of dispersal, the seed is the stage of the sporophyte generation (the generation of a plant that has two sets of chromosomes and is the asexual, spore-producing generation) of flowering plants that withstands the desiccation of the dry season or the frost of the cold season. The seed may remain in the soil for a number of years, or it might germinate immediately. In deserts it is common for seeds to remain in the seed bank in the soil for several years until conditions are appropriate for growth, that is, when the moisture and temperature regimes are equitable. In the desert the seed coat usually contains inhibitors that prevent germination until the inhibitory chemicals are leached out by heavy rain, even if conditions are otherwise favorable. This ensures that adequate water resources are present to support germination and subsequent growth.

Seeds have only trace levels of moisture, but shortly before germination the seed takes up water and swells. The radicle (embryonic root) swells most rapidly, commences growth first, and bursts the seed coat. That bursting is the moment of germination, but it is best to think of the establishment of seedlings as a continuous process. The emerging root begins to absorb water, which is used to assist in the enzymatic digestion of stored food reserves in the remaining endosperm or other storage organs. In desert plants the root often produces extensive growth before the hypocotyl (lower embryonic shoot) emerges. It becomes green when chlorophyll is synthesized and commences to photosynthesize (produce its own nourishment).

If the seed has reached a suitable location, then the new sporophyte will develop, flower, and produce new fruit and seed. Spores are of two kinds: (1) meiospores, which are produced as a result of meiosis (reduction division of cells wherein the number of chromomes is reduced by half), and (2) vegetative spores, which are the result of mitotic division (which produces identical cells with a full complement of chromosomes). In higher plants meiospores germinate within the mature sporophyte; however, in nonseed plants, such as mosses and ferns, they germinate when they reach a suitable substrate, and only after dormancy is broken. Meiospores germinate to produce gametophytes, which are haploid (containing half of the full complement of chromosomes). Meiospores are the progenitors of pollen and embryo sacs of flowering plants, and in these plants they germinate within the tissue of the sporophyte. In nonseed plants the gametes must have a moist substrate for fertilization to take place. Therefore, nonseed plants are found only in wet habitats in deserts. Vegetative spores are common in fungi. Zygotes of some algae and fungi (often termed zygospores) are also dispersed. They germinate when they break dormancy and reach a suitable location, usually a pond or river.—James R. Estes

See also **ANNUAL PLANTS; BULBS; FLOWERS; FRUITS; DESERT BLOOM; GROWING SEASON;** **PERENNIAL PLANTS; PHOTOSYNTHESIS; PLANT ADAPTATIONS; PLANT DISPERSAL BY WIND (ANEMOCHORY); PLANT ROOTS, ADVENTITIOUS; PLANTS; PRIMARY PRODUCTIVITY; PSAMMOPHYTES; PSAMMOPHYTIC SCRUB; RESURRECTION PLANT**

Further Reading

Rost, T. L., M. G. Barbour, R. M. Thornton, T. E. Weier, and C. R. Stocking. 1984. *Botany*. 2d ed. New York: John Wiley.

GERONIMO

Prominent warrior of the Bedonkohe band of the Chiricahua Apaches. Geronimo (ca. 1820–1909) was a brilliant leader of men in combat. Although some observers thought of him as cruel and treacherous, they conceded he was a man of courage and determination. In later years he displayed a shrewd business sense and a remarkable sense of humor.

The Apaches, in general, had difficult relations with the colonizing Spaniards, and later with Mexicans and Americans. There was a pattern of treaty making, followed by violations by one party or the other, dating from the second decade of the 19th century when Mexico gained its independence from Spain. In 1846 the United States went to war against Mexico, and by 1848 the Mexican nation was forced to cede approximately half of its territory to the United States, selling additional territory in 1854. Known as the Gadsden Purchase, this land included the northern portion of the Apache homeland. By 1854 the Apaches were a nomadic, raiding tribe composed of many bands straddling an international frontier between the United States and Mexico.

Around 1850, near the small town of Janos in the Mexican state of Chihuahua, Geronimo's wife and children, as well as many other members of his band, were attacked and slain by Mexican soldiers. This inspired in Geronimo a lifelong hatred of Mexicans. It should be noted, however, that the Apaches' preferred lifestyle of raiding at that time incurred the deep hostility of Mexicans and later of Americans.

Nevertheless, after the Gadsden Purchase, American settlers entered the traditional southern New Mexico and Arizona lands of the Apaches in ever-increasing numbers, and this incursion soon became the principle source of anxiety for the tribe. Finding their age-old hunting and gathering way of life threatened with extinction, the Apaches retaliated by raiding settlers, villages, and supply routes.

In 1861 a Union force moving east out of California combined a thrust against Confederate forces in the Southwest with an attempt to gain control over the Apaches. On 14 July 1861 at Apache Pass in Arizona, Geronimo probably participated in a surprise attack led by Cochise and Mangas Coloradas against the Union soldiers, but the Apaches were unable to cope with Union artillery. Gen. James Henry Carleton, the Union Army commander, issued orders for the extermination of all Apache adult males and for the roundup and resettlement of the women and children.

What followed, in 1864, was the infamous Long Walk of the Navajo and Apache nations to the Bosque Redondo in southeastern New Mexico. For four years the United States tried to force the Navajos and Apaches to live together, even though they were not historically on the best of terms, and to become farmers, even though this was culturally alien to them. Eventually the failure was acknowledged and the Native Americans were allowed to return to specified reservations. Although the Navajos returned to what had been part of their traditional lands, not all the Apaches fared so well. Some of their bands at first were relocated to the Chiricahua reservation in southern Arizona, while others went to the Warm Springs Reservation near present-day Truth or Consequences, New Mexico.

Geronimo had avoided the Long Walk and for many years lived at the Warm Springs Reservation. In 1875, however, there was another shift in U.S. Indian policy, and the decision was made to consolidate all Apaches on the harsh terrain of the San Carlos Reservation in Arizona. Between 1876 and 1886 Geronimo, seeing the appalling living conditions of his people and suffering frustration and humiliation at the hands of unsympathetic Indian agents, led his band in a series of brilliant hit-and-run raids against settlers and communities on both sides of the U.S.-Mexican border. Geronimo's raids were punctuated by brief periods of surrender alternating with renewed warfare after perceived betrayals by the United States.

By 1886 Geronimo was in his sixties and tired of running and fighting. He entered into negotiations with Gen. Nelson Miles, who falsely promised Geronimo that he would be allowed to return to his ancestral home. Instead Geronimo and his Apaches were sent to Fort Marion, near Saint Augustine, Florida, where they suffered from tropical heat and diseases. Most of the Apache children were separated from their parents and forced to go to the Indian boarding school at Carlisle, Pennsylvania. Many died from tuberculosis.

Eventually, in 1894, the Chiricahua Apaches were transferred to Fort Sill, Oklahoma. In his later years Geronimo was the object of public curiosity at gatherings such as at the World's Fair in Saint Louis, Missouri, in 1904. Fortunately he was able to dictate his memoirs during 1905–1906, and they were published under the title *Geronimo's Story of His Life* in 1906. Even after death Geronimo was never allowed to return to his native Southwest. He died of tuberculosis at Fort Sill in 1909, where he is buried.—E. A. Mares

See also **APACHES; CHIHUAHUAN DESERT; DESERT PEOPLES; HOPI; JORNADA DEL MUERTO; NAVAJO (DINE'É); NEW MEXICO DESERT; RIO GRANDE; SONORAN DESERT**

Further Reading

Ball, E. 1988. *Indeh: An Apache Odyssey.* Norman: University of Oklahoma Press.

Debo, A. 1976. *Geronimo: The Man, His Time, His Place.* Norman: University of Oklahoma Press.

Geronimo, with S. M. Barrett. 1989. *Geronimo's Story of His Life.* Williamstown, Mass.: Cornerhouse Publishers.

Smith, P. C. 1996. Geronimo. *In* P. C. Smith and P. G. Allen, eds., *As Long As The River Flows*, 34–71. New York: Scholastic Books.

GIBBER PLAINS. *See* DURICRUSTS; STONE PAVEMENT

GILA MONSTER

Venomous lizard (*Heloderma suspectum*; family Helodermatidae) with a very heavy body and small beadlike scales; a member of the only lizard family containing venomous species. The geographic range of the Gila monster extends from southwestern Utah in the United States, south through southern Nevada and Arizona, into Sonora, Mexico, and reaching the northern part of the state of Sinaloa. It also has a limited range in southeastern California and southwestern New Mexico. Gila monsters occur in a variety of habitats, from creosote flats to desert grasslands in the United States and in deciduous thorn forest in Mexico. Adults may exceed 50 centimeters in length but are usually about 35 cen-

Gila monster (*Heloderma suspectum*) from the Sonoran Desert north of Mesa, Arizona. (Photo: L. J. Vitt)

timeters. Colors on the body, head, and limbs are black with orange or pink. The color pattern is variable geographically, ontogenetically, and among individuals within a population but can be described as reticulate (having a pattern of rings). Usually there are about four dark saddlelike markings that cross the dorsal surface of the body. The eyes are small, or "beady," and black. The tail is thick and bulbar and is used for fat storage between meals. Gila monsters, like snakes, can consume enormous amounts of food in a single meal and fast for many months.

Gila monsters have long, snakelike tongues that are extruded while active. The tongue is part of the vomeronasal sensing system (sensing system associated with the mouth and nose) used to detect chemical signals associated with food or to locate other Gila monsters. Their diet consists of bird and reptile eggs, nestling birds, and small mammals. Birds and small mammals are usually swallowed whole, whereas eggs are broken and lapped up with the tongue. Gila monsters in southwestern Utah spend more than 95 percent of their time underground in rodent burrows. Most surface activity occurs during spring. During the breeding season males engage in combat in which individuals nudge each other with the head, wrap the tail around the competitor, lash the opponent with the tail, and, occasionally, bite each other.

Gila monsters are venomous but do not have movable fangs with well-developed venom delivery systems like pit vipers. Incidences of Gila monsters

biting humans are rare, but the venom is considered dangerous. These lizards appear to be slow and lethargic while active but can turn and bite quickly when disturbed. When they bite, they hold on and chew, working the venom from glands in the rear of the mouth along grooves in the teeth of both jaws and into the wound. Because of their powerful jaws and a propensity to hold on to the animal they have bitten, they can be extremely difficult to remove.—Laurie J. Vitt

See also **ARIZONA DESERT; CALIFORNIA DESERT; DEFENSIVE ADAPTATIONS, ANIMALS; LIZARDS; MEXICO, DESERTS OF; POISONOUS ANIMALS; REPTILES; SONORAN DESERT; VENOM**

Further Reading

Beck, D. D. 1990. Ecology and behavior of the Gila monster in southwestern Utah. *Journal of Herpetology* 24:54–68.

Bogert, C. M., and R. Martín del Campo. 1956. The Gila monster and its allies. The relationships, habits, and behavior of the lizards of the Family Helodermatidae. *Bulletin of the American Museum of Natural History* 109:1–238.

Campbell, J. A., and W. W. Lamar. 1989. *The Venomous Reptiles of Latin America.* Ithaca: Cornell University Press.

GILA WOODPECKER

Species of woodpecker (*Melanerpes uropygialis*; bird order Piciformes, family Picidae) resident in arid and semiarid habitats from southwestern New Mexico through Arizona to southeastern California, extending southward into Mexico. This medium-sized woodpecker (length 20–25 centimeters) is characteristic of Sonoran Desert environments dominated by saguaro cacti (*Carnegiea gigantea*), which it uses as both a food source and a nesting site. Adult males, as is the case in many other picids, possess a red cap, a feature that is absent in females and juveniles. Diet is varied, consisting of insects, fruit, bird eggs, acorns, and occasionally cactus pulp. Dry washes are preferred foraging areas.

Clutch sizes usually range from three to four. Nesting cavities are excavated in the year prior to their use and are commonly located four to nine meters above the ground in saguaro cacti. Gila woodpeckers appear to be monogamous, and both sexes incubate. When food is plentiful, pairs may nest two to three times per year. Parental care extends after fledging. Gila woodpeckers perform an integral role in desert communities by providing holes for other bird species such as owls (e.g., the elf owl, *Micrathene whitneyi*) and the purple martin (*Progne subis*). Some populations of *M. uropygialis* are threatened by the encroachment of human development, by the loss of mature saguaro cacti suitable for breeding, and by competition for nest cavities with the introduced European starling (*Sturnus vulgaris*).—Stephen C. Lougheed

See also **BIRDS; CACTUS, COLUMNAR; FEATHERS; NESTS; SAGUARO; SONORAN DESERT; WOODPECKERS**

Further Reading

Bent, A. C. 1939. Life histories of North American woodpeckers. *U.S. National Museum Bulletin* No. 174.

Ehrlich, P. R., D. S. Dobkin, and D. Wheye. 1988. *The Birder's Handbook: A Field Guide to the Natural History of North American Birds Including All Species That Regularly Breed North of Mexico*. New York: Simon and Schuster.

Kerpez, T. A., and N. S. Smith. 1990. Nest-site selection and nest-cavity characteristics of Gila woodpeckers and northern flickers. *Condor* 92:193–198.

Korol, J. J., and R. L. Hutto. 1984. Factors affecting nest site locations in Gila woodpeckers. *Condor* 86:73–78.

Short, L. L. 1982. *Woodpeckers of the World*. Greenville: Delaware Museum of Natural History.

GIRAFFE

Long-necked, tall (the world's tallest mammal), spotted, herbivorous African ungulate in the family Giraffidae (order Artiodactyla). The family contains but two living species, the giraffe (*Giraffa camelopardalis*) and the okapi (*Okapia johnstoni*). Giraffes are found throughout the semiarid regions of Africa; however, they are absent in true deserts, forests, and mountains. Giraffes were known to occur in North Africa but were probably extirpated from the region about 14 centuries ago. Giraffes also have been transplanted to areas where they were not known to occur previously.

Giraffes inhabit areas of scattered trees and bushes. Because they prefer to eat acacia leaves, giraffes are most often found in regions dominated by acacia savannas. The distribution of giraffes has also been affected by increasing desertification, hunting, farming, and outbreaks of disease, particularly rinderpest.

Giraffes may reach six meters in height, with the legs and the neck more than 1.5 meters in length.

Giraffe (*Giraffa camelopardalis*) browsing in the semi-arid thorn scrub of the Itala Game Reserve, northern Kwazulu-Natal Province, South Africa. (Photo: M. A. Mares)

Females are somewhat smaller than males. Two unbranched horns are present in both sexes. Coloration is buff with irregularly shaped brown spots (depending on the subspecies). The tail has long, coarse hairs at the tip which almost reach the ground; the mane consists of short, stiff, brown hairs.

Giraffes have the same number of cervical (neck) vertebrae (7) as other mammals. Each cervical vertebra is lengthened, as is the first thoracic vertebra. The dorsal spines of the thoracic vertebrae are long and form the hump on the upper back. It is these spines that serve as the attachment for the muscles and ligaments that support the neck and head. To pump blood to the brain, which may be two to three meters above the heart during browsing, or below the heart during drinking, adjustments in blood pressure (adaptive hypertension) are necessary. Pressure in the brain is regulated by a rete mirabile, a network of small blood vessels that have elastic walls. This elasticity allows the accommodation of excess blood when the head is lowered and retention of blood when the head is raised. In addition, a number of veins have numerous valves that serve to counteract the effects of gravity.

Giraffes have well-haired prehensile lips and a long tongue (up to 54 centimeters). Both enable giraffes to forage on leaves and twigs of plants (primarily species of *Acacia*) that are covered with spines and thorns and that are generally avoided by other animals. There are two primary aspects of the relationship between giraffe and acacia: the presence of thorns and the flat-topped shape of the tree. Whereas acacia in Australia lack thorns and spines (and also large browsing mammals), acacia in Africa are heavily "armed" with spines. Moreover, the size and number of spines decreases above the height at which giraffes can reach. Both of these facts suggest a possible evolution of thorns in response to browsers such as the giraffe. The flat-topped acacias are characteristic trees of Africa. This growth form provides an advantage to the tree, in that browsing is limited to the edges of the tree, and the leaves toward the center remain unbrowsed (unless the tree is very short, in which case the center could be reached by a tall browser such as the giraffe). Acacia also are associated with stinging ants (*Crematogaster*). Ants, which may be concentrated at the plant tips, will bite browsers. Young giraffes generally show more agitation to the stings of the ants than do the adults, but the ants deter some browsing of the plant by giraffes (even adults may shorten the time they browse on ant-protected acacias).—Janet K. Braun

See also **ACACIA; AFRICA, DESERTS OF; ANTS; HEAT BALANCE; HEAT EXCHANGE; HEAT STRESS; HERBIVORY; MAMMALS; NAMIBIA, DESERTS OF; SAVANNA; SOUTH AFRICA, DESERTS OF; UNGULATES; WATER BALANCE; XEROPHYLLOUS FOREST**

Further Reading

Dagg, A. I. 1971. Giraffa camelopardalis. *Mammalian Species* 5:1–8.

Dagg, A. I., and J. B. Foster. 1976. *The Giraffe: Its Biology, Behavior, and Ecology.* New York: Van Nostrand Reinhold.

Estes, R. D. 1991. *The Behavior Guide to African Mammals.* Berkeley: University of California Press.

GLACIAL PERIODS

Time periods of cold climate, repeated occasionally during the earth's history (notably in the late Precambrian, Ordovician-Silurian, Pennsylvanian-Permian, and Quaternary), during which glaciers covered large portions of some continents.

Two types of glaciers occur, relatively small alpine glaciers (or valley glaciers) and huge continental glaciers. Alpine glaciers can exist in montane regions at all latitudes, from equatorial to polar. Continental glaciers extending much beyond the Arctic and Antarctic circles require sufficiently heavy snowfall and climatic cooling to prevent seasonal melting and to promote the accumulation of year-round ice. Glaciers are a powerful geologic force, depressing by their tremendous mass the continental crust on which they rest. They also eliminate the biota from the regions they cover and profoundly change the landscape of a region by scouring away soil, loose rock fragments, and bedrock from some areas and transporting and depositing these rock materials in other areas at the melting ends of the flowing ice.

Because of their relative recency, we know most about the glaciations of the Pleistocene epoch. This latest series of ice ages and their intervening interglacial periods began between three and two million years ago, during the latter part of the Pliocene epoch, and continued throughout the Pleistocene. Based largely on oxygen isotope studies of drill cores of ocean-bottom sedimentary deposits around the world, during the last 900,000 years there appear to have been approximately 11 cold periods alternating every few thousand years with relatively warm periods.

Not all the cold periods necessarily represent major glaciations. Although the last continental glaciers of the Northern Hemisphere began to recede between 15,000 and 20,000 years ago, it is not yet possible to predict when the next cold or glacial period will return, or whether the cycle of Pleistocene ice ages has ended and the earth will return to a warm climate for more than just a few millennia—a long time by human standards but merely an instant in geologic time.

Continental glaciers develop at the earth's polar regions, which have changed in position through time, as have the continents themselves. During part of the Ordovician period, the region that now comprises the northern part of Africa was centered over the South Pole. Evidence of the Ordovician glaciers that spread across the region is preserved in the rocks in what is now the central Sahara. During the existence of the supercontinents Laurasia and Gondwana in the late Paleozoic, much of Gondwana lay in the southern high latitudes, including the South Pole, while the northern landmass, Laurasia, was in the middle and low latitudes. At that time a Pennsylvanian-Permian glacial period affected parts of what are now South America, Africa, Antarctica, Australia, and the Indian subcontinent. This was the longest and most extensive glaciation of the last 570 million years. During the Pliocene and Pleistocene epochs, the bulk of the earth's high-latitude landmasses prone to the buildup of continental glaciers have been in the Northern Hemisphere. For this reason the major Pliocene-Pleistocene glaciations occurred mostly in northern Europe and northern North America.

Major glaciations have an effect on the earth's hydrologic (water) system, locking up enormous amounts of water in ice and lowering sea level (as much as 150–200 meters during some Pleistocene glaciations). Thus large areas of continental shelves become exposed during glacial periods and flooded during interglacial periods. Where continental shelves are contiguous between continents, land bridges are formed (such as the Bering Land Bridge that connected, and likely will connect again, Siberia and Alaska), allowing the intercontinental migrations of animals and plants in both directions for periods of thousands of years. The Bering Land Bridge provided a means for the first humans to enter North America from Asia during the late Pleistocene, as it had done during different earlier glaciations for mammoths, bison, and many other animals.—Nicholas J. Czaplewski

See also **CENOZOIC; CRETACEOUS; EOCENE; FOSSILS; INTERGLACIALS; MIDDEN; MIOCENE; NEOGENE; OLIGOCENE; PALEOCENE; PALEOCLIMATE; PLATE TECTONICS; PLEISTOCENE; PLIOCENE; QUATERNARY; RECENT (HOLOCENE)**

Further Reading

Frakes, L. A., J. E. Francis, and J. I. Syktus, eds. 1992. *Climate Modes of the Phanerozoic: The History of the Earth's Climate over the Past 600 Million Years.* Cambridge: Cambridge University Press.

Hambrey, M. J., and W. B. Harland, eds. 1981. *Earth's Pre-Pleistocene Glacial Record.* Cambridge: Cambridge University Press.

Imbrie, J., and K. P. Imbrie. 1979. *Ice Ages.* Hillside, N.J.: Enslow.

GOAT

Domesticated mammal (order Artiodactyla, family Bovidae) in the genus *Capra* that is an important source of meat, wool, and milk in deserts. Goats have strong, stout bodies. Coat color varies widely. Both males and females can have horns that vary considerably in shape and size. Males may have longer hair on their front legs and chin forming pantaloons and a beard.

All the members of the genus *Capra* are generally considered goats. *Capra* has 10 wild species (the wild goat, *Capra hircus*; west Caucasian turs;, *Capra caucasia*; east Caucasian tur;, *Capra cylindricornis*; markhor, *Capra falconeri*; ibex, *Capra ibex*; Nubian ibex, *Capra nubiana*; Spanish ibex, *Capra pyrenaica*; Asiatic ibex, *Capra sibirica*; and Ethiopian ibex, *Capra walie*), and 1 domesticated form. All of the wild species of goats prefer steep mountainous terrain, but most can be found in a variety of habitats. Only the ibexes, the markhor, and domesticated and wild goats are frequently found in deserts.

The markhor ranges throughout southern Asia and occurs in a variety of localized forms. The most distinctive feature of the markhor is the male's spirally twisted horns. Markhors can be found in habitats varying from lightly forested slopes to steep barren areas above the tree line. In the high deserts in which they occur, markhors browse on trees and bushes. Because of fragmentation of markhor habitat and increased pressure from hunting and human intrusion, the markhor is listed as a species vulnerable to extinction.

The wild goat, from which the domesticated goat is derived, has a range extending from the Mediterranean to Pakistan in the south and the Caucasus Mountains in the north. The wild goat has been widely hunted by people, and its populations have declined over much of its range, with many local populations having become extinct. Wild goats are also threatened by competition from their domesticated relatives.

Goats, domesticated more than 9,000 years ago, are among the earliest domesticated animals. The early evidence for domestication of the goat can be found in the Near East. This long history of domestication has led to more than 200 breeds, which differ in size (10–100 kilograms), hair length and texture, horn shape and size, ability to produce milk, and hardiness. Goats were excellent candidates for domestication because they require little care and provide meat, milk, hair, and leather. Goats survive in areas where pasture and water are too poor for other livestock. Goats eat grasses and herbaceous plants and will even climb trees to reach leaves.

Feral goats or poorly managed herds of goats can devastate a region, and they have an enormous negative influence in many deserts. They kill many plants by cropping them close to the ground or stripping away leaves and bark. The loss of the plants, particularly their roots, encourages soil erosion. Goats have been implicated in the desertification of the Mediterranean region and other desert areas as well. The foraging efficiency of goats makes them fierce competitors for native wildlife and could push sensitive native species to extinction.—Rob Channell

See also **DOMESTIC ANIMALS; JORDAN, DESERTS OF; MAMMALS; MIDDLE EAST, DESERTS OF; MONTE DESERT; SAUDI ARABIA, DESERTS OF; UNGULATES**

Further Reading

Cole, H. H., and M. Ronning. 1974. *Animal Agriculture: The Biology of Domestic Animals and Their Use by Man*. San Francisco: Freeman.

Isaac, E. 1970. *Geography of Domestication*. Englewood Cliffs, N.J.: Prentice-Hall.

GOBABEB. *See* NAMIBIA, DESERTS OF

GOBI DESERT. *See* ASIA, DESERTS OF

GOPHER

Fossorial (living underground) rodent (mammalian family Geomyidae, order Rodentia), also called pocket gopher. Five genera and approximately 33 species are distributed from southern Canada to Panama. They inhabit many habitat types, including high-elevation montane meadows, plains, grasslands, tropical forests, and all of the major North American desert systems—Great Basin, Mojave, Sonoran, and Chihuahuan.

Pocket gophers have small, flat heads, no appreciable neck, small eyes and ears, strong, muscular forearms and shoulders, loose-fitting fur, a short, naked tail, and long, stiff hairs on the wrists. Close-fitting eyelids and ears with closable valves keep out sand and dirt. Furred lips that close behind the incisors prevent the ingestion of dirt. Cheek pouches, or "pockets," are fur lined, external to the mouth, and used to gather food (roots, forbs, and grasses). Some species have grooved incisors.

When digging, gophers use the long claws on their forefeet to loosen dirt and push it backward beneath their body. Gophers must turn around to push the dirt into an unused tunnel section or out of the burrow, thereby creating a mound. Mound openings are later plugged with dirt. Mima mounds are mound formations possibly created by gophers. Burrow systems placed sufficiently deep underground (about 50 centimeters) provide nearly constant levels of humidity, temperature, and gases, regardless of the outside climatic conditions.

Gophers generally are intolerant of other gophers; only one species usually is found in an area, and only one animal of the same species (except for very young individuals) is usually found in a burrow. They exhibit great variability, especially in coloration and genetics. Pelage color may reflect soil color. For example, a pale-colored gopher lives in each major desert area, and in areas of black lava soils, the gophers are very dark. Gophers are sometimes considered a pest or nuisance animal by farmers, ranchers, and gardeners.—Janet K. Braun

See also **ANIMAL ADAPTATIONS; BURROWING ANIMALS; CHIHUAHUAN DESERT; CONVERGENT EVOLUTION; GREAT BASIN DESERT; HERBIVORY; MAMMALS; MEXICO, DESERTS OF; MOJAVE DESERT; RODENTS; ROOTS; SONORAN DESERT; TUCU-TUCO**

Further Reading

Chase, J. D., W. E. Howard, and J. T. Roseberry. 1982. Pocket gophers. *In* J. A. Chapman and G. A. Feldhamer, eds., *Wild Mammals of North America*, 239–255. Baltimore: Johns Hopkins University Press.

Macdonald, D., ed. 1984. *The Encyclopedia of Mammals*. New York: Facts on File.

GOURDS

Large fleshy fruits of the trailing or climbing plants in the family Cucurbitaceae. The word *gourd* is specifically the fruit of the bottle gourd (*Lagenaria siceraria*) but is commonly applied to a variety of fruits that are hard shelled and durable and that are grown for ornament, utensils, and general interest.

The cucurbit family has more than 100 genera and almost 1,000 species, most of which are tropical. The fruit is produced from female, unisexual flowers and usually contains many seeds, which are often eaten because of their high fat content. The family has many cultivated species, including pumpkins, squashes, cucumbers, and watermelons, as well as gourd-producing species. In the United States very few species grow in the wild, but an exception is the buffalo gourd (*Cucurbita foetidissima*) of the Southwest. The scientific name of the buffalo gourd indicates that the plant is "fetid," and most parts of the plant are in fact foul smelling. The yellow fruits may reach 15 centimeters at maturity but are usually about the size of a tennis ball. Its many seeds were sometimes eaten by Native Americans of the region, and pieces of the root and fruit were used as a hand and laundry soap, although the soap could be somewhat irritating to the skin. The gourds were sometimes used as rattles but were inferior to the bottle gourd because of their thin shell.—Gordon E. Uno

See also **DESERT PEOPLES; ECONOMIC VALUE OF DESERT PRODUCTS; FRUITS; HOHOKAM; HOPI; NAVAJO (DINE'É); PLANT ADAPTATIONS; PLANTS**

Further Reading

Heiser, C. B., Jr. 1979. *The Gourd Book*. Norman: University of Oklahoma Press.

GRAND CANYON

Large gorge in northwestern Arizona cut by the Colorado River. The drier portions of the Grand Canyon lie in the Great Basin Desert-Colorado Plateau Semidesert. The Grand Canyon is known for its immense size, interesting shapes, and varied colors. It begins where the Little Colorado River joins the Colorado near the northern boundary of Arizona and stretches for 440 kilometers to Grand Wash Cliffs near the Nevada state line. Along its course the canyon varies from 0.2 to 29 kilometers in width and is up to 1.5 kilometers in depth. Grand Canyon National Park encompasses 90 kilometers of the canyon's most spectacular vistas. The general color of the canyon is red, but specific layers may be colored brown, green, buff, gray, or pink. The strata that make up the canyon's walls are an important part of the earth's geologic record. Portions of the lowest uncovered strata are composed of 2-billion-year-old schist (crystalline, layered rock) and granite. The canyon was created when the formation of

Grand Canyon of the Colorado River in Grand Canyon National Park, Arizona (the river, more than a mile below the photographer, is visible at the lower right and left of the photograph). (Photo: M. A. Mares)

the western mountains uplifted northern Arizona and increased the velocity and gravel content of the Colorado River. This increased the river's eroding of the plateau and created the Grand Canyon. The Grand Canyon also owes its existence to the aridity of the region in which it is located. The reduced precipitation in the area keeps the erosive forces that created the canyon from wearing away the canyon walls and leaving a less spectacular valley.

The habitats of the Grand Canyon are quite variable and extend from spruce-fir communities (*Picea-Abies*) at the higher elevations (above 2,500 meters) on the north rim through ponderosa pine (*Pinus ponderosa*) communities (lying between 2,134 and 2,256 meters elevation on the south rim and between 2,195 and 2,500 meters elevation on the north rim). There is a pine-juniper (*Pinus-Juniperus*) habitat that occurs between the ponderosa pine community and the desert scrub areas that are found at lower elevations. Two major desert scrub communities are found in the Grand Canyon. The first is the desert scrub of the (Tonto) plateau, which is composed of blackbrush (*Coleogyne ramosissima*), desert thorn (*Lycium pallidum*), bur sage (*Franseria*), and yucca (*Yucca*). This community is a part of the Great Basin Desert-Colorado Plateau Semidesert and lies mostly below 1,372 meters elevation. The second desert plant community is the desert scrub of the inner gorge, which is found at elevations around 760 meters elevation and includes plants such as catclaw acacia (*Acacia greg-*

gii), mesquite (*Prosopis juliflora*), and saltbush (*Atriplex canescens*).

People probably have been aware of the Grand Canyon as long as they have occupied the Southwest, but its discovery by Europeans has been credited to members of Francisco Vásquez de Coronado's 1540 expedition. John Wesley Powell directed the survey of some of the western portions of the United States and in 1869 explored the Green and Colorado rivers by canoe. It was Powell who named and began to popularize the Grand Canyon. Lake Powell, at the north end of the canyon, was named in his honor.

Development of the Colorado River threatens many aspects of the environment of the Grand Canyon. Water released from Lake Powell comes from the coldest and least productive portions of the lake. This cold and unproductive water is a shock to the native fishes that have evolved in the warm, productive waters of the canyon's lower reaches. Many species of fish native to the canyon are threatened by extinction because of the alterations that have accompanied development of the Colorado River. The control of the yearly floods has altered the patterns of erosion and sand deposition in the canyon. Large sandbars and banks that once edged the river inside the canyon are now being lost as the river no longer carries enough sand to replenish the sand that it takes away.—Rob Channell

See also **ARIZONA DESERT; COLORADO RIVER; CONSERVATION IN DESERTS; DURICRUSTS; IRRIGATION DRAINAGE; LANDSCAPE; RIVERS; WEATHERING, DESERT; WIND EROSION**

Further Reading

Beus, S. S., and M. Morales. 1990. *Grand Canyon Geology*. New York: Oxford University Press.

Carothers, S. W. 1991. *The Colorado River through Grand Canyon: Natural History and Human Change*. Tucson: University of Arizona Press.

Hoffmeister, D. F. 1971. *Mammals of the Grand Canyon*. Urbana: University of Illinois Press.

MacDougall, W. B. 1947. *Plants of Grand Canyon National Park*. Grand Canyon, Ariz.: Grand Canyon Natural History Association.

GRANIVORY

Consumption of seeds; by animals; usually distinct from frugivory, the consumption of fleshy fruit (including seeds). Seeds are an important food resource for many desert animals because they are abundant, they provide a concentrated source of energy and nutrients, and consumers obtain water when the fats in seeds are metabolized. In addition, because seeds decompose very slowly, they can be stored by animals for use during winter or during periods of drought when other food sources are scarce.

The main sources of seeds eaten by granivores are annual plants (which can produce large quantities of seeds during wet years) and ephemeral and perennial plants. Although seed production in deserts can vary tremendously from year to year (with maximum production rates varying from 80 to 1,480 kilograms per hectare), many seeds remain in the soil and thus are available to granivores for years. Seed densities in some desert soils have been estimated to remain above 1,000 seeds per square meter.

The most important desert granivores are ants, birds, and rodents. A diversity of harvester ants occurs in the deserts of North America, including *Pogonomyrmex*, *Veromessor*, and *Pheidole*. Ants forage during the day in cooler seasons, shifting their activity to crepuscular (dawn and dusk) or nocturnal (nighttime) periods during hot weather. They typically collect one seed at a time and bring it back to the colony's nest for storage. In a semiarid shrub community in Australia, one-fifth to one-third of the entire seed crop was harvested by ants. Seeds are also consumed by other desert insects, including weevils, moth larvae, and sucking bugs. Bruchid beetles are important consumers of legume (pea family) seeds.

Most desert-dwelling birds are insectivores, but a few granivorous species are desert residents, and several species migrate to the desert during periods of high seed production to take advantage of this energy-rich food resource. Granivorous birds forage diurnally. They are adept at locating patches of seeds, and their mobility allows them to move between new patches rather than rely on storage of seeds, as do ants and rodents. Granivorous birds include mourning doves, quail, sparrows, towhees, finches, sandgrouse, and budgerigars.

Rodents are the most important granivores in many arid regions. Most granivorous desert rodents; are nocturnal (active at night), relatively small, and quadrupedal. In North America the most specialized desert granivores, kangaroo rats and pocket mice (family Heteromyidae), are bipedal (walk or run using the hind legs). Heteromyids form burrow systems and typically forage near the burrow. They probably locate seeds under the soil surface by olfaction (smell), and can detect seeds up to 20 centimeters underground. They use their forepaws to rapidly stuff seeds into fur-lined cheek pouches, which are external to the mouth. Kangaroo rats can place up to 60 seeds per second in their pouches. When the pouches are full, they return to their burrows and empty the pouch contents for long-term storage. The pouches allow these rodents to make fewer trips to seed patches, reduce the amount of time they are exposed to predators, and help conserve water because the dry seeds are kept separate from the moist oral cavity. Kangaroo rats also choose moist soil pockets to temporarily store seeds and then eat the seeds after they have absorbed water from the soil.

In South America no desert rodents are specialized for feeding on seeds. An extinct family of marsupials (Argyrolagidae) may have filled this niche previously. Leaf-eared mice (*Phyllotis*) and highland desert mice (*Eligmodontia*) eat seeds along with other foods. Australia also has fewer granivorous mammals than North American deserts, but Australian hopping mice (*Notomys*) are desert-adapted granivores and Australian native mice (*Pseudomys*) eat seeds. Granivores in Old World (African, Arabian, and Asian) deserts include a variety of gerbils, hamsters, jerboas, and jirds. In the Namib Desert African pouched rats (*Saccostomus*) are similar to the North American kangaroo rats in size, as well as in possessing external cheek pouches and in their habit of caching seeds, although they are not bipedal.

In North American deserts several species of granivorous rodents may coexist in local areas. The large rodents tend to eat larger seeds than do smaller rodents, but coexisting species compete for seeds. When larger rodents are removed, the smaller granivores become more abundant. Over the long term, however, larger rodent species may indirectly benefit smaller rodents by decreasing the density of annual plants that produce large seeds, thereby allowing densities of small-seeded annuals to increase.

Within deserts several different types of granivores may coexist and therefore may affect one another directly by competing for seeds or indirectly by influencing the vegetation. For example, ant densities in North American deserts increased when rodents were removed, and rodent densities increased when ants were excluded. Birds and rodents likely also compete for seeds over the short term. Over the long term, however, ants and rodents (and birds and rodents) may have reciprocal positive effects through their effects on competing plants. By evolving together over extended periods in deserts, these diverse seed predators may force plants to develop different strategies of seed design and toxicity, thus not permitting a plant to specialize at escaping predation by any single group of seed predators (e.g., developing seeds that are too large for ants to eat). Seeds specialized to escape a single type of predator (e.g., ants) might be particularly attractive to a very different kind of predator (e.g., rodents), so plants are caught in an evolutionary struggle between diverse seed predators. This means that different mixes of seed predators (birds, ants, mammals), although competitors in ecological time, may be mutualists (mutually beneficial) over evolutionary time.

The importance of granivory varies among the world's deserts. Rates of seed consumption tend to be higher in the Sonoran Desert of North America than in South America's Monte Desert. In both regions seeds are eaten at low rates by birds compared with ants and rodents. The diversity of granivorous birds and ants appears to be higher at arid Australian sites than in North America, but the diversity of granivorous rodents is considerably lower in Australia.—Kristina A. Ernest

See also **ANIMAL ADAPTATIONS; ANNUAL PLANTS; ANTS; ARTHROPODS; AUSTRALIA, DESERTS OF; BIPEDALITY; BIRDS; BURROWING ANIMALS; DOVE; FINCH; GERBIL; HAMSTER; HETEROMYIDS; JERBOA; KANGAROO RAT; MONTE DESERT; POCKET MOUSE; QUAIL; RODENTS; SANDGROUSE; SEED DISPERSAL BY ANIMALS (ZOOCHORY); SEEDS; SONORAN DESERT; SPARROW**

Further Reading

Brown, J. H., O. J. Reichman, and D. W. Davidson. 1979. Granivory in desert ecosystems. *Annual Review of Ecology and Systematics* 10:201–227.

Mares, M. A. 1993. Heteromyids and their ecological counterparts: a pandesertic view of rodent ecology. *In* H. H. Genoways and J. H. Brown, eds., *The Biology of the Family Heteromyidae*, 652–713. Special Publication No. 10, American Society of Mammalogists.

Mares, M. A., and M. L. Rosenzweig. 1978. Granivory in North and South American deserts: rodents, birds, and ants. *Ecology* 59:235–241.

GRASSES

Members of the plant family Poaceae. Although they lack succulent water storage structures, spines, or other characteristics normally associated with desert plants, grasses are important members of many different desert ecosystems. However, they are not found in the driest deserts or in the most arid portions of other deserts. Their distribution is primarily in riparian areas (next to creeks and rivers) or in other sites that can capture and hold moisture. They are also found extensively in some of the milder desert environments, where they form desert grasslands.

Grasses are highly evolved monocotyledonous plants (flowering plants having only one seed leaf) with fibrous roots and unique stem structures known as culms, or tillers. These stems grow from buds at the base of the plant, which does not elevate as the stem elongates. This means that the actual growing point of grasses (meristem) remains at or below the soil surface. All tillers and leaves grow from these basal meristems.

The adaptations that grasses use for survival are primarily physiological rather than morphological. Depending on whether the region is a warm or cool desert, grasses will use either the C_3 or C_4 photosynthetic pathways. Desert grasses are also known to have very good stomatal (leaf pore) control, keeping their internal water level above lethal limits. Most desert grass species are short to medium in stature, with heights below 30 centimeters, and many have very narrow leaves. This reduces their exposure to desiccating winds. Also, many of these species are tolerant of burial by sand, having buds that can show rapid growth responses if sand or silt accumulates around or over the plant. Few, if any, desert grass species are tolerant of herbivory (grazing). Any loss of leaf surface results in a reduction of photosynthetic surface area, followed by reductions in growth of the plant. Some grasses in other habitats have been shown to have positive growth responses to herbivory, but this is a rare response in deserts.

One reproductive advantage that most grass species have in desert environments is that they are wind pollinated, rather than requiring insects or other animal vectors for pollination. Therefore, grass flowers are not large, showy structures that can lose a great deal of water. Considerable energy is spent creating sufficient pollen, but water loss from highly reduced floral structures is minimal. Also, the plants are not dependent on variable animal populations for successful reproduction, making wind pollination a very useful strategy in desert environments.

Some of the common genera of grasses found in deserts are *Aristida*, *Distichlis*, *Stipa*, *Eragrostis*, and *Panicum*. Many of these genera are represented in several different deserts. Some genera that are found in only a few specific locales are *Blepharidachne* and *Willkommia*: both are found only in southern Texas desert grasslands in the United States.—Linda L. Wallace

See also **C₃ PLANTS; C₄ PLANTS; DESERT GRASSLAND; FLOWERS; GRASSHOPPER MOUSE; GRASSHOPPERS; HERBIVORY; OVERGRAZING; PLANT ADAPTATIONS; PRAIRIE; PRAIRIE DOG; SAVANNA; STEPPE**

Further Reading

Bourlière, F., ed. 1983. *Ecosystems of the World.* Vol. 13: *Tropical Savannas.* New York: Elsevier.

Coupland, R. T.. ed. 1992. *Ecosystems of the World: Natural Grasslands.* Vol. 8A: *Introduction and Western Hemisphere.* New York: Elsevier.

Estes, J. R., R. J. Tyrl, and J. N. Brunken. eds. 1982. *Grasses and Grasslands: Systematics and Ecology.* Norman: University of Oklahoma Press.

Sears, E. 1935. *Deserts on the March.* Norman: University of Oklahoma Press.

Sims, P. L. 1988. Grasslands. *In* M. G. Barbour and W. D. Billings, eds., *North American Terrestrial Vegetation*, 265–286. New York: Oxford University Press.

GRASSHOPPER MOUSE

Rather stocky mouse (mammalian family Muridae, order Rodentia) with grayish or brownish upper parts, white belly, and a short, thick tail which is noteworthy for its predatory habits. Although most mice (especially in the North American deserts) eat vegetation or seeds, grasshopper mice eat insects and vertebrates, including other small rodents. Another fascinating behavior of these small rodents is their high-pitched whistles (or barks) that can be heard in the desert night.

Grasshopper mice eat a variety of invertebrates, including spiders, scorpions, grasshoppers, crickets, and beetles, and small vertebrates, especially other mice and lizards. Seed hoarding by captive grasshopper mice suggests that stored food may provide wild mice with food during the winter when invertebrates are scarce.

Grasshopper mice occur throughout the deserts of western North America. The northern grasshopper mouse (*Onychomys leucogaster*) occurs in the Great Basin, prairies, grasslands, and dune areas over much of the west central portion of the United States and barely into Canada and Mexico. The southern grasshopper mouse (*Onychomys torridus*) inhabits much of the Mojave, Sonoran, and Chihuahuan deserts and adjacent plains. In areas where their ranges overlap, the southern species usually resides at lower elevations in more arid habitats. A third species, *Onychomys arenicola*, occurs from southern New Mexico to north central Mexico.

Population densities of grasshopper mice tend to be fairly low, perhaps one or two per hectare. The home ranges (area in which the animal carries out its daily activities) are about two to three hectares, fairly large for a mouse. Individuals live alone or with a mate. Males defend territories, which they announce by emitting high-pitched vocalizations. Grasshopper mice produce a variety of other vocalizations, including sharp squeaks for hunting, shrill whistles for hunting or mating, and low chirps for warning competitors away from food.

Grasshopper mice build their own burrows, or occupy burrows that have been abandoned by other small mammals. Their reproductive potential is quite high: females can produce 3–12 litters per year, with one to six young per litter. The gestation period is usually 27–32 days but may be as long as 47 days for lactating females. Both males and females care for the young, which are weaned by the age of 23 days.—Kristina A. Ernest

See also **MAMMALS; PREDATION; RODENTS**

Further Reading

Burt, W. H., and R. P. Grossenheider. 1976. *A Field Guide to the Mammals*. 3d ed. Boston: Houghton Mifflin.

McCarty, R. 1975. Onychomys torridus. *Mammalian Species* 59:1–5.

———. 1978. Onychomys leucogaster. *Mammalian Species* 87:1–6.

Zeveloff, S. I. 1988. *Mammals of the Intermountain West*. Salt Lake City: University of Utah Press.

GRASSHOPPERS

Common name for insects in several families of the insect order Orthoptera. The name refers to the ability of these insects to hop, often long distances, from perches on stems of grass or other vegetation. Because "grasshoppers" constitutes an assemblage of insect families sharing sets of characteristics with the insects we call crickets and katydids (which in themselves are an assemblage of families), the common name serves only as a descriptor. All members of the Orthoptera have very enlarged hind legs that are used for jumping. One family, the Acrididae, is particularly conspicuous in deserts of the world.

Members of the family Acrididae, known as short-horned grasshoppers, typically have very short antennae and a short ovipositer (females). They are herbivorous and occur on many species of desert plants. This family includes the lubber grasshoppers, which are typically large, robust grasshoppers with short, often brightly colored hind wings. It also includes the migratory grasshoppers commonly called locusts, which may experience incredible population explosions and migrate in hordes of millions of individuals eating nearly all vegetation encountered. Also in this family are the band-winged grasshoppers, which are particularly conspicuous in open areas of deserts. These grasshoppers have long wings, and the rear wings have a broad band of color across them such that when they fly, the bright colors are exposed. While sitting on the ground, the dull-colored forewings cover the rear wings and the insect becomes nearly invisible against its background. Among the more interesting species are those that specialize on specific plants, such as *Bootettix punctatus* and *Ligurotettix coquilletti*, which feed nearly exclusively on creosote bush leaves. Males of *Ligurotettix coquilletti* defend individual creosote bushes as mating territories.

Many desert grasshoppers are extremely cryptic in coloration and morphology. For example, the gomphocerine acridid grasshoppers very closely mimic the color and texture of the soil on which they sit.—Laurie J. Vitt

See also **ARTHROPODS; CREOSOTE BUSH; CRYPSIS; INSECTS; LOCUSTS**

Further Reading

Anderson, R. V., C. R. Tracy, and Z. Abramsky. 1979. Habitat selection in two species of grasshoppers: The role of thermal and hydric stress. *Oecologia* 49:67–72.

Borror, D. J., C. A. Triplehorn, and N. F. Johnson. 1992. *An Introduction to the Study of Insects*. New York: Harcourt Brace.

Greenfield, M. D., T. E. Shelly, and K. R. Downum.

1987. Variation in host-plant quality: Implications for territoriality in a desert grasshopper. *Ecology* 68:828–838.

Polis, G. A., ed. 1991. *The Ecology of Desert Communities*. Tucson: University of Arizona Press.

Wisdom, C. S. 1991. Patterns of heterogeneity in desert herbivorous insect communities. *In* G. A. Polis, ed., *The Ecology of Desert Communities*, 151–179. Tucson: University of Arizona Press.

GRASSLAND

Vegetation type dominated by species of grasses (vascular plants of the family Poaceae). Grasslands tend to occur in climates wherein most of the precipitation falls during the growing season when evapotranspiration is high. Thus the area is too dry to support forest, but it has higher levels of moisture than deserts. The regions are considered subhumid to semidry, and they are climatologically and geographically intermediate between deserts and forests. Most grasslands are midcontinental, and many, such as the Great Plains, are in the lee of mountain ranges. There are also extensive desert grasslands in the Chihuahuan Desert of North America and at the western limits of the Great Plains. Grassland soils are deep, nutrient-rich, and heavy. Water binds tightly to clay particles of grassland soils so that not all water in the soil is available for plant use. As a consequence, some grassland types occur in humid regions that otherwise have sufficient precipitation to support forests. Fire is also a major element of grassland ecology. Perennial grasses maintain the following year's buds below ground, whereas the buds of trees are borne above ground, where they can be damaged by fire.

Grasslands dominated by tall grasses occur at the moister end of the grassland climatic spectrum, whereas steppe vegetation, dominated by short grasses, occurs at the drier end. An intermediate class, mixed grasslands, includes grasses of midheight; often these grasses are the best competitors from the steppes and the most drought-tolerant members of the tall grasslands. Grasses are the dominant plants of some desert areas, such as the deserts of North Africa and the higher elevations in the Chuhuahuan Desert. In these desert grasslands, grasses are more sparse than in a true grassland, however, and bare soil is common. In Australia grasslands of *Triodia* are common, and in southern Africa desert grasslands can be extensive (e.g., in the Arid Savanna Biome, where grasses make up more than 50 percent of the ground cover).

Most major grasslands have evolved along with a suite of grazing animals, including mammals and insects. The epidermis (outer cell layer) of grass leaves is heavily impregnated with silica bodies (silica dioxide). The chewing mouthparts of most animals cannot withstand the abrasive nature of the silica bodies. However, the native grazers often have teeth or mouthparts that are capable of continued growth and are composed of hardened materials that withstand the grinding of the silicaceous grass leaves.

In 1824 Maj. Stephen Long led a scientific and military exploration of the region from the Platte River in what is now Nebraska, down the front range of the Rocky Mountains, through the grasslands of southeastern Colorado and northeastern New Mexico, to the Canadian River. They followed the Canadian River through the present-day Texas Panhandle and Oklahoma. The expedition passed through the semiarid grasslands of the Great Plains, an area dominated by short grasses. The Great Plains has one of the least diverse floras of North America. Productivity is relatively high, but the region is prone to periodic drought. The expedition passed through the southern reaches of the region during a period of extreme drought; the Canadian River apparently did not have any running water. Water, game, and forage were all scarce. Perhaps because of the desolation of that year and the hardships his group endured, Long designated this grassland the Great American Desert. In his journal he suggested that it would never be conducive to settlement or agriculture. That view became popular, but ultimately the land gave way to European settlers. The climate and native vegetation of the region, which supported millions of bison, is well suited for migratory grazing or grazing agriculture.

However, as successive droughts during the 20th century have demonstrated, the Great Plains is subject to desertification if the ground is plowed for grains or row crops. Nevertheless, farmers in the region have exploited (or even overexploited) underground aquifers to produce bountiful crops of cotton, wheat, sorghum, and corn in Long's Great American Desert.

Grasses are variable with respect to their ability to withstand intensive grazing. Many grass species (known as decreasers) decline rapidly under grazing pressure, whereas others (increasers) grow well under similar conditions. Only unpalatable grasses can withstand excessively heavy grazing. Overgrazing of semiarid grasslands permits the invasion of desert species, a process known as desertification. Twice in the 20th century, during extensive droughts, the grassland-desert margin moved far to the east to encompass much of the Texas and Oklahoma panhandles, eastern Colorado, and western Kansas.—James R. Estes

See also **ANDEAN STEPPES; BADGER; DESERTIFICATION; FOREST; GRASSES; GREAT AMERICAN DESERT; KANGAROO RAT; PALEOCLIMATE; PAMPAS; PLANT ADAPTATIONS; PLANT GEOGRAPHY; PLANTS; POCKET MOUSE; PRAIRIE; PRAIRIE DOG; RODENTS; SAVANNA; SEMIDESERT; SOILS, DESERT; STEPPE**

Further Reading

Bourlière, F., ed. 1983. *Ecosystems of the World.* Vol. 13: *Tropical Savannas.* New York: Elsevier.

Coupland, R. T.. ed. 1992. *Ecosystems of the World: Natural Grasslands.* Vol. 8A: *Introduction and Western Hemisphere.* New York: Elsevier.

Estes, J. R., R. J. Tyrl, and J. N. Brunken. eds. 1982. *Grasses and Grasslands: Systematics and Ecology.* Norman: University of Oklahoma Press.

Joern, A., and K. H. Keeler, eds. 1995. *The Changing Prairie.* New York: Oxford University Press.

Lovegrove, B. 1993. *The Living Deserts of Southern Africa.* Vlaeberg: Fernwood.

McClaran, M. P., and T. R. Van Devender. 1995. *The Desert Grassland.* Tucson: University of Arizona Press.

Samson, F. B., and F. L. Knopf, eds. 1996. *Prairie Conservation.* Washington D.C.: Island Press.

Sears, E. 1935. *Deserts on the March.* Norman: University of Oklahoma Press.

Sims, P. L. 1988. Grasslands. *In* M. G. Barbour and W. D. Billings, eds., *North American Terrestrial Vegetation*, 265–286. New York: Oxford University Press.

Weaver, J. E. 1954. *North American Prairie.* Lincoln, Neb.: Johnsen Publishing Company.

Weaver, J. E., and F. W. Albertson. 1956. *Grasslands of the Great Plains.* Lincoln, Neb.: Johnsen Publishing Company.

GRAVEL DESERT. *See* STONE PAVEMENT

GRAY GULL

Moderate-sized gull species (*Larus modestus*) found along the Pacific coast of South America (bird order Charadriiformes, family Laridae). Total length is 40–55 centimeters. The plumage is predominantly dull gray, a color that may reduce radiative heat loads in the hot, windy environments where gray gulls occur. *Larus modestus* is commonly found feeding along rock and sandy beaches or scavenging in the wake of fishing boats. Its diet consists of fish and various intertidal organisms such as burrowing crabs. Almost all social activities, including courtship and copulation, have been observed among birds found on the coast. The gray gull does not nest on or near the Pacific coast but in the interior deserts of northern Chile, one of the most arid regions in the world. This somewhat bizarre behavior probably arose because *L. modestus* originally nested around Pleistocene lakes that have long since disappeared. One of the most obvious advantages to continued nesting in the desert is the paucity of predation. Usually one or two eggs are laid in shallow scrapes and are attended at all times. During the hottest part of the day an adult shades the eggs by standing over them, a behavior that is carried over in the chick stage. Incubation is undertaken by both parents, but changeovers between parents occur only at night. At dawn numerous adults leave for the coast and then return at sunset. Chicks are fed regurgitated fish. Other larids nest in dry areas (e.g., Heermann's gull, *Larus heermanni*, which nests on desert islands off the coast of northwestern Mexico), but only the gray gull breeds a significant distance from a major body of water.—Stephen C. Lougheed

See also **BIRDS; CHILE, DESERTS OF; LAKES, PLUVIAL; PLAYA; PLEISTOCENE**

Further Reading

Goodall, J. D., R. A. Philippi, and A. W. Johnson. 1945. Nesting habits of the Peruvian gray gull. *Auk* 62:450–451.

Howell, T. R., B. Araya, and W. R. Millie. 1974. Breeding biology of the gray gull, *Larus modestus. University of California Publication in Zoology* Vol. 104.

Johnson, A. W. 1965. *The Birds of Chile and Adjacent Regions of Argentina, Bolivia and Peru.* Vol. 1. Buenos Aires: Platt.

Moynihan, M. 1962. Hostile and sexual behavior patterns of South American and Pacific Laridae. *Behaviour Supplement* 8:1–365.

Murphy, R. C. 1936. *Oceanic Birds of South America.* New York: American Museum of Natural History.

GRAZING. *See* OVERGRAZING

GREASEWOOD

Common evergreen shrub of the desert Southwest, also known as the creosote bush (*Larrea tridentata*), and member of the caltrop family (Zygophyllaceae). Another common name for this species, hediondilla, comes from the Spanish word for "little stinker," because of the musty, resinous odor resembling that of creosote which the plants give off after a rain. The greasewood reaches a height of one to three meters and possesses leaves covered with a shiny resinlike material that reduces transpiration, helping the plant survive in the arid conditions. Greasewood is one of the most abundant species in the basin areas of the Chihuahuan Desert, ranging from California to western Oklahoma and Texas and south into Mexico. In some parts of its range, greasewood covers thousands of square miles in pure stands or with a variety of other shrubs. Greasewood plants often appear to be spaced at regular intervals and, due to their extensive root system, have a great ability to absorb water. The resin from the plant has been used by Native Americans to mend pottery, cement arrowheads, and coat baskets. Because of its abundance, greasewood is important as a soil stabilizer; however, it has few economic uses today and is virtually worthless as a forage plant to all livestock.—Gordon E. Uno

See also **BAJA CALIFORNIA, DESERTS OF; CALIFORNIA DESERT; CHIHUAHUAN DESERT; CHUCKWALLA; CREOSOTE BUSH; DESERT GRASSLAND; ECONOMIC VALUE OF DESERT PRODUCTS; IGUANA, DESERT; JACKRABBIT; MOJAVE DESERT; MONTE DESERT; NEW MEXICO DESERT; PLANT ADAPTATIONS; SONORAN DESERT; UNITED STATES, DESERTS OF**

Further Reading

Mabry, T. J., J. H. Hunziker, and D. R. DiFeo Jr., eds. 1977. *Creosote Bush: Biology and Chemistry of Larrea in New World Deserts.* Stroudsburg, Pa.: Dowden, Hutchinson, and Ross.

McClaran, M. P., and T. R. Van Devender. 1995. *The Desert Grassland.* Tucson: University of Arizona Press.

Wickens, G. E., J. R. Goodin, and D. V. Field, eds. 1985. *Plants for Arid Lands.* London: Unwin Hyman.

GREAT AMERICAN DESERT

Arid region of central and western North America dominated by the influence of the deserts of the southwestern United States and northwestern Mexico and including the drier grasslands of North America. In 1821, after having explored the central and western United States, Maj. Stephen Long first applied the description "Great American Desert" to the region between the 98th meridian and the Rocky Mountains. Later uses of the term have expanded the region to include the Mojave, Chihuahuan, and Sonoran deserts, the Great Basin, portions of the mountainous West, and the Great Plains. In the report of his explorations Major Long doubted that the region he explored, now more commonly referred to as the Great Plains, would ever support any number of people and noted that it was unfit for cultivation. Later explorers and pioneers passing through the region reinforced the idea of the American West as a desert. The majority of the region referred to as the Great American Desert is not by strict definition a desert, but the seasonality of the precipitation, the ephemeral nature of its streams and rivers, and its expansiveness and isolation accentuate the aridity of the region.

Despite the early characterization of the American West, its central grasslands, including the desert grassland located at the westernmost limit of the Great Plains, as well as many of its arid regions have been settled. Portions of the "Great American Desert" have become some of the world's most productive regions for growing grains and raising livestock. Several of the cities of the Southwest are among the fastest-growing cities in the United States and are considered to be among the most livable. However, the entire development of this region depends on acquiring and distributing water.

Much of the water in this region comes from the depletion of aquifers or the diversion of rivers. In some parts of the Great Plains the water extracted in one year for grain cultivation will require 100 years to be replaced. The difficulty of extracting water from these aquifers continues to increase.

Despite the overall growth and progress in the Great American Desert, the entire region is not prospering. Portions of the northern and eastern edges of the region have low and decreasing human populations. In 1890 the U.S. government declared that the frontier in the nation had ceased to exist, based on the definition of a frontier as a region having an average of fewer than two people per square mile. Today, in much of the Great Plains, the frontier is returning, as the people die from old age or move to the cities of the East or West Coast, or even those of the Southwest, and are not replaced through birth or immigration. The economy of this region has always been dependent on agriculture and, especially, on the family farm. However, the cyclic nature of precipitation on the Great Plains dictates that for every year of ample rain and prosperity, there will be one of drought and loss. The economies of scale dictate that small operations cannot function under such a variable environment, and the farms in the region that still exist are large, increasing in size, and becoming increasingly incorporated. These large farms require fewer workers, and, lacking jobs, the people move away. The future of this region is unclear.—Rob Channell

See also **AN INTRODUCTION TO DESERTS; COLORADO RIVER; DESERT GRASSLAND; DESERTS; GRASSLAND; PAMPAS; PLANT GEOGRAPHY; PRAIRIE; SAVANNA; UNITED STATES, DESERTS OF**

Further Reading

Brown, D. E., ed. 1994. *Biotic Communities: Southwestern United States and Northwestern Mexico*. Salt Lake City: University of Utah Press.

Dick, E. 1975. *Conquering the Great American Desert: Nebraska*. Lincoln: Nebraska State Historical Society.

Hollon, W. E. 1966. *The Great American Desert: Then and Now*. New York: Oxford University Press.

Joern, A., and K. H. Keeler, eds. 1995. *The Changing Prairie*. New York: Oxford University Press.

Matthews, A. 1992. *Where the Buffalo Roam*. New York: Grove Weidenfeld.

Samson, F. B., and F. L. Knopf, eds. 1996. *Prairie Conservation*. Washington D.C.: Island Press.

Unruh, J. D. 1979. *The Plains Across*. Urbana: University of Illinois Press.

GREAT BASIN DESERT

Arid region in the northwestern United States that includes more than 500,000 square kilometers of area from the Sierra Nevada range on the west to the Wasatch Mountains on the east and from north of the Snake River valley on the north to the Colorado River on the south. The Great Basin encompasses the western portion of Utah, the southwest part of Wyoming, the southeast corner of Idaho, southeastern Oregon, parts of south central Washington, part of southern California, and almost all of Nevada, including most of the Intermountain Sagebrush (*Artemisia*) Steppe vegetation. As defined, this desert includes the Blackbrush (*Coleogyne*

ramosissima) Semidesert that occurs along the Colorado, Green, and San Juan rivers in Arizona and Utah, as well as adjoining parts of Nevada, California, and western Arizona where blackbrush is dominant and the Colorado Plateau Semidesert of Colorado, Utah, Arizona, and New Mexico. More restrictive definitions of the Great Basin Desert limit it to an area that mainly includes almost all of Nevada, eastern Utah, southern Oregon and adjacent California, and southeastern California. (See map of U.S. deserts, p. 573.)

The topography of the Great Basin consists of numerous smaller basins separated by many mountain ranges, which have a general north-south orientation. The elevations of the basins range from sea level or lower to 1,200–1,500 meters; many of the mountains have peaks above 2,700 meters. The climate of the entire area is greatly influenced by the rain shadow of the Sierra Nevada range, which intercepts much of the moisture-laden winds from the Pacific Ocean. The region generally has an average annual rainfall of 250 millimeters or less.

The Great Basin (excluding the northernmost portions in Washington) is noted for having an internal drainage system in which the rain that falls usually drains into closed valleys and does not reach the ocean. This phenomenon leads to the creation of shallow, temporary lakes referred to as playas. These lakes usually have water only during the winter or after thunderstorms. The water in most playas evaporates during the summer, leaving hard, smooth, and often alkaline valley floors. The Great Salt Lake region of Utah and Death Valley in California are classic examples of the drainage patterns of the Great Basin region.

The Great Basin Desert, which occupies most of the Great Basin Physiographic Province, is the largest of the North American deserts and is the only "cold" desert on the continent. In the Great Basin Desert the ubiquitous creosote bush, which is so prevalent in the hot deserts of North America, is replaced by the soft gray of the sagebrush. The most common sagebrush is the big sagebrush (*Artemisia tridentata*), which is the state flower of Nevada. When found on well-drained gravelly soils, big sagebrush grow to a height of a meter or more and often forms pure stands over immense areas. The foliage of big sagebrush is sometimes heavily grazed by livestock, and the large clumps of this shrub provide habitat for numerous animals such as chipmunks, gophers, kangaroo rats, harvest mice, deer mice, jackrabbits, coyotes, badgers, and packrats. A considerable number of bird species are also found in this northernmost desert, including the turkey vulture (*Cathartes aura*), red-tailed hawk (*Accipiter velox*), marsh hawk (*Circus hudsonius*), killdeer (*Oxyechus vociferus*), and broad-tailed hummingbird (*Selasphorus platycercus*). In parts of the Great Basin Desert where pinyons and junipers are found, the pinyon jay (*Cyanocephalus cyanocephalus*) is also common.

Closely associated with the sagebrush is the shadscale shrub (*Atriplex confertifolia*). This low-growing and spiny saltbush is commonly found on heavy-textured alkaline basins that are common in the Great Basin. As with sagebrush, the shadscale often forms almost pure stands covering large areas of the landscape. In fact, sagebrush and shadscale are so dominant over much of the Great Basin Desert that the region is sometimes referred to as the sagebrush-shadscale desert. In addition to these two dominant shrubs, there are many other shrubs, including hopsage (*Grayia spinosa*), winterfat (*Eurotia lanata*), greasewood (*Sarcobatus vermiculatus*), gray molly (*Kochia vestita*), pickleweed (*Allenrolfea occidentalis*), glasswort (*Salicornia*), desert teas (*Ephedra*), and rabbit brush (*Chrysothamnus*). There are also numerous other species of both *Artemisia* and *Atriplex*.

In distinct contrast to the hot Sonoran Desert to the south, cacti are a relatively unimportant feature of the Great Basin Desert. Cacti are highly sensitive to cold temperatures and require warm soils for seed germination. The cold winters, in which most of the precipitation is received, are not conducive to the growth and development of most species of cacti. Only two species are relatively common, *Opuntia polyacantha* and *Opuntia fragilis*.

Some portions of the Great Basin, particularly in southern Nevada, are dominated by blackbrush (*Coleogyne ramosissima*), which forms a shrub community possibly transitional to the hotter Mojave Desert. Northern portions are mainly made up of sagebrush.

Because of the long cold winters, reptiles are not as common in the Great Basin Desert as in the hotter Mojave, Sonoran, and Chihuahuan deserts.

The Great Basin Desert is relatively young on the geologic time scale, and has not always been a desert. During the Pleistocene, when glaciers moved far to the south, there was increased precipitation and meltwater runoff into the Great Basin, which created numerous lakes in many of the smaller basins within the region. These conditions produced two spectacular lakes: in the eastern part of the Great Basin, Lake Bonneville; and in the western Great Basin, Lake Lahontan. The Great Salt Lake of Utah represents a remnant of Lake Bonneville, and Pyramid Lake in Nevada is a remnant of Lake Lahontan.

Because of the overwhelming dominance by shrubs and the vastness of the landscape, the Great Basin Desert has a repetitious or even monotonous appearance to some people. However, to the naturalist, this unique ecological region has a rugged beauty and character that is not displayed by any other region of North America. A large portion of the Great Basin Desert is public land and is managed by the Bureau of Land Management, the Bureau of Indian Affairs, and the U.S. Forest Service. Considerable political controversy has developed in the past two decades regarding the management and ultimate ownership of these lands. This controversy has pitted the livestock industry of the Great Basin region against various governmental agencies and environmental groups in what is sometimes referred to as the "Sagebrush Rebellion."

In 1986 President Ronald Reagan signed into law an act of Congress providing for the establishment of Great Basin National Park, the nation's 49th reservation to be so designated. This park, consisting of about 31,000 hectares, is located in eastcentral Nevada and was established to preserve a representative example of the regional geology, biologic diversity, and scenic grandeur of the area.—Gary K. Hulett and Amanda Renner Charles

See also **AN INTRODUCTION TO DESERTS; ARTEMISIA; BIRDS; BONNEVILLE; CALIFORNIA DESERT; CHENOPODIACEAE; COLORADO DESERT; CREOSOTE BUSH; DEATH VALLEY; DESERTS; DESERTS, MONTANE; DESERTS, TEMPERATE; LIZARDS; MAMMALS; MOJAVE DESERT; MONTANA DESERT; NEVADA DESERT; OREGON DESERT; PAINTED DESERT; PLANT GEOGRAPHY; PLAYA; PLEISTOCENE; PRONGHORN; PSAMMOPHYTIC SCRUB; REPTILES; SAGEBRUSH; SALTBUSH; SALT PAN; SEMIARID ZONES; SNAKES; SONORAN DESERT; UNITED STATES, DESERTS OF; UTAH DESERT**

Further Reading

Bender, G. L., ed. 1982. *Reference Handbook on the*

Deserts of North America. Westport, Conn.: Greenwood Press.

Grayson, D. K. 1993. *The Desert's Past: A Natural Prehistory of the Great Basin.* Washington, D.C.: Smithsonian Institution Press.

Houghton, S. G. 1976. *A Trace of Desert Waters: The Great Basin Story.* Glendale, Calif.: A. H. Clark.

Unrau, H. D. 1990. *Basin and Range: A History of Great Basin National Park.* U.S. Department of the Interior, National Park Service.

GREAT KAVIR. *See* IRAN, DESERTS OF

GREAT SANDY DESERT. *See* AUSTRALIA, DESERTS OF

GREAT VICTORIA DESERT. *See* AUSTRALIA, DESERTS OF

GROOMING

Common behavior throughout the animal kingdom, from insects to vertebrates, that functions to remove debris and ectoparasites from the body. Animals groom themselves frequently; this self-grooming is also called autogrooming. In mammals autogrooming is a highly ritualized behavior. Animals use their forelimbs, mouth, and hind feet, often in an orderly sequence. Usually the face and ears are cleaned by the forepaws while the animal sits upright. The forepaws are cleaned by the tongue and teeth, and the mouth also is used to clean the venter, rump, and hind limbs. Finally, hind limbs are used to scratch the fur on the sides, on the head, and behind the ears. This general sequence is employed in many species of small mammals.

Allogrooming, or the grooming of others, is also a common social behavior in many different taxa. Allogrooming appears to serve both a hygienic and a social function. In primates allogrooming is concentrated on the more inaccessible areas of the body, such as the back and neck. However, allogrooming also serves as a deterrent to overt aggression. Animals in tense situations will either offer to groom or present their bodies for grooming; aggressive activity seldom escalates after such behavior.

Sand bathing is a type of grooming behavior observed in desert-adapted rodents and marsupials. Animals roll and writhe in sandy areas; this behavior has the dual function of cleaning the pelage and

leaving chemical signals deposited by scent or sebaceous glands on the substrate.—Thomas E. Lacher, Jr.

See also **ANIMAL ADAPTATIONS; ANTELOPE; BABOON; MAMMALS; RODENTS; SAND BATHING**

Further Reading

Eisenberg, J. F. (1963) The behavior of heteromyid rodents. *University of California Publications in Zoology* 69:1–100.

Wilson, E. O. 1975. *Sociobiology.* Cambridge, Mass.: Belknap.

Wittenberger, J. F. 1981. *Animal Social Behavior.* Boston: Duxbury.

GROUND SQUIRREL

Term with no clear functional or taxonomic meaning which refers to a loose grouping of terrestrial, short-legged, medium-sized rodents of the mammalian squirrel family, Sciuridae (order Rodentia), having relatively short or thin tails and primarily active during the day. "Ground squirrel" can be taken to mean two different kinds of animals. Many species of the family Sciuridae, such as marmots, prairie dogs, and chipmunks, are exclusively or primarily terrestrial (live on the ground, as opposed to in the trees), but they are not called ground squirrels by mammalogists. Also, prairie dogs have a close morphological and phylogenetic (evolutionary) affinity to "ground squirrels" but are not referred to as such.

Thus defined, there are five genera and 49 species of ground squirrels, the great majority concentrated in the genus *Spermophilus*. Using this genus as the "typical" ground squirrel, these terrestrial mammals range in size from 154 to 406 millimeters in body length, with a tail that ranges from 38 to 254 millimeters. Adults weigh from 85 to 1,000 grams. They tend to be colored a uniform yellowish gray or grayish brown, but several species have striking markings of spots and stripes, for example, the thirteen-lined ground squirrel (*Spermophilus tridecemlineatus*) of the central United States or the golden-mantled ground squirrel (*Spermophilus lateralis*) of the western mountains of North America. Ground squirrels either dig their own burrows or live in rock piles or among fallen logs. They forage primarily on seeds, roots, bulbs, and other plant material, although most species are opportunistic (taking whatever they happen to come across) and will take some animal material. Seeds and nuts are stored in their cheek pouches and taken to below-ground storage chambers. They have large litters (2–13 young) once per year. Most species are gregarious to loosely colonial.

Ground squirrels are among the most arid adapted of all sciurids. The genera *Atlantoxerus, Spermophilopsis,* and *Ammospermophilus* are all arid-land species, as are several species in the African genus *Xerus.* A great number of species in the genus *Spermophilus* prefer dry grasslands.—Thomas E. Lacher, Jr.

See also **BULBS; BURROWING ANIMALS; CHIHUAHUAN DESERT; GRASSLAND; MAMMALS; MOJAVE DESERT; PLAGUE; PRAIRIE; PRAIRIE DOG; RODENTS; ROOTS; SONORAN DESERT; TORPOR**

Further Reading

Macdonald, D., ed. 1984. *The Encyclopedia of Mammals*. New York: Facts on File.

Murie, J. O., and G. R. Michener. 1984. *The Biology of Ground-dwelling Tree Squirrels*. Lincoln: University of Nebraska Press.

Nowak, R. M. 1991. *Walker's Mammals of the World*. 5th ed. Baltimore: Johns Hopkins University Press.

GROUNDWATER

Fraction of rainwater penetrating the soil and distributed in it through the action of various physical forces, such as molecular attraction, capillary force, osmotic pressure, and gravity. These forces act in such a way that two zones of water are established below the surface (subsurface water): an upper layer that is not saturated and a lower, saturated layer. In general water descends vertically through the soil until it reaches an impermeable layer, or a layer that is already saturated, at which time it will proceed to saturate the upper layer. Water in the saturated layer is known as subterranean water, although it is not retained in that layer. Rather it circulates freely and moves horizontally.

The geologic formation that contains underground water is called an aquifer; the depth that the water reaches at each point in the aquifer is the piezometric level. Water from underground aquifers may be in contact with the air through pores in the rocks; when this occurs it is called unconfined water in a free aquifer, or it may be prevented from reaching the atmosphere by an impermeable layer, in which case it is called confined water and is contained in an artesian aquifer.

Groundwater has large quantities of dissolved materials in ionic (charged particles) form, including chloride (Cl-), sulfates (SO_4—), bicarbonates (CO_3H-), sodium (Na+), calcium (Ca++), and magnesium (Mg++). Other ions may also be present but generally occur at low levels. There are also dissolved gases in groundwater (mainly carbon dioxide and oxygen). Groundwater that is considered freshwater contains less than 2,000 parts per million of dissolved substances. Groundwater that is considered brackish may contain up to 5,000 parts per million; salt water contains up to 40,000 parts per million; and brine groundwater contains more than 40,000 parts per million. Such high salt levels are generally associated with saline areas, petroleum areas, or fossil waters that are at great depth.

Groundwaters have been used by humans since long before the time of Christ, and in the Middle East wells that reach groundwater have been used extensively for very long periods. Well drilling was not common in Western countries until the Middle Ages, although China was known to have developed wells at least 1,500 years ago.—Alberto I. J. Vich and Juana Susana Barroso

See also **ARTESIAN BASIN; FIELD CAPACITY OF SOILS; HYDROLOGICAL CYCLE; HYDROLOGY; PRECIPITATION; RIVERS; RUNOFF; WATER; WATER OF RETENTION; WATER POTENTIAL**

Further Reading

Bates, R. L., ed. 1987. *Glossary of Geology*. 3d ed. Alexandria, Va.: American Geological Institute.

Davis, S. N. 1974. Hydrogeology of arid regions. *In* G. W. Brown, Jr., ed., *Desert Biology: Special Topics on the Physical and Biological Aspects of Arid Regions*, 2:1–30. New York: Academic Press.

Moore, G. W. 1978. *Dictionary of Geography: Definitions and Explanation of Terms used in Physical Geography*. New York: Harper and Row.

The New Encyclopaedia Britannica. 15th ed. 1974. Groundwater. Vol. 8:432–444. Chicago: University of Chicago Press.

Nir, D. 1974. *The Semi-arid World: Man on the Fringe of the Desert*. London: Longman.

Suh-Shiaw, Lo. 1992. *Glossary of Hydrology*. Taipei: Sheng Te.

Walter, H. and E. Stadelmann. 1974. A new approach to the water relations of desert plants. *In* G. W. Brown Jr., ed., *Desert Biology: Special Topics on the Physical and Biological Aspects of Arid Regions*, 2:213–310. New York: Academic Press.

GROWING SEASON

Period of the year when conditions are favorable for plant growth. In temperate zones the growing year is considered to extend from the last frost of spring to the first frost of autumn. In temperate deserts it is the number of consecutive frost-free days that determines the length of the growing season. However, physiological and morphological characteristics of particular species or populations may permit longer or shorter specific growing seasons. In tropical or subtropical drylands the growing season is determined by precipitation, and tropical semideserts have pronounced wet and dry seasons. However, some tropical areas are aseasonal, so that growth and reproduction may occur year-around. Each of the southern deserts of North America has a different rainfall pattern: Chihuahuan Desert, summer rains; Sonoran Desert, summer and winter rains; Colorado or Mojave Desert, winter rains. Therefore, they have distinct growing seasons and the vegetation of each is also distinctive.—James R. Estes

See also **CHIHUAHUAN DESERT; COLORADO DESERT; DESERTS; GERMINATION; MOJAVE DESERT; PLANT ADAPTATIONS; PLANT GEOGRAPHY; PLANTS; SONORAN DESERT**

Further Reading

Barbour, M. G., and W. D. Billings, eds. 1988. *North American Terrestrial Vegetation*. Cambridge: Cambridge University Press.

Rost, T. L., M. G. Barbour, R. M. Thornton, T. E. Weier, and C. R. Stocking. 1984. *Botany*. 2d ed. New York: Wiley.

GUAJIRA

Tropical dry peninsula stretching along a portion of the western Caribbean coast of South America in northern Colombia and parts of western Venezuela. In Colombia this area is known as the Desierto Guajiro. Rainfall occurs mainly over a two-month period (October and November) and is often less than 400 millimeters annually; mean annual temperature is 28°C. The region supports xerophyllous (dry-adapted) vegetation, made up of low trees, stunted shrubs, and arborescent cacti. The most common tree species are *Caesalpinia coriacea, Prosopis juliflora, Bulnesia arborea, Pithecellobium ligustrinim, Acacia tortuosa*, and *Cercidium praecox*. Common cacti are *Lemaireocereus griseus, Acanthocereus columbianus*, and *Cephalocereus*

Tropical desert scrubland with arborescent cactus on the Guajira Peninsula, northern Colombia. (Photo: N. J. Czaplewski)

russelianus. There are also terrestrial thorny bromeliads (Bromeliaceae), such as *Bromelia pinguin*, and palms, *Copernicia sanctae-marthae*.

The avifauna of the Guajira is quite distinctive from the other bird faunal groupings in the country and includes approximately 25 bird species that are typical of the region, although none is endemic (limited to the area). Among the characteristic species are the crested bobwhite (*Colinus cristatus*), a small dove (*Columbina passerina*), a hummingbird (*Chlorostilbon mellisuga*), several parrots (*Aratinga pertinax, Brotogeris*), a puffbird (*Hypnelus*), several woodpeckers (*Piculus chrysochlorus, Chrysoptilus punctigula, Picumnus cinnamoneus*), two flycatchers (*Empidonax*), a wren (*Troglodytes*), a mockingbird (*Mimus gilvus*), a tanager (*Thraupis*), and the bananaquit (*Coereba flaveola*).

In the Maracaibo Basin, whose northwestern arid extreme extends into the Guajira Peninsula, 16 species of amphibians in the following genera have been reported, including *Rana, Bufo, Leptodactylus, Hyla, Pipa, Colostethus, Pleurodema*, and *Pseudopaludicola*. Six species were widespread, and two, *Pipa parva* and *Hyla venulosa ingens*, seem to be endemic. Four other species were found along the Colombian coast and were associated with the Guajira Phytogeographic Province: *Eupemphix pustulosus ruthveni, Pleurodema brachyops*, and two species in the genus *Pseudopaludicola*.—Virgilio G. Roig

See also **AMPHIBIANS; BIRDS; CACTI; CACTUS, COLUMNAR; CARDÓN; MAMMALS; MESQUITE; REPTILES; SOUTH AMERICA, DESERTS OF**

Further Reading

Allan, T., and A. Warren, eds. 1993. *Deserts: The Encroaching Wilderness*. New York: Oxford University Press.

Camacho, J. H. 1995. *Desiertos: Zonas áridas y semiáridas de Colombia*. Cali: Banco de Occidente Credencial.

GUANACO. *See* CAMELS, SOUTH AMERICAN

GUAYULE

Long-lived, slow-growing perennial shrub (*Parthenium argentatum*) less than one meter tall with potential commercial value (sunflower family Asteraceae) found in arid regions of the southwestern United States. Guayule is native to the Chihuahuan Desert of southwestern Texas and north central Mexico. It produces a natural rubber similar to that of the *Hevea* rubber plant, the most common source of natural rubber, but guayule rubber is inferior because of its relatively high resin content. Another drawback to its use is that guayule plants cannot be harvested until they are about seven years old. The rubber is found within cells of all guayule stem and root tissues and is extracted by macerating the tissues and separating the rubber that is released through flotation methods. The entire plant is destroyed in the process, as opposed to the collection of *Hevea* rubber, whereby the latex can be collected from a plant each year for many years.

In 1910 guayule supplied about 10 percent of the world's natural rubber. During World War II, when supplies of *Hevea* rubber were cut off, the U.S. government tried to increase guayule rubber production. After the war manufacturers returned to using rubber from the *Hevea* tree. In wild guayule plants the average yield of rubber is about 7–10 percent of dry weight and, through breeding practices, can be raised to 20 percent. Historically guayule stems were chewed by Native Americans of the region to extract the rubber and make balls used in various games.—Gordon E. Uno

See also **CHIHUAHUAN DESERT; ECONOMIC VALUE OF DESERT PRODUCTS; JOJOBA; PLANT ADAPTATIONS; PLANTS**

Further Reading

Goodin, J. R., and D. K. Northington, eds. 1985. *Plant Resources of Arid and Semiarid Lands: A Global Perspective*. New York: Academic Press.

Wickens, G. E., J. R. Goodin, and D. V. Field, eds. 1985. *Plants for Arid Lands*. London: Unwin Hyman.

GUINEA FOWL

Family of robust, plump, terrestrial game birds endemic to Africa (family Numididae, order Galliformes). Six species from four genera are recognized. Species range from 40 to 55 centimeters in length and from approximately 1 to 1.5 kilograms in weight. The small head, topped by a casque in some species, is supported by a long slender neck. The bare skin of the head and neck is often richly pigmented. Guinea fowl, although capable of flying, do so only reluctantly. All species are reported to roost at night, usually on elevated perches. Robust legs and feet are adapted for their primarily terrestrial existence. Sexes are similar in appearance, although females are slightly smaller than males. *Agelastes* and *Guttera* species are found in dense forests, woodlands, and scrub, usually in areas of higher rainfall. The helmeted guinea fowl (*Numida meleagris*) ranges throughout open country of central and southern Africa, from forest edge to semiarid environments; it has been domesticated, and is found on farms around the world. Vulturine guinea fowl (*Acryllium vulturinum*) inhabit semiarid *Acacia* woodlands in east central Africa, and are apparently entirely independent of freestanding water. Heavy bills and feet are used to excavate food items. Food consists of a variety of fruits, seeds, leaves, and small invertebrates and vertebrates. Vulturine guinea fowl are reported to follow monkey troops, taking advantage of fruit the monkeys drop to supplement their diet. Long intestinal caecae (outpouchings of the intestine) aid in digestion of food with high cellulose content, and in *Acryllium vulturinum* probably aid in water conservation.

Although otherwise gregarious, guinea fowl disperse during the breeding season and form apparently monogamous breeding pairs. Nests are located on the ground. Females generally lay between 4 and 12 exceptionally hard-shelled eggs per clutch. The incubation period ranges from 23 to 28 days. Incubation duties and posthatch care of young are shared by both sexes. Chicks are precocial and can forage on their own at two to three days of age.—Stephen C. Lougheed

See also **BIRDS; OMNIVORY; NAMIBIA, DESERTS OF; SOUTH AFRICA, DESERTS OF; WATER BALANCE**

Further Reading

Ayeni, J. S. O. 1983. Home range size, breeding behaviour, and activities of the helmeted guineafowl, *Numida meleagris* in Nigeria. *Malimbus* 5:37–43.

Cramp, S., and K. E. L. Simmons, eds. 1980. *Handbook of the Birds of Europe the Middle East and North Africa. The Birds of the Western Palearctic.* Vol. 2. Oxford: Oxford University Press.

Skead, C. J. 1962. A study of the crowned Guinea fowl *Numida meleagris coronata* Gurney. *Ostrich* 33:51–65.

Urban, E. K., C. H. Fry, and S. Keith, eds. 1986. *The Birds of Africa.* Vol. 2. New York: Academic Press.

GULLY. *See* ARROYO

GUM ARABIC TREE. *See* LEGUMES

GUNDI

Diurnal, herbivorous, rock-inhabiting desert rodent that strongly resembles the guinea pig (mammalian order Rodentia, family Ctenodactylidae) occurring from sea level to more than 2,400 meters elevation across much of arid Africa. Gundis occur over most of North Africa, including the western Sahara Desert and Sahel west of 15° east longitude, from Mauritania to Libya and Chad. A second portion of their distribution is in northeastern Africa (Ethiopia, Somalia, and Djibouti). There are four genera and five species of gundis. Gundis have long, lax fur; a small, compact body (head-body length varies from 160 to 240 millimeters); a short, bushy tail (the tail is fanlike in some species); short, rounded ears; inflated tympanic bullae; kidneys with long renal tubules; and other traits common to many desert-specialized rodents. Gundis take refuge in rock crevices, where they flatten their bodies to avoid predation. They use the heat of the sun to help them digest their food, which is mainly green vegetable matter. When the heat of the day becomes intense, they move into the cool, shady rock crevices, remaining there until the temperature drops. Like many desert rodents, they do not need free water to drink. They obtain all of their moisture needs from their diet, from their ability to produce concentrated urine, and by avoiding water loss through behavioral means.

Gundis are unusual rodents that have not been well studied in the field. Their evolutionary lineage is uncertain, and it is unknown whether they evolved from the line of rodents that led to squirrels or from other ancient groups, such as the line that led to Old World porcupines. Their fossils are known from as early as the Oligocene in Eurasia, and there are 15 genera that are known only as fossils. Gundis manage to exist on arid rocky outcrops occurring in one of the most hostile habitats on earth, the vast Sahara Desert.—Michael A. Mares

See also **AFRICA, DESERTS OF; ANIMAL ADAPTATIONS; CAATINGA; CAVY; EXCRETORY SYSTEM; HERBIVORY; HYRAX; KIDNEY FUNCTION, DESERT RODENTS; KIDNEYS; MAMMALS; PHYSIOLOGY; RESPIRATORY WATER LOSS; RODENTS; SAHARA DESERT; URINE; WATER BALANCE**

Further Reading

Anderson, S., and J. K. Jones, Jr. 1984. *Orders and Families of Recent Mammals of the World.* New York: Wiley.

Macdonald, D., ed. 1984. *The Encyclopedia of Mammals.* New York: Facts on File.

Nowak, R. M. 1991. *Walker's Mammals of the World.* 5th ed. Baltimore: Johns Hopkins University Press.

Rosevear, D. R. 1969. *The Rodents of West Africa.* London: British Museum (Natural History).

GYPSUM

Common mineral with the chemical formula $CaSO_4 \cdot 2H_2O$, often found in sedimentary deposits. Alternate terms used for gypsum are alabaster, selenite, and satin spar. Gypsum is often grouped with other evaporite minerals formed as surface water evaporates. Gypsum may be formed by the total evaporation of a body of water, resulting in precipitation as the solution reaches saturation. An alternative process occurs when an isolated portion of a body of water evaporates, concentrating the salts in the surface water. This concentrated solution is dense and therefore moves downward where precipitation occurs. Large beds of gypsum are formed by this process.

Gypsum is approximately 100 times less soluble than other sulfate minerals found in soils. It is the most common sulfate found in soils and may occur in several forms. The dominant form is gypsum with the formula given above; however, in soils formed under extremely dry conditions it may occur as hemihydrate ($CaSO_4 \cdot 1/2H_2O$).

Gypsic and petrogypsic soil horizons are soil layers in which there is an accumulation of calcium sulfate in excess of that in layers deeper in the soil profile. A gypsic horizon has at least 5 percent more calcium sulfate than the underlying material and is at least 15 centimeters thick. Petrogypsic horizons are cemented, indurated (hard) layers occurring in arid climates. They are not common in the United States but occur in regions of Africa and Asia. Gypsic horizons sometimes develop below calcic horizons.

Gypsum crusts form at or near the soil surface in warm desert regions. These crusts are restricted to low rainfall regions (less than 250 millimeters annually) because they are subject to dissolution in higher rainfall areas. They may range in thickness from 0.1 to 5 meters, contain at least 15 percent gypsum and at least 5 percent more gypsum than the underlying material. There is a gradation from calcretes to gypsum crusts and then to halide (salt) crusts as the average annual rainfall decreases. Halide crusts are more prevalent in areas where the average rainfall is below 25 millimeters. In some desert areas of the world (e.g., White Sands in New Mexico), gypsum crystals produce extensive dune systems.

Gypsum has been used as a fertilizer since Greco-Roman times. It provides calcium and sulfur for plant growth but also serves to increase the water intake rate of soil by replacing sodium with calcium on the cation exchange complex, resulting in increased aggregation of the soil. Gypsum used for fertilizer may be mined from natural deposits and is also a by-product of some manufacturing processes, including the production of phosphoric acid.

The addition of gypsum at very high rates is used in the reclamation of sodic soils (a soil with the cation exchange complex containing more than 15 percent exchangeable sodium). Sodic soils, frequently induced by irrigation without sufficient leaching, occur primarily in arid and semiarid regions. Sodium saturates the cation exchange complex resulting in soil dispersion and plugging of soil pores. Exchanging the sodium with calcium facilitates flocculation (loose grouping in a suspension) of clay particles, causing aggregation and increasing infiltration rates.

Limestone and gypsum mixtures are used in producing plaster and plasterboard for construction. The material is dehydrated by heating and then mixed with water and applied to walls or formed into wallboard. The resulting construction is relatively low cost and fire resistant.—Dan R. Upchurch and Ted M. Zobeck

See also **DUNES; ECONOMIC VALUE OF DESERT PRODUCTS; IRRIGATION DRAINAGE; LIMESTONE; NUTRIENTS; PLAYA; PSAMMOPHYTES; PSAMMOPHYTIC SCRUB; SALT; SALT CRUST; SOILS, DESERT; SOILS, DESERT, CALCAREOUS; SOILS, DESERT, CALCRETE; WHITE SANDS NATIONAL MONUMENT**

Further Reading

Allen, B. L. 1977. Mineralogy and soil taxonomy. *In* J. B. Dixon, S. B. Weed, J. A. Kitterick, M. H. Milford, and J. L. White, eds., *Minerals in Soil Environments*, 771–796. Madison, Wis.: Soil Science Society of America.

Bohn, H. L., B. L. McNeal, and G. A. O'Connor. 1985. *Soil Chemistry*. 2d ed. New York: Wiley.

Buol, S. W., F. D. Hole, and R. J. McCracken. 1980. *Soil Genesis and Classification*. 2d ed. Ames: Iowa State University Press.

Soil Survey Staff. 1975. *Soil Taxonomy: A Basic System of Soil Classification for Making and Interpreting Soil Surveys*. Agriculture Handbook No. 436, Soil Conservation Service, U.S. Department of Agriculture. Washington, D.C.: U.S. Government Printing Office.

Thomas, D. S. G. 1989. *Arid Zone Geomorphology*. London: Belhaven Press.

HABITAT DEGRADATION

Decline of quality and persistence of the system of biological interactions of plants and animals and the nonliving parts of their environment in a particular area, frequently as the result of activities by humans. From the perspective of biodiversity, habitat degradation is any conversion or alteration of natural habitats (e.g., selective culling of trees, collection of fruits and nuts from native plants, or the introduction of agriculture into arid lands). The latter could alter the abundance of resources available to wildlife, thereby affecting their population size; this could then have cascading effects throughout the ecosystem. Defined in this manner, preventing habitat degradation would preclude virtually all human use of the landscape. This is clearly impossible, and the major challenge facing environmentalists, economists, and developers is how to continue to allow for the improvement of economic and social conditions for human populations while minimizing the level of attendant habitat destruction.

Nearly all discussions of the impact of habitat degradation on biodiversity deal with tropical regions. When temperate regions are considered, temperate forests, wetlands and other freshwater aquatic systems, and marine communities are discussed, but semiarid and arid regions are either cursorily mentioned or ignored. Arid lands are often considered to be wastelands with little importance for human use or global biodiversity. In reality fully one-third of the total land surface of the world is classified as semiarid or arid, and these lands are home to about 14 percent of the world's human population. In addition, temperate and tropical deserts and semideserts have surprisingly high species diversity, often exceeding that of temperate forests. More important, deserts are home to many endemic species of plants and animals with specialized morphological and physiological adaptations to drought. An important aspect of the preservation of species is the preservation of genetic diversity. The unique nature of desert organisms argues that they should be a focus of conservation activities and not be virtually neglected.

The major cause of habitat degradation in arid regions is the expansion of agriculture and livestock ranching. Agriculture is a more serious problem in semiarid regions and in arid lands adjacent to rivers or other sources of irrigation, for example, the Colorado River valley in the southwestern United States. Not only is the desert converted to crops, but the water table and adjacent rivers are often contaminated with the runoff of agricultural chemicals and sediment. Poorly managed arid-land agriculture often results in salinization—the deposition of mineral salts on the soil surface caused by the rapid evaporation of the water applied during irrigation.

Desert habitats are also rapidly degraded by overgrazing by livestock, especially goats. Desertification is defined as the conversion of habitat to desertlike conditions via human activities. The term is unfortunate, however, in that there is little resemblance between a thriving natural desert ecosystem and the heavily degraded land that remains after years of abuse of the landscape. Overgrazing has been indicated as the single most important factor in the desertification of the Sahel region south of the Sahara Desert. During the severe droughts in the West African Sahel in 1968–1973, 6 million people were affected and 100,000 people died. Up to 40 percent of the 25 million cattle in the region died. The recurring famines in Ethiopia and Somalia have been caused, at least in part, by increasing desertification in the region.

Other causes of habitat degradation include mining, urbanization, and petroleum exploration, though all of these activities tend to be more localized than agriculture and livestock. Nevertheless, where they do occur they can cause irreversible damage to the landscape.

It is important that environmentalists arguing for the conservation of the earth's flora and fauna give full consideration to the diversity of landscapes present on the earth. Tropical forests are clearly important, but arid ecosystems also harbor abundant and unique diversity. Habitat degradation in arid lands is a severe threat to this biodiversity, and human activities in deserts must be monitored as closely as tropical deforestation.—Thomas E. Lacher, Jr.

See also **BIOSPHERE RESERVE; COLORADO RIVER; CONSERVATION IN DESERTS; CONTAMINATION; DESERTIFICATION; DIRT BIKES; DIVERSITY; DUNE BUGGIES; DUNES; ECOLOGY; ECOSYSTEM; INSECTICIDES; IRRIGATION DRAINAGE; MIDDLE EAST, DESERTS OF; OFF-ROAD VEHICLES; PESTICIDES; POLLUTION; SALINIZATION; WILDLIFE**

Further Reading

Glantz, M. H. 1977. *Desertification: Environmental Degradation in and Around Arid Lands.* Boulder, Colo.: Westview Press.

Heathcote, R. L. 1983. *The Arid Lands: Their Use and Abuse.* New York: Longman.

Heywood, V. H., and R. T. Watson, eds. 1995. *Global Biodiversity Assessment.* Cambridge: Cambridge University Press.

Mares, M. A. 1992. Neotropical mammals and the myth of Amazonian biodiversity. *Science* 255:976–979.

McNeely, J. A., K. M. Miller, W. V. Reid, R. A. Mittermeier, and T. B. Werner. 1990. *Conserving the World's Biodiversity.* Gland: IUCN Publication Services.

World Resources Institute. 1994. *World Resources 1994–1995: A Guide to the Global Environment.* New York: Oxford University Press.

HABOOB

Sandstorm that forms because of cold descending air that has originated in a thunderstorm that had previously caused large amounts of dust and sand to be lifted into the air. Haboobs tend to be most frequent along the edges of great deserts. The name habiib, is Sudanese, and these storms are common along the southern edge of the Sahara Desert in Sudan. They are most common after several days of high temperatures and low atmospheric pressure in the Northern Hemisphere during summer between May and September and especially in June, although they may occur in almost any month of the year. Haboobs are fairly short-lived and seldom last more than three hours. They may come from any direction, depending on the thunderstorm from which they originally developed, and may move at up to 100 kilometers per hour. Haboobs are frequently preceded by many dust devils. A great amount of sand can be deposited during a haboob, and it is this type of dust storm that became the symbol of the dust bowl in the Great Plains of the

Wall of sand (right half of photograph) associated with a haboob in the Monte Desert of Argentina. (Photo: M. A. Mares)

United States, particularly in Oklahoma, in the 1930s.—Federico Norte

See also **AN INTRODUCTION TO DESERTS; ANTICYCLONE; CLIMATE; CLIMATE CLASSIFICATION; CONVECTIVE STORM; DESERTS; DUST DEVIL; SAHARA DESERT; SANTA ANA WINDS; WIND**

Further Reading

Day, J. A., and V. J. Schaefer. 1991. *Clouds and Weather.* Boston: Houghton Mifflin.

Oliver, J. E., and R. W. Fairbridge, eds. 1987. *The Encyclopedia of Climatology.* New York: Chapman and Hall.

Schaefer, V. J., and J. A. Day. 1981. *A Field Guide to the Atmosphere.* Boston: Houghton Mifflin.

Schneider, S. H., ed. 1996. *Encyclopedia of Climate and Weather.* 2 vols. New York: Oxford University Press.

HADZA. *See* DESERT PEOPLES

HAIL

Type of solid precipitation that forms as irregularly shaped pellets of ice and is always produced within the clouds of convective storms (generally in cumulonimbus clouds). Hailstones are usually larger than 5 millimeters in diameter, although some giant hailstones may exceed 14 centimeters. Hailstones contain concentric rings, somewhat like the inner construction of an onion, that are composed of clear ice and opaque ice being laid down in alternating bands. Various theories have been put forth to explain why these bands should develop; several involve the temperature at which the ice is laid down on the hailstone. As convective storms raise water droplets to higher and higher levels, eventually these reach the freezing point and ice crystals begin to develop. Since the convective storm is so powerful, the small hailstones may remain high in the atmosphere for long periods and are able to grow very large. Even very large hailstones may remain aloft for long periods, continuing to grow and develop until they are released from the cumulonimbus cloud and crash to earth. Hailstone formation is most common in temperate areas in storms that develop near the interior of continents. They are less common in tropical and polar areas. Hail damage can be extreme and is related to both the size and the amount of hail as well as to the velocity with which it falls to earth.—Federico Norte

See also **CLIMATE; CLIMATE CLASSIFICATION; CLOUDS; CONVECTIVE STORM; PRECIPITATION**

Further Reading

Day, J. A., and V. J. Schaefer. 1991. *Clouds and Weather.* Boston: Houghton Mifflin.

Oliver, J. E., and R. W. Fairbridge, eds. 1987. *The Encyclopedia of Climatology.* New York: Chapman and Hall.

Schaefer, V. J., and J. A. Day. 1981. *A Field Guide to the Atmosphere.* Boston: Houghton Mifflin.

Schneider, S. H., ed. 1996. *Encyclopedia of Climate and Weather.* 2 vols. New York: Oxford University Press.

HALOCLASTIC WEATHERING. *See* WEATHERING, DESERT

HALOPHYTES

Plants adapted to saline (salty) conditions. The roots of terrestrial vascular plants absorb water from the soil through the root hairs, and that absorption is influenced by differences in water potentials (water flows from a higher water potential to a lower water potential) between the soil and the root hairs. Dissolved salts lower water potential and can create negative potentials so low that water is lost from the roots into the soil, rather than the reverse. This has disastrous effects on the root hairs: the protoplast (living part of a cell) becomes condensed and pulls away from the cell wall (plasmolysis). If the cells are plasmolyzed for sufficient time, they cannot recover and will die. The death of root hairs deprives a plant of its capacity to take up

soil water, and if enough root hairs are damaged, wilting and ultimately death of the plant results.

High levels of salinity in the soil affect water potentials of the soil and have the same effect as a drier climate. Thus desertlike conditions can occur at levels of precipitation that are otherwise sufficient to support a grassland or forest.

Most salt deposits originated as sediments of ancient seas that evaporated when they lost contact with the oceans. Evaporation removed the water, but the salts remained. Evaporites tend to be either sodium chloride ($NaCl$) or gypsum ($CaSO_4$). Deposits are often eroded into level plains called salt flats or alkali flats (also called salinas) as the salts are washed downstream, and most desert rivers, when they flow, carry salty water.

Many deserts have salty soils due to the high rates of soil moisture evaporation, which leaves behind dissolved minerals and salts. However, even the warmest, saltiest desert has some plants that are indigenous (native) to the area and adapted to high salt concentrations (halophytes). Wadi Araba south of the Dead Sea and Death Valley in California both have diverse, if sparse, floras. Acacia forests appear in the Arava, where rainfall is less than 50 millimeters per year. Species of capers (members of the family Capparidaceae) actually flower during the height of summer in Death Valley.

Adaptation to salty conditions results from (1) the ability of some plant species to take up salts and to secrete them into salt-bearing hairs (salt glands) on the epidermis; (2) the use of the energy contained in the cell's chemistry (ATP energy) to affect solute levels; or (3) structural differences in membranes.—James R. Estes

See also **CHENOPODIACEAE; DEAD SEA; DEATH VALLEY; DURICRUSTS; GREAT BASIN DESERT; IRRIGATION DRAINAGE; KAVIR; MOJAVE DESERT; PLANT ADAPTATIONS; PLANTS; PLAYA; SAGEBRUSH; SALINITY; SALINIZATION; SALT BALANCE; SALTBUSH; SALT CRUST; SALT PAN; SONORAN DESERT; UNITED STATES, DESERTS OF**

Further Reading

Fuller, W. H. 1974. Desert soils. *In* G. W. Brown Jr., ed., *Desert Biology: Special Topics on the Physical and Biological Aspects of Arid Regions,* 2:31–101. New York: Academic Press.

Poljakoff-Mayber, A., and J. Gale. 1975. *Plants in Saline Environments.* New York: Springer.

Walter, H. and E. Stadelmann. 1974. A new approach to the water relations of desert plants. *In* G. W. Brown

Jr., ed., *Desert Biology: Special Topics on the Physical and Biological Aspects of Arid Regions*, 2:213–310. New York: Academic Press.

HAMADA. *See* STONE PAVEMENT

HAMSTER

Term referring to various genera and species of seed-eating (granivorous) rodents (mammalian family Cricetidae, order Rodentia). There are about 20 species of hamsters in two separate subfamilies. The genus *Calomyscus* (subfamily Calomyscinae) has six species of mouselike hamsters found in Iran, Afghanistan, Pakistan, and several of the former Russian republics. The other four genera are in the subfamily Cricetinae. The six species of the genus *Cricetulus*, or the ratlike hamsters, range from southeastern Europe to northern Asia. The common, or black-bellied, hamster,, *Cricetus cricetus* occurs in central Europe to Russia and northern China. The golden hamsters, genus *Mesocricetus*, range from eastern Europe to the Middle East; this genus contains the common pet store hamster, *Mesocricetus auratus*. Finally, the genus *Phodopus* contains three species of dwarf hamsters, including *Phodopus sungorus*, another species that has become a popular pet.

Not all hamsters resemble the domesticated form. The mouselike hamsters and ratlike hamsters are aptly named and have long tails. *Calomyscus* also have very large ears, an adaptation to their desert habitat. It is also the only genus of hamster that does not have the cheek pouches so typical of other species. All species are primarily herbivorous (plant eating) and are especially fond of seeds, which they collect in their cheek pouches and carry to their burrows to store for the winter. They are solitary and mutually aggressive, joining only to mate. Females reach sexual maturity quickly and give birth to large litters, up to 18 in some species. They are considered to be agricultural pests in some areas but do not appear to be endangered.

All golden hamsters (*Mesocricetus auratus*) sold in pet stores are derived from a single female and her twelve young that were captured in Syria in 1930. They were first sold in the United States in 1938.—Thomas E. Lacher, Jr.

See also **ANIMAL ADAPTATIONS; ASIA, DESERTS OF; BURROWING ANIMALS; CONVERGENT EVOLUTION; GERBIL; GRANIVORY; HETEROMYIDS; IRAN, DESERTS OF; JERBOA; KANGAROO RAT; MAMMALS;** **MIDDLE EAST, DESERTS OF; PINNAE; RODENTS; WATER BALANCE**

Further Reading

Macdonald, D., ed. 1984. *The Encyclopedia of Mammals*. New York: Facts on File.

Nowak, R. M. 1991. *Walker's Mammals of the World*. 5th ed. Baltimore: Johns Hopkins University Press.

HARDPAN. *See* DURICRUSTS

HARE

Member of the mammalian order Lagomorpha, family Leporidae, which includes both rabbits and hares. Several genera in the family are referred to by the common name "hare" (e.g., the hispid hare, *Caprolagus hispidus*, and the red rockhares, genus *Pronolagus*), but the term generally refers to the approximately 30 species in the genus *Lepus*. Hares occur in a variety of habitats, including tundra (*Lepus timidus*, *Lepus othus*) and temperate forest (*Lepus mandshuricus*, *Lepus americanus*); however, most species occur in open savanna habitats or arid lands.

Hares that are specialized for arid existence include the three species of *Pronolagus*, which live in rock outcrops in semiarid to arid grasslands of southern, eastern, and central Africa. Many species of *Lepus* have broad habitat tolerance, but a few are fairly specialized for an arid existence. In particular, the antelope jackrabbit (*Lepus alleni*), the black-tailed jackrabbit (*Lepus californicus*), the white-sided jackrabbit (*Lepus callotis*), and the black jackrabbit (*Lepus insularis*), all of the western United States and northern Mexico, are restricted primarily to arid and semiarid habitats. Two African species, the Cape hare (*Lepus capensis*) and the African savanna hare (*Lepus victoriae*), are found in deserts as well as in a wide range of open formation habitats. The Indian hare (*Lepus nigricollis*) also occurs in deserts but can be found in more mesic habitats as well.

Hares are herbivorous and consume grasses when available. Many species will switch to shrubs and even cacti under more arid conditions. Litter sizes vary with latitude: northern species will produce one litter of six to eight young per year, and species near the equator will produce up to eight litters of one or two young each.

Several species of hares are now quite rare and merit serious conservation efforts. The white-sided jackrabbit of southern New Mexico and Mexico is currently declining because of habitat disturbance. The Hainan hare of Hainan Island, China (*Lepus hainanus*) and the Yarkand hare of the steppes of Turkestan (*Lepus yarkandensis*) are both considered rare, and the Tehuantepec jackrabbit (*Lepus flavigularis*), which is restricted to coastal dune habitats and the riparian vegetation of saltwater lagoons in Oaxaca and Chiapas, Mexico, is considered endangered.—Thomas E. Lacher, Jr.

See also **AFRICA, DESERTS OF; ANIMAL ADAPTATIONS; ASIA, DESERTS OF; CHIHUAHUAN DESERT; DESERT GRASSLAND; DESERTS; GRASSLAND; GREAT AMERICAN DESERT; GREAT BASIN DESERT; HERBIVORY; JACKRABBIT; MAMMALS; MARA; MIDDLE EAST, DESERTS OF; MOJAVE DESERT; NAMIBIA, DESERTS OF; PINNAE; PRAIRIE; RABBIT; SAVANNA; SONORAN DESERT; SOUTH AFRICA, DESERTS OF; UNITED STATES, DESERTS OF**

Further Reading

Chapman, J. A., and J. E. C. Flux, eds. 1990. *Rabbits, Hares and Pikas: Status Survey and Conservation Action Plan.* Gland, Switzerland: International Union for Conservation of Nature and Natural Resources.

Macdonald, D., ed. 1984. *The Encyclopedia of Mammals.* New York: Facts on File.

Nowak, R. M. 1991. *Walker's Mammals of the World.* 5th ed. Baltimore: Johns Hopkins University Press.

HARTEBEEST

Species of antelope (*Alcelaphus buselaphus*) native to sub-Saharan Africa;. The hartebeest varies over its range in pelage (hair) color and length, body size, and shape and size of horns. Hartebeests are easily distinguished from other antelopes because of their massive chests, sharply sloping backs, and long, narrow faces. Males and females are difficult to distinguish by color or horn shape. Color varies from yellow to red-brown, but head and legs are usually marked in black. Juveniles are often lighter in color than are adults. Hartebeests' curved horns are less than 70 centimeters long and have horizontal ridges. The horns attach to the head in a pedicel that accentuates the length of the head. Hartebeests run with a bouncing trot and the head reared back.

The largest herds are found in steppes (grasslands) and dry savannas (grasslands with scattered trees). Herds of 20 animals are common, but some herds are much larger. Hartebeests feed on grasses and herbaceous plants. They will stand on termite mounds and survey the surrounding area, reportedly to look for predators. While hartebeests drink daily when water is available, they are capable of surviving relatively long periods without free water.

Mating takes place year-round, but individual herds are often synchronous. One calf is born after an eight-month gestation period. Weaning occurs at eight months, and sexual maturity is achieved at two years. Individuals reaching maturity can have a life span of 20 years.

In Afrikaans *hartebeest* is said to mean "tough beast." Early settlers must have been impressed with the animals' running ability, as well as a reputed ability to survive multiple gunshots.

One subspecies of hartebeest is exceptionally plentiful, but two subspecies are considered endangered and one subspecies is extinct. Hunting and habitat destruction constitute the major threats to the endangered subspecies.—Rob Channell

See also **AFRICA, DESERTS OF; ANIMAL ADAPTATIONS; ANTELOPE; HERBIVORY; MAMMALS; SAVANNA; STEPPE; SOUTH AFRICA, DESERTS OF; THERMOREGULATION; UNGULATES; WATER BALANCE**

Further Reading

Estes, R. D. 1991. *The Behavior Guide to African Mammals.* Berkeley: University of California Press.

Skinner, J. D., and R. H. N. Smithers. 1990. *The Mammals of the Southern African Subregion.* Pretoria: University of Pretoria.

HAWK. *See* RAPTORS

HAWKMOTH

Moth in the family Sphingidae (insect order Lepidoptera), also known as the sphinx moth (the larvae are often referred to as hornworms). Hawkmoths are large (often larger than 160 millimeters), furry moths with narrow, pointed front wings that move very rapidly during flight. Some have clear wings. They are often called hummingbird moths because they hover above flowers beating their wings rapidly in a manner similar to hummingbirds. Most are nocturnal, but some rather conspicuous species are diurnal. Adults feed on nectar. Some of the largest North American species of sphingid moths (in the genus *Pachysphinx*) occur in the southwestern deserts. The larvae of most hawkmoths are large and have a hornlike spine on the dorsal surface of the posterior end of the body. Like other caterpillars, they feed on leaves, and some species (e.g., the tomato hornworm) cause considerable damage to commercially grown plants.—Laurie J. Vitt

See also **ARTHROPODS; BUTTERFLIES; CATERPILLARS; FLOWERS; HUMMINGBIRD; INSECTS; MOTHS; PLANTS; POLLINATION**

Further Reading

Borror, D. J., C. A. Triplehorn, and N. F. Johnson. 1992. *An Introduction to the Study of Insects*. New York: Harcourt Brace.

Borror, D. J., and R. E. White. 1970. *A Field Guide to the Insects*. Boston: Houghton Mifflin.

HEAT

Form of energy that is transmitted in a system from one point to another based on differences in temperature, existing only as a process of transformed energy (also called thermal energy). From the first law of thermodynamics, heat that is absorbed by a system can be used by it to produce work or to raise its internal energy. The heat index developed by Thornthwaite in his system of climatic classification was designed to be low in cold conditions and to increase exponentially as temperature increased. The equator of temperature, or the thermal equator, is the line that connects all of the points having the warmest mean annual temperature for their longitude. Its trajectory varies from one continent to another and across the oceans, not exactly parallel with the geographic equator but varying from about 20° north latitude in Mexico to as far south as 14° south latitude in Brazil. From western Africa to eastern India the thermal equator is north of the geographic equator; from New Guinea to 120° west longitude it is south of the geographic equator. The warmest latitude is along the parallel of 10° north latitude. Although the mean annual temperature reflects year-round temperature, many desert areas reach extreme values during summer. The highest official temperature ever recorded is 57.8°C for the Libyan Desert, which is part of the Sahara Desert. Temperatures above 50°C in summer are not uncommon in the hot deserts of the world.—Federico Norte

See also **AN INTRODUCTION TO DESERTS; BIOME; CLIMATE; CLIMATE CLASSIFICATION; DEAD SEA; DEATH VALLEY; DESERTS, HOT; DROUGHT; HOLDRIDGE LIFE ZONES**

Further Reading

Day, J. A., and V. J. Schaefer. 1991. *Clouds and Weather*. Boston: Houghton Mifflin.

Oliver, J. E., and R. W. Fairbridge, eds. 1987. *The Encyclopedia of Climatology*. New York: Chapman and Hall.

Schaefer, V. J., and J. A. Day. 1981. *A Field Guide to the Atmosphere*. Boston: Houghton Mifflin.

Schneider, S. H., ed. 1996. *Encyclopedia of Climate and Weather*. 2 vols. New York: Oxford University Press.

HEAT BALANCE

Thermal balance of an organism. Heat balance is determined by the net exchange of heat via radiation, convection (transfer of heat energy through the movements of many particles at once, as in the flow of a liquid), conduction (transfer of heat energy from particle to particle), and evaporation, as well as via metabolic heat production and heat storage. If organisms are in heat balance, heat gain equals heat loss and body temperature remains stable. If heat gain exceeds heat loss, body temperature rises and the organism is considered to be in a state of positive heat balance. Conversely, if heat loss exceeds heat gain, body temperature drops and the organism is in negative heat balance. In heat imbalances the changes in body temperature represent changes in the storage of heat. The amount of stored heat depends on the change in body temperature, the mass of the body, and the specific heat capacity of the body (amount of heat required to heat one gram of tissue by 1°C).

If an organism is placed into a hot environment such as a desert during midday hours, then a heat balance equation can be written as

$$H_{store} = H_{met} + H_{rad} + H_{cond} + H_{conv} - H_{evap}$$

which shows that under these conditions it gains heat from its own metabolism and from the environment via radiation, conduction, and convection. Evaporation is always a heat loss term, whereas the heat stored by the body is typically a gain in hot environments. Radiation, conduction, and convection can either be heat gains (+), as shown in the above formula, when body surface temperatures are below the relevant environmental temperature, or heat losses (-) at cooler environmental temperatures. Frequently conditions exist in which heat flows into the organism via one process, say, radiation, yet flows out of the organism via another, say, convection. Desert organisms exhibit a variety of adaptations to optimize these avenues of heat exchange.

It is clear from the equation that organisms in hot conditions can only maintain a stable body temperature by evaporating water to cool the body. If the amount of heat lost through evaporation is less than the heat gained, the organism will store heat by increasing its body temperature. Allowing body temperature to increase has two distinct advantages for an organism in the desert heat. First, it allows storage of excess heat, and second, it reduces the thermal gradient, which in turn reduces the amount of heat flowing into the body. This ultimately reduces the amount of water required for cooling. Of course, there are limits to how high an organism can allow body temperature to rise. When such limits are reached, survival demands either evaporating water to cool the body or dramatically reducing or reversing the heat gain terms.

Body size is an important factor in heat balance because it relates to surface area, a major component in all of the terms of the balance equation. The smaller an organism, the greater the ratio of surface area to volume; therefore, small organisms gain (and lose) heat more rapidly than do large ones. Small endotherms (warm-blooded animals) that attempt to maintain a stable body temperature must evaporate water at rates that simply cannot be supported. Thus, to survive in deserts, they avoid the heat of the day primarily by being active at night.—David S. Hinds

See also **ANIMAL ADAPTATIONS; BODY TEMPERATURE; COUNTERCURRENT HEAT EXCHANGE; DEHYDRATION; DESICCATION; ECTOTHERMY; ENDOTHERMY; ESTIVATION; EXCRETORY SYSTEM; EXPLOSIVE HEAT DEATH; HEAT EXCHANGE; HEAT STRESS; HEATSTROKE; HIBERNATION; HUMAN PHYSIOLOGY IN DESERTS; HYPERTHERMIA; HYPOTHERMIA; KIDNEY FUNCTION, DESERT RODENTS; KIDNEYS; METABOLISM; PERSPIRATION; PHYSIOLOGY; RENAL PAPILLA; RESPIRATORY WATER LOSS; SALT BALANCE; SHIVERING; SUNSTROKE; SURVIVAL IN DESERTS; SWEAT GLANDS; THERMOREGULATION; TRANSPIRATION; VAN'T HOFF EFFECT; WATER BALANCE; WATER STRESS**

Further Reading

Bartholomew, G. A. 1982. Body temperature and energy metabolism. In M. S. Gordon, ed., Animal Physiology, 333–406. 4th ed. New York: Macmillan.

Eckert, R. 1988. Animal Physiology: Adaptation and Environment. 3d ed. New York: Freeman.

Schmidt-Nielsen, K. 1990. Animal Physiology: Adaptation and Environment. 4th ed. New York: Cambridge University Press.

Withers, P. C. 1992. Comparative Animal Physiology. Philadelphia: Saunders.

HEAT EXCHANGE

Interchange of energy in the form of heat between an organism and its environment. Organisms continually produce metabolic heat and also evaporate water, which removes heat. Heat is exchanged via three major avenues: conduction, convection, and radiation. Heat always flows from higher to lower temperatures, and an organism can gain or lose heat through conduction (transfer of energy from particle to particle), convection, and radiation depending on the relevant environmental temperatures. Hot deserts are characterized by organisms gaining heat via all three mechanisms during at least the midday hours. Heat transfer occurs via conduction when there is direct contact between the organism and the environment (e.g., sand) and via convection through the movement of air or water. Heat exchange by radiation occurs through electromagnetic radiation transfer between the organism and the environment without direct contact, and this is an important avenue of energy loss and gain in many desert animals. Unlike these three avenues, evaporation always transfers heat away from an organism because the source of energy to change water from liquid to gas comes from the evaporating surface, thus cooling the body.

Organisms cannot avoid heat exchange but can make adjustments to influence the amount of heat exchanged. Basically the rate of heat transfer increases with increased temperature difference, increased surface area, and greater heat conductivity of the tissues. Allowing body temperature to increase toward a warmer air temperature results in a decreased temperature difference, which thereby lowers organismic heat gain. Large organisms have a smaller ratio of surface area to volume than do small organisms; therefore, large organisms gain (or lose) heat at a slower rate than do small ones. Mechanisms to decrease heat conductivity have evolved in homeotherms (e.g., the insulative coat of fur of mammals or the feathers of birds).—David S. Hinds

See also **ANIMAL ADAPTATIONS; BODY TEMPERATURE; COUNTERCURRENT HEAT EXCHANGE; DEHYDRATION; DESICCATION; ECTOTHERMY; ENDOTHERMY; ESTIVATION; EXCRETORY SYSTEM;**

EXPLOSIVE HEAT DEATH; HEAT BALANCE; HEAT STRESS; HEATSTROKE; HIBERNATION; HUMAN PHYSIOLOGY IN DESERTS; HYPERTHERMIA; HYPOTHERMIA; KIDNEY FUNCTION, DESERT RODENTS; KIDNEYS; METABOLISM; PERSPIRATION; PHYSIOLOGY; RENAL PAPILLA; RESPIRATORY WATER LOSS; SALT BALANCE; SHIVERING; SUNSTROKE; SURVIVAL IN DESERTS; SWEAT GLANDS; THERMOREGULATION; TRANSPIRATION; VAN'T HOFF EFFECT; WATER BALANCE; WATER STRESS

Further Reading

Bartholomew, G. A. 1982. Body temperature and energy metabolism. *In* M. S. Gordon, ed., *Animal Physiology*, 333–406. 4th ed. New York: Macmillan.

Eckert, R. 1988. *Animal Physiology: Adaptation and Environment*. 3d ed. New York: Freeman.

Schmidt-Nielsen, K. 1984. *Scaling: Why Is Animal Size so Important?* New York: Cambridge University Press.

———. 1990. *Animal Physiology: Adaptation and Environment*. 4th ed. New York: Cambridge University Press.

Withers, P. C. 1992. *Comparative Animal Physiology*. Philadelphia: Saunders.

HEAT STRESS

Term referring to the interaction of an organism and its environment, or to the thermal state of the organism alone, especially suggesting an increase in body temperature above neutral levels. The term "heat stress" is usually employed in two different senses: (1) it may indicate environmental conditions wherein heat flowing into an organism rises above neutral levels, thereby producing a response from the organism; or (2) it may describe the resultant change in condition of the organism (e.g., an increase in body temperature). The neutral levels of heat exchange of an organism would be that set of environmental conditions (e.g., air temperature) in which the organism exhibits none of the reactions that characterize its response to undue heat. When these environmental conditions increase above the neutral zone, they constitute a stress, as the organism responds functionally to maintain its condition the same as in the neutral zone. For example, in resting humans environmental conditions of relatively dry air at 28°C cause functional responses of increased cutaneous blood flow and evaporation to keep body temperature from rising. The organismic response is often referred to as "the strain," with an analogy being a spring subjected to a stress from the outside (a force or load), which then induces a strain in the spring (a change of length).

Much work has been done to produce a reliable measurement of environmental heat stress in humans and various domesticated homeothermic (warm-blooded) animals. This work has focused on understanding heat exchange and has led to the development of several indexes based on environmental variables alone, physiological effects alone, and a combination of both. Environmental variables of importance include wind velocity and air temperature measurements taken from shaded dry and wet bulbs and an unshaded black bulb. Information concerning convection is provided by the wind velocity, conduction by the dry bulb temperature, evaporation by the wet bulb, and radiation by the unshaded black bulb. Important physiological effects include metabolism, evaporation, heart rate, and temperatures of body and skin.

The argument for using physiological responses to determine heat stress is that the organism more readily integrates the total heat effect of the environment than do purely physical measurements. Typically it is assumed that the greater the physiological response, the nearer the organism is to collapse and death. Physiological responses to heat are relatively easy to ascertain in mammals and birds because of various mechanisms used to keep body temperature stable and because the neutral zone of physiological responses is clearly delineated. However, in poikilothermic (cold-blooded) organisms body temperature is not stabilized and the neutral zone is not clearly delineated. Because of this, heat stress is often associated with changes that are much more dramatically apparent as being inimical for survival. For example, heat stress in a lizard has frequently been described by the body temperature at which the animal can no longer right itself.

Heat stress varies within an individual, between individuals, and between various species. For example, the rate of evaporation in an individual endotherm (warm-blooded organism) exposed to the same hot conditions can increase with acclimatization to heat. It can also vary between similarly sized individuals within the same species and between species.

Heat stress is also affected by a variety of factors, including body size. Larger body size results in a smaller ratio of surface area to volume, which leads to a relatively reduced heat exchange with the environment. Also, a larger body has higher thermal inertia and stores large quantities of heat with only a slight rise in body temperature. Finally, in animals increased mobility is associated with large size, and this allows the individual to escape the heat or to obtain water.—David S. Hinds

See also **ANIMAL ADAPTATIONS; BODY TEMPERATURE; COUNTERCURRENT HEAT EXCHANGE; DEHYDRATION; DESICCATION; ECTOTHERMY; ENDOTHERMY; ESTIVATION; EXCRETORY SYSTEM; EXPLOSIVE HEAT DEATH; HEAT BALANCE; HEAT EXCHANGE; HEATSTROKE; HIBERNATION; HUMAN PHYSIOLOGY IN DESERTS; HYPERTHERMIA; HYPOTHERMIA; KIDNEY FUNCTION, DESERT RODENTS; KIDNEYS; MELANIN; METABOLISM; PERSPIRATION; PHYSIOLOGY; PIGMENT; RENAL PAPILLA; RESPIRATORY WATER LOSS; SALT BALANCE; SHIVERING; SUNSTROKE; SURVIVAL IN DESERTS; SWEAT GLANDS; THERMOREGULATION; TRANSPIRATION; VAN'T HOFF EFFECT; WATER BALANCE; WATER STRESS**

Further Reading

Baker, P. T. 1974. An evolutionary perspective on environmental physiology. *In* N. B. Slonim, ed., *Environmental Physiology*, 510–522. Saint Louis: Mosby.

Bradshaw, S. D. 1986. *Ecophysiology of Desert Reptiles.* New York: Academic Press.

Folk, G. E. Jr., 1966. *Introduction to Environmenal Physiology.* Philadelphia: Lea and Febiger.

Ingram, D. L., and L. E. Mount 1975. *Man and Animals in Hot Environments.* New York: Springer.

Kerslake, D. 1972. *The Stress of Hot Environments.* London: Cambridge University Press.

HEATSTROKE

Explosive rise in body temperature resulting from failure of the thermal regulation mechanisms to maintain body temperature at a relatively constant level. It is invariably fatal unless the rise is checked artificially. Heatstroke is the most serious of a gradation of illnesses or disorders associated with rises in body temperature and is not to be confused with heat exhaustion.

Body temperature rises when the heat gain of an animal exceeds the heat lost. Animals gain or lose heat to the environment via conduction (transfer of heat energy from particle to particle), convection (transfer of heat energy through the movements of many particles at once, as in the flow of a liquid), and radiation, depending on the thermal gradient. Heat is always gained from heat produced by the animal's metabolism, whereas heat is always lost via the evaporation of water through sweating or panting.

Increased heat gains are incurred by animals exercising or exposed to high temperatures. If an animal cannot avoid either exercise or exposure, then evaporation is the only mode of dissipating the additional heat. Typically evaporation is sufficient to cope with heat gains normally incurred, and body temperature is stabilized at some higher value proportional to the magnitude and duration of the exposure. An increase in body temperature itself causes an increase in metabolism and thus heat gain. Fortunately heat gained is normally matched by heat lost through evaporation.

When prolonged periods of increased heat gain are matched by increased evaporation, levels of energy, water, and salts can become reduced. If critical levels are reached, then a state of collapse can occur which is referred to as heat exhaustion. Heat exhaustion is characterized by a moderate elevation in body temperature ($< 2.5°C$ in humans), fatigue, and a disrupted mental state. Heat exhaustion can be thought of as a safety valve that forces escape from the exposure if possible.

Unfortunately there are limits to the rate at which any animal can evaporate water and thus lose heat. If those limits are exceeded, body temperature will rise rapidly. Furthermore, when the brain's thermal regulation center (the hypothalamus) becomes excessively heated, its heat-regulating ability becomes depressed, diminishing the evaporation rate and thus lowering the cooling ability of the organism. A vicious cycle ensues, with higher body temperatures causing greater internal heat production (gain) and decreased evaporation (heat loss), with a resultant body temperature that is higher still. Thus once body temperature rises above some critical value (about $42°C$ in humans), the excessive heat being produced can no longer be dissipated by the heat-regulating mechanisms. Body temperature then rises explosively.

This complete breakdown in the heat regulation system of the animal is termed heatstroke. A key and striking characteristic is a failure to evaporate water actively coupled with an elevated body temperature ($> 2.5°C$ above normal in humans). Heatstroke typically comes as the end stage of prolonged untreated heat exhaustion, although in elderly animals it may appear with no previous period of severe evaporation. It also typically does not occur in response to exercise, as heat exhaustion usually prevents the animal from continuing the exercise to this point.

Animals typically avoid heatstroke by either tolerating elevated body temperatures or avoiding exposure. However, animals that typically avoid exposure (e.g., nocturnal mammals) can suffer heat exhaustion, heatstroke, and death if they are unable to avoid exposure and are exposed to high temperatures. The extent to which this happens in nature is not known.—David S. Hinds

See also **ANIMAL ADAPTATIONS; BODY TEMPERATURE; COUNTERCURRENT HEAT EXCHANGE; DEHYDRATION; DESICCATION; ECTOTHERMY; ENDOTHERMY; ESTIVATION; EXCRETORY SYSTEM; EXPLOSIVE HEAT DEATH; HEAT BALANCE; HEAT EXCHANGE; HEAT STRESS; HIBERNATION; HUMAN PHYSIOLOGY IN DESERTS; HYPERTHERMIA; HYPOTHERMIA; KIDNEY FUNCTION, DESERT RODENTS; KIDNEYS; METABOLISM; PERSPIRATION; PHYSIOLOGY; RENAL PAPILLA; RESPIRATORY WATER LOSS; SALT BALANCE; SHIVERING; SUNSTROKE; SURVIVAL IN DESERTS; SWEAT GLANDS; THERMOREGULATION; TRANSPIRATION; VAN'T HOFF EFFECT; WATER BALANCE; WATER STRESS**

Further Reading

Guyton, A. C. 1981. *Textbook of Medical Physiology.* Philadelphia: Saunders.

Ingram, D. L., and L. E. Mount 1975. *Man and Animals in Hot Environments.* New York: Springer.

Vander, A. J., J. H. Sherman, and D. S. Luciano. 1994. *Human Physiology: The Mechanisms of Body Function.* 6th ed. New York: McGraw-Hill.

HEDGEHOG

Members of an insectivorous group of mammals in the family Erinaceidae (order Insectivora) characterized by, among other things, the modification of hair into spines. Although hedgehogs are relatively widespread in the Old World, only three genera are found in deserts (*Erinaceus,* western hedgehogs; *Hemiechinus,* long-eared hedgehogs; and *Paraechinus,* desert hedgehogs). The backs of hedgehogs are covered with spines (three centimeters long), and the rest of the body is covered with coarse hair. Spines vary from a sandy brown to a dark brown. The mobile ears and elongated snout of the hedgehog help it find and root out insects. The ears of species of hedgehogs that live in the desert are often longer than those of their relatives in less extreme environments. The longer ears are presumed to help the animal better regulate its body temperature by radiating excess heat to the environment. However, they may also function in predator avoidance by making the detection of predators more likely.

Hedgehogs feed largely on insects, but small snakes and rodents, lizards, birds' eggs, earthworms, and scavenged carrion are also eaten. Some species of hedgehogs will eat vegetable matter while others reject it completely.

The majority of hedgehogs that frequent deserts are nocturnal (active at night) and remain in burrows during the day. Hedgehogs may dig their own burrows or use a burrow dug by another animal. During periods of extreme temperatures, or low water or food supply, many species of hedgehogs enter torpor or hibernate (extended period of reduced activity characterized by a low rate of metabolism). In the wild hedgehogs are solitary and only seek another member of their species to mate.

Long-eared hedgehogs (genus *Erinaceus*) are found across southern Asia, desert hedgehogs occur in the Near East and northern Africa, and western hedgehogs are found throughout Europe. The Algerian hedgehog (*Erinaceus algirus*) is the only member of the genus to occur in a desert, where it is restricted to North Africa.—Rob Channell

See also **AFRICA, DESERTS OF; BURROWING ANIMALS; HEAT BALANCE; IRAN, DESERTS OF; MAMMALS; MIDDLE EAST, DESERTS OF; PINNAE; SPAIN, DESERTS OF; THERMOREGULATION; WATER BALANCE**

Further Reading

Jessop, J. 1990. *Hedgehogs.* Hove, U.K.: Wayland.

Nowak, R. M. 1991. *Walker's Mammals of the World.* 5th ed. Baltimore: Johns Hopkins University Press.

HERBIVORY

Consumption of living plant material by animals. Herbivory usually refers to an interaction in which animals (herbivores) consume the vegetative (green) portions of the plant; consumption of fruits and seeds is typically considered frugivory (fruits) or granivory (seeds). Plants provide a diversity of food resources to herbivores: leaves, stems, roots, flowers, sap, pollen, nectar, and fruits. These tissues often differ in physical and chemical traits, including water content, nutrient concentrations, and concentrations of toxic chemicals.

Belowground plant tissues can be especially important food resources for desert herbivores because more than half of all plant production may be allocated to belowground tissues. In addition, herbivores feeding on these tissues are protected from the heat and aridity of the aboveground environment. Animals that feed on subterranean (underground) tissues include burrowing mammals, such as the pocket gophers of North America, tucutucos of South America, and mole rats of Africa; nematodes; larvae of beetles, moths, and butterflies that feed on roots and tubers; and gall midges that form root galls.

Herbivory is an important process in deserts because herbivores remove valuable tissues from plants whose productivity is already limited by low precipitation and nutrient-poor soils. An estimated 2–10 percent of the biomass of leaves and stems is lost to herbivores in deserts, but occasionally individual plants are almost completely consumed. One of the potential consequences of tissue loss is that the reproductive capacity of plants is severely impaired.

Plants are not necessarily passive participants while their tissues are being consumed, however. Most plants have characteristics that deter herbivores or cause them harm. In desert plants two defensive mechanisms are common: production of chemical compounds; and possession of spines or thorns. The aromatic terpenes (complex hydrocarbons commonly found in oils or resins of plants) in sagebrush, poisonous amines (hydrocarbons derived in part from ammonia) in mesquite, cyanogenic glycosides in acacias, tannins in mesquite and ironwood, and phenolic resins in creosote bush are examples of the chemical defenses of woody perennials, which typically contain higher chemical concentrations than do grasses and herbaceous plants. Herbaceous desert plants commonly contain alkaloids (e.g., locoweed, ragwort); chemicals that sensitize mammalian herbivores to solar radiation occur in the sunflower family. The possession of spines or thorns by arid-land plants (e.g., members of the cactus and pea families) may act to deter vertebrate herbivores or slow the rate at which they feed. A third way in which desert plants minimize herbivore damage lies in the timing of plant growth. Many annual plants may escape severe herbivory simply by being ephemeral: they are not available long enough for herbivore populations to build to damaging levels.

The most common herbivores are insects and mammals, but many other types of animals have herbivorous representatives. Grasshoppers are among the most important insect herbivores in deserts. Densities can fluctuate tremendously between years and among sites. In an Arizona desert grassland, grasshopper densities reached 48 per square meter during outbreaks. In hot deserts of the Old World, locusts, a specialized gregarious form of grasshopper, can have drastic effects on the vegetation. Desert locusts (*Schistocerca gregaria*) form large, dense, mobile swarms that were recorded as agricultural pests as early as the Book of Exodus. Other important species are African migratory locusts (*Locusta migratoria*) and the Australian locust (*Chortoicetes terminifera*). Locusts are always present in African habitats, but populations explode and become more mobile under favorable conditions. They eat a wide variety of plants, and can become pests of crops. A locust can consume more than its body weight in food daily; a moderate swarm can eat 1,000 tons of plant matter each day.

Other common insect herbivores in deserts are beetles, true bugs, flies, butterflies, and moths. Leaf beetles, flies, and moth and butterfly larvae are typical leaf feeders. Thrips and blister beetles are common flower feeders. Plant sap; is consumed by mites, sucking bugs (e.g., cicadas, treehoppers), and thrips. Wasps, flies, psyllids, and butterfly and moth larvae form various galls. Leaf-cutting ants occur in American arid regions. In the Sonoran Desert, leaf-cutters form long lines carrying leaves of creosote bush and other plants.

Desert insects (notably grasshoppers) may be highly specialized, feeding on only one or a few plant species. Creosote bush, saltbush, and cacti are plants whose herbivores tend to have quite specialized diets. Some desert insects that feed on plants containing toxic chemicals are able to sequester those chemicals in their bodies, which in turn defend the insects against their predators. Some butterfly larvae that feed on milkweeds containing cardenolides are able to do this, as are some grasshoppers, beetles, and sucking bugs.

Few reptiles are herbivorous, but there are several exceptions in the desert. The desert tortoise; of the Sonoran and Mojave deserts eats mainly grasses and annual plants. Three American members of the iguana family are desert herbivores: chuckwallas, desert iguanas, and *Phymaturus* (mountain lizards) eat leaves or flowers of *Larrea* (creosote bush and relatives). *Uromastix* (called mastigures, members of the agamid family) is an herbivorous lizard of Old World deserts.

Except for nectar-feeding hummingbirds, birds are represented by few herbivores. The ostrich of the Namib Desert eats mainly grasses. Rheas (*Rhea, Pterocnemia*) of South American deserts are also herbivores. In the Great Basin Desert, sage grouse feed on sagebrush and other plants.

Rodents, rabbits and hares, and hoofed mammals are of particular importance as herbivores in arid regions. Among the herbivorous rodents are woodrats, porcupines, pocket gophers, voles, viscacha rats, Patagonian hares, cavies, and tucu-tucos in New World deserts; and gerbils and their relatives, gundis, jirds, jerboas, sand rats, springhares, and porcupines in Old World deserts. Probably because of the higher energy expenditures of small endothermic animals, herbivorous rodents (with their lower-energy diets) typically are larger than the granivorous species.

The lagomorphs constitute a very important group of desert herbivores. In North American deserts, jackrabbits and cottontails are among the most abundant and conspicuous. Wild European rabbits, once established in Australia, quickly became widespread and abundant. Most rabbits have broad diets.

Large herbivores are represented in arid regions by kangaroos and wallabies and a wide variety of ungulates, including mule deer;, bighorn sheep;, pronghorn, bison, camels and guanacos, oryx, addax, and gazelles. Many of these larger herbivores are dietary generalists. Pronghorn in the Chihuahuan Desert, for example, feed on at least 200 different plant species. During wetter seasons herbivores can take advantage of a diversity of grasses and forbs; the foliage and stems of shrubs and trees provide food during drier seasons. More specialized feeders are peccaries, which consume primarily prickly pear cacti, and giraffes, whose diets are composed largely of acacia leaves. Although large mammalian herbivores are generally not abundant in New World deserts, former residents during the Pleistocene, including giant ground sloths;, horses, glyptodonts, and camels, may have been important consumers of desert vegetation.—Kristina A. Ernest

See also **ADDAX; ANNUAL PLANTS; ANTELOPE; ANTS; ARTHROPODS; ASS; BEETLES; BIGHORN SHEEP; CAMEL; CAMELS, SOUTH AMERICAN; CAVY; CHUCKWALLA; CREOSOTE BUSH; DEER; ECOLOGY; ECOSYSTEM; ENERGY FLOW; GAZELLE; GEMSBOK; GERBIL; GOAT; GOPHER; HAMSTER; HARE; HARTEBEEST; IBEX; IGUANA, DESERT; INSECTS; JACKRABBIT; JERBOA; KANGAROO; MAMMALS; MOLE RAT; MOTHS; ORYX; OSTRICH; PECCARY; PLANT ADAPTATIONS; PLANTS; PORCUPINE; PRAIRIE DOG; PRIMARY PRODUCTIVITY; PRONGHORN; RABBIT; RHEA; RODENTS; SAGEBRUSH; SAND RAT; SPRINGBOK; SPRINGHARE; THORN; TORTOISE; TUCU-TUCO; UNGULATES; VOLE; WOODRAT**

Further Reading

Cloudsley-Thompson, J. L. 1996. *Biotic Interactions in Arid Lands*. Berlin: Springer.

Meyer, M. W., and W. H. Karasov. 1991. Chemical aspects of herbivory in arid and semiarid habitats. *In* R. T. Palo and C. T. Robbins, eds., *Plant Defenses Against Mammalian Herbivores*, 167–187. Boca Raton, Fla.: CRC.

Orians, G. H., R. G. Cates, M. A. Mares, A. Moldenke, J. Neff, D. F. Rhoades, M. L. Rosenzweig, B. B. Simpson, J. C. Schultz, and C. S. Tomoff. 1977. Resource utilization systems. *In* G. H. Orians and O. T. Solbrig, eds., *Convergent Evolution in Warm Deserts*, 164–224. Stroudsburg, Pa.: Dowden, Hutchinson, and Ross.

HERBS

Vascular plants (plants with conducting tissues such as xylem and phloem) that lack woody, aboveground tissue with shoots that die back to the ground at the end of the growing season. Herbs may be annuals, biennials, or perennials. Annual herbs grow from seed, and the plants develop, flower, produce seed, and die at the end of the same season. Therefore, the seed is the only structure that survives until the next growing season. California poppy (*Eschscholzia*) is an example of a Sonoran Desert annual herb that flowers following heavy winter rains. In years when the monsoon rains are abundant, the desert floor is carpeted with these golden poppies.

In biennials the seeds germinate and produce a basal rosette of leaves during the first growing season. The rosette may remain green through the nongrowing season. The next year the stem grows rapidly in height (bolts) and the plant produces flowers, sets seed, and dies at the close of the second year. Many members of the carrot family (Apiaceae or Umbelliferae) are biennials.

Perennial herbs have belowground structures that survive the nongrowing season and resprout the next year. These belowground perenniating organs must bear buds that produce the next season's stems. An example of a perenniating organ is the bulb of an onion. Some perennial herbs flower the first season, but others may persist for several years before they begin to flower. An example of an herbaceous perennial is wormwood, which occurs in the arid lands of western North America and is related to sagebrush, which is an example of a desert woody shrub. The distinction between annuals and perennials is not always straightforward. Some annuals, such as annual sunflower (*Helianthus annuus*), persist and become woody if the winter is mild. Some perennial herbs are weak perennials and may live for only two to three years.—James R. Estes

See also **ANNUAL PLANTS; BULBS; CARRYING CAPACITY; ECOLOGY; ECOSYSTEM; GROWING SEASON; LEGUMES; PERENNIAL PLANTS; PHOTOSYNTHESIS; PLANT ADAPTATIONS; PLANTS; PRIMARY PRODUCTIVITY**

Further Reading

Rost, T. L., M. G. Barbour, R. M. Thornton, T. E. Weier, and C. R. Stocking. 1984. *Botany*. 2d ed. New York: Wiley.

HERON

Moderate- to very large-sized conspicuous wading bird (family Ardeidae, order Ciconiiformes) with an almost cosmopolitan (worldwide) distribution and absent from high latitudes. From 61 to 69 species in 10–17 genera are recognized. Maximum species diversity is in the tropics. All herons depend on aquatic habitats, although some species inhabit regions with low annual precipitation. Herons are slim of body and vary in length from 25 to 140 centimeters. The neck, bill, and legs are long. Herons have long, broad wings and can travel over long distances. Plumage varies from drab grays to the very colorful, sometimes with ornamental plumes on the head, back, or chest. Males are larger than females. Diet is dependent to a large extent on body size and bill morphology and usually consists of fish, amphibians, and insects but may include crustaceans, mollusks, and small terrestrial vertebrates. Three heron species frequently feed in dry regions: the black-headed heron (*Ardea melanocephala*) of Africa south of the Sahara; the whistling heron

(*Syrigma sibilatrix*) of the Neotropics; and the cattle egret (*Bubulcus ibis*), which probably originated in the tropics of Africa but now has an almost cosmopolitan distribution. This latter species is of particular interest because it is a commensal (lives in close association) with some herd-living ungulates. Adaptations of herons to hot environments include gular fluttering (whereby the flap of skin at the base of the mouth and throat is vibrated) for heat dissipation.

The majority of species have monogamous pairbonds of seasonal duration. Breeding may be colonial or solitary, with nests located close to water, either in dense vegetation or in trees. The nest, built primarily by the female, is a pile of vegetation or sticks. Clutch size usually ranges from three to five. Incubation lasts 20–30 days, with hatching occurring asynchronously. Typically both sexes participate in incubation and care of young.—Stephen C. Lougheed

See also **AFRICA, DESERTS OF; BIRDS; HEAT BALANCE; RIVERS; THERMOREGULATION**

Further Reading

Brown, L. H., E. K. Urban, and K. Newman. 1982. *The Birds of Africa*. Vol. 1. New York: Academic Press.

Cramp, S., and K. E. L. Simmons, eds. 1977. *Handbook of the Birds of Europe the Middle East and North Africa. The Birds of the Western Palearctic*. Vol. 1. Oxford: Oxford University Press.

Curry-Lindahl, K. 1971. Systematic relationships in herons (Ardeidae), based on comparative studies of behaviour and ecology. *Ostrich Supplement* 9:53–70.

Hancock, J., and J. Kushlan. 1984. *The Herons Handbook*. New York: Harper and Row.

Marchant, S., and P. J. Higgins, eds. 1990. *Handbook of Australian, New Zealand and Antarctic Birds*. Vol. 1 (pt. A). Melbourne: Oxford University Press.

HETEROMYIDS

Term applied to rodents belonging to the mammalian family Heteromyidae (order Rodentia) that are largely confined to North America (some genera extend into northern South America). Heteromyids are classically grouped into six genera consisting of the pocket mice, kangaroo rats, and kangaroo mice. Members of this family are characterized by the possession of externally opening fur-lined cheek pouches. This feature is diagnostic for both the New World pocket gophers (family Geomyidae) and the Heteromyidae; both families belong to the superfamily Geomyoideae. Within the Heteromyidae, the pocket mice exhibit a moderately long hind foot but travel by quadrupedal ricochetal locomotion (bounding from forefeet to hind feet, with the forefeet and hindfeet striking the ground in pairs; i.e., the animal jumps off both hind feet at the same time, lands on both front feet at the same time, and then lands on both hind feet at the same time, and so on). The kangaroo mice and kangaroo rats have extremely long hind feet (the hindfoot is about 30 percent of the head and body length) and can locomote bipedally (bound using only the hind feet together; i.e., the animal bounds off the ground with both hind feet striking the ground together, then the feet are moved forward while the animal is in the air so that it lands on both hind feet at the same time, and so on). All members of the family construct burrows as sites for refuge and for storing food. All species forage on the surface, returning to the vicinity of the burrow to cache food (seeds and fruits), and in many cases they cache food within the chambers of the burrow system itself.

Some heteromyid genera are adapted to tropical habitats in Central America and northern South America. *Liomys* is found in dry tropical forest and savannas, whereas *Heteromys* occurs in the more mesic (wetter) tropical habitats. The dorsal pelage contains spinelike hairs, a character shared with the genus *Chaetodipus*.

Many species of pocket mice (*Chaetodipus, Perognathus*), kangaroo rats (*Dipodomys*), and kangaroo mice (*Microdipodops*) are adapted to extremely arid habitats, including sagebrush deserts, pebble deserts, and even sand dune habitats, where they forage on the surface for windblown seeds. The desert heteromyids have the ability to exist without free water for drinking. They maintain their water balance by the recovery of metabolic water by means of a highly specialized kidney. The kangaroo rats and kangaroo mice, together with their distant relatives from the Asian deserts (the jerboas and gerbils), are among the most highly adapted rodents for existence in desert habitats.—John F. Eisenberg

See also **ANNUAL PLANTS; ARIZONA DESERT; BAJA CALIFORNIA, DESERTS OF; BIPEDALITY; BURROWING ANIMALS; CHIHUAHUAN DESERT; CONVERGENT EVOLUTION; DESERT BLOOM; DESERT GRASSLAND; GRANIVORY; GRASSLAND; GREAT BASIN DESERT; HAMSTER; KANGAROO MOUSE; KANGAROO RAT; KIDNEY FUNCTION, DESERT RODENTS; KIDNEYS; GERBIL; JERBOA; MEXICO, DESERTS OF; PHYSIOLOGY; POCKET MOUSE; PRAIRIE; RODENTS; SEED DISPERSAL BY ANIMALS (ZOOCHORY); SEEDS; SONORAN DESERT; UNITED STATES, DESERTS OF; WATER BALANCE**

Further Reading

Genoways, H., and J. H. Brown, eds. 1993. *Biology of the Heteromyidae.* Special Publication No. 10, American Society of Mammalogists. Lawrence, Kan.: Allen Press.

Nowak, R. M. 1991. *Walker's Mammals of the World.* 5th ed. Baltimore: Johns Hopkins University Press.

Schmidt-Nielsen, K. 1964. *Desert Animals: Physiological Problems of Heat and Water.* New York: Oxford University Press.

HETEROTHERMS. *See* BODY TEMPERATURE

HIBERNATION

Seasonal torpor employed by mammals and birds during the winter. Such torpor is typically accompanied by substantial reductions of body temperature and energy metabolism for prolonged periods (greater than 24 hours) and is correlated with equally substantial savings of energy. The period of hibernation coincides with the winter period of greatest thermoregulatory energy demand and of lowest food-energy accessibility and therefore may be viewed as a seasonal adaptation for energy conservation. Among desert mammalian hibernators are bats and rodents, the most thoroughly studied being the North American species. The Great Basin pocket mouse (*Perognathus parvus*), an inhabitant of the cold, high-elevation Great Basin Desert of North America, appears to be an obligate hibernator, retreating to its underground burrow all winter. While torpid in simulated winter burrow conditions with temperatures near freezing, pocket mice allow their body temperatures to drop to 5°C, but not lower, controlling them very precisely with metabolic adjustments to avoid lethal freezing of body tissues; this profound torpor is accompanied by enormous energy savings during times when their diet of seeds is least available on the surface. The only desert bird known to hibernate is the insect-eating poorwill of southwestern North America; it employs torpor periodically during the winter when insects are least abundant. As in mammals, this torpor is also accompanied by substantial lowering of body temperature and metabolism, resulting in significant energy conservation.—Richard E. MacMillen

See also **ACTIVITY CYCLES, ANIMALS; ANIMAL ADAPTATIONS; BODY TEMPERATURE; BURROWING ANIMALS; COUNTERCURRENT HEAT EXCHANGE; DEHYDRATION; DESICCATION; ECTOTHERMY; ENDOTHERMY; ESTIVATION; EXCRETORY SYSTEM; EXPLOSIVE HEAT DEATH; GREAT BASIN DESERT; HEAT BALANCE; HEAT EXCHANGE; HEAT STRESS; HEATSTROKE; HUMAN PHYSIOLOGY IN DESERTS; HYPERTHERMIA; HYPOTHERMIA; KIDNEY FUNCTION, DESERT RODENTS; KIDNEYS; METABOLISM; PERSPIRATION; PHYSIOLOGY; RENAL PAPILLA; RESPIRATORY WATER LOSS; SALT BALANCE; SHIVERING; SUNSTROKE; SURVIVAL IN DESERTS; SWEAT GLANDS; THERMOREGULATION; TORPOR; TRANSPIRATION; VAN'T HOFF EFFECT; WATER BALANCE; WATER STRESS**

Further Reading

Gordon, M. S., G. A. Bartholomew, A. D. Grinnell, C. B. Jorgensen, and F. N. White. 1982. *Animal Physiology: Principles and Adaptations.* New York: Macmillan.

MacMillen, R. E. 1983. Adaptive physiology of heteromyid rodents. *Great Basin Naturalist Memoirs* 7:65–76.

Withers, P. C. 1977. Respiration, metabolism, and heat exchange of euthermic and torpid poorwills and hummingbirds. *Physiological Zoology* 50:43–52.

HIMALAYA MOUNTAINS

Mountain system in Asia separating the Indian alluvial plains (formed from erosion caused by water) and the Tibetan Plateau. The Himalaya Mountains extend 2,500 kilometers from northwestern Pakistan to the great bend of the Brahmaputra River and include the world's tallest mountain, Mount Everest at 8,848 meters, more than 25 mountains reaching 7,300 meters, and few passes lower than 4,570 meters.

The Great Himalayas, the central mountain range, are relatively young, snowcapped mountains that impede cold continental air from northern Asia from entering India, thereby raising the average temperature in the subcontinent. Arid conditions on the Tibetan Plateau are exacerbated by the Himalaya Mountains, which force the moist monsoonal winds to expend their water before crossing the range. This increased aridity of the Tibetan Plateau is partially responsible for the Gobi Desert. The diversion of the monsoonal rains increases the snow and rain on the Indian side of the range. The seasonal deposition of rain and snow on the mountains causes the river systems draining the Himalaya Mountains, the Indus and Brahmaptura rivers,

to flood seasonally. The periodic flooding of the Indus River was historically very important in the cultivation of parts of the Thar Desert. Today flooding of the Indus River is prevented by dams, and cultivation is supported by irrigation.—Rob Channell

See also **ASIA, DESERTS OF; CLIMATE; DESERTS; DESERTS, MONTANE; INDO-PAKISTAN DESERTS; MONSOON; SNOW**

Further Reading

Shirakawa, Y. 1973. *Himalayas.* New York: Abrams.

West, N. E., ed. 1983. *Ecosystems of the World: Temperate Deserts and Semi-deserts.* Vol. 5. New York: Elsevier.

HOHOKAM

Piman word variously translated as "ancient ones" or "those who went away" which has been adopted by archaeologists to designate the prehistoric culture that existed in southern Arizona during the last millennium prior to the arrival of the Spanish. Many of the Hohokam were very successful desert dwellers. The Hohokam sequence was established in the 1930s, based primarily on a typological and stratigraphic analysis of pottery at Snaketown, the largest and best-known pre-Classic Hohokam site, combined with data from a number of Classic period sites. The sequence, as proposed by Emil Haury in 1976, is as follows:

Period	Phase	Dates
Classic	Civano	A.D. 1300–1450
	Soho	1100–1300
Sedentary	Sacaton	900–1100
Colonial	Santa Cruz	700–900
	Gila Butte	550–700
Pioneer	Snaketown	350–550
	Sweetwater	200–350
	Estrella	1–200
	Vahki	300 B.C. to A.D. 1

A disagreement surrounds the dating of Hohokam origins; some authors have suggested as early as 300 B.C., others as late as A.D. 500. The core of the Hohokam area is the middle Gila River and Salt River valleys in south central Arizona. It is here, on the middle Gila, where the Snaketown site is found. The *Pioneer Period* is marked by the advent of irrigation agriculture, ceramics, and life in pithouse villages, distinguishing it from a preceding archaic tradition known as the Cochise. Irrigation canals appear as early as the Vahki phase and show a continuous expansion of the canal system through time until the end of the Civano phase; these canals stand out as the hallmark of Hohokam desert adaptation.

Ceramics appear in the Vahki phase, in the form of a plain brown utility ware, a red-slipped ware, and pottery decorated with red paint in geometric to curvilinear designs. Hohokam pottery has similarities with ceramics to the south, in Mexico, and stands in contrast to the Puebloan pottery to the north and west, both stylistically and technologically. The decorated pottery is covered with a buff wash from Colonial times onward, and throughout the Colonial and Sedentary periods the red designs become increasingly complex, with numerous animal and anthropomorphic design elements appearing in addition to an elaboration of geometric motifs.

The Hohokam are also noted for their abundant use of shells, imported primarily from the Sea of Cortez but also from the Pacific Coast and, very rarely, from the Gulf of Mexico. In the Pioneer Period shell beads, bracelets, rings, and tessera (mosaic pieces) were produced. In the Colonial and Sedentary periods numerous shell objects appear in effigy form, representing frogs, snakes, birds, and a variety of unidentified mammals. Simple stone paint palettes occur in the Pioneer Period, becoming more elaborate in the succeeding Colonial and Sedentary Periods, some in effigy form. In addition, simple ceramic figurines occur, as well as stone bowls, often in the form of frog and snake effigies.

The *Colonial Period* is so called because components of the Hohokam culture appear in sites well beyond the core area of the middle Gila and Salt River valleys, suggesting a territorial expansion of Hohokam people. Evidence suggesting Hohokam occupation occurs northward in the Verde Valley, southward in the Santa Cruz and San Pedro valleys, eastward along the Gila Valley, and downstream along the Gila as far as the Gila Bend. Concurrent with this expansion is the appearance of platform mounds of West Mexican type and ball courts suggestive of the widespread Mesoamerican ball game.

The *Sedentary Period* was a continuation of Colonial Period trends but with stylistic differences. Ceramic decoration lacks the abundant animal motifs, concentrating instead on complex geometric patterns, and the formerly elaborately carved paint palettes now appear in simpler bordered designs. The period has been described as conservative, hence its name. However, a number of new cultural elements appear. Whole marine bivalve shells are decorated with animal figures by painting and acid etching, the latter being the earliest examples of this technique. Mosaic plaques, using shell, turquoise, pyrites, and other minerals, appear in forms reminiscent of Mesoamerican types, and copper bells of West Mexican origin suggest continued contact with cultures to the south. In addition, whereas the platform mounds of earlier periods appear to have been made by reshaping and plastering former trash mounds, those of the Sedentary Period were deliberately constructed as ceremonial platforms, and often show evidence of periodic rebuilding, as in Mesoamerica.

The *Classic Period* is marked by the most radical changes in Hohokam culture. There is a contraction in the territorial distribution of the Hohokam down to the core area in the middle Gila and Salt River valleys. Most Classic Period sites are new, often farther from the rivers than in previous periods, a situation made possible by an expansion of the canal system to as much as six miles from the river, and few Classic Period sites overlie Sedentary Period deposits. The most prominent change is in architecture. From Vahki phase through Sacaton phase, Hohokam houses were perishable, wattle and daub (twigs and mud) structures built over shallow pits. The Classic Period is marked by the construction of adobe-walled structures consisting of several rooms arranged in rectangular fashion around an inner courtyard. In some cases several such units are joined in a single, large rectangular structure consisting of numerous rooms arranged around several inner courts, each courtyard and its associated rooms possibly representing a separate household or lineage unit. Several large sites, such as Casa Grande and Los Muertos, include large compounds consisting of massive, adobe-walled enclosures inside of which there is at least one freestanding platform and multiple ground-level rooms. The platforms are rectangular, and were constructed by building an enclosure with puddled adobe walls as much as six feet thick and filling the interior with dirt, often mixed with trash, which was then plastered over. Atop the platforms were perishable structures, which seem to have been periodically rebuilt. One such platform, that of Casa Grande, features a multistoried massive adobe structure atop an adobe platform.

Various crafts also show sharp changes in the Classic Period. Red-on-buff pottery; becomes much simpler in geometric decoration and is reduced to a small percentage of the total ceramic inventory. Red wares and a variety of polychrome styles that are characteristic of the Salado culture, a variant Mogollon culture to the northeast, appear in quantity, suggesting to some scholars an actual migration of Salado peoples into the area. Most shell work is in the form of mosaic pieces, and different species are represented. Much of the elaboration in small crafts so prevalent in earlier periods is absent.

Finally, there is a noticeable change in burial custom. Throughout the early Hohokam sequence, disposal of the dead was primarily by cremation, although occasional inhumation (interment) also was practiced. In the Classic Period a marked shift occurred, with inhumation becoming the dominant mode. In addition, burials by inhumation often are accompanied by red ware pottery, reinforcing the suggestion of a migration of Salado peoples into the area.

The Hohokam sequence ends with the termination of the Civano phase around A.D. 1450. The reasons for the disappearance of Hohokam culture are unknown. However, it was not an isolated occurrence, as abandonment of large areas of neighboring Anasazi and Mogollon cultures occurred at about the same time.

Some controversy surrounds the relationship of the antecedent hunting-and-gathering Cochise tradition and the Hohokam. Some scholars see the Hohokam as derived directly from the Cochise, while others contend the Hohokam culture represents an intrusion of peoples from northern or western Mesoamerica displacing the indigenous Cochise.

Archaeologists recognize two major groups of the Hohokam, associated with riverine and desert environments, respectively. The Riverine Hohokam tradition was the more complex of the two, its most notable feature being the early appearance and considerable development of irrigation systems in both the Gila River and Salt River basins and a concomitant greater reliance on agriculture. Conversely, the Desert Hohokam relied on natural floodwater farming in a nonriverine desert environment and were more dependent on wild resources. This closely parallels the adaptive distribution of the Pima and Papago, who are generally believed to be descendant from the Hohokam. However, a discrepancy exists in this hypothesis in that the middle Gila and lower Salt River basins were clearly the core area of the Hohokam tradition, but do not seem to have been occupied by the Pima in historic times until after the arrival of the Spanish.

Alternative interpretations of the Hohokam phenomena are based on the Riverine and Desert distinctions. During the Pioneer Period there is little difference between the Riverine and Desert Hohokam, and Charles Di Peso attributes this period to the prehistoric indigenous O'otam. He interprets the Colonial and Sedentary periods as an intrusion from western Mexico, occupying the core area as the Hohokam. The O'otam continue in the periphery of the Hohokam, represented by various sites described as Desert Hohokam in the Papaqueria as well as sites in the Santa Cruz and San Pedro valleys, usually cited as peripheral Hohokam. He interprets the Classic Period as a reassertion of a Hohokam-influenced indigenous O'otam culture, when the Mesoamerican Hohokam either leave or are absorbed by the O'otam. A similar interpretation by Albert H. Schroeder sees the Hohokam as a Mesoamerican intrusion arriving about A.D. 500 to displace the indigenous inhabitants from the core area of the middle Gila and Salt River valleys. He calls the indigenous culture Hakataya, which he sees as ancestral Yuman-speaking tribes of the Lower Colorado area, southern California, and northern Baja California but which he claims formerly extended as far as the Mogollon Rim in eastern Arizona.—Richard A. Pailes

See also **ARIZONA DESERT; DESERT PEOPLES; DESERTS; HOPI; NAVAJO (DINE'É); O'ODHAM; SONORAN DESERT**

Further Reading

Di Peso, C. 1956. The Upper Pima of San Cayetano del Tumacacori: An archeohistorical reconstruction of the O'otam of Pimeria Alta. *Amerind Foundation Publication* No. 8. Dragoon, Ariz.

Fontana, B. L. 1974. Man in arid lands: The Piman Indians of the Sonoran Desert. *In* G. W. Brown, ed., *Desert Biology: Special Topics on the Physical and Biological Aspects of Arid Regions,* 2:489–528. New York: Academic Press.

Haury, E. 1967. *The Hohokam, Desert Farmers and Craftsmen: Excavations at Snaketown, 1964–1965.* Tucson: University of Arizona Press.

Schroeder, A. H. 1957. The Hakataya cultural tradition. *American Antiquity* 30 (3):297–309.

———. 1960. The Hohokam, Sinagua, and Hakataya. *American Archaeology, Archives of Archaeology* 5.

Warren, S. S. 1997. *Desert Dwellers: Native People of the American Southwest.* San Francisco: Chronicle Books.

HOLDRIDGE LIFE ZONES

Hierarchical system of classification of world ecosystems based on climatic factors, originally outlined by Leslie R. Holdridge in 1947. Major latitudinal and altitudinal zones of the world are delineated according to mean annual precipitation, biotemperature (sum of the mean temperatures for those months in which monthly mean exceeds 0°C, divided by 12), and evapotranspiration (the sum of evaporation and transpiration). In Holdridge's diagram each polygon relates to a climatically determined life zone. The system assumes that mature, stable vegetation types exist and may be classified into reasonably discrete categories worldwide and that the patterns of climate and major plant associations are closely associated. For example, deserts in this scheme are defined as those zones with less than 250 millimeters annual precipitation and greater than 3°C biotemperature. Holdridge's classification also allows for further subdivision of life zones according to actual vegetation cover, land use, and faunal composition.—Stephen C. Lougheed

See also **BIOME; CLIMATE; CLIMATE CLASSIFICATION; DESERTS; ECOLOGY; ECOSYSTEM; PLANT GEOGRAPHY; PLANTS**

Further Reading

Holdridge, L. R. 1947. Determination of world plant formations from simple climatic data. *Science* 105:367–368.

———. 1959. Simple method for determining potential evapotranspiration from temperature data. *Science* 130:572.

Holdridge, L. R. 1967. *Life Zone Ecology.* Tropical Science Center, San José, Costa Rica.

Holdridge, L. R., W. C. Grenke, W. H. Hatheway, T.

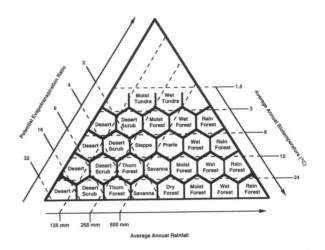

The Holdridge Life Zone System for classification of world plant formations (modified from Holdridge 1947).

Liang, and J. A. Tosi. 1971. *Forest Environments in Tropical Life Zones: A Pilot Study.* New York: Pergamon.

HOLOCENE. *See* RECENT (HOLOCENE)

HOPI

A people (the Hopi) who speak a language (Hopi) that is one of a large family of related languages called Uto-Aztecan found from eastern Oregon to Central America. From central Mexico to Oregon this language phylum is interrupted only by the recent intrusion of Athapascan speakers in Arizona. The Hopi live in several villages clustered for the most part on fingerlike projections of Black Mesa in northern Arizona, with a small outer settlement to the west on Moenkopi Wash, at what is now Tuba City. Although part of the larger Black Mesa, the projections are themselves named First, Second, and Third Mesa, numbered from east to west, as they are encountered when traveling from Keams Canyon, the location of the Indian agency several miles east of the Hopi. Prehistoric remnants of ancestral Hopi culture can be found in the canyon and mesa country throughout northern Arizona, dating back at least 1,500 years. The mesa-top villages overlook the barren landscape of the Painted Desert, and water resources are critically scarce throughout the entire region. Yet the Hopi have developed expert skills in eking out an agricultural subsistence in this dry land, including the development of varieties of corn uniquely adapted to their environment. Sand dune formations along the washes below the mesa hold moisture and nutrients for Hopi crops, and intermittent stream runoff from the mesa is diverted to crops; springs at the base of the cliffs provide additional water.

Hopi social organization is dominated by a strong corporate matrilineal (descent or kinship through the mother) and matrilocal clan system and associated religious societies preoccupied with weather control (not surprising in this climatically challenging environment). The indigenous political system was acephalous ("without a head"), lacking communitywide centralized leadership, and each village was itself an autonomous community. Clan leaders come from the dominant lineage and play a role in government, religion, and economic activity. The lineage has a ceremonial room with ritual paraphernalia, under the custody of the oldest lineage woman. The oldest male, or a close relative of the oldest woman, is the lineage head. Although membership in ceremonial associations cuts across clan lines, the associations are controlled by individual clans, or the dominant lineage within the clan, and each has at least one important ceremony to perform during the year, directed by the lineage.

The ceremonial organization includes the Katchina cult, various men's societies concerned with tribal initiation and the winter solstice ceremony, and a number of societies concerned with rain, war, clowning, and curing. Ceremonies are performed in accordance with a ritual calendar that marks important events, such as the solstice, planting time, and harvest time. The Katchina cult is tribewide, although the public performances are conducted only by men. Katchinas are supernatural spirits, including the spirits of the ancestors, and are thought to reside in nearby canyons and springs and particularly on the San Francisco peaks of northern Arizona, which can be seen in the distance from the Hopi villages. Katchina dances are impersonations of the spirits and occur between February and July, when the Katchina spirits are thought to visit the pueblos.

The modern Hopi are governed by a tribal council and constitution formed in 1936. They share in the energy resources of Black Mesa with the Navajo; they have modern schools, and many work off the reservation in the nearby towns of Holbrook, Winslow, and Flagstaff. However, they continue to practice their ancient religion and strive to maintain their distinctive culture.—Richard A. Pailes

See also **ARIZONA DESERT; DESERT PEOPLES; NAVAJO (DINE'É); PAINTED DESERT; SONORAN DESERT**

Further Reading

Dutton, B. 1983. *American Indians of the Southwest.* Albuquerque: University of New Mexico Press.

Eggan, F. 1950. *Social Organization of the Western Pueblos.* Chicago: University of Chicago Press.

Ortiz, A., ed. 1979. *Handbook of North American Indians.* Vol. 9. *Southwest.* Washington, D.C.: Smithsonian Institution Press.

Warren, S. S. 1997. *Desert Dwellers: Native People of the American Southwest.* San Francisco: Chronicle Books.

HORNBILL

Member of a group of medium to large-sized Old World bird species distinguished by an exceptionally robust bill with a large casque (horny protuberance on the upper bill) in the family Bucerotidae (order Coraciiformes). Fifty species from nine genera are recognized. Approximately half of these species are found south of the Sahara in Africa; the remainder, with the exception of one species that is restricted to New Guinea, range throughout southern Asia. The majority of bucerotids are associated with tropical habitats, primarily forest; but approximately half of African hornbills occur in drier savanna, open woodland, and thorn scrub. Total length ranges from 40 (*Tockus* spp.) to 160 centimeters (ground hornbills, genus *Bucorvus*).

Hornbills generally have short, stout tarsi (lower leg bones) and broad wings. The skeleton is highly pneumatized (filled with air spaces), and, a feature unique among birds, the first two neck vertebrae are fused. Casque structure is variable across species and between sexes within species. The casque has been reported to serve a number of functions, including individual recognition within species; aggressive intraspecific male-male interactions; amplification of calls; and possibly, in some species, facilitating digging in the ground. Feeding habits across species range from primarily frugivorous, or fruit eating (e.g., large forest-dwelling African hornbills of the genus *Ceratogymna*), to carnivorous, or meat eating (e.g., *Bucorvus* spp.), to omnivorous, both plant and animal eating, (e.g., *Tockus* spp.).

Breeding systems of hornbills vary from monogamous to communal, wherein groups of birds share a nest (e.g., the southern ground hornbill, *Bucorvus cafer*, of south central Africa; most species are monogamous. Nests occur in natural cavities in trees and in rock faces and earth banks. Clutches (groups of eggs in a nest) in larger bucerotids consist of one or two eggs, and in smaller species can include up to seven. One aspect of hornbill breeding biology is unique among birds; in all but two species (genus *Bucorvus*) the female is sealed in the nest chamber for the entire incubation period and is fed by the male through a narrow slit at the chamber entrance. In some genera the male will bring food for both female and young for the entire nesting period; in other genera the female will leave the nest when the chicks are half grown and aid in their provisioning.—Stephen C. Lougheed

See also **AFRICA, DESERTS OF; ASIA, DESERTS OF; BIRDS; SAVANNA; XEROPHYLLOUS FOREST**

Further Reading

Fry, C. H., S. Keith, and E. K. Urban. 1988. *The Birds of Africa*. Vol. 3. New York: Academic Press.

Kemp, A. C. 1979. A review of the hornbills: Biology and radiation. *Living Bird* 17:105–136.

Kemp, A. C., and T. M. Crowe. 1985. The systematics and zoogeography of Afrotropical hornbills (Aves: Bucerotidae). *In* K.-L. Schuchmann, ed., *African Vertebrates: Systematics, Phylogeny and Evolutionary Ecology*. Bonn: Selbstverlag.

HORNED LIZARD (HORNED "TOAD")

North American lizard in the genus *Phrynosoma* (family Phrynosomatidae). The misnomer "horned toad" stems from the rounded, squat morphology of these flattened lizards. Fourteen species are currently recognized. Horned lizards have a relatively short body and tail, and the body is wide and flat, giving the appearance of being ovoid in shape. All species have an enlarged crest at the posterior margin of the head, and most species have a series of sharp, pointed horns extending upward from the crest. There is a series of pointed, fringelike scales along each side of the body.

As a group horned lizards specialize on ants. Individuals frequently wait along ant trails and eat worker ants as they pass. The coloration and morphology of horned lizards renders them cryptic (camouflaged) against most backgrounds, as long as

Regal horned lizard (*Phrynosoma solare*) of the Sonoran Desert. (Photo: L. J. Vitt)

they remain immobile. When they do move they become conspicuous, and, because they are not fast runners, they can be easy to capture. Some species of horned lizards squirt blood from sinuses surrounding the eyes when grasped. It has recently been shown by Dr. Wade Sherbrooke and his colleagues that blood squirting is effective in fending off predation attempts by certain carnivorous (meat-eating) mammals (e.g., canids—members of the dog family, including foxes and coyotes).

Some horned lizards are viviparous, with females producing live young that are fully developed when born. Other horned lizards are oviparous, depositing leathery-shelled eggs in burrows in the ground. Fully formed hatchlings appear a couple of months after eggs are laid.—Laurie J. Vitt

See also **ANTS; CHIHUAHUAN DESERT; CRYPSIS; DEFENSIVE ADAPTATIONS, ANIMALS; GRASSLAND; LIZARDS; REPTILES; SONORAN DESERT**

Further Reading

Sherbrooke, W. C. 1981. *Horned lizards: Unique Reptiles of Western North America*. Tucson: Southwest Parks and Monuments Assoc.

Stebbins, R. C. 1985. *A Field Guide to Western Reptiles and Amphibians*. Boston: Houghton Mifflin.

HOWLING

Means of auditory or vocal communication in a few members of the dog family Canidae, including coyotes (*Canis latrans*), wolves (*Canis lupus*), domestic dogs, dingoes, golden jackals (*Canis aureus*), and black-backed jackals (*Canis mesomelas*). Calls are distinctive among different species and individuals and usually occur at dusk or dawn. Howling appears to serve several functions. It may act as a means of maintaining or reestablishing contact between members of a group who are separated and of facilitating activity coordination. Howling also may serve in social bonding. It is contagious and will often unite members of a group in a common activity, choral howling. A characteristic sound in the deserts of the southwestern United States is the nocturnal howling of the coyote packs. Wolves, whose captivating howls were once heard throughout the deserts of the United States, are no longer found in the vast arid spaces of North America.

Howling in golden jackals functions as social bonding among family members and as a territorial announcement. Golden jackals howl in succession and not in unison. After one group finishes, other groups will follow.—Janet K. Braun

See also **AN INTRODUCTION TO DESERTS; ARMADILLO; CARNIVORES; COYOTE; FOX; JACKAL; MAMMALS**

Further Reading

Bueler, L. E. 1973. *Wild Dogs of the World*. New York: Stein and Day.

Ewer, R. F. 1973. *The Carnivores*. London: Weidenfeld and Nicolson.

Sheldon, J. W. 1992. *Wild Dogs: The Natural History of the Nondomestic Canidae*. San Diego: Academic Press.

HUEMUL

Two species of deer in the family Cervidae (mammalian order Artiodactyla) found in South America. They are also called guemals. The Peruvian huemul, or taruca, *Hippocamelus antisensis*, inhabits the dry, steep, rocky slopes and mountains of the high Andes in northern Ecuador, Peru, Chile, Argentina, and Bolivia. The Chilean huemul, *Hippocamelus bisulcus*, is found in the dense, moist, temperate forests of southern Chile and Argentina. Both species prefer habitats at elevations from 1,400 to 1,700 meters. The common name derives from the Araucaria Indian verb *huemin*, meaning "to follow one another." This describes the animal's behavioral tendency to follow each other in single file. The Chilean coat of arms depicts the huemul and the Andean condor.

Huemuls are relatively small, standing approximately 90 centimeters at the shoulder and weighing 45–65 kilograms. Males have simple antlers with only one branch. Coarse, brittle guard hairs and dense, soft underfur comprise the pelage. The hair, which provides insulation from the cold and repels water, has hollow shafts and serrated edges. Both males and females have canine teeth, although the tusks are not usually visible. Unlike many deer, the young lack spots.

The Peruvian huemul is considered vulnerable to extinction, and the Chilean huemul is endangered. Populations of huemuls have decreased due to hunting, habitat modification, competition with domestic animals, and the introduction of nonnative species. The relative tameness of huemuls and their approachability, unfortunately, encourage hunting. Huemuls have few predators, although they are susceptible to diseases of domestic livestock.

Peruvian huemuls mate in June (dry season), and young are born between February and April (end of rainy season). Males shed their antlers in September and October (onset of rainy season). Huemuls are generally found in small groups of two or three individuals.—Janet K. Braun

See also **ALTIPLANO; ANDEAN GRASSLANDS; ANDES; DEER; HERBIVORY; MAMMALS; PERU, DESERTS OF; PUNA; SOUTH AMERICA, DESERTS OF; UNGULATES**

Further Reading

Merkt, J. R. 1987. Reproductive seasonality and grouping patterns of the North Andean deer or taruca (*Hippocamelus antisensis*) in southern Peru. *In* C. M. Wemmer, ed., *Biology and Management of the Cervidae*, 388–401. Washington, D.C.: Smithsonian Institution Press.

Thornback, J., and M. Jenkins. 1982. *The IUCN Mammal Red Data Book*. Pt. 1: *The Americas and Australasia*. Gland: IUCN.

HUMAN PHYSIOLOGY IN DESERTS

Study of the normal function of humans in very dry and often hot environments. The functions of most interest in such settings are the maintenance of water, salt, and heat balances. Humans can withstand high environmental temperatures as long as water and salt balances are maintained. Man's ability to tolerate high temperatures was aptly demonstrated two hundred years ago by a scientist who spent 45 minutes in an environment with a temperature of 126°C and was unaffected, though his steak was thoroughly cooked (water boils at 100°C). In hot environments the body heats up both from the environment and from its own production of metabolic heat. If escape is impossible, the only way for humans, or any organism, to prevent a rise in body temperature is to be cooled by evaporation of water. Some water is evaporated from the respiratory tract, but the majority of water evaporated in humans appears as sweat. The change of water from the liquid to the vapor state (evaporation) removes about 580 calories per gram of water when the water vapor is removed from the surface.

In dry desert air sweat evaporates as rapidly as it is formed, and a person is typically unaware of the act of sweating. However, sweating rates can be astonishingly high, with maximum rates for workers in desert conditions averaging about 1.5 liters (3.3 pounds) per hour. (Maximum rates of 4.2 liters per hour have been recorded under hot and humid conditions.) These high rates are impressive, given that the total water present in the blood of a human is about 3 liters.

Sweating rates increase with repeated exposure to high temperatures (acclimation) and are sufficient in any desert condition normally encountered. Sweating is not altered by moderate dehydration or hydration, and people cannot train themselves to use less water, as sweating adjusts to meet the need for adequate heat dissipation. However, sweating can be reduced by decreasing the heat gain from the environment, for example, by wearing appropriate clothing.

Aside from water, the most important constituents of sweat are sodium (Na) and chloride (Cl), salts that are present in sweat in lower concentrations than in the blood, but at high sweating rates, their loss can amount to as much as 30 grams per day—a heavy drain on the body's total resources of 165 grams. The effects of salt loss become readily apparent when only water is replenished. Drinking water without adequate salt dilutes the body fluids and can lead to heat cramps and even death. Salt needs to be replenished with the water, and is typically done in humans in food or mildly salted fluids (e.g., Gatorade).

Drinking to satisfy thirst does not suffice to replenish water. This is not changed even by enhancing the taste of the water by adding flavors, salts, and so on. The usual pattern is replacement of about half the water lost with drinking and replacement of the remainder with a meal.

Even when a human is water deprived, sweating continues unabated if needed for heat dissipation. Water loss in urine is decreased by making a more concentrated urine, but volumes typically cannot be reduced below about 400 milliliters per day. The immediate source of the water for sweating is the blood. Removal of water concentrates blood cells, making the blood thicker, and thus making it harder for the heart to pump. Pulse rate increases, and blood flow becomes inefficient. Heat from deep in the body cannot be transported to the surface for dissipation, so body temperature begins to rise. When dehydration is about 10 percent of the body weight, humans lose the ability to cope, both physically and mentally. Death, due to circulatory failure, ensues with a water loss of about 18 percent of body weight.—David S. Hinds

See also **CLOTHING; EXPLOSIVE HEAT DEATH; HEAT BALANCE; HEAT EXCHANGE; HEAT STRESS; HEATSTROKE; HYPERTHERMIA; HYPOTHERMIA; METABOLISM; PERSPIRATION; RESPIRATORY WATER LOSS; SALT BALANCE; SUNBURN; SUNSTROKE; SURVIVAL IN DESERTS; SWEAT GLANDS; WATER BALANCE; WATER STRESS**

Further Reading

Adolph, E. F. 1969. *Physiology of Man in the Desert.* New York: Hafner.

Folk, G. E., Jr. 1974. *Introduction to Environmental Physiology.* 2d ed. Philadelphia: Lea and Febiger.

Langeley, L. L., and E. Cheraskin. 1965. *Physiology of Man.* New York: Van Nostrand Reinhold.

Schmidt-Nielsen, K. 1964. *Desert Animals: Physiological Problems of Heat and Water.* New York: Oxford University Press.

HUMBOLDT CURRENT

Cold ocean current that moves from the Antarctic and northward along the west coast of South America. The Humboldt Current, also known as the Peru Current, helps form a thermal inversion in Chile (cold air below, warm air above) and intensifies the aridity of the Atacama Desert, in much the same manner as the Benguela Current off the coast of Namibia affects the desert there. The Humboldt Current creates a mass of cool air that becomes trapped by the Andes over Chile to the east. This cold air mass against the Andes forms a wedge of air that excludes warm, wet air masses from the South Pacific. The cold air above the current also forms morning fogs along the coast; much of the precipitation in this area is thus in the form of fog. The movement of the current from the deep ocean onto the continental shelf causes an upwelling of water rich in nutrients. This nutrient-rich water is ideal for the development of plankton. The high concentration of oxygen and plankton makes the Humboldt Current a particularly productive fishery for cold water species, such as the anchovy.—Rob Channell

See also **AN INTRODUCTION TO DESERTS; ATACAMA DESERT; CHILE, DESERTS OF; CLIMATE; DESERTS; DEW; FOG DESERT; PERU, DESERTS OF; PRECIPITATION; SECHURA DESERT**

Further Reading

Borgel, R. O. 1973. The coastal desert of Chile. *In* D. H. K. Amiran and A. W. Wilson, eds., *Coastal Deserts: Their Natural and Human Environments*, 111–114. Tucson: University of Arizona Press.

Neumann, G. 1968. *Ocean Currents*. Amsterdam: Elsevier.

HUMIDITY. *See* RELATIVE HUMIDITY

HUMMINGBIRD

Small, often brilliantly colored and iridescent bird of North and South America (family Trochilidae, order Apodiformes). More than 300 species in approximately 112 genera are recognized. Hummingbirds range throughout a diversity of habitats from sea level up to 4,500 meters above sea level, essentially wherever nectar-producing flowers are found. Maximum species diversity occurs in the subtropical zones of the Andes Mountains. As an example, in Ecuador, a country dominated by the Andes, 163 hummingbird species have been recorded. A number of species breed in arid and semiarid habitats. For example, the largest species in the Trochilidae, the giant hummingbird (*Patagona gigas*) with a wingspan of 30 centimeters, is found in arid shrub-steppe and high altitude puna vegetation from Peru to central Chile and Argentina. Diversity in the United States and Canada is markedly lower than in the Neotropics; maximum diversity in this region occurs in the dry mountains and foothills of southeastern Arizona where at least seven species have been reported breeding. Only a few species are migratory, primarily those of temperate latitudes (e.g., the ruby-throated hummingbird, *Archilochus colubris*), but many will undertake local movements in response to flowering seasons of preferred plant species.

Total length varies from approximately 6 to 20 centimeters, and weight varies from 2 to 20 grams. Hummingbirds are acrobatic fliers and can both hover and fly backward. Their wings are highly modified with long flight feathers. In forward flight the wings of some smaller species may beat up to 80 times a second. The predominant plumage coloration is metallic green. Iridescent patches of varied colors are often found on the throat, head, or breast. Males are typically much brighter than females and sometimes have crests or elongated tails. Bills are long and often decurved. Hummingbirds are nectarivorous and insectivorous. Many species specialize on particular flowering plant species, and hummingbird bill and plant blossom shapes are considered to have co-evolved in many cases. Some species of hummingbirds, notably the Andean hillstars (genus *Oreotrochilus*), become torpid (undergo a period of inactivity with associated metabolic changes) at night to conserve energy.

Most hummingbirds do not exhibit pair-bonding and are promiscuous. Males advertise for mates from either dispersed singing posts or singing assemblages (leks). Males generally do not contribute either to nest building or to parental care. The nest is a small cup usually placed on a horizontal twig. Clutches consist of one or two eggs. The eggs themselves are very small, ranging from approximately 5 by 7 millimeters up to 12 by 20 millimeters. Incubation varies from 14 to 21 days. The young are born helpless and blind and remain at the nest until fledging (20–40 days after hatching).—Stephen C. Lougheed

See also **ALTIPLANO; ANDES; BIRDS; CACTI; CACTUS, COLUMNAR; CARDÓN; CHACO; FLOWERS; METABOLISM; MONTE DESERT; ORGAN PIPE CACTUS; POLLINATION; PUNA; SONORAN DESERT; SOUTH AMERICA, DESERTS OF; TORPOR**

Further Reading

Bucher, T. L., and M. A. Chappell. 1989. Energy metabolism and patterns of ventilation in euthermic and torpid hummingbirds. *In* C. Bech and R. E. Reinertzen, eds., *Physiology of Cold Adaptation in Birds*, 187–195. New York: Plenum.

Calder, W. A., and L. L. Calder. 1992. Broad-tailed hummingbird (*Selasphorus platycercus*). *In* A. Poole, P. Stettenheim, and F. Gill, eds., *The Birds of North America*, No. 16. Philadelphia: Academy of Natural

Sciences; Washington, D.C.: American Ornithologists' Union.

Fjeldså, J., and N. Krabbe. 1990. *Birds of the High Andes.* Svendborg, Denmark: Apollo.

Grant, K. A., and V. Grant. 1968. *Hummingbirds and Their Flowers.* New York: Columbia University Press.

Greenewalt, C. H. 1960. *Hummingbirds.* Garden City, N.Y.: Doubleday.

Johnsgard, P. A. 1983. *The Hummingbirds of North America.* Washington, D.C.: Smithsonian Institution Press.

HUMUS

Organic matter that accumulates in the soil. Humus is derived from the remains of plants, animals, fungi, and microorganisms. It forms an important link in the chemical cycling of carbon, nitrogen, phosphorus, and sulfur. In many regions humus is the primary source of these nutrients for plants. The presence of organic matter in the soil increases the soil's ability to resist changes in pH (level of acidity) and to inactivate organic pesticides.

Humus influences the volume of water in the soil, its infiltration, and its evaporation from the soil surface. Soils with high humus content are generally darker than soils with low humus content. It this dark color that many people associate with rich or productive soils.

Deserts generally have pale soils with low (less than 1 percent) humus content. The lack of humus in desert soils causes water to run off and evaporate readily. This ready exchange of water prevents desert soils from holding water. Soil nutrient concentrations in deserts are also low because of low humus content.

The depletion of humus content in once-fertile soils has been implicated in the desertification of many of the longest-settled regions of the world. Humus can be depleted by overproduction of crops without compensating the soil for the organic material removed, removing native vegetation through grazing or harvest and not allowing the natural accumulation of organic material, or through increased erosion. With declines in the humic component of a soil, the ability of that soil to hold water declines and the productivity of the region decreases.—Rob Channell

See also **ECOLOGY; DECOMPOSITION; DESERTIFICATION; HYDROLOGICAL CYCLE; PESTICIDES; RUNOFF; SOILS, DESERT**

Further Reading

Fuller, W. H. 1975. *Soils of the Desert Southwest.* Tucson: University of Arizona Press.

Stevenson, F. J. 1982. *Humus Chemistry: Genesis, Composition, Reactions.* New York: Wiley.

Tate, R. L., III. 1987. *Soil Organic Matter: Biological and Ecological Effects.* New York: Wiley.

HUNTER-GATHERERS. *See* DESERT PEOPLES

HYDROLOGICAL CYCLE

Complete cycle through which water passes as it moves from the oceans to the atmosphere by evaporation, through the atmosphere to the earth's surface, and back to the oceans. The cycle is also known as the water cycle. It is a closed system, without new water inputs of any significance anywhere in the cycle. Water evaporating from the oceans and other moist surfaces enters the atmosphere and forms clouds, which yield their water as rain, snow, hail, and fog drip. Most of the precipitation from the clouds falls to the ground or to the ocean surface, but some of it evaporates along the way or strikes leaves and then evaporates. Precipitation reaching the ground can evaporate directly and return to the atmosphere. A small part becomes surface runoff to rivers, lakes, and other lower-lying places. Much of the precipitation infiltrates the soil and is retained there by attractive soil forces or continues to percolate downward to a water table and ultimately emerges to feed springs, rivers, and lakes by lateral subsurface flow. About two-thirds of the world's land surface has external drainage to the oceans through rivers and streams. One-third (mostly drylands) has no permanent surface drainage to the sea. Water collects in these closed basins and evaporates or percolates down to a water table (zone of water saturation), where it may remain for hundreds or even thousands of years before returning to the oceans.

Oceans occupy about 70 percent of the earth's surface, so most of the precipitation returns directly to the source. Oceans also contain 96.5 percent of the earth's water, all of it salty to varying degrees. Of the 3.5 percent that is freshwater (low in salt), about 75 percent of this amount is tied up more or less permanently in polar ice and glaciers. Of the remainder, nearly all is in groundwater. Only a very small amount is in lakes, streams, soil, vegetation, and the atmosphere. That very small amount is the part of the hydrological cycle that humans use and manage.—Harold E. Dregne

See also **CLIMATE; CLOUDS; CONVECTIVE STORM; CYCLONE; DESERTIFICATION; DEW; DESERTS; DROUGHT; EL NIÑO; FIELD CAPACITY OF SOILS; FLOOD; FLOODPLAIN; GROUNDWATER; IRRIGATION DRAINAGE; LITHOSPHERE; MIDDLE EAST, DESERTS OF; MONSOON; PRECIPITATION; RIVERS; RUNOFF; SNOW; WATER OF RETENTION; WATER POTENTIAL; WIND**

Further Reading

Black, P. E. 1991. *Watershed Hydrology.* Englewood Cliffs, N.J.: Prentice-Hall.

HYDROLOGY

Study of the distribution, circulation, and composition of the earth's water. The coordinating committee of the International Hydrological Decade, which was initiated in 1965 by UNESCO, adopted the following definition: "It is the science that deals with terrestrial waters, with their appearance, their circulation and distribution in the world, and with their physical and chemical properties, their interactions with the physical and biological environment, without forgetting their reactions to human activities." Hydrology includes all of the sciences related to the study of water on earth; however, in its strictest form, it refers to the study of the water cycle in the world, that is, the continuous circulation of water between the lithosphere (the terrestrial portion of the earth) and the atmosphere.

Some factors that influence the water cycle may take place over very long periods, for example, the formation of glaciers during ice ages. In the shorter term, human activities such as agriculture, fertilization, reforestation, deforestation, pumping of underground aquifers, dam building, and use of pesticides affect the circulation and quality of the planet's water.—Alberto I. J. Vich and Juana Susana Barroso

See also **CLIMATE; CLOUDS; CONVECTIVE STORM; CYCLONE; DESERTIFICATION; DEW; DESERTS; DROUGHT; EL NIÑO; FIELD CAPACITY OF SOILS; FLOOD; FLOODPLAIN; GROUNDWATER; IRRIGATION DRAINAGE; LITHOSPHERE; MIDDLE EAST, DESERTS OF; MONSOON; PRECIPITATION; RIVERS; RUNOFF; SNOW; WATER OF RETENTION; WATER POTENTIAL; WIND**

Further Reading

Custodio, E. 1976. *Hidrología subterránea.* Barcelona: Omega.

Davis, S. N. 1974. Hydrogeology of arid regions. *In* G. W. Brown, Jr., ed., *Desert Biology: Special Topics on the Physical and Biological Aspects of Arid Regions,* 2:1–30. New York: Academic Press.

Moore, G. W. 1978. *Dictionary of Geography: Definitions and Explanation of Terms used in Physical Geography.* New York: Harper and Row.

The New Encyclopaedia Britannica. 15th ed. 1974. Hydrologic Science. Vol. 9:116–125. Chicago: University of Chicago Press.

Suh-Shiaw, Lo. 1992. *Glossary of Hydrology.* Taipei: Sheng Te.

Walter, H. and E. Stadelmann. 1974. A new approach to the water relations of desert plants. *In* G. W. Brown Jr., ed., *Desert Biology: Special Topics on the Physical and Biological Aspects of Arid Regions,* 2:213–310. New York: Academic Press.

HYENA

Family (Hyaenidae) of the mammalian order Carnivora that includes the true hyenas (genera *Hyaena* and *Crocuta*) as well as the aardwolf (genus *Proteles*).

The true hyenas possess a typical carnivore (meat-eater) dentition, with large canines and premolars and molars that are adapted for both shearing and crushing. Jaw musculature is massive. The forequarters are long and the hindquarters short. The tail is often bushy and reduced in length. The aardwolf (*Proteles*) differs from other hyenas in that the dentition is much weaker in its structure and the musculature of its jaw is not nearly as well developed. Otherwise it has the appearance of a miniature striped hyena. *Proteles* is specialized for feeding on ants and termites, hence the reduction in the masticatory (chewing) structure.

The true hyenas are scavengers, although they also kill live prey. This is especially true for the spotted hyena, *Crocuta*, which commonly hunts wild game in packs. The two species belonging to the genus *Hyaena* (the brown hyena of Southwest Africa and the striped hyena of the Middle East and Asia) are more solitary in their behavior and are primarily scavengers rather than hunters of large game.

The spotted hyena is entirely African in its distribution and occurs primarily in savanna habitats from East Africa to South Africa. The brown hyena inhabits the more arid areas of Southwest Africa and may be considered desert adapted. The striped hyena occurs from East Africa across the Middle East onto the great plains of northcentral India and

Pakistan. It inhabits both forested and arid habitats. The aardwolf is confined to semiarid savanna habitats supporting large numbers of colonial termites in the southern and southwestern parts of Africa.

In their role as scavengers, the true hyenas prey on carcasses left by large predators. The activities of hyenas serve to scatter the remains of large desert ungulates, thus quickening the cycle of nutrient recovery by the impoverished soils of the desert. Species of *Hyaena* construct burrows or use natural cavities as denning sites. The young (2–4) are born with their eyes closed after a three-month gestation period. *Crocuta* females, in contrast, give birth to a smaller litter (2) after a gestation period of 110 days; the young are born with their eyes open. *Crocuta* females are organized into matriarchal clans and use a communal denning site.—John F. Eisenberg

See also **AARDWOLF; AFRICA, DESERTS OF; ANTS; CARNIVORES; CARRION EATERS; MAMMALS; MIDDLE EAST, DESERTS OF; NAMIBIA, DESERTS OF; SAHARA DESERT; SOUTH AFRICA, DESERTS OF; TERMITES**

Further Reading

Anderson, S., and J. K. Jones, Jr. 1984. *Orders and Families of Recent Mammals of the World.* New York: Wiley.

Estes, R. D. 1991. *The Behavior Guide to African Mammals.* Berkeley: University of California Press.

Gittleman, J. L., ed. 1989. *Carnivore Behavior, Ecology, and Evolution.* Ithaca: Cornell University Press.

Nowak, R. M. 1991. *Walker's Mammals of the World.* 5th ed. Baltimore: Johns Hopkins University Press.

HYMENOPTERA

Order of insects (class Insecta) containing most of the pollinating insects, all of the stinging insects, and several groups with complex social systems, including bees, wasps, hornets, ants, velvet ants, and sawflies. Many have wings as adults, and, when present, there are always two pairs that are unequal in size (flies have one pair, winged termites have two equal pairs, and most other insects lacking elytra or hemelytra have two pairs of wings that are relatively similar in size). Moreover, the hind wings of Hymenoptera are bordered on the front edge by a series of tiny hooks that attach to a groove in the front wing. Most have mandibles for mouthparts, but in some, such as bees, the mouthparts are modified into tonguelike structures that are used to lap nectar. Most hymenopterans have relatively long antennae, whereas flies usually have short antennae.

Hymenopterans are extremely important in desert ecosystems of the world. Many flying hymenopterans, such as bees and wasps, pollinate flowers of desert trees, shrubs, and annual plants. Interestingly, the honeybee (*Apis mellifera*) has been introduced into deserts of North America. Others, such as the chalcidoids, are parasitic on other insects and effectively reduce populations of insects that otherwise would cause great harm to plants. Some wasps, such as the sphecid and pompilid wasps, prey on spiders and other arthropods, which they paralyze, store in burrows, and use as food sources for their developing larvae. Ants are important in deserts as seed dispersers, and many live in large social colonies.—Laurie J. Vitt

See also **ANNUAL PLANTS; ANTS; ARTHROPODS; BEES; FLOWERS; INSECTS; VELVET ANT; VENOM; WARNING COLORATION; WASPS**

Further Reading

Bohart, R. M., and A. S. Menke. 1976. *Sphecid Wasps of the World.* Berkeley: University of California Press.

Borror, D. J., C. A. Triplehorn, and N. F. Johnson. 1992. *An Introduction to the Study of Insects.* New York: Harcourt Brace.

La Sall, J., and I. D. Gauld. 1993. *Hymenoptera and Biodiversity.* Wallingford, U.K.: CAB International.

Piek, T. 1986. *Venoms of the Hymenoptera: Biochemical, Pharmacological and Behavioural Aspects.* New York: Academic Press.

Spradbery, J. P. 1973. *Wasps: An Account of the Biology and Natural History of Solitary and Social Wasps.* Seattle: University of Washington Press.

Wilson, E. O. 1971. *The Insect Societies.* Cambridge, Mass.: Harvard University Press.

HYPERTHERMIA

Condition in which body temperature is higher than normal; a term best associated with endothermic (warm-blooded) birds and mammals. The normal body temperature of an endotherm is that measured when resting metabolic rate is lowest (thermal neutrality). Hyperthermia, experienced as a gradual rise in body temperature above thermal neutrality, is common in small desert birds; this is accompanied by a concomitant increase in evaporative water loss until evaporative cooling equals heat gained, resulting in stabilization of body temperature at a higher level. Such controlled hyperthermia may be extremely costly as it involves water loss, especially from the respiratory surfaces. However, birds are highly mobile because of flight and therefore can usually replenish water that has been expended for cooling. Hyperthermia in small desert mammals occurs commonly under laboratory conditions of high environmental temperatures but likely is of little ecological relevance; most of these animals are active during the cooler nights and avoid hotter daytime surface conditions that might promote hyperthermia by retreating to cool underground burrows. Hyperthermia in larger desert birds and mammals is usually less pronounced, because of reduced surface areas for heat gain from the environment relative to their body volume and lower rates of metabolic heat production; mild hyperthermia may be tolerated and controlled by either behavioral means or evaporative cooling, or combinations of both. The heat retained while hyperthermic by day can readily be dissipated in the cooler night air. Some African antelopes tolerate hyperthermic body temperatures (more than 43°C) during the day through a vascular cooling system termed the brain rete that provides cooler blood (39°C) to the brain, thus conserving water by not lowering the overall body temperature through evaporative cooling. In contrast, humans have almost no tolerance for hyperthermia and must either control their body temperatures at or near the thermal neutral level (37°C) when subjected to high environmental temperatures or suffer debilitating heat rise.—Richard E. MacMillen

See also **ANIMAL ADAPTATIONS; BODY TEMPERATURE; COUNTERCURRENT HEAT EXCHANGE; DEHYDRATION; DESICCATION; ECTOTHERMY; ENDOTHERMY; ESTIVATION; EXCRETORY SYSTEM; EXPLOSIVE HEAT DEATH; HEAT EXCHANGE; HEAT STRESS; HEATSTROKE; HIBERNATION; HUMAN PHYSIOLOGY IN DESERTS; HYPOTHERMIA; KIDNEY FUNCTION, DESERT RODENTS; KIDNEYS; METABOLISM; MELANIN; PERSPIRATION; PIGMENT; PHYSIOLOGY; RENAL PAPILLA; RESPIRATORY WATER LOSS; SALT BALANCE; SHIVERING; SUNSTROKE; SURVIVAL IN DESERTS; SWEAT GLANDS; THERMOREGULATION; TRANSPIRATION; VAN'T HOFF EFFECT; WATER BALANCE; WATER STRESS**

Further Reading

Gordon, M. S., G. A. Bartholomew, A. D. Grinnell, C. B. Jorgensen, and F. N. White. 1982. *Animal Physiology: Principles and Adaptations*. New York: Macmillan.

MacMillen, R. E., and C. H. Trost. 1967. Thermoregulation and water loss in the Inca dove. *Comparative Biochemistry and Physiology* 20:263–273.

Schmidt-Nielsen, K. 1964. *Desert Animals: Physiological Problems of Heat and Water*. New York: Oxford University Press.

HYPOTHERMIA

Condition in which the body temperature of birds and mammals is lower than normal (below thermal neutrality). Natural hypothermia is commonly associated with torpor and is typically more pronounced during hibernation (winter inactivity with lowered metabolic rate) than during estivation (inactivity with lowered metabolic rate that occurs during the summer) due to differences in prevailing environmental temperatures during winter and summer, respectively. Such controlled hypothermia is accompanied by reductions in energy metabolism and is generally viewed as an energy-conserving mechanism. Hypothermia during hibernation is usually prolonged, with lowered body temperature persisting for days at a time; the one North American desert estivator that is known (the cactus mouse, *Peromyscus eremicus*) is hypothermic during the normal daytime period of rest and normothermic (maintains a body temperature that is common for a mammal of its body size and metabolism) at night, even while secluded in its burrow for a week or more at a time.

Certain desert birds become hypothermic during their usual nocturnal (nighttime) period of sleep and resume normothermic activity by day: (1) tiny hummingbirds may become hypothermic each night, thus reducing thermoregulatory energy costs and ensuring an ample energy supply for foraging the next morning; and (2) the Sonoran Desert's Inca dove becomes hypothermic at night in response to water restriction, resulting in decreased rates of water loss.

Endotherms (warm-blooded animals) incapable of entering controlled states of hypothermia may become hypothermic if faced with periods of low environmental temperatures and an inadequate energy supply, resulting in an inability to maintain normal body temperature with endogenous heat production. Unless normal body temperature is restored almost immediately, this kind of hypothermia is usually lethal and is not uncommon in humans exposed to prolonged cold, inadequate clothing, and lack of food.—Richard E. MacMillen

See also **ANIMAL ADAPTATIONS; BODY TEMPERA-TURE; COUNTERCURRENT HEAT EXCHANGE; DEHYDRATION; DESICCATION; ECTOTHERMY; ENDOTHERMY; ESTIVATION; EXCRETORY SYSTEM; EXPLOSIVE HEAT DEATH; HEAT EXCHANGE; HEAT STRESS; HEATSTROKE; HIBERNATION; HUMAN PHYSIOLOGY IN DESERTS; HYPERTHERMIA; KID-NEY FUNCTION, DESERT RODENTS; KIDNEYS; MELANIN; METABOLISM; PERSPIRATION; PHYSI-OLOGY; PIGMENT; RENAL PAPILLA; RESPIRATORY WATER LOSS; SALT BALANCE; SHIVERING; SUN-STROKE; SURVIVAL IN DESERTS; SWEAT GLANDS; THERMOREGULATION; TRANSPIRATION; VAN'T HOFF EFFECT; WATER BALANCE; WATER STRESS**

Further Reading

Gordon, M. S., G. A. Bartholomew, A. D. Grinnell, C. B. Jorgensen, and F. N. White. 1982. *Animal Physiology: Principles and Adaptations*. New York: Macmillan.

MacMillen, R. E. 1965. Aestivation in the Cactus Mouse, *Peromyscus eremicus*. *Comparative Biochemistry and Physiology* 16:227–247.

MacMillen, R. E., and C. H. Trost. 1967. Thermoregulation and water loss in the Inca dove. *Comparative Biochemistry and Physiology* 20:243–253.

Schmidt-Nielsen, K. 1964. *Desert Animals: Physiological Problems of Heat and Water*. New York: Oxford University Press.

HYRAX

Unusual, herbivorous, rodentlike mammal (family Procaviidae, order Hyracoidea) grouped with two other orders of terrestrial ungulates, the elephants (order Proboscidea) and the aardvark (order Tubulidentata), as well as with the freshwater and marine manatees (order Sirenia). The relatedness is speculative, and the fossil record indicates that all of these orders have been separated for more than 50 million years.

There are three genera of hyraxes: *Procavia*, the rock hyrax, with one species; *Heterohyrax*, the bush hyraxes, with two species; and *Dendrohyrax*, the tree hyraxes, with three species. All genera have similar external morphology. Hyraxes have the general external appearance of guinea pigs, with a stout, oblong body, short legs, and a rudimentary tail. The feet are covered with leathery pads (an adaptation for running on the rocks), and, unlike guinea pigs, hyraxes are equipped with a set of long, sharp incisors that are used in fighting. The smaller bush hyraxes weigh about two kilograms, and the larger rock hyraxes can weigh over five kilograms.

Both rock and bush hyraxes dwell in isolated rock outcrops, called kopjes, in the East African savannas. Tree hyraxes live both in trees and in rocky areas. They are herbivores and feed on grasses and leaves. Rock and bush hyraxes form extended family groups with a single dominant male, several adult females, and their offspring. Small kopjes usually contain only one family group, but larger kopjes might contain several. This kind of harem-based mating system is called resource defense polygyny.; It is fairly common in rock-dwelling species in which a single male can effectively defend an important resource, that is, the rocks. Rock hyraxes are still fairly common, but tree hyraxes are becoming increasingly rare because of high rates of deforestation.

More than 3,000 years ago Phoenician sailors, while exploring the Mediterranean Sea, passed a landmass that was populated by a large number of mammals that appeared to be hyraxes (they were, in fact, rabbits), so they named the landmass Ishaphan, the Island of the Hyrax. Roman explorers latinized the name to Hispania; this later became Spain. Thus a country that has never been home to a hyrax is named for these animals.—Thomas E. Lacher, Jr.

See also **ANIMAL ADAPTATIONS; CAVY; ELEPHANT; INSELBERG; KOPJE; NAMIBIA, DESERTS OF; SAVANNA; SOUTH AFRICA, DESERTS OF; SPAIN, DESERTS OF**

Further Reading

Estes, R. D. 1991. *The Behavior Guide to African Mammals*. Berkeley: University of California Press.

Hoeck, H. N. 1982. Population dynamics, dispersal and genetic isolation in two species of hyrax (*Heterohyrax brucei* and *Procavia johnstoni*) on habitat islands in the Serengeti. *Zeitschrift für Tierpsychologie* 59:177–210.

Hoeck, H. N., H. Klein, and P. Hoeck. 1982. Flexible social organization in hyrax. *Zeitschrift für Tierpsychologie* 59:25–298.

Kingdon, J. 1984. *East African Mammals: An Atlas of Evolution in Africa*. Vol. 1. Chicago: University of Chicago Press.

Macdonald, D., ed. 1984. *The Encyclopedia of Mammals*. New York: Facts on File.

IBEX

Native goat (*Capra ibex*) of Europe, Asia, and northeastern Africa, closely related to the wild goat (order Artiodactyla, family Bovidae). Ibexes inhabit steep, rocky mountains throughout their range. Both sexes have a short, sturdy build, but they are easily distinguishable. Males have beards and are considerably larger (50–120 kilograms) than females (25–60 kilograms). The massive horns of the males (1 meter) may have knobs on their fronts and are considerably larger than the more delicate and smoother horns of the females (35 centimeters). Along with the differences between males and females, ibexes also vary among subspecies in body size, horn size and shape, and pelage color, texture, and length. Ibexes can vary in color from a chestnut brown to white but usually are gray or white on their undersides. Juveniles are notable by their lighter coloration. Black-and-white markings on the front legs characterize the Ethiopian ibex.

Ibexes can survive on relatively little food but require more water than most desert animals. They feed on grasses, herbaceous plants, and the foliage of trees and bushes. In mountainous regions ibexes will migrate to higher elevations during the summer and to lower elevations during the fall. These migrations allow ibexes to utilize different food resources and avoid high temperatures.

Ibexes form male groups and groups of females with young during most of the year, coming together only during the mating season. Over the majority of their range, mating takes place from December through February. In North Africa, however, mating takes place throughout the year, and males and females do not form separate groups. Males often compete for dominance by head butting and occupying higher ground. Dominance does not determine which males get to mate; all males court the same females. One kid, occasionally two, is born after a gestation period of five to six months. Juveniles reach sexual maturity at two years of age. The estimated life expectancy of an ibex in the wild is 10–15 years.—Rob Channell

Ibex (*Capra ibex*) in the Negev Desert, Israel. (Photo: M. A. Mares)

See also **AFRICA, DESERTS OF; ASIA, DESERTS OF; GOAT; HERBIVORES; ISRAEL, DESERTS OF; MAMMALS; MIDDLE EAST, DESERTS OF; SAHARA DESERT; SHEEP; SPAIN, DESERTS OF; THERMOREGULATION; UNGULATES; WATER BALANCE**

Further Reading

Nievergelt, B. 1981. *Ibexes in an African Environment: Ecology and Social System of the Walia Ibex in the Simen Mountains, Ethiopia*. Berlin: Springer.

Nowak, R. M. 1991. *Walker's Mammals of the World*. 5th ed. Baltimore: Johns Hopkins University Press.

IBIS

Medium to large-sized terrestrial and wading bird distributed widely in tropical, subtropical, and warm-temperate regions of the world (family Threskiornithidae, order Ciconiiformes). Approximately 30 species in about 15 genera are recognized. The group is sometimes subdivided into "typical ibises" (14 genera) and spoonbills (genus *Platalea*). Most species inhabit the shallows of freshwater habitats, including lakes, marshes, floodplains, and deltas. Some species forage in arid and semiarid upland habitats. The threatened bald ibis (*Geronticus eremita*), for example, may be found on dry washes, semidesert, and rocky slopes of north-

Puna ibis (*Plegadis ridgwayi*). (Photo: M. A. Mares)

western Africa and Turkey during the breeding season. Examples of New World species that may be associated with drier habitats are the black-faced ibis (*Theristicus melanopis*) and the puna ibis (*Plegadis ridgwayi*). The former species may be found foraging in a variety of open terrains in west central and southern South America, ranging from wet meadows to arid rangeland. The puna ibis ranges from 3,500 to 4,800 meters above sea level in the dry altiplano of west central South America, and is often found feeding in dry bunchgrass heath some distance from a water source.

Ibises usually have rather long bodies, long broad wings, and short tails. Lengths range from approximately 50 to 110 centimeters. The bill of "typical ibises" is long and decurved (bent downward). In *Platalea* the bill is also long but characteristically flattened at the distal end. Ibis plumage is generally white, black, or brown, although there are some notable exceptions (e.g., the scarlet ibis, *Eudocimus ruber*). The face region is often bare or partially so. Adaptations for dissipation of heat include gular fluttering (rapid vibration of the upper air passages of the throat) and excretion of urine onto the legs. Ibises are usually quite gregarious, often foraging and roosting in groups. Their diet consists of a wide variety of small invertebrates and vertebrates, and in some species (e.g., the sacred ibis, *Threskiornis aethiopica*) includes carrion.

Most species are colonial breeders. A seasonally monogamous pair-bond is probably the norm. Nests consist of platforms of various types of vegetation and are built primarily by the female. Nest sites include trees, dense vegetation, and, in some species, cliffs or the ground. Clutch size is usually two to five. Incubation (lasting 20–30 days) and parental duties are undertaken by both sexes.—Stephen C. Lougheed

See also **AFGHANISTAN, DESERTS OF; AFRICA, DESERTS OF; ALTIPLANO; BIRDS; CARRION EATERS; CHILE, DESERTS OF; INDO-PAKISTAN DESERTS; IRAN, DESERTS OF; MIDDLE EAST, DESERTS OF; PATAGONIA; PUNA; SOUTH AMERICA, DESERTS OF**

Further Reading

Brown, L. H., E. K. Urban, and K. Newman. 1982. *The Birds of Africa*, Vol. 1. New York: Academic Press.

Cramp, S., and K. E. L. Simmons, eds. 1977. *Handbook of the Birds of Europe the Middle East and North Africa. The Birds of the Western Palearctic*, Vol. 1. Oxford: Oxford University Press.

Fjeldså, J., and N. Krabbe. 1990. *Birds of the High Andes*. Svendborg, Denmark: Apollo.

Johnson, A. W. 1965. *The Birds of Chile and Adjacent Regions of Argentina, Bolivia and Peru*. Vol. 1. Buenos Aires: Platt.

Soothill, E., and R. Soothill. 1989. *Wading Birds of the World*. London: Blandford.

IBP. *See* INTERNATIONAL BIOLOGICAL PROGRAM

IGUANA, DESERT

Pale gray to cream-colored lizard (family Iguanidae) of the American Southwest with a dorsal row of enlarged, keeled (ridged) scales that extend down the back of the lizard. They are herbivores (plant eaters) as adults, active in the morning, at midday, and, often, in the late afternoon; they are most commonly observed in sandy, open, flatland desert habitats containing creosote bush (*Larrea*). They also occur in areas where fine windblown sand forms dunes, as long as there is vegetation available.

Desert iguanas vary in size from approximately 10 to 15 centimeters from snout to vent (tip of nose to cloaca). The tail is considerably longer than the body, and the head is relatively small for a lizard of its size. When inactive, desert iguanas seek refuge in mammal burrows, such as that of the kangaroo rat, or dig their own burrows in sandy areas. Often when they enter a burrow for the night they plug the entrance, presumably to reduce the probability that nocturnal predators, particularly snakes, will be able to find them. Mating occurs during spring and early summer, and eggs are deposited during summer. The number of eggs produced varies from three to eight, depending on the size of the female. Although considered a terrestrial lizard, desert iguanas frequently climb into vegetation while feeding. It is not uncommon, for example, to observe desert iguanas in the canopy of ironwood or mesquite trees feeding on flowers. Desert iguanas have a well-developed chemosensory system that is used for finding and identifying food as well as for social recognition.—Laurie J. Vitt

See also **ARIZONA DESERT; BODY TEMPERATURE; BURROWING ANIMALS; CALIFORNIA DESERT; CREOSOTE BUSH; DESICCATION-RESISTANT SPECIES; ECTOTHERMY; HERBIVORY; IRONWOOD; KANGAROO RAT; LIZARDS; MESQUITE; MOJAVE DESERT; PHYSIOLOGY; REPTILES; SONORAN DESERT; THERMOREGULATION; YUMA DESERT; WATER BALANCE**

Further Reading

Cooper, W. E., Jr., and A. C. Alberts. 1990. Responses to chemical food stimuli by an herbivorous actively foraging lizard, *Dipsosaurus dorsalis*. *Herpetologica* 46:259–266.

Glinski, T. H., and C. O. Krekorian. 1985. Individual recognition in free-living adult male desert iguanas, *Dipsosaurus dorsalis*. *Journal of Herpetology* 19:541–544.

Krekorian, C. O. 1989. Field and laboratory observations on chemoreception in the desert iguana, *Dipsosaurus dorsalis*. *Journal of Herpetology* 23:267–273.

INDIA, DESERTS OF. *See* INDO-PAKISTAN DESERTS

INDO-PAKISTAN DESERTS

Arid area extending from central Pakistan to northwestern India and including the Thar Desert and its various subdivisions. The major deserts are located between 68.5°–75° east longitude and 23°–30° north latitude in the Indo-Pakistan subcontinent. The deserts of Pakistan are situated at the western border of India between 68.5°–72.5° east longitude and 23.5°–29° north latitude, encompassing an area of about 69,000 square kilometers. The desert located in the southern portion of this vast region, in Sind Province is called the Thar Desert (sometimes called the Sind Desert) and encompasses an area of 43,000 square kilometers; the desert situated in the northern part of this region, in Punjab Province, is called the Cholistan Desert and encom-

Sand-scrub habitat in the Rajasthan Desert of northwestern India near Jodhpur. (Photo: M. A. Mares)

passes an area 26,000 square kilometers. In addition, there is another area of sandy desert, called the Thal Desert, located in Pakistan in Punjab Province, which lies between the Indus and Jehlum rivers and extends over an area of about 23,000 square kilometers (between 70.8°–72° east longitude and 30°–32.5° north latitude). It bears alluvial sediments from the adjoining rivers and is covered with loose sand. Its physiography, soil, and plant cover are like that of the Thar Desert. The Indian part of the desert is located between 69.3°–75° east longitude and 23.3°–30° north latitude at the western border of India. It covers an area of 195,091 square kilometers in western Rajasthan state and is called the Rajasthan Desert (it is also called the Great Indian Desert or the Indian portion of the Thar Desert).

These deserts are situated at the eastern end of the Sahara-Sindian region. Their boundary in the east is demarcated by the presence of the Aravalli Range, which extends southwest to northeast in Rajasthan, India. The arid zone lies to the west of the Aravallis and is overlain by a vast stretch of sand intercepted by eroded hills of low elevation. This great sandy desert extends northward to the undulating piedmont plains of the Indus Valley. Foothills of the Aravalli Range in the west merge with the 325-meter-high plateau characterized by the presence of complex sandstone ridges intercepted with sand-filled depressions. Bedrocks are raised in the form of sandstone hills and heaps of igneous metamorphic rocks at irregular intervals. The elevation

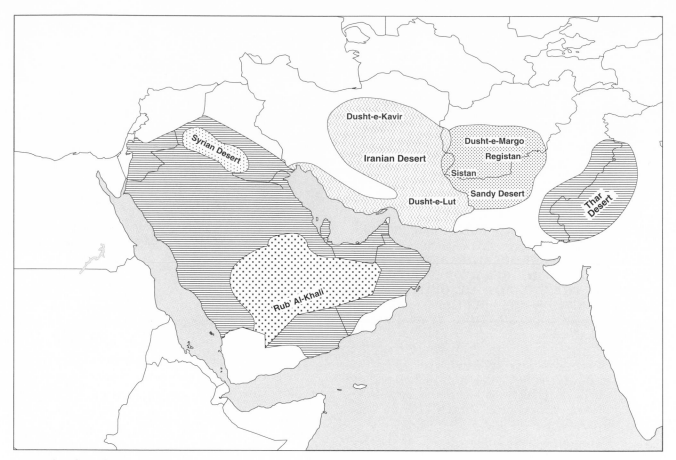

Map of Indo-Pakistan region and Southwest Asian deserts. Crosshatching in Saudi Arabia and adjoining countries indicates aridity. Shading indicates desert and semidesert limits.

near the Indo-Pakistan border drops to 150 meters, where aeolian (windblown) sand covers most of the desert in that part of India.

Soil degradation in the area is caused by wind erosion, excessive salt accumulation, physical and climatic factors, and overgrazing. Aeolian dunes include transverse ridges and parabolic and rakelike sand dunes that form perpendicular to the direction of the prevailing wind. Many sand dunes have been stabilized by xerophytic shrubs and perennial grasses due to favorable moisture regimes in localized areas. Flat plains of hard metamorphic rocky material intercept sandy dunes in the Cholistan Desert. A premonsoon period of hot weather characterizes the entire region from April to June during which mean maximum summer temperatures vary from 40°C to 42°C and mean minimum summer temperatures vary from 23°C to 27°C. Maximum summer temperatures occasionally reach 50°C. Mean maximum temperatures during the winter months (December–February) range from 18°C to 24°C, whereas mean minimum temperatures range from 3.5°C to 10°C. Temperatures as low as 2°C have been recorded in winter.

More than 90 percent of the rainfall of this region is received from southwest monsoons that occur from mid-June to mid-September. Annual rainfall varies from 100 to 300 millimeters, but precipitation is so erratic, scanty, and unpredictable that periods of several years without rain have been recorded. The depth of the water table varies from 10 to 40 meters, and the quality of water is brackish to very saline (EC: 2–20 dS/m [unit of electrical conductivity in deci-Siemens per meter; a scale for measuring the salinity of a medium, e.g., soil or water based on resistance offered by the salt; 1 dS/m is about 640 parts per million of total salts]). Rainwater reservoirs known as *tobas* have been constructed at different places for human and animal consumption. Natural vegetation is scanty and confined in low areas. Some trees grow in low-lying depressions, including *Acacia nilotica*, *Prosopis cin-*

eraria, Prosopis juliflora, Tamarix aphylla, Zizyphus jujuba, and *Capparis decidua.* Xerophytic shrubs (*Calligonum polygonoides, Calotropis procera, Aerva javanica, Alhagi maurorum, Dipterygium glaucum, Crotalaria burhia, Haloxylon salicornicum, Fagonia cretica*) and grasses (*Aristida depressa, Cenchrus pennisetiformis, Cympogon jwarancusa, Cyperus, Eleusine flagelliflora, Lasiurus scindicus, Panicum antidotale, Sporobolus*) are found growing in various parts of the desert, depending on moisture and substrate conditions. Halophytic plants such as *Haloxylon recurvum, Salsola baryosma,* and *Suaeda fruticosa* are harvested, dried, burned, and powdered to obtain soluble bicarbonates (locally called *sajji*) that are used to wash clothes. The nomadic lifestyle prevails across this desert, and the economy is based on keeping herds of domestic animals, mainly sheep and goats, for commercial purposes.—Rafiq Ahmad

See also **AN INTRODUCTION TO DESERTS; CHENOPODIACEAE; DESERT GRASSLAND; DESERTIFICATION; DOMESTIC ANIMALS; DUNES; GAZELLE; GERBIL; GOAT; GRASSES; HIMALAYA MOUNTAINS; INDUS RIVER; IRRIGATION DRAINAGE; JERBOA; MESQUITE; MAMMALS; PLAYA; PSAMMOPHYTES; PSAMMOPHYTIC SCRUB; RODENTS; SALINITY; SALT; SALT PAN; STONE PAVEMENT; UNGULATES**

Further Reading

Chouhan, T. S., ed. 1993. *Natural and Human Resources of Rajasthan.* Jodhpur: Scientific Publishers.

———. 1995. *Indian Desert: Resources and Perspective of Development.* Jaipur, India: Printwell (Rupa Books).

Ghosh, A. K., Q. H. Baquri, and I. Prakash, eds. 1996. *Faunal Diversity in the Thar Desert: Gaps in Research.* Jodhpur: Scientific Publishers.

Gupta, R. K. 1986. The Thar Desert. *In* M. Evenari, I. Noy-Meir, and D. W. Goodall, eds., *Ecosystems of the World: Hot Deserts and Arid Shrublands,* 12B:55–99.

McGinnies, W. G., B. J. Goldman, and P. Paylore, eds. 1968. *Deserts of the World: An Appraisal of Research into Their Physical and Biological Environments.* Tucson: University of Arizona Press.

Nir, D. 1974. *The Semi-arid World: Man on the Fringe of the Desert.* London: Longman.

Petrov, M. P. 1976. *Deserts of the World.* New York: Wiley.

Walter, H. 1983. *Vegetation of the Earth.* Berlin: Springer.

INDUS RIVER

Largest river system of southwestern Asia; begins at the edge of the Tibetan Plateau at 5,180 meters and flows west by northwest parallel to the Himalaya Mountains, around their western edge, and then turns southwest between the Hindu Kush and the Thar Desert to the Arabian Sea. The Indus River system flows over 2,900 kilometers and drains over 1,165,500 square kilometers. After rounding the western edge of the Himalaya Mountains, the Panjnad, a river system consisting of the Jhelum, Chenab, Ravi, Beas, and Sutlej rivers, merges with the Indus River, significantly increasing its flow.

Most of the water from the Indus River is from the melting snow and glaciers of the Himalaya Mountains, whereas most of the water flowing from the Panjnad comes from rain falling on the south side of the mountains and monsoonal rains. Increased melting of snow and frequent rains in July through September often cause portions of the river to flood and occasionally change channels.

The Indus and Punjnad River valleys are fertile valleys within an arid region. The Indus Valley served as the site of one of the earliest human civilizations, the Indus Civilization, or Harappan, of 2700–1750 B.C. Increased damming of the Indus River has decreased the degree and frequency of flooding, allowed increased irrigation, and prevented large boats from using lower portions of the river because of insufficient water flow.—Rob Channell

See also **ASIA, DESERTS OF; HIMALAYA MOUNTAINS; INDO-PAKISTAN DESERTS; RIPARIAN COMMUNITIES; RIVERS**

Further Reading

Possehl, G. L. 1979. *Ancient Cities of the Indus.* Durham: Carolina Academic Press.

INSECTICIDES

Pesticides developed specifically to control insects. Insecticides date from the mid-19th century. The first compounds were inorganic derivatives of arsenic, such as lead arsenate and calcium arsenate. They function as stomach poisons in insects. Hydrogen cyanide was first used as a crop fumigant in the 1880s to treat citrus trees in California. A cyanide-based compound, dithiocyanodiethyl ether, was the first synthetic insecticide, released in 1929 as a fly spray. There were also two early insecticides derived from natural plant compounds. Pyrethrum, found in chrysanthemums, and nicotine, from the tobacco plant, are effective neurotoxic insecticides that were recognized as such in the late 1700s.

After World War II synthetic insecticides, especially organochlorines, dominated the market. These compounds were persistent and soluble in lipids (fats) and often bioaccumulated in the food chain (became concentrated by living organisms). One of the first was DDT(dichlorodiphenyltrichloroethane), produced in 1939, which was extremely effective in killing insects at low doses by interfering with nerve transmission. It also caused eggshell thinning in birds, especially raptors, and was criticized by Rachel Carson in her book, *Silent Spring*. DDT has subsequently been banned in much of the world.

Most contemporary pesticides are either organophosphates or carbamates. Both types work by interfering with nerve transmission, essentially overstimulating the nervous system. These compounds do not bioaccumulate, and they biodegrade rapidly (are broken down into constituent compounds through the actions of living organisms). They have much higher acute toxicity than compounds like DDT, however. Development of new insecticides continues, and researchers are seeking other effective natural insecticides as an alternative to synthetic products.

Insecticide use in deserts poses special problems. When insecticides are applied in an arid or a semiarid region they often persist longer because many compounds break down via hydrolysis, which requires contact with water. Desert agriculture requires irrigation, and frequently insecticides are applied directly to irrigation canals. Insecticides can then be transported to streams or rivers where they can kill aquatic invertebrates and affect fish populations. There is also the possibility of the contamination of important groundwater sources through the leaching of insecticides into the soil.—Thomas E. Lacher, Jr.

See also **CLOUDS; CONSERVATION IN DESERTS; CONTAMINATION; ECOLOGY; ECOSYSTEM; FISHES; GROUNDWATER; IRRIGATION DRAINAGE; HABITAT DEGRADATION; HYDROLOGICAL CYCLE; HYDROLOGY; MIDDLE EAST, DESERTS OF; PESTICIDES; POLLUTION; WATER; WILDLIFE**

Further Reading

Brown, A. W. A. 1978. *Ecology of Pesticides*. New York: Wiley.

Moriarity, F. 1988. *Ecotoxicology: The Study of Pollutants in Ecosystems*. 2d ed. London: Academic Press.

Zakrzewski, S. F. 1991. *Principles of Environmental Toxicology*. Washington, D.C.: American Chemical Society.

INSECTS

Animals in the class Hexapoda (formerly called the Insecta). Hexapoda derives from *hexa* meaning six and *poda* meaning foot. Insects share the following characteristics: (1) a body with three distinct regions, head, thorax, and abdomen; (2) a head, usually with one pair of antennae, one pair of mandibles, one pair of maxillae, a hypopharynx, and a labium; (3) a thorax with three pairs of legs; (4) an abdomen with the gonopore located at the posterior end and, in most instances, no appendages for locomotion in adults.

Insects likely represent the most diverse group of animals on earth, with nearly a million described species and estimates that as many as 30 million may exist. Their taxonomic diversity is rivaled only by their ecological diversity. Insects can be found in nearly every microhabitat on earth with the possible exception of the oceans. Some insects live at the edge of seas, and larvae of a few flies actually live in seawater. For the most part, however, insects have simply not diversified in the oceans as they have in terrestrial and freshwater ecosystems. The evolutionary origins of insects date back at least 400 million years to the Devonian. The first insects were believed to be springtails (order Collembola). Phylogenetic relationships of insects remain controversial, and as a result, classifications vary depending on author, even at the ordinal level. Nevertheless, there is considerable agreement with respect to general relationships among insect groups.

Taxonomy and Diversity

There are currently 31 recognized orders of insects, most of which contain species living in deserts of the world. Most people recognize insect orders even though they may not know their names. These orders are described below.

Protura. Tiny, nondescript, white-colored insects that are associated with decomposing organic matter and fungus. The abdomen consists of nine segments, there are no eyes or antennae, and they have scraping mouthparts. The first pair of walking legs is raised off the ground and apparently function like antennae.

Collembola. Also called springtails, these insects have a forked structure distal to the abdomen that can be flicked, propelling the insects into the air (hence the name springtail). Springtails can be extremely common, are usually associated with decomposing organic matter, and are most often found in moist areas.

Diplura. Tiny larvaelike insects with two caudal filaments and retractable mandibulate mouthparts. These also are associated with damp microhabitats. They lack eyes.

Microcoryphia. Commonly known as bristletails, these brown, cylindrical insects have an arched thorax, compound eyes, and a bristlelike structure extending from the abdomen. Superficially they resemble silverfish. They are typically associated with crevices in wood or rocks, and they are nocturnal.

Thysanura. Known by most people as silverfish, these moderate-sized insects are silver in color, are flattened, and have three taillike appendages extending from the abdomen. Although some species are common in human habitations, others live in caves, mammal burrows, and even ant or termite nests. They feed on dead organic matter.

Ephemeroptera. These are the mayflies that are easily recognized by their frail bodies; long, thread-like tail filaments; and large, transparent, and triangular forewings that are held vertically above the body while at rest. Mayflies have aquatic larvae, so desert species are restricted to riparian habitats.

Odonata. Relatively large, fast-flying insects commonly known as damselflies and dragonflies. In deserts damselflies and dragonflies are usually associated with permanent water, including streams, rivers, lakes, and stock ponds. Adults are easily recognized by their four large wings and their ability to hover like helicopters and dart around with astonishing speed and agility. The larvae are aquatic. Both larvae and adults are predaceous. The larvae prey on other invertebrates, as well as on small fish and frog larvae, and the adults feed primarily on small flies. In many areas adult dragonflies are commonly called mosquito hawks because they capture small flying insects from the air.

Grylloblattaria. These strange, flattened, pale-colored insects are commonly known as rock crawlers. There are very few known species; none occurs in deserts, and all seem to be associated with cold places. They resemble early instars of some crickets but lack jumping legs.

Phasmida. These are the walkingsticks, a common name that accurately describes their morphology. Walkingsticks have elongate bodies, may or may not have wings, and have long, spindly legs. When not moving, they resemble twigs. They are herbivorous. Although often difficult to find because of their cryptic coloration and morphology, walkingsticks can occur in great numbers under the right climatic conditions.

Orthoptera. This large insect group contains crickets, grasshoppers, and katydids, in all of which the third pair of walking legs is enlarged and used for jumping. Depending on species, orthopterans may be winged or wingless, and some are good fliers. Mouthparts are designed for chewing. Most are herbivores, some are scavengers, and a few are omnivores. Orthopterans are very common in deserts, particularly grasshoppers in the family Acrididae (the locusts, lubbers, and spur-throated grasshoppers).

Mantodea. Commonly referred to as the mantises, these are elongate, slow-moving, predaceous insects that have the first pair of walking legs modified into grasping structures. When waiting for prey, mantises hold the front legs off the substrate in a folded and raised position, which has led to common names such as "praying" mantis. Although many tropical species are quite large with well-developed wings, species inhabiting deserts are usually smaller and with poorly developed wings.

Blattaria. These are the roaches, also known as cockroaches. These fast-running insects are flattened in morphology, the head is concealed from above by the pronotum, the antennae are long, and none of the legs is modified for digging or grasping. Although there are many species of roaches that live in deserts of the world, some of the more interesting ones are the molelike roaches in the family Polyphagidae, which have wingless females. The polyphagids spend most of their time burrowing in sand.

Isoptera. This order consists of the termites, which live in large social colonies and feed on cellulose. Termites in the family Termitidae are particularly diverse and common in deserts. Social colonies of termites are composed of castes that perform very different functions within the colony. These include reproductives, workers, and soldiers.

Reproductives consist of males and females that are initially winged and may disperse. Workers take care of young, feed the reproductives and soldiers, and construct and maintain the nest. Soldiers defend the nest from potential predators, among the most important being ants. Soldiers of many termites have large mandibles that form scissorslike jaws. Others have an elongate, pointed head with an opening at the terminus of the structure. These soldiers spray chemicals at invaders that either entangle or repel them.

Dermaptera. These are the earwigs, which is a misnomer: earwigs do not enter the ears of humans, at least on their own. Earwigs are slender, elongate insects with appendages at the distal end of the abdomen that resemble forceps. The shortened front wings appear as wing covers, and the hind wings are folded under the front wings. Earwigs have extended parental care, with females attending their nest of eggs. In deserts earwigs are nocturnal and tend to occur under surface debris during the day.

Embiidina. The web-spinners, a small group of tiny insects that occurs primarily in tropical and subtropical environments, live in webs that they spin in crevices. They feed primarily on dead plant material.

Plecoptera. These are the stoneflies, few species of which enter deserts. When they do it is only along relatively permanent streams. Stoneflies have four membranous wings that are folded over the back in a flat position while at rest. Stoneflies are poor fliers, and the adults do not wander far from water. The larvae live on surfaces under the water.

Zoraptera. These small, termitelike insects have no common name. They are typically darker colored than termites and live in smaller groups. Usually associated with rotting wood, zorapterans typically do not live in deserts.

Psocoptera. As a group these insects have no common name. Because the wingless forms are licelike in appearance, they are often called barklice and book-lice. The winged forms superficially resemble aphids, holding the wings in a tentlike fashion over the body. In deserts psocopterans are most common in leaf litter or within the root region (rhizosphere) of plants, an area rich in microorganisms.

Pthiraptera. These wingless ectoparasites of mammals and birds are commonly known as lice.

There are two suborders, the Mallophaga, or chewing lice, and the Anoplura, or sucking lice. These are found on many of the mammals and birds that inhabit deserts of the world.

Hemiptera. The "true" bugs are insects with thickened, leathery front wings having a membranous apex (called hemelytra) and completely membranous hind wings. The wings are held flat against the dorsal surface of the abdomen except during flight. Mouthparts are of the piercing-sucking type, and there is great diversity in feeding habits of the Hemiptera. Hemipterans are very common and diverse in deserts. Many, such as those in the family Pentatomidae (stinkbugs), live on plants, whereas others, such as the Reduviidae (assassin bugs), are predaceous, feeding on a variety of other insects and spiders. Many species of true bugs inhabit both temporary and permanent water in deserts.

Homoptera. A diverse group including aphids, cicadas (e.g., 17-year locusts), leafhoppers, planthoppers, and scale insects. Although very similar to true bugs, the sucking mouthparts of the Homoptera originate from the rear of the head rather than the front as in true bugs. Homopterans feed exclusively on plant materials and can be serious pests. Leafhoppers, planthoppers, and cicadas are very common in deserts. The loud buzzing heard during summer months is the call of the cicada.

Thysanoptera. Commonly called thrips, winged forms of these tiny, slender-bodied insects have four narrow wings fringed with long hairs and little or no membranes. They feed on plants. These tiny insects are common on desert grasses and desert shrubs.

Neuroptera. A diverse group of winged insects, including antlions, alderflies, lacewings, dobsonflies, snakeflies, and owlflies. Adults of these soft-bodied insects have four membranous wings usually held rooflike over the body while at rest. Although some superficially resemble damselflies, they are relatively poor fliers and never hold the wings vertically over the body as damselflies do. Most have predaceous larvae and adults, and some are very common in deserts. Antlions in the subfamily Myrmeleontinae in particular can be observed easily in most deserts. Adults will fly to lights at night, and the larvae, called doodlebugs or antlions, can readily be found by searching sandy areas—particularly those just under the edge of a rock overhang or under the canopy of a plant—for the funnellike pits they construct to trap insects, especially ants. The larvae remain at the apex of the pit, and when an insect falls into it, the larva throws sand at the insect with flicks of its head and thorax, causing the prey to fall to the bottom of the pit. The larvae then grasps the prey with its elongate mandibles and pulls it under the sand. Depending on family, larvae of other neuropterans may be terrestrial, arboreal, or even aquatic.

Coleoptera. These are the beetles, a highly diverse group of insects containing about 40 percent of known insect species. Most beetles are easily recognized by the thickened front wings (elytra) that meet at the midline of the back and cover the abdomen. The rear wings remain folded under the elytra except during flight. Mouthparts are typically designed for chewing but are modified in some for prey capture. Many feed on plant material, including seeds, whereas others are predaceous. Beetles are found in nearly every microhabitat available in deserts, with some species even occurring in the most barren sand dunes.

Strepsiptera. This is a relatively small group of insects known as the twisted-wing parasites. Strepsipterans are parasitic on other insects; males are free-living and have wings, whereas females are wingless and often legless and live only on other insects. Larvae live in the bodies of their hosts, metamorphose, and, depending on the sex, either leave the host (males) or remain on the surface of the host (females) to produce eggs.

Mecoptera. The scorpionflies, a rather strange-looking group of insects with four wings of nearly equal size held vertically above the body and a head with an elongate beaklike structure. The genital segment of the abdomen is turned up, pointed, and bulbous, similar to the sting of a scorpion, hence the name scorpionfly. These appear to be relatively rare in deserts.

Siphonoptera. These are the fleas, small, parasitic insects with the body laterally flattened and containing numerous spinelike structures and bristles directed backward. As in other habitats of the world, desert fleas live on desert mammals and birds.

Diptera. This order is composed of the flies, another extremely diverse insect group, both taxonomically and ecologically. Flies have only one pair of wings (front); the rear wings have been reduced to a small, knobbed structure called the halteres.

The front wings are used for flight, and the halteres are used for equilibrium. Flies are very diverse in deserts and easily observable. Some of the more obvious ones are the robber flies (family Asilidae), which are predaceous on other insects, usually capturing them while flying. They frequently capture insects as large or larger than they are. Flower flies (family Syrphidae) are usually conspicuous around flowers, where they hover, helicopterlike, changing position frequently with rapid bursts. These can often be found by the thousands at rest during hot times of day under the edges of cliffs or under overpasses constructed in deserts.

Trichoptera. Insects known as caddisflies, the adults of which are soft-bodied, feeble fliers that hold their wings above the body in a tentlike manner when not flying. The larvae are aquatic and cover themselves with a tubelike structure constructed of rocks, sticks, or other debris. In deserts these are restricted to riparian areas, usually where there is permanent water.

Lepidoptera. These are the butterflies and moths, most easily distinguished from other insects by the large wings covered with tiny scales. They typically have sucking mouthparts and well-developed compound eyes. Most butterflies are diurnal and hold the wings vertically above the body while at rest; most moths are nocturnal and hold the wings over the abdomen in a tentlike manner. Common in deserts, butterflies and moths are usually associated with flowers.

Hymenoptera. This is a large group of insects that includes bees, wasps, ants, parasitic wasps, and sawflies. Easily distinguished from flies, hymenopterans have four membranous wings (when present), with the front wings larger than the rear ones. Hymenopterans are diverse and common in deserts. Some are predaceous on spiders and other insects (e.g., families Specidae and Pompilidae), some are parasitic on larvae and pupae of wasps and bees (e.g., family Mutilidae, the velvet ants), and others form large social colonies (e.g., Apidae, Formicidae, Vespidae).

Life Histories

Life histories of insects vary depending on the group. In some there is no larval form: eggs hatch and the juvenile insects appear similar to the adults but wingless. Their development is called simple metamorphosis. In others the immature stages are drastically different from the adult (e.g., caterpillars of butterflies), there is a pupa stage, and the pupa transforms into a winged adult. This is called complete metamorphosis. There are also some intermediate forms of metamorphosis. In all types of life histories, the insects pass through a series of molts in which the exoskeleton is shed and replaced by a new one from underneath, and the insect either increases in size or changes body form. The period between each molt is called an instar. Also, depending on the insect group, larvae (when present) differ considerably. Eruciform larvae are those that are caterpillarlike, having a cylindrical body with both thoracic legs and prolegs on the abdomen. Scarabaeiform larvae are grublike, with a curved body and no abdominal prolegs. Campodeiform larvae are elongate and flattened with thoracic legs and are relatively active. Elateriform larvae, also called wireworms, are stiff, elongate, and cylindrical; the legs are very short, and the exoskeleton is thick. Vermiform larvae are maggotlike, lacking legs and a well-defined head.—Laurie J. Vitt

See also **ANIMAL ADAPTATIONS; ANTS; ANTLIONS; ARTHROPODS; BAGWORMS; BEES; BEETLES; BREEDING SEASON; BUGS; BUTTERFLIES; CATERPILLARS; CICADA; CRYPSIS; DECOMPOSITION; DEFENSIVE ADAPTATIONS, ANIMALS; DORMANCY; EARWIGS; FLIES; FLOWERS; GRASSHOPPERS; HAWKMOTH; HYMENOPTERA; LIFE HISTORY STRATEGY (ITEROPARITY); LOCUSTS; METAMORPHOSIS; MOSQUITOES; MOTHS; POISONOUS ANIMALS; POLLINATION; TENEBRIONIDAE; TERMITES; VELVET ANT; VENOM; WARNING COLORATION; WASPS**

Further Reading

Borror, D. J., C. A. Triplehorn, and N. F. Johnson. 1992. *An Introduction to the Study of Insects.* New York: Harcourt Brace.

Borror, D. J., and R. E. White. 1970. *A Field Guide to the Insects.* Boston: Houghton Mifflin.

CSIRO. 1986. *The Insects of Australia.* Melbourne: Melbourne University Press.

Daly, H. V., J. T. Doyen, and P. R. Ehrlich. 1978. *Introduction to Insect Biology and Diversity.* New York: McGraw-Hill.

Huffaker, C. B., and R. L. Rabb. 1984. *Ecological Entomology.* New York: Wiley.

Polis, G. A., ed. 1991. *The Ecology of Desert Communities.* Tucson: University of Arizona Press.

Price, P. W. 1984. *Insect Ecology.* 2d ed. New York: Wiley.

Seeley, M. K. 1991. Sand dune communities. *In* G. A. Polis, ed., *The Ecology of Desert Communities*, 348–382. Tucson: University of Arizona Press.

Tauber, M. J., and C. A. Tauber. 1986. *Seasonal Adaptations of Insects.* New York: Oxford University Press.

Wilson, E. O. 1971. *The Insect Societies.* Cambridge, Mass.: Harvard University Press.

Wisdom, C. S. 1991. Patterns of heterogeneity in desert herbivorous insect communities. *In* G. A. Polis, ed., *The Ecology of Desert Communities*, 151–179. Tucson: University of Arizona Press.

Isolated rock inselberg (kopje) in the Namib Desert near Gobabeb, Namibia. (Photo: M. A. Mares)

INSELBERG

Isolated hill that rises abruptly from the surrounding terrain in arid and semiarid regions. Inselbergs are of two major types: "boulder inselbergs," also referred to as tors, koppies (kopje), or nubbins; and "domed inselbergs," also known as bornhardts. The term is also sometimes used to denote any isolated, erosional remnant of a mountain or mountain range, without distinction as to process. Their formation most likely involves a combination of parallel mountain front retreat and subsurface fracture-controlled weathering and erosion.

Boulder inselbergs form either in heavily jointed substrate (most commonly granite) or from the extensive weathering of the larger domed inselbergs. Subsurface weathering along joints and fractures results in the formation of corestones (unweathered rock surrounded by weathered debris), which often end up stacked on each other as weathering and erosion removes the overlying materials, thus resulting in the formation of a boulder inselberg. This process is believed to be extremely slow, requiring long periods of subsurface weathering and the eventual stripping of the overlying materials. Some boulder inselbergs are thought to be 30 million–40 million years old.

Domed inselbergs form in more sparsely jointed lithologies (types of rocks) than the surrounding bedrock. The widely spaced joints prevent weathering in the area of the future inselberg, while weathering of the highly jointed surroundings proceeds at a much faster rate. The result is a massive, isolated domed hill once the surrounding weathered material has been removed by weathering, mass movement, and fluvial (related to water) processes. As with boulder inselbergs, domed inselbergs, or bornhardts, typically form in granitic bedrock, although they are also common in other lithological units, such as gneiss (a type of metamorphic rock that shows a banded or foliated structure), conglomerate, and sandstone. Examples are Ayers Rock and the Olgas in Australia, composed of coarse sandstone (arkose) and conglomerate, respectively. The steep slopes associated with bornhardts are the result of exfoliation or unloading. Domed inselberg surfaces also display a variety of cavernous weathering features, such as tafoni (cavernous hollows produced on rock faces, most likely by weathering and wind abrasion), pits (very small weathering hollows on a rock), and rills (small channels a few centimeters wide which act as a conduit for water and sediments on slopes).—Vatche P. Tchakerian

See also **CAATINGA; CAVY; KOPJE; HYRAX; LANDSCAPE; NAMIBIA, DESERTS OF; SOUTH AFRICA, DESERTS OF**

Further Reading

Twidale, C. R. 1982. The evolution of bornhardts. *American Journal of Science* 70:268–276.

Twidale, C. R. and E. M. Campbell. 1993. *Australian Landforms*. Adelaide: Gleneagles.

INSOLATION

Term used to identify the amount of solar radiation reaching the surface of the earth. This may be direct radiation transmitted through the atmosphere to the surface of the earth without interacting with other components of the atmosphere. However, it may also be diffuse insolation, which is the solar radiation that is absorbed or reflected by atmospheric components such as clouds and particulate matter in the atmosphere before it reaches the earth. Actinometry is the science of measuring radiant energy, particularly from the sun, and an actinometer is the apparatus used to measure radiant energy coming from the sun.—Federico Norte

See also **AN INTRODUCTION TO DESERTS; CLIMATE; CLIMATE CLASSIFICATION; DESERTS, HOT; HEAT**

Further Reading

Day, J. A., and V. J. Schaefer. 1991. *Clouds and Weather.* Boston: Houghton Mifflin.

Oliver, J. E., and R. W. Fairbridge, eds. 1987. *The Encyclopedia of Climatology.* New York: Chapman and Hall.

Schaefer, V. J., and J. A. Day. 1981. *A Field Guide to the Atmosphere.* Boston: Houghton Mifflin.

Schneider, S. H., ed. 1996. *Encyclopedia of Climate and Weather.* 2 vols. New York: Oxford University Press.

INSULATION

Material that retards the flow of heat. Heat diffuses along a gradient from warm areas to cool areas. By placing an insulating material between a heat source and a heat sink, the rate of this diffusion can be slowed.

Biologically, insulation helps animals reduce the energy needed for heating or cooling. Normally insulation is viewed as separating a warm object (e.g., a person) from a cool environment (e.g., cold air). In this case the insulation could be the insulation in a home or a coat. Similarly, the opposite use for insulation is equally important, protecting a cool object from a warm environment (e.g., a person's hand from a hot baking pan). Here the insulation would be an oven mitt or pot holder. In deserts insulation can serve both of these purposes. During the evening hours, which are often quite cool in deserts, even in summer, an animal may experience conditions that require it to be insulated from the cool environment to conserve energy that it would otherwise have to use to warm itself. During daylight hours the same animal might need to insulate itself from a hot environment to conserve energy that it would otherwise have to expend to cool itself. This situation is analogous to the need to air-condition a home in summer and heat it in winter; both require a significant expenditure of energy.

Heat diffuses in two ways that are of concern for desert animals. The first is by conduction. When a cooler object comes into contact with a warmer one, the heat contained in the warmer object can transfer to the cooler object. Many species of desert animals have become adapted so that their feet or other body parts that come in contact with the hot desert ground are covered with insulating hair or pads. This use of insulation reduces the heat transferred to the animal by conduction.

The second method of heat transfer of concern for desert animals is radiation. Radiation is important both for how it can increase the heat of the animal and for how it can cool the animal, depending on initial conditions. The heat radiated by the sun that can be absorbed by the animal is an important potential source for excess heat. However, one of the most efficient ways for animals to rid their bodies of excess heat is to radiate it back into the environment.

Some animals are adapted to reflect external sources of radiation or to maximize their ability to radiate excess body heat, or have developed a compromise between both strategies. Camels and some species of sheep use a heavy coat of hair or wool to insulate themselves from radiated heat and have difficulty regulating their body temperature if shorn. The temperature of a camel's coat may reach 70°C while its body temperature remains at 40°C. The black-tailed jackrabbit; (*Lepus californicus*) has a light coat and relies on shade to limit its absorption of radiated heat, but it is also able to radiate its excess body heat through its large well-veined ears, a strategy similar to that of the African elephant. The wild ass; (*Equus asinus*) has a thin yet effectively insulating coat on its back and a sparse coat on its lower sides and underside. The coat on the back of the ass insulates it from radiated heat, and its large ears and relatively naked underside allow it to radiate excess body heat back to the environment. The light colors of the coats of desert animals are characteristic of insulation that blocks radiated heat while also likely conferring protection from predators by making the animals more closely match the light-colored desert surroundings.—Rob Channell

See also **ACTIVITY CYCLES, ANIMALS; ANIMAL ADAPTATIONS; ASS; BODY TEMPERATURE; BURROWING ANIMALS; CLOTHING; COUNTERCURRENT HEAT EXCHANGE; DEHYDRATION; DESICCATION; ECTOTHERMY; ENDOTHERMY; ESTIVATION; EXCRETORY SYSTEM; EXPLOSIVE HEAT DEATH; FEATHERS; GREAT BASIN DESERT; HEAT BALANCE; HEAT EXCHANGE; HEAT STRESS; HEATSTROKE; HIBERNATION; HUMAN PHYSIOLOGY IN DESERTS; HYPERTHERMIA; HYPOTHERMIA; KIDNEY FUNCTION, DESERT RODENTS; KIDNEYS;**

METABOLISM; PERSPIRATION; PHYSIOLOGY; PINNAE; RENAL PAPILLA; RESPIRATORY WATER LOSS; SALT BALANCE; SHIVERING; SUNSTROKE; SURVIVAL IN DESERTS; SWEAT GLANDS; THERMOREGULATION; TORPOR; TRANSPIRATION; VAN'T HOFF EFFECT; WATER BALANCE; WATER STRESS

Further Reading

Allan, T., and A. Warren, eds. 1993. *Deserts: The Encroaching Wilderness*. New York: Oxford University Press.

Schmidt-Nielsen, K. 1964. *Desert Animals: Physiological Problems of Heat and Water*. New York: Oxford University Press.

INTERGLACIALS

Periods of relative warmth and glacial retreat that alternate with cold periods (glacials or glacial advances) during an ice age. During the approximately three million years of the last (and ongoing) ice age, and extending from the end of the Tertiary throughout the Quaternary period, there have been a number of interglacials. The last was relatively short, lasting only about 10,000 years. By contrast, the last glacial period lasted about 110,000 years.

Although the earth is currently experiencing an interglacial, the overall ice age persists: about 27 million cubic kilometers of ice still blanket the Arctic regions. Of this, most, about 25 million cubic kilometers, covers Antarctica and the adjacent seas; more than 2 million cubic kilometers cover Greenland and other areas in the Arctic. Were all the ice on earth to melt, global sea level would rise by more than 60 meters, flooding coastal areas where many of the world's major cities are located.

When the earth is glaciated at high latitudes, periglacial and midlatitude continental regions seem to experience pluvial (relatively high rainfall) conditions, while at the same time low-latitude regions experience aridification. The reverse is true during interglacials; that is, when high-latitude ice sheets retreat, midlatitude deserts expand and low-latitude deserts may experience greater rainfall. For example, during the last glacial maximum, pluvial conditions in southwestern North America allowed widespread woodlands to grow at low elevations. These woodlands were dominated by pygmy conifers (e.g., *Juniperus*, *Pinus*) but also included oaks (*Quercus*) and succulents (e.g., cacti, *Agave*). During the present interglacial, the same region is occupied by drier Mojave, Sonoran, and Chihuahuan desert vegetation. However, in the subtropical and tropical latitudes of North Africa, the last glacial maximum caused expansion of the Sahara Desert (greater in size than the huge Sahara Desert of today) into what is now the Sahel. Correspondingly, several of the late Pleistocene interglacials and the early Holocene interglacial brought increased precipitation and paleolake-forming episodes to the Sahara Desert.

Climatic perturbations such as ice ages are coincident with cycles of variations in the geometry of the earth's orbit. These climatic perturbations are often linked to major steps in the evolution of diverse kinds of living organisms, including humans. Some scientists have suggested that even the evolution of civilization is due to the glacial advances and retreats of the last ice age. Anthropogenic (human-influenced) phenomena, in turn, effect further perturbations of climate and enhancements of extinction and evolution.—Nicholas J. Czaplewski

See also **CLIMATE; FOSSILS; GLACIAL PERIODS; MADRO-TERTIARY GEOFLORA; MIDDEN; PALEOCLIMATE; PLEISTOCENE; PLIOCENE; QUATERNARY; RECENT (HOLOCENE); SAHARA DESERT**

Further Reading

Clark, P. U., and P. D. Lea, eds. 1992. *The Last Interglacial-Glacial Transition in North America.* Boulder, Colo.: Geological Society of America.

Frakes, L. A., J. E. Francis, and J. I. Syktus, eds. 1992. *Climate Modes of the Phanerozoic: The History of the Earth's Climate over the Past 600 Million Years.* Cambridge: Cambridge University Press.

Spaulding, W. G., and L. J. Graumlich. 1986. The last pluvial climatic episodes in the deserts of southwestern North America. *Nature* 320:441–444.

Vogel, J. C., ed. 1984. *Late Cainozoic Palaeoclimates of the Southern Hemisphere.* Rotterdam: A. A. Balkema.

Vrba, E., G. Denton, L. Burckle, and T. Partridge, eds. 1996. *Paleoclimate and Evolution with Emphasis on Human Origins.* New Haven, Conn.: Yale University Press.

INTERNATIONAL BIOLOGICAL PROGRAM

International research program conceived in the 1960s in response to the need for coordinated international cooperation in various aspects of biology and partly as a successor to the International Geophysical Year. The International Biological Program (IBP) was originally developed by the International Council of Scientific Unions (ICSU) in 1966 and was to be a five-year nongovernmental research program ending in 1972. More than 70 countries ultimately participated to various degrees in the IBP; the information obtained through this massive effort has proven invaluable in understanding various biological phenomena.

In the United States the IBP was sponsored by the National Academy of Sciences, and major funding was through the National Science Foundation. The U.S.-IBP program focused primarily on productivity of freshwater and terrestrial communities, with particular emphasis on the Analysis of Ecosystems (AOE) subprogram. In the AOE there were plans for detailed studies on six biomes: grassland, tundra, deciduous forests, coniferous forests, tropical forests, and deserts. Specific objectives of the AOE program were to study (1) productivity and its utilization within each biome; (2) nutrient-cycling patterns, with emphasis on decomposition processes; (3) pollution and disturbances that might affect the composition and production of ecosystems; and (4) methods for incorporating collected data into systems simulation and other statistical models.

The IBP sponsored an extensive comparative study of the Sonoran Desert of North America and the Monte Desert of Argentina. This Structure of Ecosystems subprogram resulted in extensive research in these two disparate, but apparently similar, desert ecosystems. The research attempted to quantify whether or not similar ecosystems developed in regions of generally similar climates, even if their floras and faunas and their histories were different. Results suggested that convergent evolution was pronounced at some levels and hardly noticeable at others. In general, however, there was an overall similarity in form and function among plants and animals that evolved in the two deserts, suggesting that there are functional and morphological constraints placed on organisms that adapt to very dry conditions.

The legacy of the International Biological Program is in its multidisciplinary approach to studying whole ecosystems. Ecologists, chemists, statisticians, geologists, climatologists, mathematicians, systematists, and other scientists were engaged in a coordinated effort to grasp the intricate workings of nature. The IBP formally ended in 1974, but the knowledge gained from this significant scientific program continues to influence the understanding of the environment.—Gary K. Hulett and Amanda Renner Charles

See also **BIOME; CHIHUAHUAN DESERT; ECOLOGY; ECOSYSTEM; ENERGY FLOW; DESERT GRASS-LAND; LANDSCAPE; MONTE DESERT; SONORAN DESERT; SOUTH AMERICA, DESERTS OF; UNITED STATES, DESERTS OF**

Further Reading

Blair, W. F. 1977. *Big Biology.* Stroudsburg, Pa.: Dowden, Hutchinson, and Ross.

Golley, F. B. 1993. *A History of the Ecosystem Concept in Ecology.* New Haven, Conn.: Yale University Press.

IRAN, DESERTS OF

Arid region occurring mainly within the geographic limits of Iran and extending into neighboring Afghanistan. Most of Iran is situated on the Irano-Afghanistan Plateau occupying an overall area of about 1,648,000 square kilometers. The country possesses many features that contribute to its geomorphological identity. The Elburz-Kopt Dagh mountain ranges in the north, the northwest to southeast orientation of the Zagros Mountains in the west, and the Makran ridges in the southeast lend Iran a special character. The central plateau is spread over scattered chains of low mountains, intermittent calcareous plains, closed undrained valleys, medium to coarse sand deposits, gently sloping river basin, highly saline depressions of solonchak deserts (enclosed depressions in which salts accumulate), sand dunes, and areas of shifting sand. Elevation of the solonchak desert is about 1,300 meters. Mean monthly winter temperature across the desert portions of the country range from 1°C to 6°C, and mean monthly summer temperatures range from 28°C to 32°C. Hence this desert has cold winters and warm to hot summers. Annual precipitation ranges from 50 to 120 millimeters, except in the foothills of the Elburz and Zagros mountains where it ranges from 350 to 800 millimeters or more. (See map of central Asian deserts, p. 292.)

Brief descriptions of some major Iranian deserts follow. (Note that *dusht* is a Persian translation of the English word meaning "desert.")

The Dusht-e-Kavir Desert (also Dasht-e-Kavir Desert) is part of the central plateau situated in northwestern Iran where the southern slopes of the Elburz and Khorasan mountains level off and enter

Iran desert habitat in the Dasht-e-Kavir with the 400-year-old caravanserai Ein-ol-Rashid in the background, Kavir Protected Region, north central Iran. (Photo: M. A. Mares)

an alluvial gravelly plain forming a flat depression. The lowest elevation in this desert is about 800 meters. The area is characterized by the presence of hamadas (pebbly steppes), kavirs (salt deserts), and sand dunes. The mountain ridge and basin system is intercepted by shallow sandy-clayey wadis (valleys or arroyos) and salt beds. Gray-colored calcareous soil occurs over almost all of the desert. There are crusted, puffed solonchaks in the central portion, which is the lowest elevation in the desert. Sand dunes accompanied by shifting sand are found in the northern part of the desert.

The Dusht-e-Lut Desert (also Dasht-e-Lut Desert) is a hyperarid region of mostly empty gravelly and sandy desert extending south and southeast from the southern fringe of the Dusht-e-Kavir for about 1,100 kilometers. The geomorphology of the area consists of folded mountain ranges, parallel ridges of weathered limestone, enclosed basins with indurated (hard) crusts, riverbeds and deltas, rocky foothills extending into the plains, sand ridges, and pyramidal dunes and shifting loose sand. Many rivers in this region dry up in summer and terminate in blind deltas filled with pebbles and sand. Strong northern and northwestern winds blow sand masses southward, thus forming a brachen chain (an arm-like spreading of sand dunes, like the rays of a starfish). Major dunes are situated in the southern parts of this desert, giving an impression of a solidified sand sea complete with waves 10–15 meters high. The Dasht-e-Naumid is another clayey-pebbly and solonchak desert extending into the Makran Hills (elevation 450–1,000 meters) located in an intermountain depression.

The coastal belt and the inland plateau adjacent to Pakistan are composed of several rows of sandy hills intercepted with sandy-clayey lowlands, dry riverbeds, loose sand dunes, and salt lakes. This topography extends to the Kharan Desert and coastal belt of Pakistan. Irano-Turan elements (subtropical, extremely arid continental climate with low precipitation, hot dry summers, and cold harsh winters) are responsible for the bulk of the natural vegetation in Iran; these elements are also found in Kirgizistan, Tadzhikistan, Turkmenistan, Iraq, and Afghanistan.

The flora of the Afghano-Iranian sector of the central plateau is fairly well known. Dominant plants along the southern foothills of the Elbur and Khurasan mountains are *Artemisia herba-alba, Stipa hohenackeriana, Stachys inflata, Convolvulus chondrilloides, Astragalus glaucanthus, Pteropyrum olivieri, Echinophora plalyloba, Dianthus tabrisianus, Bromus danthoniae, Zygophyllum atriplicoides,* and *Peganum harmala.* Vegetation on loesslike soil surfaces covered with pebbles and coarse gravel includes *Artemisia herba-alba, Stellora lessertii, Astraglus glaueacanthus, Launaea acanthodes,* and *Stipa hohenackeriana.* The dominant plants of the alluvial plains of gray pebbly soil (hamada plains) are *Ephedra intermedio, Artemisia herba-alba, Buffonia oliveriana, Stachys infflata, Euphorbia cannata,* and *Zygophyllum atriplicoides.* The *Artemisia herba-alba—Zygophyllum atriplicoides* association is one of the most common in southern Iran. Plants of higher elevations (including subalpine areas) are *Artemisia herba-alba, Daphne angustifolia, Astragalus jubatus, Herlia intermedia, Amygdalus harride, Convolvulus kermanesis,* and *Rheum ribes. Pistacia altantica* and (rarely) *Pistacia khinjuk* are widely distributed across the desert on some plants of the central plateau. *Holocnemum strobilaceum* is the most common halophytic species of the Great Kavir Desert.—Rafiq Ahmad

See also **AN INTRODUCTION TO DESERTS; ASIA, DESERTS OF; BIRDS; CHENOPODIACEAE; CLIMATE; CONSERVATION IN DESERTS; DESERTIFICATION; GAZELLE; INDUS RIVER; IRRIGATION DRAINAGE; KAVIR; LIZARDS; PLANTS; PLAYA; REPTILES; SABKHA; SALT; SALT PAN; STONE PAVEMENT**

Further Reading

Breckle, S. W. 1983. The temperate deserts and semi-deserts of Afghanistan and Iran. *In* N. E. West, ed., *Ecosystems of the World: Temperate Deserts and Semi-deserts,* 5:271–319. New York: Elsevier.

McGinnies, W. G., B. J. Goldman, and P. Paylore, eds. 1968. *Deserts of the World: An Appraisal of Research into Their Physical and Biological Environments.* Tucson: University of Arizona Press.

Petrov. M. P. 1976. *Deserts of the World.* New York: Wiley.

Walter, H. 1983. *Vegetation of the Earth.* Berlin: Springer.

Zohary, M. 1963. *On the Geobotanical Structure of Iran.* Research Council of Israel. Vol. 11D. Supplement, sec. D, Botany. Jerusalem: Weizman Science Press.

IRAQ, DESERTS OF. *See* MIDDLE EAST, DESERTS OF

IRONWOOD

Characteristic tree, *Olneya tesota,* of the Sonoran Desert named for its very hard, dense wood. Ironwood (*palofierro* or *palo de hierro* in Mexico) grows 5–10 meters tall, with a wide crown and spiny branches. The bluish or grayish leaves are pinnate with 2–12 pairs of leaflets. The leaves are essentially evergreen except after severe drought or frost. The beautiful lavender flowers in short racemes often appear concurrently with the new leaves. The pods are glandular pubescent, two to seven centimeters long, each with one seed (more rarely up to six). Individual trees do not reproduce every year.

Ironwood occurs in the Lower Sonoran Zone of the Sonoran Desert in Arizona, California, Sonora, and Baja California, from sea level to 800 meters. It grows in sandy, silty, or gravelly soils of washes, canyons, and foothills.

Many ironwoods are infested by mistletoe, which causes large swellings and stunted growth. The leaves are browsed by bighorn sheep and horses, and the seeds are harvested by rodents. Ironwood also serves as a nesting site for a few desert birds.

Ironwood is restricted to warm areas, rendering it useful as an indicator of sites suitable for citrus groves. The wood is used for firewood, and by Indians for arrowheads, tool handles, and carvings (made famous by the Seris). Roasted seeds are eaten by the Pima Indians. Juice of this tree is used by the Seri Indians for intestinal parasites and muscular spasms.

Olneya tesota is distinct from Catalina ironwood, an unrelated species of *Lyonothamnus* in the rose family.—Kristina A. Ernest

See also **ARIZONA DESERT; BAJA CALIFORNIA, DESERTS OF; CALIFORNIA DESERT; LEGUMES; SONORAN DESERT**

Further Reading

Benson, L., and R. A. Darrow. 1981. *Trees and Shrubs of the Southwestern Deserts*. Tucson: University of Arizona Press.

Kearney, T. H., and R. H. Peebles. 1960. *Arizona Flora*. Berkeley: University of California Press.

Shreve, F., and I. L. Wiggins. 1964. *Vegetation and Flora of the Sonoran Desert*. Vols. 1 and 2. Stanford: Stanford University Press.

IRRIGATION DRAINAGE

Process of applying water to crops, usually through a system of aqueducts, such as canals, that move the water from its source to the point at which it will be used; also the process of dealing with problems that develop when water is applied to croplands. Irrigation is essential to support agricultural production in most arid regions of the world. Intensive irrigation places high demands on available water supplies and may lead to the production of drainage water that is toxic to fish and wildlife. The lifeline of scarce but important wetlands present in arid regions is cut when ground and surface water is removed for agricultural use. In the western United States major losses of native wetlands have occurred due to agricultural irrigation.

Agricultural irrigation practices commonly use water applications that total about 60–80 centimeters during the growing season. This is several times greater than the natural precipitation, and two types of wastewater can be produced in the process: surface runoff and subsurface drainage. Surface runoff, also known as irrigation tailwater, occurs because of operational spillage as water is pumped into canals or pipelines for distribution to fields, or because application rates exceed infiltration rates of the soil. This water can contain high concentrations of pesticides and herbicides if aerial spraying is being done, or if recent land-based applications of these materials have occurred. Shortages of water during the 1985–1992 drought in the United States, coupled with increasing demands for water by other economic sectors, led to on-farm conservation measures that curtailed much of the surface runoff in the western United States, particularly in California.

The other type of irrigation wastewater, subsurface drainage, results from a specific set of soil conditions and cannot be eliminated through water conservation. Shallow (3–10 meters) subsurface clay lenses, or layers, impede the vertical and lateral movement of irrigation water as it percolates downward. This causes waterlogging of the crop root zone and subsequent buildup of salts as excess water evaporates from the soil surface. The accumulated subsurface water must be removed in order for crop production to continue.

Several methods of removing excess shallow groundwater were attempted in the mid- to late 1800s, including the use of wells and surface canals to pump and drain the water away. The method of choice became the installation of permeable clay pipes spaced three to seven meters apart and two to three meters below the surface. Once these drains were in place, irrigation water could be applied liberally, thus satisfying the needs of crops and also flushing away excess salts. More recently perforated plastic pipe has replaced earthen clay tile as the conduit in agricultural drainage collector systems. The resultant subsurface wastewater is pumped or allowed to drain into surface canals and ditches and is eventually discharged into ponds for evaporative disposal, or into creeks and sloughs that are tributaries to major streams and rivers.

Subsurface irrigation drainage is characterized by alkaline pH, elevated concentrations of salts, trace elements, nitrogenous compounds, and low concentrations of pesticides. The conspicuous absence of pesticides may seem to be unusual as surface runoff can contain high concentrations of these chemicals. However, the conditions responsible for producing subsurface drainwater also result in the removal of these potentially toxic compounds. The natural biological and chemical filter provided by the soil effectively degrades and removes pesticides as irrigation water percolates downward to form subsurface drainage. At the same time naturally occurring trace elements in the soil, such as selenium and boron, are leached out under the alkaline, oxidizing conditions prevalent in arid climates and are carried in solution in the drainwater.

When subsurface irrigation drainage is discharged into surface waters, a variety of serious impacts can occur. The immediate impact is degradation of surface water and groundwater quality through salinization and contamination with toxic or potentially toxic trace elements (e.g., arsenic, boron, chromium, molybdenum, selenium). This water quality degradation can in turn affect irrigation, livestock watering, industrial processing, recreational use, and drinking water supplies. Human health warnings not to eat contaminated waterfowl and fish have been issued in some drainwater-affected areas.

Elevated concentrations of trace elements in irrigation drainage can severely affect wetlands and their fish and wildlife populations. Many of these wetlands are closed aquatic systems with no outflow, formed at the terminus of the drainage. Such closed-basin systems are particularly susceptible to water quality degradation. With no outlet, incoming contaminants are effectively trapped and accumulated; the exposure of fish and wildlife is thereby maximized. The arid climate also contributes to water quality problems. Contaminants and salts can become concentrated as large quantities of water evaporate. Thus inflows carrying low concentrations of contaminants may become toxic as evaporative losses occur.

In 1985 subsurface irrigation drainage was implicated as the cause of death and deformities in thousands of waterfowl and shorebirds at Kesterson National Wildlife Refuge in California. Naturally occurring trace elements and salts were leached from soils on the west side of the San Joaquin Valley and carried to the wildlife refuge in irrigation return flows that were used for wetland management. One of the trace elements, selenium, bioaccumulated in aquatic food chains and contaminated 500 hectares of shallow marshes. Elevated selenium was found in every animal group coming into contact with these wetlands—from fish and birds to insects, frogs, snakes, and mammals. Selenium caused reproductive failure and congenital malformations in young waterbirds and fish. Some of these deformities were severe, for example, missing eyes and feet, protruding brains, and grossly deformed spines, beaks, legs, and wings. Several species of fish were eliminated due to the combined effects of high salinity, elevated selenium, and other contaminants; a high frequency (30 percent) of still-

births occurred in those species that survived. Studies conducted by the U.S. Fish and Wildlife Service confirmed that irrigation drainage was the cause of the fish and wildlife problem.

The findings at Kesterson National Wildlife Refuge led to a new awareness of the dangers posed by agricultural irrigation drainage. In 1986 the U.S. Department of the Interior established a multiagency program to investigate irrigation-related drainwater problems. Eleven study areas in nine states were found to be seriously contaminated by selenium. The concentrations present at these eleven sites exceeded toxicity thresholds for fish and wildlife. Selenium-induced deformities in bird embryos and hatchlings were found in five states: California, Utah, Wyoming, Nevada, and Montana.

The biogeochemical conditions leading to the production of subsurface irrigation drainage, culminating in death and deformities in wildlife, have been termed the "Kesterson Effect." The Kesterson Effect is prevalent throughout the western United States and is caused by these conditions: (1) a marine sedimentary basin that contains Cretaceous soils that have high concentrations (several parts per million) of selenium, boron, or other elements; (2) alkaline, oxidized soils that promote the formation of water-soluble forms of these elements; (3) a dry climate in which evaporation greatly exceeds precipitation, leading to salt buildup in soils; (4) subsurface layers of clay that impede downward movement of irrigation water and cause waterlogging of the crop root zone; and (5) subsurface drainage, by natural gradient or buried tile drainage networks, into migratory bird refuges or other wetlands.

Before the discovery of problems at Kesterson National Wildlife Refuge, irrigation drainage was viewed as being acceptable for wetland management. It was thought that agricultural wastewater could be recycled and used to supplement freshwater supplies. Kesterson National Wildlife Refuge was developed under this concept as a joint venture between the U.S. Bureau of Reclamation, which used the refuge as a site for drainwater disposal, and the U.S. Fish and Wildlife Service, which used the drainage to create shallow marshes for waterfowl. Viewed in light of the research findings of the past decade, this practice carries great environmental risk. Seasonal or permanent wetlands supported by irrigation drainage experience salt buildup as evaporative losses of water occur, thereby changing the species diversity and yield of native marsh plants that are important producers of wildlife food. Moreover, contaminants in the drainwater can bio-accumulate and cause mortality and reproductive failure in fish and wildlife.

Historically wide year-to-year fluctuations in rainfall and freshwater inflow to wetlands occurred as a consequence of natural hydrological cycles in the arid western United States. This resulted in varying salinities and produced a mixture of fresh and brackish wetlands. Irrigated agriculture has changed the natural hydrologic regime and greatly accelerated the rate of salt deposition in wetlands. Diversion of water for use by agriculture has meant that freshwater inflows to wetlands are inadequate to flush away excess salts, as would periodically occur under natural conditions.

From an environmental perspective, one obvious solution to the problem of wetland contamination is restoration of freshwater inflows. However, putting water back into wetlands means that less water will be going somewhere else, and there seems to be too little to satisfy all demands.

Resolving the dilemma over water rights of humans and water needs of native wetlands will not be easy. The situation at Kesterson National Wildlife Refuge was resolved after several years of scientific and political debate, at a cost of well over $100 million. Kesterson was declared a toxic waste dump, taken out of the national wildlife refuge system, and partially buried. Effectively managing and restoring wetlands will require creative thinking by wetlands managers, cooperation between water authorities and natural resource agencies, and increased conservation by water users.

The possibility that irrigated agriculture could produce subsurface drainage and wildlife problems in other countries is very likely. Several of the factors contributing to the formation of toxic drainwater in the western United States—a marine sedimentary basin containing soils with elevated concentrations of trace elements, alkaline conditions that favor the formation of water-soluble forms of trace elements, soil salinization problems that require the use of irrigation to flush away excess salts—occur in many other arid and semiarid regions of the world. It is not clear how widespread the other key element necessary for producing subsurface drainage is, that is, the presence of layers of clay or other impermeable soil materials that impede downward movement of irrigation water. However, drainage or salinity problems have been reported from virtually every arid region where intensive irrigation occurs, which suggests that the phenomenon may be common. Moreover, soils with elevated concentrations of trace elements prone to leaching by irrigation, such as selenium and molybdenum, are known to occur in many countries.

Heavy use of freshwater for agricultural irrigation has led to water shortages and associated wildlife problems in many locations around the world. For example, the Aral Sea, located in the driest part of Russia, was once the world's fourth-largest freshwater lake and supported vast fish and wildlife populations and extensive delta wetlands. It is now disappearing. From 1960 to 1987 its level dropped 13 meters and its area decreased by 40 percent, primarily because of withdrawals of water for irrigation. Severe environmental problems have occurred, including salinization, loss of biological productivity, deterioration of deltaic ecosystems, and major changes in native aquatic and wetland communities. The large area of exposed former sea bottom along the eastern shore is a source for major dust and salt storms that are causing significant ecological and agricultural damage for hundreds of kilometers inland. The former major shipping ports of Aral'sk and Muynak are now tens of kilometers from the sea. Correcting this problem will be very difficult and expensive, necessitating a change in the lifestyle and water usage of some 40 million people in the region. Preservation of the Aral will likely require implementation of a major, and controversial, project to divert water from western Siberia into the Aral Sea basin, a distance of more than 1,000 kilometers. The possible economic gains related to this project are brought into serious question by the huge environmental and economic losses already suffered.

With human populations and associated water demands continuing to grow in many arid and semiarid regions of the world, the potential for changes in nature's water balance is increasing. These hydrological changes can cause a variety of unforeseen negative environmental and economic impacts. In some cases the effects may occur suddenly and with little warning. In others the effects may be quite subtle, resulting in a gradual degradation of water quality and wetland ecosystems over several years or even decades. It is important for resource managers and water authorities to recognize the high potential for negative impacts and take steps to prevent them from occurring. Prevention is likely to be much easier than trying to find and choose among difficult and perhaps unpopular alternatives once environmental damage has occurred. Lessons learned in the western United States can provide valuable information for other countries to use in their water management policies.—A. Dennis Lemly

See also **AGRICULTURE IN DESERTS; COLORADO RIVER; CONTAMINATION; DAM; DESERTIFICATION; DURICRUSTS; GROUNDWATER; HYDROLOGICAL CYCLE; HYDROLOGY; INSECTICIDES; MIDDLE EAST, DESERTS OF; PLAYA; POLLUTION; RIVERS; SALINITY; SALT; SALT CRUST; SALT DESERT; SALT PAN; SOILS, DESERT; SOILS, DESERT, CLAY; WATER**

Further Reading

Hallock, R. J., and L. L. Hallock. 1993. Detailed study of irrigation drainage in and near wildlife management areas, west-central Nevada, 1987–90. *Water-Resources Investigations Report* 92–4024B. Carson City, Nevada: U.S. Geological Survey.

Harris, T. 1991. *Death in the Marsh*. Covelo, Calif.: Island Press.

Howard, A. Q. 1989. *Selenium and Agricultural Drainage: Implications for San Francisco Bay and the California Environment*. Proceedings of the Fourth Selenium Symposium. Sausalito, Calif.: Bay Institute of San Francisco.

Kingsford, R. T., and R. F. Thomas. 1995. The Macquarie Marshes in arid Australia and their waterbirds: A 50-year history of decline. *Environmental Management* 19:867–878.

Lemly, A. D. 1994. Agriculture and wildlife: Ecological implications of subsurface irrigation drainage. *Journal of Arid Environments* 28:85–94.

Lemly, A. D., S. E. Finger, and M. K. Nelson. 1993. Sources and impacts of irrigation drainwater contaminants in arid wetlands. *Environmental Toxicology and Chemistry* 12:2265–2279.

Letley, J., C. Roberts, M. Penberth, and C. Vasek. 1986. *An Agricultural Dilemma: Drainage Water and Toxics Disposal in the San Joaquin Valley*. Special Publication No. 3319, University of California, Berkeley.

Livingstone, A. J., and I. A. Campbell. 1992. Water supply and urban growth in southern Alberta: Constraint or catalyst? *Journal of Arid Environments* 23:335–349.

Micklin, P. P. 1988. Desiccation of the Aral Sea: A water management disaster in the Soviet Union. *Science* 241:1170–1174.

Moore, S. B., J. Winckel, S. J. Detwiler, S. A. Klasing, P. A. Gaul, A. R. Kanim, B. E. Kesser, A. B. Debevac, A. Beardsley, and L. A. Puckett. 1990. *Fish and Wildlife Resources and Agricultural Drainage in the San Joaquin Valley, California*. Sacramento, Calif.: San Joaquin Valley Drainage Program.

National Research Council. 1989. *Irrigation-induced Water Quality Problems: What Can Be Learned from the San Joaquin Valley Experience*. Washington, D.C.: National Academy Press.

Reisner, M. 1986. *Cadillac Desert: The American West and Its Disappearing Water*. New York: Viking Penguin.

Summers, J. B., and S. S. Anderson. 1986. *Toxic Substances in Agriculture Water Supply and Drainage: Defining the Problems*. Denver: U.S. Committee on Irrigation and Drainage.

Zahm, G. R. 1986. Kesterson Reservoir and Kesterson National Wildlife Refuge: History, current problems, and management alternatives. *Transactions of the North American Wildlife and Natural Resources Conference* 51:324–329.

ISOHYET

Line on a map based on geographic points that depict an equal amount of precipitation, or other climatic factor, such as wind speed, insolation, or atmospheric pressure, during a particular time or during particular storms. Desert climates are generally situated within the 200-millimeter isohyet (i.e., they receive less than 200 millimeters of rain each year). Plotting isohyets from month to month throughout the year, or in different seasons, provides an important tool for visualizing the climate of a particular habitat.—Federico Norte

See also **AN INTRODUCTION TO DESERTS; BAROMETRIC PRESSURE (ATMOSPHERIC PRESSURE); CLIMATE; CLIMATE CLASSIFICATION; CONVECTIVE STORM; LOW PRESSURE**

Further Reading

Day, J. A., and V. J. Schaefer. 1991. *Clouds and Weather*. Boston: Houghton Mifflin.

Oliver, J. E., and R. W. Fairbridge, eds. 1987. *The Encyclopedia of Climatology*. New York: Chapman and Hall.

Schaefer, V. J., and J. A. Day. 1981. *A Field Guide to the Atmosphere*. Boston: Houghton Mifflin.

Schneider, S. H., ed. 1996. *Encyclopedia of Climate and Weather*. 2 vols. New York: Oxford University Press.

ISRAEL, DESERTS OF

Arid lands contained within the geographic limits of the nation of Israel. Israel is a small nation in southwestern Asia (66 kilometers wide by 450 kilometers long; 20,770 square kilometers, or about one-third larger than Connecticut) bordered by Jordan and Syria on the east, Lebanon on the north, the Mediterranean Sea on the northwest, and Egypt on the southwest, composed mainly of nonmountainous arid and semiarid habitats (most of the country is desert or semidesert; the highest point is Mt. Meron, 1,290 meters, and the lowest point is the Dead Sea, 396 meters below sea level). The northern Negev Desert on the Sinai Peninsula makes up much of the southern part of the country. Rainfall in northern Israel averages about 700 millimeters, but over most of the country and particularly in the south (the Negev) rainfall is sparse (25–200 millimeters), with years during which no rain falls, and total rainfall seldom exceeds 150 millimeters. Temperatures over most of the country are mild (summer temperatures average 32°C or less; winter temperatures average 9°C or more). The Syrian-African Rift Valley, which contains the Dead Sea and the Negev Desert proper, includes areas that experience extremely high temperatures (mean monthly July temperature at the Dead Sea is 39°C; and a temperature of 47° was recorded near Eilat in July 1996). (See map of Middle East deserts, p. 361.)

The Negev is that portion of the westernmost Arabian Desert located on the Sinai Peninsula that extends into Israel. The Negev lacks trees due to the sparse and unpredictable precipitation. Common plants are *Anabasis*, *Acacia*, *Aerva*, *Artemisia*, *Balanites*, *Calotropis*, *Fagonia*, *Haloxylon*, *Lycium*, *Panicum*, *Poa*, *Salvadora*, *Ziziphus*, and *Zygophyllum*. In the northern Negev, along the Mediterranean Coast, there are sand dunes, but as the desert continues southward dunes give way to rolling plains and eroded hills. In the central Negev there are arid mountains (2,000 square kilometers in area) dissected by numerous valleys, and areas of desert pavement are common. The southern Negev is mountainous as well, with strikingly colored mountains composed of igneous rock of various dark hues, overlain by multicolored sandstones. In the southern Negev in the Arava Valley (which is

part of the Syrian-African Rift Valley) sand dunes are common.

Because Israel is an ancient land that has supported significant civilizations over many millennia, most of the natural habitats of the country were destroyed long ago. In recent years there have been attempts at reforestation (mainly with introduced pine trees) and increased levels of agricultural activity, although Israel has only a small amount of quite marginal agricultural land.

The arid lands of Israel are rather depauperate in fauna. Mammals are the hedgehog (*Hemiechinus auritus*), dormouse (*Eliomys melanurus*), mole rat (*Spalax ehrenbergi*), jird (*Meriones tristrami*, *Sekeetamys caliurus*), gerbil (*Gerbillus pyramidum*), spiny mouse (*Acomys russatus*), porcupine (*Hystrix africaeaustralis*), Dorcas gazelle (*Gazella dorcas*), ibex (*Capra nubiana*), striped hyena (*Hyaena hyaena*), Rueppell's fox (*Vulpes rueppelli*), caracal (*Caracal caracal*), and wild cat (*Felis sylvestris*). Birds include, among others, a babbler (*Turdoides squamiceps*), wheatear (*Oenanthe leucopyga*), desert partridge (*Ammoperdix heyé*), and vulture (*Aegypius tracheliotus*). Reptiles include the hardoun lizard (*Agama stellio*), snake-eyed lizard (*Ophisops elegans*), fringe-toed leopard lizard (*Acanthodactylus pardalis*), striated desert lizard (*Eremias olivieri*), gecko (*Tropiocolates studneri*), Egyptian dabb lizard (*Uromastix aegyptius*), Sinai agama (*Agama sinaita*), sidewinder (*Cerastes cerastes*), and pygmy sand viper (*Aspis vipera*). There is even an amphibian, the green toad, *Bufo viridis*, in mesic (moist) parts of the desert.—Michael A. Mares

See also **AFRICA, DESERTS OF; AN INTRODUCTION TO DESERTS; DESERTS; LEBANON, DESERTS OF; MIDDLE EAST, DESERTS OF; PALESTINE, DESERTS OF; SAHARA DESERT; SAINT CATHERINE'S MONASTERY; SAUDI ARABIA, DESERTS OF; SYRIA, DESERTS OF**

Further Reading

Evenari, M., I. Noy-Meir, and D. W. Goodall, eds. 1985. *Ecosystems of the World, Hot Deserts and Arid Shrublands*. Vol. 12 (2 pts.). New York: Elsevier.

Evenari, M., L. Shanan, and T. Naphtali. 1971. *The Negev*. Cambridge, Mass.: Harvard University Press.

JACKAL

Four species in the dog family Canidae (mammalian order Carnivora, genus *Canis*) that occur in Africa and are closely related to the gray wolf, the red wolf, and the coyote; they are also closely related to the domestic dog (currently treated as a subspecies of the gray wolf). The four species of jackals occupy different habitats. The sidestriped jackal (*Canis adustus*) is the most forest-adapted species and is largely restricted to moist woodlands. The Simien or Ethiopian jackal (*Canis simensis*) is a highlands species of the mountains of Ethiopia. They are highly endangered. The golden jackal (*Canis aureus*) has a broad distribution from eastern Africa; through southeastern Europe into Burma and Thailand. They inhabit both wooded and open habitats but seem to prefer dry grasslands. They are also tolerant of human activity and can be found in cities and villages at night. The black-backed or silver-backed jackal; (*Canis mesomelas*) is found in dry brush woodlands in eastern and southern Africa.

The arid-land jackals (*C. mesomelas* and *C. aureus*) have similar natural history. Where the two species occur together, they segregate by habitat. Golden jackals are slightly larger and heavier than black-backed jackals. Both species are highly opportunistic foragers and select a wide range of plant and animal foods. They also exhibit cooperative hunting, and small groups are capable of killing adults of some of the smaller antelope species. Jackals also are scavengers, though carrion generally represents less than 10 percent of their diet. Peak activity is in the early morning and early evening hours. Social behavior in the two species is also similar. The basic social unit is the mated pair and offspring. Adult jackals maintain breeding territories, which they mark with scent and defend.

Although jackals are often hunted as agricultural pests, their numbers appear to be stable (with the exception of the Simien jackal). Golden jackal populations appear to be increasing in Europe.—Thomas E. Lacher, Jr.

Black-backed jackal (*Canis mesomelas*) along the Etosha Pan in Etosha National Park, northern Namibia. (Photo: M. A. Mares)

See also **AFRICA, DESERTS OF; CARNIVORES; CARRION EATERS; DESERT GRASSLAND; DIET; GRASSLAND; HOWLING; KALAHARI DESERT; KAROO; MAMMALS; NAMIBIA, DESERTS OF; PINNAE; SAHARA DESERT; SAVANNA; SOUTH AFRICA, DESERTS OF**

Further Reading

Estes, R. D. 1991. *The Behavior Guide to African Mammals*. Berkeley: University of California Press.

Kingdon, J. 1989. *East African Mammals: An Atlas of Evolution in Africa*. Vol. 3A. Chicago: University of Chicago Press.

Macdonald, D., ed. 1984. *The Encyclopedia of Mammals*. New York: Facts on File.

Nowak, R. M. 1991. *Walker's Mammals of the World*. 5th ed. Baltimore: Johns Hopkins University Press.

Sheldon, J. W. 1992. *Wild Dogs: The Natural History of the Nondomestic Canidae*. San Diego: Academic Press.

JACKRABBIT

Species of hare in the genus *Lepus* (mammalian order Lagomorpha, family Leporidae) common in the deserts, semiarid grasslands, and plains of western North America. Jackrabbits are relatively large (average 2.5–3.5 kilograms), slender hares with long ears, long legs, and large hind feet. They are fleet

Black-tailed jackrabbit (*Lepus californicus*) in the Sevilleta National Wildlife Refuge, 60 miles south of Albuquerque, New Mexico. (Photo: K. A. Ernest)

runners, achieving speeds of up to 70 kilometers per hour and horizontal leaps of three to seven meters. The black-tailed jackrabbit (*Lepus californicus*) has the broadest distribution, covering all four major deserts of North America; other common species include the white-tailed jackrabbit (*Lepus townsendii*), the antelope jackrabbit (*Lepus alleni*), and the white-sided jackrabbit (*Lepus callotis*). Related hares, *Lepus victoriae* and *Lepus fagani*, inhabit the Sahara Desert and other arid areas and savannas of Africa, and *Lepus capensis* is found in southern Africa, eastern Africa, and parts of northern Africa.

Jackrabbits avoid overheating by restricting their activity to night and twilight hours. During the day they rest in shallow depressions in the soil (called forms) near shrubs, cacti, or clumps of grass. Although they lack sweat glands, they reduce body heat in another way: the enlarged ears radiate heat away from the body. Jackrabbits regularly travel two to three kilometers in a day to foraging areas, occasionally making round trips of 16 kilometers. They use trails and runways and have an average home range of about 600 hectares. The diet of jackrabbits consists of a variety of grasses, shrubs, and cacti.

Black-tailed and white-tailed jackrabbits are generally solitary, though they may share foraging areas. Antelope jackrabbits tend to be more social, forming groups of several to 25 animals. The reproductive season is nearly year-round in some areas, and females may reproduce three to four times

each year. Males fight for access to females by boxing on their hind legs. The gestation period is 30–47 days, depending on the species. Females give birth to one to eight young in nests constructed in shallow depressions or deeper pockets in the soil. The leverets (young) are fully haired, open-eyed, and able to hop around within a couple of days after birth.

Jackrabbits have very good senses of smell, vision, and hearing. Rather than finding shelter in burrows, they avoid being eaten by early detection of their predators and quick flight. Their primary predators are coyotes, but they are also frequently eaten by bobcats, foxes, hawks, and eagles. Jackrabbits are susceptible to rabbit plague, mangelike skin disease, and a variety of ectoparasites, including fleas and botflies. Though mortality rates can be high, jackrabbits can be important components of the ecosystem by contributing large numbers of individuals or high biomass.—Kristina A. Ernest

See also **ANIMAL ADAPTATIONS; ARIZONA DESERT; BAJA CALIFORNIA, DESERTS OF; BODY TEMPERATURE; CHIHUAHUAN DESERT; COLORADO DESERT; COUNTERCURRENT HEAT EXCHANGE; CREOSOTE BUSH; HARE; HEAT BALANCE; HEAT EXCHANGE; HERBIVORY; MAMMALS; MEXICO, DESERTS OF; PHYSIOLOGY; PINNAE; PREDATION; RABBIT; SONORAN DESERT; WATER BALANCE**

Further Reading

Best, T. L., and T. H. Henry. 1993. Lepus alleni. *Mammalian Species* 424:1–8.

Dunn, J. P., J. A. Chapman, and R. E. Marsh. 1982. Jackrabbits. *Lepus californicus* and allies. *In* J. A. Chapman and G. A. Feldhamer, eds., *Wild Mammals of North America. Biology, Management, and Economics*, 124–145. Baltimore: Johns Hopkins University Press.

Hoffmeister, D. F. 1986. *Mammals of Arizona*. Tucson: University of Arizona Press.

JAGUAR

New World cat (*Panthera onca*; mammalian family Felidae, order Carnivora) equivalent to Old World leopards and historically found from the southern United States (Arizona, California, New Mexico, Texas, and Louisiana) to Argentina. Habitat destruction, unrestricted hunting, and the illegal skin trade threaten this species throughout its range. Jaguars have been extirpated from Uruguay and virtually extirpated from the United States, Mexico, Argentina, and parts of Central and South

America (although a jaguar was recorded in southern New Mexico in the mid-1990s).

Jaguars usually are found near water in tropical and subtropical forests, mangroves, swamps, savannas, and deserts at elevations below 1,000 meters. They were uncommon in the Sonoran Desert of Arizona and the drylands of southern New Mexico, where peccaries and other prey were present.

Size, coloration, and fur pattern vary. Generally jaguars are yellowish brown with dark rosettes on the back and black spots on the belly, but they may be black or completely white. Weight ranges from 57 to 113 kilograms. The broad chest, compact body, short legs, and broad paws provide speed and stamina on the ground and good swimming ability in the water.

Jaguars hunt at dawn or at night and stalk their prey on the ground; a wide variety of vertebrates are eaten. Unlike mountain lions, jaguars do not bury their prey. They are secretive, good climbers, and generally have large home ranges (10–76 square kilometers). Jaguars do not roar but emit a bark, followed by loud, short, hoarse, coughlike noises. This "growling" is only found in jaguars, leopards, and lions.—Janet K. Braun

See also **CARNIVORES; CATS; CHACO; CHIHUAHUAN DESERT; DEER; MAMMALS; NEW MEXICO DESERT; PAMPAS; PECCARY; PREDATION; SONORAN DESERT; XEROPHYLLOUS FOREST**

Further Reading

Bailey, V. 1971. *Mammals of the Southwestern United States (With Special Reference to New Mexico)*. New York: Dover.

Hoffmeister, D. F. 1986. *Mammals of Arizona*. Tucson: University of Arizona Press.

Kitchener, A. 1991. *The Natural History of the Wild Cats*. Ithaca: Comstock.

Seymour, K. L. 1989. Panthera onca. *Mammalian Species* 340:1–9.

Thornback, J., and M. Jenkins. 1982. *The IUCN Mammal Red Data Book*. Pt. 1: *The Americas and Australasia*. Gland: IUCN.

JEDDAH

Saudi Arabian city situated in the eastern coastal plain along the Red Sea (21° north latitude, 39°10' east longitude) and occupying an area of about 1,200 square kilometers. *Jeddah* means "flat littoral plain" in Arabic. It is an old city (2,500 years). Originally a small humble village whose population lived mainly by fishing, the city is now considered the main caravan station for people coming to visit the Moslem holy places and represents the most important center for sea-borne commodities reaching Saudi Arabia.

The region of Jeddah is divided into three major edaphic subdivisions that run parallel to the shoreline in the west and the mountain ranges in the east. The eastern slopes of the western montain range are mainly made up of sandstone and clay. The middle region is made up of mixed igneous and marine sediments. The coastal subdivision is made up of clayey sand mixed with shell debris.

The population of Jeddah numbers two million. The city's people consume more than 40,000 cubic meters of freshwater per day from natural and desalinized waters. The climate is hot, with low or negligible rainfall and high relative humidity. The maximum temperature at Jeddah reaches 48.4°C in June, the minimum is 11.4°C in January, and the mean annual temperature is about 27.8°C. The relative humidity may reach 100 percent in autumn, with mean annual humidity of 57 percent.

The scarcity of water in Jeddah continued until the 16th century, when reservoirs were constructed to collect rainwater. The underground water in Jeddah is highly saline and not fit for drinking. Recently, due to the increased pressing need for water, in addition to the water produced from wells and springs, desalinization projects were established with high production capacity.

As a major port, Jeddah has multiple and complex environmental pressures. The rapid growth and development of Jeddah over the past few decades was accompanied by several environmental problems. These include increased air pollution and noise; depletion in the quantity and quality of water resources; increased sewage and biologically nondegradable solid wastes; and degradation of many terrestrial, coastal, and marine habitats.

The desert park is a characteristic natural reserve in Jeddah. The park was established as a biosphere reserve on an area of about six square kilometers close to King Abdulaziz University and includes on its grounds a zoo and an aviary. The vegetation of the desert park is formed mainly of *Dipterygium glaucum*, *Leptadenia pyrotechnica*, *Farsetia longisiliqua*, and *Capparis decidua* and is confined to the valley and tributary habitats.—Ahmad K. Hegazy

See also **AFRICA, DESERTS OF; AGRICULTURE IN DESERTS; ARABIAN GULF, DESERTS OF; CHENOPODIACEAE; CONTAMINATION; DESERTIFICATION; MIDDLE EAST, DESERTS OF; OVERGRAZING; PLAYA; SAHARA DESERT; SALINIZATION; SALT DESERT; SALT PAN; SAUDI ARABIA, DESERTS OF**

Further Reading

Al-Ansari, A. 1980. *The History of Jeddah: An Encyclopedia.* 2d ed. Vol. 1. Jeddah: Al Roda Press. (In Arabic)

Anonymous. 1980. *Jeddah Old and New.* London: Stacey International.

Barbor, P. *Desert Treks from Jeddah.* London: Stacey International.

Hoye, P. F. Man in arid lands: North from Jiddah. *In* G. W. Brown, ed., *Desert Biology: Special Topics on the Physical and Biological Aspects of Arid Regions,* 2:530–550. New York: Academic Press.

Municipality of Jeddah Research Department. 1983. *Jeddah: A Changing Ecosystem.* Dar Al Asfahani, Jeddah, Publication No. 4.

JERBOA

Term generally applied to species of the desert-adapted, Old World rodent family Dipodidae (mammalian order Rodentia). The genera *Jaculus, Allactaga, Dipus, and Salpingotus* typify this family. These rodents are characterized by the possession of extremely elongated hind limbs and, usually, a long tufted tail. The forepaws are extremely short, and the incisors are procumbent (projected forward). The long hind legs are an adaptation for bipedal locomotion. Rapid locomotion involves a series of hops, with the long tail acting as a counterweight. Jerboas are confined to the arid regions of Africa and Asia; they are most speciose in central Asia.

Jerboas are nocturnal in their habits and shelter during daylight hours in burrows of their own construction. They are herbivorous, feeding on subterranean roots of desert-adapted plants, especially those that store moisture in the root cells, as well as on seeds. Many species of jerboas do not need to drink water but obtain most of their moisture from their food. They have adaptations of the kidney to recover metabolic water. The litter size of the larger jerboas tends to be small, with two to three young the average. The young are born in an underground nest in an extremely undeveloped state, with the eyes and ears closed. Their process of physical maturation is lengthy; they are usually not weaned before six weeks of age. Jerboas are preyed on by

Five-toed jerboa (*Allactaga elator*). (Photo: J. F. Eisenberg)

owls and snakes as well as desert foxes and the sand cat. Some species of jerboas can enter torpor during periods of reduced food availability.—John F. Eisenberg

See also **AFRICA, DESERTS OF; ANIMAL ADAPTATIONS; ASIA, DESERTS OF; BIPEDALITY; BURROWING ANIMALS; CONVERGENT EVOLUTION; GRANIVORY; HERBIVORY; IRAN, DESERTS OF; KIDNEY FUNCTION, DESERT RODENTS; KIDNEYS; MIDDLE EAST, DESERTS OF; PINNAE; PREDATION; RODENTS; SAHARA DESERT; TYMPANIC BULLAE; WATER BALANCE**

Further Reading

Nowak, R. M. 1991. *Walker's Mammals of the World.* 5th ed. Baltimore: Johns Hopkins University Press.

Prakash, I., and P. K. Ghosh, eds. 1975. *Rodents in Desert Environments.* Monographiae Biologicae. The Hague: Junk.

JOJOBA

Common shrub (*Simmondsia chinensis*; also called goatnut) of the family Buxaceae native to the Sonoran Desert and found in lower elevations of desert mountain ranges in Arizona, California, and northern Mexico. This species includes male and female plants, both of which are one to two meters tall and possess leathery, gray-green leaves that persist throughout the year. Although the acornlike nuts are bitter in taste because of their high tannin content, they were eaten by Native Americans and early settlers of the region without preparation. The nuts contain an edible odorless and colorless oil (actually a liquid wax) that has potential use as a lubricant of fine machinery. The seeds contain up to 60 percent wax, which has led to the plant's nickname, "botanical whale," because the jojoba seed oil is similar to that obtained from sperm whales. The development of jojoba as an oil crop has been encouraged since the sperm whale became an endangered species and the import of its oil was banned in the United States. Attempts have been made to bring jojoba into cultivation as a new crop for the southwestern United States in the hope that its products could be used to replace the oil from animal sources. Jojoba oil has been used to produce antifoaming agents in the fermentation industry, protective coatings, shampoo, hair conditioners, and a variety of cosmetics including lipstick. Jojoba also has been used to lubricate motors, wax floors, soften leather, moisturize skin, cool transformers, and feed livestock.

The Cahuila Indians of the desert Southwest also used jojoba nuts to make a drink by first grinding the nuts, boiling the meal, and then straining the liquid. Mexicans also made a beverage from the jojoba nuts by roasting them, grinding them together with the yolk of a hard-boiled egg, and then boiling the paste with water, milk, sugar, and a vanilla bean. A tea from the leaves has been used to treat mucous membrane inflammations, and in Mexico jojoba plants have been widely used to treat asthma and emphysema.—Gordon E. Uno

See also **ARIZONA DESERT; COLORADO DESERT; DESERT PEOPLES; DESERTS, MONTANE; ECONOMIC VALUE OF DESERT PRODUCTS; FRUITS; MEXICO, DESERTS OF; PLANT ADAPTATIONS; PLANTS; SONORAN DESERT**

Further Reading

Goodin, J. R., and D. K. Northington, eds. 1985. *Plant Resources of Arid and Semiarid Lands: A Global Perspective.* New York: Academic Press.

Wickens, G. E., J. R. Goodin, and D. V. Field, eds. 1985. *Plants for Arid Lands.* London: Unwin Hyman.

JORDAN, DESERTS OF

Arid regions lying within the geographic boundaries of the nation of Jordan in western Asia, bordered by Israel, Syria, Iraq, and Saudi Arabia and composed largely of arid and semiarid habitats. Despite the small size of the country (90,650 square kilometers), the deserts of Jordan display a remarkable variation in climate. The climate generally belongs to the Mediterranean type, with mild, rainy winters and dry, hot summers. Six climatic types are recognized. First is the cool temperate rainy climate of the mountainous regions around Ajlum in the north and Shobak in the south, with an average annual rainfall of 296 millimeters and an annual mean temperature of 12.5°C. Second is the warm temperate rainy climate around the Irbid and Balqa mountains, where summers are hot; the average annual rainfall exceeds 400 millimeters, and mean annual temperature is 13.9°C. Third is the cool steppe or semiarid climate along the lee slopes of the eastern mountains, with an average annual rainfall of less than 300 millimeters and an annual mean temperature that does not exceed 18°C. Fourth, a warm semiarid climate occurs along the Jordan Rift Valley. The average annual rainfall in this region is 350 millimeters, and the mean annual temperature is 23°C. Fifth, a cool desert climate occurs along the eastern slopes of the country's mountainous ranges, with average annual rainfall ranging from 38 to 164 millimeters and average annual temperature less than 18°C. Sixth a warm desert climate exists across most of the eastern and southern portions of Jordan, with trace amounts of rain and an average annual temperature of 19.2°C. (See map of Middle East deserts, p. 361.)

The diverse climates support a rich array of plant communities. At higher elevations (above 1,000 meters, where snow falls regularly in winter), the Mediterranean climate of the western mountains supports *Juniperus* forests. Plant species include *Juniperus phoenicea, Cupressus sempervrens, Globularia arabica,* and *Helianthemum vesicarium.* At elevations of 700–1,000 meters, pine and oak forests predominate. Indicator species in these forests are *Pinus halepensis, Quercus calliprinus,* various *Helianthemum, Limodorum abortivum, Fumana arabica, Crataegus azarolus, Asparagus aphyllus, Dactylis glomerata,* and *Urginea maritima.*

The Mediterranean nonforest vegetation supports plant communities of *Rhamnus palestinus, Dactylis glomerata, Tecrium polium, Noaea mucronata, Artemisia herba-alba,* and *Asphodelus ramosus.* This semiarid steppe vegetation surrounds most of the mountainous regions. Common species also include *Ziziphus lotus, Retama raetam, Capparis spinosa,* species of *Haloxylon,* and *Astragalus spinosus.*

The arid deserts found in the east and along the borders with Saudi Arabia and Iraq support several different types of plant communities, depending on substrate and other factors. The rock and gravelly habitats have *Acacia tortilis* and *Acacia raddiana, Haloxylon scoparium, Zygophyllum dumosum, Helianthemum lippii*, and *Herniaria hirsuta*. The sandy plains support *Seidlitzia rosmarinus, Anabasis articulata, Ephedra transitoria, Calligonum tetrapterum*, and *Zilla spinosa*. Sand dunes are found in Wadi Ram and Wadi Araba with sparse vegetation dominated by *Holoxylon persicum, Retama raetam, Calligonum comosum, Panicum turgidum, Pancratium sickenbergeri, Hyoscyamus pusillus*, and *Cakile maritima*. Depressions with fine alluvial soils support various shrubby species, such as *Ziziphus spina-christi, Calotropis procera, Ochradenus baccatus*, various species of *Acacia*, and *Cocculus pendulus*.

Wadi Araba is a valley (about 170 kilometers long and 5–20 kilometers wide) bounded on the west by the mountains of the far Negev Desert and on the east by the Edumean Mountains. Elevation of the valley varies from -396 meters (southern shore of the Dead Sea) to about 240 meters (north of the Gulf of Aqaba). The valley represents an extremely dry desert characterized by long dry summers and short winters with average annual precipitation less than 80 millimeters. Habitat types include salt marshes, sand formations, and gravel lands with diverse vegetation.

The biodiversity of Jordan is rich, as might be expected given its diverse climates and habitats. About 2,200 species of flowering plants are known from Jordan. Agriculture contributes 9 percent of the GNP, and only 3 percent of the workforce is employed in agriculture. The area of cropland is 414,000 hectares, which is estimated at 13 percent of the country's land area. About 11 percent is irrigated; the rest is used for dryland farming supported partly by irrigation from the Jordan River and from streams and springs. Due to scarcity of water, aridity of the climate, the topography of the country with its depressions and low-lying areas, and the increasing demand for agricultural development, soil degradation from salinization has been increasing. There is little room to expand agricultural lands. Large areas of pine and oak forests in the mountains have been cut for firewood and land use. *Juniperus* forests and semiarid deserts are also subjected to overgrazing. Jordan has 30,000 cattle, 1.6 million sheep and goats, and 15,000 camels.

Two kinds of pastoralism are practiced in Jordan: sedentary and seminomadic. Sedentary pastoralism is associated with agriculture in the western parts of Jordan, where large areas of pasturelands may support natural vegetation. This kind of pasture is subject to rapid deterioration. The seminomadic pastoralism is common in the semidesert areas of the eastern parts of the country, where sporadic and patchy marginal grain sowing is possible in wadi and depression habitats.—Ahmad K. Hegazy

See also **ACACIA; AFRICA, DESERTS OF; AGRICULTURE IN DESERTS; AN INTRODUCTION TO DESERTS; CHENOPODIACEAE; CONSERVATION IN DESERTS; DOMESTIC ANIMALS; IRRIGATION DRAINAGE; MIDDLE EAST, DESERTS OF; OVERGRAZING; PSAMMOPHYTES; PSAMMOPHYTIC SCRUB; SAHARA DESERT; SALINIZATION; SAUDI ARABIA, DESERTS OF**

Further Reading

Dutton, R., J. I. Clarke, and A. Batticki. eds. 1998. *Arid Land Resources and Their Mangement: Jordan's Desert Margin*. New York: Kegan Paul.

El-Eisawi, D. M. 1985. *Studies in History and Archaeology of Jordan*. Amman: Department of Antiquities.

Evenari, M., L. Shanan, and T. Naphtali. 1971. *The Negev*. Cambridge, Mass.: Harvard University Press.

Feinbrun, M., and M. Zohary. 1955. A geobotanical survey of Trans Jordan. *Bulletin of the Research Council of Israel* 50:5–35.

Jenny, M., U. Smettan, and M. Facklam-Moniak. 1990. Soil-vegetation relationship at several arid microsites in the Wadi Araba (Jordan). *Vegetatio* 89:149–164.

Zohary, M. 1962. *Plant Life of Palestine (Israel and Jordan)*. Chronica Botanica, New Series, No. 33.

JORNADA DEL MUERTO

Spanish name meaning "dead man's journey," given by the Spaniards to a stretch of land in southern New Mexico, about 90 miles long and 25 miles wide (although the width varies greatly), from Rincon in the south to San Marcial in the north and between the San Andrés Mountains on the east and the Caballo and Fray Cristobal mountains on the west. Geologically, the Jornada del Muerto is the northern extension of the Chihuahuan Desert that runs in a northwesterly direction from the Mexican states of Coahuila and Chihuahua into southern New Mexico. The Jornada is considered a part of the Rio Grande rift.

In the 16th and 17th centuries the Spanish Empire operating out of Mexico City, the capital of New Spain, sent many parties of exploration and conquest to New Mexico. The explorers and conquistadors gave way by the late 16th century to colonizing settlers. Many of these expeditions tried to shorten the route north by at least a day or more by abandoning the course of the Rio Grande at Rincon, where the river made a great bend to the west, and heading in a more direct, northerly journey across the arid Jornada del Muerto.

The Jornada del Muerto owed its name to the many real dangers that earlier travelers encountered. There was always the threat of extreme heat and lack of water. For the Spaniards and Mexicans, as well as for the Anglos who entered this area in the early decades of the 19th century, there was the added danger of possible attacks from Apaches who resented the unwanted incursion of Europeans and their partially Europeanized subjects into their homelands.

Because so many persons, including women and children, perished in the Jornada del Muerto in those early years, T. M. Pierce has made a good case for translating the term as "journey of death," which is historically accurate, although not as literal as "dead man's journey."

Trinity Site, where the first atomic bomb was detonated on 16 July 1945, is in the northern reaches of the Jornada del Muerto, about 35 miles south of Carthage, New Mexico.—E. A. Mares

See also **CHIHUAHUAN DESERT; CREOSOTE BUSH; DESERTS; DESERT GRASSLAND; LLANO ESTACADO; NEW MEXICO DESERT; PLANT ADAPTATIONS; PLANT GEOGRAPHY; PLANTS; RIVERS; RIO GRANDE; RIPARIAN COMMUNITIES**

Further Reading

Chronic, H. 1987. *Roadside Geology of New Mexico.* Missoula, Mont.: Mountain Press.

Crouch, B. 1989. *Jornada del Muerto: A Pageant of the Desert.* Spokane, Wash.: Arthur H. Clark.

Horgan, P. 1954. *Great River: The Rio Grande in North American History.* New York: Holt, Rinehart and Winston.

Pierce, T. M. 1965. *New Mexico Place Names.* Albuquerque: University of New Mexico Press.

Szasz, F. M. 1984. *The Day the Sun Rose Twice: The Story of the Trinity Site Nuclear Explosion, July 16, 1945.* Albuquerque: University of New Mexico Press.

Joshua tree (*Yucca brevifolia*). (Photo: D. Beck)

JOSHUA TREE

Treelike member (*Yucca brevifolia*) of the lily family (Liliaceae) with succulent leaves clustered at the ends of branches. *Yucca brevifolia*, as the name suggests, has shorter leaves than other species of yucca; and it is taller than most. This is one of the characteristic and very striking plants of the Mojave Desert. Early Mormon settlers named the tree for the resemblance of its branches to the outstretched arms of Joshua pointing the Israelites toward the Promised Land.

Joshua trees attain heights of 6–12 meters and canopy diameters of up to 6 meters. The trunk, with a corky bark, is usually branched rather high above the ground. The rigid, linear leaves are less than 50 centimeters long and have toothed margins. Greenish white flowers are borne in short, dense inflorescences. Joshua trees reproduce sexually only during years with adequate moisture and freezing temperatures. They may also reproduce asexually by sprouting new plants from the underground stems. The root system consists of many small, fibrous roots that extend both laterally and vertically.

The geographic range of the Joshua tree coincides very closely with the limits of the Mojave Desert, and the plant is particularly abundant in Joshua Tree National Park, California. This species does not occur in the center of the Mojave Desert, where temperatures are higher at the lower elevations, but does extend into the western edge of the Sonoran Desert. Joshua trees may form extensive forests, or may co-dominate communities with creosote bush, juniper, Mormon tea, saguaro, blackbrush, or other perennials. They grow on sandy, loamy, or gravelly soils on plains or bajadas near the bases of high mountains.

The Joshua tree serves as food or a home for many desert animals. Larvae of the Navajo yucca borer (*Scyphophorus yuccae*) feed on aboveground fibers and underground stems. Woodrats collect leaves of Joshua trees for their nests. The night lizard (*Xantusia vigilis*) uses fallen Joshua trees for shelter, where it feeds on insects under the bark. Many bird species, including flickers, flycatchers, wrens, and owls, build nests in Joshua trees.

The smaller, red roots are used by Indians to weave designs into baskets. A tea prepared from the roots is used to treat gonorrhea, and the fruits have emetic properties.—Kristina A. Ernest

See also **AN INTRODUCTION TO DESERTS; ARIZONA DESERT; BIOSPHERE RESERVE; CACTI; COLORADO DESERT; CONSERVATION IN DESERTS; CREOSOTE BUSH; DESERTS; FLICKER; GECKO; JOSHUA TREE NATIONAL PARK; LIZARDS; MOJAVE DESERT; PLANT ADAPTATIONS; PLANT GEOGRAPHY; PLANTS; SAGUARO; SUCCULENTS; WOODPECKERS; WOODRAT; YUCCA**

Further Reading

Benson, L., and R. A. Darrow. 1981. *Trees and Shrubs of the Southwestern Deserts*. Tucson: University of Arizona Press.

Webber, J. M. 1953. *Yuccas of the Southwest*. Department of Agriculture, Agriculture Monograph No. 17. Washington, D.C.: U.S. Government Printing Office.

JOSHUA TREE NATIONAL PARK

U.S. national monument established in 1936 in southern California to preserve the large (up to 12 meters) treelike yucca, the Joshua tree or praying plant (*Yucca brevifolia*), that is common in the region. In 1994 President Bill Clinton signed the California Desert Protection Act, which changed the status of Joshua Tree National Monument to a national park.

The Joshua tree is the largest of the yuccas and is generally found at higher elevations (1,000–1,700 meters). In the Mojave Desert it is distributed along its periphery, essentially outlining its borders. In the national park Joshua trees are found in the western portion.

This 321,457-hectare national park (80 percent of which is designated as wilderness) contains portions of both the Colorado and Mojave deserts. Altitude in the park ranges from 305 meters in the Pinto Basin to 1,772 meters at the summit of Quail Mountain in the Little San Bernardino Mountains. Annual rainfall averages less than 5 inches (120 millimeters), and temperatures range from -18°C to above 38°C.

The primary flora consists of creosote bush in the low desert, at elevations of from 305 to 914 meters; yucca in the high desert, at elevations of from 914 to 1,280 meters; and pinyon woodlands at higher elevations, from 1,280 to 1,772 meters. More than 670 species of plants have been recorded in the park.

The fauna is diverse: 2 species of amphibians; 37 species of reptiles (1 tortoise, 1 gecko, 15 lizards, and 20 snakes); 46 species of mammals and 12 of probable occurrence (1 shrew, 19 bats, 2 rabbits, 23 rodents, 10 carnivores, and two ungulates); and 219 species of birds.—Janet K. Braun

See also **AN INTRODUCTION TO DESERTS; ARIZONA DESERT; BIOSPHERE RESERVE; CACTI; COLORADO DESERT; CONSERVATION IN DESERTS; CREOSOTE BUSH; DESERTS; FLICKER; GECKO; JOSHUA TREE; LIZARDS; MOJAVE DESERT; PLANT ADAPTATIONS; PLANT GEOGRAPHY; PLANTS; SAGUARO; SUCCULENTS; WOODPECKERS; WOODRAT; YUCCA**

Further Reading

MacMahon, J. A. 1985. *Deserts*. New York: Knopf.

Rowlands, P, H. Johnson, E. Ritter, and A. Endo. 1982. The Mojave Desert. *In* G. L. Bender, ed., *Reference Handbook on the Deserts of North America*, 103–162. Westport, Conn.: Greenwood.

Weir, K. 1998. *Southern California Handbook: Including Greater Los Angeles, Disneyland, San Diego, Death Valley and other Desert Parks*. Emeryville, Calif.: Moon Publications.

KALAHARI DESERT

Refers to the geologic "system" of the Kalahari Depression, which extends northward from northwestern South Africa through Botswana as far as 1° north latitude in Zaire; the semiarid, southwestern region of the Kalahari Depression is known locally as the Kalahari Desert. In the west this huge basin has extensions into eastern Namibia, whereas in the east it borders on western Zimbabwe as far as Victoria Falls. The entire Kalahari System is flat and sandy and probably represents the largest continuous surface of sand in the world. The red sands are of Pleistocene origin and overlay a vast sheet of calcareous sandstone topped with a hard crust of white limestone. This limestone sheet is often exposed along watercourses (e.g., the Molopo, Nossob, Auob, and Kuruman rivers) and wherever characteristic pans (salt flats), such as the Etosha Pan in Namibia, occur.

The word *Kalahari* comes from the indigenous black tribe, Kgalagadi, whose tribal area once included parts of the region. Scientifically it is known as the Arid Savanna Biome. It was the last region to be explored in southern Africa because of its widespread lack of surface water. It stretches from 12° south latitude in Angola, diagonally across northern and central Namibia, into Botswana as far as about 26° east longitude, and south into north central South Africa. The sand in this semiarid region of the Kalahari System has been piled by the prevailing northwesterly winds into an extensive system of long, roughly parallel dunes lying in a northwest to southeast orientation. (See map of African deserts, p. 12.)

For the most part the drainage of the Kalahari Depression is internal, ending in the Okavango Swamps, Lake Ngami, and the Makarikari Pan. In the south the Molopo River (into which drain the Nossob, Auob, and Kuruman rivers) at one time drained the Kalahari Depression via the Orange River, but for the past 1,000 years its path has been blocked by sand dunes. When the Molopo does flow a few times every century following exceptionally high rainfall, the water is diverted into the Abiquas Pan. In most years the rivers of the Kalahari Desert remain dry.

The average annual rainfall of the Kalahari Desert ranges from 200 to 500 millimeters and occurs in summer in the form of strong convective thundershowers. There is a strong gradient of increasing rainfall from west to east. There is also a strong west-east gradient of increasing annual rainfall reliability (coefficient of variation, a measure of predictability, of mean annual rainfall decreases from 50 to 25 percent).

The Kalahari Desert experiences some of the highest and lowest mean maximum and minimum temperatures in southern Africa. In midsummer mean maximum temperatures exceed 35°C (January), whereas in midwinter the mean minimum temperatures are around 2.5°C (July). Absolute maxima exceed 40°C throughout the region, whereas absolute minima fall well below freezing. In addition to this huge annual temperature range, the daily temperature ranges are also large; the range between the monthly absolute maximum and minimum usually exceeds 30°C, often reaching 39°C during winter in May and June. This high daily range in temperature is a consequence of low prevailing atmospheric vapor pressures (low relative humidity) throughout the year, which increases the amount of radiation reaching the ground surface and does not effectively impede reradiation at night.

Botanically, the biome is characterized by two co-dominant plant life forms; hemicryptophytes (buds at ground level) in the form of perennial grasses and phanerophytes (buds well above the ground) in the form of trees (usually fine leafed) and shrubs. Typical grasses throughout the vegetated sand dunes are *Eragrostis lehmanniana* and *Stipagrostis uniplumis*, whereas *Stipagrostis amabilis* is specific to the crests of the flat-topped sand dunes. Parallel dunes may have different species of grasses growing on different parts of the dunes (e.g., slope versus crest). The most common trees in these dune habitats are the camelthorn (*Acacia erioloba*), the shepherd's tree (*Boscia albitrunca*), and the grey camelthorn (*Acacia haematoxylon*). A very distinct vegetation zonation can be found lining the banks of the various dry watercourses and surrounding calcrete pans (flats with hard calcium-based crusts). The dominant shrubs are *Rhigozum trichotomum* and *Monechma incanum*.

Thanks mostly to the presence of the Kalahari Gemsbok National Park in South Africa and Botswana, the Kalahari Desert has retained a surprisingly rich and abundant animal life considering its aridity. About 72 vertebrates (15 endemic to the Arid Savanna Biome) are resident within the Kalahari Desert. These include the top African predators, such as the lion (*Panthera leo*), leopard (*Panthera pardus*), cheetah (*Acinonyx jubatus*), spotted and brown hyenas (*Crocuta crocuta* and *Hyaena brunnea*), and wild dog (*Lycaon pictus*). These predators prey on the resident herds of gemsbok (*Oryx gazella*), springbok (*Antidorcas marsupialis*), red hartebeest (*Alcelaphus buselaphus*), blue wildebeest (*Connochaetes taurinus*), steenbok (*Raphicerus campestris*), and eland (*Taurotragus oryx*). Whereas the gemsbok, springbok, steenbok, and perhaps eland can survive without access to freestanding water, blue wildebeest and red hartebeest are dependent on surface water. These latter ungulates are therefore migratory, moving seasonally between sources of drainage water in Botswana (Okavango Swamps, Botete River, Lake Ngami, Makarikari Pan) in winter and the interior of the Kalahari Desert during the rainy season in summer. Unfortunately, though, the recent erection of veterinary fences (e.g., Kuke fence) aimed at controlling foot-and-mouth disease in cattle has interrupted these ancient migratory routes and has resulted in the yearly deaths of hundreds of thousands of wildebeest in particular.

The sociable weaver (*Philetairus socius*) is the most characteristic bird of the Kalahari Desert because of the large, conspicuous communal nest structures that these highly gregarious birds build in trees (mostly *Acacia erioloba*), on telephone poles, and on windmills. The distribution pattern of the smallest falcon in southern Africa, the pygmy falcon (*Polihierax semitorquatus*), is identical to that of the sociable weavers. The pygmy falcons are totally dependent on the thermally buffered nests of the weavers for roosting and nesting. The largest bird in the world, the ostrich (*Struthio camelus*), is

well adapted to aridity and is a common resident throughout the Kalahari Desert.

Wherever cattle and small stock ranching is practiced on the fringes and within the Kalahari Desert, there are clear signs of desertification. This mostly takes the form of bush encroachment by *Acacia mellifera* at the expense of palatable, perennial grasses.—Barry G. Lovegrove

See also **ACACIA; AFRICA, DESERTS OF; AFRICAN LION; ANIMAL ADAPTATIONS; AN INTRODUCTION TO DESERTS; ANTELOPE; BIOSPHERE RESERVE; BIRDS; CATS; CHEETAH; CONSERVATION IN DESERTS; DESERTIFICATION; DOG, WILD; DUNES; DURICRUSTS; GEMSBOK; GRASSES; GRASSLAND; HARTEBEEST; HEAT; HEAT BALANCE; HEAT EXCHANGE; HEAT STRESS; HYENA; KAROO; LIMESTONE; LION; MAMMALS; NAMIBIA, DESERTS OF; PLAYA; OSTRICH; ORYX; PLANT ADAPTATIONS; PLEISTOCENE; RAPTORS; SALINITY; SALT PAN; SAND RAMP; SAVANNA; SOUTH AFRICA, DESERTS OF; SPRINGBOK; WATER BALANCE; WEAVER**

Further Reading

Dougill, A. 1995. *Land Degradation and Grazing in the Kalahari: New Analysis and Alternative Prospectives*. London: Overseas Development Institute.

Leistner, O. A. 1967. *The Plant Ecology of the Southern Kalahari*. Botanical Survey Memoir No. 38. Pretoria, South Africa: Government Printer.

Lovegrove, B. G. 1993. *The Living Deserts of Southern Africa*. Vlaeberg: Fernwood.

Owens, M., and D. Owens. 1984. *Cry of the Kalahari*. Glasgow: HarperCollins.

Thomas, D. S. G., and P. A. Shaw. 1991. *The Kalahari Environment*. New York: Cambridge University Press.

KANGAROO

Member of a diverse group of about 60 species of marsupial mammals (family Macropodidae, order Diprotodontia) found in a wide variety of habitats in Australia and New Guinea, with one-third of all macropods occurring in arid and semiarid environments. Kangaroos were first seen by Europeans in 1629 but were unknown to the general public until their rediscovery in 1770 by Capt. James Cook.

Kangaroos vary greatly in size. The smallest is the size of a rat, the largest larger than a human. The term "kangaroo" refers to the largest macropods; small to medium-sized kangaroos are called wallabies. All kangaroos have a pouch to transport their young, hind legs that are longer than their forelegs, and long and muscular tails used for balance. The fourth toe on the hind foot is large; the second and third are joined (syndactyl) and minute and are used to comb the fur; the fifth toe is minute. All kangaroos hop on their hind legs; there are varying degrees of this ability, however, and in some species the ability has been reduced (e.g., the tree kangaroo). All species have a single pair of lower incisors that extend forward (procumbent). Between the three pairs of upper incisors is a leathery pad that assists the lower incisors in pulling vegetation for forage.

Kangaroos that live in arid and semiarid environments exhibit behavioral, physiological, and morphological adaptations that enable their survival. Many kangaroos seek out daytime resting shelters during the hottest hours. These shelters may be burrows (burrowing bettong), under bushes or within clumps of vegetation (spectacled hare wallaby), in caves or under rock shelters (euro), or under small desert trees (red kangaroo). In areas having boreholes that can hold rainwater for long periods, kangaroo populations can reach higher levels than in areas lacking such a water resource.

There is a strong correlation between "licking" behavior and increase in ambient temperature. Saliva is spread over parts of the body, and when it evaporates the body is cooled. Kangaroos also may change from a lying down posture to a crouching posture during periods of high temperatures. The increased exposure to a higher wind velocity may facilitate heat loss, especially on those areas that have been licked.

Kangaroos, like most marsupials, have a basal metabolic rate that is about 30 percent lower than that of placental mammals. Unlike some desert placentals (camel, oryx), kangaroos do not allow their body temperature to increase markedly to store heat for later dissipation. Panting is their primary mechanism of heat loss.—Janet K. Braun

See also **AUSTRALIA, DESERTS OF; BIPEDALITY; GRASSLAND; HEAT BALANCE; HEAT EXCHANGE; HEAT STRESS; HERBIVORY; MALLEE; MAMMALS; MARSUPIALS; THERMOREGULATION; WATER BALANCE**

Further Reading

Grigg, G., P. Jarman, and I. Hume, eds. 1989. *Kangaroos, Wallabies and Rat-kangaroos.* Vols. 1 and 2. Chipping Norton, NSW, Australia: Beatty.

McCarron, H. C. K., and T. J. Dawson. 1989. Thermal relations of Macropodoidea in hot environments. *In*
G. Grigg, P. Jarman, and I. Hume, eds., *Kangaroos, Wallabies and Rat-kangaroos,* 1:255–263. Chipping Norton, NSW, Australia: Beatty.

Walton, D. W., and B. J. Richardson, eds. 1989. *Fauna of Australia. Mammalia,* 1B:401–1227. Canberra: Australian Government Publishing Service.

KANGAROO MOUSE

Common name applied to rodents (mammalian order Rodentia) of the family Heteromyidae and genus *Microdipodops*. There are only two species of kangaroo mice, and they are confined to the Great Basin Desert of Arizona, Nevada, and Oregon and to adjacent portions of California. They are adapted for extremely arid habitats. In common with other heteromyid rodents, they possess externally opening fur-lined cheek pouches. Kangaroo mice are rather small, weighing less than 20 grams as adults. The hind feet are elongated and the forelimbs short, a trait held in common with all other bipedal ricochetal rodents. The tail exceeds the head and body in length but does not bear a terminal tuft. The tissues of the tail may become thickened, thus serving as a fat storage organ. The tympanic bullae (the bony shell surrounding the inner ear bones) are vastly inflated, a trait shared with the kangaroo rats.

Kangaroo mice are considered by some to be closely allied to the pocket mice, and by other authors to be closely related to the kangaroo rats. Morphologically, they share characteristics with both. Litter size averages three, and the young are born in a nest built within an underground tunnel system. These mice construct elaborate burrows, a characteristic held in common with other members of the heteromyid family. They forage for seeds on the surface and include a considerable amount of insect matter in their diet.—John F. Eisenberg

See also **ANIMAL ADAPTATIONS; ARIZONA DESERT; BIPEDALITY; BURROWING ANIMALS; CALIFORNIA DESERT; COLORATION; CONVERGENT EVOLUTION; DIET; GRANIVORY; GREAT BASIN DESERT; HETEROMYIDS; KANGAROO RAT; KIDNEY FUNCTION, DESERT RODENTS; NEVADA DESERT; OREGON DESERT; POCKET MOUSE; RODENTS; SALT BALANCE; SEEDS; SONORAN DESERT; TYMPANIC BULLAE; WATER BALANCE**

Further Reading

Genoways, H., and J. H. Brown, eds. 1993. *Biology of the Heteromyidae.* Special Publication No. 10, American Society of Mammalogists. Lawrence, Kan.: Allen Press.

Nowak, R. M. 1991. *Walker's Mammals of the World.* 5th ed. Baltimore: Johns Hopkins University Press.

KANGAROO RAT

Common name applied to the larger bipedal desert rodents (mammalian order Rodentia) belonging to the genus *Dipodomys* of the family Heteromyidae. Kangaroo rats vary in body size, with small species weighing as little as 35 grams and the larger species approaching 150 grams. Kangaroo rats include some 25 species confined to the more arid portions of western North America, extending north to the state of Montana and south to the northern portions of the Mexican Central Plateau. Dorsal coat color varies from rich chocolate brown to pale blond. In part coat color varies with the reflectant properties of the soil type for which the species is adapted. Paler forms tend to be associated with sandy deserts. The darker forms are often associated with dry brushland, such as the coastal races of kangaroo rats in California.

They have externally opening fur-lined cheek pouches in which they place fruits, green vegetation, grains, and seeds that they glean from the substrate or pick from shrubs. Although they consume a varied array of food items, they are strongly granivorous, being among the world's most specialized seed eaters. The forelimbs are reduced in length and the hind limbs long, with the hind foot greater than 30 percent of the head and body length. The tail is longer than the head and body and has a terminal tuft. The common form of locomotion is bipedal—a bipedal walk when moving slowly and a bipedal ricochet for rapid movement. The external ears are reduced in size, but the eyes are relatively large. The skull is modified in that the mastoid bone is inflated. This characteristic enables kangaroo rats to detect low-amplitude (low-frequency) sounds. Apparently this enhanced auditory ability allows them to detect the movements of potential predators, such as snakes and owls, and thereby avoid them. Since kangaroo rats search for grains and seeds in the soil at some distance from shrubs, they are often exposed and without cover. The ability to detect the wing beats of an owl, or the movements of a snake, would seem to be vital given the risks that are inherent in their foraging strategy.

The animals construct burrows in the soil; these may be quite complex, including a sleeping chamber and, frequently, a chamber for storing seeds and other dried foodstuffs. Kangaroo rats can subsist without drinking water by utilizing water derived from metabolic processes, although they require green vegetation to reproduce and to lactate. They are not known to hibernate, and their seed hoards provide a predictable food resource during periods when aboveground foraging is not profitable or when the weather is extremely cold. The young are born in a rather undeveloped state after a gestation period of approximately 28–30 days. Aboveground activity usually does not commence until the young are nearly four weeks old.—John F. Eisenberg

See also **ANIMAL ADAPTATIONS; ARIZONA DESERT; BAJA CALIFORNIA, DESERTS OF; BIPEDALITY; BURROWING ANIMALS; CALIFORNIA DESERT; CHIHUAHUAN DESERT; COLORATION; CONVERGENT EVOLUTION; DESERT GRASSLAND; DIET; GRANIVORY; GREAT BASIN DESERT; HETEROMYIDS; KANGAROO MOUSE; KIDNEY FUNCTION, DESERT RODENTS; MEXICO, DESERTS OF; NEVADA DESERT; NEW MEXICO DESERT; OREGON DESERT; PHYSIOLOGY; POCKET MOUSE; PRAIRIE; RODENTS; SALT BALANCE; SEEDS; SONORAN DESERT; TYMPANIC BULLAE; WATER BALANCE**

Further Reading

Genoways, H., and J. H. Brown, eds. 1993. *Biology of the Heteromyidae.* Special Publication No. 10, American Society of Mammalogists. Lawrence, Kan.: Allen Press.

Nowak, R. M. 1991. *Walker's Mammals of the World.* 5th ed. Baltimore: Johns Hopkins University Press.

KARAKUM DESERT. *See* ASIA, DESERTS OF

KAROO

Long, coastal desert 100–150 kilometers wide extending south from Lüderitz (26° south latitude), Namibia, to Lambert's Bay (32° south latitude), South Africa. The Karoo covers more than 50 percent of the landmass of South Africa and is divided into two biomes, the Succulent Karoo Biome and the Nama Karoo Biome, based on vegetation composition. The Succulent Karoo Biome is a winter rainfall desert with a mean annual rainfall of 20–290 millimeters. East of Lambert's Bay it extends inland for about 400 kilometers along valleys bordered by the Roggeveld Mountains to the north and the Cedarberg, Koue Bokkeveld, and Swartruggens mountain ranges to the south. Despite its low mean annual rainfall, it receives the most reliable rainfall of all the African deserts. However, in summer it is the driest of the southern African deserts. (See map of African deserts, p. 12.)

The biome is also known as Namaqualand, encompassing regions known locally as the Richtersveld, Namaqualand Klipkoppe, Sandveld, and Knersvlakte. It is bisected by the perennial Orange River, which passes through the only mountainous region in the biome, the Richtersveld. The Richtersveld is extraordinarily rich in succulent plants despite its mean annual rainfall of less than 50 millimeters. The rest of the biome is mostly flat, although the Namaqualand Klipkoppe (Rocky Hills) region between the towns of Steinkopf and Bitterfontein is dotted with distinctive, round, rocky, granite hills that are separated by sandy plains. The 30-kilometer-wide coastal strip stretching south from Port Nolloth to the Oliphant's River is known as the Sandveld because of its loose, calcareous sand and distinctive vegetation.

The Succulent Karoo has by far the highest plant species diversity of all the world's deserts. Together with the high incidence of coastal fog generated over the adjacent cold Benguela Current, the predictable winter rainfall is thought to be the primary cause of the high diversity of succulent plants that have evolved in this region and from which the biome derives its name. The succulents are particularly well represented within the families Aizoaceae, Crassulaceae, Liliaceae, and Euphorbiaceae. Two subfamilies, the Mesembryanthemoideae and the Ruschiodeae, are represented by a minimum of 2,500 species of nonflowering plants, ranging in form from cryptic ground-hugging "stone" plants, such as species in the genus *Lithops*, to the most characteristic plant life form in the biome, dwarf shrubs, such as species in the genera *Ruschia* and *Lampranthus*.

The Succulent Karoo is also well known for the spectacular irruptions of flowering annuals in spring. The annuals are mostly members of the family Asteraceae and include the Namaqualand daisy, *Dimorphotheca sinuata*, and many other daisylike annuals belonging to genera such as *Osteospermum*, *Ursinia*, *Arctotis*, and *Gorteria*. Being therophytes (annual plants enduring the stressful season in the form of seeds in the soil), the annuals are well adapted to unpredictable desert climates. Unfortunately, however, being pioneer plants as well, the irruptions of the daisies are often associated with areas that have been severely disturbed by overgrazing, soil erosion, or poor land management. Nevertheless, the spring daisies generate an important source of local income through ecotourism as tourists are attracted from all over the world to view the annual displays.

Despite its plant diversity and high degree of endemism, the conservation status of the Succulent Karoo compared with other biomes in southern Africa is disturbing. Less than 2 percent of the biome is under direct conservation management. Some reserves, such as the Richtersveld National Park, have been proclaimed in cooperation with local nomadic pastoralists who continue to graze their sheep and goats there under controlled management. Other regions that have been identified as intense hot spots of species diversity, such as the Kamiesberg, Western Mountain Karoo, and Knersvlakte, have yet to be conserved and yet continue to be overgrazed by small stock farmers.

The Nama Karoo is predominantly a summer rainfall, interior, plateau desert, so named after its indigenous Namaqua inhabitants. It is the largest desert in South Africa, covering about one-half of its total landmass, stretching from the interior borders of the Succulent Karoo in the west to about 27° east longitude. It forms an ecotone (the boundary overlap between biomes) with the Arid Savanna Biome in the north, the Fynbos Biome in the south, and the Grassland Biome in the east. It extends northward through Namibia as far as southern Angola (17° south latitude).

The biome is mostly flat but is dotted with characteristic "koppies" (small, conical hills, also termed inselbergs). In southern Namibia it is bisected by the spectacular Fish River Canyon, through which flows the Fish River, one of the tributaries of the Orange River.

The mean annual rainfall varies from 100 millimeter in the west to 520 millimeter in the east. Low prevailing humidity results in large day-night temperature fluctuations. Mean minimum monthly winter temperatures drop to -9°C, whereas mean maximum monthly temperatures can exceed 40°C in summer.

The main floral characteristics of the Nama Karoo Biome are the occurrence of dwarf shrubs (e.g., *Osteospermum sinuatum* or species of *Ruschia*) and, in the eastern regions of the biome, perennial grasses. The grass to shrub ratio is lowest in the west but increases along the west-east rainfall gradient.

Extensive areas of the Nama Karoo have been desertified through selective overgrazing by European small stock farmers (people who farm sheep and goats). This process is characterized by a replacement of palatable shrubs (e.g., *Osteospermum sinuatum, Limeum aethiopicum*) and grasses (e.g., *Themeda triandra, Cenchus ciliaris*) with unpalatable shrubs (e.g., *Galenia africana, Pteronia pallens*).

As recently as 120 years ago the Nama Karoo was home to enormous herds of nomadic springbok (*Antidorcas marsupialis*). These gazelles were reliably reported to congregate in herds numbering several million mammals and which periodically embarked on "treks" (movements) to and from the Succulent Karoo during severe winter droughts. Extensive hunting for biltong (dried meat) and the erection of fences have since decimated the herds. The Nama Karoo has a rich vertebrate fauna (131 species), including, in addition to the springbok, kudus, elephants, and ostriches. The biome supports the endangered riverine rabbit (*Bunolagus monticularis*) and endemic birds (i.e., the cinnamonbreasted warbler, *Euryptila subcinnamomea*, and Sclater's lark, *Spizocorys sclateri*).

The Nama Karoo is well known for its abundance of well-preserved mammallike reptiles. These synapsids roamed the Karoo during the late Permian and Triassic, before the domination of the terrestrial environment by the dinosaurs during the Jurassic and Cretaceous eras.—Barry G. Lovegrove

See also **ACACIA; AFRICA, DESERTS OF; AFRICAN LION; ANIMAL ADAPTATIONS; AN INTRODUCTION TO DESERTS; ANTELOPE; BENGUELA CURRENT; BIOSPHERE RESERVE; BIRDS; CATS; CHEETAH; CONSERVATION IN DESERTS; CRETACEOUS; DESERTIFICATION; DOG, WILD; DOMESTIC ANIMALS; DUNES; DURICRUSTS; FYNBOS; GEMSBOK; GRASSES; GRASSLAND; HARTEBEEST; HEAT; HEAT BALANCE; HEAT EXCHANGE; HEAT STRESS; HYENA; HYRAX; INSELBERG; KALAHARI DESERT; LIMESTONE; LION; MAMMALS; NAMIBIA, DESERTS OF; PLAYA; OSTRICH; ORYX; OVERGRAZING; PLANT ADAPTATIONS; PLEISTOCENE; RAPTORS; SALINITY; SALT PAN; SAND RAMP; SAVANNA; SOUTH AFRICA, DESERTS OF; SPRINGBOK; WATER BALANCE; WEAVER**

Further Reading

Court, D. 1981. *Succulent Flora of Southern Africa.* Cape Town, South Africa: Balkema.

Cowling, R. M., D. M. Richardson, and S. M. Pierce. 1997. *Vegetation of Southern Africa.* Oxford: Cambridge University Press.

Dean, W. R. J., M. T. Hoffman, M. E. Meadows, and S. J. Milton. 1995. Desertification in the semi-arid Karoo, South Africa: Review and reassessment. *Journal of Arid Environments* 30:247–264.

Hoffman, M. T., and R. M. Cowling. 1990. Vegetation change in the semi-arid eastern Karoo over the past 200 years: An expanding Karoo—fact or fiction? *South African Journal of Science* 86:286–294.

Le Roux, A., and T. Schelpe. 1988. *Namaqualand: South African Wild Flower Guide.* Vol. 1. Cape Town, South Africa: Botanical Society of South Africa.

Lovegrove, B. 1993. *The Living Deserts of Southern Africa.* Vlaeberg: Fernwood.

KAVIR

Salt-encrusted dry lake similar to playa, salt flat, or continental sabkha-type deposits found in the interior desert basins of Iran, including the Dasht-e-Kavir and Dasht-e-Lut in central Iran. These immense desert basins are located between the tectonically uplifted ranges of the Elburz Mountains to the north and the Zagros Mountains to the south. The largest concentration of kavirs is found in the Dasht-e-Kavir (Kavir Desert), an extremely large depression filled with salt flats, mudflats, and dune fields, with an area greater than 51,000 square kilometers, of which 20,000 square kilometers are salt-crusted surface with numerous features indicating desiccation, salt wedges, thrust polygons, and blisters and mud pinnacles.—Vatche P. Tchakerian

See also **IRAN, DESERTS OF; IRRIGATION DRAINAGE; PLAYA; SALINITY; SALT; SALT CRUST; SALT DESERT; SALT PAN**

Further Reading

Firouz, E. 1974. *Environment Iran.* Tehran: National Society for the Conservation of Natural Resources and Human Environment.

Krinsley, D. B. 1970. A geomorphological and paleoclimatological study of playas of Iran. *U.S. Geological Survey Final Scientific Report*, Contract PRO CP70-800. Bedford, Mass.: U.S. Air Force Cambridge Research Laboratories.

KAZAKHSTAN. *See* ASIA, DESERTS OF

KIDNEY FUNCTION, DESERT RODENTS

Use of the kidneys of desert rodents to balance water, salts, and other materials in internal body fluids through urine production and blood filtration. Mammals and birds can produce a urine that is more concentrated in ions than the blood itself. In birds and mammals the kidney tubules exhibit long loops, termed the loop of Henle. In desert-dwelling mammals the loops are long and densely packed within the renal medulla. The long loops permit the concentration of urine by means of countercurrent exchange, wherein urine concentration is increased as blood travels along the tubules and ion exchange (and increase) takes place. Active transport of ions to be excreted can be built up within the loop structure because material within the ascending portion of the loop can be passed to the descending portion, resulting in an increased concentration in the descending loop which is ultimately excreted. Desert rodents thus possess some of the most highly specialized kidneys among mammals for producing concentrated urine.—John F. Eisenberg

See also **ANIMAL ADAPTATIONS; COUNTERCURRENT HEAT EXCHANGE; DEHYDRATION; DESICCATION; ENDOTHERMY; ESTIVATION; EXCRETORY SYSTEM; GRASSHOPPER MOUSE; GROUND SQUIRREL; HEAT BALANCE; HEAT EXCHANGE; HEAT STRESS; HYPERTHERMIA; HYPOTHERMIA; KANGAROO MOUSE; KANGAROO RAT; KIDNEYS; MAMMALS; METABOLIC WATER; PERSPIRATION; PHYSIOLOGY; POCKET MOUSE; RENAL PAPILLA; RESPIRATORY WATER LOSS; RODENTS; SALT BALANCE; SQUIRREL; URINE; WATER BALANCE; WATER STRESS; WOODRAT**

Further Reading

Degan, A. A. 1997. *Ecophysiology of Small Desert Mammals.* New York: Springer.

Eckert, R. 1988. *Animal Physiology: Adaptation and Environment.* 3d ed. New York: Freeman.

Schmidt-Nielsen, K. 1964. *Desert Animals: Physiological Problems of Heat and Water.* New York: Oxford University Press.

———. 1990. *Animal Physiology: Adaptation and Environment.* 4th ed. New York: Cambridge University Press.

KIDNEYS

Primary organs of excretion in vertebrates responsible for the formation of urine and the removal of metabolic wastes. The main nitrogenous waste products in blood are urea in mammals and uric acid and urates in birds and reptiles. These are transferred to the kidneys for removal.

The kidneys also help to maintain water balance. An outstanding feature of the kidneys of many desert animals is their ability to produce a concentrated urine with high levels of urea, salts, and other waste products, thereby preventing excess water loss. Functional equivalents are found throughout the animal kingdom, though the term "kidney" is mostly used for vertebrates. The following description relates to kidneys of terrestrial vertebrates, with emphasis on desert mammals.

Three basic processes are involved in kidney function: filtration of small molecules out of the blood and into kidney tubules, reabsorption from the filtrate of important molecules to be saved, and active secretion into the filtrate of additional molecules to be excreted in the urine. Each process is associated with a particular region of the nephron, the functional unit of the kidney. The nephron is composed of a Bowman's capsule, a renal tubule with proximal and distal portions separated by a U-shaped segment (the loop of Henle), and a collecting duct that empties into the ureters and, ultimately, into the urinary bladder. A blood capillary network, the glomerulus, is found within each Bowman's capsule; the combined structure is called a Malpighian body. Another capillary network surrounds the tubular structures. A cross-section of a kidney would show an outer cortex layer, consisting of the Malpighian bodies and the proximal and distal tubules, and an inner layer, the medulla, containing the descending and ascending portions of the loops of Henle and most of the length of the collecting duct.

It is clearly advantageous for desert species to possess kidneys with modifications that improve water-saving potential. The kidneys of desert mammals contain nephrons with long loops of Henle, the length of which is correlated with urine-concentrating ability. In birds the percentage of nephrons with loops is reduced, as is urine-concentrating ability. Tubules of reptiles, fishes, and amphibians do not have the loop of Henle, and therefore these animals, including desert reptiles, cannot produce urine more concentrated than plasma. However, reptiles (as well as birds) are suited to the desert because they excrete nitrogenous wastes in the form of uric acid and urates, insoluble compounds that do not require water for elimination. Reptiles also have extrarenal salt glands that regulate potassium and sodium levels with very little water loss.

Urine is concentrated as a result of the architecture and function of the loop of Henle and the collecting ducts relative to the surrounding tissues. The loop and collecting ducts descend into surrounding tissues in the medulla that are progressively more concentrated toward the bend of the loop. Water passively diffuses out in response to this gradient; therefore, the urine is concentrated. The gradient itself is maintained because of active transport of osmotic particles, particularly sodium chloride, from the ascending limb of the loop out to the surrounding tissues. This complex system is referred to as a countercurrent multiplier.

Regulation of the final concentration of urine as it leaves the kidney is controlled by antidiuretic hormone (ADH) released by the posterior pituitary gland in the brain. When an organism is dehydrated, ADH is released. This increases the water permeability of the collecting duct, resulting in greater reabsorption of water and increased concentration of the urine.

Urine-concentrating ability is remarkable in many mammalian desert species. The record is seemingly held by the Australian hopping mouse, which can produce urine as much as 25 times more concentrated than blood plasma. Also noteworthy are the kangaroo rat and the camel, which have urine to plasma ratios of 14 and 8, respectively. Humans, by comparison, have a ratio of 4, and birds a ratio of 2.—E. Annette Halpern

See also **AMPHIBIANS; ANIMAL ADAPTATIONS; BIRDS; CAMEL; COUNTERCURRENT HEAT EXCHANGE; DEHYDRATION; DESICCATION; ENDOTHERMY; ESTIVATION; EXCRETORY SYSTEM; HEAT BALANCE; HEAT EXCHANGE; HEAT STRESS; HYPERTHERMIA; HYPOTHERMIA; KANGAROO RAT; KIDNEY FUNCTION, DESERT RODENTS; MAMMALS; METABOLIC WATER; PERSPIRATION; PHYSIOLOGY; RENAL PAPILLA; RESPIRATORY WATER LOSS; SALT BALANCE; SURVIVAL IN DESERTS; URINE; WATER BALANCE; WATER STRESS**

Further Reading

Degan, A. A. 1997. *Ecophysiology of Small Desert Mammals*. New York: Springer.

Eckert, R. 1988. *Animal Physiology: Adaptation and Environment*. 3d ed. New York: Freeman.

Schmidt-Nielsen, K. 1964. *Desert Animals: Physiological Problems of Heat and Water*. New York: Oxford University Press.

———. *Animal Physiology: Adaptation and Environment*. 4th ed. New York: Cambridge University Press.

Templeton, J. R. 1972. Salt and water balance in desert lizards. *In* G. M. O. Maloiy, ed., *Comparative Physiology of Desert Animals*, 61–77. New York: Academic Press.

KLIPSPRINGER

Species of antelope (*Oreotragus oreotragus*) in the mammalian family Bovidae, order Artiodactyla, that is specialized for living on rocky hills in Africa from Angola to Mozambique and in East Africa from Somalia and the Sudan south to the Cape. There are also small, isolated populations in Nigeria and the Central African Republic. Klipspringers live in dry habitats ranging from semidesert to dry woodlands and can be found in open plains as well as mountains. The one requirement is the presence of rocks; these antelopes are never found away from rocky habitat. The stoutly built klipspringer has several morphological adaptations to this habitat, including hooves with the consistency of hard rubber, thick heavy fur to protect the skin against abrasion from the rock, and protective coloration of the fur that closely matches the color of the rocks. In addition to rocks, klipspringers also require the presence of thick brush for cover.

Klipspringers feed on most plant material and can go without drinking water during the dry season. They occur in pairs and appear to mate for life, though frequently males are associated with more than one female. Klipspringers give a loud whistle or snort when they perceive danger, and the male and female will often give the call in a duet. Females give birth to a single young, which matures in less than one year. Their most important predators are the medium and large cats, hyenas, and jackals. Humans hunt klipspringers for their meat, leather, and hair, which is used to stuff saddlebags. They are rare or locally extinct in parts of Nigeria, the Sudan, and South Africa.—Thomas E. Lacher, Jr.

See also **ANTELOPE; HERBIVORY; KALAHARI DESERT; KAROO; MAMMALS; NAMIBIA, DESERTS OF; SOUTH AFRICA, DESERTS OF; UNGULATES**

Further Reading

Dorst, J., and P. Dandelot. 1980. *A Field Guide to the Larger Mammals of Africa*. London: Collins.

Estes, R. D. 1991. *The Behavior Guide to African Mammals*. Berkeley: University of California Press.

Goss, R. 1986. *Maberly's Mammals of Southern Africa: A Popular Field Guide*. Craighall, South Africa: Delta.

Haltenorth, T., and H. Diller. 1980. *A Field Guide to the Mammals of Africa, Including Madagascar*. London: Collins.

Kingdon, J. 1989. *East African Mammals: An Atlas of Evolution in Africa*. Vol. 3C. Chicago: University of Chicago Press.

Nowak, R. M. 1991. *Walker's Mammals of the World*. 5th ed. Baltimore: Johns Hopkins University Press.

KOCHUR. *See* PLAYA

KOPJE

Isolated rock outcrop that dots the plains of East Africa. Kopjes, also called koppies, inselbergs, or tors, most commonly occur in the extensive plain that runs from the eastern shore of Lake Victoria to the Rift Valley. The Serengeti National Park sits in the middle of this expansive and relatively featureless peneplain. The peneplain was formed by already deeply weathered and impoverished debris that accumulated on the basement rock and by ash blown westward from the volcanoes of the highlands. Wind and water erosion over this flat area of lakeshore has left the plain virtually free of relief with the exception of the presence of the kopjes.

Because of the great age of the peneplain, the underlying basement rock has weathered and chemically rotted, at times up to depths of more than 100 meters. This weathering is very irregular, so that subsurface towers and valleys are present. As the peneplain slowly erodes away, these towers of weathered basement rock become exposed above the surface as isolated rock outcrops, or kopjes. These kopjes dot the landscape of the Serengeti in an irregular pattern. Kopjes are often separated from one another by a substantial distance.

Kopjes are important for a number of different species of wildlife, primarily because they serve as catchments. Soil and debris trapped in the crevices of kopjes allow tree seeds to take root and grow. Many species of plants unable to tolerate the drought of the savanna can survive in the kopjes. Leopards favor kopjes in the Serengeti, and several

species of antelopes are also associated with them. The most conspicuous and regular residents of the kopjes are the hyraxes—the rock hyrax (*Procavia johnstoni*) and the bush hyrax (*Heterohyrax brucei*).—Thomas E. Lacher, Jr.

See also **HYRAX; INSELBERG; KAROO; KLIPSPRINGER; NAMIBIA, DESERTS OF; SOUTH AFRICA, DESERTS OF**

Further Reading

Hoeck, H. N., H. Klein, and P. Hoeck. 1982. Flexible social organization in hyrax. *Zeitschrift für Tierpsychologie* 59:25–298.

Lind, E. M., and M. E. S. Morrison. 1974. *East African Vegetation*. London: Longman.

Matthiessen, P. 1972. *The Tree Where Man Was Born*. New York: Dutton.

Morgan, W. T. W. 1973. *East Africa*. London: Longman.

KUDU

Large antelope in the family Bovidae (mammalian order Artiodactyla) that inhabits much of Africa, particularly the drier habitats. There are two species of kudus (genus *Tragelaphus*): the greater kudu (*Tragelaphus strepsiceros*) and the lesser kudu (*Tragelaphus imberbis*). The greater kudu is found in dry woodland and acacia thickets, especially those with rocky ground, from southern Chad to South Africa. Greater kudus are very large, and the adult males can weigh as much as 315 kilograms. Coloration is variable and ranges from reddish brown to bluish gray with thin white stripes running from the back down the sides. Both sexes have a crest running down the middle of the back. The males have a mane and a large dewlap on the throat. The horns of the male are perhaps the most spectacular of all the antelopes. The lesser kudu occurs in dry thorn–bush habitat from Ethiopia to Tanzania. They are more slender than the greater kudu, and males weigh only about 100 kilograms. Coloration is a bluish gray with stripes like the greater kudu.

Greater kudus are browsers and are active at all times. They have excellent senses of smell and hearing and are very wary. They have a tremendous leaping ability and can clear obstacles 2.5 meters high. The females form groups of five or six adults; males are more solitary but occasionally form loose-knit bachelor groups. Males establish territories during the breeding season that overlap several female territories. The females give birth to one off-

Greater kudus (*Tragelaphus strepsiceros*) in semiarid shrubland of Etosha National Park, northern Namibia. (Photo: M. A. Mares)

spring. Lesser kudus are also browsers and do not appear to require drinking water. Lesser kudus are more nocturnal than greater kudus. Their social behavior is similar to the greater kudu.

Greater kudus are prized by hunters for their impressive spiraling horns. Both species are declining because of the conversion of their habitat to agriculture.—Thomas E. Lacher, Jr.

See also **AFRICA, DESERTS OF; ANTELOPE; CONSERVATION IN DESERTS; DESERTIFICATION; HERBIVORY; KALAHARI DESERT; KAROO; MAMMALS; NAMIBIA, DESERTS OF; SOUTH AFRICA, DESERTS OF; UNGULATES; WATER BALANCE; XEROPHYLLOUS FOREST**

Further Reading

Dorst, J., and P. Dandelot. 1980. *A Field Guide to the Larger Mammals of Africa*. London: Collins.

Estes, R. D. 1991. *The Behavior Guide to African Mammals*. Berkeley: University of California Press.

Goss, R. 1986. *Maberly's Mammals of Southern Africa: A Popular Field Guide*. Craighall, South Africa: Delta.

Haltenorth, T., and H. Diller. 1980. *A Field Guide to the Mammals of Africa, Including Madagascar*. London: Collins.

Kingdon, J. 1989. *East African Mammals: An Atlas of Evolution in Africa*. Vol. 3C. Chicago: University of Chicago Press.

Nowak, R. M. 1991. *Walker's Mammals of the World*. 5th ed. Baltimore: Johns Hopkins University Press.

!KUNG BUSHMEN. *See* DESERT PEOPLES

KUWAIT, DESERT OF. *See* ARABIAN GULF, DESERTS OF

LAKES, PLUVIAL

Lakes that had fluctuating water levels during periods of greater moisture availability, occurring primarily during the Quaternary Era, a time when climatic oscillations between wetter and drier episodes were widespread, especially during the last 30,000 years.

The term "pluvial" refers to increased amounts of rainfall. However, the definition of the original term is limited, as other factors such as temperature, evapotranspiration, wind, cloud cover, watershed characteristics, groundwater, and humidity are also important for the formation and maintenance of lake levels. Most pluvial lakes are located in tectonically (having active faults/earthquakes) enclosed basins in drylands, such as those found in the American Southwest. Block faulting (a type of normal fault) and crustal warping (warping of the surface owing to internal forces within the earth) have left the basins with no outlets and enabled the continuous accumulation of clastic (sands, silts—pieces of former rock) and chemical sediments. Both tectonism and aridity are thus important in the formation and distribution of pluvial lakes. Basins (and subbasins) can be also isolated or cut off by volcanic activity, such as the damming of the basin by lava flows, aeolian deflation (lowering of a surface by wind), mass movements (landslides), and alluvial fans/bajadas acting as sills to block water movement, thereby creating lakes.

Lake level fluctuations are controlled primarily by the amount of precipitation on the drainage area and directly on the lake. Other important direct contributions to lake level variations are discharge from rivers and their tributaries, springs, overland flow, throughflow, and groundwater inflow. In addition to direct inputs, evaporation also plays a key role in the water budget. Lower temperatures, higher precipitation amounts, higher humidities, and lower solar radiation values tend to lower evaporation; increased wind velocities and lower salinities increase evaporation. Past evaporation amounts can be reasonably estimated from modern-day temperature and evaporation data. Also, paleoprecipita-

tion amounts can be calculated provided the above information can be collected from lake geomorphology, hydrology, and present climatic data. Numerous methods and equations are available for reconstructing past lake water balance values.

Pluvial lakes contain and are surrounded by a plethora of geomorphic evidence in the form of high shoreline strands (marks left as a result of high lake level shoreline edges), wave-cut cliffs (sharp cliffs left standing because of undercutting by lake waves), barrier bars and spits (depositional features, generally of sand, that form parallel to a coast because of active sand movement along that coast, probably the result of longshore transport), deltas (depositional plains, similar in shape to the Greek letter D, formed as a result of a river reaching an area of a lake and depositing its sediments), and lake sediments, as well as remains of organisms and archaeological materials. In addition, deflation (lowering of a surface by wind) of playa surfaces leads to the development of dunes and lunettes (crescent-shaped, vegetated, lakeshore dunes) found on the lee side of the many dry lakes. Because pluvial lakes had no outlets, thick deposits of evaporites and chemical sediments were accumulated, along with clastic sediments from the nearshore. The paleoclimatic information from these sediments is useful for reconstructing past temperatures, salinities, and microfaunas, among others. For example, sediment cores from the deepest (central) portions of the lake might contain alternating sequences of muds (wetter periods/deeper waters), evaporites and brines (drier periods/shallow waters), and transitional sediments, indicating one or more alternating periods of conditions that were drier or wetter than present conditions. The cycles from freshwater to brackish to saline to hypersaline and back to freshwater can be reconstructed by using the remains of organisms that lived in lakes. For example, the study of diatoms can provide information about the paleochemistry of the lake waters.

The highest concentration of pluvial lakes in North America is in the Basin and Range Province of the western United States. During the Late Wisconsin, 25,000–10,000 years ago, more than 120 endoreic (internal drainage) basins contained pluvial lakes. The two largest, including their interconnected subbasins, were Lakes Bonneville and Lahontan. Lake Bonneville, with an area greater than 50,000 square kilometers and a maximum depth of 330 meters, was centered in Utah, with the present Great Salt Lake being only a small remnant of the original lake. Lake Lahontan, with an area of 23,000 square kilometers and a maximum depth of more than 275 meters, was centered in northwestern Nevada. Geomorphic evidence from the Great Basin indicates that lake levels were highest 20,000–12,000 years ago. Beginning around 9,000 years ago lake levels in the Great Basin dropped significantly with more arid conditions and warmer than present temperatures, and by the time of the mid-Holocene Climatic Optimum (also referred to as the Altithermal), about 5,000 years ago, the majority of the lakes were dry.

The pluvial (wet) periods in the middle latitudes coincide with the glacial (cold) stages, particularly in the American Southwest, when most pluvial lakes reached their greatest extent 20,000–12,000 years ago. However, during the same time in the intertropical belt, extending between 23.5° north and south latitude, climatic conditions were reversed, with aridity widespread and pluvial lake levels low to dry. Between 12,000 and 5,000 years ago the situation was reversed, with the intertropical belt experiencing wetter conditions and high lake stands, the latter exemplified by Lake MegaChad in the Saharan Desert. Lush tropical vegetation and savanna animals (as seen in the rock petroglyph drawings) were found in the interior of the present-day arid Sahara Desert. Therefore, fluctuations in lake levels were not synchronous between the intertropical regions and the middle and high latitudes. The earlier notion that worldwide pluvial conditions were synonymous with glacial stages is no longer tenable.—Vatche P. Tchakerian

See also **ALLUVIAL FAN; ALLUVIAL SOILS; AQUATIC HABITATS; BONNEVILLE; CLIMATE; DESERTS; DUNES; GLACIAL PERIODS; GREAT BASIN DESERT; GROUNDWATER; HOLDRIDGE LIFE ZONES; HYDROLOGICAL CYCLE; HYDROLOGY; IRRIGATION DRAINAGE; NEOGENE; PALEOCLIMATE; PLATE TECTONICS; PLAYA; PLEISTOCENE; PRECIPITATION; PRODUCTIVITY, AQUATIC ECOSYSTEMS; QUATERNARY; RELATIVE HUMIDITY; RIVERS; RUNOFF; WATER; WATER OF RETENTION; WEATHERING, DESERT; WIND EROSION; WIND TRANSPORT**

Further Reading

Street, F. A. 1981. Tropical paleoenvironments. *Progress in Physical Geography* 5:157–185.

Smith, G. I., and F. A. Street-Perrott. 1983. Pluvial lakes of the western United States. *In* H. E. Wright, Jr., ed., *Late Quaternary Environments of the United States*, 190–212. Minneapolis: University of Minnesota Press.

LANDSCAPE

Term emphasizing the spatial and temporal biotic patterns, interrelations, connections, and processes of the various ecosystems that compose a relatively large region, and which is commonly used in describing the physiography (geology, topography, soils, terrain) of that region. Landscape is a classification concept that has recently been receiving much attention in the areas of ecology, conservation biology, and natural resource management. In its current scientific usage the landscape concept emphasizes the next level of organization above smaller and more local ecosystems. A landscape, which may be hundreds of kilometers in size, represents a heterogeneous mosaic of interacting ecosystems.

One advantage of the landscape concept is that it does not view ecosystems as isolated compartments in nature but instead stresses that such ecosystems as lakes and forests, ponds and grasslands, deserts and streams are interconnected by a variety of complex and dynamic ecological processes. The concept of a landscape is not new. The biome classification used by ecologists also emphasizes the interrelations present in larger regions that are composed of many smaller interacting biotic communities. However, the recent interest in the landscape concept has led to the development of a new field called landscape ecology. Also, the field of landscape architecture has used many of the concepts of landscape ecology for several decades.

Landscape ecology emphasizes a holistic perspective that views landscapes as more than the mere sum of the biotic and abiotic components. At the landscape level of organization, new processes such as regional disturbances (human effects, fires, storms), intersystem migration of organisms, and energy and nutrient transport between systems begin to emerge. The exchange of energy and nutrients between ecosystems means that a landscape is a functional level of organization. Landscape ecology is the study of biotic communities or ecosystems on a larger spatial scale and involves examining patterns of habitats, species distributions, and ecological processes inherent in large and heterogeneous mosaics of ecosystems.

The landscape concept is being widely used in modern conservation biology, particularly in the design of nature preserves, the establishment of parks, and habitat preservation or restoration. Such decisions as habitat size and number, habitat shape and boundaries, buffer zones, populations sizes, and corridors and networks connecting diverse habitats, as well as other management decisions, demand a more holistic approach by resource managers. Landscape ecology attempts to provide resource managers with such relevant information, thus allowing them to make more holistic resource management decisions.

Landscape ecology and conservation biology rely heavily on remote sensing and GIS (geographic information systems) as tools, because these new techniques have tremendous capacity for collecting, analyzing, and displaying ecological information for large, complex, and integrated systems of nature.—Gary K. Hulett and Amanda Renner Charles

See also **BIOME; BIOSPHERE RESERVE; CONSERVATION IN DESERTS; DESERTIFICATION; ECOLOGY; ECOSYSTEM**

Further Reading

Edwards, P. J., R. M. May, and N. R. Webb. 1994. *Large-Scale Ecology and Conservation Biology*. Boston: Blackwell.

Forman, R. T. T. 1995. *Land Mosaics: The Ecology of Landscapes and Regions*. Cambridge: Cambridge University Press.

Hansson, L., L. Fahrig, and G. Merriam, eds. 1995. *Mosaic Landscapes and Ecological Processes*. New York: Chapman and Hall.

McHarg, I. 1969. *Design with Nature*. New York: Natural History Press.

Pickett, S. T. A,. and M. L. Cadenasso. 1995. Landscape Ecology: Spatial Heterogeneity in Ecological Systems. *Science* 269:331–334.

LARK

Small, predominantly Old World terrestrial songbird (family Alaudidae, order Passeriformes). Approximately 80 species in about 15 genera are recognized. Larks reach maximum species diversity in Africa but are also found in Eurasia, and a few representatives are found in Australia and the New World. Larks are generally associated with open country, often in semiarid and arid habitats. The body is somewhat robust. The wings are generally long and pointed. Plumage usually consists of rather muted, cryptic shades of brown, often with streaking on the breast. Some species are characterized by contrasting black-and-white markings. A number of species possess short crests. Plumage coloration is usually not sexually dimorphic, although males are often larger than females. Leg length is variable, but most species have relatively long legs. Many taxa have long straight hind claws, especially those that prefer areas with a soft soil substrate and short vegetation. Bill morphology is variable across species and even within species or between sexes. Shapes range from long and curved to short and finchlike, reflecting different modes of foraging. Diet generally includes seeds and insects, although the proportion of each food type depends on the species.

Larks are generally described as being solitary, territorial, and monogamous, although cases of polyandry (e.g., calandra lark, *Melanocorypha calandra*), cooperative breeding (e.g., spike-heeled lark, *Chersomanes albofasciata*), and semicoloniality (e.g., chestnut-backed sparrow lark, *Eremopterix leucotis*) have been reported. Onset of breeding in many regions is strongly correlated with the rainy season. In many species males advertise for a mate with intricate aerial displays and singing. Nests are usually placed on the ground and are concealed by and lined with vegetation. A few desert species build nests that are slightly elevated, presumably to allow for greater air circulation. Clutch size ranges from two to seven. Incubation periods last from 11 to 16 days.—Stephen C. Lougheed

See also **AFRICA, DESERTS OF; ANIMAL ADAPTATIONS; BIRDS; BREEDING SEASON; DIVERSITY; SPAIN, DESERTS OF**

Further Reading

Cramp, S., ed. 1988. *Handbook of the Birds of Europe the Middle East and North Africa: The Birds of the Western Palearctic*. Vol. 5. Oxford: Oxford University Press.

Dean, W. R. J., and P. A. R. Hockey. 1989. An ecological perspective of lark (Alaudidae) distribution and diversity in the southwest arid zone of Africa. *Ostrich* 60:27–34.

Keith, S., E. K. Urban, and C. H. Fry, eds. 1992. *The Birds of Africa*. Vol. 4. New York: Academic Press.

Willoughby, E. J. 1968. Water economy of the Stark's lark and grey-back finch-lark from the Namib Desert of South West Africa. *Comparative Biochemistry and Physiology* 27:723–745.

Willoughby, E. J. 1971. Biology of larks (Aves: Alaudidae) in the central Namib Desert. *Zoologica Africana* 6:133–176.

LAVA

Rocky material of magmatic origin (molten rock from deep in the earth) that emerges to the surface through the action of volcanoes or through fissures in the crust of the earth at temperatures of from 700°C to 1,200°C. When termed "magma," the material is in a semifluid stage and forms in regions at great depths below the lithosphere (the terrestrial portion of the earth), where it is subjected to high pressure and temperature, factors that give it unique properties corresponding neither to liquids nor solids. After cooling and consolidating, lava forms igneous rocks that are rich in aluminum and aluminum oxides, silica, iron, calcium, and sodium.

Depending on the amount of silica, lavas may be classified as acidic lavas, which are rich in silica, are fluid, and solidify slowly; and basic lavas, which are low in silica, are viscous, and solidify quickly. The physicochemical characteristics of the lava define its morphology. *Pahoehoe* lavas are characterized by a ridged surface and are laid down in concentric bands. These originate by rapid cooling and solidifying of a superficial layer of lava that forms over lava that is still in the fluid state and moving below it. *Malpais* lavas are characterized by a chaotic agglomeration of blocks that occurs when gases are escaping through the surface of the lava as it consolidates and solidifies. Some lavas that form below the ocean assume a pattern of rounded concentric blocks; these are termed *pillow lavas.*

Since many desert areas form in the shadow of major mountain ranges, lavas are common formations in arid areas, where they often develop their own unique flora and fauna.—Alberto I. J. Vich and Juana Susana Barroso

See also **ANIMAL ADAPTATIONS; BAJA CALIFORNIA, DESERTS OF; COLORATION; DESERTS; DURICRUSTS; ECOTYPES; ENDEMISM; LITHOSPHERE; PLANT GEOGRAPHY; PLATE TECTONICS; SPECIATION**

The Rio Grande flowing through lava more than 8 meters thick in the Valley of the Volcanoes (Valle de los Volcanes), in the Monte Desert of southernmost Mendoza Province, Argentina. (Photo: M. A. Mares)

Further Reading

Bates, R. L., ed. 1987. *Glossary of Geology*. 3d ed. Alexandria, Va.: American Geological Institute.

Cooke, R., A. Warren, and A. Goudie. 1993. *Desert Geomorphology*. London: University College London Press. Pp. 114–142.

Moore, G. W. 1978. *Dictionary of Geography: Definitions and Explanation of Terms Used in Physical Geography*. New York: Harper and Row.

LEACHING. *See* IRRIGATION DRAINAGE

LEAVES

Lateral organs of vascular plants formed by the shoot apical meristem. Leaves have two primary parts: blades and petioles. The latter, which may be lacking, is the leaf stalk. When present it extends leaves away from the stem. In cross-section petioles may be round or flat, as in cottonwoods, which occur along streams in arid lands and whose leaves

Microphyllous (tiny) leaves of the palo verde tree (*Cercidium microphyllum*); note the hand in the foreground for scale. (Photo: M. A. Mares)

rustle or quake in the breeze. Often the petiole is swollen at the base. Leaves may also exhibit accessory structures called stipules at the base of the petiole. Stipules may be leaflike or modified to form spines, and they may fall immediately after the leaf opens.

Leaf blades are the primary organ of photosynthesis in most vascular plants. Therefore, the blades are usually broad and flat to intercept the maximum available light and to capture atmospheric carbon dioxide. Their arrangement on the stem may aid in total plant light capture. Shape and structure of the blades varies widely. They may be long and slender (such as pine needles), lance shaped, or rounded. The leaves of junipers, common shrubs of western North American semideserts, are small and cover the stem like the scales of fish. Margins of leaf blades may be lobed or toothed, and the blade may even be dissected to form multiple blades (compound leaves versus simple leaves with a single blade). The leaflets of a compound leaf can be distinguished from simple leaves because they lack buds in the axils. The blade has veins that carry water and dissolved food. Blades are surrounded by a protective layer of cells called the epidermis. The epidermis is often waxy, especially on the upper surface. This reduces water loss. The epidermis is punctuated by pores (stomata) for gas exchange between the leaf's interior and the atmosphere. Gas exchange is a passive, diffusion-driven process. The cells of the central tissue (mesophyll) have chloro-

plasts and are green. The mesophyll is the photosynthetic tissue.

Leaves of desert plants are often highly modified. These modifications may reduce water loss via transpiration (loss of water vapor from the stomata and surfaces of leaves) or provide protection from herbivores, a means of reducing water loss to animals. One modification, especially for trees and shrubs, is for the plant to drop its leaves during drought. This is accomplished through the development of a corky water-impermeable layer of cells at the base of the petiole. Unable to obtain water from the root/stem axis, the leaf dies and falls from the plant. In the striking desert plant ocotillo (*Fouquieria splendens*), the blade falls away, leaving the midvein, which becomes a spine. The leaves of ocotillo may fall several times during the year, depending on rainfall. Leaf shape and size might also have been modified through natural selection to reduce the surface area and thus reduce transpiration. As an example, the leaf surface of sagebrush (*Artemisia tridentata*) is much less than that of its close relative, *Artemisia ludoviciana*, which occurs in moist areas in the Great Basin Desert. Frequently leaves of desert plants are small or linear. They also have a heavy cuticle on the upper surface, and many have long epidermal hairs. The hairs, which are abundant in sagebrush, for example, are colorless and reflect light, which probably lowers surface temperatures and reduces water loss. Desert leaves also are often hardened, making them less desirable as forage, and may be covered with spines. In some plant groups leaves have been replaced completely by spines, as in cacti. Finally, less obvious is the presence of bitter-tasting compounds that act as a deterrent to consumption of the leaves by animals.—James R. Estes

See also **ARTEMISIA; CACTI; HERBIVORY; OCOTILLO; PHOTOSYNTHESIS; PLANT ADAPTATIONS; PLANTS; SAGEBRUSH; STOMA; THORN**

Further Reading

Rost, T. L., M. G. Barbour, R. M. Thornton, T. E. Weier, and C. R. Stocking. 1984. *Botany.* 2d ed. New York: Wiley.

LEBANON, DESERTS OF

Arid lands lying within the geographic boundaries of the nation of Lebanon, a Middle Eastern country (area: 10,400 square kilometers) bordered by Syria and Israel and located at the eastern end of the

Mediterranean Sea. The mountainous landscape of Lebanon is divided into three major regions: the northern region, in which the highest peaks attain elevations of about 3,000 meters at Qurnet es Sauda and Jebel Makmal; the central region, whose highest peak is 2,620 meters at Jebel Sannin; and the southern region, which extends into the Galilean Mountains, with the highest peak being Jebel Baruk at 1,950 meters. These mountains are composed mainly of limestone and some sandstone. (See map of Middle East deserts, p. 361.)

The climate of Lebanon belongs to the general Mediterranean pattern characterized by cool to mild rainy winters and hot dry summers. Mean annual temperature is about 15°C, and annual rainfall is about 900 millimeters; extreme minimum and maximum temperatures, respectively, are -13°C and 36°C.

Due to water scarcity, as well as geopolitical factors that limit access to the country's sparse water resources, Lebanon's deserts are considered to have very limited agricultural potential. In some areas artificially enriching the soil permits limited agriculture, and there is some seasonal grazing possible in a few areas during years of elevated rainfall.

The littoral sand dune communities found along the Mediterranean coast support populations of *Ammophila arenaria* and *Retama raetam*. Ascending into the mountains from the sandy lowlands, a lower western altitudinal belt of vegetation (the Eu-Mediterranean Belt) occurs at 200–300 meters elevation. This zone supports such plants as *Hyperrhenia hirta*, *Myrtus communis*, and *Pinus brutia*. Above the Eu-Mediterranean Belt and extending up to 1,500 meters elevation is the Oro-Mediterranean Belt, a plant zone containing *Quercus calliprinos*, *Pistacia palaestina*, and various species of pines (*Pinus*). At elevations of 1,500–2,000 meters cedar forests are common, with *Cedrus libani* and other trees such as *Abies cilicica* and *Juniperus excelsa*. The subalpine and alpine belts (above 2,000 meters) are characterized by species of *Astragalus*, *Acantholimon armenum*, *Salsola canescens*, *Minuartia libanotica*, *Festuca pinifolia*, and *Marrubium libanoticum*. Above 2,500 meters elevation, vegetation is very poor with only a sparse cover of such plants as *Heracleum humile*, *Cistopteris fragilis*, *Oxyria digyna*, *Potentilla geranioides*, *Ranunclus*, and *Scorzonera alpina*. In general, the western mountain slopes support true Mediterranean vegetation, whereas the eastern slopes do not.

Biodiversity in terrestrial ecosystems is rich in relation to the small size of the country—about 2,000 species of flowering plants, 52 mammals, and 130 birds have been recorded. Agriculture contributes about 12 percent to Lebanon's GNP and employs about 12 percent of the workforce. The total arable land in Lebanon is only 301,000 hectares, and of this, 29 percent is irrigated. There are 51,000 cattle, 604,000 sheep and goats, and a few camels maintained as domestic stock.

Land use and deforestation have been accelerated in the mountainous areas due to sylvicultural practices, food crops and fodder production, wood production (including fuelwood), and intensive livestock grazing. War in the southern part of Lebanon over the past two decades has resulted in the collapse and degradation of the natural ecosystems and increasing desertification. The major manifestations of this desertification are soil erosion, damage to water resources, deterioration of vegetation, and loss of biodiversity.—Ahmad K. Hegazy

See also **ACACIA; AFRICA, DESERTS OF; AGRICULTURE IN DESERTS; CATS; CHENOPODIACEAE; CONTAMINATION; CONSERVATION IN DESERTS; DESERTIFICATION; DESERT PEOPLES; DIRT BIKES; DOMESTIC ANIMALS; FOX; GAZELLE; GERBIL; IBEX; IRRIGATION DRAINAGE; ISRAEL, DESERTS OF; LEGUMES; MAMMALS; MIDDLE EAST, DESERTS OF; OFF-ROAD VEHICLES; OVERGRAZING; PALESTINE, DESERTS OF; POLLUTION; RODENTS; SAHARA DESERT; SHEEP; SYRIA, DESERTS OF**

Further Reading

Evenari, M., I. Noy-Meir, and D. W. Goodall, eds. 1986. *Ecosystems of the World: Hot Deserts and Arid Shrublands*. Vol. 12B. New York: Elsevier.

Food and Agriculture Organization. 1994. A systems perspective for sustainable dryland development in the Near East region. Cairo: Near East Regional Office.

Zohary, M. 1973. *Geobotanical Foundations of the Middle East*. Vols. 1 and 2. Amsterdam: Gustav Fischer.

———. 1983. Man and vegetation in the Middle East. *In* W. Holzner, M. J. A. Werger, and I. Ikusima, eds., *Man's Impact on Vegetation*, 287–295. The Hague: Junk.

LEGUMES

Individuals of the pea family (Fabaceae or Leguminosae; either name is permissible in the International Code of Botanical Nomenclature), with the dry-fruit type having a single chamber that splits at maturity along both sutures and may be straight, curved, or spiraled; the fruits have two to many seeds that are inserted in two alternating rows. Members of the family have nodules on the roots that contain nitrogen-fixing bacteria of the genus *Rhizobium*. The family is one of the two or three largest plant families (approximately 700 genera and 17,000 species) and contains herbs, shrubs, trees, and vines. Fabaceae has three subfamilies (Mimosoideae, Caesalpinoideae, and Papilionoideae), all of which have fruits that are legumes. The subfamilies differ with respect to floral characteristics. Some scientists have elevated each of the subfamilies to the family level (Mimosaceae, Caesalpinaceae, and Papilionaceae).

Species of the legume family have alternate (usually compound) leaves with stipules. The flowers have five petals, all of them free, or two of them fused; they also have five or ten (or occasionally more) stamens (pollen-bearing structure), and one pistil (pollen-receiving, seed-producing structure). Papilionoideae flowers are bilaterally symmetrical with petals that form a lower keel, two wings, and an upper banner and are said to resemble insects. The stamens and pistils are completely enclosed by the keel. Examples of papilionoid species are peas and bluebonnets. The family includes trees, shrubs, and herbs.

Fabaceae has a large number of cultivated species: alfalfa, broad beans, chick peas, clover, common beans, cowpeas, garden peas, green beans, lentils, lima beans, peanuts, soybeans, and vetch. The pods and leaves are often rich in protein. The family also includes several cultivated ornamentals, and numerous drugs and gums are extracted from legume species. The family is worldwide and well represented in deserts of the world, where shrubby legumes are often armed with thorns, spines, and/or prickles.

Acacia, a shrubby genus (some species are trees) of Mimosoideae, is especially abundant in warm deserts of the world. In Latin America, in the dry tropical forest, some species of ants and acacias live in a mutualistic relationship. These acacia species produce large, paired, hollow spines (formed from stipules) at the base of the compound leaves. Ants of the genus *Pseudomyrmex* live in the hollow spines. Workers of the ant colony attack herbivores that alight on or brush against the shrubs, and they cut away branches of competing trees, thereby protecting the plant from herbivores, fire, and shading. In return the acacias produce nectar on the leaves and protein-rich structures at the tips of leaflets, both of which are consumed by the ants. Acacias in the Sinai Desert probably provided food for the Israelites during the Exodus when they wandered in the wilderness for forty years. One species of *Acacia* provides gum arabic, a resin used in glues. A species of *Acacia* is represented on the Australian coat of arms, and some members in Australia are valuable sources of timber.

Prosopis (commonly called mesquite in North America and algarrobo in South America) is also a common mimosoid genus of warm deserts of North America, South America, North Africa, and the Middle East. The genus has more than 40 species, the majority of which are native to the New World. The natural habitat of all the species is along desert washes, where they are phreatophytes (plants that exploit water-rich microhabitats in the desert). In this case the plants have deep taproots (up to 50 meters) that enter the water table (the water table is shallower under streams, even dry streams, in desert regions). Many phreatophytes do not conserve water, but mesquite species that have been studied share many water conservation traits with true xerophytes. In addition to the taproot, *Prosopis glandulosa* has a broad and shallow root system that may extend up to 20 meters from the main stem. Roots of the plants are capable of extracting water from the soil at negative water potentials of 15 atmospheres. Their abundant and very sharp spines probably deter some mammals from grazing, although these may have evolved to protect against larger mammals that are long extinct.

The introduction of grazing to the Great Plains allowed mesquite to invade the shortgrass steppes and the Chihuahuan Desert grassland. Virtually no grassland in the Chihuahuan Desert is free from mesquite today. Mesquite has become a pest because of its superior competitive ability under intense grazing. Areas of north central Texas and southwestern Oklahoma are now dominated by mesquite and buffalo grass (in the mesquite grassland savanna), whereas it may have been rare or absent there prior to A.D. 1500.

Fungi are associated with the roots of mesquite, and often the fungal flora varies with depth in the soil; the fungi probably assist in water uptake. Characteristic of legumes, mesquite has root nodules that can fix nitrogen. Interestingly, in some exceptionally dry deserts the leaves do not decompose (conditions are too arid for decomposition to occur) and return nitrogen to the soil.

Mesquite plants flower abundantly in the spring and may flower again if there are heavy rains following a drought. The profusion of flowers that are nectar-rich contributes considerable calories to the bee and butterfly fauna (bees are major pollinators of the plants). The beans are high in protein and are useful fodder. The seeds germinate readily after passage through the digestive tract of ungulates. This permits migration of the plants as they are eaten in one spot, carried off in the gut of large herbivores, and dropped with excrement at another, more distant, spot. When the seed germinates most of the early energy for growth is devoted to the root, an adaptation that is undoubtedly useful in the dry conditions of the desert.—James R. Estes

See also **ACACIA; ANTS; BEES; BUTTERFLIES; DECOMPOSITION; DESERT PEOPLES; ECONOMIC VALUE OF DESERT PRODUCTS; FLOWERS; FOREST; FRUITS; FUNGI; GERMINATION; LEAVES; MESQUITE; NITROGEN-FIXING PLANTS; PHOTOSYNTHESIS; PHREATOPHYTES; PLANT ADAPTATIONS; PLANTS; ROOTS; SEEDS; THORN; XEROPHYLLOUS FOREST; XEROPHYTES**

Further Reading

Heywood, V. H., ed. 1993. *Flowering Plants of the World.* Updated ed. New York: Oxford University Press.

Simspon, B. B., ed. 1977. *Mesquite: Its Biology in Two Desert Ecosystems.* Stroudsburg, Pa.: Dowden, Hutchinson and Ross.

LIBYA, DESERTS OF

Arid areas situated within the geographic boundaries of Libya, located on the Mediterranean coast of North Africa and bordered by Tunisia, Algeria, Niger, Chad, Sudan, and Egypt. Libya occupies an area of about 1,760,000 square kilometers; 94.7 percent of the area is arid desert. The country possesses a rather wide range of climate, varying from a subhumid Mediterranean climate to an extremely arid inland desert climate. There are no regular rivers, but the deeply eroded wadis (gullies or arroyos) may form torrential streams during periods of heavy rainfall. The inland deserts receive a mean annual rainfall ranging from 0.9 to 71.0 millimeters, with the rainy season occurring from October to April. The mean minimum temperature of the coldest month varies from 2.3° to 10.2°C, and the mean maximum of the hottest month varies from 28.3° to 42.5°C. (See map of African deserts, p. 12.)

Few studies have been carried out on the biotic and abiotic components of the desert ecosystems of Libya. Some parts of the country were studied in connection with other vast areas of the Sahara, or with subjects devoted to special topics, for example, pasture, savanna, and esparto lands (steppe land characterized by loamy soils and covered by the esparto grass, *Lygeum spartum*). Most of these studies have not been published. The landscape exhibits many well-defined landforms. The main phyto-, eco-, or geomorphological systems are sand formations, rocky and gravel deserts, depressions, salt-affected lands, fallow lands, wadis (or water runnels), escarpments, and mountains.

Biodiversity of Libya the country is not as rich as might be expected considering its vast size. Libya supports an estimated 1,800 species of flowering plants, 80 species of mammals, and 85 species of birds in the major desert ecosystems. Of these species, a number are threatened, including 4 percent of the flowering plants, 15 percent of the mammals, and 11 percent of the birds. Biological diversity in the Tibesti Plain facing the Chad frontier is mainly restricted to wadis and sandy depressions. Common plants are *Centropodia forsskalii, Stipagrostis plumosa,* and *Monosonia nivea.* Desert savanna vegetation occurs in the southeastern portions in wadi terraces, depressions, and escarpments. Among the common woody plants are *Acacia raddiana, Balanites aegyptiaca,* and *Ziziphus mauritiana,* which are interspersed with the perennials *Cymbopogon schoenanthus, Lasiurus scindicus,* and *Panicum turgidum.* Generally the depressions accumulate fine soils and runoff water and harbor a denser vegetation than the more arid surroundings. The main sand formations are represented by the Great Sand Sea of Calanscio and the Rebiana Sand Sea in the eastern part of the country, while the Ubari and Murzuq sand seas are found in the southwest. Occasional showers may produce an ephemeral, or short-lived, annual vegetation. The mountainous landscapes have a characteristic arid vegetation with strong Mediterranean affinities.

The history of land use and human impact on desert ecosystems is attested to by the presence of Libyan "predesert" towns, for instance, the town of Bani Walid in western Libya. Ancient runoff-water farming systems (sometimes referred to as wadi agriculture) were introduced almost two millennia ago. Relics of man-made terraces and dams can still be observed in many desert areas. The tribal disputes between the nomadic populations and agricultural interests over ownership of grazing lands, grain fields, and oases have forced the agricultural settlers to retreat to mountainous areas such as Jabal Nefusah in northwestern Libya. In these arid mountains they developed rather sophisticated land use practices for desert agriculture.

In rural areas where firewood is used extensively, overgrazing, clearing of natural vegetation for cultivation, and drought have led to desertification, loss of biodiversity, accelerated land erosion, and deterioration of the ecological balance in many parts of the country. Agricultural development has been a governmental goal for the past two decades. In Tripolitania, Yeffren Area, and the Libyan Desert itself, thousands of hectares of sand formations have been developed. The large fossil aquifer of Al Kufrah in the Libyan Desert, which is being pumped into a great man-made covered river, yields about 4.3 cubic meters per second of water that is 20,000–30,000 years old. Currently agriculture contributes 5 percent of the GNP and employs about 14 percent of the workforce. The area of arable land is estimated at about 2.1 million hectares; of this, about 11 percent is irrigated and the rest is fed by rainwater. There are about 212,000 cattle, 6.6 million sheep and goats, and 182,000 camels supported in the country as domestic livestock.—Ahmad K. Hegazy

See also **ACACIA; AFRICA, DESERTS OF; AGRICULTURE IN DESERTS; CATS; CHENOPODIACEAE; CONTAMINATION; CONSERVATION IN DESERTS; DESERTIFICATION; DESERT PEOPLES; DIRT BIKES; DOMESTIC ANIMALS; FOX; GAZELLE; GERBIL; IBEX; IRRIGATION DRAINAGE; ISRAEL, DESERTS OF; LEGUMES; MAMMALS; MIDDLE EAST, DESERTS OF; OFF-ROAD VEHICLES; OVERGRAZING; PALESTINE, DESERTS OF; POLLUTION; RODENTS; SAHARA DESERT; SALINIZATION; SHEEP; SYRIA, DESERTS OF**

Further Reading

Barker, G. 1996. *Farming the Desert: The UNESCO Libyan Valleys Archaeological Survey.* Paris: UNESCO.

Boulos, L. 1972. Our present knowledge of the flora and vegetation of Libya: Bibliography. *Webbia* 26:365–400.

Brown, E. S. 1947. The distribution and vegetation of

egg-laying sites of the desert locust (*Schistocerca gregaria* Forsk) in Tripolitania in 1946. *Bulletin of the Society Fouad 1er Entomology* 31:287–306.

Gilbertson, D. D., C. O. Hunt, N. R. J. Fieller, and G. W. W. Barker. 1994. The environmental consequences and context of Ancient floodwater farming in the Tripolitanian Pre-desert. *In* A. C. Millington and K. Pye, eds., *Environmental Change in Drylands,* 229–251. New York: Wiley.

Kassas, M. 1995. Desertification: A general review. *Journal of Arid Environments* 30:115–128.

Le Houerou, H. N. 1986. The desert and arid zones of Northern Africa. *In* M. Evenari, I. Noy-Meir, and D. W. Goodall, eds., *Ecosystems of the World: Hot Deserts and Arid Shrublands,* 12A:101–147. New York: Elsevier.

LICHENS

Organisms defined by (and composed of) a symbiotic association of a fungus and an autotrophic species that form a mutualistic relationship. The photosynthetic (green) member of the pair often is a species of green algae (Chlorophyta) or bluegreen bacteria (Cyanobacteria). In the majority of lichens the fungus belongs to the Ascomycetes (sac fungi) but may also be a member of the Basidiomycetes (club fungi). The fungal member is dependent on the relationship, but the algae can exist free of the lichen association.

The chlorophyll-containing element provides photosynthate (organic molecules) to the fungal member, whereas the fungus provides a moist habitat. The fungus forms the outer and inner layers of the thallus (nonvascular plant body), and the photosynthetic member is between the two. Reproduction is usually vegetative (nonsexual) with the thallus breaking up and both parts growing, or a lichen may produce small sporelike bodies that have fungal and algal cells. Sexual reproduction and true spore production involve each member reproducing independently and reestablishment of the lichen thallus. Lichens are abundant in both hot and cold deserts of the world. They form crusts on exposed rock and through the release of chemicals, dissolve the substrate to form soil. High levels of lichen biodiversity appear to be an excellent measure of air quality. During periods of extreme drought lichens become dry and appear to be dead, but with rain they absorb water and become green again.—James R. Estes

See also **BACTERIA; PLANTS; RESURRECTION PLANT; ROCK VARNISH**

Further Reading

Friedmann, E. I., and M. Galun. 1974. Desert algae, lichens, and fungi. *In* G. W. Brown, ed., *Desert Biology: Special Topics on the Physical and Biological Aspects of Arid Regions*, 2:166–212. New York: Academic Press.

Nash, T. H., and T. J. Moser. 1982. Vegetational and physiological patterns of lichens in North American deserts. *J. Hattori Botanical Laboratory* 53:331–336.

Rost, T. L., M. G. Barbour, R. M. Thornton, T. E. Weier, and C. R. Stocking. 1984. *Botany.* 2d ed. New York: Wiley.

LIFE HISTORY STRATEGY (ITEROPARITY)

Life history term that refers to the repeated production of offspring during an individual's lifetime. In contrast, an organism that is semelparous produces all of its offspring in a single reproductive event, after which it dies. Organisms must meet various challenges of their environments, and natural selection has favored a variety of life history patterns to meet these challenges. Life histories include an organism's pattern of growth and differentiation, its storage of nutrients, and perhaps most important, its reproductive pattern. Iteroparous species allocate less energy to reproduction during any one time period, but they generally have a reasonable chance to survive to produce future offspring. Iteroparity may be overlapping or continuous. In overlapping iteroparity, individuals breed repeatedly but nevertheless have a distinct breeding season. In continuous iteroparity, breeding is continuous throughout the year, and these species typically live in aseasonal environments.

Most vertebrates tend to be iteroparous; in general long-lived species tend to breed repeatedly. Iteroparous species must be able to survive from one reproductive event to the next; thus if environmental conditions are harsh, such as in a desert, the risk of dying may be greater. As an individual organism ages, an increase in reproductive effort is predicted. This is because the cost of present reproduction diminishes as the future expectation of reproduction declines. In general life history patterns are complicated responses to a suite of environmental and biotic factors, and organisms have solved these problems in many ways. The study of life history patterns is an area of ecology in which basic concepts are just beginning to emerge.—Janalee P. Caldwell

See also **ACTIVITY CYCLES, ANIMALS; AMPHIBIANS; ANIMAL ADAPTATIONS; ECOLOGY; REPRODUCTION**

Further Reading

Begon, M, J. L. Harper, and C. R. Townsend. 1990. *Ecology: Individuals, Populations, and Communities.* Boston: Blackwell.

Stearns, S. C. 1992. *The Evolution of Life Histories.* Oxford: Oxford University Press.

LIMESTONE

Sedimentary rock composed principally of calcium carbonate that is very soluble in water containing dissolved carbon dioxide (CO_2). Limestone dissolves very slowly at cold temperatures but more rapidly as the water becomes warmer. It is also affected by acids, especially nitric acid in the air after a rain and organic acids in the soil. Limestones may be of either organic or mineral origin. Those of organic origin are formed primarily from calcareous elements that have been left behind from the remains of organisms such as corals, algae, and gastropods. Material formed in this manner is called chalk (e.g., the white cliffs of Dover are chalk formations). When limestone is of mineral origin, it will occasionally contain some silica. Certain limestones (dolomites) have large amounts of bicarbonates of calcium and magnesium. Depending on the proportion of calcium carbonate that is dissolved and the amount of insoluble magnesium carbonate, the limestone may erode at different rates in different places, causing a wide variety of stone forms to appear. Dolomites are very porous and offer little resistance to pressure; they are easily eroded by water.—Alberto I. J. Vich and Juana Susana Barroso

See also **ARTESIAN BASIN; CARBONATES; CRETACEOUS; DURICRUSTS; FOSSILS; GROUNDWATER; LAKES, PLUVIAL; LITHOSPHERE; MINERALS; PRECIPITATION; RUNOFF; SANDSTONE; SOILS, DESERT; SOILS, DESERT, CALCAREOUS; SOILS, DESERT, CALCRETE; WEATHERING, DESERT**

Further Reading

Bates, R. L., ed. 1987. *Glossary of Geology.* 3d ed. Alexandria, Va.: American Geological Institute.

Cooke, R., A. Warren, and A. Goudie. 1993. *Desert Geomorphology.* London: University College London Press.

Derruau, M. 1966. *Geomorfología.* Barcelona: Ariel.

Moore, G. W. 1978. *Dictionary of Geography: Definitions and Explanation of Terms used in Physical Geography.* New York: Harper and Row.

The New Encyclopaedia Britannica. 15th ed. 1974. Limestones and dolomites. Vol. 10:979–985. Chicago: University of Chicago Press.

Suh-Shiaw, Lo. 1992. *Glossary of Hydrology.* Taipei: Sheng Te.

Termier, H., and G. Termier. 1960. *Erosion et sedimentation. Introduction a la géologie générale et a la paléogeographie.* Paris: Masson.

LION

Large cat, *Panthera leo* (mammalian family Felidae, order Carnivora), that is one of the most familiar and admired animals in the world (the "King of Beasts"). Although normally associated with the savannas of East Africa, the lion at one time occurred throughout Africa, including North Africa, eastward across Asia to India and Sri Lanka, and throughout much of Europe as recently as 15,000 years ago. Lions are mentioned as a part of the fauna of Greece in the writings of Aristotle (300 B.C.). Lions are now restricted to the Gir Forest in western India and to Africa south of the Sahara, except for the rain forests of western Africa and extreme southern Africa. Lions are important predators and the largest of the cats; males attain weights of 250 kilograms. The two forms associated with arid lands are the Barbary lion (now extinct) and the African lion.

Lion populations occur in arid habitats in southern Africa. A notable population inhabits the arid Kalahari Gemsbok National Park on the border between Botswana and Namibia. Lions are active in very arid regions of the park; however, the population density there is about one-tenth of that in savanna woodlands such as in Kruger National Park. Temperatures in the Kalahari can dip to -0°C at night, but lions will continue to hunt even at cold temperatures. Ectoparasite loads also appear to be lower in desert lions than in lions in more mesic (moister) habitats.—Thomas E. Lacher, Jr.

See also **AFRICA, DESERTS OF; BARBARY LION; CARNIVORES; CATS; KALAHARI DESERT; KAROO; MAMMALS; NAMIBIA, DESERTS OF; PREDATION; SAVANNA; SOUTH AFRICA, DESERTS OF; XEROPHYLLOUS FOREST**

Further Reading

Dorst, J., and P. Dandelot. 1980. *A Field Guide to the Larger Mammals of Africa.* London: Collins.

Estes, R. D. 1991. *The Behavior Guide to African Mammals.* Berkeley: University of California Press.

Haltenorth, T., and H. Diller. 1980. *A Field Guide to the Mammals of Africa, Including Madagascar.* London: Collins.

Nowak, R. M. 1991. *Walker's Mammals of the World.* 5th ed. Baltimore: Johns Hopkins University Press.

Smuts, G. L. 1982. *Lion.* Johannesburg, South Africa: Macmillan.

LITHOSOL. *See* SOILS, DESERT, LITHOSOL

LITHOSPHERE

Outermost fragile, thin, and least dense of the layers that form the internal structure of the earth, varying in thickness from 8 to 40 kilometers, encircling the mantle and separated from it by a thin layer that is called the Moho, short for Mohorovicic discontinuity. The lithosphere is composed of three zones. The first, and deepest layer, is the inferior or basaltic-sima zone and is named after the rocks that form it, which have the chemical composition of basalts, the principal components of which are silica and magnesium. The next is the intermediate layer, which is also called the granitic-sial layer, and is composed principally of silica and aluminum. The last layer is the superficial layer, or sedimentary zone, and is formed by material that derives from the destruction of rocks in the inferior and intermediate layers and includes intruded materials from the deeper layers that have been transported to the surface through volcanic action.

The thickness of the two deepest layers varies from one point to another, generally being denser below mountains than under plains and oceans. The thickness of the sedimentary zone is even more variable than the other two, and in some places this zone may be missing entirely.

The crystalline rocks of the mantle behave as a very viscous material, permitting the lithosphere, which is rigid and lighter than the inner layers, to float in an equilibrium on the mantle. Should this equilibrium be disturbed, it reequilibrates by vertical movements whereby blocks rendered lighter by erosion are elevated and the rocks that are weighted down by ice or sediments sink. Convective currents are generated within the mantle which give rise to the tangential motions of the lithosphere. Because of this, continental blocks are displaced horizontally, leading to the "drifting" of continents.—Alberto I. J. Vich and Juana Susana Barroso

See also **ARTESIAN BASIN; CARBONATES; CRETA-CEOUS; DURICRUSTS; FOSSILS; GROUNDWATER; LAKES, PLUVIAL; MINERALS; PLATE TECTONICS; PRECIPITATION; RUNOFF; SANDSTONE; SOILS, DESERT; SOILS, DESERT, CALCAREOUS; SOILS, DESERT, CALCRETE; WEATHERING, DESERT**

Further Reading

Bates, R. L., ed. 1987. *Glossary of Geology.* 3d ed. Alexandria, Va.: American Geological Institute.

Hamblin, W. K. 1992. *Earth's Dynamic Systems.* 6th ed. New York: Macmillan.

Moore, G. W. 1978. *Dictionary of Geography: Definitions and Explanation of Terms Used in Physical Geography.* New York: Harper and Row.

The New Encyclopaedia Britannica. 15th ed. 1974. Continents, Development of. Vol. 5:119–128. Chicago: University of Chicago Press.

Suh-Shiaw, Lo. 1992. *Glossary of Hydrology.* Taipei: Sheng Te.

LITTER. *See* HUMUS

LIVESTOCK. *See* DOMESTIC ANIMALS

LIZARDS

Tetrapod vertebrates with four legs (usually), external ear openings (usually), movable eyelids (usually), scales on the entire body, a well-developed tongue, a scale-covered tail, and a mandibular symphysis (anterior bony connection between each lower jaw), such that the alternate sides of the lower jaw are solidly connected anteriorly. The last feature separates lizards from snakes, as do any of the first three, if present. However, as different as snakes may seem, their evolutionary origin lies within the lizards, and thus snakes should be considered to be a group of lizards rather than a taxon of equal evolutionary rank. There are approximately 3,000 species of lizards (excluding snakes), and they occur on nearly every continent and in nearly every habitat type. The greatest diversity of lizards occurs in tropical rain forests and in the deserts of Australia.

There are 22 recognized families of lizards and several additional groups that represent distinct lineages, including the bizarre limbless amphisbaenians. The following families have species that occur in deserts: Agamidae, Chamaeleonidae, Iguanidae, Phrynosomatidae, Crotaphytidae, Gekkonidae, Eublepharidae, Teiidae, Gymnoph-

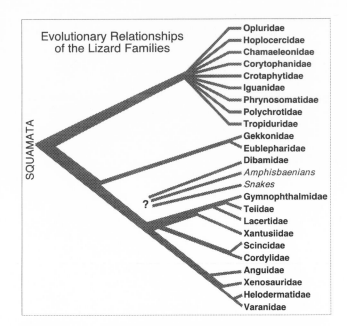

Evolutionary relationships of the lizard families of the world.

thalmidae, Scincidae, Xantusiidae, Helodermatidae, Pygopodidae, and Varanidae. Indeed, lizards are often among the most conspicuous vertebrates in desert environments, especially as many species are diurnal.

The Australian outback contains more species of lizards than any other desert area in the world. The diversity of lizards in Australia is such that lizards are equaled only by birds in terms of numbers of species in any particular locality: as many as 42 species of lizards can be found at a particular site. Even tropical forests in the Amazon Basin support fewer species of lizards than do the Australian deserts. Two reasons for such elevated lizard species diversity in Australian deserts are (1) the presence of a remarkably high food biomass in the form of subterranean termites and (2) a history of burning across vast areas that has repeatedly dissected the habitat into ecologically different patches, thus permitting many species in a defined area to select different habitat patches in which to exist. In contrast, North and South American deserts are rather depauperate in terms of lizard species found in any single locality, averaging only 4–11. Recent research in southwestern New Mexico, however, has revealed that as many as 19 species may occur at a single site, thus making this desert area one of the continent's richest for lizards.

Among the many reasons lizards are so successful in deserts is that they feed primarily on insects and spiders, prey items that not only provide nourishment and water but also are extremely abundant and diverse in deserts. A few species of lizards are herbivores. The relatively low energetic demands of lizards and other ectothermic (cold-blooded) vertebrates make it possible for them to exist in areas where resource levels are too low to support endothermic animals, such as mammals, which have higher energy requirements. During extended drought conditions, when water is unavailable and invertebrate density is reduced, most desert lizards cease activity and avoid the extreme conditions.

Among the more common lizards observed in North American deserts are the zebra-tailed lizard (*Callisaurus draconoides*), the western whiptail (*Cnemidophorus tigris*), the side-blotched lizard (*Uta stansburiana*), and the desert iguana (*Dipsosaurus dorsalis*). Common Kalahari Desert lizards include *Eremias lineo-ocellata*, *Meroles suborbitalis*, *Mabuya variegata*, and *Chondrodactylus angulifer*. Conspicuous Australian desert lizards are *Ctenophorus isolepis*, *Ctenophorus inermis*, *Ctenotus grandis*, *Ctenotus pantherinus*, *Moloch horridus*, *Gehyra variegata*, and *Rhynchoedura ornata*.—Laurie J. Vitt

See also **AFRICA, DESERTS OF; ANIMAL ADAPTATIONS; ASIA, DESERTS OF; AUSTRALIA, DESERTS OF; BAJA CALIFORNIA, DESERTS OF; CHIHUAHUAN DESERT; CHUCKWALLA; DEFENSIVE ADAPTATIONS, ANIMALS; ECTOTHERMY; GECKO; GILA MONSTER; IGUANA, DESERT; MOJAVE DESERT; PHYSIOLOGY; REPTILES; SAHARA DESERT; SONORAN DESERT; SOUTH AFRICA, DESERTS OF; SOUTH AMERICA, DESERTS OF; UNITED STATES, DESERTS OF; URIC ACID; WATER BALANCE**

Further Reading

Cogger, H. G. 1992. *Reptiles and Amphibians of Australia*. Ithaca: Cornell University Press.

Estes, R., and G. Pregill, eds. 1988. *Phylogenetic Relationships of the Lizard Families*. Stanford: Stanford University Press.

Pianka, E. R. 1986. *Ecology and Natural History of Desert Lizards: Analyses of the Ecological Niche and Community Structure*. Princeton: Princeton University Press.

LLANO ESTACADO

Geographic feature of a southern extension of the Great Plains encompassing part of New Mexico from the eastern slopes of the Rocky Mountains to the high plains of West Texas where the eastern border of this area is formed by the Cap Rock Escarpment. The northern border of the Llano Estacado corresponds roughly with the northern border of New Mexico, whereas its southern border extends into southwestern Texas to the Mexican border region.

The Spanish term "Llano Estacado" usually is translated as "Staked Plain," although perceptive historians have argued for "Stockaded Plain" or "Palisaded Plain," because of how the Cap Rock appeared to the Spanish explorers, beginning with the Coronado expedition in spring 1541. The Spaniards were the first Europeans to discover and cross this area, and the name they gave it has endured.

Rugged and arid, the Llano Estacado has been historically and remains today a relatively thinly populated area. By 1706 the Comanches, having acquired the horse from the Spaniards in the previous century, made their earliest appearance on the Llano Estacado. By 1750 the Comanches had succeeded in driving out the Apaches from these southern plains and were to dominate the Llano Estacado for the next century.

By 1848 the United States had gone to war with Mexico, defeated the Mexican nation, and incorporated Mexico's far northern frontier into its own territory. This became the American Southwest and included the Llano Estacado. Despite trade along the Santa Fe Trail after 1821, from Missouri to Santa Fe, most of the traffic on the Llano Estacado was military. Even this military presence became less pronounced during the American Civil War (1861–1865).

For the New Mexican Hispanos (people of Spanish/Mexican descent), the reduction of U.S. Army forces on the Llano Estacado offered an opportunity to engage in a lucrative trade with the Comanches. The traders were known as comancheros. They traded agrarian and domestic products from the Rio Grande region for buffalo hides, French rifles, horses, and other articles acquired from the Comanches. Since the horses were stolen from Texas ranchers, the comanchero trade on the whole worsened relations between Texans and New Mexicans.

After the end of the American Civil War, the comanchero trade declined. The Comanches came under considerable pressure from the U.S. Army as well as from the arrival of ever-larger numbers of American settlers. In 1875 the surrender of the great chief of the Comanches, Quanah Parker, brought to an end the nomadic lifestyle of these inhabitants of the Llano Estacado.

From the end of the 19th century until now, the Llano Estacado has been home to flourishing cattle ranches and both irrigation and dry farming, including an extensive cotton industry and, more recently, a wine industry. Abundant oil deposits have also been found in this region. The area is also a major flyway for migrating waterfowl. Important cities in the Llano Estacado are Amarillo and Lubbock, Texas, and Clovis and Hobbs, New Mexico.—E. A. Mares

See also **CHIHUAHUAN DESERT; DESERT GRASS-LAND; DURICRUSTS; JORNADA DEL MUERTO; NEW MEXICO DESERT; RIO GRANDE; TEXAS DESERT**

Further Reading

Bolton, H. E., and A. L. Hurtado. 1996. *The Spanish Borderlands: A Chronicle of Old Florida and the Southwest.* Albuquerque: University of New Mexico Press.

Chipman, D. E. 1992. *Spanish Texas, 1519–1821.* Austin: University of Texas Press.

Meinig, D. W. 1971. *Southwest.* New York: Oxford University Press.

Noyes, S. 1993. *Los Comanches.* Albuquerque: University of New Mexico Press.

LOCOMOTION

Activity of animals that moves them from place to place and consists of propulsion and control. Propulsion is the activity of the animal's body that results in it being moved. Control is the coordination of propulsion to reach a particular place or accomplish a particular task. Most modes of locomotion can be loosely grouped into being either axial or appendicular. When animals change the shape of their body to generate propulsion it is called axial locomotion. The best examples of axial locomotion are the "jet propulsion" of jellyfish and squids, but the crawling of snakes is another good example. When animals use their appendages for propulsion it is called appendicular locomotion. Appendicular locomotion includes walking, running, flying, and some forms of swimming and digging, to name but a few. Animals move through the air and over the surface of earth and its waters, as well as through them, in myriad ways, but the desert provides special challenges to locomotion and animals have developed distinctive ways of coping.

The low precipitation and often extreme temperatures of deserts result in sparse vegetation in which moving animals are particularly conspicuous to predators. Many of the locomotor adaptations possessed by animals are a response to this increased predation threat. Most deserts of the world are inhabited by at least some mammals that are bipedal, that is, hop on their hind legs without the forefeet contacting the ground. This bipedal locomotion is thought to be primarily an adaptation to avoid being caught by predators. Besides being a method of moving extremely rapidly during escape maneuvers, bipedal species frequently make rapid ricocheting movements that are unpredictable. Bipedal locomotion, or bipedality, may also function to permit the animal to forage at food sources that are great distances apart, such as one might expect in the sparse desert habitat.

Another way that many desert species have attempted to avoid the harsh desert conditions and alleviate predation is to burrow. The pocket gopher;, a desert resident in the southwestern United States, burrows throughout its territory feeding on the roots and tubers of desert plants. The pocket gopher is highly specialized for burrowing; it has small eyes, reduced ears, and broad shovel-like paws with long claws for digging.

Some lizards and snakes have also become specialized at burrowing into desert sand dunes. These burrowing reptiles are not only avoiding the animals that may feed on them, they are waiting to ambush prey of their own. The snakes move through the sand with an undulating motion that the lizards also use, but in lizards this is frequently accompanied by a "swimming" stroke of the rear legs. The hind feet of these lizards are often edged with a fringe of modified scales to broaden the foot. These lizards also may have specialized scales to protect their ears and eyes from the fine sand. Both the snakes and the lizards often have special scales on their nose or chin for protection as they force themselves through the sand.

Although a wide variety of birds can be found in many deserts, one group commonly identified with deserts is the vultures. Vultures are capable fliers, but they often rely on soaring. A vulture begins soaring by finding an area that is being heated more rapidly than the area around it. This uneven heating could be caused by shadows, angle of the ground relative to the sun, or color of the soil. This warmer earth heats the air above it rapidly, and the warm air begins to rise. The vultures position themselves in these rising columns of air and gain considerable altitude. They then glide over relatively cool ground to reach another warm spot where they again gain altitude. Soaring allows these scavengers to traverse the large distances between carcasses using a minimum of energy.—Rob Channell

See also **AMPHIBIANS; ANIMAL ADAPTATIONS; ARTHROPODS; BAT; BIPEDALITY; BIRDS; BURROWING ANIMALS; BUZZARD; CONDOR; FISHES; INSECTS; JERBOA; KANGAROO; KANGAROO RAT; LIZARDS; MAMMALS; PREDATION; REPTILES; RODENTS; SNAKES; VULTURE**

Further Reading

Hertel, H. 1966. *Structure, Form, Movement*. New York: Van Nostrand Reinhold.

Radinsky, L. 1987. *The Evolution of the Vertebrate Design*. Chicago: University of Chicago Press.

LOCOWEED

Low-growing perennial plants in the legume family (Fabaceae or Leguminosae; either name is permissible in the International Code of Botanical Nomenclature) that resemble clover or small pea plants but have much more robust flowers and leaves; they belong to the genera *Oxytropis* and *Astragalus*. These species survive well in desert environments due to their deep taproot and their low-growing morphology. In addition, they produce several chemicals that deter herbivores. These chemicals are concentrated in both the leaves and the fruits, the latter resembling large swollen bean pods. Few animal species are capable of detoxifying these compounds, and thus few, if any, plants suffer damage due to herbivory. The plant "advertises" the presence of these toxic compounds by having a flavor that is extremely bitter to most grazing animals.

Large grazing animals such as cattle sometimes feed on the members of these genera despite the bitter flavor. Usually hunger lowers flavor rejection thresholds in livestock species. Following ingestion of these plants, animals then respond with erratic behavior, sickness, or death. The strange behaviors that accompany grazing on these plants were considered to be crazy, or "loco," by western ranchers.

Hence the name locoweed was coined for these plant species.

Species of both *Astragalus* and *Oxytropis* are usually slow-growing and minor members of most plant communities. However, overgrazing by livestock removes more palatable species that compete with the locoweeds. In this circumstance locoweeds may become the dominant members of the plant communities, thus reducing the grazing value of the area.—Linda L. Wallace

See also **DESERT GRASSLAND; DOMESTIC ANIMALS; ECONOMIC VALUE OF DESERT PRODUCTS; GREAT BASIN DESERT; HERBIVORY; LEAVES; LEGUMES; OVERGRAZING; PLANT ADAPTATIONS; PLANTS; PRAIRIE**

Further Reading

Valentine, J. E. 1990. *Grazing Management*. San Diego: Academic Press.

LOCUSTS

Certain grasshoppers in the family Acrididae which may migrate in dense flocks containing millions of individuals. These large flocks can cause considerable damage to crops as well as to the natural vegetation, in addition to being hazards along roadways. Under normal circumstances population levels remain low enough that the flocking behavior is not observed. Following a combination of favorable conditions for population increases, the large flocks move from place to place eating nearly all edible vegetation.

Underlying the massive migrations of locusts is a phenomenon known as *phase polymorphism*. Depending on the physical and biotic conditions that nymph stage locusts experience as they grow and reach maturity, they may become solitary or gregarious. The proximate trigger determining whether the solitary or gregarious phases will develop appears to be density. At high densities the gregarious phase develops. Often the solitary and gregarious phases are colored differently and differ in morphology, depending on species. The solitary phase locusts are much less mobile as they develop than are the gregarious phase locusts. When adulthood is attained the solitary phase locusts remain in much the same area in which they were born. Adults of the gregarious phase locusts form giant swarms, often exceeding 10,000 individuals. Some of the larger swarms have been estimated to weigh as much as 50,000 tons. These swarms migrate and are carried by prevailing winds over great distances. The locust *Shistocerca*, for example, can migrate up to 2,000 miles in a season. When the swarm of locusts lands, it consumes virtually all the available vegetation.—Laurie J. Vitt

See also **ARTHROPODS; GRASSES; GRASSHOPPERS; GRASSLAND; HERBIVORY; INSECTS; METAMORPHOSIS**

Further Reading

Borror, D. J., C. A. Triplehorn, and N. F. Johnson. 1992. *An Introduction to the Study of Insects*. New York: Harcourt Brace.

Borror, D. J., and R. E. White. 1970. *A Field Guide to the Insects*. Boston: Houghton Mifflin.

Daly, H. V., J. T. Doyen, and P. R. Ehrlich. 1978. *Introduction to Insect Biology and Diversity*. New York: McGraw-Hill.

LOESS. *See* SOILS, DESERT, LOESS

LOW PRESSURE

Measurement of atmospheric pressure (barometric pressure) taken at a particular elevation (either high or low) where minimum atmospheric pressure is detected ("minimum" is based on comparing the low pressure to a standard reference pressure, such as one standard atmosphere, which is 1,013.3 millibars). Lows are also known as cyclonic centers or cyclones, as low pressure is associated with these phenomena. Pressure is measured in isobars and plotted on a map to show areas within which low pressure develops. Low pressure is the antithesis of high pressure or a center of high pressure. In general the lowest atmospheric pressures on the planet are found in the ocean over the eye of a hurricane (as low as 920 millibars).—Federico Norte

See also **AN INTRODUCTION TO DESERTS; ANTICYCLONE; BAROMETRIC PRESSURE (ATMOSPHERIC PRESSURE); CLIMATE; CLIMATE CLASSIFICATION; CONVECTIVE STORM; CYCLONE; ISOHYET**

Further Reading

Day, J. A., and V. J. Schaefer. 1991. *Clouds and Weather*. Boston: Houghton Mifflin.

Oliver, J. E., and R. W. Fairbridge, eds. 1987. *The Encyclopedia of Climatology*. New York: Chapman and Hall.

Schaefer, V. J., and J. A. Day. 1981. *A Field Guide to the Atmosphere*. Boston: Houghton Mifflin.

Schneider, S. H., ed. 1996. *Encyclopedia of Climate and Weather*. 2 vols. New York: Oxford University Press.

LUNETTE. *See* DUNES, LUNETTE

LYNX. *See* BOBCAT; CARACAL

MADAGASCAR (MALAGASY REPUBLIC)

Island country off the coast of southeastern Africa colonized by humans in several separate migrations commencing about A.D. 1100 and ruled for most of its history as an independent kingdom. In the 19th century, during the era of colonialism, the island was dominated by the nations of Western Europe. The island received its independence from France in 1962, declaring itself the Malagasy Republic, with its capital at Tananarive (Antananarivo).

Madagascar was formerly attached to the continent of Africa but separated 60 million years ago, with the subsequent development of a flora and fauna dominated by endemic taxa. Madagascar is situated in the southwestern portion of the Indian Ocean, lying approximately 400 kilometers from the coast of East Africa. It has an area of 588,000 square kilometers between the latitudes of 11°57' and 25°38' south. The island is approximately 1,600 kilometers long and has a maximum width of approximately 563 kilometers. A central plateau with a variable elevation of 762–1,371 meters dominates the island. On the eastern coast the plateau drops off abruptly. At lower elevations the east coast originally supported a true tropical evergreen forest (which has been largely eliminated due to human activities), because this area receives a high annual rainfall. To the west the central plateau gradually decreases in altitude and originally supported a dry deciduous forest and, in the vicinity of permanent rivers, tropical evergreen forest. Currently in the southwest there is an area of extreme aridity. The vegetation of the southwest is characterized by scrub and spiny succulents.

The natural vegetation of Madagascar has been altered greatly through human activities. During the last 1,000 years the vegetation of the central plateau has been extensively degraded by humans, with widespread burning and overgrazing by cattle herds being primarily responsible for the loss of vegetation. The result has been the loss of humus and extensive exposure of the underlying red lateritic clay. The deforestation of the central plateau was accompanied by the extermination of the giant lemurs and a giant ostrichlike bird (*Aepyornis*), as well as the extermination of giant land tortoises. The tropical forests of the eastern coastal region and foothills of the plateau have also been cut extensively primarily to create clear areas for the cultivation of rice. Most of the habitat destruction resulting from human occupancy has occurred in the last 600 years.

Because of the poor agricultural prospects for the arid southwest, it comprises the least disturbed vegetation zone at present. The plants and animals of the arid southwest indicate a long history of aridity in this portion of the island, and, although long-term global climatic changes may reduce or expand the arid zone's flora and fauna, a dry adapted vegetational component has been present since before the Miocene.—John F. Eisenberg

See also **AN INTRODUCTION TO DESERTS; ARIDITY; CACTI; CONSERVATION IN DESERTS; CONVERGENT EVOLUTION; DESERTIFICATION; EUPHORBIACEAE; MADAGASCAR, DESERTS OF; MAMMALS; MIOCENE; PLANT ADAPTATIONS; PLANTS; PRECIPITATION; SEMIARID ZONES; SUCCULENTS; XEROPHYLLOUS FOREST; XEROPHYTES**

Further Reading

Battestini, R., and G. Richard-Vindard. 1972. *Biogeography and Ecology of Madagascar.* The Hague: Junk.

MADAGASCAR, DESERTS OF

Southwestern semiarid portion of Madagascar. Much of this region lies to the south of the Tropic of Capricorn. The area is not a true desert; rainfall ranges from 500 to 900 millimeters per year with a seven-month dry season. Although the mean annual temperature is approximately 25°C, the maximum temperature that has been recorded in this region is 44°C. The most extreme arid portion in the southwest region occurs in a narrow strip along the coast, roughly 30 kilometers wide, from Morombe to Tulear. Here the average rainfall is only 350 millimeters per year, and the timing of precipitation is extremely irregular. The mean annual temperature is about 26°C, and the recorded maximum is 40°C. The soils are extremely complex and include temporary alluvial depositions, saline soils, and calcimorphic soils. (See map of African deserts, p. 12.)

The vegetation is characterized by xerophyllous bush with spines. Over much of the region baobab trees (*Adansonia*) dominate, and seven species of this genus have been recorded from the island. The dense dry woodlands of the westcentral region grade imperceptibly into the xeric southwest. The southwestern vegetation is referred to as "bush," and consists of small shrubs from one to two meters high and occasional trees up to four meters high. Finally, extremely xeric-adapted plant forms may reach 10 meters in height (these are members of the endemic family Didiereaceae). Intermediate-size tree forms up to 5 meters in height include various species of the Didiereaceae, as well as the Euphorbiaceae. The Didiereaceae includes woody plants, many of them succulents, that are highly adapted to withstand aridity. The branches bear deciduous leaves and are often quite slender, hence the common name octopus tree. The Euphorbiaceae also exhibit extreme adaptation to aridity. Trunks and twigs may bear spines. Some species are leafless. Many take grotesque forms reminiscent of the branching corals of a marine reef. Others are very similar in structure to succulent cacti of American deserts (examples of convergent evolution).

The trees and shrubs of southwestern Madagascar have been under strong selective pressure to adapt to a climate in which water loss governs plant growth. Thus swollen underground roots as water storage organs, or swollen trunks that retain water during adverse conditions, are reminiscent of desert plants from other parts of the world. The trees exhibit a high degree of endemism, with 18 endemic genera recorded for the southwest.—John F. Eisenberg

See also **AN INTRODUCTION TO DESERTS; ARIDITY; CACTI; CONVERGENT EVOLUTION; DESERTIFICATION; EUPHORBIACEAE; MADAGASCAR (MALAGASY REPUBLIC); PLANT ADAPTATIONS; PLANTS; PRECIPITATION; SEMIARID ZONES; SUCCULENTS; XEROPHYLLOUS FOREST; XEROPHYTES**

Further Reading

Battestini, R., and G. Richard-Vindard. 1972. *Biogeography and Ecology of Madagascar*. The Hague: Junk.

Jolly, A., P. Oberlé, and R. Albignac, eds. 1984. *Key Environments: Madagascar*. Oxford: Pergamon.

United Nations Environment Programme. 1992. *World Atlas of Desertification*. London: Edward Arnold.

MADRO-TERTIARY GEOFLORA

Hypothetical paleovegetation during the Tertiary period in parts of western North America that is thought to have given rise to the modern semiarid and desert vegetation in the southwestern part of the continent. The Madro-Tertiary Geoflora is believed to have developed gradually during the early and middle Tertiary in a relatively dry zone between a more northern, temperate, mixed deciduous Arcto-Tertiary Geoflora and a southern, broad-leafed evergreen Neotropical-Tertiary Geoflora.

The Madro-Tertiary Geoflora is considered to be derived from elements (families, genera, and species of plants) of the Neotropical-Tertiary Geoflora. The ideas about the existence of these geofloras were championed by Daniel I. Axelrod during the 1950s. Axelrod based them on the evidence reconstructed from hundreds of western North American localities in which fossil floras are preserved. The Madro-Tertiary Geoflora is named for the Sierra Madres of Mexico, where relictual members of the Geoflora survive in enclaves today.

Early in the development of the Madro-Tertiary Geoflora its plants consisted of small trees, shrubs, and grasses. Many of these were microphyllous (small-leafed) and sclerophyllous (leaves with tough cuticles) descendants of plants of the Neotropical-Tertiary Geoflora. They became increasingly adapted to arid conditions and may have developed first as subtropical savannas in the rain shadow of the mountains flanking the central plateau of Mexico. In the western United States, uplift of the Rocky Mountains may have enabled the northward spread of some elements of this flora. Later, uplift of the Sierra Nevada and Cascade mountain ranges occurred, further increasing the rain shadow effects. As the mountains became more elevated, they blocked moisture-laden prevailing winds from the Pacific Ocean and extensive aridity developed on their leeward sides. As xeric conditions became widespread, the Madro-Tertiary Geoflora occupied the drier regions of southern California, the Great Basin, and the western parts of the Great Plains.

By the late Tertiary and Quaternary the Madro-Tertiary Geoflora is believed to have differentiated regionally under varying conditions of topography and climate into a number of derivative plant communities. These include semiarid oak-conifer woodland, chaparral, arid subtropical scrub, plains and desert grassland, and subdesert and desert scrub. According to Axelrod, the most xerophytic (arid-adapted) communities in southwestern North America were among the latest to assemble, not developing until the Pleistocene.

Axelrod further believed that the general pattern of desert development elsewhere in the world seemed to parallel closely that of western North America, with respect both to age and to origin, from ancestral species of more mesic communities that dominated the same regions in the Tertiary. Thus modern cold deserts largely derived their species from regional Arcto-Tertiary and Antarcto-Tertiary Floras; warm deserts found their sources chiefly in the Tropical-Tertiary Floras. The latter developed around the globe in the northern and southern margins of the tropics as drier climate expanded over low to middle latitudes during the Tertiary.

A contrasting view is held by modern paleobotanists, who do not subscribe to Axelrod's views of stable, relatively homogeneous geofloras existing in discrete portions of North America over millions of years of the Tertiary. Instead they view the plants as forming intricate, dynamic community relationships through the Tertiary and as responding on a species-by-species basis to millions of years of changes in temperature and precipitation and in the seasonality of temperature and precipitation.—Nicholas J. Czaplewski

See also **CENOZOIC; CHIHUAHUAN DESERT; CRETACEOUS; DESERTS; EOCENE; FOSSILS; GLACIAL PERIODS; GREAT BASIN DESERT; INTERGLACIALS; MEXICO, DESERTS OF; MIDDEN; MIOCENE; MOJAVE DESERT; NEOGENE; OLIGOCENE; PALEOCLIMATE; PERMIAN; PLANT GEOGRAPHY; PLATE TECTONICS; PLEISTOCENE; PLIOCENE; QUATERNARY; RECENT (HOLOCENE); SONORAN DESERT; TERTIARY; XEROPHYLLOUS FOREST**

Further Reading

Axelrod, D. I. 1950. Evolution of desert vegetation in western North America. *Contributions to Paleontology, Carnegie Institution of Washington Publication* 590:215–306.

———. 1958. Evolution of the Madro-Tertiary Geoflora. *Botanical Review* 24:433–509.

Wolfe, J. A. 1975. Some aspects of plant geography of the Northern Hemisphere during the late Cretaceous and Tertiary. *Annals of the Missouri Botanical Garden* 62:264–279.

MALAGASY REPUBLIC. *See* MADAGASCAR (MALAGASY REPUBLIC)

MALLEE

Descriptive term applied both to a plant community and a life form of multistemmed, dwarf species of *Eucalyptus* that occur in a broad vegetational belt across southern Australia in the 20–43 centimeters annual winter rainfall region of semiarid scrublands. This belt stretches from Western Australia through parts of south Australia to New South Wales and Victoria. In the higher rainfall regions of its distribution, much of the mallee has been cleared and replaced by winter wheat, whereas the more arid mallee is grazed intensively by sheep. The main species of mallee are *Eucalyptus oleosa*, *Eucalyptus dumosa*, *Eucalyptus socialis*, *Eucalyptus sideroxylon*, *Eucalyptus fruticetorum*, and *Eucalyptus viridis*, and they are often accompanied by a secondary layer of shrubs in the genera *Acacia*, *Atriplex*, *Kochia*, and *Bassia*, with a frequent ground cover of the spinifex grass, *Triodia*.

As a plant community, mallee is prone to periodic wildfire but regenerates readily both by resprouting from undamaged underground biomass and from seedling recruitment. Among the mallee's rare and unusual animals, one of the best known is the malleefowl, a turkey-sized bird that is one of the mound-nesting megapodes, laying its eggs in large mounds constructed of sand and leaf litter.

Because mallee occupies a bioclimatic zone that is attractive to agriculture and is near the most densely settled areas of Australia, it has been badly decimated and deserves protection as a sensitive, if not endangered, habitat. The traveler may still observe mallee in relatively undisturbed states in either Big Desert National Park or Little Desert National Park in eastern Victoria, Australia.—Richard E. MacMillen

See also **ACACIA; AN INTRODUCTION TO DESERTS; AUSTRALIA, DESERTS OF; BIRDS; CLIMATE; MALLEEFOWL; PLANT ADAPTATIONS; PLANTS; XEROPHYLLOUS FOREST; XEROPHYTES**

Further Reading

Leigh, J. H., and J. C. Noble. 1969. Vegetation and resources. *In* R. O. Slatyer and R. A. Perry, eds., *Arid Lands of Australia*, 73–92. Canberra: Australian National University Press.

Noble, J. C. 1982. The significance of fire in the biology and evolutionary ecology of mallee *Eucalyptus* populations. *In* W. R. Barker and P. J. M. Greenslade, eds., *Evolution of the Flora and Fauna of Arid Australia*, 153–159. Frewville, South Australia: Peacock.

Pizzey, G. 1988. *A Field Guide to the Birds of Australia.* Sydney: Collins.

MALLEEFOWL

Large ground-dwelling bird (*Leipoa ocellata*) found in the semiarid mallee woodlands of southern Australia. The malleefowl is one of 12–19 species in six genera of the family Megapodiidae (order Galliformes). Malleefowl are approximately 60 centimeters in length and weigh from 1.5 to 2.5 kilograms. They are primarily terrestrial and have strong, powerful legs and short, rounded wings. Sexes are similar, although males generally are slightly larger than females. The bill is short and of simple shape. Malleefowl are primarily granivorous, although they will eat invertebrates and various types of herbaceous material when it becomes available.

Malleefowl are primarily sedentary. Monogamous pair-bonds are of long duration. The breeding season may be long, although breeding may not occur at all during drought. *L. ocellata*, like other megapodes, is unusual in that it does not directly incubate its eggs. Instead, malleefowl (primarily the male) construct mounds of sand, soil, leaf litter, sticks, and pebbles. Eggs are laid in chambers excavated primarily by males. Clutch sizes are quite variable, with a mean of 15–20 eggs. Heat for incubation results from decomposition of organic matter and by solar radiation. Males adjust temperatures of the mound by varying the depth of the material covering the eggs, and on extremely hot days may even uncover the eggs entirely. Mean incubation is approximately 62–64 days. On hatching, the young burrow to the surface. The chicks are independent of the adults almost immediately after emergence from the mound.—Stephen C. Lougheed

See also **ACACIA; ANIMAL ADAPTATIONS; AN INTRODUCTION TO DESERTS; AUSTRALIA, DESERTS OF; BIRDS; CLIMATE; PLANT ADAPTATIONS; XEROPHYLLOUS FOREST; XEROPHYTES**

Further Reading

Booth, D. T. 1987. Effects of temperature on development of malleefowl *Leipoa ocellata* eggs. *Physiological Zoology* 60:437–445.

Diamond, J. 1983. The reproductive biology of mound-building birds. *Nature* 301:288–289.

Frith, H. J. 1962. *The Malleefowl: The Bird That Builds an Incubator.* Sydney: Angus and Robertson.

Marchant, S., and P. J. Higgins, eds. 1990. *Handbook of Australian, New Zealand and Antarctic Birds.* Vol. 1 (pt. A). Melbourne: Oxford University Press.

MALPAIS. *See* BAJA CALIFORNIA, DESERTS OF

MAMMALS

Members of the class Mammalia characterized by, among other things, the presence of mammary glands used in producing milk to nourish young and the presence of greater or lesser amounts of hair. The class Mammalia has had a long evolutionary history; mammals are first detected in the fossil record of the late Triassic. All contemporary mammals possess hair at some stage in their life cycle, and in most species the hair persists throughout life, although in some aquatic forms the hairs have been reduced to remnant bristles or are lost in adults. All female mammals possess functional mammary glands that produce milk, which in turn serves as nourishment for the newborn. In males these glands are present but rudimentary. The chest and abdominal cavities are separated by a muscular diaphragm. In most mammals the brain is considerably enlarged relative to comparably sized reptiles. The top of the forebrain, or the neopallium, is proportionately larger in mammals when compared with other vertebrates.

In skeletal anatomy all recent mammals are defined by the fact that the lower jaw comprises a single pair of bones, the dentaries, which articulate directly with the cranium. Most species of mammals possess heterodont dentition (i.e., the teeth are differentiated into functional types: incisors, canines, premolars, and molars). Some living mammals, such as anteaters and pangolins, have secondarily lost their teeth, whereas others (e.g., dolphins and armadillos) have reverted to a homodont condition (all teeth are similar in shape). In contrast to the reptilian condition of continual tooth replacement, mammal teeth usually are replaced only once (diphyodonty). The base of the skull possesses two occipital condyles by which it articulates with the spinal column. This differs from the reptiles, in which only one condyle is typically present.

Living mammals are descended from reptiles. Approximately 320 million years ago, the reptilian order Synapsida began to diversify into several different lineages. One of these, the Cotylosauria, gave rise to the Therapsida, which first show the beginnings of the evolution of heterodont dentition and the development of two occipital condyles. Approximately 200 million years ago, in the Triassic, the oldest-known fossil mammals appear. These usually are grouped in the family Morganucodontidae. In these forms the articulation of the dentition with the cranium is nearly complete, thus setting the stage for the typical mammalian jaw articulation. Toward the end of the Jurassic two other mammalian orders appeared, the Multituberculata and Docodonta. The Multituberculata was an exceedingly diverse group of rodentlike animals that persisted for 80 million years, until the Eocene. About 150 million years ago the Pantotheria appeared; this group exhibited a basic molar tooth with a three-cusp triangular pattern. They are believed to be the stem group that gave rise to modern mammals. Marsupials and placentals appeared in the late Cretaceous, perhaps 100 million years ago.

In the transition from the mammallike reptiles to the earliest mammals, there are several observable trends. First, there is a separation of hearing and mastication. That is to say, in the mammallike reptiles the jawbone comprised several bones: the dentary, angular, articular, and quadrate. The quadrate and articular not only formed part of the jaw joints but also conducted sonic vibrations from the ear drum, which was supported by the angular bone, to the stapes (the first inner ear bone). Clearly, bone conduction was involved in the hearing process in these early forms, but as mammals evolved the hearing function was separated completely from the jaw, such that the quadrate bone became the incus (the second inner ear bones of mammals), the angular bone became the tympanic bone, and the articular bone became the malleus (the third inner ear bone). Thus the classical three inner ear ossicles (bones) of mammals came to be enclosed in their own skull chamber, away from direct contact with the jaw. It is speculated that refinements in hearing went hand in hand with the evolution of nocturnality, when both hearing and olfaction became the primary senses locating prey and avoiding predators at night.

The evolution of more complex teeth and the specialization of teeth into different types are associated with increased feeding efficiency, both in terms of grasping prey and mastication. Greater masticatory efficiency facilitated an increase in metabolic rate. One might assume, therefore, that endothermy (maintenance of an elevated body temperature), as well as specializations in food processing, probably accompanied the adaptation to a nocturnal habit.

If early mammals were nocturnal, then competition with the coexisting smaller therapsid reptiles was reduced. If, as is believed, early mammals preyed on insects, then selection may well have favored a small body size. No doubt hair evolved at some point in the sequence of adapting for nocturnality and insectivory, although therapsids themselves may have had hair. Hair would have been a great advance for providing insulation to small-bodied mammals to assist in thermoregulation.

The evolutionary trend away from multiple tooth replacement with restriction to two sets of teeth may have accompanied the evolution of lactation. Lactation by females could have resulted in the rapid growth of young to near-adult size, thus relieving the necessity for multiple tooth replacement and, in effect, confining tooth replacement to shortly after weaning and the attainment of adult size. Although modern manatees and elephants do replace teeth throughout life, this involves delayed eruption of molars. The loss of the milk teeth in some mammals (e.g., living marsupials) may have been a secondary adaptation to the condition of obligate teat attachment, which accompanies the development of a pouch. This would also have been a departure for marsupials from producing eggs (see below). The egg-laying condition, still retained by the echidna and platypus, was likely characteristic of all mammals prior to the marsupial and eutherian split in the Cretaceous.

The great diversification of the Mammalia began at the close of the Cretaceous and the beginning of the Paleocene, some 70 million years ago. Marsupials first appear in the fossil record in North America but shortly thereafter are present in the South American fossil record. Marsupials appear in the fossil record of the Oligocene of Australia, and it is assumed that marsupial stocks transited from South America to Australia via Antarctica before the final breakup of Gondwanaland.

Living mammals represent three major subclasses defined by profound differences in their mode of reproduction. The Prototheria, repre-

Orders of Mammals, including Numbers of Species and Geographic Distribution

Order	Common Name	No. of Species	Geographic Distribution
Monotremata	platypus and echidna	3	Aus
Marsupialia	opossums, kangaroos, phalangers, etc.	282	Aus, SA, NA
Xenarthra (Edentates)	sloths, anteaters, and armadillos	29	SA, NA
Insectivora	shrews, moles, hedgehogs, tenrecs	365	Af, As, NA, SA, Eu
Scandentia	tree shrews	16	SE Asia
Dermoptera	flying lemur	2	SE Asia
Chiroptera	bats	977	Worldwide
Primates	monkeys, apes, baboons	201	S Asia, Af, SA
Carnivora	cats, dogs, civets, weasels, bears, allies	235	Af, Asia, Eu, NA, SA
Pinnipedia	seals, sea lions, walruses	34	Marine, freshwater
Cetacea	whales, porpoises, dolphins	77	Marine, freshwater
Sirenia	dugongs, manatees	5	Marine, freshwater
Proboscidea	elephants	2	Af, S Asia
Perissodactyla	rhinos, equines, tapirs	16	Asia, CA, SA
Hyracoidea	hyraxes	8	Af, ME
Tubulidentata	aardvark	1	Af
Artiodactyla	deer, camels, swine, giraffes, bovines	194	NA, SA, Eu, Asia, Af
Pholidota	pangolins	7	Af, S Asia
Rodentia	rodents	1,793	Worldwide
Lagomorpha	hares, rabbits, pikas	65	Eu, Af, Asia, SA, NA
Macroscelidea	elephant shrews	15	Af

Key to abbreviations: Aus (Australia), NA (North America), Af (Africa), SA (South America), Asia, SE Asia (Southeast Asia), Eu (Europe), S Asia (Southern Asia), CA (Central America), ME (Middle East).

sented by the platypus and spiny anteaters, reproduce by means of laying eggs. The marsupials, or Metatheria, retain the egg within the uterus, where early embryonic development proceeds. A shell is not formed, but the shell membrane remains intact. Nutrient exchange can occur between the embryo and the mother through a yolk sac placenta or, in the case of the bandicoots, a true chorioallantoic placenta.

Marsupials are lactation specialists in that the intrauterine development is brief. At birth the young attach to a teat, and lactation is a long process. In most marsupials teat areas are enclosed within a pouch. The Eutheria generally have reduced the relative duration of lactation in favor of retaining the embryos for a prolonged period in the uterus. The elaboration of the embryonic tropho-

blast and chorioallantoic placenta with a long functional duration in eutherians means that a great deal of nutrient exchange can take place between the mother and the young. From this standpoint, eutherians may be viewed as gestational specialists.

Members of the various living mammalian orders exhibit an astonishing array of adaptation. Some species show a rather conservative morphology and occupy ecological niches that probably differ very little from their original ancestral stock (e.g., shrews). However, the forces of natural selection have molded many taxa for increasing specializations for the exploitation of particular habitats and particular feeding habits. The modern whales represent one such extreme specialization; the bats, with their flapping flight, represent another.

Mammals live in every major habitat on earth, including the seas, the Arctic, the Antarctic, and the air. They are found in caves, in the most humid tropical zones, in the coldest polar zones, and in the driest deserts. They are clearly a remarkably adapted group of animals. Their feeding adaptations are manifold and include carnivory (meat eating), insectivory (insect eating), frugivory (fruit eating), nectarivory (nectar eating), piscivory (fish eating), and sanguinivory (blood feeding), to mention some.

If the marsupials are considered to be a single order (some authors consider them to be five orders), then the current mammals may be divided into 21 orders. There are approximately 4,500 living species of mammals, and 70 percent of the named species belong to just two orders, the Rodentia (rodents) and the Chiroptera (bats).—John F. Eisenberg

See also **AARDVARK; AARDWOLF; ADDAX; AFRICAN LION; ANTELOPE; ARGALI; ARMADILLO; ASS; BABOON; BADGER; BARBARY DEER; BARBARY LION; BARBARY SHEEP; BAT; BIGHORN SHEEP; BLACKBUCK; BOBCAT; CAMEL; CAMELS, SOUTH AMERICAN; CARACAL; CARNIVORES; CATS; CAVY; CHEETAH; COATI; COYOTE; DASSIE RAT; DEER; DIK-DIK; DINGO; DOG, WILD; ECHIDNA; ELAND; ELEPHANT; ENDOTHERMY; FENNEC; FERRET; FOX; GAZELLE; GEMSBOK; GENET; GERBIL; GERENUK; GIRAFFE; GOPHER; GRASSHOPPER MOUSE; GROUND SQUIRREL; GUNDI; HAMSTER; HARE; HARTEBEEST; HEDGEHOG; HETEROMYIDS; HUEMUL; HYENA; HYRAX; IBEX; JACKAL; JACKRABBIT; JAGUAR; JERBOA; KANGAROO; KANGAROO MOUSE; KANGAROO RAT; KLIPSPRINGER; KUDU; MARA; MARSUPIALS; MEERKAT; MELANIN; MOLE, GOLDEN; MOLE RAT; MONGOOSE; MONKEYS IN DESERTS; NYALA; ORYX; PANGOLIN; PECCARY; PIGMENT; PIKA; POCKET MOUSE; PORCUPINE; PRAIRIE DOG; PRONGHORN; PUMA; QUOKKA; RABBIT; RHINOCEROS; RINGTAIL; RODENTS; SAND RAT; SEA LION; SEAL; SERVAL; SHREW; SPRINGBOK; SPRINGHARE; SQUIRREL; TUCU-TUCO; UNGULATES; VOLE; WARTHOG; WEASEL; WOODRAT; ZEBRA**

Further Reading

Corbett, G. B., and J. E. Hill. 1991. *A World List of Mammalian Species.* 3d ed. Natural History Publications. Oxford: Oxford University Press.

Eisenberg, J. F. 1981. *The Mammalian Radiations.* Chicago: University of Chicago Press.

Nowak, R. M. 1991. *Walker's Mammals of the World.* 5th ed. Baltimore: Johns Hopkins University Press.

Wilson, D. E., and D. M. Reeder. 1993. *Mammal Species of the World: A Taxonomic and Geographic Reference.* Washington, D.C.: Smithsonian Institution Press.

Mara, or Patagonian "hare" (*Dolichotis patagonum*). (Photo: M. A. Mares)

MARA

Spanish common name for large rodents of the mammalian family Caviidae (order Rodentia) that occur in arid and semiarid parts of southernmost South America. They are also known as Patagonian hares because of their external resemblance to hares and jackrabbits. There are two species in two genera (although some authors only recognize the single genus *Dolichotis*): *Dolichotis patagonum*, restricted to central and southern Argentina, and *Pediolagus salinicola*, found in northwestern Argentina and parts of Paraguay and Bolivia. Both species inhabit arid grasslands and sparsely vegetated shrub lands.

Maras are large rodents that can weigh as much as 16 kilograms. They have a harelike body with long, rabbitlike ears. Their legs are long and thin and resemble those of a small deer or antelope. They are adapted to open, arid regions. The large ears facilitate the radiation of excess heat, and the long legs enable them to run at speeds of up to 45 kilometers per hour, making them the fastest rodent in the world. Maras have a white patch of fur on the rump that they flash when running, an adaptation they share with several species of deer and antelopes. They feed on short grasses and herbs.

Maras are unusual among mammals in that they are strictly monogamous. Males and females form lifelong pairs, and the males vigorously defend their mates from the advances of other males. However, during the breeding season up to 15 pairs of maras will congregate at a communal den where the females give birth. The den is dug by the females, and no adults enter after it is completed. The females give birth at the mouth of the den to up to three highly precocial young, which immediately enter the burrow. The young emerge to nurse. The adult males maintain a truce during this time, but the pair-bonds are maintained. It is believed that the communal den is an adaptation to reduce the loss of young to predators in the open habitat.—Thomas E. Lacher, Jr.

See also **CAVY; CONVERGENT EVOLUTION; LOCO-MOTION; MAMMALS; MONTE DESERT; PATAGONIA; PINNAE; PRAIRIE; RODENTS; SOUTH AMERICA, DESERTS OF**

Further Reading

Macdonald, D., ed. 1984. *The Encyclopedia of Mammals*. New York: Facts on File.

Nowak, R. M. 1991. *Walker's Mammals of the World*. 5th ed. Baltimore: Johns Hopkins University Press.

Redford, K. H., and J. F. Eisenberg. 1992. *Mammals of the Neotropics: The Southern Cone, Chile, Argentina, Uruguay, Paraguay*. Vol. 2. Chicago: University of Chicago Press.

Taber, A. B., and D. W. Macdonald. 1992. Spatial organization and monogamy in the mara *Dolichotis patagonum*. *Journal of Zoology London* 227:417–438.

———. Communal breeding in the mara, *Dolichotis patagonum*. *Journal of Zoology London* 227:439–452.

MARSUPIALS

The "pouched mammals," one of the three major groups of mammals (monotremes, marsupials, and placentals), with species found in the New World and Australian Region. Three families, about 19 genera, and 69 species are found in the New World, but marsupial diversity is highest in the Australian Region, where 16 families, about 64 genera, and 203 species occur. The name of the group derives from the Latin word *marsupium*, meaning "pouch," which is a reference to the fold of skin covering the teats that provides protection to the young during development. While some marsupials have a pouch (e.g., kangaroos and the North American opossum), others do not, and in some it is a temporary structure. Pouches may open anteriorly or posteriorly. A pouch is not restricted to marsupials, as it also is present in echidnas (monotremes, which are egg-laying mammals).

New World marsupials include such animals as the water opossum (*Chironectes*), mouse opossums (*Marmosa, Thylamys*), short-tailed opossums (*Monodelphis*), and four-eyed opossums (*Philander*). Although some species are found in deserts and semideserts, most are common in forested habitats. Species in several genera are common in arid areas, including *Didelphis* (opossums), *Thylamys, Lestodelphis* (Patagonian opossum), and *Monodelphis*, most of which are found in the semiarid parts of Argentina, Chile, Paraguay, and Bolivia.

In the Australian Region marsupials include the bandicoots, bilbies, koalas, wombats, possums, kangaroos, wallabies, potoroos, bettongs, rat kangaroos, numbats, marsupial moles, and dasyurids (e.g., quolls, *Antechinus*). Fewer than one-third of Australia's marsupials inhabit arid and semiarid habitats, and even fewer are restricted to arid zones. Species of the family Dasyuridae are most likely to be found in arid and semiarid areas, with about 47 percent of species inhabiting such areas (a higher percentage than for any other family of marsupials). Other genera common in arid areas are *Notoryctes* (marsupial moles), *Chaeropus* (bandicoots), *Macrotis* (bilbies), and a number of kangaroos and potoroos.

Marsupials have two uteri; young are born small, blind, hairless, and with partially formed hind limbs. After birth the young climb up the mother's abdomen and attach to a teat. Although most marsupials lack a placenta, some (e.g., bandicoots and koalas) possess one. In all but one family (the fossorial, i.e., burrowing, marsupial moles, family Notoryctidae), the testes are contained in a scrotum that is anterior (rather than posterior) to the penis. Most species have an opposable hallux (big toe) on the hind foot; this structure is lost in the kangaroos and is absent or obsolete in the bandicoots and dasyurids.

Marsupials have diversified, especially in the Australian Region, into many forms. There are gliding, terrestrial, burrowing, sand swimming, aquatic, and bipedal marsupials. Marsupials may be insectivorous (insect eating), myrmecophagous (ant eating), carnivorous (meat eating), omnivorous (have a wide range of dietary items), herbivorous (plant eating), frugivorous (fruit eating), and nectarivorous (nectar eating).

As with many inhabitants of deserts and semideserts, marsupials use a number of mechanisms to avoid excessive heat loads. Compared with placental mammals, they generally have a lower body temperature and metabolic rate. This may allow them to expend less energy for maintenance. They are nocturnal or crepuscular (active at dawn and dusk); during the day, when temperatures are highest, they rest in burrows or under shelter.—Janet K. Braun

See also **AUSTRALIA, DESERTS OF; BIPEDALITY; BODY TEMPERATURE; CONVERGENT EVOLUTION; ECHIDNA; ENDOTHERMY; HEAT BALANCE; HEAT STRESS; KANGAROO; MAMMALS; MELANIN; METABOLISM; PIGMENT; QUOKKA; THERMOREGULATION; WATER BALANCE**

Further Reading

Dyne, G. R., and D. W. Walton, eds. 1987. *Fauna of Australia.* Canberra: Australian Government Publishing Service.

Lee, A. K., and A. Cockburn. 1985. *Evolutionary Ecology of Marsupials.* Cambridge: University of Cambridge Press.

Nowak, R. M. 1991. *Walker's Mammals of the World.* 5th ed. Baltimore: Johns Hopkins University Press.

Ride, W. D. L. 1980. *A Guide to the Native Mammals of Australia.* Oxford: Oxford University Press.

Strahan, R., ed. 1983. *The Complete Book of Australian Mammals.* London: Angus and Robertson.

MECCA. *See* SAUDI ARABIA, DESERTS OF

MEERKAT

Species of mammal, *Suricata suricatta*, also known as the suricate or slender-tailed meerkat, in the civet family (order Carnivora, family Viverridae) which inhabits arid and semiarid areas in southern Africa from Angola to South Africa. Meerkats live in colonies in burrows and forage mainly on insects and other arthropods and lizards. This small (weight less than 1 kilogram), diurnal mongoose is light gray with a grizzled appearance. It has dark bands posteriorly on the back, a white face with dark ears, large eyes with a dark eye ring (making the eyes appear exceptionally large), a broad head, and a pointed muzzle; the tail, which is about three-fourths as long as the head and body, is light colored and tipped with black. The forefeet have long curved claws, reflecting the propensity to dig. The ears (pinnae) are capable of being closed to protect the inner ear from dirt when the animals are digging. Burrows are shared with other mammals, including ground squirrels (*Xerus*) and the yellow mongoose (*Cynictis*).

The animals spend a good deal of time basking in the sun, particularly in the early morning. They appear outside their burrows shortly after sunrise, bask and groom one another, then begin feeding. They sleep during the heat of the day in the shade of desert plants or in their burrows. Ever alert, the meerkats convey an impression of great nervousness and high anxiety, racing away to their burrows en masse and screaming after being alerted to potential predators by the cry of a sentry. After taking refuge in the burrow, barking all the time, they cautiously reemerge, assume alert positions, and eventually begin foraging again. Suricates race around through the desert and semidesert habitats for up to six kilometers in groups of 30 or more searching for food. A group may move to a new location if food supplies dwindle.

Meerkats have become popular in recent years due to extensive media coverage of their colonial behavior and propensity for an entire group to sit erect on their haunches while being alert for predators, giving them an especially large-eyed, doleful, and appealing appearance. They tame easily and are commonly used as pets.—Michael A. Mares

See also **AFRICA, DESERTS OF; BURROWING ANIMALS; CARNIVORES; GROUND SQUIRREL; KALAHARI DESERT; KAROO; MAMMALS; NAMIBIA, DESERTS OF; SOUTH AFRICA, DESERTS OF**

Further Reading

Estes, R. D. 1991. *The Behavior Guide to African Mammals.* Berkeley: University of California Press.

Nowak, R. M. 1991. *Walker's Mammals of the World.* 5th ed. Baltimore: Johns Hopkins University Press.

Skinner, J. D., and R. H. N. Smithers. 1990. *The Mammals of the Southern African Subregion.* Pretoria: University of Pretoria.

MELANIN

Substance in the skin of animals that is made up of brown pigment granules and, depending on its concentration, imparts a darker or lighter skin color. Melanin develops from specialized epidermal skin cells called melanocytes. Humans vary enormously in the amounts of melanin in their skin epidermis, from near or complete absence (albinism) to superabundance (melanism). In addition, the amount of melanin in the epidermis of an individual human will vary with the degree of exposure of the skin to solar radiation. The ultraviolet component of solar radiation, if exposure is gradual, will stimulate melanocytes to produce more melanin, resulting in a tanning of the skin. This tanning, in turn, protects the deeper skin layers from harmful ultraviolet radiation that might otherwise result from overexposure, a major cause of skin cancer. Dark skin in desert-dwelling humans is a mixed blessing, however, as it not only protects the skin from sunburn but also serves, when exposed to solar radiation, as an effective absorber of heat in an already hot environment; lighter skin is more reflective of solar heat.

Many desert animals are less melanistic than their nondesert counterparts, which probably is an adaptation geared more to protective coloration and predator avoidance than to promoting efficiency in heat exchange. However, in some desert animals, especially lizards that behaviorally thermoregulate, melanin is packed in specialized epidermal cells called melanophores. These cells are under hormonal control and/or control through the nervous system, and, although each melanophore contains a discrete number of melanin granules, these can be dispersed to make the cell (and skin) darker or concentrated to make the cell (and skin) lighter. This capacity is employed during behavioral thermoregulation in lizards by darkening the skin (dispersal of melanin granules within melanophores) when the body temperature is lower than the preferred level, thereby enhancing solar heat absorption. Conversely, when the body temperature is at or above the preferred level, the skin blanches (pigment granules within melanophores are concentrated), thereby minimizing solar absorption.—Richard E. MacMillen

See also **AMPHIBIANS; BIRDS; COLORATION; ECTOTHERMY; HEAT EXCHANGE; HEAT STRESS; MAMMALS; METABOLISM; PIGMENT; PHYSIOLOGY; THERMOREGULATION; WATER BALANCE**

Further Reading

Gordon, M. S., G. A. Bartholomew, A. D. Grinnell, C. B. Jorgensen, and F. N. White. 1982. *Animal Physiology: Principles and Adaptations*. New York: Macmillan.

Huge algarrobo (mesquite) tree (*Prosopis*) in Monte Desert habitat of westernmost Tucuman Province, Argentina. (Photo: M. A. Mares)

MESA. *See* DESERT SLOPES

MESQUITE

Common name for a group of small desert trees or shrubs of the genus *Prosopis* in the legume family (Fabaceae or Leguminosae). Most mesquites live in warm, dry subtropical or tropical climates, although they are abundant in parts of the southwestern United States. Here the honey mesquite, the velvet mesquite, and the common mesquite grow along streams and desert washes, often in extensive thickets.

The branches of the tree have sturdy, straight thorns and compound leaves. Like all members of the family, mesquites produce legumes, long fruits resembling string beans that ripen in the autumn and are eaten by livestock and wild animals. Mesquite pods are sweet, rich in protein, and nutritious, and were eaten by Native Americans of the region who sometimes ground them to make a meal called pinole.

Mesquite is very drought tolerant and can withstand heavy grazing, invading grasslands after overgrazing. One explanation for its aggressiveness is its deep roots; some root systems grow to depths of more than 20 meters below the surface of the ground. In some sandy soils honey mesquite is considered to be a valuable soil binder; blowing dirt and sand frequently collect around mesquite trees and eventually form hummocks of soil.

Pioneers built corrals, furniture, and utensils with the very hard wood of the mesquite, and burned its wood as fuel. Native Americans of the region used mesquite fires to bake pottery, and the wood was used to make weapons. The honey mesquite exudes a gum similar to gum arabic that is used in the production of confections and mucilage, and was eaten directly by Native Americans like a candy. The common mesquite was an important plant to California tribes in providing food, housing, and some clothing. The long yellow legume pods were collected and stored for later use. The beans were often ground to a coarse meal and then left to stand in water for a few hours, during which time the concoction fermented. Nectar from the flowers produces a fine-quality honey with a distinctive flavor, and because it gives off a characteristic aroma as it burns, mesquite wood is still used today to flavor barbecued meats. *Prosopis* is also an important plant in South American arid areas and occurs in the Old World as well.—Gordon E. Uno

See also **AFRICA, DESERTS OF; AUSTRALIA, DESERTS OF; CHACO; CHIHUAHUAN DESERT; ECONOMIC VALUE OF DESERT PRODUCTS; FOREST; FRUITS; LEAVES; LEGUMES; MEXICO, DESERTS OF; MONTE DESERT; NEW MEXICO DESERT; PLANT ADAPTATIONS; PLANT GEOGRAPHY; PLANTS; RIPARIAN COMMUNITIES; RIVERS; ROOTS; SONORAN DESERT; SOUTH AMERICA, DESERTS OF; TEXAS DESERT; THORN; UNITED STATES, DESERTS OF**

Further Reading

Balls, E. K. 1970. *Early Uses of California Plants*. Berkeley: University of California Press.

McClaran, M. P., and T. R. Van Devender. 1995. *The Desert Grassland*. Tucson: University of Arizona Press.

Simpson, B. B., ed. 1977. *Mesquite: Its Biology in Two Desert Ecosystems*. Stroudsburg, Pa.: Dowden, Hutchinson, and Ross.

METABOLIC WATER

Water produced in animals as a by-product of oxidative metabolism; may also be termed water of oxidation. The amount of metabolic water formed depends on the amount of hydrogen present in the foodstuff, with the oxidation of fat (rich in hydrogen) producing the most, followed by carbohydrates, then protein metabolism. However, the value of metabolic water to an animal also depends on the caloric content of the foodstuff, and fat has more than twice the calories of carbohydrates or protein. Thus, at a given metabolic rate, an animal will use as an energy source only half as much fat per unit time as carbohydrate or protein, the net result being that carbohydrate has the largest metabolic water yield per unit of metabolism of the three basic foodstuffs.

It should not be surprising, then, that some of the most efficient desert animals with regard to water regulation are granivorous (seed eating); they rely largely on carbohydrate-rich seeds for both energy and metabolic water. Included among these granivores are certain insects, small birds, and many rodents. In fact, some of these granivores can be essentially independent of exogenous water, by reducing their water losses through behavioral and physiological means to the extent that the losses are more than offset by metabolic water production alone. Further, it has now been demonstrated in both granivorous birds and mammals that small size confers an advantage for water independence, with the higher metabolic rates of these small endotherms yielding maximal amounts of metabolic water relative to water losses. While there are small, water-independent granivores in most of the world's deserts, perhaps the most renowned of these seed-eating wonders (but not necessarily the most desert specialized) is the North American Merriam kangaroo rat, *Dipodomys merriami*, which may be kept in captivity in good health indefinitely on a diet of air-dry seeds.—Richard E. MacMillen

See also **ANIMAL ADAPTATIONS; BODY TEMPERATURE; COUNTERCURRENT HEAT EXCHANGE; DEHYDRATION; DESICCATION; ECTOTHERMY; ENDOTHERMY; ESTIVATION; EXCRETORY SYSTEM; HEAT BALANCE; HEAT EXCHANGE; HEAT STRESS; HEATSTROKE; HIBERNATION; HYPERTHERMIA; HYPOTHERMIA; KANGAROO RAT; KIDNEY FUNCTION, DESERT RODENTS; KIDNEYS; METABOLISM; PERSPIRATION; PHYSIOLOGY; RENAL PAPILLA; RESPIRATORY WATER LOSS; SALT BALANCE; SHIV-**

ERING; SWEAT GLANDS; THERMOREGULATION; TORPOR; TRANSPIRATION; VAN'T HOFF EFFECT; WATER BALANCE; WATER STRESS

Further Reading

MacMillen, R. E. 1990. Water economy of granivorous birds: a predictive model. *Condor* 92:379–392.

MacMillen, R. E., and D. S. Hinds. 1983. Water regulatory efficiency in heteromyid rodents: A model and its application. *Ecology* 64:152–164.

Schmidt-Nielsen, K. 1990. *Animal Physiology: Adaptation and Environment.* 4th ed. New York: Cambridge University Press.

METABOLISM

Sum total of all the chemical reactions that occur in an organism, which includes provision of energy for cell function and the synthesis and breakdown of molecules required for cell structure and function. All of these reactions involve energy in some manner; therefore, many studies of metabolism focus on measurement of the metabolic rate or overall energy use by organisms per unit of time. Metabolic rate generally is determined by measuring the amount of oxygen consumed, since the vast majority of energy expended by organisms is derived from reaction of oxygen with different foods.

Metabolic rate varies with many factors, including activity, developmental stage, hormonal balance (including sex), photoperiod, diet, taxonomy, and climate. However, three of the most important factors affecting metabolism are body size, temperature, and activity.

As organisms increase in size their total need for energy increases. A striking observation is that the increase in total energy use is not directly proportional to the increase in body size. The metabolic rate of large organisms is considerably lower than would be predicted by extrapolating in direct proportion from metabolic rate in small organisms. Conversely, small organisms have higher rates than would be predicted from studying large ones. It is also important that smaller animals have a higher mass-specific metabolic rate than do large animals. Mass-specific metabolic rate is the amount of energy per unit time required to support a single unit of body mass. Small animals require much more energy to support one unit of body mass than do large animals.

Metabolism increases in all animals with increasing body temperature. In ectotherms (poikilo-

therms, or cold-blooded animals), body temperature and metabolism increase with increasing environmental temperatures. Endotherms (homeotherms, or warm-blooded animals) have physiologically regulated, relatively high body temperatures (e.g., 36°C). This regulation is quite costly, and an endotherm expends about seven times more energy than an ectotherm of the same body size at the same body temperature.

In endotherms metabolism shows three distinct relationships with air temperature. Metabolism increases with colder temperatures (e.g., below 18°C in humans) as the body requires more energy to maintain a stable temperature. At thermoneutral temperatures (e.g., 18°–28°C) metabolism does not change with increasing temperature, as the animal adjusts by reducing its insulation, which does not cost additional energy. At higher temperatures metabolism increases with increasing temperature due to the cost of cooling and the effect of slightly elevated body temperatures.

Metabolism increases with increased activity. For running animals, metabolism typically increases in direct proportion to the speed of running, with a fascinating exception being large kangaroos. A typical way of comparing the cost of various forms of locomotion is to determine the cost of transport, or the amount of energy it takes to move one unit of body mass over one unit of distance. Surprisingly, large animals have a lower cost of transport than do small animals, and the cost of transport for same-sized animals is highest for those that run, lowest for those that swim, and intermediate for those that fly.

It can be advantageous for desert animals to have a reduced metabolism, which would generate less internal heat and require less energy while also necessitating lowered amounts of water for cooling. There is some evidence that at least some desert animals (e.g., desert rodents) do indeed have a reduced metabolism when compared to nondesert species.—David S. Hinds

See also ANIMAL ADAPTATIONS; BODY TEMPERATURE; COUNTERCURRENT HEAT EXCHANGE; DEHYDRATION; DESICCATION; ECTOTHERMY; ENDOTHERMY; ESTIVATION; EXCRETORY SYSTEM; HEAT BALANCE; HEAT EXCHANGE; HEAT STRESS; HEATSTROKE; HIBERNATION; HYPERTHERMIA; HYPOTHERMIA; INSULATION; KANGAROO RAT; KIDNEY FUNCTION, DESERT RODENTS; KIDNEYS; METABOLISM; PERSPIRATION; PHYSIOLOGY;

RENAL PAPILLA; RESPIRATORY WATER LOSS; RODENTS; SALT BALANCE; SHIVERING; SWEAT GLANDS; THERMOREGULATION; TORPOR; TRANSPIRATION; VAN'T HOFF EFFECT; WATER BALANCE; WATER STRESS

Further Reading

Bartholomew, G. A. 1982. Energy metabolism. *In* M. S. Gordon, ed., *Animal Physiology*, 46–93. 4th ed. New York: Macmillan.

———. Body temperature and energy metabolism. M. S. Gordon, ed., *Animal Physiology*, 333–406. 4th ed. New York: Macmillan.

Schmidt-Nielsen, K. 1984. *Scaling: Why Is Animal Size so Important?* New York: Cambridge University Press.

———. *Animal Physiology: Adaptation and Environment*. 4th ed. New York: Cambridge University Press.

Withers, P. C. 1992. *Comparative Animal Physiology*. Philadelphia: Saunders.

METAMORPHOSIS

Process of changing from one body form to another during the life cycle of an animal. Metamorphosis occurs in a variety of organisms but is best known in insects and amphibians. Certain insects undergo simple metamorphosis, in which the young are similar to the adults in form and are called nymphs, whereas others undergo complete metamorphosis, in which the immature and adult forms are very different and the young are called larvae. Immature larvae are often wormlike in form. Prior to metamorphosis to the adult form, the immatures of most insects undergo from four to eight molts as they grow and develop. At the final molt, when the last stage (known as the pupa) changes into the adult, the insect is pale and soft, but within a few hours its wings expand and harden, pigmentation develops, and the insect becomes an adult capable of flight.

In amphibians metamorphosis of tadpoles occurs after a variable period of from one or two weeks to several years, depending on species. The process involves numerous physiological and morphological changes, with the thyroid gland playing a key role in initiation of the change. The change from tadpole to adult frog is most dramatic; in the other two major groups of amphibians, salamanders and caecilians, juvenile forms are similar to adults. In frogs metamorphosis is an abrupt transition, as the animal is changing not only its morphology but also its diet, feeding behavior, and even habitat, generally moving from an aquatic existence to a terrestrial one. Because of the narrow window of time in which water is available in deserts, the larval period in desert frogs is usually very short (less than two weeks), and the tadpoles metamorphose in synchrony. Opportunistic predators may take advantage of this mass exodus of thousands of toadlets or froglets. For example, on one occasion many metamorphosing and newly metamorphosed spadefoot toads were observed to be pulled into the mud around the edge of the pond as they attempted to leave. They were being captured and eaten by horsefly larvae, *Tabanus punctifer*, which were submerged in the mud by the hundreds with only their powerful hooked mandibles flush with the surface.—Janalee P. Caldwell

See also **AMPHIBIANS; ANIMAL ADAPTATIONS; ARTHROPODS; BREEDING SEASON; DORMANCY; FOAM NEST; FROGS; INSECTS; REPRODUCTION; SPADEFOOT TOAD; SPIDERS; TADPOLES; TOADS**

Further Reading

Borror, D. J., C. A. Triplehorn, and N. F. Johnson. 1992. *An Introduction to the Study of Insects*. New York: Harcourt Brace.

Duellman, W. E., and L. Trueb. 1986. *Biology of Amphibians*. New York: McGraw-Hill.

Fox, H. 1984. *Amphibian Morphogenesis*. Clifton, N.J.: Humana Press.

Jackman, R., S. Nowicki, D. J. Aneshansley, and T. Eisner. 1983. Predatory capture of toads by fly larvae. *Science* 222:515–516.

MEXICO, DESERTS OF

Arid and semiarid areas lying within the boundaries of the nation of Mexico. The area of these habitats is estimated to be 99 million hectares, or about half Mexico's total territory. Arid habitats, or true deserts, are defined as those that receive less than 250 millimeters of annual precipitation and have 8–12 months without rain. Semiarid regions receive from 250 to 700 millimeters of annual precipitation, and the number of dry months is 6–8. Both deserts and semiarid habitats are extremely important biologically. There are more than 6,000 species of plants found in these two classes of ecosystems in Mexico, and about 60 percent of the plant species are endemic (found nowhere else). Arid and semiarid habitats are the second most important, in terms of endemism, in Mexico (the temperate subhumid zone has the highest percentage of endemism). (See map of North American deserts, p. 356.)

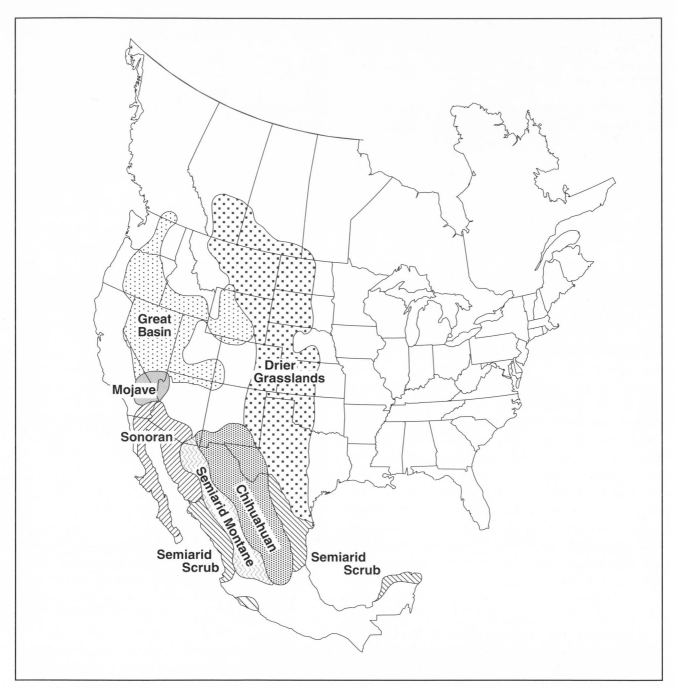

Map of the deserts, semideserts, and drier grasslands of the United States and Mexico. Shading indicates desert and semidesert limits.

Two major deserts, the Chihuahuan and Sonoran, dominate the northern border of Mexico with the United States. The Chihuahuan Desert of Mexico extends from the border of Arizona, New Mexico, and Mexico east along the Rio Grande valley to Reynosa and then south past Monterrey to the outskirts of Mexico City; the limits extend west to Guadalajara, then north again to the U.S. border.

There is a central arid core in this desert, and the habitat becomes semiarid as one moves to the peripheries. The total area of the Chihuahuan Desert within Mexico is approximately 362,000 square kilometers. This is primarily a high-elevation desert, with most of the region lying between 1,000 and 1,500 meters elevation in the Mesa del Norte. To the east and west, the desert is bordered by highly degraded grasslands and dry woodlands. The plateau on which the desert occurs is under the rain shadow of the Sierra Madre Oriental and Sierra Madre Occidental ranges, and mean annual precipitation varies from 77 millimeters in the central valley to 513 millimeters in the higher elevations. Most rain falls in summer. Areas of the plateau can have several days of below-freezing temperatures in mid-winter. Vegetation is dominated by creosote bush (*Larrea tridentata*), which co-occurs with tarbush (*Flourensia cernua*). Prickly pears (*Opuntia*) are the most common species of cacti. Common trees are mesquite (*Prosopis glandulosa*) and ocotillo (*Fouquieria splendens*), with saltbush (*Atriplex canescens*) and several species of *Acacia* occurring along washes. The genera *Agave* and *Yucca* are found at higher elevations.

The Sonoran Desert of Mexico begins at Nogales (south of Tucson) and extends west to Baja California; most of the Baja Peninsula is Sonoran Desert. This desert also extends south from Nogales to Ciudad Obregón and includes the entire western coast of the Gulf of California between these two cities. The area of Sonoran Desert within Mexico is roughly 184,000 square kilometers. About 28 percent of the total area of Mexico (1,967,183 square kilometers) lies within either the Chihuahuan or Sonoran Desert. The Sonoran Desert is primarily a lowland desert, with most of the area below 600 meters elevation. The region is dominated by large basins that serve as drainage basins for seasonally flowing rivers. Between the basin and plains there are a series of mountain ranges with a north-south orientation. Several areas, in particular the headlands of the Gulf of California and the Gran Desierto of the state of Sonora, are dominated by extensive dune formations. Rainfall varies greatly with topography; the west is in the rain shadow of the Pacific Coast Ranges, but the east receives precipitation moving westward from the Gulf of Mexico. The mean annual precipitation in the east (254–395 millimeters) is substantially higher than the west (as low as 51 millimeters). Temperature extremes in the Sonoran Desert are somewhat greater than in the Chihuahuan Desert. Below-freezing temperatures are common in winter, and summer temperatures can stay at 38°C for up to 90 consecutive days, reaching a maximum of 41.3°C.

The vegetation of the Sonoran Desert is quite complex, and botanists divide the region into seven subregions. The Lower Colorado Valley, for example, is extremely arid and mostly barren. Scattered plants include bur sage (*Ambrosia dumosa*) and creosote bush. The area most typically associated with the Sonoran Desert is the Arizona Upland region. Distinctive species of this region are paloverde (*Cercidium floridum*), many species of prickly pear and cholla (*Opuntia*), and the most famous of Sonoran species, the saguaro cactus (*Carnegiea gigantea*). The region that forms the two shores of the Gulf of California is the Central Gulf Coast region. Unusual species include the elephant tree (*Bursera microphylla*) and the boojum (*Idria columnaris*). The other four vegetation regions of the Sonoran Desert are Plains of Sonora, Foothills of Sonora, Vizcaíno, and Magdalena.

These arid regions are important to the ecology, culture, and history of Mexico. Indeed, much of what is presented as the image of Mexico in film and popular media derives from the deserts of the northern parts of the country. Both Mexican deserts are basically subtropical, with exceptionally rich floras compared to more temperate deserts like the Great Basin of the western United States. The two Mexican deserts differ from one another in climate and flora. However, both the Sonoran and Chihuahuan deserts share their faunas to some degree. Rattlesnakes (*Crotalus*) occur in both deserts, but the copperhead (*Agkistrodon contortrix*) is found only in the Chihuahuan Desert. At least two species of birds in these deserts survive entirely on water obtained from their food: Gambel's quail (*Callipepla gambeli*) and the black-throated sparrow (*Amphispiza bilineata*). The Gila woodpecker (*Centurus uropygialis*), the gilded flicker (*Colaptes chrysoides*), and the elf owl (*Micrathene whitneyi*) all use the saguaro cactus in the Sonoran Desert for nests. The woodpeckers actually peck a hole in the cactus to construct their burrow, and the elf owl moves into abandoned woodpecker holes. Bobcats (*Lynx rufus*) and kit foxes (*Vulpes macrotis*) are important predators of small vertebrates in both deserts, and the black-tailed jackrabbit (*Lepus californicus*) is an important small herbivore across the arid lands of northern Mexico. Large herbivores like the javelina or peccary (*Pecari tajacu*), the pronghorn (*Antilocapra americana*), and the desert bighorn (*Ovis canadensis*) are found to some degree in both deserts as well, although the latter two are more common in the Sonoran Desert than the Chihuahuan.

Semiarid ecosystems occur in several regions of Mexico, and there are several types of habitat within these ecosystems. Parts of the northern Baja Peninsula are semiarid, especially in the zone of transition between the chaparral habitat of southern California and the true desert in the extreme southern part of the peninsula. This zone is complex, with pinyon-juniper woodlands at higher elevations, desert scrub in the lowlands, and riparian woodlands along the Colorado River floodplain. There is an extensive semiarid zone that extends along the Pacific slope of Mexico, from southern Sinaloa, through Nayarit, Jalisco, Colima, and Michoacán, to Guerrero, north of Acapulco. Most of this region is covered by a dry thorn forest, dominated by *Acacia* trees. There is another extensive dry thorn forest along the northeastern edge of Mexico, referred to as the Tamaulipian Biotic Province. This habitat runs along the Gulf Coast from Tamaulipas south to northern Veracruz, and the most dominant tree species is mesquite (*Prosopis glandulosa*), with an extensive grass understory in many areas. This region has a fauna with many tropical elements, including several species of parrots, the coati (*Nasua narica*), and several tropical cats, such as the ocelot (*Leopardus pardalis*), jaguarundi (*Herpailurus yaguarondi*), and jaguar (*Panthera onca*). Other isolated semiarid regions are a small area along the north coast of the Yucatan Peninsula and the Coahuila grasslands south of Saltillo.

The northern arid regions were home to native peoples such as the Sari of Sonora and the Tarahumara of Chihuahua until the 1500s, when the Spanish exploration began. Colonists were drawn to the region in search of minerals and land for livestock. Much of the grassland habitat that bordered the core desert of Chihuahua was degraded by overgrazing. The construction of irrigation canals led to the expansion of agriculture in many desert valleys; indeed much of the winter lettuce and tomatoes consumed in the United States come from these areas.—Thomas E. Lacher, Jr.

See also **AMPHIBIANS; BAJA CALIFORNIA, DESERTS OF; BIOSPHERE RESERVE; BOOJUM; CACTI; CACTUS, COLUMNAR; CARDÓN; CHIHUAHUAN DESERT; CREOSOTE BUSH; DESERT PEOPLES; DESERTS; FROGS; GRASSHOPPER MOUSE; JACK-RABBIT; JORNADA DEL MUERTO; LLANO ESTACADO; KANGAROO RAT; LIZARDS; MESQUITE; MOVIES IN DESERTS; ORGAN PIPE CACTUS; OVERGRAZING; PIT VIPER; PLANT GEOGRAPHY; POCKET MOUSE; PRONGHORN; RABBIT; RATTLESNAKE; REPTILES; SAGUARO; SEMIARID ZONES; SONORAN DESERT; SNAKES; SPADEFOOT TOAD; TOADS; XEROPHYLLOUS FOREST**

Further Reading

Allan, T., and A. Warren, eds. 1993. *Deserts: The Encroaching Wilderness*. New York: Oxford University Press.

Arritt, S. 1993. *The Living Earth Book of Deserts*. New York: Reader's Digest Assoc.

Dice, L. R. 1943. *The Biotic Provinces of North America*. Ann Arbor: University of Michigan Press.

McGinnies, W. G., B. J. Goldman, and P. Paylore, eds. 1968. *Deserts of the World: An Appraisal of Research into Their Physical and Biological Environments*. Tucson: University of Arizona Press.

Nir, D. 1974. *The Semi-arid World: Man on the Fringe of the Desert*. London: Longman.

Ramamoorthy, T. P., R. Bye, A. Lot, and J. Fa. 1993. *Biological Diversity of Mexico: Origins and Distribution*. New York: Oxford University Press.

Wauer, R. H. 1992. *Naturalist's Mexico*. College Station: Texas A&M University Press.

MICE. *See* RODENTS

MICROHABITAT

The microspatial complexity of the environment at a local scale. The physical characteristics of the environment at different points on the surface of the ground differ from those at some depth in the soil or at some height above ground. Plants and animals add a biological component to the structure of the environment. For example, foliage complexity is a measure of the stratification of the vegetation in a particular place or in a particular microhabitat and is an important factor in determining the composition and abundance of animal species. Trees and shrubs may produce a stratification or gradient of temperature, humidity, light intensity, soil moisture, and mineral content. This in turn influences the kind and abundance of species that might occur in any particular site. The concepts of habitat and microhabitat are sometimes fuzzy and should be used with caution. In general, the term "microhabitat" is used when referring to finer distributions within a particular habitat. The significance of a microhabitat is determined in part by the size and mobility of the organism under consideration. Thus an insect might be restricted to a particular plant species (habitat), or even to a particular portion of that plant, such as the underside of young leaves (microhabitat), whereas a larger species, such as an antelope, might be restricted to areas of low desert scrub (habitat), or to sandy areas within a desert scrub area (microhabitat).

Microhabitat selection, which is the choice made by organisms (plants or animals) to live in a particular place, might be determined by, among other things, physiological requirements, food abundance, predation, competition with other organisms for scarce resources, or the availability of nesting sites. The cactus wren, for example, inhabits the deserts of the southwestern United States and is adapted to face the demands of the hot desert by foraging during the day in cooler microhabitats (i.e., within the shade of shrubs and trees) in the desert habitat. Desert rodents are adapted to different microhabitats in response to competition with other species, predation, food composition, food abundance, soil texture, and density of conspecifics. Thus some species live mainly in the open spaces between shrubs, others are active primarily under shrubs, some stay near rock piles, and others may favor spiny vegetation. This also is known as habitat partitioning, a mechanism that promotes the coexistence of closely related species within the same general environment.—Ricardo A. Ojeda

See also **BIOME; DIVERSITY; ECOLOGY; ECOSYSTEM; ECOTYPE; ENDEMISM; HABITAT DEGRADATION; LANDSCAPE**

Further Reading

Kotler, B. P., and J. S. Brown. 1988. Environmental heterogeneity and the coexistence of desert rodents. *Annual Review Ecology and Systematics* 19:281–307.

Partridge, L. 1978. Habitat selection. *In* J. R. Krebs and N. B. Davies, eds., *Behavioural Ecology: An Evolutionary Approach*, 351–376. Oxford: Blackwell.

Ricklefs, R. E. 1990. *Ecology.* 3rd ed. New York: Freeman.

MICROPHYLLY. *See* LEAVES

MIDDEN

Dung pile or refuse heap, here especially meaning the refuse including fecal pellets and plant and animal fragments accumulated by certain mammals (particularly by desert-inhabiting woodrats, genus *Neotoma*). (The term "kitchen midden" is sometimes used in archaeological contexts wherein it refers to trash piles left by humans near prehistoric dwellings.)

Woodrats are herbivorous rodents of western and southern North America that habitually collect twigs, cactus joints, leaves, flowers, seeds, animal bones, insect parts, and other small objects within a radius of about 50–100 meters of their dens. Their dens may be in rock piles, cliffs, caves, or at the bases of trees or cacti and are used by generations of woodrats. The debris includes plant clippings, both used and unused, collected while foraging and cached in or near the den. In addition to the plant debris, generations of rats leave their fecal pellets; these materials may be mixed by periodic cleanings of the dens. Over time the mixture of these and other items becomes cemented with residues of the rats' viscous, mineral-containing urine.

These midden accumulations are excellent samples of the local vegetative community (and to a lesser extent, the vertebrate and insect communities) at a point in time. Long sequences of successive, stratified, cemented midden deposits can span thousands of years. The crystallized urine even includes a record of past levels of bombardment by cosmic rays, which are indicated by a radioactive isotope of chlorine preserved in the chloride salts excreted by the woodrats. In arid regions the cemented middens may be protected from weathering in dry rock crevices, ledges, or caves, and are often preserved there for additional thousands or tens of thousands of years. Many of the organic materials preserved in the middens can be readily dated by radiocarbon, and hundreds of middens throughout the North American deserts provide abundant paleontological data for the reconstruction of ancient plant communities.

In western North America ancient woodrat middens have been collected mostly in the lowest, driest parts of the Sonoran, Chihuahuan, and Mojave deserts. Overall they date back from the present through the last glaciation (40,000 or 45,000 years). Studies of plant macrofossils, pollen, and animal fossils (bones and arthropod exoskeletal fragments) in these middens revealed that before and during the last glacial maximum these low desert regions were largely occupied by pygmy conifer woodlands of juniper and pinyon pine instead of desert scrub.

The valuable and detailed biotic record preserved in ancient woodrat middens is limited to the late Pleistocene epoch and to North American deserts, but similar kinds of middens are left by other kinds of mammals in arid regions of other continents. Although middens have not been investigated extensively on continents other than North America, their presence elsewhere indicates their potential paleontological usefulness on a greater scale. Middens are also made by chinchilla rats (*Abrocoma*) in South America, stick-nest rats (*Leporillus*) in Australia, hyraxes (*Procavia*) in the Middle East and South Africa, dassie rats (*Petromus*) in South Africa, porcupines (*Erethizon dorsatum*) in North America, and possibly by still other mammals in these same areas.—Nicholas J. Czaplewski

See also **CENOZOIC; CHIHUAHUAN DESERT; GLACIAL PERIODS; INTERGLACIALS; MADRO-TERTIARY GEOFLORA; MIOCENE; MOJAVE DESERT; PALEOCLIMATE; PLEISTOCENE; PLIOCENE; QUATERNARY; RECENT (HOLOCENE); SONORAN DESERT; WOODRATS**

Further Reading

Betancourt, J. L., T. R. Van Devender, and P. S. Martin. 1990. *Packrat Middens: The Last 40,000 Years of Biotic Change*. Tucson: University of Arizona Press.

Mead, J. I., T. R. Van Devender, and K. L. Cole. 1983. Late Quaternary small mammals from Sonoran Desert packrat middens, Arizona and California. *Journal of Mammalogy* 64:173–180.

Wells, P. V., and C. D. Jorgensen. 1964. Pleistocene wood rat middens and climatic change in Mojave Desert—A record of juniper woodlands. *Science* 143:1171–1174.

MIDDLE EAST, DESERTS OF

Arid and semiarid parts of Libya, Egypt, Israel, Palestine, Jordan, Lebanon, Syria, Iraq, and northern Arabia. Middle Eastern countries have always been difficult to delineate as a geographic region because the definition of their boundaries has varied. Deserts represent the major part of this region, and climates range from semiarid (150–300 millimeters rain per year) over most of the region to arid (rainfall below 150 millimeters) and to extremely arid (annual rainfall less than 80 millimeters) in the inland regions. The climate is characterized by low and irregular winter rainfall and hot dry summers. Temperatures below freezing may occur occasionally, and snow may even fall at times, although snow cover is of short duration. Soils consist of the erosion products of the underlying rocks, altered by the action of wind and water. Several soil types are recognized, including sandy, clayey, and stony soils. Salt-affected soils (or saline areas) occur in coastal or inland regions that are subjected to a continuous cycle of periodic moisture followed by evaporation. (See map of Middle East, p. 361.)

The Middle East is a point of intersection for four biogeographic regions: the Mediterranean, the Irano-Turanian, the Saharo-Arabian, and the Sudanian. These regions give the Middle East its diverse habitat types and a rich biological diversity. Vegetation differs depending on the level of aridity of the desert. The semideserts are found on the upper slopes of the Jordan Valley in Israel and Jordan, on high mountains of the Sinai, and in the central Negev. They are also found in Syria, northwestern Iraq, and in northern Egypt and Libya. Vegetation of the semidesert areas provides relatively high ground cover. Scattered trees and shrubs dominate these areas. Where rainfall is greater, the lower plant layer is dominated by herbaceous perennials. With increasing aridity, the semideserts are replaced by arid deserts with open vegetation (less ground cover) dominated by dwarf shrubs. However, even in the arid areas during the rainy season the ground surface may be completely covered by short-lived ephemeral plants (annuals).

In the extremely arid deserts rainfall is irregular and may be lacking for several consecutive years. Vegetation cover decreases and becomes contracted or restricted to more favorable microhabitats, for example, runoff-fed depressions, runnels (or gullies), and valleys. These extremely arid deserts are found in the Libyan Desert, southern and western Egypt, the Sinai, Arabia, and the Negev.

Salt-affected lands are also a common feature of the Middle Eastern deserts. Desert salines (or salt flats) are formed by various interactions of high water table, poor drainage, and inundation by seawater. The saline habitats are relatively less diverse in plant life than other habitat types.

The desert landscapes of the Middle East have historical, archaeological, aesthetic, and environmental significance beyond their habitat and wildlife diversity. The Middle East was settled very early by humans, and is usually considered the cradle of human civilization. As might be expected, inhabitants of the ancient settlements completely changed

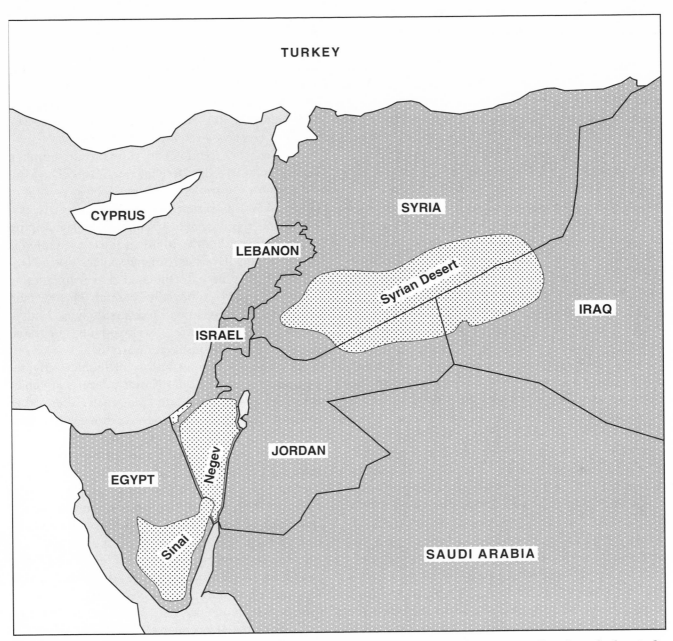

Map of the major deserts of the Middle East. Dark shading extends over a region of pronounced aridity. Shading indicates desert and semidesert limits.

the landscape. In areas that were once fertile the intervening thousands of years have led to a disruption of the natural vegetation and its associated fauna, and deserts now predominate. More recently the impact of humans on desert landscapes includes urban expansion and related road constructions and vehicle traffic, mining operations and related industrial activities, land reclamation for agricultural purposes, discharge of sewage into the open desert, and, lately, eco-tourism and tourism activities associated with coastal and inland resorts. In all cases habitat disturbance or habitat destruction has become a common feature in the desert. Moreover, the habitat types include sand plains and dunes, valleys, depressions, oases, mountains, salt marshes, and seaside landscapes. Fortunately, portions of many of these habitats now enjoy protected status as parks and reserves and are under professional management and development, particularly in Arabia, Egypt, and Israel.

The human population in the Middle East has multiplied more than sevenfold since the beginning of this century. The consequences of this demographic explosion have magnified the environmental problems in the region. Foremost among these may be the process of human-related desertification—the degradation of terrestrial ecosystems by increasing drought and salinity, careless development, overexploitation of land resources, and loss of biological diversity. Climate change is only a supporting factor in desertification of the Middle Eastern deserts. The leading cause of desertification is overcultivation of desert lands: as the arable lands are used up, agricultural practices are extended into unproductive lands that receive less than 150 millimeters of annual rainfall. Under such conditions crop expectancy is very low. The high-risk crops result in destruction of native vegetation, with the many wild species replaced by weeds that infest all newly reclaimed desert lands. Reclamation of desert lands by industry and agriculture, urban and rural expansion, and canal and road construction have caused the deserts of the Middle East to change radically.

Many of the Middle Eastern countries have proven to be quite effective in utilizing desert lands. The construction of the Aswan High Dam, the Industrial 10th of Ramadan City, the digging of the Al-Salam Canal that will divert the waters of the Nile to the Sinai in Egypt, the great covered manmade river in Libya, the development of advanced technology for desert reclamation in Israel, particularly in the fields of water use and solar energy, and the application of modern technology in many countries of the Middle East, all have proven the ability of people to make deserts a more productive and valuable resource. But such interventions do not come without ecological consequences, particularly in fragile desert ecosystems. The question is then raised, Can such large-scale development projects be maintained in a sustainable manner without causing widespread damage to the desert system? At present, there is no clear answer to this question.

For the more distant future, the major consequences of the expected rise in sea levels due to global warming for the deserts of the Middle East will be confined to the coastal marshes, including the Nile Delta, the arid coastal marshes in the Arabian Gulf, and many sites on the Red Sea coast, which are all potentially highly vulnerable to a rise in sea level. This is particularly true where extensive areas of the coastline are bounded by low-lying salt marshes, or sabkhas. The major impacts of the anticipated climate change will be manifested by interruptions of the hydrological cycle, increased desertification, penetration of seawater into coastal aquifers, and accelerated coastal erosion.

As a concept, biodiversity refers to the number, variety, and variability of living organisms. The Middle Eastern deserts are rich in species. A total of about 15,500 flowering plants, 250 mammals, 950 birds, 350 reptiles, and 15 amphibian species are found in these deserts. Many of these are endemic to the region. However, many species are threatened and may be exterminated due to increasing human impacts, especially habitat change and destruction. To conserve biodiversity, most Middle Eastern countries have developed an integrated development and conservation strategy.

Because of the long history of human activities in the region, the Middle Eastern deserts are characterized by a rarity of large mammals. Many other wild animals occur in the deserts, however, including smaller herbivores and carnivores, rodents, birds, reptiles, arthropods, and gastropods. Unfortunately, populations of many species are severely declining due to environmental pressures, hunting and poaching activities, and other impacts associated with human actions. Domestic animals also have a negative impact on wild species, and are common in the deserts of the Middle East. These include camels, horses, donkeys, goats, and sheep. The impact of humans on vegetation and plant resources includes cutting woody species for fuel and other uses, overgrazing, obtaining minerals or other raw materials, and introducing exotic species that adversely affect the natural vegetation.

Modern human impacts in deserts of the Middle East come mainly from the petroleum industry and eco-tourism. Most current exploration and development is for oil and natural gas. During the exploration, development, production, and transportation phases of oil and gas operations, much of the environmental concern centers on the impact on landscapes and wildlife resources. However, in some Middle Eastern countries there are no environmental regulations pertaining to the different phases of oil and gas production. International and domestic tourism activities have also put increased pressures on the natural resources, increased the degradation of sensitive ecosystems, and threatened the environmental stability of the deserts.

In Egypt, Israel, and Lebanon, because of mild winters, sunny summers, beaches, varied and accessible landscapes, diverse marine life, sport hunting and fishing, desert adventures, archaeological sites, health tourism, and the holy sites for the world's three great religions, millions of visitors come each year from around the world. International and domestic tourism has put increased pressures on the natural resources, increased the degradation of sensitive ecosystems, and threatened the environmental stability of the deserts.

The Middle East has also been subjected to war and other hostilities for a long period. Perhaps the most environmentally destructive was the war between Iraq and Kuwait in August 1990 which expanded into the Gulf War. The impacts of hostilities on the biotic and abiotic components of the terrestrial ecosystems of the region were extensive: bombing, shelling, camping, discharge of garbage, placing of mines, use of track and wheeled vehicles on fragile desert soils, tank battles, digging of trenches and tunnels, burning of oil wells, and massive oil spills.

Cleanup measures after the war, such as minefield clearance and other reconstruction activities, also have a considerable impact on desert ecosystems. Among the long-term impacts of war on the soil were severe soil compaction and erosion. Soil cover disappeared, and new habitats such as craters, scars, embankments, and ruts were created. These new microsites led to the appearance or disappearance of some species, as well as a change in their patterns of distribution.

Soils saturated with oil became badly aerated, and pore spaces were lost. The formation of lakes of oil and oil pools from smaller spills eradicated all living organisms on those sites. The impact on the vegetation caused by mechanical damage and the uprooting of standing plants was extensive. The seed content of the soil (the seed bank that supports the future vegetative cover) was also disturbed. In addition, direct killing of plants by oil spills or changes in metabolic activities and productivity due to soot and airborne pollutants from oil burning was widespread. The impact of war on the fauna included the direct killing of animals, habitat destruction, and interrupted animal behavioral cycles, such as breeding. Crude oil spills damaged the feathers, fur, and skin of animals, leading to death. Seawater-spreading on burning oil wells during capping may create severely salinized lands. Smoke and soot fallout increased the acidic deposition and chemical contamination of the desert. Ironically, recovery of disturbed ecosystems is encouraged in zones of uncleared mines, which deter human activities and land use. A similar situation obtained in the Egyptian and Libyan deserts after World War II.

The deserts of the Middle East are strongly affected by the aridity of the area and the rapid social, agricultural, and industrial development that also characterizes the region. Scarcity of natural resources and land degradation have provoked the demand for development of modern environmental technology, particularly in the fields of water use, agriculture, reducing desertification, and controlling pollution. To ensure food security, agriculture in Egypt, Israel, and Arabia stand in the forefront of desert agriculture by using sophisticated and efficient irrigation systems to reduce water loss. Seawater desalination plants are used in Israel and Arabia to supply water for agricultural, industrial, and municipal installations. Technologies for wastewater treatment and recycling of water are successfully used in almost all Middle Eastern countries.—Ahmad K. Hegazy

See also **AFRICA, DESERTS OF; AGRICULTURE IN DESERTS; ANNUAL PLANTS; ANTELOPE; ARABIAN GULF, DESERTS OF; CATS; CHENOPODIACEAE; CONSERVATION IN DESERTS; CONTAMINATION; DESERTIFICATION; DESERT PEOPLES; DIVERSITY; DOMESTIC ANIMALS; DUNES; GAZELLE; GERBIL; INSECTS; IRRIGATION DRAINAGE; ISRAEL, DESERTS OF; JEDDAH; JERBOA; JORDAN, DESERTS OF; LEBANON, DESERTS OF; LEGUMES; LIBYA, DESERTS OF; LIZARDS; MAMMALS; OVERGRAZING; PALESTINE, DESERTS OF; PLANT ADAPTATIONS; PLANTS; PLAYA; REPTILES; SAHARA DESERT; SALINIZATION; SALT DESERT; SALT PAN; SAND RAT; SAUDI ARABIA, DESERTS OF; SNAKES; SHEEP; SYRIA, DESERTS OF; TIGRIS-EUPHRATES; UNITED ARAB EMIRATES, DESERTS OF; YEMEN, DESERTS OF**

Further Reading

Boulos, L. 1985. The arid eastern and south-eastern Mediterranean region. *In* Gomez-Campo, C., ed., *Plant Conservation in the Mediterranean Area*, 123–140. The Hague: Junk.

Danin, A. 1983. *Desert Vegetation of Israel and Sinai.* Jerusalem: Cana Publishing.

Evenari, M., I. Noy-Meir, and D. W. Goodall, eds. 1986. *Ecosystems of the World: Hot Deserts and Arid Shrublands*. Vol. 12B. New York: Elsevier.

Evenari, M., L. Shanan, and T. Naphtali. 1971. *The Negev*. Cambridge, Mass.: Harvard University Press.

Glantz, M. H. 1977. *Desertification: Environmental Degradation in and Around Arid Lands*. Boulder, Colo.: Westview Press.

McNeely, J. A., and V. M. Neronov, eds. 1991. *Mammals in the Palaeoarctic Desert: Status and Trends in the Sahara-Gobian Region*. Moscow: UNESCO Man and Biosphere Programme (MAB).

Millington, A. C., and K. Pye, eds. 1994. *Environmental Change in Drylands: Biogeographical and Geomorphological Perspectives*. New York: Wiley.

Nir, D. 1974. *The Semi-arid World: Man on the Fringe of the Desert*. London: Longman.

Orshan, G. 1986. The deserts of Middle East. *In* M. Evenari, I. Noy-Meir, and D. W. Goodall, eds., *Ecosystems of the World: Hot Deserts and Arid Shrublands*, 12B:1–28. New York: Elsevier.

Swearingen, W. D., and A. Bencherifa. 1996. *The North African Environment at Risk*. Boulder, Colo.: Westview Press.

Zahran, M. A., and A. J. Willis. 1992. *The Vegetation of Egypt*. New York: Chapman and Hall.

Zohary, M. 1973. *Geobotanical Foundations of the Middle East*. Vols. 1 and 2. Amsterdam: Gustav Fischer.

———. 1983. Man and vegetation in the Middle East. *In* W. Holzner, M. J. A. Werger, and I. Ikusima, eds., *Man's Impact on Vegetation*, 287–295. The Hague: Junk.

MILLIPEDES

Moderate-sized (2–12 centimeters), elongate, segmented, terrestrial arthropods with two pairs of legs on each body segment, giving the impression that they have 1,000 legs. The body is cylindrical or flat, depending on the species. Millipedes make up the class Diplopoda. Species in this primitive group have chewing mouthparts, which are used to masticate dead and living plant matter. There are many species, some of which have been discovered recently and thus are unnamed. They can occur in remarkably large populations, particularly after rains, yet during periods of drought they can be extremely rare. They retreat underground to avoid desiccation.

A common species in deserts of North America is *Orthoporus ornatus*, often referred to as the rainworm. Although millipedes appear harmless owing to their lack of apparent structural weaponry, many species produce potentially lethal chemicals

Rhinocricid millipede (***Rhinocricus albidolimbatus***) from the Brazilian Caatinga. (Photo: L. J. Vitt)

through pores in the exoskeleton. The chemicals cause dark stains on human skin and, depending on the species, may contain cyanide compounds that are potentially lethal to predators. Although many millipedes are drab in coloration, some are brightly ringed with red, yellow, or white against a background color of dark brown or black. This bright color pattern is believed to be aposematic coloration (warning coloration), signaling potential predators that the millipede is toxic. Certain small, elongate vertebrates (including some snakes) have taken advantage of this signal by mimicking the color pattern of the millipedes.—Laurie J. Vitt

See also **ANIMAL ADAPTATIONS; ARTHROPODS; DECOMPOSITION; DEFENSIVE ADAPTATIONS, ANIMALS; DESICCATION-RESISTANT SPECIES**

Further Reading

Hopkin, S. P., and H. J. Read. 1992. *Biology of Millipedes*. Oxford: Oxford University Press.

Vitt, L. J. 1992. Mimicry of millipedes and centipedes by elongate terrestrial vertebrates. *Research Exploration* 8:76–95.

MINERALS

Substance meeting the following six criteria: (1) occurs naturally; (2) is formed by inorganic processes; (3) is a solid; (4) is crystalline; (5) has a definite chemical composition; and (6) has a characteristic crystal structure. Exhaustive tests and observations of a given specimen are required to establish that all of these requirements have been met. Some substances may be produced in nature by both inorganic and organic processes; however, a substance with the same chemical formulation and physical characteristics may be produced artificially. Therefore, in practice, a less restrictive definition may be applied once it has been established that a specimen has the above characteristics.

A second definition of this term applies to mining of materials for use by humans. Any naturally occurring, homogenous substance is considered a mineral. In the United States "mineral rights" also apply to oil, coal, and natural gas. Under some circumstances underground and surface water may also be considered a mineral.

Within the confines of the science of mineralogy we can consider the six characteristics and identify exceptions. Although the material must occur naturally, a substance having the same chemical and physical properties but produced artificially is also considered a mineral. Examples of artificially produced minerals are diamonds, mica, ruby, and quartz. Synthetic minerals are often given unique names to differentiate them from the naturally occurring material. Minerals may be synthesized to enhance desirable properties or because their synthesis is less costly than mining of the natural mineral.

Under the strict definition of a mineral the substance must be produced through inorganic processes. Some naturally occurring minerals may also be formed in the life cycle of animals or plants. An example is the formation of calcite in seawater by organisms producing shells and skeletons. Oil, coal and natural gas are by-products of deposition and transformation of organic material.

It can easily be determined that a material is a solid; therefore, this characteristic is consistently used within the science of mineralogy. However, when the definition is extended to include any material mined for human use, a mineral may be solid, liquid (oil), or gaseous (natural gas).

The crystalline nature of a substance refers to an ordered, repeating, three-dimensional arrangement of the atoms within the substance. This repeating structure forms "faces" or "cleavage planes" within the body of the crystal. Depending on the conditions during formation of the crystal, these faces may extend to the surface and produce visible external planes. Independent of the surface of the material the planes within the material can be detected using certain analysis procedures, such as X-ray diffraction. Conditions during crystallization will also affect the size of individual crystals. Some naturally occurring minerals may appear to be powders or aggregates; however, the internal structure of individual particles maintains a definite crystal structure. Again, an extended definition that includes oil and natural gas does not apply the crystalline requirement.

Most naturally occurring minerals have a certain amount of substitution of atoms within their chemical formulation. This may lead to a family of materials having similar properties but with slight variations in the atoms they contain. Some variation in chemical formulation is allowed within the description of a particular mineral. An example is the family of feldspars, aluminosilicates with varying amounts of sodium, potassium, and calcium included in the crystal structure.

The characteristic crystal structure can be used to identify minerals. Although there may be considerable variation and distortions in the naturally occurring material, crystal structures can be grouped into six systems: isometric, hexagonal, tetrahedral, orthorhombic (three unequal axes at right angles), monoclinic (three unequal axes with one oblique intersection), and triclinic (three unequal axes intersecting at oblique angles). The groups can be further divided into classes based on their symmetry, with the symmetry of a crystal being relative to a point, a line, or a plane.

Within the U.S. Soil Classification System, ten of the eleven orders (the highest category) are defined as mineral soils. These are Alfisols, Andisols, Aridisols, Entisols, Inceptisols, Mollisols, Oxisols, Spodosols, Ultisols, and Vertisols. In the remaining order, Histisols, the dominant material is organic.—Dan R. Upchurch and Ted M. Zobeck

See also **CARBONATES; COLLUVIAL DEPOSITS (COLLUVIUM); DURICRUSTS; FELDSPAR; GYPSUM; NUTRIENTS; PLANTS; POTASH; ROOTS; SEDIMENTATION; SOILS, DESERT; SOIL TAXONOMY; WEATHERING, DESERT**

Further Reading

Allen, B. L. 1977. Mineralogy and soil taxonomy. *In* J. B. Dixon, S. B. Weed, J. A. Kitterick, M. H. Milford, and J. L. White, eds., *Minerals in Soil Environments*, 771–796. Madison, Wis.: Soil Science Society of America.

Judson, S., K. S. Deffeys, and R. B. Hargraves. 1976. *Physical Geology*. Englewood Cliffs, N.J.: Prentice-Hall.

Nir, D. 1974. *The Semi-arid World: Man on the Fringe of the Desert*. London: Longman.

Tennissen, A. C. 1974. *Nature of Earth Materials*. Englewood Cliffs, N.J.: Prentice-Hall.

MIOCENE

Epoch of the Cenozoic era and of the Neogene period that lasted from about 22 million years ago until 5 or 6 million years ago, and which was characterized in general by global cooling and drying that began earlier in the Cenozoic. The early part of the Miocene was relatively warm, but by the middle Miocene irregular cooling led to a massive buildup of ice at the southern end of the world, particularly in eastern Antarctica. By the end of the Miocene and early Pliocene, the earth experienced an intense cooling pulse evidenced by further cyclical, glacial development in the Southern Hemisphere. This cooling was accompanied by a major drop in sea level known as the Messinian Low or Messinian Salinity Crisis which might have led to the isolation from global oceans and the drying of the Mediterranean Sea.

While polar temperatures decreased, tropical temperatures increased. As a result of this steepening temperature gradient from low to high latitudes, there was an intensification of subtropical high-pressure weather systems and summer droughts along the western sides of continents. This led to further spread of low-latitude savannas and grasslands that had begun in the Oligocene. The increased low-latitude aridity supported expansion of the Namib and Sahara regions in Africa and of the interior of Australia. Andean uplift (and attendant rain shadow) plus offshore cold-weather upwelling created hyperarid conditions in the Atacama Desert of South America by the middle Miocene.

Prior to the Miocene, the major biochemical pathway for photosynthesis among plants was that known as the C_3 pathway, which is found in most trees, shrubs, and forbs and in grasses that are adapted to cool, wet growing seasons. During the Miocene the C_4 photosynthetic pathway evolved. It is found mostly in grasses that are adapted to the hot, dry growing seasons that were then becoming more widespread at low latitudes. Some still more xeric-adapted plants (cacti and others) utilize a third photosynthetic pathway, called CAM (for Crassulacean Acid Metabolism), the evolution of which is unknown.—Nicholas J. Czaplewski

See also ANDES; C_3 PLANTS; C_4 PLANTS; CACTI; CAM PLANTS; CENOZOIC; CRETACEOUS; EOCENE; FOSSILS; GLACIAL PERIODS; GRASSLAND; MADROTERTIARY GEOFLORA; MIOCENE; NAMIBIA, DESERTS OF; NEOGENE; OLIGOCENE; PALEOCENE; PALEOCLIMATE; PERMIAN; PHOTOSYNTHESIS; PLATE TECTONICS; PLEISTOCENE; PLIOCENE; PRECAMBRIAN; QUATERNARY; RECENT (HOLOCENE); SAHARA DESERT; TERTIARY

Further Reading

Alpers, C. N., and G. H. Brimhall. 1988. Middle Miocene climatic change in the Atacama Desert, northern Chile: Evidence from supergene mineralization at La Escondida. *Geological Society of America Bulletin* 100:1640–1656.

Drooger, C. W. 1973. *Messinian Events in the Mediterranean*. Amsterdam: North-Holland.

Frakes, L. A., J. E. Francis, and J. I. Syktus, eds. 1992. *Climate Modes of the Phanerozoic: The History of the Earth's Climate over the Past 600 Million Years*. Cambridge: Cambridge University Press.

Morgan, M. E., J. D. Kingston, and B. D. Marino. 1994. Carbon isotopic evidence for the emergence of C4 plants in the Neogene from Pakistan and Kenya. *Nature* 367:162–165.

Swart, P. K., K. C. Lohmann, J. McKenzie, and S. Savin, eds. 1993. *Climate Change in Continental Isotopic Records*. Washington, D.C.: American Geophysical Union.

Van Zinderen Bakker, E. M., and J. H. Mercer. 1986. Major late climatic events and paleoenvironmental changes in Africa viewed in a world wide context. *Palaeogeography, Palaeoclimatology, Palaeoecology* 56:217–235.

Vogel, J. C., ed. 1984. *Late Cainozoic Palaeoclimates of the Southern Hemisphere*. Rotterdam: A. A. Balkema.

Wolfe, J. A. 1985. Distribution of major vegetational types during the Tertiary. *In* E. T. Sundquist and W. S. Broecker, eds., *The Carbon Cycle and Atmospheric CO2: Natural Variations Archean to Present*, 357–375. Washington, D.C.: American Geophysical Union.

MISTLETOE

Small shrubby plants in the mistletoe family (Loranthaceae; sometimes considered two families, Loranthaceae and Viscaceae) that is parasitic on the branches of other shrubs or trees. The family is mainly tropical but ranges worldwide and contains more than 600 species. The American mistletoe (genus *Phoradendron*) includes many of the desert dwellers as well as species in other habitats. Other desert species belong to the genera *Struthanthus*, *Phrygilanthus* (one species parasitizes the giant *Cereus* cacti in South America), or *Psitticanthus*. The European mistletoe (*Viscum album*) is commonly used as a Christmas decoration (as are some of the American *Phoradendron* species). Dwarf mistletoes (*Arceuthobium*) parasitize conifers.

Some mistletoes have chlorophyll and produce some of their own food (e.g., *Phoradendron*); others are without chlorophyll and are totally dependent on the host plant for nutrition (e.g., *Arceuthobium*). They may be scarce on the host plant and cause little observable change or may be so large and numerous that they eventually kill the host. Mistletoes reproduce sexually, and male and female flowers are usually on separate plants. They are usually pollinated by insects or birds, or in some cases by wind. The small, round, white or reddish berry contains one seed enclosed in a sticky covering. When a berry is carried by rain or birds to a new branch, the seed sticks and germinates there. Mockingbirds, cedar waxwings, and robins are known to eat mistletoe berries; in the southwestern deserts of the United States the phainopepla is famous for its consumption of these berries.

Host plants for *Phoradendron* in the Sonoran, Mojave, and Chihuahuan deserts include a wide variety of trees and shrubs, such as mesquite, ironwood, acacia, paloverde, cottonwood, sycamore, and willow. Mistletoes often blend in with the leaves of their host trees, but their evergreen leaves are easy to spot on deciduous hosts (plants that shed their leaves) during the winter.

Branches and leaves of mistletoes are used to treat diarrhea and enteritis and as an aid during childbirth by the Seri Indians.—Kristina A. Ernest

See also **CACTI; CHIHUAHUAN DESERT; FLOWERS; IRONWOOD; MESQUITE; MOJAVE DESERT; PLANT ADAPTATIONS; PLANTS**

Further Reading

Benson, L., and R. A. Darrow. 1981. *Trees and Shrubs of the Southwestern Deserts*. Tucson: University of Arizona Press.

Kuijt, J. 1969. *The Biology of Parasitic Flowering Plants*. Berkeley: University of California Press.

Shreve, F., and I. L. Wiggins. 1964. *Vegetation and Flora of the Sonoran Desert*. Vols. 1 and 2. Stanford: Stanford University Press.

MOCKINGBIRD

Common name for species in the New World family Mimidae (order Passeriformes). Approximately 30 species in 9–13 genera are recognized including the catbirds, the mockingbirds, and the thrashers. Most or part of the ranges of many of the mockingbirds (genera *Mimus* and *Nesomimus*) and *Toxostoma* thrashers include desert or semiarid scrub. For example, the Bendire's thrasher (*Toxostoma bendirei*) ranges throughout the deserts of the southwestern United States and northwestern Mexico. The brown-backed mockingbird (*Mimus dorsalis*), a Neotropical species, breeds in arid Andean scrub, from 2,300 to 3,500 meters above sea level in Bolivia and Argentina. The mimids have slender bodies with long tails, ranging in total length from 20 to 30 centimeters. Plumage usually consists of drab brown and gray colors, often streaked on the underside. The wings are short and rounded. Many species are highly terrestrial in habit. The bill is quite robust and generally long, sometimes notably down curved. Diet for most taxa consists of a variety of invertebrates and some fruit. Many of the mimids, notably some of the desert thrashers, forage by digging in the earth with their bills.

Most species appear to be monogamous, although both polygyny and polyandry have been reported as rare occurrences in some. The Galapagos mockingbirds (*Nesomimus* spp.) breed cooperatively, with related adults from previous years helping a breeding pair feed young and defend territories. Mimid nests are untidy twig cups placed in trees, shrubs, or cacti, usually at or close to the ground. Clutch size usually varies from two to five. Incubation either is performed by the female or is shared. Hatching is asynchronous in many North American mimids. In most species females brood the young, although feeding duties are shared.—Stephen C. Lougheed

See also **BIRDS; CHIHUAHUAN DESERT; MEXICO, DESERTS OF; SONORAN DESERT; SOUTH AMERICA, DESERTS OF; UNITED STATES, DESERTS OF**

Further Reading

Bent, A. C. 1948. Life histories of North American nuthatches, wrens, thrashers, and their allies. *U.S. National Museum Bulletin* 195.

Curry, R. L., and P. R. Grant. 1990. Galápagos mockingbirds: Territorial cooperative breeding in a climatically variable environment. *In* P. B. Stacey and W. D. Koenig, eds., *Cooperative Breeding in Birds*, 291–331. Cambridge: Cambridge University Press.

Derrickson, K. C., and R. Breitwisch. 1992. Northern mockingbird (*Mimus polyglottos*). *In* A. Poole, P. Stetteheim, and F. Gill, eds., *The Birds of North America*, No. 7. Philadelphia: Academy of Natural Sciences; Washington, D.C.: American Ornithologists' Union.

England, A. S., and W. F. Laudenslayer. 1993. Bendire's thrasher (*Toxostoma bendirei*). *In* A. Poole and F. Gill, eds., *The Birds of North America*, No. 71. Philadelphia: Academy of Natural Sciences; Washington, D.C.: American Ornithologists' Union.

Fischer, D. H. 1983. Growth, development, and food habits of nesting mimids in south Texas. *Wilson Bulletin* 95:97–105.

Reynolds, T. D., and T. D. Rich. 1978. Reproductive ecology of the sage thrasher (*Oreoscoptes montanus*) on the Snake River Plain in southeastern Idaho. *Auk* 95:580–582.

Ricklefs, R. E. 1965. Brood reduction in the curve-billed thrasher. *Condor* 67:505–510.

MOHAVE DESERT. *See* MOJAVE DESERT

MOISTURE INDEX

Amount of water vapor or moisture in the atmosphere (humidity) or the total amount of water in whatever form (gaseous, liquid, or solid) that is contained within a given volume of air. In climatology humidity refers to the amount of precipitation or the effectiveness of precipitation (efficiency of precipitation) utilized for plant growth. The humidity index (moisture index) used by Thornthwaite in his climatic classification system is a measurement that takes into account both excess water and scarcity of water from some norm that has been established for a particular region. Thornthwaite used this aridity index with two goals in mind: (1) as a component of his humidity index; and (2) as a base for a more detailed definition of humid days. The humidity index measured the amount of excess water above the amount of water that was required for plant growth at any given point. It is calculated independently of the aridity index and is the sum of the monthly differences in rainfall and potential evapotranspiration for those months in which normal precipitation exceeds potential evapotranspiration, and where necessary water is the sum of the monthly potential evapotranspiration for those months having excess rain. The humidity index has two uses in Thornthwaite's classification: (1) as a component of

the moisture index; and (2) as a base for detailed classification of arid climates.—Federico Norte

See also **ARIDITY; CLIMATE; CLIMATE CLASSIFICATION; HOLDRIDGE LIFE ZONES; PRECIPITATION**

Further Reading

Day, J. A., and V. J. Schaefer. 1991. *Clouds and Weather.* Boston: Houghton Mifflin.

Gates, D. M. 1972. *Man and His Environment: Climate.* New York: Harper and Row.

Oliver, J. E., and R. W. Fairbridge, eds. 1987. *The Encyclopedia of Climatology.* New York: Chapman and Hall.

Schaefer, V. J., and J. A. Day. 1981. *A Field Guide to the Atmosphere.* Boston: Houghton Mifflin.

Schneider, S. H., ed. 1996. *Encyclopedia of Climate and Weather.* 2 vols. New York: Oxford University Press.

MOJAVE DESERT

Smallest of the North American deserts, found mainly in southeastern California, southern Nevada, northwestern Arizona, and extreme southwestern Utah and blending biotically with the Great Basin Desert to the north and the Sonoran Desert to the south; generally thought to be transitional between these two larger North American deserts. The Mojave is most distinctive from adjacent deserts at elevations of between 600 and 1,200 meters.

The Mojave Desert exhibits a typical basin and range physiography with several north-south mountain ranges, extensive bajadas, and numerous undrained basins. The Colorado River adjoins portions of the eastern border of the Mojave. As is the case with much of the region, the Mojave was wetter and had many lakes at the end of the last ice age, one of which was located in present-day Death Valley. The elevation is variable, ranging from 1,200 meters on the west to near sea level on the east. The soils are primarily aridosols, which are characteristically formed under arid climatic conditions. (See map of U.S. deserts, p. 573.)

Annual precipitation is extremely low, ranging from 25–50 millimeters in the east to 125 millimeters in the west. Summer temperatures are very hot, and frost occurs mainly at higher elevations in the western part of the region. Most moisture in the Mojave Desert is brought by cool westerly winds in the form of winter rains from the Pacific Ocean.

The vegetation of the Mojave is primarily open stands of creosote bush (*Larrea tridentata*) and bur sage (*Franseria dumosa*); as much as 70 percent of the vegetational cover in the Mojave consists of these two important shrub species. Although the Mojave is shrub dominated, as is the Great Basin Desert, the former is considerably more arid and hotter. It has been suggested that the transition from the Mojave Desert to the Great Basin Desert may result from increased precipitation and lower temperatures in the Great Basin, which apparently leads to the elimination of creosote bush and replacement by big sagebrush (*Artemisia tridentata*).

There are also a variety of shrub and woodland communities that occur below the coniferous woodlands, which are found only at higher elevations. The creosote bush scrub, which is excluded from heavier soils near playas, is found mainly on well-drained sites, sandy flats, and gravelly bajadas. Saltbush scrub also occurs on such xerophytic (dry) soils and is dominated by *Atriplex polycarpa*, *Atriplex confertifolia*, and *Atriplex hymenolytra*, which do well on xerophytic sites but have limited tolerance to salty conditions. Saltbush scrub is also present on saline soils, where there are many associated halophytic (salt-loving) species, such as *Allenrolfea occidentalis*, *Salicornia subterminalis*, *Suaeda*, and *Sarcobatus vermiculatus*, which are generally found at lower elevations in the Mojave. In some areas creosote bush clones may achieve ages of several thousand years as a result of vegetative fragmentation, making this plant one of the oldest living organisms on earth. At higher elevations blackbrush (*Coleogyne ramosissima*), a shrub in the Rose family, is common, as are shadscale scrub and the Joshua tree woodlands.

The Mojave Desert has a lower diversity of perennial species than the Sonoran Desert to the south but a much great diversity of annual species. Cacti are also not as diverse as in the Sonoran Desert; the main species are the prickly pear and cholla (*Opuntia*). The Mojave is generally poor in succulent plants when compared to the Sonoran Desert. About 25 percent of species in the Mojave are endemic (restricted to this desert region).

Small trees, so common in much of the Sonoran Desert, are less prevalent except for the Joshua tree (*Yucca brevifolia*), which is the indicator species of the Mojave at higher elevations. The distribution of the Joshua tree, which is also known as the dagger tree, is often used to delineate the boundary of the Mojave Desert. The Joshua tree is perhaps the best-known plant from the Mojave Desert and is commonly shown in photographs depicting the region. Although the Joshua tree is endemic to the Mojave, it is generally restricted to the edge of the desert where the transition to cooler and better moisture conditions occurs. Stands of Joshua trees develop best on sandy, loamy, and gravelly soils, where moisture conditions are more favorable.

The transitional nature of the Mojave Desert between the Great Basin Desert and the Sonoran Desert is also reflected in the distribution of the fauna of the region. Amphibians, birds, mammals, and reptiles found in the Mojave occur, for the most part, in the Great Basin Desert to the north and the Sonoran Desert to the south, with very few species being characteristic, or indicative, of the Mojave Desert.—Gary K. Hulett and Amanda Renner Charles

See also **ACACIA; AMPHIBIANS; AN INTRODUCTION TO DESERTS; ARTHROPODS; BIRDS; CACTI; CALIFORNIA DESERT; CHENOPODIACEAE; COLORADO DESERT; COLORADO RIVER; CREOSOTE BUSH; DEATH VALLEY; DESERTS; DESERTS, HOT; DESERTS, TEMPERATE; GLACIAL PERIODS; GREAT BASIN DESERT; HALOPHYTES; HEAT; INSECTS; LIZARDS; JOSHUA TREE; JOSHUA TREE NATIONAL PARK; MAMMALS; NEVADA DESERT; PIT VIPER; PLANT GEOGRAPHY; PLANTS; REPTILES; SALTBUSH; SEMIARID ZONES; SIDEWINDER; SNAKES; SONORAN DESERT; UNITED STATES, DESERTS OF**

Further Reading

Bassett, A. M., and D. H. Kupfer. 1964. *A Geologic Reconnaissance in the Southeastern Mojave Desert, California*. Special Report 85. San Francisco: California Division of Mines and Geology.

Bender, G. L., ed. 1982. *Reference Handbook on the Deserts of North America*. Westport, Conn.: Greenwood Press.

Brown, D. E., ed. 1994. *Biotic Communities: Southwestern United States and Northwestern Mexico*. Salt Lake City: University of Utah Press.

Caruthers, W. 1951. *Loafing along Death Valley Trails: A Personal Narrative of People and Places*. Palm Desert: Desert Magazine Press.

Darlington, D. 1997. *The Mojave: A Portrait of the Definitive American Desert*. New York: Henry Holt.

Jaeger, E. C. 1938. *The California Deserts: A Visitor's Handbook*. Stanford: Stanford University Press.

Leadabrand, R. 1966. *A Guidebook to the Mojave Desert of California, including Death Valley, Joshua Tree National Monument, and the Antelope Valley*. Los Angeles: Ritchie Press.

Rundel, P. W., and A. C. Gibson. 1996. *Ecological Communities and Processes in a Mojave Desert Ecosystem: Rock Valley, Nevada.* Cambridge: Cambridge University Press.

Weir, K. 1998. *Southern California Handbook: Including Greater Los Angeles, Disneyland, San Diego, Death Valley and Other Desert Parks.* Emeryville, Calif.: Moon Publications.

MOLE, GOLDEN

Family of insectivorous, burrowing molelike rodents (mammalian family Chrysochloridae, order Rodentia) having compact bodies with no visible tail and native to sub-Saharan Africa. The iridescent shine of the golden mole's pelage gives it its name. A thickened pad of skin protects the nose while burrowing. Individuals are solitary and will aggressively defend their burrow from other members of their species. Evolution has reduced the size and function of the eyes and greatly altered that of the ears. Modification of the ear has increased its sensitivity to ground-transmitted vibrations. To locate food the golden mole relies on touch while burrowing and smell when above ground. They will leave their burrows for the surface when they are unable to find food underground, when trying to establish a new burrow system, or when looking for a mate. In compactable soils they construct burrow systems, but in the fine soils of deserts they swim through the sand.

Of the 18 species of golden moles, only Grant's golden mole (*Eremitalpa granti*) and De Winton's golden mole (*Cryptochloris wintoni*) enter a desert to any significant degree. Both are found in the Namib Desert and surrounding sandy regions. The small size (15–20 grams) and yellow-gray pelage of Grant's golden mole distinguish it from the larger (20–30 grams), pale yellow De Winton's golden mole.

The golden mole lies motionless under the surface of the sand and waits for prey. Vibrations on the sand's surface alert it to the presence of prey. The predator then quickly emerges from the sand, seizes the prey, and drags it away under the sand before consuming it. Major food items for Grant's golden mole are beetles and lizards. The rarity of desert golden moles, the difficulty in observing them, and the harshness of their habitat discourages study of these animals.—Rob Channell

See also **BURROWING ANIMALS; CONVERGENT EVOLUTION; DUNES; MAMMALS; NAMIBIA, DESERTS OF; SOUTH AFRICA, DESERTS OF**

Further Reading
Gorman, M. L., and R. D. Stone. 1990. *The Natural History of Moles.* Ithaca: Comstock.

MOLE RAT

Common name applied to burrowing rodents (mammalian order Rodentia) of the families Bathyergidae and Spalacidae. These two families are Old World in their distribution. The spalacids occur from the Middle East northward into the steppes of Russia. The bathyergids are found in arid to semi-arid habitats of South Africa, although some species of this family may be adapted to more mesic (moister) environments.

In common with most rodents adapted to a burrowing way of life, the eye is reduced in size, the external ear is reduced, the claws of the forefeet are enlarged, the neck and tail are shortened, and the fur is dense but short. The incisor teeth may be procumbent (projected forward) to varying degrees. Both families are typically herbivorous and forage for succulent roots beneath the surface of the soil.

One of the most specialized members of this group is the naked mole rat, *Heterocephalus*. The naked mole rat has virtually no eyes, and, as its name implies, its fur is vastly reduced, with only a few sparse sensory hairs still prominent. These rodents occupy the extremely dry portions of Kenya and Tanzania in East Africa. They are colonial, a trait not commonly associated with adaptation for a burrowing life. Nevertheless, these colonies exploit the underground roots of certain desert-adapted plants; they cooperatively dig chambers and rear their young communally. Usually only a single pair within a colony reproduces and the other members show retarded growth and gonadal development, thus serving effectively as "workers" in support of the breeding pair. In many ways their social system is similar to that of such colonial insects as ants or bees.

Other species of mole rats, such as *Spalax*, typically lead a solitary, noncolonial existence, dwelling in burrows of their own construction and gathering foodstuffs for exclusive use and storage in their tunnel systems. Varying degrees of social tolerance may be noted when species of the Bathyergidae are compared, but *Heterocephalus* is unique in the degree of communal living displayed.—John F. Eisenberg

See also **AFRICA, DESERTS OF; ASIA, DESERTS OF; BURROWING ANIMALS; CONVERGENT EVOLUTION; GOPHER; MAMMALS; MIDDLE EAST, DESERTS OF; NAMIBIA, DESERTS OF; RODENTS; SAHARA DESERT; SOUTH AFRICA, DESERTS OF; TUCU-TUCO**

Further Reading

Nowak, R. M. 1991. *Walker's Mammals of the World.* 5th ed. Baltimore: Johns Hopkins University Press.

Sherman, P. W., J. U. M. Jarvis, and R. D. Alexander, eds. 1991. *Biology of the Naked Mole Rat.* Princeton: Princeton University Press.

MOLT

Periodic shedding and replacement of feathers in birds, hair in mammals, skin in reptiles and amphibians, and the exoskeleton in arthropods. This process is under hormonal control of the pituitary and thyroid glands.

In arthropods molting, or ecdysis, occurs when growth is needed. After a new skeleton is produced, the old skeleton is shed. This new skeleton is soft but later hardens. The time periods between molts are termed instars and may be fixed, as in insects and spiders, or may continue throughout the animal's life, as in lobsters.

Birds shed and replace their plumage according to a definite sequence. Each plumage and molt is named. Adult birds molt no more than twice per year—a prenuptial (a limited molt occurring in relatively few species) and a postnuptial molt (a nearly complete molt occurring in all species). For most birds, the postnuptial molt takes place during the summer when high temperatures preclude the need for many feathers. Molting generally is a continuous, sequenced process involving a few feathers at a time. For example, tail feathers are molted from the center outward. In some species molting is not continuous. Many waterbirds, such as geese, lose all of their wing primary feathers at the same time, leaving them flightless. To evade predators some ducks move from their breeding grounds to sheltered marshy areas to molt and may exhibit a drab postbreeding plumage that aids in concealment.

Mammals also molt, replacing hair by a definite process and in particular patterns. Most mammals have three major pelages (juvenile, subadult, adult), each separated by a molt. Adults may molt continuously (e.g., humans), once a year (e.g., the Brazilian free-tailed bat, *Tadarida brasiliensis*) or twice a year (e.g., the ground squirrel, *Spermophilus undulatus*). Some mammals, such as the Arctic fox (*Alopex lagopus*) and the snowshoe hare (*Lepus americanus*), molt seasonally and exhibit a white winter pelage and dark summer pelage. The time of molting for variably colored species is dependent on daylight length; light affects the pituitary gland and subsequent hormone production. Evidence of molting may be seen on the inside of the skin where dark patches indicate increased blood flow and the pigmentary nuclei of the new hairs.

Amphibians and reptiles shed a layer of their epidermis (the stratum corneum) in a process known as ecdysis. This layer of horny, dead cells protects the inner epidermal layers and aids in preventing moisture loss; it is thicker in reptiles than in amphibians. In amphibians and reptiles, although the skin may be shed whole or in pieces at regular intervals ranging from a few days to months, molting occurs over the entire body at the same time. Amphibians always eat the skin. Reptiles begin shedding at the head, which enlarges due to increased blood pressure, and ruptures the old skin, which is left behind.

In desert areas molting is important because animals must not lose their protective covering during times of high water stress, or during especially cold periods. Moreover, molting requires energy, which means that the animals may find it difficult to molt during periods of food or water stress. Thus the timing of molt is critical to their survival.—Janet K. Braun

See also **AMPHIBIANS; ANIMAL ADAPTATIONS; BIRDS; FEATHERS; HARE; INSECTS; MAMMALS; PHYSIOLOGY; REPTILES; THERMOREGULATION**

Further Reading

Barnes, R. D. 1980. *Invertebrate Zoology.* 4th ed. Philadelphia: W. D. Saunders.

Cockrum, E. L. 1962. *Introduction to Mammalogy.* New York: Ronald.

Goin, C. J., and O. B. Goin. 1962. *Introduction to Herpetology.* San Francisco: Freeman.

Pettingill, Jr., O. S. 1961. *A Laboratory and Field Manual of Ornithology.* Minneapolis: Burgess.

Porter, K. R. 1972. *Herpetology.* Philadelphia: Saunders.

Welty, J. C. 1964. *The Life of Birds.* Philadelphia: Saunders.

MONGOLS. *See* DESERT PEOPLES

MONGOOSE

Common name referring to the species of small carnivores in the family Herpestidae (mammalian order Carnivora). There are two subfamilies: the Madagascar mongooses (Galidiinae, 4 genera and 5 species); and the African and Asian mongooses (Herpestinae, 14 genera and 32 species). They occur from southern Africa, north to the Mediterranean into Spain and Portugal, and east into southern Asia, including Indochina, Indonesia, Borneo, and the Philippines. Many species occur in swamps and wet forest, but several are restricted to arid and semiarid habitats.

In the Madagascar subfamily, Galidiinae, *Mungotictis decemlineata* is restricted to savannas and *Galidictis grandieri* is known only from the semiarid scrublands. The African/Asian subfamily Herpestinae includes a number of species that occupy a broad range of habitat types. Several species are exclusively or mostly restricted to semiarid and arid habitats. *Herpestes ichneumon* and *Herpestes edwardsi* are wide ranging but occur in dry regions of Africa and Asia. The closely related genus *Galerella* has four species (*Galerella flavescens*, *Galerella pulverulenta*, *Galerella sanguinea*, and *Galerella swalius*) that are restricted to semiarid and arid habitats in southern Africa. *Cynictis penicillata*, *Paracynictis selousi*, and *Suricata suricatta* are also associated with dry habitats in southern Africa, the former two in savanna and the latter in more arid regions. Two genera, each with two species, are found in savannas and savanna woodlands in eastern Africa: *Mungos gambianus* and *Mungos mungo*; and *Helogale parvula* and *Helogale hirtula*.

Mongooses are primarily insectivorous; however, several species, especially those in the genus *Herpestes*, are efficient predators of small vertebrates. Most species are nocturnal, although the more social species are active during the day. Mongooses generally are solitary, and the only social unit is the mother with her offspring. Several of the species most adapted to savanna or semiarid habitats show a high degree of sociality. The banded mongoose (*Mungos mungo*) is one of the most social of all mammals. Large packs of banded mongooses scour the savannas of East Africa in search of insects. The band is generally led by the dominant female. The banded mongoose responds to any threats as a group, and the pack will advance in coordinated unity against small predators.

The South African gray meerkat or suricate, (*Suricata suricatta*) is also highly social. This slender mongoose has become well known due to widely distributed photographs of groups standing at attention on the top of a communal burrow. Meerkats are often kept as pets to hunt rats and mice.

No species of mongoose is known to be endangered, although there is growing concern for the Galidiinae because of extensive habitat loss in Madagascar.—Thomas E. Lacher, Jr.
See also **AFRICA, DESERTS OF; ASIA, DESERTS OF; CARNIVORES; MADAGASCAR, DESERTS OF; MAMMALS; MEERKAT; NAMIBIA, DESERTS OF; PREDATION; SOUTH AFRICA, DESERTS OF**

Further Reading

Estes, R. D. 1991. *The Behavior Guide to African Mammals*. Berkeley: University of California Press.

Gittleman, J. L., ed. 1989. *Carnivore Behavior, Ecology, and Evolution*. Ithaca: Cornell University Press.

Kingdon, J. 1989. *East African Mammals: An Atlas of Evolution in Africa*. Vol. 3A. Chicago: University of Chicago Press.

Macdonald, D., ed. 1984. *The Encyclopedia of Mammals*. New York: Facts on File.

Nowak, R. M. 1991. *Walker's Mammals of the World*. 5th ed. Baltimore: Johns Hopkins University Press.

MONKEYS IN DESERTS

Occurrence of nonhuman primates in arid and semiarid habitats of the Old World. Nonhuman primates are generally thought of as being adapted to forested habitats, and indeed most living nonhuman primates occur in the tropical forests of Central and South America, Africa, and Asia. However, there are exceptions to this rule; some species have adapted to semiarid habitats in both Africa and Asia. Such adaptation can be seen in the savanna habitats of northern, central, and eastern Africa, where baboons (*Papio*) and Patas monkeys (*Erythrocebus*) typically forage in large troops at quite some distance from trees. They retire to trees for safety and for sleeping at night. In a parallel fashion, langurs of the genus *Presbytis* and, in particular, *Presbytis entellus* (the hanuman langur) have adapted to the semiarid regions of Rajasthan in northwestern India and eastern Pakistan. The extreme in adaptation to a desert habitat is dis-

Vervet (green) monkey (*Cercopithecus aethiops*) in the thorn scrub of the Itala Game Reserve, northern Kwazulu-Natal Province, South Africa; its pale color matches the pale semiarid vegetation and makes it difficult to see. (Photo: M. A. Mares)

played by the *Papio hamadryas*. This species occurs in desert regions dominated by cliffs in eastern Ethiopia and in the southwestern Arabian peninsula, in particular Yemen. The animals are able to use temporary springs for drinking and take shelter on rock cliffs, where they locate their sleeping sites. They forage in large troops for tubers, seed pods, and other edible plants among the sparse vegetation of these dry areas.

In no case are desert primates independent of water, although moisture may be obtained from dew or succulent plants. In all cases they must have access either to sleeping trees or to some safe refuge such as a cliff side for shelter and protection from predators.—John F. Eisenberg

See also **AFRICA, DESERTS OF; BABOON; INDO-PAKISTAN DESERTS; MAMMALS; SOUTH AFRICA, DESERTS OF; YEMEN, DESERTS OF**

Further Reading

Alden, P. C., R. D. Estes, D. Schlitter, and B. McBride. 1995. *National Audubon Society Field Guide to African Wildlife*. New York: Knopf.

Richard, A. 1985. *Primates in Nature*. New York: Freeman.

MONSOON

Name given to a windy season that derives from the Arabic word *mousim*, which means "season." The term was originally applied to surface winds that blew over the Arabian Sea and over southern Asia and that reversed their direction of flow from winter to summer. For six months the monsoon blows from the northeast in the northern winter; for the other six months it blows from the southeast in the northern summer. Monsoons are especially prevalent in India, Bangladesh, and Indochina. The term has been extended to winds that blow in other parts of the world as well. Thus one speaks of the stratospheric monsoon and the European monsoon, names that are assigned to winds from the west and the northwest that blow in summer on that continent. The principal cause of these winds is great annual variation in temperature between the land and the sea, which causes great pressure differences to develop in their overlying air masses. However, other factors, such as the surface relief of the land, can also have a considerable effect. Monsoon winds are particularly strong in southern and eastern Asia, where there is a great extension of land, but they also occur in tropical regions. Monsoon winds have been described for Spain, northern Australia, Africa, Texas, along the west coast of the United States, and in Chile. Monsoonal winds commonly occur during years in which the El Niño phenomenon is pronounced.

A more detailed explanation of monsoons involves the intense cold that develops over continents during the winter, leading to the development of systems of high or very high pressure while at the same time the more temperate or warm temperatures over the oceans cause low pressures to develop. This great differential in pressure between the land and the sea is a primary force leading to monsoonal winds. During the summer the situation is reversed, and the winds blow from the ocean, which is relatively cold, to the land, which is quite hot.—Federico Norte

See also **ANTICYCLONE; BAROMETRIC PRESSURE (ATMOSPHERIC PRESSURE); CLIMATE; CLIMATE CLASSIFICATION; CLOUDS; CONVECTIVE STORM; CYCLONE; EL NIÑO; FLOOD; ISOHYET; LOW PRESSURE; PRECIPITATION**

Further Reading

Day, J. A., and V. J. Schaefer. 1991. *Clouds and Weather*. Boston: Houghton Mifflin.

Schaefer, V. J., and J. A. Day. 1981. *A Field Guide to the Atmosphere*. Boston: Houghton Mifflin.

Schneider, S. H., ed. 1996. *Encyclopedia of Climate and Weather*. 2 vols. New York: Oxford University Press.

MONTANA DESERT

Portions of Montana at lower elevations below the coniferous and grassland zones of the mountains and along the border with Idaho and Wyoming which have vegetation characteristic of the Great Basin Desert dominated by sagebrush and assorted grasses. The Montana Desert is a region of winter precipitation. Most of the state of Montana is dominated by semiarid grasslands (shortgrass prairie and northern mixed prairie) in the east and coniferous forests (spruce-fir-pine) in the mountains of the west.—Gary K. Hulett and Amanda Renner Charles

See also **AN INTRODUCTION TO DESERTS; GREAT BASIN DESERT; OREGON DESERT; SEMIARID ZONES; UTAH DESERT**

Further Reading

Bourgeron, P. S., A. M. Kratz, T. Weaver, and N. Weidman. 1988. Bibliography of Montana Vegetation. *Great Basin Naturalist* 48:301–323.

MONTANE DESERTS. *See* DESERTS, MONTANE

MONTE DESERT

Geographic region comprising much of the most arid portions of Argentina lying approximately between 27° and 44° south latitude, from the province of Salta in the north to northeastern Chubut Province in the south. In a geobotanical sense the word *monte* refers to any woody (ligneous) formation, and may be called *monte bajo* (low monte) when composed of thickets or *monte alto* (high monte) when supporting tree formations. (See map of South American deserts, p. 533.)

Geomorphologically, the Monte Desert is quite diverse, consisting of sandy plains, bolsones (enclosed basins), plateaus, and low mountain slopes. The climate is dry and warm in the north and cooler and dry in the south. Rainfall ranges from 80 to 250 millimeters annually, and the mean annual temperature fluctuates between 13° and 15.5°C. Rain falls mainly as summer rains in the north, with increasingly more winter precipitation as one moves south.

Despite the great extent of this natural region, its vegetation is relatively homogeneous. Open thorn scrub is dominant, with predominance of plants such as *jarillas* (*Larrea divaricata*, *Larrea cuneifolia*, and *Larrea nitida*), *Bulnesia schicken-*

Monte Desert habitat near Andalgalá, Catamarca Province, northwestern Argentina, showing extensive cardón cactus (*Trichocereus*) forest. (Photo: M. A. Mares)

dantzii and also *retamo* (*Bulnesia retama*), *alpataco* (*Prosopis alpataco*), and other shrub species in the genera *Prosopis*, *Cercidium*, *Acacia*, and *Geoffroea*.

Several annual grass species appear after the rains. Despite the many plants that might be considered to characterize the Monte, it is species in the genus *Larrea* that identify the vegetation of the Argentine Monte, especially *Larrea cuneifolia*, which forms vast, almost single-species communities, with plants less than two meters in height, accompanied by tall cardón cacti in the northern portions of the desert on rocky slopes and bajadas. Among trees, edaphic communities of *algarrobos* (*Prosopis chilensis*, *Prosopis flexuosa*) occur, together with *chilcales* (*Baccharis*) on riverbanks.

The typical mammal fauna of the Monte includes various rodents, such as the mara (*Dolichotis*), the gerbil mouse (*Eligmodontia*), tucutucos (*Ctenomys*), and cavies (*Microcavia*). Other mammals include the mouse opossum (*Thylamys*), some bats, foxes (*Pseudalopex*), ferrets (*Galictis*, *Lyncodon*), a spotted cat (*Oncifelis geoffroyi*), the puma (*Puma concolor*), and skunks (*Conepatus*). Armadillos are also common, including the *mataco* (*Tolypeutes*), a *peludo* (*Zaedyus*), and the *piche llorón* (*Chaetophractus*). The fairy armadillo (*Chlamyphorus truncatus*) is endemic to the Monte, as are several rodents (*Salinomys*, *Tympanoctomys*, *Octomys*, *Andalgalomys*), indicating a long period of isolation for this extensive South American desert.

As for birds, Chacoan thorn scrub species are dominant, though some Patagonian and endemic species occur there as well. The most representative birds are tinamous (*Eudromia*), parrots (*Aratinga*, monk parakeet), and rhinocryptids (*Teledromus fuscus*, *Poospiza ornata*).

Reptiles are fairly abundant and include a coral snake (*Micrurus*), the *yarará* (*Bothrops neuwiedi*), and various other snakes as well as lizards of various genera (*Leisaurus*, *Liolaemus*, and *Tropidurus*), iguanas (*Tupinambis*), and a tortoise (*Geochelone*). Among the most typical fishes are several species of catfish, and the "native trout" (*Percicthys trucha*).

Invertebrates are numerous. There are two endemic genera of Neuroptera from the family Nemopteridae, and two kinds of "social wasps." The most common arthropods inhabit sandy grounds and humid gorges.—Virgilio G. Roig

See also **AMPHIBIANS; ARMADILLO; ARTHROPODS; BIRDS; CACTI; CACTUS, COLUMNAR; CARDÓN; CATS; CAVY; CHACO; CHENOPODIACEAE; CONDOR; CREOSOTE BUSH; DESERTS; INSECTS; LEGUMES; LIZARDS; MAMMALS; MARA; MESQUITE; PATAGONIA; PIT VIPER; PLANT ADAPTATIONS; PLANTS; PLAYA; PUNA; RATTLESNAKE; REPTILES; RODENTS; SNAKES; TUCU-TUCO**

Further Reading

Mares, M. A. 1993. Heteromyids and their ecological counterparts: A pandesertic view of rodent ecology. *In* H. H. Genoways and J. H. Brown, eds., *The Biology of the Family Heteromyidae*, 652–713. Special Publication No. 10, American Society of Mammalogists.

Mares, M. A., J. Morello, and G. Goldstein. 1985. The Monte Desert and other subtropical semi-arid biomes of Argentina, with comments on their relation to North American arid areas. *In* M. Evenari, I. Noy-Meir, and D. W. Goodall, eds., *Ecosystems of the World: Hot Deserts and Arid Shrublands*, 12B:203–237. New York: Elsevier.

Mares, M. A., and M. L. Rosenzweig. 1978. Granivory in North and South American deserts: rodents, birds, and ants. *Ecology* 59:235–241.

Morello, J. 1958. La provincia fitogeográfica del Monte. *Opera Lilloana* 2:1–155.

Orians, G. H., and O. T. Solbrig, eds. 1977. *Convergent Evolution in Warm Deserts*. Stroudsburg, Pa.: Dowden, Hutchinson, and Ross.

MONUMENT VALLEY

A 42-kilometer-long valley located in southeastern Utah and northeastern Arizona containing spectacularly dramatic rock formations. Monument Valley is one of the most photographed and filmed landscapes in the world, and formed the remarkable backdrop for many of the classic John Ford westerns starring John Wayne. This has led to this area's being viewed as the quintessential desert landscape of North America by millions of people throughout the world.

Monument Valley lies atop the Monument Upwarp (uplifted strata). Due to erosion beds of the Middle Pennsylvanian have been exposed in canyons of major drainages. Where the San Juan River bisects the Monument Upwarp, Permian red beds are well exposed. The bases of the formations are composed of Organ Rock Shale, a soft red shale from the Cutler red beds that was deposited through the action of water. De Chelly sandstone, a wind-deposited sand, forms the vertical walls. Moenkoepi Shale and Shinarump Conglomerate of the Chinle Formation cap the buttes and rock fingers.

During the Paleozoic the sandstone that composes the rock formations was compacted. Later, during the Cenozoic, portions of the sandstone were eroded by wind, water, and exfoliation, leaving behind the buttes, mesas, pinnacles, and rock fingers that characterize the valley today. These formations ("monuments") lie in sharp contrast to the stark blue sky and the flat, scrub desert that surrounds them. Iron oxide contributes to the reddish coloration of the sand and rock, and manganese oxide is responsible primarily for the black streaks (desert varnish) seen on the cliffs.

The earliest-known inhabitants of the area were ice age Paleo-Indian hunters (12,000–6000 B.C.), Archaic hunter-gatherers (6000 B.C.- A.D. -1), and Anasazi farmers (A.D. 1-1300). The San Juan Band Paiutes frequented the region they called "Valley or Treeless Area Amid the Rocks" after A.D. 1300. Many of the features of the landscape were given supernatural qualities or formed the basis of mythological stories. El Capitan is said to be a sky supporter. A legend suggests that Totem Pole Rock is supported by lightning. Indeed, it has been suggested that the entire area of the valley near Goulding's Trading Post is an eastward-facing hogan.

The valley is administered by the Cultural Resource Department of the Navajo Nation—it is not a national park or a national monument. It has been a part of the Navajo Reservation since 1884. Navajos continue to live in the valley; many herd sheep and goats, weave rugs, and live in traditional homes (hogans).

Monument Valley continues to be a popular backdrop for movies and for television, magazine, and newspaper advertisements. Some of the movies filmed there are *Stagecoach* (1938), *She Wore A Yellow Ribbon* (1949), *My Darling Clementine* (1946), *The Searchers* (1956), *How The West Was Won* (1962), and *Cheyenne Autumn* (1964).—Janet K. Braun

See also **CHENOPODIACEAE; DESERT SLOPES; DURICRUSTS; FLOOD; GREAT BASIN DESERT; LIMESTONE; MOVIES IN DESERTS; PAINTED DESERT; ROCK VARNISH; RUNOFF; SEDIMENTATION; WATER; WEATHERING, DESERT; WIND EROSION**

Further Reading

Chronic, H. 1983. *Roadside Geology of Arizona*. Missoula, Mont.: Mountain Press.

———. 1990. *Roadside Geology of Utah*. Missoula, Mont.: Mountain Press .

Klinck, R. 1953. *Land of Room Enough and Time Enough*. Albuquerque: University of New Mexico Press.

MOSQUITOES

Insects in the family Culcidae in the order Diptera, which contains all flies, including houseflies, botflies, midges, fruit flies, and flesh flies, among many others. Mosquitoes have become an important group of insects, primarily because they are vectors of many diseases that affect humans and other animals. They are responsible for every known case of malaria, a disease that affects a vast proportion of the world's human population. Larvae of mosquitoes are aquatic and may occur in bodies of water ranging in size from several cubic centimeters to large lakes. Most larvae are herbivorous, feeding on algae, but some are predaceous, feeding on other invertebrates and in some cases (tropical mosquitoes in the genus *Toxyrhynchites*) small vertebrates. Mosquito larvae typically breathe at the surface of the water. Pupae of mosquitoes are also aquatic. Adult females of many species of mosquitoes feed on blood of vertebrates and thereby transmit disease. In deserts mosquitoes are usually confined to riparian (riverine) habitats, where there are pools of water in which they can breed. However, there may be blooms of mosquitoes following seasonal rainstorms when water forms small pools in rocks. Mosquitoes are eaten by a wide variety of invertebrates

and vertebrates, including dragonflies, frogs, birds, and bats, and consequently play an important role in food webs.—Laurie J. Vitt

See also **AQUATIC HABITATS; ARTHROPODS; FLIES; INSECTS; METAMORPHOSIS; RIPARIAN COMMUNITIES; WATER; WATER HOLE**

Further Reading

Borror, D. J., C. A. Triplehorn, and N. F. Johnson. 1992. *An Introduction to the Study of Insects*. New York: Harcourt Brace.

Borror, D. J., and R. E. White. 1970. *A Field Guide to the Insects*. Boston: Houghton Mifflin.

Gillette, J. D. 1971. *Mosquitoes*. London: Weidenfeld and Nicolson.

MOSSES

Nonvascular plants (i.e., they have no tissues devoted to the movement of water or sugars) that have no true leaves, stems, or roots. Water moves by diffusion from cell to cell throughout the plant. This inefficient mode of water transport restricts moss growth to moist habitats. Their life cycle restricts them to moist environments, since movement of sexual propagules is water dependent. Therefore, most mosses in desert environments live near moist seeps or springs. A very few live in mats on soil between large vascular plants, where they form microphytic or cryptogamic mats. The biology of mosses has been confused somewhat through a common error: the growth form of several species of primitive vascular plants (club mosses, including species of *Selaginella* and *Lycopodium*) appears mosslike, but they are not true mosses.

Mosses that grow in the moist areas of deserts can cope very successfully with variable resource levels. If water supply is interrupted for a brief period, these species can survive desiccation through a variety of physiological adaptations, including modifications of the cellular organelles responsible for protein synthesis, modification of the proteins themselves, and modification of the amount of material dissolved in the cytoplasm. Because mosses possess no stomata, they do not control water loss via stomatal control, but they can have variable thicknesses of waxy cuticle over the surface of the leaflike portions of the plant. Being low growing, mosses can escape desiccating winds. Species in the genus *Andreaea* form soil mats and can survive much longer periods of desiccation and possess several of these adaptations.—Linda L. Wallace

See also **DIVERSITY; ECOLOGY; ECOSYSTEM; PHOTOSYNTHESIS; PLANT ADAPTATIONS; PLANTS; RESURRECTION PLANT; STOMA**

Further Reading

Burns, G. W. 1974. *The Plant Kingdom.* New York: Macmillan.

MOTHS

All insects in the order Lepidoptera (butterflies and moths) that have filiform (hairlike or threadlike), setaceous (bristlelike), or plumose (featherlike) antennae. The remainder of lepidopterans (butterflies) have antennae that are slender and knobbed at the tip. Butterflies and moths have distinctive scales on the wings such that, with few exceptions, the wings are not transparent.

There are many families and species of moths, and most are nocturnal. As a group moths are extremely important economically because many of their larvae cause large-scale damage to trees and commercially cultivated grains, fruits, and vegetables. In deserts they are most often seen at night under artificial lights, which attract the adults. During the day most species remain hidden in shady microhabitats, including crevices, hollows of trees, and holes. Moths feed on nectar (if they feed); their larvae, called caterpillars, feed on vegetation. Some moth larvae feed on leaves, some bore into stems or roots of plants, and others feed on seeds of various plants. Certain moth species are critical for pollination of desert plants. For example, moths in the family Proxidae pollinate various species of desert yuccas, and no other organisms are known to pollinate these plants. The pollination process is particularly fascinating because pollen is collected by the female moths, carried to another flower in which she lays her eggs, and finally the flower is fertilized with the pollen she carries, which results in the production of seeds on which the larvae feed.

Moth families that are found in deserts include the Aegeriidae (clearwing moths, also called the Sesiidae by some authors), the Geometridae (measuring worms), the Noctuidae (moths), the Psychidae (bagworms), the Saturniidae (royal moths and giant silkworm moths), and several families that are rather nondescript (e.g., Tineidae, Tortricidae, Cosmopterigidae). Some desert moths, for example, those in the family Gelechiidae in the Namib

Desert, form galls in perennial plants that may then be used as microhabitats for other insects.—Laurie J. Vitt

See also **ANIMAL ADAPTATIONS; ARTHROPODS; BAGWORMS; BAT; BUTTERFLIES; FLOWERS; HAWKMOTH; INSECTS; METAMORPHOSIS; POLLINATION; YUCCA**

Further Reading

Seeley, M. K. 1991. Sand dune communities. *In* G. A. Polis, ed., *The Ecology of Desert Communities*, 348–382. Tucson: University of Arizona Press.

Tilden, J. W., and A. C. Smith. 1986. *A Field Guide to Western Butterflies.* Boston: Houghton Mifflin.

Warson, A., and P. E. S. Whalley. 1975. *The Dictionary of Butterflies and Moths in Color.* New York: McGraw-Hill.

Wisdom, C. S. 1991. Patterns of heterogeneity in desert herbivorous insect communities. *In* G. A. Polis, ed., *The Ecology of Desert Communities*, 151–179. Tucson: University of Arizona Press.

MOUFLON SHEEP

Species of wild sheep (*Ovis aries*) indigenous to mountainous or arid regions of Europe, western Asia, and the Near East. Mouflon sheep vary from dark brown to straw colored. Rams have long, curved horns and may have a light-colored saddle patch and a dark neck ruff. The horns of mouflon sheep, while curved, are not spiraled like the horns of other wild sheep. Ewes may be horned or hornless. Mouflon sheep eat a variety of grasses and herbaceous plants. Rams live in herds separate from those of the ewes, lambs, and juvenile rams. During the mating season, November–January, males compete by head butting for the right to breed. A single lamb, occasionally twins, is born after a gestation period of 150 days. Lambs may begin to eat solid food early, but weaning does not take place until the lamb is four months old. Ewes reach sexual maturity in 18 months; rams, in two and a half years. The estimated life span of mouflon sheep in the wild is 13 years. Mouflon sheep were the wild precursor to domesticated sheep. Several subspecies of mouflon sheep are vulnerable to extinction because of habitat alteration, increased competition from domesticated stocks, and hunting.—Rob Channell

See also **DESERT PEOPLES; DOMESTIC ANIMALS; MAMMALS; MIDDLE EAST, DESERTS OF; SAHARA DESERT; SHEEP**

Further Reading

Isaac, E. 1970. *Geography of Domestication.* Englewood Cliffs, N.J.: Prentice-Hall.

MOUSEBIRD

Group of medium-sized, morphologically uniform bird species found in Africa south of the Sahara (family Coliidae, order Coliiformes). Coliiformes is the only order of birds endemic to Africa. Six species from two genera (*Urocolius* and *Colius*) are recognized, all of which are sedentary. Mousebirds (also known as colies) range through sub-Saharan open savannas and are often common in such areas. Total length varies from 30 to 35 centimeters; however, mousebirds have small bodies, with two-thirds of their length consisting of a long, graduated tail. Mousebirds have short, rounded wings and are not strong fliers. Foot morphology is unusual in that the outer two toes are mobile and can be moved to face forward or backward. Mousebirds are exceedingly agile on the ground and often will run quickly into the underbrush or climb among branches of thickets when disturbed. The bill is short, strong, and curved slightly downward. Plumage is a rather drab gray or brown, although punctuated in most species by a patch of color on the head, neck, or rump. The head is topped by an erectile crest. Sexes are alike.

Mousebirds are quite gregarious and usually live in small flocks of up to 20–30 individuals. This social behavior extends to communal roosting, sunbathing, and dustbathing. Mousebirds roost in a unique fashion, hanging in clusters from branches so that their "shoulders" are level with their perches. Some, if not all, species of mousebirds may undergo torpor, allowing their body temperature to drop at night and warming themselves again in the morning sunlight. Diet consists of a variety of plant matter, including fruits, leaves, and flowers.

Monogamy is generally suggested to be the norm, although both polygamy and polyandry have been reported in the speckled mousebird, *Colius striatus*. Nests are open cups of a variety of plant and animal matter constructed one to six meters above ground in trees and shrubs. Probably all mousebirds exhibit some form of cooperative breeding. Clutch size ranges from one to nine, although larger clutches are probably the result of laying by more than one female. The eggs are, relative to female body weight, the smallest among all nonparasitic birds. Both parents contribute to incubation and chick feeding.—Stephen C. Lougheed

See also **AFRICA, DESERTS OF; BIRDS; GRASSLAND; SAVANNA**

Further Reading

Fry, C. H., S. Keith, and E. K. Urban, eds. 1988. *The Birds of Africa*. Vol. 3. New York: Academic Press.

Prinzinger, R., R. Goppel, A. Lorenz, and E. Kulzer. 1981. Body temperature and metabolism in the red-backed mousebird (*Colius castanotus*) during fasting and torpor. *Comparative Biochemistry and Physiology A* 69:689–692.

Rowan, M. K. 1967. A study of the colies of southern Africa. *Ostrich* 38:63–115.

Schifter, H. 1985. Systematics and distribution of mousebirds (Coliidae). *In* K.-L. Schuchmann, ed., *International Symposium on African Vertebrates: Systematics, Phylogeny and Evolutionary Ecology*, 325–247. Bonn: Selbstverlag.

MOVIES IN DESERTS

With the possible exception of the tropical jungle, the harsh habitat of the desert—from the Sahara to the Kalahari and from the Mojave to the Arabian—has become the most depicted natural landscape in the history of world cinema. Since the 1930s both naturalistic, ethnographic documentaries and fiction films have focused attention on this desolate, apparently lifeless, environment, so hostile to the mere presence of humans. Although natural history films such as Walt Disney's *The Living Desert*, about the fauna of California's deserts, or John Walsh's *The Hunters*, about a group of Bushmen in the Kalahari, have contributed to the general public's knowledge of the flora, the fauna, and the peoples of the desert, and their unique adaptations to the arid land, it is primarily fiction films that have indelibly imprinted the popular image of the desert in our eyes and minds.

The purpose of films, like that of any other art form, is not to represent or to document reality "as it is" but rather to re-create it and present it as an expression of particular beliefs, values, and feelings. Thus in the case of movies set in the desert, the images on the screen are not real, nor were they meant to be. Whether by depicting the desert in its most traditional image as an endless extension of shifting sand dunes or in any of its rocky, shrubby, semiarid, or arid varieties, filmmakers are not really interested in providing viewers with a scientific, objective representation of the physical environment and its human population. In fact, many films are shot on locations different from the ones they purport to represent, such as *Flight of the Phoenix*, which is supposed to take place somewhere in

Partial List of Major Motion Pictures Set in a Desert

Movie	Director	Country/Year	Desert
Apache	Robert Aldrich	USA/54	White Mts.
Barren Lives	Glauber Rocha	Brazil/63	Sertão/NE Brazil
Cairo	D. W. van Dyke II	USA/63	Sahara
Casablanca	Michael Curtiz	USA/42	Sahara
Chato's Land	Michael Winner	USA/71	Sonora
The Desert Warrior	George Miller	AUS/82	Outback
Flight of the Phoenix	Robert Aldrich	USA/65	North Africa
Fort Apache	John Ford	USA/48	Monument Valley
The Four Feathers	Alexander Korda	UK/39	Sahara/Sudan
Gallipoli	Peter Weir	Aus/81	Outback
Lawrence of Arabia	David Lean	UK/62	Arabian
Lion of the Desert	Moustapha Akkad	Libya/75	Sahara/Libya
Major Dundee	Sam Peckinpah	USA/64	Sonora
Morocco	Josef von Sternberg	USA/35	Sahara
The Professionals	Richard Brooks	USA/66	Chihuahua
Sahara	Zoltan Korda	UK/43	Sahara
Sands of the Kalahari	Cy Enfield	UK/65	Kalahari
The Searchers	John Ford	USA/56	Monument Valley
Seven Years in Tibet	Jean-Jacques Annaud	USA/Fr	Argentine
Shame	Steve Jodrell	Aus/87	Outback
The Sheltering Sky	Bernardo Bertolucci	Italy/90	Sahara
Stagecoach	John Ford	USA/39	Monument Valley
Thelma and Louise	Riddley Scott	USA/91	Arizona
Treasure of the Sierra Madre	John Huston	USA/48	Chihuahua
Ulzana's Raid	Robert Aldrich	USA/71	Nogales, Ariz.
Walkabout	Nicholas Roeg	Aus/71	Outback
Wake in Fright	Ted Kotcheff	Aus/79	Outback
The Wild Bunch	Sam Peckinpah	USA/69	Chihuahua

North Africa but was actually filmed in California and Nevada; or the "spaghetti westerns" of Sergio Leone, which substitute the arid region of Extremadura, Spain, for the Mexican desert. Moreover, in low-budget comedies like Bob Hope and Bing Crosby's *The Road to Morocco*, or Laurel and Hardy's *Flying Deuces*, the Sahara Desert is re-created within the walls of the film studio set. Even when films do seem to portray the desert in a direct, unmediated manner, as would be the case of the documentary film, they are always carefully planned and staged, through the use of light filters, camera angles and movements, close-up or panoramic shots, and stage props, to create a particular scenario and a specific atmosphere rather than to capture the "true" desert landscape.

Filmmakers of different nationalities, film styles, and ideologies, such as the Americans John Ford, Robert Aldrich, and Sam Peckinpah, the Italians Michelangelo Antonioni and Bernardo Bertolucci, the Brazilian Glauber Rocha, the Australians Peter Weir and Nicholas Roeg, and the Britons David Lean and Alexander Korda, have, at some point in their careers, chosen this unique landscape as the setting for the expression of their personal interpretations of the national character and their visions of the epic struggles of men against the land, the elements, the native people, and, perhaps most important, themselves. In the process some of these visionaries, like Ford and later Lean, have changed forever the way we look at the desert.

Although each director uses the landscape of the desert in different ways and with different meanings, it is nevertheless possible to find some basic underlying common reasons for their choice of landscape that stem from the natural features of the desert: its aridity and climatic extremes, its openness and vastness, its great extremes of light and shadows, and its contrasts of plains and towering rocky hills. In the first place these topographic and climatic properties allow filmmakers greater freedom of cinematic experimentation in the area of photography—wide and deep focus, panoramic views, widescreen projection—and provide them with an incomparable canvas for the representation of visual contrasts of terrain and movement and the depiction of a beautiful yet menacing environment. Some of the most memorable images of the desert are precisely those in which a lone rider, a stagecoach, a column of wagons, or a troop of soldiers is seen crossing the immense, colorful landscape, as in the John Wayne westerns shot by John Ford in Monument Valley, Arizona, which became the model for later westerns.

Most important, these features also support the basic dramatic functions of the deserts in movies: (1) to isolate people and settlements; (2) to threaten their survival; (3) to become the meeting place of savagery and civilization; and (4) to test men's abilities and values. These functions are found inextricably combined to different degrees in virtually all film genres dealing with the desert.

Isolation, probably the most basic and common of all functions, assumes many forms and variations—from the single individual, the government official like James Stewart in *The Man from Laramie*, an army scout like Gregory Peck in *The Stalking Moon*, Indian fighters like Hondo and Ethan Edwards, both portrayed by John Wayne, to small groups like the family of homesteaders in *The*

Searchers. Larger human groups can also be isolated in precarious towns and military outposts like the U.S. Cavalry and the French Foreign Legion forts. Surrounded by the vast expanse of the desert—a sea of sand or of towering mountains—these settlements in the wilderness, while offering the relative safety of an organized community, are nevertheless either completely cut off from the rest of the world or, in the case of the western, linked to civilization by precarious yet vital trails, stagecoaches, and the railroad.

When isolated physically from the rest of civilization, people become vulnerable to destruction by either natural or cultural causes. The first emanate from the physical characteristics of the environment itself; the very vastness of the desert provides a serious obstacle for people crossing it, distances are incredibly long and often without even recognizable routes, and its arid climate and barren terrain add the ever-present danger of lack of water and food for travelers and explorers. The latter threat has been exploited by many movies, in which characters are always on the brink of death from dehydration and journeys are usually measured as the space from water hole to oasis. In fact, the need for and possession of water often becomes the center of the story and controls the actions of characters, for example, Josef von Sternberg's *Greed* and D. W. Griffith's *The Last Drop of Water*, John Ford's *3 Godfathers*, or Sam Peckinpah's *The Ballad of Cable Hogue*.

The sun itself is sometimes shown as a malevolent force that either toys with people's emotional and mental stability by creating false hopes through the illusion of the mirage, a typical desert phenomenon, as in *Treasure of the Sierra Madre*, or destroys them outright, as in *The Four Feathers*, where it actually blinds Lieutenant Dorrance (Ralph Richardson). Desert movies also often include sandstorms, both because of the story—they tend to separate people from each other or make them lose their way—and because of their spectacular image. The heat and the merciless sun, as well as a blinding sandstorm, were used in Richard Brooks's film *The Professionals*, in which an unforgiving desert is a major factor in the development of the film.

Most films have remained very limited in their depiction of desert fauna and flora. They are usually represented by the ever-present camel and the palm trees in North African settings, kangaroos and dingoes in Australian films, and venomous creatures and flying vultures in westerns, thus contributing to the generalized perception of the desert as a generally lifeless or, at best, dangerous and evil environment. A curious example of this constant threat is found in westerns, which rarely fail to include coyotes and wolves howling in the distance as ominous signals to settlers and pioneers, but audiences do not actually get to see them. In short, any depiction of life is restricted to showing little more than the aforementioned animals, all of which have become part of the iconography of the desert. Some notable exceptions to this trend are *The Treasure of the Sierra Madre*, in which a Gila monster threatens Humphrey Bogart's gold, and *Sands of the Kalahari*, in which a pack of baboons shares quarters with the plane-wrecked survivors and even becomes crucial in the resolution of the drama.

This leads to the next function of the desert in movies: to serve as the stage for the confrontation between two radically opposed cultures, one bent on expansion and colonization, the other on resistance and protection of a traditional way of life. The plots are strikingly similar in the case of the three major genres—the American western, the British film of empire, and the Foreign Legion movie. These usually involve some agent of European civilization—settlers, soldiers, administrators, explorers—claiming ownership of new territories, trying to protect trade routes and places of strategic military importance. In the case of the Western especially, an attempt is made to turn some desolate, barren expanse of desert into a prosperous and law-abiding community. A good example is John Ford's *The Man Who Shot Liberty Valence*, in which John Wayne and James Stewart represent force and law, respectively, and together bring civilization to a desert land by eliminating lawlessness, represented by Lee Marvin's Liberty Valence.

On-screen military confrontations against the background of the desert landscape are an integral part of films depicting heroic defenders battling against overwhelming numbers of bloodthirsty attackers. The majority of these movies, especially in the early 20th century, portrayed the different peoples of the desert as anonymous, faceless masses who lacked a distinct cultural identity and who were irrationally bent on destroying Europeans. With the general rejection of colonialism in the 1940s, film-makers began to change their perspective and portray native people as complex individuals and groups who may have been wronged by innocent and well-intentioned colonists, as in *Apache*, *Chato's Land*, and *Lawrence of Arabia*.

Long established by religion as the classical place of temptation through the stories of Jesus and Muhammad, the desert subjects people to all kinds of trials that test their ethical principles, as well as their capacity for survival. Consequently the desert is often presented as a burning hell that must be crossed before people reach their goal, whether it be the safety of the settlement, the fertile land of California for American homesteaders, or some hidden treasures—maybe even the Fountain of Youth itself—of a lost African or Middle Eastern city for the adventurous explorer, as in the Indiana Jones trilogy.

Actually films show that life in the desolate environment of the desert requires not so much extraordinary physical powers as successful adaptation. The few successful Europeans who survive do so by learning from the native inhabitants and by imitating them, creating memorable characters, such as the army scouts McIntosh (Burt Lancaster) in *Ulzana's Raid* and Potts (James Coburn) in *Major Dundee*, who actually live halfway between the Indian and the American way, but also those like Major Kirby (John Wayne) in *Fort Apache* who while fighting against the Indians has learned to respect them. Some of those who learn how to survive in the desert also manage to maintain a guiding set of ethical principles that prizes values such as loyalty, solidarity, compassion, and honesty above greed and personal gain, like plane crash survivors in *Flight of the Phoenix* who pull together to build a plane or the team of experts in *The Professionals* who break their lucrative contract to throw in their lot with the oppressed Mexicans.

Unfortunately for every one of these principled characters, we find many others whose effort at survival assumes the form of Social Darwinism and whose values become similar to those of the savages they fight. In *The Searchers*, Ethan Edwards, for all his skill as a desert Indian fighter, is, or becomes during the story, almost as bloodthirsty as his enemy, the Comanche chief Scar, whom he scalps in the end. Humprhey Bogart, suffering the heat and aridity of the desert, betrays friendship for gold in *Treasure of the Sierra Madre*. In *Sands of the*

Kalahari, Stuart Whitman methodically and ruthlessly eliminates his companions, one by one, to ensure his own supply of water and food. One of the best films to show the complete process of a European's successful adaptation to desert life and subsequent transgression of his own code of values is *Lawrence of Arabia*. In the first half of the movie, Lawrence, portrayed by Peter O'Toole, learns the ways of the Bedouins and actually becomes one of them but is later corrupted by his own success when he defiantly declares to Ali (Omar Sharif), after rescuing the lost Arab from the Anvil of the Sun, "Nothing is written . . . except in here," pointing at his head, implying that his will is superior to the will of God as the Arabs had said. Soon after, he discovers that he enjoys killing and having the power to decide over men's lives. He eventually orders the massacre of Turkish troops at Desra.

Outside the United States, Australia is probably the only country where the outback has become a symbol of the national character, which came of age in World War I, and where the landscape has helped to forge the values and the special qualities of "Australianness." Some films, like *Gallipoli* and *The Light Horsemen*, explore the historical roots of the Australian character, while others, like *Walkabout* and the Crocodile Dundee films, create the myth of the "bushman" in his relation to the land and the Aborigines. Australian films are responsible for popularizing the newest image of the desert as an apocalyptic wasteland, a man-made product of erroneous environmental policies that will eventually provoke a new struggle for the survival of the fittest. The best of these futuristic films are the Mad Max series, called in America *The Desert Warrior* and *Beyond the Thunderdome*.

The reason for such radically contrasting interests in the desert lies equally in the cinematographic possibilities and the philosophical implications it offers to Western eyes, which have continued to be drawn to and intrigued by its exoticism. For other cultures, particularly those that have to contend with deserts on a daily basis, the myths are more easily dispelled. These contrasting attitudes are summed up well in a scene from *Lawrence of Arabia* in which Prince Faisal (Alec Guinness) tells Lawrence during their first meeting, "You Englishmen have a great hunger for vast desolate spaces. We Arabs do not like the desert. There is nothing *in* the desert. My heart, instead, longs for the lost gardens of Córdoba."—Orlando Ocampo

See also **AUSTRALIA, DESERTS OF; CHUIHUAHUAN DESERT; DEATH VALLEY; MOJAVE DESERT; MONTE DESERT; MONUMENT VALLEY; SAHARA DESERT; SONORAN DESERT; UNITED STATES, DESERTS OF**

Further Reading

Buscombe, E., ed. 1988. *The British Film Industry Companion to the Western*. New York: Da Capo Press.

King, J. 1990. *Magical Reels: A History of the Cinema in Latin America*. New York: Verso.

Landy, M. 1991. *British Genres: Cinema and Society, 1930–1960*. Princeton: Princeton University Press.

Matthews, L. 1984. *History of Western Movies*. New York: Crescent Books.

Murray, S., ed. 1994. *Australian Cinema*. Sydney: Southwood Press.

Schatz, T. 1985. *Hollywood Genres: Formulas, Filmmaking and the Studio System*. New York: Random House.

NABKHA. *See* DUNES, NABKHA

NAMIBIA, DESERTS OF

Arid and semiarid areas lying within the geographic boundaries of the nation of Namibia. Namibia is home to one of the driest, oldest deserts in the world, the Namib Desert. In addition, the country has two other desert biomes: the Nama Karoo Biome, which extends northward in a fingerlike pattern from its main distribution in South Africa to the south of Angola; and the western limits of the Arid Savanna Biome (Kalahari Desert). (See map of African deserts, p. 12.)

The Namib Desert is an extremely arid, cool, coastal strip desert roughly 100 kilometers wide on the west coast of Namibia and Angola. It is sandwiched between the Atlantic Ocean and the southern African escarpment on its eastern fringes. It stretches south from the San Nicolai River (14°20' south latitude) in southern Angola to southern Namibia. Its southern limit is a matter of debate: some authors claim it is the Orange River, whereas others suggest Lüderitz, a delimitation based on recent biome classifications in southern Africa. Lüderitz is the northern limit of the Succulent Karoo Biome and the winter rainfall in southern Africa. South of the Kuiseb River the Namib consists predominantly of sand dunes, whereas the northern regions are made up mostly of gravel plains.

The average yearly rainfall in the Namib ranges from nearly zero on the coast to a maximum of about 100 millimeters on its eastern borders. However, the predominantly summer rainfall is extremely unpredictable and irregular. For example, stations such as Walvis Bay and Gobabeb, with yearly averages of about 15 millimeters, have recorded years with zero precipitation as well as years with more than 100 millimeters of rainfall. The coefficient of variation (an index of predictability) of mean annual rainfall is 70–80 percent.

Coastal fog generated over the cold Benguela Current, which travels northward up the coast of the Namib at 40 kilometers per day, is common

Sparse Namib Desert habitat near Gobabeb, Namibia, at the Namib Desert Research Station. (Photo: M. A. Mares)

throughout the year. As a source of condensed water in the form of dew, the fog is generally considered to be more important biologically than the sporadic rainfalls. The fog is carried inland over the Namib at night by sea breezes and dissolves slowly during the day as the desert surface is heated. It occurs on more than 100 days per year on the coast (Swakopmund), but this frequency decreases to about 5–10 days per year at the eastern limits of the Namib.

Air temperatures in the Namib tend to be ameliorated by the cool air generated over the Benguela Current and are not as extreme as they are in the other southern African deserts, the Nama Karoo and the Kalahari. Mean monthly maximum temperatures may reach 33°C (Gobabeb, March), whereas mean monthly minimum temperatures seldom fall below 7°C. Mean monthly relative humidity ranges from about 85 percent on the coast to about 30 percent on the eastern fringes of the Namib in winter.

The formation and age of the Namib has been a subject of much scientific debate. Its existence is best understood as a five-stage model of events that started with the breakup of Gondwana during the early Cretaceous (about 130 million years ago) and the subsequent formation of the South Atlantic

Ocean. With the exception of several igneous rock complexes that remained as inselbergs (e.g., Brandberg and Spitzkoppe), several kilometers of the surface of what is now the Namib were eroded away during this wetter period, leading to the formation of the great escarpment in southern Africa. This post-Gondwana erosion phase was followed by the first phase of aridity (Proto-Namib Desert Phase), which persisted from the Paleocene during the early Tertiary (about 65 million years ago) to the late Oligocene (about 22 million years ago). During this phase unequivocal evidence of desert conditions and a southerly paleowind regime can be dated to the early Eocene, 55 million years ago. Aridity during this arid phase can be attributed, as it is today, to the establishment of the South Atlantic anticyclonic circulation that followed the complete opening of the South Atlantic Ocean. Briefly, this circulation takes the form of high-altitude air returning from the tropics which descends over the semitropics as stable, dry air masses. This phase was followed by a relatively short lived, wetter, more semiarid Pluvial Phase during the early to middle Miocene (about 22–14 million years ago) and a late middle Miocene Pedogenic Phase during which the annual rainfall was 350–450 millimeters per year and occurred mainly in summer. The last Namib Desert phase of extreme aridity, and that which exists today, was initiated once the Benguela Cold Water Upwelling Current System was fully established in the late Miocene (11–7 million years ago). This dry, windy phase led to the formation of the dune fields and the great Namib dune sea that lies between Lüderitz and the Kuiseb River.

As a consequence of a long evolutionary history of aridity, the Namib supports a high diversity of endemic plants and animals that display some extraordinary adaptations to aridity. On the gravel plains hemicryptophytes (annuals) in the form of annual *Stipagrostis* grasses are the dominant plant life form. They respond rapidly to rainfall exceeding about 20 millimeters. Trees such as *Acacia erioloba* grow along drainage lines and washes. The most unusual and well-known plant of the Namib, if not the world, is *Welwitschia mirabilis*, an ancient evolutionary relict from the era when flowering trees (angiosperms) were evolving from the cone-bearing trees (gymnosperms). Some plants are estimated to be in excess of 2,000 years old. In the dune sea characteristic plants are the nara plant (*Acan-*

thosicyos horridus), common at the bases of sand dunes, the perennial grass *Stipagrostis sabulicola*, and one of the few succulents in the Namib, *Trianthema hereroensis*. The large riverbeds, such as those of the Kuiseb and Ugab rivers, are lined by large ana trees (*Faidherbia albida*) and the wild tamarisk (*Tamarix usneoides*).

The Namib has a very rich and diverse invertebrate fauna, especially beetles of the family Tenebrionidae. There are 29 vertebrate species endemic to the Namib: 23 reptiles, 3 mammals, and 3 birds. Ostriches (*Struthio camelus*) and a number of desert-adapted mammals such as springbok (*Antidorcas marsupialis*), gemsbok (*Oryx gazella*), and Hartmann's mountain zebra (*Equus zebra hartmannae*) roam the Namib but also occur in adjacent desert biomes (Karoo and Kalahari).—Barry G. Lovegrove

See also **ACACIA; AFRICA, DESERTS OF; AFRICAN LION; ANIMAL ADAPTATIONS; AN INTRODUCTION TO DESERTS; ANTELOPE; BENGUELA CURRENT; BIOSPHERE RESERVE; BIRDS; CATS; CHEETAH; CONSERVATION IN DESERTS; CRETACEOUS; DESERTIFICATION; DOG, WILD; DUNES; DURICRUSTS; EOCENE; GEMSBOK; GRASSES; GRASSLAND; HARTEBEEST; HEAT; HEAT BALANCE; HEAT EXCHANGE; HEAT STRESS; HYENA; KAROO; LIMESTONE; LION; MAMMALS; MIOCENE; NAMIBIA, DESERTS OF; PLAYA; OCEAN CURRENTS; OLIGOCENE; OSTRICH; ORYX; PALEOCENE; PLATE TECTONICS; PLANT ADAPTATIONS; PLEISTOCENE; RAPTORS; SALINITY; SALT PAN; SAND RAMP; SAVANNA; SOUTH AFRICA, DESERTS OF; SPRINGBOK; TERTIARY; WATER BALANCE; WEAVER; WELWITSCHIA; ZEBRA**

Further Reading

Augustinus, P. 1997. *Desert Adventure: In Search of Wilderness in Namibia and Botswana*. Randburg, South Africa: Acorn Books.

Cowling, R. M., D. M. Richardson, and S. M. Pierce. 1997. *Vegetation of Southern Africa*. Oxford: Cambridge University Press.

Lovegrove, B. 1993. *The Living Deserts of Southern Africa*. Vlaeberg: Fernwood.

Seely, M. K. 1990. *Namib Ecology*. Pretoria, South Africa: Transvaal Museum.

Walter, H. 1986. The Namib Desert. *In* M. Evenari, I. Noy-Meir, and D. W. Goodall, eds., *Ecosystems of the World: Hot Deserts and Arid Shrublands*, 12B:245–282. New York: Elsevier.

NATUFIANS. *See* DESERT PEOPLES

NAVAJO (DINE'É)

Ethnic subdivision of a much larger family of Native American groups known as Nadene speakers. The Nadene were the last wave of migrants to cross the Bering Strait from Siberia to the North American continent before the arrival of Europeans. The time of their arrival in the New World has been estimated to be about 3,000 years ago. They soon spread along the coast of southern Alaska and northwestern Canada through the interior and as far east as Hudson's Bay. In the process they differentiated into culturally and linguistically distinguishable groups. In linguistic taxonomy the Nadene constitute a phylum with three families, the Tlingit, Haida, and Athapascan. The Tlingit and Haida are found on the coastal islands of the Alaskan Panhandle and British Columbia. The Athapascan family is further divided into twenty groups. Nine of these are in the interior of Alaska and Canada. Another five are found in coastal northern California and southern Oregon. Finally, there are six southern Athapascan groups, found in the southwestern United States and southern Plains. In addition to the Navajo, these are five Apache groups, the San Carlos, Chiricahua-Mescalero, Jicarilla, Lipan, and Kiowa Apache.

The southern Athapascans are estimated to have separated from the northern Athapascans and begun their drift southward some 1,000–1,300 years ago. It is not certain what route they took, but most evidence indicates that they migrated southward through the high plains, hugging the eastern base of the Rocky Mountains. Along the way some bands may have encountered peoples living in permanent or semipermanent settlements and practicing horticulture. These would have been the westernmost representatives of eastern Woodland cultures, variants of which extended, fingerlike, deep into the plains along river valleys. As a result, by the time the Athapascans reached the Southwest, some bands may already have been practicing horticulture. This would include the Navajo, who also made a crude form of pointed-bottom pottery remarkably similar to Woodland pottery.

The arrival of Athapascans in the Southwest is generally placed at about A.D. 1500, although some authorities believe they were present as early as A.D. 1000. The Navajo were first encountered by Spanish explorers in northern New Mexico in 1582–1583. From there they gradually spread westward and southward, and by the middle of the 17th century they occupied a territory stretching from the Chama River in northcentral New Mexico to the Little Colorado River in Arizona, across many arid and semiarid landscapes of the southwestern United States.

The Navajos call themselves Dine'é; the name Navajo was given to them by the Spanish. Initially unfamiliar with the various Indian groups that they encountered, the Spanish often referred to them by Hispanicized native words and descriptive terms. The word *Apache* is derived from a Zuñi word denoting enemies, to which the Spanish attached a term denoting some attribute that distinguished one group from another. Hence Apache noted for their basketry were Jicarilla Apache, those who used agave, or mescal, for food were Mescalero Apache, and so on. In this vein those Apaches in northern New Mexico who practiced some horticulture became Apaches de Navaju, "Apaches with cultivated fields."

Traditional Navajo social organization was based on the family, the clan, and a localized cooperative entity called an outfit, usually consisting of several extended families but cutting across clan lines. Descent was reckoned along matrilineal lines, and while postmarital residence was loosely defined, there was a tendency toward matrilocality. Although clans do not seem to have any clear function other than determining descent, the matrilineal principle is strongly exhibited in the residence group, which is organized around a mother, her children, and relatives. Each biological family occupies a separate hogan, which will usually have a corral, some sheds, and an outdoor cooking shelter associated with it. Many also include a sweat lodge.

In the past there were apparently twelve recognized chiefs, who functioned as six war chiefs and six peace chiefs. The war chiefs were determined by their ability and held authority only on war parties. Peace chiefs were chosen by the community and were always medicine men who knew the rituals, particularly the Blessingway. However, there is contradictory data as to their actual authority.

Initially the Navajo had a mixed subsistence economy consisting of simple agriculture combined with hunting and gathering. Unlike their Puebloan neighbors, who were concentrated in compact villages, the Navajo settlement pattern was dispersed and seasonal. They spent the winter in higher elevations, such as the Chuska-Lukachukai Mountains or Black Mesa, where hunting was better, pinyon nuts could be harvested, and winter fuel was available. In the summer they moved to lower elevations where they planted their cornfields. As a result of this dispersed pattern and seasonal movement, they were ideally suited to adopt sheep herding after the introduction of domesticated animals by the Spanish, and by the middle of the 19th century sheep had become a major part of their economy.

Navajo religious beliefs and rituals focus on the well-being of the individual, although rituals include public gatherings. Rituals revolve around chants, which are grouped according to mythological associations. There are six main groups: Blessingway, a series of chants designed to place the individual in harmony with the Holy People, mythological supernatural beings; war ceremonials, now obsolete; Gameway, chants relating to hunting and associated animals; Holyway, a series of chants believed to attract good and ward off evil; Evilway, designed to exorcise evil; and Lifeway, chants involved in curing bodily injuries.

The latter three groups constitute curing rituals. Beautyway, of the Holyway group, is performed if snakes have been offended; Shootingway is when lightning or thunder must be appeased. Many chants have multiple functions. Enemyway, which used to be associated with wars, is performed to cure illness contracted from non-Navajo people. However, it also serves the social function of announcing women of marriageable age. Nightway, another curing ritual, which lasts nine days, also serves to initiate boys and girls into ceremonial life. More than 58 distinct ceremonies have been recorded, and there are probably many more.

In addition to chants, a centerpiece of all rituals is the sand painting. These are elaborate stylized representations of Yei figures (Holy People) and associated ritual symbols, drawn with dry colored sand and crushed minerals on a bed of clean white sand.

During the Pueblo Revolt of 1680, many Puebloan people fled the Rio Grande area in fear of Spanish reprisal and took refuge with several Navajo groups. As a result there was considerable acculturation of Navajo and Pueblo traditions, which is clearly reflected in ritual. As an example, the graphic depiction of Yei figures in Navajo sand paintings is clearly derived from Pueblo representations of Katchina figures, and much of Navajo mythology reflects Pueblo influence.

Relations with Europeans have been typical of most Indian peoples. Their relations with the Spanish consisted of intermittent peace and raiding. Since the Navajo settlement pattern was dispersed over a wide area, Spanish retaliation for raids on Spanish settlements often was directed at the wrong parties, thereby exacerbating already hostile relations. Similar problems continued with the coming of the Anglos and U.S. domination. Finally, many Navajo were rounded up in a campaign led by Kit Carson in 1863 and incarcerated in a reservation at Fort Sumner, New Mexico. Conditions at Fort Sumner, where some 8,000 Navajo were confined, were deplorable, promoting disease and death. Finally, in 1868, a treaty was concluded granting the Navajo a 3.5-million-acre reservation in Arizona and New Mexico.

Since their return to their old homeland, conditions have changed considerably for the Navajo. Through land grants and purchase, their reservation has grown to 16,000,000 acres. In 1922 they formed a modern government under the Indian Reorganization Act, consisting of an elected tribal council and chairman, and a local chapter system was added in 1927. A dam on the San Juan River in New Mexico has enabled the irrigation of 110,000 acres, and more recently the tribe receives benefits from the construction of Glen Canyon Dam and Lake Powell. The reservation is rich in energy resources. The Burnham area of northwestern New Mexico has an estimated 824.5 million tons of minable coal, and Black Mesa has another 350 to 400 million tons of strippable coal; and a coal mining operation at Fruitland, New Mexico, produces approximately 8.5 million tons annually. In addition, there are extensive oil, gas, and uranium leases on Navajo land. The tribe operates its own utilities company, runs its own public schools and community college, and, through the tribally owned Navajo Forest Products Industries, is developing a successful forestry program with two operating sawmills and sustainable yields.—Richard A. Pailes

See also **ARIZONA DESERT; COLORADO RIVER; DESERT PEOPLES; GRAND CANYON; GREAT BASIN DESERT; HOHOKAM; HOPI; LLANO ESTACADO;**

JORNADA DEL MUERTO; NEW MEXICO DESERT;
RIO GRANDE; SONORAN DESERT

Further Reading

Downs, J. F. 1972. *The Navajo*. New York: Holt, Rinehart, and Winston.

Dutton, B. 1983. *American Indians of the Southwest*. Albuquerque: University of New Mexico Press.

Kluckhohn, C., and D. Leighton. 1962. *The Navajo*. Garden City, N.Y.: Doubleday.

Warren, S. S. 1997. *Desert Dwellers: Native People of the American Southwest*. San Francisco: Chronicle Books.

NEGEV DESERT. *See* ISRAEL, DESERTS OF; JORDAN, DESERTS OF

NEOGENE

Subdivision of the Cenozoic era and of the Tertiary period ranging in geologic time from 24 million to 1.6 million years ago and including the Miocene and Pliocene epochs. By some definitions the Tertiary is divided into an earlier Paleogene period extending from 67 million years ago to 24 million years ago and the later Neogene period. Some scholars consider the Neogene to include the Quaternary period, in which case the Neogene extends from 24 million years ago to the present day.

A general cooling trend in the earth's climate characterizes much of the Cenozoic, especially during the Neogene. This trend is manifested in widespread, high-latitude glaciations that occurred earlier in the Southern Hemisphere than in the Northern Hemisphere. The strong circum-Antarctic ocean current, first developed during the Oligocene, began the Cenozoic glaciation of Antarctica. This glaciation continued into the Neogene, spreading across all of Antarctica by the end of the Miocene. By the middle Pliocene, about 3.5 million years ago, extensive evidence of glaciation appears also in South America and possibly northern Asia and Alaska, although plant fossils indicate that mixed boreal forests still grew in parts of Siberia, northern Alaska, and Arctic Canada. By the late Pliocene (about 3 million years ago), large volumes of ice had built up in Greenland and Iceland.

The global drying trend that began during the Oligocene continued through the Neogene, and is reflected in many continental regions at middle latitudes by the change from seasonally arid savanna woodlands to grasslands or other open habitats with herbaceous vegetation. By the Miocene (or late Oligocene in South America), grazing, hoofed mammals reach their acme in the fossil record of most continents.

Many complex factors contributed to the global climate changes of the Cenozoic. A few that have been proposed include the tectonic closure of the Isthmus of Panama, which may have affected Atlantic Ocean circulation in such a way as to produce sufficient atmospheric moisture to build the large volumes of ice in Greenland and Iceland, and the uplift of the Tibetan Plateau, which affected atmospheric circulation in the Northern Hemisphere. Phenomena such as these in turn had a profound effect on biotic evolution in the Neogene. Steven Stanley proposed the term "cascading radiation" for a chain reaction in which the radiation of one group of organisms promotes the radiation of another, which in turn promotes the radiation of a third group. This idea was partly based on the Neogene diversification of grasses and herbaceous plants, which could have substantially promoted the diversification of murid rodents (members of the rodent family Muridae) and songbirds, which in turn could have led to the radiation of predatory colubrid snakes (members of the snake family Colubridae).—Nicholas J. Czaplewski

See also ANDES; C_3 PLANTS; C_4 PLANTS; CACTI; CENOZOIC; CRETACEOUS; EOCENE; FOSSILS; GLACIAL PERIODS; GRASSLAND; MADRO-TERTIARY GEOFLORA; MIDDEN; MIOCENE; NAMIBIA, DESERTS OF; OCEAN CURRENTS; OLIGOCENE; PALEOCENE; PALEOCLIMATE; PERMIAN; PHOTOSYNTHESIS; PLATE TECTONICS; PLEISTOCENE; PLIOCENE; PRECAMBRIAN; QUATERNARY; RECENT (HOLOCENE); SAHARA DESERT; TERTIARY

Further Reading

Cocks, L. R. M. 1981. *The Evolving Earth*. London: British Museum (Natural History).

Frakes, L. A., J. E. Francis, and J. I. Syktus, eds. 1992. *Climate Modes of the Phanerozoic: The History of the Earth's Climate over the Past 600 Million Years*. Cambridge: Cambridge University Press.

Stanley, S. M. 1990. Adaptive radiation and macroevolution. *In* P. D. Taylor and G. P. Larwood, eds., *Major Evolutionary Radiations*, 1–16. Oxford: Clarendon Press.

Sugden, D. E., D. R. Marchant, N. Potter, Jr., R. A. Souchez, G. H. Denton, C. C. Swisher III, and J.-L. Tison. 1995. Preservation of Miocene glacier ice in East Antarctica. *Nature* 376:412–414.

Vogel, J. C., ed. 1984. *Late Cainozoic Palaeoclimates of the Southern Hemisphere.* Rotterdam: A. A. Balkema.

NESTS, BIRD

Generally refers to structures constructed or excavated by birds to house and protect their eggs and young. Nests vary from the exceedingly simple (e.g., eggs laid directly on the ground) to elaborate and substantial. Nests can enhance effectiveness of incubation by providing insulation and shielding from the sun, protection from predation, and allowing for optimal positioning of the eggs. In hot environments various adaptations serve to reduce overheating of the developing embryos. Nonpasserines tend to have simpler nests than do the passerines, the former often laying eggs directly on the ground. For example, eggs of lesser nighthawks (*Chordeiles acutipennis*) are laid in unlined nest scrapes; excess heat from the eggs is removed via the body of the incubating adults, who in turn dissipate heat by gular fluttering. Many nonpasserine birds nest in burrows (e.g., many penguins of tropical latitudes) or tree cavities (e.g., the hornbills), ensuring that humidity is usually higher and temperatures typically lower than external ambient conditions. Some desert nonpasserines build quite flimsy nests that may be of some adaptive value. For example, the white-winged dove (*Zenaida asiatica*) of the southwestern United States typically build loosely constructed nests of 100–150 twigs, usually in exposed locations. The flimsy nest structure may allow for evaporative cooling from the brood-patch of the incubating adults. At the other end of the nest structure spectrum are the often-complex roofed structures of many tropical and subtropical passerines. For example, the weavers (family Ploceidae, subfamily Ploceinae) of Africa build suspended, woven, domed nests of various types of vegetation that provide a micro-environment in which daily fluctuations in temperature are markedly reduced. The rufous hornero (*Furnarius rufus*) of southern South America constructs a domed nest of hardened mud with an entrance at the side that also helps to control the incubation environment and that resembles the clay ovens used widely in desert areas throughout the southwestern United States and Argentina.—Stephen C. Lougheed

See also **ANIMAL ADAPTATIONS; BIRDS; BURROWING ANIMALS; ENDOTHERMY; FINCH; HEAT BAL-**

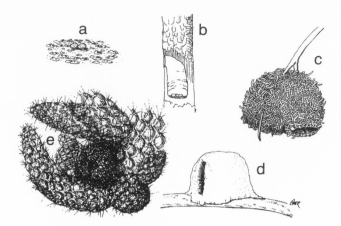

Some examples of different designs of bird nests: A, lesser nighthawk (*Chordelles acutipennis*); B, woodpecker; C, village weaver (*Ploceus cucullatus*); D, rufous hornero (*Furnarius rufus*); E, cactus wren (*Campylorhynchus brunneicapillus*) in a cholla cactus. (Artist: Ken Otter)

ANCE; OVENBIRD; PENGUIN; PIGEON; REPRODUCTION; WATER BALANCE

Further Reading

Collias, N. E. 1964. The evolution of nests and nest-building in birds. *American Zoologist* 4:175–190.

Collias, N. E., and E. C. Collias. 1984. *Nest Building and Bird Behavior.* Princeton: Princeton University Press.

Drendt, R. 1975. Incubation. *In* D. S. Farner and J. R. King, eds., *Avian Biology,* 5:333–420. New York: Academic Press.

Goodfellow, P. 1977. *Birds as Builders.* New York: Arco.

Grant, G. S. 1982. Avian incubation: Egg temperature, nest humidity and behavioral thermoregulation in a hot environment. *Ornithological Monographs* No. 30.

NEVADA DESERT

Arid and semiarid areas within the state of Nevada in the western United States. Much of Nevada lies within the Great Basin Desert, which extends from the Sierra Nevada on the west almost to the Rocky Mountains on the east and consists of an assortment of undrained basins separated by north-south oriented mountain ranges. Some ecologists refer to this area as the Nevada Desert, but technically it is a part of the only cold desert that occurs in North America. The climate of the entire area is greatly influenced by the rain shadow of the Sierra Nevada Range, which intercepts much of the moisture-laden winds from the Pacific Ocean. This arid region has an average annual rainfall of 10 inches or less.

The vegetation of the Nevada Desert is dominated by the big sagebrush (*Artemisia tridentata*), the state flower of Nevada. This gray and aromatic shrub is found on well-drained gravelly soils, often forming pure stands over large areas. The foliage of big sagebrush is sometimes heavily grazed by livestock, and the large clumps of this shrub provide habitat for numerous wild animals.

Closely associated with the sagebrush is shadscale (*Atriplex confertifolia*). This low-growing and spiny saltbush is commonly found on heavy-textured alkaline basins that are so common in the Great Basin. As with sagebrush, shadscale often forms almost pure stands covering large areas of the landscape. In fact, sagebrush and shadscale are so dominant over much of the Great Basin Desert that the region is sometimes referred to as the sagebrush-shadscale desert. Cacti are a relatively unimportant feature of the Nevada Desert because of their susceptibility to cold temperatures. Some portions of the southern Nevada Desert are dominated by blackbrush (*Coleogyne ramosissima*).—Gary K. Hulett and Amanda Renner Charles

See also **AN INTRODUCTION TO DESERTS; CALIFORNIA DESERT; CHENOPODIACEAE; DESERTS; GREAT BASIN DESERT; PLANT GEOGRAPHY; PLANTS; SAGEBRUSH; SALTBUSH; SEMIARID ZONES; UNITED STATES, DESERTS OF; UTAH DESERT**

Further Reading

Allred, D. M., D. E. Beck, and C. D. Jorgensen. 1963. Biotic communities of the Nevada test site. *Brigham Young University Science Bulletin* 2:1–52.

Billings, W. D. 1949. The shadscale vegetation zone of Nevada and eastern California in relation to climate and soils. *American Midland Naturalist* 42:87–109.

Bradley, W. G., and J. E. Deacon. 1965. *Biotic Communities of Southern Nevada*. University of Nevada, Desert Research Institute, Preprint 9.

Brown, D. E., ed. 1994. *Biotic Communities: Southwestern United States and Northwestern Mexico*. Salt Lake City: University of Utah Press.

Hall, E. R. 1946. *Mammals of Nevada*. Berkeley: University of California Press.

Young, J. A., R. A. Evans, and P. T. Tueller. 1976. Great Basin plant communities—pristine and grazed. *In* R. Elston, ed., *Holocene Environmental Change in the Great Basin*, 186–215. Nevada Archeological Survey Research Paper No. 6.

NEW MEXICO DESERT

Southern portion of New Mexico, on either side of the Rio Grande Valley, with a flora and fauna characteristic of the more extensive Chihuahuan Desert farther south in the Mexican states of Chihuahua, Coahuila, Nuevo León, Zacatecas, Durango, San Luis Potosí, and Hidalgo. The New Mexico Desert occurs primarily along the Pecos River in the southeastern part of the state and along and west of the Rio Grande northward to about the middle of the state.

This hot desert biome consists of rolling grasslands at higher elevations, creosote bush plains, and cactus and agave on rocky limestone soils. Large expanses of the outwash plains and low hills of the New Mexico Desert are dominated by the creosote bush (*Larrea tridentata*), which gives the biome a distinctive and somewhat monotonous appearance. Other characteristic plants are lechuguilla (Spanish for "little lettuce") (*Agave lechuguilla*), sotol (*Dasylirion wheeleri*), tarbush (*Flourensia cernua*), mesquite (*Prosopis*), and numerous species of soapweed, including *Yucca elata*, which is the state flower of New Mexico. This narrow-leafed yucca, or soapweed in reference to the saponaceous (soaplike) qualities of its crushed roots, is a beautiful and conspicuous sight on the open New Mexican grasslands and desert. It is actually a small "tree," often attaining a height of three meters, with tall panicles of prominent white flowers.

In the northernmost part of the New Mexico Desert, near Alamogordo, New Mexico, is the unique and geologically fascinating Tularosa Basin (sometimes referred to as the Tularosa Desert). One of the most interesting aspects of the Tularosa Basin is the extensive dunes of dazzling white gypsum known as White Sands National Monument. These shifting, snow white dunes cover more than 1,000 square kilometers and are home to a diversity of plant and animal life that is adapted to this unusual habitat.

North of White Sands is another New Mexico Desert area of geological and ecological interest. The Tularosa Malpais (Spanish for "badland") is an extensive area of congealed lava beds that support a variety of plants and animals. To the northwest of White Sands is the famous Valle Jornada del Muerto (Valley of the Journey of Death), so named because of the early Spanish travelers who died there in 1690 while in flight south toward Old Mexico.

There is evidence that much of the present-day New Mexico Desert was at one time a desert grassland and that overgrazing by domestic livestock caused a deterioration of the grassland and the invasion of species more typical of the drier Chihuahuan Desert. Animal life in the New Mexico Desert is similar to the Chihuahuan Desert.—Gary K. Hulett and Amanda Renner Charles

See also **BIRDS; CACTI; CHIHUAHUAN DESERT; CREOSOTE BUSH; DESERTS; DESERTS, HOT; DESERTS, TEMPERATE; LIZARDS; MAMMALS; MESQUITE; MEXICO, DESERTS OF; PLANT GEOGRAPHY; REPTILES; SALTBUSH; SALT CEDAR; SEMIARID ZONES; SNAKES; SONORAN DESERT; WHITE SANDS NATIONAL MONUMENT; YUCCA**

Further Reading

Brown, D. E., ed. 1994. *Biotic Communities: Southwestern United States and Northwestern Mexico.* Salt Lake City: University of Utah Press.

Castetter, E. F. 1956. The vegetation of New Mexico. *New Mexico Quarterly* 26:257–288.

Donart, G. B., D. Sylvester, and W. Hickey. 1978. *A vegetation classification system for New Mexico. In Proceedings of the First International Rangeland Congress,* 488–490. Denver, Colo.

Reid, R. L. 1998. *America, New Mexico.* Tucson: University of Arizona Press.

Shields, L. M., and L. J. Gardner. 1961. *Bioecology of the Arid and Semiarid Lands of the Southwest.* New Mexico Highlands University Bulletin 212.

York, J. C., and W. A. Dick-Peddie. 1969. Vegetation changes in southern New Mexico during the past hundred years. *In* W. G. McGinnies and B. J. Goldman, eds., *Arid Lands in Perspective,* 155–166. Tucson: University of Arizona Press.

NICHE

Abstract concept in which the role of a species is envisioned to include the sum total of its biotic and abiotic interactions with the environment. The concept of the niche was formalized by G. Evelyn Hutchinson in 1957, although it was used with various meanings in the ecological literature before that time. The niche of a species can be defined as the range of activity along every dimension of its environment, including, for example, temperature, salinity, pH, humidity, and oxygen concentration at which the species is able to exist. The length of the breeding season, the prey eaten, the predators that consume the species, and the species' competitors are additional attributes of the niche, as are various characteristics of the species' behavior. The niche is usually visualized as occupying a volume with n dimensions, where each dimension is one aspect of the biotic or abiotic environment. Thus a species is said to occupy an n-dimensional hypervolume, within which viable populations of the species exist. Hutchinson further divided the niche into the fundamental niche and the realized niche. The fundamental niche is the hypothetical range of conditions under which a species can exist without interference from other species. In the real world, however, all species interact with other species in a variety of ways; the hypervolume used by a species that is limited (= reduced) by other species is the realized niche.

The concept of the niche has allowed community ecologists to make great strides in formulating and understanding questions related to the organization and diversity of communities of organisms. A fundamental axiom of ecology is that no two species can occupy the same niche. This has led to many studies designed to elucidate which dimensions of the niches of closely related species differ and thus to infer how these species can coexist in a given environment. Many mathematical and statistical techniques have been developed to examine various parameters of the niche among species comprising a community.—Janalee P. Caldwell

See also **AQUATIC HABITATS; BIOME; ECOLOGY; ECOSYSTEM; ECOTYPE; ENERGY FLOW; LANDSCAPE; PREDATION; PRIMARY PRODUCTIVITY; PRODUCTIVITY, AQUATIC ECOSYSTEMS; SPECIATION; SUCCESSION**

Further Reading

Cody, M. L. 1974. *Competition and the Structure of Bird Communities.* Princeton: Princeton University Press.

Hutchinson, G. E. 1957. Concluding remarks. *Cold Spring Harbor Symposium on Quantitative Biology* 22:415–427.

———. 1978. *An Introduction to Population Ecology.* New Haven: Yale University Press.

Pianka, E. R. 1981. Competition and niche theory. *In* R. M. May, ed., *Theoretical Ecology: Principles and Application,* 114–141. Philadelphia: Saunders.

Whittaker, R. H., and S. A. Levin. 1975. *Niche: Theory and Application.* Stroudsburg, Pa.: Dowden, Hutchinson, and Ross.

NIGHTJAR

Moderate-sized nocturnal insectivorous bird (family Caprimulgidae, order Camprimulgiformes) with an almost cosmopolitan distribution, absent only from New Zealand, the northern holarctic zone, Antarctica, and many oceanic islands. Approximately 80 species in 18 genera are grouped into two subfamilies: the nightjars (subfamily Caprimulginae) and the New World nighthawks (subfamily Chordeilinae). Nightjars are found in a range of vegetation types, from humid forests to various open habitats. Numerous species inhabit deserts. For example, the lesser nighthawk (*Chordeiles acutipennis*) occurs in desert scrub, savanna, mangrove forests, and humid woodlands from the southwestern United States to southern Brazil. An Old World example of a caprimulgid that inhabits arid habitats is the Nubian nightjar (*Caprimulgus nubicus*); this species breeds in arid scrub and semidesert zones of the Middle East and northeastern Africa. Most temperate zone species are migratory.

Nightjars are delicately built, ranging in length from 20 to 30 centimeters, and in weight, from 40 to 80 grams. Plumage is generally cryptic, consisting of mottled grays and browns. Males sometimes have elongated tail or wing plumes. Adaptations for nocturnal activities include enlarged eyes and heightened visual acuity. The bill is small, but the gape is enormous, facilitating capture of insects while flying. Heat is dissipated by gular fluttering. Some species, notably the common poorwill (*Phalaenoptilus nuttallii*), are capable of undergoing torpor.

Most nightjars are described as monogamous, although a few species are polygynous. Eggs are usually laid directly on the ground with little or no nest. Clutches usually consist of one or two eggs. Incubation periods last from 16 to 20 days, and the nestling period is of approximately the same duration. In some desert nightjars (e.g., the lesser nighthawk) the female ensures that her eggs do not overheat by directly incubating and allowing her body to carry away excess heat.—Stephen C. Lougheed

See also **AFRICA, DESERTS OF; ASIA, DESERTS OF; ANIMAL ADAPTATIONS; BIRDS; DIET; NESTS, BIRD; SOUTH AMERICA, DESERTS OF; UNITED STATES, DESERTS OF**

Further Reading

Bent, A. C. 1940. Life histories of North American cuckoos, goatsuckers, hummingbirds and their allies. *U.S. National Museum Bulletin* 176.

Brigham, R. M. 1992. Daily torpor in a free ranging goatsucker, the common poorwill (*Phalaenoptilus nuttallii*). *Physiological Zoology* 65:457–472.

Csada, R. D., and R. M. Brigham. 1992. Common poorwill (*Phalaenoptilus nuttallii*). In A. Poole, P. Stettenheim, and F. Gill, eds., *The Birds of North America*, No. 32. Philadelphia: Academy of Natural Sciences; Washington, D.C.: American Ornithologists' Union.

Fry, C. H., S. Keith, and E. K. Urban. 1988. *The Birds of Africa*. Vol. 3. New York: Academic Press.

Grant, G. S. 1982. Avian incubation: Egg temperature, nest humidity and behavioral thermoregulation in a hot environment. *Ornithological Monographs* No. 30.

NILE RIVER

River in eastern Africa that flows for 6,671 kilometers from its source in the tropical humid highlands of Burundi and Rwanda to the Mediterranean coast of Egypt—the longest river in the world. From springs in the snowcapped mountains west of Lake Victoria, the Nile passes through Lake Victoria on its way to Uganda, Sudan, and Egypt. At Khartoum, the capital of Sudan, the Nile—there called the White Nile—is joined by the Blue Nile. Although the Blue Nile, at 1,720 kilometers, is shorter than the White Nile, it supplies 58 percent of the water that enters Egypt from Sudan. The Blue Nile begins at Lake Tana in the highlands of Ethiopia.

In southern Sudan the Nile River enters an immense swamp called the Sudd. There is no defined channel for the river in the Sudd, which is about 400 kilometers in length. During the flood season river water spreads out across the swamp. To capture the water lost in the Sudd, construction of a canal to channelize the Nile was begun. Water saved by such a canal will be used in northern Sudan and Egypt for cities, industries, and agriculture.

The major user of Nile water in Sudan is the 800,000-hectare irrigated Gezira Scheme in the triangle at Khartoum where the Blue and White Niles come together. High-quality cotton is grown in the Gezira, and exported cotton is the principal source of foreign exchange in Sudan.

By far the largest dam on the Nile is the High Dam at Aswan in Egypt (built in 1970), near the Sudanese border, which impounds water in Lake Nasser. The lake stores water for agriculture, generating electricity, and flood control. When full the lake is about 310 kilometers in length, extending into Sudan. A Herculean international effort to preserve massive stone Pharaonic temples about to be submerged under Lake Nasser's waters was undertaken successfully while the High Dam was being constructed. In a remarkable engineering feat, the temples of Ramses II and Queen Nefertari were raised—in blocks—and reassembled 64 meters above their original sites at Abu Simbel.

Retention of Nile silt in Lake Nasser has had several major impacts. Damaging floods have ended, but the silt that formerly enriched farm soils must now be replaced with commercial fertilizers. Also, soils that have become salty no longer are leached regularly. Now elaborate drainage systems attempt to do the job that floods did before the dam was built. Silt that once reached the mouth of the Nile near Alexandria helped to reduce erosion of the coastline in the Mediterranean Sea east of Alexandria. Now serious scouring is threatening to breach the narrow strip of land that separates several freshwater lakes from the more saline Mediterranean. Such an occurrence would adversely affect the thriving fishing industry.

Practically all of the 60 million people of Egypt live in or along the narrow Nile Valley and the broad delta that fans out between Cairo and the Mediterranean Sea. Ninety-seven percent of Egypt is uninhabited desert. The Nile River divides into two branches a short distance north of Cairo. The eastern branch is called the Damietta and the western, the Rosetta. The famous Rosetta Stone that enabled archaeologists to decipher hieroglyphic writing was discovered along the Rosetta branch. Egypt can truly be said to be the "Gift of the Nile."—Harold E. Dregne

See also **AFRICA, DESERTS OF; DESERTIFICATION; DESERT PEOPLES; FLOOD; FLOODPLAIN; HYDROLOGICAL CYCLE; HYDROLOGY; MIDDLE EAST, DESERTS OF; RIVERS; RUNOFF; SAHARA DESERT; WATER**

Further Reading

Brander, B. 1966. *The River Nile*. Washington, D.C.: National Geographic Society.

NITROGEN-FIXING PLANTS

Plants that live mutualistically with bacteria that are capable of converting atmospheric nitrogen (N_2), which cannot be used by plants, to ammonia (NH_3), which can. The most thoroughly studied example is the relationship between members of the legume family and *Rhizobium*. However, other plant groups also gain from an association with nitrogen-fixing bacteria. The bacteria occur in nodules, which form on the roots following invasion by the microbes. Nitrogen-fixing bacteria may also exist in specialized regions of leaves or be associated with plants in the soil or water.

Nitrogen-fixing bacteria are scattered throughout the bacterial kingdom, but many are cyanobacteria (blue-green bacteria). Nitrogen fixation in the bluegreen bacteria occurs in heterocysts, which are specialized cells in the cyanobacteria filaments. Cyanobacteria are facultative nitrogen fixers. Thus when nitrogen is in good supply they do not produce the specialized nitrogen-fixing cells, but if ambient nitrogen levels are low, then heterocysts are formed. The remaining nitrogen-fixing bacteria are anaerobic (living in the absence of free oxygen). Bacteria gain energy in the form of ATP when they convert nitrogen to ammonia.

$$N_2 \rightarrow NH_3$$

Other soil bacteria convert NH_3 to nitrites and nitrates, which are the primary sources of nitrogen for many plant groups.

In cultivated ecosystems, nitrogen is often depleted from the soil, but planting legumes can replenish it.—James R. Estes

See also **BACTERIA; LEGUMES; PLANT ADAPTATIONS; PLANTS**

Further Reading

Rost, T. L., M. G. Barbour, R. M. Thornton, T. E. Weier, and C. R. Stocking. 1984. *Botany*. 2d ed. New York: Wiley.

NOCTURNAL

Refers to an animal's activity period that occurs during the night, or to an animal that is active at night. Thus an animal that exhibits a nocturnal period of activity is a nocturnal animal. Animals active during the day are diurnal; those active at dawn or dusk are crepuscular. Most animals have a daily activity cycle. Differences in time of activity among ecologically similar animals are thought to have the effect of reducing resource competition, but only if the resources are available at different times. In deserts many animals are nocturnal so as to conserve water, cope with the heat, and take advantage of the dew and fog that may condense on plants and plant parts. Examples of animal pairs with different times of activities are hawks and owls, swallows and bats, and grasshoppers and crickets.—Janet K. Braun

See also **ACTIVITY CYCLES, ANIMALS; ANIMAL ADAPTATIONS; BURROWING ANIMALS; CREPUSCULAR; NICHE; WATER BALANCE**

NOMADS. *See* DESERT PEOPLES

NULLARBOR PLAIN. *See* AUSTRALIA, DESERTS OF

NUTRIENTS

Essential elements required for normal development of plants that are obtained principally from the soil and must be available not only in sufficient quantity but also in a form that permits them to be absorbed by the plants. Nutrients are transferred from plants to animals, often in the same form in which they were taken up by the plants but sometimes in different form after being involved in plant metabolic pathways. In general, depending on the quantities required by the plants, nutrients are classified as macronutrients (required in large quantities) and micronutrients (required only in traces). The essential macronutrient minerals are nitrogen, which makes up plant proteins, chlorophyll, and nucleic acids; phosphorus, important in the transportation of energy and protein structure, nucleic acids, and metabolic substrates; potassium, which functions in photosynthesis and protein synthesis; calcium, a component of cell walls and other structures; magnesium, a component of chlorophyll and an enzyme activator; and sulfur, a component of proteins. The most important micronutrients are boron, which plays a role in metabolism; iron, used in chlorophyll synthesis; manganese, which controls some of the oxidative reduction processes of the cell; copper and zinc, which are involved in enzyme structure; molybdenum and cobalt, which help to fix nitrogen; and chlorine, used in photosynthesis. Without proper nutrients, both plants and animals die.—Alberto I. J. Vich and Juana Susana Barroso

See also **DECOMPOSITION; MINERALS; PHOTOSYNTHESIS; PLANT ADAPTATIONS; PLANTS; PRIMARY PRODUCTIVITY; ROOTS; SOILS, DESERT**

Further Reading

Baber, S. A. 1984. *Soil Nutrient Bioavailability: A Mechanistic Approach.* New York: Wiley.

Buckman, H. O. 1968. *The Nature and Properties of Soils: A College Text of Edaphology.* New York: Macmillan.

Foth, H. D. 1984. *Fundamentals of Soil Science.* New York: Wiley.

Walter, H. and E. Stadelmann. 1974. A new approach to the water relations of desert plants. *In* G. W. Brown Jr., ed., *Desert Biology: Special Topics on the Physical and Biological Aspects of Arid Regions,* 2:213–310. New York: Academic Press.

NYALA

Antelope of the species *Tragelaphus angasi* (mammalian family Bovidae, order Artiodactyla) that is closely related to kudu but has a much more limited distribution. Nyalas are restricted to the southeastern corner of the African continent, from Malawi and Zimbabwe through Mozambique and eastern South Africa;. They are not found in xeric deserts but occur in plains and hills and in dry savannas, primarily in dense woody thickets near water. They are large-bodied antelopes that can weigh as much as 280 kilograms. The coat of males is a purplish dark brown. Thin whitish stripes (8–13 in number), which extend down the sides of the body, are present in both sexes; however, they may be reduced or absent in older males. Females are browner and smaller than males. Males have horns that are curved (1.5–2.5 twists) and may reach more than 800 millimeters. Females lack horns. There are other significant differences between the sexes, including the presence of a heavy whitish mane on the neck (dorsal and ventral), back, stomach, and haunches of the male. The female lacks this pronounced fringe of hair.

Nyalas are browsers and will stand on their hind legs to reach higher foliage. When disturbed they will give a barking call as an alarm signal. They have been observed to be both solitary and gregarious in small groups. Groups are generally composed of females; the males tend to be solitary. During the mating season the older males will attempt to join the female groups. Females give birth to a single calf.

Leopards are the most important predator of nyalas. The males are known to be aggressive and will attempt to fight if cornered or wounded. Nyalas are protected in several parks, and their numbers appear to be stable.—Thomas E. Lacher, Jr.

See also **AFRICA, DESERTS OF; AN INTRODUCTION TO DESERTS; ANTELOPE; HERBIVORES; KUDU;**

MAMMALS; SOUTH AFRICA, DESERTS OF; UNGU-
LATES; XEROPHYLLOUS FOREST

Further Reading

Dorst, J., and P. Dandelot. 1980. *A Field Guide to the Larger Mammals of Africa*. London: Collins.

Estes, R. D. 1991. *The Behavior Guide to African Mammals*. Berkeley: University of California Press.

Goss, R. 1986. *Maberly's Mammals of Southern Africa: A Popular Field Guide*. Craighall, South Africa: Delta.

Haltenorth, T., and H. Diller. 1980. *A Field Guide to the Mammals of Africa, Including Madagascar*. London: Collins.

Nowak, R. M. 1991. *Walker's Mammals of the World*. 5th ed. Baltimore: Johns Hopkins University Press.

O

OASIS. *See* WATER HOLE

OCEAN CURRENTS

Patterns of water circulation within the ocean. Gravity, wind, and Coriolis forces can cause ocean currents. An individual current cell is called a gyre.

Gravity acts on water masses of different densities and is primarily responsible for currents in a vertical plane. The density of a water mass is dependent on its temperature and salinity. Water reaches maximum density relative to temperature at 4°C. High concentrations of salt in water also increase its density. If a dense water mass occurs over a low-density water mass, it will sink, and the low-density water mass will rise, causing a vertical circulation of water. Vertical circulation of water can be important in the movement of nutrients from deep to shallow water.

Wind blowing on the surface of the ocean, particularly prevailing winds, can generate ocean currents. Ocean currents caused by wind friction are most often in a horizontal direction, but wind can also cool surface water, causing its density to increase and develop a vertical circulation.

The Coriolis effect causes most of the large horizontal currents in oceans. Horizontal ocean currents moving from deep ocean and up onto the continental shelf can often cause an upwelling of cold nutrient-rich water from ocean depths near the coasts. These rich waters support dense populations of plankton, microscopic plants and animals that form the base of many oceanic food chains.

The temperature of horizontal ocean currents depends on the temperature of the region in which the current originates. Currents originating in the tropics are typically warm, whereas those originating at high latitudes are cold. Because increased temperature increases evaporation, warm currents are considered moist currents, and cool currents are dry.

Coastal deserts are associated with cool ocean currents. The temperature of the current causes the air above the current to be cool and relatively dry, providing little precipitation along the coast. The cool temperature over the water often causes the formation of morning fog in coastal deserts. Because cold water can hold more oxygen, and is often associated with coastal upwellings, increased nutrient levels, and high plankton density, many cool current deserts are adjacent to some of the world's finest and most important fishing areas.—Rob Channell

See also **AN INTRODUCTION TO DESERTS; ATACAMA DESERT; BAJA CALIFORNIA, DESERTS OF; BENGUELA CURRENT; CHILE, DESERTS OF; CLIMATE; EL NIÑO; FOG DESERT; HUMBOLDT CURRENT; NAMIBIA, DESERTS OF; PERU, DESERTS OF; SECHURA DESERT; SOUTH AFRICA, DESERTS OF**

Further Reading

Neumann, G. 1968. *Ocean Currents*. Amsterdam: Elsevier.

OCOTILLO

Large shrub (*Fouquieria splendens*) in the boojum family Fouquieriaceae with many long, slender, spiny, unbranched stems radiating from the base. Ocotillos exhibit an unusual growth form and have beautiful displays of bright red flowers near the branch tips during the spring and following summer rains. They are one of the characteristic species of both the Sonoran and Chihuahuan deserts but also extend into the eastern Mojave Desert, desert grassland, and oak woodland. A closely related species, the tree ocotillo (*Fouquieria macdougalii*), occurs in the Sonoran Desert in Mexico.

Ocotillos are drought tolerant. The roots are shallow and wide spreading, allowing these plants to respond quickly to rainfall. The shrubs are leafless much of the year but may produce new leaves within days after rains, up to seven times per year. The leaves, which are not particularly adapted to prevent water loss, are then dropped as the soil dries. The petioles left on the stems after the leaves drop become stout spines. The stems have a hardened surface, with resins, gum, and wax in the bark, but plants can absorb water from the surface of the buds. The tubular red flowers are visited by hummingbirds and bees.

Ocotillo (*Fouquieria splendens*) near Red Rock, New Mexico. (Photo: D. Beck)

Ocotillos are common on the shallow soils (especially limestone-derived soils) of rocky slopes but also grow on gravelly or sandy plains and mesas. They occur at elevations up to 2,100 meters.

Cuttings from ocotillos are used to construct living fences. The flowers and seeds are eaten by Indians. Concoctions from the roots and flowers are used to treat coughing, inflammation, hemorrhoids, and fatigue.—Kristina A. Ernest

See also **ARIZONA DESERT; BAJA CALIFORNIA, DESERTS OF; BOOJUM; CALIFORNIA, DESERTS OF; LEAVES; MEXICO, DESERTS OF; PLANT ADAPTATIONS; PLANTS; SONORAN DESERT**

Further Reading

Benson, L., and R. A. Darrow. 1981. *Trees and Shrubs of the Southwestern Deserts*. Tucson: University of Arizona Press.

Shreve, F., and I. L. Wiggins. 1964. *Vegetation and Flora of the Sonoran Desert*. Vols. 1 and 2. Stanford: Stanford University Press.

OFF-ROAD VEHICLES

All means of motorized transportation that allow the user to leave paved or prepared road beds and enter roadless areas. Off-road vehicles (ORVs) include trail or dirt bikes, dune buggies, four-wheel-drive jeeps and trucks, all-terrain vehicles, swamp buggies, air boats, and other miscellaneous modes of transportation.

The use of off-road vehicles was quite limited in the United States until the 1960s. Their use began to grow dramatically in the 1970s and 1980s, and in 1972 President Richard Nixon signed Executive Order 11644 to control the use of off-road vehicles on public lands. A number of major concerns were expressed in the executive order. Use was restricted to minimize the damage to soils, watersheds, vegetation, and other resources on the public lands. Use was also regulated to minimize the disturbance of wildlife and wildlife habitats. Finally, regulations were imposed to reduce conflicts between the users of off-road vehicles and other recreational users of the public lands, such as campers, hikers, and persons engaged in fishing and hunting. A second executive order was signed by President Jimmy Carter in 1977 which gave agency personnel the authority to close areas to ORV use when adverse effects had been demonstrated.

Arid habitats have received a disproportionate use by operators of off-road vehicles, partly because of the ease of riding in sparsely vegetated regions. The vehicles most heavily used in deserts are trail or dirt bikes and dune buggies. In both cases the damage produced is similar. There is direct damage to the vegetation caused by vehicles passing over and through fragile desert plants. Another major concern is the alteration of the soil. Direct soil damage includes the disruption of the soil surface and the compaction of the soil. These effects can lead to increased levels of wind and water erosion, loss of soil organic material, increased runoff, and a reduction in the ability of water to penetrate the soil. This soil damage also indirectly affects the vegetation by decreasing the amount of available organic material, reducing the availability of water in the soil, and inhibiting the germination and growth of new seedlings.

Less is known about the effects on desert animals. There will be some direct mortality as a result of vehicles passing over small vertebrates in or on the sand. Another concern is the effect of high noise levels on the behavior of mammals, reptiles, and amphibians. Studies have demonstrated a significant impact of ORV noise on the hearing acuity of Mojave fringe-toed lizards (*Uma scoparia*) and desert kangaroo rats (*Dipodomys deserti*). The reduction in hearing acuity was severe enough to reduce the ability of these animals to find food or avoid predators.

The potential and real impacts of off-road vehicles have resulted in increased management of the public lands for multiple uses, with pressure to have ORV users bear the cost of their activities. Other regulations include having proper mufflers to prevent excessive noise. In addition, many desert areas that have been heavily damaged by vehicle use have been, or are in the process of being, restored.—Thomas E. Lacher, Jr.

See also **ARABIAN GULF, DESERTS OF; BIOSPHERE RESERVE; CONSERVATION IN DESERTS; CONTAMINATION; DESERTIFICATION; DUNES; ECOLOGY; MIDDLE EAST, DESERTS OF; POLLUTION**

Further Reading

Andrews, R. N. L., and P. F. Nowak, eds. 1980. *Off-Road Vehicle Use: A Management Challenge*. Washington, D.C.: Office of Environmental Quality, U.S. Department of Agriculture.

Heath, R. 1974. *The Environmental Consequences of the Off-Road Vehicle: With Profiles of the Industry and the Enthusiast*. Washington, D.C.: Defenders of Wildlife.

Webb, R. H., and H. G. Wilshire, eds. 1983. *Environmental Effects of Off-Road Vehicles: Impacts and Management in Arid Regions*. New York: Springer.

OIL IN DESERTS. *See* ARABIAN GULF, DESERTS OF

OLIGOCENE

Geologic epoch spanning the time from 34 million years ago to about 24 million years ago. Tectonically, the American continents were moving westward; South America was isolated, and North America was connected to Asia but separated from Europe. Africa (including the present Arabian Peninsula) was rotating slightly and moving northward, closing off the eastern portion of the ancient Tethys Sea. The Indian subcontinent, separate from Africa, had closed the easternmost portion of Tethys and contacted southern Asia. India's continued subduction beneath Asia began uplifting the region that would become the Himalayas during the Neogene. Australia, which exited Gondwana by splitting from Antarctica in the Eocene, continued moving northward.

Prior to the Oligocene the Scotia Arc (connecting the southern Andes and the Antarctic Peninsula) diverted cooler high-latitude waters near Antarctica and allowed them to mix with warmer, lower-latitude waters. The Oligocene opening up of the Drake Passage between South America and Antarctica and the widening separation of Australia and Antarctica allowed cold water circulation around Antarctica that isolated it and led to its more extensive glaciation (than in the Eocene) and an attendant drop in global sea level. However, a cool-temperate flora of low species diversity still grew on some parts of Antarctica throughout the Oligocene. Australian Oligocene plant assemblages also reflect cool-temperate conditions, including plants indicative of greater seasonality; parts of the continent underwent increasing drying that gave a more open aspect to the forests. This sort of development of semiarid habitats probably also occurred in South America, based on the fossil record there of mammals adapted to grazing on coarse vegetation.

In the Northern Hemisphere the Arctic region remained free of ice, but the global cooling trend caused plant zones to shift such that the warmer and more mesic-adapted ones narrowed and moved to lower latitudes and were replaced at high latitudes by cool-temperate forests. Increasing aridity in the rain shadow of the Rocky Mountains in central North America resulted in changes from the forests of the Eocene to dry woodland, wooded shrubland with gallery forest, and even open scrubland or possibly grassland with gallery woodland by the middle Oligocene. In Asia Eocene forests were replaced with Oligocene woody savanna in Kazakhstan; but in China the deserts of the northwest were replaced by woody savanna.—Nicholas J. Czaplewski

See also **AN INTRODUCTION TO DESERTS; CENOZOIC; CRETACEOUS; DESERTS; EOCENE; FOSSILS; GLACIAL PERIODS; MADRO-TERTIARY GEOFLORA; MIOCENE; PALEOCENE; PALEOCLIMATE; PERMIAN; PLATE TECTONICS; PLEISTOCENE; PLIOCENE; PRECAMBRIAN; QUATERNARY; RECENT (HOLOCENE); TERTIARY**

Further Reading

Barker, W. R., and P. J. M. Greenslade. 1982. *Evolution*

of the Flora and Fauna of Arid Australia. Adelaide: Peacock.

Frakes, L. A., J. E. Francis, and J. I. Syktus, eds. 1992. *Climate Modes of the Phanerozoic: The History of the Earth's Climate over the Past 600 Million Years.* Cambridge: Cambridge University Press.

Pascual, R., and E. Ortiz Jaureguizar. 1990. Evolving climates and mammal faunas in Cenozoic South America. *In* J. G. Fleagle and A. L. Rosenberger, eds., *The Platyrrhine Fossil Record*, 23–60. London: Academic Press.

Prothero, D. R., and W. A. Berggren, eds. 1992. *Eocene-Oligocene Climatic and Biotic Evolution.* Princeton: Princeton University Press.

Wolfe, J. A. 1978. A paleobotanical interpretation of Tertiary climates in the Northern Hemisphere. *American Scientist* 66:694–703.

OMNIVORY

Feeding relationship in which an organism (animal) consumes a wide range of food types; usually refers to consumption of both plants and animals. Omnivores are food generalists;: they often have unspecialized morphology and physiology as well as generalized dietary preferences. Omnivory occurs in all types of environments but seems to be particularly common in desert systems. Some desert animals eat mainly other animals (insects and vertebrates) but consume plant materials as a source of water. Others eat mainly seeds or vegetation but eat insects as a source of protein. In some beetles, flies, and wasps, adults feed on plants while immature stages are predaceous on other insects.

An important advantage of omnivory in deserts is that in times of food scarcity the diet can be broadened, or another type of food can serve as a substitute for the more usual dietary items. In fact, omnivory can result when organisms consume the most abundant food source available. Many species we call omnivores have more restricted diets within seasons but switch food types seasonally as the availability of foods changes. One of the consequences of more frequent omnivory in desert communities is that food webs are highly interconnected, with many direct and indirect links among organisms and trophic levels. This makes the desert ecosystem a very complex and highly interrelated system. This is unusual in that deserts, which are in fact highly complex, are often thought to be simple systems.

There are a variety of omnivorous desert organisms, including insects (e.g., cockroaches, many ants), a few reptiles (e.g., collared lizards), and birds (e.g., ravens). Among the most conspicuous are the mammalian omnivores, especially rodents. The diets of desert mice (deer mice and harvest mice in North America; *Eligmodontia* and *Phyllotis* in South America) may include equal parts of insects and plants (seeds and green vegetation). Ground squirrels eat a broad range of plant materials (seeds, fruits, green vegetation), insects, small vertebrates, and carrion. Many mammals that are classified as carnivores are actually omnivorous. Coyotes are dietary generalists, feeding on vertebrates, insects, fruits, and green vegetation. Some fox species and skunks have similarly mixed diets. Jackals are typically scavengers but also consume crop plants like sugarcane and corn. Some armadillos eat vegetation and fruit as well as insects, small vertebrates, and carrion. Two desert-dwelling primates; are omnivores: humans and the baboon, which feeds on leaves, flowers, fruits, grass seeds, locusts, and perhaps carrion.—Kristina A. Ernest

See also **ANIMAL ADAPTATIONS; ARMADILLO; BABOON; CARNIVORES; CARRION EATERS; COYOTE; CROW; DIET; ECOLOGY; ENERGY FLOW; HERBIVORY; INSECTS; JACKAL; MAMMALS; MONKEYS IN DESERTS; NICHE; PRIMARY PRODUCTIVITY; RODENTS; SQUIRREL**

Further Reading

Polis, G. A., ed. 1991. *The Ecology of Desert Communities.* Tucson: University of Arizona Press.

O'ODHAM

Desert farmers of southern Arizona, known to non-Indians as Pima and Papago, and also known as Pima Alto, to distinguish them from the Pima Bajo, closely related peoples in the sierras of eastern Sonora. The first Europeans to encounter the O'odham were members of Coronado's expedition in 1540. Later they became known through the Jesuit priest Eusebio Kino, who established many missions in their country between 1687 and 1711. Originally they were found in the Sonoran Desert in what is now north central Sonora and south central Arizona.

Father Kino recognized five divisions of Pima: those whom he called Pimas, in the Rio San Miguel and upper Rio Sonora valleys in Sonora, Mexico; the Sobas, in the Rio Magdelena and Rio Altar valleys of north central Sonora; the Sobaipuris in the Rio San Pedro and Rio Santa Cruz valleys of southern Arizona; the Gileños, on the south banks of the Gila River in central Arizona; and the Papagos and Sand Papagos, in the desert lands west of the Rio Santa Cruz and extending into extreme northwestern Sonora.

After the U.S. war with Mexico and the subsequent Gadsden Purchase, which established the present border with Mexico, relations between the O'odham and Mexicans deteriorated, and many Pimas and Sobas moved north to join the Papago, with whom they are now identified. In the 19th century Apache raids forced the Sobaipuris to abandon the San Pedro and Santa Cruz valleys and join the Gileños on the Gila River, and, with the Gileños, they make up the present population of the Gila River Reservation. Today the few O'odhams remaining in Sonora have been completely Hispanicized and are no longer recognizable as anything but Mexican.

The Sand Papagos, also known as the Areneños, were found in the extreme northwestern portion of Sonora and southwestern Arizona, in the vicinity of the Cerro Pinacate in the Altar Desert, a subdivision of the Sonoran Desert. The Altar Desert is extremely barren and dry. It has the distinction of having what may be the highest officially recorded temperature in the world, in San Luis, Sonora, 58°C (136.4°F) in the shade, on 11 August 1933. The Sand Papagos, who never numbered more than a few hundred, were living in a desolate area that neither Spanish nor Americans wanted and hence were left alone to follow their meager hunting-gathering way of life until late in the 19th century, when the few remaining are reported to have all died from an epidemic disease.

Geographically, the area occupied by the O'odham is known as the Pimeria, which includes the entire area; that part of it occupied by the Papago is known as the Papagueria. Today the Papago occupy three reservations that were originally created by executive order and later enlarged by acts of Congress. The largest of these is the Sells Reservation, west of the Rio Santa Cruz and Tucson, with 1,122,772 hectares, all tribally owned. Close to Tucson is the San Xavier Reservation of 28,815 hectares, which was allotted in 1890. The Gila Bend Reservation, on the Gila River, has 4,213 hectares that are tribally owned.

The combined Sobaipuri and Gileños, who can no longer be distinguished and are collectively the Pima, are found on the Gila River Reservation, all that remains to them after Euro-Americans began settling the Gila and Salt River valleys in the mid-18th century and expropriated much of the land and water. The Gila River Reservation consists of 58,681 hectares on both sides of the Gila River, extending from near Coolidge, Arizona, downstream to the junction with the Salt River.

The O'odham are generally considered to be the descendants of the prehistoric Hohokam who occupied south central Arizona and practiced irrigation agriculture. However, this connection has never been established archaeologically with certainty, and is based primarily on superficial similarities in certain crafts, such as pottery, and the fact that the Pimas in Arizona were said to be practicing irrigation agriculture in the same geographic area when first contacted by Spanish explorers.

Another way in which the O'odham have been described is as the no-village, two-village, and one-village Pimas. The no-village Pimas would be the Sand Papago in the extreme southwestern portion of the Pimeria, in a desolate zone lacking water or substantial vegetation. Lacking sufficient water or fertile soil, the Sand Papago relied on hunting-gathering and had no permanent habitations. The most complex structures attributed to them are simple circles of rocks erected as windbreaks, sometimes referred to as sleeping circles.

The one-village are the riverine Pimas who practiced irrigation agriculture in the middle Gila and Salt River valleys. They inhabited villages consisting of an aggregation of post and thatch houses, ramadas, and brush shelters scattered throughout the community, interspersed with unclaimed land in no formal arrangement. Each village had a single public structure, a round post and thatch house and ramada, which served as a council meeting place and as the locale for some ritual occasions.

Indigenous irrigation technology consisted of run-of-the-river irrigation. A headgate was constructed on the river far enough upstream so that the intended farmland would be at a lower elevation. Ditches were dug directly from the river, following the contour with a gradual slope as the ditch was carried farther and farther from the river until the fields were reached. Indigenously, such ditches were hand dug, using a digging stick and baskets, and as they had to begin several miles upstream from the cultivated fields, they must have been community projects, which would have required some type of formal organization.

Given the warm climate and long growing season, two crops per year were possible. Between May and March the irrigation canals filled with the melting of the snowpack in the mountainous watershed, and the first crop was planted in mid-March. By mid-June the first crop could be harvested. About this time the saguaro cactus fruit ripened and was harvested, much of it to make a wine that figured in some public rituals. In mid-July a second crop was planted as the irrigation canals filled with summer storm waters of the Gila River. In September the mesquite beans were harvested, and in late October the second agricultural crop was harvested.

In addition to agriculture, the Pima continued to rely heavily on wild resources. As with most desert peoples, the Pimas were experts on botanical resources and gathered a wide variety of seeds, cactus fruits, herbs, and succulents. It has been said that 600 Papago could live where 60 Anglos would starve. The riverine Pima gained approximately 50–60 percent of their subsistence from agriculture and the remainder from wild resources. In contrast, the Papago relied on agriculture for only 20 percent of their subsistence.

The continued reliance on wild resources in spite of their practicing of irrigation agriculture was an important feature of Pima adaptation. A failure in the irrigation system was always a possibility. Heavy winter snows in the mountain watershed and an early warm spell could cause flooding downstream, ripping out floodgates and also causing erosion of the riverbed, lowering the water level to below the headgates. This would necessitate extending the canal farther upstream and constructing a new headgate, but such work would take time. Conversely, insufficient runoff in the spring could result in low water, again leaving the headgates high and dry. Summer rains in desert areas are highly variable, and a dry summer could result in low water or none at all in the irrigation ditches.

But while variable precipitation patterns could cause a failure in the irrigation system, they could also render the system unnecessary. According to 17th-century Spanish accounts, the Gileños practiced floodwater farming on the Gila and had no need for ditch irrigation. Subsequent studies indicate that the 17th-century rainfall was above normal.

The Pima are known to have cultivated corn, beans, squash, and cotton. Their corn, of which there were three colors, white, yellow, and blue, had small ears that matured early, an advantage in an environment with an uncertain water supply. They obtained 4–5 bushels per hectare. The cotton raised by the Pima, known as pima cotton, is a very fine, long staple variety of such good quality that it has replaced other varieties as a major cotton crop around the world. While there were no community fields, families worked reciprocally. Clearing ground, planting, cultivating, and irrigation were men's work; harvesting was women's work.

Father Kino introduced wheat, chickpeas, lentils, cowpeas, cabbage, lettuce, onions, leeks, garlic, anise, pepper, mustard, mint, melons, watermelons, cane, grapevines, plums, pomegranates, and figs and a variety of domesticated livestock, including cattle, oxen, horses, mules, burros, goats, sheep, and chickens. As a result when the Americans began to cross the continent on their way to California during the gold rush, they found Pima villages and well-ordered productive farms with bountiful harvests, and the Pimas became known as suppliers of desert travelers. The main route of travel to California and the first stage lines went across southern Arizona specifically to take advantage of the supplies that could be had in the Pimeria.

The two-village O'odham are the Papago. The Papagueria lacks flowing streams, and water came from springs, tinajas (pools in natural rock basins), and runoff from the summer rains. Consequently the Papago relied much more on wild resources, and only about 20 percent of their subsistence came from agriculture. During the summer they inhabited villages near their fields and broke up into family groups to winter in the mountains. Their agricultural techniques included various devices for concentrating runoff water to their fields, such as rock alignments across hill slopes, check dams across arroyos, and a practice called akchin field farming after the Papago village of Ak Chin. This consists of locating a cultivated field at the mouth of an arroyo where it will be watered by runoff from rains upstream. The system is based on the fact that there is a low probability of rain falling on any one spot but a good probability that it will fall somewhere in the total drainage area of an arroyo and that water will eventually be concentrated at the arroyo's mouth. During extremely dry years the Papago left the area entirely, and different families went to different refuge areas where they lived with relatives or worked for other Piman farmers. Areas of refuge are the Casa Grande Valley to the north, in riverine Pima territory; Gila Bend to the northeast, where the Maricopa are to be found; the Altar Valley and the Sonoita River Valley to the south and southwest, which are no longer viable alternatives, since they are across the international border.

Much of O'odham native culture has been lost over the 400-plus years that elapsed between the earliest Spanish contact and the careful observation of Pima culture. Hence our knowledge of Pima social organization and ceremonialism is meager and often contradictory. For example, the Pimas are reported to have a moiety, wherein the society is divided into two parts, or units, called moieties, and everyone in the society belongs to one or the other. Moieties have various functions; sometimes they are economic, sometimes ritual, sometimes political, and so forth. Among the Tanoan Pueblos in New Mexico moieties have political and religious functions; among some Indian groups in South America moieties function solely in death rituals, the members of one moiety being responsible for the burial arrangements of members of the opposite moiety. Moieties exist among the O'odham, but they no longer have any function. Because much of O'odham ritual culture has been lost, we do not know the functions of their moieties, but they seem to be remnants of former social organization. organization, but it seems to have no real function, and a patrilineal clan system, but again with no real functions.

When first encountered by Anglo-Americans, the O'odham in the Gila and Salt River valleys were prosperous farmers able to supply Euro-American immigrants and military personnel alike. They are famous, among other things, for having supplied the Mormon Battalion on its way to California. Unfortunately, with white settlement in the Gila and Salt River valleys, the Pima lands were largely expropriated, along with their water. The first canal built by whites on the Gila was in operation in 1867, and by 1887 the white settlers' canal used the entire flow of the Gila River, leaving the Pima lands dry. By the end of the 19th century the Pima were poverty stricken. Only recently has the future begun to

look much brighter for them. With the Central Arizona Project coming on line, bringing much-needed water from the Colorado River to central Arizona, the O'odham lands will again have an adequate supply, since the U.S. Supreme Court has ruled that Native American water rights will have priority in access to the water.—Richard A. Pailes

See also **APACHE; COCHISE; DESERT PEOPLES; GERONIMO; HOHOKAM; HOPI; NAVAJO (DINE'É); SAGUARO; SONORAN DESERT**

Further Reading

Ortiz, A., ed. 1983. *Handbook of North American Indians.* Vol. 10. Washington, D.C.: Smithsonian Institution Press.

Russell, F. 1908. *The Pima Indians.* 26th Annual Report of the Bureau of American Ethnology for the Years 1904–1905. Washington, D.C.

Warren, S. S. 1997. *Desert Dwellers: Native People of the American Southwest.* San Francisco: Chronicle Books.

OREGON DESERT

Southern portion of the state of Oregon; a starkly beautiful desert region that is considered the northernmost extension of the Great Basin Desert, America's only cold desert (some authors extend the Great Basin into the state of Washington). The Great Basin Physiographic Province extends from the Sierra Nevada on the west almost to the Rocky Mountains on the east and consists of a number of undrained basins separated by mountain ranges having a north-south orientation. The climate of the region is influenced by the rain shadow of the Sierra Nevada range, which intercepts much of the moisture-laden winds from the Pacific Ocean. This area has an average annual rainfall of 10–15 inches throughout most of the region, almost all of which comes in the winter in the form of rain or snow.

The vegetation of the Oregon Desert is composed principally of small shrubs, with scattered perennial grasses and other herbaceous plants occurring in the open spaces between the shrubs. In composition this desert is similar to that found in much of the Great Basin and is dominated by the ever-present big sagebrush (*Artemisia tridentata*). This important shrub species is found on well-drained gravelly soils and forms extensive and homogeneous stands over large areas.

In parts of southern Oregon there are spectacular cones of black or reddish volcanic cinders, extensive black lava flows, and upraised blocks of basalt. In the nutrient-rich soils formed by the disintegration of lavas in southern Idaho and eastern Oregon, the growth of the vegetation can be luxurious considering the aridity of the area.

Associated with the sagebrush are a variety of shrubs and grasses. Portions of the southern Oregon area are used extensively for sheep grazing, and the grasslands are often termed bunchgrass steppe or Palouse Prairie. The dominant grass species is bluebunch wheat grass (*Agropyron spicatum*). Cacti are a relatively unimportant feature of the Oregon Desert.

In south central and eastern Oregon there is a large area sometimes referred to as the Great Sandy Desert or the Harney High Desert. This is an area of picturesque buttes and mesas, few streams, and numerous undrained basins that alternate between shallow ephemeral lakes and white alkaline-encrusted playas.—Gary K. Hulett and Amanda Renner Charles

See also **AN INTRODUCTION TO DESERTS; DESERT GRASSLAND; DESERTS; GREAT BASIN DESERT; MONTANA DESERT; NEVADA DESERT; PLAYA; SAGEBRUSH; SALTBUSH; SEMIARID ZONES; UTAH DESERT; WASHINGTON DESERT**

Further Reading

Daubenmire, R. F. 1969. Ecological plant geography of the Pacific Northwest. *Madrono* 20:11–128.

Franklin, J. F., and C. T. Dyrness. 1973. *Natural Vegetation of Oregon and Washington.* USDA Forest Service General Technical Report. PNW-8. Pacific Northwest Forest and Range Experiment Station, Portland, Ore.

ORGAN PIPE CACTUS

Large cactus, *Stenocereus thurberi*, with many branches arising from the main plant and suggesting the appearance of organ pipes; common in Mexico, it only extends into the United States in southern Arizona. In 1937 the United States designated 133,925 hectares as the Organ Pipe National Monument to protect this unusual cactus. This species may also be found listed in the genera *Lemaireocereus* and *Cereus*.

The organ pipe cactus is one of the indicator cacti of the Sonoran Desert and is common on the southwestern slopes of desert mountains, at elevations from 1,000 to 3,000 feet, in south central Arizona, north central Sonora, and the southern one-third of Baja California, Mexico. The distribution of

Organ pipe cactus (*Cereus thurberi*) in the Arizona Sonoran Desert at Organ Pipe Cactus National Monument. (Photo: M. A. Mares)

this cactus is most likely limited by its sensitivity to frost, which may kill the tips of the branches, the portion of the cactus that experiences growth.

This cactus is a large cluster of branches and usually lacks a trunk. The branches, which are ribbed, can be 3–6.7 meters high and 13–20 centimeters in diameter. The clustered, ribbed branches emerge from a common base and may serve to channel rain to the plant's base, where large numbers of roots are located. Branches sometimes also have roots located farther up from the base; these branches may break off during storms and form new plants. The structure of the plant, with many branches emerging from a common base, may also increase the photosynthetic area of the plant, thereby increasing the energy level, promoting more active growth, and increasing the production of the juicy fruits, which have a high sugar content.

The greenish brown, greenish white, or pinkish purple flowers present from May to June bloom at night and close after sunrise. The flowers are located on the tips and sides of the branches. The juicy red fruits are covered with black spines, which are lost as the fruit matures. A candy, *dulce pitahaya*, is made from a combination of the fruits of the organ pipe cactus and the prickly pear cactus.—Janet K. Braun

See also **BAJA CALIFORNIA, DESERTS OF; CACTI; CACTUS, COLUMNAR; COLORADO DESERT; FRUITS; ORGAN PIPE CACTUS NATIONAL MONUMENT; SAGUARO; SONORAN DESERT; SUCCULENTS**

Further Reading

Crosswhite, F. S., and C. D. Crosswhite. 1982. The Sonoran Desert. *In* G. L. Bender, ed., *Reference Handbook on the Deserts of North America,* 163–319. Westport, Conn.: Greenwood.

Earle, W. H. 1966. Cacti of the Southwest. *Desert Botanical Garden of Arizona, Scientific Bulletin* 4:1–111.

Little, E. L. 1976. Southwestern trees: A guide to the native species of New Mexico and Arizona. *U.S. Department of Agriculture Handbook* 9:1–109.

ORGAN PIPE CACTUS NATIONAL MONUMENT

National monument established in 1937, located in southwestern Arizona and sharing its southern border with Mexico; the monument protects about 134,000 hectares of Sonoran Desert and is the third-largest national monument in the United States.

Organ Pipe Cactus National Monument is located in the Arizona Upland Division, or paloverde-cactus desert, of the Sonoran Desert. Much of the area consists of small granitic hills or volcanic mountains; there are no large areas of sand, although there are expansive arid valleys. Rain occurs during two periods, winter and summer, resulting in two blooms of annual plants.

One of the major features of the region is the organ pipe cactus, *Stenocereus thurberi*. Although many species of cacti are found in the monument, organ pipe cactus and senita (*Lophocereus schottii*) are more common in Mexico and extend into the United States only in the area of the monument. Other common plants are saguaro cactus (*Carnegiea gigantea*), prickly pear and cholla (*Opuntia*), agave, elephant tree (*Bursera microphylla*), paloverde (*Cercidium*), ironwood (*Olneya tesota*), and ocotillo (*Fouquieria splendens*).

The animals of the monument are typical of those that inhabit the Sonoran Desert, although many are rare or are transients from Mexico. Common mammals are antelope, ground, and rock squirrels; coyotes; kit and gray foxes; desert cottontails; antelope and black-tailed jackrabbits; spotted, striped, and hog-nosed skunks; collared peccaries; bighorn sheep; mule and white-tailed deer; pronghorns; bobcats; and woodrats. Some mammals that are rare or transient are: gray wolves, hooded skunks, pumas, jaguars, and coatis. Characteristic birds are Wied's crested flycatcher, Gila woodpecker, gilded flicker, cactus wren, Gambel's quail, and turkey vulture.—Janet K. Braun

See also **ARIZONA DESERT; CACTI; CACTUS, COLUMNAR; COLORADO DESERT; FRUITS; ORGAN PIPE CACTUS; SAGUARO; SONORAN DESERT; SUCCULENTS; UNITED STATES, DESERTS OF**

Further Reading

Crosswhite, F. S., and C. D. Crosswhite. 1982. The Sonoran Desert. *In* G. L. Bender, ed., *Reference Handbook on the Deserts of North America,* 163–319. Westport, Conn.: Greenwood.

MacMahon, J. A. 1985. *Deserts.* New York: Knopf.

ORIOLES

Two evolutionarily distinct groups of moderate-sized perching birds (order Passeriformes), including the Old World orioles (family Oriolidae), which are not explicitly associated with arid habitats and the New World orioles (family Emberizidae, subfamily Icterinae), which consist of 25 species in the genus *Icterus*. Although distributed throughout a variety of environments in North and South America, many New World orioles are found in arid and semiarid habitats. For example, Scott's oriole (*Icterus parisorum*) occurs in dry woodland, arid oak scrub, and pinyon-juniper woodlands of the southwestern United States and Mexico. Another example of a desert-dwelling species is the white-edged oriole (*Icterus graceannae*); it is found in desert scrub and mesquite woodlands of westcentral South America at altitudes below 1,500 meters.

New World orioles are slender of body with long tails, ranging in total length from approximately 17 to 23 centimeters. Plumage coloration basically consists of orange or yellow and black. Sexes may exhibit plumage dimorphism (temperate species) or may be similar. Bills are relatively long and pointed. New World orioles are primarily insectivorous, but the diet may include fruit and nectar in some species.

The distinctive nests of orioles are elongated structures woven of fine twigs and grass, with an entrance at the top. The nests are suspended from the tips of branches, often high up in trees. The breeding system is described as monogamous for those species that have been investigated. Clutch size usually varies from two to five. Incubation periods are from 12 to 15 days, and these duties are undertaken by the female. Both sexes participate in feeding of the nestlings.—Stephen C. Lougheed

See also **ANIMAL ADAPTATIONS; BIRDS; NESTS, BIRD; DESERTS; MEXICO, DESERTS OF; SOUTH AMERICA, DESERTS OF; UNITED STATES, DESERTS OF**

Further Reading

Bent, A. C. 1958. Life histories of North American blackbirds, orioles, tanagers, and allies. *U.S. National Museum Bulletin* 211.

Oberholser, H. C. 1974. *The Bird Life of Texas*. Austin: University of Texas Press.

Orians, G. H. 1985. *Blackbirds of the Americas*. Seattle: University of Washington Press.

Pleasants, B. Y. 1993. Altamira oriole (*Icterus gularis*). *In* A. Poole and F. Gill, eds., *The Birds of North America*, No. 56. Philadelphia: Academy of Natural Sciences; Washington, D.C.: American Ornithologists' Union.

Skutch, A. F. 1960. *Life Histories of Central American Birds*. Vol. 2. Pacific Coast Avifuana No. 34. Berkeley: Cooper Ornithological Society.

ORYX

Genus (*Oryx*) consisting of three species of antelopes (mammalian family Bovidae, order Artiodactyla) indigenous to Africa and the Arabian Peninsula. Oryxes are large antelopes with lightly colored bodies and dark brown or black markings on the head and chest. The closely related members of this genus are characterized by the obvious muscle mass over their shoulders, short mane, long horns, and large hooves. The large hooves are an adaptation allowing them to walk easily over sand. Males and females are hard to distinguish by size, color, or shape and size of horns.

All oryxes use their horns to defend their food or water resources, and the males use them to establish dominance through fights with other males. Most fighting does not cause bloodshed, however.

Oryxes can survive for prolonged periods without having to drink water, but they drink regularly when water is available. During dry periods oryxes will dig into dried riverbeds with their hooves to reach groundwater. To conserve water oryxes can withstand increases in their body temperature while differentially cooling the blood that flows to the brain, thereby reducing the need for perspiring in order to cool the body. Oryxes eat grass, herbaceous plants, and occasional fruits or tuberous roots.

Herds consisting of both males and females can number up to 100 animals. All the breeding in a herd is done by the dominant male. A single calf is born after a gestation period of 8–10 months. The calf hides away from the herd until it is weaned at 14 weeks. Juveniles reach sexual maturity in two years.

The endangered scimitar-horned oryx (*Oryx dammah*) once inhabited most of North Africa, but is now extinct north of the Sahara. The scimitar-shaped horns of this species distinguish it from the two other straight-horned species. The distribution of the gemsbok (*Oryx gazella*) covers most of southern Africa. This species is found in several national parks in Africa and is the most numerous of the three oryxes. The Arabian oryx (*Oryx leucoryx*), the smallest of the oryxes, originally occupied the Arabian and Sinai peninsulas. Hunting from vehicles and long-range rifles drove this species to extinction in the wild, but it was preserved in zoos and private collections. Despite being reintroduced in Oman, this species is listed as endangered.—Rob Channell

See also **ANIMAL ADAPTATIONS; ANTELOPE; COUNTERCURRENT HEAT EXCHANGE; ENDOTHERMY; GEMSBOK; HEAT BALANCE; HEAT STRESS; HERBIVORY; KALAHARI DESERT; KAROO; MAMMALS; NAMIBIA, DESERTS OF; SAVANNA; SOUTH AFRICA, DESERTS OF; UNGULATES; WATER BALANCE**

Further Reading

Alden, P. C., R. D. Estes, D. Schlitter, and B. McBride. 1995. *National Audubon Society Field Guide to African Wildlife*. New York: Knopf.

Estes, R. D. 1991. *The Behavior Guide to African Mammals*. Berkeley: University of California Press.

Nowak, R. M. 1991. *Walker's Mammals of the World*. 5th ed. Baltimore: Johns Hopkins University Press.

Price, M. R. S. 1989. *Animal Reintroductions: The Arabian Oryx in Oman*. Cambridge: Cambridge University Press.

OSMOTIC POTENTIAL

Fraction of water potential that originates from the presence of solutes in the soil. Dissolved salts in soil water affect its thermodynamic properties and reduce its energy level; in particular, solutes decrease the vapor pressure of water at the interface of liquid and air which modifies the surface tension of water. For example, if a semipermeable membrane is placed between pure water (water lacking dissolved salts) and water containing solutes, molecules will move from the pure-water side to the water that contains the solutes, indicating that work is being performed in transporting the molecules across the membrane. This indicates a greater water potential in the water that contains the solutes. The osmotic potential is important in the movement of water from the soil into the roots of plants. It also influences the movement of vapor from water in the soil. It does not, however, have a great effect on the movement of water in the liquid state from one point to another in the soil, because the dissolved salts move with the water in its liquid phase.—Alberto I. J. Vich and Juana Susana Barroso

See also **FIELD CAPACITY OF SOILS; SOILS, DESERT; WATER**

Further Reading

Fuller, W. H. 1974. Desert soils. *In* G. W. Brown Jr., ed., *Desert Biology: Special Topics on the Physical and Biological Aspects of Arid Regions*, 2:31–101. New York: Academic Press.

Walter, H. and E. Stadelmann. 1974. A new approach to the water relations of desert plants. *In* G. W. Brown Jr., ed., *Desert Biology: Special Topics on the Physical and Biological Aspects of Arid Regions*, 2:213–310. New York: Academic Press.

OSTRICH

The only species (*Struthio camelus*) in the family Struthionidae (order Struthioniformes) and the largest of living birds, distributed throughout arid, open habitats of Africa. The ostrich, like the rhea and the emu, is a ratite because it lacks a prominent keel on the sternum, the site of flight-muscle attachment in flying birds. Males (2.1–2.8 meters) differ from females (1.8–1.9 meters) in stature, and plumage coloration (males are black; females are brown). The weight of large males can exceed 150 kilograms. Of five described subspecies, one (*S. c. syriacus*), previously ranging throughout northern Arabia, is extinct.

Adaptations to desert environments include barbless feathers for insulation, panting for temperature regulation, and production of concentrated urine to minimize water loss. Ostriches, however, are exceptionally tolerant of dehydration and can endure up to a 25 percent reduction of body weight due to water loss. Their long powerful legs and feet with two robust toes are ideally suited for ranging over long distances. Ostriches are purported capable of attaining speeds of up to 50 kilometers per hour. Diet consists of fruit, roots, shoots, foliage of desert plants, insects, and small reptiles. Much of their water requirements are met through consumption of succulent foliage, although freestanding water is essential for long-term survival.

Nests consist of shallow scrapes some three meters in diameter. The mating system ranges from monogamy through promiscuity and varies across habitats with population density and resource abundance. The breeding unit is usually composed of a male, a "major" hen, and two to three subordinate hens. Clutch sizes range from 20 to 25, the "major" hen laying six to eight eggs and "minor" hens contributing fewer. *S. camelus* lay the largest eggs of any living bird, up to 18 centimeters in length and 14 centimeters across. Incubation duties, lasting approximately 40 days, are performed by the male at night and by the "major" hen during the day. The young are precocial (helpless) and generally remain with parents for a year or more.—Stephen C. Lougheed

See also **ANIMAL ADAPTATIONS; BIRDS; COUNTERCURRENT HEAT EXCHANGE; ENDOTHERMY; HEAT BALANCE; HEAT STRESS; KALAHARI DESERT; KAROO; MAMMALS; NAMIBIA, DESERTS OF; OMNIVORY; SAVANNA; SOUTH AFRICA, DESERTS OF; WATER BALANCE**

Further Reading

Bertram, B. C. R. 1992. *The Ostrich Communal Nesting System*. Princeton: Princeton University Press.

Brown, L. H., E. K. Urban, and K. Newman. 1982. *The Birds of Africa*. Vol. 1. New York: Academic Press.

Cramp, S., and K. E. L. Simmons, eds. 1977. *Handbook of the Birds of Europe the Middle East and North Africa. The Birds of the Western Palearctic*. Vol. 1. Oxford: Oxford University Press.

Freitag, S., and T. J. Robinson. 1993. Phylogeographic patterns in mitochondrial DNA of the ostrich (*Struthio camelus*). *Auk* 110:614–622.

Handford, P., and M. A. Mares. 1985. The mating systems of ratites and tinamous: An evolutionary perspective. *Biological Journal of the Linnean Society* 25:77–104.

Sauer, E. G. F., and E. M. Sauer. 1966. The behavior and ecology of the South African ostrich. *Living Bird* 5:45–75.

OVENBIRD

Member of a diverse group of small to medium-sized perching birds found exclusively in the New World south of central Mexico (family Furnariidae, order Passeriformes). Approximately 215 species in 56 genera are currently recognized. Ovenbirds occur in a wide array of habitats, ranging from closed forest to desert and from sea level to the high Andes. Examples of desert-dwelling furnariids are plentiful and include members of the genera *Geositta* (the miners), *Upucerthia* (the earthcreepers), *Phacellodomus* (the thornbirds), *Leptasthenura* (the tit-spinetails), *Asthenes*, (the canasteros), and *Furnarius* (the horneros).

Total length varies from 10 to 25 centimeters, and weight ranges from approximately 9 to 45 grams. The majority of species have short, rounded wings and, correspondingly, rather labored flight. The plumage typically consists of drab hues of rufous, brown, or gray. In contrast to this uniformity in color, the furnariids exhibit an astonishing array of tail shapes, bill morphologies, and breeding and foraging habits. For example, the tit-spinetails often feed in small flocks, moving with great agility through vegetation and using their short, fine bills to glean insects from leaves, flowers, and bark. Alternatively, the earthcreepers are primarily terrestrial in habit and use their robust curved bills to probe in crevices and low-lying vegetation for insects. The majority of furnariids are insectivorous, although some species have been reported to eat other types of invertebrates (e.g., earthworms) and seeds.

The nest structure is exceptionally variable across taxa. The horneros build oven-shaped mud nests that give the family its name. Many species build enormous, sometimes multichambered nests of sticks (e.g., the thornbirds). Some furnariids nest in burrows that they have excavated (e.g., *Upucerthia*) or that they have appropriated from rodents or other birds (e.g., some miner species). These elaborate structures may help to maintain a more constant micro-environment for incubation in extreme environments and may also have an antipredator function. Furnariids are usually described as being monogamous. Clutch size varies between two and five. Duration of incubation, for those species where it is known, is about 15 days. Both sexes are involved in nest building and in caring for the young.—Stephen Lougheed

See also **BIRDS; CHACO; MONTE DESERT; NESTS, BIRD; SOUTH AMERICA, DESERTS OF**

Further Reading

Fjeldså, J., and N. Krabbe. 1990. *Birds of the High Andes*. Svendborg, Denmark: Apollo.

Feduccia, A. 1973. Evolutionary trends in neotropical ovenbirds and woodhewers. *Ornithological Monographs* 13:1–69.

Ridgely, R. S., and G. Tudor. 1994. *The Birds of South America*. Vol. 2. Austin: University of Texas Press.

Short, L. L. 1975. A zoogeographic analysis of the South American chaco avifauna. *Bulletin of the American Museum of Natural History* 154:163–352.

Vaurie, C. 1971. *Classification of the Ovenbirds (Furnariidae)*. London: Witherby.

———. 1980. Taxonomy and geographical distribution of the Furnariidae (Aves, Passeriformes). *Bulletin of the American Museum of Natural History* 166:1–357.

OVERGRAZING

Use or removal of plant tissue by herbivores to such an extent that habitat damage occurs. Herbivores are usually arthropods, reptiles, the tadpoles of some amphibians, or mammals. Plant response to tissue loss varies from severe reductions in growth to dramatic increases in growth. Plants that increase growth in response to herbivory are said to compensate for tissue loss, whereas those species that show decreased growth are said to undercompensate for tissue loss. Most desert species undercompensate for tissue loss.

The definition of overgrazing is tightly integrated with the predominant plant response to herbivory. However, overgrazing is not defined simply. Range managers, wildlife managers, and ecologists all have different indicators that they look for before determining that a habitat is overgrazed. For example, for range managers, when vegetation vigor and biomass (weight/unit area) are reduced, the area is overgrazed. They do not accept the notion that vegetation in the area may be the result of herbivore regulation of the plants, that is, a zootic climax. Some ecologists do consider that vegetation is in a zootic climax and that reductions in biomass may be transient phenomena due more to changing weather conditions than overgrazing. Wildlife managers would agree with these ecologists but disagree with other ecologists who feel that grazing pressures should track changes in regional weather.

All three groups disagree about the role livestock grazing may play in irreversible declines in range condition. Some ecologists feel that livestock grazing is one of the most critical factors in the decline of desert grasslands. Over time areas that were previously dominated by grass and scattered trees have become practically denuded of all vegetation, a process known as desertification. Many range managers disagree with this viewpoint and believe that livestock grazing contributes only to reversible declines in vegetation abundance, a process known as degradation. Wildlife managers believe that wildlife certainly do not contribute to desertification but can contribute to degradation.

Despite the fine points of disagreement, most people agree that livestock grazing in desert environments has harmed those habitats. Photographic documentation has repeatedly shown where grass cover has diminished due to grazing pressures, resulting in increased wind erosion of sand and silt. The blowing sand abrades trees and kills them, causing a further decrease in vegetative cover. Species that are adapted to grow on shifting substrates such as loose sand are very slow growing. Hence total vegetative cover is reduced in these areas.

Essentially all desert plant species respond negatively to herbivory, a fact that leads some ecologists to suggest that deserts should never be used for livestock grazing because their plant species do not appear to have evolved in the presence of consistent or heavy grazing. In fact, many desert species allocate a great deal of energy to secondary plant compounds that deter herbivory through their bitter taste or poisonous qualities. In communities where these species dominate the plant community, the animal community is dominated by frugivores (fruit eaters), granivores (seed eaters), and root-feeding species. A few animal species such as the North American pronghorn, *Antilocapra americana*, have evolved complex mechanisms for coping with secondary compounds. This ungulate has the capability of persisting on several different shrub species, all known to have high concentrations of secondary compounds in their leaves.

An additional consequence of overgrazing is a change in the structure of the plant community. Plant species that are highly preferred by herbivores disappear first, followed by less desirable species. Ultimately only inedible species remain. This can have one of two effects. Due to the loss of spe-cies from the community, a number of unfilled ecological niches develop. Other plant species could then enter the community to fill these niches. If these colonizing species are also unpalatable, they will remain in the community. Species such as these are known as "increasers" with respect to grazing. Species that do not tolerate herbivory are known as "decreasers."

Increaser species can be plants that are indigenous to the affected habitat, or they can be exotic species that have moved into the habitat by various vectors, usually humans. Because of increased human travel and commerce, exotic plant species are increasingly common throughout the world. Lacking some of the constraints on their growth that native species may have, exotic species can flourish and overrun their new habitats. Examples of this phenomenon are found worldwide, in Australian, North American, South American, Asian, and African deserts. In western North America the process has advanced to the point where some exotics are even capable of invading less disturbed habitats than the original overgrazed habitat in which they were introduced. An example of this process is the movement of *Agropyron cristatum*, crested wheat grass, throughout the Great Basin Desert. Another species that is covering large areas of disturbed ground is the thorny herb *Tribulus terrestris*, a native of South African deserts.

Loss of native species to overgrazing also has important ramifications in the world biodiversity crisis. As the number of living species declines globally, a decline in the available genetic resources occurs. For example, some desert species have unique adaptations to water stress or to salinity. Plant breeders might be able to use genetic engineering techniques to transfer the genes that convey such stress resistance to other plant species, including agriculturally important plants. Desert species that deter herbivory with secondary compounds might also be useful to genetic engineers looking for ways to make crop species less susceptible to insect pests. In addition, species loss within the plant community has a ripple effect, causing losses within the animal community. This could include losses of insect species, most of which have not yet even been cataloged.—Linda L. Wallace

See also **CONSERVATION IN DESERTS; DESERT GRASSLAND; DESERTIFICATION; DESERTS; DOMESTIC ANIMALS; ECOLOGY; ECOSYSTEM; GRASS-**

LAND; GRASSES; GREAT BASIN DESERT; HER-
BIVORY; LOCOWEED; PAMPAS; PLANT ADAP-
TATIONS; PLANTS; PRAIRIE

Further Reading

Coughenour, M. B., and F. J. Singer. 1991. The concept
of overgrazing and its application to Yellowstone's
northern range. *In* R. B. Keiter and M. S. Boyce,
eds., *The Greater Yellowstone Ecosystem*, 209–230.
New Haven: Yale University Press.

Dodd, J. L. 1994. Desertification and degradation in
Sub-Saharan Africa. *BioScience* 44:28–34.

Hastings, J. R., and R. M. Turner. 1965. *The Changing
Mile.* Tucson: University of Arizona Press.

Heitschmidt, R. K., and J. W. Stuth. 1991. *Grazing Management: An Ecological Perspective.* Portland, Ore.:
Timber.

Schlesinger, W. J., J. F. Reynolds, G. L. Cunningham, L.
F. Huenneke, W. M. Jarrell, R. A. Virginia, and W. G.
Whitford. 1990. Biological feedbacks in global deser-
tification. *Science* 247:1043–1048.

OWL

Small to large-sized predatory bird species, often
nocturnal or crepuscular, with almost cosmopolitan
distribution (families Strigidae and Tytonidae, order
Strigiformes). More than 130 species in 24–29 genera are recognized. The majority of owls are termed
"typical owls;" (the approximately 120 species of the
family Strigidae), while the tytonid species include
barn owls or bay owls (genera *Tyto* and *Phodilus*).
Strigiformes occupy a diversity of habitats ranging
from forests and woodlands through grasslands to
true deserts and tundra. Numerous species are
quite specialized and are found closely associated
with desert habitats. For example, the elf owl
(*Micrathene whitneyi*) breeds in deserts supporting
saguaro cacti, arid scrub, and wooded canyons from
southeastern California to Texas and south to central Mexico. Other strigiformes show quite catholic
habitat preferences as illustrated by the great
horned owl (*Bubo virginianus*), which ranges
throughout North and South America. Across this
immense range, *B. virginianus* may be found
breeding in virtually every habitat type, including
desert and semidesert, and is absent only from tundra and tropical rain forest.

Although ranging in length from about 12 to 70
centimeters, owls are quite homogeneous in form.
The body is densely feathered, the tail is generally
short, and the wings are quite broad. Flight is efficient and silent. Owls, when perched, have a char-

Owl. (Photo: M. A. Mares)

acteristic vertical stance. The head, often topped by
"ear tufts," is rounded and large with prominent
forward-facing eyes. Plumage is often intricately
patterned in shades of brown, white, gray, and
black. Owls that inhabit desert and other open habitats are typically paler than strigiformes that
occupy more humid forests and woodlands. Sexes
are similarly marked, but females typically exceed
males in size. Ear openings are long vertical slits,
often asymmetrical (e.g., the barn owl, *Tyto alba*),
an adaptation for locating prey using auditory cues.
The densely feathered facial disks may function to
funnel sound and improve hearing acuity. The bill is
short, decurved, and powerful. Owls possess strong
legs and feet equipped with sharp curved talons.
Diet is dictated by habitat and the body size of the
species, and prey may include small rodents, birds,
reptiles, frogs, fish, earthworms, and large insects.
Small owls tend to be more insectivorous than their
larger counterparts. Prey is usually consumed
whole, and a pellet of indigestible items such as
bones, fur, teeth, and claws is subsequently regurgitated (these are termed owl pellets;).

Many owl species are not migratory and are quite territorial, often year-round. The majority of strigiformes do not build a nest but rather co-opt the nest of other birds, or lay eggs in depressions in trees, on rock ledges, or on the ground. A few open country species will nest in burrows. For example, the burrowing owl (*Athene cunicularia*), found in many dry open-country habitats of North and South America including deserts, either excavates its own nest or appropriates the burrows of other animals (e.g., prairie dogs in North America and vizcachas in Argentina). Clutch sizes typically vary from 2 to 7 but may range up to 14. Incubation duties are usually undertaken by the female, although she is often fed by the male. A single annual brood is the norm; however, some species will produce multiple broods when prey is plentiful. Incubation begins with the laying of the first egg; thus hatching is asynchronous, and in years of food shortages the youngest chicks may perish. Chicks hatch blind and helpless and are initially brooded by the female.

Once owlets no longer require brooding, both parents provide food.—Stephen C. Lougheed

See also **BIRDS**; **PREDATION**; **SAGUARO**

Further Reading

Burton, J. A. 1973. *Owls of the World: Their Evolution, Structure and Ecology.* London: Oxford University Press.

Cramp, S., ed. 1985. *Handbook of the Birds of Europe the Middle East and North Africa: The Birds of the Western Palearctic.* Vol. 4. Oxford: Oxford University Press.

Fry, C. H., S. Keith, and E. K. Urban. 1988. *The Birds of Africa.* Vol. 3. New York: Academic Press.

Karalus, K. E., and A. W. Eckert. 1974. *The Owls of North America.* Garden City, N.Y.: Doubleday.

Marti, C. D. 1992. Barn Owl (*Tyto alba*). *In* A. Poole, P. Stettenheim, and F. Gill, eds., *The Birds of North America*, No. 1. Philadelphia: Academy of Natural Sciences; Washington, D.C.: American Ornithologists' Union.

Voous, K. H. 1989. *Owls of the Northern Hemisphere.* Cambridge, Mass.: MIT Press.

P

PACKRAT. *See* WOODRAT

PAINTED DESERT

Geologic formation lying within the Colorado Plateau Semidesert, Navahoan Desert, and (part of) the Great Basin Desert, located in the Intermountain West of southeastern Utah, southwestern Colorado, northeastern Arizona, and northwestern New Mexico—an area known as the Four Corners. It occupies the arid portions of the Colorado Plateau and includes most of the Little Colorado River drainage, portions of the upper Colorado River, and part of the San Juan River in southeastern Utah.

Geologically, the area is composed of stacked layers of sedimentary rock (sandstones), which may be uplifted but are generally flat. These sandstone layers exhibit brilliant colors of reds, oranges, yellows, and browns. Many have been cut by rivers and streams to form spectacular canyons, flat-topped mesas, and rock formations. Volcanic cones and lava flows may also be present. In some areas the soil is made up of large amounts of water-absorbing volcanic ash. When wet these soils puff up to form what prospectors called self-rising soil. The region is surrounded by mountain ranges. Elevations within the Painted Desert itself range from 1,000 to 1,700 meters.

The Painted Desert is not a true desert but a semidesert. The winters are cold, and the summer can be hot. Rains usually fall in summer and can be intense. Approximately one-fourth of the region receives less than 250 millimeters of precipitation per year, mostly in the form of snow.

Both the flora and the fauna show affinities to the Great Basin Desert, and many believe it to be a southeastern extension of this desert. Yet because it is surrounded by mountain ranges and is thus relatively isolated, a number of endemic plant species have evolved: locoweeds (*Astragalus*), cryptanthas (*Cryptantha*), and buckwheats (*Eriogonum*), among others. The vegetation is dominated by pinyon pine (*Pinus edulis*), juniper (*Juniperus*), and sagebrush (*Artemisia*). The plants are generally midelevational woodland species, grassland species, and some that are found in the Great Basin Desert.

Most species of vertebrates also are found in the grasslands or in the surrounding deserts.

A number of well-known areas are found in the Painted Desert, including Monument Valley, Petrified Forest National Park, Canyon de Chelly, Sunset Crater, and the Navajo National Monument. The spectacular scenery of Monument Valley was immortalized on film in many classic John Ford westerns starring John Wayne.

The red sandstone cliffs of Canyon de Chelly exhibit some of the best-preserved cliff-dwelling ruins in the southwestern United States. The high mesas and cliffs, into which Native Americans built their adobe and stone pueblos, protected the inhabitants.

Petrified Forest National Park contains several fossil log and forest areas. Estimated to be 160 million years old, many of the trees now are found only in the Andes of South America or New Zealand. The trees were preserved because they were washed into a swamp and buried under layers of volcanic ash and then supersaturated with a silicon solution. Staining by small amounts of iron and manganese accounts for the characteristic coloration.—Janet K. Braun

See also **COLORADO RIVER; DESERT GRASSLAND; DESERTS; GREAT BASIN DESERT; MONUMENT VALLEY; MOVIES IN DESERTS; NAVAJO (DINE'É); SAGEBRUSH; UNITED STATES, DESERTS OF; UTAH DESERT**

Further Reading

Jaeger, E. C. 1957. *The North American Deserts*. Stanford: Stanford University Press.

MacMahon, J. A. 1985. *Deserts*. New York: Knopf.

West, N. E. 1983. Colorado Plateau-Mohavian blackbush semi-desert. *In* N. E. West, ed., *Ecosystems of the World: Temperate Deserts and Semi-deserts*, 5:399–411. New York: Elsevier.

———. 1983. Great Basin-Colorado plateau sagebrush semi-desert. *In* N. E. West, ed., *Ecosystems of the World: Temperate Deserts and Semi-deserts*, 5:331–349. New York: Elsevier.

———. 1983. Intermountain salt-desert shrubland. *In* N. E. West, ed., *Ecosystems of the World: Temperate Deserts and Semi-deserts*, 5:375–397. New York: Elsevier.

PAIUTE. *See* DESERT PEOPLES

PAKISTAN, DESERTS OF. *See* INDO-PAKISTAN DESERTS

PALEOCENE

First epoch of the Tertiary period, extending from 65 million to 58 million years ago. During this epoch warm, humid climates present since the early Cretaceous period continued to prevail over most of the earth's continents, although there was a mild cooling in the late Paleocene. Based on the distribution of fossils of warmth-loving foraminifera (one-celled animals with calcite tests), ocean water temperatures also were warm at least during much of the Paleocene. As a result of the warm and globally uniform climate, vegetational zones were broad and simple. Temperatures were high enough to allow temperate and subtropical forests (including diverse and widespread palms) to grow at high latitudes, but ice might have been present seasonally in northern high latitudes. Tropical rain forests occupied a broad zone from equatorial latitudes to about 50° north and south latitude. Succeedingly higher latitudes were occupied by paratropical broad-leafed evergreen and polar broad-leafed deciduous forests. How these plants could grow at such high latitudes without direct sunlight for a large part of the year is unexplained. Humid tropical forests and mangroves occurred in southern South America and Antarctica, although arid, or at least drier, climates occurred farther north in the southern portion of South America.—Nicholas J. Czaplewski

See also **CENOZOIC; CRETACEOUS; EOCENE; FOSSILS; GLACIAL PERIODS; MADRO-TERTIARY GEOFLORA; MIOCENE; NEOGENE; OLIGOCENE; PALEOCLIMATE; PERMIAN; PLATE TECTONICS; PLEISTOCENE; PLIOCENE; PRECAMBRIAN; QUATERNARY; RECENT (HOLOCENE); TERTIARY**

Further Reading

Behrensmeyer, A. K., J. D. Damuth, W. A. DiMichele, R. Potts, H.-D. Sues, and S. L. Wing. 1992. *Terrestrial Ecosystems Through Time.* Chicago: University of Chicago Press.

Creber, G. T., and W. G. Chaloner. 1985. Tree growth in the Mesozoic and early Tertiary and the reconstruction of palaeoclimates. *Palaeogeography, Palaeoclimatology, Palaeoecology* 52:35–60.

Frakes, L. A., J. E. Francis, and J. I. Syktus, eds. 1992. *Climate Modes of the Phanerozoic: The History of the Earth's Climate over the Past 600 Million Years.* Cambridge: Cambridge University Press.

Wolfe, J. A. 1985. Distribution of major vegetational types during the Tertiary. *In* E. T. Sundquist and W. S. Broecker, eds., *The Carbon Cycle and Atmospheric CO2: Natural Variations Archean to Present*, 357–375. Washington, D.C.: American Geophysical Union.

PALEOCLIMATE

Hypothetical reconstruction of the generalized weather of a given region in the geologic past that is based on many and highly varied kinds of evidence, mainly in the geologic, geochemical, and fossil records. Different extremes of climate (i.e., cold, hot, humid, arid) are evidenced by different geologic indicators, including isotopes of various elements. One widely applied method involves the ratio of two isotopes of oxygen, ^{18}O and ^{16}O, found in the calcium carbonate of fossil shells of marine organisms. This ratio depends partly on the chemical composition of the seawater, but it is also temperature-dependent and reflects the temperature of the surface water in which the carbonate shell was secreted during the life of the organism. Cores drilled in ocean bottom sediments all around the world contain the tiny sunken shells of these organisms in which the ratio can be measured over long periods of geologic time and compared over broad regions and among oceans. The oxygen isotope ratios have been applied also to freshwater and land snail shells, and even to soil carbonate nodules. The size, shape, and distribution of oceans, as well as ocean currents and circulation patterns, have strong effects on earth's climate. Similarly for continents, the size, shape, and distribution of landmasses, as well as their topographic relief and interactions with the atmosphere and its circulation, strongly affect climate.

The most common evidence for recognizing hot, arid climates in the past is the existence of deposits of evaporites. Evaporites are sediments that are precipitated from aqueous solution as a result of the evaporation of the water. Evaporite minerals include halite (rock salt), gypsum, potash, and other salts. They occur today in ephemeral lakes, salt pans, alkali flats, playas, and hypersaline lakes in arid zones around the world. Thick, extensive beds of evaporites are recorded throughout geologic time, especially since the Precambrian. Other kinds of salt deposits (e.g., caliche or calcrete) can occur below the surface in arid and semiarid regions.

Sand dunes are characteristic of many deserts, and paleodunes often can be recognized in the rock record and differentiated from water-laid sands. However, prior to the Silurian-Devonian periods (when plant life first invaded the land surface), the lack of terrestrial vegetation and soils suggests aeolian dunes might have occurred then in humid environments as well as arid ones.

Plant and animal fossils can sometimes be indicators of past climates. Some organisms have particular morphological features that in modern habitats are associated with a particular climatic feature (e.g., leaves with entire margins and drip-tips in areas of heavy rainfall, or leaves with varying densities of stomata depending on the atmospheric concentration of CO_2). Other fossil organisms may be related to living organisms with known, narrow physiological or ecological tolerances. The climatic requirements of the living organisms are extrapolated to their extinct relatives and used to infer approximate paleoclimatic parameters. The extrapolation must be cautiously applied, however, and the conclusions are necessarily indefinite. In some instances Quaternary fossil biotas include faunal elements that give conflicting environmental or paleoclimatic interpretations. These have been termed nonanalogue communities or disharmonious faunas, and it should be recognized that it might actually be the recently remodeled, living communities on which the comparison is based that are "disharmonious" relative to a given species' evolutionary history. The low rainfall in desert environments lessens the likelihood of burial of the already sparse organisms and their preservation as fossils in sedimentary rocks. Hence fossils of desert plants and animals are only infrequently encountered.—Nicholas J. Czaplewski

See also **CENOZOIC; CRETACEOUS; DESERTS; DUNES; EOCENE; FOSSILS; GLACIAL PERIODS; GRASSLAND; MADRO-TERTIARY GEOFLORA; MIDDEN; MINERALS; MIOCENE; NAMIBIA, DESERTS OF; NEOGENE; OCEAN CURRENTS; OLIGOCENE; PALEOCENE; PALEOCLIMATE; PERMIAN; PHOTOSYNTHESIS; PLATE TECTONICS; PLEISTOCENE; PLIOCENE; PRECAMBRIAN; QUATERNARY; RECENT (HOLOCENE); SAHARA DESERT; SALT; SOILS, DESERT, CALCRETE; SOILS, DESERT, CALICHE; TERTIARY**

Further Reading

Cocks, L. R. M. 1981. *The Evolving Earth*. London: British Museum (Natural History).

Frakes, L. A., J. E. Francis, and J. I. Syktus, eds. 1992. *Climate Modes of the Phanerozoic: The History of the Earth's Climate over the Past 600 Million Years*. Cambridge: Cambridge University Press.

Leinen, M., and M. Sarnthein, eds. 1989. *Paleoclimatology and Paleometeorology: Modern and Past Patterns of Global Atmospheric Transport*. Boston: Kluwer.

Magaritz, M., and A. Kaufman. 1983. Paleoclimate in desert regions. *American Scientist* 71:514–521.

Nairn, A. E. M., ed. 1961. *Descriptive Paleoclimatology*. New York: Interscience.

Swart, P. K., K. C. Lohmann, J. McKenzie, and S. Savin, eds. 1993. *Climate Change in Continental Isotopic Records*. Washington, D.C.: American Geophysical Union.

Van Der Burgh, J., H. Visscher, D. L. Dilcher, and W. M. Kürschner. 1993. Paleoatmospheric signatures in Neogene fossil leaves. *Science* 260:1788–1790.

PALESTINE, DESERTS OF

Arid areas lying within the likely state of Palestine. According to the recent Israeli-Palestinian agreement for establishment of a Palestinian state in the Gaza Strip and Jericho, the former is situated in the southwest of Israel on the Mediterranean with a coastline of about 45 kilometers and extends up to 8 kilometers in width. Jericho (known as Ariha) is located in the West Bank. Because of the difficulty of obtaining detailed and specific official information, the present definition is based on limited sources, most of it from journal articles and media reports. (See map of Middle East deserts, p. 361.)

The climate of Palestine is mostly Mediterranean with a hot dry summer and a cool wet winter. Mean annual temperature is about 20°C in the Gaza Strip and 25°C in Jericho. Annual rainfall averages 250 millimeters in Gaza and about 200 millimeters in Jericho. Water aquifers and the River Jordan contribute significantly to the sources of freshwater in this zone. Agricultural land occupies most of the total land area (more than 50 percent), and about 40 percent is irrigated. About 25 percent of the land is devoted to urban and rural constructions. Both land and water are scarce resources in Palestine, and their availability and accessibility is a matter of crucial importance to human existence. The scarcity of water and land resources has created many environmental problems, including reduction of arable land, degradation of natural vegetation, soil erosion, and increasing desertification.

Desert vegetation of Palestine is difficult to describe in such a geographically limited area. It has been included as a part of many botanical studies dealing with Israel, Sinai, Jordan, and the Middle East. The district contains diverse habitat types within its relatively small area, ranging from arid to semiarid deserts. Among these habitats are coastal dunes, inland sand formations, stony and gravelly habitats, chalk outcrops, and salt marshes. These habitat types support diffused and contracted vegetation types. Natural vegetation is mainly restricted to the fallow lands and to a very few undisturbed sites. Large areas have been cleared for agricultural developments. Overexploitation and use of underground water has led to increased soil salinity, and wastewater seepage has seriously polluted underground water in many areas.

Despite heavy human pressures on water and heavy land use related to agriculture, grazing, and the clearing of woody vegetation for fuel and for the construction of huts, the stumps of many species of trees have resprouted, and dense stands of such regrowth forests occur in some areas. Modern scientific information on species and habitat diversity and nature conservation are crucial and urgently needed to ensure the recovery and sustainability of the ecosystems of Palestine, including the few forested areas that remain.

The extensive military activities over the decades, related to the Israeli-Palestinian situation, have adversely affected the natural ecosystems of the region. An integrated Israeli-Palestinian ecological restoration program is needed. The recently proposed Israeli plan to build a canal linking the Mediterranean Sea to the Dead Sea may have an adverse effect on the Gaza Strip and the adjoining territories. These impacts include disturbance of farmlands, deterioration of groundwater through seepage of salt water, damage to the shoreline in the region, damage to the coastal sand dune ecosystem, and other disturbances related to the construction of the project itself.—Ahmad K. Hegazy

See also **AFRICA, DESERTS OF; AGRICULTURE IN DESERTS; ARABIAN GULF, DESERTS OF; CHENOPODIACEAE; CONTAMINATION; DESERTIFICATION; DESERT PEOPLES; DOMESTIC ANIMALS; IRRIGATION DRAINAGE; ISRAEL, DESERTS OF; MIDDLE EAST, DESERTS OF; PLAYA; POLLUTION; SALINIZATION; SALT DESERT; SALT PAN; OVERGRAZING; SAHARA DESERT; SHEEP**

Further Reading

Danin, A. 1983. *Desert Vegetation of Israel and Sinai.* Jerusalem: Cana Publishing.

Palestine National Report. 1992. *The Environment in the Occupied Palestinian Territories.* Rio de Janeiro: Report to United Nations Conference on Environment and Development (UNCED).

United Nations Environment Programme (UNEP). 1983. *Report on the Environmental Consequences of the Israeli Project to Build a Canal Linking the Mediterranean Sea to the Dead Sea.* Nairobi: United Nations Environment Programme (UNEP) Governing Council, No. 11/3/Add.4.

———. (1991) *Report on the Environmental Situation in the Occupied Palestinian and Other Arab Territories.* Nairobi: United Nations Environment Programme (UNEP) Governing Council, No. 16/5.

PALMS

Plants of varying life form (ranging from vines to shrubs to trees) in the worldwide family Arecaceae (= Palmae), with more than 3,400 species in 236 genera occurring principally in tropical and subtropical regions. Palms are especially common in wet forested habitats, but some species occur in arid and semiarid areas. For example, in North America the fan palm (*Washingtonia filifera* in California and Mexico; *Washingtonia sonorae* in the Sonoran Desert) and the blue palm (*Erythea*) are common in desert areas of southern California, Arizona, and Baja California, Mexico. Palm leaves, or fronds, may range up to 15 meters in length, and the leaf morphology varies greatly among taxa. As might be expected with a large, diverse family, other traits, such as reproductive morphology, also vary (e.g., some species have bisexual flowers, others unisexual ones). Palms may form forests in areas that support dry scrub, such as *Copernica alba* across parts of the semiarid Chacoan thorn scrub of Argentina. *Butia yatay* fills a similar role in the thorny Espinal scrubland of Argentina. Palms may also be major tree components in open grassy areas, such as *Arecastrum romanzoffianum*, which is a significant member of the grassland savannas in eastern Argentina. In the Sahara Desert native palms, such as the Doum palm (*Hyphaene thebaica*) were once common in wadis (arroyos), around oases, or in areas having a high water table, but through

Palm trees in the dry coastal forest of Mexico near Puerto Vallarta. (Photo: M. A. Mares)

human activities over millennia they have been largely eliminated, often being replaced with date palms. *Hyphaene* species also occur in Madagascar and India.

Date palm oases (*Phoenix dactylifera*) have had great importance in the history of the Sahara Desert across all of North Africa as a plant species offering both shelter and food. Date palms were cultivated as early as 6000 B.C., and all parts of the tree, from fruit to leaves to wood, have been used by desert peoples. Thus date palms have come to dominate water holes and other areas across much of arid North Africa. Palms have enormous economic importance. Indeed, after the grass family, Poaceae, palms are likely the most economically important plant family in the world.—Michael A. Mares

See also **AFRICA, DESERTS OF; ARABIAN GULF, DESERTS OF; ASIA, DESERTS OF; CHACO; DESERT PEOPLES; ECONOMIC VALUE OF DESERT PRODUCTS; INDO-PAKISTAN DESERTS; MADAGASCAR, DESERTS OF; MIDDLE EAST, DESERTS OF; MOJAVE DESERT; PLANT ADAPTATIONS; PLANTS; SAHARA DESERT; SAUDI ARABIA, DESERTS OF; WATER HOLE**

Further Reading

Blombery, A., and T. Rodd. 1982. *Palms*. London: Angus and Robertson.

Corner, E. J. H. 1966. *The Natural History of Palms*. Berkeley: University of California Press.

Jaeger, E. C. 1957. *The North American Deserts*. Stanford: Stanford University Press.

Langlois, A. C. 1980. *Supplement to Palms of the World*. Stuart, Fla.: Horticultural Books.

Foothill paloverde (*Cercidium microphyllum*) near Yuma, Arizona. (Photo: M. A. Mares)

McCurrach, J. C. 1960. *Palms of the World*. New York: Harper and Brothers.

PALOVERDE

Large shrub or small tree of the legume family (Leguminosae or Fabaceae) with smooth green bark. These desert plants are unusual in having branches capable of photosynthesis. Paloverde (Spanish for "green stick") usually refers to the genus *Cercidium* but is also used for *Parkinsonia* (and locally for *Canotia holocantha*). Trees of both genera lose their leaves during dry periods. Paloverdes are drought tolerant and have deep, widespreading roots.

Cercidium is a strictly New World genus with 8–10 species ranging from the southern United States to South America. In North America it occurs in the Mojave and Sonoran deserts and desert grassland at elevations up to 1,200 meters. One species inhabits the Monte Desert of Argentina and the Chacoan thorn scrub of south central South America. *Cercidium* trees grow up to 10 meters tall, with a main trunk up to 50 centimeters in diameter. The branches bear thorns and compound leaves with small leaflets. Profuse yellow flowers can produce a showy desert scene in the spring, and supply nectar for honeybees. The pods, which are constricted between the seeds, are eaten by cattle during drought. The wood is soft and not useful as fuelwood. The seeds are ground into a meal by Native Americans, and the cortex is used in treatment of sprains and to aid expulsion of the placenta after childbirth.

Blue paloverde (*Cercidium floridum*) grows along washes and canyons and sometimes on slopes. Seeds of the blue paloverde germinate after they are abraded by rocks and sand in flowing washes. Littleleaf, or foothill paloverde (*Cercidium microphyllum*), is a smaller tree, more abundant on bajadas in association with saguaro, ironwood, ocotillo, cholla, and prickly pear. This species is more xerophytic than the blue paloverde and lives up to 400 years.

Parkinsonia grows up to 15 meters tall. The branches have paired spines. The yellow flowers have red spots. The pods are strongly constricted between the seeds. The Mexican paloverde (*P. aculeata*), also called horse bean, occurs on plains and bajadas and in canyons in the Sonoran Desert and in the subtropical and tropical areas of the New World. Mexican paloverde is cultivated for landscaping. One species of *Parkinsonia* occurs only in South Africa.—Kristina A. Ernest

See also **LEAVES; LEGUMES; MONTE DESERT; PHOTOSYNTHESIS; PLANT ADAPTATIONS; PLANTS; SONORAN DESERT; UNITED STATES, DESERTS OF**

Further Reading

Benson, L., and R. A. Darrow. 1981. *Trees and Shrubs of the Southwestern Deserts*. Tucson: University of Arizona Press.

Shreve, F., and I. L. Wiggins. 1964. *Vegetation and Flora of the Sonoran Desert*. Vols. 1 and 2. Stanford: Stanford University Press.

PAMIR DESERT. *See* ASIA, DESERTS OF

PAMPAS

Temperate grassland (500,000 square kilometers) of east central Argentina in the provinces of Buenos Aires, Santa Fé, Córdoba, La Pampa, and San Luis, between 32° and 38° south latitude. The Pampas is continuous with grasslands to the north in Uruguay and Brazil, with which it forms a grassland region termed the Rio de La Plata Grasslands. Rainfall varies across the Pampas from as much as 1,600 millimeters to as little as 400 millimeters per year. In the drier portions, in southern Buenos Aires and La Pampa provinces, dunes are present. Actual evapotranspiration rates are high in the Pampas (mean temperature approximatly 20°C), and the vegetation is more xerophytic (drier) than might be supposed from the rainfall. In the driest portions rainfall deficits can approach 700 millimeters per year. At its southwestern extreme (e.g., San Luis Province) the Pampas becomes wetter and ponds are common, whereas in northeastern Buenos Aires Province there are many marshes. The Pampas supports a great diversity of grasses (190 native species), including *Andropogon*, *Axonopus*, *Bothriochloa*, *Panicum*, and *Paspalum*, and up to 1,000 species of vascular plants. In many regions dry lakes (playas) may form as water accumulates and evaporates. Like the southern Great Plains of North America, the Pampas lacks trees except in areas of drainage, or where there is a high water table with suitable soil. In general terms the Pampas occupies a broad flat plain with fertile, loessial soils and is covered by dense grass. Soils are complex across the temperate grasslands of South America, and different soil types give rise to different grassland and herbaceous plant communities. (See map of South American deserts, p. 533.)

The Pampas, while not as extensive as the North American grasslands, is one of the richest grazing lands in the world. As a consequence it has been severely affected by domestic livestock and farmers. No pristine Pampas remains, and there are only a few remnants left of the original "sea of grass" that covered this portion of the South American continent. Today it is considered one of the most endangered habitats on earth.

The Pampas supports a rich and diverse fauna of wildlife, including many amphibians (22 species), reptiles, birds (more than 390 species), and mammals. Among the more notable species are the rhea (*Rhea americana*), a large ostrichlike flightless bird; the now-extirpated pampas deer (*Ozotoceros bezoarticus*); the maned wolf (*Chrysocyon*); the guanaco (*Lama guanicoe*, a South American camelid); and an array of rodents (including the vizcacha, *Lagostomus maximus*), carnivores (including the now-extirpated jaguar, *Panthera onca*), bats, and armadillos.

The Pampas is famous in Argentine folklore as the original home of the gauchos, legendary cowboys that helped to settle the country during its early days. The gauchos were remarkably adept horsemen and used *boleadoras* (rawhide thongs with stones attached that were used in place of a lariat) for hunting while also being masters with the long knife (*facón*). They personified freedom from societal norms, much as the cowboy did in the United States, and there are many legendary tales about gauchos that are told to this day in Argentina. The gaucho was inseparably associated with the Pampas.—Michael A. Mares

See also **CAMELS, SOUTH AMERICAN; CLIMATE; DESERT GRASSLAND; GRASSLAND; GREAT AMERICAN DESERT; HOLDRIDGE LIFE ZONES; PLAYA; PRAIRIE; SALT PAN; RHEA; SAVANNA; SOUTH AMERICA, DESERTS OF**

Further Reading

Cabrera, A. L., and A. Willink. 1973. *Biogeografía de América Latina.* Organization of American States, Monograph No. 13. Washington, D.C.

Soriano, A. 1992. Río de La Plata Grasslands. *In* R. T. Coupland, ed., *Ecosystems of the World: Natural Grasslands*, 8A:367–407. New York: Elsevier.

Walter, H. 1983. *Vegetation of the Earth.* Berlin: Springer.

PAN. *See* PLAYA

PANGOLIN

Member of the mammalian family Manidae of the order Pholidota with extremely large claws on the forepaws that are employed in digging burrows and excavating ant and termite nests and with the dorsal surface of the body covered by overlapping epidermally derived scutes of scales. There are seven living species: three are Asian and four are African in distribution. The tail of pangolins usually exceeds the head and body in length. Although sparse hairs are present on the belly, and hairs protrude between the scutes, the overall appearance is that of a mammal covered with large scales. Most species of pangolins are associated with tropical forests, but one species, *Manis temminckii*, penetrates to the more arid regions of southern Africa.

All pangolins are highly specialized for feeding on ants and termites. They have an extremely long tongue, which can be extruded into the tunnel systems of their prey. The tongue is usually coated with a sticky saliva produced from enlarged salivary glands. The pangolin has no teeth and in its form and function is convergent with the New World anteaters of the family Myrmecophagidae.—John F. Eisenberg

See also **ANTS; ARMADILLO; CONVERGENT EVOLUTION; MAMMALS; SOUTH AFRICA, DESERTS OF; TERMITES**

Further Reading

Nowak, R. M. 1991. *Walker's Mammals of the World.* 5th ed. Baltimore: Johns Hopkins University Press.

PAPAGO. *See* O'ODHAM

PARALLEL EVOLUTION

In evolutionary theory, when the descendants of two lineages of related organisms that are reproductively isolated from one another resemble one another because of common heritage and similar selection pressures. Thus, for example, the different lineages of pocket mice constituting the genera *Perognathus* and *Chaetodipus* resemble each other, although they are reproductively isolated. Presumably in their adaptation to desert habitats they have been subjected to similar selective pressures throughout their separate evolutionary histories.—John F. Eisenberg

See also **CONVERGENT EVOLUTION; HETEROMYIDS; RODENTS; SPECIATION**

PARROT

Group of robust, highly vocal, and gregarious birds in the family Psittacidae (order Psittaciformes) distributed throughout Central and South America, Africa, southern Asia, and Australia. Approximately 330 species of psittacids in about 80 genera are recognized, although these numbers vary somewhat depending on the author cited. Parrots range in length from 8 to 100 centimeters but are quite homogeneous in appearance. The body is compact and the neck short. Tail length is variable across species, and wings are usually rounded and strong. Most taxa are nonmigratory, although some are nomadic. Parrots possess short tarsi and powerful zygodactylous feet (the two outer toes pointing forward and the two inner toes pointing backward). The bill is short, broad, and strongly curved downward. The upper mandible is articulated at the skull, allowing for some movement, and the tongue

Monk parakeet (*Myiopsitta monacha*) in the Chacoan thorn scrub of Córdoba Province, Argentina. This is the only species of parrot that nests communally, and the large stick nests constructed of branches from thorn trees are a significant feature of the Argentine thorn scrub. (Photo: M. A. Mares)

is thick and fleshy. The most common plumage color is green, although some psittacids are brightly colored. Sexes are usually similar in appearance, but in some species sexual dimorphism in size is evident (the sexes are of markedly different sizes). The diet is variable; fruit usually predominates, but it also includes seeds, pollen, and nectar in some species.

Most parrot taxa are found in tropical regions and are especially plentiful in lowland tropical forests. Some psittacids, although dependent on water sources, have become well adapted to arid and semiarid environments. Many of the parrots that occur in xeric environments are common and abundant and are often seen in large, highly vocal flocks. For example, the budgerigar, *Melopsittacus undulatus*, and the cockatiel, *Nymphicus hollandicus*, are prominent members of the avifauna of drier Australian habitats. Both species are somewhat nomadic, a characteristic of parrots of arid zones, and their breeding cycles are tied to patterns of food abundance and consequently rainfall. A number of South American psittacid taxa are also associated with dry habitats, either in the Andes Mountains (e.g. parakeets of the genus *Bolborhynchus*) or in lower-altitude, open arid lands (e.g., the monk parakeet, *Myiopsitta monacha*, of south central South America, and the burrowing parrot, *Cyanoliseus*

patagonus, of central Chile and northwestern through central Argentina).

Knowledge of breeding behavior of most psittacids is limited. Parrots appear to be primarily monogamous, and pair-bonds seem to be of long duration. The majority nest in unlined, natural tree cavities. Some arid-land species nest in burrows (e.g., burrowing parrots). The monk parakeet is unique among parrots in that it builds a large, often multichambered, twig nest that can exceed 200 kilograms in weight. These nests are often constructed of the branches of thorny desert trees and are placed on the tops of trees, or nowadays on telephone poles.

Psittacid clutch sizes are small, generally ranging from two to five eggs. Length of incubation is loosely correlated to body size of the species and varies from 17 to 35 days. Usually only the female incubates the eggs, and during this period she is fed by the male. Chicks are born blind and naked and generally develop slowly. Parental duties are shared by both members of the pair, except that only the female broods the young.—Stephen C. Lougheed

See also **AUSTRALIA, DESERTS OF; BIRDS; MEXICO, DESERTS OF; MONTE DESERT; NESTS, BIRD; SOUTH AMERICA, DESERTS OF**

Further Reading

Fjeldså, J., and N. Krabbe. 1990. *Birds of the High Andes*. Svendborg, Denmark: Apollo.

Forshaw, J. M. 1989. *Parrots of the World*. 3d ed. Melbourne: Lansdowne.

PASTORALISTS. *See* DESERT PEOPLES

PATAGONIA

Cold desert shrub steppe with almost constant wind that extends southward in Argentina from the mid-Andean precordillera in Mendoza Province, gradually widening across western Neuquén and Rio Negro provinces, and over much of the Chubut Basin, reaching as far south as Santa Cruz Province and northern Tierra del Fuego; in Chile it penetrates the pre-Andean regions of Chiloé and Aisén and extends along the northeastern portion of the Magellan Strait in the south. This region is one of the largest and most diverse xeric (dry) landscapes in South America. Physiographically, Patagonia is usually divided into eastern Patagonia and western Patagonia. The former encompasses the vast Argen-

Desert habitat of central Patagonia, Chubut Province, Argentina. (Photo: M. A. Mares)

tine plains around the middle courses of the Negro, Chubut, and Chico rivers, Sarmiento Lake, and the Deseado, Santa Cruz, and Turbio rivers. The latter includes the territory on either side of the Andes, mostly on the eastern side of the mountain range.

Due to its extent and diversity Patagonia has a varied climate that is difficult to define. Mean annual temperature ranges from 13.4°C in Chos Malal in the north to 5°C in Rio Grande in the south. Annual rainfall ranges from 100 to 260 millimeters, although significant increases are likely to occur in the bordering areas, especially on the western border near the cold rain forest slopes of the Andes. In the more humid western portions of Patagonia, the shrub steppe yields to stiff grasses, or bunchgrasses, including several endemic genera such as *Ameghinoa*, *Pantacantha*, *Benthamiella*, and *Lepidophyllum*. The most important plant family is that of composites (Asteraceae), with nearly 50 genera and numerous species of *Senecio*, *Naussavia*, *Perezia*, and *Chuquiraga*. Other important plants are legumes (*Adesmia*) and members of the families Verbenaceae and Solanaceae.

Six phytogeographic districts within the Patagonian Domain have been described:

1. *Payunia*. Extreme northern Patagonia, with volcanic soils and thickets of *Ephedra ochreata*, *Chuquiraga rosulata*, or *Mulinum spinosum*.

2. *Western Patagonia*. A narrow strip on the western border of Patagonia, with steppes of *Mulinum spinosum*, *Trevoa patagonica* (malaspina), or *Nassauvia axillaris*, or steppes of *Stipa*, *Poa*, *Bromus*, and *Festuca*.

3. *Central Patagonia*. Located in the central basins of the Rivers Negro and Chubut and including almost the entire province of Santa Cruz, with steppes of *Chuquiraga avellanedae* (quilembai), *Naussavia glomerulosa* (cola-piche), or *Junella tridens* (mata negra).

4. *District of Saint George Gulf (Golfo de San Jorge)*. Steppes of *Trevoa patagonica* (malaspina) and *Colliguaya integerrima* (duraznillo).

5. *Sub-Andean Patagonia*. Covering a narrow strip along the southern Andes, south of 51° south latitude, and spreading out to the west in the southernmost part of the continent. It is a landscape of grass steppes where the dominant species is *Festuca pallescens*.

6. *Fuegian District*. Northern Tierra del Fuego, with bunchgrass steppes of *Festuca gracillina*, *Hordeum jubatum* var. *pilosum*, and *Agropyron magellanicum*.

In all the above districts, different plant communities may appear in valley bottoms, with mesic or riparian (riverine) vegetation and dwarf *Nothofagus* in western Patagonia. *Lepidophyllum cupressiforme* occurs on the sand dunes by the sea.

There is an abundance of animal species in Patagonia that are frequently associated with the shrubby plants that dominate the region (an association that is beneficial given the strength and frequency of the winds). Among mammals, there are marsupials (*Thylamys* and the endemic *Lestodelphis*); numerous bats (*Lasiurus*, *Tadarida*, *Histiotus*, *Eumops*); and various carnivores, the gray fox (*Pseudalopex griseus*) and red fox (*Pseudalopex culpaeus*), the weasel (*Galictis cuja*), the puma (*Puma concolor*), two skunks (*Conepatus*), and the pampas cat (*Oncifelis colocolo*). Rodents are abundant, both in numbers of species and numbers of individuals, and include the mara, or Patagonian hare (*Dolichotis patagonum*), the vizcacha (*Lagostomus*), mountain vizcachas (*Lagidium*) on rocky hillsides, several tucu-tucos (*Ctenomys*), and numerous mice and rats. Among the armadillos, the *peludo* (*Chaetophractus*) and the *piche* (*Zaedyus pichiy*) are common. Guanacos (family Camelidae: *Lama guanicoe*) are common throughout the region. Sea lions (*Otaria flavescens*) are common along the coast.

Birds are remarkably numerous: *pato vapor*, or steamer ducks (*Tachyeres*), other ducks (*Anas*, *Oxyura*, *Marganetta*), geese (*Chloephaga*), swans (*Coscoroba*, *Cygnus*), grebes (*Podiceps*), and gulls (*Larus*). Enormous colonies of penguins (*Spheniscus magellanicus*) are found on the coast, with the birds building nesting burrows in the desert scrubland, leading to the unusual sight of penguins in the desert. Birds of prey are very abundant, as are rhinocryptids (*Pteroptochos* and *Scelorchilus*).

Reptile species include some poisonous snakes, such as the *yarará ñata* (*Bothrops ammodytoides* and *Bothrops alternata*), as well as various other snakes and lizards.

The fishes that are found most frequently in Patagonia are some catfishes (*Hatcheria*), bagres sapos (*Dyplomystes*), peladillas, the *trucha criolla* (*Percichthys*), and the *pejerrey patagónico*, or Patagonian atherine (*Brasilichthys*). A viviparous (live-bearing) fish (*Jenysia lineata*) reaches as far south as Chubut.

As for insects, there are many Coleoptera (beetles) of the families Tenebrionidae, Curculionidae, and Carabidae. Various genera of Hymenoptera (wasps) are present, some of which are endemic: *Ephebomyrmex*, *Paponomyrmex*, *Camponotus*, and *Dorymyrmex*. Numerous Diptera (flies) are found as well: tabanids, simulids, and chironomids, many of them related to similar forms in Australia and New Zealand. There are also many Lepidoptera (butterflies and moths) and various scorpions and spiders. Mollusks are also well represented in this southern cold desert.—Virgilio G. Roig

See also **ARMADILLO; BIRDS; CAMELS, SOUTH AMERICAN; CATS; CHACO; CHILE, DESERTS OF; DESERTS; DESERTS, TEMPERATE; LIZARDS; INSECTS; MAMMALS; MARA; MONTE DESERT; PENGUIN; REPTILES; SEA LION; SEMIDESERT; SNAKES; SOUTH AMERICA, DESERTS OF**

Further Reading

Cabrera, A. L. 1976. *Regiones fitogeográficas Argentinas: Enciclopedia Argentina de Agricultura y Jardinería.* Buenos Aires: ACME.

Cabrera, A. L., and A. Willink. 1973. *Biogeografía de América Latina.* Organization of American States, Monograph No. 13. Washington, D.C.

Mares, M. A., J. Morello, and G. Goldstein. 1985. The Monte Desert and other subtropical semi-arid biomes of Argentina, with comments on their relation to North American arid areas. *In* M. Evenari, I. Noy-Meir, and D. W. Goodall, eds., *Ecosystems of the World: Hot Deserts and Arid Shrublands*, 12B:203–237. New York: Elsevier.

Mares, M. A. 1993. Heteromyids and their ecological counterparts: a pandesertic view of rodent ecology. *In* H. H. Genoways and J. H. Brown, eds., *The Biology of the Family Heteromyidae*, 652–713. Special Publication No. 10, American Society of Mammalogists.

Simpson, G. G. 1934. *Attending Marvels: A Patagonian Journal.* New York: Macmillan.

Soriano, A., W. Volkheimer, H. Walter, E. O. Box, A. A. Marcolin, J. A. Vallerini, C. P. Movia, R. J. C. León, J. M. Gallardo, M. Rumboll, M. Canevari, P. Canevari, and W. G. Vasina. 1983. Deserts and semi-deserts of Patagonia. *In* N. E. West, ed., *Ecosystems of the World: Temperate Deserts and Semi-deserts*, 5:423–460. New York: Elsevier.

PATAGONIAN "HARE." *See* MARA

PATHOGENS

Organisms, including bacteria, viruses, mites, yeasts, and other fungi, that act parasitically on their host organism, causing debilitation or death. Since most pathogens are microorganisms, factors limiting their growth and development include the proper substrate, temperature, and water.

Because of their need for moisture, the desert environment has small populations of pathogens. However, many of the pathogenic microbes can enter a physiologically dormant stage within specialized structures such as cysts or spores. These are usually cells surrounded by very thick walls that protect the cell from water loss and enable it to reactivate in an environment more conducive to growth. Even given this option, most pathogens in desert environments are found in the soil, as the environment above ground is usually too harsh for them to be supported.

These soil-borne organisms primarily attack roots and other belowground structures. A number of fungi, such as species of *Fusarium*, are responsible for severe wilting and death of desert plants that live in relatively mesic (moist) environments.

There are some critically important aboveground pathogens, however. When succulent plants such as cacti are injured, an opening into the very moist, warm environment provided by their internal structure will promote the growth of both pathogenic and nonpathogenic microbes. This is implicated in a decline of the very large cactus *Carnegiea gigantea*, or saguaro, in the Sonoran Desert of North America, where many of the very largest members of the species are dying. Bacterial necrosis has been found in a number of these individuals.—Linda L. Wallace

See also **BACTERIA; CACTUS, COLUMNAR; DIVERSITY; ECOLOGY; ECOSYSTEM; PLANT ADAPTATIONS; PLANTS; SAGUARO; SONORAN DESERT**

Further Reading

Keasey, M. S., III. 1981. *The Saguaro Book*. Dubuque, Iowa: Kendall/Hunt.

Niering, W. A., R. H. Whittaker, and C. H. Lowe. 1963. The saguaro: A population in relation to environment. *Science* 142:15–23.

Steenbergh, W. F., and C. H. Lowe. 1977. *Ecology of the Saguaro: 2. Reproduction, Germination, Establishment, Growth, and Survival of the Young Plant*. Scientific Monograph Series, No. 8. Washington, D.C.: National Park Service.

PEBBLE DESERT. *See* STONE PAVEMENT

PECCARY

Piglike member of the mammalian family Tayassuidae of the order Artiodactyla (which also includes deer and other even-toed ungulates) that has a large head, bristly fur, a snout, and a short tail. Unlike pigs, the upper and lower canines are not curved but are short and pointed. The two genera and three species found in the New World differ in color and size. The collared peccary, smallest, has a white collar, the white-lipped peccary has white lips, and the large Chacoan peccary has a white collar and white lips. All three species are highly vocal.

The Chacoan peccary (*Catagonus wagneri*) was thought to be extinct until it was found in 1972 in northwestern Paraguay. This species inhabits the Gran Chaco region of Paraguay, Argentina, and Bolivia, a flat, xerophytic thorn scrub. It has long legs for running, and the dewclaws are absent; both are adaptations for a cursorial (running) life in open, semiarid habitats. Large nostrils and a long snout serve to filter dust in this dry habitat and provide a good sense of smell. Chacoan peccaries primarily eat cactus parts. They form herds of up to 10 individuals, are generally diurnal, and use communal areas for defecation. This species is considered threatened. All three species of peccary are found in the Chaco region but have different activity patterns and forage on different food types.

The white-lipped peccary (*Tayassu pecari*) ranges from southern Mexico to northern Argen-

Collared peccary (*Pecari tajacu*) photographed in captivity in the Caatinga scrubland of eastern Brazil. (Photo: M. A. Mares)

tina, overlapping the distributions of the Chacoan and collared peccaries. Although generally found in humid tropical forests, it also occurs in Venezuelan savannas and the Paraguayan Chaco. It feeds on plant and animal material and is active at night. Herds of 5–200 animals are common; this species may be the most aggressive peccary and has been known to attack humans.

The collared peccary (*Pecari tajacu*) is distributed from the Chihuahuan and Sonoran deserts of the southwestern United States (Texas, Arizona, and New Mexico) to northern Argentina. It inhabits both tropical forest and dry scrublands. This species ranges farther north than the other peccary species. Although a tropical animal, certain adaptations and behaviors allow this species to live in the desert Southwest. In the winter the pelage thickens, and the peccary feeds during the day to utilize the heat from the sun; heat acquisition is maximized by the black bristles of the pelage. At night groups huddle together to conserve heat. During the heat of the summer collared peccaries feed in the mornings and evenings and rest during the hottest part of the day. The bristles that are black in winter break off. The resulting pelage is lighter in color and is better at reflecting the sun's rays. Collared peccaries form groups of 2–20 individuals and feed on plant material.—Janet K. Braun

See also **ANIMAL ADAPTATIONS; CACTI; CHACO; HEAT BALANCE; MAMMALS; MEXICO, DESERTS OF; MONTE DESERT; OMNIVORY; SONORAN DESERT; UNGULATES**

Further Reading

Bissonette, J. A. 1982. Collared peccary. *In* J. A. Chapman and G. A. Feldhamer, eds., *Wild Mammals of North America: Biology, Management, and Economics,* 841–850. Baltimore: Johns Hopkins University Press.

Grzimek's Encyclopedia of Mammals. Vol. 5. 1990. New York: McGraw-Hill.

Mayer, J. J., and P. N. Brandt. 1982. Identity, distribution, and natural history of the peccaries, Tayassuidae. *In* M. A. Mares and H. H. Genoways, eds., *Mammalian Biology in South America,* 433–455. Linesville, Pa.: Pymatuning Laboratory of Ecology, University of Pittsburgh.

Mayer, J. J., and R. M. Wetzel. 1986. Catagonus wagneri. *Mammalian Species* 259:1–5.

———. 1987. Tayassu pecari. *Mammalian Species* 293:1–7.

PEDOCAL. *See* SOILS, DESERT, PEDOCAL

PENGUIN

Medium- to large-sized flightless marine bird of the Southern Hemisphere (family Spheniscidae, order Sphenisciformes). Sixteen to 18 species in six genera are recognized. Penguins are an ancient group of birds, fossils having been described from the late Eocene (about 45 million years ago). Tropical and warm-temperate species are predominantly nonmigratory. In contrast, those species that breed on sub-Antarctic islands and on the Antarctic coast spend a significant portion of the year at sea or at the edge of the pack ice.

Obviously, an important component of the habitat of all penguins is seawater. Breeding habitats, always close to a marine coast, range from the Antarctic sea ice (e.g., the emperor penguin, *Aptenodytes forsteri*) through lava-covered regions of equatorial islands (e.g., the Galapagos penguin, *Spheniscus mendiculus*) and the desert scrublands of Patagonia ;(the Magellanic penguin, *Spheniscus magellanicus*) to temperate rain forests (e.g., the fiordland penguin, *Eudyptes pachyrhynchus*, of New Zealand).

Penguins are streamlined and well adapted for movement through water. Propulsion in water is provided by the narrow, powerful wings, while the feet and tail act as rudders. Swimming speeds of up to 60 kilometers per hour have been claimed for larger penguin species, but a speed of 5–10 kilometers per hour is probably more representative. Pen-

Two burrow-nesting Magellanic penguins (*Spheniscus magellanicus*) in the Patagonian Desert of Chubut Province, Argentina. (Photo: M. A. Mares)

guins have both a dense covering of feathers and a well-developed layer of subcutaneous fat to provide insulation against the sometimes frigid seawater. Heights range from approximately 40 to 110 centimeters. Plumage is primarily gray or black above and white below. Plumage differences across species include crests, bands on the neck and chest, and coloration on the face and crown. Sexes are usually similar. The bills are generally short and robust. The diet consists of crustaceans, fish, and squid.

Many penguins are colonial when breeding, with colonies in some species (e.g., the Magellanic penguin of the Patagonian Desert) numbering several million pairs. Seasonal monogamy is the norm, but bonds may persist for longer. Clutches consist of either one (the king and emperor penguins, genus *Aptenodytes*) or two eggs (all others). Nests range from burrows in the desert to loose groupings of pebbles to bare ground. In the highly colonial Magellanic penguin, the nesting burrows may be located up to a kilometer or more from the ocean shore, thus providing the unusual experience of penguins living in burrows in desert scrubland.—Stephen C. Lougheed

See also **BIRDS; MONTE DESERT; NESTS, BIRD; PATAGONIA; SEA LION; SEAL; SOUTH AMERICA, DESERTS OF**

Further Reading

Boersma, P. D. 1976. An ecological and behavioral study of the Galapagos penguin. *Living Bird* 15:43–93.

Davis, L. S., and J. T. Darby. eds. 1990. *Penguin Biology.* New York: Academic Press.

Marchant, S., and P. J. Higgins, eds. 1990. *Handbook of Australian, New Zealand and Antarctic Birds.* Vol. 1 (pt. A). Melbourne: Oxford University Press.

Simpson, G. G. 1976. *Penguins: Past and Present, Here and There.* New Haven: Yale University Press.

Stonehouse, B., ed. 1975. *The Biology of Penguins.* London: Macmillan.

PERENNIAL PLANTS

Plants that live for more than one year or growing season. Perennials may be one of the following four forms: (1) trees or shrubs, plants with woody stems in which new growth emerges from buds on the woody stem, usually at the onset of the growing season; (2) perennial herbs, plants with herbaceous stems that die back to the ground at the end of the growing season and new growth emerges from belowground stems; (3) monocarpic herbs, plants that live over many years but flower only once; and (4) succulents, plants with spongy tissue that stores water. Examples of trees and shrubs that occur in North American deserts are mesquite, creosote bush, and sagebrush. Perennial herbs are not as common in desert settings as in grassland and forest biomes; examples are wormwood and tobosa grass. The century plant is an example of a perennial, monocarpic plant that occurs in the warm deserts of North America. Desert succulents include cacti and sedum.

Perennials may be contrasted with annuals, plants that emerge from the seed and die at the end of the first growing season after setting seed, and biennials, plants that produce a basal rosette the first year and then flower at the end of the second or third year of growth.—James R. Estes

See also **ANNUAL PLANTS; BULBS; CACTI; CHENOPODIACEAE; COTTONWOOD; HERBS; LEGUMES; PLANT ADAPTATIONS; PLANTS; SHRUBS**

Further Reading

Rost, T. L., M. G. Barbour, R. M. Thornton, T. E. Weier, and C. R. Stocking. 1984. *Botany.* 2d ed. New York: Wiley.

PERMIAN

Subdivision of geologic time spanning the interval from 286 million to 245 million years ago and named for rocks exposed over much of the province of Perm, Russia, west of the Ural Mountains. In this portion of the late Paleozoic era the earth's continental crust was configured as the supercontinent of Gondwana mostly south of the equator. Several other landmasses were beginning to merge with each other (as Laurasia in the Northern Hemisphere) and with Gondwana to form Pangea by the end of the Permian and the beginning of the Triassic period.

In the east Gondwana was separated from the northern continents by the Tethys Sea but was connected in the west between what are now eastern North America and northwestern Africa. The equator passed through the Tethys Sea and what are now southeastern North America and extreme northwestern Africa. Low-latitude deserts occurred during the Permian and part of the preceding Pennsylvanian period throughout central Laurasia and in northwestern Gondwana, as evidenced by evaporites and desert dune deposits in the stratigraphic record.

At the same time, at high latitudes, the earth experienced its most extensive and longest glaciation of the last 570 million years. Continental glaciers spread across most of Gondwana, which spanned the south polar region. Because of its mid- to low-latitude position, Laurasia apparently was unaffected by continental glaciation.—Nicholas J. Czaplewski

See also **CENOZOIC; CRETACEOUS; EOCENE; FOSSILS; GLACIAL PERIODS; MINERALS; MIOCENE; NEOGENE; OCEAN CURRENTS; OLIGOCENE; PALEOCENE; PALEOCLIMATE; PLATE TECTONICS; PLEISTOCENE; PLIOCENE; PRECAMBRIAN; QUATERNARY; RECENT (HOLOCENE); TERTIARY**

Further Reading

Harland, W. B., R. L. Armstrong, A. V. Cox, L. E. Craig, A. G. Smith, and D. G. Smith. 1990. *A Geologic Time Scale 1989.* New York: Cambridge University Press.

Stanley, S. M. 1986. *Earth and Life Through Time.* New York: Freeman.

PERSIAN DESERT. *See* IRAN, DESERTS OF

PERSPIRATION

A means of body temperature regulation that transfers heat away from the body when surface water is evaporated (sweating). Although all animals can lose water by diffusion through the skin, few animals have sweat glands. Therefore, sweating is not a prerequisite for desert survival, but it is an important mechanism in temperature regulation for some animals, including camels, donkeys, cattle, and humans. The risks from profuse sweating in a desert environment are loss of body water and salts, both of which must ultimately be replaced. In humans there is usually little effect from salt loss during sweating, although excessive loss of salts can lead to heat stroke. However, with rapid rehydration body fluids may become dilute and cause symptoms such as cramps. Salt replacement by normal foods is usually sufficient to deal with this problem; salt replacement with drinking water is rarely needed.

Water from perspiration is important because heat is dissipated when water on the skin surface evaporates. Conversion of liquid water to water vapor transfers heat to the surroundings as the latent heat of vaporization. The quantity of heat transferred varies with temperature but is about 0.58 kcal per gram of water evaporated.

A person exposed to the sun on a hot desert day can lose from one to one and a half liters of water per hour from perspiration. If a person continued sweating at that rate without replacing the water, death could ensue from dehydration in one day. For small desert animals with a much larger surface area to volume ratio than humans, heat regulation and evaporation are more difficult. If a small desert animal were to stay in the hot sun, it would have to perspire at a rate of 15 to 30 percent of its body weight per hour. Such a rate is intolerable, and therefore small desert animals must avoid the heat of the day by staying in underground burrows.—E. Annette Halpern

See also **ANIMAL ADAPTATIONS; BODY TEMPERATURE; COUNTERCURRENT HEAT EXCHANGE; DEHYDRATION; DESICCATION; ECTOTHERMY; ENDOTHERMY; ESTIVATION; EXCRETORY SYSTEM; HEAT BALANCE; HEAT EXCHANGE; HEAT STRESS; HEATSTROKE; HIBERNATION; HYPERTHERMIA; HYPOTHERMIA; KANGAROO RAT; KIDNEY FUNCTION, DESERT RODENTS; KIDNEYS; METABOLISM; PHYSIOLOGY; RENAL PAPILLA; RESPIRATORY WATER LOSS; SALT BALANCE; SHIVERING; SWEAT GLANDS; THERMOREGULATION; TORPOR; TRANSPIRATION; VAN'T HOFF EFFECT; WATER BALANCE; WATER STRESS**

Further Reading

Ingram, D. L., and L. E. Mount. 1975. *Topics in Environmental Physiology and Medicine*. New York: Springer.

Schmidt-Nielsen, K. 1990. *Animal Physiology: Adaptation and Environment*. 4th ed. New York: Cambridge University Press.

Whitney, E. N., and S. R. Rolfes. 1993. *Understanding Nutrition*. New York: West.

PERU, DESERTS OF

Peru contains both a lowland desert along the Pacific Coast and the high-altitude altiplano in the Andes, a high-elevation scrub desert that includes the puna. (The high-altitude deserts are discussed in detail in separate accounts: Altiplano, Andean Grasslands, Andes, and Puna). The most arid desert in the country is a narrow, rugged desert extending 2,350 kilometers along Peru's entire coast; it is a northward continuation of the Atacama Desert of Chile. In the north, between Piura and Chiclayo, the desert is a wide lowland largely covered by migrating sand dunes and is known as the Sechura Desert. (See map of South American deserts, p. 533.)

From Chiclayo south to Pisco forbidding Andean slopes reach the sea. Near Pisco several alluvial fans coalesce to a narrow, irregular lowland that is interrupted in places by rocky mountain spurs. Farther south a low range of mountains rises from sea level. A deeply eroded rocky surface rises east of these mountains, and its elevation increases gradually to the base of the Andes.

Most of this desert is so dry that only 10 or 15 rivers that drain the Andean slopes to the Pacific have sufficient volume to maintain their flow across the desert and reach the coast. The Peruvian section of the Atacama Desert is a narrow strip divided into more than 40 transverse valleys, where considerable volumes of water descending from the Andes flow from October to April. This desert is almost devoid of vegetation, except along the courses of rivers and streams. On the talus slopes, moistened by fog or rare winter drizzle, a thin cover of *Tilland-*

sia is likely to grow, associated with several lichens. This desert, like other coastal deserts, is one of the few deserts on earth where most precipitation is received in the form of fog.—Virgilio G. Roig

See also **ALLUVIAL FAN; ANDES; AN INTRODUCTION TO DESERTS; ARIDITY; ATACAMA DESERT; CHILE, DESERTS OF; CLIMATE; DESERTS, TEMPERATE; FOG DESERT; HUMBOLDT CURRENT; OCEAN CURRENTS; SECHURA DESERT; SOUTH AMERICA, DESERTS OF**

Further Reading

Allan, T., and A. Warren, eds. 1993. *Deserts: The Encroaching Wilderness*. New York: Oxford University Press.

Amiran, D. H. K., and A. W. Wilson, eds. 1973. *Coastal Deserts: Their Natural and Human Environments*. Tucson: University of Arizona Press.

Cabrera, A. L., and A. Willink. 1973. Biogeografía de América Latina. Organization of American States, Monograph No. 13. Washington, D.C.

Rauh, W. 1985. The Peruvian-Chilean deserts. *In* M. Evenari, I. Noy-Meir, and D. W. Goodall, eds., *Ecosystems of the World: Hot Deserts and Arid Shrublands*, 12B:239–267. New York: Elsevier.

PESTICIDES

Chemicals designed as poisons to protect plants grown for agricultural or decorative purposes from a variety of pests. Some pesticides are also applied to livestock. Pests are insects and other invertebrates, vertebrates, fungi, rusts and molds, and other competing plants. Although some pesticides have been in use since the mid-1800s, most widely used products have been developed since the end of World War II. Pesticides have gained wide acceptance because they are cost-effective, representing about three dollars in losses saved for every dollar spent. This does not take into account any environmental costs associated with the application of pesticides, however.

Pesticides are generally broken into three categories, depending on the target pests. Insecticides are used to kill insect pests. The first insecticides were inorganic compounds, like arsenates and hydrogen cyanide, and date to the mid-1800s. One of the first important synthetic insecticides was DDT, an organochlorine first developed in 1939. Most modern pesticides are organophosphates (OPs) or carbamates, which are less persistent than organochlorines and degrade more quickly in the environment. Herbicides are used for weed control

in agriculture and gardening. Herbicides date to 1900, but the variety of available herbicides expanded greatly in the 1940s and 1950s. They have many different modes of action on plants. Fungicides were developed first in 1851 to protect the ornamental shrubs and trees at Versailles. As with other pesticides, many new compounds were developed during the mid-20th century. They are currently widely used on fruits and vegetables.

Although environmental concerns have restricted pesticide use to some degree, they are still heavily used the world over on crops, forests, lawns, gardens, and golf courses. Pesticide use in deserts is primarily for agriculture, turf (including golf courses), and livestock. Agriculture and turf in desert environments both require irrigation; when pesticides are sprayed near or onto watercourses, they can become concentrated in the limited water that is available. The heavy use of herbicides in dryland agriculture can also affect soil texture and make the land difficult to seed. The use of toxins for rodent (primarily prairie dogs) and predator control in livestock grazing lands is a serious problem in some arid grasslands. Hawks and vultures are occasionally killed by consuming tainted bait set out in predator control programs.—Thomas E. Lacher, Jr.

See also **CONSERVATION IN DESERTS; CONTAMINATION; DESERTIFICATION; ECOLOGY; ECOSYSTEM; INSECTICIDES; IRRIGATION DRAINAGE; POLLUTION; PREDATION**

Further Reading

Brown, A. W. A. 1978. *Ecology of Pesticides*. New York: Wiley.

Moriarity, F. 1988. *Ecotoxicology: The Study of Pollutants in Ecosystems*. 2d ed. London: Academic Press.

Zakrzewski, S. F. 1991. *Principles of Environmental Toxicology*. Washington, D.C.: American Chemical Society.

PHOTOSYNTHESIS

Absorption of light energy by membrane-bound chlorophyll, or related molecules, and the use of the absorbed energy to convert carbon dioxide (CO_2) and a hydrogen source to simple organic compounds. A broad array of organisms are capable of photosynthesis—green plants, photosynthetic bacteria, Cyanobacteria (= blue-green bacteria), true algae, and assorted flagellated protistans. The details of photosynthesis may vary from group to group, but a generalized equation is possible:

$CO_2 + 2H_2A$ (+ energy from light) $\rightarrow (CH_2O) + H_2O + 2A$,

with A varying between the photosynthetic bacteria and the green plants. In green plants A is oxygen, and the summary reaction is

$CO_2 + 2H_2O$ (in the chloroplast + energy from light) $\rightarrow (CH_2O) + H_2O + O_2$.

The significance of photosynthesis to life on earth cannot be overstated: (1) the capture of solar energy by chlorophyll provides the earth with massive levels of biological energy, and permitted the evolution of biological complexity at the molecular, cellular, organismal, community, and biome levels; (2) carbohydrates produced in the photosynthetic reaction provide the backbone for all organic compounds and most metabolism; (3) all free oxygen in the atmosphere originated with photosynthesis, and oxygen is necessary both for oxidative respiration and for filtering ultraviolet light from the solar energy that strikes the earth's surface; (4) photosynthesis fixes carbon dioxide and removes it from the atmosphere, and, because CO_2 is a major greenhouse gas, its concentration in the atmosphere affects global temperatures; (5) photosynthesis also permitted the evolution of multicellular plants, which provide human society with sources of food, fuel, fiber, and pharmaceuticals. Thus life as we know it on earth would not be feasible without photosynthesis and plants, and human society could not have flourished without this chemical reaction. Some authors have speculated that reduced levels of photosynthesis resulting from a large meteor striking the earth resulted in mass extinction of dinosaurs.

Photosynthesis and oxidative respiration are highly interrelated and global; annual levels of the two are in equilibrium. One of the essential elements of photosynthesis is the use of solar energy in the reduction of carbon dioxide to store energy in the form of carbohydrates $[(CH_2O)_x]$. Respiration, in contrast, is primarily an oxidation event in which foods, including carbohydrates, utilize oxygen to release stored energy in the form of the energy-rich molecule ATP (adenosine triphosphate). In the process carbon dioxide is released. Thus, under usual circumstances, global levels of CO_2 and O_2 should remain constant, but over the span of geologic time there have been significant fluctuations of these two atmospheric gases.

Reduction reactions store energy when a target molecule accepts an electron (e^-). In biological reduction reactions, the electron is often affiliated with the nucleus of a hydrogen atom. Oxidation reactions store energy, and they involve the release of an e^- with its hydrogen nucleus in biological systems.

Among the eukaryotic organisms, photosynthesis takes place in the chloroplast. Chloroplasts are variously shaped cellular organelles with an external double membrane, a liquid phase (stroma), and flattened membrane systems embedded within the stroma (thylakoids). Thylakoids contain the chlorophyll and accessory pigments.

Photosynthesis is composed of two processes. The first is a light-dependent, photochemical reaction that occurs within the thylakoids. The pigments of the thylakoids harvest or capture light in two separate membrane-bound systems: Photosystem I and Photosystem II. In each the energy is passed to a reaction center, where the chlorophyll molecules are raised to a higher energy state (excited state) through the acceptance of an electron. The excited chlorophyll molecules can then accomplish work. Photosystem II carries out the photolysis (breaking down) of water molecules to produce free oxygen and a hydrogen nucleus. It also passes the e^- it received when it absorbed light to a chain of e^- acceptors. Energy is lost with each conversion in the chain, and the free energy is used to synthesize the high-energy molecule ATP. Ultimately the e^- is passed to Photosystem I, which also absorbs light energy. Consequently, Photosystem I is boosted to an even higher energy state. That e^- also flows down an electron chain where it finally reduces NADP (nicotine adenine dinucleotide phosphate) to produce $NADPH_2$ (reduced NADP), the final e^- acceptor in the light reaction. NADP also receives the hydrogen nucleus that originated with photolysis. The products of the light-dependent phase of photosynthesis are therefore free oxygen, ATP, and reducing power in the form of an electron carrier with an attendant hydrogen atom with its electron ($NADPH_2$).

The second phase of photosynthesis is the light-independent, biochemical reaction, also called the Calvin cycle. In the stroma of the chloroplast, ATP and $NADPH_2$ from the light-dependent reaction are used by the plant to fix CO_2, that is, to reduce the molecule and to form carbohydrate. This is accomplished when the CO_2-acceptor molecule, ribulose 1-5 biphosphate (RuBP), encounters a carbon dioxide molecule in the presence of the enzyme ribulose biphosphate carboxylase. In the process the five-carbon RuBP and the single-carbon CO_2 are converted to two three-carbon sugars (C_3), which are the first organic products of photosynthesis:

$$5C + 1C \rightarrow 2C_3.$$

Repeating this reaction six times, requires six carbon dioxide molecules and generates enough new carbohydrate for a newly minted glucose molecule. Glucose is a 6C sugar ($C_6H_{12}O_6$), and it is the basic building block for all carbohydrates, amino acids, and lipids—it is the most fundamental food for most organisms. Note that a molecule of glucose includes six carbon atoms, one for each CO_2 molecule:

$$6(5C + 1C) \rightarrow 12C_3 \text{ or } 36C.$$

When six carbon atoms are used enzymatically to synthesize glucose, 30 remain (36 - 6 = 30). The 30Cs could, of course, be enzymatically refashioned to synthesize five glucose molecules. However, more often they are used to resynthesize the original six RuBP that were initially used to begin the production of glucose. This capacity to recycle a vital primer contributes to the overall efficiency of photosynthesis and green plants.

The photosynthetic reaction with glucose as the primary carbohydrate product can be summarized as follows:

$$6CO_2 + 12H_2O \text{ (in the chloroplast + energy from light)} \rightarrow C_6H_{12}O_6 + 6H_2O + 6O_2.$$

When O_2 levels are high or when CO_2 levels are low, RuBP preferentially binds with oxygen and photosynthesis is restricted. This situation often occurs at high temperatures or during drought conditions because the stomata close, restricting access to carbon dioxide. Plants of arid and semiarid habitats are especially susceptible. Many tropical, warm grassland, and warm desert plants, however, have evolved systems to counter what is effectively a loss of RuBP. In this process the first organic product of photosynthesis is a four-carbon organic acid, hence the name C_4 photosynthesis in contrast to C_3 photosynthesis. In C_4 plants, the organic acid is eventually shunted to the Calvin cycle.

C_4 plants are especially abundant in the warm deserts of southwestern North America and in the southern Great Plains. Many of these plants are members of the grass family (Poaceae), the genera of which exhibit several variations on this common theme.

Succulent plants (e.g., cacti and sedum) have yet another mechanism termed Crassulacean Acid Metabolism (CAM) in which CO_2 is fixed at night rather than in the daylight. The products are likewise shunted into the Calvin cycle. CAM plants are very common in the Sonoran and Coloradan deserts of the Southwest.

Regardless of the variations in carbon fixation, it is clear that photosynthesis is the "key that winds the spring of life" (Walker).—James R. Estes

See also **AQUATIC HABITATS; BACTERIA; C_3 PLANTS; C_4 PLANTS; CARRYING CAPACITY; DECOMPOSITION; ENERGY FLOW; FUNGI; GROWING SEASON; LEAVES; LICHENS; MOSSES; PATHOGENS; PLANT ADAPTATIONS; PLANTS; PRIMARY PRODUCTIVITY; PRODUCTIVITY, AQUATIC SYSTEMS; STOMA; SUCCESSION; TRANSPIRATION**

Further Reading

Budyko, M. I., A. B. Ronov, A. L. Yanshin. 1987. *History of the Earth's Atmosphere.* New York: Springer.

Hall, D. O., and K. K. Rao. 1987. *Photosynthesis.* 5th ed. London: Edward Arnold.

Walker, D. 1992. *Energy, Plants, and Man.* 2d ed. Brighton, U.K.: Oxygraphics.

PHREATOPHYTES

Plants with long taproots that extend into the water table. Phreatophytes avoid the desiccating conditions of deserts through their ability to gain access to deep water. They often occur along desert watercourses, because the water table is higher there, even under dry streambeds. They may also grow along the banks of running streams in deserts and grasslands. These plants are so effective at extracting water that water tables can be depleted seriously when they are abundant, especially because most phreatophytes are inefficient at water conservation. Mesquite, a phreatophyte of American, Asian, and African deserts, successfully has invaded vast acreages in the arid and semiarid lands of North America, and in the process uses valuable water resources. Mesquite is effective, in part, because it has characteristics both of phreatophytes and of true xerophytes. Salt cedar (*Tamarix*) was introduced into the United States from the steppes of Asia. Salt cedar is a halophyte (salt-loving plant) and a phreatophyte. It is now the dominant tree along many permanent streams in the western United States. It appears to have reduced the flow of water in many of these streams, such as the Arkansas, Canadian, and Red rivers, and to have lowered water tables in many parts of the Southwest.—James R. Estes

See also **COTTONWOOD; GRASSLAND; HALOPHYTES; LEGUMES; MESQUITE; PHOTOSYNTHESIS; ROOTS; RIO GRANDE; RIPARIAN COMMUNITIES; RIVERS; SALT CEDAR; STOMA; XEROPHYLLOUS FOREST; XEROPHYTES**

Further Reading

Paylore, P., ed. 1974. *Phreatophytes: A Bibliography.* Washington, D.C.: Department of the Interior.

Simpson, B. B., ed. 1977. *Mesquite: Its Biology in Two Desert Ecosystems.* Stroudsburg, Pa.: Dowden, Hutchinson, and Ross.

PHYSIOLOGY

The study of the normal function or actions of living organisms or their parts. Physiology in desert settings is concerned primarily with organismic responses to environmental conditions of high aridity, with concomitant high levels of potential organismic evaporation and dehydration. Responses to heat are also of great interest in desert physiology, because the high temperatures exacerbate the effects of aridity in two major ways: high temperatures increase the drying potential of the air, and they increase the need of an organism to cool evaporatively to maintain body temperature below damaging limits. For animals, an additional problem for living in the desert is the typically sparse and scattered vegetation, resulting in reduced shelter and food.

Studies in desert physiology tend to focus on the avenues involved in three major balances that organisms must maintain to survive: water, heat, and nutrition. Tolerance and adjustments to excessive losses (e.g., water) or gains (e.g., heat) are frequently the first parameters examined. Determinations are then made of the input and output avenues and actual organismic quantities under varying environmental conditions. As an example, in water balance analyses of animals, the inflows via drinking, free water in food, and metabolic or oxidative water are compared relative to the outflows in feces, urine, and evaporation through the skin (e.g., sweat) and respiratory organs (e.g., panting). Similarly, avenues of thermal balance are determined, including metabolism and evaporation, which are always heat input and output terms, respectively. The avenues of radiation, convection, and conduction can be either input or output terms, depending on organismic and environmental attributes.—David S. Hinds

See also **ANIMAL ADAPTATIONS; BODY TEMPERATURE; CAMEL; CAMEL'S HUMP; CLOTHING; COUNTERCURRENT HEAT EXCHANGE; DEHYDRATION; DESICCATION; ECTOTHERMY; ENDOTHERMY; ESTIVATION; EXCRETORY SYSTEM; EXPLOSIVE HEAT DEATH; HEAT BALANCE; HEAT EXCHANGE; HEAT STRESS; HEATSTROKE; HIBERNATION; HUMAN PHYSIOLOGY IN DESERTS; HYPERTHERMIA; HYPOTHERMIA; KANGAROO RAT; KIDNEY FUNCTION, DESERT RODENTS; KIDNEYS; METABOLISM; PERSPIRATION; RENAL PAPILLA; RESPIRATORY WATER LOSS; SALT BALANCE; SHIVERING; SUNBURN; SUNSTROKE; SURVIVAL IN DESERTS; SWEAT GLANDS; THERMOREGULATION; TORPOR; TRANSPIRATION; VAN'T HOFF EFFECT; WATER BALANCE; WATER STRESS**

Further Reading

Batholomew, G. A. 1982. Body temperature and energy metabolism. *In* M. S. Gordon, ed., *Animal Physiology*, 333–406. 4th ed. New York: MacMillan.

Bradshaw, S. D. 1997. *Homeostasis in Desert Reptiles.* New York: Springer.

Degan, A. A. 1997. *Ecophysiology of Small Desert Mammals.* New York: Springer.

Gosh, P. K., and I. Prakash. 1988. *Ecophysiology of Desert Vertebrates.* Jodhpur: Scientific Publishers.

Heatwole, H. 1996. *Energetics of Desert Invertebrates.* New York: Springer.

Maclean, G. L. 1996. *Avian Adaptations to Deserts of the Northern and Southern Hemispheres: A Comparison.* Perth, Western Australia: Curtin University of Technology.

Schmidt-Nielsen, K. 1990. *Animal Physiology.* 4th ed. New York: Cambridge University Press.

Smith, S. D. 1997. *Physiological Ecology of North American Desert Plants.* New York: Springer.

Somme, L. 1995. *Invertebrates in Hot and Cold Arid Environments.* New York: Springer.

Warburg, M. R. 1997. *Ecophysiology of Amphibians Inhabiting Xeric Environments.* New York: Springer.

PIGEON

Generally refers to all species of the avian family Columbidae (order Columbiformes). The term "pigeon" is often used in a more restricted sense to include only larger columbids, while "dove" refers to smaller species of the family. Approximately 300 species of columbids from 42 genera have been described. Pigeons have an almost cosmopolitan distribution, absent only from Antarctica and northern portions of Eurasia and North America. Columbids inhabit a wide variety of habitats, from rain forest to desert. New World taxa that are found in arid habitats include members of the genera *Columbina* and *Metriopelia* (ground doves) and *Leptotila* and *Columba*. For example, the Inca dove (*Columbina inca*) occupies savanna, arid scrub, and second growth woodlands, ranging from the southwestern United States through Central America to northern South America. A number of African genera are also associated with arid habitats. For example, the ring-necked dove (*Streptopelia capicola*) is widespread in most types of semiarid and arid zones of eastern and southern Africa. The now-widespread rock pigeon (*Columba livia*) is believed to have evolved in arid zones of the Old World. The crested pigeon (*Ocyphaps lophotes*) is an example of an Australian columbid that inhabits various types of open arid country.

Generally pigeons have short legs, compact bodies, relatively small heads, and thin, flexible bills. Wing shape varies, but columbids generally are strong fliers, and some taxa undertake migrations of substantial distances. Species range in total length from 14 centimeters (e.g., dwarf fruit dove, *Ptilinopus nanus*) to 80 centimeters (e.g., crowned doves, genus *Goura*). Most species possess plumage that is relatively drab and cryptically colored except for iridescent patches on the wings or head; a few tropical species are brightly colored with dramatic ornamentation. Degree of sexual dimorphism in plumage varies, although in most species sexes are colored similarly.

Pigeons are generally gregarious and often feed, fly, and roost in groups. There is a continuum of feeding habits across species ranging from mainly arboreal (e.g., fruit doves) to foraging almost completely on the ground (e.g., ground doves). Food items include seeds, fruit, buds, leaves, and flowers. For some taxa, invertebrates make up part of the diet. Digestion of hard seeds is aided through abrasion by the muscular gizzard containing grit. All columbids require ready access to water, and even desert species are almost always found, sometimes in substantial numbers, close to permanent water sources.

Most columbids nest in trees or bushes, although a few arid country species nest on the ground (e.g., flock pigeons, *Phaps histrionica*, of Australia) or use cliff ledges (e.g., rock pigeons) or burrows (e.g., bare-faced ground doves *Metriopelia ceciliae*, of the South American Andes). Where availability of nesting sites is limited, pigeons may nest colonially. Nests are insubstantial, consisting of small twigs and grasses. The majority of pigeons lay two eggs per clutch, and a smaller number of species lay only a single egg. Incubation duties and care of young are shared by both sexes. Incubation times tend to be quite short (10–30 days), and numerous species are capable of producing many broods per year. The young are altricial; for the first few days after hatching they are fed protein-rich secretions from the parents' crop ("crop milk"). Crop milk is gradually supplanted by the natural food of the adults. The young grow rapidly and fledge 10–36 days after hatching.—Stephen C. Lougheed

See also **ANIMAL ADAPTATIONS; BIRDS; GRANIVORY; NESTS, BIRD; SEEDS**

Further Reading

Goodwin, D. 1983. *Pigeons and Doves of the World*. 3d ed. Ithaca: Cornell University Press.

Johnston, R. F. 1992. Rock dove (*Columba livia*). *In* A. Poole, P. Stetteheim, and F. Gill, eds., *The Birds of North America*, No. 13. Philadelphia: Academy of Natural Sciences; Washington, D.C.: American Ornithologists' Union.

McLelland, J. 1979. Digestive system. *In* A. S. King and L. McLelland, eds., *Form and Function in Birds*, 1:69–181. New York: Academic Press.

Mueller, A. J. 1992. Inca dove (*Columbina inca*). *In* A. Poole, P. Stetteheim, and F. Gill, eds., *The Birds of North America*, No. 28. Philadelphia: Academy of Natural Sciences; Washington, D.C.: American Ornithologists' Union.

PIGMENT

Classes of biological molecules that impart color to an organism and typically serve other vitally important metabolic functions as well. The number of molecules that are colored is relatively small compared to the total number of molecules present in living organisms; however, these thousands of colored molecules are crucial to many physiological and metabolic functions in plants and animals. In addition, these molecules are responsible for the majority of colors and color patterns in living organisms that are so aesthetically valuable. Some of the most common pigments in plants and animals are porphyrins and carotenoids. Numerous types of biological compounds are formed from porphyrins, including the chlorophylls, which play a critical role in photosynthesis, the process by which plants convert water and inorganic carbon to carbohydrates, the ultimate source of food for all living organisms. Another porphyrin is hemoglobin, the protein molecule that transports oxygen in the blood and imparts the red color to blood. Carotenoids are synthesized only by plants, yet are crucial to numerous metabolic functions in both plants and animals; thus animals are entirely dependent on the consumption of plants as a source of carotenoids. In animals carotenoids, particularly vitamin A, are central to the many chemical reactions necessary to produce vision. Another major class of pigments present in nearly all living organisms is melanin. Melanins are responsible for the black, brown, buff, and tawny colors of the feathers, skin, and plumage of many organisms. The many black organisms found in cooler deserts owe their coloration to the presence of melanin. In contrast, mammals that have white fur have the hair shaft filled with a pithy substance in place of concentrated melanins.

Arid-adapted African frogs in the genus *Hyperolius* have an unusual adaptation in which the pigment guanine is used for slowing the rate of water loss across the skin. During dry periods these frogs show an increase in the number of iridophores found in their skin. Approximately 80–90 percent of iridophores are composed of the purine pigment guanine, which in turn has a large amount of nitrogen. Thus these frogs are able to store part of the nitrogen in their bodies in this form as opposed to excreting it, which would require the expenditure of valuable water. Iridophores can store enough nitrogen to be of significant osmoregulatory benefit to these frogs.—Janalee P. Caldwell

See also **AMPHIBIANS; ANIMAL ADAPTATIONS; ARTHROPODS; BIRDS; COLORATION; CRYPSIS; FEATHERS; FROGS; INSECTS; LIZARDS; MAMMALS; MELANIN; MOLT; PHOTOSYNTHESIS; REPTILES; SNAKES; TOADS; WARNING COLORATION**

Further Reading

Fox, D. L. 1979. *Biochromy: Natural Coloration of Living Things*. Berkeley: University of California Press.

Herman, C. A. 1992. Endocrinology. *In* M. E. Feder and W. W. Burggren, eds., *Environmental Physiology of the Amphibians*, 40–54. Chicago: University of Chicago Press.

Schmuck, R., and K. E. Linsenmair. 1988. Adaptations of the reed frog *Hyperolius viridiflavus* (Amphibia, Anura, Hyperoliidae) to its arid environment: 3. Aspects of nitrogen metabolism and osmoregulation in the reed frog, *Hyperolius viridiflavus taeniatus*, with special reference to the role of iridophores. *Oecologica* 75:354–361.

Shoemaker, V. H., S. S. Hillman, S. D. Hillyard, D. C. Jackson, L. L. McClanahan, P. C. Withers, and M. L. Wygoda. 1992. Exchange of water, ions, and respiratory gases in terrestrial amphibians. *In* M. E. Feder and W. W. Burggren, eds., *Environmental Physiology of the Amphibians*, 125–150. Chicago: University of Chicago Press.

PIKA

Rodentlike member of the family Ochotonidae (mammalian order Lagomorpha) in the genus *Ochotona* (with one recently extinct genus and 22 species). Although in the same order as rabbits and hares, pikas resemble guinea pigs in form (length of head and body 125–300 millimeters). Limbs are short, and the soles of the feet are heavily furred. The tail is absent, and the ears are short and rounded. The grayish brown hair is long and soft. Like other members of the order, two pairs of incisors are present in the upper jaw; the cheek teeth are high crowned, rootless, and continually growing.

Pikas are distributed in Eurasia (from sea level to 6,000 meters) and western North America (at elevations of 90–4,100 meters). They inhabit open plains, deserts, and grassy steppes. In open country they live primarily in rocks and talus. Most species inhabit talus slopes or piles of rocks. They occur in the Iranian Desert above 3,000 meters and in the high-altitude desert of the Himalayas.

Pikas are noted for the haystacks they construct, which sometimes reach a height of more than a half meter and which are the animals' food supply throughout the year; the stacks are made of grasses, sedges, weeds, and other plants. In areas where snow does not cover the ground during winter, pikas may not construct haystacks.

Pikas are active during the day (diurnal); they do not hibernate, and they may be seen basking in the sun during the winter. Their body temperature is high (40.1°C); to reduce the amount of body heat produced, they reduce their activity in higher temperatures.

Pikas may form large colonies (the steppe-dwelling species) or may live in pairs or small family groups (rock-dwelling species). Dens are excavated burrows or natural crevices and contain passages, a nesting chamber, food stores, and areas for defecation. Pikas are very vocal, and one of their common names is the whistling hare.—Janet K. Braun

See also **ANIMAL ADAPTATIONS; ASIA, DESERTS OF; DESERTS, MONTANE; GRASSLAND; HARE; RABBIT; SAVANNA; STEPPE**

Further Reading

Grzimek's Encyclopedia of Mammals. Vol. 4. 1990. New York: McGraw-Hill.

Macdonald, D., ed. 1984. *The Encyclopedia of Mammals.* New York: Facts on File.

Nowak, R. M. 1991. *Walker's Mammals of the World.* 5th ed. Baltimore: Johns Hopkins University Press.

PIMA. *See* O'ODHAM

PINNAE

External auditory structures, found only in mammals, that function to intercept and focus sounds and that may be independently directed, as when attempting to determine the direction of a particular sound. Pinnae may be present or absent (as in some insectivores, cetaceans, and the "earless" seals).

When present pinnae may be large (as in some bats or rabbits) or small (as in many fossorial, or burrowing, mammals). Pinnae are important in temperature regulation and echolocation. Mammals that live in hot, arid environments generally have elongated extremities, including ears (Allen's Rule). This elongation increases the surface area (in the case of ear pinnae) and thus increases the heat loss. Vessels in the large ears of the black-tailed jackrabbit (*Lepus californicus*) vasodilate to dissipate heat rapidly when the ambient temperature is less than the body temperature.

Mammals inhabiting cold regions have small, poorly insulated pinnae. Heat loss may be reduced by allowing the ears to cool using a vasoconstriction or countercurrent heat exchange system, thereby reducing the difference between the ambient temperature and the ear temperature.—Janet K. Braun

See also **ASS; BODY TEMPERATURE; ENDOTHERMY; ELEPHANT; FOX; HEAT BALANCE; HEAT STRESS;**

Large pinnae (ears) of a Chacoan thorn scrub species, the brown brocket deer (*Mazama gouazoupira*). (Photo: M. A. Mares)

JACKRABBIT; JERBOA; MARA; METABOLISM; PHYSIOLOGY; THERMOREGULATION; WATER BALANCE

Further Reading

Schmidt-Nielsen, K. 1964. *Desert Animals: Physiological Problems of Heat and Water.* New York: Oxford University Press.

———. 1972. *How Animals Work.* London: Cambridge University Press.

Vaughan, T. A. 1986. *Mammalogy.* 3d ed. Philadelphia: Saunders.

PIT VIPER

Snake in the family Viperidae possessing a pair of heat sensory pits located between the nostrils and eyes. All pit vipers are in the subfamily Crotalinae of the family Viperidae, and a vast majority of species are restricted to the New World. At least 144 species in 16 genera are currently recognized, and they occur in an amazing diversity of habitats, including montane forests, deserts, plains, tropical lowland forests, cloud forests, and coastal sand dunes. The geographic range of pit vipers encompasses parts of Asia, North America, Mexico, Central America, and most of South America. Although most species are terrestrial, some are arboreal, aquatic, or even somewhat fossorial (burrowing), partially burying themselves in sand. All pit vipers are venomous and have large, movable front fangs capable of delivering potentially lethal doses of primarily hemolytic venom. Venom is used for capturing prey as well as for defense. Bites of pit vipers are considered dangerous to man, with disfiguration and death occurring in extreme cases of envenomation.

Pit vipers are considered by most herpetologists to be among the most fascinating of reptiles because of their remarkable sensory capabilities, the great diversity of habitats and microhabitats they use, the variation in their life histories (some species deposit eggs, while most are viviparous), the medicinal importance of their venoms, and the overall impact that these snakes have had on humans, including their importance in folklore and art. As higher-order predators in a diversity of ecosystems, pit vipers are important components of the natural biota within their extensive geographic range.

The best-known pit vipers are the rattlesnakes (genera *Crotalus* and *Sistrurus*) and the lance-headed pit vipers (genus *Bothrops*). Most species of rattlesnakes occur in North America and Mexico, whereas most species of lance-headed pit vipers occur in South America. The largest pit viper is the bushmaster (*Lachesis muta*), which occurs from Nicaragua southward through tropical South America, including southeastern Brazil. Bushmasters may reach lengths as great as four meters.

Most pit vipers occurring in deserts are rattlesnakes in the genus *Crotalus*. The most obvious adaptations of pit vipers to desert habitats are behavioral and oriented toward avoiding extremes of temperature and desiccation. Desert pit vipers are usually nocturnal or crepuscular (active at dawn and dusk), except in early spring and late fall, when temperatures are cooler. They spend most of their time underground in rodent burrows, or deep in rock crevices, where temperatures are relatively low and humidity is relatively high. Most desert pit vipers feed on warm-blooded prey (mammals and birds) as adults, but juveniles often feed on lizards, and some may even eat large centipedes. Pit vipers identify prey by a combination of chemical and thermal cues. The tongue and vomeronasal organs are involved in chemoreception, and the infrared heat sensory pits are involved in heat detection. The pit organs are extremely sensitive to relatively rapid changes in the thermal landscape surrounding a snake's head, so much so that the snake can accurately strike a small mammal that walks by, even when the snake is blindfolded.—Laurie J. Vitt

See also **CROTALUS; DEFENSIVE ADAPTATIONS, ANIMALS; POISONOUS ANIMALS; PREDATION; RATTLESNAKE; SIDEWINDER; SNAKES; VENOM**

Further Reading

Campbell, J. A., and E. D. Brodie, Jr. 1992. *Biology of the Pitvipers*. Tyler, Tex.: Selva.

Campbell, J. A., and W. W. Lamar. 1989. *The Venomous Reptiles of Latin America*. Ithaca: Cornell University Press.

Minton, S. A., and M. R. Minton. 1969. *Venomous Reptiles*. New York: Scribner's.

PLAGUE

Disease, also known as bubonic plague or the black death, which is caused by the bacillus *Yersinia pestis* and that has led to millions of deaths and greatly influenced human history. Many mammals can serve as a reservoir for the plague bacillus, but the most commonly associated animals are rats and other rodents. Rodents that live closely with people are often the source of outbreaks of plague. The bacillus is transmitted from rats to people by fleas. Fleas become infected when they bite an infected animal. The fleas either abandon the animal when it dies, often from the plague itself, or leave the living rodent and adopt a nearby human for a host. A person can become infected when bitten by an infected flea. Whether the person develops the disease depends on the strain of the bacillus, the magnitude of the exposure, and the physical condition of the infected person. Plague symptoms differ from person to person but often include combinations of high fever; pains in the chest, abdomen, and head; general weakness; chills; blue coloration of the face, lips, or skin under the finger- and toenails; inflammation of the lungs with shallow breathing; nausea; racing pulse; and painful swellings of the lymph nodes (termed bubos). The death rate from plague is estimated to be 40–60 percent of those infected. Antibiotics have been effective in treating several strains of plague. Plague vaccines have been only moderately successful. Plague is most common in arid regions, but the reason for this is not known.—Rob Channell

See also **ARTHROPODS; BACTERIA; ECOLOGY; MAMMALS; PATHOGENS; PRAIRIE DOG; RODENTS**

Further Reading

Gregg, C. T. 1978. *Plague: An Ancient Disease in the Twentieth Century*. Albuquerque: University of New Mexico Press.

PLANT ADAPTATIONS

Evolutionary structures, strategies, functions, and devices developed by plants to be able to exist in particular environments. Plants adapt to a desert environment using one of two major strategies, stress tolerance or stress avoidance. Species that remain physiologically and metabolically active during periods of stress are said to tolerate that stress, whereas species that enter dormancy in one form or another may avoid the stressful period. Within each of these major categories are several different modes of behavior.

Stress tolerance in deserts consists of an ability to either procure or store water during dry periods, as well as an ability to tolerate extremes in temperature. Water procurement depends on the physical structure or morphology of the plant, particularly its rooting structure. Typically most desert species are either very deeply rooted, with roots extending several meters into the soil, or they are very shallow rooted, with roots found only in the upper 10–20 centimeters of soil. Deeply rooted species may tap into sources of groundwater and thus be able to obtain water during extreme dry periods. Species with shallow roots are dependent on rainfall for their moisture. These species quickly absorb surface moisture whenever it is available. Although their rooting structure is not deep, it is extensive, with roots extending in the surface soil layers for several meters in all directions away from the aboveground shoot. After these species absorb moisture from occasional rainfall or runoff, it is stored in succulent tissue, such as is found in cactus stems or in fleshy leaves.

In addition to water procurement and storage, it is important for these stress tolerators to reduce their loss of water as much as possible. Plants undergo the process of transpiration, the evaporation of water through specialized pores called stomata. These pores operate as the location for gas exchange for plants; they take in CO_2 in the process of photosynthesis (the fundamental chemical equation of life, wherein carbon dioxide and water, in the presence of chlorophyll, are combined with energy from light to form carbohydrates and release oxygen). As plants absorb CO_2 they also lose water vapor. Desert species have to strike a delicate balance between procuring the CO_2 that is necessary for their survival and losing water through transpi-

ration. There are structural and physiological mechanisms whereby plants can reduce their water loss.

Desert species generally use structural mechanisms to reduce water loss. Reduction of leaf size reduces the heat load on the leaf and thus lessens the need for transpiration to help cool the leaf. Some species actually can move their leaves with respect to the angle of the sun so that they minimize heat buildup over the course of a day. For example, creosote bush, *Larrea cuneifolia*, orients its leaves in a north-south direction to minimize heat load, a characteristic that leads to one of its common names, compass plant. Other species, such as *Encelia farinosa*, brittlebush, grow large spines, hairs, or other reflective coverings on the surface of the leaf that also act to keep leaves cool.

On a microscopic scale some species have "sunken" stomata where the pores are found at the bottom of microscopic pits on the leaf surface. The pit acts to hold water vapor close to the stomatal surface, thus reducing the rate of diffusion of water vapor from the interior of the leaf to the outside. Other species have waxy coatings on the leaf surface that reduce nonstomatal evaporation and may reflect light as well.

Species of large cacti have combinations of all the above structures and an additional mechanism of "self-shading." If one took a cross-section of a cactus stem, the edges would appear fluted due to the occurrence of ribs. The angle of the ribs and their depth create shadows on the surface of the cactus stem. By cooling the stem, there is less evaporative loss of water. These mechanisms for reducing water loss have drawbacks in that they reduce the amount of light absorbed, which will reduce the rate of photosynthesis. Thus the plant "pays" for its ability to reduce water loss with a reduction in growth rate.

A physiological mechanism to reduce the rate of water loss is employed by plants using a unique form of photosynthesis termed Crassulacean Acid Metabolism (CAM). This was first discovered in succulent members of the family Crassulaceae, the stone crops. In this form of photosynthesis, CO_2 is taken in during the night through open stomata and then stored in plant cells in the form of four-carbon acids (acids containing four carbon atoms). During the daylight hours the stomata close and the plant uses light energy to take a CO_2 molecule off of each four-carbon acid (decarboxylation) and then run it through the usual metabolic pathways to make sugar. This form of photosynthesis is extremely costly in energetic terms. It takes a great deal of energy to keep cell membranes intact in the presence of large quantities of acid, and it takes a lot of energy to decarboxylate acid molecules. Thus employing this mechanism to reduce water loss also causes plants to pay a price in decreased rate of growth, since the plant's energy is being used for other things. This form of photosynthesis is frequently found in cactuslike plants and plants that have succulent leaves. Many of these species may also have several of the structural mechanisms for reducing water loss, such as spines, ribs, or hairs. These species are typically very slow growing and therefore do not grow where they may have to compete with faster-growing species for nutrients.

Another physiological mechanism for the reduction of water loss is known as stomatal control. Species with high levels of stomatal control can quickly close stomata when their internal water content starts to get too low, a situation known as water stress. Surprisingly, many species outside of arid environments do not exercise stomatal control but leave stomata open until water stress reaches lethal levels. The stomatal control exercised by many desert species ensures that stomata are closed long before lethal levels of stress are reached.

The level of stress that a plant can tolerate is determined through a unique measure of the water inside that plant. This measure includes both the amount of water in the plant and the availability of that water for plant use. This is termed water potential. The potential of "pure water" (water that lacks minerals or other materials) is zero. As more material is dissolved in water, it becomes more difficult for plants to procure and transport it. The water potential then has a negative value, becoming increasingly negative as more material is dissolved in it. The water potentials of tissues of stress tolerators have been found to be very low. Plants in less arid habitats would suffer cell collapse (plasmolysis) at these low potentials. One mechanism used by stress tolerators to avoid this fate is to have extremely thick cell walls that maintain cell structure even when the cell cytoplasm starts to collapse due to low water potentials. Plants whose leaves have this thick cell wall structure are said to have xerophyllous leaves.

In addition to water stress, species in warm desert environments need to cope with thermal stress. Species that tolerate high temperatures can do so through either acclimation or homeostasis. Acclimation (adjusting to temperature changes) is shown by a number of species over the course of a year, with their temperature optimum for photosynthesis being higher in summer than in spring. Plants can acclimate by making enzymes (specialized proteins that catalyze chemical reactions) that can tolerate and operate at different temperature levels. Thus in the cool spring these species will make enzymes that operate best at cool temperatures. In summer enzymes that operate best at high temperatures are used. Species using the homeostasis approach (maintenance of relatively constant temperature) use the mechanisms discussed above which reduce the amount of light striking the leaf to keep leaf temperature within a narrow temperature range, rather than make different types of enzymes.

Stress avoiders enter dormancy when temperature or moisture stress becomes severe. Perennial species that lose their leaves are termed drought deciduous, and many desert shrub species are drought deciduous. Some nonvascular plants (plants lacking vascular tissues) have no true leaves but have leaflike structures (thalli) that will curl up into dense protective mats during drought stress. Although the thalli of these species appear dead due to their blackened color and brittle texture, they will rehydrate in the next rainfall, becoming green and supple again, hence the common name resurrection plant given to many of these species.

Drought-deciduous species (species that lose their leaves during times of drought) enter a state of dormancy similar to that experienced by species in temperate deciduous forests (forests that lose their leaves each year and occur in the climatic zone located between the tropics and the Arctic or Antarctic). Species that use this strategy include ocotillo, *Fouquieria splendens*, catclaw, *Acacia greggii*, and paloverde, *Cercidium floridum*. The tissue remaining after leaves are lost is protected from water loss by a reduction in metabolic activity. The living cells in that tissue slow their metabolic rate so much that the cell no longer needs large quantities of water to maintain itself. Thus it can exist in a state of low hydration. Drought-deciduous plants can offer further protection to these cells by placing them inside structures on the plant (buds) or by burying them below ground. Living cells placed within buds are protected by thick, waxy scales called bud scales. This protects the living tissue from water loss very effectively when the living tissue is elevated above the soil surface. Nonwoody species such as grasses bury their buds beneath the soil. The entire aboveground portion of the plant dies back during drought periods, leaving the living buds below ground carefully protected from evaporation and possible damage from animals. Species with elevated buds face desiccation from desert winds. Thus most desert species that have elevated buds do not elevate them very far above the soil surface. This is one of the reasons that many deserts are populated by a variety of species of low-growing shrubs.

Drought-deciduous species emerge from dormancy when temperatures moderate or water becomes available. Given that their growth is limited to these periods, many of these species lack some of the special adaptations discussed above for stress-tolerant plants. However, several do have morphological adaptations, such as reflective hairs, to reduce the rate of water loss so that the period for growth is maximized. Also, some species exhibit stronger stomatal control as the soil starts to dry but lack stomatal control during periods of high soil moisture. This also can act to lengthen the period of time during which these species can remain physiologically active.

These perennial plants also have the problem of storage of photosynthetically fixed sugars from year to year. Most species store excess sugars as starch in specialized belowground structures. The root systems of many drought-deciduous species are quite extensive, not only for successful water procurement, but also to provide sufficient space for starch storage. When the plant emerges from dormancy, these starches are mobilized, that is, chemically changed back into sugars, which are then transported above ground to help support the growth of the newly emerging leaves.

Annual plants (also known as ephemerals) do not enter dormancy in the same way as perennial species but avoid drought through rapid growth and reproduction during the wet period. Thus by the time the water supply is gone these species will have already formed seeds and will survive as seeds during the dry period. The seeds formed by these species will not germinate until sufficient water is

present to support growth. The growth period of annuals depends on the timing of rainfall in the desert in which they are found. Thus in the North American Sonoran Desert, where rainfall occurs primarily in late summer, most of the annual species are "summer annuals." These species primarily use the C_4 photosynthetic pathway, which has a high temperature optimum and supports extremely rapid growth. Examples are *Tidestromia lanuginosa* and *Atriplex elegans*. In the Mojave Desert most of the annuals are "winter annuals" since rainfall is concentrated in the late winter or early spring months. These species use the C_3 photosynthetic pathway, which has a lower temperature optimum and does not support the extremely high growth rates seen in summer annuals. Winter annuals typically do not achieve the stature seen in summer annuals and require a longer time to complete their growth cycle. Examples are *Salvia columbariae* and *Festuca octoflora*. Neither winter nor summer annual species are known for having many of the structural adaptations for reducing water loss that have been discussed above. This is because their growth occurs only during a period of adequate water supply. However, summer annuals are known for having highly dissected leaves (fernlike) rather than entire (nondissected) leaves. The dissection of the leaves into small subunits helps to keep the summer annual's leaves from overheating. Because heat accumulation rather than avoidance may be a problem for winter annuals, having leaves that are entire helps them to heat up above the level of the ambient air temperature, which in turn helps to speed the rate of photosynthesis and possibly the growth rate of these plants.

Seeds of desert annuals face the challenge of determining when sufficient water is present. Germinating after a brief shower could be fatal. They possess both structural and physiological mechanisms to ensure that germination does not occur until large quantities of water are present. Seeds will not germinate until their protective covering, known as a seed coat, is no longer intact. Breakage of the seed coat then allows the embryonic plant inside of the seed to expand, extend its root, and start to grow. Desert species can use this restriction to their advantage by placing water-repelling (hydrophobic) substances in the seed coat. In the presence of sufficient water these hydrophobic compounds are washed from the seed coat; water can then enter the seed and cause swelling and breakage of the seed coat. This ensures germination in the presence of large quantities of water, as a short shower will not generate enough water to wash all the hydrophobic compounds from the seed coat. Other species have extremely thick seed coats that gradually get worn down by the abrasion caused by water moving the seed past stones, pebbles, and other hard objects.

Of all of the plant groups discussed above, only summer annuals do not look like desert plants. They have few of the spines, hairs, or succulent tissues that we have come to associate with life in desert environments. In addition, they may be among the species that are physiologically least closely tied to the desert environment, as their entire life cycle is timed closely to the average length of the wet period in the particular desert community they inhabit. All the other plant types described above may possess one or more morphological and physiological traits that are usually associated with desert life.

Regardless of the structural or physiological adaptations employed by desert species, all share one important trait in terms of their life history. (Life history is defined as how long and when a particular species is in different life stages. The stages could include prereproductive, reproductive, and postreproductive portions of the life cycle.) Desert species, regardless of their tolerance to stress, time the reproductive portion of their life cycle to occur during an optimal period for growth. This strategy is employed because reproduction is energetically costly, and may be extremely costly in terms of water use, depending on the type of flower used by the species. Large, showy flowers that attract pollinators with the promise of excess pollen or nectar are typically delicate structures that lose a great deal of water through both evaporation and transpiration. These flowers are usually very short lived but can be supported by the plant during times of adequate soil moisture and moderate temperatures. Smaller, nonshowy flowers that may depend on wind pollination (such as grass flowers) are less costly in terms of water loss but will still be costly energetically. This is due to the large quantities of pollen produced, as well as the large amount of energy spent on the flowers and seeds themselves. Seeds and fruits require large quantities of energy,

both to store sufficient quantities of food for the survival of the embryo and to provide any specialized structures such as thick seed coats.—Linda L. Wallace

See also **ANIMAL ADAPTATIONS; ANNUAL PLANTS; ARIDITY; BACTERIA; C$_3$ PLANTS; C$_4$ PLANTS; CACTI; CAM PLANTS; CRYPTOGAMS; DEHYDRATION; DESERT BLOOM; DESERTS; DROUGHT; EPIPHYTES; FLOWERS; FRUITS; GOURD; GRASSES; GROWING SEASON; HERBS; LEAVES; LEGUMES; LICHENS; MOSSES; NITROGEN-FIXING PLANTS; OVERGRAZING; PALOVERDE; PERENNIAL PLANTS; PHREATOPHYTES; PLANT COVER; PLANT DISPERSAL BY WIND (ANEMOCHORY); PLANT GEOGRAPHY; PLANT ROOTS, ADVENTITIOUS; PLANTS; POLLINATION; PRIMARY PRODUCTIVITY; PRODUCTIVITY, AQUATIC SYSTEMS; PSAMMOPHYTES; RESURRECTION PLANT; ROOTS; SALTBUSH; SEED DISPERSAL BY ANIMALS (ZOOCHORY); SEEDS; SHRUBS; STOMA; SUCCESSION; THORN; TRANSPIRATION; WATER BALANCE; WATER LOSS; XENOPHYTES; XEROPHYLLOUS FOREST**

Further Reading

Cloudsley-Thompson, J. L. 1996. *Biotic Interactions in Arid Lands*. Berlin: Springer.

Chabot, B. F., and H. A. Mooney. 1985. *Physiological Ecology of North American Plant Communities*. New York: Chapman and Hall.

MacMahon, J. A., and F. H. Wagner. 1985. The Mojave, Sonoran and Chihuahuan deserts of North America. *In* M. Evenari, I. Noy-Meir, and D. W. Goodall, eds., *Ecosystems of the World: Hot Deserts and Arid Shrublands*, 12A:105–202. New York: Elsevier.

Mulroy, T. W., and P. W. Rundle. 1977. Annual plants: Adaptations to desert environments. *BioScience* 27:109–114.

Smith, S. D. 1997. *Physiological Ecology of North American Desert Plants*. New York: Springer.

Wickens, G. E. 1998. *Ecophysiology of Economic Plants in Arid and Semi-arid Lands*. New York: Springer.

PLANT COVER

Amount of ground area covered by a plant or group of plants. It is usually expressed as a percentage of the total area within a defined region and particular plant community.

Cover is determined in several ways. The most common method is to estimate visually the aerial (aboveground) coverage of each plant. The entire aerial portion of the plant is considered to cover the soil surface, even if that portion is not touching the soil surface. Another estimation procedure, based on basal coverage, measures or estimates how much area is covered by the basal portion of the plant in contact with the soil surface.

In desert communities plant cover is usually quite low. In the warm deserts of western North America total coverage estimates range from 20 to 40 percent of the soil surface occupied by plants in a community. This leaves a great deal of bare soil uncovered by any plant portion, the "interstitial" spaces. In some communities this area is occupied by cryptogamic mats of nonvascular plants, lichens, cyanobacteria, and algae. In most communities this area is unoccupied.

In desert communities that are dominated by shrubs, plant cover values are usually much greater and can actually exceed 100 percent due to overlapping aerial plant parts. However, in the shrub steppe communities of western North America and other "semideserts," cover values are more typically in the range from 60 to 70 percent. Interstitial spaces in these communities can also be either bare or occupied by cryptogamic mats.

In any environment low coverage values are felt to be due to intense competitive interactions that exist between plant species. The widely spreading roots of many species are capable of drawing down soil moisture to levels that are incapable of supporting additional plant life. Also, nutrient levels in these interstitial spaces are extremely low.

In addition to the intense competition that exists between established plants, extremely intense competition occurs between an established plant and a seedling attempting to gain a foothold in an environment, especially in a very dry area such as a desert. The advantage lies with the established plant because of its existing root network. Seedlings have much shorter roots that occupy only the very superficial soil layers. These layers are subject to rapid drying and nutrient loss. Therefore, seedling establishment in interstitial spaces is rare. This leads to the retention of the open aspect of the appearance (physiognomy) of desert plant communities.

In specialized cases cover provided by plants is critical to the establishment of seedlings. For example, saguaro cacti (*Carnegiea gigantea*) seedlings actually require shading from plants to prevent overheating or photobleaching. The plants providing the shade are termed nurse plants. As the cactus grows it eventually displaces or causes reduced growth of the nurse plant.

Plant cover is also essential to animals in desert communities. Many species use larger shrubs for shade and protection from predators, as well as for food or nest materials. Indeed, several species actually dig their burrows underneath shade plants to help cool the burrow entrance as well as to conceal it from predators. Many desert animals will spend the entire day underneath shade plants or in burrows and will venture forth only after sunset.—Linda L. Wallace

See also **BACTERIA; BURROWING ANIMALS; ECOLOGY; ECOSYSTEM; ENERGY FLOW; HERBS; LICHENS; MOSSES; PLANT ADAPTATIONS; PLANTS; PRIMARY PRODUCTIVITY; SAGUARO; SHRUBS; SUCCESSION; WOODRAT**

Further Reading

MacMahon, J. A. 1988. Warm deserts. *In* M. G. Barbour and W. D. Billings, eds., *North American Terrestrial Vegetation*, 231–264. Cambridge: Cambridge University Press.

Walter, H. 1983. *Vegetation of the Earth*. 3d ed. Berlin: Springer.

West, N. E. 1988. Intermountain deserts, shrub steppes, and woodlands. *In* M. G. Barbour and W. D. Billings, eds., *North American Terrestrial Vegetation*, 209–230. Cambridge: Cambridge University Press.

PLANT DISPERSAL BY WIND (ANEMOCHORY)

Wind-assisted dispersal of plant seeds and other propagules, a common pattern of dispersal by plants in sparse, windy deserts. The seeds of plants that use anemochory tend to be very small or dust-like. Anemochorous plants also produce seeds in large quantities, up to several million. Adaptations that facilitate anemochory include plumes, winglike appendages, tumbling, and ballooning. Plumes are the most common adaptation for anemochory among plants with small fruits and seeds. The common dandelion (*Taraxacum officinale*) is one of several plants in the sunflower family (Asteraceae) that have developed plumes to aid in dispersal. Other examples are members of the milkweed family (Asclepiadaceae) and cottonwood trees (*Populus*). Winged fruits are more prominent in plants with heavy seeds. Fruits with winglike appendages are common in the maple (Aceraceae) and elm (Ulmaceae) families. Tumbling is a form of anemochory that requires the wind to move the whole plant or large portions of the inflorescence. Russian thistle, or tumbleweed (*Salsola kali*), an introduced species in the southwestern United States, best exemplifies this form of anemochory. Ballooning is a rarer form of anemochory than those cited above. It involves the swelling or inflation of appendages on the fruit or portions of the inflorescence. *Kochia scoparia* and *Suaeda*, members of the goosefoot family (Chenopodiaceae), are desert and steppe species that employ this mode of dispersal.—Bruce W. Hoagland

See also **CHENOPODIACEAE; COTTONWOOD; ECOLOGY; ECOSYSTEM; PLANT ADAPTATIONS; PLANTS; SEED DISPERSAL BY ANIMALS (ZOOCHORY); SEEDS; SUCCESSION; TUMBLEWEED**

Further Reading

Howe, H. F., and J. Smallwood. 1982. Ecology of seed dispersal. *Annual Review of Ecology and Systematics* 13:201–228.

Pijl, L. van der. 1972. *Principles of Dispersal in Higher Plants.* 2d ed. New York: Springer.

Ridely, H. N. 1930. *The Dispersal of Plants throughout the World.* London: Ashford.

PLANT GEOGRAPHY

Study of the distribution of plants through space and time, including factors affecting the distribution (and co-occurrence) of species. A number of environmental factors exert an influence on the survival of plants, and the distribution of those factors plays a role in influencing the geographic dispersal of plant species. The following nonexhaustive, nonordered list provides a sample of environmental factors, both biotic and abiotic: (1) climate, with all its ramifications; (2) soil type; (3) day length; (4) pathogenic agents; (5) other plants; (6) soil moisture; (7) available minerals; (8) periodicity of fire; (9) herbivores; and (10) periodicity of drought.

It is obvious to even the most casual traveler that the vegetation varies across North America and other continents. Traveling from Cape Hatteras to the California coast just north of Santa Barbara along the 35th parallel, for example, the vegetation changes dramatically from the sparse vegetation of the sand dunes of the Outer Bank to the pine-dominated forests of the sand hills of Carolina and then to a deciduous forest that extends across the Great Smoky Mountains to central Oklahoma. The forest gradually diminishes in height, density, and number of species from eastern Oklahoma to its terminus in central Oklahoma. Then the great Eastern Deciduous Forest is replaced by the grasslands of central

North America. There is a brief interlude of tallgrass prairie, but the vegetation quickly passes into a midgrassland that extends westward to the Texas Panhandle.

From the 100th meridian into Texas and almost to Albuquerque, New Mexico, the High Plains, or American Steppes, are a semiarid grassland whose grasses average less than a foot tall. However, on the flanks of the buttes and mountains the mixed coniferous forests of the eastern Rocky Mountains begin and continue to the western flank of the range. In northern Arizona there is a long stretch of the Great Basin Desert, which gives way with declining elevation to the Mojave Desert at the Arizona-California border. Crossing the southern limits of the Sierra Nevadas is another coniferous forest; then the interior valley grasslands of California appear and are followed by the chaparral scrublands (Mediterranean climate) of the southern Coast Range. Finally, there are the sparsely vegetated dunes of the California coast.

A north-to-south transect across North America from Guatemala to Baffin Island in the Arctic Ocean would reveal even greater differences in vegetation types. Four basic types of terrestrial vegetation emerge: (1) forest, (2) shrubland, (3) grassland, and (4) desert. On this scale, forests generally receive the highest levels of precipitation, and deserts the lowest.

The continuity of vegetation types across broad geographic areas led early plant geographers to define these large vegetation zones as biomes. Eastern Deciduous Forest, Southern Pine Forest, Subtropical Forest, Central Grasslands, Western Coniferous Forest, Great Basin, Southwestern Deserts, and California Chaparral are biomes in the United States. Some investigators divided the vegetation more finely, separating, for instance, the hot deserts of the Southwest into two to four biomes. Because these biomes could be correlated with differences in climate (or, in a few instances, soils), it was often concluded that climate determined the vegetation of a region. This dominant vegetation type was termed the climax vegetation. If the area were disturbed by geologic, meteorological, or human influences, the climatic vegetation type for that region would gradually become reestablished. The vegetation might, however, pass through several stages (termed successional stages) before the climax was attained. The climax stage can be identified because the plants that exist in the climax reproduce themselves, and all age classes of all the species are represented in the same proportions, meaning that a stable, self-replicating community had developed in a region.

More recently most plant geographers have concluded that the boundaries are not as exact among the biomes or their subdivisions as was first thought and that the species are distributed as individuals, rather than being components of a larger, organic whole. Thus a more detailed examination would reveal that the Eastern Deciduous Forest varies across its range, and the observed variance depends on the physiological limits of each of the individual species that make up the community. Furthermore, the intergradation between biomes is gradual rather than abrupt. This view, referred to as the continuum concept, is now widely accepted.

Plant distributions may also be discontinuous (i.e., disjunct distributions). In general wide discontinuities result from two historical causes: (1) long-range dispersal and subsequent establishment of the newly founded populations and (2) segregation of a once larger distribution into a fragmented one through the extinction of individuals in the intermediate zones (i.e., vicariance). Both undoubtedly occur in nature. Many species of New World desert shrubs, such as creosote bush (*Larrea*) and mesquite (*Prosopis*), occur in similar habitats in North and South American deserts. The intermediate geographic zone is tropical, and much of it is tropical rain forest, where these two desert endemics would be unable to survive. There is considerable evidence that the tropical vegetation is older than the desert types; therefore, these instances almost certainly involve long-range dispersal. In contrast, the genus *Platanus* exists in India, the Mediterranean, the eastern United States, and along streams in the desert Southwest of the United States. Fossil records provide evidence that this genus once had a much greater range. The present disjunct distribution is therefore the result of vicariance events, presumably the opening of the North Atlantic Ocean, which resulted from plate tectonics, and the emergence of drier conditions in North America. These two examples reveal the need to use historical evidence to comprehend distributional patterns, and it is vital that the phylogenetic history of the taxa also be taken into account if one is to understand how species came to be distributed where they are found today.—James R. Estes

See also **AN INTRODUCTION TO DESERTS; BIOME; CLIMATE; DESERT GRASSLAND; DESERTS; GRASSES; GRASSLAND; GREAT BASIN DESERT; HOLDRIDGE LIFE ZONES; MADRO-TERTIARY GEOFLORA; MOJAVE DESERT; PAINTED DESERT; PALEOCLIMATE; PLANT ADAPTATIONS; PLATE TECTONICS; PLEISTOCENE; PLIOCENE; PRIMARY PRODUCTIVITY; SPECIATION; SONORAN DESERT; SUCCESSION; UNITED STATES, DESERTS OF**

Further Reading

Barbour, M. G., and W. D. Billings. 1988. *North American Terrestrial Vegetation*. Cambridge: Cambridge University Press.

Brown, J. H., and A. C. Gibson. 1983. *Biogeography*. St. Louis: Mosby.

Gleason, H. A., and A. Cronquist. 1964. *The Natural Geography of Plants*. New York: Columbia University Press.

PLANT ROOTS, ADVENTITIOUS

Roots that develop from stems or leaves. "Adventitious" refers to any plant part that develops in an unusual manner or position. The plant axis consists of the shoot (the aerial portion, including stems and leaves) and the root (the belowground component). Primary roots develop from the radicle, the basal segment of the axis and the first part of the embryo to emerge when seeds germinate. Primary roots may branch to form secondary roots, which may also branch to form tertiary roots. This process of rebranching may continue an indeterminate number of times.

Adventitious roots may be produced in response to injury, and horticulturists may induce their production by cutting or treating stems with a plant hormone. However, adventitious roots are natural features of many species. In maize (*Zea mays*) and many species of palms (family Arecaceae), roots develop from the lower stem; these prop roots provide support for the stem and angle away from the stem entering the soil. The banyan tree (*Ficus benghalensis*), also called strangling fig, is an epiphyte (a plant that grows on another plant but not as a parasite) that produces roots, which originate from branches. Adventitious roots of banyan trees extend to the ground and enter the soil; they also become woody and support the branches.

Most vascular plants' roots are anchored in soil, from which they obtain water, oxygen, and minerals (e.g., nitrogen). Adventitious roots function normally in water uptake and are structurally similar to other roots. In deserts the additional water absorption capacity they provide is probably of some importance.—James R. Estes

See also **GERMINATION; PLANT ADAPTATIONS; PLANTS; SEEDS**

Further Reading

Davis, T. D., and B. E. Haissig, eds. 1994. *Biology of Adventitious Root Formation*. New York: Plenum.

PLANTS

Any individuals or species that are members of the plant kingdom. From the classical period until the middle of the 20th century, the biological world was considered to be composed of two kingdoms, plant and animal. In this classification scheme plants were circumscribed (delimited or defined) on the basis of their immotility (in contrast to the ability of animals to move) and the presence of a cell wall (animal cells lack walls). The plant kingdom contained bacteria, fungi, algae, and higher, or multicellular, plants.

The traditional classification has been substantially revised during the past three decades. This alteration was based on the realization that (1) each of the two kingdoms was highly diverse and (2) many species could not be unequivocally placed in either kingdom. As an example, dinoflagellates have cell walls, but they are highly motile. One widely accepted solution was to circumscribe kingdoms on the basis of overall similarity, organizational and cellular complexity, and ecological function. In the resultant classification five kingdoms were recognized: (1) bacterial kingdom, (2) protistan kingdom, (3) fungal kingdom, (4) animal kingdom, and (5) plant kingdom. Plants were defined as multicellular, photosynthetic organisms (capable of using light energy from the sun to synthesize food from inorganic molecules) with cells that have cell walls, chloroplasts, and membrane-bound nuclei. Plants in this scheme include multicellular algae, mosses, and vascular plants. This classification of kingdoms, however, also has serious conceptual and practical weaknesses: (1) Protista is highly heterogeneous and includes groups of organisms that are clearly not closely related, (2) several major groups of organisms are difficult to place in any of the kingdoms, and (3) the classification is not based on phylogeny (patterns of evolutionary divergence or branching), the commonly accepted conceptual basis for classification. In addition, the plant kingdom remained highly diverse.

Methods of analysis have since been developed which permit more rigorous hypotheses of phylogenetic relationships. One element of this method (cladistic analysis) is to define taxa on the basis of shared, derived characters. Cladistics makes it possible to infer whether individuals share a common origin. One phylogenetic lineage that has been recognized involves the stoneworts (family Characeae); mosses, hornworts, and liverworts (phylum Bryophyta), wisk ferns (phylum Psilotophytes), club mosses (phylum Lycophyta); horsetails (phylum Equisetophyta); ferns (phylum Polypodiophyta), cycads (phylum Cycadiophyta), gingkoes (phylum Gingkophyta), conifers (phylum Pinophyta), *Gnetum* and its relatives (phylum Gnetophyta), and flowering plants (phylum Magnoliophyta). These organisms share the following characters: (1) multicellular organization; (2) the presence of chlorophylla and chlorophyllb as light-absorbing molecules; (3) alternating sexual and asexual generations; (4) starch as the primary form of stored energy; (5) cellulose cell walls; and (6) immotility. This group of taxa (kingdom Plantae) are thus considered plants. The kingdom Plantae is closely related to the green algae (phylum Chlorphyta), and the two groups share all of these characters, with the exception of multicellular organization and lack of motility. Therefore, the plants probably arose from within the green algae. Some botanists even consider the plant kingdom to involve the first group of multicellular forms plus the green algae, but most biologists place the green algae within the protistan kingdom. Investigations are being conducted to explore the phylogeny of the plants and phylogenetic relationships of the included taxa based on molecular and structural data.

Plants have the capacity to synthesize their own energy-rich food from carbon dioxide (CO_2) and water (H_2O) through the absorption of solar energy by chlorophyll molecules, which are located in chloroplasts. Chlorophyll absorbs energy most effectively in the blue and red regions of the visible spectrum. Therefore, plant tissues often reflect green wavelengths and appear green. The phrase "green plants" is often used to refer to the plant kingdom, but it is somewhat redundant and, as noted below, not entirely accurate.

Animals, fungi, and many bacteria are incapable of using light to synthesize food. Some organisms, such as broom-rape, dodder, and some orchids, that are otherwise clearly plants also cannot carry out photosynthesis. These are still considered plants because they share all the remaining features and their closest living relatives are green and photosynthetic. It has been hypothesized that these plants lost their photosynthetic capacity rather recently, and many of them retain chloroplasts that produce chlorophyll molecules that are incapable of photosynthesis.

Most algae and many bacteria and protistans photosynthesize, but among these groups only the green algae utilize both chlorophylla and chlorophyllb as light-absorbing pigments. Thus only the green algae are related to the higher plants and may be included within the plant kingdom. In addition, many algae, other than the green algae, store food in forms other than starch and have cell walls based on molecules other than cellulose.

Alternation of generations is restricted to plants. Plants that are members of a sexual generation (gametophyte) reproduce through production of gametes (sex cells) that unite (fertilization) to produce a zygote—the first cell in the asexual generation (sporophyte). Sporophytes are diploid, and they undergo meiosis to produce haploid, asexual reproductive cells (spores) that germinate without fertilization to produce a gametophyte. Gametophytes are haploid. In most plants the gametophyte and sporophyte are structurally very different. As an example, the sporophytes and gametophytes of ferns could easily be mistaken for members of different phyla. However, in some green algae the sporophytes and gametophytes are similar.

In animals gametes are products of meiosis, but in plants gametes are produced by mitotic division. In all the plant groups meiotic division produces spores, sometimes referred to as meiospores.

Bacteria, fungi, some unicells, and plants all produce cell walls. Only plants use cellulose as the primary building material of the walls. Cellulose is a long-chain polymer of glucose, a product of photosynthesis.

Plants are largely immobile, a consequence of their ability to synthesize food from sunlight. Sunlight is generally available across the surface of the globe, and there is no advantage to changing locations to capture light. Rather, obtaining water is a more crucial necessity, and water may be obtained more dependably from the soil, even in deserts. Hence the vast majority of plants are rooted firmly in the earth. In arid and semiarid regions water may be a limiting factor in plant growth. Therefore, competition for water is a factor in desert biomes.

Higher plants (vascular plants) maintain an embryonic region (meristem) at the terminus of stems and roots. Meristems continue to produce new shoot and root tissue. These plants are therefore able to grow continuously, and they have an open growth plan.

The lack of available water is the defining feature of deserts, and four different strategies are used by plants to survive this paucity:

1. *Annual or ephemeral plants*. Such plants germinate and grow from seed or underground perenniating organs only when moisture is abundant following a rain and then die or become dormant when drought conditions return; such plants essentially avoid desert conditions.

2. *Succulents*. This group of plants, which includes cacti, geophytes (low-growing plants that have the appearance of rocks), sedum, and euphorbias, has effective water-gathering root systems, and the water is then stored in spongy tissue at the center of the stem or the root. They tend to have highly reduced leaves and carry on photosynthesis in the stem, features that also reduce water loss.

3. *Phreatophytes*. Plants that grow in microhabitats that are wet and effectively extract the available moisture. The most common mechanism is to produce deep taproots that extend to the water table. Mesquite and tamarisk (salt cedar) are both effective phreatophytes.

4. *Xerophytes*. Plants that rely on their capacity to extract water from the soil against high negative water potentials and concomitantly to reduce transpiration (loss of water vapor from the leaf surface). Extracting water from the soil against low water potentials requires the expenditure of considerable cellular energy. Mechanisms for reducing water loss include closing stomates and varying the time of closing, sinking stomates at the base of pits in the leaf surface, surface hairs to reflect light and slow wind flow across the leaves, increasing the thickness of the waxy

cutin, reducing the surface area of leaves, producing leaves that roll or curl under dry or hot conditions, dropping leaves during extreme drought, and inhibiting loss of water-laden tissue to predators. Examples of desert xerophytes are mesquite in the Western Hemisphere and acacia in the Eastern Hemisphere and *Artemisia* in both.

Primary productivity of desert ecosystems is low relative to plants in other major vegetation types (e.g., grasslands, forests), because vegetation is sparse. Hence there is a low concentration of chlorophyll per hectare. Not surprisingly, the vegetation cover is governed largely by water availability, with the hot, dry deserts—for instance, the Sahara and Middle Eastern deserts—having little vegetation and the cooler, wetter deserts—for instance, the Great Basin and Gobi deserts—being relatively productive.

Although the abundance of plants is reduced in desert biomes, plant diversity (number of species per unit area) may be quite high. Thus Wadi Araba of Israel and Jordan is exceptionally dry but has a fairly high level of endemic plant species. The Sonoran Desert of the southwestern United States and northwestern Mexico has a very high level of plant diversity, in part because of the number of habitats that are available.—James R. Estes

See also **ANNUAL PLANTS; BACTERIA; BIOME; BULBS; CACTI; CARRYING CAPACITY; CRYPTOGAMS; ECOLOGY; ECOSYSTEM; ECOTYPE; EPIPHYTES; FLOWERS; FOREST; FRUITS; GERMINATION; GROWING SEASON; HALOPHYTES; HERBS; LANDSCAPE; LEAVES; LEGUMES; LICHENS; MOSSES; NITROGEN-FIXING PLANTS; OVERGRAZING; PATHOGENS; PERENNIAL PLANTS; PHOTOSYNTHESIS; PLANT ADAPTATIONS; PLANT COVER; PLANT DISPERSAL BY WIND (ANEMOCHORY); PLANT ROOTS, ADVENTITIOUS; POLLINATION; PRIMARY PRODUCTIVITY; PSAMMOPHYTES; RESURRECTION PLANT; ROCK VARNISH; ROOTS; SEED DISPERSAL BY ANIMALS (ZOOCHORY); SEEDS; SUCCESSION; STOMA; THORN; TRANSPIRATION; XENOPHYTES**

Further Reading

Anonymous. 1978. *Plant-Water Relationships in Arid and Semi-arid Conditions*. Paris: UNESCO.

Bilbrough, C. J., and J. H. Richard. 1993. Growth of sagebrush and bitterbrush following simulated winter browsing. *Ecology* 74:481–493.

Ehleringer, J. R., H. A. Mooney, P. W. Rundel, R. D. Evans, and B. Palma. 1992. Lack of nitrogen cycling in the Atacama Desert. *Nature* 359:316–319.

Friedmann, E. I., and M. Galun. 1974. Desert algae, lichens, and fungi. *In* G. W. Brown, ed., *Desert Biology: Special Topics on the Physical and Biological Aspects of Arid Regions*, 2:166–212. New York: Academic Press.

Kamenetsky, R. 1994. Life-cycle, flower initiation, and propagation of the desert geophyte *Allium rothii*. *International Journal of Plant Science* 155:597–606.

Margulis, L. 1982. *Five Kingdoms: An Illustrated Guide to the Phyla of Life on Earth*. San Francisco: W. H. Freeman.

Semft, D. 1995. Success secrets of desert plants. *Agricultural Research* 43:12–15.

Simpson, B. B., ed. 1977. *Mesquite: Its Biology in Two Desert Ecosystems*. Stroudsburg, Pa.: Dowden, Hutchinson, and Ross.

Wiley, E. O., D. R. Brooks, and A. V. Funk. 1993. *The Compleat Cladist: A Primer of Phylogenetic Procedures*. Lawrence: University of Kansas Museum of Natural History, Special Publication No. 19.

PLATE TECTONICS

Theory in which the lithosphere, or crust, of the earth is shown to be fractured into several segments (plates) that are formed by volcanic activity along midoceanic ridges, that slowly move in response to convection in the earth's mantle, and that are subducted or thrust back down into the mantle along oceanic trenches. The lithosphere of the earth is its relatively rigid outer shell and includes the denser oceanic crust and the lighter, thicker continental crust. The less dense continental crust "floats" atop the deeper oceanic crust, just as the whole lithosphere floats above the asthenosphere of the molten mantle. Significant geologic activity, including earthquakes, volcanism, and mountain building, typifies the margins of tectonic plates. The theoretical mechanism proposed as the driving force moving the plates is convection currents within the outer mantle that drag the plates along or push from beneath.

The process has probably been ongoing since the Precambrian inception of the first small continental landmasses that developed as a result of the slow density separation of the materials making up the accreting planet earth. There is strong evidence that similar volcanic and tectonic activity occurred or continues to occur on other planets and their satellites in our solar system. The oldest-known continental crust on earth, discovered in Australia, has been radiometrically dated as 3.5 billion years old.

Older continental crust might have existed but could have been recycled by the process of subduction into the mantle. A "fossil" subduction zone (now long inactive) that is 2.7 billion years old is known in Canada.

As lithospheric plates move they change the relative positions and orientation of the continents. At times some masses of continental crust have coalesced to form larger landmasses, while others have been (and, like Africa, Iceland, and parts of California, are being) rifted into smaller pieces. In the late Precambrian and early Paleozoic most of the early continents merged to form a supercontinent called Pangea. In time the plates that made up Pangea started to split up to form Laurasia (which was mostly in the Northern Hemisphere) and Gondwana (which was mostly southern). This split began in the Mesozoic and continues with still greater fragmentation to the present day.

The dynamism of plate tectonics and the drift of the continents have significant effects on climate, including the existence and occurrence of deserts. As crustal plates move some ocean basins open and others close or are otherwise altered. As a result the circulation patterns of oceans and the atmosphere can be drastically changed; this in turn strongly alters regional climates. Upwelling of cold ocean water alongside continents, as in coastal Namibia in Africa, can contribute to aridification of the adjacent continental area. As tectonic plates converge or collide, mountains are squeezed up (and down into the mantle). Mountains also alter the circulation patterns of the atmosphere, sometimes creating a rain shadow protecting the leeward side of the mountain range from precipitation. Occasionally both upwelling and rain shadow effects act together, as in the Atacama Desert of coastal Peru and northern Chile, to form extreme deserts.

Plate tectonics and the movement of continents also have had tremendous effects on the earth's biota over time. As ocean basins, shorelines, paleocurrents, and sea levels have changed, marine organisms have been forced into extinctions, evolutionary radiations, or competition with species from which they had previously been isolated. Similar occurrences have characterized organisms evolving on the continents, as evidenced in the fossil record. And as the continents have been rafted across latitudinal belts of climate, pronounced climatic changes have occurred.—Nicholas J. Czaplewski

See also **AUSTRALIA, DESERTS OF; CLIMATE; CRETACEOUS; EOCENE; FOSSILS; GLACIAL PERIODS; LITHOSPHERE; OCEAN CURRENTS; OLIGOCENE; PALEOCENE; PALEOCLIMATE; PRECAMBRIAN**

Further Reading

Bambasch, R. K., C. R. Scotese, and A. M. Ziegler. 1980. Before Pangea: The geographies of the Paleozoic world. *American Scientist* 68:26–38.

Briggs, J. C. 1987. *Biogeography and Plate Tectonics.* Amsterdam: Elsevier.

Buick, R., J. R. Thornett, N. J. McNaughton, J. B. Smith, M. E. Barley, and M. Savage. 1995. Record of emergent continental crust ~3.5 billion years ago in the Pilbara Craton of Australia. *Nature* 375:574–577.

Flessa, K. W. 1980. Biological effects of plate tectonics and continental drift. *BioScience* 30:518–523.

Habicht, J. K. A. 1979. *Paleoclimate, Paleomagnetism and Continental Drift.* Tulsa, Okla.: American Association of Petroleum Geologists.

Hamblin, W. K. 1992. *Earth's Dynamic Systems.* 6th ed. New York: Macmillan.

Kröner, A., and P. W. Layer. 1992. Crust formation and plate motion in the early Archean. *Science* 256:1405–1409.

Levin, H. L. 1988. *The Earth Through Time.* 3d ed. Philadelphia: Saunders.

Smith, A. G., D. G. Smith, and B. M. Funnell. 1994. *Atlas of Mesozoic and Cenozoic Coastlines.* Cambridge: Cambridge University Press.

Windley, B. F. 1995. *The Evolving Continents.* 3d ed. New York: Wiley.

PLAYA

Flat basin common in arid and semiarid regions subject to inundation by ephemeral surface waters and groundwater fluctuations. Playas occupy regional or topographic lows in enclosed drainage basins, where evaporation greatly exceeds moisture inputs. Playa surfaces are composed of fine-grained sediments such as silts, clays, or evaporites (salts) and are generally free of vegetation, except for halophytic (salt-tolerant) plants near their margins. Desiccation features, such as cracks and polygons, are found on playas dominated by silts and clays, while salt crusts, blisters, and mounds are found in saline playas. In mountainous desert regions playas grade into sand flats and mudflats, the distal (lowermost) deposits of alluvial fans.

The formation of playas is the result of a number of interrelated factors, including climatic change, tectonic activity, and aeolian deflation (lowering of a surface by wind). During wet periods the depres-

The salt-encrusted Etosha Pan (or playa) in Etosha National Park, northern Namibia, with a black-backed jackal (*Canis mesomelas*) visible at right. (Photo: M. A. Mares)

sions are filled with water and a lake is present. During drier periods the waters evaporate, leaving behind various dessication features, salt, or mud. Playas also form as a result of tectonic activities such as faulting, folding, and subsidence. These tectonic activities create an enclosed drainage basin (a bolsón) from a previously open drainage system.

Some playas have been attributed to aeolian deflation of fine-grained sediments or to solutional and animal activities. These depressions are generally referred to as pans, with lunettes (clay dunes) formed on their lee side. Extensive pans can be found in eastern New Mexico and the Panhandle region of West Texas and in the Kalahari Desert of southern Africa.

Playas are important for two primary reasons. Playa deposits have numerous evaporites (salts) such as chlorides, sulfates, nitrates, carbonates, and trona, which have economic value. In addition, playa sediments contain paleoenvironmental information that can be used to study past climate change in deserts.

Playas are prominent in the Basin and Range Province of the western United States, the Sahara and the Kalahari deserts, Iran, Mongolia, Argentina, and Western Australia. Regional synonyms for playa are salt pan (United States), salar or salina (South America), continental sabkha (North Africa and Middle East), chott (North Africa), pan (southern Africa and Australia), kavir (Iran), and nor (Mongolia).—Vatche P. Tchakerian

See also ALLUVIAL FAN; BOLSÓN; BONNEVILLE; CHENOPODIACEAE; DUNES, LUNETTE; HALOPHYTES; IRRIGATION DRAINAGE; KAVIR; LAKES, PLUVIAL; SABKHA; SALINITY; SALT; SALTBUSH; SALT CRUST; SALT DESERT; SALT PAN; SALT POLYGON; SOILS, DESERT, CALICHE; WEATHERING, DESERT

Further Reading

Cooke, R., A. Warren, and A. Goudie. 1993. *Desert Geomorphology.* London: University College London Press. Pp. 202–217.

Goudie, A., and G. L. Wells. 1995. The nature, distribution and formation of pans in arid zones. *Earth Science Reviews* 38:1–69.

Shaw, P. A., and D. S. G. Thomas. 1989. Playas, pans and salt lakes. *In* D. S. G. Thomas, ed., *Arid Zone Geomorphology*, 184–205. London: Belhaven.

PLEISTOCENE

Final epoch of the Cenozoic era, encompassing the time period from about 1.6 million years ago to 10,000 years ago. The Pleistocene spans much of the last ice age up to the end of the last glacial maximum. It is followed by the Holocene, or Recent, epoch, which probably does not warrant distinction from the Pleistocene epoch. The Holocene is considered by climatologists to be an interglacial interval, and the ice age of the Pliocene-Pleistocene is still ongoing.

The Pleistocene epoch is frequently characterized by long-term cold climates influenced by the existence of landmasses in the polar regions and of continental glaciers. But in fact Pleistocene climates fluctuated dramatically and abruptly between glacial periods and relatively warm interglacials. Similar fluctuations probably characterized some of the much earlier ice ages in earth history, but detailed evidence of them is only available for the Pleistocene glaciations. The evidence is preserved in "fossil" ice in Antarctica and in the Arctic (especially Greenland), in seafloor sediments, and in certain kinds of continental deposits. Major factors that exert control on earth's climate, or that "force" the glacial-interglacial fluctuations, are variations in the tilt of the earth's spin axis and in the shape of the earth's orbit around the sun.

Much has been learned in recent years about high-latitude Pleistocene glacial cycles and their interrelatedness with orbital forcing (the astronomical influences on earth's climates mentioned above), ocean circulation, and sea surface temperatures through computer modeling. Much less, however, is understood about middle- and low-latitude continental patterns of aridity and humidity during the Pleistocene. Whereas certain glacial events are nearly global and synchronous in nature, patterns of aridity on some continents are not necessarily in phase with the glacial events, and they differ within and among continents in complex ways.

Continental aridification in tropical and subtropical latitudes is partly determined by monsoonal circulation patterns and their variability. Some of the most important factors that affected monsoonal variability during the Pleistocene are thought to be the amount of incoming solar radiation at different latitudes, boundary conditions (geographic and climatic parameters under which either glacial or interglacial conditions are considered to have existed), and the transport of heat from one hemisphere to the other. While glaciers are present at high latitudes, they have strong effects on the climate of middle and low latitudes, altering aridity, temperature, and wind strength.

Some of the earth's present-day deserts (e.g., Australian, southwestern North American, Sahara) began as semiarid regions in the Tertiary period that developed greater aridity during the Pleistocene epoch. Certainly during the Pleistocene low-latitude deserts fluctuated in extent, normally enlarging during high-latitude glacial periods and shrinking during interglacial periods.—Nicholas J. Czaplewski

See also **AN INTRODUCTION TO DESERTS; CENOZOIC; CRETACEOUS; DESERTS; EOCENE; FOSSILS; GLACIAL PERIODS; MADRO-TERTIARY GEOFLORA; MIDDEN; MIOCENE; NEOGENE; PALEOCENE; PALEOCLIMATE; PERMIAN; PLATE TECTONICS; PLIOCENE; PRECAMBRIAN; QUATERNARY; RECENT (HOLOCENE); TERTIARY**

Further Reading

Cocks, L. R. M. 1981. *The Evolving Earth*. London: British Museum (Natural History).

Frakes, L. A., J. E. Francis, and J. I. Syktus, eds. 1992. *Climate Modes of the Phanerozoic: The History of the Earth's Climate over the Past 600 Million Years*. Cambridge: Cambridge University Press.

Spaulding, W. G., and L. J. Graumlich. 1986. The last pluvial climatic episodes in the deserts of southwestern North America. *Nature* 320:441–444.

Vogel, J. C., ed. 1984. *Late Cainozoic Palaeoclimates of the Southern Hemisphere*. Rotterdam: A. A. Balkema.

Wright, H. E., Jr., J. E. Kutzbach, T. Webb III, W. F. Ruddiman, F. A. Street-Perrott, and P. J. Bartlein, eds. 1993. *Global Climates Since the Last Glacial Maximum*. Minneapolis: University of Minnesota Press.

PLIOCENE

Last and briefest epoch of the Neogene or Tertiary period representing geologic time between 5–6 million years ago and 1.8 million years ago. The Pliocene is preceded by the Miocene epoch and followed by the Pleistocene epoch. Global cooling that had begun earlier in the Cenozoic era continued through the Pliocene; glacial ice that began to build up in Antarctica in the Oligocene-Miocene covered most or all of that continent by the middle Pliocene. While southern beech (Nothofagus) forests were present in parts of the Transantarctic Mountains, a cold desert was present 4 million years ago adjacent to these mountains, as evidenced by a buried desert pavement, salt pan, and ultraxeric soil in Arena Valley, Victoria Land. The area remains a cold desert to this day.

For the first time in the Cenozoic, ice began to form in the Arctic during the early to middle Pliocene. This north polar ice produced the Labrador Current, which forced the Gulf Stream southward, altering the climate of northern Europe. By 3 million years ago glaciers covered parts of Greenland and Iceland. Vegetation in the Arctic included taiga (coniferous forests) by about 5 million years ago and tundra by 2 million years ago. The most intense phase of uplift of the Himalayas occurred in the late Miocene and Pliocene; these mountains had an effect on atmospheric circulation, which, in turn, possibly also contributed to glaciation in the Northern Hemisphere. In association with the onset of the Northern Hemisphere glacial cycles, the cooling of the North Atlantic resulted in more arid conditions in Africa by 2.8 million years ago. Sea-bottom cores drilled in the North Atlantic west of Africa and in the Gulf of Aden and the Arabian Sea contain a sedimentary record including increased aeolian dust blown off northern Africa and the Arabian Peninsula at 2.8, 1.7, and 1.0 million years ago. These Pliocene-Pleistocene events contributed not only to the enhanced desertification of the Sahara and Arabian deserts but also to the drying and opening of woodlands and savannas in much of the rest of Africa. Over the course of geologic time relatively major and abrupt climate changes have often spurred the evolution of species. The Pliocene-Pleistocene aridification events of Africa may have contributed to the speciation of hominids. Australopithecines first appeared in Africa about 4 million years ago: *Homo* appeared about 2 million years ago.

Although the Isthmus of Panama was presaged by a chain of ephemeral volcanic islands, it rose to become a land connection between North and South America in the late Pliocene, about 3 million years ago. Prior to the existence of this land connection, South America had been isolated from other continents for at least 40 million years, and only a few kinds of terrestrial vertebrates had made their way from either of these landmasses to the other. After the land connection appeared, large-scale reciprocal migrations of organisms, termed the Great American Interchange, occurred. Factors that began in the Miocene to produce the Atacama Desert along the Peruvian-Chilean coast of South America continued throughout the Pliocene. These factors included changes in ocean circulation (in the circum-Antarctic and southern Pacific, which were in turn affected to some extent by continental drift and the closing of the marine portal between the Americas by the Isthmus of Panama and the opening of the Drake Passage between South America and the Antarctic Peninsula), cold-water upwelling, and continued uplift of the Andes and attendant rain shadow effects.—Nicholas J. Czaplewski

See also **AN INTRODUCTION TO DESERTS; CENOZOIC; CRETACEOUS; DESERTS; EOCENE; FOSSILS; GLACIAL PERIODS; MADRO-TERTIARY GEOFLORA; MIDDEN; MIOCENE; NEOGENE; OCEAN CURRENTS; PALEOCENE; PALEOCLIMATE; PERMIAN; PLATE TECTONICS; PLEISTOCENE; PRECAMBRIAN; QUATERNARY; RECENT (HOLOCENE); TERTIARY**

Further Reading

Cocks, L. R. M. 1981. *The Evolving Earth*. London: British Museum (Natural History).

deMenocal, P. B. 1995. Plio-Pleistocene African climate. *Science* 27:53–59.

Frakes, L. A., J. E. Francis, and J. I. Syktus, eds. 1992. *Climate Modes of the Phanerozoic: The History of the Earth's Climate over the Past 600 Million Years*. Cambridge: Cambridge University Press.

Marchant, D. R., C. C. Swisher III, D. R. Lux, D. P. West, Jr., and G. H. Denton. 1993. Pliocene paleoclimate and East Antarctic ice-sheet history from surficial ash deposits. *Science* 260:667–670.

Simpson, G. G. 1980. *Splendid Isolation: The Curious History of South American Mammals*. New Haven: Yale University Press.

Stehli, F. G., and S. D. Webb, eds. 1985. *The Great American Biotic Interchange*. New York: Plenum.

Vrba, E., G. Denton, L. Burckle, and T. Partridge, eds. 1996. *Paleoclimate and Evolution with Emphasis on Human Origins*. New Haven: Yale University Press.

POCKET MOUSE

Common name applied to mice of the family Heteromyidae of the genera *Liomys*, *Heteromys*, *Chaetodipus*, and *Perognathus*. Pocket mice are endemic to North and South America. The genera *Chaetodipus* and *Perognathus* are predominately North American, extending from the plains of Saskatchewan to northern Mexico. The tropical heteromyids are the *Liomys* and *Heteromys*, which extend from Mexico south through Panama to northern South America. The tropical pocket mice occupy both humid and xeric habitats, with *Heteromys* predominately in the former and *Liomys* in the latter habitat types. *Chaetodipus* and *Perognathus* exhibit varying degrees of adaptation to aridity, with some forms extremely specialized for both high- and low-elevation desert habitats. The pocket mice of the high altitudes or high latitudes often hibernate during the winter months.

The dorsal color is usually some shade of brown, and the venter is white. Species found on pale sands in desert environments have a pale dorsal pelage. Species of *Heteromys*, *Liomys*, and *Chaetodipus* possess spiny hairs on the dorsum.

They are called pocket mice because they possess external fur-lined cheek pouches, a characteristic shared with all members of the family Heteromyidae, as well as with the true gophers (family Geomyidae). Members of the genera *Chaetodipus* and *Perognathus* are rather small, some species of *Perognathus* being as small as 7 grams as adults and no member of the genus exceeding 40 grams as an adult. The genera *Liomys* and *Heteromys* tend to be somewhat larger than 40 grams but rarely exceed 80 grams.

All pocket mice construct burrows, which they use for dens and shelter. The burrows often include storage chambers for food gathered on the surface. All pocket mice feed primarily on seeds and fruits, which they gather on the surface and transport in their capacious cheek pouches to their dens. Desert species of pocket mice can subsist their entire lives without drinking water, obtaining all necessary water as a by-product of metabolism. They exhibit specializations in the kidney for efficient recovery of water produced during the process of excretion.

Pocket mice produce rather altricial (poorly developed and helpless) young in an underground chamber after a gestation period of 23–27 days. The young are usually mature enough to appear above ground at approximately three to four weeks of age. All species are primarily nocturnal, avoiding extremes of temperature in desert habitats and diurnal predators in the tropical habitats. Nevertheless, they are frequently preyed on by owls and snakes.—John F. Eisenberg

See also **ANIMAL ADAPTATIONS; BIPEDALITY; BURROWING ANIMALS; ESTIVATION; GRANIVORY; HETEROMYIDS; KANGAROO MOUSE; KANGAROO RAT; KIDNEY FUNCTION, DESERT RODENTS; KIDNEYS; PHYSIOLOGY; RODENTS; SALT BALANCE; SEEDS; THERMOREGULATION; TORPOR; WATER BALANCE**

Further Reading

Genoways, H., and J. H. Brown, eds. 1993. *Biology of the Heteromyidae*. Special Publication No. 10, American Society of Mammalogists. Lawrence, Kan.: Allen Press.

PODSOL. *See* SOILS, DESERT, PODSOL

POISONOUS ANIMALS

Animals that produce chemicals used to subdue prey or defend themselves against predators. Among poisonous animals in deserts are certain spiders (black widows and the brown recluse), centipedes, scorpions, whipscorpions, blister beetles, bombardier beetles, darkling beetles, certain caterpillars, some true ants, velvet ants, numerous wasps and bees, toads and frogs, the Gila monster, some rear-fanged snakes in the family Colubridae, rattlesnakes and coral snakes (New World), vipers and cobras (Old World), and tiger snakes and many other species in the family Elapidae (Australia). Poisons produced by animals may be injected (scorpions, ants, wasps, snakes), sprayed (whipscorpions, beetles, spitting cobras), or simply secreted on the surface of the body to be tasted or smelled (millipedes, frogs, toads).

Poisonous chemicals frequently have more than one function. For example, snake venoms are used for defense as well as for subduing and digesting prey. The reason that some animal poisons cause such extensive tissue damage in humans is because the chemicals composing the venoms were designed through natural selection to aid in the breakdown of tissue of small-bodied prey for digestive purposes. Venoms of many rattlesnakes, for example, contain proteolytic enzymes (enzymes that break down proteins) important in the digestion of the prey after it has been swallowed. Other poisons, like that of the bark scorpion, are designed to kill prey rapidly. These neurotoxins act directly on the nervous system, rendering prey helpless. Used in defense, they can cause excruciating pain, numbness, and death.

Venoms of many stinging insects, particularly social insects, are used primarily for defense, and all stinging individuals are females (workers). Most of these venoms cause immediate pain but are rarely dangerous except to people with allergic reactions to insect stings. With the exception of Africanized bees, most stinging insects sting only when the nest is threatened or when an individual insect is held.

Chemicals produced by beetles and frogs are generally not lethal; their primary role is defense. These chemicals usually cause localized pain, or taste bad, affording the animal that produces the toxin the opportunity to escape while the potential predator is reacting to the chemicals. Some chemicals produced by blister beetles and bombardier beetles can cause lesions or burns on the skin, eyes, or other soft tissues. It is interesting that some defense chemicals of desert animals have recently attracted interest as hallucinogens (e.g., skin secretions of the Colorado River toad, *Bufo alvarius*).—Laurie J. Vitt

See also **ADDER; ANIMAL ADAPTATIONS; ARTHROPODS; BEES; CENTIPEDE; COBRA; CORAL SNAKE; GILA MONSTER; INSECTS; LIZARDS; MILLIPEDES; PIT VIPER; RATTLESNAKE; REPTILES; SCORPIONS; SNAKES; SPIDERS; TOADS; WASPS**

Further Reading

Bücherl, W., and E. Buckley. eds. 1968. *Venomous Animals and Their Venoms*. 2 vols. New York: Academic Press.

Campbell, J. A., and E. D. Brodie, Jr. 1992. *Biology of Pitvipers*. Tyler, Tex.: Selva.

Campbell, J. A., and W. W. Lamar. 1989. *The Venomous*

Reptiles of Latin America. Ithaca: Cornell University Press.

Cloudsley-Thompson, J. L. 1996. *Biotic Interactions in Arid Lands*. Berlin: Springer.

Smith, R. L. 1982. *Venomous Animals of Arizona*. Tucson: Cooperative Extension Service, University of Arizona.

POLAR DESERTS. *See* AN INTRODUCTION TO DESERTS

POLLINATION

Transfer of pollen from one plant to another, usually by wind or animals; a prelude to fertilization in seed plants. Pollination involves the movement of pollen grains from one reproductive structure of a cone-bearing or flowering plant to another reproductive structure on the same or different plant. Pollen grains carry sperm nuclei, and pollination is a necessary precursor to fertilization and sexual reproduction in which a sperm fuses with the egg cell located inside the ovule of the flower or cone-bearing plant. For pollination to occur, pollen grains must be carried by the wind or by animal agents from one plant to another, promoting cross-pollination. In harsh environments, such as deserts, vegetative reproduction may replace sexual reproduction, or plants may pollinate themselves, thus limiting the importance of pollination agents.

Yucca plants (*Yucca*) grow throughout the deserts of the southwestern United States and are pollinated by the yucca moth (*Tegeticula*). The female moth lays its eggs inside the ovary of the yucca flower and then pollinates the flower. This behavior ensures its developing young, the moth larvae, will have seeds on which to feed. The larvae eat some, but not all, of the yucca seeds. The giant saguaro cactus, *Carnegiea*, in Arizona is pollinated by a bat, *Leptonycteris nivalis*. Bats visit cactus flowers in the evening, attracted by the musty smell of the large white flowers and the copious amounts of nectar and pollen that are used as food by the animals. The bat then flies between cacti, pollinating flowers with the uneaten pollen that still clings to its body.—Gordon E. Uno

See also **ARTHROPODS; BAT; BEES; BIRDS; BUTTERFLIES; ECOLOGY; FLIES; FLOWERS; HAWKMOTH; HUMMINGBIRD; MOTHS; PLANT ADAPTATIONS; PLANTS; SAGUARO; YUCCA**

Further Reading

Cloudsley-Thompson, J. L. 1996. *Biotic Interactions in Arid Lands*. Berlin: Springer.

Faegri, K., and L. van der Pijl. 1979. *Principles of Pollination Ecology*. Oxford: Pergamon.

Proctor, M., and P. Yeo. 1972. *The Pollination of Flowers*. New York: Taplinger.

POLLUTION

Refers to the contamination of the air, water, soil, or biological components of an ecosystem by human activities which results in a harmful effect on biological systems. The products of human activities include solid waste, chemicals, human waste, and the by-products of the combustion of fuels. The heaviest pollution is generally found near major population and industrial centers. Pollution has not been as important an issue in arid lands as other kinds of environmental disturbance because population density is low, there are few large cities, and industries tend to locate near abundant sources of freshwater.

There are several kinds of pollution that are of concern in deserts. Water is a limiting resource in deserts, and much available water is used for the irrigation of crops. This water can become quickly contaminated with the residues of agricultural chemicals. In addition, water used for agriculture can become salty due to high rates of evaporation in the desert climate, resulting in the concentration of mineral salts in the remaining water. Water found downstream from an agricultural area can therefore be of very low quality and can require desalinization, an expensive process, if it is to be used further.

Mining activities can also lead to pollution in arid lands. More than 80 percent of the world's copper and almost 90 percent of the gold is extracted from arid and semiarid lands. Toxic residues from mines can pollute limited water supplies and the surface soil. Some of the world's largest petroleum reserves are located in deserts. Natural gas is burned as a by-product in many countries, creating atmospheric pollution. Pipeline construction is often done without regard to important natural areas, and spills can cause soil and groundwater pollution. The potential for more serious pollution associated with the exploration of petroleum was realized at the conclusion of the 1990–1991 Gulf War, when Iraqi troops destroyed wells throughout Kuwait, spilling oil in the desert and causing fires to burn out of control for weeks.—Thomas E. Lacher, Jr.

See also **AGRICULTURE IN DESERTS; ARIDITY; COLORADO RIVER; CONSERVATION IN DESERTS; CONTAMINATION; DAM; DESERTIFICATION; DIRT BIKES; DUNE BUGGIES; INSECTICIDES; IRRIGATION DRAINAGE; MIDDLE EAST, DESERTS OF; MINERALS; OFF-ROAD VEHICLES; SALINIZATION; WILDLIFE**

Further Reading

Heathcote, R. L. 1983. *The Arid Lands: Their Use and Abuse.* New York: Longman.

Moriarity, F. 1988. *Ecotoxicology: The Study of Pollutants in Ecosystems.* 2d ed. London: Academic Press.

Southwick, C. H. 1976. *Ecology and the Quality of Our Environment.* New York: Van Nostrand.

Williams, M., ed. 1993. *Planet Management.* New York: Oxford University Press.

POLYGON. *See* SALT POLYGON

POPPY

Annual or perennial herb (or less commonly a shrub) in the family Papaveraceae, often with milky or yellow sap in the stems. Poppies are famous for their beautiful flowers and narcotic seeds. The true poppies (*Papaver*) are the source of opium and are used as ornamental flowers. This genus is widespread in the Old World. Several annual species of *Papaver* occur in the Negev and Judean deserts, on sandy soils and in fields. The true poppies have showy red, violet, yellow, or white flowers.

Poppies in other genera are common inhabitants of the New World deserts. The California poppy is a brilliant example of the gold poppies (*Eschscholzia*), which have bright yellow or orange flowers. This genus of mostly annual poppies occurs in the Sonoran, Mojave, Chihuahuan, and Great Basin deserts (and in other biomes), on sandy or gravelly soils of plains or slopes. Cattle graze *E. mexicana* when other forage is not available. The sap of *E. californica* has narcotic effects, and has been used by Indians for toothache.

Prickly poppies (*Argemone*) are annual, biennial, or perennial herbs with spiny leaves, white or yellow sap, and white, yellow, or orange flowers. Prickly poppies (*chicalote* in Spanish) have fairly broad distributions in North and South America and occur in deserts as well as subtropical and tropical areas. These plants grow in sandy, dry soils and disturbed areas. Because they are not palatable to

A desert poppy (*Arctomecon humilis*). (Photo: D. Beck)

cattle, they can become abundant on overgrazed rangelands. The seeds of prickly poppies are narcotic and are used medicinally as a sedative and cathartic.

Desert poppies (*Arctomecon*) are biennial or perennial herbs with large white or pale yellow flowers. These plants have a large taproot. They occur on open gravelly slopes in the Mojave Desert. The pygmy poppy (*Canbya*) is a tiny plant, only two to three centimeters tall, with white flowers. This poppy is endemic to the Mojave Desert, where it can be found on the sandy soils of mesas.—Kristina A. Ernest

See also **CHIHUAHUAN DESERT; ECONOMIC VALUE OF DESERT PRODUCTS; HERBS; ISRAEL, DESERTS OF; JORDAN, DESERTS OF; LEBANON, DESERTS OF; LIBYA, DESERTS OF; MEXICO, DESERTS OF; MOJAVE DESERT; PALESTINE, DESERTS OF; PLANT ADAPTATIONS; PLANTS; SONORAN DESERT**

Further Reading

Kearney, T. H., and R. H. Peebles. 1960. *Arizona Flora.* Berkeley: University of California Press.

Shreve, F., and I. L. Wiggins. 1964. *Vegetation and Flora of the Sonoran Desert.* Vols. 1 and 2. Stanford: Stanford University Press.

Zohary, M. 1966. *Flora Palaestina.* Vol. 1. Jerusalem: Israel Academy of Sciences and Humanities.

PORCUPINE

Large, stocky, rather odd-looking rodent with relatively stout body, short limbs, and an armor of quills. "Porcupine" refers to animals in either of two families, the New World Erethizontidae and the Old World Hystricidae. These two families show convergent evolution in both having sharp-tipped quills and similar jaw musculature, yet they are not closely related evolutionarily.

The quills are modified hairs, which have become thick and stiff. They can reach a length of 35 centimeters in the Old World porcupines but range from very short to 7.5 centimeters in New World porcupines. Despite popular belief, porcupines cannot throw their quills; rather the quills become embedded in attackers on contact with the body or from a quick tail swipe. Old World porcupines can become quite agitated if encountered, stamping their feet, rattling the quills, and backing into the intruder with their quilled rumps.

Porcupines occupy a variety of habitats, including desert, savanna, and forest. Of the New World forms only the North American porcupine (*Erethizon dorsatum*) occurs in deserts, but even this species is more common in woodlands and forest. North American porcupines are mainly terrestrial, but their modified feet (long claws and naked foot pad are opposable) allow them to climb shrubs and trees in search of food. They are chiefly herbivorous, feeding on buds, roots, leaves, and fruits during the summer and bark and conifer needles during the winter. These porcupines are generally solitary but may congregate at feeding areas. They mate during the fall or early winter, and females give birth to one (or rarely two) precocial young after a gestation period of seven months. Population densities may be cyclic in some areas; densities in Arizona ranged from one to six per square kilometer.

Old World porcupines (genus *Hystrix*) occupy a variety of habitats, including forest, steppe, and desert. Like North American porcupines, they are nocturnal, but unlike their New World counterparts, they rarely climb trees. Their diet is a bit more varied, including insects and small vertebrates as well as plant material. Old World porcupines find shelter in burrows or crevices, which they share with a family group. Females may produce two litters per year, usually with one or two young per litter. The gestation period is 16 weeks.—Kristina A. Ernest

See also **ANIMAL ADAPTATIONS; CHIHUAHUAN DESERT; CONVERGENT EVOLUTION; DEFENSIVE ADAPTATIONS, ANIMALS; HERBIVORY; MAMMALS; SONORAN DESERT; RODENTS**

Further Reading

Costello, D. F. 1966. *The World of the Porcupine*. Philadelphia: Lippincott.

Woods, C. A. 1973. Erethizon dorsatum. *Mammalian Species* 29:1–6.

POTASH

Term generally used for potassium oxide (K_2O). However, potassium oxide does not occur naturally. The potassium oxide equivalent of material is used as an indication of the potassium-supplying property of the material. Within the agricultural industry, "potash" refers to any fertilizer applied as a source of potassium. Sometimes the term is applied to potassium carbonate, KCO_3, derived from wood ash and used as fertilizer.

Any naturally occurring deposit of materials containing potassium may be called potash. For example, commercially mined deposits of sylvite (KCl), langbeinite ($K_2Mg_2(SO_4)_3$), carnallite ($KMgCl_3\cdot 6H_2O$), and kainite ($KCl\cdot MgSO_4\cdot 3H_2O$) exist in various locations around the globe.

Mining procedures are dependent on the ore material and the depth of the deposit. Solid ore mining is used when the deposit is within 1,200 meters of the surface. Solution mining has been used in highly soluble deposits. Water is pumped into the deposit, and the brine is then extracted and the potash recovered, usually by evaporation. Limited quantities of potash material are also recovered from the flue dust and gases released in the production of cement.—Dan R. Upchurch and Ted M. Zobeck

See also **FELDSPAR; MINERALS; NUTRIENTS; SOILS, DESERT; SOIL TAXONOMY; WEATHERING, DESERT**

Further Reading

Soil Science Society of America. 1987. *Glossary of Soil Science Terms*. Madison, Wis.: Soil Science Society of America.

Tennissen, A. C. 1974. *Nature of Earth Materials*. Englewood Cliffs, N.J.: Prentice-Hall.

Tisdale, S. L., and W. L. Nelson. 1975. *Soil Fertility and Fertilizers*. 3d ed. New York: Macmillan.

PRAIRIE

Term referring to a treeless grassy area; most frequently applied to grasslands of North America. These communities are not classified as deserts, but in the early European history of North America they were once called the "Great American

Desert." For early settlers crossing these vast expanses on foot or on horseback, they must have appeared as foreboding as any true desert.

The prairies of North America include the tallgrass prairies at the eastern boundary of the grasslands. These grasslands interdigitate with forested areas along their eastern border. At the western edge of the central grasslands, shortgrass prairie is found. These areas are immediately east of the Rocky Mountains and are most influenced by the orographic effect (rain shadow) of the mountains. There is a broad region, the mixed grass prairie, in the middle of the central grasslands where short- and tallgrass prairies mingle.

The tallgrass prairies are dominated by four genera of grasses, *Andropogon*, *Schizachyrium*, *Panicum*, and *Sorghastrum*. The shortgrass prairies are dominated by *Bouteloua*, *Stipa*, and *Buchloë*.

In regions where overgrazing has degraded plant communities, grass dominance is reduced and other species now dominate. These species are known as "increasers" with grazing, whereas the grass and grasslike (graminoid) plants are "decreasers." In the shortgrass prairie, common increasers include cacti such as *Opuntia* and introduced species such as Japanese brome grass (*Bromus*) and Russian thistle (*Salsola iberica*). In the tallgrass prairie introduced species such as *Bromus* can increase also.

Fire is an important component of prairie ecosystems. Because fire suppression has become common, there has been an increase of woody species, particularly in the tallgrass prairies. In the southern portions of the tallgrass prairies *Prosopis* (mesquite) is also increasing in dominance due both to fire suppression and to overgrazing.—Linda L. Wallace

See also **DESERTIFICATION; DESERT GRASSLAND; GRASSES; GRASSLAND; GREAT AMERICAN DESERT; MESQUITE; PAMPAS; PLANT ADAPTATIONS; PLANT GEOGRAPHY; OVERGRAZING**

Further Reading

Chabat, B. F., and H. A. Mooney. 1985. *Physiological Ecology of North American Plant Communities*. New York: Chapman and Hall.

Collins, S. L., and L. L. Wallace, eds. 1990. *Fire in North American Tallgrass Prairies*. Norman: University of Oklahoma Press.

Prairie dog (*Cynomys ludovicianus*). (Photo: M. A. Mares)

PRAIRIE DOG

Large, ground-dwelling squirrel (mammalian family Sciuridae, order Rodentia) found in North America from southern Canada to northern Mexico. One genus and five species are recognized. Length of head and body ranges from 280 to 330 millimeters, length of tail from 30 to 115 millimeters, and weight from 0.7 to 1.4 kilograms. All species are yellowish or buffy in coloration and have short legs and a short, flattened black- or white-tipped tail.

Prairie dogs inhabit plains, mountain valleys, and plateaus. They occur in portions of the Great Basin Desert and in semiarid scrublands, although they are not generally found in deserts. They may be found in desert grasslands. Their extensive burrow systems are used for shelter and hibernation. Prairie dogs have a highly organized social system; "towns" can cover up to 100 hectares and contain millions of prairie dogs. Grasses and herbs, eaten during the day, are preferred food. Prairie dogs were considered economic pests, and control projects greatly reduced the populations. Some species are now threatened or endangered. Prairie dog burrows provide shelter for numerous species of vertebrates and invertebrates, including other mammals, snakes, turtles, scorpions, spiders, and birds.—Janet K. Braun

See also **BADGER; BURROWING ANIMALS; DESERT GRASSLAND; FERRET; GRASSES; GRASSLAND; MAMMALS; PLAGUE; PRAIRIE; RATTLESNAKE; RODENTS; SQUIRREL**

Further Reading

Ceballos-G., G., and D. E. Wilson. 1985. *Cynomys mexicanus*. *Mammalian Species* 248:1–3.

Clark, T. W., R. S. Hoffmann, and C. F. Nadler. 1971. *Cynomys leucurus*. *Mammalian Species* 7:1–4.

Murie, J. O., and G. R. Michener, eds. 1984. *The Biology of Ground-Dwelling Squirrels*. Lincoln: University of Nebraska Press.

Pizzimenti, J. J., and G. D. Collier. 1975. *Cynomys parvidens*. *Mammalian Species* 52:1–3.

Pizzimenti, J. J., and R. S. Hoffmann. 1973. *Cynomys gunnisoni*. *Mammalian Species* 25:1–4.

PRECAMBRIAN

Major informal division of geologic time between the origin of the earth, 4.5 billion years ago, and the appearance of most phyla of multicellular animals, 570 million years ago. This era represents more than 80 percent of the earth's history. It is divided into two eons: the Archean and the Proterozoic, which began 2.5 billion years ago.

During the Precambrian the earth and other planets originated by accretion (growth by gradual accumulation of solid material from asteroids, meteorites, and planetesimals) and condensation of material from a primordial, swirling cloud of dust and gases. Rocks from space (meteorites, still accreting to the earth at a much-reduced rate today) and from the earth's moon are not subjected to the weathering and tectonic alteration as those on earth have been. Thus they provide the best estimate of the age of the earth and the solar system; lunar rocks and meteorites have been dated radiometrically to about 4.6 billion years old. Earth's accreting materials underwent their fundamental density separation and stratification into core, mantle, crust, oceans, and atmosphere. The earliest continents began to form late in the Archean, 3.5–2 billion years ago, as evidenced by the oldest known cratonic rocks in several modern continents. The chemical evolution and origination of life on earth occurred during the Archean probably by 3.4–3.6 billion years ago based on the presence of stromatolitelike structures (fossil structures consisting of stacked hemispheres or flat layers of limestones). These structures are thought to result from the communal growth of blue-green algae in mats or layers in rocks of that age in what is now Australia, where the oldest fossils yet known are about 3.5 billion years old. Early forms of life included prokaryotic bacteria;, single-celled organisms that later in the Precambrian evolved the ability to photosynthesize and began to generate free oxygen into the earth's atmosphere. In the Proterozoic eukaryotic, unicellular plants evolved, followed by unicellular animals. Multicellular animals appeared by 680 million years ago.—Nicholas J. Czaplewski

See also **BACTERIA; CENOZOIC; CRETACEOUS; DESERTS; EOCENE; FOSSILS; GLACIAL PERIODS; MADRO-TERTIARY GEOFLORA; MIDDEN; MIOCENE; NEOGENE; PALEOCENE; PALEOCLIMATE; PERMIAN; PLANTS; PLATE TECTONICS; PLEISTOCENE; QUATERNARY; RECENT (HOLO-CENE); TERTIARY**

Further Reading

Newsome, H. E., and J. H. Jones. eds. 1990. *Origin of the Earth*. New York: Oxford University Press.

Schopf, J. W. 1993. Microfossils of the early Archean Apex Chert: New evidence of the antiquity of life. *Science* 260:640–646.

Schopf, J. W. ed. 1983. *Earth's Earliest Biosphere: Its Origin and Evolution*. Princeton: Princeton University Press.

Stanley, S. M. 1986. *Earth and Life Through Time*. New York: Freeman.

PRECIPITATION

Any form of water, whether solid or liquid (e.g., dew, drizzle, fog, hail, ice, rain, snow), that falls from the atmosphere to the surface of the earth. Various forms of moisture reach the surface, but these are not considered precipitation unless they fall from the atmosphere. Precipitation is measured by rain gauges and is usually expressed as inches or millimeters of liquid that has fallen to the surface. Most precipitation in arid areas develops from cumulonimbus or nimbostratus clouds, but the majority of clouds that form in arid areas do not produce rain. Indeed, in arid areas it is not uncommon for rain to fall from a cloud but to evaporate before it reaches the surface of the desert; these long, wispy streamers of rain are called virga.

There are various physical parameters of clouds that are necessary to produce rain. Some clouds are considered to be warm; that is, they are clouds with temperatures above the freezing point of water. In these clouds water droplets may develop and grow in size through the process of collision and coalescence. As the water droplets continue to collide and grow, they eventually become so large that they fall from the sky in the form of rain.

There are also cold clouds, which have a temperature below the freezing point of water. Precipitation in these requires a coexistence of water vapor, ice crystals, and supercooled water droplets. Clouds with temperatures between 0° and -9°C are primarily composed of supercooled water droplets. From -10° to -20°C, clouds are a mix of supercooled water and ice crystals. Below -20°C, clouds are formed primarily of ice crystals. Through complex physical mechanisms and differential movement of the supercooled water droplets and ice crystals, the water droplets are deposited on the ice crystals and the crystals begin to grow. As the ice crystals continue to grow and become heavier, their terminal velocities increase and they collide with tiny droplets of supercooled water as well as other ice crystals and continue to enlarge. Eventually the ice crystals are so large that they fall from the base of the clouds in the form of snow or hail, or if the air below the cloud is quite warm, they may melt as they fall and be converted into rain.

Although deserts are areas that receive small amounts of rain, occasionally large amounts can fall over short periods from convective storms, and the desert can be subjected to flash floods. Some deserts also receive significant amounts of snow.—Federico Norte

See also **AN INTRODUCTION TO DESERTS; ANTICYCLONE; BAROMETRIC PRESSURE (ATMOSPHERIC PRESSURE); CLIMATE; CLIMATE CLASSIFICATION; CLOUDS; CONVECTIVE STORM; CYCLONE; DESERTS; EL NIÑO; FLOOD; GROUNDWATER; HAIL; RIVERS; RUNOFF; SNOW; WATER**

Further Reading

Day, J. A., and V. J. Schaefer. 1991. *Clouds and Weather.* Boston: Houghton Mifflin.

Gates, D. M. 1972. *Man and His Environment: Climate.* New York: Harper and Row.

Oliver, J. E., and R. W. Fairbridge, eds. 1987. *The Encyclopedia of Climatology.* New York: Chapman and Hall.

Schaefer, V. J., and J. A. Day. 1981. *A Field Guide to the Atmosphere.* Boston: Houghton Mifflin.

Schneider, S. H., ed. 1996. *Encyclopedia of Climate and Weather.* 2 vols. New York: Oxford University Press.

PREDATION

The act of consuming an animal by killing it to obtain essential nutrients or other materials. True predators are defined as those animals that consume other animals for survival. The animals consumed are termed the prey. Some ecologists broaden the definition of predation to include parasitoids (insects that lay their eggs in other organisms that the hatching larvae consume and kill), parasites (organisms that infect a host and harm but generally do not kill it), and herbivores (animals that consume plants). Predation is one of the most important of all ecological processes, yet it is one of the most rarely observed.

Much of the published literature on predation concerns either the behavior and natural history of predators or mathematical models of the ecological effects of predation. Large predators, like cheetahs and lions, have been studied, and their hunting and prey selection is well documented. Many observational studies suggest that predator and prey populations exhibit long-term cycles in abundance. When prey increase, the predator populations, after a lag, follow suit. When predator abundance increases, prey population declines. These dynamics have been described with great realism by mathematical models of predator-prey dynamics. Other factors could cause these cycles (climate, for example), and few studies of natural populations have been conducted for a sufficiently long period to provide a definitive answer concerning the causes of predator-prey cycles.

Predators can have an impact on ecosystem processes as well. Predation can lower the density of prey populations, which in turn affects the organisms that the prey consumes. If the prey are heavy consumers of a particular plant species, then as a result of a decline in prey abundance the plant can become more common. Thus carnivores indirectly can have effects on the abundance of plant species.

Predation, as a process, functions in deserts as in other ecosystems. There are some aspects unique to deserts, however. Desert habitats are extremely open, affording little cover for foraging prey. Many desert species have behavioral and morphological adaptations for avoiding predators. Desert species tend to be nocturnal and avoid full moons. Many species of desert rodents have enlarged tympanic bullae that allow them to detect very low frequency sounds, such as the wing beats of an approaching owl. In addition, there are a large number of bipedal rodents in the desert, an adaptation that might confer an enhanced ability to flee from a predator in open habitats. The species of predators in deserts are not unlike those of other habitats; however, venomous reptiles are particularly abundant in arid areas.—Thomas E. Lacher, Jr.

See also **ANIMAL ADAPTATIONS; ARTHROPODS; BIPEDALITY; BIRDS; CATS; CARNIVORES; DOG, WILD; ECOLOGY; ECOSYSTEM; FOX; GRASSHOPPER MOUSE; HYENA; MEERKAT; MONGOOSE; NICHE; POISONOUS ANIMALS; RAPTORS; RATTLESNAKE; SNAKES; SEA LION; SEAL; VENOM**

Further Reading

Begon, M., and M. Mortimer. 1986. *Population Ecology.* 2d ed. Sunderland, Mass.: Sinauer.

Cloudsley-Thompson, J. L. 1996. *Biotic Interactions in Arid Lands.* Berlin: Springer.

Ricklefs, R. E. 1990. *Ecology.* 3d ed. New York: Freeman.

Taylor, R. J. 1984. *Predation.* New York: Chapman and Hall.

PREVAILING WESTERLIES

Winds that blow predominantly from the west in the middle latitudes of both the Northern and the Southern hemispheres in a westerly "belt" that extends between 35° and 60° latitude. At the higher levels of the atmosphere the westerlies extend from the equator to the poles, but the surface winds are generally limited to the belt delineated above. The equatorial limit of the prevailing westerlies is well defined by the subtropical high pressure zone, whereas the polar limits are more diffuse and variable. The principal source of energy for the prevailing westerlies is the thermal gradient (from north to south) between the warm tropical atmosphere and the cold polar atmosphere. This horizontal thermal gradient, known in meteorology as baroclinic instability, is formed because of the nonuniform distribution of the annual solar radiation that reaches the earth-atmosphere system. This results in much lower pressures developing at tropospheric altitudes of the atmosphere in the cold polar regions than at the equator. As a consequence tropical air flows toward the polar regions at high altitudes. Because of the Coriolis force that results from the rotation of the earth, the air masses that are moving toward the pole are bent from west to east. The seasonal variation in the prevailing westerlies is not equal in each hemisphere. In the Northern Hemisphere the westerlies show great seasonal variation related to the differential heating and cooling in the high latitudes. Because there is more land surface in the Northern Hemisphere, heating and cooling of this large surface are more extreme and thus pro-

duce greater gradients in temperature and circulation of the westerlies. This situation contrasts with the Southern Hemisphere, where there is less land surface at the higher latitudes and the thermal gradient is concentrated during summer when the land surface is much warmer than the ocean surface. In the Southern Hemisphere the westerlies are commonly known as the Roaring Forties.—Federico Norte

See also **ANTICYCLONE; BAROMETRIC PRESSURE (ATMOSPHERIC PRESSURE); CLIMATE; CLIMATE CLASSIFICATION; CYCLONE; EL NIÑO; ROARING FORTIES; WIND**

Further Reading

Day, J. A., and V. J. Schaefer. 1991. *Clouds and Weather.* Boston: Houghton Mifflin.

Oliver, J. E., and R. W. Fairbridge, eds. 1987. *The Encyclopedia of Climatology.* New York: Chapman and Hall.

Schaefer, V. J., and J. A. Day. 1981. *A Field Guide to the Atmosphere.* Boston: Houghton Mifflin.

Schneider, S. H., ed. 1996. *Encyclopedia of Climate and Weather.* 2 vols. New York: Oxford University Press.

PRICKLY PEAR

Plant species within the genus *Opuntia* that have numerous branches formed from flattened stem segments (members of the subgenus *Platyopuntia*). These succulent-stemmed cacti may be shrubby, treelike, or prostrate and trailing but in all forms are composed entirely of flat, spiny pads (joints). In large individuals the oldest pads become woody and circular in cross-section, functioning as supporting trunks. Prickly pears are in the same genus as the cylindrical-jointed chollas.

Prickly pears have large showy flowers, often yellow but sometimes orange or reddish. The plant is named for the spiny, oval fruit, the size of a small pear. The pads and fruits bear both spines and glochids (barbed bristles).

Prickly pears are broadly distributed from Canada to southern South America, occupying a variety of habitats including deserts, grasslands, pinyon-juniper woodlands, oak woodlands, tropical deciduous forest, thorn forest, and beaches. They grow best on well-drained soils: sandy, gravelly, or rocky. In some areas of Mexico prickly pears form dense thickets called nopaleras. Prickly pears tend to be less frost and drought tolerant than are chollas and columnar cacti.

Prickly pears are cultivated in Mexico, Europe, India, and Australia. One species was introduced to Australia in the mid-1800s and became a widespread weed by the early 1900s. Biological control by the *Cactoblastis* moth curtailed the spread of this pest plant.

The pads (*nopales* in Mexico) provide water for desert dwellers and are cooked or pickled in brine. The sweet fruits (*tunas*) are also edible, and can be made into jelly. Juice from prickly pears is used by Indians in mortar and to treat scrapes and wounds. Other parts of the plant are used medicinally for arthritis, ulcers, mumps, gout, headaches, insomnia, asthma, fever, diarrhea, gonorrhea, diabetes, and other maladies.—Kristina A. Ernest

See also **C₃ PLANTS; C₄ PLANTS; CACTI; CAM PLANTS; CHOLLA; MOTHS; SONORAN DESERT; SUCCULENTS**

Further Reading

Benson, L. 1981. *The Cacti of Arizona*. 3d ed. Tucson: University of Arizona Press.

Bravo-Hollis, H. 1978. *Las Cactáceas de México*. 2d ed. Vol. 1. México, D. F.: Universidad Nacional Autónoma de México.

PRIMARY PRODUCTIVITY

The measure of photosynthetic rates per unit area for a specific time. The important parameter is the amount of carbon dioxide (CO_2) fixed or carbohydrate synthesized. However, it is often easier to measure the amount of oxygen (O_2) released. Gross primary productivity is the total production of biomass, whereas net primary productivity is the biomass produced beyond what is used by the primary producers (plants) in their own respiration. Plant cells conduct cellular respiration in a series of reactions that are identical or similar to those that occur in animal and fungal cells:

$$CH_2O + O_2 \rightarrow CO_2 + H_2O.$$

In full sunlight and with adequate levels of water, photosynthesis occurs so rapidly in green plants that all the carbon dioxide they release in the respiratory reaction is used within the plants. Therefore, there is no net CO_2 production. However, in the evening hours, when photosynthesis has ceased, plants continue to respire and CO_2 gas is released through the stomata via diffusion.

Plants are sparse in deserts, primarily because water is a limiting factor; therefore, primary productivity is low. However, deserts have a massive influx of solar energy, and desert soils are often fertile. This has prompted irrigated agriculture in deserts throughout the world, and initial productivity (measured in agricultural terms as yield per hectare per year) is often dramatically high. Unfortunately, the high evapotranspiration rates of warm deserts leads to high rates of water vapor loss from the soil and leaves. As a consequence, dissolved salts build up in the soil. Most plants are intolerant of salty soils, and on numerous historical occasions yield began to decline after years of irrigation. This agricultural system permitted a significant increase in the size of the local human population, which then dropped dramatically with the rapid decline in agricultural productivity.

In ecological terms primary productivity is usually expressed as net production of organic matter (biomass) per unit area per year. Net productivity is measured by obtaining a sample of the dry weight (biomass) of the plant tissue. The derived information permits land managers to calculate carrying capacity of the plant community, for example, the number of cattle that can be managed on a pasture.—James R. Estes

See also **CARRYING CAPACITY; DECOMPOSITION; DESERTS; ENERGY FLOW; HERBIVORY; HOLDRIDGE LIFE ZONES; IRRIGATION DRAINAGE; PHOTOSYNTHESIS; PLANT COVER; PLANT GEOGRAPHY; PLANTS; SALINIZATION; STOMA**

Further Reading

Odum, E. P. 1983. *Basic Ecology*. Philadelphia: Saunders.

Whittaker, R. H. 1975. *Communities and Ecosystems*. New York: Macmillan.

PRODUCTIVITY, AQUATIC ECOSYSTEMS

Rate at which energy is transformed and fixed into biomass of species that live in aquatic ecosystems in desert environments. Primary production by algae and other plants serves as the energy base in desert aquatic ecosystems, accounting for 36–100 percent of all input of organic matter. This situation is in contrast to that in nondesert stream systems where input of terrestrial plants and food items is more important in determining the available energy in the system than is aquatic primary production.

Algal primary productivity may be extremely high in desert springs due to warm water, an extended growing season, high nutrient availability, and lack of shade. Despite simple food webs in most desert aquatic systems (with only one or two dominant consumer species), secondary productivity can also be quite high. Overall high annual productivity may occur in spite of low efficiencies of energy transfer between trophic (feeding) levels. In Tecopa Bore, a desert stream in California, pupfish are the only consumers of the blue-green algae *Oscillatoria*. The pupfish consume 17 percent of the annual algal production, and of that, 6.5 percent is assimilated (taken into the body) and 10.5 percent is lost as feces. Of the assimilated energy, most is used for metabolism (which is quite high due to the warm environment of Tecopa Bore), with only 1.1 percent of the annual primary production being converted to fish biomass through growth. The high productivity of fish biomass results from the extended growing season for both *Oscillatoria* and the pupfish consumers.—Edie Marsh-Matthews

See also **AQUATIC HABITATS; BACTERIA; ECTOTHERMY; ENERGY FLOW; FISHES; METABOLISM; PRIMARY PRODUCTIVITY; WATER**

Further Reading

Naiman, R. J. 1981. An ecosystem overview: Desert fishes and their habitats. *In* R. J. Naiman and D. L. Soltz, eds., *Fishes in North American Deserts*, 493–531. New York: Wiley.

PRONGHORN

Species (*Antilocapra americana*) of antelopelike animal in the mammalian family Antilocapridae, order Artiodactyla, that inhabits rocky deserts, dry scrublands, and grasslands from west central Canada to northern Mexico. Pronghorn are not true antelopes, which are in the same family as cattle (Bovidae), but are in their own family. Although not a true desert animal, pronghorns are associated with grassland habitats in the Great Basin Desert, Sonoran Desert, and Chihuahuan Desert. This is one of only two families of mammals that is geographically restricted to North America (along with the burrowing rodent the mountain beaver, family Aplodontidae, of the Pacific Northwest).

Males and females have horns that are shed and regrown annually. Females have small, stunted horns, or they may be absent. The horns consist of a basal portion, short forward-projecting branches (anterior prongs), and terminal hooks.

The body coloration is a distinctive tan and white. Large eyes protrude from the skull, permitting 360° vision. Long eyelashes serve as sun visors. When threatened, hairs on the distinctive white rump patch are raised to alert other pronghorn; these patches are visible for up to two miles. Both males and females have numerous skin glands that are used in communication.

Pronghorn are the fastest North American mammals, reaching speeds up to 80 kilometers per hour; they can also leap six meters in a single bound. Pronghorn usually form small herds. They are curious animals and will approach humans, objects, or predators. When anxious or angry, they blow air through their nostrils. Fawns are born from May to June; twins are common.

Pronghorns have large kidneys for water conservation and excretion of toxic plant substances. They are active both day and night but on the hottest days are active at dusk and dawn. Pronghorns are well adapted to life in the grasslands. To insulate themselves from harsh winters, the sparse undercoat is covered by long, coarse, stiff and dense bristle hairs that have large central air spaces. These hairs function like a down jacket. To aid in thermoregulation, the hairs can be maintained at different angles by flexing the skin muscles.

Pronghorns have adapted to deal with the results of prairie fires. They prefer the high protein forbs and grasses that germinate quickly after a fire; shrubs and cactus are also eaten. Pronghorns are generally water independent and, except in extremely dry periods, obtain all needed water from their diet.

Pronghorns are short-lived, early maturing, prolific, and fast-moving animals. They have a large heart and lungs for running and a large liver for storing glycogen as a source of energy. They open their mouths and gulp air when they begin to run and have a large trachea for the rapid exchange of oxygen. The small stomach enhances their ability for fast movement but also necessitates use of nutritious, high-protein food.

Before the arrival of settlers, up to 35 million pronghorns may have inhabited North America. These numbers decreased to fewer than 20,000 by the 1920s. Populations have now increased to approximately 500,000 due to conservation and management, restricted hunting, and reintroductions.—Janet K. Braun

See also **DESERT GRASSLAND; ENDOTHERMY; GREAT BASIN DESERT; HEAT BALANCE; HEAT STRESS; HERBIVORY; MAMMALS; METABOLISM; SAGEBRUSH; UNGULATES; WATER BALANCE; WILDLIFE**

Further Reading

Grzimek's Encyclopedia of Mammals. Vol. 5. 1990. New York: McGraw-Hill.

Kitchen, D. W., and B. W. O'Gara. 1982. Pronghorn. *In* J. A. Chapman and G. A. Feldhamer, eds., *Wild Mammals of North America: Biology, Management, and Economics,* 960–971. Baltimore: Johns Hopkins University Press.

Macdonald, D., ed. 1984. *The Encyclopedia of Mammals.* New York: Facts on File.

O'Gara, B. W. 1978. Antilocapra americana. *Mammalian Species* 90:1–7.

Van Wormer, J. 1968. *The World of the Pronghorn.* Philadelphia: Lippincott.

PROSOPIS. *See* MESQUITE

PSAMMOMYS. *See* SAND RAT

PSAMMOPHYTES

Specialized plant species capable of living in the midst of shifting sands. These species are capable of survival in the extremely inhospitable environment that is common in desert ecosystems. Active dunes cover approximately one-tenth of the continental areas between 30° north and 30° south latitude.

Adaptations for survival in an active dune include rapid seed germination with very rapid growth of substantial root systems. Many species have rhizomes, underground stems from which new aboveground portions can readily sprout. The buds borne on the surface of the rhizomes can tolerate burial but also are capable of producing new stems that can grow very rapidly back to the surface. Some species also possess roots and rhizomes that are covered with very thick, corky bark that allows those structures to survive exposure when the sand is blown away and uncovers them. Examples of common psammophytes are found in the genus *Stipagrostis,* a group of perennial grasses.

Cyanobacteria represent another type of psammophyte. These small bacteria are photosynthetic organisms that grow in thick mats on the sand surface. They frequently cover themselves with a thick mucilaginous layer that allows the cells to resist desiccation and abrasion by blowing sand. Older mats can also support the growth of other microphytes (small plants) such as mosses. These microphytic mats help to increase the nutrient content of impoverished dune soils by fixing atmospheric nitrogen into forms that are usable by plants.—Linda L. Wallace

See also **BACTERIA; DUNES; LICHENS; MOSSES; PLANT ADAPTATIONS; PLANTS; PSAMMOPHYTIC SCRUB; WIND EROSION**

Further Reading

Danin, A. 1991. Plant adaptations in desert dunes. *Journal of Arid Environments* 21:192–212.

———. 1996. *Plants of Desert Dunes.* New York: Springer.

Sykes, M. T., and J. B. Wilson. 1990. Dark tolerance in plants of dunes. *Functional Ecology* 4:799–805.

PSAMMOPHYTIC SCRUB

Communities in which sand dunes are stabilized by collections of shrubs and grasses. In sand dunes that have undergone some initial stabilization by grasses and microphytic mats, larger plant species can gain a foothold. Many of these shrub species can grow in dune systems where there is more than 100 millimeters of rainfall during the year. Deserts that support this type of plant community growth include those found on the northern coast of Venezuela, the fog desert of the Namib, the western Negev Desert, the Sinai Desert, and the Red Desert of north central Wyoming in the United States. Of course, many coastal dune communities throughout the world support psammophytic scrub, but these communities also must deal with salt stress from oceanic salt spray. Most deserts have dunes, and in the majority of these there are psammophytic scrub communities that act as a stabilizing force and reduce, or stop altogether, the movement of sand dunes. In noncoastal areas such stabilized dunes are common, for example, in the southwestern United States and in central Argentina.

Following dune formation, several successional steps occur in which different vegetation types start to grow on the dune and act to slow the movement of free sand grains. The first invaders, or pioneer species, are perennial grasses and cyanobacteria. These slow the movement of sand both through a reduction in wind speed at the sand surface (grasses) and through accretion of the sand particles (cyanobacteria).

Shrub species are usually the next group of organisms to invade dunes. These include members of the genera *Artemisia*, *Halocnemum*, *Salsola*, and *Salvadora*. The larger shrubs act to reduce wind speed even further and allow more extensive areas of the dune surface to become stabilized. Some of these species may actually act to capture moving sand and form isolated hillocks on the dune surface. This increases their ability to reduce air movement.

Once a dune is stabilized by psammophytic scrub, it can easily become destabilized. Any activity that results in the death or uprooting of a group of plants in a specific site can allow sand in that site to become mobile once again. Once the vegetation cover is gone, the sand can be blown away from the disturbed site; this small-scale phenomenon is known as a blow out. The initial cause of plant death or uprooting does not necessarily have to be from excess wind, however. Often the proximal cause is the activities of burrowing animals or large grazing animals or off-road vehicles.

The psammophytic scrub community in the Namib Desert is unique in that the primary source of water in this site is fog. Plant species are adapted to obtain usable moisture from the condensate. In most of the remaining psammophytic scrub types, water is from either deep underground sources or occasional rainfall. Hence many of the shrub species have deep taproots that can take advantage of underground sources. However, other species have extensive superficial roots that rapidly absorb chance rainfall. Both root types are found in stabilized dune systems.—Linda L. Wallace

See also **BACTERIA; DESERTIFICATION; DUNES; GRASSES; OFF-ROAD VEHICLES; NAMIBIA, DESERTS OF; PLANT ADAPTATIONS; PLANTS; PSAMMOPHYTES; SUCCESSION; WIND**

Further Reading

Danin, A. 1991. Plant adaptations in desert dunes. *Journal of Arid Environments* 21:192–212.

———. 1996. *Plants of Desert Dunes.* New York: Springer.

Walter, H. 1983. *Vegetation of the Earth.* Berlin: Springer.

PUMA

Species of large cat, *Puma concolor* (mammalian family Felidae, order Carnivora), ranging from Canada to the tip of South America—the widest distribution of any cat species. Pumas occur in most habitats, including rain forests, semideserts, wetlands, grasslands, and high mountains, at elevations up to 4,500 meters (areas with humans are generally avoided). The puma is also known as the cougar, mountain lion, silver lion, catamount, panther, painter, lion, Mexican lion, mountain demon, mountain devil, mountain screamer, brown tiger, red tiger, deer killer, Indian devil, purple feather, king cat, sneak cat, and varmint.

The general shape is that of a large domestic cat. The ears are round and short, the tail is long, and the claws are retractile. The muzzle, backs of the ears, and tail tip are blackish. The chin, tip of the muzzle, and belly are whitish. Adults vary in coloration. In the northern and southern parts of their distribution pumas are grayish; elsewhere they are reddish. All black and all white pumas have been reported.

Pumas vary greatly in size. In the northern and southern extremes of their range they are large (weighing up to 110 kilograms) and have a uniform, compact body. In the center of their range they are small, slender, and weigh about 50 kilograms. Young pumas have black spots extending in irregular lines, a coloration that disappears after three or four months of age. The eyes change from blue to brown in four months and are golden by nine months. The pupils are round. Pumas have stereoscopic vision.

Pumas are polygamous and first breed at two and a half years. Breeding is nonseasonal, although most births occur in the summer. Gestation lasts 82–96 days. Litter size ranges from one to six but averages two to four. Wild pumas live about 12 years. In captivity they may live longer than 20 years. A simple den is used by the female to raise the young; pumas do not use a permanent den.

The preferred food items in western North America are mule deer (usually old males and young individuals) and porcupines. Rabbits, European hares;, pacas, agoutis, elk, peccaries, guanacos, huemuls, birds, rodents, and even other carnivores are also eaten. Pumas also will prey on domestic livestock. They generally eat on six out of nine days and need 860–1,300 kilograms of meat per year (5–7 elk or 14–20 deer). Hunting success for the puma may be as high as 82 percent. A puma will drag a kill to a secluded spot, feed for a while, and cover the carcass. It may return to the carcass to feed for several days until it is all consumed.

Adults are solitary. Density estimates indicate one puma every 25–50 square kilometers. A small home range is used for resting and a second, larger home range is used for feeding. Home ranges vary in size from 96 to 575 square kilometers, and by season, year, sex, density, and location of prey. North American pumas have large summer ranges and smaller winter ranges that are determined by elk and mule deer migration patterns. Home ranges are maintained by mutual avoidance. Boundaries are marked by scrapes—small piles of dirt, leaves, or other items, including urine or feces.

Pumas have excellent eyesight and good hearing, but their sense of smell may be poorly developed. They are good swimmers but are shy of water. The female's "love call" has been described as a long, undulating scream that sounds like the frightened cry of a human. They will attack humans occasionally.

Once common throughout the eastern United States and Canada, hunting pressure and land use changes have restricted their range to western North America. Pumas are possibly extinct in the eastern United States and Canada, although occasional sightings have been reported. An endangered population exists in southern Florida. Conservation and protection have allowed population recovery and some expansion into previous ranges.—Janet K. Braun

See also **CARNIVORES; CATS; CHACO; CHIHUAHUAN DESERT; MAMMALS; MOJAVE DESERT; MONTE DESERT; PREDATION; SONORAN DESERT; SOUTH AMERICA, DESERTS OF; UNITED STATES, DESERTS OF**

Further Reading

Currier, M. J. P. 1983. Felis concolor. *Mammalian Species* 200:1–7.

Dixon, K. R. 1982. Mountain lion. *In* J. A. Chapman and G. A. Feldhamer, eds., *Wild Mammals of North America: Biology, Management, and Economics*, 711–727. Baltimore: Johns Hopkins University Press.

Young, S. P., and E. A. Goldman. 1946. *The Puma.* New York: Dover.

PUNA

Native South American word referring to the dry plateau of the high Andes (3,200–4,400 meters elevation) that lies between the western Andean mountain ranges and the Cordillera Real in the east and extends from Peru to the Tropic of Capricorn. The puna is dominated by a shrub steppe formed of low, scattered shrubs in the shape of thorny cushions and separated by stretches of permanently bare soil. Summer temperatures may be fairly high, but the rarefied air and the strong winds increase water loss and relative aridity and bring about great thermal fluctuations. Freezing may occur at any time of year, and the ground is likely to be covered with frost due to high levels of radiation. Snowfalls are more frequent in summer than in winter, but summer snow cover does not usually persist, even though it may reach a depth of 20–30 centimeters. Aridity is the overriding feature of the puna. (See map of South American deserts, p. 533.)

During the rainy season (summer) some annual species appear, as do species having plant organs that are perennially subterranean (geophytes). As a group puna plants are unable to cover the ground completely. Plant communities are fairly uniform and grow poorer in diversity of species as the climate grows drier. There are also areas of natural grasslands on more humid soils, as well as open forests of *queñoa* (*Polylepis australis*) on slopes and gorges that do not exceed 4,200 meters in elevation.

In the northern and eastern puna, where precipitation exceeds 400 millimeters, the *tola* steppe is dominant (*Parastrephia lepidophyla, Parastrephia phylicaefolia*). To the south and west of the *tolar* lies a drier region, with dominance of *chijua* (*Psila boliviensis*), *tolilla* (*Fabiana densa*), *añagua* (*Adesmia horridiuscula*), and other shrubs. This vegetation grows poorer toward the Chilean sector, where precipitation is lower.

Some endemic plant genera occur in the puna, including *Parastrephia* (family Asteraceae), *Lampaya* (family Verbenaceae), *Chersodoma* (family Asteraceae), *Anthobrym* (family Frankeniaceae), *Oreocereus* (family Cactaceae), *Chiliotrichiopsis* (family Asteraceae), and *Lophopappus* (family Poaceae). Humid and somewhat salty soils support grasslands, mainly of *Festuca scirpifolia*, which, on humid sandy soils, is replaced by *Pennisetum chilense*. The only tree present in the puna, *Polylepis australis*, grows on slopes and gorges lying between elevations of 3,800 and 4,300 meters. This tree, which can reach a height of four meters, is slow growing and has a twisted trunk. In the eastern puna there are communities of tree-sized cacti (*Oreocereus celsianus*). The fauna of the Puna Domain is characterized by numerous endemics. Among mammals, South American camelids common, with the vicuña (*Vicugna*) being found throughout the puna and the guanaco (*Lama guanicoe*) being more widely distributed toward the south. In addition, the domesticated llama (*Lama glama*) is widely used by people of the puna. The taruca or huemul deer (*Hippocamelus antisensis*) is also present. Among carnivores, there are foxes (*Pseudalopex*), the puma (*Puma concolor*), the pampas cat (*Oncifelis colocolo*), the *gato lince*, or Andean cat (*Oreailurus jacobita*), a skunk (*Conepatus rex*), and a weasel (*Galictis cuja*). Rodents are numerous, and there are various endemic species, including chinchillas (*Chinchilla*) and *chinchillones*, or mountain vizcachas (*Lagidium*), several species of rats and field mice (the Andean rat, *Andinomys*, *Akodon*, *Phyllotis*, *Chinchillula*), *cuis*, or cavies (*Cavia* and *Microcavia*), *tucu-tucos* (*Ctenomys*), *rata chinchilla*, or chinchilla rat (*Abrocoma*), an armadillo (*Chaetophractus*), and several bats.

The bird fauna is also diverse and includes the following species: the *ñandú petiso*, or Darwin's rhea (*Pterocnemia*), tinamous (*Nothoprocta*, *Attagis*, *Tinamotis*), four doves (*Metriopelia*), some rhinocryptids, two woodpeckers (*Colaptes*), and two grebes (*Centropelma micropterum*, *Podiceps occipitalis*). Other large birds are the Andean condor (*Vultur gryphus*), two vultures (*Coragyps* and *Cathartes*), the *carancho* (*Polyborus*), and the black-chested buzzard-eagle (*Geranoaetus*).

Various amphibians are present in the puna (e.g., *Pleurodema marmorata*, *Telmatobius atacamensis*, *Telmatobius marmoratus*), and there is an endemic fish (*Orestia*) in Lake Titicaca, as well as several other fish genera (*Pygidium*, *Ancistrus*, *Astroblepus*). The invertebrate fauna, which has not been studied in detail, is also diverse and includes ants (*Pogonomyrmex longibaris*, *Dorymyrmex joergenseni*) and an array of beetles (families Tenebrionidae, Carabidae, Scarabidae, and Curculionidae).—Virgilio G. Roig

See also **ALTIPLANO; AMPHIBIANS; ANDEAN GRASS-LANDS; ANDES; AN INTRODUCTION TO DESERTS; ARMADILLO; ARTHROPODS; BIRDS; CAMELS, SOUTH AMERICAN; CHILE, DESERTS OF; CONDOR; DESERTS; DESERTS, MONTANE; DESERTS, TEMPERATE; HUEMUL; INSECTS; LIZARDS; MAMMALS; PERU, DESERTS OF; REPTILES; SNAKES**

Further Reading

Cabrera, A. L. 1957. La vegetación de la puna, Argentina. *Revista de Investigaciones Agrícolas*. Buenos Aires.

Cabrera, A. L., and A. Willink. 1973. Biogeografía de América Latina. Organization of American States, Monograph No. 13. Washington, D.C.

Fjeldså, J., and N. Krabbe. 1990. *Birds of the High Andes*. Svendborg, Denmark: Apollo.

Morello. J. 1984. *Pérfil ecológico de Sudamérica*. Barcelona: Ediciones Cultura Hispánica, Instituto de Cooperación Iberoamericana.

Ojeda, R. A., and M. A. Mares. 1989. A biogeographic analysis of the mammals of Salta Province, Argentina: Patterns of species assemblage in the Neotropics. *Special Publications, The Museum, Texas Tech University* 27:1–66.

QUAIL

Small to moderate-sized, compact game birds with wide distribution across Eurasia, the Americas, Africa, and Australia (family Phasianidae, order Galliformes). Two distinct groups of quail are recognized. The New World quail are distributed from Paraguay to southern Canada; this group, sometimes placed in a family separate from other phasianids (Odontophoridae), is composed of approximately 30 species in 8 to 10 genera. The Old World quail encompass approximately 11 species in three genera and occur in open habitats of southern Eurasia, Africa, and Australia. Various species in both groups are found in desert habitats. For example, the common quail (*Coturnix coturnix*) breeds throughout semiarid, perennial grasslands of Africa, the Malagasy region, and Eurasia east to central Siberia and south into India. Similarly, a number of New World species prefer arid habitats. For example, the range of the Gambel's quail, *Lophortyx gambelii*, centers largely on the Sonoran Desert of the southwestern United States and northwestern Mexico.

Quail possess rounded wings and are largely terrestrial; they fly reluctantly and only for short distances. Most species undertake only local movements, although some of the Old World *Coturnix* species do migrate. The plumage coloration of New World quail consists of various shades of black, white, brown, and gray. Some species have crests. In Old World taxa plumage is similarly varied with markings of blue, brown, black, and white. Sexes are generally dimorphic. The bill is relatively short and stout. Diet consists largely of vegetable matter, primarily seeds and shoots, but may include some invertebrates. Some quail species have adapted quite well to an agricultural setting (e.g., the northern bobwhite, *Colinus virginianus*, and the common quail), feeding on such crops as corn and soya. Other taxa appear to have been adversely affected by human activities; for example, population declines in the North American scaled quail (*Callipepla squamata*) have probably been brought about by habitat degradation caused by livestock overgrazing.

Quail are generally gregarious, and in the non-breeding season some species may form flocks (coveys) of up to 300 birds; however, they appear to be largely socially monogamous. Nests consist of concealed shallow scrapes placed on the ground. Clutch size ranges from approximately 3 to 14. Incubation is usually performed by the female, although in some species the male has been reported to share these duties. The young are precocial and capable of self-feeding almost immediately after hatching. The chicks are initially predominantly insectivorous but soon switch to the vegetarian diet of the adults.—Stephen C. Lougheed

See also **BIRDS; CHIHUAHUAN DESERT; GRANIVORY; MEXICO, DESERTS OF; MOJAVE DESERT; OVERGRAZING; SEEDS; SONORAN DESERT**

Further Reading

Bent, A. C. 1932. Life histories of North American gallinaceous birds. *U.S. National Museum Bulletin* 162.

Cramp, S., and K. E. L. Simmons, eds. 1980. *Handbook of the Birds of Europe, the Middle East and North Africa: The Birds of the Western Palearctic*. Vol. 2. Oxford: Oxford University Press.

Johnsgard, P. A. 1988. *The Quails, Partridges and Francolines of the World*. Oxford: Oxford University Press.

Marchant, S., and P. J. Higgins. eds. 1993. *Handbook of Australian, New Zealand and Antarctic Birds*. Vol. 2. Melbourne: Oxford University Press.

Schemnitz, S. D. 1994. Scaled quail (*Callipepla squamata*). *In* A. Poole and F. Gill, eds., *The Birds of North America*, No. 106. Philadelphia: Academy of Natural Sciences; Washington, D.C.: American Ornithologists' Union.

Urban, E. K., C. H. Fry, and S. Keith, eds. 1986. *The Birds of Africa*. Vol. 2. New York: Academic Press.

QUATERNARY

Period of geologic time beginning 1.8–1.6 million years ago and continuing to the present day. The Quaternary period is made up of two epochs, Pleistocene and Holocene (or "Recent"). The Pleistocene makes up more than 99 percent of elapsed geologic time of the Quatern

10,000 years ago; the Holocene makes up the remaining small percentage. The Quaternary represents the culmination of the long-term, Cenozoic global climatic deterioration in which continental glaciers developed when polar temperatures dropped, and low-latitude temperatures increased, contributing to the development of deserts. Thus the latest of the earth's great ice ages (times of frequent, widespread continental glaciations) began in the late Pliocene and possibly ended with the end of the Pleistocene. However, if the present, relatively warm temperate epoch (Holocene) is simply an interglacial, as most scientists believe, this ice age may not yet have ended. During the Quaternary some 21–27 cold periods have occurred, alternating with relatively warm interglacial periods. Extensive continental glaciations did not necessarily occur during all the cold periods.

During the times of glacial maxima, even the climates of many unglaciated regions were affected by pluvial periods (relatively wet and cool climate) due to the presence of the glaciers elsewhere. For example, in those parts of North America presently occupied by deserts, the vegetation and climate was very different during the late Quaternary. Between 15,000 and 10,000 years ago, much of the low-lying regions of southwestern North America were covered with juniper and pinyon pine woodlands, and basins such as Death Valley and other huge areas of the Great Basin held pluvial lakes. The same is true of other continents: more abundant vegetation grew, and pluvial lakes were present in what are now barren deserts or desert scrub with saline lakes or dry lake basins. These are found in the present Sahara and Kalahari deserts of Africa, the Atacama and Monte deserts of South America, the interior desert of Australia, and many parts of central Asia. The lakes dried up and desert vegetation appeared (or returned) to these lowland areas during the warmth and aridity of the Holocene interglacial. The wh͏ abouts of desert scrub vegetation during the ͏s glacial/pluvial periods are largely ͏ern deserts and desert vegetation ͏nly present in many parts of the the Holocene, but there is ͏olocene evidence of them ͏gies of remote sensing ͏adar have dramatically ͏e of streams and northern Africa

that are now covered by the barren sands of the eastern Sahara.—Nicholas J. Czaplewski

See also **CENOZOIC; CRETACEOUS; DEATH VALLEY; DESERTS; EOCENE; FOSSILS; GLACIAL PERIODS; GREAT BASIN DESERT; INTERGLACIALS; MADRO-TERTIARY GEOFLORA; MIDDEN; MIOCENE; NEOGENE; PALEOCENE; PALEOCLIMATE; PERMIAN; PLANTS; PLATE TECTONICS; PLAYA; PLEISTOCENE; PLIOCENE; RECENT (HOLOCENE); TERTIARY**

Further Reading

Behrensmeyer, A. K., J. D. Damuth, W. A. DiMichele, R. Potts, H.-D. Sues, and S. L. Wing. 1992. *Terrestrial Ecosystems Through Time*. Chicago: University of Chicago Press.

Bradley, R. S. 1985. *Quaternary Paleoclimatology: Methods of Paleoclimatic Reconstruction*. Boston: Allen and Unwin.

Flint, R. F. 1971. *Glacial and Quaternary Geology*. New York: Wiley.

Szabo, B. J., C. V. Haynes, Jr., and T. A. Maxwell. 1995. Ages of Quaternary pluvial episodes determined by uranium-series and radiocarbon dating of lacustrine deposits of eastern Sahara. *Palaeogeography, Palaeoclimatology, Palaeoecology* 113:227–242.

QUOKKA

Species of wallaby (*Setonix brachyurus*), a marsupial relative of kangaroos, found only in the extreme western corner of the Australian mainland and on two small offshore islands. It is the only species in the genus. The population on the mainland is restricted to thick, swampy forests; however, the island populations, especially the one on Rottnest Island, have survived in an extremely harsh, seasonally dry environment. The quokka was the first studied of all Australian marsupials, and the knowledge of its biology formed the foundation for future zoological research on marsupials in Australia.

Quokkas are approximately the size of a domestic cat. They have coarse, short, brownish gray fur and short, rounded ears. The tail is short with little fur. They are active day and night but tend to be more nocturnal during the dry months of the year. They are terrestrial and move by walking or with short hops. Quokkas are herbivores (plant eaters) and forage on a wide range of plants. On Rottnest Island they forage on coastal dune vegetation. During the dry season food becomes scarce and many animals starve. The quokkas have an excellent ability to regulate their body temperature, especially for an animal adapted to such humid conditions on the mainland, but they still must seek shelter during the hottest part of the day. The island has few suitable shelters, and defense of suitable refuges from the heat is an important part of their social behavior. Females give birth to one offspring, which remains in the pouch for up to 10 months.

Quokkas at one time were almost eliminated from the mainland, but recently their numbers have increased somewhat. The population on Rottnest Island is under threat from expanding development of recreational and vacation facilities.—Thomas E. Lacher, Jr.

See also **AUSTRALIA, DESERTS OF; KANGAROO; MALLEE; MAMMALS; MARSUPIALS**

Further Reading

Nowak, R. M. 1991. *Walker's Mammals of the World.* 5th ed. Baltimore: Johns Hopkins University Press.

Ride, W. D. L. 1980. *A Guide to the Native Mammals of Australia.* Oxford: Oxford University Press.

Strahan, R., ed. 1983. *The Complete Book of Australian Mammals.* London: Angus and Robertson.

RABBIT

Small, furry mammal of the order Lagomorpha (family Leporidae) superficially similar to rodents but distinguished from them by having two (rather than one) pairs of upper incisors. Rabbits range nearly worldwide across a variety of habitats. Most desert rabbits belong to the genus *Sylvilagus*, the cottontails. Another desert dweller, the Bushman rabbit (*Bunolagus*) lives in the Karoo Desert of South Africa, and the rock rabbit, *Pronolagus*, inhabits rocky areas in deserts of southern, eastern, and central Africa.

Most rabbits are crepuscular, resting in burrows or depressions during the day and night and coming out to feed at dawn and dusk. Rabbits eat a variety of plant parts; their diet consists of grasses, herbs, shrubs, and young trees. Two types of fecal pellets are produced: soft, green pellets that still have nutrients available and are reingested (a process called coprophagy); and hardened, brown pellets that are produced after most of the nutrients have been extracted.

Some rabbits dig burrows, whereas others find shelter in abandoned burrows of other small mammals, among rocks, or beneath shrubs. Nests are usually constructed in protected areas, and may be lined with fur. Rabbits are known for their high reproductive potential. Although some species have relatively few young, more typical are litters of three to six, and several litters may be produced each year. Most rabbits can swim, and some can even climb trees. Bobcats, weasels, foxes, coyotes, owls, hawks, and rattlesnakes are some of their main predators. Rabbits are afflicted by a variety of parasites (including fleas) and various diseases.

Rabbits are distinguished from the related hares and jackrabbits (*Lepus*) by their shorter hind limbs. Newborn rabbits are altricial and naked, and their eyes are closed. Hares have precocial young that are ready to move about within hours after birth. Rabbits often live in brushy areas or forests; hares occupy more open areas. Some rabbits excavate burrows, an activity seldom engaged in by hares, which may dig simple depressions for rest sites.

Desert cottontail (*Sylvilagus audubonii*) near Red Rock, New Mexico. (Photo: D. Beck)

Rabbits often freeze to avoid detection by predators, or may run short distances to the shelter of a shrub; jackrabbits are more difficult to approach, as they bound away at high speeds.

One of the most common of the desert-dwelling rabbits is the desert cottontail (*Sylvilagus audubonii*). This species occupies all four major North American deserts as well as grassland, shrubland, pinyon-juniper forest, and riparian areas. The diet of desert cottontails consists largely of grasses but also shrubs (including sagebrush) and other plants. Home range size varies up to six hectares for males and four hectares for females.

The pygmy rabbit (*Sylvilagus idahoensis*) is the smallest rabbit of North America. It resides primarily in the Great Basin Desert, from 1,300 to 2,100 meters elevation. Pygmy rabbits construct fairly extensive burrows with several entrances at the bases of sagebrush. They feed mainly on sagebrush, especially in the winter, but include grasses in their summer diet. Nuttall's or mountain cottontails (*Sylvilagus nuttallii*) also inhabit the Great Basin Desert, but their range extends into coniferous forests. This is another species that relies heavily on sagebrush for food. They also eat grasses and juniper berries. The eastern cottontail (*Sylvilagus floridanus*) occurs primarily in the eastern United

States but overlaps with desert cottontails on arid slopes with grass and mesquite in the Southwest.—Kristina A. Ernest

See also **GREAT BASIN DESERT**; **HARE**; **HERBIVORY**; **JACKRABBIT**; **MAMMALS**; **PHYSIOLOGY**; **PINNAE**; **SAGEBRUSH**; **SOUTH AFRICA, DESERTS OF**; **SOUTH AMERICA, DESERTS OF**; **UNITED STATES, DESERTS OF**

Further Reading

Chapman, J. A. 1975. Sylvilagus nuttallii. *Mammalian Species* 56:1–3.

Chapman, J. A., J. G. Hockman, and W. R. Edwards. 1982. Cottontails: *Sylvilagus floridanus* and allies. *In* J. A. Chapman and G. A. Feldhamer, eds., *Wild Mammals of North America: Biology, Management, and Economics*, 83–123. Baltimore: Johns Hopkins University Press.

Chapman, J. A., and G. A. Willner. 1978. Sylvilagus audubonii. *Mammalian Species* 106:1–4.

RAINFALL. *See* PRECIPITATION

RAIN SHADOW DESERTS. *See* DESERTS, RAIN SHADOW

RAJASTHAN DESERT. *See* INDO-PAKISTAN DESERTS

RAPTORS

Diverse group of small to very large diurnal birds of prey (order Falconiformes). The term "raptors" is sometimes extended to include owls (order Strigiformes), but for purposes of this discussion it will be limited to the Falconiformes. The phylogenetic history of the Falconiformes is still not clearly delineated, although it is generally agreed that the raptors do not constitute a monophyletic group (i.e., with a single common ancestor). Morphological and ecological similarities between some raptor groups are apparently due to convergent evolution (e.g., the Old and New World vultures). The Falconiformes include approximately 270–290 species from 70 to 80 genera in five families: the Accipitridae (eagles, kites, buzzards, Old World vultures), the Cathartidae (New World vultures), Falconidae (falcons, falconets, caracaras), Pandionidae (osprey), and the Sagitariidae (secretary bird). Raptors, distributed worldwide in virtually all habitat types including deserts, are absent only from Antarctica and some oceanic islands.

Crested caracara (*Polyborus plancus*) in the Pantanal, Mato Grosso, Brazil. (Photo: M. A. Mares)

Raptors share a variety of adaptations for a primarily carnivorous existence. Bills are generally strong and hooked, facilitating tearing of the flesh from captured animals. Most species have strong legs and feet with powerful talons for grasping prey. Generally both visual and auditory senses are highly developed. As one would expect from such a cosmopolitan group, Falconiformes fill a variety of ecological roles and are specialized to varying degrees. For example, the red-tailed hawk (*Buteo jamaicensis*) of North and Central America is found in a wide variety of habitats including desert scrub. Its diet is correspondingly varied and, depending on the season and the geographic location, may include small mammals, reptiles, birds, fish, crustaceans, and carrion. At the other end of the spectrum are species with highly specialized dietary requirements. For example, the Everglade kite (*Rostrhamus sociabilis*), which ranges from Florida to South America, feeds exclusively on freshwater snails of the genus *Pomacea*. Many birds of prey will include at least some carrion in their diets. For some species (e.g., the vultures), carrion constitutes the majority of the diet.

Raptors show various adaptations to a desert existence. For example, the cathartids have a variety of mechanisms for dissipation of heat, including gular fluttering, the raising of their wings to expose the sparsely feathered flanks and underwings, and excretion of dilute urine onto the legs to facilitate evaporative cooling. Other birds of prey pant to dissipate heat. Many birds of prey do not appear to require standing sources of water and undoubtedly gain much of their requirements from prey.

Breeding systems vary from socially monogamous through cooperative breeding, with juveniles assisting adult pairs (e.g., the merlin, *Falco columbarius*) to polyandrous, with females breeding with more than one male (e.g., the Galapagos hawk, *Buteo galapagoensis*). Raptors may be highly territorial and solitary, or may breed in loose colonies. Nests locations include trees (the majority of raptors), cliff ledges, buildings, caves, or, rarely, the ground (notably harriers, genus *Circus*). The majority of raptors build their own nest of sticks and branches, often lined with fresh green vegetation (most accipitrids and caracaras). Alternatively, New World vultures and most falcons either build no nest or use the nests of other bird species. In the majority of Falconiformes, most of the nest building duties are undertaken by the female. Clutch sizes typically range from one to five. Incubation in most species is solely or largely undertaken by the female with males providing food. Incubation periods last approximately 20–50 days. Hatching is asynchronous, and younger chicks often perish. Generally only the female will brood and directly feed the nestlings, while males perform hunting duties. Fledging periods range from as few as 20 up to 100 days or more.—Stephen C. Lougheed

See also **AFRICA, DESERTS OF; BIRDS; BUZZARD; CARRION EATERS; CONDOR; CONVERGENT EVOLUTION; HEAT BALANCE; LOCOMOTION; NESTS, BIRD; PHYSIOLOGY; PREDATION; SOUTH AFRICA, DESERTS OF; SOUTH AMERICA, DESERTS OF; UNITED STATES, DESERTS OF; VULTURE**

Further Reading

Bent, A. C. 1937. Life histories of North American birds of prey. Pt. 1. *U.S. National Museum Bulletin* 167.

———. 1938. Life histories of North American birds of prey. *U.S. National Museum Bulletin* No. 170.

Brown, L. H. 1970. *African Birds of Prey*. London: Collins.

Brown, L., and D. Amadon. 1968. *Eagles, Hawks and Falcons of the World*. Vol. 2. London: Country Life.

Cade, T. J. 1982. *The Falcons of the World*. Ithaca: Cornell University Press.

Cook, W. E. 1997. *Avian Desert Predators*. New York: Springer.

Hollands, D. 1984. *Eagles, Hawks and Falcons of Australia*. Melbourne: Nelson.

Johnsgard, P. A. 1990. *Hawks, Eagles and Falcons of North America: Biology and Natural History*. Washington, D.C.: Smithsonian Institution Press.

Mundy, P., D. Butchart, J. Ledger, and S. Piper. 1992. *The Vultures of Africa*. New York: Academic Press.

Newton, I. 1979. *Population Ecology of Raptors*. Berkhamsted: Poyser.

Newton, I., and R. D. Chancellor, eds. 1985. *Conservation Studies on Raptors*. ICBP Technical Publication No. 5.

RATTLESNAKE

Snake in the family Viperidae (subfamily Crotalinae) possessing a series of interlocking cornified structures at the end of the tail that make a buzzing sound when vibrated. The 29 species of rattlesnakes occur only in the New World; there are two genera (*Crotalus* and *Sistrurus*), and all are venomous, injecting venom through retractable fangs located in the front of the upper jaw. Rattlesnakes are heavy bodied and range in size from about 0.5 to 2.5 meters.

The segmented rattle contains a single button at birth that is not capable of making any sounds. Following the first shedding of the skin, the second rattle is produced, and rubbing of adjacent segments when the tail is rapidly vibrated produces the characteristic buzzing sound, or rattle. Contrary to popular belief, rattlesnakes do not gain a new rattle every year; rather they gain a new segment each time the skin is shed. Shedding may occur two or more times per year depending on season length and food levels. Rattlesnakes that feed frequently and grow rapidly shed their skins more often than those that feed infrequently.

Prey include lizards, mammals, and birds, but other animals, including centipedes, are sometimes eaten. In addition to locating prey by sight and smell, rattlesnakes and other pit vipers use a highly evolved infrared detection system that involves sensors located in "pits" just posterior to and below the nostrils, as well as complex neural structures. Prey are usually killed by envenomation and are then swallowed whole. Rattlesnakes, like many other heavy-bodied snakes, can eat nearly their own weight at a single feeding.

During the breeding season males of many species of rattlesnakes undergo ritualistic male-male combat in which males intertwine their bodies with the anterior portion of the body raised high off the ground. The winner is the individual that maintains its position the longest. Mating occurs when the male inserts one lobe of its double-lobed intromit-

Great Basin rattlesnake (*Crotalus viridis lutosus*) from southern Idaho. (Photo: L. J. Vitt)

tent organ, the hemipenes, into the cloaca of the female. All rattlesnakes are viviparous, producing live young that are nearly identical to adults except for size.

Although many species of rattlesnakes occur in deserts, others do not. Desert species in North America include the western diamondback rattlesnake (*Crotalus atrox*), the red diamond rattlesnake (*Crotalus ruber*), the Mojave rattlesnake (*Crotalus scutulatus*), the prairie rattlesnake (*Crotalus viridis viridis*), the Hopi rattlesnake (*Crotalus viridis nuntius*), the sidewinder (*Crotalus cerastes*), the speckled rattlesnake (*Crotalus mitchelli*), and the tiger rattlesnake (*Crotalus tigris*). A number of other species may occur in deserts but are usually found at the periphery of desert habitats. These include the black-tailed rattlesnake (*Crotalus molossus*), the Arizona black rattlesnake (*Crotalus viridis cerberus*), the southern Pacific rattlesnake (*Crotalus viridis helleri*), and the rock rattlesnake (*Crotalus lepidus*). The only species of *Sistrurus* that occurs in deserts is *Sistrurus catenatus edwardsii*, the desert massasauga, which is found in grassy areas of the Chihuahuan Desert. Some of the rattlesnakes typically associated with deserts may occur elsewhere as well. For example, the western diamondback occurs in parts of Oklahoma and Arkansas, and one species, the cascabel (*Crotalus durissus*), occurs in a variety of tropical habitats as well as the deserts of northern and central Argentina and the semiarid Caatinga of northeastern Brazil. A number of rattlesnake species appear to be distributed mainly in deserts based on range maps in popular field guides. However, some of these, including the ridge-nosed rattlesnake (*Crotalus willardi*) and the twin-spotted rattlesnake (*Crotalus pricei*), occur only in montane forest habitats of mountain ranges isolated within surrounding deserts.

The venom delivery system of rattlesnakes, used for killing prey and for defense, is among the most complex and evolutionarily advanced known in reptiles. The fangs are elongate, hollow teeth located on a movable bone (the maxillary) in the front of the upper jaw. When not in use, the fangs are folded up against the upper palate. Behind each fang is a series of fangs at various stages of development—the fangs are shed and replaced periodically. Fangs are connected to large poison glands on either side of the rear of the head by venom ducts, which carry the venom from the glands to the fangs. During a biting sequence the fangs are erected as the snake strikes with its mouth open so that the fangs are forced into the victim. Muscles contracting around the glands send venom through the ducts and fangs and into the victim. Venoms of rattlesnakes are primarily hemolytic. Hemolytic venoms are complex compounds containing enzymes that break down muscle and blood tissues. Rattlesnake venoms are very effective for killing and subduing prey. Used in defense, rattlesnake venoms cause excruciating pain and without proper medical treatment bites to humans can be disfiguring or fatal. However, like most naturally occurring animals, rattlesnakes are beneficial in the control of small mammal populations.

Rattlesnakes, because of their often beautiful color patterns, impressive set of defensive adaptations, and an interesting history of inclusion in human folklore, have caught the attention of entrepreneurs in numerous small towns across their broad geographic range. As a result many species are heavily exploited as tourist attractions during "rattlesnake roundups." At numerous tourist shops, skins, dried heads, rattles, fangs, and rattlesnake meat can be purchased. The widespread slaughter of these snakes associated with this rapidly expanding exploitative industry is very likely having long-range deleterious effects on rattlesnake populations.—Laurie J. Vitt

See also **AFRICA, DESERTS OF; CROTALUS; DEFENSIVE ADAPTATIONS, ANIMALS; ECTOTHERMY; HEAT BALANCE; LOCOMOTION; PHYSIOLOGY;**

POISONOUS ANIMALS; PREDATION; REPTILES; SIDEWINDER; SNAKES; SOUTH AFRICA, DESERTS OF; SOUTH AMERICA, DESERTS OF; UNITED STATES, DESERTS OF; VENOM

Further Reading

Campbell, J. A., and E. D. Brodie, Jr. 1992. *Biology of the Pitvipers.* Tyler, Tex.: Selva.

Campbell, J. A., and W. W. Lamar. 1989. *The Venomous Reptiles of Latin America.* Ithaca: Cornell University Press.

Greene, H. W. 1990. A sound defense of the rattlesnake. *Pacific Discovery* 43:10–19.

Greene, H. W. 1997. *Snakes: The Evolution of Mystery in Nature.* Berkeley: University of California Press.

Klauber, L. M. 1972. *Rattlesnakes: Their Habits, Life Histories and Influence on Mankind.* 2d ed. 2 vols. Berkeley: University of California Press.

RAVEN. *See* CROW

RECENT (HOLOCENE)

The geologic epoch at the end of the Pleistocene that is often termed Holocene and that denotes only the last 10,000 years of geologic time. The Recent epoch began approximately during the melting of the last continental glaciers of the Northern Hemisphere. It is considered by climatologists simply to represent another interglacial, or relatively warm period, interspersed between the glacial periods (ice ages) that have been occurring cyclically in at least the Northern Hemisphere since the late Pliocene.

Conditions affecting earth's climate at any given time are extremely complex and include astronomical, atmospheric, hydrospheric, and lithospheric factors. Because of its recency, much more paleoclimatic and climatic data are available for the Holocene epoch than for any period in the more remote past. Pertinent data include many environmental conditions, ice sheet extents and volumes, ocean surface temperatures and boundaries of water masses, continental topographic effects, amelioration effects by continental lakes, atmospheric concentrations of CO_2 and other gases, insolation (amount of sunlight), and albedo (reflectivity). Studies also have shown that cycles of global climate change during the last 600,000 years—termed Milankovitch climate cycles—are linked to astronomical changes or variations in the earth's orbit. The latter include variation in eccentricity of the earth's orbit (which varies on a 100,000-year cycle),

in tilt of the earth's spin axis (40,000–41,000-year cycle), and in precession (variation in direction that the spin axis points when the earth is at its position of perihelion, the part of its orbit when earth is closest to the sun; 22,000–23,000-year cycle).

Based on such complex data as these, modeling by supercomputers of atmospheric general circulation has been relatively successful at simulating climates of the last several thousand years. Refinements of the computer models are frequently being added, and predictions have even been made for a few thousand years into the future. However, human population growth and modification of environment and climate are increasingly perturbing the global system.

By the Holocene most of the earth's present-day deserts had been long established (since Miocene-Pliocene times). One exception may be the deserts of southwestern North America. Although the North American Southwest may have begun to feel rain shadow effects from uplift of the Sierra Nevadas in the Pliocene, true deserts might have appeared there only in the Holocene. Through at least the last glacial period, much of the area now occupied by the Sonoran, Mojave, and Chihuahuan deserts was occupied in the late Pleistocene and early Holocene by pygmy conifer woodland (*Juniperus* and pinyon pines). The driest areas of desert during the Pleistocene might have retreated to a "core" area in the lowest elevations of the Colorado River valley near the river's mouth at the head of the Gulf of California, and possibly to refugia in Mexico.

In the world's other, earlier-established deserts, the Holocene has been a time of fluctuation between hyperarid and semiarid conditions, as was probably true throughout the histories of these deserts. In northern Africa the Sahara Desert already existed in the Plio-Pleistocene as a hyperarid region with almost no plant life. But during the early Holocene there was sufficiently increased precipitation there to produce small lakes and to allow thorn scrub and savanna to grow.—Nicholas J. Czaplewski

See also **CENOZOIC; CRETACEOUS; DEATH VALLEY; DESERTS; EOCENE; FOSSILS; GLACIAL PERIODS; GREAT BASIN DESERT; INTERGLACIALS; MADRO-TERTIARY GEOFLORA; MIDDEN; MIOCENE; NEOGENE; PALEOCENE; PALEOCLIMATE; PERMIAN; PLANTS; PLATE TECTONICS; PLAYA; PLEISTOCENE; PLIOCENE; TERTIARY**

Further Reading

Betancourt, J. L., T. R. Van Devender, and P. S. Martin. 1990. *Packrat Middens: The Last 40,000 Years of Biotic Change.* Tucson: University Arizona Press.

CLIMAP Project Members. 1976. The surface of the ice-age earth. *Science* 191:1138–1144.

COHMAP Members. 1988. Climate changes of the last 18,000 years: Observations and model simulations. *Science* 241:1043–1052.

Frakes, L. A., J. E. Francis, and J. I. Syktus, eds. 1992. *Climate Modes of the Phanerozoic: The History of the Earth's Climate over the Past 600 Million Years.* Cambridge: Cambridge University Press.

Gasse, F. 1978. Quaternary changes in lake-levels and diatom assemblages on the southeastern margin of the Sahara. *Palaeoecology of Africa* 12:333–350.

Heine, K. 1978. The main stages of the late Quaternary evolution of the Kalahari region, southern Africa. *Palaeoecology of Africa* 15:53–76.

Imbrie, J., and J. Z. Imbrie. 1980. Modeling the climatic response to orbital variations. *Science* 207:943–953.

Maley, J. 1977. Paleoclimates of Central Sahara during the early Holocene. *Nature* 269:573–577.

Thorne, R. F. 1986. A historical sketch of the vegetation of the Mohave and Colorado Deserts of the American Southwest. *Annals of the Missouri Botanical Garden* 73:642–651.

Van Devender, T. R. 1977. Holocene woodlands in the south-western deserts. *Science* 198:189–192.

Wright, H. E., Jr., J. E. Kutzbach, T. Webb III, W. F. Ruddiman, F. A. Street-Perrott, and P. J. Bartlein, eds. 1993. *Global Climates Since the Last Glacial Maximum.* Minneapolis: University of Minnesota Press.

Zubakov, V. A., and I. I. Borzenkova. 1990. *Global Palaeoclimate of the Late Cenozoic.* Amsterdam: Elsevier.

RED VELVET MITE

Giant mite in the arthropod family Trombidiidae that occurs in deserts of the southwestern United States and is brilliant red in color with a velvety covering of hairs. Although other species of *Dinothrombium* occur in Africa, Europe, and Asia, the species that are found in the deserts of the southwestern United States, *Dinothrombium pandorae*, *D. magnificum*, and *D. superbum*, are the best known ecologically. The most impressive features of these desert mites are their size, color, and abundance. Individuals may reach a centimeter in length—larger than any other known mites. Moreover, populations of these brilliant red, velvety animals numbering in the tens of thousands may appear on the surface.

These large mites are solitary during most of the year, remaining underground in areas with sandy substrate. Depending on locality, they may become active on the surface following certain winter rains (e.g., Coachella Valley of southern California) or after the beginning of summer monsoon rains (e.g., southeastern Arizona). Individuals emerge from the ground by first exposing their legs and sensing the substrate, presumably to assess moisture level. If conditions are appropriate, they emerge and wander on the surface for as long as three hours or more. While they are active on the sparse desert soils, they may engage in social interactions or feed, but the frequency with which such activity occurs is apparently very low. When social interactions occur, males spin webs on the ground in a ritualized manner, constituting a courtship sequence of behaviors. Later, females deposit eggs in burrows. The eggs apparently hatch after about 30 days. Larvae are parasitic on grasshoppers, whereas the adults are predaceous, feeding exclusively on alate termites (termites whose males and females have developed wings). Presumably the same set of conditions that triggers the release of alate termites also triggers the surface activity of the giant red velvet mites. The mites capture the termites as the insects rain down from the sky. Synchronized emergence of these mites is so impressive that some emergences have been visible even from satellites. Paradoxically, because of their reclusive habit of spending the vast majority of their time awaiting the very specialized conditions that trigger their emergence, it is generally extremely difficult to find even a single individual giant red velvet mite in the desert.—Laurie J. Vitt

See also **AFRICA, DESERTS OF; ARACHNIDS; ARTHROPODS; ASIA, DESERTS OF; CALIFORNIA DESERT; FLOOD; GRASSHOPPERS; INSECTS; MOJAVE DESERT; MONSOON; PREDATION; TERMITES; UNITED STATES, DESERTS OF**

Further Reading

Tevis, L., Jr., and I. M. Newell. 1962. Studies on the biology and seasonal cycle of the giant red velvet mite, *Dinothrombium pandorae* (Acari, Trombidiidae). *Ecology* 43:497–505.

RELATIVE HUMIDITY

Commonly termed humidity, it is an adimensional ratio (usually expressed as a percentage) of the water vapor of the air to the saturation point of the air. The saturation point of water in the atmosphere is that point at which, for a given temperature (saturation point is directly proportional to the temperature of the air), water vapor is in gaseous equilibrium over a planar surface (of water) and at which an increase in the amount of water vapor would cause the water to pass from a gaseous to a liquid state, thus exceeding the saturation point and leading to the formation of rain or some other type of precipitation. Relative humidity is expressed as a percentage, determined by using a psychrometer, which measures the temperature differential between a wet bulb (evaporation) and a dry bulb, converting these values to the percent relative humidity.—Federico Norte

See also **BAROMETRIC PRESSURE (ATMOSPHERIC PRESSURE); CLIMATE; CLIMATE CLASSIFICATION; CLOUDS; CONVECTIVE STORM; HAIL; PRECIPITATION; SNOW**

Further Reading

Day, J. A., and V. J. Schaefer. 1991. *Clouds and Weather.* Boston: Houghton Mifflin.

Oliver, J. E., and R. W. Fairbridge, eds. 1987. *The Encyclopedia of Climatology.* New York: Chapman and Hall.

Schaefer, V. J., and J. A. Day. 1981. *A Field Guide to the Atmosphere.* Boston: Houghton Mifflin.

Schneider, S. H., ed. 1996. *Encyclopedia of Climate and Weather.* 2 vols. New York: Oxford University Press.

RELIGION IN DESERTS

Refers to the fact that at least three of the world's major religions have had desert origins. Judaism, Christianity, and Islam all sprang from desert visionaries in the Middle East. These desert religions, monotheistic in nature, have had a global impact out of proportion to their origins in thinly populated deserts. The very idea of one god, or monotheism, can itself be traced back to Akhenaten, ruler of ancient Egypt in the Sahara Desert from 1379 to 1362 B.C.

Judaism traces its origins to a biblical patriarch, Abraham, who instituted monotheism among the Jews. Descendants of Abraham came under Egyptian rule for many generations. Eventually, led by Moses, the Jews left Egypt and wandered for forty years in the desert until Moses came down from Mount Sinai (located in the desert Sinai Peninsula) with the Ten Commandments and the Torah (a parchment scroll that contained the Five Books of Moses) and led the Jews into the promised land of Israel. These holy scriptures of Judaism would later be referred to as the Old Testament by Christians. From their desert origins, Jews are able to trace their ethnic, cultural, and religious history at least back to around 2000 B.C. in biblical texts.

Christianity has Jewish origins. Its founder, Jesus of Nazareth, was probably born between 4 B.C. and 2 B.C. At about age 30 he was baptized by a prophet, John the Baptist, who came out of a long Jewish ascetic and prophetic tradition. Jesus became an itinerant rabbi and developed his message based on love and the idea of physical resurrection from the dead. He was accused of blasphemy (for using the Davidic title Messiah), condemned to death, and executed. His followers, particularly the eleven apostles, believed he rose from the dead and ascended into heaven. From its desert origins, the Christian movement at first came into conflict with and was persecuted by Rome but gradually spread throughout the Roman Empire. By the 4th century A.D. Christianity became the state religion of Rome and finally a major international religion. Also by the 4th century A.D. hermits began to form in desert communities in Egypt. These "desert fathers" played an influential role in the development of Western monasticism.

Early on, Christian beliefs were formalized and gathered, from about the end of the 2d century A.D., into the New Testament. Just as Judaism was a "religion of the book," based on the Ten Commandments and the Torah, so Christianity was a religion of the book based on the New Testament. There would be one more religion of the book: Islam.

Islam is the third major desert religion. Muhammad, the prophet of Islam, was born in Mecca, an Arabian desert oasis, about A.D. 570. As a young man Muhammad went into the desert to pray, and there, on Mount Hira in 610, he believed he had a vision revealing the word of God to him. In July 622 Muhammad left Mecca and moved to Medina. This journey is called the Hejira, and the year 622 marks the first year of the Islamic calendar. Islam, which means "the perfect peace that comes when one's life is surrendered to God [Allah]," like Christianity, emphasizes prayer, good works, and charity and is a monotheistic religion. Unlike Christianity or Judaism, Islam views Muhammad as the last of the prophets, not as a deity.

Muhammad died in 632. Within two decades of his death the statements of Muhammad and his immediate followers, which were believed to be divinely inspired, were gathered into the sacred text of Islam, the Koran, written in Arabic. The Koran thus joins the Hebrew Scriptures and the Christian New Testament as sacred texts that grew out of the profound religious experience of desert cultures.

The successors to Muhammad were known as the caliphs. They were strikingly successful in expanding the geopolitical domain of Arabic and Islamic domination. From the 7th century through the 8th century, under the leadership of the Umayyad caliphs from their capital at Damascus, Syria, Islam spread from the Arabian Peninsula throughout the Middle East and the Mediterranean world. The Arabs greatly reduced the territory of the Byzantine Empire by conquering large stretches of Syria, Persia, and Armenia, far north into the Caucasus Mountains. The Arabs also spread the Islamic empire eastward across Egypt and North Africa. In 711 the Berbers, or Moors as they are also called, led by Arabs, crossed into Spain at Gibraltar and initiated a 700-year domination of Spain. There is a link, then, between desert habitats, the rise of religions, and the spread, in some cases, of enormous geopolitical influence.—E. A. Mares

See also **DESERT PEOPLES; HOHOKAM; HOPI; JEDDAH; JORNADA DEL MUERTO; MIDDLE EAST, DESERTS OF; NAVAJO (DINE'É); O'ODHAM; PALESTINE, DESERTS OF; RIO GRANDE; SAINT CATHERINE'S MONASTERY; SAUDI ARABIA, DESERTS OF**

Further Reading

Cahill, T. 1998. *The Gifts of the Jews: How a Tribe of Desert Nomads Changed the Way Everyone Thinks and Feels.* New York: Nan A. Talese.

Doorn-Harder, N. van, and K. Vogt, eds. 1997. *Between Desert and City: The Coptic Orthodox Church Today.* Oslo: Novus Forlag, Instituttet for Sammenlignende Kulturforskning.

Hobbs, J. 1995. *Mount Sinai.* Austin: University of Texas Press.

Lane, B. C. 1998. *The Solace of Fierce Landscapes: Exploring Desert and Mountain Spirituality.* Oxford: Oxford University Press.

Lewis, B. 1996. *The Middle East: 2000 Years of History from the Rise of Christianity to the Present Day.* New York: Simon and Schuster.

Merton, T. 1970. *The Wisdom of the Desert.* New York: New Directions.

RENAL PAPILLA

The apex of the renal pyramid in the inner medulla of the kidney. It is into the papilla (pl., papillae) that urine flows from the collecting ducts of the nephron. From the papillae urine is released into the pelvis, the central cavity of the kidney, and ultimately transferred to the ureters. Depending on the species of animal, the papillae may project to a varying degree into the pelvis of the kidney.

There is a close correlation between the concentrating power of the kidney and the length of the renal papilla, which in turn correlates with the length of the loop of Henle, a U-shaped portion of some nephrons. It is the length of the loop of Henle that is associated with an organism's ability to produce a concentrated urine. Only birds and mammals have a loop of Henle, and therefore only these animals are able to produce a urine much more concentrated than their plasma.

The loops of Henle of many desert animals are so long as to extend into the renal papillae. By contrast, the loops in the kidneys of organisms from less arid environments are usually short or absent; these animals do not need to conserve body water by producing a concentrated urine. A particularly long renal papilla is found in the Australian hopping mouse, *Notomys alexis*, a species with perhaps the most highly developed ability to produce a concentrated urine. Its urine can be concentrated to a factor 25 times that of its blood.—E. Annette Halpern

See also **ANIMAL ADAPTATIONS; BODY TEMPERATURE; CAMEL; CAMEL'S HUMP; COUNTERCURRENT HEAT EXCHANGE; DEHYDRATION; DESICCATION; ECTOTHERMY; ENDOTHERMY; ESTIVATION; EXCRETORY SYSTEM; EXPLOSIVE HEAT DEATH; HEAT BALANCE; HEAT EXCHANGE; HEAT STRESS; HEATSTROKE; HIBERNATION; HUMAN PHYSIOLOGY IN DESERTS; HYPERTHERMIA; HYPOTHERMIA; KANGAROO RAT; KIDNEY FUNCTION, DESERT RODENTS; KIDNEYS; METABOLISM; PERSPIRATION; RESPIRATORY WATER LOSS; SALT BALANCE; SURVIVAL IN DESERTS; SWEAT GLANDS; THERMOREGULATION; TORPOR; TRANSPIRATION; WATER BALANCE; WATER STRESS**

Further Reading

Eckert, R. 1988. *Animal Physiology: Adaptation and Environment.* 3d ed. New York: Freeman.

Folk, G. E., Jr. 1974. *Introduction to Environmental Physiology.* 2d ed. Philadelphia: Lea and Febiger.

Gordon, M. S., G. A. Bartholomew, A. D. Grinnell, C. B.

Jorgensen, and F. N. White. 1982. *Animal Physiology: Principles and Adaptations*. New York: Macmillan.

Schmidt-Nielsen, K. 1990. *Animal Physiology*. 4th ed. New York: Cambridge University Press.

REPRODUCTION

Process by which the genes of an organism are passed on to form individuals of the next generation. Reproduction may be sexual or asexual by means of binary fission or budding. Asexual reproduction occurs in bacteria when the DNA of a single bacterium replicates, after which the cell divides to form two daughter cells that are nearly identical to the parent cell (except when genetic mutations occur). Sexual reproduction is much more complex, involving the union of sperm and egg (gametes) from a male and female parent, respectively. Because the chromosome numbers must remain the same from generation to generation within each species of organism, an elaborate cell division process called meiosis must occur to form the gametes. Meiosis reduces the chromosome number of the gametes by one-half, so that the resulting zygote (developing organism) has the same number of chromosomes as each of the parents. Sexual reproduction is advantageous over asexual reproduction because it involves numerous mechanisms for increasing genetic variability. Genetic variation is often referred to as the raw material on which natural selection and evolution can act. A large amount of genetic variation allows populations of organisms to adapt more readily to changes in the environment should they occur. Organisms that are adapted to their environment are more likely to contribute offspring to future generations.

Some desert lizards in the genus *Cnemidophorus* (family Teiidae) reproduce by parthenogenesis. There are no males in these populations, and females produce viable female offspring that are genetically identical to their mothers, grandmothers, and other female ancestors without inclusion of male genetic material. Chromosome numbers are maintained because there is a premeiotic doubling of chromosomes, and genetic variation attributable to chromosomal crossovers is of no consequence because the chromosomes in which crossovers would occur are identical.—Janalee P. Caldwell

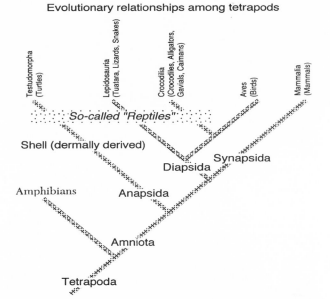

Evolutionary relationships among tetrapods

Cladogram of relationships among tetrapods. From the above, it can be seen that the set of organisms historically referred to as "reptiles" does not form a monophyletic group, rather, the entire set of tetrapods across the top, including birds and mammals, forms a monophyletic group based on presence of a single shared derived character, the amnion (from Pough et al. 1989, *Vertebrate Life*).

See also **AMPHIBIANS; ANIMAL ADAPTATIONS; ARACHNIDS; ARTHROPODS; BIRDS; BREEDING SEASON; DORMANCY; FOAM NEST; INSECTS; LIFE HISTORY STRATEGY (ITEROPARITY); LIZARDS; MAMMALS; NESTS, BIRD; REPTILES; SNAKES; SPADEFOOT TOAD; TADPOLES**

Further Reading

Begon, M., J. L. Harper, and C. R. Townsend. 1990. *Ecology: Individuals, Populations, and Communities*. Boston: Blackwell.

Cole, C. J. 1984. Unisexual lizards. *Scientific American* 250:94–100.

REPTILES

Term historically used to include all of the dinosaurs ("giant reptiles"), the tuatara (Rhynchocephalia), turtles (Testudines), crocodilians (Crocodilia), and lizards, amphisbaenians, and snakes (Sauria). The word *reptile* derives from the class Reptilia, an out-of-date taxonomic term that included the above groups but was based on a set of shared characters that, unfortunately, have little importance in the evolutionary relationships of these diverse groups. With the advent of cladistic methodology of characteristics, in which hierarchical evolutionary relationships are based on shared derived traits, it has become clear that the "old" taxonomy is invalid. "Reptile," at best, is thus a lay term usually referring to turtles, crocodilians, *Sphenodon*, lizards, and snakes.—Laurie J. Vitt

See also **ADDER; ANIMAL ADAPTATIONS; CERASTES; CHUCKWALLA; COBRA; CORAL SNAKE; DEFENSIVE ADAPTATIONS, ANIMALS; GECKO; GILA MONSTER; HORNED LIZARD; IGUANA, DESERT; LIZARDS; PIT VIPER; POISONOUS ANIMALS; RATTLESNAKE; SNAKES; TORTOISE; VENOM**

Further Reading

Pough, F. H., J. B. Heiser, and W. N. McFarland. 1989. *Vertebrate Life*. New York: Macmillan.

Stoops, E. D. 1997. *Snakes and Other Reptiles of the Southwest*. Phoenix: Golden West Publishers.

RESPIRATORY WATER LOSS

Loss of water from an organism due to evaporation from respiratory surfaces. It is a major component of evaporative water loss in most terrestrial animals, the other component being cutaneous water loss, water loss through the skin. Because gas exchange occurs most readily on moist surfaces, all respiratory surfaces are kept moist, from the nasal and oral membranes to the bronchioles and alveoli of the lungs in vertebrates; or from the spiracular openings through the tracheae to the tracheoles in arthropods.

Particularly for desert animals, this condition represents potentially a very high avenue of water loss through the inhalation of dry air, which becomes saturated with water vapor as it passes down the respiratory tract for gas exchange. On exhalation this saturated air is expelled to the external environment, resulting in water loss. Since the amount of water vapor the air may hold when saturated is positively related to the temperature of that air, animals with high body temperatures are particularly at risk of high rates of respiratory water loss. In endothermic birds and mammals, and at least in some heliothermic lizards with high body temperatures, this high potential of respiratory water loss is ameliorated somewhat by the presence of a mechanism in the upper respiratory tract that cools the air as it is expired to several degrees Celsius below the core body temperature. This promotes condensation along the airway, followed by reabsorption and reclamation of this condensed water, thereby reducing respiratory water loss.

In desert arthropods the apertures to the respiratory passages, the spiracles, are opened only intermittently for gas exchange, thereby reducing rates of water loss. Nearly all desert animals are quite effective in reducing rates of respiratory water loss through behavior that places them in microenvironments that are more moderate than the surrounding desert. An example of this behavioral amelioration is seen in nocturnal desert rodents that avoid the desiccating desert surface during the day, living in underground humid burrows, inspiring air that approaches saturation, and thereby reducing respiratory water loss to a mere fraction of that which would be expended in diurnal surface activity.—Richard E. MacMillen

See also **ANIMAL ADAPTATIONS; BODY TEMPERATURE; CAMEL; CAMEL'S HUMP; COUNTERCURRENT HEAT EXCHANGE; DEHYDRATION; DESICCATION; ECTOTHERMY; ENDOTHERMY; ESTIVATION; EXCRETORY SYSTEM; EXPLOSIVE HEAT DEATH; HEAT BALANCE; HEAT EXCHANGE; HEAT STRESS; HEATSTROKE; HIBERNATION; HUMAN PHYSIOLOGY IN DESERTS; HYPERTHERMIA; HYPOTHERMIA; KANGAROO RAT; KIDNEY FUNCTION, DESERT RODENTS; KIDNEYS; METABOLISM; PERSPIRATION; RENAL PAPILLA; SALT BALANCE; SHIVERING; SUNBURN; SUNSTROKE; SURVIVAL IN DESERTS; SWEAT GLANDS; THERMOREGULATION; TORPOR; TRANSPIRATION; VAN'T HOFF EFFECT; WATER BALANCE; WATER STRESS**

Further Reading

Gordon, M. S., G. A. Bartholomew, A. D. Grinnell, C. B. Jorgensen, and F. N. White. 1982. *Animal Physiology: Principles and Adaptations*. New York: Macmillan.

Schmidt-Nielsen, K. 1990. *Animal Physiology*. 4th ed. New York: Cambridge University Press.

RESURRECTION PLANT

Common name given to several species of plants that are capable of surviving extended droughts by allowing their body structures to dry out and enter a dormant state; when moisture again becomes available, these structures resorb water and resume activity. While dormant, because of its blackened, dry appearance and easily crumbled texture, the plant seems to be dead. Thus, following resorption a "dead" plant seemingly becomes "alive," hence the common name.

Most resurrection plants are primitive vascular plants that produce no true flowering structures. The most common species are members of the genus *Selaginella*. This genus belongs to a group of plants known as club mosses, but they are not true mosses. They are more closely related to ferns. Another club moss genus that can behave as a resurrection plant is *Lycopodium*. There are mosses that also behave as resurrection plants. These are components of microphytic mats that grow on the soil surface in many deserts and include members of the genera *Pterygoneurum* and *Aloina*.

Even some true ferns can act as resurrection plants. These include the resurrection fern, *Polypodium polypoides*, and the cliff brake, *Pellaea atropurpurea*.

The plants that use this adaptation to arid conditions do not have any one morphological (physical) feature in common. Some have true vascular systems; some (e.g., mosses) do not. Some have stomata (pores) on their leaves through which they can control their rate of water loss; others (mosses) do not. They all share the same general physiological traits, however. All are capable of protecting their cellular structures and keeping them from destruction during severe water loss. This allows them to resume physiological activity rapidly when rehydrated.—Linda L. Wallace

See also **DESERT BLOOM; DORMANCY; DROUGHT; MOSSES; PLANT ADAPTATIONS; PLANTS; PRECIPITATION**

Further Reading

Burns, G. W. 1974. *The Plant Kingdom.* New York: Macmillan.

RHEA

A member of two monotypic genera of large flightless birds endemic to South America (family Rheidae, order Rheiformes). The greater rhea; (*Rhea americana*) inhabits grasslands and open thorn scrub from southern Brazil to northern Patagonia. The lesser rhea (or Darwin's rhea; *Pterocnemia pennata*) ranges throughout arid, high-altitude Andean regions of northwestern Argentina, Bolivia, and Chile and the Patagonian scrub of Argentina. Rheas, like ostriches and emus, are ratites, lacking the keel on which flight muscles attach in flying bird species. Adult *Rhea americana* stand approximately 1.3–1.4 meters high and weigh 20–25 kilograms. Mature *Pterocnemia pennata* average 0.9–1.0 meter

Rhea (*Rhea americana*), a flightless bird of the South American drylands. (Photo: M. A. Mares)

in height and weigh 15–25 kilograms. The rhea's long powerful legs and feet with three strong toes are ideally suited for ranging over great distances.

Rheas are largely vegetarian, preferring broadleafed plants including obnoxious weeds like thistles. They will also eat insects and small vertebrates if the opportunity presents itself. Rheas may form flocks in winter but disperse into smaller groups during the breeding season. Breeding behavior is poorly studied. Rheas nest in sparsely lined scrapes on the ground. The mating system for both species is probably promiscuous. In *Rhea* a male maintains a harem, usually of six to seven females; however, females may switch mates when another harem is encountered. The situation in *Pterocnemia* is probably similar. Clutch sizes in *Rhea* usually range from 25 to 35, with eggs contributed by the various females of the harem. Incubation lasts 36–37 days in *Rhea*, and in *Pterocnemia* it is probably in this range. Both incubation and posthatching care of the chicks are undertaken solely by the male.

Although relatively common in some areas, many populations of both species are considered threatened. Declines can be attributed to extensive hunting for both meat and feathers and to egg collecting by local peoples. Moreover, although rheas adapt well to agricultural settings, they have often been killed because they will forage on most crops.—Stephen C. Lougheed

See also **ALTIPLANO; ANDEAN GRASSLANDS; ANDES; ANIMAL ADAPTATIONS; BIRDS; CHACO; MONTE DESERT; OSTRICH; PAMPAS; PATAGONIA; SOUTH AMERICA, DESERTS OF**

Further Reading

Bruning, D. F. 1974. Social structure and reproductive behavior of the greater rhea. *Living Bird* 13:251–294.

Handford, P., and M. A. Mares. 1985. The mating systems of ratites and tinamous: An evolutionary perspective. *Biological Journal of the Linnean Society* 25:77–104.

Johnson, A. W. 1965. *The Birds of Chile and Adjacent Regions of Argentina, Bolivia and Peru*. Vol. 1. Buenos Aires: Platt.

Raikow, R. J. 1968. Maintenance behavior of the common rhea. *Wilson Bulletin* 80:312–319.

———. 1969. Sexual and agonistic behavior of the common rhea. *Wilson Bulletin* 81:196–206.

RHINOCEROS

Immense herbivorous mammal (family Rhinocerotidae) in the order Perissodactyla (which also includes horses and tapirs). There are four genera and five species of rhinoceroses that share a common character: the weight of the body is carried on the third digit of the foot, which is always the longest, and sometimes the only, functional digit.

Rhinos do not inhabit true deserts, although they do occur in very dry scrubland habitats such as those found in Namibia and South Africa. The African rhinos (*Diceros bicornis* and *Ceratotherium simum*) historically are distributed south of the Sahara and also possibly occurred in North Africa. *Ceratotherium* prefers open forest or woodlands interspersed with grasslands, whereas *Diceros* prefers edges of thick bush or scrub between grassland and forest. Two genera (*Dicerorhinus* and *Rhinoceros*) are found in forests of south central and Southeast Asia.

Rhinos have a large body and head (length of head and body, 200–420 centimeters; height at shoulder, 100–200 centimeters; weight, 1,000–3,500 kilograms), a bristled tail (length, 60–75 centimeters), and short legs. The skin is thick and sparsely covered with hair. Coloration varies from

White rhinoceros (*Ceratotherium simum*) in the thorn scrub of the Itala Game Reserve, northern Kwazulu-Natal Province, South Africa. (Photo: M. A. Mares)

grayish to brownish. Rhinos have one or two horns, which are not made of bone but of a compressed fibrous keratin. Females are smaller than males. *Diceros* and *Rhinoceros* have a prehensile lip. The eyes are small, and vision is poor; hearing and smell are well developed. Incisors and canines are vestigial; cheek teeth are high crowned in *Ceratotherium*, a grazer, and low crowned in the other species, which are browsers.

In Africa distributions are restricted by a dependence on water. Most activity is confined to the evening, night, and early morning. Muddy pools and riverbanks are used as wallows for thermoregulation and parasite control. Tick birds and egrets, often seen in the company of rhinos, act as sentinels and feed on their parasites. A single young is born after a gestation period of 420–570 days; rhinos may live up to 50 years.

All rhinos are endangered by hunting and habitat disruption. The horn is used for folk medicine and by artists in Eastern cultures.—Janet K. Braun

See also **AFRICA, DESERTS OF; HEAT BALANCE; HEAT STRESS; HERBIVORY; MAMMALS; PHYSIOLOGY; SOUTH AFRICA, DESERTS OF; THERMOREGULATION; UNGULATES; WATER BALANCE; XEROPHYLLOUS FOREST**

Further Reading

Estes, R. D. 1991. *The Behavior Guide to African Mammals*. Berkeley: University of California Press.

Groves, C. P. 1972. Ceratotherium simum. *Mammalian Species* 8:1–6.

Groves, C. P., and F. Kurt. 1972. Dicerorhinus sumatrensis. *Mammalian Species* 21:1–6.

Kingdon, J. 1989. *East African Mammals: An Atlas of Evolution in Africa. (Large Mammals)*. Vol. 3B. Chicago: University of Chicago Press.

Laurie, W. A., E. M. Lang, and C .P. Groves. 1983. Rhinoceros unicornis. *Mammalian Species* 211:1–6.

Nowak, R. M. 1991. *Walker's Mammals of the World*. 5th ed. Baltimore: Johns Hopkins University Press.

Skinner, J. D., and R. H. N. Smithers. 1990. *The Mammals of the Southern African Subregion*. Pretoria: University of Pretoria.

RINGTAIL

Species of carnivorous mammals in the genus *Bassariscus* that are found in North and Central America. The North American ringtail, *Bassariscus astutus*, generally occurs in semiarid deserts, rocky areas, and canyons of the southwestern United States and Mexico but is usually never found far from water. Ringtails are also known as ring-tailed cats (for the ringed tail and catlike behavior), miner's cat (for their skill in hunting mice in mining camps), and cacomistles (from an Aztec word, which in Spanish means "nimble thief").

Ringtails are in the same family as raccoons (Procyonidae) but are smaller and more slender, with pointed faces, large eyes and ears, and a bushy tail approximately as long as the body. Total length varies from 616 to 811 millimeters, length of tail from 310 to 438 millimeters, and weight from 870 to 1,110 grams. The black-tipped tail is annulated (ringed) with alternating black and white bands. Because the bands are not completely closed, the underside of the tail is white.

Of the raccoonlike animals, ringtails are the most adapted to arid habitats. They are generally nocturnal. During the day they take refuge in caves, rock crevices, burrows, hollow parts of trees, and buildings. Ringtails are dependent on free water, but in arid regions they maintain their water balance by eating high-protein foods or foods having a high water content. Water loss is further reduced by their ability to produce the highest reported urine concentrations for any carnivore.

Ringtails are the most carnivorous of the procyonids. In addition to birds and mammals, they will eat cacti, acorns, mistletoe, juniper berries, persimmons, wild figs, insects, and arachnids. They are very curious and may be seen in parks, camping areas, or buildings. They can climb easily into trees and cacti and onto rocks. When threatened, ringtails may snarl, hiss, bark, bristle the tail hair, and bend the tail forward over the body, or release musk from the paired anal glands.

Ringtails mate between February and June. After approximately 50 days, one to four young are born. The young can sometimes be seen following the female in single file as they search for food. In the wild they may live for 7 years, and in captivity up to 16 years.—Janet K. Braun

See also **CARNIVORES; CHIHUAHUAN DESERT; COATI; MAMMALS; MEXICO, DESERTS OF; PREDATION; SONORAN DESERT**

Further Reading

Grzimek's Encyclopedia of Mammals. Vol. 3. 1990. New York: McGraw-Hill.

Kaufmann, J. H. 1982. Raccoon and allies. *In* J. A. Chapman and G. A. Feldhamer, eds., *Wild Mammals of North America: Biology, Management, and Economics*, 567–585. Baltimore: Johns Hopkins University Press.

Poglayen-Neuwall, I., and D. E. Toweill. 1988. Bassariscus astutus. *Mammalian Species* 327:1–8.

RIO GRANDE

River, called the Rio Bravo in Mexico, whose headwaters are in the San Juan Mountains of southern Colorado and which flows from its source more than 3,200 kilometers through its basin generally south and southeast through southern Colorado, the rift valley in the heartland of New Mexico, and then on to form the boundary between Texas and Mexico from El Paso to the Gulf of Mexico.

The river is of great historical importance. Desert people of the Southwest may have lived in close proximity to the banks of the Rio Grande as early as 10,000 B.C. The ancient Anasazi were in this area by 200 B.C., and their descendants were building their villages, called *pueblos* by the Spaniards, near the Rio Grande and its tributaries by A.D. 700. After 1540 the Spanish and Mexican settlers built their villages in close proximity to the Pueblos for the obvious reason that in an arid and semiarid environment, water was a scarce, needed, and highly desirable resource. Later, with the arrival of the United States in 1821 and particularly after the U.S. war against Mexico (the Mexican-American War, 1846–1848), new and heavy demands were placed on the Rio Grande. Thus in addition to its critical geographic and geologic significance, the river is also a great cultural divide. The ethnically and culturally diverse populations of the United States and Mexico interface at many different levels and in a complex variety of interactions along the entire length of the river.

Today the river is under increasingly heavy stress. Recreational businesses dot its banks in northern New Mexico; radioactive wastes from Los Alamos and industrial and urban pollution from such sizable cities as Santa Fe, Albuquerque, Las Cruces, El Paso, and Juárez (Mexico), in addition to the impact of the Texas cities below El Paso, including but not limited to Del Rio, Ciudad Acuna (Mexico), Eagle Pass, Piedras Negras (Mexico), Laredo, and Nuevo Laredo (Mexico), place the future of the Rio Grande in jeopardy. Untreated wastes are of particular concern because they are dumped into the river all along the border. The greatest contamination occurs, as would be expected, in the stretches of the river just below major urban areas. Environmental concerns for the Rio Grande also focus on toxic chemical contamination, particularly pesticides and heavy metals, that may contribute to birth defects and fish deformities. The *maquiladoras* (assembly factories located on the Mexican side of the border where labor is cheap) may also contribute to the environmental degradation of the Rio Grande and to the health hazards of the people who live on both sides of the border.

The Rio Grande, in addition to its historic and current geopolitical significance, is a vital and scarce water resource for two nations whose demands far exceed the capacity of the river.—E. A. Mares

See also **COLORADO RIVER; CONTAMINATION; COTTONWOOD; FLOOD; FOREST; HYDROLOGICAL CYCLE; HYDROLOGY; IRRIGATION DRAINAGE; JORNADA DEL MUERTO; MEXICO, DESERTS OF; NAVAJO (DINE'É); NEW MEXICO DESERT; PESTICIDES; POLLUTION; RIPARIAN COMMUNITIES; RIVERS; RUNOFF; SALT CEDAR; WATER**

Further Reading

Bowman, J. A. 1993. *The Rio Grande: A Confluence of Waters, Nations & Cultures.* College Station: Texas Water Resource Institute.

Eaton, D., and J. Anderson. 1987. *The State of the Rio Grande/Rio Bravo.* Tucson: University of Arizona Press.

Horgan, P. 1954. *Great River: The Rio Grande in North American History.* New York: Rinehart.

Riparian forest of cottonwood trees (*Populus*) along a river in the Sonoran Desert of Pima County, Arizona. (Photo: M. A. Mares)

RIPARIAN COMMUNITIES

Vegetation within or immediately adjacent to stream channels or on floodplains, often referred to as the riparian zone. Riparian communities are regarded as an ecotone between the true aquatic environment and the surrounding desert uplands. The transition from riparian to desert communities is rapid. In arid regions riparian zones are linear, narrow landscape features. As a result riparian zones link different regions within the desert and provide corridors for the movement of species between regions. Characteristic woody plants of riparian zones in the southwestern United States include boxelder (*Acer negundo*), ashes (*Fraxinus pennsylvanica*), alders (*Alnus oblongifolia*), sycamores (*Platanus wrightii*), cottonwoods (*Populus angustifolia, Populus fremontii*), and willows (*Salix goodingii, Salix exigua, Salix bebbiana*).

The species composition and structure of the riparian community is closely linked to the flow of water and channel dynamics of the adjacent stream. Early spring floods and high water tables produce lush vegetation in the riparian zone that is typically taller than the surrounding desert vegetation. However, available moisture decreases as the summer progresses. Although increased moisture availability is beneficial, riparian plants must also be able to tolerate excess water. The duration of flooding, or length of time that water saturates the soil, is an important determinant of which plant species will be present. As the duration of flooding increases, the amount of oxygen in the soil decreases. These conditions are detrimental to the roots of many species, but specialized adaptations allow riparian plants to tolerate periods of low soil oxygen concentration. In fact, species are organized in riparian communities based on their ability to tolerate flooding. Species that are tolerant of flood conditions grow adjacent to the stream, and those least tolerant are found farther from the channel. Also, most desert streams flood rapidly and violently, which uproots riparian plants. The increased productivity of riparian communities is also a product of nutrient-rich sediments deposited by floodwaters. Riparian soils are often coarse and poorly developed. Nutrients enter the soil through direct deposition or evaporation of floodwaters. However, in desert environments the concentration of deleterious salts can increase as a result of evaporation.

Riparian communities are imperiled by a number of factors. The introduction of exotic, or nonnative, species decreases species diversity and ecosystem functions. Since their introduction into the southwestern United States 50 years ago, salt cedar (*Tamarix chinensis*) and Russian olive (*Elaeagnus angustifolia*) have displaced many native plant species, resulting in a decline of bird species associated with riparian communities. The construction of dams has decreased in-stream flow and interrupted the natural cycle of flooding that is crucial for the maintenance of riparian communities. The vast majority of riparian communities in the southwestern United States have been grazed by domestic livestock. The adverse effects of livestock overgrazing include decreased riparian plant biomass, decreased species diversity, and accelerated streambank erosion.—Bruce W. Hoagland

See also **COLORADO RIVER; CONTAMINATION; DAM; DESERTIFICATION; FLOOD; FLOODPLAIN; FOREST; IRRIGATION DRAINAGE; INDUS RIVER; MESQUITE; NILE RIVER; OVERGRAZING; PESTICIDES; PHREATOPHYTES; PLANT ADAPTATIONS; PLANTS; RIO GRANDE; RIVERS; RUNOFF; SALT CEDAR; SOILS, DESERT; TIGRIS-EUPHRATES; WATER**

Further Reading

Brinson, M. M., B. L. Swift, R. C. Plantico, and J. S. Barclay. 1981. *Riparian Ecosystems: Their Ecology and Status*. Washington, D.C.: U.S. Fish and Wildlife Service OBS-81/17.

MacMahon, J. A. 1988. Warm deserts. *In* M. G. Barbour and W. D. Billings, eds., *North American Terrestrial Vegetation*, 231–264. Cambridge: Cambridge University Press.

Malanson, G. P. 1993. *Riparian Landscapes*. Cambridge Studies in Ecology. Cambridge: Cambridge University Press.

Mitsch, W. J., and J. G. Gosselink. 1993. *Wetlands*. 2d. ed. New York: Van Nostrand Reinhold.

Szaro, R. C. 1989. Riparian forest and scrubland community types of Arizona and New Mexico. *Desert Plants* 9:70–138.

RIVERS

Natural streams of water occurring within defined boundaries known as beds and which have a particular flow and volume and empty into another river, lake, or ocean. Rivers are the natural collectors of the waters that form from glacial melt, overland flow from rains, and water from underground aquifers that reaches the surface. They are a vital part of the hydrological cycle, circulating water across the surface of the earth, evaporating water into the atmosphere as they carry it along, and transporting water into lakes and oceans.

Rivers have always formed an important means of communication in human societies and have provided access to the interior of continents. Great civilizations have often developed alongside rivers throughout the world, including the earliest civilizations along the Nile, Euphrates, and Indus rivers.

Each river has three major sections: upper, middle, and lower. In the upper section, the river is "young," the slope is more pronounced than at lower levels, and the river is characterized by its erosional action. In such areas rivers detach and transport large amounts of solid materials. In the middle section the slopes are more moderate, and the materials carried by the river are much smaller than at the upper levels. This is also an area of deposition of some of the coarser materials. In the lowest part of the river the slope is minimal, and the river can no longer carry many of the smaller particles that are in suspension; thus it deposits fine materials along its edges, at times forming deltas. Along with its tributaries, the river forms a drainage net that collects waters over an area known as a watershed.

Rivers are one of the most important factors influencing terrestrial landscapes. They constantly alter the profile of their watercourses, carving new and deeper channels, forming alluvial plains, filling lakes with sediments, and depositing enormous amounts of sediments where they empty into oceans. Through the action of rivers, deep valleys are formed, rich valleys are developed, and mountains are eroded.

A great majority of the freshwater on earth is contained in polar ice, glaciers, and subterranean water in aquifers. Only 0.006 percent (or approximately 2,120 cubic kilometers) of freshwater is in rivers. Although the percentage of freshwater contained in rivers is small, they transport immense quantities of water. Sixty-one percent of the rain that falls on the land is evaporated back into the atmosphere. The remaining 39 percent is carried in rivers to the oceans at the rate of 44,700 cubic kilometers of water per year.

The longest river in the world is the Nile at 6,650 kilometers, followed by the Amazon at 6,437 kilometers. There are approximately 100 rivers that exceed 1,600 kilometers in length. Generally the area that is drained by a river's system as well as the length of the river and the amount of water carried by it vary greatly. Although the Amazon is not the longest river in the world, for example, it drains the largest area and carries the largest amount of water of any of the world's rivers. Indeed, the annual water that is discharged by this single river is 19.2 percent of the total freshwater carried by all the rivers of the world. The Congo in Africa and the Paraná–La Plata in South America are among the five longest rivers that carry the greatest amount of water in the world. The Mississippi–Missouri river system is the third longest in the world, the fifth in drainage area, and seventh in total amount of water discharged. The 20 principal rivers in the world drain 30 percent of the earth's land surface, carrying approximately 40 percent of the total water runoff.

Rivers in deserts may be permanent, like the Nile of North Africa or the Rio Grande of the southwestern United States; or they may be ephemeral, like the Kuiseb of the Namib Desert, carrying water only during times of snowmelt or rain. Whether they carry water permanently or only during a short period of the year, rivers provide special mesic (moist) riverine habitats within arid areas and often support lush forests or other vegetation along their length.—Alberto I. J. Vich and Juana Susana Barroso

See also **COLORADO RIVER; CONTAMINATION; DAM; DESERTIFICATION; FLOOD; FLOODPLAIN; FOREST; INDUS RIVER; IRRIGATION DRAINAGE; MESQUITE; NILE RIVER; OVERGRAZING; PESTICIDES; PHREATOPHYTES; PLANT ADAPTATIONS; PLANTS; RIO GRANDE; RIPARIAN COMMUNITIES; RUNOFF; SALT CEDAR; SOILS, DESERT; TIGRIS-EUPHRATES; WATER**

Further Reading

Bates, R. L., ed. 1987. *Glossary of Geology.* 3d ed. Alexandria, Va.: American Geological Institute.

Davis, S. N. 1974. Hydrogeology of arid regions. *In* G. W. Brown, Jr., ed., *Desert Biology: Special Topics on the Physical and Biological Aspects of Arid Regions,* 2:1–30. New York: Academic Press.

Leopold, L. B., M. G. Wolman, and J. P. Miller. 1964. *Fluvial Processes in Hydrology.* San Francisco: Freeman.

Moore, G. W. 1978. *Dictionary of Geography: Definitions and Explanation of Terms used in Physical Geography.* New York: Harper and Row.

The New Encyclopaedia Britannica. 15th ed. 1974. Rivers and Rivers Systems. Vol. 15:874–891. Chicago: University of Chicago Press.

Suh-Shiaw, Lo. 1992. *Glossary of Hydrology.* Taipei: Sheng Te.

Walter, H. and E. Stadelmann. 1974. A new approach to the water relations of desert plants. *In* G. W. Brown Jr., ed., *Desert Biology: Special Topics on the Physical and Biological Aspects of Arid Regions,* 2:213–310. New York: Academic Press.

ROADRUNNER

Genus (*Geococcyx*) of robust, largely terrestrial cuckoos native to the southern United States to as far south as Central America (family Cuculidae, order Cuculiformes). The greater roadrunner (*Geococcyx californianus*) ranges throughout desert scrub and chaparral of the southern United States and northern Mexico. The lesser roadrunner (*Geococcyx velox*) occurs in more tropical regions from Mexico to Nicaragua. Roadrunners are largely carnivorous, consuming insects, reptiles, rodents, and small birds, but will also eat fruit. The greater roadrunner (length 50–60 centimeters; weight 300–350 grams) possesses a number of adaptations for desert existence. Heat is dissipated through gular fluttering (rapid vibration of the upper air passages of the throat). A nasal gland allows for efficient elimination of salt; from the body. Adults will often consume nestling fecal material, deriving a significant proportion of their water needs from this source. Finally, body temperatures of nonincubating males and females fall at night; at dawn the darkly pigmented dorsal skin is exposed, allowing for the efficient absorption of radiant solar energy. This process is presumably a mechanism for energy conservation.

Two distinct breeding seasons are evident in greater roadrunners, coincident with increased rainfall and corresponding increase in prey density. The cuplike nests are constructed in low trees, shrubs, or clumps of cacti. Greater roadrunner pairs are probably monogamous and highly territorial. Clutch size is variable (two to seven) and is probably dependent on food supply. Male *G. californianus* incubate during the night, while such duties are shared by both sexes during the day. The altricial young (i.e., naked, blind, and helpless) hatch after approximately 20 days and are cared for by both parents. Hatching is not synchronous, and this may be an adaptation to allow for reduction of brood size during times of decreased food supply.

These colorful and highly visible birds have come to be synonymous with the deserts of the southwestern United States. The popularization of this species in the roadrunner and coyote cartoons has also endeared it to the public.—Stephen C. Lougheed

See also **BIRDS; BREEDING SEASON; CHIHUAHUAN DESERT; DESERT GRASSLAND; ENDOTHERMY; HEAT BALANCE; HEAT EXCHANGE; HEAT STRESS; MELANIN; MEXICO, DESERTS OF; NESTS, BIRD; PHYSIOLOGY; PIGMENT; SALT BALANCE; SONORAN DESERT; THERMOREGULATION; WATER BALANCE**

Further Reading

Bent, A. C. 1939. Life histories of North American cuckoos, goatsuckers, hummingbirds and their allies. *U.S. National Museum Bulletin* 176.

Calder, W. A. 1968. Nest sanitation: A possible factor in the water economy of the roadrunner. *Condor* 70:279.

Ehrlich, P. R., D. S. Dobkin, and D. Wheye. 1988. *The Birder's Handbook: A Field Guide to the Natural History of North American Birds Including All Species That Regularly Breed North of Mexico.* New York: Simon and Schuster.

Ohmart, R. D. 1973. Observations on the breeding adaptations of the roadrunner. *Condor* 75:140–149.

Ohmart, R. D., and R. C. Lasiewski. 1971. Roadrunners: Energy conservation by hypothermia and absorption of sunlight. *Science* 172:67–69.

Vehrencamp, S. L. 1982. Body temperatures of incubating versus non-incubating roadrunners. *Condor* 84:203–207.

Whitson, M. 1975. Courtship behavior of the greater roadrunner. *Living Bird* 14:215–255.

ROARING FORTIES

Popular term used by mariners to identify the regions of storms over the ocean at 40° and 50° south latitude. It refers primarily to the Southern Hemisphere because there is a belt of ocean that is uninterrupted by land surface at those latitudes, permitting the prevailing westerlies to reach very high velocities. This is one reason such dangerous stormy areas are found at the Strait of Magellan and Drake Passage in South America. The Tasmanian Sea and the confluence of the Atlantic and Indian oceans off Capetown in South Africa are similar zones where the Roaring Forties can lead to great storms at sea. These areas are subject to great cyclonic storms having very low pressure systems (some as low as 950 hecto-Pascals on the ocean surface at the storm centers). The Roaring Forties are particularly pronounced in far southern arid areas, such as the Patagonian region of Argentina.—Federico Norte

See also **ANTICYCLONE; BAROMETRIC PRESSURE (ATMOSPHERIC PRESSURE); CLIMATE; CLIMATE CLASSIFICATION; CLOUDS; CONVECTIVE STORM; CYCLONE; LOW PRESSURE; WIND**

Further Reading

Day, J. A., and V. J. Schaefer. 1991. *Clouds and Weather.* Boston: Houghton Mifflin.

Oliver, J. E., and R. W. Fairbridge, eds. 1987. *The Encyclopedia of Climatology.* New York: Chapman and Hall.

Schaefer, V. J., and J. A. Day. 1981. *A Field Guide to the Atmosphere.* Boston: Houghton Mifflin.

Schneider, S. H., ed. 1996. *Encyclopedia of Climate and Weather.* 2 vols. New York: Oxford University Press.

ROCK VARNISH

Thin (less than 300 millimeters [micron] thick) coating of manganese and iron oxides and hydroxides, clay minerals, and trace elements on rock surfaces. The color ranges from black manganese-rich varnish to orange iron-rich varnish. Rock varnish covers an estimated 75 percent of all bare rock in the southwestern United States.

Rock varnish is derived from both biological and physiochemical processes. In the biological model microorganisms such as microcolonial lichens or bacteria attach to the surface of airborne dust particles, which settle on rock surfaces. To obtain energy the microorganisms oxidize incoming manganese during brief wet periods. The manganese oxide subsequently accumulates on the rock surface as a smooth patina or veneer. The physiochemical process leads to the formation of both iron- and manganese-rich varnishes. Iron and manganese from aeolian dust and the rock are mobilized in solution. During evaporation the iron and manganese are precipitated onto the rock surface. Iron-rich varnishes will form in areas where the redox potential (Eh) fluctuates wildly, the pH is too high, the mosses or higher plants outcompete microcolonial lichens and bacteria, dust-trapping microenvironments are present, there is excessive wetness or dryness, and there are small amounts of manganese. Scanning electron microscopy (SEM) X-ray analysis of varnish indicates that manganese is concentrated on rock surfaces by bacteria, while biotic and physiochemical processes appear to contribute to the enhancement of iron on rock surfaces. Alternating iron-rich and manganese-rich laminae have been inferred to imply changes from arid to semiarid or subhumid climates.

Based on the premise that with time the leachable cations in rock varnish, such as sodium, magnesium, potassium, and calcium, are gradually replaced by and/or depleted relative to the less mobile cations, such as titanium, rock varnish may be used as a relative dating tool. Varnish cation ratio (VCR) dating, using the potassium and calcium to titanium ratio (K+Ca/Ti), provides an indicator of the length of time that the rock varnish has been exposed to cation leaching. The smaller the ratio, the older the varnish. Because rock varnish is susceptible to both mechanical and chemical weathering, dissolution under wet conditions, wind abrasion, or change in Eh or pH, precautions are taken when using the rock varnish as a relative dating tool. The simultaneous accumulations of barium and titanium (which could mask the titanium signal), the incorporation of titanium from volcanic sources, and variations in the rates at which microorganisms concentrate varnish have led some scientists to caution the use of VCR curves until there is a better understanding of rock varnish diagenesis (changes that affect sediments after they have been deposited).

The organic matter in rock varnish consists mostly of bacteria and pollen and plant debris within the clays and the iron and manganese oxides. Small amounts of subvarnish organics have been dated by the accelarator mass spectrometer radio-carbon dating method (14C AMS) to better calibrate the ages of surfaces. VCR and 14C AMS, along with chemical microanalysis of rock varnish laminae, are useful tools for deciphering paleoenvironmental fluctuations in deserts and, with current limitations in mind, provide a valuable dating method for geomorphic surfaces and lithic artifacts such as petroglyphs and other types of rock art, art that is frequently found in arid or semiarid regions.—Vatche P. Tchakerian

See also **BACTERIA; LICHENS; MINERALS; PALEO-CLIMATE; PLANT ADAPTATIONS; PLANTS; PRECIPI-TATION; WEATHERING, DESERT**

Further Reading

Dorn, R. I. 1991. Rock varnish. *American Scientist* 79:542–553.

Oberlander, T. M. 1994. Rock varnish in deserts. *In* A. D. Abrahams and A. J. Parsons, eds., *Geomorphology of Desert Environments*, 106–119. London: Chapman and Hall.

RODENTS

Order (Rodentia) of mainly gnawing mammals. This is the largest order of mammals, with more than 1,700 species. Almost one in every two mammals is a rodent. The Rodentia has a worldwide distribution, especially when species such as the house mouse *(Mus)* or rat *(Rattus)* are considered, because they occur wherever people occur. Rodents are an important faunal component in most deserts of the world. In the deserts of Africa, Asia, Australia, North America, or South America, rodents are faced with unpredictable food resources, sparse plant cover, and a lack of free water. To cope with these limiting factors, rodents possess a wide array of adaptations in terms of morphology, physiology, behavior, and ecology. Thus it is common to find rodents from different deserts showing similar adaptations in response to these limiting conditions, a situation resulting from convergent evolution. Among the most well known desert rodents are the kangaroo rats and the pocket mice (family Heteromyidae) of North American deserts and the jerboas (family Dipodidae) and gerbils (family Muridae) of Old World deserts.

Desert rodents have adapted to a wide array of microhabitats, including rocky areas, sand dunes, and salt flats, and have developed specializations that permit existence underground. Rodents may be diurnal (active during the day, such as ground squirrels or maras) or nocturnal (active at night, such as kangaroo rats and jerboas), and their diet may include seeds, shrubs, grasses, succulent halophytic plants, and insects. Rodents that specialize on seeds (granivores) are able to obtain water directly from the products released when the seeds are digested, while also obtaining their food needs in packets that are amenable to long-term storage. In fact, seed eating is a particularly successful foraging strategy for desert rodents.

Desert rodents are generally gray or pale in color, matching the substrate where they live (a phenomenon called crypsis). Such coloration may function as a protection against predators. Most of the highly adapted desert rodents live a solitary existence, although there are notable exceptions, such as mole rats, that live communally. Among the most conspicuous adaptations to desert life is the habit of being bipedal or saltatorial (i.e., hopping on the hind feet by species; e.g., *Jaculus*, *Pedetes*, *Notomys*, *Microdipodops*). This adaptation is thought to function primarily as a predator-avoidance mechanism, and has evolved repeatedly in the sparse desert environment. It is evidenced externally by elongated hind feet and a long tufted tail that acts as a balance or rudder for the animal as it hops.

Many desert rodents also are characterized by elongate pinnae (external ears) or large tympanic bullae (capsules containing the inner ear). These serve as adaptations for detecting the approach of predators. Desert rodents also have evolved physiological adaptations to obtain water and maintain stable body temperatures in an environment characterized by high temperature and low water supply. Most rodents escape excessive daytime heat by restricting activity to the nighttime (nocturnal), when temperatures are cooler. During the hours of heat stress they remain in their humid burrows or in the shade of vegetation (diurnal species). Another way some rodents reduce exposure to heat is by becoming inactive and lowering metabolism during stressful periods (e.g., estivation; North America pocket mice are examples of desert rodents that use this strategy). Some species may change their circadian rhythm during summer (being more nocturnal) and winter (being more diurnal) in response to heat or water stress. Desert rodents lose water through urine, feces, and evaporation but are able to keep such losses to a minimum using kidneys that produce remarkably concentrated urine. This minimizes water loss and permits many species to survive without access to free water, or to obtain water from solutions of high salt concentration, such as from the tissues of halophytic plants. Examples of desert species that use a strategy of specializing on salt-loving plants are the sand rat (*Psammomys*) of North African deserts, the chisel-toothed kangaroo rat (*Dipodomys microps*) of the Great Basin Desert of North America, and the red vizcacha rat (*Tympanoctomys*) of the Monte Desert of Argentina.—Ricardo A. Ojeda

See also **ANIMAL ADAPTATIONS; BIPEDALITY; BURROWING ANIMALS; CONVERGENT EVOLUTION; DASSIE RAT; ESTIVATION; GERBIL; GOPHER; GRANIVORY; GRASSHOPPER MOUSE; GROUND SQUIRREL; GUNDI; HAMSTER; HETEROMYIDS; JERBOA; KANGAROO MOUSE; KANGAROO RAT; KIDNEY FUNCTION, DESERT RODENTS; KIDNEYS; MAMMALS; MARA; METABOLIC WATER; MICROHABITAT; MOLE RAT; MONTE DESERT; PHYSIOLOGY; PINNAE; POCKET MOUSE; PORCUPINE; PRAIRIE DOG; RESPIRATORY WATER LOSS; SAND RAT; SQUIRREL; TORPOR; VOLE; WATER BALANCE; WOODRAT**

Further Reading

Degan, A. A. 1997. *Ecophysiology of Small Desert Mammals*. New York: Springer.

Eisenberg, J. F. 1963. The behavior of heteromyid rodents. *University of California Publications in Zoology* 69:1–100.

Mares, M. A. 1993. Desert rodents, seed consumption, and convergence: The evolutionary shuffling of adaptations. *BioScience* 43:372–379.

———. 1993. Heteromyids and their ecological counterparts: A pandesertic view of rodent ecology. *In* H. H. Genoways and J. H. Brown, eds., *The Biology of the Family Heteromyidae*, 652–713. Special Publication No. 10, American Society of Mammalogists.

Prakash, I., and P. K. Ghosh, eds. 1975. *Rodents in Desert Environments*. Monographiae Biologicae. The Hague: Junk.

ROOTS

Central axis of a plant that develops from the descending pole of the embryo (radicle) and the lateral structures that develop from it. Similar structures (adventitious roots) may develop from other sources. For most vascular plants, the root serves as an anchor and absorbs water and dissolved minerals from the soil. Roots have a meristem at the tip of the primary and lateral roots. The meristem divides and produces new root cells. It also has a central vascular system for transporting water, dissolved minerals and food. Roots have storage cells, which may accumulate extensive amounts of carbohydrates, usually starch. Water absorption is accomplished by the cells at the tips of all the roots. In this zone, just behind the meristem, the epidermal cells are extended to form many long hairs that increase the surface area. Behind this zone the root is covered with a corky layer, which prevents the loss and uptake of water.

Plants that have adapted to arid conditions use three basic strategies for obtaining water: (1) limit growth to periods of rainfall; (2) have a highly diffuse root system that is close to the soil surface to capture rainfall percolating into the soil; or (3) use deep roots to absorb water from the water table. Desert annuals are proficient in the first of these, cacti have diffuse root systems, and mesquite has a deep taproot. Some desert plants may have both surface and deep roots.—James R. Estes

See also **ACTIVITY CYCLES, PLANTS; ANNUAL PLANTS; BULBS; CACTI; CREOSOTE BUSH; DECOMPOSITION; HERBS; HUMUS; GRASSES; GROWING SEASON; LEGUMES; MESQUITE; NITROGEN-FIXING PLANTS; PERENNIAL PLANTS; PHOTOSYNTHESIS; PHREATOPHYTES; PLANT ADAPTATIONS; PLANT COVER; PLANT ROOTS, ADVENTITIOUS; PLANTS; PRECIPITATION; PRIMARY PRODUCTIVITY; PSAMMOPHYTES; RUNOFF; XEROPHYTES**

Further Reading

Rost, T. L., M. G. Barbour, R. M. Thornton, T. E. Weier, and C. R. Stocking. 1984. *Botany*. 2d ed. New York: Wiley.

RUB' AL KHĀLI. *See* SAUDI ARABIA, DESERTS OF

RUNOFF

Fraction of rain or snowmelt that reaches and is circulated by a river, usually expressed in terms of total volume or volume per period of time or depth of a layer of water distributed uniformly over the entire drainage area of the river.

Waters that reach the river channel come through various paths; some in the form of rain, others through overland flow or surface runoff, subsurface runoff, and groundwater runoff. The flow of water over the surface until a drainage channel is reached is called surface runoff. A drainage channel is any longitudinal depression that is capable of transporting water from one point to another. When it reaches a channel, surface runoff is transported rapidly, leading to flood peaks. A fraction of the water that infiltrates the soil may move laterally through superficial soil layers until it reaches the drainage channel. This subsurface water and its amount are characteristics of the subsoil. Such subsoil movement of water occurs much more slowly than surface runoff. Should the process of water infiltration into the soil continue to greater soil depths, it will increase the levels of the groundwater storage. This water may eventually discharge into the river as subterranean water. Subterranean water does not fluctuate greatly in its rate of flow into rivers as it is roughly a constant.

In deserts surface runoff can be quite rapid and pronounced after sudden rainstorms because the soil and the sparse vegetation may not absorb much moisture over a short time. This surface runoff contributes to the flash floods that characterize many deserts.—Alberto I. J. Vich and Juana Susana Barroso

See also **DAM; FIELD CAPACITY OF SOILS; FLOOD; GROUNDWATER; HYDROLOGICAL CYCLE; HYDROLOGY; RIVERS; WATER**

Further Reading

Davis, S. N. 1974. Hydrogeology of arid regions. *In* G. W. Brown, Jr., ed., *Desert Biology: Special Topics on the Physical and Biological Aspects of Arid Regions*, 2:1–30. New York: Academic Press.

Eagleson, P. 1974. *Dynamic Hydrology*. New York: McGraw-Hill.

Huggins, L. F., and J. R. Burney. 1982. Surface Runoff, storage and routing. *In* C. T. Hann, H. P. Johnson, and D. L. Brackensiek, eds., *Hydrologic Modeling of Small Watersheds*, 169–225. Monograph No. 5. St. Joseph, Mo.: ASAE.

Moore, G. W. 1978. *Dictionary of Geography: Definitions and Explanation of Terms used in Physical Geography*. New York: Harper and Row.

Suh-Shiaw, Lo. 1992. *Glossary of Hydrology*. Taipei: Sheng Te.

Ven, T. C. 1964. Runoff. *In* T. C. Ven, ed., *Handbook of Applied Hydrology: A Compendium of Water-Resources Technology*. New York: McGraw-Hill.

Walter, H., and E. Stadelmann, 1974. A new approach to the water relations of desert plants. *In* G. W. Brown Jr., ed., *Desert Biology: Special Topics on the Physical and Biological Aspects of Arid Regions*, 2:213–310. New York: Academic Press.

RUSSIAN DESERTS. *See* ASIA, DESERTS OF

SABKHA

Coastal sand flats; found slightly above the high tide level, in arid and semiarid environments. Sabkhas (sebkhas) are located along coastlines characterized by gentle slopes, high sea surface temperatures, high evaporation rates, and pronounced intertidal and supratidal zones. The high rates of evaporation combined with the salinity of the coastal waters and the capillary rise of saline shallow groundwaters lead to the development of extensive salt-crusted (evaporite) surfaces. Halite and gypsum crusts are common, as are muddy carbonate sediments and algal mats. Generally their seaward sides are characterized by shallow lagoons and offshore bars; they grade inland into salt marsh or mangrove type ecosystems or low-gradient beach ridges and coastal dunes.

Sabkhas are especially well developed along the Arabian Gulf, the Gulf of Aqaba (Sinai), and Baja California, Mexico. A 320-kilometer-long and up to 25-kilometer-wide series of sabkhas and interconnected salt marshes and beach ridges characterize the northeastern section of the Arabian Peninsula, between Bahrain and the United Arab Emirates.

"Continental sabkha" is the term sometimes used to refer to playas in interior drylands with extensive salt deposits.—Vatche P. Tchakerian

See also **ARABIAN GULF, DESERTS OF; BAJA CALIFORNIA, DESERTS OF; CHENOPODIACEAE; COLLUVIAL DEPOSITS (COLLUVIUM); DUNES; DUNES, NABKHA; DURICRUSTS; GYPSUM; KAVIR; MIDDLE EAST, DESERTS OF; PLAYA; SALINITY; SALINIZATION; SALT CRUST; SALT PAN; SAUDI ARABIA, DESERTS OF; SOILS, DESERT, CALCAREOUS; UNITED ARAB EMIRATES, DESERTS OF**

Further Reading

Cooke, R., A. Warren, and A. Goudie. 1993. *Desert Geomorphology*. London: University College London Press. Pp. 217–219.

Viles, H., and T. Spenser. 1995. *Coastal Problems: Geomorphology, Ecology and Society at the Coast*. London: Arnold.

Sagebrush (*Artemisia*) desert near Mono Lake, California, with the Sierra Nevada in the background. (Photo: M. A. Mares)

SAGEBRUSH

Common name applied to members of the genus *Artemisia* (tansy tribe, sunflower family Asteraceae or Compositae), which includes an assortment of annual, biennial, or perennial herbs or shrubs and which are usually aromatic; there are 10 or more woody species that occur primarily in the Great Basin Desert. Relatives within the tribe include yarrow, tansy, and chrysanthemum. The genus name is from the Latin Artemisia, the ancient name of the mugwort, in memory of the wife of Mausolus, king of Caria, a province of Asia Minor. All species of the genus *Artemisia* are wind pollinated, in contrast to other members of the tribe, which are insect pollinated. The clusters of flowers that compose the composite head (equivalent to a single sunflower with the yellow rays and brown center) are reduced in size and gray-green. The species of sagebrush have only one flower form, but the other groups of *Artemisia* have two types of flowers in the composite heads. The clusters of heads are difficult to see against the gray-green foliage. Therefore, they are not attractive to insects. As with most wind-pollinated plants, the pollen is smooth and nonoily. It is buoyant and produced in great abundance, both of which are essential features of wind-pollinated species.

Many species of this genus are common to western North America, but big sagebrush (*Artemisia tridentata*) is often the species referred to as sagebrush. Big sagebrush, also known as black sage, purple sage, and sagebrush, is one of the most abundant and widely distributed shrubs over much of the Great Basin Desert, and there is considerable evidence that it has increased to its current levels in response to overgrazing. Pronghorns eat the leaves and twigs, but most other wildlife and domestic cattle appear to avoid browsing the shrubs, probably because of the bitter taste that results from the aromatic compounds. However, when it is the only forage available, cattle and deer will eat the leaves. Big sagebrush is one of the largest shrubs of the genus and can attain a height of almost three meters. It is the state flower of Nevada.

Sagebrush is a xerophyte, and it is effective in conserving water. The leaves are gray-green owing to the heavy growth of hairs on the epidermis. The hairs reflect light, cooling the leaves to reduce transpiration. Air currents near the stomata are also disrupted by the hairs, probably also slowing the loss of water vapor. Surface area of the leaves is rather small because the leaves are narrow. They have three teeth at the apex, hence the scientific name of big sagebrush, *Artemisia tridentata*. The plants are evergreen and produce two leaf sizes; the larger ones drop during drought, but the smaller ones remain on the plant in winter.

Although big sagebrush is characteristic of the Great Basin region, it also occurs south into California, north into Canada, and at higher elevations in the Great Basin in association with spruce-fir forests. The plant is well adapted to the semiarid conditions found in the Great Basin and other desert regions, with long and deep roots to secure water in times of drought. There is also evidence that big sagebrush steadily decreases phosphorus and potassium in its leaves as the leaves age, thereby conserving and reusing these nutrients in flowering. Members of the genus contain oil, waxes, resins, volatile oils, and other substances that enable them to resist temperature fluctuations and moisture deficiencies.

Other species of *Artemisia* that are commonly referred to as sagebrush are Bigelow sagebrush (*Artemisia bigelovii*), black sagebrush (*Artemisia nova*), three-tip sagebrush (*Artemisia tripartita*), sand sagebrush (*Artemisia filifolia*), and fringed sagebrush (*Artemisia frigida*).

Efforts have been made to control the growth of sagebrush with herbicides to increase grass growth and livestock production.—James R. Estes, Gary K. Hulett, and Amanda Renner Charles

See also **AN INTRODUCTION TO DESERTS; CHENOPODIACEAE; DESERTS; GREAT BASIN DESERT; HALOPHYTES; MONTANA DESERT; NEVADA DESERT; OREGON DESERT; PRONGHORN; SEMIARID ZONES; UTAH DESERT; WASHINGTON DESERT; UNITED STATES, DESERTS OF; XEROPHYTES**

Further Reading

Beetle, A. A. 1960. *A Study of Sagebrush, the Section Tridentatae of* Artemisia. Bulletin of the University of Wyoming Experimental Station.

Tisdale, E. W., and M. Hironaka. 1981. *The Sagebrush-Grass Region: A Review of the Ecological Literature.* University of Idaho Forest and Range Experiment Station, No. 29.

SAGUARO

Large, columnar cactus endemic to the Sonoran Desert. The saguaro (*Carnegiea gigantea*) is the largest succulent plant in the United States and the species of columnar cactus having the northernmost distribution. Older individuals usually have several branches ("arms") arising from high on the trunk. The stems have many prominent ribs covered with stout spines. The skeleton of woody ribs remains standing after the cactus has died and decayed. Saguaros reach heights of 15 meters or more and weights of up to 8,200 kilograms (9 tons). Ages of 150–200 years have been recorded. These magnificent cacti bloom during the dry spring, with large whitish flowers displayed on the ends of the arms.

Saguaros occur only in Arizona, extreme southeastern California, and Sonora, Mexico;, at elevations up to 1,500 meters. Their distribution coincides with areas where freezing temperatures last less than 24 hours. Plants exposed to longer freezing periods may be killed and subsequently subject to rot caused by the bacterium *Erwinia carnegieana*; the young and very old plants are especially vulnerable to frost damage. Saguaros grow on coarse, well-drained soils, often on bajadas or rocky south-facing slopes. They do not generally occur on valley floors.

Giant saguaro cactus (*Carnegiea gigantea*) in the Arizona Sonoran Desert. (Photo: M. A. Mares)

The stem serves for water storage, expanding and contracting in wet and drought years, respectively. The water content of the plant ranges from 75 to 95 percent. The roots are shallow but may extend laterally for 30 meters.

Reproduction occurs primarily during the hot, dry late spring to early summer. Flowers open mainly at night and are pollinated by honeybees and other insects, white-winged doves, and long-nosed bats. Most mature plants can produce fruits every year, essentially regardless of moisture availability. A single plant may produce up to 200 fruits a year, each fruit bearing about 1,000–2,000 seeds. The lifetime seed production of a saguaro is about 40 million, and in a steady-state population, only one seed must reach adulthood over a period of perhaps two centuries, suggesting that successful germination and growth of the seeds is an especially rare event. Fruits and seeds are eaten by a variety of animals, which also act as seed dispersers. They include ants, white-winged doves, mourning doves, quail, thrashers, ground squirrels, pocket mice, kangaroo rats, long-nosed bats, coyotes, and peccaries.

Seeds germinate when the summer rains begin in July and August. Seedlings become established under the canopies of shrubs and small trees that serve as nurse plants, protecting the young saguaros from extreme temperatures (both hot and cold) and possibly from herbivore damage. Seedlings are susceptible to feeding damage by insects (moth larvae, grasshoppers, beetles), woodrats, other rodents, and rabbits. Cattle grazing may indirectly affect saguaro establishment by reducing the cover provided by nurse plants.

Branching begins when the plant is about 50 years old and four to five meters tall. An unusual growth form is the crowned, or cristate, saguaro, in which mutation, fungal infection, or mechanical injury causes the plant to grow an expanded crown rather than branches.

Gila woodpeckers and flickers create nest holes in the trunks. The saguaro responds to this damage by forming a hardened callus lining in the cavity. These cavities later become nest sites for elf owls, and are used by purple martins, woodrats, and lizards. After the saguaro dies and decays, the cavity lining is often left behind as a "boot."

Dried ribs are used in frames, lances, and fences. The fruits, which ripen in June and July, are eagerly collected by Tohono-O'odam and other Indians and eaten raw or cooked for syrup, preserves, and wine. The seeds can be ground into a paste for use in cooking.—Kristina A. Ernest

See also **BAT; BEES; C₃ PLANTS; C₄ PLANTS; CACTI; CACTUS, COLUMNAR; CAM PLANTS; CARDÓN; CHOLLA; DESERT PEOPLES; ECONOMIC VALUE OF DESERT PRODUCTS; FLIES; FLOWERS; FRUITS; GILA WOODPECKER; O'ODHAM; PHOTOSYNTHESIS; PLANT ADAPTATIONS; PLANTS; POLLINATION; PRICKLY PEAR; SONORAN DESERT; SUCCULENTS; THORN**

Further Reading

Keasey, M. S., III. 1981. *The Saguaro Book.* Dubuque, Iowa: Kendall/Hunt.

Niering, W. A., R. H. Whittaker, and C. H. Lowe. 1963. The saguaro: A population in relation to environment. *Science* 142:15–23.

Steenbergh, W. F. 1974. *The Saguaro Giant Cactus: A Bibliography.* San Francisco: U.S. Department of Interior, National Park Service, Western Region.

Steenbergh, W. F., and C. H. Lowe. 1976. *Ecology of the Saguaro: 1. The Role of Freezing Weather in a Warm-desert Plant Population.* Scientific Symposium Series, No. 1. Washington, D.C.: National Park Service.

———. 1977. *Ecology of the Saguaro: 2. Reproduction, Germination, Establishment, Growth, and Survival of the Young Plant.* Scientific Monograph Series, No. 8. Washington, D.C.: National Park Service.

———. 1977. *Ecology of the Saguaro: 3. Growth and Demography.* Scientific Monograph Series, No. 17. Washington, D.C.: National Park Service.

Barren Sahara Desert habitat near the Step Pyramid of Saqqara—the oldest Egyptian pyramid, built in 2650 B.C.—south of Cairo. (Photo: M. A. Mares)

SAHARA DESERT

World's largest desert (deriving its name from the plural of the Arab word *sahra*, meaning "wilderness"), extending across the African continent in a broad band of unbroken aridity from the Atlantic Ocean to the Red Sea, its maximum length exceeding 4,800 kilometers, and separating North Africa from tropical Africa. From north to south its width varies from 1,280 to 2,560 kilometers. Only the Nile River crosses this desert in its eastern portion, transferring water from the equatorial highlands of Africa to the Mediterranean Sea. The total area of the Sahara is approximately 7,387,000 square kilometers, nearly one quarter of the African continent. For the most part it is a true desert, with large parts falling into the category of hyperarid desert. In the central core years may pass without any rainfall, and the vegetation that is present there is sparse and stunted. Over most of its vast expanse, the desert's surface consists of shifting sand, pebbles, and broken rock exposed to clear skies and a scorching sun. (See map of African deserts, p. 12.)

The Sahara is characterized by frequent winds and high temperatures but experiences a great range of daily high and low of temperatures during any season. Large areas experience mean July temperatures of above 37°C. Clear skies favor unbroken sunshine, and the air in the desert is very dry. Dry, northerly currents of descending air (associated with the 30° latitudinal band) prevail much of the time, and by midday the sky tends to be hazy, with even light breezes having raised large amounts of dust. Temperatures greater than 43°C may occur for many consecutive days, but as the air is dry, the ground cools rapidly when the sun sets and the nights are cold. Daily ranges of more than 27°C are normal. In winter daytime temperatures may be around 16°C, but severe frosts can occur at night. Occasional violent dust storms, known by local names such as simoom, sirocco, and khamsin, occur periodically, being most frequent and severe in the Northern Hemisphere spring.

The geographic limits of the desert are rather arbitrary; however, the northern limit is usually drawn to coincide with the 100-millimeter isohyet and the southern limit with the 150-millimeter isohyet. The latter is much less abrupt than the former due to the scarcity of pronounced features of geographic relief, whereas the transition zone between Saharan and Sahelian elements occurs in a mosaic over a wide area. northern, central, and southern climatic zones can be identified on the basis of rainfall, which, throughout the desert, is irregular and usually occurs in the form of short, often violent, storms. In the north rain falls during the colder months, with rainfall maxima occurring in autumn and spring. Rainfall is unpredictable from year to year in both distribution and quantity. In the central region rain is episodic in nature and low in amount. Between 18° and 30° north latitude, mean annual rainfall is less than 20 millimeters, except in the high mountains, where rainfall may be higher. Large areas of the Libyan Desert are virtually rainless. In the south rainfall increases and falls mainly in summer.

The Sahara consists of several large basins, mostly isolated from the sea and lacking outward drainage. The substrate over most of the desert consists of Cretaceous and Tertiary deposits; crystalline bedrock only breaks through to form the summits of the higher mountains, which include the Tibesti Mountains (3,415 meters), the Ahaggar Mountains (2,918 meters), and the Jebel Uweinat (1,900 meters). The depressions are filled with Pleistocene deposits that form either sand deserts (ergs) or gravel deserts (regs). Between the depressions the stratified terraced landscape forms a stone desert (hamada) incised by dry valleys (wadis). Oases occur wherever water of low salt content discharges as springs. Saline soils play a minor role in the Sahara proper as the rainfall is so low that salts are neither removed by leaching nor accumulated in depressions. Oases are also relatively scarce in the Sahara. The original vegetation of oases consisted of Doum palms, *Hyphaene thebaica* (Aceraceae), *Citrullus colocynthis* (Cucurbitaceae), species of *Acacia* (Leguminosae), and *Maerua* and *Capparis* (Capparidaceae). This vegetation has been almost completely displaced by the date palm, *Phoenix dactylifera* (Aceraceae), and other cultivated plants. Stands of *Typha latifolia* (Typhaceae), *Phragmitis australis* (Poaceae), and *Scirpus holoschoenus* (Cyperaceae) may also be found in the desert.

Aside from oases, wadis are the only habitats in the Sahara where trees and large bushes are found. Communities consisting of *Tamarix* (Tamaricaceae), *Acacia* (Leguminosae), and *Hyphaene* (Aceraceae) occur in the wadi (arroyo) ecosystem, much as riparian forests occur along drainage systems in other deserts. In the central Sahara *Tamarix* communities occur in larger sandy wadis radiating from mountainous massifs wherever the water table is within 7 or 8 meters of the surface. Under favorable conditions *Tamarix* may form a closed riparian forest with large individuals up to 10 meters in height and boles (trunks) nearly 2 meters in diameter.

Acacia communities are very widespread and grow in rocky beds of wadis. They are characteristic of the tropical Sahara below 1,800 meters elevation and wherever the annual rainfall exceeds 30 millimeters. They are widely distributed from coastal Mauritania to the Tibesti Mountains and beyond. Of the larger woody plants, the most important are *Acacia tortilis*, *Acacia ehrenbergiana* (Leguminosae), *Maerua crassifolia*, *Capparis decidua* (Capparidaceae), and *Salvadora persica* (Salvadoraceae). Large wadis radiating from the southwestern slopes of the Tibesti support several tree species forming *Hyphaene* communities. Locally these communities form significant forests, including *Hyphaene thebaica* (Arecaceae), *Salvadora persica* (Salvadoraceae), and *Acacia nilotica* and *Acacia albida* (Leguminosae).

Sand covers more than one-third of the surface of the western Sahara and a somewhat smaller area farther east. More than half of the desert sands are without perennial vegetation, especially in hyperarid zones, although some annual plants may appear on some dunes. Two principal psammophilous (sand-loving) vegetation habitats can be recognized:

1. *Desert dunes (ergs)* are generally completely devoid of plants. However, some dunes may have up to half of their surface covered by vegetation (although the number of plant species that grow on these dunes is low). Apart from *Malcolmia aegyptiaca* (Cruciferae), annuals are rarely encountered due to the constant movement of the surface sand by wind action. Two species—*Stipagrostis pungens* (Poaceae), with sclerophyllous, spine-tipped leaves, and *Cornulaca monacantha* (Chenopodiaceae)—occur throughout the western Sahara. In the northern Sahara several other shrubs are characteristic of dunes areas, for example, three species of *Calligonum* (Polygonaceae), *Retama raetam*, and *Genista saharae* (Leguminosae). In the central and southern Sahara the shrub *Leptadenia pyrotechnica* (Asclepiadaceae) is common.

2. *Sandy regs* are frequent throughout the Sahara, especially in the hyperarid zone. Although regs are gravelly, sometimes sand is deposited among the pebbles and stones so that sandy regs are formed. The vegetation is homogeneous, with *Asthenatherum forskallii* (Poaceae), *Plantago ciliata* (Plantaginaceae), *Polycarpaea repens* (Caryophyllaceae), *Neurada procumbens* (Neuradaceae), and *Fagonia glutinosa* (Zygophyllaceae) being most common. In the driest parts of the western Sahara episodic rainfall of 10–20 millimeters that occurs in certain years is sufficient for the development of ephemeral vegetation on sandy regs.

The finer components of erosion that result from weathering processes are removed by the wind from the tops of plateaus, resulting in a predominantly stony pavement called hamadas appearing on the plateau. The plateau surfaces of hamadas are usually devoid of vegetation because of the paucity of water and a relatively high salt content. Plants only occur in rock crevices and water-retaining depressions. Among the widespread species typical of hamadas are *Forskahlea tenacissima* (Urticaceae), *Astericus graveolens* (Asteraceae), *Reseda villosa* (Resedaceae), *Fagonia latifolia* (Zygophyllaceae), *Enneapogon scaber*, *Enneapogon desvauxii* (Poaceae), and *Anastatica hierochuntica* (Cruciferae).

Gravel deserts, or regs (not to be confused with sandy regs), have compacted superficial gravel surfaces, often underlain by gypsum accumulations that may form a hardpan at a deeper level. In the northern Sahara *Haloxylon scoparium* (Chenopodiaceae) is a characteristic species of regs; regs of the central Sahara are mostly devoid of vegetation, although *Stipagrostis obtusa* (Poaceae) may appear after rain. In the eastern Sahara the vast pebble desert between Cairo and Suez virtually lacks vegetation except in small, sand-filled drainage channels where *Haloxylon salicornicum* (Chenopodiaceae) is dominant on very shallow sand and on deeper sands where communities of *Lasiurus hirsutus*, *Panicum turgidum* (Poaceae), and *Zilla spinosa* (Cruciferae) occur. Regs are preferred habitat for bipedal jerboas (family Dipodidae: *Jaculus* and *Allactaga*), which feed on bits of leaves, seeds, and other plant material that is lodged among the larger gravel, but the animals are poor burrowers and need the softer sand if they are to build burrows. Fat-tailed gerbils (family Muridae: *Pachyuromys*) also inhabit regs, where they feed on insect and detritus and burrow into the gravelly ground for their shelter. The frequent winds are an important factor in the lives of these rodents and of spiny mice (family Muridae: *Acomys*), as they move food matter over the gravel habitat, replenishing the food that has been consumed by the animals.

Above 1,800 meters elevation the vegetation on the high mountains of the Sahara is markedly different from that of lower elevations. The summits receive more rain than the lowlands, as much as 150 millimeters annually, often falling as a fine rain for several consecutive days both in summer and in winter. The flora is rich and diversified, and Mediterranean, Saharan (playing a subordinate role), Sahelian, and Afromontane elements are represented.

In the Sahara salt accumulation takes place when water evaporates from depressions without drainage. Salt pans, or chotts, are filled during winter rains and are often covered with a white crust after the moisture evaporates in the hot summer. Although large chotts occur toward the northern limits of the Sahara, they are more common outside the Sahara proper. Halophytic (salt-loving) and gypsophilous (gypsum-loving) plant communities inhabiting the chotts are more diversified and better developed in northern and northwestern parts of the western Sahara and along the Atlantic Coast than in the central or southern parts of the desert. In the northern Sahara three main types of halogypsophylous (gypsum/salt-loving) vegetation can be found. In chotts in southern Tunisia *Halocnemum strobilaceum* (Chenopodiaceae), an extreme halophyte, occurs as a low shrub, covering some 55–70 percent of the surface of the desert, and is always the dominant plant in the area. The larger chotts at the northern rim of the Sahara are fringed with halogypsophilous vegetation on drier soils, characterized by the low shrubs *Salsola sieberi* (Chenopodiaceae) and *Zygophyllum cornutum* (Zygophyllaceae). Vegetation of gypsaceous loamy sands occur locally in the beds of wadis and on ancient alluvial terraces, characterized by the low shrubs *Suaeda vermiculata* and *Salsola baryosma* (Chenopodiaceae). This vegetation occurs along the Atlantic Coast of the Sahara but is rare in the central Sahara.

Absolute desert areas occur where episodic rainfall is less than 20 millimeters annually, resulting in many consecutive years without rain. Such hyperarid desert is more extensive in the east than in the west. In places in the southern Libyan Desert not a single plant may be seen for distances of more than 200 kilometers.

There are some 1,620 plant species in the Sahara, of which 12 percent are endemic. Endemic genera are few and mostly monospecific (one species/genus). The latter include *Foleyola* (Cruciferae), *Monodiella* (Gentianaceae), and *Tibestina* and *Warionia* (Asteraceae). The Atlantic coastal Sahara and the Sahara's mountains are relatively rich in endemic species. In contrast, the southern Sahara has very few. The vegetation of the western Sahara is more diversified and probably better known than that of the eastern Sahara.

The three major floristic zones of the Sahara tend to coincide with the rainfall zones. In the northern Sahara elements with a Mediterranean affinity predominate, the latter being almost totally absent in the southern Sahara, where the flora shows tropical characteristics. The flora of the central zone is mixed.

The Sahara is fringed by two transitional zones, one in the north and another in the south. In the north the Maghreb consists essentially of the folded mountains at the northwestern portion of the continent, covering an area of approximately 330,000 square kilometers. The landscape is dominated by the Atlas Mountains, the products of Tertiary folding and uplifting of sediments deposited over long periods in the ocean. The Atlas Mountains extend for about 1,000 kilometers from northern Morocco to Tunisia, roughly parallel to the Mediterranean coast where the coastal lowlands are fairly narrow. They are best developed in Morocco, where Mount Toubkal reaches an altitude of 4,165 meters in the High (Great) Atlas, a range with many snowcapped peaks. In Tunisia mountain elevations do not exceed 1,500 meters. The Rif Atlas, oldest of the folded mountains, forms a coastal range extending from Tangier eastward into Algeria, where it is known as the Tell Atlas. The High Atlas extends eastward from the Atlantic Coast near Agadir and in Algeria becomes the Saharan Atlas, rarely exceeding 2,000 meters elevation. In Morocco the formidable Middle Atlas, which diverges from the High Atlas in a northeasterly direction, consists mainly of a plateau bordered by mountain chains on the south and east. The highest peak of the Anti-Atlas is nearly 3,900 meters above sea level. The different ranges of the Atlas Mountains are separated by plateaus and basins. The geology of the montane region is diverse, with prevalent rocks consisting of sediments, sometimes metamorphosed, of Triassic, Jurassic, and Cretaceous age.

Most rain (250–1,000 millimeters per year) falls in winter in the mountains of the northern Sahara, and the summer is dry. Frosts are frequent, and the high mountains maintain snowpack for long periods. Some 4,000 species of plants occur in this region. Of these, about 2,900 are Mediterranean endemics, though only about 800 are confined to North Africa. There are no endemic plant families in the mountainous region.

South of the Magreb the Mediterranean-Saharan transition zone is encountered from the southwestern corner of Morocco eastward to the Suez Canal. The largest area, with an elevation of 750–1,000 meters, is occupied by the High Plateau, an undulating landscape between the Tell Atlas and the Sahara Atlas, principally in Algeria. On the plateau are many semipermanent salt lakes, or chotts. The total area of this transition zone is about 366,000 square kilometers. Rain falls in winter and totals from 100 to 250 millimeters per year. On the High Plateau the mean annual temperature is 13°–17°C, and the season with severe frosts may last up to eight months. Otherwise frosts are not very severe in the transition zone, and east of Tunisia the coastal belt is frost-free.

Overall the flora of this zone is relatively poor, with no more than 2,500 species of plants, of which only a few are endemic. The monotypic genus *Argania* (Sapotaceae) is almost confined to the western end of the zone in Morocco, while others, such as *Euphorbia resinifera*, *Euphorbia beaumierana*, and *Euphorbia echinus* (Euphorbiaceae), show a similar distribution. These are taxa that are absent from the typical Mediterranean vegetation. The vegetation in the west is much more diversified. The prevalent vegetation types in western Morocco are scrub forest and bush land dominated by *Argania spinosa* (Sapotaceae) and *Euphorbia*-dominated succulent shrub land. From eastern Morocco to Tunisia the landscape is dominated by a mosaic of grassland consisting almost entirely of *Stipa tenacissima* or *Lygeum spartum* (Poaceae) alternating with patches of dwarf *Artemisia* (Asteraceae) shrub land. About 1,095 species of plants are known from the coastal strip of Egypt, but few are typical Mediterranean species. The coastal strip of Libya is slightly richer, with some 1,440 species. Tussock grassland of economic importance covers large parts of the zone. On the High Plateau of Algeria and Morocco this grassland dominates the landscape, which it shares with two species of *Artemisia* (Asteraceae). In western Morocco the landscape is dotted by wheat fields and pastures for cattle and sheep. The coastal plain of Tunisia is a rich agricultural area noted for its olive groves. Indigenous forests have been totally eradicated. Farther east, toward Egypt, the region has been intensively cultivated since Roman times and grazed for an even longer period, resulting in continual degradation of grazing land while unpalatable species remain.

The Sahel Transitional Zone, situated on the southern fringes of the Sahara Desert, receives low rainfall that is insufficient for permanent agriculture based on rain-fed crops. The unreliable rainfall (mostly 150–500 millimeters annually) usually falls in three to four summer months, and the dry season is long and severe. Mean temperature is 26°–30°C. Livestock production in the form of pastoralism is the main source of livelihood, involving common ownership of grazing lands based on nomadism.

The Sahel is a relatively narrow band, some 400 kilometers wide, extending across North Africa south of the Sahara proper from the Atlantic Coast to the Red Sea. The massifs of Adrar des Iforas (727 meters), Air (1,900 meters), and Ennedi (1,450 meters) lie along the northern fringe of the Sahel. The former two are composed of Precambrian crystalline rocks; the latter is capped by horizontal Devonian sandstone. The Sahel is a flat or undulating landscape 2,482,000 square kilometers in area, usually lying below 600 meters elevation. Large areas are covered with Pleistocene clays. In the Sudan there are two late Tertiary volcanic mountains: Jebel Gurgeil (2,400 meters) and Jebel Marra (3,057 meters).

The flora of the Sahel consists of some 1,200 species of plants, of which fewer than 40 are endemic. These figures exclude species confined to the high Sahelian mountains. There are no endemic families, and endemic species include *Ammania gracilis* (Lythraceae), *Chrozophora brocchiana* (Euphorbiaceae), *Indigofera senegalensis* (Leguminosae), *Nymphoides ezannoi* (Menyanthaceae), and *Tephrosia gracilipes* (Leguminosae). The extended sand sheets of the Sahel support wooded grassland in the south and semidesert grassland in the north. Bush land is limited to rocky outcrops.

The Sahel transition to the Sahara is gradual. The northern Sahel grassland is a prevalent vegetation on deep sandy soils where rainfall is less than 250 millimeters per year. The whole region has been subjected to intense human activity for thousands of years, and woody plants are therefore scarce. The chief woody elements include species of *Acacia* (Leguminosae), *Balanites* (Balanitaceae), and *Boscia* (Capparidaceae). The most characteristically Sahelian dominant grasses (Poaceae) that occur in the Sahel are all annual species, such as *Cenchrus biflorus*, *Aristida stipoides*, and *Tragus racemosus*. In the northern Sahel certain grass species, such as *Panicum turgidum* and *Stipagrostis pungens*, that are absent from the southern Sahel are locally dominant and increase in abundance as one moves northward.

In total, human-related activity in the Saharan transitional zones, such as grazing, woodcutting, and agriculture, have had a profound impact. Many areas that formerly were a bread basket are now barren lands, unfit even for grazing.

The Sahara is relatively depauperate in animal species, with the number of species declining toward the central core of the desert. Many formerly widespread vertebrate species either have been extirpated (eliminated from the area) or are rare. Among mammals, lions, cheetahs, scimitar-horned oryx, aoudad, and various gazelles are included in this group, while others, such as hippos, elephants, giraffes, hartebeest, and even an extinct giant buffalo, are known to have occurred in the Sahara based on numerous and widespread prehistoric cave paintings. Many species of desert-adapted rodents, such as bipedal jerboas, gerbils, jirds, and spiny mice, occur across the Sahara. Rocky outcrops, in addition to providing refuges for various rats and mice, also harbor isolated populations of gundis (family Ctenodactylidae), a group of rodents represented in the Sahara by three endemic genera, and hyraxes (family Procaviidae), rodentlike relatives of elephants that are represented in the Sahara by a single widespread genus. Among carnivores, golden jackals and striped hyenas may occur in the desert; and two foxes, the sand fox and the fennec, are both adapted to the extensive sand seas of the Sahara.

Ostriches and greater bustards are birds that have been eliminated from the desert. Although many birds pass through the Sahara on their annual migration from Europe to sub-Saharan Africa, the resident bird population is also depauperate, with most species being found only in peripheral areas. Various birds of prey and larks occur in the central regions.

Among reptiles, an unusual species found in the Sahara is the large herbivorous lizard, *Uromastix*, which has a heavy, spiked tail. There are various other snakes and lizards that are found throughout the desert.

Common invertebrates include beetles, especially members of the family Tenebrionidae, and various arachnids. Scorpions are represented by two of the six known families. Only a single species of the family Scorpionidae, *Scorpio maurus*, noted for its bulbous claws, occurs commonly across the northern Sahara. Most scorpions of the Sahara belong to the family Buthidae, with over 13 genera and 29 species occurring throughout. These scorpions possess venoms that cause intense pain and may be dangerous to humans. Scorpions are able to survive easily in the intense heat and dryness of the desert by a combination of traits—burrowing, nocturnal activity, and a tolerance for high temperatures. Even more typical of the Sahara than scorpions are the sun spiders, or camel spiders, of the order Solifugae. These secretive animals, with their lateral chelicerae used in masticating insects, scorpions, and other solifugids, are most common in bare and broken soils. Avoiding the high temperatures by burrowing deeply and hunting for prey at night with a rapid running movement but random search pattern, adults exhibit an aggressiveness unparalleled in other invertebrates.—Duane A. Schlitter

See also **ACACIA; AFRICAN LION; ANIMAL ADAPTATIONS; AN INTRODUCTION TO DESERTS; ANTELOPE; ARABIAN GULF, DESERTS OF; ARROYO; ARTEMISIA; ARTHROPODS; BARBARY LION; BARBARY SHEEP; BEETLES; BIPEDALITY; BIRDS; CATS; CHEETAH; DESERTIFICATION; DESERT PEOPLES; DESERTS; DUNES; DURICRUSTS; ELEPHANT; FENNEC; FOX; GERBIL; GIRAFFE; GUNDI; GYPSUM; HALOPHYTES; HERBIVORY; HYENA; HYRAX; INSECTS; JACKAL; JERBOA; LIBYA, DESERTS OF; LIZARDS; MAMMALS; MIDDLE EAST, DESERTS OF; OSTRICH; PALMS; PLAYA; POISONOUS ANIMALS; RODENTS; SALT CEDAR; SALT CRUST; SALT PAN; SAND RAT; SAUDI ARABIA, DESERTS OF; SCORPIONS; SNAKES; SPIDERS; STONE PAVEMENT; SUN SPIDER; UNGULATES; VENOM; WATER HOLE; WIND TRANSPORT**

Further Reading

Alden, P. C., R. D. Estes, D. Schlitter, and B. McBride. 1995. *National Audubon Society Field Guide to African Wildlife.* New York: Knopf.

Boulos, L. 1975. The Mediterranean element in the flora of Egypt and Libya. *In La Flore du Bassin Mediterraneen,* 119–124. Colloquium in Compte Rendu de Researche Scientifique, No. 235.

Cloudsley-Thompson, J. L., ed. 1984. *Key Environments: Sahara Desert.* New York: Pergamon Press, in collaboration with the International Union for the Conservation of Nature and Natural Resources.

Grenot, C. J. 1974. Physical and Vegetational aspects of the Sahara Desert. *In* G. W. Brown Jr., ed., *Desert Biology: Special Topics on the Physical and Biological Aspects of Arid Regions,* 2:103–164. New York: Academic Press.

Guerzoni, S., and R. Chester. 1996. *The Impact of Desert Dust across the Mediterranean.* Boston: Kluwer.

Hollom, P. A. D., R. F. Porter, S. Christensen and I. Willis. 1988. *Birds of the Middle East and North Africa.* Calton, England: T. and A. D. Poyser.

Kassas, M., and W. A. Girgis. 1964. Habitat and plant communities in the Egyptian desert. 5. The limestone plateau. *Journal of Ecology* 52:107–119.

Kassas, M. and M. Imam. 1954. Habitat and plant communities in the Egyptian desert. 3. The wadi bed ecosystem. *Journal of Ecology* 42:424–441.

———. 1959. Habitat and plant communities in the Egyptian desert. 4. The gravel desert. *Journal of Ecology* 47:289–310.

Mortimore, M. 1998. *Roots in the African Dust: Sustaining the Sub-Saharan Drylands.* New York: Cambridge University Press.

Quezel, P. 1965. *La vegetation du Sahara, du Tchad a la Mauritanie.* Stuttgart: Gustav Fischer.

———. 1978. Analysis of the flora of Mediterranean and Saharan Africa. *Annals of the Missouri Botanical Garden* 65:479–534.

Stuart, C., and T. Stuart. 1995. *Africa: A Natural History.* Halfway House, South Africa: Southern Book Publishers.

Swearingen, W. D., and A. Bencherifa. 1996. *The North African Environment at Risk.* Boulder, Colo.: Westview Press.

Walter, H. 1971. *Ecology of Tropical and Subtropical Vegetation.* Translated by D. Mueller-Dombois. New York: Van Nostrand Reinhold.

White, F. 1983. *The Vegetation of Africa: A Descriptive Memoir to Accompany the UNESCO/AETFAT/UNSO Vegetation Map of Africa.* Paris: UNESCO.

SAHEL. See SAHARA DESERT

SAINT CATHERINE'S MONASTERY

Monastery situated at Mount Sinai supposedly on the spot of the burning bush, where Moses received the Ten Commandments. The monastery was built about the time of the reign of the Byzantine emperor Justinian (Eastern Roman Emperor, A.D. 527–565) and was named after Catherine, apparently a Christian martyr of Alexandria, who possibly lived in the 4th century A.D. It is one of the oldest, if not the oldest, monastery in Christendom. So little is known about Catherine that her name was removed from the liturgical calendar in 1969. According to one tradition, the emperor Justinian built a tomb for Catherine on Mount Sinai.

Justinian inherited a weakened Byzantine state and, aided by his wife, Theodora, set about to strengthen it in all spheres. Militarily, he secured his eastern border with Persia, drove the Vandals out of North Africa, and reconquered old imperial territories from the Visigoths in southern Spain and the Ostrogoths in southern Italy. He also organized Roman law into the Code of Justinian and instituted other legal reforms. Another area of major accomplishment for Justinian was that of church construction throughout the empire. Although not as well known as the churches he built at Ravenna or the church of Hagia in Constantinople, Saint Catherine's Monastery remains as one of the oldest sites of Christian worship, and has been occupied for

1,400 years, during which time it was never conquered or looted. Today it is a functioning monastery and maintains a remarkable collection of Byzantine icons dating from before the 15th century. The monastery also contains a library of rare manuscripts, some dating to the 4th century.—E. A. Mares

See also **ISRAEL, DESERTS OF; JEDDAH; PALESTINE, DESERTS OF; MIDDLE EAST, DESERTS OF; RELIGION IN DESERTS**

Further Reading

Anson, P. 1932. *The Quest for Solitude*. London: J. M. Dent.

Clark, K. W. 1952. *Checklist of Manuscripts in St. Catherine's Monastery, Mount Sinai*. Microfilmed for the Library of Congress. Washington, D.C.: Library of Congress, Library of Congress Photo Duplication Service.

Forsyth, G. H., and K. Weitzman. 1973. *The Monastery of Saint Catherine at Mount Sinai: The Church and Fortress of Justinian*. Ann Arbor: University of Michigan Press.

SALINA. *See* PLAYA

SALINITY

Concentration of soluble salts in soil and water. Excess salinity in soil solutions has a harmful effect on plant growth. Salinity usually is a significant problem only in deserts and other arid regions, but low-lying coastal areas in humid regions may also be saline. The dominant soluble salts in deserts are the chlorides and sulfates of sodium, calcium, and magnesium. Well waters frequently are salty in deserts and other arid regions, such as the Great Artesian Basin of eastern Australia and lowlands in the southwestern United States. High salinity in the closed basins that are called playas in the United States, in conjunction with standing water that exists after rains, usually leaves the center of the basin barren of vegetation. Frequently the barren playas are covered with a white salt crust representing the accumulation over decades or centuries of small amounts of salt brought in by runoff water from the surrounding slopes. The ultimate source of soluble salt is the dissolution of minerals in rocks, their transport in solution to lower elevations, and evaporation of the water, leaving salts behind.

Salt accumulation in soil and water in deserts is a natural process because of the low rainfall and the high rates of evaporation. Human-induced salinity is the result of improper soil and water management in irrigated land. Lack of adequate drainage to prevent rising groundwater tables is a common cause of increases in salinity. In the special case of what is called dryland salinity, the cause is removal of deep-rooted trees and other plants from sloping lands in semiarid regions. Dryland salinity is a problem in croplands and grazing lands in Australia, Canada, Thailand, and the United States.

Salinity control in irrigated croplands is accomplished by applying sufficient water to wash salts out of the soil. Good drainage is essential.—Harold E. Dregne

See also **ARTESIAN BASIN; CHENOPODIACEAE; COLLUVIAL DEPOSITS (COLLUVIUM); DURICRUSTS; HALOPHYTES; IRRIGATION DRAINAGE; PLAYA; SALINIZATION; SALT; SALTBUSH; SALT CRUST; SALT DESERT; SALT PAN; SALT POLYGON; WEATHERING, DESERT**

Further Reading

Ghassemi, F., A. J. Jakeman, and H. A. Nix. 1995. *Salinization of Land and Water Resources*. Wallingford, U.K.: CAB International.

SALINIZATION

Process of increase of dissolved salts in soil and water. Primary salinization is caused by natural physical and chemical processes that concentrate soluble salts in coastal zones, marine sediments, and closed depressions. Secondary salinization is the result of human action, most commonly seen in irrigated soils having a groundwater table within two meters of the soil surface. Chlorides and sulfates of sodium, calcium, and magnesium are the dominant soluble salts. Salinization is a continuing threat to the permanence of irrigated agriculture because soluble salts impede water absorption by plants, which reduces crop yields. Sodium salts can do additional damage by reducing soil permeability to water. Salinized soils are classified as saline, saline-sodic, or sodic. Saline soils contain high levels of soluble salts, saline-sodic soils have high levels of sodium salts, and sodic soils are low in soluble salts but high in what is called adsorbed or exchangeable sodium.

About 25 percent of irrigated soils in the western United States are affected by salinization to the point where crop yields are reduced. Globally 25–30 percent of irrigated soils in arid regions are salinized. Human-induced soil salinization usually is the result of applying excessive amounts of water to irrigated lands and raising water tables. Evaporation of groundwater concentrates the salts that are always present in soils and can ultimately produce a saline soil. Irrigating nonsaline soils with salty irrigation water also can produce a saline soil. Saline-sodic soils are less common in irrigated land than are saline soils, and human-induced sodic soils are even less common.—Harold E. Dregne

See also **ARTESIAN BASIN; CHENOPODIACEAE; COLLUVIAL DEPOSITS (COLLUVIUM); DURICRUSTS; GROUNDWATER; HALOPHYTES; IRRIGATION DRAINAGE; MIDDLE EAST, DESERTS OF; PLAYA; SALINITY; SALT; SALTBUSH; SALT CRUST; SALT DESERT; SALT PAN; SALT POLYGON; WEATHERING, DESERT**

Further Reading

Ghassemi, F., A. J. Jakeman, and H. A. Nix. 1995. *Salinization of Land and Water Resources*. Wallingford, U.K.: CAB International.

SALT

Chemical combinations of cations (an atom or group of atoms having a positive electrical charge) and anions (an atom or group of atoms having a negative electrical charge). Salts can be inorganic (combinations of mineral cations and anions; e.g., table salt is sodium chloride) or organic (combinations of mineral cations and organic anions; e.g., aspirin is sodium salicylate). In soils and surface and ground waters, inorganic salts dominate; organic salts are usually present in very small amounts and have no significant effect on plant growth. The original source of inorganic salts in nature are primary minerals such as micas and feldspars. As chemical weathering occurs in the presence of water, inorganic salts form from the weathering products of the minerals. Different salts may have different degrees of solubility in water. Soluble salts adversely affect plant growth; salts of very low solubility do not. Salt damage to plants is due to the reduced intake of water that occurs, as well as a few direct effects of certain ions such as sodium and chloride.

Under natural conditions the principal soluble salts in soil and water are the chlorides and sulfates of sodium, calcium, and magnesium. Two very common—but of low solubility—salts in desert soils are calcium carbonate (lime) and hydrated calcium sulfate (gypsum). Gypsum is sufficiently soluble to adversely affect growth of a few very salt-sensitive plants. However, gypsum generally has favorable effects on soil properties and plant growth. Lime is so insoluble that it presents no salinity problem.

The world's oceans are the source of thick and thin salt beds in the outer mantle of the earth. Those marine deposits that emerge from the sea during continent formation are mined for commercial salts such as borax, potash, table salt, and nitrate and fertilizer.—Harold E. Dregne

See also **ARABIAN GULF, DESERTS OF; CARBONATES; CHENOPODIACEAE; COLLUVIAL DEPOSITS (COLLUVIUM); CHIHUAHUAN DESERT; DEAD SEA; DUNES; DURICRUSTS; GROUNDWATER; GYPSUM; HALOPHYTES; IRRIGATION DRAINAGE; KAVIR; MIDDLE EAST, DESERTS OF; PALEOCLIMATE; PLAYA; SABKHA; SALINITY; SALTBUSH; SALT CRUST; SALT DESERT; SALT PAN; SALT POLYGON; SOILS, DESERT, CALCAREOUS; SYRIA, DESERTS OF; WEATHERING, DESERT**

Further Reading

Petrucci, R. H., and W. S. Harwood. 1993. *General Chemistry*. 6th ed. New York: Macmillan.

SALT BALANCE

Condition in animals and plants in which the vital salts (especially sodium and potassium salts) are maintained at some constant, tolerable level such that salt gains are offset by losses. Many desert soils are either salty or alkaline, and often support salt-tolerant (halophytic) plants that absorb salty water through their root systems to provide the necessary water and nutrients for growth. Best known among these plants are species of saltbush (genus *Atriplex*) that maintain a fairly low and constant internal salt concentration that may be less than that of the water absorbed by the roots. In *Atriplex* salt balance is maintained by excreting excess salt as salt crystals that are stored in specialized cells in the outermost leaf layers; these cells are otherwise metabolically inactive, serving primarily for salt storage to aid in regulating internal fluid salt concentration.

In animals, including desert forms, salt balance is achieved concomitantly with water balance, through combinations of behavioral and physiological mechanisms. In all instances the ultimate goal is to maintain a constant fluid volume, consisting of a balanced ratio of solutes (salts) to solvent (water). Nearly all salt intake in desert animals occurs in the process of eating, and its amount depends on the quality of the food, including the degree of succulence. Behaviorally, animals may simply avoid foods whose salt concentrations would result in a salt/fluid imbalance. Physiologically, all animals possess excretory organs that eliminate excess salts while at the same time retaining necessary body water, thereby achieving both salt and fluid balance. In terrestrial arthropods the excretory system is made up of numerous Malpighian tubules that extract excess salts from the blood (hemolymph) and excrete them to the outside, maintaining hemolymph salt concentrations at a low, constant level. Depending on the succulence or dryness of the food, the excreted, excess salts may form a urine of low concentration, or they may be excreted as highly concentrated urine or as urate salts and uric acid, the latter two being nearly dry precipitates.

In vertebrate animals the primary excretory organ is the kidney, which excretes excess dissolved substances, including salts, as urine. In reptiles the kidney is incapable of forming urine that is more concentrated than the blood, and some excess salt is voided as precipitated urate salts. At least in most desert lizards, salt balance is aided by the presence of nasal salt-secreting glands that concentrate excess salts (either sodium or potassium salts) from the blood and excrete them to the outside through the nostrils, thereby augmenting the kidneys in achieving salt balance. Birds are able to produce urine that is somewhat more concentrated than the blood, but, in addition, they can excrete urate salts and uric acid as insoluble precipitates, thereby voiding excess salts and nitrogenous waste without expending precious water. In this manner desert birds are able to maintain salt balance.

Mammalian kidneys are incapable of producing precipitated urates and uric acid. Instead they can produce extremely concentrated urine made up of combinations of dissolved salts and urea, voiding excesses of each as needed. Thus desert mammals rely primarily on the physiological capacities of the kidney and prudent dietary choices to achieve salt balance.

In humans salt balance is so carefully controlled that fluid volume may be sacrificed in achieving it. This can be particularly critical in the desert, where large amounts of water and salt are voided as perspiration, reducing internal fluid volume but, at the same time, maintaining a constant salt concentration. So precise is this regulation that unless salt is ingested along with drinking water, the water will be eliminated at the expense of maintaining salt balance, leading to progressive dehydration. For this reason it is wise for humans in the desert to take salt pills periodically as well as drink large amounts of water to maintain both salt balance and fluid volume.—Richard E. MacMillen

See also **DEHYDRATION; HALOPHYTES; HEAT BALANCE; HEAT EXCHANGE; HEAT STRESS; HEATSTROKE; HUMAN PHYSIOLOGY IN DESERTS; KIDNEY FUNCTION, DESERT RODENTS; KIDNEYS; PERSPIRATION; PHYSIOLOGY; RENAL PAPILLA; SURVIVAL IN DESERTS; SALT; SALTBUSH; SALT DESERT; SALT PAN; SUNSTROKE; TRANSPIRATION; URIC ACID; URINE; WATER BALANCE**

Further Reading

Gordon, M. S., G. A. Bartholomew, A. D. Grinnell, C. B. Jorgensen, and F. N. White. 1982. *Animal Physiology: Principles and Adaptations*. New York: Macmillan.

Schmidt-Nielsen, K. 1990. *Animal Physiology: Adaptation and Environment*. 4th ed. New York: Cambridge University Press.

SALTBUSH

Common name applied to members of the genus *Atriplex*, an assortment of annual or perennial herbs or shrubs common to the deserts of western North America in the family Chenopodiaceae (Goosefoot family). *Atriplex* is found on all continents and many oceanic islands; however, only seven species are truly cosmopolitan in distribution. The genus has maximum diversity and endemism (taxa that are found nowhere else) in the arid regions of North America, South Africa, and Australia. Many species of *Atriplex* are dominants in the deserts of the southwestern United States, the drylands of Argentina (Monte Desert, Patagonia, Pampas), the Karoo region of South Africa, southern Australia, and the steppes of central Asia. There is a remarkable similarity in the growth forms of this important desert plant throughout its range of distribution.

Although many species of this genus are called saltbush, the name usually refers to four-wing saltbush (*Atriplex canescens*) or shadscale (*Atriplex confertifolia*). Saltbush is also called chamiso (chamiza). Saltbush is one of the most abundant and widely distributed shrubs over much of the Great Basin Desert, but it also occurs south into California, north into Canada, and at higher elevations in the Great Basin in association with spruce-

Saltbush scrubland (*Atriplex*) in the Patagonian Desert of southern Argentina. (Photo: M. A. Mares)

fir forests. Saltbush is well adapted to the saline and/or alkaline soils and semiarid conditions found in the Great Basin Desert and other desert regions, and the salt that is concentrated in its leaves helps it reduce herbivory by mammals, although a few species (e.g., rodents in North America [*Dipodomys microps*] and South America [*Tympanoctomys barrerae*], and in North Africa [*Psammomys obesus*]) have managed to develop the ability to strip away its protective salt-filled tissues before consuming the green leaves.

Many members of this genus exhibit the characteristic "Krantz" leaf anatomy and the correlated C_4 photosynthetic pathway, an evolved anatomical and physiological adaptation to hot and sunny desert environments. In addition, many species of saltbush are well adapted to the cold winters of the Great Basin through the accumulation of salts in their tissues; higher osmotic (intracellular) concentrations of salts confers additional resistance to cold temperatures and also allow these hardy shrubs to extract moisture from saline and alkaline soils.

One species of *Atriplex*, shadscale, occurs in nearly pure stands throughout much of northern Arizona and the Great Basin and is an essential forage plant for livestock in the region. It is less common in the southern part of Arizona. The widely distributed four-wing saltbush is one of the most preferred forage shrubs in the desert Southwest. The leaves, stems, flowers, and seeds are grazed by all livestock. Shadscale is also palatable to livestock but is particularly valuable as fall, winter, and spring

browse for sheep. This species has an extensive root system and is very drought resistant.—Gary K. Hulett and Amanda Renner Charles

See also **ARABIAN GULF, DESERTS OF; ARTEMISIA; CHENOPODIACEAE; COLLUVIAL DEPOSITS (COLLUVIUM); CHIHUAHUAN DESERT; DEAD SEA; DUNES; DURICRUSTS; GROUNDWATER GREAT BASIN DESERT; GYPSUM; HALOPHYTES; IRRIGATION DRAINAGE; KAVIR; MIDDLE EAST, DESERTS OF; PALEOCLIMATE; PAMPAS; PLAYA; RODENTS; SABKHA; SALINITY; SALTBUSH; SALT CRUST; SALT DESERT; SALT PAN; SALT POLYGON; SAND RAT; SOILS, DESERT, CALCAREOUS; SYRIA, DESERTS OF; WEATHERING, DESERT**

Further Reading

Billings, W. D. 1949. The shadscale vegetation zone of Nevada and eastern California in relation to climate and soils. *American Midland Naturalist* 42:87–109.

Branson, F. A., R. F. Miller, and I. S. McQueen. 1967. Geographic distribution and factors affecting the distribution of salt desert shrubs in the United States. *Journal of Range Management* 29:287–296.

Freeman, D. C., E. D. McArthur, S. C. Sanderson, and A. R. Tiedemann. 1993. *Influence of Topography on Cumulative Pollen Flow of Fourwing Saltbush.* U.S. Department of Agriculture, Intermountain Research Station, Research Note INT-413.

———. 1993. The influence of topography on male and female fitness components of *Atriplex canescens.* *Oecologia* 93:538–547.

Mares, M. A., R. A. Ojeda, C. E. Borghi, S. M. Giannoni, G. B. Diaz, and J. K. Braun. 1997. How desert rodents overcome halophytic plant defenses. *BioScience* 47:699–704.

Osmond, C. B., O. Bjorkman, and D. J. Anderson. 1980. *Physiological Processes in Plant Ecology: Toward a Synthesis with Atriplex.* New York: Springer.

SALT CEDAR

Large shrub or tree (genus *Tamarix*) with long, slender, drooping branches covered by small, scale-like leaves and commonly called tamarisk. The small, pink flowers are clustered on short stalks at the tips of small branches. When not flowering, these trees resemble cypress.

Salt cedars are native to the Eastern Hemisphere, from western and southern Europe to northern Africa, India, China, and Japan. They occur in the Sahara, Negev, and other deserts, as well as nondesert areas. Several species were introduced to North America as ornamentals, shade trees, and windbreaks, but some have become naturalized. They now have a wide distribution along streams and rivers and at the edges of marshes in the deserts of the southwestern United States, where they sometimes form dense thickets.

Salt cedars are phreatophytes, water-spending (rather than water-conserving) plants with deep taproots that absorb water from the permanent water table. They can also obtain water by absorbing it from humid air, and from fog trapped by branches which drips onto the ground around the tree. Salt cedars commonly grow on sandy or saline soils. They are both halophytes (salt tolerant) and salt accumulators, excreting salt from glands on the leaf surface.

Many insects feed on salt cedars. The tamarisk manna scale insect (*Trabutina mannipara*) excretes honeydew, which forms a sugary material called manna (possibly that of biblical fame) when it dries on the leaves.

In North America salt cedars have displaced some native species (e.g., willow) and are difficult to control. Moreover, in some areas (e.g., southern New Mexico) they are responsible for a general lowering of the water table, which has led to efforts to control the salt cedar populations. They have important uses, however, in erosion control and for binding dunes;. Although not good browse, salt cedars do provide cover for cattle. The wood has potential use in cabinetry and for fence posts. The flowers are a source of honey, and medicines and tannin can be extracted from the insect galls.—Kristina A. Ernest

See also **ARABIAN GULF, DESERTS OF; CHENOPODIACEAE; COLLUVIAL DEPOSITS (COLLUVIUM); CHIHUAHUAN DESERT; FOREST; GROUNDWATER; HALOPHYTES; IRRIGATION DRAINAGE; KAVIR; MIDDLE EAST, DESERTS OF; PLANT ADAPTATIONS; PLANTS; PLAYA; PHREATOPHYTES; RIPARIAN COMMUNITIES; ROOTS; SABKHA; SALINITY; SALT PAN**

Further Reading

Baum, B. R. 1978. *The Genus* Tamarix. Jerusalem: Israel Academy of Sciences and Humanities.

Christensen, E. M. 1962. The rate of naturalization of *Tamarix* in Utah. *American Midland Naturalist* 68:51–57.

Kunzmann, M. R., R. R. Johnson, and P. S. Bennett. eds. 1989. *Tamarisk Control in Southwestern United States*. Tucson: National Park Service, Cooperative National Park Resources Studies Unit, Special Report No. 9.

Salt crust and formations of precipitated salts in the Dead Sea, Israel. (Photo: M. A. Mares)

SALT CRUST

Mixture of inorganic salts of varying composition and solubilities forming a surface crust on desert soils. Crusts can be several centimeters thick or quite thin. They usually are a grayish white color and may contain organic or inorganic soil particles. Most commonly natural soil crusts are found in closed basins having no permanent outflow. Dissolved salts are carried into the basin in runoff water from the surrounding uplands or by lateral movement of groundwater. Subsequent evaporation of water, either surface water or groundwater, concentrates the salts and builds up a crust. The White Sands of New Mexico are the result of continuous crust formation in a basin upwind from the present "sand" dunes. Strong winds break the crust and carry the precipitated salt downwind, where it forms sparkling white dunes 10 or more meters high. The "sand" actually is almost pure gypsum, a hydrated calcium sulfate. The White Sands are so extensive and white that astronauts use them as an unmistakable landmark from space.

In closed basins the salt crust is often composed of a clearly defined sequence of particular salts in concentric rings around the basin. The outermost ring will consist of the least soluble salts, such as calcium carbonate, and the innermost ring will contain the most soluble salts, such as chlorides and nitrates. The rings form by differential precipitation of dissolved salts as the water recedes following rains.

Salt crusts also form in irrigated land that is heavily salinized. The crusts, however, tend to be thin and occur in generally circular spots a few or several meters across. Crusts in furrow-irrigated fields frequently occur as white strips on top of the beds between the furrows. Furrow irrigation carries dissolved salts toward the center of the beds, where they are precipitated as the water evaporates.—Harold E. Dregne

See also **ARABIAN GULF, DESERTS OF; CARBONATES; CHENOPODIACEAE; CHIHUAHUAN DESERT; COLLUVIAL DEPOSITS (COLLUVIUM); DEAD SEA; DUNES; DURICRUSTS; GREAT BASIN DESERT; GROUNDWATER; HALOPHYTES; IRRIGATION DRAINAGE; KAVIR; MIDDLE EAST, DESERTS OF; PALEOCLIMATE; PLAYA; SABKHA; SALINITY; SALTBUSH; SALT DESERT; SALT PAN; SALT POLYGON; SOILS, DESERT, CALCAREOUS; SOILS, DESERT, CALICHE; WEATHERING, DESERT; WHITE SANDS NATIONAL MONUMENT**

Further Reading

Ward, S. M. 1970. *Geology and Hydrology of Selected Playas in Western United States.* Amherst: University of Massachusetts, Geology Department.

SALT DESERT

Desert in which the high levels of soil salinity result in desertlike conditions and vegetation in areas outside the desert latitudes. Plant roots absorb water from the soil through the root hairs, and that absorption is influenced by differences in water potentials (water flows from high potentials to lower water potentials) between the soil and the root hairs. Dissolved salts lower water potentials and create a scenario in which water might be lost from the roots into the soil, rather than the reverse. This has disastrous effects on the root hairs. The protoplast (living part of a cell) becomes condensed and pulls away from the cell wall (plasmolysis). If the cells are plasmolyzed for sufficient time, they cannot recover. High levels of salinity in the soil affect water potentials of the soil and have the effect of a drier climate. Thus desertlike conditions can occur at levels of rainfall that are otherwise sufficient to support a grassland or forest.

Salts generally originated as sediments of ancient seas that evaporated when they lost contact with the sea. Evaporation removed the water, but the salts remained. Evaporites tend to be either sodium chloride (NaCl) or gypsum (CaSO$_4$).

Deposits are often eroded into level plains called salt flats or alkali flats.

The vegetation of most salt deserts is dominated by members of the plant family Chenopodiaceae, and the vegetation of an area is often dominated by a single shrub species, usually of the genus *Atriplex* (saltbush). Saltbush is capable of absorbing salt and moving it through the plant to hairs on the leaf epidermis that accumulate salt until they burst. In the process they leave salt deposits on the leaf surface. Therefore, *Atriplex* and other halophytes (plants adapted to grow in ecosystems with high levels of ambient salt) often taste salty themselves.

Many true deserts also have salty soils, because of the high rates of evaporation, and even the warmest, saltiest desert has some plants that are indigenous (native) to the area and adapted to high salt concentrations. Wadi Araba south of the Dead Sea and Death Valley in California both have diverse, if sparse, floras. Acacia forests appear in the Arava, where rainfall is less than 50 millimeters per year. One group of plants, the genera *Oxystylis* and *Wislizenia* of the family Capparidaceae, actually flower in the blistering temperatures and low moisture levels of the height of summer in Death Valley.—James R. Estes

See also **ARABIAN GULF, DESERTS OF; CARBONATES; CHENOPODIACEAE; COLLUVIAL DEPOSITS (COLLUVIUM); CHIHUAHUAN DESERT; DEAD SEA; DEATH VALLEY; DUNES; DURICRUSTS; GROUNDWATER; GYPSUM; HALOPHYTES; IRRIGATION DRAINAGE; ISRAEL, DESERTS OF; KAVIR; LEGUMES; MIDDLE EAST, DESERTS OF; PALEOCLIMATE; PLAYA; ROOTS; SABKHA; SALINITY; SALTBUSH; SALT CRUST; SALT PAN; SALT POLYGON; SOILS, DESERT, CALCAREOUS; SOILS, DESERT, CALICHE; SYRIA, DESERTS OF; WEATHERING, DESERT**

Further Reading

Vanderpool, S. S., W. J. Elisens, and J. R. Estes. 1991. Pattern, tempo, and mode of evolutionary and biogeographic divergence in *Oxystylis* and *Wislizenia* (Capparaceae). *American Journal of Botany* 78:925–937.

West, N. E. 1983. Intermountain salt-desert shrubland. In N. E. West, ed., *Ecosystems of the World: Temperate Deserts and Semi-deserts*, 5:375–397. New York: Elsevier.

SALT PAN

Shallow natural depression in which rainfall and runoff water accumulate and evaporate, leaving a salt deposit on the land surface. The depressions are variously called salt flats, playas, salinas, salares, chotts, sabkhas, and pans. Salt pans usually are devoid of vegetation because of their salinity. Because most pans consist of heavy clay, water can stand on them for weeks and months, depending on their permeability, the amount of water in the depression, and the weather. The term "salt pan" is also used to refer to the shallow lakes of brackish water that occupy the pans during relatively wet years. The Makarikari Pan in northern Botswana is a very large but shallow depression with a salt marsh covering much of the pan. The groundwater table is close to the surface. Salt-tolerant plants grow in the perennially wet marshlands, but the drier margins of the pan are barren of vegetation. The smaller—but still large—Etosha Pan is located in northern Namibia.

Salt pans are the source of many salts of commercial value, including table salt (sodium chloride), gypsum, borax, and nitrates. Different salts have differential solubility. In a salt lake where there is a mixture of different kinds of salts, calcium carbonate is precipitated first as the salt pan water evaporates, forming a ring around the perimeter of the pan. Halite (sodium chloride) is a highly soluble salt that precipitates last and is concentrated in the lowest part of the pan. In some cases lake waters will consist largely of a single salt, which precipitates in a nearly pure form. An example is the gypsum that makes up the White Sands dune field in New Mexico. Gypsum in runoff water from the surrounding mountains precipitates in Lake Lucero, a salt pan lake, and the white crystals are blown out by strong southwest winds during the periodic dry periods, forming the White Sands.—Harold E. Dregne

See also **ARABIAN GULF, DESERTS OF; CARBONATES; CHENOPODIACEAE; COLLUVIAL DEPOSITS (COLLUVIUM); CHIHUAHUAN DESERT; DUNES; DURICRUSTS; GROUNDWATER; GYPSUM; HALOPHYTES; IRRIGATION DRAINAGE; KAVIR; MIDDLE EAST, DESERTS OF; NAMIBIA, DESERTS OF; PALEOCLIMATE; PAMPAS; PLAYA; SABKHA; SALINITY; SALT; SALTBUSH; SALT CRUST; SALT DESERT; SALT POLYGON; SOILS, DESERT, CALCAREOUS; SYRIA, DESERTS OF; WEATHERING, DESERT; WHITE SANDS NATIONAL MONUMENT**

Further Reading

Ward, S. M. 1970. *Geology and Hydrology of Selected Playas in Western United States.* Amherst: University of Massachusetts, Geology Department.

Salt polygons along the Dead Sea, Israel. (Photo: M. A. Mares)

SALT POLYGON

Polygonal structure of salt crusts on the surface of highly saline playas (salt flats, salt pans, chotts, sabkhas, salinas, etc.). Polygons have three to eight sides marked by ridges of salt and soil formed by the expansive force of crystallizing salt. They range in width from several centimeters to 30 or more meters. Salt polygons form in playas having thick salt crusts and saturated brine solutions under the crusts. Saline groundwater is close to the surface. Salts dissolved in the capillary water moving to the surface during dry periods are deposited as the water evaporates. Typically salt crusts at the boundaries of the polygons curl upward when the surface is dry. The upward curl may be 15 centimeters or more in height. Where runoff water from surrounding uplands accumulates in the playa, the curls collapse and disappear as the salts are dissolved. With recrystallization during subsequent dry periods, the curls re-form. The location of the edges of the polygons remain relatively constant during the cycles of crystallization and solution. Sometimes polygons in small areas are of roughly the same size and shape, but commonly they vary considerably from polygon to polygon.

Polygons are ubiquitous in playa soils. Most of them are the result of repeated wetting and drying of the surface and the development of cracks along fracture lines in the clays that are found in playas. Salt polygons are also formed by thermal expansion and contraction during the crystallization and solution processes associated with the very high salt content. When the playa salt content is low, polygons are hard and dry. The surface becomes softer as the salt content increases. In many playas part of the surface will be hard and part will be soft and friable (crumbly).—Harold E. Dregne

See also **ARABIAN GULF, DESERTS OF; CARBONATES; CHENOPODIACEAE; COLLUVIAL DEPOSITS (COLLUVIUM); CHIHUAHUAN DESERT; DEAD SEA; DUNES; DURICRUSTS; GROUNDWATER; GYPSUM; HALOPHYTES; IRRIGATION DRAINAGE; KAVIR; MIDDLE EAST, DESERTS OF; PALEOCLIMATE; PLAYA; SABKHA; SALINITY; SALT; SALTBUSH; SALT CRUST; SALT DESERT; SALT PAN; SOILS, DESERT, CALCAREOUS; SYRIA, DESERTS OF; WEATHERING, DESERT**

Further Reading

Ward, S. M. 1970. *Geology and Hydrology of Selected Playas in Western United States.* Amherst: University of Massachusetts, Geology Department.

SAND BATHING

Behavior shared by most desert-adapted rodents and many desert birds that functions both as a method of grooming the pelage (or fur in mammals) and plumage (or feathers in birds) and of marking territories in mammals. Among rodents most desert-specialized species in the genera *Gerbillus, Tatera, Meriones, Pachyuromys, Allactaga, Jaculus, Microdipodops, Perognathus,* and *Dipodomys,* to list only a few, exhibit this behavior. Among birds such groups as tinamous, quail, roadrunners, larks, sandgrouse, ostriches, and bustards sand bathe. Grooming or dressing of the pelage or plumage is a necessity for many desert species. Rodents have thick fur, and birds have dense plumage. Both possess large numbers of sebaceous glands. In rodents sebaceous glands are a necessary protection against the cold nighttime and winter temperatures of the desert, as well as a means to reduce epidermal water loss. In birds the oils keep the feathers waterproof and weatherproof.

Sand bathing behavior possibly is derived from a basic behavior, that of drying the fur or cleaning the feathers. In sand bathing a rodent digs into the sand with the forefeet, then rubs the venter (belly) or side of the body in the sand. Some species use both venter and side rubs (Heteromyidae); others (*Jaculus* and *Allactaga*) exhibit only the side rub. Birds will use the wings to toss sand into the feathers and work it through the feathers with the bill. They may also roll in the sand. It helps to keep the feathers in good condition and to remove parasites.

During sand bathing in rodents, the area is marked with chemical cues. Kangaroo rats (*Dipodomys*) will investigate and sand bathe in those areas used by other kangaroo rats. Males of some kangaroo rat species are able to determine the reproductive condition of females by examining the cues left in the sand. A single site will be used for several consecutive days by an individual of some species of *Meriones, Gerbillus,* and *Perognathus*; this site also may be used by other individuals of the same species.—Janet K. Braun

See also **ANIMAL ADAPTATIONS; GERBIL; HETEROMYIDS; KANGAROO MOUSE; KANGAROO RAT; MAMMALS; POCKET MOUSE; RODENTS; SAND RAT**

Further Reading

Eisenberg, J. F. 1963. The behavior of heteromyid rodents. *Universitiy of California Publications in Zoology* 69:1–100.

———. 1967. A comparative study in rodent ethology with emphasis on evolution of social behavior, 1. *Proceedings U.S. National Museum* 3597:1–51.

Jones, W. T. 1993. The social systems of heteromyid rodents. *In* H. H. Genoways and J. H. Brown, eds., *Biology of the Heteromyidae.* Special Publication No. 10, American Society of Mammalogists. Lawrence, Kan.: Allen.

SAND DEVIL. *See* DUST DEVIL

SANDGROUSE

Medium-sized, pigeonlike terrestrial bird found in Afro-Asian arid habitats (order Pterocliformes, family Pteroclididae). Two genera are recognized: *Pterocles* (14 species found primarily in Africa) and *Syrrhaptes* (2 species confined to colder deserts of central Asia). Sandgrouse have compact bodies, short bills reminiscent of a pigeon's, short, densely feathered legs, and long, pointed wings. Species vary in length from 27 to 48 centimeters. Sexes are similar in size. Plumage is cryptically colored, but sexual dimorphism is usually evident. Diet consists almost exclusively of small dry seeds. Sandgrouse are dependent on permanent supplies of freshwater and often occur in large congregations around water holes. Location of breeding sites is largely determined by distribution of this limiting resource.

Sandgrouse appear to be monogamous and generally nest in solitary pairs. Nests consist of scrapes on the ground, either unlined or sparsely lined with stones and dry vegetation. Clutch size is usually three. Incubation periods last 21–31 days. Chicks begin to feed on seeds almost immediately after hatching. Belly feathers of the male parent are uniquely configured so as to provide a means of carrying water to the nestlings. The unique belly-feather barbules are kidney shaped in cross-section (compared to wedge shaped in most birds); they are helically coiled for about two complete turns and end in a straight filament. When dry the coils of adjacent barbules are intertwined; however, when wet, the barbules uncoil and the terminal filaments stand up and form a dense mat in which water is retained. Aside from water transport, incubation duties and nestling care are shared equally by the male and female.—Stephen C. Lougheed

See also **AFRICA, DESERTS OF; ANIMAL ADAPTATIONS; ASIA, DESERTS OF; BIRDS; FEATHERS; IRAN, DESERTS OF; NESTS, BIRD; SAHARA DESERT; WATER BALANCE**

Further Reading

Cramp, S., ed. 1985. *Handbook of the Birds of Europe, the Middle East and North Africa: The Birds of the Western Palearctic*. Vol. 4. Oxford: Oxford University Press.

Johnsgard, P. A. 1991. *Bustards, Hemipodes and Sandgrouse: Birds of Dry Places*. Oxford: Oxford University Press.

Maclean, G. L. 1983. Water transport by sandgrouse. *BioScience* 33:365–369.

Thomas, D. H. 1984. Adaptations of desert birds: Sandgrouse (Pteroclididae) as highly successful inhabitants of Afro-Asian arid lands. *Journal of Arid Environments* 7:157–181.

Urban, E. K., C. H. Fry, and S. Keith, eds. 1986. *The Birds of Africa*. Vol. 2. New York: Academic Press.

SAND RAMP

Topographically controlled accumulation of aeolian (windblown) sands along the windward side of desert mountain ranges. The mountains act as barriers to aeolian transport, thus reducing wind velocities and enabling the deposition of the windblown sands. Sand ramps are generally located astride well-defined regional and local sand transport corridors. The sand ramps are covered by talus (weathered rock debris) and entrenched by ephemeral streams. Excellent examples are found in the Mojave Desert of California and in parts of North Africa and the Middle East. In the Mojave Desert sand ramps generally extend from the middle to upper slopes of the mountains and range over 25–40 percent of the local relief.

Owing to their proximity to the mountain fronts, sand ramp deposits also contain an amalgamation of fluvial (river), colluvial (slope), and talus deposits. The aeolian units are capped by paleosols (buried soils) with calcrete and calcified root rhizoliths, indicating multiple periods of aeolian deposition interspersed with periods of geomorphic stability and the establishment of vegetation and soils. The association of buried soils and fluvial/talus units suggests that periods of soil formation occurred under conditions of somewhat wetter climates than today.

Most sand ramps are relict features, and formed during past periods when sediment supply was high and/or desert lake levels were low or dry. Because of their unique nature, sand ramps are useful for the study of paleoenvironments in deserts and provide a long-term record of the response of aeolian processes to climate change.—Vatche P. Tchakerian

See also **COLLUVIAL DEPOSITS (COLLUVIUM); DESERT SLOPES; DUNES; MOJAVE DESERT; SOILS, DESERT; WEATHERING, DESERT; WIND EROSION; WIND TRANSPORT**

Further Reading

Lancaster, N., and V. P. Tchakerian. 1996. Geomorphology of sediments of sand ramps in the Mojave Desert. *Geomorphology* 17:151–165.

Tchakerian, V. P. 1991. Late Quaternary geomorphology of the Dale Lake sand sheet, southern Mojave Desert, California. *Physical Geography* 12:347–359.

SAND RAT

Herbivorous rodent in the genus *Psammomys* (family Muridae) that is related to gerbils and is most common in sandy deserts but also occurs in rocky habitats. There are two species of sand rats: *Psammomys obesus*, found from Libya to Saudi Arabia, and *Psammomys vexillaris*, which occurs in Algeria and Libya. Sand rats are stocky rodents, about the size of a common gerbil, with a hairy tail that has a terminal tuft. They are primarily diurnal but are also active at night. They forage on a number of desert plants and obtain their moisture from desert succulents, especially those of the family Chenopodiaceae. These plants contain water but also have very high concentrations of salt. Sand rats are able to forage on them because of special adaptations that they possess in urine concentrating capacity. Their kidneys produce a very salty urine and retain the water. They also wipe the leaves before eating them; this might function to remove salt. They also consume large amounts of grain and are considered agricultural pests in some areas.

Sand rats dig extensive burrow systems with numerous openings and food storage chambers. The nest area is lined with cut grass. Little is known about their social organization, but they are believed to be colonial. Males have much larger home ranges than females. Sand rats sit on their hind legs at the burrow entrance when they emerge, apparently looking for predators. They communicate through high-pitched squeaks and foot drumming. Females give birth to an average of three offspring and appear to reproduce year-round.—Thomas E. Lacher, Jr.

See also **CHENOPODIACEAE; HALOPHYTES; KANGA-ROO RAT; KIDNEY FUNCTION, DESERT RODENTS; KIDNEYS; MAMMALS; MIDDLE EAST, DESERTS OF; PHYSIOLOGY; PLAYA; RENAL PAPILLA; RODENTS; SALT BALANCE; URINE; WATER BALANCE**

Further Reading

Harrison, D. L., and P. J. J. Bates. 1991. *The Mammals of Arabia*. Kent, U. K.: Sevenoaks: Harrison Zoological Museum.

Nowak, R. M. 1991. *Walker's Mammals of the World*. 5th ed. Baltimore: Johns Hopkins University Press.

SANDSTONE

Sedimentary rocks with cemented grains composed of various types of minerals which are produced by the disintegration of preexisting rocks through various weathering processes; these sediments are then transported through water or wind and tend to separate into materials based on their size, with the soft minerals being eliminated through chemical alteration. The most common component of sandstone is quartz, which is highly resistant to chemical and mechanical attack. Sandstone also contains dark minerals and mica.

Sandstones owe their hardness to the process of cementation. Over enormous periods of time deposits of oxides of silica and calcium carbonate accumulate in the porous spaces between the sand grains, leading to the development of solid rock. These cementing substances are carried in solution by the water that circulates through the pores. When cementation is incomplete sandstones are easily eroded through wind and water.

Sandstone bluffs and other formations, such as those seen at Arches National Park in Utah or in Monument Valley in Arizona, characterize many of the world's deserts.—Alberto I. J. Vich and Juana Susana Barroso

See also **BADLANDS; DESERT SLOPES; DURICRUSTS; MINERALS; MONUMENT VALLEY; SEDIMENTA-TION; WEATHERING, DESERT; WIND EROSION**

Further Reading

Bates, R. L., ed. 1987. *Glossary of Geology*. 3d ed. Alexandria, Va.: American Geological Institute.

Cooke, R., A. Warren, and A. Goudie. 1993. *Desert Geomorphology*. London: University College London Press.

Fuller, W. H. 1974. Desert soils. *In* G. W. Brown Jr., ed., *Desert Biology: Special Topics on the Physical and Biological Aspects of Arid Regions*, 2:31–101. New York: Academic Press.

Moore, G. W. 1978. *Dictionary of Geography: Definitions and Explanation of Terms used in Physical Geography*. New York: Harper and Row.

The New Encyclopaedia Britannica. 15th ed. 1974. Sandstone. Vol. 16:212–216. Chicago: University of Chicago Press.

Pomerol, C., and R. Forut. 1964. *Las rocas sedimentarias*. Buenos Aires: Eudeba.

SANTA ANA WINDS

Type of local wind that is hot and dry; characteristic of desert areas in California. The equivalent of this is the Chinook in the Rocky Mountains, the foehn in the Swiss Alps, the zonda in Andean Argentina, and other winds associated with mountainous areas in other deserts of the world. The Santa Ana winds generally come from the northeast or from the east, especially in mountain passes and valleys. In California the canyons near Santa Ana are noteworthy for developing these mountain-gap winds, which reach very high velocities as they drop into the lowland deserts from the mountains in the Sierra Nevada. The winds may bring with them large amounts of dust as well as very hot dry air (e.g., air temperature increases of more than 16°C have been recorded over a seven-minute period; more than 1.5 meters of snow melted in 12 hours when exposed to a Santa Ana wind). These winds are more common in winter. Should they occur in springtime, they can cause great damage to the fruit orchards by damaging trees and buds. Los Angeles is also affected by these hot dry winds, and should they coincide with fires in the chaparral scrub lands of southern California, they can help to move the advancing fires and lead to great conflagrations. In California in 1991 a fire that was greatly influenced by the Santa Ana winds destroyed 484 homes and cost $25 million in damage.

Santa Ana winds have their ultimate origin in the formation of a high-pressure system at higher elevations in Nevada. The clockwise rotation of the air around an anticyclone or a center of high pressure forces the air to descend to lower elevations. The air is dry because it developed over a desert, and it warms adiabatically as it descends, picking up large amounts of dust and other matter. Santa Ana winds and winds of similar types in other deserts can have great effects on the human populations of those areas, as low pressure and very dry air can cause great discomfort and even affect human behavior.—Federico Norte

See also **ANTICYCLONE; BAROMETRIC PRESSURE (ATMOSPHERIC PRESSURE); CLIMATE; CLIMATE CLASSIFICATION; CLOUDS; CONVECTIVE STORM; CYCLONE; LOW PRESSURE; WIND**

Further Reading

Day, J. A., and V. J. Schaefer. 1991. *Clouds and Weather.* Boston: Houghton Mifflin.

Oliver, J. E., and R. W. Fairbridge, eds. 1987. *The Encyclopedia of Climatology.* New York: Chapman and Hall.

Schaefer, V. J., and J. A. Day. 1981. *A Field Guide to the Atmosphere.* Boston: Houghton Mifflin.

Schneider, S. H., ed. 1996. *Encyclopedia of Climate and Weather.* 2 vols. New York: Oxford University Press.

SAUDI ARABIA, DESERTS OF

Arid areas occurring within Saudi Arabia, a Middle Eastern country situated on the Arabian Peninsula and bordered by Kuwait, Iraq, Jordan, Yemen, Oman, the United Arab Emirates, and Qatar. Saudi Arabia covers an area of about 2,253,000 square kilometers between latitudes 32°34'–16°83' north and longitudes 34°36'–56°00' east, with maximum length (N–S) about 2,500 kilometers and a maximum width (E–W) of about 1,700 kilometers. The climate is hot and dry and affected by two climatic types: the monsoon climate, which affects the south, and the Mediterranean climate, which affects the north. The country is divided into five major geomorphological regions: the Red Sea coastal region (Tihama Plains), the Hijaz and Asir mountains, the central region, the eastern region, and the Empty Quarter (Rub' Al-Khāli). (See map of Middle East deserts, p. 361.)

The Red Sea coastal region varies in width, reaching a maximum of about 45 kilometers in the south near Jizan, and almost disappears in the north along the Gulf of Aqaba. Soils are of alluvial origin and transported by runoff water from the adjacent mountains. The climate is hot and dry, with a mean annual temperature of about 30°C and annual rainfall of only 30 millimeters. There are many major habitat types, including mangroves, salt marshes, sand formations, valleys, depressions, and gravel habitats. The mangrove vegetation is dominated by *Avicennia marina*. Salt marshes of the southern region support *Aeluropus lagopoides, Halopeplis perfoliata, Halocnemum strobilaceum, Limonium axillare*, and *Atriplex farinosa*; toward the north *Arthrocnemum glaucum, Suaeda pruinosa, Nitraria retusa*, and *Zygophyllum coccineum* dominate. The sand formations are covered by various species of *Acacia, Leptadenia pyrotechnica, Dipterygium glaucum, Panicum turgidum, Lasiurus scindicus*, and *Cadaba rotundifolia*. The valleys and water runnels (gullies) are occupied by *Acacia, Hyphaena thebaica, Calotropis procera*, and *Ziziphus spina-christi*. The depressions harbor dense vegetation of species that grow in surrounding habitat types.

The Asir and Hijaz mountains constitute the western mountainous landscape of Saudi Arabia. The mountain peaks south of Jeddah reach an altitude of more than 3,000 meters in the Asir and Sarawat highlands, while north of Jeddah they do not exceed 1,500 meters. Generally they are less continuous, less precipitous, and lower in the north. They are composed of granite, crystalline, and eruptive rocks. The southern mountains are subjected to both summer and winter rain. Vegetation at the high elevations of the Asir Mountains is dominated by *Juniperus procera, Clutia myricoides, Euryops arabicus, Lavandula dentata*, and *Dodonaea viscosa*. The cushion-plant communities of

Cichorium bottae, Argrolobium confertum, and *Minuartia filifolia* predominate on the dry exposed rocky slopes. Vegetation of the high elevations in the Hijaz Mountains north of Jeddah and around Mecca is dominated by *Acacia asak, Acacia tortilis, Maerua crassifolia,* and *Lycium persicum.* Climatic variation associated with different elevations leads to changes in plant associations and plant species diversity in the mountains, although substrate discontinuities and the entire escarpment between the dry, hot Tihama Plains and the wet, cold highlands play an important role as well. At intermediate elevations the vegetation forms broad ecotones of mixed communities.

The central region is characterized by low and irregular winter rainfall. The soil is mainly sedimentary sandstone, limestone, or siltstone with medium gravelly texture. Vegetation on sandy habitats is dominated by *Artemisia monosperma, Calligonum comosum, Monosonia nivea,* and *Scrophularia deserti.* Steppe vegetation is developed on limestone plains overblown with sand and is dominated by *Rhanterium epapposum* and *Artemisia monosperma.* The dominant species on gravelly plains are *Gymnocarpos decander* and *Stipa capensis.* The shallow silty depressions are occupied by *Artemisia herba-alba* and *Achillea fragrantissima.* The deep depressions are covered by *Helianthemum lippii* and *Helianthemum kahiricum.* In the wadi habitats *Aristida obtusa, Heliotropium luteum, Rhazya stricta, Pergularia tomentosa, Zilla spinosa,* and *Polycarpaea repens* are common.

The eastern region along the Arabian Gulf has soils composed mainly of marine sediments. The landscape is flat and interrupted by shallow depressions. The surface is often covered by aeolian deposits in the form of mobile or static sand dunes that give the landscape an irregular topography. The salt-affected coastline habitats are usually sandy and support the following plant species: *Aeluropus logopoides, Juncus maritimus, Cressa cretica,* and *Limonium axillare.* South of Kuwait the steppe vegetation is represented by *Panicum turgidum, Rhanterium epapposum, Calligonum comosum,* and *Leptadenia pyrotechnica.* Continuing southward, *Helianthemum lippii, Hippocrepis bicontorta, Lasiurus scindicus, Salsola tetrandra, Anabasis setifera,* various species of *Aristida, Cyperus conglomeratus,* and *Zygophyllum quatarense* become common.

The Empty Quarter covers about 640,000 square kilometers in the southern part of Saudi Arabia and is nearly devoid of human inhabitants. It is considered the largest area of continuous sand cover in the world. Its sands are underlain in the western part by gravels. In portions of the eastern Rub' Al-Khāli the substrate grades into evaporites with salt marshes exposed amid the massive dunes. The dunes themselves range from parallel linear dunes about one kilometer in length to rounded sand mountains up to 250 meters high. The major sand dune forms are shaped largely by local wind conditions. The climate is extremely arid, and no rain may fall for several consecutive years. The mean annual rainfall is less than 10 millimeters, and the absolute maximum temperature exceeds 52°C.

Vegetation of the Rub' Al-Khāli is sparse and seldom exceeds 30 species of plants. The major plant species include *Calligonum crinitum, Calligonum comosum, Cornulaca arabica, Suaeda monoica, Cyperus Conglomeratus, Stipagrostis drarii, Limonium arabicum, Tribulus arabicus,* and *Zygophyllum mandavilliei.* The plant life forms demonstrate that phanerophytes (shrubs) and chamaephytes (dwarf shrubs) constitute about 32 percent and 36 percent of the flora, respectively. The therophytes (annual plants) constitute only about 19 percent. The rest of the flora consists of hemicryptophytes (plants with buds at ground level) and cryptophytes (plants with perennating organs below the ground surface).

The major environmental stresses on the plant life of sand dunes are due to poor nutrient content and the availability of water, which is strongly affected by the mobile coarse sand that has very low water-holding capacity. The mobility of sand and strong winds lead to burial of plants or exposure of their roots and interfere with seed germination and seedling establishment. Windborne sand particles may injure the aerial organs of plants.

Nomadic pastoralism has been the traditional form of land use practice and a major lifestyle for people in the deserts of Saudi Arabia before the discovery and exploitation of oil occurred. In recent years the desert nomads are facing difficulties due to the shrinkage of rangelands as a result of urban and rural expansions, degradation of ecosystems, desertification, and severe drought. Wealth accruing from oil revenues has exerted rapid social, industrial, and agricultural developments in the region. Oil-related activities, road construction, urbanization, and industrialization have increased the human impacts on different parts of the country. The traditional relationship between the desert people and their environment is thus being neutralized. The landscape of the holy places and neighboring areas in Mecca is severely affected by the visiting pilgrims every year. Constructing accommodations, paving roads, and related activities have disrupted the natural ecosystem in the three major sites, Mena, Muzdalifah, and Arafat, where local vegetation has been eradicated. Recently plant species, including *Melia azedarach*, *Tamarindus indicus*, and *Ziziphus spina-christi*, have been cultivated in these holy sites to shade the visiting pilgrims from exposure to direct sun, where air temperature may exceed 50°C during summer months.

Saudi Arabia is the largest country in the world without a river. Rainfall is scanty and irregular over most of the country and rarely exceeds an annual mean of 100 millimeters. The highest rainfall occurs on the southwestern highlands of the Asir and Hijaz mountain ranges and may reach 500 millimeters annually. About two-thirds of the country is underlain by sedimentary formations that may have been buried with underground water of nonmarine origin. The urgent need for water has made drilling for oil and groundwater associated processes. However, there is a depletion in natural water resources due to the uncontrolled use of fossil water in agriculture, in industry, and for municipal purposes. To improve the water supplies, many dams and dikes have been constructed for holding and spreading runoff water and floods. A seawater desalination program was initiated in 1965. Many desalination plants were constructed on the Red Sea and Arabian Gulf coasts.

The land use for agriculture depends largely on suitable soils and water availability. Agriculture is a major consumer of groundwater. About 1.2 million hectares have been classified as arable land; of these, 37 percent is irrigated. Agricultural and rangelands support 323,000 cattle, 11 million sheep and goats, and 415,000 camels. However, even where irrigation water may be available, agriculture may be limited by high temperature and high evaporation, which lead to great stresses on domestic animals and crops.

The traditional *hema* (Arabic for "protected land") system of vegetation in Saudi Arabia goes back to the pre-Islamic era, and has continued since then as a respected tradition for conservation and restoration of degraded ecosystems, particularly the rangeland resources. Management and use of hema systems was controlled by tribal communities, villages, or individuals. At present the establishment and management of protected national parks are under governmental control to combat the degradation of desert ecosystems and the loss of biodiversity.—Ahmad K. Hegazy

See also **AFRICA, DESERTS OF; AGRICULTURE IN DESERTS; AN INTRODUCTION TO DESERTS; ARABIAN GULF, DESERTS OF; BIRDS; CHENOPODIACEAE; CONTAMINATION; DESERTIFICATION; DESERT PEOPLES; DOMESTIC ANIMALS; DUNES; HEAT; JEDDAH; LIZARDS; MAMMALS; MIDDLE EAST, DESERTS OF; OVERGRAZING; PLAYA; RELIGION IN DESERTS; REPTILES; SAHARA DESERT; SALINIZATION; SALT; SALT CEDAR; SALT DESERT; SAND RAT; SNAKES; SHEEP**

Further Reading

Abd El-Rahman, A. A. 1986. The deserts of the Arabian peninsula. *In* M. Evenari, I. Noy-Meir, and D. W. Goodall, eds., *Ecosystems of the World: Hot Deserts and Arid Shrublands*, 12B:29–54. New York: Elsevier.

Brooks, W. H., and K. S. D. Mandil. 1983. Vegetation dynamics in the Asir woodlands of south-western Saudi Arabia. *Journal of Arid Environments* 6:357–362.

Draz, O. 1969. *The Hema System of Range Reserves in the Arabian Peninsula: Its Possibilities in Range Improvement and Conservation Projects in the Middle East*. Rome: Food and Agriculture Organization/PL, PFC/13.11.

El-Demerdash, M. A., A. K. Hegazy, and A. M. Zilay. 1994. Distribution of plant communities in Tihamah coastal plains of Jazan region, Saudi Arabia. *Vegetatio* 112: 141–151.

Mandaville, J. P. 1990. *Flora of Eastern Saudi Arabia*. London: Kegan Paul.

McNeely, J. A., and V. M. Neronov, eds. 1991. *Mammals in the Palaeoarctic Desert: Status and Trends in the Sahara-Gobian Region*. Moscow: UNESCO Man and Biosphere Programme (MAB).

Migahid, A. M. 1989. *Flora of Saudi Arabia*. 3d ed. Vols. 1 and 2. Riyadh: King Saud University Press.

Schmid, H. 1997. *The Desert Sea: Fauna of the Saudi-Arabian Red Sea Coast*. 2d rev. ed. Hong Kong: Paramount.

Schulz, E., and J. W. Whitney. 1986. Vegetation in north-central Saudi Arabia. *Journal of Arid Environments* 10:175–186.

Younes, H. A., M. A. Zahran, and M. E. El-Qurashy. 1983. Vegetation-soil relationships of a sea landward transect, Red Sea coast, Saudi Arabia. *Journal of Arid Environments* 6:349–356.

SAVANNA

Region having equal amounts of cover from grasses (and grasslike plants) and trees. Some authors suggest that savannas are located only in South America and Africa, with no true savanna forms found elsewhere, but most have a more relaxed definition that includes open, parklike forests. These authors recognize savanna associations on nearly all continents. The broader definition is used here.

The existence of savannas represents an enigma to those ecologists who feel that grasslands are fire-maintained ecosystems. Fire is a common occurrence in some savannas. Obviously there is sufficient rainfall to support trees, as savannas, by definition, have trees present. Why, then, do savannas exist, with their open, parklike vegetational aspect? Why does fire not destroy the trees and return the area to a grassland?

Several savanna tree species are fire-resistant as mature trees. Species such as *Acacia* spp. and *Banalities* spp. can tolerate fire due to thick bark and elevated branches. However, when young these species are susceptible to fire. Therefore, in order for savannas to exist, the intervals over which fires occur must be sufficiently long so that some tree saplings can reach maturity.

In addition to fire, browsing animals can play a major role in the maintenance of savanna type-vegetation. As with fires, small trees are more susceptible to damage from browsers, whereas the elevated foliage of mature trees will escape all but the largest browsing animals. Thus a constant level of browsing will keep the woody vegetation from becoming dominant as long as some members manage to escape.

Other savanna types are maintained due to unique soil formations that allow growth of trees in some locations but not others. The Llanos region of the Orinoco Basin of Venezuela is an example of this process, as are the vast Cerrado savannas of central Brazil.

Some of the desert grasslands in the southwestern portions of North America could be considered to be savannas. Due to heavy grazing pressure on the grass component, shrubs and small trees have

The cerrado grassland of central Brazil, a tropical savanna with a pronounced dry season. (Photo: M. A. Mares)

been able to invade this habitat with great success. A common example of such an invader is the mesquite tree, *Prosopis*.

However, many of the savanna vegetation types that are recognized around the globe may be transitional vegetation types rather than a climax stage. Ecologists have recognized that many grasslands are undergoing a process of woody plant invasion. This has been caused by the processes described above, along with shifts in climatic patterns in these regions as well. Thus it has been argued that the savanna stages that are recognized, particularly in the southwestern portions of North America, are merely steps in the process of forming a scrub woodland vegetation. Computer simulation models have used past woody growth to predict future vegetation trends in these communities and have found that these areas are switching from herbaceous dominance (grasses) to woody shrub and tree dominance.

Savannas are not true desert vegetation types but are considered to be either semidesert or semiarid vegetation. As is the case for other semidesert vegetation types, savannas can occur within desert areas in sites where water accumulates or on specialized soils. However, their distribution within deserts is rare.—Linda L. Wallace

See also **AFRICA, DESERTS OF; ASIA, DESERTS OF; BIOME; CAATINGA; DESERT GRASSLAND; GRASSES; GRASSLAND; GREAT AMERICAN DESERT; PAMPAS; PLANT ADAPTATIONS; PLANT GEOGRAPHY; PLANTS; PRAIRIE; OVERGRAZING;**

SOUTH AFRICA, DESERTS OF; SOUTH AMERICA, DESERTS OF; STEPPE; SUCCESSION; UNITED STATES, DESERTS OF

Further Reading

Archer, S. 1989. Have southern Texas savannas been converted to woodlands in recent history? *American Naturalist* 134:545–561.

Camacho, J. H. 1994. *Sabanas naturales de Colombia.* Cali, Colombia: Banco de Occidente Credencial.

Joern, A., and K. H. Keeler, eds. 1995. *The Changing Prairie.* New York: Oxford University Press.

Martinez, D. S., C. C. Ortegón, E. G. Afanador, and G. G. Monroy. 1995. *Llanos.* Bogotá: Diego Samper Ediciones.

Samson, F. B., and F. L. Knopf, eds. 1996. *Prairie Conservation.* Washington D.C.: Island Press.

Solbrig, O. T., E. Medina, and J. F. Silva, eds. 1996. *Biodiversity and Savanna Ecosystem Processes.* Berlin: Springer.

Walter, H. 1983. *Vegetation of the Earth.* Berlin: Springer.

SCAVENGERS. *See* CARRION EATERS

SCORPIONS

Flattened nocturnal arthropods with four pairs of walking legs, a set of large pincers located on the first apparent set of appendages (pedipalps), and an elongate, segmented, taillike structure called a telson, harboring a bulbous final segment containing a sharp recurved stinger. Many species are yellow in coloration, although some of the largest species are black. Most species are small (less than 5 centimeters total length), but some are much larger. During the day scorpions remain hidden in crevices, under rocks, and in the burrows or nests of other animals. Although they were among the first groups of animals to colonize terrestrial environments, they have reproductive characteristics that are considered advanced in higher organisms such as mammals. Females have a complex placenta that nourishes young through development. Young scorpions are born alive (no egg stage) and remain on the female's back for an extended period.

Scorpions feed on small, soft-bodied arthropods, such as spiders. They grab their prey with the pincers and, by whipping the telson over the body, inject venom into the constrained prey. Death occurs rapidly. The pincers are then used to help masticate the prey, which is thus liquified and ingested.

A scorpion (*Rhopalurus roachi*) from the semiarid Caatinga of northeastern Brazil (Photo: L. J. Vitt)

The bark scorpion (*Centruroides sculpturatus*) of the Sonoran Desert is the most dangerous species in North America and has caused deaths.—Laurie J. Vitt

See also ANIMAL ADAPTATIONS; ARACHNIDS; ARTHROPODS; DEFENSIVE ADAPTATIONS, ANIMALS; POISONOUS ANIMALS; RED VELVET MITE; VENOM

Further Reading

Polis, G. ed. 1990. *Biology of Scorpions.* Stanford: Stanford University Press.

Smith, R. L. 1982. *Venomous Animals of Arizona.* Tucson: Cooperative Extension Service, University of Arizona.

SEA LION

Ocean-dwelling species of carnivores that belong to the mammalian family Otariidae, which also includes fur seals. Five genera and five species are known: New Zealand sea lion (*Phocarctos hookeri*), South American sea lion (*Otaria byronia*), California sea lion (*Zalophus californicus*), Australian sea lion (*Neophoca cinerea*), and Steller sea lion (*Eumetopias jubatus*). In the Pacific Ocean they are distributed along the coastlines of Hokkaido Island, islands of the North Pacific, including Alaska, and western North America to the tip of South America, including the Galápagos Islands. In the Atlantic Ocean they are found from the tip of South America to Uruguay, including the Falkland Islands (Islas Malvinas). Sea lions also occur along the southern coast of Australia and around the southern islands of New Zealand. As with other marine mammals,

Southern sea lions (*Arctocephalus australis*) along the desert coast of Patagonia, Argentina. (Photo: M. A. Mares)

sea lions are threatened by hunting, fishing, and pollution.

Sea lions have large streamlined bodies, a small tail that is not used in swimming, elongate foreflippers (with very small claws) that are used to propel the animal through the water, and hind flippers with two small outer claws and three long central claws. The hind flippers can be turned forward at the ankle and are not used for locomotion. The external ear or pinna is small. Males are much larger than females and have a thick neck with a dense mane of hair. Total length ranges from 2.3 to 3 meters in males and from 1.6 to 2.2 meters in females. Weight ranges from 300 kilograms to one tonne in males and from 80 to 270 kilograms in females. Fishes, squid, octopuses, penguins, crustaceans, and occasionally other seals and sea otters compose the diet.

Although extensive data are not available, it appears that sea lions, especially *Zalophus*, are not well adapted to high temperatures. Tolerance of high temperatures cannot exceed more than a few hours, and they cannot maintain equilibrium at temperatures over 30°C. At high temperatures sea lions will breathe through the mouth, salivate, and sweat. They will remain near water to keep the body damp and to take advantage of the sea breezes that cause evaporative cooling. South American sea lions are common along the coast of the Patagonian Desert of Argentina, where they coexist with Magellan's penguins.—Janet K. Braun

See also **CARNIVORES; MAMMALS; MONTE DESERT; PATAGONIA; PENGUIN; SEAL; SOUTH AMERICA, DESERTS OF**

Further Reading

Grzimek's Encyclopedia of Mammals. Vol. 4. 1990. New York: McGraw-Hill.

King, J. E. 1991. *Seals of the World*. Ithaca: Comstock.

Macdonald, D., ed. 1984. *The Encyclopedia of Mammals*. New York: Facts on File.

Peterson, R. S., and G. A. Bartholomew. 1967. *The Natural History and Behavior of the California Sea Lion*. Special Publication No. 1, American Society of Mammalogists.

Ridgway, S. H., and R. J. Harrison, eds. 1981. *Handbook of Marine Mammals: The Walrus, Sea Lions, Fur Seals and Sea Otter*. Vol. 1. New York: Academic Press.

Ronald, K., J. Selley, and P. Healey. 1982. Seals. *In* J. A. Chapman and G. A. Feldhamer, eds., *Wild Mammals of North America: Biology, Management, and Economics*, 769–827. Baltimore: Johns Hopkins University Press.

SEAL

Ocean-dwelling species of mammalian carnivores that belong to the family Phocidae and are worldwide in distribution, including coastal areas in deserts. This diverse family, containing 19 species and 10 genera, is divided into a northern and a southern group. Northern seals (gray seal, harbor seal, ringed seal, Caspian seal, Baikal seal, harp seal, ribbon seal, hooded seal, and bearded seal) are generally found in and around the North Pole. Northern seals may range as far south as the Yellow Sea in the Pacific and to the state of New York in the Atlantic.

Southern seals include monk seals, elephant seals, and Antarctic seals (Weddell seal, Ross seal, crabeater seal, and leopard seal). The four Antarctic seals are generally restricted to the Antarctic and divide the region according to their distribution and feeding preferences.

Seals have a number of characteristics that distinguish them from other mammals. They lack an external ear (pinna), are unable to raise themselves up on their foreflippers, have hind flippers that are furred on both sides and that cannot be turned forward, have a streamlined body, lack a clavicle (collarbone), and move on land by "humping," or moving caterpillarlike.

Of all the seals only monk and elephant seals can be considered as inhabiting desert environments. Monk seals (*Monachus*) are found in the Mediterranean Sea, around the Hawaiian Islands, and in the West Indies. The West Indian monk seal may be extinct, as monk seals are especially sensitive to human disturbance. The Hawaiian monk seal has adapted behaviorally to the tropical climate. They lie in shade, wet sand, or in the surf during the day and feed at night. The Mediterranean monk seal eats fishes and octopuses; the Hawaiian monk seal feeds on eels, fishes, cephalopods, and octopuses.

The prominent proboscis present in adult males gives the elephant seal (*Mirounga*) its name. Southern elephant seal males are four to five meters in length and weigh three to six tonnes. Females and northern elephant seals are smaller. In northern elephant seals (found from San Francisco southward along the Baja Peninsula coast) the long proboscis, when inflated, presses against the roof of the mouth. Snorts are directed into the open mouth and pharynx, which resonates the sound. In the southern elephant seal (found in the Antarctic, New Zealand, and along the coasts of southern South America) the smaller proboscis functions as the resonating chamber. Along the desert coastline of Patagonia in southern Argentina elephant seals, sea lions, and penguins are common inhabitants of the desert's edge.—Janet K. Braun

See also **CARNIVORES; MAMMALS; MONTE DESERT; PATAGONIA; PENGUIN; SEA LION; SOUTH AMERICA, DESERTS OF**

Further Reading

Grzimek's. Encyclopedia of Mammals. Vol. 4. 1990. New York: McGraw-Hill.

King, J. E. 1991. *Seals of the World*. Ithaca: Comstock.

Macdonald, D., ed. 1984. *The Encyclopedia of Mammals*. New York: Facts on File.

Ridgway, S. H., and R. J. Harrison, eds. 1981. *Handbook of Marine Mammals: The Walrus, Sea Lions, Fur Seals and Sea Otter*. Vol. 1. New York: Academic Press.

Ronald, K., J. Selley, and P. Healey. 1982. Seals. *In* J. A. Chapman and G. A. Feldhamer, eds., *Wild Mammals of North America: Biology, Management, and Economics*, 769–827. Baltimore: Johns Hopkins University Press.

SECHURA DESERT

Warm desert along the northwestern Peruvian coast between the provinces of Piura in the north and Lambayeque in the south. It reaches a maximum width of 150 kilometers from the Pacific Ocean to the Andes Mountains. This desert consists of an extensive plateau made up of Tertiary sediments which has been dissected in numerous blocks. It is a part of the Peruvian Desert. (See map of South American deserts, p. 533.)—Virgilio G. Roig

See also **AN INTRODUCTION TO DESERTS; ARIDITY; ATACAMA DESERT; CHILE, DESERTS OF; FOG DESERT; HUMBOLDT CURRENT; OCEAN CURRENTS; PERU, DESERTS OF**

Further Reading

Allan, T., and A. Warren, eds. 1993. *Deserts: The Encroaching Wilderness*. New York: Oxford University Press.

Amiran, D. H. K., and A. W. Wilson, eds. 1973. *Coastal Deserts: Their Natural and Human Environments*. Tucson: University of Arizona Press.

Cabrera, A. L., and A. Willink. 1973. Biogeografía de América Latina. Organization of American States, Monograph No. 13. Washington, D.C.

Rauh, W. 1985. The Peruvian-Chilean deserts. *In* M. Evenari, I. Noy-Meir, and D. W. Goodall, eds., *Ecosystems of the World: Hot Deserts and Arid Shrublands*, 12B:239–267. New York: Elsevier.

SEDIMENTATION

Settling out or deposition of solid materials of various sizes (sediment) from a suspension to produce an accumulation of sediment. Sediment may be derived from biological, geological, or soil materials and be physically deposited by air, water, or glaciers or chemically deposited in bodies of water. Prior to physical sedimentation, erosive agents (wind, running water, or glaciers) pick up and transport the sediment. The sediment is deposited when the erosive agent no longer provides the energy needed to keep the sediment in motion. In desert environments air and water can act as fluids to produce sedimentation and transport particles. Sediment moves downhill in running water in response to gravity but may be transported to higher elevations by the wind. As the sediment moves sorting of the particles by size tends to occur. For example, particles that were held aloft by rapidly moving air may settle when the wind velocity is slightly reduced while still smaller particles remain aloft. The process of physical sedimentation is responsible for creating many desert landforms, ranging from a variety of sand dunes to alluvial fan and valley fill deposits. In chemical sedimentation sediments are deposited in response to chemical differences in bodies of water, most notably seawater. Chemical sedimentation of dissolved geologic material occurs when the solution becomes saturated. Sometimes microorganisms play an important role in promoting production and sedimentation of chemical sediment. For example, diatoms produce silica-rich sediments and certain bacteria promote sulfide sedimentation in some oxygen-depleted bodies of water.—Ted M. Zobeck and Dan R. Upchurch

See also **ALLUVIAL FAN; BACTERIA; DESERT SLOPES; DUNES; LIMESTONE; ROCK VARNISH; RUNOFF; SOILS, DESERT; SOIL TAXONOMY; WATER; WEATHERING, DESERT**

Further Reading

Press, F., and R. Siever. 1978. *Earth*. 2d ed. San Francisco: Freeman.

Pye, K. 1994. *Sediment Transport and Depositional Processes*. Oxford: Blackwell Scientific.

SEED DISPERSAL BY ANIMALS (ZOOCHORY)

Animal-assisted dispersal of seeds and other propagules. There are two modes of zoochory: endozoochory and epizoochory. In both cases sophisticated adaptations have been developed among plants to ensure that a seed enters or attaches to an animal. Endozoochory is the dispersal of seeds that have been carried internally by an animal. Typically an animal ingests a fleshy fruit containing seeds. In exchange the fruit provides a nutritional and/or energetic reward for the animal. Once ingested the seeds are carried by the animal until excreted. As an added benefit to the seed, the excrement often provides a moist, nutrient-rich substrate in which the seed can germinate. Some plant species have thick seed coats that must pass through the abrasive environment of the animal's digestive system before it germinates (e.g., the mesquite plant, genus *Prosopis*).

Epizoochory is the external transport of seeds by an animal. The process is involuntary and provides none of the rewards associated with endozoochory. The fruits of epizoochoric plants have developed barbs, hooks, or sticky chemical substances that attach the seed to a passing animal. Epizoochoric fruits are often referred to as stick-tights, burrs, or hitchhikers. Fruits and seeds carried in this manner may travel greater distances than endozoochoric fruits, but the probability of a seed arriving at a site

where it can successfully germinate is much lower. A novel form of epizoochory involves the voluntary removal of fruits and seeds from the parent plant by animals. For example, squirrels and nutcrackers will place hundreds of seeds in underground caches. Many of these seeds will be eaten, but others will not be eaten and will germinate. A final adaptation to epizoochory, which involves ants, is the development of a small edible appendage attached to an inedible seed. Ants carry the entire fruit to their nest, eat the appendage, and discard the seed.—Bruce W. Hoagland

See also **ANNUAL PLANTS; BIRDS; CHOLLA; DESERT BLOOM; DESERT GRASSLAND; DESERTIFICATION; DOMESTIC ANIMALS; FLOWERS; FRUITS; GERBIL; GERMINATION; GRANIVORY; KANGAROO MOUSE; KANGAROO RAT; LEAVES; MESQUITE; PLANT ADAPTATIONS; PLANT DISPERSAL BY WIND (ANEMOCHORY); PLANTS; POCKET MOUSE; SEEDS; SQUIRREL; THORN**

Further Reading

Howe, H. F., and J. Smallwood. 1982. Ecology of seed dispersal. *Annual Review of Ecology and Systematics* 13:201–228.

Pijl, L. van der. 1972. *Principles of Dispersal in Higher Plants*. 2d ed. New York: Springer.

Ridely, H. N. 1930. *The Dispersal of Plants Throughout the World*. London: Ashford.

SEEDS

Mature ovule composed of a seed coat, an embryo, and, typically, nutritive tissue. In seed plants ovules hold the female gametophyte (the haploid, sexual generation of plants); they are produced in cones and in the pistils of flowers. The gametophyte is much reduced in seed plants and completely supported by the sporophyte generation. In seed plants seeds are reproductive structures that are produced following pollination and fertilization. The embryo develops from the zygote (fertilized egg) and represents the first stage of the new sporophytic generation.

Seeds provide the means of dispersal of the species, and they are dormant through seasons that are unfavorable for growth. This latter feature is especially important in desert biomes, where precipitation is undependable. As young, tender seedlings are unable to survive during drought, seeds of most desert plants germinate only when there is ample moisture to sustain growth through the early vulnerable stages. This occurs after soaking rains.

Inhibitory chemicals in the seed coat that prevent the seeds from germinating in dry periods leach from the seed when soaked for several days.

Seeds of some desert perennials, such as mesquite (*Prosopis*), must pass through the gut of larger herbivores to have the seed coats scarified (partially broken) by digestive action before they can germinate. This permits the seeds to disperse away from the parent plant (thus minimizing competition for water) before developing into a new plant.—James R. Estes

See also **ANNUAL PLANTS; BIRDS; DESERT GRASSLAND; FLOWERS; FRUITS; GERBIL; GERMINATION; GRANIVORY; KANGAROO MOUSE; KANGAROO RAT; MESQUITE; PLANT ADAPTATIONS; PLANT DISPERSAL BY WIND (ANEMOCHORY); PLANTS; POCKET MOUSE**

Further Reading

Raven, P. H., and G. B. Johnson. 1986. *Biology*. St. Louis: Mosby.

Simpson, B. B., ed. 1977. *Mesquite: Its Biology in Two Desert Ecosystems*. Stroudsburg, Pa.: Dowden, Hutchinson, and Ross.

SEMIARID ZONES

Climatic belt that receives 250–375 millimeters of precipitation per year and undergoes frequent droughts. As much as one-fourth of the annual rainfall may occur in a single day. These areas, sometimes referred to as steppes, usually occur in the center of large landmasses, occasionally aided or abetted by a rain shadow. Semiarid zones typically support shortgrass vegetation with the most competitive of any adjoining desert floras also present. The terrain in shortgrass steppes is usually a plain because the annual precipitation is too low to induce extensive water erosional patterns.

The most prominent global semiarid zone is the Eurasian steppes, which extend from Hungary well into Siberia. This extensive grassland also has a shrub component, of which species of the genus *Artemisia* are prominent members.

The North American steppe is the Great Plains, which occurs in the lee of the Rocky Mountains. This area is grassland, rather than desert, because of the incursion of limited levels of moisture from the Gulf of Mexico. Although the grasses of the Great Plains are short—generally less than three centimeters—they are abundant and nutritious. Furthermore, the nutrients in the species of short-grass cure in the aboveground leaves rather than the roots. Therefore, this grassland could be grazed throughout the year and supported enormous numbers of bison and pronghorns as well as their predators.

The Great Plains intergrade into each of the North American desert formations.—James R. Estes

See also **AN INTRODUCTION TO DESERTS; ARTEMISIA; DESERT GRASSLAND; DESERTS; GRASSES; GRASSLAND; GREAT AMERICAN DESERT; PRAIRIE; PRONGHORN; SAGEBRUSH; SAVANNA; SEMIDESERT; XEROPHYLLOUS FOREST**

Further Reading

Weaver, J. E., and F. W. Albertson. 1956. *Grasslands of the Great Plains*. Lincoln, Neb.: Johnsen Publishing Company.

SEMIDESERT

Vegetation type intermediate between grasslands and deserts. These ecotones may be dominated by the most competitive of the xerophytic desert grasses or shrubs and the most drought-tolerant species from the shortgrass prairie. Precipitation is either lower than in the shortgrass prairie or very sporadic with periodic long droughts. Although annual rainfall is lower than in true grasslands, it is sufficient to provide vegetative cover, and hence the area is not a true desert. Many authors consider the Great Basin to be a semidesert because the area has extensive plant cover. However, many areas within this sagebrush-dominated region, such as the Alvord Desert, fall well within the strictest definition of a desert vegetation type.—James R. Estes

See also **AN INTRODUCTION TO DESERTS; ARTEMISIA; DESERT GRASSLAND; DESERTS; GRASSES; GRASSLAND; GREAT AMERICAN DESERT; PRAIRIE; PRONGHORN; SAGEBRUSH; SAVANNA; SEMIARID ZONES; XEROPHYLLOUS FOREST**

Further Reading

Neilson, R. P. 1991. Climatic constraints and issues of scale controlling regional biomes. *In* M. M. Holland, P. G. Risser, and R. J. Naiman, eds., *Ecotones: The Role of Landscape Boundaries in the Management and Restoration of Changing Environments*, 31–51. New York: Chapman and Hall.

West, N. E. 1988. Intermountain deserts, shrub steppes, and woodlands. *In* M. G. Barbour and W. D. Billings, eds., *North American Terrestrial Vegetation*, 209–230. Cambridge: Cambridge University Press.

SERVAL

Small cat (family Felidae, mammalian order Carnivora) that generally weighs less than 15 kilograms and is restricted in distribution to Africa south of 20° north latitude. The serval is largely absent from extreme southern Africa, and an isolated population that occurred in northwestern Africa is believed to be extinct. Servals are dark golden brown above and paler below with either dark spots or stripes on the back. They occur in a wide variety of habitats, including savannas, open woodlands, and gallery forests; they do not occur in dense forest. Servals require proximity to water and a cover of dense vegetation, and they are especially common near the vegetated banks of streams. There are two morphs or ecotypes of servals—the "serval" type and the "servaline" type. The serval type is larger, spotted, and the most arid adapted. It is more likely to occur in dry grasslands, bush, or open savannas. The servaline type is smaller and darker and is a forest species. Servals are nocturnal and solitary.

Servals prey on small mammals and birds and have also been observed to consume lizards and some grasses and fruits. They have the longest legs for their size of all the cats, an adaptation for hunting in tall grass. They often take poultry from populated regions and are heavily hunted as pests. They are also hunted for their skins. Females give birth to two to four young, often in abandoned aardvark burrows. Although not endangered, servals are heavily persecuted and appear to be declining in numbers throughout their range.—Thomas E. Lacher, Jr.

See also **AFRICA, DESERTS OF; CARNIVORES; CATS; MAMMALS; PREDATORS; SAHARA DESERT**

Further Reading

Dorst, J., and P. Dandelot. 1980. *A Field Guide to the Larger Mammals of Africa.* London: Collins.

Haltenorth, T., and H. Diller. 1980. *A Field Guide to the Mammals of Africa, Including Madagascar.* London: Collins.

Kingdon, J. 1989. *East African Mammals: An Atlas of Evolution in Africa.* Vol. 3A. Chicago: University of Chicago Press.

Nowak, R. M. 1991. *Walker's Mammals of the World.* 5th ed. Baltimore: Johns Hopkins University Press.

SHEEP

Major herd animal (genus *Ovis*; subfamily Caprinae, family Bovidae, order Artiodactyla) found in desert regions and represented by diverse domesticated stock and six wild species. Of the wild species, the argali (*Ovis ammon*), mouflon (*Ovis aries*), bighorn (*Ovis canadensis*), and urial (*Ovis vignei*) occur in arid regions.

The wild species of sheep vary in their pelage color and texture within a species as well as between species. Rams are larger than ewes and have curved horns that can approach two meters in length. Ewes are hornless or have horns that are much smaller (10 centimeters) and less curved. Sheep are quite adaptable in their food selection but graze mostly on grasses and herbaceous plants. Sheep are gregarious, sometimes coming together to form herds of more than 100 individuals. However, males and females form separate herds. Herds of ewes also include lambs and juvenile rams. Rams and ewes come together only during the mating season. Rams establish dominance and breeding rights by ritualized matches of head butting. A dominant male separates a breeding female from the ewe herd and mates with her until she is no longer willing to continue. A rutting ram will protect a breeding female from other males. Wild sheep are threatened by competition from domesticated sheep and goats, habitat alteration, hunting, and diseases and parasites introduced with livestock.

Domesticated sheep were derived from mouflon sheep more than 10,000 years ago in the Near East. Other species of wild sheep may have contributed to some local variants, but all domesticated breeds share a common ancestry with mouflon sheep. Sheep are able to survive harsh environmental conditions, poor food, and water scarcity. This hardiness, their ability to exploit regions of low productivity, and the wealth of resources that they can provide make them very useful to inhabitants of deserts. Products derived from sheep include meat, wool, hides, and milk. There are more than 800 breeds of domesticated sheep. Most are adapted to their local environments and to fill the particular needs of the local people. Breeds of sheep vary considerably in their shapes, size, color, wool texture, ears, and presence or shape of horns. Herds of domesticated sheep compete with native grazing species and may alter native vegetation. The potential to alter the vegetation of an area has implicated sheep and goats in the expansion of several deserts around the world.—Rob Channell

See also **ARGALI; AWASSI SHEEP; BARBARY SHEEP; BIGHORN SHEEP; DESERT PEOPLES; DOMESTIC ANIMALS; GOAT; MAMMALS; MIDDLE EAST, DESERTS OF; MOUFLON SHEEP; OVERGRAZING; UNGULATES**

Further Reading

Cole, H. H., and M. Ronning. 1974. *Animal Agriculture: The Biology of Domestic Animals and Their Use by Man.* San Francisco: Freeman.

Isaac, E. 1970. *Geography of Domestication.* Englewood Cliffs, N.J.: Prentice-Hall.

SHIVERING

Muscular contractions used to liberate heat rather than to effect movement. There are three major ways that animals increase heat production (metabolism) for thermoregulation: movement, shivering, and nonshivering thermogenesis. In shivering motor units of groups of antagonistic skeletal (locomotory) muscles are stimulated by nervous signals from the hypothalamus in the brain. Because the muscle contractions are improperly timed and the antagonistic muscles work against one another, no net movement or locomotion occurs. However, the process warms the body because the inefficient contractions release heat from the hydrolysis of ATP (adenosine triphosphate), which provides the chemical energy for the contractions.

Shivering is practiced by insects and vertebrates. Many flying insects warm up prior to flight through shivering contractions of thoracic flight muscles until the body temperature is high enough to sustain flight. Honeybees also practice shivering thermogenesis to keep the hive warm. At least one ectothermic vertebrate, the brooding female Indian python, also uses shivering thermogenesis. The python uses shivering to provide warmth for incubating its eggs, around which it coils.

All endothermic vertebrates practice shivering to raise heat production at air temperatures below their thermal neutral temperature. Shivering is evoked in endotherms by a decrease in core or skin temperatures, and it need not be visible to be effective. Vigorous shivering can increase metabolism by four to five times the resting values. However, the efficiency of shivering in terms of maintaining body temperature is much less, which means the amount of heat transferred to the air must increase during shivering (i.e., insulation must decrease). The major cause of decreased insulation is increased connective heat loss caused by body movement, coupled with increased circulation to skeletal muscles near the body surface.—David S. Hinds

See also **BAT; CLOTHING; DEHYDRATION; ENDOTHERMY; ESTIVATION; HEAT BALANCE; HEAT EXCHANGE; HEAT STRESS; HEATSTROKE; HIBERNATION; HUMAN PHYSIOLOGY IN DESERTS; HUMMINGBIRD; HYPERTHERMIA; HYPOTHERMIA; KIDNEY FUNCTION, DESERT RODENTS; KIDNEYS; METABOLISM; PERSPIRATION; PHYSIOLOGY; RENAL PAPILLA; SALT; SUNBURN; SUNSTROKE; SURVIVAL IN DESERTS; THERMOREGULATION; TORPOR; TRANSPIRATION; WATER BALANCE**

Further Reading

Carlson, L. D., and A. C. L. Hsieh. 1974. Temperature and humidity. Pt. A: Cold. *In* N. B. Slonim, ed., *Environmental Physiology*, 61–84. St. Louis: Mosby.

Eckert, R. 1988. *Animal Physiology: Adaptation and Environment.* 3d ed. New York: Freeman.

Hill, R. W., and G. A. Wyse. 1989. *Animal Physiology.* 2d ed. New York: Harper and Row.

Withers, P. C. 1992. *Comparative Animal Physiology.* Philadelphia: Saunders.

SHOSHONI. *See* DESERT PEOPLES

SHREW

Member of a diverse group (22 genera, 246 species) of small (3.5–29 centimeters), invertebrate-eating mammals in the family Soricidae (order Insectivora) which occur throughout North America, the northern part of South America, and across Europe, Asia, India, and Africa. Shrews have long, pointed noses, small eyes and ears, and well-developed senses of hearing and smell. Shrews generally communicate by touch, but vocalizations are also used; some species (genera *Blarina* and *Sorex*) use ultrasound. Their life span is generally about one year.

Most shrews inhabit forests and grasslands, but some occur in semideserts and deserts. Several species live in water; webbed feet and fringes of stiff hairs on the tail, feet, and digits are some of the adaptations for an aquatic life. There are few desert-inhabiting shrews. *Notiosorex crawfordi* is distributed in the south central and southwestern United States and northern and central Mexico and occurs in the Chihuahuan, Mohave, and Sonoran deserts. Throughout its distribution *Notiosorex* uses many types of cover but is frequently found in the dens of woodrats, *Neotoma*. In Eurasia and Africa some species of *Crocidura* are adapted to desert life. The piebald shrew, *Diplomesodon*, which lives in the sandy soil of the Turkestan Desert, has a short tail, long claws for digging, and fringes of hair on the feet and digits that increase the surface area and aid in propelling it through the sand.

Shrews are voracious eaters and feed both day and night. Their high metabolic rate requires that they consume large amounts of food in relation to their body size. Desert-adapted shrews have a lower metabolic rate than those that inhabit forests. Some desert shrews can lower their body temperature when food is scarce, are more efficient at dissipating heat, and may enter torpor during the hottest parts of the day.—Janet K. Braun

See also **AFRICA, DESERTS OF; ASIA, DESERTS OF; CHIHUAHUAN DESERT; ENDOTHERMY; ESTIVATION; MAMMALS; METABOLISM; MOJAVE DESERT; SONORAN DESERT; SOUTH AFRICA, DESERTS OF; SPAIN, DESERTS OF; TORPOR; VENOM; WOODRAT**

Further Reading

Armstrong, D. M., and Jones, J. K., Jr. (1972) Notiosorex crawfordi. *Mammalian Species* 17:1–5.

Churchfield, S. 1990. *The Natural History of Shrews.* Ithaca: Comstock.

Grzimek's Encyclopedia of Mammals. Vol. 1. 1990. New York: McGraw-Hill.

Macdonald, D., ed. 1984. *The Encyclopedia of Mammals.* New York: Facts on File.

SHRIKE

Fairly small to moderate-sized carnivorous songbird (order Passeriformes). The taxonomic limits of the shrikes are unclear. Some authorities include the true shrikes, helmet shrikes, and bush shrikes as subfamiles within the family Laniidae (Laniinae, Prionopinae, and Malaconotinae, respectively). Other taxonomists consider the helmet shrikes to be a distinct family. The true shrikes are composed of some 28–30 species in three genera found in Africa, Eurasia, Papua New Guinea, and North America. The bush shrike group contains 39–44 species almost wholly confined to the Afrotropics. Approximately 9 species of helmet shrikes are recognized, ranging throughout Africa south of the Sahara. The vanga shrikes, with about 13 species in nine genera, are restricted to Madagascar.

Regardless of their taxonomic rank, it is clear that these groups share a number of ecological attributes, including the fact that a number of taxa within each group inhabit arid environments. For example, the fiscals, true shrikes of the genus *Lanius*, occur in dry thorn brush of northeastern Africa. The three-streaked tchagra (*Tchagra jamesi*), a bush shrike, and the grey-crested helmet shrike (*Prionops poliolophus*) also inhabit dry thorn scrub in northeastern and eastern Africa, respectively. Finally, the Lafresnaye's vanga (*Xenopirostris xenopirostris*) is an example of a vanga shrike that inhabits arid brushland of southwestern Madagascar.

Shrikes range in total length from 15 to 38 centimeters. True shrikes are predominantly gray or brown, often with a black mask. Bush shrikes generally have brightly colored plumage of black, black and white, or with yellow, red, or green. Most vanga shrikes are metallic black above and white below. Helmet shrikes are usually boldly marked with brown or black and white. The majority of shrikes do not exhibit sexual dimorphism in coloration, although in a few species (e.g., many bush shrikes) the sexes are markedly different. The legs and feet are strong, the latter equipped with sharp claws for grasping prey.

The bill of most taxa is characteristically robust and hooked. However, vanga shrikes show an exceptional diversity of bill shapes and sizes, ranging from the "typical" laterally compressed shrike shape through a long down-curved bill; foraging behaviors are correspondingly variable. The majority of shrike taxa are insectivorous, although some true shrikes will also eat small vertebrates. Shrikes are often highly visible, seen perching at the top of bushes or trees to scan for potential prey. The true shrikes search for prey animals from such a vantage and then swoop down on them to make the capture. Many of the true shrikes impale their prey on thorns and for this reason are sometimes referred to as "butcher birds."

The breeding biology of many taxa is still undescribed; this is especially true of most of the vanga and helmet shrikes. Those species that have been studied display a range of breeding systems, including apparent monogamy, polygyny, and cooperative breeding (e.g., with other adults birds helping at the nest). Nests, placed in bushes or trees, are usually cup-shaped structures constructed of various types of vegetation. Clutch sizes range from two to seven.—Stephen C. Lougheed

See also **AFRICA, DESERTS OF; BIRDS; CHIHUAHUAN DESERT; MADAGASCAR, DESERTS OF; MEXICO,**

DESERTS OF; MOJAVE DESERT; NESTS, BIRD; SEMIARID ZONES; SONORAN DESERT; XEROPHYLLOUS FOREST

Further Reading

Bent, A. C. 1950. Life histories of North American wagtails, shrikes, vireos and their allies. *U.S. National Museum Bulletin* 197.

Cramp, S., and C. M. Perrins, eds. 1993. *Handbook of the Birds of Europe, the Middle East and North Africa: The Birds of the Western Palearctic*. Vol. 7. Oxford: Oxford University Press.

Yosef, R., and B. Pinshow. 1988. Polygyny in the northern shrike (*Lanius excubitor*) in Israel. *Auk* 105:581–582.

Zack, S. 1986. Behaviour and breeding biology of the cooperatively breeding grey-backed fiscal shrike, *Lanius excubitorius*. *Ibis* 128:214–233.

SHRIMP, DESERT

Crustaceans (phylum Arthropoda, class Crustacea) that are further divided into the subclass Branchiopoda, consisting of the fairy shrimp and brine shrimp (order Anostraca), tadpole or shield shrimp (order Notostraca), and clam shrimp (order Diplostraca, suborder Conchostraca). All are fairly small, ranging in length from several millimeters to several centimeters. Paradoxical as it may seem, shrimp occur in deserts worldwide, although their conspicuous presence is limited to periods when surface water is available, either in the form of ephemeral ponds or permanent saline lakes. During periods of surface water absence, desert shrimp exist as heat- and desiccation-resistant "eggs," which are actually early embryonic stages encased in a protective "shell," buried in the bottoms of dry playas (salt flats) and clay pans. There they may rest for months or even years until rainfall and runoff again fill their ephemeral aquatic habitats, stimulating "hatching" and renewed development to adult stages.

Fairy shrimp are dwellers in fresh to brackish water of lower salinities and therefore are present as adults in only the earlier stages of ephemeral desert waters. As these waters recede by evaporation and salinity increases the adults die, leaving their eggs to settle to the bottom, awaiting the next return of freshwater. As salinities increase fairy shrimp may be replaced by the salinity-tolerant brine shrimp that commonly occur in desert waters that approach or exceed the salt concentration of seawater. The salinity tolerance record is apparently held by an Australian brine shrimp that can withstand salinities up to 10 times the concentration of seawater. The dormant eggs of brine shrimp are commonly sold in pet stores and catalogs as "Sea Monkeys," whose development may be stimulated and observed by placing them in a saline solution; they also are commonly available as adults for feeding aquarium fish, either in the living or the frozen state. Both adult fairy shrimp and brine shrimp look like little shrimp, except that they swim upside down as they move through the water.

Tadpole or shield shrimp look like miniature versions of the marine horseshoe crab, with flattened head shields and two or three compound eyes mounted dorsally near the front of the shield. They are primarily inhabitants of ephemeral waters and seem to have remarkable powers of dispersal, which must be due to wind or waterfowl carrying their drought-resistant eggs to new temporary pools of water. This author and his family saw developing shield shrimp in temporary pockets of water following rainstorms on the sheer face of Uluru (Ayers Rock), a sandstone monolith in central Australia that rises almost vertically about 1,000 meters from the surrounding desert floor.

Clam shrimp, as their name implies, are encased as adults in a pair of leathery valves, strongly resembling a small shrimp packed into an equally small clamshell. The enclosing valves must serve as protection from predators, for, in addition to ephemeral waters, these shrimp are found in less temporary waters, together with predatory fish and other aquatic animals.—Richard E. MacMillen

See also **ANIMAL ADAPTATIONS; ARTHROPODS; AUSTRALIA, DESERTS OF; DORMANCY; FLAMINGO; FLOOD; PLAYA; PRECIPITATION; SALINIZATION; SALT BALANCE; SALT PAN; WATER BALANCE; WATER HOLE**

Further Reading

Barnes, R. D. 1980. *Invertebrate Zoology*. 4th ed. Philadelphia: W. D. Saunders.

Hadley, N. F., ed. 1975. *Environmental Physiology of Desert Organisms*. Stroudsburg, Pa.: Dowden, Hutchinson, and Ross.

Van Oosterzee, P. 1991. *The Centre*. Balgowlah, NSW: Reed.

Williams, W. D. 1980. *Australian Freshwater Life*. Melbourne: Macmillan.

SHRUBS

Woody plants that have more than one main stem and that are shorter than three meters in height. The shoots remain viable during the nongrowing season, and in the spring or the start of the wet season, the buds burst and leaves and flowers are produced. The buds contain a meristematic tissue (a region of cell division that produces new growth); therefore, the stems grow longer at the tip. As with trees, the stems grow in diameter through the action of a vascular cambium, which is also a meristem. (Plants such as cacti and bamboo are sometimes considered shrubs, but actually they defy the age-old classification of higher plants into trees, shrubs, and herbs.)

Shrubs are the dominant plants of North American desert communities and of many of the world's deserts. Generally there is insufficient precipitation in deserts to support a true forest, unless abundant groundwater is present. In cold deserts, such as the Great Basin, the shrubs tend to be silvery green because the leaf epidermis is covered with long, tangled hairs that reflect light. In warm deserts shrubs are often armed with spines or thorns and have small, green, resinous leaves. These are adaptations to prevent against water loss and grazing.

Many desert shrubs produce chemicals that deter grazing. They also produce chemicals that inhibit the germination and growth of competing plants (allelopathy). Allelopathy often is the cause of the wide dispersal pattern of shrubs in desert habitats.

Important shrubs of the American deserts include *Acacia* (which may grow into trees), creosote bush, mesquite (which may grow into trees), ocotillo, paloverde (which may grow into trees), rabbit brush, and sagebrush.—James R. Estes

See also **ASIA, DESERTS OF; CHENOPODIACEAE; GREAT BASIN DESERT; HALOPHYTES; LEGUMES; MESQUITE; PALOVERDE; PLANT ADAPTATIONS; PLANTS; PERENNIAL PLANTS; PSAMMOPHYTIC SCRUB; PSAMMOPHYTES; ROOTS**

Further Reading

Rice, E. L. 1984. *Allelopathy*. 2d ed. Orlando: Academic Press.

Rost, T. L., M. G. Barbour, R. M. Thornton, T. E. Weier, and C. R. Stocking. 1984. *Botany*. 2d ed. New York: Wiley.

North American sidewinder rattlesnake (*Crotalus cerastes*). (Photo: L. J. Vitt)

SIBERIA, DESERTS OF. *See* ASIA, DESERTS OF

SIDEWINDER

Species of relatively small (up to about 80 centimeters snout-vent length) desert rattlesnake (*Crotalus cerastes*; family Viperidae) that uses a characteristic sidewinding locomotion. It is light in color, often nearly white, with darker blotches distributed down the dorsal surface. A ridge of scales over each eye gives the impression of a small "horn," hence the common name horned rattlesnake.

The sidewinder is most frequently found in desert flats and arroyos, often on sand. It appears most common in areas of fine, windblown sand such as dunes and is frequently associated with mammal burrows, including those of kangaroo rats (genus *Dipodomys*). In areas of fine-grained sand sidewinders leave a characteristic imprint that allows them to be tracked easily. The tracks result from the type of locomotion that characterizes this species of snake and several others in similar habitats of the Old World. One end of the body is lifted off the sand and set down a short distance to the side of the original position. The snake moves through the points of contact with the ground such that entire prints of the snake's body in the form of a *J* are left in the sand in a series of parallel tracks. Most activity occurs at night when individuals move from site to site in search of good places to ambush prey. Food includes lizards and small mammals, which are killed by envenomation. During the day sidewinders either retreat to rodent burrows or partially bury themselves in the sand. These snakes are poisonous but only bite humans in self-defense.

Sidewinders occur in northern Mexico and the southwestern United States. A morphologically and ecologically similar snake species, *Cerastes cerastes*, the horned viper, occurs in deserts of northern Africa.—Laurie J. Vitt

See also **ADDER; CERASTES; CROTALUS; DEFENSIVE ADAPTATIONS, ANIMALS; POISONOUS ANIMALS; RATTLESNAKE; SNAKES; VENOM**

Further Reading

Brown, T. W., and H. B. Lillywhite. 1992. Autecology of the Mojave desert sidewinder (*Crotalus cerastes cerastes*) at the Kelso Dunes, Mojave Desert, California. *In* J. A. Campbell and E. D. Brodie, Jr., eds., *Biology of Pitvipers*, 279–308. Tyler, Tex.: Selva.

Secor, S. M. 1992. A preliminary analysis of the movement and home range size of the sidewinder, *Crotalus cerastes*. *In* J. A. Campbell and E. D. Brodie, Jr., eds., *Biology of Pitvipers*, 389–393. Tyler, Tex.: Selva.

SILT. *See* SOILS, DESERT, SILT

SINAI. *See* MIDDLE EAST, DESERTS OF

SIND DESERT. *See* INDO-PAKISTAN DESERTS

SISTAN DESERT. *See* AFGHANISTAN, DESERTS OF

SNAKES

Elongate, limbless vertebrates with a spectacle (a transparent scale) covering the eye (if present), no external eardrums, relatively short tail, scales on the body, dry skin, and a long, forked tongue. Snakes are in fact an evolutionary lineage within lizards, believed to be most closely related evolutionarily to monitor lizards. The actual number of snake "families" varies depending on the authority, but approximately 14 families are recognized by most herpetologists. The primary problem in understanding relationships of snakes at the family level is a paucity of good fossil material. Snakes are known to date to the early Cretaceous period, making them among the most recently evolved reptilian group. Their recent diversification is the best evidence for their relative success in environments saturated with highly diversified lizards, amphibians,

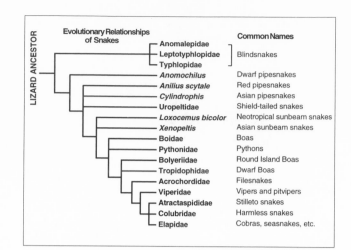

Evolutionary relationships of the snakes of the world. (Redrawn from Greene 1997.)

mammals, and birds. One likely reason for this success is that snakes, as a group, feed only on animals, and they are capable of eating large prey and fasting for long periods. Most other species of animals in the various environments occupied by snakes are unlikely to be competitors but are likely to be prey for at least some snake species.

Ecological diversity of snakes is astonishing considering the relative lack of morphological diversity within the group. Two families, the Hydrophiidae and Laticaudidae, are restricted to oceans of the world, with most species actually giving birth to live young at sea. The highest diversity of sea snakes is in shallow seas of the tropical Pacific region, but one species is truly pelagic, with a distribution that includes the west coast of North, central, and South America. All of the sea snakes (family Elapidae) are highly venomous, producing neurotoxic venoms that are injected through fixed fangs in the upper jaw. Three families of subterranean blind snakes (Typhlopidae, Leptotyphlopidae, and Anomalepidae) are predators on social insects; they live in the chambers of underground termite and ant nests and feed on eggs, larvae, and pupae. They produce chemicals that protect them from attacks by the insects. Most blind snakes are small-bodied and have poorly developed eyes. Boas and pythons are among the largest snakes in the world, and the longest terrestrial vertebrate is a snake. Whether the longest snake is a reticulated python or an anaconda remains uncertain, but both can exceed nine meters. The aquatic anaconda is certainly the largest species in terms of total mass. Within boas and pythons there is considerable ecological diversity, with species living below ground (fossorial), in water, on land, and in trees. Boas and pythons are perhaps best known for their ability to swallow very large prey, including deer, pigs, and, on rare occasions, humans. The most diverse group of snakes is the family Colubridae, with about 1,800 known species (66 percent of all known snake species).

The most common snakes occurring in deserts of both the Old and the New World are in the families Colubridae, Viperidae, Leptotyphlopidae, Boidae, Pythonidae, and Elapidae. Although most snakes in New World deserts are colubrids, most in Australian deserts are elapids, indicating very different evolutionary histories of the snake faunas of these areas. Probably the single most important feature of the biology of snakes that has permitted their success in desert environments is the ability to withstand long periods without food: some species can survive without nourishment for a year or more. Most snakes in deserts are nocturnal, thus avoiding the heat and desiccation associated with diurnal activity. Some species, such as banded sand snakes (*Chilomeniscus cinctus*), literally swim through the sand and spend most of their lives under the surface. Still others, like the various species of blind snakes (family Leptotyphlopidae), live within social insect colonies, thereby avoiding extremes of desert environments. Although snake faunas of deserts throughout the world have originated independently of one another for the most part, there are some striking convergences in morphology, behavior, and ecology that are evident when faunas are compared. One of the most unusual involves the set of adaptations to life in a habitat composed of fine-grained sand. Snakes on different continents have independently evolved similar strategies for living in such dunes. A comparison of sidewinders (North America), horned adders (southwestern Africa), and horned vipers (Arabian Peninsula) shows that these species are similar in size and coloration, use the unusual sidewinding locomotion, and rapidly disappear into the sand when threatened.—Laurie J. Vitt

See also **ADDER; CERASTES; COBRA; CORAL SNAKE; CROTALUS; PIT VIPER; POISONOUS ANIMALS; PREDATION; RATTLESNAKE; REPTILES; SIDEWINDER; VENOM**

Further Reading

Greene, H. W. 1997. *Snakes: the Evolution of Mystery in Nature.* Berkeley: University of California Press.

Mara, W. P. 1996. *Desert Snakes of North America.* Neptune City, N.J.: T. F. H. Publications.

Mehrtens, J. M. 1987. *Living Snakes of the World in Color.* New York: Sterling.

Seigel, R. A., and J. T. Collins. 1993. *Snakes: Ecology and Behavior.* New York: Macmillan.

Seigel, R. A., J. T. Collins, and S. S. Novak. 1987. *Snakes: Ecology and Evolutionary Biology.* New York: Macmillan.

Shine, R. 1991. *Australian Snakes: A Natural History.* Sydney: Reed.

Stoops, E. D. 1997. *Snakes and Other Reptiles of the Southwest.* Phoenix: Golden West.

SNOW

Atmospheric moisture that reaches the earth in solid form as crystalline water, formed via condensation of atmospheric water vapor when air temperatures are below freezing. The ice crystals are prismatic in form and have a wide variety of shapes. Snow precipitates in two ways, as individual crystals or as flakes formed from an amalgam of a large number of individual smaller crystals. At times snow may fall and melt as it reaches warmer layers of air, thus reaching the surface of the earth as rain. At other times raindrops may freeze, forming a mix of water and snow that reaches the earth as sleet. (In the United States "sleet" is used exclusively to describe rainwater that is partially frozen, whereas in other parts of the world "sleet" is used to describe a mix of snow and rain as well as partially frozen rainwater). Snow in subtropical deserts is an uncommon occurrence and is unknown in tropical drylands. However, it may be common in temperate deserts at high latitudes, such as the Patagonian Desert, or in montane deserts, such as the Andean puna or the great high-altitude deserts of Asia. There snow may be a primary source of precipitation for desert organisms.—Alberto I. J. Vich and Juana Susana Barroso

See also **ALTIPLANO; ANDES; AN INTRODUCTION TO DESERTS; ASIA, DESERTS OF; DESERTS; DESERTS, MONTANE; DESERTS, TEMPERATE; GREAT BASIN DESERT**

SODIUM. *See* SALT

SOILS, DESERT

Complex and dynamic body of material overlying the earth's crust containing living material and capable of supporting life. In some cases the upper boundary of the soil is delimited by the atmosphere; in other cases, by superficial waters; and at its sides, by other soils, ice, or deep waters. Its lower level is determined by the depth reached by plant roots. Soils are a complex medium characterized by their own internal atmosphere, elemental minerals, particular flora and fauna in different parts of the world, and a characteristic water regimen.

Soil is a dynamic medium because it owes its structure to continually changing and interacting environmental factors. Soil both develops and evolves. Its prime constituent is the parent material, which is altered by climate and vegetation and broken down into smaller particles. There are interactive effects between the minerals deriving from the breakdown of the parent material and organic matter that is developed in the biosphere. When this evolution is completed it gives rise to a stable equilibrium state in which the organomineral complexes, with their physical, chemical, and biological properties, are well defined and give the soil its individuality. Like all natural systems, soils are polyphasic and heterogeneous, with properties that are not easily described within single phases but which also include interphases. The soil's phases are (1) the solid phase, which consists of organic particles and minerals of different sizes and shapes that can be encountered as individual small particles or aggregates; (2) the liquid phase, which is the soil water that carries many materials in solution; and (3) the gaseous phase, which is the air in the soil that has a composition similar to that of the atmosphere, frequently with lower levels of oxygen and higher levels of carbon dioxide. Soil is also a dispersed system, particularly as its solid phase is composed of many particles that have a huge surface area. The disposition of the particles determines the porous space of the soil through which air and water are transmitted or retained. The liquid and gaseous phases of the soil are also variable in time and space.

Soil formation is ultimately based on rocks that are eroding due to the forces of water and biological processes. These processes lead to the successive breakdown of the rocks and the formation of smaller particles arranged in successive layers of the soil. These materials are very low in organic content and contain numerous rock fragments that give rise to the young soil. Continual action of these factors develops a transformation and a mixing of these elements. The movement of soluble and colloidal substances between the layers enriches some of them with those materials and causes other areas to become poor. This leads to the stratification of the soil into different layers, known as horizons, and the development of a characteristic soil profile, which is a set of horizons.

These horizons may be well differentiated such that they are described by letters A, B, and C. In the A horizon, which is the most superficial, the soil is characterized by the accumulation of organic matter; it is also the zone of maximum biological activity and removal of extremely fine materials. The B horizon is the site of accumulation of elements from the upper horizon as well as from the lower horizon. The C horizon is characterized by a greater alteration of the underlying rock.

In dry regions soils are poorly evolved, poorly developed, very superficial, and generally closely allied to the underlying rock material. Generally the decomposition of rock is based on mechanical factors, rather than biological ones, and desert soils have very low organic matter, particularly because of the small amount of rainfall and the limit this places on plant diversity and abundance. Desert soils are often brilliantly colored, reflecting their mineral origin, and they show little or no color difference between horizons.—Alberto I. J. Vich and Juana Susana Barroso

See also **DESERT SLOPES; FIELD CAPACITY OF SOILS; GROUNDWATER; LITHOSPHERE; MINERALS; NUTRIENTS; SOILS, DESERT, ARENOSOL; SOILS, DESERT, ARIDOSOL; SOILS, DESERT, ARKOSIC SAND; SOILS, DESERT, CALCAREOUS; SOILS, DESERT, CALCRETE; SOILS, DESERT, CALICHE; SOILS, DESERT, CLAY; SOILS, DESERT, FLUVISOL; SOILS, DESERT, LITHOSOL; SOILS, DESERT, LOESS; SOILS, DESERT, PEDOCAL; SOILS, DESERT, PODSOL; SOILS, DESERT, SILT; SOIL TAXONOMY; WEATHERING, DESERT; WIND EROSION; WIND TRANSPORT**

Further Reading

Baber, S. A. 1984. *Soil Nutrient Bioavailability: A Mechanistic Approach*. New York: Wiley.

Bates, R. L., ed. 1987. *Glossary of Geology*. 3d ed. Alexandria, Va.: American Geological Institute.

Cooke, R., A. Warren, and A. Goudie. 1993. *Desert Geomorphology*. London: University College London Press.

Dochaufour, P. 1978. *Manual de edafología*. Barcelona: Toray-Masson.

Fuller, W. H. 1974. Desert soils. *In* G. W. Brown Jr., ed., *Desert Biology: Special Topics on the Physical and Biological Aspects of Arid Regions*, 2:31–101. New York: Academic Press.

Moore, G. W. 1978. *Dictionary of Geography: Definitions and Explanation of Terms Used in Physical Geography*. New York: Harper and Row.

The New Encyclopaedia Britannica. 15th ed. 1974. Soils. Vol. 16:1018–1028. Chicago: University of Chicago Press.

Suh-Shiaw, Lo. 1992. *Glossary of Hydrology*. Taipei: Sheng Te.

Walter, H., and E. Stadelmann. 1974. A new approach to the water relations of desert plants. *In* G. W. Brown Jr., ed., *Desert Biology: Special Topics on the Physical and Biological Aspects of Arid Regions*, 2:213–310. New York: Academic Press.

SOILS, DESERT, ARENOSOL

Soils having a loamy sand or coarser texture with slight to moderate profile development to a depth of at least 100 centimeters from the surface or to bedrock, whichever is shallower; one of eleven orders of the U.S. Soil Classification System. Arenosols also contain less than 35 percent rock fragments with diameters greater than two millimeters. The name is derived from the Latin word *arena*, meaning "sand." Shifting sands and active dunes are not included in this group. Arenosols have no soil horizons diagnostic of other soils, except a moderate alteration of the surface horizon or a bleached horizon below the surface horizon. They may also have a dense horizon cemented with silica or a salty horizon, if it occurs at a depth greater than 50 centimeters. The sandy nature of these soils dominates their behavior and characteristics. These soils have been recognized as a major soil group in the *World Reference Base of Soil Resources*, developed by the International Society of Soil Science. Arenosols were recognized as coarse-textured soils on the *Soil Map of the World*, developed by the Food and Agriculture Organization (FAO) of the United Nations. They are classified as Psamments or Psammaquents in the *Soil Taxonomy* of the U.S. Department of Agriculture, Natural Resource Conservation Service. Arenosols are widely distributed and have been estimated to cover 900 million hectares, or 7 percent of the land surface, by FAO. Although arenosols can be found in very arid to very humid climates, as well as in cold to hot climates, they are usually found in arid and semiarid regions. Extensive areas of arenosols are found in South America, Africa, the Middle East, the northwest region of the Indian subcontinent, and Australia.—Ted M. Zobeck and Dan R. Upchurch

See also **DESERT SLOPES; FIELD CAPACITY OF SOILS; GROUNDWATER; LITHOSPHERE; MINERALS; NUTRIENTS; SOILS, DESERT; SOILS, DESERT, ARIDOSOL; SOILS, DESERT, ARKOSIC SAND; SOILS, DESERT, CALCAREOUS; SOILS, DESERT, CALCRETE; SOILS, DESERT, CALICHE; SOILS, DESERT, CLAY; SOILS, DESERT, FLUVISOL; SOILS, DESERT, LITHOSOL; SOILS, DESERT, LOESS; SOILS, DESERT, PEDOCAL; SOILS, DESERT, PODSOL; SOILS, DESERT, SILT; SOIL TAXONOMY; WEATHERING, DESERT; WIND EROSION; WIND TRANSPORT**

Further Reading

FAO-UNESCO-ISRIC. 1990. *Soil Map of the World. Rev. Leg.* World Soil Resources Report No. 60. Rome: Food and Agriculture Organization of the United Nations.

Soil Survey Staff. 1975. *Soil Taxonomy: A Basic System of Soil Classification for Making and Interpreting Soil Surveys*. Agriculture Handbook No. 436, Soil Conservation Service, U.S. Department of Agriculture. Washington, D.C.: U.S. Government Printing Office.

Spaargaren, O. C. 1994. *World Reference Base for Soil Resources-Draft*. Wageningen/Rome: International Society of Soil Science/International Soil Reference and Information Center, Food and Agriculture Organization.

SOILS, DESERT, ARIDISOL

Mineral soils of arid regions that do not have water available to plants for long periods during the growing season; one of eleven soil orders of the U.S. Soil Classification System. These soils do not have water above the wilting points of plants for more than half the cumulative time when the soil is above 5°C at a depth of 50 centimeters. They also have no period of 90 consecutive days or more when water is available for plants and the soil temperature is greater than 8°C. Some aridisols have water at shallow depths that is not available to most plants because it is too salty. In addition, some aridisols are in semiarid regions but are dry due to slow water infiltration or runoff. Aridisols may occur in very cold to very warm climates. The surfaces of aridisols are generally light in color and have from a soft to a very hard consistency. The soil layers that develop in aridisols are formed by movement and accumulation of carbonates, salts, or clays, or by simple alteration of the original earthen parent material. Aridisols differ from other soils in desert environments because they have one or more characteristic horizons. In many soils horizons are cemented with carbonates, silica, or other agents. Some aridisols have complex horizons that were developed in different climates than exist at present. In the 1938 U.S. classification of soils, aridisols of hot regions were called Red Desert Soils, aridisols in temperate regions were Desert Soils, and aridisols in temperate to cool regions were Sierozems.—Ted M. Zobeck and Dan R. Upchurch

See also **DESERT SLOPES; FIELD CAPACITY OF SOILS; GROUNDWATER; LITHOSPHERE; MINERALS; NUTRIENTS; SOILS, DESERT; SOILS, DESERT, ARENOSOL; SOILS, DESERT, ARKOSIC SAND; SOILS, DESERT, CALCAREOUS; SOILS, DESERT, CALCRETE; SOILS, DESERT, CALICHE; SOILS, DESERT, CLAY; SOILS, DESERT, FLUVISOL; SOILS, DESERT, LITHOSOL; SOILS, DESERT, LOESS; SOILS, DESERT, PEDOCAL; SOILS, DESERT, PODSOL; SOILS, DESERT, SILT; SOIL TAXONOMY; WEATHERING, DESERT; WIND EROSION; WIND TRANSPORT**

Further Reading

Baldwin, M., C. E. Kellog, and J. Thorp. 1938. Soil classification. *In Soils and Men*, 979–1001. Washington, D.C.: U.S. Government Printing Office.

Buol, S. W., F. D. Hole, and R. J. McCracken. 1980. *Soil Genesis and Classification*. 2d ed. Ames: Iowa State University Press.

Nettleton, W. D., and F. F. Petersonk. 1983. Aridisols. *In* L. P. Wilding, N. E. Smeck, and G. F. Hall, eds., *Pedogenesis and Soil Taxonomy. 2. The Soil Orders*, 165–215. Developments in Soil Science, 11B. New York: Elsevier.

Soil Survey Staff. 1975. *Soil Taxonomy: A Basic System of Soil Classification for Making and Interpreting Soil Surveys*. Agriculture Handbook No. 436, Soil Conservation Service, U.S. Department of Agriculture. Washington, D.C.: U.S. Government Printing Office.

SOILS, DESERT, ARKOSIC SAND

Unconsolidated sediment composed of 85 percent or more individual grains 0.05–2 millimeters in diameter and derived from sandstone with more than 25 percent (but not commonly more than 50 percent) feldspar and 40–80 percent quartz (arkose). The individual grains often have a subangular or angular shape and are moderately to poorly sorted by size. Arkose is sandstone derived from acid igneous rocks (granites) that have undergone erosion under arid conditions. The chemical composition of arkosic sand suggests weak weathering because the sand is very similar in composition to the source material. The composition of weathered geologic material may depart significantly from the composition of the source material when it has undergone strong weathering conditions or has weathered for a long time. At stronger weathering intensities feldspar grains tend to weather to silicate clays.—Ted M. Zobeck and Dan R. Upchurch

See also **DESERT SLOPES; FELDSPAR; FIELD CAPACITY OF SOILS; GROUNDWATER; LITHOSPHERE; MINERALS; NUTRIENTS; SAND RAMP; SOILS, DESERT; SOILS, DESERT, ARIDOSOL; SOILS, DESERT, ARENOSOL; SOILS, DESERT, CALCAREOUS; SOILS, DESERT, CALCRETE; SOILS, DESERT, CALICHE; SOILS, DESERT, CLAY; SOILS, DESERT, FLUVISOL; SOILS, DESERT, LITHOSOL; SOILS, DESERT, LOESS; SOILS, DESERT, PEDOCAL; SOILS, DESERT, PODSOL; SOILS, DESERT, SILT; SOIL TAXONOMY; WEATHERING, DESERT; WIND EROSION; WIND TRANSPORT**

Further Reading

Chorley, R. J., S. A. Schumm, and D. E. Sugden. 1985. *Geomorphology*. New York: Methuen.

Press, F., and R. Siever. 1978. *Earth*. 2d ed. San Francisco: Freeman.

SOILS, DESERT, CALCAREOUS

Widely distributed carbonate-rich mineral soils occurring in desert, arid, semiarid, and Mediterranean-type climates. Calcareous soils contain sufficient calcium or magnesium carbonate in one or several horizons to produce effervescence when treated with cold dilute hydrochloric acid (HCL) (1:10 solution of concentrated hydrochloric acid). The amount of effervescence depends on the type, amount, and particle size of the carbonate material present. With cold dilute HCL, calcite will readily effervesce, whereas dolomite does not readily effervesce. Calcareous soils usually contain an amount of carbonate equivalent to 10–200 grams per kilogram of pure calcium carbonate. The carbonate in calcareous soils may originate from weathering of carbonate-rich geologic deposits or from soil formation processes. Calcification is the accumulation of carbonates in soils due to soil formation processes.

Calcareous soils often have subsoil horizons with substantial accumulations of carbonates, gypsum, or salts that may or may not be strongly cemented. Management of calcareous soils often presents enormous challenges as surface crusts limit plant emergence and water infiltration, subsoil horizons are cemented, and there is low nutrient and water availability for plants.—Ted M. Zobeck and Dan R. Upchurch

See also **DESERT SLOPES; FELDSPAR; FIELD CAPACITY OF SOILS; GROUNDWATER; LITHOSPHERE; MINERALS; NUTRIENTS; SAND RAMP; SOILS, DESERT; SOILS, DESERT, ARIDOSOL; SOILS, DESERT, ARENOSOL; SOILS, DESERT, ARKOSIC SAND; SOILS, DESERT, CALCRETE; SOILS, DESERT, CALICHE; SOILS, DESERT, CLAY; SOILS, DESERT, FLUVISOL; SOILS, DESERT, LITHOSOL; SOILS, DESERT, LOESS; SOILS, DESERT, PEDOCAL; SOILS, DESERT, PODSOL; SOILS, DESERT, SILT; SOIL TAXONOMY; WEATHERING, DESERT; WIND EROSION; WIND TRANSPORT**

Further Reading

Buol, S. W., F. D. Hole, and R. J. McCracken. 1980. *Soil Genesis and Classification*. 2d ed. Ames: Iowa State University Press.

Food and Agriculture Organization of the United Nations. 1973. *Calcareous Soils*. FAO Soils Bulletin No. 21. Rome.

SOILS, DESERT, CALCRETE

Zone of accumulation of almost pure calcium carbonate ($CaCO_3$) ranging in physical properties from powdery to highly indurated (hard). Calcretes are prominent features of many arid and semiarid regions and range in thickness from 15 centimeters to 10 meters. These accumulations form at the surface of the landscape or up to several meters below the soil surface. Magnesium may be substituted for calcium, to some degree.

Calcrete has been used interchangeably with caliche in describing zones of calcium carbonate accumulation. The term "calcrete" is usually reserved for material that is almost pure calcium carbonate and is indurated, whereas the term "caliche" is applied to any zone where the calcium carbonate equivalent is at least 15 percent within a 15-centimeter layer. The soil science term most closely related to calcrete is "petrocalcic horizon."

As with calcic horizons, two processes have been proposed for the formation of these layers. Weathered materials that originate near surface soil are moved in the soil solution and precipitate deeper in the profile, forming the zone of accumulation. Alternatively, the carbonates can originate from aeolian (windblown) sources and are deposited on the soil surface and moved downward in the soil solution. In both cases the depth of the layer is determined by the depth of infiltration of rain. It has also been proposed that calcretes form through the evaporation of water containing dissolved calcium carbonate that has risen from a water table by capillary action.

Calcrete formation generally is limited to regions such as deserts in which the annual evaporation exceeds annual precipitation. Also, because the formation of calcretes involves precipitation of calcium carbonate from the soil solution, they generally form on flat to gently sloping landscapes. On steeply sloped areas the calcium carbonate would be transported and deposited downslope. However, calcretes may be exposed through erosion and appear on steeply sloped areas that have been subsequently uplifted. In desert regions calcretes form a protective layer, or duricrust, of resistant material that tends to prevent erosion of the landscape and exposure of underlying layers. An example is the Ogallala caprock, which is an extensive calcrete with its southern edge located in West Texas and eastern New Mexico and extending over the high plains of the United States.—Dan R. Upchurch and Ted M. Zobeck

See also **DESERT SLOPES; FELDSPAR; FIELD CAPACITY OF SOILS; GROUNDWATER; LITHOSPHERE; MINERALS; NUTRIENTS; SAND RAMP; SOILS, DESERT; SOILS, DESERT, ARIDOSOL; SOILS, DESERT, ARENOSOL; SOILS, DESERT, ARKOSIC SAND; SOILS, DESERT, CALCAREOUS; SOILS, DESERT, CALICHE; SOILS, DESERT, CLAY; SOILS, DESERT, FLUVISOL; SOILS, DESERT, LITHOSOL; SOILS, DESERT, LOESS; SOILS, DESERT, PEDOCAL; SOILS, DESERT, PODSOL; SOILS, DESERT, SILT; SOIL TAXONOMY; WEATHERING, DESERT; WIND EROSION; WIND TRANSPORT**

Further Reading

Cooke, R., A. Warren, and A. Goudie. 1993. *Desert Geomorphology*. London: University College London Press.

Thomas, D. S. G. 1989. *Arid Zone Geomorphology*. London: Belhaven.

SOILS, DESERT, CALICHE

Soil layer with an accumulation of calcium carbonate ($CaCO_3$) in excess of the amount found in adjacent layers. In the caliche layer the soil is cemented by secondary carbonates of both calcium and magnesium that precipitate from the soil solution. Caliche is widespread in soils of arid and semiarid regions. Two processes have been proposed for the formation of this layer. In one mechanism weathered materials from the near-surface soil are moved in the soil solution and precipitate deeper in the profile, forming the zone of accumulation. Alternatively, the carbonates arise from aeolian (wind-blown) sources and are deposited on the soil surface and moved downward in the soil solution. In both cases the depth of the layer is determined by the depth of rain infiltration.

Caliche layers may be classified as calcic or petrocalcic horizons, depending on the thickness and hardness of the layer. Calcic soil horizons are at least 15 centimeters thick and have a calcium carbonate equivalent of at least 15 percent. There may or may not be identifiable pebbles or concretions. Petrocalcic horizons are cemented into hard, massive, continuous layers (indurated, or hard, layers) that cannot be penetrated with a spade or auger.

"Caliche" is the common term equivalent to the scientific term "calcic horizon" used in soil classification. The term was introduced in geology from Spanish-speaking countries. It has also been used to describe the rock and gravel deposits of sodium nitrate, sodium chloride, and other salts in Chile and Peru.

Calcrete is sometimes used interchangeably with caliche. "Calcrete" is the geologic term equivalent to the soil science term "petrocalcic horizon."—Dan R. Upchurch and Ted M. Zobeck

See also **DESERT SLOPES; FELDSPAR; FIELD CAPACITY OF SOILS; GROUNDWATER; LITHOSPHERE; MINERALS; NUTRIENTS; SAND RAMP; SOILS, DESERT; SOILS, DESERT, ARIDOSOL; SOILS, DESERT, ARENOSOL; SOILS, DESERT, ARKOSIC SAND; SOILS, DESERT, CALCAREOUS; SOILS, DESERT, CALCRETE; SOILS, DESERT, CLAY; SOILS, DESERT, FLUVISOL; SOILS, DESERT, LITHOSOL; SOILS, DESERT, LOESS; SOILS, DESERT, PEDOCAL; SOILS, DESERT, PODSOL; SOILS, DESERT, SILT; SOIL TAXONOMY; WEATHERING, DESERT; WIND EROSION; WIND TRANSPORT**

Further Readings

Allen, B. L. 1977. Mineralogy and soil taxonomy. *In* J. B. Dixon, S. B. Weed, J. A. Kitterick, M. H. Milford, and J. L. White, eds., *Minerals in Soil Environments*, 771–796. Madison, Wis.: Soil Science Society of America.

Buol, S. W., F. D. Hole, and R. J. McCracken. 1980. *Soil Genesis and Classification*. 2d ed. Ames: Iowa State University Press.

Elias, M. K. 1948. Ogallala and Post-Ogallala sediments. *Geologic Society of America Bulletin* 59:609–612.

Soil Science Society of America. 1987. *Glossary of Soil Science Terms*. Madison, Wis.: Soil Science Society of America.

Soil Survey Staff. 1975. *Soil Taxonomy: A Basic System of Soil Classification for Making and Interpreting Soil Surveys*. Agriculture Handbook No. 436, Soil Conservation Service, U.S. Department of Agriculture. Washington, D.C.: U.S. Government Printing Office.

SOILS, DESERT, CLAY

Soil particles of a size less than 0.002 millimeter (clay-sized) based on the U.S. and International soil classification systems. Clay-sized particles have a large surface area and are therefore the most reactive component of most soils. The surface area of 4.5 kilograms of 0.001-millimeter-diameter particles is approximately one hectare.

The same term is used to describe a soil that contains at least 40 percent clay-sized particles, less than 45 percent sand-sized particles (0.05–2 millimeters diameter), and less than 40 percent silt-sized particles (0.05–0.002 millimeters diameter). These percentage values are based on the weight of material in each size class, excluding any material larger than 2 millimeters in diameter. Clay is the finest textural class for soils. A moist clay soil will form a ribbon that is flexible when squeezed between the thumb and fingers. When dry, clay soils usually are very hard and form large clods.

Clay-sized particles (clay minerals) form in the normal weathering process of soils. The mineralogy of the clay fraction of the soil is determined by the parent material from which the soil formed. Clay particles are primarily aluminosilicate crystals that form sheets or platelets. These platelets are formed from unit tetrahedrons of silica surrounded by three oxygen atoms or octahedrons of aluminum surrounded by hydroxyls (OH). Aluminum may substitute for silicon in the tetrahedron resulting in a net negative charge on the surface of the crystal plates. The degree of substitution defines the type of clay; for example, kaolinite ($Al_2Si_5(OH)_4$) is a clay mineral in which there is essentially no substitution.

The plates form layers with other cations (positively charged molecules) held between the plates by the charges on the surfaces. The layers may be all tetrahedron, or may alternate with some combination of tetrahedron and octahedron layers. Hydrated ions entering the space between the crystal layers can cause the plates to be pushed apart, this being the process responsible for the swelling of some clays on wetting.—Dan R. Upchurch and Ted M. Zobeck

See also **DESERT SLOPES; FELDSPAR; FIELD CAPACITY OF SOILS; GROUNDWATER; LITHOSPHERE; MINERALS; NUTRIENTS; SAND RAMP; SOILS, DESERT; SOILS, DESERT, ARIDOSOL; SOILS, DESERT, ARENOSOL; SOILS, DESERT, ARKOSIC SAND; SOILS, DESERT, CALCAREOUS; SOILS, DESERT, CALCRETE; SOILS, DESERT, CALICHE; SOILS, DESERT, FLUVISOL; SOILS, DESERT, LITHOSOL; SOILS, DESERT, LOESS; SOILS, DESERT, PEDOCAL; SOILS, DESERT, PODSOL; SOILS, DESERT, SILT; SOIL TAXONOMY; WEATHERING, DESERT; WIND EROSION; WIND TRANSPORT**

Further Reading

Buol, S. W., F. D. Hole, and R. J. McCracken. 1980. *Soil Genesis and Classification*. 2d ed. Ames: Iowa State University Press.

Fanning, D. S., and V. Z. Keradimas. 1977. Micas. *In* J. B. Dixon, S. B. Weed, J. A. Kitterick, M. H. Milford, and J. L. White, eds., *Minerals in Soil Environments*, 195–258. Madison, Wis.: Soil Science Society of America.

Soil Science Society of America. 1987. *Glossary of Soil Science Terms*. Madison, Wis.: Soil Science Society of America.

Soil Survey Staff. 1975. *Soil Taxonomy: A Basic System of Soil Classification for Making and Interpreting Soil Surveys*. Agriculture Handbook No. 436, Soil Conservation Service, U.S. Department of Agriculture. Washington, D.C.: U.S. Government Printing Office.

SOILS, DESERT, FLUVISOL

Soil unit in the FAO-UNESCO classification system which develops on recently deposited alluvial (waterborne) materials from rivers, lakes, and oceans containing organic material of varying depth and receiving sediments at regular intervals characterized by a sequence of fine strata, often containing sulfur. Fluvisols are generally permanently saturated with water containing many salts in solution. If such soils are drained artificially, the sulfides are oxidized and form sulfuric acid that causes the pH of the soils to descend from the neutral level to as low as 3.5, indicating a high degree of acidity.

These soils have been considered azonal or mineralized supporting soils (Class I, French Soil Classification, 1967) if they lack a differentiated profile. (Fluvisols are roughly equivalent to the soil suborder fluvent of the order entisols in the U.S. Soil Classification, 1967).—Alberto I. J. Vich and Juana Susana Barroso

See also **DESERT SLOPES; FELDSPAR; FIELD CAPACITY OF SOILS; GROUNDWATER; LITHOSPHERE; MINERALS; NUTRIENTS; SAND RAMP; SOILS, DESERT; SOILS, DESERT, ARIDOSOL; SOILS, DESERT, ARENOSOL; SOILS, DESERT, ARKOSIC SAND; SOILS, DESERT, CALCAREOUS; SOILS, DESERT, CALCRETE; SOILS, DESERT, CALICHE; SOILS, DESERT, CLAY; SOILS, DESERT, LITHOSOL; SOILS, DESERT, LOESS; SOILS, DESERT, PEDOCAL; SOILS, DESERT, PODSOL; SOILS, DESERT, SILT; SOIL TAXONOMY; WEATHERING, DESERT; WIND EROSION; WIND TRANSPORT**

Further Reading

Cooke, R., A. Warren, and A. Goudie. 1993. *Desert Geomorphology*. London: University College London Press.

Dochaufour, P. 1978. *Manual de edafología*. Barcelona: Toray-Masson.

FAO-UNESCO-ISRIC. 1990. *Soil Map of the World. Rev. Leg.* World Soil Resources Report No. 60. Rome: Food and Agriculture Organization of the United Nations.

Fuller, W. H. 1974. Desert soils. *In* G. W. Brown Jr., ed., *Desert Biology: Special Topics on the Physical and Biological Aspects of Arid Regions*, 2:31–101. New York: Academic Press.

SOILS, DESERT, LITHOSOL

Poorly developed soil lacking humus and approximating the original rock material from which it is derived, including the presence of fragments of the primary rock material; also a soil unit in the FAO-UNESCO Classification System of 1974. Fragments may be coarse or fine and are products of mechanical disintegration. Its origin is not climatic and is typical of mountainous regions and representative of erosional soils with a very poorly developed profile that is not easily classified. It is variously considered to be an azonal soil (FAO-UNESCO Classification System, 1967) and a mineral soil derived from erosional materials (French Soil Classification System). In some classifications it is placed in the suborder ortents and the order entisols (U.S. Soil Classification System).—Alberto I. J. Vich and Juana Susana Barroso

See also **DESERT SLOPES; FELDSPAR; FIELD CAPACITY OF SOILS; GROUNDWATER; LITHOSPHERE; MINERALS; NUTRIENTS; SAND RAMP; SOILS, DESERT; SOILS, DESERT, ARIDOSOL; SOILS, DESERT, ARENOSOL; SOILS, DESERT, ARKOSIC SAND; SOILS, DESERT, CALCAREOUS; SOILS, DESERT, CALCRETE; SOILS, DESERT, CALICHE; SOILS, DESERT, CLAY; SOILS, DESERT, FLUVISOL; SOILS, DESERT, LOESS; SOILS, DESERT, PEDOCAL; SOILS, DESERT, PODSOL; SOILS, DESERT, SILT; SOIL TAXONOMY; WEATHERING, DESERT; WIND EROSION; WIND TRANSPORT**

Further Readings

Bates, R. L., ed. 1987. *Glossary of Geology.* 3d ed. Alexandria, Va.: American Geological Institute.

Dochaufour, P. 1978. *Manual de edafología.* Barcelona: Toray-Masson.

FAO-UNESCO-ISRIC. 1990. *Soil Map of the World. Rev. Leg.* World Soil Resources Report No. 60. Rome: Food and Agriculture Organization of the United Nations.

Fuller, W. H. 1974. Desert soils. *In* G. W. Brown Jr., ed., *Desert Biology: Special Topics on the Physical and Biological Aspects of Arid Regions,* 2:31–101. New York: Academic Press.

Suh-Shiaw, Lo. 1992. *Glossary of Hydrology.* Taipei: Sheng Te.

SOILS, DESERT, LOESS

Well-sorted, unstratified, blanketlike, wind-deposited (aeolian) silt and clay up to 100 meters thick. The dominant mineral is quartz, with lesser amounts of calcium carbonate, feldspar, and heavy minerals, although carbonate content increases in arid regions. Typically loess sediments consist of about 50 percent silt, 5–30 percent clay, and the rest sand. Grain sizes are 0.02–0.05 millimeter. In the United States large accumulations of loess are found in the Mississippi Valley and other parts of the Midwest, immediately south of the great Pleistocene ice sheets. Loess deposits typically blanket landscapes, filling topographic lows with flat sheets and covering slopes. Because of its strong interparticle cohesion, loess deposits can maintain steep slopes. Spatial depositional patterns and thicknesses result from variations in topography, vegetation cover, slope, and soil moisture conditions.

The two primary mechanisms for the production of silt-sized quartz particles are mechanical grinding and abrasion in glacial and periglacial environments and salt weathering and aeolian abrasion in deserts. The extensive deposits of loess found in areas bordering the Pleistocene ice sheets in eastern Europe, the United States, and central Asia led to the notion that loess deposits originate from outwash plains and other fluvioglacial environments. They are subsequently entrained by the wind and deposited farther down. However, silt-sized quartz can also be produced by aeolian abrasion during desert dust storms and as a by-product of salt weathering. Desert dust accumulates around vegetation, in rock fissures, and on desert pavements and playas. Significant desert-type loess deposits occur in the Negev Desert in Israel, in the Tunisian Sahara, and in the deserts of Pakistan, India, and China. The dating and analysis of the various soil horizons and the fossil fauna and flora preserved in the loess deposits have been invaluable for deciphering Pleistocene environmental changes.—Vatche P. Tchakerian

See also **DESERT SLOPES; FELDSPAR; FIELD CAPACITY OF SOILS; GLACIAL PERIODS; GROUNDWATER; LITHOSPHERE; MINERALS; NUTRIENTS; PLEISTOCENE; SAND RAMP; SOILS, DESERT; SOILS, DESERT, ARIDOSOL; SOILS, DESERT, ARENOSOL; SOILS, DESERT, ARKOSIC SAND; SOILS, DESERT, CALCAREOUS; SOILS, DESERT, CALCRETE; SOILS, DESERT, CALICHE; SOILS, DESERT, CLAY; SOILS, DESERT, FLUVISOL; SOILS, DESERT, LITHOSOL; SOILS, DESERT, PEDOCAL; SOILS, DESERT, PODSOL; SOILS, DESERT, SILT; SOIL TAXONOMY; WEATHERING, DESERT; WIND EROSION; WIND TRANSPORT**

Further Reading

Cooke, R., A. Warren, and A. Goudie. 1993. *Desert Geomorphology.* London: University College London Press.

Goudie, A. 1989. Weathering processes. *In* D. S. G. Thomas, ed., *Arid Zone Geomorphology,* 11–24. London: Belhaven.

Mabbutt, J. A. 1977. *Desert Landforms.* Cambridge, Mass.: MIT Press.

Pye, K. 1987. *Aeolian Dust and Dust Deposits.* London: Academic Press.

SOILS, DESERT, PEDOCAL

Soils characterizing arid zones where evaporation exceeds precipitation and the soils are dry during extended periods of the year; water from lower saturated soil zones ascends through capillary action to near the soil surface, where it evaporates and leaves dissolved salts in the upper layers of the soil. Calcium carbonate is the most common salt found as surface deposits, giving rise to a white coating on the soil. In the United States such areas are called "caliche." Gypsum (a hydrated calcium sulfate) forms similar coatings. In zones of intermediate rainfall calcium carbonate appears in one of the soil profiles as small nodules. According to the degree that carbonates are washed from the soil, pedocals can be classified as chestnut soils, brown steppe soils, and gray subdesertic soils.—Alberto I. J. Vich and Juana Susana Barroso

See also **DESERT SLOPES; FELDSPAR; FIELD CAPACITY OF SOILS; GLACIAL PERIODS; GROUNDWATER; LITHOSPHERE; MINERALS; NUTRIENTS; PLEISTOCENE; SAND RAMP; SOILS, DESERT; SOILS, DESERT, ARIDOSOL; SOILS, DESERT, ARENOSOL; SOILS, DESERT, ARKOSIC SAND; SOILS, DESERT, CALCAREOUS; SOILS, DESERT, CALCRETE; SOILS, DESERT, CALICHE; SOILS, DESERT, CLAY; SOILS, DESERT, FLUVISOL; SOILS, DESERT, LITHOSOL; SOILS, DESERT, LOESS; SOILS, DESERT, PODSOL; SOILS, DESERT, SILT; SOIL TAXONOMY; WEATHERING, DESERT; WHITE SANDS NATIONAL MONUMENT; WIND EROSION; WIND TRANSPORT**

Further Reading

Bates, R. L., ed. 1987. *Glossary of Geology.* 3d ed. Alexandria, Va.: American Geological Institute.

Fuller, W. H. 1974. Desert soils. *In* G. W. Brown Jr., ed., *Desert Biology: Special Topics on the Physical and Biological Aspects of Arid Regions,* 2:31–101. New York: Academic Press.

Moore, G. W. 1978. *Dictionary of Geography: Definitions and Explanation of Terms Used in Physical Geography.* New York: Harper and Row.

Suh-Shiaw, Lo. 1992. *Glossary of Hydrology.* Taipei: Sheng Te.

SOILS, DESERT, PODSOL

Soil found in cold, humid regions associated with the sub-Arctic climate and developing under coniferous forests; it is high in acid and of low fertility, the result of the low temperatures that inhibit bacterial action in the A horizon (outermost layer of the soil). This soil is characterized by a thick layer of dead or partially decomposed vegetation in its outermost layer; below this is a thin layer of highly acidic humus-rich soil that forms a zone of chemical interaction of acids and bases and a layer that is strongly leached and from which soluble materials are removed and descend to lower soil layers. The B horizon (the second major layer of the soil) is a zone rich in materials that accumulate from the upper horizon and cause this layer to have a heavy

claylike consistency. At times the deposition of large amounts of oxides can cause this layer to cement, in which case an extremely hard layer known as hardpan develops.—Alberto I. J. Vich and Juana Susana Barroso

See also **DESERT SLOPES; FELDSPAR; FIELD CAPACITY OF SOILS; GLACIAL PERIODS; GROUNDWATER; LITHOSPHERE; MINERALS; NUTRIENTS; PLEISTOCENE; SAND RAMP; SOILS, DESERT; SOILS, DESERT, ARIDOSOL; SOILS, DESERT, ARENOSOL; SOILS, DESERT, ARKOSIC SAND; SOILS, DESERT, CALCAREOUS; SOILS, DESERT, CALCRETE; SOILS, DESERT, CALICHE; SOILS, DESERT, CLAY; SOILS, DESERT, FLUVISOL; SOILS, DESERT, LITHOSOL; SOILS, DESERT, LOESS; SOILS, DESERT, PEDOCAL; SOILS, DESERT, SILT; SOIL TAXONOMY; WEATHERING, DESERT; WHITE SANDS NATIONAL MONUMENT; WIND EROSION; WIND TRANSPORT**

Further Readings

Baber, S. A. 1984. *Soil Nutrient Bioavailability: A Mechanistic Approach.* New York: Wiley.

Bates, R. L., ed. 1987. *Glossary of Geology.* 3d ed. Alexandria, Va.: American Geological Institute.

Dochaufour, P. 1978. *Manual de edafología.* Barcelona: Toray-Masson.

FAO-UNESCO-ISRIC. 1990. *Soil Map of the World. Rev. Leg.* World Soil Resources Report No. 60. Rome: Food and Agriculture Organization of the United Nations.

Fuller, W. H. 1974. Desert soils. *In* G. W. Brown Jr., ed., *Desert Biology: Special Topics on the Physical and Biological Aspects of Arid Regions,* 2:31–101. New York: Academic Press.

Gedroits, K. K. 1966. *Genetic Soil Classification Based on the Absorptive Soil Complex ans Absorbed Soil Cations.* Jerusalem: Israel Program for Scientific Translations, Agricultural Chemistry, No. 47.

Moore, G. W. 1978. *Dictionary of Geography: Definitions and Explanation of Terms Used in Physical Geography.* New York: Harper and Row.

Stralher, A. 1974. *Geografía física.* Barcelona: Omega.

SOILS, DESERT, SILT

Silt-sized particles having a diameter of 0.05–0.002 millimeter (U.S. Soil Classification System). The International system of soil classification defines the silt size as a diameter of 0.02–0.002 millimeter. The same term is used to describe a soil that contains at least 80 percent silt-sized particles and less than 12 percent clay-sized particles (less than 0.002 millimeter diameter). These percentage values are based on the weight of material in each size class, excluding any material larger than 2 millimeter in diameter.

The term "silt" is also used to describe the deposit of sediment such as that of a river (alluvial deposits) or windblown material (aeolian deposits). In this case it does not necessarily refer to particles of a particular size range but to all material being deposited.

Airborne particles derived from desert regions include particles in the silt-sized range. Such particles generally remain airborne long enough to be transported up to 100 kilometers. Silt-sized particles contribute more than 50 percent of the total particles in desert "dust." They are generated in desert environments through wind and water abrasion of larger particles, release from parent material during chemical weathering, and physical weathering caused by freezing. It is not clear that one process dominates over another, with the exception that abrasion in flowing water in a desert climate would be minimal and weathering by freezing would be limited to deserts at higher latitudes and elevations.

Sedimentary deposits of silt-sized particles are lithified (hardened) into silty shale by compaction, generally without other cementing agents. Siltstone is indurated (hard) material derived from sedimentary deposits primarily including silt-sized particles.—Dan R. Upchurch and Ted M. Zobeck

See also **ALLUVIAL FAN; DESERT SLOPES; DUNES; FELDSPAR; FIELD CAPACITY OF SOILS; GLACIAL PERIODS; GROUNDWATER; LIMESTONE; LITHOSPHERE; MINERALS; NUTRIENTS; PLEISTOCENE; RUNOFF; SAND RAMP; SANDSTONE; SOILS, DESERT; SOILS, DESERT, ARIDOSOL; SOILS, DESERT, ARENOSOL; SOILS, DESERT, ARKOSIC SAND; SOILS, DESERT, CALCAREOUS; SOILS, DESERT, CALCRETE; SOILS, DESERT, CALICHE; SOILS, DESERT, CLAY; SOILS, DESERT, FLUVISOL; SOILS, DESERT, LITHOSOL; SOILS, DESERT, LOESS; SOILS, DESERT, PEDOCAL; SOILS, DESERT, PODSOL; SOIL TAXONOMY; WEATHERING, DESERT; WHITE SANDS NATIONAL MONUMENT; WIND EROSION; WIND TRANSPORT**

Further Reading

Buol, S. W., F. D. Hole, and R. J. McCracken. 1980. *Soil Genesis and Classification*. 2d ed. Ames: Iowa State University Press.

Soil Science Society of America. 1987. *Glossary of Soil Science Terms*. Madison, Wis.: Soil Science Society of America.

Soil Survey Staff. 1975. *Soil Taxonomy: A Basic System of Soil Classification for Making and Interpreting Soil Surveys*. Agriculture Handbook No. 436, Soil Conservation Service, U.S. Department of Agriculture. Washington, D.C.: U.S. Government Printing Office.

Tennissen, A. C. 1974. *Nature of Earth Materials*. Englewood Cliffs, N.J.: Prentice-Hall.

Thomas, D. S. G. 1989. *Arid Zone Geomorphology*. London: Belhaven.

SOIL TAXONOMY

Systematic ordering of soil types into groups or categories based on their fundamental properties and presented in the form of a pyramid, with the upper units being fewer in number and making up the top and the lower units being continually subdivided and more numerous and making up the base. The classification of the upper soil units is based exclusively on one or more factors that determine the processes of soil formation. Some suggest that climate is the ultimate factor in soil formation (leading to "climatic" classifications of soils) and divide soils into zonal soils, azonal soils, and intrazonal soils. These are subdivided into orders and suborders, with the suborders described by the letters A, B, C, and so on. Other classification systems are related to the chemical aspect of the horizons (known as chemical classification systems); these generally include information on the absorption rate of the soil or its degree of washing of salts and other materials through the action of water. There are also mixed classifications, which tend to combine chemical and climatic soil classifications; these would include such types as pedalfers (soils that are completely washed of their carbonates and generally occur in humid climates), pedocals (soils that are partially washed of their carbonates and generally formed in dry climates), and intrazonal soils (which have washing of carbonates impeded by water).

The most recent classifications are based on a combination of morphological, biological, physico-chemical, and mineralogical characteristics of the soil profiles, all of which integrate the developmental process of the soil. There are three of these so-called synthetic genetic classifications. In the American classification, for example, soils are divided into order, suborder, great group, subgroup, family, and series. The ten fundamental orders are entisols, vertisols, inceptisols, aridosols, molisols, spodosols, alphisols, ultisols, oxysols, and histosols. In the soil classification used by the UN Food and Agricultural

Organization, 23 different soil divisions are given, including such soil types as fluvisols, regosols, arenosols, xerosols, halosols, and chernozems. In the French system of soil classification, 11 classes are described which are based on the degree of evolution of the soil profile, as well as other characteristics.—Alberto I. J. Vich and Juana Susana Barroso

See also **DESERT SLOPES; FELDSPAR; FIELD CAPACITY OF SOILS; GLACIAL PERIODS; GROUNDWATER; LITHOSPHERE; MINERALS; NUTRIENTS; PLEISTOCENE; SAND RAMP; SOILS, DESERT; SOILS, DESERT, ARIDOSOL; SOILS, DESERT, ARENOSOL; SOILS, DESERT, ARKOSIC SAND; SOILS, DESERT, CALCAREOUS; SOILS, DESERT, CALCRETE; SOILS, DESERT, CALICHE; SOILS, DESERT, CLAY; SOILS, DESERT, FLUVISOL; SOILS, DESERT, LITHOSOL; SOILS, DESERT, LOESS; SOILS, DESERT, PEDOCAL; SOILS, DESERT, SILT; SOIL TAXONOMY; WEATHERING, DESERT; WHITE SANDS NATIONAL MONUMENT; WIND EROSION; WIND TRANSPORT**

Further Reading

Buol, S. W., F. D. Hole, and R. J. McCracken. 1980. *Soil Genesis and Classification*. 2d ed. Ames: Iowa State University Press.

Cooke, R., A. Warren, and A. Goudie. 1993. *Desert Geomorphology*. London: University College London Press.

Dochaufour, P. 1978. *Manual de edafología*. Barcelona: Toray-Masson.

Fuller, W. H. 1974. Desert soils. *In* G. W. Brown Jr., ed., *Desert Biology: Special Topics on the Physical and Biological Aspects of Arid Regions*, 2:31–101. New York: Academic Press.

Soil Conservation Service-USDA. 1975. *Soil Taxonomy: A Basic System of Soil Classification for Making and Interpreting Soil Surveys*. Washington, D.C.: USDA Agriculture Handbook No. 436.

SOLAR RADIATION. *See* INSOLATION

SONORAN DESERT

Extensive arid region west of the Sierra Madre Occidental that arcs from the western half of Sonora, Mexico, around the upper reaches of the Gulf of California through portions of southeastern California and southwestern Arizona and extends into the northern part of Baja California, representing one of the most fascinating and ecologically significant hot deserts found in North America. (See map of North American deserts, p. 356.)

Sonoran Desert habitat near Gila Bend, Arizona. (Photo: L. J. Vitt)

The Sonoran Desert is one of the most complex desert biomes in the world. Its huge cacti, drought-resistant plants, high temperatures, and extremely low precipitation make it the quintessential North American desert For many, its significance is enhanced by its importance in the early history of Mexico and the United States and the many images of its stark beauty in numerous motion pictures.

The Sonoran Desert occurs in four states with approximate areas (in square kilometers) as follows: Sonora, Mexico, 48,000; Arizona, U.S.A., 40,000; Baja California, Mexico, 24,000; and California, U.S.A., 6,000. This vast region, which spans 12 degrees of latitude from 23° to 35° north, has varied topography consisting of plains, bajadas, and isolated mountain ranges, although it lies mainly below 600 meters elevation. The latitudinal extent and elevational variations produce a wide assortment of environmental conditions and likely contribute to the biotic diversity of this desert. Although much of the Sonoran Desert is within the Basin and Range Physiographic Province, it has a well-developed drainage pattern into the Gulf of California. The Colorado River bisects a large portion of the region and greatly influences the region's vegetational patterns and agricultural economy.

The Sonoran Desert is the hottest and most arid of the four North American Deserts. Nevertheless, it has the greatest diversity of plants and animals of any of the North American deserts. Rainfall in the region ranges from traces of winter precipitation in some of the western parts to more than 250 millimeters along the eastern edge, where biannual (summer and winter) rains occur. In general the proportion of summer to winter rainfall increases from west to east, and along the eastern edge the distribution of rainfall is about half in summer and half in winter.

The Sonoran Desert is most characteristically developed in the western half of the state of Sonora, Mexico, where it consists of a mixture of broad sandy flats, isolated mountains, bajadas, dry arroyos, and a few intermittent streams. The North American desert ecologist Forrest Shreve described the Sonoran Desert in great detail and is the source of much of the information on this fascinating and historically important ecosystem.

Seven major subdivisions are commonly recognized: the Plains and Foothills of Sonora, the Arizona Upland Desert (also called the Saguaro Desert), the Yuman Desert, the Colorado Desert of California, the Vizcaino Desert of Baja California, the Magdalena Desert of Baja California, and the Gulf Coast Desert of Baja California and western Sonora.

The lower Colorado Valley is the largest, lowest, and hottest of these Sonoran Desert regions, extending around the head of the Gulf of California and along both sides of the Sea of Cortez. Vast areas of this subdivision are dominated by creosote bush (*Larrea tridentata*) and white bur sage (*Franseria dumosa*). The hot, dry conditions of this region are perfect for these two shrubs, and in some locations they make up 80–90 percent of the plant cover. In contrast to the low shrub vegetation of the Great Basin Desert farther to the north, the Sonoran Desert contains an abundance of small and large evergreen trees, a remarkable array of succulents, and some outstanding tree cacti that create an arborescent (treelike) desert.

Many of the trees are found along the dry washes that are common in the region. These include mesquites (*Prosopis*), paloverde (*Cercidium*), ironwood (*Olneya tesota*), and smoke tree (*Dalea spinosa*). The mesquites are particularly widespread and are significant plants in all of the southwestern deserts of North America; their seed pods are a valuable forage for livestock and wildlife, and the wood is used for firewood, construction, and fence posts. However, the aggressive growth of mesquite has resulted in deterioration of the grazing value of much of the area. As a result range

management practices have focused on chemical and mechanical control of mesquite. The trees of the Sonoran Desert seldom exceed nine meters in height but are especially adapted to the harsh desert environment. Many have very small leaves, which reduces water loss, and green stems for photosynthesis. In addition, the root systems of many species are shallow and extensive and thereby make optimum use of the scant and episodic rainfall.

The fauna of the Sonoran Desert is less closely tied to specific habitats, as is the case with the vegetation. Most of the animal species are found in one or more of the distinctive vegetational subdivisions. The animal life is rich in diversity and also abundant in numbers. Some examples (and these are only a few) of typical Sonoran Desert animals are the desert tortoise (*Gopherus agassizi*), the Gila monster (*Heloderma suspectum*), the collared lizard (*Crotophytus collaris*), the zebra-tailed lizard (*Callisaurus draconoides*), the glossy snake (*Arizona elegans*), the Arizona coral snake (*Micruroides euryxanthus*), the sidewinder (*Crotalus cerastes*), and the Mojave rattlesnake (*Crotalus scutulatus*). Just a few of the numerous bird species are the roadrunner (*Geococcyx californianus*), the phainopepla (*Phainopepla nitens*), the cactus wren (*Campylorhynchus brunneicapillus*), the white-winged dove (*Zenaida asiatica*) and the Gila woodpecker (*Centurus uropygialis*). Some of the mammals found in the Sonoran Desert are the pocket gopher, grasshopper mouse, shrew, woodrat, kangaroo rat, various ground squirrels, cottontail, jackrabbit, coyote, bobcat, peccary, mule deer, puma (mountain lion), and pronghorn.—Gary K. Hulett and Amanda Renner Charles

See also **AN INTRODUCTION TO DESERTS; ANZA-BORREGO DESERT; APACHE; ARIZONA DESERT; BAJA CALIFORNIA, DESERTS OF; BIRDS; CACTI; CACTUS, COLUMNAR; CALIFORNIA DESERT; COCHISE; COLORADO DESERT; COTTONWOOD; CREOSOTE BUSH; DEATH VALLEY; DESERT PEOPLES; DESERTS; DESERTS, HOT; DESERTS, TEMPERATE; FISHES; GERONIMO; LIZARDS; MAMMALS; MEXICO, DESERTS OF; MOJAVE DESERT; MOVIES IN DESERTS; O'ODHAM; PALOVERDE; PLANT GEOGRAPHY; REPTILES; SALTBUSH; SALT CEDAR; SEMIARID ZONES; SNAKES; UNITED STATES, DESERTS OF; YUMA DESERT**

Further Reading

Alcock, J. 1985. *Sonoran Desert Spring*. Chicago: University of Chicago Press.

Bender, G. L., ed. 1982. *Reference Handbook on the Deserts of North America*. Westport, Conn.: Greenwood Press.

Brown, D. E., ed. 1994. *Biotic Communities: Southwestern United States and Northwestern Mexico*. Salt Lake City: University of Utah Press.

Dunbier, R. 1968. *The Sonoran Desert*. Tucson, Arizona: University of Arizona Press.

Dykinga, J. W. 1997. *The Sonoran Desert*. New York: Abrams.

George, J. C. 1983. *One Day in the Desert*. New York: Crowell.

Jaeger, E. C. 1957. *The North American Deserts*. Stanford: Stanford University Press.

Shreve, F., and I. L. Wiggins. 1964. *Vegetation and Flora of the Sonoran Desert*. Vols. 1 and 2. Stanford: Stanford University Press.

Stone, C. L. 1986. *Deceptive Desolation: Prehistory of the Sonoran Desert in West Central Arizona*. Phoenix: Arizona State Office of the Bureau of Land Management.

Turner, R. M. 1995. *Sonoran Desert Plants: An Ecological Atlas*. Tucson: University of Arizona Press.

SOUTH AFRICA, DESERTS OF

Arid and semiarid areas lying within the geographic boundaries of the nation of South Africa and extending into neighboring countries. Aridity in South Africa is caused primarily by persistent, dry, stable air masses characteristic of the semitropical regions of continents. There are three recognized desert biomes in South Africa, the Succulent Karoo Biome, the Nama Karoo Biome, and the Arid Savanna Biome (Kalahari Desert). Each biome is characterized by its vegetation composition and the climatic adaptations displayed by the vegetation. (See map of African deserts, p. 12.)

The Succulent Karoo, which receives a mean annual rainfall of 20–290 millimeters, is the only winter rainfall desert in South Africa. Coastal fog is common and is an important source of water for many plants and animals. The rainfall is the most reliable (least variability) of all the African deserts. It is a narrow coastal desert about 100–150 kilometers wide stretching from Lüderitz (26° south latitude), Namibia, to Lambert's Bay (32° south latitude), South Africa. Also known as Namaqualand, the biome has the highest plant species diversity for any desert in the world. This can be attributed to the estimated minimum 3,500 species of succulent plants within the families Aizoaceae, Crassulaceae, Liliaceae, and Euphorbiaceae that are endemic to the biome.

The Nama Karoo Biome lies on a plateau within the western interior of South Africa, covering nearly one-half of South Africa's landmass. It receives 100–520 millimeters of rain, predominantly during summer. The rainfall can be very variable from year to year in response to climatic phenomena such as the El Niño Southern Oscillations. The latter cause negative rainfall anomalies (droughts), often for several consecutive years. The biome is characterized by dwarf shrubs and perennial grasses in grass to shrub ratios that increase along the strong west–east rainfall gradient. The entire Nama Karoo has been subjected to extensive overgrazing by European small stock (sheep and goat) farmers during the past 200 years which has resulted in widespread desertification—an increase in unpalatable shrubs at the expense of palatable grasses and shrubs. The Nama Karoo has the richest deposits of well-preserved Permian and Triassic mammallike reptile (synapsids) fossils in the world.

A small part of the Arid Savanna Biome, known locally as the Kalahari Desert, extends into northwestern South Africa from Botswana and Namibia from 20° to 26° east longitude. It is a summer rainfall desert that receives a mean annual rainfall of 235–500 millimeters in violent, convective thunderstorms. Most of the Kalahari Desert consists of vegetated undulating red sand dunes interspersed with flat calcrete pans (desert flats with a hard calcium-based crust). The biome is characterized by perennial grasses, such as species of *Eragrostis*, and trees, such as the camelthorn (*Acacia erioloba*) and the shepherd's tree (*Boscia albitrunca*). The conservation status of the Arid Savanna Biome is excellent owing to the Kalahari Gemsbok National Park. The park supports the top carnivores, such as African lion (*Panthera leo*), leopard (*Panthera pardus*), cheetah (*Acinonyx jubatus*), brown hyena (*Hyaena brunnea*), and spotted hyena (*Crocuta crocuta*), as well as large herds of arid-adapted ungulates, such as springbok (*Antidorcas marsupialis*), gemsbok (*Oryx gazella*), red hartebeest (*Alcelaphus buselaphus*), blue wildebeest (*Connochaetes taurinus*), and eland (*Taurotragus oryx*). Desertification in the form of bush encroachment by *Acacia mellifera* is caused by overgrazing by cattle on the southern fringes of the Kalahari Desert.—Barry G. Lovegrove

See also **AFRICA, DESERTS OF; AFRICAN LION; AN INTRODUCTION TO DESERTS; ANTELOPE; CATS; CHEETAH; DOMESTIC ANIMALS; DUNES; DURICRUSTS; GEMSBOK; KALAHARI DESERT; KAROO; PLAYA; NAMIBIA, DESERTS OF; SPRINGBOK**

Further Reading

Cowling, R. M., D. M. Richardson, and S. M. Pierce. 1997. *Vegetation of Southern Africa*. Oxford: Cambridge University Press.

Lovegrove, B. 1993. *The Living Deserts of Southern Africa*. Vlaeberg: Fernwood.

Werger, M. J. A. 1986. The Karoo and southern Kalahari. *In* M. Evenari, I. Noy-Meir, and D. W. Goodall, eds., *Ecosystems of the World: Hot Deserts and Arid Shrublands*, 12B:283–359. New York: Elsevier.

SOUTH AMERICA, DESERTS OF

Arid and semiarid habitats lying within the continent of South America. The South American continent is perhaps best known for its extensive tropical rain forest, but it also contains a great diversity of arid deserts and semiarid scrublands and grasslands. The continent largely is rimmed by arid and semiarid areas, both inside and outside of the tropics, and few countries lack drylands. In the far northwest of the continent, in Venezuela and Colombia, is the Pericarribean Arid Belt, which contains relatively limited areas of hyperaridity as well as more extensive semiarid habitats. This region includes the Guajira Desert of Colombia and Venezuela, an extremely arid region located on the Guajira Peninsula.

There are also semiarid scrublands situated in the complex vegetation of the mountains of northwestern South America. Characteristically, extensive dry areas may appear wherever there are high mountains with resultant rain shadows that lead to reduced rainfall. Thus arid and semiarid highlands extend largely unbroken from Colombia in the north to southernmost Argentina along the west coast of South America. These would include the Andean scrublands and grasslands of high elevations as well as the hyperarid lowland coastal deserts of Ecuador, Peru, and Chile (the Sechura and Atacama deserts).

Arid and semiarid areas are also quite extensive inland from the west coast of South America in Bolivia, Paraguay, and Argentina. These include the Chaco, or thorn scrub, the Monte Desert, and the Patagonian Desert. The Patagonian and Monte

Tropical desert scrubland near Mérida, Venezuela, with columnar cacti in the background. (Photo: M. A. Mares)

deserts grade into the grasslands of the Pampas of eastern Argentina.

In northeastern Brazil, situated entirely within the tropics, is the semiarid Caatinga scrubland, a zone of periodic and extensive droughts that encompasses more than 650,000 square kilometers. The Caatinga is an ancient zone of semiaridity. Along its western boundaries it grades into the high plains savanna of the Brazilian Cerrado, an area that undergoes significant yearly droughts. The Cerrado adjoins the Chaco.

Over the huge expanse of South America it is almost possible to move from one zone of aridity or semiaridity to the other without having to cross intermediate areas of rain forest or mesic forest habitats. (see map, p. 533.)—Michael A. Mares

See also **ALTIPLANO; ANDEAN GRASSLANDS; ANDES; AN INTRODUCTION TO DESERTS; ATACAMA DESERT; CAATINGA; CHACO; CHILE, DESERTS OF; DESERTS, MONTANE; GUAJIRA; MONTE DESERT; PAMPAS; PATAGONIA; PERU, DESERTS OF; PUNA; SECHURA DESERT**

Further Reading

Arritt, S. 1993. *The Living Earth Book of Deserts*. New York: Reader's Digest Assoc.

Camacho, J. H. 1995. *Desiertos: Zonas áridas y semiáridas de Colombia*. Cali: Banco de Occidente Credencial.

Evenari, M., I. Noy-Meir, and D. W. Goodall, eds. 1985. *Ecosystems of the World, Hot Deserts and Arid Shrublands*. Vol. 12 (2 pts.). New York: Elsevier.

McGinnies, W. G., B. J. Goldman, and P. Paylore, eds. 1968. *Deserts of the World: An Appraisal of Research*

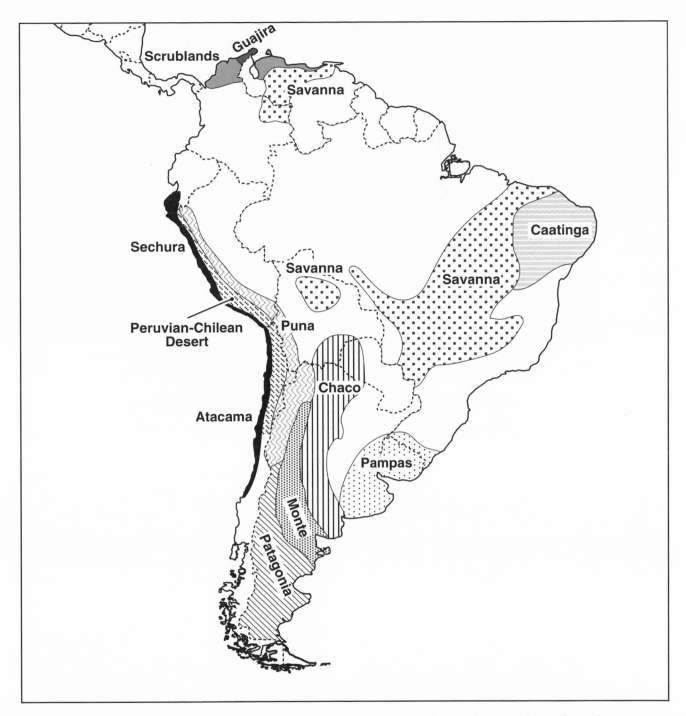

Map of the major arid and semiarid habitats of South America. Shading indicates desert and semidesert limits.

into Their Physical and Biological Environments. Tucson: University of Arizona Press.

Morello. J. 1984. *Pérfil ecológico de Sudamérica.* Barcelona: Ediciones Cultura Hispánica, Instituto de Cooperación Iberoamericana.

United Nations Environment Programme. 1992. *World Atlas of Desertification.* London: Edward Arnold.

SPADEFOOT TOAD

Small toad in the subfamily Pelobatinae of the family Pelobatidae that is a common inhabitant of desert environments in the southwestern United States. Spadefoot toads should not be confused with "true toads," which are in the family Bufonidae. Spadefoot toads derive their common name from a

Spadefoot toad (*Scaphiopus couchi*) near Portal, Arizona. (Photo: J. P. Caldwell)

spadelike tubercle on the foot, which they use to bury themselves in the soil. They are smooth-skinned, fossorial toads with unusual vertical pupils. Three genera of spadefoot toads are recognized. One, *Pelobates*, consists of four species that occur in Europe, parts of Asia, and northwestern Africa. Two others, *Scaphiopus* and *Spea*, consisting of two and four species, respectively, occur primarily in deserts and grasslands of the western United States, although one species occurs in the eastern United States. *Scaphiopus* and *Spea* have many unusual adaptations for life in desert environments, including rapidly developing tadpoles. Some species in the genus *Spea* have tadpoles that have the ability to become carnivorous morphs. Adults spend much of the year beneath the ground in individual self-excavated burrows. They generally emerge when summer rains begin to fall and breed explosively for only a few days. The tadpole stage is rapid, lasting approximately two weeks, depending on pond drying time. Larger metamorphs lose water more slowly than smaller ones and have a higher chance of survivorship, possibly because they are able to move over larger arid areas to reach patches of moist desert soil.—Janalee P. Caldwell

See also **AMPHIBIANS; ANIMAL ADAPTATIONS; BREEDING SEASON; DORMANCY; FLOOD; FROGS; LIFE HISTORY STRATEGY (ITEROPARITY); METAMORPHOSIS; PRECIPITATION; TADPOLES; TOADS; WATER HOLE**

Further Reading

Bragg, A. N. 1965. *Gnomes of the Night*. Philadelphia: University of Pennsylvania Press.

McClanahan, L. L. 1967. Adaptations of the spadefoot toad, *Scaphiopus couchi*, to desert environments. *Comparative Biochemistry and Physiology* 20:73–99.

Newman, R. A., and A. E. Dunham. 1994. Size at metamorphosis and water loss in a desert anuran (*Scaphiopus couchi*). *Copeia* 1994:372–381.

Ruibal, R., L. Tevis, Jr., and V. Roig. 1969. The terrestrial ecology of the spadefoot toad *Scaphiopus hammondii. Copeia* 1969:571–584.

Wiens, J. J., and T. A. Titus. 1991. A phylogenetic analysis of *Spea* (Anura:Pelobatidae). *Herpetologica* 47:21–28.

Woodward, B. D., and S. L. Mitchell. 1991. The community ecology of desert anurans. *In* G. Polis, ed., *The Ecology of Desert Communities*, 223–248. Tucson: University of Arizona Press.

SPAIN, DESERTS OF

Semiarid region lying within the nation of Spain. Extensive areas of Spain lying mainly in the southeastern part of the country and in the region of the Ebro (River) Depression receive less than 400 millimeters of annual precipitation, and the vegetation in these areas is semidesertic in nature. If the semiarid zone is expanded to include areas receiving less than 600 millimeters of annual precipitation, most of the Spanish Peninsula is included, with the exception of Galicia and far northern Spain (Cantabria, Principado de Asturias, and País Vasco). Because the country is also quite mountainous, with peaks exceeding 3,400 meters, general rainfall is affected by topography and can vary greatly from one point to another. Certain areas can be significantly drier than the general precipitation pattern of the region might suggest (an example is the Ebro Depression, the driest zone in the country).

The climate is predominantly Mediterranean, with a long period of drought (4–7 months) and most of the rain occurring in fall and spring. Rains in the driest parts of Spain are torrential, and there is great variation in annual precipitation; for example, in 1959 in Buñuel, 850 millimeters of rain fell in one year, whereas the same locality received only 186 millimeters of rain in 1985. Maximum temperatures range from 35° to 45°C, and lows are below 4°C. Traveling inland from the Mediterranean Sea, the climate changes to one that is more continental (i.e., drier and with seasonal and daily temperature extremes that are more pronounced).

The vegetation is similar to the semiarid Mediterranean steppes of North Africa and is characterized by great floristic heterogeneity and diversity at taxonomic, structural, and ecological levels. This diversity in vegetation types is a response to climate, topography, and soil variation. As with most semiarid areas, the flora of this region is sensitive to environmental changes and vulnerable to human-related ecological impacts. Plants have the typical arid-land adaptations found in other drylands of the world, including long roots that extend to underground water sources, hirsute (hairy) leaves that reflect sunlight, and reduced leaf size. In areas that receive less than 400 millimeters of annual precipitation, vegetation is largely limited to shrubs (e.g., rosemary, *Rosmarinus officinalis*, thyme, *Thymus vulgaris*, *Genista scorpius*, lavender, *Lavandula latifolia*, saltwort, *Salsola vermiculata*, and white sage, *Artemisia herba-alba*) and grasses (e.g., *Stipa parviflora* and *Brachypodium retusum*). In areas of higher precipitation an arborescent (forested) flora develops, including sclerophyllous (thick-leafed) species. These are the juniper (*Juniperus oxycedrus*), the mastic tree (*Pistacia lentiscus*), and two species of oaks (*Quercus rotundifolia*, *Quercus coccifera*). As in other xeric areas of the world, low-lying habitats will have areas of salt deposition due to leaching, including saline flats, such as the Bardenas Reales (Navarra), which support halophytic (salt-loving) vegetation, such as *Atriplex halimus*, *Limonium ruizii*, and *Limonium viscoso*.

The semiarid steppes of Spain support a fauna that is specially adapted to its sparse vegetation and dry climate. Amphibians are uncommon, as with many arid areas, although a frog, *Rana ridibunda*, is common in moist areas. Reptiles are common and include lizards (*Lacerta lepida*, *Acanthodactylus erythrurus*, *Podarcis hispanica*, *Psammodromus hispanicus*, and the amphisbaenid *Blanus cinereus*) and snakes (*Coronella girondica*, *Vipera latastei*, *Elaphe scalaris*). The most common vertebrates are birds, including *Pterocles alchata*, *Pterocles orientalis*, *Otis tarda*, *Alectoris rufa*, *Carduellis cannabina*, *Aquila chrysaetos*, and *Athene noctua*. Mammals in this area include the rabbit, *Oryctolagus cuniculus*, the fox, *Vulpes vulpes*, and rodents such as *Microtus duodecimcostatus*, *Microtus cabrerae*, *Rattus rattus*, *Apodemus sylvaticus*, and *Eliomys quercinus*.

The xeric areas of Spain have been greatly affected by human activities throughout the centuries. Grasses and shrublands have been overgrazed by sheep and goats, and other areas have been converted for agricultural purposes. Indeed, in areas where water for irrigation can be obtained from rivers or other sources, the semiarid region has become an economically important agricultural area. Poorly managed croplands and grazing lands have led to increased desertification in the region (25 percent of the land area of Spain has serious problems with soil erosion and desertification, and an additional 25 percent has moderate levels of erosion).

Spain has developed a number of protected areas in its xeric region to preserve the flora and fauna, including the natural park Cabo de Gata Nijar and the natural desert reserve Tabernas in Almería Province, and the national Refugio de Caza de la Lomada de Belchite in Aragón.—Antonia Paniza Cabrera

See also **AMPHIBIANS; AN INTRODUCTION TO DESERTS; BIRDS; CHENOPODIACEAE; DESERTS; MAMMALS; PLANT ADAPTATIONS; REPTILES; PLAYA**

Further Reading

Gomez, J. M. 1996. Predispersal reproductive ecology of an arid land crucifer *Moricandia moricandioides*— effect of mammal herbivory on seed production. *Journal of Arid Environments* 33:425–437.

Hodar, J. A., F. Campos, and B. A. Rosales. 1996. Trophic ecology of the ocellated lizard *Lacerta lepida* in an arid zone of southern Spain: Relationships with availability and daily activity of prey. *Journal of Arid Environments* 33:95–107.

Moro, M. J., Pugnaire, F. I., Haase, P., and Puigdefabregas, J. 1997. Effect of the canopy of *Retama sphaerocarpa* on its understorey in a semiarid environment. *Functional Ecology* 11:425–431.

———. 1997. Mechanisms of interaction between a leguminous shrub and its understorey in a semiarid environment. *Ecography* 20:175–184.

Pinero, F. S. 1997. Analysis of spatial and seasonal variability of carrion beetle (Coleoptera) assemblages in two arid zones of Spain. *Environmental Entomology* 26:805–814.

Roldan, A., I. Quereteja, J. Albaladejo, and V. Castillo. 1996. Survival and growth of *Pinus halapatensis* Miller seedlings in a semiarid environment after forest soil transfer, terracing and organic amendments. *Anales des Sciences Forestieres* 53:1099–1112.

Williams, M., ed. 1993. *Planet Management*. New York: Oxford University Press.

SPARROWS

Two evolutionarily distinct but ecologically convergent groups of small to moderate-sized songbirds.

The Old World sparrows (order Passeriformes, family Passeridae) are composed of some 34–37 species in three genera, with a center of distribution in the Afrotropics. The New World sparrows and buntings (order Passeriformes, family Emberizidae, subfamily Emberizinae) contain approximately 280 species in 69 genera. The Emberizinae are believed to have originated in the New World, where they reach maximum species diversity, and subsequently spread to their present-day almost cosmopolitan distribution (absent from Southeast Asia and Australasia). The taxonomic extent of both groups is unclear. The weavers (Ploceidae) and the waxbills (Estrildidae) are grouped together with the Old World sparrows within the Passeridae by some authorities. DNA-DNA hybridization data suggest that many of the Neotropical "emberizines" may be more closely related to tanagers than to other New World sparrows.

Taxa in both groups occupy a wide diversity of habitats ranging from open woodlands to true deserts. The majority of passerids, however, are found in xeric or semiarid open country. For example, the desert sparrow (*Passer simplex*) occurs in desert scrub of the Sahara region from Morocco east to Egypt. Examples of Northern Hemisphere emberizine species that occupy arid habitats over a portion or all of their range include various genera of sparrows (e.g., *Aimophila*, *Amphispiza*), buntings (genus *Emberiza*), and towhees (genus *Pipilo*). For example, the black-chinned sparrow (*Amphispiza bilineata*) inhabits cactus and sagebrush deserts of the American Southwest and northern Mexico. In the Old World many of the buntings breed in drier environments. For example, the chestnut-breasted bunting (*Emberiza stewarti*) is found in dry, sparsely vegetated regions of the Himalayan foothills in south central Asia. South American exemplars of desert-dwelling taxa are similarly numerous and include some members of the yellow finches (genus *Sicalis*), the sierra finches (genus *Phrygilus*), the warbling finches (genus *Poospiza*), grassquits (genus *Tiaris*), and diuca finches (genus *Diuca*). The mourning sierra finch (*Phrygilus fruticeti*) is an example of one of these, inhabiting arid and semiarid brushy slopes of the Andes Mountains from Peru south to southern Argentina and Chile.

Total length of the New World sparrows ranges from 10 to 20 centimeters and of the passerids from 10 to 18 centimeters. Wing shape is highly variable across species in both groups, reflecting differences in migratory status. Many of the emberizines of higher latitudes are migratory. The majority of *Passer* species are sedentary, but some members of the other passerid genera are wholly or partially migratory. The plumage of the passerids and many of the emberizines is brown, gray, gray and black, or black. Some emberizines, especially some of the buntings, are exceptionally colorful. Most taxa in both groups have typical seed-eater bills, short and conical. Diet typically consists of seeds but may also include other vegetable matter (e.g., fruit) and insects. Some desert taxa can derive a substantial proportion of their water needs from their food. Many emberizines use their strong toes and claws to scratch through leaf litter in search of food, while this behavior is not exhibited by their Old World counterparts.

The majority of both passerids and emberizines are reported to be monogamous, although some species are polygynous. In passerid species both sexes build the bulky domed nest that is usually placed in a bush, a tree, a hole, or a nest box. The emberizine nest is typically a small woven cup placed on the ground or low at the base of a shrub. Clutch size ranges from three to seven in passerids and usually from four to six in emberizines. In New World sparrows the female is usually solely responsible for incubation and brooding of the young; males may make substantial contributions to feeding. In most passerids incubation and feeding duties are shared.—Stephen C. Lougheed

See also **ANIMAL ADAPTATIONS; BIRDS; FINCH; FEATHERS; GRANIVORY; SEED DISPERSAL BY ANIMALS (ZOOCHORY); SEEDS**

Further Reading

Bent, A. C. 1968. Life histories of North American cardinals, grosbeaks, buntings, towhees, finches, sparrows, and allies. *U.S. National Museum Bulletin* No. 237.

Cramp, S., and C. M. Perrins, eds. 1994. *Handbook of the Birds of Europe, the Middle East and North Africa: The Birds of the Western Palearctic.* Vol. 8. Oxford: Oxford University Press.

———. 1994. *Handbook of the Birds of Europe, the Middle East and North Africa: The Birds of the Western Palearctic.* Vol. 9. Oxford: Oxford University Press.

Ehrlich, P. R., D. S. Dobkin, and D. Wheye. 1988. *The Birder's Handbook: A Field Guide to the Natural History of North American Birds Including All Species That Regularly Breed North of Mexico.* New York: Simon and Schuster.

Ridgely, R. S., and G. Tudor. 1989. *The Birds of South America*. Vol. 1. Austin: University of Texas Press.

Tweit, R. C., and D. M. Finch. 1994. Albert's towhee (*Pipilo alberti*). *In* A. Poole and F. Gill, eds., *The Birds of North America*, No. 111. Philadelphia: Academy of Natural Sciences; Washington, D.C.: American Ornithologists' Union.

SPECIATION

Process by which new species arise. A species is defined as a group of populations that can interbreed with each other and therefore share a common gene pool. Thus for new species to arise from existing populations, some form of genetic isolation must occur. The most widely accepted model of speciation is that initially proposed by Ernst Mayr and referred to as the allopatric model of speciation. Since its initial proposition, biologists have confirmed many aspects of this model. *Allopatric* literally means "living in different places" and refers to the chance geographic separation of populations of a single species that is necessary to begin the process of speciation. Geographic isolation may occur, for example, when a river changes its course, or, over geologic time, when a colder climatic period permits only remnants of tropical forest to survive, thus isolating tropical species therein, or when deserts are encroached on by grasslands during a wetter climatic period. Once populations become separated and no longer have the opportunity to interbreed, chance genetic changes caused by genetic drift or bottlenecks begin to accumulate. Eventually enough genetic changes occur that should the separated populations reunite, they are no longer capable of interbreeding and are now distinct species. Biologists have determined that most speciation in the animal kingdom occurs in this manner.

A different method of speciation has been discovered to account for much speciation in plants, although allopatric speciation also gives rise to new plant species. The entire complement of chromosomes in a single individual may become multiplied during one reproductive event because the chromosomes fail to separate correctly during cell division. This method (polyploidy) is sometimes called instant speciation because it happens in only one generation, not over expansive periods of time as in allopatric speciation. When polyploidy occurs, the new offspring can interbreed because they have the same number of chromosomes; however, these individuals cannot interbreed with the parental population that gave rise to the new individuals. Thus a genetic barrier has occurred and a new species has formed.

With the advent of sophisticated molecular techniques, biologists have begun to investigate the amounts and kinds of changes that are necessary in the DNA of individuals in order for reproductive isolation to occur. The relative importance of changes in structural and regulatory genes is also being examined. Regulatory genes differ from structural genes in that regulatory genes control the activation of complexes of structural genes. Thus the timing of when regulatory genes turn structural genes off and on can have major consequences over large parts of an organism's body, such as the number of body segments or the orientation of certain appendages. Mutations or changes in regulatory genes may be one way in which relatively large changes can occur and lead to somewhat different body forms over a relatively short period.

Biologists have long believed that the proliferation of species that has existed in the past and currently exists on earth has resulted from the gradual accumulation of genetic changes and the slow development of one species giving rise to daughter species. In recent years, however, scientists, particularly Stephen Jay Gould of Harvard University, have been debating a new theory called punctuated equilibrium. The changes that come about in speciation are basically the same as described above, but the timing of these events is different. Proponents of punctuated equilibrium believe that there are long periods during which populations remain relatively unchanged; then, in response to some major environmental or other change, speciation and evolution occur relatively rapidly, giving rise to radiations of large numbers of new species.—Janalee P. Caldwell

See also **BIOME; CONVERGENT EVOLUTION; CREOSOTE BUSH; ECOLOGY; ECOTYPE; ENDEMISM; FLOWERS; PARALLEL EVOLUTION; PLANT GEOGRAPHY; PLANTS**

Further Reading

Hillis, D. M., and C. Moritz. 1990. *Molecular Systematics*. Sunderland, Mass.: Sinauer.

Mayr, E. 1966. *Animal Species and Evolution*. Cambridge, Mass.: Belknap Press.

Otte, D., and J. A. Endler. 1989. *Speciation and its Consequences*. Sunderland, Mass.: Sinauer.

SPIDER, BLACK WIDOW. *See* BLACK WIDOW SPIDER

SPIDERS

Variably sized arthropods with the first body segment, the prosoma, covered by a single plate, the mouthparts (chelicerae) in two segments with poison glands, the abdomen (opisthosoma) consisting of 12 united segments with appendages modified as spinnerets, and book lungs or tracheae for respiration. Spiders have four pairs of walking legs preceded by a pair of appendages, the pedipalps, usually modified in males for mating. The prosoma is connected to the opisthosoma by a thin pedicel. Spiders have up to eight eyes.

Spiders make up the arachnid order Araneae, and species are known to occur in nearly every habitat on earth, with the possible exception of oceans. There are even aquatic spiders. Although about 26,000 species have been described, many remain to be discovered, particularly in tropical rain forests of the world. Spider density can be high, with more than 2,200,000 individuals found in a single acre of a grassy field. Spiders vary in size both within and among species. Some species are nearly invisible to the naked eye, whereas others may reach more than nine centimeters in total length. The most impressive (but not most toxic) spiders, the tarantulas, are in the family Theraphosidae and are typically recognized by their large size and hairy body and legs. Some of the more toxic spiders are black widows (family Theridiidae), brown recluses (family Loxoscelidae), and some of the tropical species in the family Ctenidae.

Many spiders produce webs that are used primarily for capturing prey. The structures that spiders use to produce webs, spinnerets, are known from the earliest fossil spiders, indicating that webs were produced by spiders during the Devonian as long ago as 385 million years. This also indicates that web production was evolutionarily "lost" in those present-day species that do not construct webs. Webs are constructed of silk and vary greatly in size and shape, depending on species.

Spiders are exceedingly diverse ecologically. All are predators on other invertebrates, and some are even known to take vertebrates. Large tarantulas, for example, can easily feed on lizards, small snakes, and baby mice. Even smaller species of spiders, like black widows, can capture juvenile lizards in their webs.

Common spiders in deserts of the world are tarantulas, black widows, crab spiders (several families), and wolf spiders (family Lycosidae). Ecology and life histories of spiders vary among species, but most produce large numbers of small eggs that hatch into minute spiderlings that are morphologically very similar to adults. The spiderlings may live in the same burrow with adult females (as in tarantulas), ride on the back of the females (as in wolf spiders), or live in the webs of the parents (many of the remaining spiders) until they are large enough to survive on their own. Tarantulas are among the most conspicuous spiders of deserts because of their large size and migratory habits during the breeding season. Males typically search for burrows of females by walking considerable distances, both at night and during the day. They are common sights in deserts after rains. Males typically live for only about a year. Once males find and mate with a female, the female retreats to her burrow, where eggs are laid between layers of webbing. Females typically live many years and reproduce repeatedly.—Laurie J. Vitt

See also **ARACHNIDS; ARTHROPODS; BLACK WIDOW SPIDER; DEFENSIVE ADAPTATIONS, ANIMALS; POISONOUS ANIMALS; SCORPIONS; SUN SPIDER; TARANTULA; VENOM**

Further Reading

Gertsch, J. W. 1979. *American Spiders*. 2d ed. New York: Van Nostrand Reinhold.

Kaston, B. J. 1978. *How to Know the Spiders*. Dubuque, Iowa: W. C. Brown.

Shear, W. A., ed. 1986. *Spiders, Webs, Behavior, and Evolution*. Stanford: Stanford University Press.

Shear, W. A., J. M. Palmer, J. A. Coddington, and P. M. Bonamo. 1989. A Devonian spinneret: Early evidence of spiders and silk use. *Science* 246:479–481.

SPRINGBOK

Species of antelope (*Antidorcas marsupialis*; mammalian family Bovidae, order Artiodactyla) inhabiting the open, dry savannas and grasslands of Angola, Namibia, Botswana, and South Africa. These small antelopes, also called springbucks, have a head and body length of 120–140 centimeters, tail length of 15–30 centimeters, shoulder height of 73–87 centimeters, and weight of 30–48 kilograms. They are brownish, with a reddish brown horizontal

Springbok (*Antidorcas marsupialis*) in Etosha National Park, northern Namibia. (Photo: M. A. Mares)

stripe on the sides, and a white belly and tail. Both males and females have horns.

Light-colored hairs cover a fold of skin that extends along the midline of the back to the base of the tail. When the animal is alarmed these hairs and the white hairs of the rump are erected. Springbok exhibit a behavior when alarmed or playing called springing or stotting that may serve to confuse predators or act as a warning to other springbok. While leaping to heights of 3.5 meters, the body is curved, the legs are stiff, and the head is held down—a most unusual behavior that is highly visible at great distances.

This is one of the most arid-adapted small antelopes in southern Africa. They are generally inactive during the hottest part of the day and may seek shade if it is available. Springbok do not need free water but will drink if it is available. They are able to detect rainfall at distances of several hundred kilometers. Several physiological mechanisms and types of behavior help to keep water loss to a minimum. Evaporative cooling by sweating is limited. When temperatures are above 30°C, springbok will orient the long axis of their bodies to the sun, minimizing the amount of solar heat hitting the body. The white hairs of the belly, back, and tail reflect up to 75 percent of the radiation, and if they are oriented properly, reflectance increases up to 90 percent. Springbok have the shortest hairs known for a desert ungulate. Although the short, thin fur allows the rapid "off-loading" of heat and prevents over-

heating during cool nights, springbok must shiver to keep warm.

Springbok are both browsers and grazers, switching between the wet and the dry season. Their small body size and high metabolic rate necessitates very high fermentation rates. They eat plants with high protein and water content and feed at night.

Reproduction is not seasonal but appears to be concentrated during the wet season. A single young is born after a gestation of 24 weeks. Females reach sexual maturity at seven months, males at one year.

Springbok are gregarious and form large herds during the wet season. During the dry season smaller groups of 100 females and some adult males are common. Massive seasonal migrations of springbok, or trekbookken, have been recorded. These migrations, which probably occurred every 10–40 years, with increasing frequency during droughts, may have followed a natural 18-year rainfall cycle. Herds numbering in the millions migrated from the Nama Karoo and the southern Kalahari to the Succulent Karoo as vegetation deteriorated. Populations of springbok are now much reduced due to hunting pressure, and such migrations are rare.—Janet K. Braun

See also **ANTELOPE; ENDOTHERMY; HEAT BALANCE; KALAHARI DESERT; KAROO; MAMMALS; NAMIBIA, DESERTS OF; SOUTH AFRICA, DESERTS OF; UNGULATES; WATER BALANCE**

Further Reading

Estes, R. D. 1991. *The Behavior Guide to African Mammals.* Berkeley: University of California Press.

Grzimek's Encyclopedia of Mammals. Vol. 5. 1990. New York: McGraw-Hill.

Kingdon, J. 1989. *East African Mammals: Atlas of Evolution in Africa (Bovids).* Vol. 3D. Chicago: University of Chicago Press.

Lovegrove, B. 1993. *The Living Deserts of Southern Africa.* Vlaeberg: Fernwood.

Macdonald, D., ed. 1984. *The Encyclopedia of Mammals.* New York: Facts on File.

Nowak, R. M. 1991. *Walker's Mammals of the World.* 5th ed. Baltimore: Johns Hopkins University Press.

Skinner, J. D., and R. H. N. Smithers. 1990. *The Mammals of the Southern African Subregion.* Pretoria: University of Pretoria.

SPRINGHARE

Unusual bipedal species of rodent, *Pedetes cafer* (family Pedetidae, order Rodentia), resembling a small kangaroo and inhabiting open arid or semiarid habitats and savannas of southern Africa and East Africa (Kenya, Tanzania, Angola, Zimbabwe, Botswana, Namibia, South Africa). The single living species prefers sandy areas with little vegetation. Where they occur they are generally common. Decreases in available food resources as a result of overgrazing by domestic livestock may negatively affect population sizes of springhares.

These large rodents (length of body 35–45 centimeters, weight three to four kilograms) are brownish or pale colored, with a whitish belly; the area in front of the thighs and the inside of the legs is whitish. The tail (length 37–48 centimeters) has a black tuft and is used to maintain balance when hopping. The ears are long (seven to nine centimeters) and can be folded. They have a backward folding flap of skin (tragus) that closes the ear opening to keep out sand when digging. The nostrils can also be closed. The forelimbs are small and have five toes with long, curved claws for digging. The long hind limbs have four toes; the third is elongated (the first is absent, the second is small); the claws are wider than those on the forefeet and resemble small hooves. The eyes are large. The auditory bullae are greatly inflated. The molars are rootless and grow throughout life.

Springhares are herbivores and prefer grass and roots that are high in water and protein content; they will also eat agricultural crops. Water is obtained from dew and from leaves and fruits of plants. At night they may be seen foraging in groups of two to six individuals; this behavior may reduce the possibility of a predatory attack on any single individual.

During the day springhares remain in their tunnels and burrows, which may be up to 80 centimeters below the surface. Each burrow system has multiple entrances, some marked with piles of excavated dirt. The entrances are plugged with dirt for protection and control of airflow. Nest chambers or food storage areas are lacking. When resting springhares place their head and forelegs between the hind legs and their head on the ground; the ears are folded back, and the tail is curled around the head. This position may allow detection of vibrations made by predators while the animal is sleeping.

In general springhares are solitary; only one adult occupies each burrow. Reproduction occurs year-round, and females may have up to three pregnancies per year. One large, well-developed young is born after a gestation period of 72–82 days. Young leave the nest after reaching about 1.5 kilograms and are sexually mature at 2.5 kilograms. In captivity springhares may live up to 14 years.— Janet K. Braun

See also **BIPEDALITY; CONVERGENT EVOLUTION; HERBIVORY; KALAHARI DESERT; KAROO; MAMMALS; NAMIBIA, DESERTS OF; PINNAE; RODENTS; SOUTH AFRICA, DESERTS OF**

Further Reading

Grzimek's Encyclopedia of Mammals. Vol. 3. 1990. New York: McGraw-Hill.

Kingdon, J. 1984. *East African Mammals: Atlas of Evolution in Africa (Hares and Rodents)*. Vol. 2B. Chicago: University of Chicago Press.

Macdonald, D., ed. 1984. *The Encyclopedia of Mammals*. New York: Facts on File.

Nowak, R. M. 1991. *Walker's Mammals of the World*. 5th ed. Baltimore: Johns Hopkins University Press.

Skinner, J. D., and R. H. N. Smithers. 1990. *The Mammals of the Southern African Subregion*. Pretoria: University of Pretoria.

SQUIRREL

Term applied to a variety of species of rodents in the mammalian family Sciuridae, a diverse family with 50 genera and 273 species that is nearly global in distribution. Sciurids are absent only from the southern tip of South America, extreme northern latitudes, Antarctica, Australia, New Zealand, and other Pacific islands. The family includes tree squirrels, ground squirrels, chipmunks, marmots, woodchucks, prairie dogs, flying squirrels, and giant flying squirrels. The term "squirrel" is generally used to refer only to the tree squirrels; the other species in this genus are generally referred to with the appropriate modifiers (e.g., ground squirrel or flying squirrel).

Tree squirrels alone are an extremely diverse group and account for nearly two-thirds of the species in the family. They are mostly forest-dwelling animals with long, bushy tails that act as a counterweight as these agile animals scramble among the tree branches. They are abundant in coniferous, temperate deciduous, and tropical forests. Tree squirrels occur in arid regions where there are trees along watercourses. None of the species are truly desert adapted but are found in fairly dry forests in parts of their range.

Ground squirrels are the most common representatives of the sciurids in arid habitats.—Thomas E. Lacher, Jr.

See also **GROUND SQUIRREL; PHYSIOLOGY; PRAIRIE DOG; RODENTS; SALT BALANCE; WATER BALANCE**

Further Reading

Macdonald, D., ed. 1984. *The Encyclopedia of Mammals.* New York: Facts on File.

Murie, J. O., and G. R. Michener. 1984. *The Biology of Ground-dwelling Tree Squirrels.* Lincoln: University of Nebraska Press.

Nowak, R. M. 1991. *Walker's Mammals of the World.* 5th ed. Baltimore: Johns Hopkins University Press.

STAR DUNE. *See* DUNES

STEPPE

Treeless area whose vegetation consists of grasses and grasslike (graminoid) plants with a significant small shrub and subshrub component. In western North America many of the intermountain grasslands are actually steppes due to the presence of large amounts of the shrub *Artemisia tridentata* and the subshrub *Artemisia frigida*. There, as in many of the world's steppes, grazing has reduced the dominance of the graminoids, causing an increase in the shrub components.

The Asian steppes in Siberia and Mongolia also have increasing shrub populations in response to increased grazing pressure. In some portions of the autonomous province of Inner Mongolia, heavy grazing has reduced plant diversity to a single species. The steppes of northern Asia are felt to be relics of a glacial era, as pollen analysis of deep lakes and bogs shows that a similar steppe community was found in the region during active glacial periods.

One of the best-known steppes is the Pampas of eastern Argentina. However, it can be considered to be a grassland, because the shrub component is so small. The humid nature of this region separates it from other true steppes. Because rainfall averages from 500 to 1,000 millimeters per year, it was once thought that fires set by European settlers were the reason that trees do not grow in this area. However, the vegetation is now considered to be of natural origin.—Linda L. Wallace

See also **AFRICA, DESERTS OF; ANDEAN GRASSLANDS; ANDES; AN INTRODUCTION TO DESERTS; ASIA, DESERTS OF; CLIMATE; DESERTS; DESERT GRASSLAND; GRASSES; GRASSLAND; GREAT AMER-ICAN DESERT; GREAT BASIN DESERT; HOLDRIDGE LIFE ZONES; PAMPAS; PATAGONIA; PLANT GEOGRAPHY; SAVANNA; SEMIARID ZONES; SOUTH AMERICA, DESERTS OF; UNITED STATES, DESERTS OF**

Further Reading

Walter, H. 1983. *Vegetation of the Earth.* Berlin: Springer.

West, N. E. 1988. Intermountain deserts, shrub steppes, and woodlands. *In* M. G. Barbour and W. D. Billings, eds., *North American Terrestrial Vegetation*, 209–230. Cambridge: Cambridge University Press.

STOMA

Pore in the shoot epidermis of plants and surrounding associated guard cells. (The plural of stoma is stomata; colloquial terms are stomate and stomates.) The shoot epidermis is a single layer of cells that covers stems, leaves, flower parts, fruits, and seeds. It provides protection against desiccation, and in most plants and plant organs it secretes a cuticle (waxy covering) that is an effective barrier to water (H_2O) loss. However, green tissues must extract carbon dioxide (CO_2) from the surrounding atmosphere to carry out photosynthesis. In the process of photosynthesis, free oxygen (O_2), a waste product of photosynthesis, is liberated into the atmosphere. This exchange of gases (CO_2, O_2, and H_2O) occurs via stomata in the epidermis. These stomata can be opened or closed through the activity of two guard cells that surround the pore.

Guard cells in all plants except grasses are sausage or kidney shaped; in all members of the grass family they are dumbbell shaped. Guard cells, in contrast to other epidermal cells, have chloroplasts and thus are photosynthetic. The inner wall adjacent to the pore is thicker than the walls away from the pore. That permits the guard cells to become distended, or bow, when they are engorged with water (turgid). Turgor pressure causes the pore to open and permits gas exchange between the interior of the plant and the atmosphere. When the guard cells lose water and become flaccid, the stomata are closed.

Plants use cellular energy to control guard cell turgor by pumping solutes into (when the stomata are open) or out of (when the stomata are closed) the guard cells. Potassium ions (K^+), and perhaps sucrose, are important in the solute balance. Opening and closing of stomata is significant in conserving H_2O and CO_2 balances. When leaves begin to wilt the guard cells become flaccid and the stomata close, thereby restricting water loss. Many plants have the ability to close stomata before they become severely wilted. Stomata distribution may also assist in water retention; the stomata of the vast preponderance of plants are more abundant on the lower surfaces of leaves, where temperatures, and thus transpiration rates, are lower. However, photosynthesis is restricted when the stomata are closed. CO_2 buildup in the leaf or stem induces the stomata to close, which conserves water. Light, which initiates photosynthesis, causes the stomata to open.

In deserts and grasslands water is often a limiting factor for plant survival, and water conservation is important in plants adapted to these biomes. In desert succulents (plants with spongy, water-retaining tissues, such as cacti) stomatal opening occurs during the cooler evening hours when transpiration is reduced. In these plants a mechanism for the storage of CO_2 has evolved.

Stomata are rare on the epidermis of seeds, but two groups of plants of the American southwestern deserts (California poppies and capers) do have seed stomata. These stomata might permit the seed to absorb atmospheric moisture, which is often higher than levels of water in desert soils.

All members of the plant kingdom (mosses through flowering plants), including the oldest fossil representatives, bear stomata. Therefore, the presence of stomata is a shared derived character and ancestral plants most likely also had stomata.—James R. Estes

See also **LEAVES; PHOTOSYNTHESIS; PLANT ADAPTATIONS; PLANTS; SALT BALANCE; TRANSPIRATION; WATER BALANCE**

Further Reading

Esau, K. 1977. *Anatomy of Seed Plants.* 2d ed. New York: Wiley.

Jarvis, P. G, and T. A. Mansfield, eds. 1981. *Stomatal Physiology.* Cambridge: Cambridge University Press.

Zeiger, E., G. D. Farquhar, and I. R. Cowan, eds. 1987. *Stomatal Function.* Stanford: Stanford University Press.

STONE PAVEMENT

Surface feature of concentrated stones ranging in size from boulder to finest gravel and overlying a layer of sand, silt, or clay. Stone pavements are typically one to two clasts thick (a clast is an individual

Stone pavement near Yuma, Arizona, with ocotillo (*Fouquieria splendens*) in the background. (Photo: M. A. Mares)

grain or pebble in a sedimentary rock), devoid of vegetation and fine sediments, and, in some cases, smooth. *Hamada*, *reg*, and *serir* are Arabic terms for stone pavements. Hamadas are pavements of larger rocks and boulders that were most likely eroded in place or transported short distances as indicated by the lack of sorting and angularity of the clasts and their similarity in composition to the underlying bedrock. Regs and serirs are gravel- and pebble-sized pavements consisting of stones that are smooth, sorted, and of mixed composition. "Serir" and "reg" are terms that are used preferentially in different regions. Serir is more commonly used to describe pavements in the central Sahara, such as in the Libyan Desert, whereas reg is commonly used in Algeria. In the Australian Desert stone pavements are referred to as gibber plains and are composed primarily of silcrete (a rock containing a great deal of silica) or other duricrust fragments. Stony plains in the deserts of central Asia are known as gobis. The term "desert pavement" is more commonly used in the southwestern United States to refer to very smooth, flat, pebble-sized pavements that develop on the lower sections of alluvial fan surfaces after prolonged periods of weathering. Desert pavements are often covered with rock varnish.

Four explanations for the formation of stone pavements have been proposed. First, fines (clay- and silt-sized particles such as in desert dust or dunes) may be concentrated by deflation (lowering of a surface by wind), which continues until the stones are sufficiently closely spaced and protuberant to act as a protective desert armor and are subsequently cemented. explains the pavement as being a lag or veneer left by the deflation. However, deflation may be less effective than originally thought because of the lack of fine materials, since most fines form protective crusts as a result of wetting and drying. Second, overland flow of water, including rainsplash (raindrops hitting a surface and causing erosion) and sheetwash (the minimum amount of water needed to initiate any type of sediment movement or erosion), produces concentration as it erodes fine-textured soil on sloping desert pavements. This appears to be more effective than wind, as desert thunderstorms produce large, high-impact raindrops that dislodge fine particles from the crust. In addition, the relative impermeability of the surface crusts can increase the erosive capabilities of overland flow. Third, materials may be concentrated by the upward displacement of stones. Soils may contain expansive clays that are subject to swelling and heaving on wetting and to shrinking and deep cracking on drying. A net upward displacement of stones results from the filling of cracks beneath the stones by the fine particles that were once above them, followed by cementation. Fourth, pedogenic (soil-forming) and aeolian (wind) processes may be responsible for the concentration of stones in place. Desert pavements are formed and maintained on the surface via aeolian deposition of silts and clays and simultaneous development of soils beneath the stone mantles. Silts, sands, and clays form a soil on which larger rocks fall and are cemented, or aeolian debris settles between loose stones and forms a soil layer beneath the stones. As additional sand, silt, and clay are deposited, the soil will accumulate, producing a layer on which the stones will settle evenly, forming the level surface common on desert pavements.

Stone pavements have been recognized as being important for a variety of reasons. In the absence of vegetation, stone pavements provide surface stability and protection for desert soils. If the pavements are destroyed, the underlying soil can be subject to accelerated erosion. This is a major concern in arid lands where off-road vehicle use has increased.—Vatche P. Tchakerian

See also **DIRT BIKES; DURICRUSTS; MIDDLE EAST, DESERTS OF; MINERALS; OFF-ROAD VEHICLES;**

Jabiru (*Jabiru mycteria*), a common inhabitant of the Chacoan thorn forest of Argentina. (Photo: M. A. Mares)

ROCK VARNISH; SOILS, DESERT; WEATHERING, DESERT; WIND EROSION

Further Reading

Cooke, R. 1970. Stone pavements in deserts. *Annals of the Association of American Geographers* 60:560–577.

Mabbutt, J. A. 1977. *Desert Landforms.* Cambridge, Mass.: MIT Press.

STORK

Large to very large wading bird with almost cosmopolitan distribution (family Ciconiidae, order Ciconiiformes). Seventeen species in six to nine genera are recognized. Ciconiids reach maximum species diversity in tropical Asia (nine species) and tropical Africa (eight species). Two other taxa, the hammerhead (*Scopus umbretta*) and the whale-headed stork (*Balaeniceps rex*) are commonly referred to as "storks," but each is a representative of a monotypic family (Scopidae and Balaenicipitidae, respectively) within the Ciconiiformes. Total length ranges from 80 to 150 centimeters and weight from two to nine kilograms. Storks have long legs and long robust bills, both adaptations for feeding. Plumage is primarily white, gray, black, or gray and black and is often strikingly patterned. The head is either partly or wholly bare and often brightly colored. The broad, long wings are well suited for soaring, although storks are also strong fliers.

All storks frequent aquatic habitats. A number of species may be found inhabiting permanent water bodies or visiting ephemeral wetlands in arid regions. Some taxa, notably the marabou (*Leptoptilos crumeniferus*) of Africa, may range far from water into dry savannas. Diet usually consists of insects, crustaceans, amphibians, fish, and other small vertebrates. Carrion is a prominent component of the diet of *Leptoptilos* species, including the marabou. Adaptations for dissipation of heat include panting and excretion of dilute urine over the legs.

All storks are strongly territorial when nesting, although this may be in either a solitary or a colonial setting, depending on the species. Seasonal monogamous pair-bonds are probably the case for most ciconiids. The nests, which are often reused annually, are generally constructed in trees and on cliff ledges. Nests are generally rather untidy, composed of substantial piles of branches and earth. Clutch sizes range from one to seven. Both sexes contribute to nest building, incubation (30–50 days), and parental care.—Stephen C. Lougheed

See also **AFRICA, DESERTS OF; AQUATIC HABITATS; ASIA, DESERTS OF; BIRDS; CHACO; SAVANNA; MONTE DESERT; RIPARIAN COMMUNITIES; RIVERS; SHRIMP, DESERT; SOUTH AMERICA, DESERTS OF**

Further Reading

Brown, L. H., E. K. Urban, and K. Newman. 1982. *The Birds of Africa*. Vol. 1. New York: Academic Press.

Cramp, S., and K. E. L. Simmons, eds. 1977. *Handbook of the Birds of Europe, the Middle East and North Africa: The Birds of the Western Palearctic*. Vol. 1. Oxford: Oxford University Press.

Kahl, M. P. 1966. Comparative ethology of the Ciconiidae. Pt. 1: The marabou stork, *Leptoptilos crumeniferus* (Lesson). *Behaviour* 27:76–106.

———. 1971. Social behavior and taxonomic relationships of the storks. *Living Bird* 10:151–170.

———. 1972. Comparative ethology of the Ciconiidae. Pt. 4: The "typical" storks (genera *Ciconia, Sphenorhynchus, Dissoura,* and *Euxenura*). *Zeitschrift für Tierpsychologie* 30:225–252.

Soothill, E., and R. Soothill. 1989. *Wading Birds of the World*. London: Blandford.

SUBTROPICAL DESERTS. *See* DESERTS, SUBTROPICAL

SUCCESSION

Theory stating that changes that occur in plant and animal community structure following a disturbance or on a newly available substrate proceed in a directional, or predictable, pattern. All ecosystems are dynamic; that is, they go through processes of change over time and space. Succession can be classified into two major types. If a newly available substrate has never before supported life, then primary succession will occur. This consists of the invasion of "pioneer" organisms onto the new surface, usually bare rock, cooled lava, or newly exposed soil. Pioneer plant species usually include lichens on rock or lava and grasses or grasslike plants (graminoids) on new soil. As the growth processes of these organisms alter and stabilize the surface, new groups of organisms become capable of tolerating the newly altered environment. Usually they grow more rapidly than the original pioneer species and will thus supersede them. In turn this group of colonizing organisms will also alter the substrate and will allow yet another, and different, community to gain a foothold. This continues until a community forms which is constrained more by climatic factors than by substrate alteration and competition. This community is termed the climatic climax. It is felt that this community will continue to occupy the site either until climate shifts occur or until the site is disturbed.

After disturbance another form of succession occurs. This is termed secondary succession and follows much the same scenario, except that substrate alteration and stabilization requirements are not nearly so stringent. Thus a series of replacement communities, also known as seres, forms until a climatic climax community is reached.

The above description assumes that the ecosystem in which this process is occurring is capable of coming to some form of equilibrium, the climatic climax. There are a number of ecologists who feel that ecosystems, particularly ecosystems in stressful environments such as deserts, never reach a true equilibrium. In this case variable climatic factors intervene and a stable climax is never formed. A series of different community types may supersede one another over time as the climate varies within certain limits. Thus the end product of succession is a series of communities that vary about an equilibrium but never reach it.

Regardless of which viewpoint ecologists espouse, all agree that rates of succession in desert environments are quite slow. Most desert plant species are slow growing, and the chance of successful establishment of new seedlings in this harsh environment is quite low. Thus, in deserts, effects of disturbances that may have occurred in the past and resulted in the loss of plants are very long lasting.

Disturbances in deserts which can trigger secondary succession include animal burrows and diggings, scouring floods, fires, and human activities, such as construction, farming, ranching, and transportation. Of these, the incidence of human activities is increasing, particularly the popularity of off-road vehicle use. These vehicles can be driven over a variety of terrains and frequently destroy the vegetation by either direct uprooting or increasing soil erosion. The effects of their passage will be seen for an extremely long time.—Linda L. Wallace

See also **BIOME; CONSERVATION IN DESERTS; DESERTIFICATION; DIRT BIKES; ECOLOGY; ECOSYSTEM; LANDSCAPE; OFF-ROAD VEHICLES; PLANT ADAPTATIONS; PLANT GEOGRAPHY; PLANTS; SPECIATION**

Further Reading

Polis, G. A., ed. 1991. *The Ecology of Desert Communities*. Tucson: University of Arizona Press.

VanKat, J. L. 1979. *The Natural Vegetation of North America*. New York: Wiley.

SUCCULENTS

Plants with swollen or fleshy tissues that store water for use when environmental water is unavailable. Succulents occur in habitats with periodic drought, including deserts, rock outcrops, and rain forest canopies. They are uncommon in extremely arid environments or where growing season frost occurs. Many halophytes (plants of salty environments) are succulents because water is physiologically unavailable in salty habitats, even if soil is wet as in salt marshes. Cells of water-storage organs, commonly leaves, stems, and roots, are generally large with large vacuoles. Succulents occur in a variety of growth forms including annuals, geophytes, deciduous perennials, and leafless perennials. Plant families

Succulent euphorbs in the Rajasthan Desert of northwestern India near Jodhpur. (Photo: M. A. Mares)

with many succulents are the Agavaceae, Bromeliaceae, Cactaceae, Chenopodiaceae, Crassulaceae, Euphorbiaceae, Mesembryanthemaceae, Orchidaceae, and Piperaceae.

Most succulents have extensive shallow root systems to take advantage of light rainfalls. Water uptake is enhanced in succulents by low tissue water potentials. Some succulents (e.g., *Crassula*) absorb dew or fog condensate through hydathodes, special structures at the ends of veins in leaves. Succulent tissues can expand rapidly as water is absorbed, then gradually contract as water is lost. Succulents often possess other adaptations to reduce water loss, including a thick waxy cuticle, light coloration, hairiness, and few stomates or stomates that are sunken. Leaves may be positioned to reduce light interception, absent altogether, or reduced to spines (e.g., cacti). Many succulents are CAM plants, although others use C_3 or C_4 photosynthesis. CAM plants conserve water by opening stomates at night rather than during the day.— Ernest M. Steinauer

See also **C_3 PLANTS; C_4 PLANTS; CACTI; CACTUS, COLUMNAR; CAM PLANTS; CHOLLA; CRYPTOGAMS; DEW; FOG DESERT; HALOPHYTES; PHOTOSYNTHESIS; ORGAN PIPE CACTUS; PRICKLY PEAR; ROOTS; SALT DESERT; STOMA; THERMOREGULATION; THORN; TRANSPIRATION**

Further Reading

Eppele, D. L. 1996. *Cactus and Succulents for the High Deserts*. Bisbee: Arizona Cactus and Succulent Research.

Gibson, A. C. 1982. The anatomy of succulence. *In* I. P. Ting and M. Gibbs, eds., *Crassulacean Acid Metabolism*, 1–16. Baltimore: Waverly.

Nobel, P. S. 1994. *Remarkable Agaves and Cacti*. New York: Oxford University Press.

Von Willert, D. J., B. M. Eller, M. J. A. Werger, E. Brinckmann, and H. Ihlenfeldt. 1992. *Life Strategies of Succulents in Deserts*. Cambridge: Cambridge University Press.

SUNBURN

Skin injury resulting from excessive exposure to solar ultraviolet radiation in the wavelength range of 290–320 nanometers (1×10^{-9} meters). Exposure is influenced by many factors, including environmental conditions as well as the use of protective clothing and sunscreens. The intensity of solar radiation diminishes with increasing latitude and decreasing altitude, and the effects of exposure vary with duration, time of day, and season.

Sunburn is different from a thermal burn in that ultraviolet radiation (UVR) also produces a photochemical effect—a chemical change initiated by the absorption of light or ultraviolet radiation. In photochemical reactions a quantity of light or radiation has the same effect regardless of whether it is absorbed over a long or short period. Therefore, cumulative sun exposure is important. In addition, susceptibility to sunburn varies with age, the young and the elderly being more sensitive.

Redness of the skin (erythema) due to capillary dilation occurs in skin areas directly exposed to solar radiation. Blood vessels in the affected areas dilate several hours after exposure, with maximum dilation occurring 8–24 hours following exposure. Other symptoms associated with sunburn are blistering, sweat suppression, and reduction of the pain threshold.

Erythema associated with sunburn is caused by the release of histamine and prostaglandins in the body. Skin cells increase in number because of an increased mitotic rate, which begins within 72 hours after sun exposure. The skin therefore becomes thicker but can return to normal if there is no further sun exposure for two months. Tanning of the skin occurs over three to four days following sun exposure and is caused by new melanin production in pigment cells (melanocytes) located in the epidermis. Thickening of the skin provides important protection against continued UVR exposure. In light-skinned people it probably confers more protection than does tanning.

Irreversible degenerative damage to both epidermal and dermal skin layers may follow repeated exposures. Damage may lead to premature wrinkling and greatly increased risk of skin cancer. Heat accelerates degeneration; therefore, the typical hot climate of deserts may compound sunburn problems. In addition, highly reflective desert sands intensify exposure.—E. Annette Halpern

See also **CLIMATE; CLOTHING; HEAT; HEAT STRESS; HEATSTROKE; HUMAN PHYSIOLOGY IN DESERTS; INSOLATION; SALT BALANCE; SUNSTROKE; SURVIVAL IN DESERTS; WATER BALANCE**

Further Reading

Diffey, B. L. 1991. Solar ultraviolet radiation effects on biological systems. *Physics in Medicine and Biology* 36:299–328.

Hawk, J. L. M., and J. A. Parrish. 1982. Responses of normal skin to ultraviolet radiation. *In* J. D. Regan and J. A. Parrish, eds., *The Science of Photomedicine*, 219–260. New York: Plenum.

Koenigsberg, R., ed. 1989. *Churchill's Medical Dictionary*. New York: Churchill Livingstone.

Slonim, N. B. 1974. *Environmental Physiology*. St. Louis: Mosby.

Stewart, W. D., J. L. Danto, and S. Maddin. 1974. *Dermatology Diagnosis and Treatment of Cutaneous Disorders*. St. Louis: Mosby.

SUNSHINE. *See* INSOLATION

SUN SPIDER

Large (up to seven centimeters) arthropod with four pairs of walking legs, a pair of leglike structures called pedipalps located anterior to the walking legs, and extremely heavy and long feeding structures called chelicerae. The front section of the body, the prosoma, is covered by two large plates. The first pair of walking legs function as tactile organs. The pedipalps have adhesive pads on the ends which serve to hold prey. The chelicerae are highly modified, forming a pair of vertically articulating pincers. The soft bulblike body is covered with fine hairs.

Sun spiders are in the arachnid order Solifugae, and there are approximately 800 species worldwide. Many species are common in deserts, including more than 50 species in deserts of the United States. They are known locally by a variety of names, including wind scorpions, camel spiders,

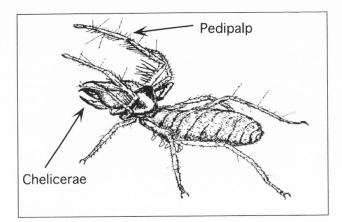

Sun spider (order Solifugae).

and solpugids. Many desert species are nocturnal but can be found by day underneath surface objects such as rocks. They occasionally are active by day, hence the name sun spiders. When active they are fast moving, giving rise to the common name wind scorpions. Sun spiders feed primarily on other arthropods but will take small vertebrates as well. Their pedipalps are used to capture prey, and their chelicerae are used to kill and masticate prey. Sun spiders produce no venoms and are harmless to humans. However, bacterial infections following bites often leave the impression that envenomation has occurred. A well-developed tracheal system is used for respiration. Eggs are deposited by females in burrows. The number of eggs ranges from about 50 to more than 200.—Laurie J. Vitt

See also **ANIMAL ADAPTATIONS; ARACHNIDS; ARTHROPODS; BLACK WIDOW SPIDER; DEFENSIVE ADAPTATIONS, ANIMALS; POISONOUS ANIMALS; SCORPIONS; SPIDERS; VENOM**

Further Reading

Barnes, R. D. 1980. *Invertebrate Zoology*. 4th ed. Philadelphia: Saunders.

Nielsen, C. 1995. *Animal Evolution: Interrelationships of the Living Phyla*. New York: Oxford University Press.

Smith, R. L. 1982. *Venomous Animals of Arizona*. Tucson: Cooperative Extension Service, University of Arizona.

SUNSTROKE

Explosive rise in body temperature resulting from failure of thermal regulation caused by exposure to the sun (= heatstroke). During or after exposure to intense sunlight in a hot environment its appearance in humans is forewarned by headache, weakness, and vertigo. Its clearest signals are elevated body temperature with little sweating; skin that is hot, red, and dry; and a hard and rapid pulse (160–180 bpm). Respiratory rate usually increases, whereas blood pressure is seldom affected. If untreated, disorientation may briefly precede sudden unconsciousness or convulsions, and death can ensue from cardiovascular failure. Survivors are likely to have brain damage if extremely high body temperatures are sustained for some hours. Susceptibility to sunstroke is increased by age, obesity, physical weakness, and a number of drugs, including alcohol, cocaine, and antihistamines.

Treatment of sunstroke requires heroic measures aimed at lowering the body temperature as rapidly as possible with whatever cooling means are available, such as wrapping the person in wet cloths or immersing the person in water. Body temperature should be monitored and care taken to avoid converting the hyperthermia (high body temperature) to hypothermia (low body temperature).

The best preventive is common sense, which dictates avoidance of prolonged exposure and strenuous exercise in hot conditions. If either is unavoidable, then care should be taken to dress properly; wide-brimmed hat and loose, lightweight, and light-colored clothing that reflects the sun and covers as much skin as possible. Such clothing allows evaporation of water (sweat) at the skin instead of at the cloth and reduces the radiant heat load by half and water loss by two-thirds relative to the unclothed state. Fluids and electrolytes are often lost imperceptibly and must be replaced by continuous intake of both fluids and foods that are slightly salty to the taste.—David S. Hinds

See also **CLOTHING; HEAT STRESS; HEATSTROKE; HUMAN PHYSIOLOGY IN DESERTS; HYPERTHERMIA; HYPOTHERMIA; PERSPIRATION; SALT BALANCE; SUNBURN; SURVIVAL IN DESERTS; TRANSPIRATION; WATER BALANCE**

Further Reading

Berkow, R. ed. 1992. *The Merck Manual*. Rahway, N. J.: Merck Research Laboratories.

Daniels, Jr., F. 1972. Radiant energy. *In* N. B. Slonim, ed., *Environmental Physiology*, 276–287. Saint Louis: Mosby.

Ingram, D. L., and L. E. Mount 1975. *Man and Animals in Hot Environments*. New York: Springer.

Schmidt-Nielsen, K. 1964. *Desert Animals: Physiological Problems of Heat and Water*. New York: Oxford University Press.

SURVIVAL IN DESERTS

Process of managing to exist in the desert despite the challenges of heat, cold, and lack of water. The deserts of the world typically straddle the 30° latitudinal belts (the horse latitudes) on major continental landmasses in both hemispheres, although they may be displaced occasionally, particularly toward higher latitudes, by the presence of north-south oriented mountain ranges that form rain shadow deserts on their lee sides. Wherever deserts occur they present challenges to their attendant organisms, for they are regions of great aridity and extreme 24-hour temperature fluctuations.

Whereas low-elevation, horse latitude deserts are characteristically dry and hot in the summer and cool in the winter, deserts of higher latitudes (e.g., the Great Basin Desert of North America) or higher elevations (e.g., the puna of South America), while dry, are more moderate in temperature in the summer and cold in the winter. Furthermore, the seasonal rainfall patterns in the various deserts of the world vary enormously. Although the North American Mojave and Sonoran deserts are geographically adjacent, the more northerly Mojave experiences a single, winter rainy season, whereas the more southerly Sonoran Desert has both winter and summer rainy seasons. Moreover, although annual rainfall amounts and seasons are quite predictable in some deserts (such as the Mojave), other deserts of the world may experience prolonged droughts of several years (or even decades) duration, which are then broken by torrential, monsoonal rains, producing extensive flooding; this latter condition is typical of Australian deserts.

Thus when one speaks of survival in deserts, it is important to understand that while all deserts are characterized by aridity and extreme daily temperature fluctuations, each of the world's deserts presents its own suite of environmental challenges to survival. In addition, the term "survival" is somewhat misleading and likely an artifact of human perceptions stemming from the Darwinian concept of a "struggle for existence." It is true that for most humans, life in deserts approaches survival, but for the many plants and animals that live there and are adapted to desert conditions, continuing existence likely offers no more challenge than life does to rain forest organisms that are adapted to that ecosystem.

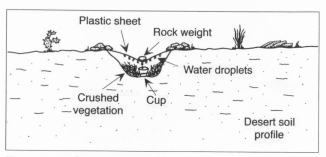

Emergency desert water still.

The universal adaptations that characterize native desert plants and animals are those that deal with aridity and temperature fluctuations. While animals may employ behavior to ameliorate these desert extremes within narrower limits that are compatible with their physiological limitations, plants are more rigidly fixed on the desert surface and must rely largely on physiological and morphological adaptations to meet the environmental challenges of the desert.

For humans, the primary challenge of desert habitation is aridity, both from the perspectives of the scarcity of drinking water and the very dry air that maximizes water lost in respiration and perspiration. Another result of aridity that affects desert people who are reliant on the desert as a food source is the low rate of primary production. Thus most native desert dwellers are nomadic people who move periodically from place to place as sparse water, food, and fuel supplies are depleted, allowing them to replenish naturally for future exploitation. Examples of such nomadic native desert inhabitants are central Australian Aboriginals; and the Bedouins of the Middle East and North Africa. At the opposite extreme are humans who are products of industrialized nations, whose behavioral innovations have allowed them to manipulate the desert into microenvironments that allow nearly complete escape from the desert macroenvironment; the North American gambling mecca of Las Vegas, Nevada, in the Mojave Desert is an example of extreme desert modification. Thus humans exploit deserts through behavioral modifications that promote survival, as the modest physiological capabilities of humans preclude a desert existence otherwise.

It is imperative for humans traveling in remote desert regions both to understand their physiological limitations and to be familiar with the behavioral adjustments that may be employed should they become temporarily stranded, thus enhancing survival possibilities. Water is of paramount importance, and should always be carried in large amounts, which is easy if one is traveling by automobile. When traveling by automobile in remote desert regions, it is equally important to have a fixed itinerary and time schedule that is filed with friends and a regional security office so that should an automobile breakdown occur and the traveler is missing from a scheduled stop, a search may commence as soon as possible. When a breakdown occurs that is beyond immediate repair, and unless an inhabited dwelling exists within a few miles, one should stay by the vehicle and use it for shelter at night and seek shade and try to remain calm and quiet during the day. Activity by day will only increase the rate of evaporative water loss and will result in displacement from the vehicle, its water supply, and from a large object (the vehicle) that is much easier for searchers to spot than a human.

Should the water supply be inadequate, a primitive water still may be fabricated which takes advantage of the cooler night air to yield small amounts of water that can prolong survival. This consists of a hole that is dug in the desert soil, partially filled with crushed vegetation of the most succulent kind available. Then a receptacle (cup or tin can) is placed in the center of the hole at the bottom and a sheet of plastic is used to cover the opening at the top, carefully sealing its sides to prevent air exchange with the outside with a weight (rock or other heavy object) placed on the outer surface in the center, immediately over the receptacle. The object is to trap water vapor evaporating from the crushed vegetation and the exposed soil within the hole which, when exposed to the cooler night air, will condense as water droplets on the under surface of the plastic sheet, flowing toward the weighted center and then dropping into the receptacle.

It must be emphasized that the human need for water in the desert far exceeds the capacity to produce it from a primitive still and that this latter measure will only help to stave off a thirst that requires the intake of water nearly as fast as it is lost from the human body. During the 1993 Gulf War in Iraq, for example, soldiers of the United States were required to consume eight quarts of water each day during normal (noncombat) activities. The role of behavioral amelioration of water loss can best be put into perspective by realizing that the bloodstream of an adult human carries about four liters of water and that a human exercising vigorously at an air temperature of about 36°C will lose about 4.2 liters of water per hour by sweating alone. Only thorough preparation combined with appropriate behavioral responses will ensure survival of humans in the desert.—Richard E. MacMillen

See also **ANIMAL ADAPTATIONS; ENDOTHERMY; HEAT; HEAT BALANCE; HEAT EXCHANGE; HEAT STRESS; HEATSTROKE; HUMAN PHYSIOLOGY IN DESERTS; KIDNEYS; PERSPIRATION; PHYSIOLOGY; PLANT ADAPTATIONS; SUNBURN; SUNSTROKE; SWEAT GLANDS; THERMOREGULATION; TRANSPIRATION; WATER BALANCE**

Further Reading

Gordon, M. S., G. A. Bartholomew, A. D. Grinnell, C. B. Jorgensen, and F. N. White. 1982. *Animal Physiology: Principles and Adaptations*. New York: Macmillan.

Hills, E. S., ed. 1966. *Arid Lands: A Geographical Appraisal*. London: Methuen.

Schmidt-Nielsen, K. 1964. *Desert Animals: Physiological Problems of Heat and Water*. New York: Oxford University Press.

Schmidt-Nielsen, K. 1990. *Animal Physiology: Adaptation and Environment*. 4th ed. New York: Cambridge University Press.

SWEAT. *See* PERSPIRATION

SWEAT GLANDS

Glands that provide water for evaporation at the skin surface to assist in heat loss from the body. Sweat glands provide an additional source of water for evaporative cooling beyond that which is normally evaporated from the respiratory and skin surfaces. The production of fluid by sweat glands is an energy-using process wherein the glands are activated during periods when heat loss by other means cannot prevent a rise in body temperature, typically occurring when the environmental temperature is high or during muscular exercise. Many mammals possess sweat glands, though they are absent from several species, especially those that are more heavily furred (including rodents, dogs, and cats). Sweat glands are also absent from birds.

Sweat glands are simple, tubular, highly coiled glands found deep within the skin which occur over much of the body. The hypothalamus is responsible for regulating the activity of the sweat glands through its sensitivity to blood temperature. Peripheral and central temperature receptors also provide neural inputs that determine sweat rate. When the body's heat load cannot be adequately dissipated, the sweat glands are activated at the motor nerve endings to release sweat at the surface of the skin. Heat is required to evaporate sweat, and when the heat is provided by the body, internal cooling results.

In addition to water, sweat contains potassium, sodium, and chloride ions and some nitrogenous wastes such as urea. When the volume of sweat is high, as on hot days or from prolonged exertion, timely replacements of fluid and electrolytes must occur. Fluids must obviously be consumed to maintain water balance. To regain osmotic balance, salts must also be consumed, and these are provided by an animal's normal food choices.—E. Annette Halpern

See also ANIMAL ADAPTATIONS; ENDOTHERMY; HEAT; HEAT BALANCE; HEAT EXCHANGE; HEAT STRESS; HEATSTROKE; HUMAN PHYSIOLOGY IN DESERTS; KIDNEYS; PERSPIRATION; PHYSIOLOGY; PLANT ADAPTATIONS; SUNBURN; SUNSTROKE; SURVIVAL IN DESERTS; THERMOREGULATION; TRANSPIRATION; WATER BALANCE

Further Reading

Craig, F. N. 1972. Sweat mechanisms in heat. In M. K. Yousef, S. M. Horvath, and R. W. Bullard, eds., Physiological Adaptations: Desert and Mountain, 53–64. New York: Academic Press.

Hickman, C. P., Jr., and L. S. Roberts. 1994. Biology of Animals. Dubuque, Iowa: Brown.

Hill, R. W., and G. A. Wyse. 1989. Animal Physiology. New York: Harper and Row.

Robinson, S., and D. L. Wiegman. 1974. Heat and humidity. In N. B. Slonim, ed., Environmental Physiology, 94–101. Saint Louis: Mosby.

SWIFT

Small to moderate-sized, highly aerial, insectivorous bird distributed throughout the Americas, Eurasia, and Africa (family Apodidae, order Apodiformes). The crested swifts of Southeast Asia are placed in a separate family, the Hemiprocnidae. Between 70 and 90 species of swifts have been described from up to 18 genera. Maximum species diversity occurs at tropical latitudes; a few migratory species breed in northern areas of Eurasia and North America. Swifts range throughout a variety of habitats, from tropical rain forest through dry deciduous woodlands to mountainous, rocky deserts. Examples of swift taxa that may be found in arid environments are the African palm swift (Cypsiurus parvus) and the Andean swift (Aeronautes andecolus). The former species inhabits human settlements, clearings in the African rain forest zone, and arid and mesic savannas in Africa south of the Sahara. The Andean swift ranges throughout semi-arid mountainous country from Peru south to northern Argentina and Chile.

Swifts have a narrow, cigar-shaped body and long slender wings. Total length ranges from 10 to 30 centimeters. Swifts spend an inordinate portion of their lives airborne, and have been reported eating, drinking, bathing, copulating, and even sleeping while in flight. Swifts perch on vertical surfaces, and adaptations to facilitate this include short robust tarsi, a strong modified foot for grasping (two toes facing forward and the other two facing backward), and, in some species, stiffened tail rectrices (feathers). The majority of the Apodidae have drab brown or black plumage, sometimes with white or pale markings. The bill is small and weak but when opened reveals a large gape to aid in the capture of insects.

Most swifts are described as being monogamous, and the pair-bond may extend over many years. Generally swifts are colonial, although some species will nest solitarily. Nests are typically small cups of various materials "glued" together with saliva and affixed to vertical or overhanging surfaces. Nest sites include crevices, caves, and hollows in trees as well as various man-made structures. Clutch size ranges from one to six. Parents share in incubation and parental duties. The incubation period is 17–28 days. The young are born naked and helpless and are fed boluses of insects. Swifts, both chicks and adults, may become semitorpid (i.e., lower core body temperature) to conserve energy.—Stephen C. Lougheed

See also AFRICA, DESERTS OF; ANIMAL ADAPTATIONS; ASIA, DESERTS OF; BIRDS; ENDOTHERMY; ESTIVATION; FEATHERS; INSECTS; LOCOMOTION; NESTS, BIRD; SOUTH AMERICA, DESERTS OF; WATER BALANCE

Further Reading

Bent, A. C. 1940. Life histories of North American cuckoos, goatsuckers, hummingbirds and their allies. U.S. National Museum Bulletin 176.

Cramp, S., ed. 1985. *Handbook of the Birds of Europe, the Middle East and North Africa: The Birds of the Western Palearctic*. Vol. 4. Oxford: Oxford University Press.

Fjeldså, J., and N. Krabbe. 1990. *Birds of the High Andes*. Svendborg, Denmark: Apollo.

Fry, C. H., S. Keith, and E. K. Urban. 1988. *The Birds of Africa*. Vol. 3. New York: Academic Press.

Lack, D. 1956. A review of the genera and nesting habits of swifts. *Auk* 73:1–32.

———. 1956. *Swifts in a Tower*. London: Methuen.

SYRIA, DESERTS OF

Arid and semiarid habitats lying within Syria, a Middle Eastern, largely desert country with an area of 185,180 square kilometers situated at the eastern end of the Mediterranean Sea and bordered by Iraq, Israel, Lebanon, Jordan, and Turkey. The climate is influenced by the Mediterranean, with rainfall decreasing as one travels eastward from the western coastal plain (which may receive rainfall of up to 1,000 millimeters or more in a year). Toward the inland desert in eastern Syria average annual precipitation decreases to less than 80 millimeters, with a mean annual temperature of about 20°C. Minimum and maximum temperatures range from 0°–47°C. (See map of Middle East deserts, p. 361.)

The western mountainous region of Syria (Ansariye Mountains) has many characteristics in common with Lebanon, including vegetation, landforms, and water resources. It is divided into two major elevational regions: the northern region, which has the country's highest peak (Jebel Akra at 1,730 meters), and the southern region, where elevation does not exceed 1,600 meters. The mountains are cut by a few watercourses that flow into the Mediterranean Sea. The western mountain range is folded toward the east, where the huge Syrian Desert begins at the eastern slopes of the Anti-Lebanon Mountains.

The western slopes of the Ansariye Mountains support various species of *Quercus* (oak), *Acer*, and *Juniperus*, as well as *Ostrya carpinifolia*, *Fraxinus ornus*, *Pyrus syriaca*, and *Eriolobus trilobatus*. The eastern slopes of the Anti-Lebanon Mountains throughout the Baqa Valley (including Homs, Hama, and Aleppo) support several species of *Amygdalus* and *Gundelia tournefortii*, *Asphodelus microcarpus*, *Rhamnus palaestinus*, and *Pistacia atlantica*.

The Syrian Desert is divided into six biogeographic regions. The northern region extends from El-Haseke to Gerablus and is used extensively for dryland agriculture; its vegetation includes *Phlomis burguieri*, *Centauria balsamitoides*, *Oliveria orientalis*, and *Cousinia chaborasica*. The northwestern region extends from southeast of Aleppo to east of Hama; vegetation there is dominated by *Poa sinaica* and *Carex stenophylla*. The eastern region along the Iraqi border covers the area from Jebel Abdul Aziz through Risafe and Es Sukhne to Abu Kemal. The region is characterized by gypsum and sandy soils. Plant communities include *Salsola spinosa*, *Scabiosa olivieri*, *Astragalus mossulensis*, *Erodium glaucophyllum*, *Achillea conferta*, *Astragalus duplostrigous*, *Cornulaca setifera*, and *Aristida plumosa*. The southeast region extends from Abu Kemal along the Iraqi-Jordanian border. The soils are calcareous and sandy. Vegetation is poor and highly degraded. The indicator species are *Poa sinaica*, *Haloxylon aticulatum*, and *Anabasis aphylla*. The southern region extends from Damascus to Suweida and includes the border with Jordan; its vegetation is made up of species of *Linum*, *Anabasis setifera*, and *Halogeton alopecuroides*. Finally, the western region covers the area from north of Damascus to the Tadmur Mountains and Selemiya. Indicator plant species of this region are *Stipa parviflora*, *Haloxylon articulatum*, and *Peganum harmala*.

Inland salt marshes and salt-affected lands are characterized by *Tamarix*, *Halocnemum strobilaceum*, *Salicornia herbacae*, *Aeluropus littoralis*, and *Juncus maritimus*. The inland mountains of the Syrian Desert support *Agropyron libanoticum*, *Phlomis damascena*, *Prunus tortusa*, *Rhamnus palaestinus*, *Amygdalus orientalis*, *Crataegus azarolus*, and *Prunus tortusa*.

Although for the most part the Syrian Desert has a continuous vegetative cover, it does not support particularly rich plant communities. This may be a result of the intensive human impact in the region over many centuries, particularly in the southern portion, which served as the main caravan route between Persia and Egypt. Also, impoverished vegetation results from heavy grazing and fuel collection by nomadic Bedouin tribes.

The major sources of freshwater in Syria are rainfall, rivers, springs, and groundwater. Problems of water resource development are many; among them are a general scarcity of water, pollution, and geopolitical factors. The increased demand on water for agricultural, industrial, and domestic purposes poses a real threat to the hydric balance in Syria. In the field of agriculture, incorporation of inappropriate lands such as saline, gypsum, and calcareous areas has caused great water wastage, low production, and severe deterioration of the arable land. Where irrigation is practiced, problems of waterlogging and salinity may occur and contribute to the land degradation. Rain-fed areas are subject to periodic drought and environmental degradation.

The country has a great deal of arable land—about 67 percent (5.6 million hectares) of the nation's total area. Agriculture contributes 27 percent to the GNP and employs 27 percent of the country's workforce. About 12 percent of the arable land is irrigated, and the rest is rain fed. There are 713,000 cattle, 13.5 million sheep and goats, and 70,000 camels in Syria. Measures have been undertaken to correct desertification, for example, restricting animal grazing on saplings, checking erosion, reforesting degraded lands, and planting fast-growing trees in denuded areas.

The establishment of the International Center for Agricultural Research in Dry Areas (ICARDA) and the Arab Center for the Studies of Arid Zones and Drylands (ACSAD) has provided new alternative technologies to the rain-fed agriculture and has reduced the loss of biodiversity in Syria. However, there remains a great need for conservation in the desert areas and associated habitats of Syria. For example, over the past few decades alone the forests of the internal Syrian mountains have been reduced from more than 300,000 hectares to only a few hundred hectares.—Ahmad K. Hegazy

See also **AFRICA, DESERTS OF; AGRICULTURE IN DESERTS; ARABIAN GULF, DESERTS OF; CHENOPODIACEAE; CONTAMINATION; DESERTIFICATION; DOMESTIC ANIMALS; DUNES; IRRIGATION DRAINAGE; ISRAEL, DESERTS OF; LEBANON, DESERTS OF; LIBYA, DESERTS OF; MIDDLE EAST, DESERTS OF; OVERGRAZING; PALESTINE, DESERTS OF; SAHARA DESERT; SALINIZATION; SAUDI ARABIA, DESERTS OF; SHEEP**

Further Reading

Arab Center for the Study of Arid Zones and Drylands (ACSAD). 1989. *The Arab Data Base for Arid Plants: Bibliography.* Damascus: ACSAD.

Sankary, M. N. 1977. *Ecology, Flora and Range Management of Arid Zones of Syria: Conservation and Development.* Aleppo, Syria: University of Aleppo Press. (In Arabic with English summary)

———. 1986. Species distribution and growth on salt affected land in Syria. *Journal of Reclamation and Revegetation* 5:125–141.

UNESCO/FAO. 1970. Ecological study of the Mediterranean zone: Vegetation map of the Mediterranean zone. *Arid Zone Research* 30:1–90.

Zohary, M. 1973. *Geobotanical Foundations of the Middle East.* Vols. 1 and 2. Amsterdam: Gustav Fischer.

TADPOLES

Nonreproductive early developmental stages of frogs and toads. Frogs and toads have a two-phase life cycle, a larval (usually aquatic) stage and an adult (usually terrestrial) stage. Indeed, the word *amphibian*, derived from Greek, means "double life." Frogs and toads (anurans) deposit eggs that develop into tadpoles, which are very different morphologically, physiologically, and ecologically from adults. Tadpoles have a globular body, usually with a long tapering tail. The mouth is very different from that of an adult anuran. It has a keratinous beak (technically referred to as labial jaws) surrounded by a fleshy disc on which are rows of tiny keratinous structures sometimes called denticles but which are not homologous with true teeth.

The ecological and morphological diversity of tadpoles is truly remarkable. Tail fin shape ranges from almost absent in stream-dwelling species to three times the body depth in pond species. Tadpoles of some species of glass frogs are fossorial (burrowing), living as far as three meters from water; these species are often bright red due to the increased epidermal vascularization and hemoglobin. Tadpoles inhabit every possible type and size of body of water, from ponds, lakes, and streams to bromeliad axils, fallen fruit husks, empty snail shells, tree holes, and ephemeral desert ponds. Length of the tadpole stage varies from two weeks to several years; those species that inhabit deserts generally have the shortest developmental periods to avoid the risk of drying ponds. Most tadpoles feed on algae and other detritus, but some are carnivorous, feeding on mosquito larvae and other small invertebrates. In some desert species in the genus *Spea*, a specialized carnivorous morph may develop and feed on invertebrates and other smaller tadpoles of the same species, thus increasing their rate of growth and shortening the time they must spend in the drying pond. Some tropical tadpoles do not feed at all, having been provisioned by the female frog with enough yolk to carry them through the tadpole stage. Others are fed unfertil-

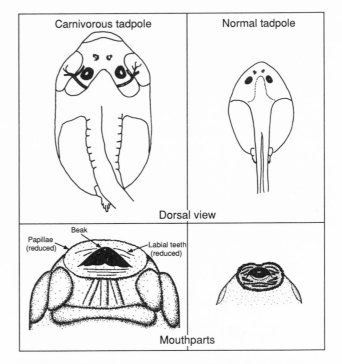

Carnivorous and noncarnivorous tadpoles and their mouthparts.

ized eggs by the female parent, who remembers where she deposited her tadpoles. Tadpoles of some species form large aggregations similar to fish schools. In a few of these species the female parent guards the tadpoles throughout their entire period of development, striking and frightening away small mammals and birds that attempt to prey on the tadpoles. Currently tadpoles of approximately 1,000 frogs and toads have been described; many more remain to be discovered.—Janalee P. Caldwell

See also **AMPHIBIANS; ANIMAL ADAPTATIONS; BREEDING SEASON; COLORATION; CRYPSIS; DIET; DORMANCY; FLOOD; FOAM NEST; FROGS; LIFE HISTORY STRATEGY (ITEROPARITY); METAMORPHOSIS; PIGMENT; SPADEFOOT TOAD; TOADS; WARNING COLORATION; WATER HOLE**

Further Reading

Altig, R. 1970. A key to the tadpoles of the continental United States and Canada. *Herpetologica* 26:180–207.

Altig, R., and G. F. Johnston. 1989. Guilds of anuran larvae: Relationships among developmental modes, morphologies, and habitats. *Herpetological Monographs* 3:81–109.

Duellman, W. E., and L. Trueb. 1986. *Biology of Amphibians*. New York: McGraw-Hill.

TAIL LOSS

Loss of the tail resulting from contraction of muscles within the tail caused by an attack on the tail by a predator. Tail autotomy occurs primarily in lizards and salamanders, although it is known in a few other vertebrates. It is a defense mechanism that involves behavior, morphology, and physiology.

Animals using tail autotomy for defense generally accomplish this by raising and moving the tail, but morphological adaptations such as bright color or large size may also be involved. When the tail is grabbed by a predator, muscles in it cause it to disconnect. The muscles and nerves are segmented so that tail loss results in little fluid or blood loss. The tail contains large energy reserves and the ability to metabolize in the absence of oxygen. Consequently the tail moves vigorously after being released by the lizard so that the attention of the predator is further distracted, allowing the lizard or salamander to escape having lost only the tail.

Tail autotomy is a common defense mechanism among desert lizards. It is so common in fact that numerous studies on the ecology of desert lizards have used frequency of tail loss as an indicator of relative predation intensity. Moreover, one desert lizard genus (*Coleonyx*) has been the model organism for studies of tail autotomy. Many desert geckos, including *Coleonyx* of the North American deserts, *Oedura, Gehyra,* and *Heteronotia* of the Australian deserts, and *Chondrodactylus* and *Pachydactylus* from the Kalahari Desert of Africa, move the tail laterally or raise it to distract the attention of a predator away from the body and toward the tail, thus increasing the probability of tail loss but reducing the probability of loss of life. Many other desert lizards in the families Teiidae, Lacertidae, Iguanidae, Phrynosomatidae, Scincidae, and Xantusiidae use tail autotomy to varying degrees to escape predation. Usually associated with tail autotomy is the subsequent regeneration of a tail that is similar in size and shape to the one that was lost. Some geckos, however, regenerate a shorter, fatter tail that may actually be a better decoy than the original one.—Laurie J. Vitt

See also **ANIMAL ADAPTATIONS; DEFENSIVE ADAPTATIONS, ANIMALS; GECKO; KANGAROO RAT; LIZARDS; PREDATION; REPTILES**

Further Reading

Arnold, E. N. 1988. Caudal autotomy as a defense. *In* C. Gans and R. B. Huey, eds. *Biology of the Reptilia, Ecology B, Defense and Life History,* 16:235–273. New York: Liss.

Greene, H. W. 1988. Antipredator mechanisms in reptiles. *In* C. Gans and R. B. Huey, eds., *Biology of the Reptilia: Ecology B, Defense and Life History,* 16:1–152. New York: Liss.

TAKLA MAKAN DESERT. *See* ASIA, DESERTS OF

TAMARISK. *See* SALT CEDAR

TAPACULO

Member of a group of small to medium-sized, largely terrestrial perching birds of Central and South America (family Rhinocryptidae, order Passeriformes). Between 29 and 35 species in approximately 12 genera are recognized. The majority of rhinocryptids are associated with cool, relatively moist Andean habitats. A few species inhabit xeric environments. The sandy gallito; (*Teledromas fuscus*) is found in arid open brushy habitats of the Andean slopes in Argentina, often some distance from open water. The crested gallito (*Rhinocrypta lanceolata*) is more widespread than the former species but is also found in open arid regions of southern South America, generally at altitudes of less than 1,800 meters. They are commonly seen running through xeric Chaco thorn scrub or along dry river gullies in the Monte Desert of Argentina. The four species of crescentchests (genus *Melanopareia*) inhabit semiarid zones of northwestern Peru, western Ecuador, eastern and central Brazil, Bolivia, and northern Argentina.

Tapaculos are large of body, with a total length of from 10 to 25 centimeters. Many rhinocryptids have small wings and are poor fliers. Most species are quite secretive and are more often heard than seen. The majority of taxa have rather cryptically colored plumage, although some (e.g., the crescentchests) are brightly colored and boldly patterned. Bills are typically robust and short. A movable flap (operculum) that covers the nostrils is a unique feature of the Rhinocryptidae. Tapaculos use their robust legs and feet to scratch through leaf litter in search of invertebrates, primarily insects, that constitute their diet. The diet of some species includes vegetable matter.

Tapaculos live in pairs and are reported to mate for life. The globular nests are placed in holes or crevices or at the end of burrows. Clutch size ranges from two to four. Incubation duties are performed by both parents.—Stephen C. Lougheed

See also **ALTIPLANO; ANDEAN GRASSLANDS; ANDES; BIRDS; CHACO; COLORATION; CRYPSIS; MONTE DESERT; PATAGONIA; PUNA; SOUTH AMERICA, DESERTS OF**

Further Reading

Fjeldså, J., and N. Krabbe. 1990. *Birds of the High Andes*. Svendborg, Denmark: Apollo.

Ridgely, R. S., and G. Tudor. 1994. *The Birds of South America*. Vol. 2. Austin: University of Texas Press.

Short, L. L. 1975. A zoogeographic analysis of the South American chaco avifauna. *Bulletin of the American Museum of Natural History* 154:163–352.

TARANTULA

Large, robust spider belonging to the arachnid family Theraphosidae with legs and abdomen covered with hair. The largest spiders in the world are tarantulas. Coloration varies, but most North American species are dark brown or black. Some Central and South American species have orange or red coloration. Although secretive during much of the year, living in burrows in the ground, summer finds sexually mature males active on the surface as they search for females. Individuals spend nearly all of their relatively long lives (females live as long as 10 years) in a single burrow.

As formidable as tarantulas appear, they are relatively harmless. They possess large fangs mounted on strong chelicerae (the first pair of appendages) but must be provoked to bite. Their bites can cause considerable pain and possible puncture wounds that can become infected, but the toxin is weak. The bite of most species is not considered dangerous to man. The hairs on the abdomen of many species are used in defense as well and can cause severe irritation. These hairs (called urticating hairs) have small barbs at the tips and can be rubbed off by the spider such that they land on the surface of the skin or eyes or are inhaled by humans or other animals that threaten it. Severe itching, and even the development of lesions, may occur. Urticating hairs appear to be effective in defense

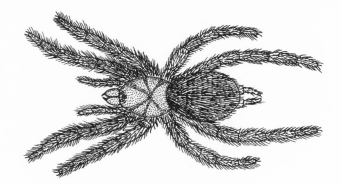

Tarantula (family Theraphosidae).

against many predators, particularly small predaceous mammals.—Laurie J. Vitt

See also **ARACHNIDS; ARTHROPODS; DEFENSIVE ADAPTATIONS, ANIMALS; POISONOUS ANIMALS; PREDATION; SPIDERS; VENOM; WASPS**

Further Reading

Kaston, B. J. 1978. *How to Know the Spiders*. Dubuque, Iowa: W. C. Brown.

Smith, R. L. 1982. *Venomous Animals of Arizona*. Tucson: Cooperative Extension Service, University of Arizona.

TARIM BASIN. *See* ASIA, DESERTS OF

TEMPERATURE IN DESERTS. *See* AN INTRODUCTION TO DESERTS

TENEBRIONIDAE

Family of beetles (order Coleoptera) characterized by the combination of a 5-5-4 tarsal formula, coxal cavities (cavities in the basal segment of the leg, or coxa) closed on the posterior edge, and antennae nearly always composed of 11 segments. These beetles are commonly known as darkling beetles. The Tenebrionidae is the fifth-largest beetle family, and a majority of species live in arid or semiarid environments. Darkling beetles are usually common and are often seen marching about in the morning, late afternoon, or at night on the surface of the ground. Size varies from very small to about 40 millimeters. The larvae of tenebrionids are elongate with a heavy exoskeleton. Larvae of many species are commonly known as mealworms.

Among the best known of the desert darkling beetles are those in the genus *Eleodes*. These large black beetles assume a defensive posture when disturbed, with the tip of the abdomen held high in the air. If bothered, they exude strong chemicals from glands near the tip of the abdomen which apparently offer protection from at least some potential predators. They are sometimes called stinkbugs. As larvae and adults, the beetles feed primarily on grains.

Desert tenebrionids avoid desiccation by restricting activity to cooler parts of the day and remaining underground during the hottest hours. The subelytral cavity (an air space under the wings) of desert species buffers the insects from extreme temperatures and aridity by providing a boundary layer of air that reduces heat exchange and water loss.—Laurie J. Vitt

See also **ANIMAL ADAPTATIONS; ARTHROPODS; BEETLES; DEFENSIVE ADAPTATIONS, ANIMALS; INSECTS; VENOM**

Further Reading

Borror, D. J., C. A. Triplehorn, and N. F. Johnson. 1992. *An Introduction to the Study of Insects.* New York: Harcourt Brace.

Borror, D. J., and R. E. White. 1970. *A Field Guide to the Insects.* Boston: Houghton Mifflin.

Hadley, N. F. 1970. Micrometeorology and energy exchange in two desert arthropods. *Ecology* 51:434–444.

———. 1972. Desert species and adaptation. *American Scientist* 3:338–347.

TERMITES

Insects in the order Isoptera characterized by front and hind wings of near equal size (when present). Termites typically are soft bodied, have white or light coloration, often appear antlike (even though they are more closely related evolutionarily to roaches than they are to ants), live in highly structured social societies, and feed on cellulose.

Termite societies are composed of primary and secondary reproductive castes, workers, and soldiers. In many termites determination of whether any individual will be a reproductive male or female versus a worker or soldier is based on chemical cues (pheromones), although sex is involved in some of the more evolutionarily advanced termites. The primary reproductive castes in a colony are kings and queens, and there is usually one of each. The large-bodied queen is essentially an egg factory producing thousands of eggs fertilized by the relatively small king. In addition to producing workers and soldiers, the queens produce winged reproductive

Enormous termitarium, approximately 3.5 meters high, in Etosha National Park, northern Namibia. (Photo: M. A. Mares)

castes (future kings and queens) that leave the nest in large swarms. Swarms are usually seasonal and often triggered by rainfall. The winged reproductives (alates) fly away from the colony and eventually drop to the ground, lose their wings, and search for mates. Once they find mates both the male and the female participate in nest construction, mate, and initiate new colonies. In instances in which kings or queens die in an established colony, additional reproductive individuals can develop within the nest and take over reproductive functions. These secondary reproductive individuals never develop wings and remain within the nest.

Interestingly, and very different from social hymenopterans (ants, bees, wasps), dominance hierarchies are nonexistent in termites. Workers and soldiers make up most of the colony and can number in the tens of thousands or more. Both of these castes are sterile and wingless. Worker castes consist of both males and females. Workers typically are the smallest individuals in the colony and have mouthparts designed for chewing. They perform most of the vital functions of the colony, including repair and construction of nests and feeding of other castes. Workers eat plant material containing cellulose, swallow the cellulose, and colonies of flagellated microorganisms (protists) in the termite gut digest the cellulose, making it available to the termite as food. Without the microorganisms termites would not be able to feed on cellulose. There are many species of flagellated microorganisms in termites, and they vary among termite species.

Soldiers typically are larger in size than workers and have enlarged jaws or other defensive weaponry. Soldiers are usually darker in coloration, partly due to the sclerotized head. The enlarged mandibles of soldiers are used to dismember small organisms that attack the colony or to inflict wounds on larger invaders. The sheer number of attacking soldiers is often enough to ward off most potential predators. Some termites also have the ability to produce chemicals that are effective in defense. Some of the chemicals are toxic to other invertebrates, and other chemicals simply disable the aggressor by covering it with a gluelike substance.

The most common termites in deserts are in the family Termitidae. Termites are extremely important ecologically in that they play a major role in the breakdown of plant material and the conversion of cellulose to products that can be used by other plants. Termites are considered keystone species in some desert ecosystems. For example, most, and in some cases all, of the organic matter produced in the Chihuahuan Desert ecosystem is ultimately consumed by termites. In addition, because many invertebrates and vertebrates eat termites, they are important in food webs. Termites are of economic importance because they are capable of causing major damage to wooden structures constructed by humans.—Laurie J. Vitt

See also **AARDVARK; AARDWOLF; AMPHIBIANS; ANTS; ARMADILLO; ARTHROPODS; BIRDS; DECOMPOSITION; HORNED LIZARD; INSECTS; LIZARDS; PANGOLIN**

Further Reading

Borror, D. J., C. A. Triplehorn, and N. F. Johnson. 1992. *An Introduction to the Study of Insects.* New York: Harcourt Brace.

Ernst, E. 1986. *A Bibliography of Termite Literature 1966–1978.* New York: Wiley.

Krishna, K., and F. M. Weesner. 1961. *Biology of Termites.* Vol. 1. New York: Academic Press.

———. 1970. *Biology of Termites.* Vol. 2. New York: Academic Press.

Lee, K. E., and T. G. Wood. 1971. *Termites and Soils.* New York: Academic Press.

MacKay, W. P. 1991. The role of ants and termites in desert ecosystems. *In* G. A. Polis, ed., *The Ecology of Desert Communities,* 111–150. Tucson: University of Arizona Press.

Weesner, F. M. 1960. Evolution and biology of the termites. *Annual Reviews of Entomology* 5:153–170.

Wilson, E. O. 1971. *The Insect Societies.* Cambridge, Mass.: Harvard University Press.

TERTIARY

Period of geologic time beginning after the great extinction event at the end of the Mesozoic era about 65 million years ago and lasting until the beginning of the Quaternary period about 1.8–1.6 million years ago. The Tertiary period makes up about 97 percent of the Cenozoic era and is subdivided into five epochs, the Paleocene, Eocene, Oligocene, Miocene, and Pliocene. Alternatively, the Tertiary is considered to be composed of two periods, the Paleogene and Neogene. The term "Tertiary" is held over from the earliest attempts to subdivide geologic time into three eras, Primary, Secondary, and Tertiary. The first two of these are no longer used, having been replaced by Precambrian, Paleozoic, and Mesozoic; Tertiary and Quaternary are now used as periods rather than eras. Following the extinction of dinosaurs and many other forms of animal life which marks the end of the Cretaceous and beginning of the Tertiary, mammals underwent major evolutionary diversifications and became the dominant members of most continental fossil records.

A number of important paleogeographic events occurred during the Tertiary. There was the opening of the North Atlantic Ocean, with Greenland and eastern coastal North America separating from Europe and northwestern Africa. The South Atlantic Ocean continued the widening that had begun in the late Cretaceous. India, which split off of Antarctica and the rest of the supercontinent Gondwana, continued its northward movement and contacted southern Asia, beginning the uplift of the Himalaya Mountains about 35–40 million years ago. At about the same time Australia separated from Antarctica and began moving northward toward southeastern Asia. South America and Antarctica remained connected by a narrow isthmus, probably until the late Eocene. North and South America, which were separated during most of the Tertiary, became joined at the Isthmus of Panama by the end of the period, about 2.5 million years ago. Westward tectonic movement of the Americas during the Tertiary resulted in the buildup of the western North American and Andean cordilleras, in the rain shadow of which some modern deserts formed.—Nicholas J. Czaplewski

See also **AN INTRODUCTION TO DESERTS; CENO-ZOIC; CRETACEOUS; DESERTS; EOCENE; FOSSILS; GLACIAL PERIODS; MADRO-TERTIARY GEOFLORA; MIOCENE; NEOGENE; OLIGOCENE; PALEO-CLIMATE; PERMIAN; PLATE TECTONICS; PLEI-STOCENE; PLIOCENE; PRECAMBRIAN; QUATER-NARY; RECENT (HOLOCENE)**

Further Reading

Cocks, L. R. M. 1981. *The Evolving Earth*. London: British Museum (Natural History).

Frakes, L. A., J. E. Francis, and J. I. Syktus, eds. 1992. *Climate Modes of the Phanerozoic: The History of the Earth's Climate over the Past 600 Million Years*. Cambridge: Cambridge University Press.

Smith, A. G., and J. C. Briden. 1977. *Mesozoic and Cenozoic Paleocontinental Maps*. Cambridge: Cambridge University Press.

TEXAS DESERT

Southwestern part of Texas, which is known as the Trans-Pecos Region, supporting desert grasslands and Chihuahuan Desert vegetation. The Chihuahuan Desert is a hot desert, and yet it is the wettest (mainly summer precipitation) of the North American desert biomes. It consists of rolling grasslands on higher elevations, creosote bush plains, and cactus and agave on rocky limestone outcrops. Large expanses of the plains and low hills of the Texas Desert are dominated by creosote bush (*Larrea tridentata*). Other characteristic plants include lechuguilla (*Agave lechuguilla*), the common name deriving from the Spanish word meaning "little lettuce," sotol (*Dasylirion wheeleri*), tarbush (*Flourensia cernua*), mesquite (*Prosopis*), and numerous species of soap weed (*Yucca*).

The most spectacular part of the Texas Desert is found in and around Big Bend National Park, at the bend of the Rio Grande, which flows between the United States and Mexico on its way to the Gulf of Mexico. This vast mix of pine forests, woodlands, desert grasslands, riparian woodlands, and Chihuahuan Desert vegetation covers about 800,000 acres and is home to a rich assortment of plant and animal life. To the west of Big Bend National Park, the state of Texas has preserved more than 121,000 hectares of desert in the Big Bend Ranch State Natural Area, which is typical of the Chihuahuan Desert that extends south into Mexico. To the north of the Big Bend region the Texas Desert occurs west of the Pecos River and in the extreme south-

eastern corner of New Mexico.—Gary K. Hulett and Amanda Renner Charles

See also **BIG BEND NATIONAL PARK; BIRDS; CACTI; CHIHUAHUAN DESERT; CREOSOTE BUSH; DESERTS; DESERTS, HOT; DESERTS, TEMPERATE; LLANO ESTACADO; LIZARDS; MAMMALS; MESQUITE; MEXICO, DESERTS OF; NEW MEXICO DESERT; PLANT GEOGRAPHY; REPTILES; RIO GRANDE; SALT CEDAR; SEMIARID ZONES; SNAKES; YUCCA**

Further Reading

Blair, W. F. 1950. The biotic provinces of Texas. *Texas Journal of Science* 2:93–117.

Cottle, H. J. 1931. Studies on the vegetation of southwest Texas. *Ecology* 12:105–155.

Schmidly, D. J. 1977. *The Mammals of Trans-Pecos Texas Including Big Bend National Park and Guadalupe Mountains National Park*. College Station: Texas A&M University Press.

Tharp, B. C. 1939. *The Vegetation of Texas*. Texas Academy of Science, Texas Academy Publications in Natural History, No. 1.

Warnock, B. H., and W. M. Kittams. 1970. *Plant Communities of Big Bend National Park: Texas*. Map. U.S. Department of Interior, National Park Service.

THAR DESERT. *See* INDO-PAKISTAN DESERTS

THERMALS

Vertical currents of air rising from a warm part of the ground. Differences in ground cover, composition, or orientation of the sun can cause uneven heating of the ground, which also causes the air above the ground to be heated unevenly. Warm air is less dense than cool air, and air that has been warmed by the ground rises through the cooler, denser air above. Thermals may reach altitudes of three kilometers. Because of the often uneven terrain and the lack of substantial vegetation, thermals are a relatively common phenomenon in deserts. Many birds use thermals to reach high altitudes with relatively little expenditure of energy. Birds commonly associated with thermals are vultures. Vultures use the altitude that thermals provide to glide from one thermal to another and in the process search for carrion or other food items. The image of vultures circling in the rising air of the thermal is often associated with deserts.—Rob Channell

See also **BAROMETIC PRESSURE (ATMOSPHERIC PRESSURE); BIRDS; BUZZARD; CLIMATE; CONDOR;**

DUST DEVIL; LOCOMOTION; RAPTORS; VULTURE; WIND

THERMOREGULATION

Process in animals of regulating body temperature. The desert surface climate is one of prevailing aridity, resulting in very low atmospheric water vapor content. Deserts also show extreme 24-hour air temperature fluctuations. It should not be surprising, therefore, that most desert animals do not let their body temperatures fluctuate passively with surface air temperatures, even though their periods of activity may be confined largely to the surface. Instead they thermoregulate, maintaining body temperatures within narrower limits than those typically experienced on the surface. This thermoregulation may be either behavioral or physiological, or a mix of the two.

Desert animals that employ largely or exclusively behavioral thermoregulation are termed ectotherms; these include most arthropods, the few amphibians that live in deserts, and reptiles. Ectotherms lack effective body surface insulation and have inherently low metabolic rates; they therefore exchange heat very rapidly with their surroundings. For this reason ectotherms generally seek out thermally moderate microclimates in which they can maintain body temperatures within rather narrow preferred and tolerable limits. Diurnal desert lizards have refined behavioral thermoregulation to an extreme degree wherein by moving between shaded and sunny microhabitats during their periods of activity they are able to maintain preferred body temperatures that do not vary more than a few degrees Celsius. When surface microclimates become either too cold or too hot, precluding maintenance of this preferred temperature, these lizards retreat under the surface where the desert soils shield them from the more extreme surface conditions.

Birds and mammals possess effective body surface insulation and have inherently high metabolic rates, resulting in heat that is produced endogenously (internally) and whose loss to the external environment is retarded by the insulative properties of feathers or fur. For this reason birds and mammals are termed endotherms; they are capable of adjusting their metabolic rates at moderate and low environmental temperatures sufficiently to offset the low, but continuous, loss of body heat through the insulation, thereby maintaining constant body temperatures. The body temperatures of birds and mammals are typically rather high (birds, 40°–42°C; mammals, 36°–38°C), usually exceeding desert surface air temperatures except during the hottest periods. Desert endotherms only infrequently experience the potential of heat gain from the environment. This potential is behaviorally avoided by most mammals that spend the days in cooler underground burrows, confining surface activity to the cooler nights. Birds are typically diurnal, but they may also avoid high surface temperatures by seeking cooler, shady refuges, or merely by flying away to cooler habitats. Some birds challenge the desert heat directly and in so doing use a combination of costly evaporative cooling and mild hyperthermia, relaxing strict body temperature maintenance by allowing body temperature to coast upward to as high as 44°–45°C, usually higher than that of the environment. Even these birds must resort to flight if it becomes hotter, however.

At night in the desert winter temperatures on the surface may frequently approach or be below freezing, requiring considerable energy output by endotherms to thermoregulate. These demands are avoided behaviorally by some birds by migrating to more moderate climates. Less mobile mammals have to either cope directly with the added energy expenses of thermoregulation by increased food consumption or give up endothermy temporarily by retreating to thermally more moderate underground burrows to hibernate until surface conditions improve. Different species of desert mammals employ either or both of these options during the winter as part of their thermoregulatory repertoires.—Richard E. MacMillen

See also **ANIMAL ADAPTATIONS; BODY TEMPERATURE; CAMEL; CAMEL'S HUMP; CLOTHING; COUNTERCURRENT HEAT EXCHANGE; DEHYDRATION; DESICCATION; ECTOTHERMY; ENDOTHERMY; ESTIVATION; EXCRETORY SYSTEM; EXPLOSIVE HEAT DEATH; HEAT BALANCE; HEAT EXCHANGE; HEAT STRESS; HEATSTROKE; HIBERNATION; HUMAN PHYSIOLOGY IN DESERTS; HYPERTHERMIA; HYPOTHERMIA; KANGAROO RAT; KIDNEY FUNCTION, DESERT RODENTS; KIDNEYS; METABOLISM; PERSPIRATION; RENAL PAPILLA; RESPIRATORY WATER LOSS; SALT BALANCE; SHIVERING; SUNBURN; SUNSTROKE; SURVIVAL IN DESERTS; SWEAT GLANDS; THERMOREGULATION; TORPOR; TRANSPIRATION; VAN'T HOFF EFFECT; WATER BALANCE; WATER STRESS**

Further Reading

Bradshaw, S. D. 1997. *Homeostasis in Desert Reptiles.* New York: Springer.

Degan, A. A. 1997. *Ecophysiology of Small Desert Mammals.* New York: Springer.

Gordon, M. S., G. A. Bartholomew, A. D. Grinnell, C. B. Jorgensen, and F. N. White. 1982. *Animal Physiology: Principles and Adaptations.* New York: Macmillan.

Schmidt-Nielsen, K. 1990. *Animal Physiology: Adaptation and Environment.* 4th ed. New York: Cambridge University Press.

THORN

Firm, sharp structure derived from a modified branch or part of a branch. Branches emerge from axillary buds (i.e., buds in the axils of leaves). A thorn might be a simple structure emerging from the axil of a leaf, or the end of a branch might become hardened and sharp. Examples of plant species that bear thorns are chittum, firethorn, osage orange, acacia, mesquite, and honey locust.

Sharp structures have three other origins: (1) superficial or epidermal appendages, called prickles, (2) modified leaves or leaf tissues, called spines, and (3) epidermal hairs. Prickles usually can be identified because they are not associated with leaves or axillary buds, and they generally are easy to break off. Examples of plants that produce prickles are blackberries and roses. Leaves are composed of stipules, petioles, and blades with veins. Spines may be produced from any part of a leaf. In black locust the two stipules are slender and very sharp. The leaf margins of many hollies are lobed, and each lobe is sharpened into a spine. Desert candle (*Fouquieria*) loses its blades when the leaves mature, but the midvein becomes hardened into a spine. In cacti the entire leaf is converted into a spine. Some plants produce hairs on the surface that are sharp; in *Cnidoscolus* (nettles) from arid and semiarid areas of the southwestern United States and Mexico, those hairs are often hollow and secrete formic acid, which burns the skin of any animal that brushes against them.

Plants with thorns, prickles, spines, or stinging hairs are said to be armed. These sharp appendages probably protect the plants that bear them from being eaten by herbivores. Many plants of warm deserts are armed, probably an adaptation to prevent the loss of tissue with its valuable water supply.—James R. Estes

See also **ACACIA; CACTI; LEAVES; MESQUITE; PLANT ADAPTATIONS; PLANTS; OCOTILLO**

Further Reading

Benson, L. 1979. *Plant Classification.* 2d ed. Lexington, Mass.: Heath.

THORN FOREST. *See* CHACO

THORNTHWAITE MOISTURE INDEX. *See* MOISTURE INDEX

TICKS

Flattened arthropods with four pairs of walking legs and a mouthpart designed for drilling into flesh. There is no distinct head, but the mouthparts appear headlike. Ticks are in the order Acari, which also includes mites. There are four stages in a tick's life cycle. Eggs (first stage) hatch into tiny larvae (second stage) that have only three pairs of walking legs. The nymphs (third stage) and adults (fourth stage) have four pairs of walking legs. All stages except the egg require blood meals for further development or, in the case of adults, for reproduction. Female ticks engorge with blood and convert the blood to several thousand tiny eggs.

Ticks are ectoparasites, living on the surface of a host's skin, with their mouthparts piercing through the skin to suck blood from their host. Because the mouthparts are hooklike, ticks can be difficult to remove. There are many species of ticks that belong in several families. Ticks position themselves on low vegetation with the first pair of legs extended. When an animal brushes against the vegetation, the tick adheres to the animal, often migrating to areas where there are folds of skin that protect the tick from removal. In addition to the fact that ticks are considered nuisance animals because of their parasitic habits, some carry potentially life-threatening diseases such as Rocky Mountain spotted fever and Lyme disease. Tick density is often greatest in areas with a long history of cattle grazing.

A variety of ticks occur in deserts, but most of them are not restricted to dry habitats. The best-known ticks in North American deserts are the Rocky Mountain wood tick, *Dermacentor andersoni*, and the brown dog tick, *Rhipicephalus sanguineus*. Another species, the adobe tick (*Argas sanchezi*), may also attack man, although it is usually associated with birds.—Laurie J. Vitt

See also **ARACHNIDS; ARTHROPODS; BIRDS; INSECTS; MAMMALS; METAMORPHOSIS; PLAGUE; PRAIRIE DOG; RED VELVET MITE; REPTILES**

Further Reading

Baker, E. W., and G. W. Wharton. 1952. *An Introduction to Acarology.* New York: Macmillan.

Smith, R. L. 1982. *Venomous Animals of Arizona.* Tucson: Cooperative Extension Service, University of Arizona.

TIGRIS-EUPHRATES

Two rivers, largely in Iraq, that originate in Turkey and join at the Shatt-al-Arab, a waterway in southern Iraq, before entering the Persian Gulf. They are the major rivers of Iraq, traversing the country from north to south. The Tigris River is 1,840 kilometers long, and the Euphrates is 2,860 kilometers long. Both rivers entered the Persian Gulf independently several thousand years ago. Sediment carried by the two rivers and deposited at the mouth of the Shatt-al-Arab extends the shoreline about 30 meters into the Persian Gulf each year. The source of the sediment is water erosion in the hills and mountains of the upper watersheds of the rivers in Turkey, Iraq, and Iran. There are many tributaries of the Euphrates in mountainous Turkey but few in the lowlands of Syria and Iraq. Several sizable rivers flow into the Tigris above Baghdad. In their lower reaches both rivers are divided into many branches that meander across the floodplain, forming marshes and lakes before they converge on the Shatt-al-Arab. Whereas the Euphrates is navigable for only a short distance, the Tigris is navigable nearly to Mosul in the north. Sandbanks impede navigation on the lower Euphrates.

The Tigris-Euphrates Basin has been occupied by humans for several thousand years. It is part of the Fertile Crescent that stretched from the hills of southwestern Iran to the uplands of Iraq, Syria, and Jordan. Irrigation has been practiced in Mesopotamia (present-day Iraq) for almost 6,000 years. Small canals diverting water to adjoining fields were first used for irrigation. Later, big canals carrying water a few hundred kilometers were built.

Two problems have plagued the region over the millennia: silt in the river water and salinization of the irrigated land. Those problems have yet to be controlled. Silt deposition in canals reduces their water-carrying capacity. It must be removed periodically. Individual farmers or small groups of them can do the job of cleaning the short canals. For cleaning long canals, however, such as the Nahrawan Canal on the Diyala branch of the Tigris (300 or more kilometers in length), a strong government was needed to bring about cooperative action among large numbers of farmers. During times of civil strife and weak governments canal cleaning tends to be neglected. This leads to shortages of water at the ends of the canals and, frequently, abandonment of the silted canals and the digging of new ones. Entire canal systems have been abandoned, along with the farmland they formerly watered. Salinization is a threat to virtually all irrigated areas in arid regions. Constructing a patterned and efficient irrigation system disrupts natural drainage flows, which leads to rising water tables and increasing soil salinization. Much of the land in the southern Tigris-Euphrates plain became badly affected with salt and had to be abandoned in past millennia.

Irrigation brought about greatly increased crop yields in Mesopotamia. The surplus food fed urban populations and allowed a nonfarm population of government officials, artisans, philosophers, priests, physicians, engineers, and scribes to develop. One product of urbanization was the formulation during the second millennium B.C. by Hammurabi of a system of laws that controlled political, social, and cultural life and also set forth the first rules on the use of water in irrigated and urban areas.

Canal siltation and salinization became permanent problems in the Tigris-Euphrates Basin because irrigation in Mesopotamia depended on canals to carry water to distant fields. In the Nile Valley, by contrast, the annual floods of the river spread out across the well-defined valley and delta. The floods provided water to the crops and also washed salts from the soil while depositing silt that helped to fertilize the land.—Harold E. Dregne

See also **AFRICA, DESERTS OF; AGRICULTURE IN DESERTS; ASIA, DESERTS OF; DESERT PEOPLES; JORDAN, DESERTS OF; MIDDLE EAST, DESERTS OF; SYRIA, DESERTS OF; IRAN, DESERTS OF; NILE RIVER; RIPARIAN COMMUNITIES; SALINIZATION**

Further Reading

Adams, R. 1981. *Heartland of Cities.* Chicago: University of Chicago Press.

Elegant crested tinamou (*Eudromia elegans*). (Photo: M. A. Mares)

TINAMOU

Member of a group of robust, largely terrestrial bird species distributed throughout Neotropical America (family Tinamidae, order Tinamiformes). The Tinamiformes, although possessing a keel on the sternum for flight muscle attachment, are most closely related to the ratites (e.g., the rheas). The number of species recognized depends on the authority, but approximately 46 species in nine genera have been identified. Tinamous inhabit a wide diversity of habitats ranging from humid forests through grassland to desert. The elegant crested tinamou (*Eudromia elegans*) is an example of an arid-land species. It is a common resident of the dry open woodlands, savannas, and mountain steppes of Chile and Argentina.

Species range in length from 20 to 50 centimeters and in weight from 0.45 to 2.3 kilograms. Tinamous have compact bodies, rounded wings, short tails, long necks, small heads, and powerful legs and feet. They are reluctant fliers and prefer to run or hide to escape detection by predators. Open-country species tend to have variegated plumage of muted brown, gray, black, and white. Forest species are generally a more uniform brown. Diet for species where it has been described consists of plant material, insects, and, occasionally, small vertebrates. Most species are solitary, except for late in the breeding season when there are family groups evident.

Breeding behavior of relatively few species has been studied. Nests consist of lined or unlined scrapes on the ground. Clutch sizes vary from 1–12 depending on whether more than one female has contributed eggs. The eggs are quite distinctive in character, hard and glossy. There is considerable variation in coloration and pattern of eggs across species. Tinamous show a broad array of mating systems, ranging from monogamy to promiscuity. Incubation and care of young is probably carried out exclusively by the male. The young are precocial, capable of running soon after hatching.—Stephen C. Lougheed

See also **ALTIPLANO; ANDEAN GRASSLANDS; ANDES; BIRDS; CRYPSIS; MONTE DESERT; NESTS, BIRD; PATAGONIA; PUNA**

Further Reading

Blake, E. R. 1977. *Manual of Neotropical Birds*. Vol. 1. Chicago: University of Chicago Press.

Fjeldså, J., and N. Krabbe. 1990. *Birds of the High Andes*. Svendborg, Denmark: Apollo.

Handford, P., and M. A. Mares. 1985. The mating systems of ratites and tinamous: An evolutionary perspective. *Biological Journal of the Linnean Society* 25:77–104.

Johnson, A. W. 1965. *The Birds of Chile and Adjacent Regions of Argentina, Bolivia and Peru*. Vol. 1. Buenos Aires: Platt.

Lancaster, D. A. 1964. Life history of the Boucard tinamou in British Honduras. 2. Breeding biology. *Condor* 66:253–276.

Olrog, C. C. 1968. *Las Aves Sudamericanas*. Tucumán, Argentina: Instituto Miguel Lillo.

TOADS

Members of the amphibian family Bufonidae. Species in certain other frog families have common names that include the word *toad*, but they are not true toads. An example is the "spadefoot toad," a common desert inhabitant in the United States, which is a member of the family Pelobatidae. The family Bufonidae is characterized by a large number of osteological features that distinguish it from all other families of frogs, such as the lack of teeth. In addition, toads typically have thick glandular skin that often appears warty. Their skin protects them from water loss much more effectively than the thin, porous skin typical of other frogs; thus toads can survive arid conditions and are more common in deserts than other frogs. Many toads are protected from their predators by large parotoid glands that can secrete copious amounts of toxins when the animal is disturbed. The eggs of toads can be recognized easily because they are deposited in long, gelatinous strings. Many species deposit extremely large numbers of eggs. For example, a single female of the South American species *Bufo guttatus* can deposit 55,000 eggs at one time. The distribution of the family is worldwide, except for Australia, the Sahara Desert, and high latitudes in the Northern Hemisphere. Herpetologists recognize 365 species of toads in 31 genera. *Bufo* is the largest genus, with 211 species. Toads range in size from 20 to 250 millimeters in snout-vent length.—Janalee P. Caldwell

See also **AMPHIBIANS; ANIMAL ADAPTATIONS; BREEDING SEASON; COLORATION; DORMANCY; FOAM NEST; FROGS; LIFE HISTORY STRATEGY (ITEROPARITY); METAMORPHOSIS; PIGMENT; REPRODUCTION; SPADEFOOT TOAD; TADPOLES; WARNING COLORATION**

Further Reading

Blair, W. F., ed. 1972. *Evolution in the Genus* Bufo. Austin: University of Texas Press.

Duellman, W. E., and L. Trueb. 1986. *Biology of Amphibians*. New York: McGraw-Hill.

TORPOR

Condition in endothermic (warm-blooded) animals (birds and mammals) in which the usual states of high body temperature and metabolism are replaced temporarily by lower body temperature and metabolism. While torpid these animals typically have body temperatures that are within a degree or two Celsius of the ambient temperature; the metabolic reduction (= energy saving) is directly related to body temperature reduction and therefore is greater during the winter than during the summer. Torpor is common in small species of desert endotherms, which, because of low levels of food production and precipitation in their habitats, often face both energy and water shortages. Because of the drastic lowering of metabolic processes during torpor, there is a concomitant reduction of energy expenditure and water loss, enabling those species with the capacity for torpor to withstand periods of shortage. This capacity is under precise endogenous control, even when body temperature approaches freezing, and torpid animals can arouse fully by "turning on" their heat-producing machinery until body temperature returns to normal. While torpid animals are typically quite lethargic, depending on the degree of body temperature lowering. This places them in a very vulnera-

South American tortoise (*Geochelone*) from the Chacoan thorn scrub of Argentina. (Photo: M. A. Mares)

ble position with respect to predation, and so it is understandable that torpor is usually employed in cryptic shelters to avoid detection. Torpor may be either long-term (seasonal) or short-term (daily) in nature, and both schedules are found among the array of desert endotherms.—Richard E. MacMillen

See also **ACTIVITY CYCLES, ANIMALS; ANIMAL ADAPTATIONS; BAT; BURROWING ANIMALS; ECTOTHERMY; ENDOTHERMY; ESTIVATION; HEAT BALANCE; HEAT EXCHANGE; HEAT STRESS; HIBERNATION; HYPERTHERMIA; HYPOTHERMIA; PHYSIOLOGY; SHIVERING; SUNSTROKE; THERMOREGULATION; WATER BALANCE; WATER STRESS**

Further Reading

Gordon, M. S., G. A. Bartholomew, A. D. Grinnell, C. B. Jorgensen, and F. N. White. 1982. *Animal Physiology: Principles and Adaptations*. New York: Macmillan.

TORTOISE

Primarily herbivorous turtle having elephantlike legs, particularly the hind legs. Tortoises are in the family Testudinidae; about 40 species in 10 genera are described. They occur in North, Central, and South America, Africa, Madagascar, the Middle East, southern Europe, and Southeast Asia.

Tortoises are terrestrial and occur in a variety of habitats, including tropical forests (e.g., the redfooted tortoise of South America), deserts (e.g., the desert tortoise of the southwestern United States), and Mediterranean areas (e.g., the Greek tortoise).

Although evolutionarily related to aquatic turtles, the tortoises that inhabit desert and semiarid regions of the world have developed a variety of adaptations allowing them to exist in arid environments. The most important of these is behavioral: desert tortoises live in burrows or other refuges so that they can avoid the high daytime temperatures and rapid water loss associated with terrestrial activity in deserts. Most desert tortoises are active early in the morning or late in the afternoon (crepuscular) when temperatures are relatively low. During extended hot and dry periods desert tortoises remain underground and avoid adverse conditions on the surface. The heavily armored shell of tortoises protects them from predators.

The best-known tortoise in desert environments is the desert tortoise (*Gopherus agassizii*), which occurs in the Mojave and Sonoran deserts of the southwestern United States and northwestern Mexico. At one time this tortoise was extremely abundant in much of the Mojave Desert, but its numbers have declined radically due to habitat loss and exploitation by man. It is now considered an endangered species.—Laurie J. Vitt

See also **AFRICA, DESERTS OF; ANIMAL ADAPTATIONS; BURROWING ANIMALS; CHACO; CHIHUAHUAN DESERT; DEFENSIVE ADAPTATIONS, ANIMALS; DESICCATION-RESISTANT SPECIES; ECTOTHERMY; HERBIVORY; PHYSIOLOGY; MIDDLE EAST, DESERTS OF; MOJAVE DESERT; MONTE DESERT; REPTILES; SONORAN DESERT**

Further Reading

Auffenberg, W. 1967. The genus *Gopherus* (Testudinidae). Pt. 1: Osteology and relationships of extant species. *Bulletin of the Florida State Museum Biological Science* 20:47–110.

Murray, R. C., and V. M. Dickinson, eds. 1996. *Management Plan for the Sonoran Desert Population of the Desert Tortoise in Arizona*. Phoenix: Arizona Game and Fish Department.

Pritchard, P. C. H. 1967. *Living Turtles of the World*. Neptune City, N.J.: THF.

TRADE WINDS

System of winds that occurs primarily within the tropics and that blows from semipermanent high pressure centers, or subtropical highs, toward the equatorial low pressure zones. Trade winds are from the southeast in the Southern Hemisphere and from the northeast in the Northern Hemisphere, where they are known as the southeasterly trades and the northeasterly trades, respectively. In the Northern Hemisphere the northeasterly trades generally extend from about 30° to 35° north latitude in July and continue as northeasterly trade winds until just a few degrees north of the equator. In the Southern Hemisphere the southeasterly trades occur over a similar latitudinal range.—Federico Norte

See also **ANTICYCLONE; BAROMETRIC PRESSURE (ATMOSPHERIC PRESSURE); CLIMATE; CLIMATE CLASSIFICATION; CLOUDS; CONVECTIVE STORM; CYCLONE; LOW PRESSURE; WIND**

Further Reading

Day, J. A., and V. J. Schaefer. 1991. *Clouds and Weather*. Boston: Houghton Mifflin.

Oliver, J. E., and R. W. Fairbridge, eds. 1987. *The Encyclopedia of Climatology*. New York: Chapman and Hall.

Schaefer, V. J., and J. A. Day. 1981. *A Field Guide to the Atmosphere*. Boston: Houghton Mifflin.

Schneider, S. H., ed. 1996. *Encyclopedia of Climate and Weather*. 2 vols. New York: Oxford University Press.

TRANSHUMANCE. *See* DESERT PEOPLES

TRANSPIRATION

Process in organisms of passing water vapor through membranes or pores. Although in a general sense transpiration may be applied to animals losing water in the act of respiring or sweating, the term is most aptly applied in a biological context to plants as they lose water while respiring. The potential for transpirational water loss is much greater in plants than in animals, because the former inspire carbon dioxide and the latter inspire oxygen as the primary metabolic gases. Carbon dioxide constitutes only 0.03 percent of the air, whereas oxygen constitutes nearly 21 percent; thus in the process of photosynthesis plants must process much greater volumes of air to extract the required amounts of carbon dioxide. Gas exchange in plants occurs through cuticular openings on photosynthetic surfaces called stomata, which may be closed during periods of nonexchange. Since photosynthesis is a daytime process, it occurs during the hottest, driest periods, thereby promoting maximal rates of transpiration.

Desert plants have evolved several ways to deal with these potentially high rates of transpirational water loss. Many desert plants are annuals that restrict germination and vegetative growth to short periods following precipitation, when soil moisture content will support high rates of transpiration. During periods of drought annuals are represented by their seeds lying dormant in the soil. Desert perennial plants have waterproofing cuticles and, during drought, open their stomata only enough to meet their photosynthetic needs. In extreme drought perennials may become photosynthetically dormant, closing the stomata and shutting down metabolically until conditions improve. Some desert perennials are drought deciduous, losing their leaves during droughts, which, combined with metabolic dormancy, reduces transpiration to a minimum.

The most remarkable desert plants are those that employ Crassulacean Acid Metabolism (CAM). These are mostly succulents of the families Crassulaceae (species of *Dudleya*), Agavaceae (agaves), Liliaceae (yuccas), and Cactaceae (cacti), which open their stomata for gas exchange only during the cooler nights when transpirational water loss is less. In these species carbon dioxide absorbed at night is stored temporarily in the plant tissues as malic acid and then is released to support photosynthesis during the daytime when the stomata are closed. Desert plants thus employ a variety of mechanisms to avoid detrimental rates of transpirational water loss.—Richard E. MacMillen

See also **ANNUAL PLANTS; CACTI; CAM PLANTS; LEAVES; PERENNIAL PLANTS; PHOTOSYNTHESIS; PLANT ADAPTATIONS; PLANTS; ROOTS; STOMA; WATER BALANCE**

Further Reading

Hadley, N. F., ed. 1975. *Environmental Physiology of Desert Organisms*. Stroudsburg, Pa.: Dowden, Hutchinson, and Ross.

MacMahon, J. A. 1985. *Deserts*. New York: Knopf.

TSAIDAM DESERT. *See* ASIA, DESERTS OF

TUCU-TUCO

Common name used in Argentina and several other South American countries for burrowing rodents (mammalian family Ctenomyidae, order Rodentia) in the genus *Ctenomys*. Almost 60 species have been described from the southern states of Brazil, Paraguay, Bolivia, Chile, Uruguay, Peru, and throughout Argentina as far south as Tierra del

Tucu-tuco (*Ctenomys opimus*) of the high puna desert of Argentina. (Photo: R. A. Ojeda)

Fuego. These are generally small rodents (most species weigh less than 300 grams) and usually occur in arid and semiarid habitats from sea level to more than 4,500 meters. The common name of these animals (*tunduque* is also used in Chile and parts of Argentina) comes from the sound that they make, which is a low, thumping "tucu-tuco" that often bubbles up from underground in South America's southern desert regions. Frequently the thumping sound proceeds in waves across the desert as different groups of animals are stimulated to call by the calls of others. Generally, tucu-tucos are solitary, with only one animal inhabiting a burrow at any one time (with the exception of mothers and young). One species, *Ctenomys sociabilis*, is colonial, with groups of animals living together. There is a great deal of taxonomic confusion concerning this genus, which may be found to contain only about 30–35 species. Even its familial affinities are questionable, with some authorities placing the genus in the family Octodontidae, a group of species that are not generally as highly specialized for fossorial (burrowing) life. *Ctenomys* look very much like North American pocket gophers and are an excellent example of convergent evolution.—Virgilio G. Roig

See also **ALTIPLANO; BURROWING ANIMALS; CONVERGENT EVOLUTION; GOPHER; MONTE DESERT; PUNA; RODENTS; TYMPANIC BULLAE**

Further Reading

Mares, M. A., J. Morello, and G. Goldstein. 1985. The Monte Desert and other subtropical semi-arid biomes of Argentina, with comments on their relation to North American arid areas. *In* M. Evenari, I. Noy-Meir, and D. W. Goodall, eds., *Ecosystems of the World: Hot Deserts and Arid Shrublands*, 12B:203–237. New York: Elsevier.

Mares, M. A., R. A. Ojeda, and R. M. Bárquez. 1989. *Guide to the Mammals of Salta Province, Argentina (Guía de los mamíferos de la Provincia de Salta, Argentina)*. Norman: University of Oklahoma Press.

Nowak, R. M. 1991. *Walker's Mammals of the World*. 5th ed. Baltimore: Johns Hopkins University Press.

Redford, K. H., and J. F. Eisenberg. 1992. *Mammals of the Neotropics: The Southern Cone, Chile, Argentina, Uruguay, Paraguay*. Vol. 2. Chicago: University of Chicago Press.

TULAROSA BASIN. *See* NEW MEXICO DESERT

TUMBLEWEED

Plant or plant infructescence (fruit cluster) that blows before the wind and in the process disperses its seed; the name is commonly applied to *Salsola kali*. The tumbleweed habit is common in flat treeless or shrubless, open landscapes usually referred to as steppes. The semiarid Great Plains of North America (defined here as the shortgrass prairie region that occupies the level, alluvial outwash of the Rocky Mountains) is such an area. One impact of the fencing of the Great Plains was to intercept tumbling plants. Once established along a fence row, later generations of the plants germinated in place and the increased vegetation intercepted blowing sands. The result, during periods of severe drought, was to bury the fences. *Salsola* is native to the steppes of Eurasia. It was introduced into North America, where it has become a serious pest.—James R. Estes

See also **ASIA, DESERTS OF; CHENOPODIACEAE; GERMINATION; PLANT ADAPTATIONS; PLANT DISPERSAL BY WIND (ANEMOCHORY); SEEDS; SHRUBS; STEPPE**

Further Reading

Heywood, V. H., ed. 1993. *Flowering Plants of the World*. Updated ed. New York: Oxford University Press.

TURANIAN DESERT. *See* ASIA, DESERTS OF

TURKESTAN DESERT. *See* ASIA, DESERTS OF

TYMPANIC BULLAE

Globose structures located between the mandibular fossae (the point in the skull where the mandible attaches to the cranium) and the occipital condyles on the mammalian skull, and consisting of an expanded tympanic bone, or the tympanic bone plus the entotympanic bone, and containing the structures of the middle ear (incus, malleus, and stapes). The tympanic membrane (eardrum) stretches across the external auditory meatus, a foramen located on the lateral side of the bullae. The tympanic bullae are also called the auditory bullae.

This bulbous structure is highly modified in some species, including especially those that inhabit deserts. Mammals living in deserts tend to have larger auditory bullae than closely related species living in cool, humid, nondesert habitats. Although the reasons for this are unclear, it is known that sound is absorbed differentially under different conditions and humidity. Bullae enlargement may compensate for the poor sound-carrying attributes of desert air.

Mammals with enlarged tympanic bullae include kangaroo rats and kangaroo mice (Heteromyidae, *Dipodomys* and *Microdipodops*), some South American hystricomorph rodents, gerbils, jerboas (Dipodidae), springhares (Pedetidae), Australian hopping mice (*Notomys*), and elephant shrews (Macroscelididae).

The extremely large tympanic bullae of kangaroo rats (*Dipodomys*) have a total bullar volume that is greater than that of the braincase. Low-frequency sounds made by predators, such as the wing beats of an owl or scales rubbing on the ground by a snake, may be easily heard by kangaroo rats, which respond by leaping into the air. Although many desert inhabitants have enlarged tympanic bullae, some have large ears (pinnae) instead (e.g., *Allactaga* and *Jaculus*); sometimes enlarged bullae and enlarged ears are major features used to characterize a species. Whether the bullae or the ear pinnae are enlarged, the function remains the same: to enhance the ability of the animals to detect low-frequency sounds.—Janet K. Braun

See also **ANIMAL ADAPTATIONS; ARMADILLO; BIPEDALITY; CONVERGENT EVOLUTION; DEFENSIVE ADAPTATIONS, ANIMALS; HETEROMYIDS; JERBOA; KANGAROO MOUSE; KANGAROO RAT; PINNAE; POCKET MOUSE; PREDATION; SAND RAT; SPRINGHARE; RODENTS**

Further Reading

Lay, D. M. 1993. Anatomy of the heteromyid ear. *In* H. H. Genoways and J. H. Brown, eds., *The Biology of the Family Heteromyidae*, 270–290. Special Publication No. 10, American Society of Mammalogists.

Vaughan, T. A. 1986. *Mammalogy.* 3d ed. Philadelphia: Saunders.

UNGULATES

Term applied to herbivorous mammals that do not bear claws at the ends of their digits but instead have hooflike structures. Living ungulates include subungulates, such as elephants, and the more typical ungulates, such as the tapirs, rhinoceroses, equines (order Perissodactyla) and swine, hippopotamuses, giraffes, deer, and bovines (order Artiodactyla).

For ungulates, plants form the primary source of nourishment. Species may have varied diets, combining plant foods such as fruits, nuts, leaves, and grasses. The swine and peccaries are exceptional in that they are highly omnivorous, feeding on a wide array of both animal and plant matter, and have rather simple digestive systems. Those ungulates specialized for feeding on plant parts, such as leaves and grasses, usually fall into two anatomical groups. Elephants, tapirs, rhinoceroses, and equines (including horses) have an elongate large intestine and enlarged caecum. The latter structure is a blind pouch of the gut opening at the junction of the large and small intestine. Within the caecum microbial fermentation of plant parts takes place, allowing nutrients to be extracted from structural carbohydrate (cellulose), which no mammal is capable of digesting without the aid of bacterial or protozoan symbionts. These species are referred to as the hindgut fermenters. The remainder of the herbivorous ungulates, such as camels, giraffes, deer, and bovines, have a specialized stomach, usually divided into four chambers. The anterior chamber is referred to as the rumen, which serves as a location for microbial fermentation of structural carbohydrates. In a manner parallel to the hindgut fermenters, energy may be extracted from structural carbohydrate with the aid of bacterial and, in some cases, protozoan symbionts.

In conjunction with the evolution of hooves, one may notice two general trends. Within the Perissodactyla, the weight is borne on the median toe, with the other toes becoming reduced in size or lost. The remaining metacarpals and metatarsals may be lost or fused. This grouping includes the tapirs, rhinoc-

Brown brocket deer (*Mazama gouazoupira*), an ungulate from the Chacoan thorn scrub of Argentina. (Photo: M. A. Mares)

eroses, and equines. In the case of the equines, toe reduction has proceeded so that only a single toe on each foot is functional. The remaining ungulates are usually grouped into the order Artiodactyla, wherein the weight is borne between the third and fourth toes. Again toe reduction is demonstrable, and in the extreme case, such as in some bovines, toe loss is pronounced with only two functional toes remaining on each foot.

Together with toe reduction, there is an increase in the length of the forefeet and hind feet, often with the fusion of the metacarpal and metatarsal bones. The animals are capable of achieving great speed in their locomotion. Obviously enhanced locomotor ability allows the possessor to locate efficiently pockets of rich food across a wide landscape, but in addition, it allows them to employ speed as an antipredator mechanism.

Many ungulates employ seasonal migration patterns, thus permitting the seasonal use of extremely arid habitats by seeking out grazing and browsing sites where recent rainfall has promoted plant growth. Extreme adaptation of ungulates to arid habitats is demonstrated by the camel family (Camelidae) both in the Old World (*Camelus*) and in the New World (e.g., the vicuña, (*Vicugna*, of the Bolivian and Peruvian plateaus). African and Asian ungulates adapted to desert environments include the wild asses (*Asinus*), gazelles (*Gazella*), *Oryx*, and gerenuk (*Litocranius*). In desert areas of Africa and parts of Asia most mammalian biomass in deserts is held in the tissues of ungulates. They are extremely important components of these desert ecosystems because of their diet, body size, and ability to modify the vegetation through browsing, grazing, and other activities, such as the propensity of elephants to destroy entire trees. Population sizes of several species, even in deserts and semideserts, can be remarkable. The vast herds of African ungulates are legendary.—John F. Eisenberg

See also **AFRICA, DESERTS OF; ANTELOPE; ARGALI; ASS; ATLAS BROWN CATTLE; AWASSI SHEEP; BARBARY DEER; BARBARY SHEEP; BLACKBUCK; CAMEL; DEER; DOMESTIC ANIMALS; ELAND; ELEPHANT; GAZELLE; GEMSBOK; GERENUK; GIRAFFE; GOAT; HARTEBEEST; IBEX; KLIPSPRINGER; KUDU; MAMMALS; MOUFLON SHEEP; NYALA; ORYX; PECCARY; PRONGHORN; RHINOCEROS; SHEEP; SPRINGBOK; WARTHOG; ZEBRA; ZEBU CATTLE**

Further Reading

Ghosh, P. K., and I. Prakash. 1988. *Ecophysiology of Desert Vertebrates*. Jodhpur: Science Publishers.

UNITED ARAB EMIRATES, DESERTS OF

Arid and semiarid habitats lying within the United Arab Emirates (UAE), a country located between latitudes 20°50'–26°00' north and longitudes 51°–56° east near the southeastern tip of the Arabian Peninsula and bordered by Saudi Arabia, Qatar, and Oman. The total area of the UAE is about 83,600 square kilometers, and the climate is characterized by low winter rainfall, high temperatures, and a dry summer. Mean annual rainfall is less than 100 millimeters, and the daily rainfall figures indicate that as much as 50 percent of the annual precipitation may be expected in a single day. Temperature extremes range from about 50°C in July to 4°C in January. There are three major bioclimatic zones in the UAE: (1) the semiarid zone, which includes steppe or tropical shrublands in the northeast along the Gulf of Oman; (2) the arid zone, which encompasses the drylands of the northern UAE (north of Dubai and Al Ain) and contains very sparse perennial vegetation; and (3) the hyperarid zone, which corresponds to extreme desert and encompasses

the rest of the country. (See map of Middle East deserts, p. 361.)

The main water resources are underground water, rainfall, and seawater desalination (desalination plants have been constructed on the Gulf). Underground aquifers generally lie 10–200 meters below the surface. Rainfall in the mountains of Oman is a major reliable source of water, with torrential rains and their runoff flooding numerous wadis that discharge onto the plains. Part of the rainfall percolates and flows as underground water.

The UAE has two distinct phytogeographic regions: the eastern mountain region, which constitutes part of the Hajar Mountains of Oman with a submontane zone of outwash (alluvial) plains, and the western desert region, which is divided into an inland desert and a coastal belt.

The eastern mountains support plant communities of *Dodonaea viscosa*, *Farsetia linearis*, *Reseda aucheri*, *Ficus carica*, *Cymbopogon parkeri*, *Eleusine compressa*, and *Launaea spinosa* at the higher elevations. At lower elevations *Jaubertia aucheri*, *Pteropyrum scoparium*, *Pulicaria glutinosa*, *Ochradenus aucheri*, *Capparis cartilaginea*, *Ficus salicifolia*, *Forskahlea tenacissima*, and species of *Trichodesma* dominate. Several species from the desert lowlands may be found at higher elevations in the mountains.

The outwash plains are covered by plant communities that are distinct from those found in the mountains. In the Jiri Plains of the north *Prosopis cinerea*, *Pulicaria undulata*, and *Ranterium eppaposum* characterize the plant communities. In the plains of Dhaid and Madam *Acacia tortilis*, *Haloxylon salicornicum*, *Tephrosia persica*, *Leptadenia pyrotechnica*, *Astenatherum forsskalii*, and species of *Cenchrus* are the major plants. In the Al Ain area, vegetation on the disturbed plains includes *Rhazya stricta*, *Aerva javanica*, *Zilla spinosa*, *Fagonia ovalifolia*, *Indigofera argentea*, and various *Centaurea*.

Several plant communities are found on the sandy and gravelly plains of the inland central desert. Among these are *Haloxylon salicornicum*, *Cornulaca monacantha*, *Cyperus conglomeratus*, *Pennisetum divisum*, *Stipagrostis plumosa*, *Panicum turgidum*, *Crotalaria aegyptiaca*, *Leptadenia pyrotechnica*, *Calligonum comosum*, and *Citrullus colocynthis*.

The inland sand dunes are formed of weathered quartz rocks. Toward the north the dunes are relatively small and support some plants, including various *Calligonum*, *Cyperus conglomeratus*, *Haloxylon salicornicum*, *Zygophyllum hamiense*, and *Heliotropium digynum*. To the south the dunes increase in height, and vegetation cover may be essentially absent.

The eastern coastal belt on the Arabian Gulf is extensive and consists of several plant community types. The sheltered lagoons and their borders (where regular flooding occurs) support *Avicennia marina*, *Arthrocnemum macrostachyum*, and *Halocnemum strobilaceum*. The sabkha (salt marshes) above the high tide are characterized by *Halopeplis perfoliata* and *Salsola baryosma*. The coastlines have *Suaeda vermiculata*, *Atriplex leucoclada*, *Zygophyllum hamiense*, and *Anabasis setifera*. Conspicuous species in older salt marshes are *Limonium axillare*, *Aeluropus lagopoides*, and *Juncus maritimus*.

The coastal sand dunes are composed of white carbonate sands of marine origin and support mixed plant communities characterized by *Halopyrum mucronatum*, *Salsola baryosma*, *Cyperus conglomeratus*, and *Seidlitzia rosmarinas*. Offshore islands have plant communities similar to those of the mainland.

Biodiversity of the country is declining due to rapid rural and urban development. About 340 species of flowering plants, 40 mammals, 300 birds, and 40 reptiles are listed for the terrestrial ecosystems of the UAE.

Patterns of land use and human impact in the UAE are diverse. Because of rapid agricultural expansion, forest plantations, and the development of inland and coastal towns, increasingly large amounts of freshwater are required and the region's water resources are overexploited. As an example, the underground water level in some regions fell by 10 meters from 1977 to 1984. As a result of aquifer depletion, salinity levels rise and seawater seeps into coastal areas. The gradual dying off of some *Prosopis* and *Acacia* trees in Ras Al Khaimah and other areas is caused by the lowering of underground water levels. Increasing salinity of underground irrigation water has caused a decline in the agricultural yields of the UAE to the point where some water wells have had to be abandoned. Construction of dams to control the erratic flash floods is not practical in the UAE because of the permeability of the underlying rock, the excessive amounts of solid materials discharged in the runoff from rain, and the high water evaporation rate.

Agriculture contributes only 2 percent to the GNP of the UAE and employs few people; the arable land in the country occupies only an estimated 19,000 hectares, of which about 27 percent is irrigated. The outwash plains are the most fertile and agriculturally productive land. There are about 12.1 million cattle, 53.2 million sheep and goats, and 543,000 camels maintained as domestic livestock in the UAE. Attempts have been made to improve agriculture in the region, and agricultural research is conducted in many experimental farms and laboratories on irrigation systems and seawater irrigation, fertilizer application, cropping systems, and new drought- and salt-tolerant plant crop introduction.

It is difficult to assess the extent to which traditional nomadic pastoralism has survived the urbanizing influence of oil wealth. Bedouin (nomads) settlements are concentrated into small villages. Vegetation near these fixed villages is subject to degradation. The extensive grazing, gathering of fuel plants, fodder use, and water transportation by vehicles have increased the pressure on rangelands.

The UAE is considered the leading country in desert afforestation among the other Arabian Gulf states. High priority is given to planting for aesthetics, wildlife parks, and along highways. There are many introduced species of exotic plants that are of economic importance, including *Eucalyptus*, *Casuarina*, *Parkinsonia*, *Bougainvillea*, and various *Prosopis*. Other indigenous species including *Acacia* and *Ziziphus spina-christi* are also used. Maintenance of these plantations consumes large amounts of water and increases soil salinity problems in the arid environment of the UAE.—Ahmad K. Hegazy

See also **AFRICA, DESERTS OF; AGRICULTURE IN DESERTS; ARABIAN GULF, DESERTS OF; CHENOPODIACEAE; CONTAMINATION; DESERTIFICATION; DOMESTIC ANIMALS; DUNES; MIDDLE EAST, DESERTS OF; OVERGRAZING; PLAYA; SAHARA DESERT; SALINIZATION; SHEEP**

Further Reading

Cantacuzino, S., and K. Browne. 1977. The United Arab Emirates. *Architectural Review* 161:325–351.

El-Ghonemy, A. A. 1985. *Ecology and Flora of Al Ain Region*. Al Ain: UAE University.

Food and Agriculture Organization (FAO). 1973. *Agricultural Development in the United Arab Emirates.* Cairo: Near East Regional Office.

―――. 1994. A systems perspective for sustainable dryland development in the Near East region. Cairo: Near East Regional Office.

FAO, UNESCO, and WHO. 1977. World map of desertification. UN Conference on Desertification, Nairobi.

Jongbloed, M. 1988. *The Living Desert.* Arabian Heritage Series. Dubai: Motivate Publishing.

Lieth, H., and A. Lieth. 1993. Seawater irrigation studies in the United Arab Emirates. *Tasks for Vegetation Science* 27:1–10.

Osborne, P. E., and al-W. Marzak, eds. 1996. *Desert Ecology of Abu Dhabi: A Review of Recent Studies.* Newbury, U.K.: Pisces, in association with the National Avian Research Center.

Satchell, J. E. 1978. Ecology and environment in the United Arab Emirates. *Journal of Arid Environments* 1:201–226.

Satchell, J. E., M. D. Mountford, and W. M. Brown. 1981. A land classification of the United Arab Emirates. *Journal of Arid Environments* 4:275–285.

Western, A. R. 1989. *The Flora of the United Arab Emirates: An Introduction.* Al Ain: UAE University.

UNITED STATES, DESERTS OF

Deserts located exclusively in the western part of the United States which are the result of their geographic location in areas of dominant high pressure systems and in the rain shadow of high mountain ranges. These deserts share many characteristics, the most common of which is the sparse xerophytic vegetation consisting primarily of widely spaced shrubs and other plants adapted to arid conditions. The physiography of the U.S. deserts consists of mountains, low hills, playas, arroyos, and bajadas and is reflective of the Basin and Range Province in which these deserts occur. The elevation is highly variable, ranging from below sea level to more than 3,000 meters. The desert soils are a complex mixture of aridisols, lithosols, and regosols.

Four major deserts are generally recognized as occurring in the United States. These are the Sonoran Desert of Arizona, the Chihuahuan Desert of southern New Mexico and western Texas, the Mojave Desert of California and southern Nevada, and the Great Basin Desert located mainly in Utah and Nevada. Two of these, the Sonoran and the Chihuahuan deserts, are portions of larger desert areas that extend into Mexico. The Sonoran, Chihuahuan, and Mojave are usually referred to as hot deserts; the Great Basin Desert is considered a cold desert. Creosote bush (*Larrea tridentata*) and big sagebrush (*Artemisia tridentata*) are the most widespread species of the hot and cold deserts, respectively.

The Sonoran Desert is a pressure system desert that is characterized by extreme aridity and high temperatures that often exceed 40°C. This is a highly variable desert with a great diversity of plants and life forms such as low shrubs, trees, and succulents—particularly large cacti, including the columnar saguaro cactus.

The Chihuahuan Desert, which is more extensive in the arid high plains between the Sierra Madre Oriental and Sierra Madre Occidental of Mexico, has a more moderate climate than the Sonoran Desert. Temperatures are usually lower; there is a longer and more predictable growing season than in the Sonoran Desert; and cacti are a less dominant life form. Vegetation in the Chihuahuan Desert is dominated by creosote bush, tarbush (*Flourensia cernua*), *Acacia*, ocotillo (*Fouquieria splendens*), mesquite (*Prosopis*), *Yucca*, and *Agave*.

The Mojave (also spelled Mohave) Desert is the smallest of the hot deserts in the United States and is generally considered to be a transition between the Sonoran and Great Basin deserts. This desert exhibits great variation in topography, ranging from high mountains to areas well below sea level. The climate is extreme, with very little precipitation and the highest temperatures ever recorded in North America. The vegetation is dominated by shrubs such as creosote bush and bur sage (*Franseria dumosa*), but the most characteristic plant is the Joshua tree (*Yucca brevifolia*).

The Great Basin Desert, located in the rain shadow of the Sierra Nevada and the Cascade Mountains, is the only cold desert in North America. It is a region of primarily winter precipitation, including snow, and freezing winter temperatures. This is the simplest desert in the United States, with relatively few species and a shrub-dominated landscape. Big sagebrush occupies the more elevated, better-drained, and less saline areas, and shadscale (*Atriplex confertifolia*) occurs at lower elevations on poorly drained and saline sites. Grasses, such as *Agropyron*, *Poa*, and *Festuca*, are important in the northern part of the Great Basin

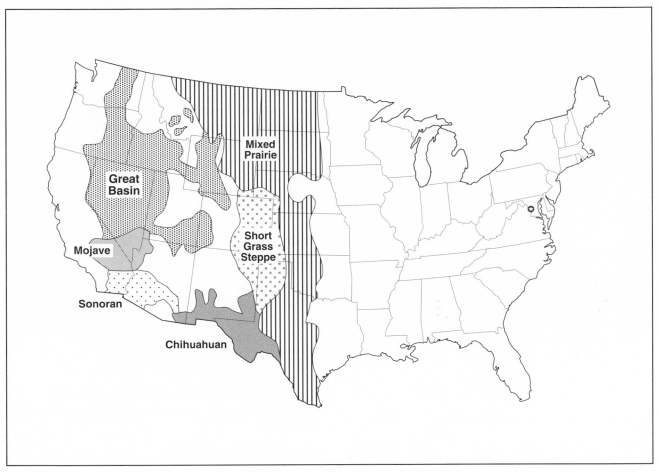

Map of the major deserts and semiarid grasslands of the United States.

Desert. In marked contrast to the hot deserts, cacti are relatively unimportant in this desert.

Characteristic animals of the deserts of the United States are peccary, woodrat, kangaroo rat, black-tailed jackrabbit, coyote, deer mouse, red-tailed hawk, doves (mourning, Inca, white-winged), desert horned lizard, Gambel's quail, sage grouse, phainopepla, pyrrhuloxia, cactus wren, Gila woodpecker, Gila monster, and roadrunner. The hot deserts also support a relatively rich fauna of snakes and lizards.—Gary K. Hulett and Amanda Renner Charles

See also **AMPHIBIANS; ANZA-BORREGO DESERT; ARIZONA DESERT; BAJA CALIFORNIA, DESERTS OF; BIG BEND NATIONAL PARK; BIRDS; BONNEVILLE; CACTI; CACTUS, COLUMNAR; CALIFORNIA DESERT; COLORADO DESERT; CREOSOTE BUSH; DEATH VALLEY; DESERT GRASSLAND; DESERTS; DESERTS, HOT; DESERTS, TEMPERATE; FISHES; GRAND CANYON; GREAT AMERICAN DESERT; JORNADA DEL MUERTO; JOSHUA TREE NATIONAL PARK; LIZARDS; LLANO ESTACADO; MAMMALS;** **MEXICO, DESERTS OF; MOJAVE DESERT; MONUMENT VALLEY; MOVIES IN DESERTS; NEVADA DESERT; NEW MEXICO DESERT; OREGON DESERT; ORGAN PIPE CACTUS NATIONAL MONUMENT; PAINTED DESERT; PALOVERDE; PLANT GEOGRAPHY; REPTILES; RIO GRANDE; SALTBUSH; SALT CEDAR; SEMIARID ZONES; SNAKES; UTAH DESERT; WASHINGTON DESERT; YUMA DESERT; WHITE SANDS NATIONAL MONUMENT**

Further Reading

Axelrod, D. I. 1950. Evolution of desert vegetation in western North America. *Contributions to Paleontology, Carnegie Institution of Washington Publication* 590:215–306.

———. 1958. Evolution of the Madro-Tertiary Geoflora. *Botanical Review* 24(7):433–509.

Bailey, R. G. 1978. *Descriptions of the Ecoregions of the United States.* Ogden, Utah: USDA Forest Service.

Brown, D. E., ed. 1994. *Biotic Communities: Southwestern United States and Northwestern Mexico.* Salt Lake City: University of Utah Press.

Dice, L. R. 1943. *The Biotic Provinces of North America.* Ann Arbor: University of Michigan Press.

Hastings, J. R., and R. M. Turner. 1965. *The Changing Mile: An Ecological Study of Vegetation Change with Time in the Lower Mile of an Arid and Semiarid Region.* Tucson: University of Arizona Press.

Hubbard, J. P. 1974. Avian evolution in the arid regions of North America. *The Living Bird* 12:155–195.

MacMahon, J. A. 1979. North American deserts: Their floral and faunal components. *In* D. W. Goodall and R. A. Perry, eds., *Arid-land Ecosystems: Structure, Functioning and Management,* 21–82. New York: Cambridge University Press.

Martin, P. S. 1963. *The Last 10,000 Years: A Fossil Pollen Record of the American Southwest.* Tucson: University of Arizona Press.

Shreve, F. 1942. The desert vegetation of North America. *Botanical Review* 8:195–246.

URIC ACID

End product of nitrogen metabolism formed during the chemical decomposition of proteins and amino acids by some animals, and composing their excreta. Uric acid has the chemical composition $C_5H_4O_3N_4$ and among desert animals is excreted most commonly by insects, land snails, most reptiles, and birds. Those organisms that excrete uric acid are referred to as being uricotelic, and this capacity is viewed as an extremely important water-conserving mechanism, as the excreta are eliminated in the form of a pasty precipitate having a very low water content. Furthermore, uric acid is both nontoxic and osmotically inert, enabling it to be held internally in a very concentrated state during its formation and prior to elimination. Although amphibians are rare in deserts, there are desert-adapted frogs and toads in nearly all the world's deserts; the vast majority of these produce urea as the end product of nitrogen metabolism, losing significant amounts of water during its elimination. Exceptions to this rule are certain arid-adapted frogs from Africa and South America that excrete uric acid and exhibit the same water-conserving benefits of other uricotelic animals.—Richard E. MacMillen

See also **AMPHIBIANS; ANIMAL ADAPTATIONS; BIRDS; EXCRETORY SYSTEM; KIDNEYS; LIZARDS; METABOLISM; PHYSIOLOGY; RENAL PAPILLA; SALT BALANCE; URINE; WATER BALANCE**

Further Reading

Schmidt-Nielsen, K. 1990. *Animal Physiology: Adaptation and Environment.* 4th ed. New York: Cambridge University Press.

URINE

Excretory material that is formed in the kidneys in vertebrates and is carried from the kidneys by the ureters to be voided into the cloaca (amphibians, reptiles, birds) or directly to the outside (mammals). In amphibians and mammals the urinary nitrogenous waste product is urea, which is water soluble, requiring the loss of water to eliminate it; the urine of reptiles and birds contains insoluble uric acid, resulting in less water loss. The kidneys of birds and mammals void urine in osmotic concentrations that exceed that of the blood, representing a significant conservation of water, particularly in certain desert rodents. The Spinifex hopping mouse of the Australian deserts (*Notomys alexis*) is independent of free drinking water and when deprived of water concentrates its urine to a level 25 times that of the blood, a concentration greater than in any other mammal. Humans are much less efficient, with maximal urine concentrations; approaching four times that of the blood, resulting in considerable urinary water loss, which, together with perspiration and respiratory water loss, results in high water requirements. Thus, for example, during the war in Iraq (Desert Storm), each soldier was expected to drink at least eight quarts of water per day. Amphibians and reptiles cannot concentrate their urine. Certain desert toads, frogs, and tortoises exploit this seeming disadvantage by storing in the bladder large volumes of very dilute urine formed during the infrequent wet periods; this serves as a reservoir from which water may be resorbed gradually back into the bloodstream, thereby retarding dehydration during dry periods.—Richard E. MacMillen

See also **AMPHIBIANS; ANIMAL ADAPTATIONS; BIRDS; EXCRETORY SYSTEM; HUMAN PHYSIOLOGY IN DESERTS; KIDNEY FUNCTION, DESERT RODENTS; KIDNEYS; LIZARDS; METABOLISM; PHYSIOLOGY; RENAL PAPILLA; SALT BALANCE; SURVIVAL IN DESERTS; URIC ACID; WATER BALANCE**

Further Reading

Schmidt-Nielsen, K. 1990. *Animal Physiology: Adaptation and Environment.* 4th ed. New York: Cambridge University Press.

MacMillen, R. E., and A. K. Lee. 1967. Australian desert mice: Independence of exogenous water. *Science* 158:383–385.

UTAH DESERT

Great Basin Desert habitat extending from the Sierra Nevada on the west almost to the Rocky Mountains on the east and encompassing most of the state of Utah. The arid climate of this region is the result of the rain shadow of the Sierra Nevada range, which intercepts much of the moisture-laden winds from the Pacific Ocean. The average annual rainfall is 250 millimeters or less throughout most of the area.

Some portions of this vast orographic (rain shadow) desert are sometimes referred to as the Utah Desert. However, the vegetation is very similar to that found in adjacent Nevada, Oregon, and Idaho, and only minor species compositional differences are present. The vegetation of the Utah Desert is dominated by big sagebrush (*Artemisia tridentata*) and shadscale (*Atriplex confertifolia*). These low-growing, soft gray shrubs are so common in the region that it is often designated the sagebrush-shadscale desert. In the Utah Desert the shadscale probably is as abundant as sagebrush because of the extensive alkaline flats that are so conducive to the growth of the saltbush. As with most of the Great Basin region, cacti are a relatively unimportant feature of the Utah Desert.

The desert of Utah is for the most part an expansive arid region of rather bleak and monotonous scenery, often lacking in trees except along the few waterways, where willow (*Salix*) and cottonwood (*Populus*) are found. On the scattered low mountain ranges of the region pinyon-juniper woodlands are common, and if the elevation is sufficiently high, pines (*Pinus*), spruce (*Picea*), and firs (*Abies*) also occur. These isolated mountains are very interesting ecologically because they serve as refugia (habitat islands) in an otherwise arid desert sea and often support distinctive biota as a result of evolutionary isolation.

The lowest parts of the Utah landscape are dominated by salt- and alkali-encrusted dry lakes or playas, which have little or no drainage to the sea. Some playas are so large, flat, and hard surfaced that they have been used extensively as automobile speed record tracks, the most famous of these being the Bonneville Salt Flats in western Utah. The

Utah Desert (Great Basin Desert) habitat in southern Utah. (Photo: M. A. Mares)

Great Salt Lake in Utah is but a remnant of the much larger Lake Bonneville that occurred in the area during wetter ice age times.—Gary K. Hulett and Amanda Renner Charles

See also **ARIZONA DESERT; BONNEVILLE; CALIFORNIA DESERT; CHENOPODIACEAE; DESERTS; GREAT BASIN DESERT; HALOPHYTES; NEVADA DESERT; PLANT ADAPTATIONS; PLANT GEOGRAPHY; PLANTS; OREGON DESERT; WASHINGTON DESERT; SEMIARID ZONES; SALTBUSH; SALT DESERT; SALT PAN; SHRUBS; STEPPE; UNITED STATES, DESERTS OF**

Further Reading

Andersen, B. A. 1996. *Desert Plants of Utah*. Logan: Utah State University.

Christensen, E. M. 1959. A comparative study of the climates of mountain brush, piñon-juniper, and sagebrush communities in Utah. *Proceedings of the Utah Academy of Science* 36:174–175.

Fautin, R. W. 1946. Biotic communities of the northern desert shrub biome in western Utah. *Ecological Monographs* 16:251–310.

Hayward, C. I. 1948. Biotic communities of the Wasatch chaparral, Utah. *Ecological Monographs* 18:473–506.

Ibrahim, K., N. E. West, and D. L. Goodwin. 1972. Phytosociological characteristics of perennial *Atriplex*-dominated vegetation of southeastern Utah. *Vegetatio* 24:13–22.

West, N. E., and K. Ibrahim. 1968. Soil-vegetation relationships in Utah. *Ecology* 49:445–456.

UTE. *See* DESERT PEOPLES

VAN'T HOFF EFFECT

Effect of increasing temperature on increasing rates of reactions and organismic functions. A temperature quotient is calculated comparing the rates of biological reactions of interest at two temperatures, typically 10°C apart. The temperature coefficient, called Q_{10}, is calculated using the van't Hoff equation:

$$Q_{10} = \left(\frac{K_2}{K_1}\right)^{\frac{10}{T_2 - T_1}}$$

where K_1 and K_2 are the rates at temperatures T_1 and T_2.

In general chemical reactions have Q_{10} values of about 2–3, whereas purely physical processes (e.g., diffusion) have lower temperature sensitivities with Q_{10}'s slightly above 1.0. Because many organismal responses are based on chemical reactions, the Q_{10} indicates these responses will double or even triple with each 10°C rise in temperature. Examples of such important responses are metabolic rate and heart and breathing rates of various ectothermic animals. The magnitude of the effect is quite startling when quantified. Imagine a desert lizard of about 100 grams with a heart rate of 20 beats per minute at a body temperature of 20°C, a typical nighttime body temperature in the desert. If the Q_{10} for heart rate for this animal is 2, the heart rate would double to 40 at a body temperature of 30°C, and it would quadruple to 80 at 40°C, a typical daytime body temperature in the desert.

Q_{10}'s are entirely empirical values with no theoretical basis. Furthermore they typically decrease with increasing temperature. It is therefore necessary to specify the range of temperatures for which a particular Q_{10} is reported.—David S. Hinds

See also ANIMAL ADAPTATIONS; ECTOTHERMY; ENDOTHERMY; HEAT STRESS; METABOLISM; PHYSIOLOGY

Further Reading

Bartholomew, G. A. 1982. Body temperature and energy metabolism. M. S. Gordon, ed., *Animal Physiology*, 333–406. 4th ed. New York: Macmillan.

Eckert, R. 1988. *Animal Physiology: Adaptation and Environment*. 3d ed. New York: Freeman.

Schmidt-Nielsen, K. 1984. *Scaling: Why Is Animal Size so Important?* New York: Cambridge University Press.

Schmidt-Nielsen, K. 1990. *Animal Physiology: Adaptation and Environment*. 4th ed. New York: Cambridge University Press.

Withers, P. C. 1992. *Comparative Animal Physiology*. Philadelphia: Saunders.

VELVET ANT

Antlike insect in the family Mutilidae. Velvet ants are in the insect order Hymenoptera, which, in addition to velvet ants, contains ants, bees, wasps, sawflies, and myriad other insects. Velvet ants are really a type of wasp. Females are wingless, covered with hairs of varying colors, depending on species. They march around on the ground in an antlike fashion, usually seeking egg deposition sites. Males have wings and fly around in search of females. Colors of velvet ants are typically reds, oranges, yellows, and occasionally white. Some, such as the "cowkillers," have black markings against a background of red.

Unlike ants, and many wasps and bees, velvet ants do not live in social groups. Individual adults vary in size from about 6 to 20 millimeters. Most impressive is the set of defense mechanisms exhibited by adult females. The bright color of these animals is aposematic warning coloration, alerting potential predators that the insect may be dangerous. The cuticle of the body is extremely thick, rendering it nearly impossible to kill a velvet ant by stepping on it or otherwise applying pressure to the body. Females produce noxious chemicals from the abdomen when disturbed, and when grabbed they bite viciously with large, sharp mandibles and sting with a long stinger that injects a painful toxin. In addition, the hairs on their bodies are like tiny spears (called urticating hairs) that cause considerable irritation to the mouth and nasal passages of animals that attack them. The stinger is coiled inside of the abdomen and may be half as long as the body. The effectiveness of these defense mechanisms has been demonstrated in experimental studies with natural predators. Velvet ants attacked by large broad-headed skinks (lizards in the genus *Eumeces*) bit and stung the lizards in the mouth, were not damaged by the powerful jaws of the lizards, and were released unharmed by the lizards. The lizards learned, usually after a single encounter, not to attack velvet ants.—Laurie J. Vitt

See also **ANIMAL ADAPTATIONS; ANTS; ARTHROPODS; DEFENSIVE ADAPTATIONS, ANIMALS; HYMENOPTERA; INSECTS; LIZARDS; POISONOUS ANIMALS; VENOM; WARNING COLORATION; WASPS**

Further Reading

Borror, D. J., and R. E. White. 1970. *A Field Guide to the Insects.* Boston: Houghton Mifflin.

Manley, D. G. 1984. Predation upon velvet ants of the genus *Dasymutilla* in California (Hymenoptera: Mutillidae). *Pan-Pacific Entomologist* 60:219–226.

Manley, D. G., and H. G. Spangler. 1983. Observations on daily activity patterns of mutillid wasps of the genus *Dasymutilla. Journal of the Georgia Entomological Society* 18:235–239.

Vitt, L. J., and W. E. Cooper, Jr. 1988. Feeding responses of broad-headed skinks (*Eumeces laticeps*) to velvet ants (*Dasymutilla occidentalis*). *Journal of Herpetology* 22:485–488.

VENOM

Chemical or mix of chemicals injected by one organism into the body of another in defense or for the purpose of immobilizing or killing potential prey. Venoms vary considerably in their chemical constitution, toxicity, and potential threat to humans. Effects of envenomation are almost as diverse as the organisms that produce venoms. Because venoms consist of complex organic molecules, most of which require the expenditure of considerable energy to produce, use of venoms for defense is usually a last resort, only after other measures have failed. Because most venoms evolved for subduction of prey, venom delivery systems are highly evolved and very effective.

Almost all major categories of terrestrial animals that produce venoms occur in deserts of the world, including insects, spiders, scorpions, centipedes, and snakes. Bees, wasps, ants, spiders, scorpions, centipedes, and some other arthropods produce venoms of various types. Social bees, wasps, and ants (all in the order Hymenoptera) produce venoms for defense. These venoms cause immediate extreme pain, thus warding off intruders, and generally cause little or no tissue damage in the immediate vicinity of the sting or bite. The greatest threat from these stings is the possibility that a systemic allergic reaction; may occur. Some solitary wasps produce neurotoxic venoms that paralyze prey; the immobilized but living prey are then used to feed the wasp's larvae. Venoms produced by spiders, scorpions, and centipedes are used to immobilize prey as well as for defense. Some, like that of the bark scorpion (*Centruroides sculpturatus*), are highly neurotoxic and potentially fatal to humans, causing convulsions, hyperactivity, numbness, and respiratory depression. Others, like that of the brown recluse spider (*Loxosceles*), can cause massive lesions at the location of the bite, resulting in tissue loss.

The most impressive venoms among terrestrial animals are those produced by poisonous snakes in the families Elapidae and Viperidae. These venoms are highly evolved and are generally considered to have been designed by natural selection to kill and aid in digestion of prey. These venoms, depending on the particular species of snake, may contain proteinases, which destroy tissues; hyaluronidase, which increases tissue permeability, thus increasing the rate at which other components of the venom spread through the victim's body; polypeptides (elapid snakes only), which interfere with neuromuscular transmission; cholinesterase (mostly in elapids), whose effects are not well known; phospholipases, which destroy cell membranes; phosphatases, which specifically affect ATP and other high-energy phosphate molecules, thus affecting metabolic activity; and L-amino acid oxidase (mostly in rear-fanged colubrid snakes), which can cause extensive tissue damage. Most of these venoms cause extreme pain when injected and consequently serve to ward off potential predators.

There has been recent controversy over the treatment of envenomation by pit vipers with the advent of a technique referred to as electroshock. There is no reliable scientific evidence that this technique is effective in snakebite treatment; controlled laboratory experiments have failed to demonstrate positive effects using electroshock. Expert medical advice should be sought in all cases of envenomation by poisonous snakes or other potentially lethal animals.—Laurie J. Vitt

See also **ADDER; ANTS; ARACHNIDS; ARTHROPODS; BEES; BLACK WIDOW SPIDER; CENTIPEDE,**

GIANT; COBRA; CORAL SNAKE; CROTALUS; DEFENSIVE ADAPTATIONS, ANIMALS; GILA MONSTER; HYMENOPTERA; PIT VIPER; POISONOUS ANIMALS; RATTLESNAKE; REPTILES; SCORPIONS; SHREW; SIDEWINDER; SNAKES; SUN SPIDER; TARANTULA; TERMITES; VELVET ANT; WARNING COLORATION; WASPS

Further Reading

Hardy, D. L., Jr. 1992. A review of first aid measures for pitviper bite in North America with an appraisal of ExtractorTM suction and stun gun electroshock. *In* J. A. Campbell and E. D. Brodie, Jr., eds., *Biology of Pitvipers*, 405–414. Tyler, Tex.: Selva.

Russel, F. E. 1980. *Snake Venom Poisoning.* Philadelphia: Lippencott.

———. 1984. Snake venoms. *Symposium of the Zoological Society of London* 52:469–480.

Smith, R. L. 1982. *Venomous Animals of Arizona.* Tucson: Cooperative Extension Service, University of Arizona.

VICUÑA. *See* CAMELS, SOUTH AMERICAN

VOLE

Member of a large group of herbivorous grazing rodents (mammalian subfamily Arvicolinae, family Muridae, order Rodentia). This subfamily includes 17 genera and more than 100 species, all limited to the Northern Hemisphere. Voles are hamsterlike. They have large heads, small feet, relatively soft fur, and tails of variable length. Coat color also differs among species. Most voles feed on grasses. The widespread abundance of grasses allows voles the potential to be as widespread as the grass on which they feed. The continuous growth and looping enamel patterns of the molars allows them to feed on tough grasses. Increases in the size of jaw musculature and the caecum have improved food processing and digestive efficiency of the voles, permitting them to survive on relatively nutrient-poor grasses. Most voles construct burrows or use abandoned burrows of other animals. Despite the diversity of voles and their wide distribution, only four genera enter arid regions.

The sagebrush vole (*Lemmiscus curtatus*) is the only member of its genus and is found in central and western North America. Its pelage is ashy gray with a buff underside. Although most active after sunset and before sunrise, this vole can be found active at any hour of the day. Breeding occurs year-round. An average of five pups is born after a gestation period of 25 days. Juveniles reach sexual maturity in 60 days.

The steppe lemmings (genera *Eolagurus* and *Lagurus*) are voles that inhabit arid regions, pastures, and cultivated fields from the Ukraine to Mongolia. *Lagurus* has a light gray pelage with a black stripe down the middle of the back; *Eolagurus* is sand colored. Both genera have white undersides. Steppe lemmings are active at night. These voles collect, dry, and store vegetation for use during the winter. The breeding season extends from April to October. Litters of 3–12 pups are born after a gestation period of 20 days. Juveniles reach sexual maturity in 28 days.

Although not limited to deserts, the largest group of voles—the meadow voles (genus *Microtus*)—has members that occur in arid regions or may enter arid regions along waterways. Size, color, and natural history of this genus exhibit variation.

Mole-voles (genus *Ellobius*) are the most fossorial (burrowing) voles. They are limited to arid and semiarid regions between the Ukraine and Mongolia. Mole-voles are noted for the reduced size of their ears and eyes. The velvetlike pelage of mole-voles is cinnamon to brown in color. Several species have a dark patch that covers their faces. Mole-voles feed on the underground parts of plants and store food in special chambers in their burrows. Breeding takes place year-round but is most frequent from April to October. Litters of two to five pups are born after a gestation period of 25 days. Juveniles attain sexual maturity in 100 days.—Rob Channell

See also ASIA, DESERTS OF; DESERT GRASSLAND; GRASSES; GRASSLAND; GREAT AMERICAN DESERT; GREAT BASIN DESERT; HERBIVORY; MAMMALS; PRAIRIE; RODENTS; SAGEBRUSH

Further Reading

Gromov, I. M., and I. Ya. Polyakov. 1992. *Voles (Microtinae), Fauna of the USSR Mammals.* Vol. 3, no. 8. New Delhi: Oxonian.

VULTURE

Two evolutionarily distinct groups of large scavenging birds of prey. Old World vultures are traditionally included in the Falconiformes with other birds of prey (15 species, family Falconidae). The New World vultures (7 species, family Cathartidae) have been placed variously in the Falconiformes, Accipitriformes, Cathartiformes, and Ciconiiformes. The Ciconiiformes includes the storks, and it now seems apparent that cathartids are closely related to these wading bird species. Cathartids are distributed throughout an array of habitats, including forests and deserts, from southern Canada to Tierra del Fuego. For example, the turkey vulture (*Cathartes aura*) is distributed throughout the Americas across many habitats, including deserts, woodlands, and open plains. Old World vultures range throughout primarily open country, often arid regions, in southern Europe, Asia, and Africa. The lappet-faced vulture (*Torgos tracheliotus*) is an example of an Old World vulture that inhabits drier environments. It ranges from the northwestern Sahara, west to Somalia, and south to South Africa and is found in thorn scrub, open plains, and deserts.

New and Old World vultures are superficially similar in morphology as a consequence of convergent evolution. Vultures are large (40–120 centimeters in length), sometimes with an impressive wingspan (three meters in condors). Fossil evidence suggests that some extinct vulture taxa greatly exceeded the condors in size; one such North American form (a "teratorn") had a wingspan of greater than seven meters. Larger vultures engage almost exclusively in passive soaring flight. Some vulture species, both New and Old World, roost communally. For example, turkey vultures roost in numbers sometimes exceeding 30 individuals. Other taxa are essentially solitary throughout the year.

New World vultures excrete liquid onto their legs to facilitate heat loss through evaporative cooling. In addition, during periods of heat stress some vultures (e.g., the black vulture, *Coragyps atratus*) may increase the surface area of exposed skin by raising their wings to expose the more sparsely feathered underwing and flank.

The heads of many species are bare, probably an adaptation to prevent feather soiling when feeding on carcasses. The hooked bill is well suited for tearing food from carcasses but is not as powerful as that of other raptors. Vultures rarely kill their prey and feed almost exclusively on carrion; thus they fill an important ecological role in many communities. Many individuals, sometimes of more than one species, may congregate at a carcass. Carrion is located visually by Old World vultures, but in some cathartids, especially turkey vultures, olfaction is

important. Many vultures use the circling flight behavior of conspecifics or of other vulture species as cues to the presence of carrion. One species of Old World vulture, the Egyptian vulture (*Neophron percnopterus*), throws rocks at ostrich (*Struthio camelus*) eggs to access their contents, one of the rare examples of tool use in birds.

Vultures generally have low reproductive rates, clutches consisting of between one and three eggs. Species may nest colonially or solitarily. Nest sites are caves, rock ledges, and trees. Females alone incubate in some taxa, whereas in others these duties are shared between sexes. Generally both sexes contribute to parental care.—Stephen C. Lougheed

See also **AFRICA, DESERTS OF; ASIA, DESERTS OF; BAJA CALIFORNIA, DESERTS OF; BIRDS; BUZZARD; CARRION EATERS; DECOMPOSITION; MIDDLE EAST, DESERTS OF; MONTE DESERT; PATAGONIA; PREDATION; RAPTORS; SAHARA DESERT; SOUTH AMERICA, DESERTS OF; SPAIN, DESERTS OF; THERMALS; UNITED STATES, DESERTS OF**

Further Reading

Brown, L., and D. Amadon. 1968. *Eagles, Hawks and Falcons of the World*. Vol. 1. London: Country Life.

Brown, L. H., E. K. Urban, and K. Newman. 1982. *The Birds of Africa*. Vol. 1. New York: Academic Press.

Cramp, S., and K. E. L. Simmons, eds. 1980. *Handbook of the Birds of Europe, the Middle East and North Africa: The Birds of the Western Palearctic*. Vol. 2. Oxford: Oxford University Press.

Gailey, J., and N. Bolwig. 1973. Observations on the behavior of the Andean condor (*Vultur gryphus*). *Condor* 75:60–68.

Houston, D. C. 1980. The adaptations of scavengers. *In* A. R. E. Sinclair and M. Norton-Griffiths, eds., *Serengeti: Dynamics of an Ecosystem*, 263–286. Chicago: University of Chicago Press.

Johnson, A. W. 1965. *The Birds of Chile and Adjacent Regions of Argentina, Bolivia and Peru*. Vol. 1. Buenos Aires: Platt.

Stager, K. 1964. The role of olfaction in food location by the turkey vulture. *Los Angeles County Museum Contributions to Science*, No. 81.

Wallace, M. P., and S. A. Temple. 1987. Competitive interactions within and between species in a guild of avian scavengers. *Auk* 104:290–295.

Wilbur, S. R., and J. A. Jackson, eds. 1983. *Vulture Biology and Management*. Berkeley: University of California Press.

Zimmerman, D. R. 1975. Vulture restaurant. *Natural History* 84:26–31.

WADI. *See* ARROYO

WARNING COLORATION

Bright colors and patterns characterizing unpalatable or dangerous animals that could potentially serve as prey for other organisms; thought to warn a predator that the brightly colored organism is not suitable for consumption. Typically warning colors are bright red, yellow, or orange but may be black and white or any bold colors or patterns that stand out against the background. These colors and patterns are referred to as aposematic. Animals with aposematic coloration have some sort of defense mechanism, such as toxic skin secretions that make it bad tasting, a sting, or some other noxious property. Aposematic coloration is common in invertebrates such as millipedes and beetles. Laurie Vitt has recently suggested that the bright red, yellow, white, and black colors and patterns of American coral snakes are mimics of similarly colored distasteful millipedes. Skunks are common desert inhabitants that have bold black-and-white warning color patterns to let potential predators know that they have protective scent glands.

For warning coloration to defend against predators, some prey animals must be sacrificed in order for a predator to learn the association between the noxious qualities and the aposematic coloration. If a population of prey organisms is large, this loss would be insignificant. However, a significant portion of a population could be lost if the population is small. Thus it is unlikely that warning coloration would be maintained in rare species. Kin selection may have favored longevity in aposematic organisms as the killing of a postreproductive animal would reduce the chances of that animal's offspring being killed.—Janalee P. Caldwell

See also **AMPHIBIANS; ANIMAL ADAPTATIONS; ANTS; ARACHNIDS; ARTHROPODS; BEES; BEETLES; BUGS; BUTTERFLIES; CENTIPEDE, GIANT; COLORATION; CORAL SNAKE; DEFENSIVE ADAPTATIONS, ANIMALS; FLIES; FROGS; HYMENOPTERA; INSECTS; PIGMENT; PLANT ADAPTATIONS; PLANTS; PREDATION; RED VELVET MITE; SCORPIONS; SNAKES; SPIDERS; SUN SPIDER; TOADS; WASPS**

Further Reading

Endler, J. A. 1989. On the measurement and classification of colour in studies of animal colour pattern. *Biological Journal of the Linnean Society* 41:315–352.

Fox, D. L. 1979. *Biochromy: Natural Coloration of Living Things*. Berkeley: University of California Press.

Hamilton, W. J., III. 1973. *Life's Color Code*. New York: McGraw-Hill.

Vitt, L. J. 1992. Mimicry of millipedes and centipedes by elongate terrestrial vertebrates. *Research and Exploration* 8:76–95.

WARTHOG

Piglike species (*Phacochoerus aethiopicus*) of mammal (family Suidae, order Artiodactyla) native to the savannas and grasslands of sub-Saharan Africa;. Three pairs of facial warts give the warthog its descriptive name. The warthog also possesses two pairs of impressive tusks; the smaller lower tusks serve as weapons; the larger upper tusks are for display. While both sexes have tusks and facial warts, in males these features are larger. Males also can outweigh females by 20 percent. Their gray skin is sparsely covered with black and white hairs or bristles. They also have manes along their necks and backs that vary from yellow to red to black.

Warthogs are active during the day. Grasses and grass seeds make up the bulk of the diet. Wallowing in mud or dust occupies much of the day when the animals are not feeding or napping. They use abandoned aardvark burrows for shelter during the night.

Warthogs have excellent senses of sight, smell, and hearing. They use these to protect themselves from numerous natural predators, such as cheetahs, leopards, or lions. Warthogs communicate to the members of their small groups (six individuals on average) by short grunts or chirps. During courtship males grunt rhythmically to the females. Mating takes place in May or June. One to four piglets are born after a gestation period of 22 weeks. They can live 12–15 years.

Warthogs have been extirpated over large portions of their range but are still relatively common where they remain. They can be carriers of the

Warthog (*Phacochoerus aethiopicus*) in the Itala Game Reserve, northern Kwazulu-Natal Province, South Africa. (Photo: M. A. Mares)

virus that causes African swine fever, a disease often fatal to domesticated pigs that has retarded the development of swine farming in southern Africa. Warthogs are also thought to sustain populations of the tsetse fly, the vector of African sleeping sickness.—Rob Channell

See also **AARDVARK; AFRICA, DESERTS OF; BURROWING ANIMALS; KALAHARI DESERT; KAROO; MAMMALS; NAMIBIA, DESERTS OF; OMNIVORY; SAVANNA; SOUTH AFRICA, DESERTS OF; STEPPE; UNGULATES; XEROPHYLLOUS SCRUB**

Further Reading

Estes, R. D. 1991. *The Behavior Guide to African Mammals*. Berkeley: University of California Press.

Haltenorth, T., and H. Diller. 1980. *A Field Guide to the Mammals of Africa, Including Madagascar*. London: Collins.

Skinner, J. D., and R. H. N. Smithers. 1990. *The Mammals of the Southern African Subregion*. Pretoria: University of Pretoria.

WASHINGTON DESERT

Eastern portions of the state of Washington influenced by the rain shadow of the Cascades which support extensive xeric (dry) vegetational communities, including a composite of bunchgrass steppe and sagebrush desert similar to that found in adjacent Idaho and Oregon, representing the northern extension of the Great Basin Desert. The driest habitats in the Washington sagebrush desert are located at lower elevations, below the coniferous forest and grassland ecological zones of the mountains. The sagebrush desert commonly occurs in a scattered pattern on the deeper soils of the flats and valleys, while grasslands and woodlands occupy the shallower soils of hills and low mountains. This is a region of winter precipitation and cold winter temperatures.—Gary K. Hulett and Amanda Renner Charles

See also **CHENOPODIACEAE; DESERTS, COLD; GREAT BASIN DESERT; HALOPHYTES; MONTANA DESERT; OREGON DESERT; SAVANNA; SEMIARID ZONES; STEPPE; UNITED STATES, DESERTS OF; UTAH DESERT**

Further Reading

Daubenmire, R. F. 1970. *Steppe Vegetation of Washington*. Washington State University Agricultural Experiment Station Technical Bulletin 62.

WASPS

Catch-all term for a wide variety of insects in many families of the insect order Hymenoptera. The term has only a partial taxonomic basis. Insects in the superfamilies Scolioidea (except ants), Vespoidea, and Sphecoidea are considered wasps. Typically "wasps" are thought of as rapidly flying social insects that respond to the presence of humans or other intruders by attacking in large numbers and inflicting painful stings. Although this is true of some wasp families, it is not true for others. Moreover, other insect families, such as the Apidae (honeybees) may exhibit similar behavior. Wasps are common in deserts. A few examples are provided below.

Vespid wasps are in the family Vespidae. Many species in this family are social and construct paper-like nests. These include the wasps commonly known as paper wasps, yellow jackets, and hornets. Typically workers construct large nests in whose cells larvae are fed by adults. When the nest is disturbed, workers attack landing on and stinging the intruder. Although the venom is not toxic, many people have allergic reactions to the stings, particularly when many stings are inflicted at one time; these allergic reactions have been known to cause death in humans and other species. Adults typically feed on insects and then feed the chewed insects to the larvae. They are occasionally pests at picnic grounds, where they land and feed on human food. Some species of vespid wasps are not social and live solitary lives. Potter wasps, for example, paralyze caterpillars, which they bring back to their mud nest. The caterpillars are fed on by the larvae of the wasp.

Spider wasps are in the family Pompilidae. These wasps may be quite large (up to 40 millimeters) and typically are dark colored with black or, in some instances, red wings. The large wasp known as the tarantula hawk (in the genus *Pepsis*) is in this family. Spider wasps search for and paralyze large spiders with their potent venom. The spiders are then carried, and sometimes dragged, back to the nest, which is usually a hole in the ground. The paralyzed spiders are placed in the nest for the larvae to feed on. Spider wasps can inflict extremely painful stings, but they typically do not attack or sting unless they are physically constrained.

Sphecid wasps are in the family Sphecidae. This is another large family of common wasps in deserts. The most familiar sphecid wasps are the thread-waisted wasps (subfamily Sphecinae), which are characterized by an abdomen that is threadlike at the base. Similar to spider wasps, many thread-waisted wasps nest in holes in the ground. Some species search for and paralyze grasshoppers and bring them back to the nest to provision the larvae. Other thread-waisted wasps construct mud nests (hence the name mud dauber) and, like spider wasps, provision the nest with paralyzed spiders.—Laurie J. Vitt

See also **ANIMAL ADAPTATIONS; ANTS; ARTHROPODS, BEES; COLORATION; DEFENSIVE ADAPTATIONS, ANIMALS; HYMENOPTERA; INSECTS; PIGMENT; POISONOUS ANIMALS; VELVET ANT; VENOM; WARNING COLORATION**

Further Reading

Bohart, R. M., and A. S. Menke. 1976. *Sphecid Wasps of the World*. Berkeley: University of California Press.

Borror, D. J., C. A. Triplehorn, and N. F. Johnson. 1992. *An Introduction to the Study of Insects*. New York: Harcourt Brace.

Borror, D. J., and R. E. White. 1970. *A Field Guide to the Insects*. Boston: Houghton Mifflin.

Ross, K. G., and R. W. Matthews. 1991. *The Social Biology of Wasps*. Ithaca: Comstock.

Spradbery, J. P. 1973. *Wasps: An Account of the Biology and Natural History of Solitary and Social Wasps*. Seattle: University of Washington Press.

Wilson, E. O. 1971. *The Insect Societies*. Cambridge, Mass.: Harvard University Press.

WATER

Molecule composed of one atom of oxygen and two atoms of hydrogen, with characteristic properties—it freezes at 0°C and boils at 100°C. Water is one of the four primary "elements" that the Greek philosopher Aristotle in the 4th century B.C. defined as a major constituent of the universe, the others being earth, air, and fire. Despite its apparent simplicity, water is a complex liquid whose properties and importance are not yet fully understood. It makes up only a small fraction of the universe but is common in the form of water vapor or ice on some stars, planets, and comets. Only on earth is it in its liquid phase, where it defines a space called the hydrosphere, a region that extends from 15 kilometers above the earth in the atmosphere to as far as 1 kilometer below the earth's surface. It circulates through this hydrosphere in a labyrinth of complex ways that make up the hydrological cycle. Oceans, lakes, rivers, ice, rain, and clouds are some of the many forms taken by water; the action of water has led to the formation of much of the earth as we see it today. It is a basic component of all living creatures. For example, the human body contains 70 percent water.

These exceptional physical and chemical properties, at the molecular level as well as in its interaction with the environment, make water among the most important elements on earth. Because of its molecular structure, it is considered to be the universal solvent. It is the finest solvent of inorganic compounds, which is of fundamental importance in all natural processes. Among the properties of water is the hydrophobic effect; that is, certain hydrocarbons have a tendency to be repelled by water molecules, and this effect is responsible in large part for the complex structures of protein molecules, DNA, and other vital molecules of life that, if they were not hydrophobic, would be unstable.

Natural water is never chemically pure; it always contains dissolved salts and gases, substances in suspension, microorganisms, and many other materials that may vary during the cycle of water. These substances are not considered impurities but are natural components of water—except for those contaminants and other materials that have been added to the water cycle by human activities or through natural processes, which drastically affect its properties or may render it useless as water.

The most important sources of water are the oceans, which generally contain elevated salinity and a variety of elements. Water that is percolated through the soils and through the earth's surface takes on chemical characteristics of the formations through which it percolates. The quantities of water on the earth are approximately as follows: oceans and seas contain 1,350,000,000 cubic kilometers; polar ice caps and glaciers contain 25 million cubic kilometers; the continents contain 8.6 million cubic kilometers, of which 66,000 cubic kilometers are in the form of soil moisture, 8.3 million cubic kilometers are subterranean water at a level of greater than 800 meters, 200,000 cubic kilometers are contained in the world's lakes and rivers, and 13,000 cubic kilometers are in the atmosphere. Only 600 cubic kilometers of water are contained in the organisms of the earth. Water is constantly transferred from one form to another, and the entire period of renovation of the hydrological cycle ranges from about 11 days for the water that is stored in the atmosphere to several thousand years for water stored in seas and oceans.—Alberto I. J. Vich and Juana Susana Barroso

See also **ALLUVIAL FAN; ARIDITY; ARTESIAN BASIN; CLIMATE; CLOUDS; CONVECTIVE STORM; CYCLONE; DAM; DEW; DRINKING WATER; FIELD CAPACITY OF SOILS; FLOOD; FLOODPLAIN; GROUNDWATER; HAIL; HYDROLOGICAL CYCLE; HYDROLOGY; MOISTURE INDEX; OSMOTIC POTENTIAL; PRECIPITATION; RELATIVE HUMIDITY; RIVERS; RUNOFF; SNOW; WATER POTENTIAL; WEATHERING, DESERT; WELL**

Further Reading

Bates, R. L., ed. 1987. *Glossary of Geology.* 3d ed. Alexandria, Va.: American Geological Institute.

Davis, S. N. 1974. Hydrogeology of arid regions. *In* G. W. Brown, Jr., ed., *Desert Biology: Special Topics on the Physical and Biological Aspects of Arid Regions,* 2:1–30. New York: Academic Press.

Eagland, D. 1990. La estructura del agua. *Mundo Científico* 10:736–742.

The New Encyclopaedia Britannica. 15th ed. 1974. Water. Vol. 19:633–643. Chicago: University of Chicago Press.

Suh-Shiaw, Lo. 1992. *Glossary of Hydrology.* Taipei: Sheng Te.

Omont, A., and J. L. Bertreaux. 1990. El agua en el cosmos. *Mundo Científico* 10:744–750.

USSR National Committee for the International Hydrological Decade. 1978. *World Water Balance and Water Resources of the Earth.* Paris: UNESCO Studies and Reports in Hydrology, No. 25.

WATER BALANCE

Condition in a water-bearing system in which an equilibrium in water content is achieved by balancing water output (or extraction) with water input (or addition). Deserts by definition are geographic settings in which, at least on an average annual basis, water balance is never achieved because the potential for water loss to the atmosphere by evaporation (output) always exceeds the water input by precipitation. Thus deserts are exceedingly dry places, imposing on their living inhabitants major challenges in maintaining water balance. The magnitude of these challenges may best be appreciated by understanding that, at least in their mature reproductive phases, desert plants and animals maintain body water contents equivalent to or in excess of two-thirds of their body masses; that is, they are mostly water. Yet in spite of these challenges, the deserts of the world teem with a diversity of living things, making the study of the means by which they achieve water balance one of the more intriguing elements in the field of physiological ecology.

The specific strategies of maintaining water balance by desert organisms are many and varied and generally consist of combinations of structural, functional, and behavioral adjustments. For desert plants that as mature individuals are fixed in place on the surface, structural and functional adaptations must serve the purpose; animals, which are more mobile, add behavioral modifications to their water balance repertoire, providing additional versatility. Among the most interesting of desert organisms are those that are ephemeral, spending most of their lives withstanding drought in the dry desert soil as desiccation-resistant reproductive propagules (i.e., spores, eggs, seeds) that are independent of requirements to remain in a positive state of water balance. When the infrequent rains occur these propagules rapidly enter a growth phase, with reproductive maturity ensuing during the brief period when water is in optimal supply, ensuring positive water balance. Included among these desert ephemerals are certain aquatic crustaceans (especially shield shrimps and fairy shrimps) and annual plants. Positive water balance during the growth and reproductive phases of desert annual plants is ensured by the presence in the seeds of water-soluble inhibitors that prevent germination until removed. For removal by leaching, these require just the amount of rainfall that will sustain positive water balance in the growing, short-lived plant until it flowers and sets seeds, to produce the next generation of drought-resistant propagules.

Another strategy employed by desert organisms to enhance maintenance of water balance during drought is periodic dormancy, accompanied by substantial metabolic reduction and reduced rates of water exchange. In desert perennial plants this dormancy is often accompanied by drought-deciduousness, in which the photosynthetic leaves with their porous stomata are shed, resulting in significant reductions in water loss at the cost of temporary abandonment of photosynthesis. These perennial plants typically possess deep taproots that extend down to soil levels where there is sufficient moisture to offset the reduced rate of water loss while dormant. With rains these plants resume metabolic activity, rapidly replace leaves, and operate with high rates of photosynthesis. This results in energy production to sustain growth, as well as in an increased rate of water loss, which is affordable until drought once again ensues. At that time another period of dormancy is required to enhance maintenance of water balance.

Among the desert animals that resort to dormancy as a water-conserving measure are several species of frogs from North American and Australian deserts and the Australian inland crab. These animals are essentially aquatic as reproductive adults, with fast-growing larval or young stages that rely on temporary aquatic habitats for early growth and development to afford optimal states of water balance. But these aquatic habitats in the desert are ephemeral by nature. When they dry up the surviving adults and newly emerged youngsters retreat to underground burrows in sand or clays with unusual water-holding capacities and become dormant with substantial metabolic reductions. There they spend most of their adult lives waiting out the periods of drought and sustaining positive water balance while in a state of suspended animation.

In desert frogs this process is aided by the storage in the blood of urea, a waste product of metabolism, which gradually increases the blood's osmotic pressure, thereby making it easier for the dormant frog to extract water from the surrounding soil; on reemergence after rains, the frog voids this excess urea and resumes temporary aquatic existence in an abundance of fresh rainwater.

The Australian inland crab occurs in low-lying desert regions of fine-grained clays, subject to periodic flooding following infrequent rains. During drought the dormant crabs are at the bottoms of burrows about a meter in depth, surrounded by moist clay soil in atmospheres saturated with water vapor, apparently resulting in the maintenance of positive water balance. With the onset of rains the crabs emerge on the surface to resume an active aquatic life until surface waters once again recede; they then retreat to their underground refugia to await, sometimes for a year or more, the next rain.

Desert succulent plants such as New World agaves and cacti and Old World aloes and euphorbs abandon strict maintenance of water balance and rely instead on rapid water uptake and storage during rains, followed by gradual but continual water loss during drought, undergoing substantial but tolerable changes in tissue water content. This process is aided by the presence of spreading shallow root systems that rapidly absorb rainwater as it accumulates at the surface, by waxy cuticles that inhibit water loss from the plant surfaces, and by exchanging photosynthetic gases during the cooler night via Crassulacean Acid Metabolism, resulting in reduced rates of stomatal water loss.

Most terrestrial desert animals, invertebrates and vertebrates alike, maintain body water contents within very narrow limits, finding ways to offset very conservative water expenditures with an equally sparse water supply. Smaller animals rely extensively on behavior to place them in microclimates that minimize water loss. Many of these avoid the daytime desiccating surface conditions in underground, moist retreats, resorting to nocturnal (nighttime) surface activity with its accompanying cooler temperatures and lessened water demands. Taken together, behavior, efficient excretory systems that minimize water expenditures while voiding metabolic wastes, respiratory systems that minimize water lost while breathing, and dry external surfaces (skins or cuticles) that repel excessive water loss combine to yield low water outputs that can be balanced (often just with the prudent choice of food) with the little water the desert has to offer. Certain small, seed-eating animals (i.e., ants, rodents, birds) have perfected these capabilities to the extent that the water that is produced as a by-product of metabolizing the seeds of desert plants, together with the very small amounts of water the seeds absorb from the soil, is sufficient under most circumstances to offset water losses, enabling the animals to maintain a constant water content of about two-thirds of body mass.

Compared to ectothermic (cold-blooded) animals (e.g., reptiles), endotherms, or warm-blooded animals (e.g., mammals and birds), have potentially high rates of water exchange with the environment. For small mammals, behavioral adjustments (e.g., nocturnality, seeking cool and moist refugia) together with food choice are of paramount importance in offsetting water that has been lost. Small desert birds add the greater mobility of flight to their water-balance repertoires, ameliorating with periodic drinking their demanding daytime habits. Large desert flightless birds (e.g., ostriches, emus) and mammals (e.g., camels, gazelles) employ behavior to a lesser extent but are relatively mobile, can tolerate partial dehydration between visits to water, and are capable of rapid rehydration. Humans, in contrast, have very narrow tolerance limits with regard to water balance and are not good desert animals. We must rely extensively on behavioral modifications of the desert environment and drinking large amounts of freshwater to offset our very high rates of water loss, together with replacement of salts lost via perspiration. Under exposure to the most demanding of daytime desert conditions humans are unable to drink water in sufficient volumes to offset losses and must tolerate uncomfortable, temporary periods of negative water balance, regaining positive water balance during the cooler nighttime, through continuing water intake. Thus it is imperative for humans in the desert to seek daytime shelter and to carry an abundant, reliable supply of water.—Richard E. MacMillen

See also ANIMAL ADAPTATIONS; BODY TEMPERATURE; CAMEL; CAMEL'S HUMP; COUNTERCURRENT HEAT EXCHANGE; DEHYDRATION; DESICCATION; DESICCATION-RESISTANT SPECIES; ECTOTHERMY; ENDOTHERMY; ESTIVATION; EXCRETORY SYSTEM; GRANIVORY; HEAT BALANCE; HEAT EXCHANGE; HEAT STRESS; HEATSTROKE; HIBERNATION; HUMAN PHYSIOLOGY IN DESERTS; HYPERTHERMIA; HYPOTHERMIA; INSULATION; KANGAROO RAT; KIDNEY FUNCTION, DESERT RODENTS; KIDNEYS; METABOLIC WATER; METABOLISM; PERSPIRATION; PHOTOSYNTHESIS; PHYSIOLOGY; PLANT ADAPTATIONS; RENAL PAPILLA; RESPIRATORY WATER LOSS; RODENTS; SALT BALANCE; SHIVERING; STOMA; SURVIVAL IN DESERTS; SWEAT GLANDS; THERMOREGULATION; TORPOR; TRANSPIRATION; URIC ACID; URINE; VAN'T HOFF EFFECT; WATER BALANCE; WATER HOLE; WATER STRESS

Further Reading

Bradshaw, S. D. 1997. *Homeostasis in Desert Reptiles*. New York: Springer.

Degan, A. A. 1997. *Ecophysiology of Small Desert Mammals*. New York: Springer.

Gordon, M. S., G. A. Bartholomew, A. D. Grinnell, C. B. Jorgensen, and F. N. White. 1982. *Animal Physiology: Principles and Adaptations*. New York: Macmillan.

Hadley, N. F., ed. 1975. *Environmental Physiology of Desert Organisms*. Stroudsburg, Pa.: Dowden, Hutchinson, and Ross. ·

MacMillen, R. E. 1990. Water economy of granivorous birds: a predictive model. *Condor* 92:379–392.

MacMillen, R. E., and P. Greenaway. 1978. Adjustments of energy and water metabolism to drought in an Australian arid-zone crab. *Physiological Zoology* 51:230–240.

MacMillen, R. E., and D. S. Hinds. 1983. Water regulatory efficiency in heteromyid rodents: A model and its application. *Ecology* 64:152–164.

Schmidt-Nielsen, K. 1990. *Animal Physiology: Adaptation and Environment*. 4th ed. New York: Cambridge University Press.

WATER HOLE

Low area that fills with water. Water holes can be temporary pools that fill after a single rain or can fill throughout the wet season and then dry when arid conditions return. They can also be relatively permanent features associated with high groundwater or rivers and streams. Water holes are an important resource for wildlife in arid regions, and many species of animals have altered their lifestyles or behavior to take advantage of them.

Some spadefoot toads; (genus *Spea*) have evolved to breed during the brief period that ephemeral water holes are filled with water. Increased soil moisture alerts the dormant adults in their underground cocoons that conditions may be favorable for breeding. The adult toads emerge and begin mating in the shallow pools. Once the eggs are laid they develop quickly. The young toads can develop from egg through tadpole to small adult in 20 days or less in some species. The young toads then burrow into the ground to await the next year's rain. The toads do not, however, have these water holes to themselves.

Small eggs of fairy shrimp; (genus *Chriocephalopsis*) are often mixed with the dirt that forms the bottom of water holes. The flooding of the water holes stimulates the eggs and causes them to hatch. These shrimp grow quickly, mate, and complete their entire life cycle in the brief existence of a temporary water hole. The eggs they release into the water remain at the bottom of the water hole when it dries. The wind blows the eggs and dirt from one water hole depression to another, ensuring that most water holes have shrimp eggs to begin the cycle. The sudden appearance of shrimp in a dry desert water hole after a rain seems an almost miraculous event to observers of desert life.

The timing of migration flights of many waterbirds coincides with periods when temporary pools are available. This gives the birds a comfortable resting spot in an arid region, and the abundant invertebrates like the fairy shrimp that occupy the shallow water are an ideal food source. To take advantage of these resources many species of birds alter their migratory paths. Migrating herds of mammals (antelope and wildebeest in Africa and, formerly, bison in North America) also often time their migrations to coincide with the presence of temporary water holes or alter their paths to take advantage of temporary and permanent sources of water in arid regions.

The effect of permanent water holes on desert faunas, while less spontaneous and spectacular, is no less profound than that of temporary pools. Many species of animals that occur in deserts are well adapted for their environment but require water. Access to water limits the distribution of many large mammals. Animals such as goats and sheep may feed over a broad region of the desert, but they are limited to the region surrounding a permanent source of water. These water holes often form a concentration of activity for many species of animals.

In an arid region the concentration of the water resource at water holes concentrates animal activity, and this attracts predators. Snakes, birds, and some small mammalian predators prey on breeding spadefoot toads or on their abundant offspring. The fairy shrimp are preyed on by birds and migrating antelopes are preyed on by lions or wild dogs that wait near water holes.—Rob Channell

See also **AMPHIBIANS; ANIMAL ADAPTATIONS; ARTHROPODS; BIRDS; BREEDING SEASON; DAM; DORMANCY; CYCLONE; FLOOD; FROGS; IRRIGATION DRAINAGE; PRECIPITATION; REPRODUCTION; RIVERS; RUNOFF; SHRIMP, DESERT; SPADEFOOT TOAD; TOADS; TADPOLES; WATER**

Further Reading

Alcock, J. 1985. *Sonoran Desert Spring*. Chicago: University of Chicago Press.

Allan, T., and A. Warren, eds. 1993. *Deserts: The Encroaching Wilderness*. New York: Oxford University Press.

Brown, G. W., Jr., ed. 1968. *Desert Biology: Special Topics on the Physical and Biological Aspects of Arid Regions*. Vol. 1. New York: Academic Press.

WATER OF RETENTION

Quantity of water adsorbed by soil particles and which owes its properties to the fact that the water molecule is polarized and acts as a small magnet attracted by electronic irregularities on the surface of various particles that make up solids in the soil. It has properties very different from free water, and it is represented in three major forms: hydroscopic water, film water, and interfilm water. Hydroscopic water is that which covers the surface and fills the micropores of the soil particles. It is maintained by forces of adsorption and can only be affected by sufficient heat to transform it into water vapor. Film water, or adhesion water, surrounds the soil particles and their hydroscopic water with a thin film of variable thickness (generally only a few microns) that can be displaced in the liquid phase by molecular attractions of soil particles. It can only be removed from the soil through centrifugation. These two forms of soil water are so strongly retained in the soil that they cannot be absorbed by the roots of plants. Interfilm water is retained by capillary forces in the partially filled soil pores and is not displaced through gravitational force.—Alberto I. J. Vich and Juana Susana Barroso

See also **FIELD CAPACITY OF SOILS; GROUNDWATER; HYDROLOGICAL CYCLE; HYDROLOGY; OSMOTIC POTENTIAL; WATER; WATER POTENTIAL**

WATER POTENTIAL

Potential energy contained in water in soil due to the internal properties of the soil. This energy is of fundamental importance in determining the movement and status of water in the soil, since the difference in potential energy between two points gives rise to the flow of water through the soil; the potential energy of water in the soil is the quantity of work that must be realized per unit volume of water to transfer an infinitesimally small amount of water from one arbitrarily selected point to another. Many factors affect the water potential of the soil, including hydration, osmotic pressure, surface tension, the presence of solutes, hydrostatic pressure, and gravity. Water potential in the soil is thus the sum of all these separate forces.—Alberto I. J. Vich and Juana Susana Barroso

See also **FIELD CAPACITY OF SOILS; GROUNDWATER; HYDROLOGICAL CYCLE; HYDROLOGY; OSMOTIC POTENTIAL; WATER; WATER OF RETENTION**

WATER QUALITY. *See* IRRIGATION DRAINAGE

WATER RELATIONS. *See* IRRIGATION DRAINAGE

WATER STRESS

Condition in plants and animals in which water balance has been disrupted and which typically refers to a state of dehydration leading to desiccation. In plants water stress occurs when transpirational water loss exceeds the capacity of the roots to extract water from the soil, resulting in wilting and eventually death if the condition is not reversed. Desert plants have many strategies to avoid water stress, from annual plants that grow vegetatively only after rainfall to perennials that are drought deciduous and drop their leaves to reduce water loss while in a photosynthetically dormant state.

Desert animals, too, have many adaptive strategies to avoid water stress, combining behavioral, physiological, and morphological mechanisms to maintain healthy states of water balance. Thus in native desert animals it is only during periods of unusually prolonged drought that water stress occurs, resulting in selection for survival of only the hardiest of individuals. Humans, however, are not very highly adapted desert animals, for they suffer water stress readily when exposed to the combined rigors of desert heat and aridity. Water stress may be avoided only by remaining quiescent in the shade, drinking copious amounts of water, and replacing the salt that is lost in perspiration.—Richard E. MacMillen

See also **ANIMAL ADAPTATIONS; HEAT; HEAT BALANCE; HEAT STRESS; HUMAN PHYSIOLOGY IN DESERTS; KIDNEYS; PERSPIRATION; PHYSIOLOGY; PLANT ADAPTATIONS; SALT BALANCE; SUNSTROKE; SURVIVAL IN DESERTS; THERMOREGULATION; TRANSPIRATION; SWEAT GLANDS; WATER BALANCE**

Further Reading

Hadley, N. F., ed. 1975. *Environmental Physiology of Desert Organisms*. Stroudsburg, Pa.: Dowden, Hutchinson, and Ross.

Schmidt-Nielsen, K. 1964. *Desert Animals: Physiological Problems of Heat and Water*. New York: Oxford University Press.

WATER TABLE. *See* GROUNDWATER

WAXBILL

Small, primarily seed-eating songbird ranging throughout southern Asia, Australia, and Africa (family Estrildidae, order Passeriformes). The taxonomic status of the estrildids is contentious, and the group is sometimes subsumed within the weaver family, Ploceidae. Approximately 120–130 species from 27 genera are recognized. Estrildids are found in a wide variety of habitats ranging from dry savanna and thorn scrub to tropical forest. Examples of estrildid taxa that inhabit arid or semiarid environments are plentiful. The zebra finch (*Taeniopygia guttata*) ranges throughout much of Australia and is found in a variety of drier open habitats. Maximum species diversity in the Estrildidae occurs in Africa, and many of these taxa are also desert dwelling. For example, the red-billed firefinch (*Lagonosticta senegala*) inhabits dry areas often dominated by *Acacia* south of the Sahara in Africa.

Body shape varies substantially from quite stocky with short tails to slender with long tails. Total length varies from 9 to 14 centimeters. Plumage ranges from quite drab to very bright coloration. Bill morphology is highly variable across species, ranging from an exceedingly robust seed-cracking bill (e.g., the seed-crackers, genus *Pyrenestes* of Africa) to a narrow, warblerlike bill (e.g., the ant-peckers, genus *Parmoptila* of central Africa). Most estrildids are granivorous but will consume some vegetable matter and insects. Some aberrant forms, however, are predominantly insectivorous (e.g., the ant-peckers). The majority of species drink several times daily, but some desert taxa, notably the zebra finch, can undergo water deprivation for long periods. Estrildids are generally gregarious and in the nonbreeding season may be seen in large flocks.

The breeding season often coincides with the period of maximum rainfall, and numerous arid-land species initiate nesting soon after substantial precipitation has fallen. Some species breed colonially, but the majority of estrildids nest solitarily. Pair-bonds in most taxa are strong and may endure throughout the nonbreeding season. All estrildids build enclosed nests constructed primarily of grasses, some with long entrance "tunnels." Many waxbills add a second structure to the top of the primary nest (a "cock-nest"). Clutch size usually ranges from four to eight eggs. In most species both members of the pair perform incubation and parental duties.—Stephen C. Lougheed

See also **AFRICA, DESERTS OF; ASIA, DESERTS OF; AUSTRALIA, DESERTS OF; BIRDS; GRANIVORY; PLANT ADAPTATIONS; PLANTS; SEED DISPERSAL BY ANIMALS (ZOOCHORY); SEEDS**

Further Reading

Cade, T., C. A. Tobin, and A. Gold. 1965. Water economy and metabolism of two estrildid finches. *Physiological Zoology* 38:9–33.

Cramp, S., and C. M. Perrins, eds. 1994. *Handbook of the Birds of Europe, the Middle East and North Africa: The Birds of the Western Palearctic.* Vol. 8. Oxford: Oxford University Press.

Goodwin, D. 1982. *Estrildid Finches of the World.* Oxford: Oxford University Press.

WEASEL

Numerous species of small carnivorous mammals in the family Mustelidaeweasels. These include several species in the widespread genus *Mustela*, the North African banded weasel (*Poecilictis libyca*), the African striped weasel (*Poecilogale albinucha*), and the lesser grison (*Galictis cuja*) and Patagonian weasel (*Lyncodon patagonicus*) from Argentina and Chile. Weasels are predominantly species of temperate and subarctic forests and prairies; however, several species occur in semiarid woodlands and grasslands, and some occur in deserts. Among the latter are three species of *Mustela* (*Mustela frenata* in North America; *Mustela nivalis* in areas bordering the Sahara in Africa; *Mustela eversmanni* in steppe and semidesert in the former Soviet Union, Mongolia, and China), and the species in the other four genera.

All species of weasels are aggressive and efficient hunters that specialize in small mammals. Several species are kept by local people to control rats in dwellings. Indeed, domesticated lesser grisons, *Galictis*, were used by hunters in the high Andes of South America to enter chinchilla burrows and drive the valuable animals out so that they could be captured and their exquisite fur used in the manufacture of coats. This caused the near-extinction of the chinchilla. Weasels will also consume large insects, small birds, and snakes; some of the bigger species will kill animals as large as rabbits. Weasels hunt by stalking and chasing their victims, and some species track their prey by scent. They generally kill by biting the throat of the prey and grasping and chewing until the victim is dead. Their long, slender bodies enable them to pursue small rodents into their burrows.

The slender body is also viewed as an energetic disadvantage. The very high surface to volume ratio results in a high rate of heat loss. This means that weasels have very high metabolic requirements, a burden for species that live in cold climates. They must be constantly active and cannot hibernate.

Weasels are generally solitary and can be active day and night. They are strongly territorial. Females give birth to fairly large liters (up to 13) of poorly developed young, which stay with the mother for three to four months. Weasels are among the most common and widespread of all carnivores.—Thomas E. Lacher, Jr.

See also **CARNIVORES; ENDOTHERMY; FERRET; MAMMALS; METABOLISM; PREDATION**

Further Reading

Gittleman, J. L., ed. 1989. *Carnivore Behavior, Ecology, and Evolution.* Ithaca: Cornell University Press.

Macdonald, D., ed. 1984. *The Encyclopedia of Mammals.* New York: Facts on File.

Nowak, R. M. 1991. *Walker's Mammals of the World.* 5th ed. Baltimore: Johns Hopkins University Press.

WEATHERING, DESERT

Erosional processes (including mechanical or physical, chemical, and biological weathering) that in deserts play a key role in breaking down rocks for subsequent transportation by water, wind, or mass movement and provide the debris for the fluvial (water) and aeolian (wind) systems that dominate deserts. Mechanical or physical weathering processes in deserts include insolation weathering or thermoclastis, salt weathering, slaking (wetting and drying), and, to a lesser degree, frost weathering. Insolation weathering involves the mechanical breakdown of rocks because of expansion and contraction from daily and annual heating and cooling cycles. Greater than 30°C daily temperature fluctuations have been recorded in the interior of some continental deserts. The volumetric changes from contraction and expansion exert enough force to lead to microcracking and ultimately to the breakdown of rocks into angular fragments. Although the effectiveness of insolation weathering has been the subject of much debate, it is more likely that significant temperature fluctuations affect the individual minerals, leading to granular disintegration (the breakdown of certain minerals, such as the silicates, in rocks) and/or making the rocks susceptible to other mechanical and chemical weathering processes.

Salt weathering is accomplished through three interrelated processes: the thermal expansion of salt crystals, hydration, and the growth of salt crystals. Many salts such as sodium chloride have high coefficients of volumetric expansion because of heating and cooling. In hydration certain salts, such as gypsum and anhydrite, hydrate and dehydrate in response to changes in moisture. As water is absorbed in the crystal lattice a volumetric change takes place, exerting pressure against the rock minerals. The most effective form of salt weathering involves pressures set up by the growth of crystals in the rock pores and cracks. Among the most potent salts are sodium carbonate, sodium sulfate, sodium nitrate, and magnesium sulfate. Because saline solutions penetrate into desiccation cracks in playas, various patterned ground and heaving phenomena, such as salt polygons, are common on playas with salt crusts.

Certain salts when subjected to repeated cycles of wetting and drying (slaking) can also expand volumetrically and exert pressure on the surrounding materials. In some interior continental deserts or in higher elevations, frost weathering or pressures exerted by the volumetric expansion of water owing to freezing (up to 9 percent), can also contribute to the mechanical breakdown of rocks. Small-scale exfoliation (peeling of rock surfaces) is also important in deserts because of both mechanical and chemical weathering processes, expansion as a result of the removal of overlying materials, and fires.

Although moisture in deserts is limited in time and space, precipitation does occur, and hence water is available for chemical weathering and decomposition. Many coastal deserts, such as the Namib Desert, Baja California, and the Atacama Desert, also receive substantial amounts of moisture from fog and dew. Thus chemical weathering processes such as hydrolysis and solution are common, although limited in extent owing primarily to a number of factors. These include the shallow penetration of water in the soil or weathered mantle, extremely high rates of evaporation, reduced chemical reaction rates because of the high alkalinity of most desert soils, and the limited presence of organic acids. Although very much limited in scope, biological weathering, such as weathering by lichens and algae, also contributes to rock disintegration and dissolution as well as to the formation of rock varnish.

Small-scale landforms produced as a result of desert weathering processes include various cavernous features such as tafoni (hollows cut into sloping rock outcrop faces) and rock honeycombs or alveoles (closely spaced weathering pits). Also present are gnammas, small depressions that could hold water, soil, and vegetation, which have dimensions ranging from about 10 centimeters wide and a few centimeters deep to more than 12 meters wide and up to 3 meters deep. Once a small pit is established, moisture, weathered debris, and vegetation facilitate biochemical weathering processes, leading to the enlargement of the gnamma hole.

Large-scale weathering landforms include arches, developed mostly on sloping sedimentary rocks such as sandstones and seen in Arches and Canyonlands national parks in Utah; large alcoves, the result of basal sapping processes; and tors, weathered boulders stacked on one another. Some desert weathering landforms are almost certainly inherited from past climate regimes and are thus relictual. In addition, certain lithologies that weather in more humid environments tend to remain behind as resistant units or caprocks in more arid environments. The majestic Egyptian pyramids;, constructed mostly of limestone blocks (limestone is highly soluble in water), have survived for more than 5,000 years owing to the scarcity of precipitation in the desert.—Vatche P. Tchakerian

See also **DESERT SLOPES; DURICRUSTS; INSEL-
BERG; LITHOSPHERE; MINERALS; ROCK VARNISH;
RUNOFF; SOILS, DESERT**

Further Reading

Cooke, R., A. Warren, and A. Goudie. 1993. *Desert Geomorphology*. London: University College London
Press.

Goudie, A. 1989. Weathering processes. *In* D. S. G. Thomas, ed., *Arid Zone Geomorphology*, 11–24. London:
Belhaven.

Mabbutt, J. A. 1977. *Desert Landforms*. Cambridge,
Mass.: MIT Press.

WEAVER

Small to medium-sized, gregarious, and highly visible songbird primarily confined to Africa (family
Ploceidae, order Passeriformes). The taxonomy of
this family is somewhat contentious. The parasitic
indigobirds and whydahs and the waxbills are sometimes included as two additional subfamilies (the
Viduinae and Estrildinae, respectively). Further,
the weaver family itself has been subsumed within
the family Passeridae (the Old World sparrows) by
some authorities. The present discussion will be
restricted to four ploceid subfamilies: Bubalornithi-
nae (buffalo-weavers, 3 species), Ploceinae (true
weavers, 105 species), Plocepasserinae (sparrow-
weavers, 8 species), and the Sporopipinae (the
scaly-weavers, 2 species).

The majority of weaver taxa are found in Africa,
although some occur in southern Asia. Ploceids
inhabit a wide variety of habitats ranging from forest to open, dry thorn scrub. Weaver taxa that occur
in arid and semiarid environments are numerous.
For example, the white-billed buffalo-weaver
(*Bubalornis albirostris*) inhabits arid thorn savanna
of sub-Saharan Africa from Senegal east to Kenya.
A number of true weavers of the genus *Ploceus*
occur in drier parts of the Afrotropics. For example,
the Speke's weaver (*Ploceus spekei*) is found in dry
thorn savanna in the highlands of northeastern
Africa.

Weavers have a robust body. The wings are generally short and rounded. Bill morphology is somewhat variable, but most species have bills that are
short and conical. Total length varies from 12 to 65
centimeters, although this range is somewhat misleading as a number of species have exceptionally
long tails (e.g., the long-tailed widow-bird,
Euplectes progne). Little sexual dimorphism in size

exists. The plumage may be patterned, with predominant coloration of white, yellow, red, or glossy
black. In some weavers the sexes are alike; in others
females are rather nondescript. Many species are
highly social and occur in huge flocks. For example,
the red-billed quelea (*Quelea quelea*), widespread
in dry savanna and thorn scrub of Africa south of
the Sahara, has been recorded in flocks estimated at
more than one million individuals. Weavers are usually granivorous, although some will include vegetable matter other than seeds, insects, and nectar in
their diet. A few species are wholly insectivorous. A
number of weaver taxa, including the red-billed
quelea, cause serious damage to cereal crops.

The majority of weavers are polygynous and
colonial, although a few species are solitary and
purported to be monogamous. Nest construction is
performed by both sexes in monogamous species
and by the male alone in polygynous ones. The
nests of most species consist of a woven domed
structure suspended from a tree or bush. The
entrance is typically a woven "tunnel," sometimes
some 60 centimeters long, located on the underside
of the nest. Clutch size usually ranges from two to
four. Incubation duties and care of the young may
be shared by both sexes or may be undertaken
solely by the female.—Stephen C. Lougheed

See also **AFRICA, DESERTS OF; BIRDS; FINCH;
GRANIVORY; KALAHARI DESERT; KAROO; NA-
MIBIA, DESERT OF; NESTS, BIRD; SEEDS; SOUTH
AFRICA, DESERTS OF; SPARROWS; WAXBILL**

Further Reading

Collias, N. E., and E. C. Collias. 1964. Evolution of nest-
building in the weaverbirds (Ploceidae). *University of
California Publications in Zoology* 73:1–162.

Cramp, S., and C. M. Perrins, eds. 1994. *Handbook of
the Birds of Europe the Middle East and North
Africa: The Birds of the Western Palearctic*. Vol. 8.
Oxford: Oxford University Press.

Crook, J. H. 1960. Nest form and construction in certain
West African weaverbirds. *Ibis* 102:1–25.

———. The evolution of social organisation and visual
communication in the weaverbirds (Ploceinae).
Behaviour Supplement 10:1–178.

WELL

Artificial excavation of variable size and depth
designed (when referring to a water well) to extend
to an underground water source to provide water
for drinking or irrigation. Wells may require a pump

to extract the water, or, in the case of a subterranean water source that is not excessively deep, the well may offer free access to the underground water. In some cases underground water will reach the surface directly (artesian well). Wells are commonly used in deserts to permit human habitations to be maintained where no free water is available.—Alberto I. J. Vich and Juana Susana Barroso

See also **ARTESIAN BASIN; DRINKING WATER; IRRIGATION DRAINAGE; WATER**

WELWITSCHIA

Endemic gymnosperm plant (*Welwitschia mirabilis*) of the Namib Desert of southern Africa, first discovered in 1859 and known for a series of unusual characteristics that it shares with such diverse groups as pine trees, flowering plants, and club mosses. These traits make its exact placement in the plant kingdom uncertain. Female plants bear cones that produce seeds, and male plants have smaller reproductive structures (thus the species is dioeceous). *Welwitschia* grows along dry riverbeds in the hyperarid Namib Desert, where the flattened plants bear two enormous, continuously growing, fibrous leaves that are usually shredded by mechanical action (e.g., wind) into many strips. Thus the plant appears to have numerous straplike leaves rather than two large leaves. The stem is large and disklike, extending as a root into the ground for up to three meters. The plant may also obtain moisture from the frequent fogs of the Namib. *Welwitschia* are long-lived, with individuals probably surviving for many centuries.—Michael A. Mares

See also **NAMIBIA, DESERTS OF; PLANT ADAPTATIONS; PLANTS; SOUTH AFRICA, DESERTS OF**

Further Reading

Bornman, C. H. 1972. *Welwitschia mirabilis*: Paradox of the Namib Desert. *Endeavor* 31(113):95–99.

Marsh, B. A. 1990. The microenvironment associated with *Welwitschia mirabilis* in the Namib Desert. *In* M. K. Seely, ed., *Namib Ecology*, 149–153. Pretoria: Transvaal Museum.

Seely, M. 1992. *The Namib*. Windhoek, Namibia: Meinert.

Welwitschia (*Welwitschia mirabilis*) near Gobabeb, Namibia, in the Namib Desert. (Photo: M. A. Mares)

WHITE SANDS NATIONAL MONUMENT

National monument established in 1933 and encompassing about 59,000 hectares of the Chihuahuan Desert in south central New Mexico, just north of Las Cruces. The monument lies in the Tularosa Basin or bolsón (a valley without an external drainage outlet), which is one of four projections of the Chihuahuan Desert into the United States. This basin was formed by geologic processes that uplifted the area of south central New Mexico about 60 million years ago (mya). About 40 mya the region was lowered and basins were formed. Processes of erosion resulted in the deposition of large amounts of gypsum and alluvial sediments from adjacent mountains into the basin. Various topographic features reflect the deposits: lava beds (malpais), alkali flats or salt beds (playas), and gypsum dune fields surrounded by mountain ranges.

The Tularosa Basin once contained a large lake (Lake Otero) that may have covered about 4,500 square kilometers. Although it no longer exists, a playa or salt marsh remains, which sometimes extends to Lake Lucero. Groundwater levels are about one meter below the surface.

White Sands National Monument is known best for its extensive gypsum dune fields, which cover about 700 square kilometers. In addition to dunes, an area of lava beds is found in the northern part of the monument. The dunes are made of sand-sized particles of gypsum (calcium sulfate), rather than of particles of silica sand or quartz. Four types of

White gypsum sand dunes supporting sparse vegetation at White Sands National Monument. (Photo: M. A. Mares)

dunes are present: low, broad, dome-shaped dunes lie at the southwestern margin of Lake Lucero, which provides the gypsum; transverse dunes up to 12 meters tall are found in the middle; barchan dunes up to 8 meters in height are located northeast of the transverse dunes; and U-shaped dunes lie at the northeastern and eastern margins of the dune field. The dunes are not stationary; rather they move about 0.7–3.9 meters per year to the east-northeast. Movement is driven by strong winds out of the west-southwest.

Sparse clumps of grass are found in the areas between the dunes, which generally have little other vegetation. The dune surfaces remain relatively free of vegetation. Vegetation is confined generally to the periphery of the dune areas. In extreme central portions of extensive gypsum areas only a few species such as *Ephedra torreyana*, *Oryzopsis hymenoides*, and the White Sands endemic, *Abronia angustifolia*, persist. Some plants, which grow about 1 meter high in other parts of their range, grow up to 10 meters high in the shifting dune environment. The three-leafed sumac (*Rhus trilobata*) or squaw bush occurs as single bushes at the crest of sand hummocks or atop a column of sand. These columns of gypsum are held together by the roots of the sumac. Although the dunes move, the plant and its pedestal remain in place. The narrow-leafed yucca (*Yucca elata*) grows with most of its stalk beneath the sand.

Many of the plants have adapted to the relatively nitrogen-free and water-free soil of the sand dunes.

"Pioneer plants," such as yucca, form part of the plant succession on the dunes. These plants are efficient at fixing nitrogen; after they die and decay other plants use the nitrogen from the organic matter. Water is obtained from the gypsum, which absorbs much of the rainfall it receives.—Janet K. Braun

See also **BOLSÓN; CHIHUAHUAN DESERT; DUNES; GYPSUM; NEW MEXICO DESERT; PLAYA; SALT DESERT; SUCCESSION; UNITED STATES, DESERTS OF; YUCCA**

Further Reading

Jaeger, E. C. 1957. *The North American Deserts*. Stanford: Stanford University Press.

Schneider-Hector, D. 1993. *White Sands: The History of a National Monument*. Albuquerque: University of New Mexico Press.

WILDLIFE

Any species of wild birds and mammals (the definition usually used by practitioners of wildlife management), all terrestrial and aquatic vertebrates, and even all wild animals and plants. The last definition often is used in the field of conservation biology but is far too broad for most people involved in wildlife biology. The definition of wildlife has changed with time. Until about 1970 "wildlife" referred almost exclusively to game animals, primarily birds and mammals that were hunted for sport. The definition has expanded progressively. Wildlife biology, as opposed to ecology, generally implies that the organisms under study have some importance for human populations and require management. This definition is broad enough to cover a wide range of species in many different ecosystems that have importance for human populations.

Wildlife management is the practice of applying scientific techniques to manage populations of wildlife. Managers pursue one or more of four options: (1) increase population size; (2) reduce population size; (3) develop a set of procedures to harvest a population in a sustainable manner; or (4) monitor population size over time with no manipulation. Game managers deal mostly with the first and third options. A good example of the effects of wildlife management involves populations of white-tailed deer in the United States. Populations of white-tailed deer are probably higher now than at any time in history. Wildlife managers have altered the landscape to favor deer populations by creating second-growth habitat and planting forage to support higher densities of deer. These inflated populations are then studied to generate estimates of maximum rates of harvest for hunters. Game managers have been effective in maintaining sustainable harvests of populations of a number of game species, particularly in North America and Europe.

Wildlife management is also a major focus in the field of conservation biology, but the emphasis is on the first and fourth options listed above. Conservation biologists are primarily concerned with the management of endangered species and with the protection of biotic communities. The recovery of endangered species involves the management of habitat, diseases, and predators in the wild in an attempt to increase population size. In extreme cases management extends to the creation of captive populations that eventually can be reintroduced when conditions in the wild improve. The protection of biotic communities has, as a component, the monitoring of indicator or keystone species. Changes in the density or abundance of these species can indicate the presence of impacts at the community level that should be investigated and remedied.

Wildlife management and conservation in arid lands does not differ in principle from techniques employed in other habitats. Deserts have a surprising abundance of plant and animal species, most of which possess specialized adaptations to the harsh desert climate. Thus many desert species are vulnerable to the adverse effects of human activities. Conservationists have been successful in establishing protected areas in virtually all of the world's major arid regions.—Thomas E. Lacher, Jr.

See also **AMPHIBIANS; BIOSPHERE RESERVE; BIRDS; CONSERVATION IN DESERT; IRRIGATION DRAINAGE; MAMMALS; REPTILES; SNAKES**

Further Reading

Allan, T., and A. Warren, eds. 1993. *Deserts: The Encroaching Wilderness*. New York: Oxford University Press.

Caughley, G., and A. R. E. Sinclair. 1994. *Wildlife Ecology and Management*. Boston: Blackwell.

Chapman, J. A., and G. A. Feldhamer. eds. 1982. *Wild Mammals of North America: Biology, Management and Economics*. Baltimore: Johns Hopkins.

Shaw, J. H. 1985. *Introduction to Wildlife Management*. New York: McGraw-Hill.

WIND

Movement of air. On a global scale air movements act as a mechanism of thermal equilibrium that helps to regulate a permanent imbalance of latitudinal energy on the earth. This imbalance is caused by the equatorial regions absorbing more radiation than they can lose effectively and the polar regions losing more radiation than they receive from the sun. These great imbalances cause the existence of wind currents on the earth. There are four fundamental factors that are responsible for producing wind. Some are important at a global level, and others, such as tornadoes, are important at a smaller scale.

Pressure gradient force is the force caused by the differences in pressure in a mass of air, with the vertical component of this force (the lifting component) being 10,000 times greater than the horizontal components of the force.

Gravity is the only other force that can initiate the movement of the atmosphere, and it operates only in the vertical dimension. All atmospheric components, regardless of size, experience a descending acceleration toward the mass of the earth, which is termed gravity, and which would collapse the atmosphere if there were not a counterbalancing force caused by the decrease in pressure with altitude that acts against gravity and permits air masses to rise (the pressure gradient force).

As the spinning earth rotates, it causes objects moving northward in the Northern Hemisphere to veer to the right (and to the left in the Southern Hemisphere). The resultant directional vector is termed the *Coriolis force*. This is an apparent force acting on the earth's circulating atmosphere, rather than a real force, because it is not related to the air mass directly (unlike the other forces just described) but is evaluated against the rotation of the earth as a point of reference.

Centrifugal force is one of the major forces that influences the movement of air, especially at the upper levels of the atmosphere, and the effect of this force varies from 30 meters to 3 kilometers above the ground. The friction between the movement of the air and the surface of the earth produces a reduction in velocity of the wind. The magnitude of this force of friction, or the viscosity, is a function of the topography of the surface. If the surface is very smooth, the air currents are slowed down by only a small amount. This is why winds over the ocean are quite strong. There may also be friction between adjoining air masses that are moving in opposite directions, although this is generally of less magnitude than the friction between the air and the land.

Deserts are subjected to high winds, and wind erosion is common in deserts. In addition, the action of wind causes desert animals and plants to deal with increased evaporation.—Federico Norte

See also **ANIMAL ADAPTATIONS; ANTICYCLONE; BAROMETRIC PRESSURE (ATMOSPHERIC PRESSURE); CLIMATE; CLIMATE CLASSIFICATION; CLOUDS; CONVECTIVE STORM; CYCLONE; DUST DEVIL; HABOOB; INSOLATION; LOW PRESSURE; PLANT ADAPTATIONS; PREVAILING WESTERLIES; ROARING FORTIES; SANTA ANA WINDS; TRADE WINDS; WATER BALANCE.**

Further Reading

Day, J. A., and V. J. Schaefer. 1991. *Clouds and Weather.* Boston: Houghton Mifflin.

Guerzoni, S., and R. Chester. 1996. *The Impact of Desert Dust across the Mediterranean.* Boston: Kluwer.

Oliver, J. E., and R. W. Fairbridge, eds. 1987. *The Encyclopedia of Climatology.* New York: Chapman and Hall.

Schaefer, V. J., and J. A. Day. 1981. *A Field Guide to the Atmosphere.* Boston: Houghton Mifflin.

Schneider, S. H., ed. 1996. *Encyclopedia of Climate and Weather.* 2 vols. New York: Oxford University Press.

WIND EROSION

Processes, including deflation and abrasion, by which wind wears away and transports materials in deserts. Deflation involves the removal of fine materials and its transport in suspension. The deflation of sediments from desert basins and dry lake surfaces can lead to the formation of depressions. Abrasion takes place when sand and silt-sized particles carried in the wind act as grinding and scouring tools (analogous to sandblasting) and mechanically wear down exposed rock surfaces, particularly soft rock lithologies and outcrops. Particle size and velocity, the angle of impact, and atmospheric density are all important parameters as to how efficient abrasion can be on rock surfaces or outcrops. Ultimately the main factor is the transfer of kinetic energy from the impacting grains to the target rock. The greater the kinetic energy as a result of larger grains or higher grain speeds, the greater the efficacy of abrasion.

Landforms that result from aeolian (wind) erosion include ventifacts, yardangs, and desert depressions. Ventifacts are small-scale aeolian erosional features and consist of grooves, flutes, etchings, and facets on rocks and outcrops, oriented with the dominant wind regime. They are found in a wide range of rock types, although certain lithologies such as schist and granite do not preserve grooves and flutes owing to their rapid disintegration in desert environments. Ventifacts form as a result of the sculpting of the windward face of a rock or an outcrop by sand and silt-sized particles, mostly because of the saltation cloud, one to two meters above the surface. Occasionally during strong dust storms some objects (such as telephone and power poles) have shown the effects of polished, etched, or frosted surfaces to heights of 10 meters. Although the majority of ventifaction takes place within the saltation cloud, there is some indirect evidence (mostly laboratory) that winds carrying dust particles (or snow) in suspension can form some of the flutes, pits, and other microscale etched or lustrous features. Ventifact morphologies and orientations can be mapped in the field to infer both current wind patterns and paleowinds (especially if the ventifacts are "fossil" and have stopped forming). Ventifacts are more common in areas where winds are topographically enhanced, either by constricting the flow, such as between mountain ranges (gaps), or by the acceleration of wind flow over the hills.

Yardangs are aerodynamically streamlined, wind-abraded landforms. Their appearance is similar to an inverted boat hull, with an abrupt, blunt-ended, steep windward side and an elongated and tapered lee side. They are composed of either homogeneous, cohesive materials (such as lake deposits) or bedrock (such as sandstones and limestones). In the deserts of western Egypt yardang lithologies range from soft lacustrine muds to resistant granites and quartzites. Typical yardang length to width ratios average 3:1 or greater. Some large bedrock yardangs in Chad in the central Sahara Desert are more than 200 meters high and two kilometers long and are spaced one kilometer apart. Most yardangs are located in areas characterized by strong and persistent wind regimes, are aligned parallel to the effective winds, and usually occur in extensive groups. They are separated by troughs or wind-eroded bedrock surfaces. They have not been studied in any great detail, and much remains to be determined about their formation, including a better understanding of wind dynamics, secondary wind flows in the lee side, sediment transport over and around them, and the deflation of the inter-yardang corridors. However, extreme hyperaridity and strong and persistent unidirectional winds and aeolian erosion are most likely involved in their formation. It is very likely that yardangs are the product of aeolian abrasion and deflation and are further modified by weathering, mass movement, and some fluvial activity.

The formation of desert depressions from deflation remains controversial. It is more likely that large-scale closed depressions in deserts (such as the Qattara in Egypt) form as a result of a combination of geomorphic processes, including fluvial processes, karst faulting (limestone solution and weathering), and wind erosion, the latter especially prominent during the more arid phases of climate. Other surfaces, such as pans (shallow closed depressions), are thought to form as a result of aeolian deflation and salt weathering, both controlled primarily by the groundwater table, although such secondary processes as solution (chemical weathering) and animal activities may also play a role. Pans are abundant in southern Africa (such as in the Kalahari Desert) and in the panhandle of Texas in the United States.—Vatche P. Tchakerian

See also **BADLANDS; COLLUVIAL DEPOSITS (COLLUVIUM); DESERT SLOPES; DUNES; DUNES, LUNETTE; DUNES, NABKHA; GROUNDWATER; LAKES, PLUVIAL; PLAYA; SAND RAMP; SOILS, DESERT; STONE PAVEMENT; WEATHERING, DESERT; WIND TRANSPORT**

Further Reading

Breed, C. S., J. F. McCauley, and M. I. Whitney. 1989. Wind erosion forms. In D. S. G. Thomas, ed., Arid Zone Geomorphology, 284–307. London: Belhaven.

Cooke, R., A. Warren, and A. Goudie. 1993. Desert Geomorphology. London: University College London Press.

Laity, J. E. 1994. Landforms of aeolian erosion. In A. D. Abrahams and A. J. Parsons, eds., Geomorphology of Desert Environments, 506–535. London: Chapman and Hall.

Tchakerian, V., ed. 1995. Desert Aeolian Processes. New York: Chapman and Hall.

WIND TRANSPORT

Processes of sand movement by wind that involve a number of interrelated physical principles, with wind speed being one of the primary factors. Wind speed increases with increasing height from a point of zero velocity just above the surface layer. This zone of "zero wind velocity" is generally equivalent to the 1/30th diameter of the grains on that surface. Air near the surface is generally turbulent because of local variations in air pressure from the unequal heating and cooling and surface roughness, such as terrain characteristics and vegetation cover, among others. Turbulent air increases the potential for sand entrainment (entrainment refers to the picking up processes of particles, such as lift and drag) and transport (similar to turbulent flow in rivers and its influence on the entrainment and transport of river sediments).

When wind velocity begins to increase there is a corresponding increase in shear stress exerted over the grains at the surface. There is a direct correlation between increasing wind velocity and shear stress. Eventually a threshold is reached whereby the driving force (wind velocity or shear velocity) is greater than the resisting forces. The resisting forces include such physical properties as grain size, sorting, packing, density, shape, and cohesion, as well as the presence or absence of vegetation, moisture, and other cementing agents such as salts. For example, removal of particles from a salt-cemented crust or wet surface would require much higher wind velocities or shear stresses. Smaller grains (such as the size of silt or clay) are harder to entrain (move) because of their small size and interparticle cohesion and chemical bonds. Larger grains are also hard to move because of their increased mass and weight. The most easily entrained particles are the fine to medium sands (roughly 0.25–0.5 millimeter), and thus the majority of aeolian (wind-blown) deposits are sand dunes. This critical velocity threshold is known as the fluid threshold (the term coined by R. A. Bagnold, a distinguished British scientist who in the late 1930s first studied in detail the nature and dynamics of sand transport and dune formation). A typical value for the fluid threshold for fine sands would be about five meters per second at a few centimeters above the ground surface.

As the wind velocity increases beyond the fluid threshold, sand grains begin to move. Four types of sediment transport or grain motion have been described: suspension, saltation, reptation, and creep. Suspension takes place when smaller grains (clay- and silt-sized particles less than 0.08 millimeter, or 60 microns) are lifted up by turbulent flow and, because of their lower densities and size, remain "suspended" in air until the velocities needed to keep them in the turbulent air column are decreased below the threshold velocities needed to maintain them in the air and deposition takes place. Suspended particles make up the majority of desert dust and loess (fine-grained loam deposited by wind) deposits and account for about 5 percent (by weight) of the total aeolian sand transport load.

The majority of aeolian transport, about 80 percent (by weight), takes place through saltation and reptation. This takes place close to the ground surface. Saltation involves the bouncing and long-leaping motion of sand grains at the surface. After an initial vertical takeoff, the sand grain is pushed forward in the air and comes down at an angle and hits another grain on the surface, setting it in motion. This "skip and hop" motion takes place within one to two meters of the surface and involves mostly fine and medium-size sand particles. Reptation involves the movement of certain coarse grains close to the surface without being displaced upward into the airstream, as well as grains that have very short saltation path lengths. Laboratory experiments indicate that an individual saltating grain dislodges 10 to 15 low-hopping grains for short distances. Creep involves the movement of coarser sands (one to two millimeters) by rolling and sliding over the surface (reptation and creep are sometimes used to infer the same process because they are rather similar). These grains do not get lifted up into the saltation cloud owing to their large sizes. They constitute about 10 percent (by weight) of the total aeolian sand transport load and tend to be left behind as lag deposits.—Vatche P. Tchakerian

See also **BADLANDS; COLLUVIAL DEPOSITS (COLLU-VIUM); DESERT SLOPES; DUNES; DUNES, LUNETTE; DUNES, NABKHA; GROUNDWATER; LAKES, PLUVIAL; PLAYA; SAND RAMP; SOILS, DESERT; STONE PAVEMENT; WEATHERING, DESERT**

Further Reading

Cooke, R., A. Warren, and A. Goudie. 1993. *Desert Geomorphology.* London: University College London Press.

Lancaster, N. 1994. Dune morphology and dynamics. *In* A. D. Abrahams and A. J. Parsons, eds., *Geomorphology of Desert Environments,* 474–505. London: Chapman and Hall.

Pye, K., and H. Tsoar. 1990. *Aeolian Sand and Sand Dunes.* London: Unwin Hyman.

WOODPECKERS

Group of small to quite large birds adapted to a primarily arboreal existence, distributed throughout Eurasia, Africa, and the Americas (subfamily Picinae, family Picidae, order Piciformes). Piculets and wrynecks, generally not considered "true woodpeckers," are placed in the subfamilies Picumninae and Jynginae, respectively. Picinae contains approximately 169 species in about 23 genera. The vast majority of woodpeckers are associated with treed habitats, ranging from rain forest through savanna to scrub deserts. Examples of desert taxa are the Gila woodpecker (*Melanerpes uropygialis*) of the Sonoran Desert of North America; the bearded woodpecker (*Dendropicos namaquus*), found in many habitats, including dry scrub of west central Africa; and the Sind woodpecker (*Dendrocopos assimilis*), resident of woodland and desert scrub of southwestern Asia. A few species, notably the flickers (genus *Colaptes*), inhabit open treeless grasslands.

Total length ranges from approximately 15 to 55 centimeters, and large species may weigh up to 600 grams. Woodpeckers possess various specializations for an arboreal existence. Tarsi are short, and the zygodactylous ("yoke-toed") feet are equipped with sharp claws for clinging to vertical surfaces; the stiffened tail feathers provide additional support. Woodpeckers primarily engage in bark foraging for insects. Adaptations for excavating in wood in search of food include a thickened skull, a strong, often chisel-shaped bill, and an extensible, barbed tongue. Most woodpeckers are sexually dichromatic, with the presence of a malar stripe ("moustache") and brightly colored crown patch on the male being the most common distinguishing features.

The majority of woodpeckers are socially monogamous. Generally picids are territorial and resident, although a few species undertake extensive migratory movements. Woodpeckers are usually rather solitary breeders and exhibit aggression to conspecifics; only a few species are social nesters (e.g., species in the genera *Colaptes and Melanerpes*). Nest cavities are typically located in trees or cacti. Excavation is performed either by both members of the pair or predominantly by either the male or the female, depending on the species. Clutch sizes range from 3 to 11. Incubation lasts 10–20 days, and these duties are generally undertaken by both sexes. Nestlings hatch blind and helpless and are fed and brooded by both parents.—Stephen C. Lougheed

See also **BIRDS; CACTI; CACTUS, COLUMNAR; CARDÓN; FLICKER; FOREST; GILA WOOD-PECKER; MESQUITE; NESTS, BIRD; ORGAN PIPE CACTUS; RIPARIAN COMMUNITIES; RIVERS; SAGUARO; XEROPHYLLOUS FOREST**

Further Reading

Bent, A. C. 1939. Life histories of North American woodpeckers. *U.S. National Museum Bulletin* 174.

Burt, W. H. 1930. Adaptive modifications in the woodpeckers. *University of California Publications in Zoology* 32:455–524.

Short, L. L. 1979, Burdens of the picid hole-nesting habit. *Wilson Bulletin* 91:16–28.

———. 1982. *Woodpeckers of the World*. Greenville: Delaware Museum of Natural History.

WOODRAT

Common, medium-sized (150–280 grams) herbivorous rodent in the genus *Neotoma* (family Muridae, order Rodentia) with a long, hairy tail that lives in diverse habitats of the western and southeastern United States and Mexico, including deserts (especially desert scrub), tropical thorn forest, pinyon-juniper woodlands, and grasslands. Because of their occasional tendency to adorn their nests with human artifacts (especially bright or shiny objects), bones, dung, and other unusual objects, woodrats are often called packrats (a term originally applied more specifically to the bushy-tailed woodrat).

Woodrats construct nests in aboveground dens (often near a cholla or prickly pear patch) or in crevices between rocks. These dens or houses may be two meters in diameter and nearly two meters high with multiple entrances and several chambers. They are usually made from cholla joints, sticks, or small chunks of wood from dead pinyon pine or juniper trees. Sticks, cactus pads, leaves, and dung are used to line the chambers, which provide shel-

Desert woodrat (*Neotoma albigula*) climbing on a cholla cactus in Arizona. (Photo: K. A. Ernest)

ter for the adult woodrat during the day and a nest site for young. The rats travel to feeding sites along runways extending from the den and may bring food back to store in caches. The runways and dens are often protected with cactus joints and spines, which do not seem to hinder in any way the movement of the rat. Woodrat dens are an important structural component of many desert communities and provide shelter for many other animals, including insects, lizards, rattlesnakes, shrews, mice, rabbits, and skunks.

The diet of woodrats consists mostly of plant material, especially the green portions and fruits of cholla and prickly pears. Other common food items are yucca, juniper, miscellaneous shrubs, grass, mesquite pods, and acorns and other fruits. Woodrats are not physiologically adapted to tolerate high water loss or to minimize water loss by concentrating urine. Instead they rely on behavioral mechanisms for reducing desiccation. Woodrats are nocturnal and usually remain in dens or rock crevices during the heat of the day, although on cooler days they may forage during daylight hours. They obtain water from succulent plants; cacti may make up as much as 90 percent of the diet during the drier times of the year. Oxalic acid in cacti is difficult for most mammals to digest, but woodrats are able to tolerate this toxic chemical compound, an adaptation for their intimate relationship with cacti.

Although the population densities of some species of woodrats are fairly stable, other species fluctuate considerably between years (from less than one to more than 30 animals per hectare). The home ranges of individual woodrats may overlap extensively, but each seems to defend its den site. An individual rat may occupy an area of 150–1,300 square meters. Litter size is commonly one to three, and females may have several litters each year. Woodrats thump their feet on the ground during the mating ritual, when alarmed by potential predators, and possibly to signal ownership of a territory. They rarely live more than two years in the wild.

Predators of woodrats include coyotes, foxes, bobcats, skunks, badgers, snakes, hawks, and owls. Incredibly, woodrats (at least some species) are resistant to the venom of western diamondback rattlesnakes, which commonly share their dens. Fleas, lice, ticks, mites, and botflies are common ectoparasites of woodrats, as are kissing bugs (*Triatoma*). In tropical areas these bugs can transmit Chagas disease to humans.

Woodrats have enabled researchers to describe the past vegetation types of desert regions. Accumulations of their food caches and dung become hardened with urine deposits over time, forming middens that effectively preserve fossil evidence of the previous plant community. These ancient middens contain nearly continuous records of the plants that were collected by these industrious rodents thousands of years ago.—Kristina A. Ernest

See also **CACTI; CHOLLA; GLACIAL PERIODS; HERBIVORY; KIDNEY FUNCTION, DESERT RODENTS; KIDNEYS; MAMMALS; MIDDEN; PALEOCLIMATE; PHYSIOLOGY; PLEISTOCENE; PRICKLY PEAR; THORN; RODENTS; WATER BALANCE**

Further Reading

Lee, A. K. 1963. The adaptations to arid environments in woodrats of the genus *Neotoma*. *University of California Publications in Zoology* 64:57–96.

Macedo, R. H., and M. A. Mares. 1988. Neotoma albigula. *Mammalian Species* 310:1–7.

Stones, R. C., and C. L. Hayward. 1968. Natural history of the desert woodrat, *Neotoma lepida*. *American Midland Naturalist* 80:458–475.

WREN

Small to moderate-sized songbird primarily distributed throughout North, Central, and South America, with one species found in the Old World (family Troglodytidae, order Passeriformes). Approximately 60–70 species in 12–14 genera are recognized. Total length ranges from 7 to 20 centimeters, although most species are at the smaller end of the spectrum. The majority of wrens are rather cryptically colored and live in dense understory vegetation of woodlands. In contrast, the cactus wren (*Campylorhynchus brunneicapillus*) of desert habitats of the southwestern United States and northwestern Mexico and its allies occupy more open, often semiarid, habitats. Wrens typically have a robust body that seems disproportionately large compared to the head. Tail lengths are variable across species, but most wrens cock their tails upward in a distinctive fashion. The bill is rather slender and usually slightly down curved. The diet consists exclusively of invertebrates.

All wrens studied to date are highly territorial, at least during the breeding season. The Troglodytidae show a range of breeding systems. Many species are monogamous; others, however, are polygynous (e.g., the marsh wren, *Cistothorus palustris*). Some of the *Campylorhynchus* wrens are cooperative breeders, with nonreproductive individuals helping to feed the nestlings. The nest of most species is a roofed structure, although some build cups in cavities. In polygynous species males may build numerous nests in their territories, but in most wrens the sexes collaborate in nest construction. Clutch size varies substantially, from two to ten, with temperate species typically laying a larger number of eggs. In all species the female incubates, with incubation periods lasting 12–20 days. Parental care may be shared between sexes or may be undertaken solely or mostly by the female.—Stephen C. Lougheed

See also **BIRDS; CACTI; CHOLLA**

Further Reading

Anderson, A. H., and A. Anderson. 1973. *The Cactus Wren*. Tucson: University of Arizona Press.

Bent, A. C. 1948. Life histories of North American nuthatches, wrens, thrashers, and their allies. *U.S. National Museum Bulletin* 195.

Rabenold, K. N. 1990. *Campylorhynchus* wrens: The ecology of delayed dispersal and cooperation in the Venezuelan savanna. *In* P. B. Stacey and W. D. Koenig, eds., *Cooperative Breeding in Birds*, 157–196. Cambridge: Cambridge University Press.

Wolf, L, R. M. Lejnieks, C. R. Brown, and J. Yarchin. 1975. Temperature fluctuations and nesting behavior of rock wrens in a high-altitude environment. *Wilson Bulletin* 97:385–387.

XENOPHYTES

Plant species that are particularly adapted for, and generally restricted to, growth in dry habitats. By having extreme adaptations for aridity, most of which result in slowed plant growth, these species cannot compete with faster-growing plants that grow in less arid habitats. Thus their range is usually constricted, with successful growth occurring only in habitats that are so dry that the faster-growing, less well adapted species cannot survive.

Examples of xenophytes are some plant species that we have come to associate with deserts, such as the giant saguaro cacti (*Carnegiea gigantea*), Joshua tree (*Yucca brevifolia*), ocotillo (*Fouquieria splendens*), and paloverde (*Cercidium microphyllum*).

The special adaptations that xenophytes may possess are small leaves, which restrict the rate of water loss; spines, thorns, fluted stems, and hairs, which reduce the amount of light that falls on the surface of the plant and thus reduce heat stress; thick waxy coatings, which help to restrict water loss; and specialized photosynthetic mechanisms in which the stomata open at night rather than during the day (Crassulacean Acid Metabolism), which also reduce water loss. These adaptations also result in slowed growth, usually because of reduced rates of photosynthesis. True xenophytes usually possess several of these adaptive mechanisms.—Linda L. Wallace

See also **CACTI; OCOTILLO; PALOVERDE; PLANT ADAPTATIONS; PLANTS; PSAMMOPHYTES; PSAMMOPHYTIC SCRUB; SAGUARO; STOMA; XEROPHYTES; XEROPHYLLOUS FOREST**

Further Reading

Barbour, M. G., and W. D. Billings, eds. 1988. *North American Terrestrial Vegetation.* Cambridge: Cambridge University Press.

Chabot, B. F., and H. A. Mooney. 1985. *Physiological Ecology of North American Plant Communities.* New York: Chapman and Hall.

XEROPHYLLOUS FOREST

Forests composed of plants that show unique adaptations to life in a dry environment (xerophyllous

Xerophyllous forest at the Itala Game Reserve, northern Kwazulu-Natal Province, South Africa. (Photo: M. A. Mares)

plants). These forests are rare, as trees are not usually found in arid locales. The best-known xerophyllous forests occur in Africa—in northern Kenya, western Ethiopia, and Somalia—and on the islands of Socotra and Madagascar. Xerophyllous forest species are truly adapted for dry environments, with bizarre succulent stems, small leaves, and a reticulating network of small branches. These include the famous baobab tree as well as members of the genera *Pyrenacantha*, *Euphorbia*, *Caralluma*, *Cissus*, *Dracena*, *Adenium*, and *Aderia*.

Rainfall in the habitats where these species grow averages only 100–200 millimeters per year. Thus these trees are living in truly xeric (dry) conditions. Many of the trees found in other desert environments actually exist in relatively mesis (moist) microclimates, such as those found along stream courses. Other species have taproots that exploit groundwater resources. The shallow-rooted xerophyllous forest species, however, do not exist in mesic microclimates.

Many of these species behave like the giant columnar cacti found in other deserts, for example, the saguaro cacti of the southwestern deserts of North America or the similar columnar cacti of the South American deserts. Their shallow roots take advantage of sporadic rainfall. Water is then stored in succulent stems or trunks. Trunk diameters for some of these species can exceed two meters. Tree height can be up to 10 meters, thus yielding a tremendous water storage volume.

The wood of these species is not useful for construction purposes. However, some of these species are in danger of local extinction due to pressures put on populations as sources of firewood.—Linda L. Wallace

See also **ACACIA; AFRICA, DESERTS OF; CACTI; CACTUS, COLUMNAR; CARDÓN; CHACO; MADAGASCAR, DESERTS OF; MESQUITE; ORGAN PIPE CACTUS; PALMS; PHREATOPHYTES; PLANT ADAPTATIONS; PLANTS; ROOTS; SAGUARO; STOMA; TRANSPIRATION; WATER BALANCE; XENOPHYTES; XEROPHYTES**

Further Reading

Walter, H. 1983. *Vegetation of the Earth*. Berlin: Springer.

XEROPHYTES

Plants adapted to dry conditions through using a strategy of reducing transpiration (loss of water vapor from their surface). Cells in the mesophyll tissue of leaves lose water continually through cell membranes and cell walls. Therefore, the intercellular spaces in a leaf exhibit high relative humidities. When stomata are open there is a net loss of water vapor to the atmosphere. In deserts this loss is exacerbated because the air is dry and hot, and it is often windy. Therefore, all other things being equal, the rate of transpiration will be high. However, a variety of mechanisms have been selected in populations of desert plants which reduce transpiration: (1) closing stomata during the periods of greatest potential transpiration; (2) sinking stomata in pits on the surface of leaves; (3) distributing stomata on the abaxial (usually underside) surface of leaves; (4) rolling or folding leaves during the heat of the day; (5) reducing the numbers of stomata; (6) reducing the sizes of leaves; (7) covering the leaf surface with wax or hairs; (8) losing leaf blades completely; (9) dropping leaves during drought conditions. None of these processes completely stops transpiration, which is necessary to maintain the water column from the roots to the leaves and perhaps to cool leaves.

Not all desert plants are xerophytes. Desert annuals, for instance, germinate only during wet periods, and the plants grow and flower before the onset of dry conditions. Plants of vernal pools in the semiarid areas of southern California bloom before the pools dry in late spring. Some plants also avoid dry conditions by producing taproots that reach the permanent water table.

Landscape architects and gardeners in dry climates are increasingly turning to xeroscapes—gardens that make extensive use of xerophytes in low-water-use gardens. Attractive varieties and selections of flowering perennials, annuals, lawn grasses, shrubs, trees, and succulents are all available in arid and semiarid landscapes of the United States. The use of native plants in the garden adds a level of hardiness that cannot otherwise be attained, and more research and plant breeding needs to be accomplished to increase the number of locally adapted races available for use in horticulture and landscape architecture. The use of xerophytic or halophytic grasses, such as buffalo grass, in lawns, parks, and playgrounds should certainly be encouraged. One result would be substantial savings in water consumption for irrigation.—James R. Estes

See also **ACACIA; AFRICA, DESERTS OF; CACTI; CACTUS, COLUMNAR; CARDÓN; CHACO; CHENOPODIACEAE; CREOSOTE BUSH; HALOPHYTES; HOLDRIDGE LIFE ZONES; MADAGASCAR, DESERTS OF; MESQUITE; ORGAN PIPE CACTUS; PALMS; PHOTOSYNTHESIS; PHREATOPHYTES; PLANT ADAPTATIONS; PLANTS; ROOTS; SAGEBRUSH; SAGUARO; STOMA; TRANSPIRATION; WATER BALANCE; XENOPHYTES**

Further Reading

MacMahon, J. A. 1988. Warm deserts. *In* M. G. Barbour and W. D. Billings, eds., *North American Terrestrial Vegetation*, 231–264. Cambridge: Cambridge University Press.

Walter, H. 1983. *Vegetation of the Earth*. Berlin: Springer.

West, N. E. 1988. Intermountain deserts, shrub steppes, and woodlands. *In* M. G. Barbour and W. D. Billings, eds., *North American Terrestrial Vegetation*, 209–230. Cambridge: Cambridge University Press.

YARDANG. *See* WIND EROSION

YEMEN, DESERTS OF

Arid and semiarid habitats within Yemen, a large country (531,872 square kilometers) located in the southwestern corner of the Arabian Peninsula and bordered by Saudi Arabia and Oman. The environment is greatly influenced by the topography of the country. The highlands and escarpment of the central and northern parts recede toward the lowlands of the eastern and western plains. The Yemen highlands have two major rainy seasons (March-April and July-September), but sporadic showers may occur year-round; frost is common in winter. The lowlands are characterized by a tropical arid to semiarid climate. Summer rains are monsoonal, whereas winter rains are of the Mediterranean type. The major deserts and semideserts of Yemen are restricted to the eastern portions of the country and the coastal lowlands. (See map of central Asia, p. 292.)

There are five phytogeographic regions recognized in Yemen: Tihama Lowlands, Tihama Foothills, Escarpment, High Mountains, and Eastern Semidesert and Desert.

The Tihama Lowlands extend as a 30- to 50-kilometer-wide belt between the coast of the Red Sea and the inland foothills at an elevation of 300 meters. Mean annual temperature is above 30°C, and rainfall is less than 200 millimeters per year. Several habitat types are distinguishable. Mangrove coastal habitats have *Avicennia marina* as the common plant. Salt marshes and salt-affected lands support halophytic vegetation, such as *Suaeda fruticosa*, *Suaeda monoica*, *Salsola spinescens*, and *Aeluropus massauensis*. Inland sand formations are characterized by several plant communities composed of *Indigofera spinosa*, *Aerva javanica*, *Panicum turgidum*, *Lasiurus scindicus*, *Cadaba rotundifolia*, *Jatropha curcas*, *Salvadora persica*, *Tephrosia purpurea*, and *Dipterygium glaucum*. The desert plains are characterized by *Dobera glabra*, *Balanites aegyptiaca*, *Acacia tortilis*, *Acacia ehrenbergiana*, and *Dactyloctenium scindicum*. The

Tihama Lowlands are crossed by wadi (gully) systems with fluvial deposits that support plant communities of *Tamarix nilotica*, *Hyphaene thebaica*, *Cassia senna*, *Calotropis procera*, *Leptadenia pyrotechnica*, and *Desmostachya bipinnata*.

The Tihama Foothills occur in the lower montane elevations between 300 and 1,000 meters. Mean annual temperature in this area is about 30°C, and annual rainfall varies from 200 to 400 millimeters. Plant communities include various species of *Acacia* and *Commiphora*, *Anisotes trisulcus*, *Abrus bottae*, *Ormocarpum yemenense*, *Idigofera spinosa*, *Adenium obesum*, *Ziziphus spina-christi*, *Dobera glabra*, and *Ficus salicifolia*.

The Escarpment landscape constitutes an elevational belt from 1,000 to 2,200 meters. Mean annual temperature is about 22°C, and annual precipitation ranges from 600 to more than 1,000 millimeters, the highest in the country. Different plant communities are associated with the different habitat types found on humid western slopes, on dry eastern slopes, and along the wadi drainage systems. The western slopes have the highest rainfall and support a dense vegetation dominated by species of *Commiphora* and *Acacia*, *Phoenix reclinata*, *Ficus salicifolia*, *Cordia abyssinica*, and *Olea chrysophylla*. The eastern dry slopes support plant communities characterized by *Acalypha fruticosa*, *Barleria bispinosa*, various species of *Acacia*, *Adenium obesum*, and *Euphorbia cactus*. In the wadi drainage systems dense tropical evergreen forests prevail, with *Ficus salicifolia*, *Cordia abyssinica*, *Carissa edulis*, and *Myrsine africana*.

The High Mountain phytogeographic area constitutes the highlands above 2,200 meters elevation. Mean annual temperature is about 16°C, and rainfall is about 400 millimeters per year. Frost, snow, and hail are common in winter. The Yemen Highlands have much in common with the Asir Highlands in Saudi Arabia and contain the highest mountain peak on the entire Arabian Peninsula, Jebel An Nabi Shu'ayb at 3,766 meters. Over the long history of Yemen the highlands have been heavily cultivated; the natural vegetation therefore has largely disappeared. Among the dominant plant species remaining are *Acacia negrii*, *Acacia gerrardii*, *Lavandula pubescens*, *Lycium shawii*, *Cichorium bottae*, *Grewia mollis*, *Rosa abyssinica*, *Myrsine africana*, *Teucrium yemense*, *Eleusine floccifolia*, and *Pennisetum setaceum*.

The Eastern Semidesert and Desert occurs on the steep rocky slopes and gravelly habitats adjacent to the eastern highlands as well as the foothills and dune fields found between 1,300 and 2,000 meters elevation. Mean annual temperature is about 25°C, and annual rainfall is less than 200 millimeters. The dry eastern slopes are gravelly and support poor vegetation cover; they are dominated by *Lycium shawii*, *Euphorbia balsamifera*, *Euphorbia schimperi*, various species of *Acacia*, *Farsetia longisiliqua*, *Stipagrostis ciliata*, *Stipagrostis obtusa*, and *Desmostachya bipinnata*. The sand dune fields support *Calligonum comosum*, *Leptadenia pyrotechnica*, and *Panicum turgidum*.

A total of about 2,300 flowering plant species are known in Yemen. The country supports about 20 million livestock animals: cattle, sheep, goats, camels, horses, and donkeys. To meet the demands of the growing population for agricultural products, fuelwood, and timber, vast areas of natural vegetation are being replaced by man-made ecosystems. Only a few relictual woodlands still remain, and these are mostly artificially planted woodlands rather than natural forestlands. Over the past two decades many agricultural fields have been abandoned, and as a result weedy communities dominate the fallow lands. Terrace walls are no longer maintained, and the subsequent soil erosion has devastated what was once a fertile land.

The seminomadic lifestyle is widespread in the desert and semidesert lowlands. These areas are subject to overgrazing as manifested by degradation of vegetation and failure of regeneration among woody plant species. This leads to the disappearance of palatable plant species and their replacement by unpalatable and toxic species, as well as the increased spread of succulent plants. In the highlands livestock are maintained in settled agricultural systems.

Agriculture on leveled terraces and in wadi basins is common in the Escarpment area, with extensive regions being highly developed. In the past few centuries coffee plantations (*Coffea arabica*) provided the characteristic crop of the Escarpment, where adequate rainfall and absence of frost provide the best growing conditions. Today coffee cultivation has lost much of its former importance, and coffee farms have been replaced by el-qat (*Catha edulis*) plantations.—Ahmad K. Hegazy

See also **ACACIA; AFRICA, DESERTS OF; AGRICULTURE IN DESERTS; ARABIAN GULF, DESERTS OF; CONSERVATION IN DESERTS; CHENOPODIACEAE; CONTAMINATION; DESERTIFICATION; DOMESTIC ANIMALS; DUNES; MIDDLE EAST, DESERTS OF; OVERGRAZING; PLANT ADAPTATIONS; SAHARA DESERT; SALINIZATION; SHEEP; XENOPHYTES; XEROPHYTES; XEROPHYTIC FOREST**

Further Reading

Al-Hubaishi, A., and K. Muller-Hohenstein. 1984. *An Introduction to the Vegetation of Yemen*. Eschborn, Germany: *Deutsche Gesellschaft für Zusammenarbeit* (GTZ).

Beskok, T. E. 1971. Forestry problems of the Yemen Arab Republic and possibilities for afforestation. Rome: Food and Agriculture Organization.

Gabali, A. S., and A. N. Al-Gifri. 1991. A survey of the vegetation of Hadramout, Republic of Yemen. *Fragmenta Floristica et Geobotania*, 36:127–134.

Hepper, F. N. 1977. Outline of the vegetation of the Yemen Arab Republic. *Publications of Cairo University Herbarium* 7–8:307–322.

Scholte, P. T., A. W. Al-Khuleidi, and J. J. Kessler. 1991. *The Vegetation of the Republic of Yemen: Western Part*. RLIP, OHV consultants.

YUCCA

Perennial plant of the lily family (Liliaceae) with a thick basal stem and numerous, elongate, semisucculent leaves with sharply pointed tips. The stems may be mostly underground or may form an aboveground trunk. The large, fleshy, whitish or greenish flowers are often conspicuously present on tall flowering stalks and open at night. Yuccas are similar in growth form to the agaves, but the leaves are not as fleshy and are generally more elongate.

The genus *Yucca* contains many species, including the arborescent Joshua tree. Yuccas are also commonly called Spanish bayonet, and the various species may be referred to as palmilla, soapweed, or datil. Yuccas occur in the Mojave, Sonoran, Chihuahuan, and Great Basin deserts and the desert grasslands. Although popularly considered typical desert plants, yuccas also occupy the chaparral, pinyon-juniper woodland, oak woodland, Great Plains, and more mesic (moist) habitats of North America. They grow in a variety of situations, including

Yuccas in full bloom in Utah. (Photo: D. Beck)

plains, rocky slopes, and sandstone outcrops at elevations up to 2,500 meters.

Individual plants do not flower every year. Pollination of yuccas by the yucca moth (*Tegeticula yuccasella*) is an example of coevolution between two species that apparently require each other's services. Female moths visit the flowers at night. After collecting pollen from several flowers, the moth flies to another flower and inserts eggs into the ovary. She then deposits pollen on the stigma of that flower. The developing moth larvae feed on the seeds as the fruit pods mature.

Larvae of the yucca weevil (*Scyphophorus yuccae*) bore into the buds and can kill the branches. Cattle seem to have voracious appetites for the flowering stalks and often prevent yuccas from successfully reproducing. Yuccas also reproduce asexually, however, sprouting new plants from the underground stems. The fruits are eaten by woodrats.

Indians find many uses for yuccas. The buds, flowers, and fruits are edible. Leaves provide fibers for rope, baskets, mats, and cloth. A soap can be made from the roots, which contain saponins. A tea made from the leaves, which contain salicylic acid, helps relieve aches and fever. The fruits have laxative properties. The root is prepared as a treatment for arthritis and inflammation.—Kristina A. Ernest

See also **CHIHUAHUAN DESERT; DESERT GRASS-LAND; DESERT PEOPLES; DESERTS; ECONOMIC VALUE OF DESERT PRODUCTS; FLOWERS; JORNADA DEL MUERTO; JOSHUA TREE; MEXICO, DESERTS OF; MOTHS; NEW MEXICO DESERT; PLANT GEOGRAPHY; POLLINATION; SUCCULENTS; WOODRAT**

Further Reading

Benson, L., and R. A. Darrow. 1981. *Trees and Shrubs of the Southwestern Deserts*. Tucson: University of Arizona Press.

Webber, J. M. 1953. *Yuccas of the Southwest*. U.S. Department of Agriculture, Monograph No. 17. Washington, D.C.: U.S. Government Printing Office.

YUMA DESERT

Extremely arid region of low sandy plains, dunes, eroded volcanic hillsides, and low dry mountain ranges in extreme southwestern Arizona and extending into the Mexican state of Sonora along the east side of the Gulf of California to the west of the Arizona Upland subdivision of the Sonoran Desert and reaching the Colorado River; rainfall may be as little as 60 millimeters a year. This ecological region known as the Yuma (Yuman) Desert lies within land originally obtained from Mexico through the Gadsden Purchase of 1854. In addition to being extremely dry, the southern part of the Yuma Desert rarely experiences freezing temperatures.

The physiography of this region is varied, although most of it consists of bajadas and nearly level plains, and the vegetation is dominated by creosote bush (*Larrea tridentata*), burro bush (*Franseria dumosa*), and brittlebush (*Encelia farinosa*). The arroyos and waterways in the Yuma Desert often support trees that are more typical of the upland desert in Arizona. These include *Prosopis juliflora*, *Cercidium floridum*, *Cercidium microphyllum*, *Olneya tesota*, *Dalea spinosa*, *Prosopis glandulosa*, and *Chilopsis linearis*. The saguaro (*Carnegiea gigantea*) and many other succulents are also found in this desert.

In isolated gorges where the microclimate is favorable, species such as California fan palm (*Washingtonia filifera*) may also be found. Interest-

Yuma Desert habitat in Yuma County, Arizona. (Photo: M. A. Mares)

One of the most ecologically interesting areas within the Yuma Desert is the Organ Pipe National Monument between Ajo, Arizona, and Sonoita, Mexico. This is an area of beautiful organ pipe cactus, senita, and, of course, the enigmatic saguaro. A considerable portion of the Yuma Desert in the United States has restricted access because of its use as military proving grounds.—Gary K. Hulett and Amanda Renner Charles

See also **ALLUVIAL FAN; BAJA CALIFORNIA, DESERTS OF; BIRDS; CACTI; CACTUS, COLUMNAR; CALIFORNIA DESERT; COLORADO DESERT; CREOSOTE BUSH; DESERTS; DESERTS, HOT; DESERTS, TEMPERATE; LIZARDS; MAMMALS; MEXICO, DESERTS OF; PALOVERDE; PLANT GEOGRAPHY; REPTILES; SEMIARID ZONES; SNAKES; SONORAN DESERT; UNITED STATES, DESERTS OF; YUCCA**

ingly, yuccas are uncommon in the area to the south of the Gila River in Arizona, although they are common in many of the other hot deserts of North America.

Further Reading

Musick, H. B. 1975. Bareness of desert pavement in Yuma County, Arizona. *Journal of the Arizona Academy of Science* 10:24–28.

ZEBRA

Striped horses (plains zebra, mountain zebra, and quagga) and striped ass (Grevy's zebra) of the mammalian family Equidae (order Perissodactyla) that occur in Africa. There are three living species, *Equus burchellii* (plains zebra), *Equus grevi* (Grevy's zebra), *Equus zebra* (mountain zebra); and one recently extinct species, *Equus quagga* (quagga).

The plains zebra inhabits the open and lightly wooded savannas, plains, and steppes of eastern Africa from Sudan and Ethiopia to southern Africa. Grevy's zebra, the largest wild equid, uses the dry savannas and semideserts of East Africa, including Kenya, Somalia, and Ethiopia. The mountain zebra is restricted to the barren, rocky uplands and arid plains of the coastal moutains of southwestern Africa. The quagga, extinct since the late 1800s, was found in the arid Karoo Desert and temperate grasslands of the interior plateau of South Africa.

Zebras and the quagga are recognizable by their distinct black-and-white striped body. Species are distinguished by different forms and patterns of striping. There also is much individual and population variation. The quagga had stripes only on the head, neck, and back. Body length is 2–3 meters, tail length is about 55 centimeters, and the height at the shoulder is 1.2–1.6 meters. Like all wild horses, zebras have an erect mane; the mountain zebra has a dewlap (flap of skin on the throat).

Species of zebras generally do not overlap in distribution, although Grevy's and plains zebras may coexist in the semidry thorny scrubland of northern Kenya during certain times of the year. Although they inhabit arid and semiarid areas, zebras are not water independent. Grevy's zebra is able to withstand drought conditions better than the plains zebra. Plains zebras are important in opening up areas for grazing, because they will forage on the tall grasses that other animals, such as wildebeest, will not eat. After the tall grass has been eaten and trampled, other species will move into the area to forage on the remaining vegetation.

Plains zebra (*Equus burchellii*) at the Itala Game Reserve, northern Kwazulu-Natal Province, South Africa. (Photo: M. A. Mares)

Zebras forage primarily on grasses. Their digestive system of hindgut fermentation allows rapid processing of food matter but incomplete digestion of plant cell walls. Thus they need to eat large quantities of grass to extract the same amount of nutrients that other ruminants would obtain from smaller amounts of vegetation. Because zebras are not dependent on forage quality, they can occupy more marginal habitats than other African herbivores.

Zebras generally have two types of social systems. Grevy's zebras form no long-lasting social bonds, but males maintain territories, usually around water holes or in good grazing lands. These territories, which are among the largest known for an herbivore (2.7–10.5 square kilometers in Kenya), are used solely for mating and are defended by a single male by his presence and behavior (e.g., urinating, defecating in dung piles).

Mountain zebras and plains zebras form groups (harems) of permanent members, which consist of a single adult male (stallion) and several mares with young. These small bands are nonterritorial and have home ranges that overlap those of other groups. This social system, in which individuals, rather than land, are defended, is thought to offer benefits to animals that lead a nomadic or migratory existence.—Janet K. Braun

See also **AFRICA, DESERTS OF; ASS; BODY TEMPERATURE; COLORATION; CRYPSIS; HERBIVORY; KALAHARI DESERT; KAROO; MAMMALS; NAMIBIA, DESERTS OF; PHYSIOLOGY; PREDATION; SOUTH AFRICA, DESERTS OF; THERMOREGULATION; UNGULATES; WATER BALANCE**

Further Reading

Alden, P. C., R. D. Estes, D. Schlitter, and B. McBride. 1995. *National Audubon Society Field Guide to African Wildlife*. New York: Knopf.

Dorst, J., and P. Dandelot. 1980. *A Field Guide to the Larger Mammals of Africa*. London: Collins.

Estes, R. D. 1993. *The Safari Companion*. White River Junction, Vt.: Chelsea Green.

Nowak, R. M. 1991. *Walker's Mammals of the World*. 5th ed. Baltimore: Johns Hopkins University Press.

Skinner, J. D., and R. H. N. Smithers. 1990. *The Mammals of the Southern African Subregion*. Pretoria: University of Pretoria.

ZEBU CATTLE

One of the two major lines of domesticated cattle. Many breeds of cattle can be described as zebu cattle, which are characterized by the hump on their backs, large, often pendulous ears, distinctive dewlap, and long foreskins or umbilical folds. While zebu cattle can now be found worldwide, they are particularly well adapted for life in the tropics and subtropics. The hump on the back of the cattle is formed by two muscles and an accumulation of fat. The concentration of fat deposits in the hump allows the cattle to use the rest of their bodies to radiate excess heat more efficiently. The radiation of heat is also aided by the extra surface area of the dewlap, ears, and foreskin or umbilical fold. The fat in the hump also allows the animal to survive in times when food may be less plentiful. The zebu cattle line was already well established in Asia more than 6,500 years ago.—Rob Channell

See also **BODY TEMPERATURE; DESERT PEOPLES; DOMESTIC ANIMALS; MAMMALS; THERMOREGULATION; UNGULATES; WATER BALANCE**

Further Reading

Rouse, J. E. 1970. *World Cattle*. Vol. 2. Norman: University of Oklahoma Press.

ZONDA. *See* SANTA ANA WINDS

INDEX

(Boldface capital letters indicate major encyclopedia accounts)

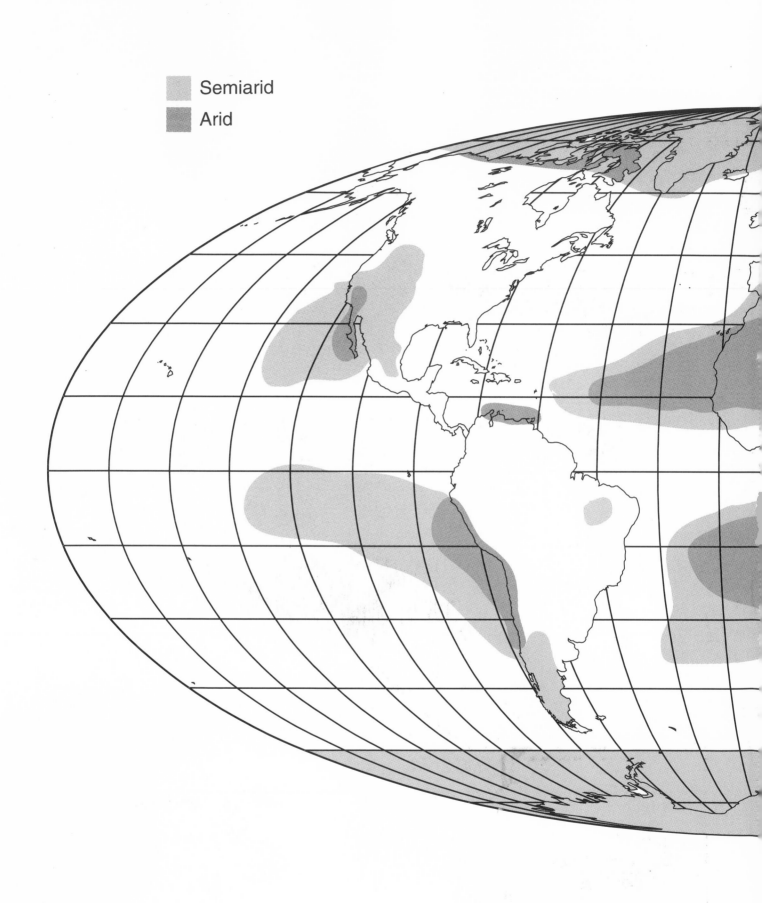